ETHICS
Revised Edition

Ethics
Revised Edition

Volume 3
Practical reason — Zoroastrian ethics
Index

Edited by

JOHN K. ROTH
Claremont McKenna College
Department of Philosophy and Religious Studies

SALEM PRESS, INC.
PASADENA, CALIFORNIA   HACKENSACK, NEW JERSEY

Editor in Chief: Dawn P. Dawson
Managing Editor: Christina J. Moose
Project Editor: R. Kent Rasmussen
Assistant Editor: Andrea Miller
Acquisitions Editor: Mark Rehn
Photograph Editor: Philip Bader
Research Assistant: Andy Perry
Production Editor: Kathy Hix
Graphics and Design: James Hutson
Layout: William Zimmerman

Library of Congress Cataloging-in-Publication Data

Ethics / edited by John Roth.— Rev. Ed.
    p. cm.
  Includes bibliographical references and index.
    ISBN 1-58765-170-X (set : alk. paper) — ISBN 1-58765-171-8 (vol. 1 : alk. paper) — ISBN 1-58765-172-6 (vol. 2 : alk. paper) — ISBN 1-58765-173-4 (vol. 3 : alk. paper)
    1. Ethics—Encyclopedias. I. Roth, John K.
    BJ63.E54 2004
    170'.3—dc22

                                                                    2004021797
                            First Printing

CONTENTS

CONTENTS

COMPLETE LIST OF CONTENTS

Volume 1

Volume II

Volume III

ETHICS
Revised Edition

Practical reason

DEFINITION: Justification for taking action
TYPE OF ETHICS: Theory of ethics
SIGNIFICANCE: Theories of practical reason try to answer such questions as why one should be moral, whether it is always rational to act on moral requirements, and if human beings are inherently selfish.

The difference between practical and theoretical reason rests on a distinction between two types of reasons. A practical reason—such as the need to help people in trouble—gives one a reason for doing something. A theoretical reason—such as "7 + 5 = 12"—gives one a reason for believing something. Some argue that by nature people act only for selfish reasons. Thomas Hobbes, the founder of modern egoism, is the most influential defender of this view. Most theories of practical reason attempt to refute egoism by proposing standards for moral decision making. These standards are supposed to show that human beings have reasons to be moral that are not based exclusively on self-interest.

Each of the three dominant theories of practical reason defends a conception of practical reason that can be traced back to its founder. The ancient Greek philosopher Aristotle argued that a virtuous person is someone who knows how to act in ways that promote the virtuous life. A benevolent person, for example, knows that it is good to help others in need. The practical reasoning of a benevolent person is motivated by the desire for beneficence and the knowledge that beneficence is a virtue. Practical reasoning thus involves putting moral knowledge into practice by acting morally.

The eighteenth century English philosopher David Hume argued that practical reason is always motivated by desire. For example, having a desire to relieve someone's suffering counts as a reason for acting. Moreover, unless a desire is present a person cannot have a reason for action. Hume and his followers believe that the reasons people have for acting morally are usually not selfish reasons. Because people are generally believed to have a natural sympathy for the plights of others, they have a natural desire to act morally.

The late eighteenth century German philosopher Immanuel Kant claimed that it is possible to act from a reason even if one has no desire to do so. According to his view, a moral reason is a requirement of rationality; a moral reason is also a practical reason because it specifies an action that a person should perform. Rational people, so far as they are rational at the moments of action, will know that they have a duty to assist those in need. Kant therefore rejects the claim that a reason for action presupposes a desire. For Kant and his followers, sometimes morality requires acting on reasons that conflict with human desires. Contemporary ethicists usually defend a version of one of these positions.

Jon Mahoney

FURTHER READING

Kant, Immanuel. *Critique of Practical Reason.* 1788. Translated and edited by Mary Gregor. Cambridge, England: Cambridge University Press, 1997.

Millgram, Elijah, ed. *Varieties of Practical Reasoning.* Cambridge, Mass.: MIT Press, 2001.

SEE ALSO: Aristotelian ethics; Golden mean; Good, the; Hobbes, Thomas; Idealist ethics; Kant, Immanuel; Morality; Nagel, Thomas; Natural law; Prudence.

Pragmatism

DEFINITION: School of philosophy which asserts that ideas should be understood as practical entities
TYPE OF ETHICS: Theory of ethics
SIGNIFICANCE: Pragmatism holds that thought is essentially a guide for action. Therefore, ideas acquire their meanings from their practical consequences, and truth is defined as whatever it is useful to believe. Pragmatist ethics tends to be situational and consequentialist, since it focuses on the useful effects of moral values in particular contexts.

Pragmatism was initiated by Charles Sanders Peirce and William James and developed by John Dewey and George Herbert Mead; it has been revived since the 1970's. Responding to Darwinism, Peirce and James viewed thought as a process within the whole context of life-activity. In his foundational essays

"The Fixation of Belief" (1877) and "How to Make Our Ideas Clear" (1878), Peirce argued that thinking arises from a disturbance in action and aims at producing a belief that more successfully guides future action. Beliefs are not mental states but organic dispositions or habits. James popularized the term "pragmatism" first in 1898 and then in the famous lectures published as *Pragmatism* (1907).

For Peirce, pragmatism was a general theory of meaning, while James stressed the view that "truth" means "workability." Mead explored the implications for social psychology. John Dewey developed it into a rich theory of human existence and conduct, including ethical, social, and political philosophy, often known as "instrumentalism" but more correctly called "Cultural naturalism." (Instrumentalism, the theory of intelligent inquiry, is part of Dewey's general theory of experience, ranging from prereflective feelings to refined aesthetic and religious meanings.)

Dewey begins by seeing humans as living organisms acting within and responding to their environments. People are neither predetermined mechanisms nor purely independent. Action is a feedback process of learning, operating within certain constraints but capable of a variety of developments. As cultural beings, people also live in a social environment in which the experience of others shapes their own conduct. The process of learning, then, offers a third alternative for moral theory. "Morals means growth of conduct in meaning," says Dewey. "It is learning the meaning of what we are about and employing that meaning in action."

For Dewey, ethics deals with all human action. It legitimately involves obtaining reliable information; broad experience; skills in communication, cooperation, and deliberation; educational and political organization; and the creation of new values and ideals. Ethics, in short, is the art of rendering human existence as meaningful and intrinsically fulfilling as possible.

REALIZING AIMS

Like any art, ethics is concerned with the techniques whereby its aims may be realized. In this sense, it is experimental and gains insight from the success of the scientific method. Dewey denied that ethical problems should be handed over to the social sciences or some managerial elite, but he hoped that the cooperative, experimental attitude of science

could be widely inculcated for framing tentative solutions to social problems that leave many human lives devoid of hope or meaning. By seeing the moral life as capable of being guided by a variety of intelligently undertaken experiments instead of as the subject matter for formal principles of ethical judgment, Dewey thought, it might be possible to improve the human condition.

Out of native impulses, desires arise, leading to actions that form habits. Habits "constitute the self," becoming one's character. They lead to certain kinds of further action that may cause reevaluation of past desires, a transformation or enlargement of them with respect to their objects, or a deepening of their meaning with broadened experience. Although Dewey agrees with Aristotle that action and habit are the basis of character, he finds no one fixed and defining virtue. The self is a process, Dewey states: It "is impossible for the self to stand still, it is becoming and becoming for better or worse. It is in the *quality* of becoming that virtue resides. We set up this and that end to be reached, but *the* end is growth itself." Although he rejects absolute values, Dewey is no subjective relativist; instead, he is a contextual pluralist. The good self is one that is informed about its world, grasps the tendencies of situations, and deliberates well about possible ends and the means required to realize them.

Deliberation includes the imaginative search for ideals of conduct and the discovery of new values. Only in a derivative sense is it understood as the mere search for means to preselected ends. Two children fighting over a ball may discover the game of catch, discovering the new value of cooperative play and friendship, transforming the old values of possessiveness and dominance. Deliberation is not primarily a private affair; one deliberates alone because one has deliberated aloud with others. Ethical reasoning, then, is no calculative or rule-bound procedure but is fraught with imagination, dialogue, and dramatic interpretation. It aims to understand the meaning of a present situation by determining its tendencies and the possible values that they realize. An event gains meaning within an overall process. By seeing the actual in the light of the possible, one can make intelligent choices and critically evaluate one's conduct. One can grow intelligently. This is Dewey's understanding of freedom.

A society incorporating such behavior would provide the most secure basis for democracy as a way of life. Civilization would be no abstract ideal but would concretely aim at every means possible to realize conditions whereby human beings could lead inherently significant lives.

Thomas Alexander

FURTHER READING

Dewey, John. *The Collected Works: The Early Works, the Middle Works, the Later Works*. 37 vols. Edited by Jo Ann Boydston. Carbondale: Southern Illinois University Press, 1967-1992.

Fesmire, Stephen. *John Dewey and Moral Imagination: Pragmatism in Ethics*. Bloomington: Indiana University Press, 2003.

Gouinlock, James. *John Dewey's Philosophy of Value*. New York: Humanities Press, 1972.

James, William. *Pragmatism, and Other Writings*. Edited by Giles Gunn. New York: Penguin Books, 2000.

Nietzsche, Friedrich. *Beyond Good and Evil*. Translated by Walter Kaufmann. New York: Vintage, 1989.

Peirce, Charles. *The Essential Peirce: Selected Philosophical Writings*. Edited by Nathan Houser and Christian Kloesel. 2 vols. Bloomington: Indiana University Press, 1992-1998.

SEE ALSO: Dewey, John; Intersubjectivity; James, William; Mean/ends distinction; Peirce, Charles Sanders; Theory and practice; Utilitarianism.

Premarital sex

DEFINITION: Sexual contacts between unmarried partners

TYPE OF ETHICS: Sex and gender issues

SIGNIFICANCE: Premarital sex is a subject of significant moral controversy; sexual ethics are used to assess the morality of sexual practices in terms of how they affect human welfare.

At the beginning of the twenty-first century, premarital sex remained one of the most controversial subjects in most cultures. Most guidelines for acceptable sexual behavior in the Western world are derived from religious teachings and cultural traditions. In most cases, the official viewpoint is that sex outside committed married relationships is discouraged if not prohibited. Despite this doctrine, the vast majority of people have sexual experiences prior to marriage.

Sexual ethics revolve around concerns about human welfare. Sexual behavior is deemed moral when it is determined that it does not harm the partners who are involved. To that end, it is essential that sexual relationships be based on mutual consent, equality, and reciprocity. Herein lies one of the challenges of sexual ethics. In cultures such as that of the United States, in which a double standard for sexual conduct prevails, mutual consent is sometimes difficult to assess. Because of taboos and religious proscriptions, some people may choose to enter sexual relationships with reservations. If one partner in a sexual encounter between two people participates with some reluctance, does that qualify as mutual consent?

Two broad ethical perspectives on premarital sex are evident in most Western cultures. The conservative ethical viewpoint is influenced by traditional religious teachings. The liberal ethical viewpoint is a secular perspective prevalent in the media.

CONSERVATIVE AND LIBERAL VIEWPOINTS

The conservative stance advocates a conventional morality that is congruent with most Judeo-Christian teachings. From this perspective, individuals are expected to conform to explicit rules. The conservative stance is viewed as absolutist and legalistic. Moral precepts should guide all sexual practices, and no person is exempt. This perspective is also viewed as restrictive in that its intent is to limit the range of acceptable sexual practices. For example, one viewpoint, consistent with traditional Christian doctrine, considers heterosexual intercourse in marriage to be the only morally acceptable form of sexual behavior.

The liberal viewpoint is less cohesive than the conservative viewpoint. In general, though, this approach is sometimes referred to as the new morality and situational ethics. From this perspective, the morality of sexual choices can only be gauged according to the situations or contexts. For example, one possible context for acceptable premarital sex is a caring committed relationship. In most Western cultures, mutually consenting sexual behavior between two adults in a committed relationship is viewed as acceptable by the majority of people.

The liberal perspective is often described as tolerant and permissive because its proponents often argue that people should be free to choose their own sexual practices rather than rely on traditional or rigid guidelines. As long as nobody is being hurt or deceived, people should feel free to engage in sexual relationships.

Sexual Ethics

Kenneth A. Strike and Pamela A. Moss have summarized five principles that are useful for evaluating moral dilemmas. The greatest good principle evaluates personal choices based on their outcomes. This principle favors choices that yield the most positive outcomes for the greatest number of people, a philosophy also known as utilitarianism. The equal respect principle is akin to the golden rule in arguing that each person merits being treated with dignity and respect. The relationship principle evaluates the morality of an action by its impact on people's relationships. Choices that promote positive relationships are viewed as morally desirable. The community principle evaluates the value of personal choices based on how these affect the community at large, which would include social groups, organizations, and other social structures. Finally, the character growth principle evaluates behavior based on how it contributes to making individuals the kinds of persons they aspire to become.

These principles can be readily adapted to some sexual situations, such as sexual infidelity. Being unfaithful to one's partner clearly violates the greatest good and the equal respect principles. Deceiving someone is likely to have an unfavorable outcome for all parties, and it suggests a lack of respect for one's partner. Deceit does not promote positive relationships, thereby violating that principle. It may also harm other relationships within a larger context. Finally, the majority of people do not aspire to become dishonest or deceitful.

Other situations are more ambiguous, and the applicability of these principles is less obvious in such cases. Premarital sex generally occurs within mutually consenting relationships between individuals of equal status, and deceit is therefore not an issue. Such relationships would conform to the equal respect principle. The extent to which such relationships promote the greatest good, character growth, and the relationship itself is debatable and is at the heart of the controversy surrounding premarital sex.

From the conservative ethical perspective, any sex outside marriage is immoral and is harmful to the parties involved and their community. According to the liberal ethical viewpoint, sexual relationships between unmarried persons are not invariably harmful. They can be morally acceptable if the partners are deeply attached and committed to each other, which would be consistent with most of the principles discussed. Premarital sex could even be morally justified, from this viewpoint, in uncommitted or casual relationships whose encounters are completely open, reciprocal, and consensual. It might be argued that it conforms to the greatest good principle because it is enjoyable for both persons. It might promote character growth by facilitating self-discovery. It could feasibly create a positive bond between the parties. Finally, in an environment free of taboos and repressive views toward sexuality, premarital sex would not have a negative impact on the community or on personal growth. Whether such an environment can ever be achieved is also the subject of controversy.

Richard D. McAnulty

Further Reading

Gallagher, Maggie. *The Abolition of Marriage: How We Destroy Lasting Love.* Washington, D.C.: Regnery, 1996.

McAnulty, Richard D., and M. Michele Burnette. *Exploring Human Sexuality: Making Healthy Decisions.* Boston: Allyn & Bacon, 2004.

Monti, Joseph. *Arguing About Sex: The Rhetoric of Christian Sexual Morality.* Albany: State University of New York Press, 1995.

Roleff, Tamera L. *Teenage Sexuality: Opposing Viewpoints.* Chicago: Greenhaven Press, 2001.

Seidman, Steven. *Embattled Eros: Sexual Politics and Ethics in Contemporary America.* New York: Routledge, 1992.

Strike, Kenneth A., and Pamela A. Moss. *Ethics and College Student Life: A Case Study Approach.* Upper Saddle River, N.J.: Prentice Hall, 2003.

SEE ALSO: Adultery; Consent; Lust; Marriage; Promiscuity; Prostitution; Sex therapy; Sexual revolution; Sexuality and sexual ethics; Sexually transmitted diseases.

Prescriptivism

DEFINITION: Theory developed by by R. M. Hare holding that the main purpose of moral language is to prescribe or command

DATE: Term coined in 1952

TYPE OF ETHICS: Theory of ethics

SIGNIFICANCE: Prescriptivism implies that ethical knowledge as such does not exist, because moral language affects action rather than containing meaning or truth.

British philosopher R. M. Hare's view has received at least five important criticisms. First, his view that morality consists only of commands implies that ethical knowledge is impossible, since a command, unlike an indicative statement, cannot be true. Second, his view that anyone who accepts a moral statement and can act on it will obey the command has counterexamples in apathetic and evil people who knowingly refuse to do what they admit is ethically required. Third, the great variety of uses of moral claims makes it unlikely that they can all be reduced to imperatives. Fourth, F. E. Sparshott believes that Hare neglects the fact that any morality must incorporate "those rules of conduct that seem necessary for communal living." Fifth, P. H. Nowell-Smith reduces Hare's theory to the absurd by exposing its implication that "Nothing that we discover about the nature of moral judgments entails that it is wrong to put all Jews in gas-chambers."

In ethics and religion, prescriptivism sometimes refers not to Hare's theory but to the theory that the only justifications for moral claims are the commands of some authority (such as God). Socrates criticized this view in Plato's *Euthyphro* (399-390 B.C.E.), where he suggested that an act was not good only because God commanded it but that God commanded the act because it was independently good.

Sterling Harwood

SEE ALSO: Cognitivism; Emotivist ethics; Hare, R. M.; Is/ought distinction; Language; *Leviathan*; Relativism.

Price fixing

DEFINITION: Agreement by competing sellers of products or services to charge the same prices

TYPE OF ETHICS: Business and labor ethics

SIGNIFICANCE: Price fixing is thought of as creating an "artificially" high price for a commodity by circumventing the "natural" deflationary effects of competition. Consumer advocates assert that it is an unfair practice because it takes advantage of consumers' lack of bargaining power.

Concepts associated with price fixing go back at least to ancient Greece. Philosophers argued about how a "just price," one that was fair to both consumers and producers, could be identified. Debates concerning the ethical issues involved in setting prices concerned the relative power of consumers and producers in the marketplace and behavior that constituted fair play. Opponents of price fixing argued that producers are likely, if allowed, to set prices that give them high levels of profit that are not justified by costs or risks taken in business.

The Sherman Antitrust Act, signed into law on July 2, 1890, forbade contracts, combinations of business, or conspiracies in restraint of trade. Exactly what constituted a restraint of trade remained to be decided by the courts, but price fixing was soon declared illegal under the act. The price fixing laws of the United States are more stringent than are those of other countries. Many countries do not forbid the practice, and some well-known trade organizations, such as the Organization of Petroleum Exporting Countries, exist primarily to fix prices. Even the United States allows some forms of price fixing, such as guaranteed minimum prices for farm products and minimum wages. These exceptions are seen as benefiting sellers of products or services that society has an interest in protecting.

A. J. Sobczak

SEE ALSO: Antitrust legislation; Consumerism; Minimum-wage laws; Monopoly; Profit economy; Sales ethics.

Pride

DEFINITION: Reasonable or unreasonable self-esteem; dignity or conceit

TYPE OF ETHICS: Personal and social ethics

SIGNIFICANCE: Justifiable pride is often accounted to be a virtue, but in ethical systems which value self-effacement, there is no such thing as justifiable pride. In traditional Christianity, pride is the worst of all the "seven deadly sins."

John Stuart Mill noted that pride is "a name which is given indiscriminately to some of the most and to some of the least estimable feelings of which mankind is capable." Pride has been identified as a proper reward for moral achievement and as a key element in a healthy psyche, and it has been blasted as a destructive emotion and as one of the "seven deadly sins."

The core of pride is a high sense of one's own moral value. One dimension of this is moral ambitiousness—a desire to achieve excellence of character. People speak, for example, of taking pride in their work; that is, of being committed to the achievement of quality. This forward-looking dimension of pride complements its backward-looking dimension as a sense of self-satisfaction for what one has achieved. People speak, for example, of feeling proud of having done a good job, of having succeeded at a challenging task.

HISTORY

Aristotle held pride, or "greatness of soul," to be the "crown" of the virtues. Pride, he argued, follows from the achievement of virtue. Anyone who has worked hard to achieve excellence of character will feel a justified sense of self-worth. Excellence of character and the pride that goes with it also translate into a certain style of action: The proud person not only does excellent things but also does them with grace and dignity. Magnificence characterizes the great-souled person in both character and action.

Aristotle's was a highly optimistic account of what was possible for human beings. Later thinkers often accepted a more pessimistic view of human nature, and therefore deemphasized pride or even condemned it as a sin. The Christian tradition has many prominent representatives of this view. Emphasizing human helplessness in the face of Original Sin, Christians argued that pride is unjustified. Since

humankind is sinful and weak, humility is proper. Pride was condemned as rebellion against God, because it involves a sense of self-worth and competence, and those who feel self-worth and competence will not feel dependent upon God to save them from sin.

The modern era has been an heir to the Greek and Christian traditions, and many modern thinkers seek a middle way between them. Between the extremes of pride and humility lies modesty—thinking oneself neither great nor worthless. Such middle ways can be found in David Hume's advocacy of a "well-regulated pride" and Adam Smith's advocacy of magnanimity tempered with self-denial and a ready sympathy for the woes of others.

CRITICISMS

Pride requires that one (a) achieve excellence of character, (b) evaluate one's character accurately, and (c) act in accordance with one's evaluation. Opponents of pride argue that one or more of these conditions cannot or should not be satisfied. As noted above, Christians argue that since humans cannot achieve moral goodness by their own efforts, (a) is impossible. Others argue that humans chronically overestimate their achievements, so (b) is wishful thinking, and a dose of modesty or humility is a useful corrective. Still others argue that one ought to be self-deprecating about oneself so as not to hurt the feelings of others, or so as not to appear to be vain or a braggart.

Defenders of pride reject these arguments. Humans have free will, so they can regulate their thoughts and actions. Accordingly, they can act consistently in a way that allows them to achieve excellence of character and a fulfilled life, and this is what one should do: Happiness depends on excellence of character, and excellence of character is acquired by one's own efforts. This process of forming one's character means objectively evaluating one's thoughts and actions throughout one's life, reaffirming those that are good and changing those that are not. Once one has achieved excellence of character, simple justice requires that one reap the reward for one's achievement: pride.

FALSE PRIDE, VANITY, AND HUBRIS

True pride should be distinguished from false pride, vanity, and hubris. Everyone knows people who never miss an opportunity to brag about some achievement, whether real or imagined. A braggart may appear to be proud, but chronic bragging indicates a lack of pride: The braggart feels a desperate need for the approval of others, feeling self-worth only when that approval is received. Therefore, the braggart publicizes his or her accomplishments or, failing that, exaggerates or invents some. Clearly, there is a huge difference between self-evaluation based on actual accomplishment and self-evaluation based on deluded praise or praise extorted from others.

Vain people depend for their feeling of self-worth upon superficial or secondary characteristics, such as having a glorious family history, a slim figure, or a wonderful head of hair. While such things can be pleasant or desirable, vain people place them at the core of their self-evaluation and therefore expect inappropriate amounts of admiration from others.

Hubris is presented in classical Greek mythology and drama as the flaw of wanton activity flowing from an overestimation of one's worth. The man of hubris acts as though he has power and worth beyond his station, and because of his flaw he inevitably meets a tragic end. Hubris is distinguished from pride by reference to the accuracy of one's self-evaluation. The man of hubris misjudges his power and worth, and since he cannot live up to or control the outcomes of his deeds, he ends in disaster. The proud woman, by contrast, judges her considerable powers accurately and has the excellence of character necessary to use her powers confidently, gracefully, and successfully.

Stephen R. C. Hicks

FURTHER READING

Aristotle. *Nicomachean Ethics*. Translated and edited by Roger Crisp. New York: Cambridge University Press, 2000.

Augustine, Saint. *The Confessions*. Translated and edited by Philip Burton. Introduction by Robin Lane Fox. New York: A. A. Knopf, 2001.

Bernard (Abbot of Clairvaux). *The Steps of Humility*. Translated by George Bosworth Burch. Notre Dame, Ind.: University of Notre Dame Press, 1963.

Kristjánsson, Kristján. *Justifying Emotions: Pride and Jealousy*. New York: Routledge, 2002.

Rand, Ayn. "The Objectivist Ethics." In *The Virtue of Selfishness: A New Concept of Egoism*. New York: New American Library, 1964.

Smith, Adam. *The Theory of Moral Sentiments*. Edited by Knud Haakonssen. New York: Cambridge University Press, 2002.

SEE ALSO: Character; Christian ethics; Egoism; Egotist; Humility; Individualism; Narcissism; Selfishness; Self-respect; Self-righteousness; Sin; Virtue.

Principles of Medical Ethics

IDENTIFICATION: American Medical Association's official guidelines on professional conduct

DATE: Adopted in 1957; revised in 1980 and 2001

TYPE OF ETHICS: Bioethics

SIGNIFICANCE: *Principles of Medical Ethics* formally codifies professional standards of conduct that are applicable to all physicians practicing in the United States.

In 1957, the AMA replaced its *Code of Ethics*—which had, since the organization's founding in 1847, stated the duties that American physicians owed to their patients, to their society, and to one another—with a statement of moral principles, supplemented by commentary. The reform was consonant with the appeal to basic moral principles by the 1948 Nuremberg Tribunal and the World Medical Association. It also lessened physicians' malpractice liability under the explicit obligations stipulated by the code and, at the same time, provided a more flexible format for advising physicians on conduct.

The *Principles* require physicians to provide competent, compassionate medical service, respectful of human dignity; to deal honestly with patients and colleagues; to expose fraud and deception; to respect the law; to respect the rights of patients and to safeguard their confidences; to respect the rights of colleagues and other health care professionals; to advance scientific knowledge; to share information with patients, colleagues, and the public; and to recognize a responsibility to contribute to the community. Revised in 1980 and again in 2001, the *Principles* are largely unchanged but have shifted in subtle ways. They have tended toward a slightly more ex-

Ethical Principles of the American Medical Association

1. A physician shall be dedicated to providing competent medical care, with compassion and respect for human dignity and rights.

2. A physician shall uphold the standards of professionalism, be honest in all professional interactions, and strive to report physicians deficient in character or competence, or engaging in fraud or deception, to appropriate entities.

3. A physician shall respect the law and also recognize a responsibility to seek changes in those requirements which are contrary to the best interests of the patient.

4. A physician shall respect the rights of patients, colleagues, and other health professionals, and shall safeguard patient confidences and privacy within the constraints of the law.

5. A physician shall continue to study, apply, and advance scientific knowledge, maintain a commitment to medical education, make relevant information available to patients, colleagues, and the public, obtain consultation, and use the talents of other health professionals when indicated.

6. A physician shall, in the provision of appropriate patient care, except in emergencies, be free to choose whom to serve, with whom to associate, and the environment in which to provide medical care.

7. A physician shall recognize a responsibility to participate in activities contributing to the improvement of the community and the betterment of public health.

8. A physician shall, while caring for a patient, regard responsibility to the patient as paramount.

9. A physician shall support access to medical care for all people.

Note: Adopted June 17, 2001.

Source: American Medical Association (http://www.ama-assn.org/ama/pub/category/2512.html).

plicit enumeration of physicians' rights as well as their responsibilities, and they have expunged certain financial rules (for example, a prohibition against referral fees).

Robert Baker

SEE ALSO: American Medical Association; Medical bills of rights; Medical ethics; Physician-patient relationship; *Principles of Medical Ethics with Annotations Especially Applicable to Psychiatry.*

Principles of Medical Ethics with Annotations Especially Applicable to Psychiatry

IDENTIFICATION: Addendum to *Principles of Medical Ethics* published by the American Psychiatric Association to address unique ethical issues confronting psychiatrists

DATE: First published in September, 1973; revised in 1981, 1986, 2001, 2003, and 2004

TYPE OF ETHICS: Psychological ethics

SIGNIFICANCE: The *Principles* sets out the issues particular to practitioners in the mental health field and codifies standards of ethical conduct in matters not covered by the American Medical Association's code.

The 1973 statement of *Principles* recognized that, although psychiatrists have the same goals as all physicians in adhering to the American Medical Association's code of ethics, psychiatrists also face particular ethical questions that differ in kind and degree from those of other medical specialties. The annotations given in the *Principles* were viewed as being open to revision from time to time to reflect current issues and problems. An extensive revision was published in 1986. The most relevant sections of the 1973 document dealt with contractual relationships with other mental health professionals and physicians, the waiving of confidentiality, and speaking out on social issues not related to psychiatry.

The thrust of the document was that psychiatrists must maintain the trust of their patients and other medical and nonmedical professionals. The 1986 revision maintains this basic thrust, but its seven sections contain much more lengthy, detailed, and specific annotations and focus in particular on the various aspects of the psychiatrist-patient relationship, such as confidentiality, consultation with other psychiatrists, and honesty. In 2001, the AMA adopted a revised version of its *Principles*. The APA followed suit and added a series of amendments in November, 2003.

Laurence Miller

SEE ALSO: Ethical Principles of Psychologists; Medical ethics; *Principles of Medical Ethics*; Psychology; Therapist-patient relationship.

Prisoner's dilemma

DEFINITION: Thought experiment designed to illustrate issues raised when individuals are expected to cooperate to achieve collective goals

TYPE OF ETHICS: Theory of ethics

SIGNIFICANCE: The prisoner's dilemma demonstrates that lack of communication breeds distrust, and that without trust mutual cooperation is difficult. It may also demonstrate the pitfalls of treating humans as rational, rather than irrational, decision makers.

The prisoner's dilemma was originally developed as a thought experiment in 1950. It has since become synonymous with a whole class of ethical and social problems involving the conflict between individual rationality and collective action aimed toward serving common goals.

STRUCTURE: TWO-PERSON PROBLEM

The problem begins with two prisoners, A and B, who are arrested for a crime. A clever district attorney, not having enough evidence to convict either defendant, offers each of them a deal separately. If both individuals confess to the crime, then both will receive a lesser sentence of three years. If neither confesses to the crime, they will be convicted of a lesser charge, which carries a five-year sentence. If one confesses and the other does not, however, then the prisoner who confesses will receive a sentence of ten years and the other prisoner will go free. It would appear that both prisoners would be well-advised to confess to the crime and receive a three-year sen-

tence; certainly, both would prefer this result to the one in which neither confesses and both receive a five-year sentence. Yet each prisoner's protection of his or her own self-interest will lead to the less preferred result.

Consider prisoner A's position. If prisoner B does not confess, prisoner A receives a sentence of ten years if he confesses and five years if he does not confess; hence, prisoner A should not confess under these circumstances. If prisoner B does confess, then prisoner A receives a sentence of five years if he confesses but goes free if he does not confess; hence, prisoner A should not confess under these circumstances either. Since prisoner B has only these two choices, prisoner A's individual rationality compels him to avoid confessing, regardless of what prisoner B does.

Similarly, prisoner B should avoid confessing, regardless of what prisoner A does. Both prisoners therefore receive five-year sentences for not confessing, even though both would prefer the three-year sentence they would receive if both confessed. Note that communication between the two prisoners will not help this problem. Even if the two could speak to each other, each would find it in his interest to try to convince the other to confess and to avoid confessing himself.

The ethical dimensions of this problem arise because both prisoners know they would be better off if they would coordinate their efforts and cooperate in their strategy, but their individual self-interest leads them to a less optimal result. One of the first applications of this problem to a real-life situation concerned the control of nuclear weapons. Consider two nations, A and B, in a nuclear arms race. Each nation knows that these weapons are horribly expensive to build and maintain; each nation also has sufficient firepower to destroy the other nation.

However, if one nation gains a significant edge in building nuclear weapons, it will be able to destroy the other nation's weapons in a first strike and dictate terms for peace by threatening the now-defenseless nation with a second destructive strike. Both nations may agree that to build new nuclear weapons is senseless, since the opposing nation will simply build more weapons to match the increase; as a result, they will have the same strategic balance but will be much poorer and will not be able to use their resources for other important domestic priorities such as social welfare and job creation.

It would seem that the two nations should agree to stop building arms. Yet consider nation A's interests. If nation B does not stop building arms, nation A can stop and risk conquest or can keep building and maintain the status quo. Under these circumstances, nation A will continue building arms. If nation B does stop building arms, nation A can stop and maintain the status quo or can keep building arms and conquer nation B. Under these circumstances, nation A will continue building arms. Since nation B must be expected to think in the same way, the arms race will escalate and both nations will waste resources to maintain the status quo, even though both sides realize they would be better off with fewer weapons (and, therefore, lower costs for the creation and maintenance of arms).

STRUCTURE: MULTIPERSON PROBLEM

A second ethical application of the general prisoner's dilemma, discussed by Mancur Olson and Russell Hardin, among others, extends the problem to more than two parties and discusses individual efforts toward collective action approved by all members of a group. In this scenario, an individual is asked to contribute to a group effort. A common example used is the placement of catalytic converters on cars to reduce pollution. Assuming that it costs $400 to add a converter to a car and that each individual believes that it is worth paying the money to clean up the air, it seems reasonable to believe that all individuals would order converters for their cars.

However, the individual contemplating this action considers two circumstances. If everyone else does not add a converter, then the individual can pay $400 to add a converter without making the air significantly cleaner (since one car produces very little pollution) or can choose not to add the converter and avoid paying the price. Under these circumstances, the individual should not order the converter. If everyone else does add a converter, then the individual can pay $400 to add a converter without adding appreciably to cleaner air (since one car produces insignificant amounts of pollution) or he can not add the converter and enjoy cleaner air without paying the price. Once again, the individual should not order the converter under these circumstances.

The one difference between the two-party situation and the multiparty situation with the prisoner's dilemma is that it would be in the interest of the individual in the second situation to order the converter only if his contribution made the difference between the success or failure of efforts to clean up the air. Unfortunately, the chances of such a situation occurring are so small in most cases of large groups that it would not provide sufficient incentive to contribute to solving the problem. As a result, all individuals agree that it would be worth the money to contribute $400 for cleaner air, but none of the individuals does so, and the effort fails.

PROPOSED SOLUTIONS

Two solutions have been posited to both situations. The first involves coercing, or forcing, all individuals to cooperate toward the common goal. In the case of pollution controls, for example, the federal government sets emission standards that must be met for individuals to drive their cars; they are forced to add catalytic converters to their cars. A problem with this solution is that it requires some authority to compel the parties to cooperate; in the example involving nuclear weapons, however, there is no authority that exists that has the power to compel nations to halt an arms race.

A second solution is to give selective incentives to only those persons who cooperate. All individuals who contribute to public television, for example, receive handbags with the PBS logo, which only contributors can obtain. Such selective incentives may include cheaper vacations, group medical or life insurance benefits, or other incentives. The problem with this solution is that in most cases a group must already exist to provide selective incentives; one cannot obtain group health insurance rates, for example, if one does not have a group to insure. This solution does not explain how groups are started in the first place.

Neither solution addresses the central ethical problem of the prisoner's dilemma: that self-interested individuals may be prevented from participating in collective action that all understand is in the general interest. Therefore, self-interest alone may not compel people to contribute to the general welfare in many cases, even when individuals realize that their self-interest would be better served if everyone contributed to the collective goal than if no one did.

Frank Louis Rusciano

FURTHER READING

Abrams, Robert. *Foundations of Political Analysis: An Introduction to the Theory of Collective Choice.* New York: Columbia University Press, 1980.

Barry, Brian, and Russell Hardin, eds. *Rational Man and Irrational Society?* Beverly Hills, Calif.: Sage, 1982.

Hardin, Russell. *Collective Action.* Baltimore: Johns Hopkins Press for Resources for the Future, 1982.

Hirsch, Fred. *The Social Limits to Growth.* Cambridge, Mass.: Harvard University Press, 1976.

Jervis, R. *The Logic of Images in International Relations.* Princeton, N.J.: Princeton University Press, 1970.

Olson, Mancur. *The Logic of Collective Action.* Cambridge, Mass.: Harvard University Press, 1965.

Rapaport, Anatol, ed. *Game Theory as a Theory of Conflict Resolution.* Boston: D. Reidal, 1974.

Sen, Amartya. *Rationality and Freedom.* Cambridge, Mass.: Belknap Press, 2002.

SEE ALSO: Common good; Dilemmas, moral; Paradoxes in ethics.

Privacy

DEFINITION: Freedom from unwarranted observation of, or intrusion into, one's domestic space, personal relationships, or intimate activities

TYPE OF ETHICS: Civil liberties

SIGNIFICANCE: As a general moral right, the right to privacy came to be discussed and debated in the Information Age far more than it had ever been before, because electronic recording, surveillance, and storage technologies rendered it far more fragile. As a legal matter, the Ninth Amendment to the U.S. Constitution makes it possible to argue that privacy is a constitutionally guaranteed right, but because it is not explicitly enumerated as such, that argument too is a source of controversy.

John Stuart Mill wrote that "there is a sphere of action in which society, as distinguished from the individual, has, if any, an indirect interest; comprehending all that portion of a person's life and conduct which affects only himself, or if it also affects others, only with their free, voluntary and undeceived consent and participation" (*On Liberty*, 1859). The "sphere of action" in which society has only an indirect interest is a matter of intense controversy. As Otis H. Stephens and John M. Schab II said in *American Constitutional Law* (1993),

> The debate over the constitutional right of privacy is ultimately a debate between two sharply divergent views of the law. In the libertarian view, the law exists to protect individuals from one another. In this view, morality is not in and of itself a legitimate basis for law. The classical conservative view, on the other hand, sees law and morality as inseparable and holds that the maintenance of societal morality is one of the essential functions of the legal system.

CONSTITUTIONAL BASIS OF PRIVACY RIGHTS

There are several provisions in the U.S. Bill of Rights that explicitly protect privacy. The Third Amendment prevents forced quartering of soldiers in people's homes. The Fourth Amendment protects against unreasonable searches and seizures. The Fifth Amendment protects the privacy of people's minds by prohibiting compulsory self-incrimination, and the First Amendment ensures freedom of conscience in political, religious, and associational matters. The due process clause of the Fifth Amendment protects substantive as well as physical liberty. Proponents of greater privacy rights have argued that the Ninth Amendment, which states that there are unspecified rights "retained by the people," provides additional justification for expanding constitutional rights of privacy.

Although Justice Louis D. Brandeis dubbed "the right to be let alone" "the most comprehensive of rights and the right most valued by civilized men," the first explicit recognition of a constitutional right of privacy by a majority of the Supreme Court took place in *Griswold v. Connecticut* (1965). An 1879 Connecticut law forbade the sale or possession of birth control devices and also made "assisting, abetting, or counselling" another in the use of such devices unlawful. Estelle Griswold, the director of Planned Parenthood in Connecticut, was arrested for violating this statute three days after Planned Parenthood opened a clinic in New Haven. Griswold was convicted and fined $100. After several intermediate appeals, the Supreme Court agreed to hear Griswold's case. After argument, the Connecticut law was declared unconstitutional.

Justice William O. Douglas, writing for the majority, found that "specific guarantees in the Bill of Rights have penumbras, formed by emanation from those guarantees that help give them life and substance. Various guarantees create zones of privacy..." In sum, Douglas's argument was that the First, Third, Fourth, Fifth, and Ninth Amendments, when taken together in the light of the Court's earlier decisions, created a new independent right of privacy that was violated by Connecticut when it attempted to deny people access to birth control devices. Although Douglas's opinion was carefully limited to "marital privacy," it was widely read to go beyond the rights of married couples, and when a similar issue arose a few years later in Massachusetts, the Court extended the *Griswold* holding to unmarried persons.

Eight years after *Griswold*, the Supreme Court enormously extended the right to privacy when it decided in *Roe v. Wade* (1973) that the right of privacy covers a pregnant woman's decision whether to have an abortion. In this case, the Court struck down a Texas statute that prohibited all abortions except for the purpose of saving the life of the mother. Justice Harry A. Blackmun's opinion recognized, however, that there is a state interest in the preservation of fetal life, and therefore the right to abortion is qualified— it is absolute only in the first trimester of pregnancy, the period in which the fetus is not yet viable. *Roe v. Wade* has occasioned immense political and juridical controversy since 1973. The American public has been sharply divided over the abortion issue, and judicial and legislative struggles still continue thirty years after the Court's decision. The right announced in *Roe v. Wade* has been slightly modified in several subsequent Supreme Court decisions, but despite several serious challenges, its fundamental principle still stands.

Roe v. Wade was the high-water mark of the constitutional right of privacy. The Supreme Court has not pressed it further and, indeed, held in *Bowers v. Hardwick* (1986) that there is no constitutional right to engage in homosexual sodomy. The Court explicitly reserved decision on whether there is a right, marital or otherwise, to engage in heterosexual sodomy.

Some public safety issues also raise privacy issues. Recreational drug use, motorcycle helmet and automobile seat belt laws, prostitution, suicide, and euthanasia are all issues that implicate privacy rights and with which courts and legislatures will increasingly have to deal.

Robert Jacobs

FURTHER READING

Allen, Anita L. *Why Privacy Isn't Everything: Feminist Reflections on Personal Accountability.* Lanham, Md.: Rowman & Littlefield, 2003.

Barendt, Eric M., ed. *Privacy.* Burlington, Vt.: Ashgate/Dartmouth, 2001.

Mill, John Stuart. *Utilitarianism, Liberty, and Representative Government.* New York: E. P. Dutton, 1951.

Stephens, Otis H., and John M. Scheb II. *American Constitutional Law.* Minneapolis: West, 1993.

SEE ALSO: Abortion; Bill of Rights, U.S.; Biometrics; Cell-phone etiquette; Civil rights and liberties; Computer databases; First Amendment; Gay rights; Information access; Invasion of privacy.

Private vs. public morality

DEFINITION: Distinction drawn between the moral codes governing private individuals in their personal and interpersonal relationships and the moral codes governing political and business leaders while acting in their official capacities

TYPE OF ETHICS: Beliefs and practices

SIGNIFICANCE: Because the decisions of public figures may significantly impact the lives of vast numbers of people, some theorists posit a fundamental dichotomy between public and private morality.

In his book *Moral Man and Immoral Society* (1932), Reinhold Niebuhr argued that there are sharp, major distinctions between the moral, ethical "rules" of behavior for individuals, on one hand, and for social groups, political and business leaders, and the state and nation, on the other hand. Actually, Niebuhr's thought on the issue was not original, for consideration of this ethical problem dates from antiquity.

The most famous philosopher to address the subject was Niccolò Machiavelli, who taught political rulers how to be "bad" ethically so that they could be "good" in their calling. Such leaders, then, may lie, break promises, use violence, engage in deceit, give and take bribes, and even commit murder if such actions are necessary to hold and augment power. Another who drew distinctions between personal morality and public morality was Martin Luther, who talked of an "earthly realm" and a "spiritual realm" as if they were absolutely different entities. Max Weber also argued that there was a sharp split between personal and public ethics, while pointing out that the public "person"—all leaders in politics, business, the military, and so on—may have to use dubious means to achieve "good."

Twentieth century political analysts such as George Kennan, Charles Frankel, and Arthur M. Schlesinger, Jr., have argued that realpolitik is the only thing that counts in government and in diplomacy. Frankel perhaps spelled it out best. He held that the moral rules of individuals in their personal lives are definitely not the rules that should guide people in performing complex social, political, or economic roles.

Interestingly, J. Fred Buzhardt, legal counsel to the morally condemned former president Richard Nixon, who resigned his office in disgrace, once asked whom the members of society would prefer as a leader—did they want a competent "scoundrel" or an "honest boob"? In this view, the picture of private versus public morality is darkly painted. Is it necessary to choose between ethically upright "boobs" and dishonest, lying, cheating criminals and near-criminals? The implication of Buzhardt's question is, of course, that the ethical, honest, sincere person is too naïve to assume a leadership role in politics, business, education, and so on. Instead, there is room in the elite leadership class only for liars and thieves.

Machiavelli and Buzhardt, then, endorse unethical public behavior as the norm and ethical behavior as bizarre. Such thinkers are themselves taking an immoral position by clinging to views that, over time, have caused much harm. Therein lies the problem. Public morality has been defined by those who speak for immorality, some of whom would tolerate all corruption and abuse if such practices were to lead to success. Actually, the later scandals in American "public" life have demonstrated that the country does not need competent scoundrels but should return to honesty, lest American civilization experience a permanent decline.

Consider a few facts. During the Vietnam War, four different presidents at some point lied to the public, as did some of their generals. Had the truth been told, might America have avoided that long, costly, and lethal imbroglio? In the Watergate scandal of the 1970's, lawyers, onetime Central Intelligence Agency operatives, and their minions committed such crimes as breaking and entering, burglary, and illegally "bugging" phones—all this for political and economic gain. When the scandal became public, lies abounded in such great number that many people think that the public may never know the exact extent of the wrongdoing.

During the late 1980's and 1990's, more scandals abounded. Corporate executives of the Chrysler Automobile Company ordered mechanics to "roll back" speedometers so that used cars could be sold as new cars. Executives of many savings and loan associations and commercial banks looted their own depositors, their own "businesses," and forced the future's taxpayers to pick up the tab. Many congresspersons also showed their true character when they corruptly mismanaged their post office, restaurant, and bank. Former presidents Ronald Reagan and George Bush were implicated in the "Irangate" arms-for-hostages controversy and a possible cover-up. A person need only read a big-city newspaper regularly to find example after example of corruption and immorality in politics, business, and other public fields.

There are those who believe that public leaders should be held morally accountable for their actions, just as individuals are held accountable in private life. Perhaps public leaders should examine their lives and ask such questions as: Have I lied, cheated, stolen, broken promises, deceived, or taken bribes today?

James Smallwood

FURTHER READING

Cahn, Edmond. *The Moral Decision: Right and Wrong in the Light of American Law.* Bloomington: Indiana University Press, 1955.

Dobel, J. Patrick. *Public Integrity.* Baltimore: Johns Hopkins University Press, 1999.

Durkheim, Émile. *Professional Ethics and Civic Morals.* Translated by Cornelia Brookfield. Preface by Bryan S. Turner. New York: Routledge, 1992.

Fleishman, Joel L., and Bruce L. Payne. *Ethical Dilemmas and the Education of Policymakers.* Hastings-on-Hudson, N.Y.: Hastings Center, Institute of Society, Ethics, and the Life Sciences, 1980.

Geuss, Raymond. *Public Goods, Private Goods.* Princeton, N.J.: Princeton University Press, 2001.

Halsey, Margaret. *The Pseudo-ethic: A Speculation on American Politics and Morals.* New York: Simon & Schuster, 1963.

Holmes, Samuel J. *Life and Morals.* New York: Macmillan, 1948.

Joad, C. E. M. *Guide to the Philosophy of Morals and Politics.* New York: Random House, 1937.

Sellers, James. *Public Ethics: American Morals and Manners.* New York: Harper & Row, 1970.

Webber, Robert E. *The Moral Majority: Right or Wrong?* Westchester, Ill.: Cornerstone Books, 1981.

SEE ALSO: Clinton, Bill; Corporate scandal; Dirty hands; Luther, Martin; Morality; Niebuhr, Reinhold; Realpolitik; Watergate scandal.

Pro-choice movement

DEFINITION: Coalition of activists working to keep abortion legal, unrestricted, and available to all women

TYPE OF ETHICS: Sex and gender issues

SIGNIFICANCE: The pro-choice movement represents one side in perhaps the most heated moral debate of the late twentieth and early twenty-first centuries. Although associated with feminists and the political left, neither of those two groups is undivided on the issue of abortion.

Throughout history, a major means by which men have controlled women and restricted their rights is the control of human reproduction. Abortion rights have become a central concern of the women's rights movement. The movement argues that women must have total control over their bodies, including their reproductive processes, if they are to be able to function as free, equal members of society.

HISTORY

Abortion has been practiced throughout history and across cultures. Formulas for abortion appear in Chinese medical texts dating from 3000 B.C.E. and in Islamic texts in the Middle Ages. Regular references to abortion appear in Greek and Roman texts and early Christian literature. Regardless of societal tolerance or prohibition, women have resorted to abortion to terminate unwanted pregnancies even though many of the techniques used have threatened their lives and health.

The modern pro-choice movement has its roots in the women's rights movements of the early twentieth century in the United States and Europe. Responding to legal prohibitions against disseminating information about birth control, women such as Margaret Sanger incorporated demands for reproductive rights into the movement. Building on this base, the feminist movement in the United States during the 1960's established a pro-choice coalition to support abortion rights. Included were demands that the legality of abortion be restored (abortion had been legal in the United States until the latter half of the nineteenth century).

In 1973, with the Supreme Court decision *Roe v. Wade,* prohibitions against abortion during the first trimester of pregnancy were ruled unconstitutional and only limited restrictions were permitted during the second trimester of the pregnancy. In the ruling, a woman's "right to privacy" in such matters was upheld as having greater legal standing than fetal rights or the right of states to intervene in the reproductive life of women. The Court's decision generated an immediate protest and the establishment of a coalition of religious groups that designated themselves as the "pro-life movement." This movement has worked to limit and even abolish the legal right to abortion. Such limitations have included the removal of federal funding for abortions, the establishment of required waiting periods before abortions can be performed, and parental and paternal notification and/or consent. A number of such restrictions were upheld by the Court during the 1980's and early 1990's.

These new restrictions have revitalized the pro-choice movement and expanded the coalition to include a number of secular and religious groups. The term "pro-choice" was consciously employed during this period to affirm the belief in the primacy of women's right to choose. While persons in this coali-

Thousands of pro-choice advocates stage a rally in Hollywood, Florida, as part of a campaign to ease the state's abortion restrictions in 1989. (AP/Wide World Photos)

tion have a wide range of viewpoints pertaining to the morality of abortion, they are united by their belief that abortion should and must remain legal. By the 1980's, the movement had become more proactive, stating that a pro-choice environment requires guaranteed medical care for expectant mothers and young children, guaranteed minimum adequate income that assures proper nutrition and housing for children, job-security guarantees for pregnant women, and federally mandated maternity leaves. Only such rights, it is argued, allow women to exercise free choice in response to pregnancy.

ETHICAL ARGUMENTS

Because of the disparity of beliefs of those who constitute the pro-choice movement, there are no moral arguments that are universally accepted. The most prominent and widely used arguments follow.

Drawing on the concept of "developmentalism," fetal life is recognized as human life and as having value. Value accrues, however, as humans develop. A woman, as a fully developed person living in a network of relationships in which she is valued, has rights that take precedence over fetal rights in situations of conflict. Since many pregnancies occur without the consent of the woman involved (rape, incest, contraceptive failure, ignorance), the fetus has no more right to use the woman's body than the state or a stranger has a right to use her organs, without consent, for transplant purposes.

Since women are the ones primarily affected by pregnancy and childbirth, they legitimately retain the right to decide whether to terminate a pregnancy. Only legal access to safe abortions assures women control of their own lives.

Confronted with unwanted pregnancies, many women will resort to abortion whether legal or not. (Between 250,000 and 1,000,000 illegal abortions were performed annually in the United States in the years prior to its legalization.) Illegal abortions are often unsafe, leading to the death or sterility of the mother. Since abortion cannot be stopped, it should be legal, medically safe, and easily accessible.

Failure to provide federal funding for low-income women is discriminatory and leads to unwanted births, further impoverishment, and in some cases life-threatening attempts at self-induced abortion. Since some pregnancies result in the development of severely defective fetuses, the mother, as the party most affected by the birth of such a child, should have the right to decide whether such a pregnancy should be continued.

In an overpopulated world suffering from resource depletion and environmental pollution, women should have the right to use abortion as a means of population control when they view it as a morally preferable choice.

Charles L. Kammer III

FURTHER READING

Boston Women's Health Book Collective. *The New Our Bodies, Ourselves: A Book by and for Women.* Rev. ed. New York: Simon & Schuster, 1992.

Feinberg, Joel, and Suan Dwyer, eds. *The Problem of Abortion.* 3d ed. Belmont, Calif.: Wadsworth, 1997.

Graber, Mark A. *Rethinking Abortion: Equal Choice, the Constitution, and Reproductive Politics.* Princeton, N.J.: Princeton University Press, 1999.

Harrison, Beverly Wildung. *Our Right to Choose: Toward a New Ethic of Abortion.* Boston: Beacon Press, 1983.

Petchesky, Rosalind Pollack. *Abortion and Women's Choice: The State, Sexuality, and Reproductive Freedom.* Rev. ed. Boston: Northeastern University Press, 1990.

Shrage, Laurie. *Abortion and Social Responsibility: Depolarizing the Debate.* New York: Oxford University Press, 2003.

Tribe, Laurence H. *Abortion: The Clash of Absolutes.* New York: W. W. Norton, 1992.

Williams, Mary E., ed. *Abortion: Opposing Viewpoints.* San Diego, Calif.: Greenhaven Press, 2002.

SEE ALSO: Abortion; Feminist ethics; Life and death; Pro-life movement; Right to life; *Roe v. Wade*; Sexism; Women's ethics; Women's liberation movement.

Product safety and liability

DEFINITION: Issues relating to questions of who is liable for products that cause harm

TYPE OF ETHICS: Business and labor ethics

SIGNIFICANCE: Two related ethics questions are integrally connected to product safety and liability issues: determination of who is responsible, *prior* to a product's purchase, for ensuring that the product is appropriately safe, and determination of who is responsible, *after* the product is purchased, if someone is injured by it.

Safety is one value among many in transactions between buyers and sellers. Products vary in their degree of riskiness—from cotton balls to butter knives to parachutes—and customers vary in the importance they attach to safety. Automobiles provide an apt example. How attractive a car is to a customer depends upon its price, style, dependability, fuel efficiency, comfort, capacity, speed, power, maker's service record, and safety features. A young man buying his first car is likely to make speed and style higher priorities, while the parents of a young child who are struggling to make ends meet are more likely to make safety and fuel efficiency their highest priorities.

Two competing ethical models of how to achieve appropriate amounts of safety have been debated. One model emphasizes that both the seller of a product and the product's buyer are self-responsible agents who negotiate appropriate levels of safety in a free market. The other model calls for government regulation of safety on the grounds that sellers do not have enough sufficient incentives to provide appropriate levels of safety, and that buyers often do not have the knowledge or power to negotiate for safety.

THE FREE MARKET MODEL

The free market model sees safety as a value no different in principle than any other value that is produced and consumed. Just as prices, styles, and quality of customer service vary among products and are negotiable between buyers and sellers, optimal amounts of safety are variable and negotiable. Both sellers and buyers are self-responsible agents with their own goals, and both have responsibilities with respect to safety.

The seller's responsibility (*caveat vendor*, let the seller beware) is to manufacture a product within the range of professional standards of competence, to research reasonably foreseeable risks associated with using the product, and, in the case of risks that might not be obvious to consumers, to inform potential buyers of the risks.

The buyer's responsibility (*caveat emptor*) is to become aware of the risks associated with using the product—either by doing firsthand research or by seeking expert advice, such as one might get from physicians or from sources such as *Consumer Reports* magazine. Buyers must then determine their own risk tolerance and learn how to use the products they purchase properly.

Ultimately, sellers and buyers seek each other out and negotiate transactions that are mutually satisfactory, including the question of how safe the products are. On this free market model, appropriate amounts of safety are fixed but vary from product to product and emerge as a result of supply and demand. Different producers emphasize the safety of their products to different degrees and attract to varying degrees customers who are interested in the amount of safety they are providing. The producers' profit motive should lead them to give to consumers the amounts of safety that satisfy them. Some cars, for example, are produced out of heavier materials and have additional safety features, while others are lighter and have extra speed or style features. How many of each kind of car are sold depends on how many customers are interested in their different features. Safety is thus a market value like any other, and the optimal levels of safety are set by supply and demand.

THE GOVERNMENT-REGULATION MODEL

The free market model assumes that customers are knowledgeable about both the relative safety of given products and their own risk tolerances, or that they can become knowledgeable by research. It also assumes that producers are responsive to consumer demands for safety. By contrast, the government-regulation model is skeptical of both assumptions, so it concludes that safety should be provided primarily via government regulation rather than through free market forces.

Producers have a profit motive, which leads some to cut corners on safety. Since safety can be costly, an obvious way to cut costs is to avoid spending money on either research or additional safety features. Correspondingly, consumers are often unaware of risks involved in using many products, particularly new or complex products, and are consequently often unwilling to pay the extra costs associated with safer products. Therefore, the government-regulation model assumes that many consumers will end up injured or worse because of an unregulated market. Therefore, to protect consumers from both themselves and producers, an informed third party with the power to regulate safety is needed. The government, therefore, should act paternalistically to shield consumers from their own lack of knowledge and poor judgment, and it should act protectively to shield consumers from careless, profit-seeking producers.

According to the government-regulation model, government experts should research products and decide uniform safety standards. The government should craft regulations and communicate them to producers. The producers should be given incentives to produce the specified amounts of safety—the incentives being the avoidance of fines, losing their licenses, or going to prison. Consumers can then purchase products confident in the knowledge that the government has made sure that their production meets adequate safety standards.

The two models of safety differ over two key ethical issues. Both agree that safety is a value but disagree over whether safety is a value that varies from consumer to consumer or is a uniform value that all products in a given category should possess equally. Both sides also agree that assigning responsibility for safety is crucial—but disagree over whether producers and consumers can be self-responsible for safety or whether government regulators can best handle that responsibility.

LIABILITY

During the 1960's, American liability law began shifting from its long-standing emphasis upon a standard of individual negligence to an emphasis upon strict liability. Common law traditionally analyzed li-

Two Relevant Legal Cases

Two key cases demonstrate the trend toward strict liability in modern courts. In 1992, a New Mexico jury awarded Stella Liebeck $2.7 million in punitive damages and $200,000 in actual damages because she was scalded by a cup of McDonald's coffee that she spilled while riding in a car. The determining factor for McDonald's guilt was the harm done to Liebeck. The large amounts were awarded to perform the two functions of strict liability. First, the $200,000 was awarded to cover Liebeck's medical costs (social insurance). Second, the judgment of $2.7 million was used to force McDonald's to lower the temperature of the coffee it served (safety incentive).

The 1980 case of *Sindell v. Abbott Laboratories* also indicates the newer concepts in strict liability. Judith Sindell brought a class action lawsuit on behalf of the daughters of women who alleged that diethylstilbestrol (DES), a drug approved by the Food and Drug Administration for pregnant women, caused their vaginal cancer. The class action lawsuit was brought against eleven DES manufacturers because the injured women could not isolate which company provided the actual drug to their mothers. Under the strict liability model, the women were not required to prove that DES was the definitive cause of their vaginal cancer—only that they were harmed. The collective liability standard held the DES manufacturers to be responsible even though some women may have never ingested their product.

ability in terms of individual responsibility. Plaintiffs were responsible to show that acts of negligence by identifiable defendants caused their injuries. Negligence is ignoring or hiding a reasonably foreseeable harm to a person. The argument for negligence-based liability relies on the concept of rational self-responsibility. Manufacturers sell goods for profit, and customers purchase them for consumption. Since no product can be completely risk-free, traditional liability requires that both sellers and buyers be responsible.

Manufacturers have two basic responsibilities to consumers. They must identify and address foresee-

able risks in their products and must inform consumers of the risks. Under traditional liability, consumers have three responsibilities to protect themselves from injury. First, they must educate themselves about the products they buy and the companies that make them. Second, they must accept the foreseeable risks associated with the products. When a company issues directions indicating proper use, the consumers' third responsibility is to use the products properly.

If someone is harmed in using a product, determining liability requires identifying who, if anyone, was negligent in upholding his or her responsibilities. However, even when producers and consumers act responsibly, accidents may still happen. If a manufacturing company provides proper warnings of a product's risks, and the consumer accepts those risks, or if the accident that occurs is not foreseeable, then the costs fall to the consumer. Part of being an ethically responsible consumer is to recognize that accidents may happen and to protect oneself through insurance. Under the negligence standard, however, a producer is liable only if the company has been negligent.

STRICT LIABILITY

Although the negligence standard of liability has a long history of solving disputes between parties, proponents of strict liability argue that that standard does not adequately address social concerns, such as large liability claims and complex products. To address these concerns, strict liability eliminates the requirement of having an identifiable negligent party as the cause of the harm. Negligence by the producer or consumer is not necessary for legal liability. Strict liability is a harm-only concept. Additionally, strict liability collectivizes the concepts of harm and liability, in contrast to the negligence standard's individual focus. Strict liability has created two new concepts in litigation, the class action lawsuit and collective liability. A group of people who have suffered the same harm can bring about a single lawsuit in which the question of plaintiff responsibility is irrelevant. Collective liability occurs when more than one producer contributes to the manufacture of the same harm-causing product. If the product cannot be isolated to one company, then all the producers may be held liable.

Strict liability's use of class action lawsuits and collective liability is intended to solve the perceived gaps left by traditional negligence liability. From the negligence-standard perspective, strict liability may seem unfair to a producer who has not been negligent; however, proponents of strict liability argue that it provides two main social benefits. First, strict liability gives manufacturers a greater incentive to make the safest possible products. If a manufacturer is liable for any of its products that causes harm, then rational economic thought dictates that the manufacturer should market only extremely safe products. Second, strict liability functions as a social insurance policy. Some people who are harmed have no way to pay their medical costs under traditional liability. If, however, companies are legally required to accept the responsibility for harm done to people, then the medical and other costs will be transferred from the victim to the manufacturers of the product. Manufacturer will then simply add liability as a cost of production. In wealthy nations such as the United States it may be easier to make everyone share the cost of liability rather than leaving it as an individual responsibility.

ETHICAL CONTROVERSIES

Proponents of traditional liability find two problems with strict liability. The first problem is with the safety incentive. Under strict liability, companies should produce safer products; however, their incentive to innovate will decline. Since innovative products involve unknown risks, manufacturers will rationally decide in some cases that the costs of innovation combined with unknowable liability exposure is not compatible with the profit motive.

The second criticism of strict liability is a result of ethical differences. Traditional liability holds self-responsibility as its ethical ideal, while strict liability demands sacrifices of some for the sake of others. Therefore, the negligence view believes strict liability is unjust to manufacturers and will lessen consumers' self-responsibility; advocates of strict liability, by contrast, believe that the negligence model is unfair to individuals who cannot pay for their medical costs.

Stephen R. C. Hicks
Todd M. Krist

FURTHER READING

Cane, Peter. *The Anatomy of Tort Law.* Oxford, England: Hart, 1997. Analysis of tort law as an ethical system.

Goldberg, Richard. *Causation and Risk in the Law of Torts: Scientific Evidence and Medicinal Product Liability.* Oxford, England: Hart, 1999. Surveys the legal and scientific issues relating to proof of causation in cases of alleged drug-induced injury.

Huber, Peter W. *Liability: The Legal Revolution and Its Consequences.* New York: Basic, 1990. Survey of the transformation of tort law since the 1960's.

Owen, David G., et al. *Products Liability and Safety.* New York: Foundation Press, 1998. Contains cases and other materials.

Vandall, Frank J. *Strict Liability: Legal and Economic Analysis.* Westport, Conn.: Greenwood Press, 1989. Discusses the legal and economic consequences arising from the expansion of strict liability.

SEE ALSO: Consumerism; Corporate responsibility; Employee safety and treatment; Genetically modified foods; Industrial research; Marketing; Nader, Ralph; Public interest; Sales ethics; Tobacco industry; Warranties and guarantees.

Professional athlete incomes

DEFINITION: Money that professional athletes make from salaries, product endorsements, appearance fees, and other sources

TYPE OF ETHICS: Business and labor ethics

SIGNIFICANCE: The dramatic rise in the earning power of professional athletes that began during the closing decades of the twentieth century raised numerous ethical questions about income distribution and the role of athletes in society.

Until the late twentieth century, financial compensation for professional athletes typically varied according to each individual athlete's level of competition, experience, and achievement. Athletes at lower levels of professional competition often earned wages that were below subsistence levels. Those at higher competitive levels typically earned comfortable salaries, while a select few were paid handsomely but not out of proportion to the top earners of other professions. In 1930, for example, baseball star Babe Ruth earned an annual salary of $80,000—approximately equivalent

Top-Earning American Athletes in 2004

Rank	Athlete	Sport	Salary	Other	Total
1	Tiger Woods	golf	$6,673,413	$70,000,000	$76,673,413
2	Shaquille O'Neal	basketball	$26,517,858	$14,000,000	$40,517,858
3	LeBron James	basketball	$4,018,920	$35,000,000	$39,018,920
4	Peyton Manning	football	$26,900,000	$9,500,000	$36,400,000
5	Kevin Garnett	basketball	$29,000,000	$7,000,000	$36,000,000
6	Oscar De La Hoya	boxing	$30,000,000	$2,000,000	$32,000,000
7	Andre Agassi	tennis	$2,530,929	$24,500,000	$27,030,929
8	Kobe Bryant	basketball	$13,498,000	$12,000,000	$25,498,000
9	Derek Jeter	baseball	$19,000,000	$6,000,000	$25,000,000
10	Grant Hill	basketball	$13,279,250	$11,000,000	$24,279,250

Source: Sports Illustrated/SI.com, May 14, 2004. Totals reflect expected total income for calendar 2004. "Salary" column includes salaries, bonuses, and winnings; "Other" column includes money from commercial endorsements, appearance fees, and other sports-related sources

to a $800,000 salary in 2003 dollars. At the same time, the average salary of Major League Baseball players was approximately $6,000, or $60,000 in 2003 dollars. Athletes competing in sports emphasizing individual excellence sometimes earned much more. In 1927, for example, heavyweight boxing champion Gene Tunney earned $990,000—equal to almost $10 million dollars in 2003—for a single boxing match against former champion Jack Dempsey. However, most rank-and-file competitors of the past earned salaries commensurate with national averages for skilled and professional workers.

After World War II, as the advent of mass media made professional athletics increasingly popular and profitable, many professional athletes began to resent team owners and event promoters who were reaping ever higher profits while restricting increases in athlete compensation. In 1966 Major League Baseball players organized the first successful professional athletes' union and, after a series of contentious court cases, won the right to negotiate with other teams when their contracts expired. Andy Messersmith and Dave McNally exercised this option in 1975 and became the first "free agents" in professional sports.

Other professional sports soon followed suit by enacting their own systems of free agency, resulting in dramatic increases in player salaries. By the end of the twentieth century, the *minimum* salary for rookie Major League Baseball players was $200,000, and the highest-paid baseball player, Alex Rodriguez, was earning approximately $25 million per year. In addition to their salaries as players, many top athletes were receiving additional money from product endorsement contracts that often paid them millions of dollars per year.

IMPACT ON SPORTS

Although most observers agree that higher compensation for athletes has exerted a profound influence upon professional sports, disagreements exist as to whether the aggregate impact has been positive or negative. Supporters maintain that higher earnings have provided athletes with increased motivation to improve their performances, resulting in more intense competition among athletes and higher overall standards of athletic excellence. Moreover, since professional athletes no longer have to work during their off-season months to supplement their incomes as they did in the past, they have more time and energy for training.

Some critics argue, however, that high salaries and lucrative endorsements negatively affect performance by compromising team loyalty, fostering jealousy and friction among team players, and diminishing the desire of individual athletes to achieve their full potentials. In order to enhance their "market value," team-sport athletes are often encouraged to prioritize individual achievement over team success. Thus, critics argue, high salaries and endorsements serve either to distract and spoil athletes or to saddle them with unrealistic expectations.

Defenders of rising compensation rates for professional athlete pay often cite past and present inequalities between athlete pay and the profits of their employers or sponsors. This argument is rooted in the assertion that team owners, event promoters, and corporate sponsors have profited handsomely from the growth of the professional sports industry, and that athletes—without whom the industry would not exist—are ethically justified in their efforts to share in the financial success of their sports.

SOCIETAL IMPLICATIONS

The ethical implications of higher athlete pay upon society have also been the subject of contentious debate. Many argue that paying athletes large amounts of money damages both sport and society by fostering gross inequalities in income, and that salaries should thus be limited through regulation. Proponents of free market capitalism insist that owners, promoters, and sponsors are ethically justified in compensating athletes according to freely conducted negotiations and the demands of the market, and that athletes reserve the right as contract employees to sell their services to the highest bidders. Proponents

With tournament winnings and endorsement income totalling more than seventy million dollars a year, golfer Tiger Woods ranked as the world's highest-paid athlete in 2004. (AP/Wide World Photos)

Average Player Salaries in Major League Sports in 2004

League	Total teams	Total players	Average salaries	Total salaries
Major League Baseball	30	850	$2,490,000	$2,116,500,000
National Basketball Association	29	375	4,900,000	1,837,500,000
National Football League	32	1,200	1,260,000	1,512,000,000
National Hockey League	30	725	1,700,000	1,232,500,000
			total payrolls	$6,698,500,000
	121	3,150	*player average*	$2,126,508

Source: Average salary figures from Associated Press, April 8, 2004. Total player numbers are estimated from average active-player rosters as of early 2004, and total salary figures are extrapolated from these estimates.

1197

of regulation argue that larger payrolls are unethical because they give sports teams in large markets—such as New York and Los Angeles—unfair advantages over those in small markets, and result in increased costs that are routinely passed along to fans in the form of much higher prices for tickets, concessions, souvenirs, and parking.

Some people view the disproportionately high earnings of top professional athletes as an example of growing disparities between rich and poor people in developed societies. Others argue that it is inequitable, and therefore unethical, to pay top athletes amounts totaling hundreds of times the salaries of persons in such essential occupations as education, health care, public safety, and social work.

EFFECTS ON YOUTH

Many critics also assert that higher athlete pay also damages society by setting a negative and unrealistic example for youth that is inherently unethical. The conspicuous presence of multimillionaire athletes, they argue, encourages youth to value athletic achievement over educational accomplishment, character, and citizenship. Moreover, the lure of immense wealth often encourages young people, especially those from disadvantaged backgrounds, to make sports a higher priority than education or personal growth in the often-unrealistic belief that they will themselves eventually succeed in professional sports. This assertion is supported by numerous examples of athletes who have interrupted their educations to "turn pro."

Proponents of the free market can cite numerous examples of athletes who emerged from modest backgrounds to become rich and famous athletes. By contrast, only a tiny minority of athletes are ever afforded the opportunity to compete professionally, and fewer still ever achieve the level of success required to command large earnings. Therefore, those who are persuaded single-mindedly to pursue careers in professional sports and do not succeed often lack the skills necessary to become healthy, productive members of society.

Michael H. Burchett

FURTHER READING

Abrams, Roger I. *The Money Pitch: Baseball Free Agency and Salary Arbitration*. Philadelphia: Temple University Press, 2000.

Gorman, Jerry, et al. *The Name of the Game: The Business of Sports*. Indianapolis, Ind.: John Wiley & Sons, 1994.

Meier, Klaus V., et al., eds. *Ethics in Sport*. Champaign, Ill.: Human Kinetics Publishers, 2001.

Simon, Robert L. *Fair Play: The Ethics of Sport*. Boulder, Colo.: Westview Press, 2003.

Staudohar, Paul. *Playing for Dollars: Labor Relations and the Sports Business*. Ithaca, N.Y.: Cornell University Press, 1996.

SEE ALSO: Betting on sports; Corporate compensation; Drug testing; Greed; Income distribution; Minimum-wage laws; Poverty and wealth; Role models; Taxes; Title IX.

Professional ethics

DEFINITION: Codes of conduct governing the performance of professional duties

TYPE OF ETHICS: Professional ethics

SIGNIFICANCE: Members of most professions are governed by ethical rules which may be formal or informal, codified or left unspoken. Such rules are designed to protect the public welfare and to encourage a high level of trust for the profession as a whole.

Professional ethics undertakes to examine the special ethical obligations and problems that people who work in professional occupations have because of their professional status. It seeks to reach normative conclusions about these; that is, it considers how professionals *ought* to behave in their professional work, not merely how they *do* conduct themselves. In order to accomplish this goal, it must consider the various professions in their historical, legal, and social contexts in society. Relative to differently organized societies, or relative to different eras in Western society, it may need to reach different conclusions concerning professional conduct.

Every legitimate occupation involves its own characteristic ethical obligations. Thus, firemen have a special obligation to rescue people from burning buildings even when it is dangerous for them to do so, and farmers have a special obligation to see that the foodstuffs that they produce are safe to consume. All such special obligations presumably could be discussed in the field of occupational ethics.

In order for professional ethics to be a distinctive field in its own right, it needs to differ from occupational ethics. The special ethical obligations of professionals need to be seen as differing in their source and character from those of nonprofessional workers. This can come about only if professional ethics is based on a conception of the professions that succeeds in demarcating them ethically from other occupations.

The term "profession" is used in a variety of ways in the English language, and most of these do not embody conceptions that are suitable for grounding professional ethics as a field in its own right. To forestall confusion that may generate doubt about the legitimacy of professional ethics, it will be useful to review several of these widespread uses before focusing on a more appropriate one.

USES OF THE TERM "PROFESSION"

When people ask "What is your profession?" this is often merely a polite way of asking one's occupation. In this usage, the terms "profession" and "occupation" are synonyms. Another frequent use, which is familiar from sports, contrasts professional with amateur standing: To be a professional in an activity is to make that activity one's principal career, from which one expects to derive income. In another sense, professional work is work that is done skillfully. "They do a professional job," people say of workers who perform knowledgeably and well.

The term "profession" generally carries a favorable connotation, and sometimes it is used merely to express the speaker's approval of an occupation and the desire that it be accorded high status. Thus, when someone says "Realtors are professionals!" often no factual information is involved, and the speaker is merely voicing approval of the occupation and seeking to enhance its standing in the minds of hearers.

In sociology, professions often have been discussed, and many descriptive criteria of professionalism have been put forward. These include the following: the work is white-collar, above-average education is required, above-average pay is received, there is an explicit code of ethics to which those in the occupation subscribe, entry is limited by licensing procedures, those in the occupation have an association that is dedicated to maintaining standards, the

service provided is indispensable for the public good, those in the occupation work as independent practitioners, and income does not depend much on the deployment of capital. Typically, a sociologist studying professionalism establishes a particular list of such factors and then stipulates that an occupation is to count as a profession only if it accords with at least several factors on that list.

None of these widespread ways of understanding the term "profession" is satisfactory as a basis for normative professional ethics, because each of these definitions picks out as professions some set of occupations that, from the standpoint of normative ethics, do not differ significantly from the occupations it classifies as nonprofessions. If professional ethics is to be viewed as a field in its own right, it is necessary to employ a conception of what professions are that is more normatively oriented than are any of the conceptions noted above.

A HISTORICALLY BASED CONCEPTION

How did certain occupations first come to be called professions? Considering the history of the term may lead toward a conception that is suitable for the purposes of professional ethics.

The Latin term *professionem* originally meant the making of a public declaration. In medieval Latin, it came to mean the taking of religious vows. The English word "profession" comes directly from the Latin, and until the sixteenth century it too meant only the public taking of religious vows. After that, however, it came to mean an occupation in which learned knowledge is applied to the affairs of others, especially medicine, law, divinity, and university teaching.

The linkage between oath taking and distinctively professional occupations arose because of the procedures of the medieval universities. In them, students prepared for one of four careers; they could become physicians, lawyers, clerics, or university teachers. At various stages in the course of study, and especially at its conclusion, the student was required publicly to take religious oaths. These oaths affirmed general loyalty to the doctrines of the Church and to the discipline of the university, and specific commitment to the special ethical standards of the learned occupation being entered into. Such oaths, devised by persons who already belonged to the occupations in question, carried with them the threat of divine retribution should they be violated; thus, they served as fairly effective means for constraining new entrants to respect the ideals of service that had been established for these occupations.

Because they had taken these oaths, members of these four occupations came to have special ethical obligations that were different in origin and nature from those incurred in other occupations.

APPLYING THE CONCEPTION TO MODERN LIFE

Downplaying its religious aspect, this conception of professions nowadays can be regarded as postulating an understanding between society and those in a profession, a bargain from which both sides benefit. This understanding may be spelled out explicitly, at least in part, but often in modern times it is left largely unstated and is taken for granted. Society accords certain valuable advantages to the members of the occupation, and they in return pledge themselves to promote certain goals that have value to society.

The chief benefit that society grants to members of the occupation is the right to a considerable measure of control over their own activities. This includes the right of those in the occupation to define for themselves the standards of performance that should be obeyed in it and their right to organize their own disciplinary procedures for enforcing those standards. They may also be granted the right to restrict entry into the occupation by imposing licensing requirements (this may well have the effect of reducing competition and keeping fees high). It will be especially appropriate for society to grant these privileges to the members of occupations that are highly technical and require extensive knowledge. Outsiders will be unable to make reliable judgments about how those in such occupations ought to conduct themselves; therefore, the setting of standards and the enforcement of discipline may best be left to the specialists within.

In return for granting these privileges, society receives from the members of the occupation higher-quality service and the curbing of certain types of self-interested exploitation of their expertise by those in the occupation. The ethical requirements that the profession imposes upon itself fall under three headings: responsibilities toward clients (or patients), responsibilities toward the profession itself, and responsibilities toward society. Usually, the interests of the client will be accorded high priority, and the pro-

fessional's technical skills will be viewed as the client's to command, for any reasonable purpose. Responsibilities toward the profession itself will aim at enhancing the excellence of the profession's services and maintaining its standing in the eyes of the public. The responsibilities to society, though not negligible, will usually be accorded a distinctly lower priority.

If all goes well, both society and those in the profession will benefit from such a bargain. The ethical status of professionals will thereby become differentiated from that of nonprofessionals, whose conduct is not governed by bargains of this type.

In U.S. society, medicine and law are traditionally the paradigmatic examples of professions in this sense. Other occupations deserve to be classified as professions if they strongly resemble medicine and law in having this type of ethical structure. Whether an occupation counts as a profession will not be a black-or-white matter, however, but will be a question of degree.

FREE ENTERPRISE VS. COMMUNISM

This contrast between the ethics of professionals and those of nonprofessionals makes sense within a society that has an individualistic ideology such as the free enterprise system, which prevails in the economic life of the United States. Such an ideology makes it ethically permissible for workers to aim at promoting their own individual advantage, when they are in occupations which have not entered into any professional-type bargain with society. Such nonprofessional workers are supposed to be ethically bound by the law and by the requirements of minimal decency (which prohibit lies, fraud, murder, assault, and the like). In addition, they are ethically bound by any explicit promises they have made to others; for example when an employee contracts to obey an employer's orders in doing work of certain kinds. Aside from these limitations, however, nonprofessional workers in an individualistic society are ethically free to act as they please, seeking their own advantage. (Society permits them this ethical latitude because doing so encourages them to work harder and more efficiently, which ultimately benefits society.) There arises a contrast between their ethical situation and that of professionals, whose conduct is constrained by self-imposed ethical commitments of the kind already mentioned, which are quite unlike employment contracts.

In a communistic society, this difference between professionals and nonprofessionals would not exist. Under communism, the ideology would be that every worker, whether physician or coal miner, always should be striving above all to promote the well-being of society. Consequently, there would be no special group of professional occupations whose ethics would contrast significantly with the ethics of other occupations.

MEDICINE AS A PROFESSION

In Western society, medicine has had a professional character since ancient Greek times, when physicians took the Hippocratic oath, pledging to protect their art and to use their medical skill only for the promotion of health. Although medicine has changed enormously over the years, modern physicians are rightly expected to retain some of the Hippocratic spirit of dedication to healing, righteousness, and service. For example, in an emergency, even a physician who is off duty is ethically bound to provide medical aid to injured persons who would not otherwise be treated (this is not the case with nonprofessional workers, such as farmers or fire fighters, who have no general obligation to provide services that have not been contracted).

Some writers who discuss medical ethics include in it wide-ranging public policy questions concerning how best to organize the delivery of health care in society. This is potentially misleading, in that it may suggest that defects in the system of health-care delivery exist only because physicians are not fully discharging their ethical responsibilities. It should not be supposed that increasing the ethical dedication of physicians will be the only, or even the best, way to perfect the structure of a health-care system. To deal with its problems, legislators must make wise public policy decisions.

A particularly controversial topic in medical ethics is whether it is permissible for physicians to end the lives of terminally ill patients who request it or to assist them in committing suicide. On one hand, the Hippocratic tradition commits the physician to using medical skill only to heal and to preserve life; on the other hand, suffering patients sometimes desire to die, and some compassionate physicians think that it would be proper to provide such service. Prevailing opinion within the American Medical Association has opposed the latter view as setting too dangerous a precedent, and U.S. law has forbidden such action by physicians. In the Netherlands, however, euthanasia has been legally accepted and has been widely practiced.

LAW AS A PROFESSION

In the United States, law as a profession has been dominated by the American Bar Association (ABA). Its Canons of Professional Conduct serve as an explicit statement of the way in which U.S. lawyers conceive of their professional responsibilities. According to this statement, the lawyer is "an officer of the court." This phrase expresses the idea that the lawyer is a part of the justice system and therefore has an obligation to uphold that system and to promote its efficient functioning.

The ABA views the lawyer as having a primary responsibility to the client, whose prerogative it is to decide what legal action is to be undertaken. The lawyer's task is to provide accurate legal information and then to carry out the client's wishes. It is the lawyer's duty to keep strictly confidential what the client has revealed in the course of consultation, and the lawyer cannot legally be forced to divulge such information.

One vexing issue in legal ethics is how far the lawyer may go in promoting the client's cause by means that seem shady yet that are not illegal. For example, in a criminal defense, may the lawyer permit the client to give testimony that the lawyer has good reason to believe is untruthful? As an officer of the court, the lawyer ought not to countenance perjury, yet the lawyer also has an obligation to advance the client's case, and the client's questionable testimony may do this. In such cases, two responsibilities clash, and lawyers differ among themselves about how far to go.

BUSINESS AS A PROFESSION

As education in business management has advanced, the field has become more and more complex and technical. Intricate mathematical analyses and strategies have become available to assist and guide the business executive. This development has encouraged some writers to say that business has now become "professionalized."

Business ethics, however, remains different from professional ethics. Under the free enterprise system as it exists in the United States, it is ethically permissible for businesspersons to make pursuit of their own advantage their primary goal, as long as they do

1201

not break the law or violate minimal standards of decency. Professionals, however, have additional ethical obligations that further limit their pursuit of self-interest; they ought not to be as single-minded in their profit-seeking as businesspersons may be.

OTHER PROFESSIONS

Architecture, engineering, accounting, military science, and many other occupations partake of the character of professions in varying degrees. Those engaged in these occupations possess technical skills and provide them to those who need them. Because these skills are so technical, it is difficult for outsiders to evaluate their use; therefore, associations in these occupations establish codes of conduct and seek to maintain high standards. The degree of professional independence is less, on the whole, than that prevailing in medicine and law, but the professional model does make sense in respect to these occupations.

When architects, engineers, or accountants (especially certified public accountants) are independent practitioners taking on clients, their status is more strongly professional. When the practitioner is an employee of a business enterprise, the employer naturally exercises considerable control over the way in which work is carried out, and independence is diminished. Even so, the practitioner who has a will to do so may be able to maintain independence by rejecting any orders that are contrary to professional canons.

JOURNALISM: A CONTROVERSIAL OCCUPATION

Journalism is an occupation whose status has been especially controversial. Many journalists have come to regard themselves as subject to very special ethical imperatives that make journalism a profession rather than a business activity. They think of themselves as charged by society with the vital task of conveying news, and, more specifically, of exposing wrongdoing by prominent persons. (They have sometimes spoken of journalism as constituting a "fourth branch of government.")

A special test of this conception of journalism as a profession arises when journalists claim a legal right to preserve the confidentiality of their sources. For example, suppose an employee in a government department reveals to a journalist classified information about improper activity within that department. The government then seeks to prosecute the leaker and demands that the journalist reveal this person's name. The journalist perhaps refuses to do so, claiming a privilege of confidentiality that is, supposedly, analogous to the lawyer's privilege of keeping confidential what clients have said in legal consultation. Many journalists have thought they ought to have such a privilege; the U.S. Congress and the courts, however, have refused to grant it to them, and journalists who refuse to cooperate with legal authorities risk criminal prosecution.

Against the view that journalism is a profession, it can be pointed out that it is not an occupation requiring extensive scholarly education. Furthermore, it would probably be imprudent for society to hand over to journalists the kind of power to set their own standards and regulate their own activities that physicians and lawyers are granted. To do so might give journalists more political control over society than they should have.

CONCLUSION

From time to time, society should ask itself whether the tacit bargains that have been struck with professional groups are working out well. If they are not, and the balance has shifted away from the best interests of society in certain areas, then renegotiation may be appropriate.

Modern trends in medicine and law have been away from the older pattern of individual practitioners. More and more physicians and lawyers are becoming employees of large organizations. As employees, they must accept direction from their employers; therefore, they tend to be less independent than was the case in the past. This decreasing independence diminishes their distinctively professional status but does not eliminate it.

Stephen F. Barker

FURTHER READING

Bayles, Michael. *Professional Ethics*. 2d ed. Belmont, Calif.: Wadsworth, 1989. Attempts to find a common structure in the ethical issues confronting many different occupations.

Callahan, Joan C., ed. *Ethical Issues in Professional Life*. New York: Oxford University Press, 1988. A wide-ranging anthology of writings about various occupations.

Cooper, David E. *Ethics for Professionals in a Multicultural World*. Upper Saddle River, N.J.: Pearson/

Prentice Hall, 2004. Provides an overview of the history of ethics and explains the necessity of well-founded ethical principles to guide decisions in a pluralistic, multicultural society.

Goldman, Alan. *The Moral Foundations of Professional Ethics.* Totowa, N.J.: Rowman & Littlefield, 1980. An opinionated but stimulating philosophical analysis of basic issues, especially those concerning law and medicine.

McDowell, Banks. *Ethical Conduct and the Professional's Dilemma.* New York: Oxford University Press, 1991. Discusses the professional's conflict of interest over providing excessive services.

Pellegrino, Edmund D., et al., eds. *Ethics, Trust, and the Professions.* Washington, D.C.: Georgetown University Press, 1991. A lively collection of essays on philosophical, sociological, and international aspects of professions.

SEE ALSO: Applied ethics; Code of Professional Responsibility; Ethical Principles of Psychologists; Hippocrates; Law; Medical ethics; Military ethics; Normative vs. descriptive ethics; Permissible acts; Whistleblowing.

Profit economy

DEFINITION: Social system designed to allocate efficiently the scarce resources of a society by allowing individuals to pursue their own self-interest and to accumulate the wealth gained from that pursuit

TYPE OF ETHICS: Politico-economic ethics

SIGNIFICANCE: The profit economy is celebrated by those who focus on the theory behind it, which indicates that the system is fundamentally just since it should lead to increased benefits for all members of the community. It is attacked by those who focus on actual examples of such economies, in which the disparity between rich and poor grows larger and larger over time.

The purpose of economic activity is the satisfaction of wants. The question of which wants and whose wants should be satisfied is a problem of social justice. A profit economy determines how resources are to be allocated, what goods will be provided, and which wants will be satisfied by encouraging individuals to act in ways that they believe will enhance their own self-interest. In a profit economy, firms will act to maximize their profits and households will act to maximize their income, since firms and households are motivated by the desire to accumulate wealth.

It is the ability to accumulate wealth that has raised questions about the justice of a system based on profit. Utopian thinking, which is based on the idea of economic equality, considers the getting of profit as the getting of more than one rightfully deserves, resulting in an unjust and preferential system. Supporters of a profit economy counter that in the real world, if profit is not to be had, little will be done. Furthermore, it is argued that a profit economy functions particularly efficiently, creating wealth that, over time, will benefit all.

Sandra L. Christensen

SEE ALSO: Advertising; Capitalism; Cost-benefit analysis; Distributive justice; Free enterprise; Greed; Monopoly; Poverty and wealth; Product safety and liability; Profit taking; Smith, Adam.

Profit taking

DEFINITION: Selling one's securities or property for more money than one expended to acquire them, especially when the sale occurs immediately after a rise in their market value.

TYPE OF ETHICS: Business and labor ethics

SIGNIFICANCE: Profit taking by many people at once is often the cause of a temporary drop in the price of the security being sold, following the laws of supply and demand. This situation raises ethical issues to the extent that profit takers harm the interests of long-term shareholders to benefit themselves. As the stock market comes less and less to be populated with long-term shareholders, however, this becomes less and less of an issue.

In its broadest context, profit taking simply refers to the action of an investor in cashing in an investment and realizing whatever profit has been made. There are at least three circumstances, however, in which profit taking raises ethical questions. Especially during the 1980's, when corporate restructuring became commonplace, insider or management buyouts and firms "going private" often meant that investors with privileged knowledge about a company would offer stockholders more than the market value for their shares but less than the true value of those shares. Then, sometimes after only a brief period of reorganization, the investors would "go public" again, sell some or all of their shares at a considerably higher price, and thus engage in profit taking.

Such practices raised questions of a conflict of interest on the part of the managers involved, who were operating in their own interest rather than upholding their fiduciary responsibility to the company's shareholders. A second circumstance that raises ethical questions occurs when an investor realizes excessive profit from a transaction based on some standard of social acceptability, and a third such circumstance occurs when an investor gains profit by using unreasonable economic power.

D. Kirk Davidson

SEE ALSO: Capitalism; Free enterprise; Greed; Insider trading; Profit economy.

Progressivism

DEFINITION: Political movement and philosophy advocating social change through governmental and institutional action

TYPE OF ETHICS: Theory of ethics

SIGNIFICANCE: Progressivism holds that social and political institutions and activist coalitions bear the burden of improving the quality of life for individuals, because an individual alone lacks the power to achieve social justice. On the political spectrum, progressives are generally to the left of liberals and to the right of radicals.

Although lacking a definitive ideology with common tenets, progressivism evolved during the late nineteenth century as a unique American philosophy that was intended to counter the economic and social ills of the Industrial Revolution and a burgeoning urban society. The philosophy formed the basis for a large-scale reform movement, led by young, educated professionals, that embraced all levels of society and encompassed diverse ideologies.

The unifying forces for this movement were a belief that humankind had evolved sufficiently to con-trol the course of human development through reform, dispelling the prevailing assumption of a fixed unalterable order beyond human control, and the belief that reform was to be accomplished through a democratically controlled government. Progressives emphasized systems, planning, management, predictability, collective action, the scientific method, and the value of expert opinion. Beginning with the Theodore Roosevelt administration in 1901, the U.S. government initiated and sponsored legislation and amendments to cure the ills of society, make society more democratic, and provide equality for all Americans.

Stephen D. Livesay

SEE ALSO: Conservatism; James, William; Liberalism; Pragmatism.

Pro-life movement

DEFINITION: Coalition of activists working to ban abortion

TYPE OF ETHICS: Sex and gender issues; bioethics

SIGNIFICANCE: The pro-life movement represents one side in perhaps the most heated moral debate of the late twentieth and early twenty-first centuries. Although associated with Roman Catholics and the political right, neither of those two groups is undivided on the issue of abortion.

Ethical conflict over abortion has grown hugely since the 1960's, when the pro-life movement began. The first members of this movement were Catholics, whose views were supported by the Roman Catholic Church. Since then, the movement has spread, and it now numbers among its proponents people from every religion, race, and walk of life. All these people view any abortion as being murder because they see the fetus as becoming a human being at the moment of conception, when sperm and egg fuse. Pro-life responses to abortions vary from peaceful methods that include demonstrations and attempts to dissuade women seeking abortions to active demonstrations at abortion clinics that sometimes lead to physical confrontations involving pro-life demonstrators, clinic staffers, and patients seeking to obtain abortions. In some cases, abortion clinic staffers have been threatened with physical violence, abducted from their homes or workplaces, and subjected to various levels of physical harm by pro-life zealots.

The end goals of the pro-life movement are to seek for the fertilized ovum the same rights that persons who have been born enjoy. It is deemed by many or most pro-lifers that the U.S. Constitution should be amended. A version of the amendment supported by several pro-life members of Congress states that "the paramount right to life is vested in each human being, from the moment of fertilization without regard to age, health or condition of dependency."

CONCEPTS AND METHODOLOGY

The basic pro-life concepts about abortion, from several sources, indicate the following ethical judgments: (1) the fetus at any stage in its growth from fertilization on is a human being in every sense of the word, (2) an abortion thus kills a person and is murder, and (3) anyone who condones abortion condones murder and is a criminal. According to some members of the movement, such people deserve "anything that happens to them." The action techniques of the pro-life movement vary greatly, and many are codified by pro-life manifestos such as *Closed: Ninety-nine Ways to Stop Abortion* (Scheidler, 1985).

Such manifestos list numerous operational procedures, including sidewalk counseling of pregnant women, picketing and demonstrations at abortion sites, disseminating leaflets and getting pro-life literature into libraries, advertising in the news media, using sit-ins, picketing the homes of abortionists, going into politics, and using horror stories to frighten women who are seeking abortions. Fortunately, many manifesto writers point out that violence should not be used, because it constitutes using evil to fight evil. Yet there have been regrettable instances in which this belief has not been shared by some pro-lifers, who have destroyed property, abducted abortionists, threatened a shooting war, and, in one case, killed a doctor who performed abortions.

HISTORICAL BACKGROUND

The conflict over abortion is as old as humankind. The ancient Greek and Roman philosophers codified the use of abortion. For example, Plato favored the use of abortion when it was for society's good, and Aristotle defined human life as beginning only forty or ninety days after the conception of a male or female fetus, respectively. With the development of Christianity, strong antiabortion sentiment arose and began to flourish. In more modern times, English common law stated that abortion was legal until mothers felt movement in the womb—"quickening"—and this view persisted well into the eighteenth century.

By the twentieth century, the abortion debate became quiescent, and many abortions were made legal by the 1950's. During the 1960's, with most Americans favoring therapeutic abortion, the pro-life movement began and evolved to include religious, medical, and lay proponents. At first, the pope and numerous Catholic functionaries preached a pro-life manifesto that was not backed by the Protestant churches. During the 1970's, however, various Protestant clerics began to support the idea.

A number of physicians, including Jack Wilke, have been long time leaders of the movement. Wilke, in fact, wrote a 1970's "abortion handbook," illustrated with pictures of mutilated fetuses, that earned eminence for his pro-life National Right to Life Committee. By the 1980's, the polarization between pro-life and pro-abortion factions had grown hugely, and the debate has since then become more and more acrimonious. It is not clear what will happen; however, verbal—and sometimes physical—battle lines have been drawn.

Pro-life lobbies in Washington, D.C., have sought to pass the amendment alluded to earlier. In addition, Randall Terry's well-known Operation Rescue has sought to prevent abortions and close abortion clinics. Documents have also been written by prominent lawyers propounding the legality of the rights of the unborn. Some splinter groups among pro-life proponents have warned their adversaries that a shooting war awaits them. A serious confrontation seems to be inevitable.

CONCLUSIONS

The ethical issue that focuses the actions of the pro-life movement is that it is never appropriate to stop the occurrence of a human life. The advocates of this viewpoint warn that if their point of view is unheeded, the consequences of such unethical decision making will lead to the practice of genocide. In contrast, those who favor abortion for "appropriate reasons" fear that its criminalization will lead to other restrictive legislation that will diminish human rights and produce many other forms of related human persecution. It seems possible that an ethical compromise could give both sides some of their desires. One model for use could be that of Western Europe, in which respect for every human life is promised and abortion is permitted under conditions that are deemed appropriate and ethical.

Sanford S. Singer

FURTHER READING

Cozic, Charles P., and Stacy L. Tipp, eds. *Abortion: Opposing Viewpoints*. San Diego, Calif.: Greenhaven Press, 1991.

Faux, Marian. *Crusaders: Voices from the Abortion Front*. Secaucus, N.J.: Carol, 1990.

Merton, Andrew H. *Enemies of Choice*. Boston: Beacon Press, 1981.

Paige, Connie. *The Right to Lifers*. New York: Summit Books, 1983.

Rice, Charles. *No Exceptions*. Gaithersburg, Md.: Human Life International, 1990.

Risen, James, and Judy L. Thomas. *Wrath of Angels: The American Abortion War*. New York: Basic Books, 1998.

Scheidler, Joseph M. *Closed: Ninety-nine Ways to Stop Abortion*. San Francisco, Calif.: Ignatius Press, 1985.

Williams, Mary E., ed. *Abortion: Opposing Viewpoints*. San Diego, Calif.: Greenhaven Press, 2002.

SEE ALSO: Abortion; Bioethics; Birth control; Christian ethics; Family; Jewish ethics; Life and death; Pro-choice movement; Right to life.

Promiscuity

DEFINITION: Sexual activity with multiple partners
TYPE OF ETHICS: Personal and social ethics
SIGNIFICANCE: Promiscuity may involve simple non-monogamy, but the term has strong connotations of a lack of discrimination in sexual partners. It is therefore judged by some to cheapen or even commodify the sexual relationship.

The change in sex habits of Americans since the end of World War II has been described as leading to unlimited sexual freedom. Contraceptive devices had provided nearly complete protection from pregnancy,

and changing and more relaxed attitudes about sex had mitigated the stigma of premarital and extramarital sex, sex with multiple partners, and having children out of wedlock. It seemed the American society had indeed become more promiscuous.

An extensive study of sexual behavior by Albert D. Klassen, Colin J. Williams, and Eugene E. Levitt (1989) concluded, however, that there was no evidence suggesting any far-reaching changes in sexual norms. Patterns of traditional sexual behavior were neither significantly reduced nor reversed. The authors concluded that a "sexual revolution" had not occurred in the United States.

PROMISCUITY

The conclusion that no sexual revolution has occurred does not imply that promiscuity does not exist. Klassen et al. pointed out that norms contradicting the traditional ones have emerged and that commitment to the traditional norms may not be as strong as in the past.

In Africa, premarital and extramarital sex are common. For example, a survey in Zimbabwe revealed that 40 percent of married men had had extramarital sex within the past year (the actual figure is probably higher). Part of the reason for this high frequency is that there is a cultural expectation that married men can have other relationships, and these relationships are accepted by the wives. (This attitude is changing because of the AIDS epidemic in Africa.) Ethically, promiscuity per se is neither good nor bad but depends on the culture in which it occurs. Unfortunately, often accompanying promiscuity are the following outcomes, which can only be viewed as negative.

Where promiscuous behavior is not condoned—for example, in marriage—it is usually conducted without the partner's awareness. Lying and deceitfulness are commonly used by the one having the relationship in order to keep it secret. This breach of trust and of the bonds of marriage is hardly noble and virtuous behavior.

ROLE MODELS

For better or worse, professional athletes are the true heroes of American culture, and therefore their behavior sets a powerful example. When, for example, famous basketball players brag publicly about having sex with more than ten thousand women or

Patterns in American Sexual Promiscuity

An extensive study of American sexual patterns and behavior by Sam Janus and Cynthia L. Janus provided a measure of how extensive promiscuity is. Their data, which suggest that promiscuous behavior occurs frequently, include these findings:

1. Twenty-six percent of women and 40 percent of men aged eighteen to thirty-eight at the time of the survey became sexually active by age fourteen.

2. Forty to 63 percent of men from ages eighteen through sixty-five and older said that their sexual experience before marriage was important. For women, the figure ranged from 25 to 56 percent.

3. Sixty percent of the men surveyed had had relations with from one to thirty partners, 21 percent with thirty-one to sixty partners, and 18 percent with sixty-one or more. For women, the figures were 81, 9, and 7 percent.

4. Eighteen percent of married men had had one extramarital affair, 38 percent had engaged in extramarital affairs rarely, and 29 percent often had extramarital sex. For women, the figures were 27, 38, and 12 percent.

5. Twenty percent of the men, regardless of income level, had had sex with prostitutes, whereas the figures for women ranged from 3 to 8 percent. Most of these people used the services of a prostitute occasionally (25 to 63 percent), rather than once (6 to 50 percent) or often (7 to 31 percent).

Source: Janus, Sam, and Cynthia L. Janus. *The Janus Report on Sexual Behavior* (1993).

about 90 percent involve people under age 25. By March of 1992, 139,269 adults and adolescents and 1,954 children had died from AIDS in the United States (not all as a result of promiscuous sex). The AIDS epidemic in Africa is even worse.

The 1993 *Kids Count Data Book* claims that the status of adolescents is "deteriorating." Aside from STDs, almost 9 percent of all babies in 1990 were born to single teenagers, and teenagers also accounted for about 25 percent of all abortions. Marilyn Gardner used these data to claim that "Early sexual activity can exact a terrible price from promising young lives . . . too many find themselves shackled by unplanned pregnancies, abortions, single motherhood, infections or infertility."

On balance, then, promiscuity is bad. To avoid the pejorative connotation of the term "promiscuity," social scientists often refer to "sexual networking" or "a pattern of multiple partners." Since promiscuity is not neutral in its effects, however, perhaps the pejorative connotation is desirable.

Laurence Miller

FURTHER READING

Janus, Sam. *The Death of Innocence*. New York: Morrow, 1981.

Janus, Sam, and Cynthia L. Janus. *The Janus Report on Sexual Behavior*. New York: J. Wiley, 1993.

Klassen, Albert D., Colin J. Williams, and Eugene E. Levitt. *Sex and Morality in the U.S.* Middletown, Conn.: Wesleyan University Press, 1989.

Posner, Richard A. *Sex and Reason*. Cambridge, Mass.: Harvard University Press, 1992.

Weeks, Jeffrey. *Sex, Politics, and Society*. 2d ed. New York: Longman, 1989.

White, Emily. *Fast Girls: Teenage Tribes and the Myth of the Slut*. New York: Scribner, 2002.

SEE ALSO: Acquired immunodeficiency syndrome (AIDS); Adultery; Lust; Premarital sex; Prostitution; Sexism; Sexual revolution; Sexual stereotypes; Sexuality and sexual ethics; Sexually transmitted diseases.

contract AIDS in the course of having sex with hundreds of women, or the mistress of a baseball player is rewarded with extensive coverage in *Playboy*, legitimate questions can be raised about the kinds of examples that these heroes provide.

SEXUALLY TRANSMITTED DISEASES (STDs)

The more persons with whom an individual has sex, the greater that individual's chance of contracting a sexually transmitted disease. According to a report released in 1993 by the Guttmacher Institute, 20 percent (56 million) of all Americans have an STD. Of the 12 million new cases diagnosed each year,

Promises

DEFINITION: Morally binding declarations that one will or will not do something; oaths

TYPE OF ETHICS: Personal and social ethics

SIGNIFICANCE: One's ability or inability to keep one's promises is often taken as a sign of one's general level of integrity or moral character. The keeping of promises is also of central theoretical importance to moral philosophers as different as Immanuel Kant and Friedrich Nietzsche.

Every society is organized according to various kinds of rules and standards for behavior. Humans' social nature, limitations, and similar needs, along with the scarcity of objects, goods, or conditions such as food, wealth, and jobs, serve to create situations of conflicts that moral and other rules seek to resolve or minimize. There are many implied agreements, or moral rules, that allow people to live safely and to have meaningful relationships with others. These include agreements not to harm one another, not to lie or cheat, to obey laws, to treat others with dignity, and to keep promises.

In earlier times, one's promise, or "word," was part of one's reputation. Many promises and agreements were made verbally or by shaking hands. Some promises, such as personal ones, are still made that way, but many are written down as formal contracts and agreements. This is because such promises tend to be more complex and because fewer and fewer people actually honor their promises.

To understand the concept of promising and the breaking of promises, two basic and opposed approaches to morality must be examined: nonconsequentialist and consequentialist views.

Nonconsequentialist views oppose the breaking of promises at any time. Whether one keeps or breaks promises has an effect on human relationships, and one of the main arguments against breaking promises

---

Promises and Kant's Categorical Imperative

In *Foundations of the Metaphysics of Morals* (1785), German philosopher Immanuel Kant argues for the existence of a categorical imperative, a universal and objectively valid moral law. Kant's first formulation of the categorical imperative is "I should never act in such a way that I could not also will that my maxim should be a universal law." In other words, in making moral decisions, one should apply the following test: Is it logically possible to universalize the maxim that guides my action? Kant uses the breaking of promises as his central example. If one were to break a promise, the maxim one followed in such a case would be something like this: "I should always keep my promises . . . unless I decide to break them." Kant argues that if this claim were to be universalized, the word "promise" would lose all meaning. "Everyone should always keep their promises, unless they decide to break them." If it is universally acknowledged that no one is obliged to keep a promise, then the promise ceases to *be* a promise, since a promise entails obligation by definition. A world in which the universal version of the maxim is accepted, then, would be one in which there is simply no such thing as a promise.

The important point about the first formulation of the categorical imperative is that it is a statement, *not* about desirability, but about logical coherence. Kant is not saying that oath-breaking is bad, because one would not want to live in a world where promises cannot be trusted. He is rather pointing out that the statement "everyone should always keep their promises unless they decide to break them" is a logically incoherent utterance, because the proposition renders its key term meaningless. Therefore, it is simply not *possible* to will that this maxim should be a universal law, whether one wants to or not. Kant is committed to this kind of analysis, because he believes that the categorical imperative derives its authority from its form rather than its content. It must have the form of law as such. Only then will it be both objective and universal.

This point raises a potential objection to Kant's formulation, however, since it is unclear that any other type of transgression fails his test in the same way. Vengeful murder, for example, does not cause similar logical inconsistencies when it is universally willed. Kant may well have chosen oath-breaking as an example, because it is the only transgression that clearly fits his point.

is that breaking them can destroy or undermine personal relationships. If a person promises to do something, most people will tend to believe that person's word. If the promise is broken, the relationship with that person is weakened, because trust is a central element of vital relationships. The lack of trust that develops makes rapport more difficult to achieve in the future.

A second argument against the breaking of promises is the idea that if a person breaks a promise and gets away with it, it becomes easier to break other promises. It can become a habit that is hard to break. Third, breaking a promise can have serious effects on other people's lives. In some situations, people make decisions that can greatly affect their lives based on promises that are made to them. For example, someone may quit one job for a promised job and end up with no job at all.

The destruction of general social trust is a fourth reason for not breaking promises. Much of what people do is based on promises and agreements. Once these promises and agreements break down, social trust breaks down. One example of such a situation is the lack of trust that people have regarding promises made during political campaigns. A final argument against breaking promises involves the loss of personal integrity of the one breaking the promise. Breaking a promise not only hurts one's reputation with others but also causes the loss of one's own self-esteem.

What if the consequences for everyone affected would be better if a promise were broken? Consequentialist theories argue that whether a promise should be kept depends on the end results. Consequentialists believe that one should always act to maximize happiness and minimize pain for all involved. Breaking a promise is acceptable if the greatest good consequences would be the result of that act.

One argument favoring the breaking of promises has to do with changed circumstances. One who has made a promise should have the right to break it if the circumstances under which it was made have changed. Another defense of promise breaking involves the arising of moral conflicts. For example, protecting human life should take precedence over keeping a promise. Promise breaking should also be allowed when promises are made in unusual situations. For example, a promise made to satisfy someone on his deathbed can be broken later for good reasons.

Finally, in the spirit of the Latin phrase *caveat emptor* ("let the buyer beware"), recipients of promises should beware. They should not assume that promises will be kept.

Cheri Vail Fisk

FURTHER READING

Adler, Mortimer J. *The Time of Our Lives: The Ethics of Common Sense.* New York: Holt, Rinehart & Winston, 1970.

Barnsley, John H. *The Social Reality of Ethics: The Comparative Analysis of Moral Codes.* London: Routledge & Kegan Paul, 1972.

Cunningham, Robert L. *Situationism and the New Morality.* New York: Appleton-Century-Crofts, 1970.

Fox, Richard M., and Joseph P. DeMarco. *The Immorality of Promising.* Amherst, N.Y.: Humanity Books, 2001.

Hare, R. M. *Applications of Moral Philosophy.* Berkeley: University of California Press, 1972.

Kant, Immanuel. *Groundwork for the Metaphysics of Morals.* Edited and translated by Allen W. Wood. New Haven, Conn.: Yale University Press, 2002.

Nietzsche, Friedrich. *On the Genealogy of Morals.* Edited and translated by Walter Kaufmann. New York: Vintage Books, 1967.

Páll S. Árdal. *Passions, Promises, and Punishment.* Edited by Mikael M. Karlsson and Jörundur Guðmundsson. Reykjavík: University of Iceland Press, 1998.

SEE ALSO: Consequentialism; Deontological ethics; Integrity; Kant, Immanuel; Nietzsche, Friedrich; Rights and obligations; Teleological ethics; Trustworthiness; Universalizability.

Property

DEFINITION: Objects, land, ideas, creative expressions, or other things over which individuals or groups enjoy ownership

TYPE OF ETHICS: Theory of ethics

SIGNIFICANCE: In traditional liberal political philosophy, ownership of property is a fundamental civil right. In socialist theory, it is an evil to be overcome.

Human beings need material goods to survive. Therefore, whoever controls the production and distribution of material goods controls human survival. The legal arrangements that societies enact for the control of material goods—property—are based on ethical principles regarding the proper relationship between the individuals who must ultimately consume the goods and the societies of which they are a part. Historically, three broad ethical approaches have shaped legal arrangements for the control of property: the individual, the collective, and the monarchic.

INDIVIDUALISM

Individualist ethics argue that each individual is an end in himself or herself. Each individual should have control of his or her own life and be responsible for his or her own well-being. Accordingly, individualists argue that each individual should have legal control over whatever property he or she produces or acquires; in other words, the right to private property should be a fundamental social principle. Economically, a free enterprise system results from the recognition of private property rights. In such a system, the moral standard at work is self-responsibility and individual achievement, and the property arrangements in the individualist society reflect this standard.

COLLECTIVISM

Collectivist ethics argue that individuals are subordinate to the larger social group of which they are a part. The larger social group varies depending on the version of collectivism that is advocated: The group may be defined in national, tribal, racial, or cultural terms. Common to all versions of collectivism is the principle that individuals exist primarily to serve the welfare of society as a whole; therefore, collectivists argue that society as a whole (or its representatives) should have legal control over all property in society. Control of a portion of society's property may be delegated to various individuals, but ultimate control remains with society as a whole. Economically, some form of socialist economy should result. In such a system, the moral standard at work is the value of the individual to the society, and the property arrangements within the collectivist society reflect this standard.

MONARCHISM

Monarchist ethics argue that some single individual (or, in aristocratic variations, a small number of individuals) is inherently superior to the rest of the individuals in the society. Accordingly, most individuals in the society exist primarily to serve the monarch (or the aristocratic class), and therefore the monarch should retain ultimate control over all property. Whether an individual has control of much, little, or no property thus depends upon the will of the monarch. Economically, some form of command economy should result. In such a system, the moral standard at work is the value of the individual to the monarch, and the property arrangements within monarchist society reflect this standard.

MIXED SYSTEMS

Historically, most societies' property arrangements have been mixtures of two or more of the above principles. In some tribal societies, for example, most property is controlled communally, while some is controlled individually. Since no individual has control over the use of enough property to ensure his or her existence, however, an individual's survival is controlled by the tribe. Individuals whom the tribe holds to be valuable are granted greater control over property, both as a sign of favor and in the hope that they will use it to benefit the tribe, while individuals for whom the tribe no longer has a use—such as the deformed, the aged, and those who are deemed troublemakers—are denied access to the tribe's property. In this way, the primary moral standard at work is the value of the individual to the tribe, and the property arrangements within the tribe reflect this standard.

Most modern Western societies are a mixture of individual and collective property arrangements. Much property is owned and controlled by private individuals, but the use to which individuals can put their property is often controlled collectively by, for example, zoning laws; in some cases, a private individual's property rights can be overridden by eminent domain.

CONNECTION TO CIVIL RIGHTS

Individual property rights are sometimes contrasted with other categories of individual rights—most often, civil rights such as the rights to freedom of religion, freedom of speech, freedom of association, and the freedom to vote. In some accounts of

rights, civil and property rights fall into two fundamentally different categories; advocates of such accounts use such a distinction to argue for a mixed system of rights—for example, that all property should
be controlled collectively, while individuals should
retain the full range of civil rights. Others argue that
there is no fundamental distinction between civil and
property rights; they will argue, for example, that the
right to freedom of speech means very little if one has
no right to own a printing press.

INTELLECTUAL PROPERTY

Most philosophical discussion has focused on
material property; for example, tools, real estate, machines, and animals. Increasingly, however, many of
the values that contribute to human life require primarily intellectual (rather than physical) work for
their production. Accordingly, individualist societies
have evolved legal mechanisms to protect individuals' rights to the fruits of their intellectual labors,
once they have been translated into physical form.
Copyrights exist to allow individuals to control the
use of the written works or art works that they have
produced, industrial trademarks are registered and
protected by law, and patents are issued to protect
individuals' control over their inventions, such as
new machines or drugs. Scientific advances continue
to raise questions about the proper scope of such
rights—for example, as biotechnology makes possible the creation of new life-forms.

Stephen R. C. Hicks

FURTHER READING

Blumenfeld, Samuel, ed. *Property in a Humane Soci-
ety.* LaSalle, Ill.: Open Court, 1974.
Hamilton, Alexander, James Madison, and John Jay.
The Federalist Papers. New York: Washington
Square Press, 1976.
Locke, John. *Two Treatises of Government.* Edited
by Peter Laslett. New York: Cambridge Univer-
sity Press, 1988.
Macpherson, C. B. *The Political Theory of Posses-
sive Individualism: Hobbes to Locke.* Oxford, En-
gland: Oxford University Press, 1988.
Marx, Karl, and Friedrich Engels. *The Communist
Manifesto.* New York: Bantam, 1992.
Rand, Ayn. "Patents and Copyrights." In *Capitalism:
The Unknown Ideal.* New York: New American
Library, 1966.
Ross, Stephen David. *The Gift of Property—Having
the Good: Betraying Genitivity, Economy, and
Ecology, an Ethic of the Earth.* Albany: State Uni-
versity of New York Press, 2001.
Singer, Joseph William. *The Edges of the Field: Les-
sons on the Obligations of Ownership.* Boston:
Beacon Press, 2000.

SEE ALSO: Capitalism; Communism; Copyright; Intellectual property; Socialism.

Prostitution

DEFINITION: Provision of sexual services for payment
TYPE OF ETHICS: Sex and gender issues
SIGNIFICANCE: The ethics of prostitution constitute
one of the most debated and controversial issues
concerning human relationships in history, and
prostitution itself is the focus of significant criminal justice resources.

Prostitution, or sex for pay, has been pervasive
throughout human history. It differs from sex slavery
because its sexual contacts are generally voluntary
and largely commercial. It also differs from marriages of convenience, or mistress-keeping, in that its
sexual contacts are relatively indiscriminate and typically involve large numbers of customers. It differs
from sexual promiscuity or sexual addiction because
payments are involved. Finally, it differs from other
sex work, such as strip shows or pornographic films,
because it provides direct physical sex contacts to its
clients.

A primary sex issue in prostitution is the contrast
between marital or romantic sex and commercial sex,
in which the physical acts tend to be more mechanical than emotional. Moreover, the sexual access that
the prostitutes provide to their clients is objectified,
depersonalized, and merely a means to satisfy their
clients' sexual needs. The prostitutes themselves
tend to be emotionally detached and even alienated
from their own sexuality, and their physical relationships with their clients are brief and utilitarian.

Other issues relating to prostitution include the
extent to which oral, anal, and genital sexual access is
granted to customers and questions of mutual con-

Mexican prostitutes in the border city of Tijuana watch for customers on a rainy afternoon. During the mid-1990's Tijuana's prostitutes—like those in other major Mexican cities—organized a labor union to protect themselves against police harassment and to secure better health care. (AP/Wide World Photos)

sent in the undertaking of such activities as bondage, sadomasochistic acts, and role playing. Gender issues include the relative rights of men and women to work as prostitutes and the sexual access each may grant, and perceptions of male domination symbolized by female prostitution.

BEYOND SEX AND GENDER ISSUES

Many people question the morality of prostitution. Prostitution tends to be judged immoral because it is usually illegal. Critics charge that prostitution does great harm to the prostitutes themselves, their customers, third parties, and society in general. Religious critics charge that prostitution promotes sexual unions that lack the sanctification of marriage, do not

serve the natural purposes of reproduction or conjugal union, and are both impersonal and mercenary. They see prostitution as sinful: Prostitutes are unclean and fallen, at least temporarily, from the grace of God. However, some ancient and primitive religions used prostitutes in religious rites. Social critics would add that prostitution is often forced upon its practitioners by economic forces and is inherently degrading to them.

Human rights advocates see prostitution as a social welfare problem with people taking up prostitution out of economic desperation, lack of skills, or social isolation. They recommend counseling, education, and training to encourage prostitutes to make other employment and human relationship choices.

Women choosing careers in prostitution even though other options are open to them are encouraged to direct themselves toward healthier and safer sexual practices and working environments.

Some civil libertarians view prostitution as a privacy issue and argue that individuals should be permitted to choose any lifestyle and profession they wish, so long as they do not harm others. Sexually transmitted disease or the psychological and economic damage done to third persons including the prostitutes' or customers' spouses and dependent children are possible types of harm.

Politico-economic rights advocates debate prostitution as both a power issue and a free-exchange issue. Those with political power define, through law, what is permissible commercial behavior. Sex is one of several regulated or prohibited commodities. Paternalists would protect the prostitute from abuse, disease, and social ostracism by either banning prostitution or regulating it with geographic zones, medical inspections, and licenses. Free market advocates believe all voluntary commercial exchange, including prostitution, should be permitted and see sex as merely another form of wage labor.

Legal ethics address the subjective and relative criminality of prostitution. Regarded as a victimless crime, prostitution is consequently an offense that is subject to considerable discretion and variance in both law enforcement and adjudication. Some communities treat prostitution permissively, while others subject it to strict, harsh, and punitive enforcement.

Some business and labor ethicists advocate extending to prostitutes and their customers the same business standards and work safety protections offered in other professions. Such a change would help relieve prostitutes from exploitation by third parties, especially pimps, public accommodations operators, and organized crime. According to this view, prostitutes deserve the same health care, insurance, banking privileges, tax paying, public accommodations, and public utility rights as other citizens.

UNINTENDED CONSEQUENCES OF PROHIBITION

Continuing efforts to stop prostitution tend to generate disrespect for both the law and law enforcement, as prostitution continues to flourish. Meanwhile, prostitution enriches pimps and members of organized crime bodies. Traffickers in prostitutes provide financial incentives for the corruption of law enforcement, the courts, and politics, adding to the burdens of the police, the courts, and the penal system. At the same time, the prostitutes themselves rarely profit financially and are increasingly marginalized socially. They and their customers also stand greatly increased chances of contracting sexually transmitted diseases, including acquired immunodeficiency syndrome (AIDS), especially because they avoid testing.

Prostitution also contributes to tensions in marriages in which one partner is more sexually demanding or adventurous than the other. Laws define as criminals people engaging in what are essentially victimless crimes, while consuming public resources that might be better used elsewhere. Criticisms of prostitution contribute to erosion of respect for religion and other institutions that try to define a relatively popular practice as immoral. Confused public attitudes toward prostitution also help to perpetuate moral, religious, and legal double standards in which the clients are less condemned than the prostitutes, and male clients of female prostitutes are less condemned than female clients of male prostitutes.

Gordon Neal Diem

FURTHER READING

Bullough, Vern, and Bonnie Bullough. *Women and Prostitution: A Social History.* Buffalo, N.Y.: Prometheus Books, 1987.

Davis, Nanette, ed. *Prostitution: An International Handbook on Trends, Problems, and Policies.* Westport, Conn.: Greenwood Press, 1993.

Jenness, Valerie. *Making It Work: The Prostitute's Rights Movement in Perspective.* New York: Aldine de Gruyter, 1993.

Perkins, Roberta, and Garry Bennett. *Being a Prostitute: Prostitute Women and Prostitute Men.* Boston: Allen & Unwin, 1985.

Roberts, Nickie. *Whores in History: Prostitution in Western Society.* London: HarperCollins, 1992.

SEE ALSO: Adultery; Agreement for the Suppression of White Slave Traffic; Lust; Promiscuity; Rape and political domination; Sexual revolution; Slavery; Vice.

Prudence

DEFINITION: Skill in judging how to achieve one's ends while avoiding danger or minimizing risk

TYPE OF ETHICS: Personal and social ethics

SIGNIFICANCE: Prudence is sometimes described as a virtue, especially to the extent that it entails avoiding conflicts that will necessarily harm oneself or others. It is also possible, however, to judge people to be overly prudent, or too cautious for their own good.

In twentieth century ethical theory, there are two quite different ways of understanding prudence and its relationship to ethics. According to one, prudence is a virtue that is essential to an ethical life. According to the other, prudence is a principle that is distinct from, and often opposed to, ethics. The best approach to understanding these two conceptions of prudence is to look at their history. Since prudence has been examined during most of its history in languages other than English, it is helpful to identify the non-English ancestors of the term "prudence."

For most of the leading ethical theorists of ancient Greece, ancient Rome, and the Roman Catholic tradition, prudence is understood to be one of the four cardinal (principal) virtues. In the *Republic* (c. 390 B.C.E.), Plato uses the Greek word *sophia*, which is usually translated into English as "wisdom," and Greek words meaning justice, courage, and temperance to name the four chief virtues (states of character) of both good persons and good communities. For Plato, persons with the virtue of *sophia* are those who exercise forethought in determining what is best, both for themselves and for the communities to which they belong, and whose rational faculties are in command of their other faculties.

Plato's student Aristotle distinguishes, in his *Nicomachean Ethics* (c. 330 B.C.E.), *sophia* and *phronīsis*. For Aristotle, a person with the virtue of *phronīsis* is able to deliberate rationally about which actions best achieve the end of a good human life. *Phronīsis* was later translated into Latin as *prudentia*, from which the English word "prudence" is derived. Philosophers in the Stoic and Epicurean traditions, both Greek and Roman, also developed theories of the cardinal virtues.

Drawing from many of his predecessors in the Greco-Roman and Judeo-Christian traditions, Thomas Aquinas provides a detailed account of the virtue of *prudentia* in his *Summa Theologica* (c. 1270). He defines *prudentia* as "right reason applied to action" and explains that it is concerned not with determining ends, but with determining the means to the end of a good, complete human life. Following Aristotle, he discusses three subvirtues of *prudentia*: *euboulia*, or good deliberation; *synesis*, or good judgment in ordinary cases; and *gnome*, or good judgment in exceptional cases. He distinguishes *prudentia* from false *prudentia*, which enables one to determine well the means to an immoral end, and from incomplete *prudentia*, which falls short of complete *prudentia* in one way or another. He explains that *prudentia* is concerned with both the good of individuals and the good of the families and communities to which they belong, and he offers a detailed analysis of the vices, or negative states of character, that are opposed to *prudentia*.

THE MIDDLE AGES AND BEYOND

The shift in the understanding of prudence that occurred between the thirteenth and twentieth centuries was part of a larger shift in the understanding of the relationship between ethical obligation and the good of persons who perform ethical actions. Whereas the dominant view in ancient and medieval ethics was that being ethical is usually good both for ethical persons themselves and for those who are affected by their actions, the history of modern ethical theories is one of increasing emphasis on the obligation to benefit other persons at the expense of self-interest.

Prussian philosopher Immanuel Kant played a major role in developing the belief that prudence (in German, *Klugheit*) and ethics often oppose one another. His *Foundations of the Metaphysics of Morals* (1785) distinguishes "rules of skill," which describe the means to ends that people could desire; "counsels of prudence," which describe the means to an end that all people do in fact desire (their own happiness); and "commands of morality," which tell people which actions they should perform because they are good actions, regardless of what ends are desired.

For Kant, what makes an action moral is that it is motivated by a desire to perform a moral action, not that it has certain intended or actual consequences. In his *Critique of Practical Reason* (1788) and *Perpetual Peace* (1795), Kant writes that there are clear boundaries between prudence and ethics, and that actions motivated by the desire to achieve happiness directly oppose morality. Kant's theory is, therefore, a departure from those traditions that understand prudence to be one of the virtues, without which one cannot be ethical.

The history of eighteenth to twentieth century ethical theory in the English-speaking world also includes a shift toward the belief that prudence and morality are in competition with, or opposed to, each other. Jeremy Bentham, in his *Introduction to the Principles of Morals and Legislation* (1789), understands ethics in terms of a distinction between duty to self and duty to others. He associates prudence with the former but is somewhat tentative in calling it a duty at all: "The quality which a man manifests by the discharge of this branch of duty (if duty it is to be called) is that of *prudence*."

In *The Methods of Ethics* (1874), Henry Sidgwick goes beyond Bentham by calling *phronīsis* "practical wisdom" and classifying it as an "intellectual virtue," and then classifying prudence as a "self-regarding virtue." Although Sidgwick allows that "prudence may be said to be merely wisdom made more definite by the acceptance of self-interest as its sole ultimate end" and that "it is a strongly supported opinion that all valid moral rules have ultimately a prudential basis," he is a contributor to the separation of prudence from ethics.

In twentieth century English-language discussions of ethics, it is common to find "prudence" used both as the name of a principle that is in competition with ethics and as the name of a virtue that is essential to an ethical life. For example, William K. Frankena writes, within a single paragraph in *Ethics* (1973), both that "morality must be contrasted with prudence" and that "it may also be that prudence is a moral virtue." Some twentieth century writers attempt to minimize confusion by following Sidgwick in using "practical wisdom" as the English name of the virtue *phronīsis/prudentia*.

David W. Lutz

FURTHER READING

Aristotle. *Nicomachean Ethics.* Translated and edited by Roger Crisp. New York: Cambridge University Press, 2000.

Hariman, Robert, ed. *Prudence: Classical Virtue, Postmodern Practice.* University Park: Pennsylvania State University, 2003.

Kant, Immanuel. *Groundwork for the Metaphysics of Morals.* Edited and translated by Allen W. Wood. New Haven, Conn.: Yale University Press, 2002.

Plato. *The Republic.* Translated by Desmond Lee. 2d ed. New York: Penguin Books, 2003.

Sidgwick, Henry. *The Methods of Ethics.* 1907. 7th ed. Foreword by John Rawls. Indianapolis: Hackett, 1981.

Thomas Aquinas, Saint. *The Summa Theologica.* Translated by Laurence Shapcote. 2d ed. 2 vols. Chicago: Encyclopaedia Britannica, 1990.

SEE ALSO: Altruism; Egoism; Negligence; Self-interest; Self-love; Virtue ethics; Wisdom.

Psychology

DEFINITION: Scientific study of the human mind and human behavior
TYPE OF ETHICS: Psychological ethics
SIGNIFICANCE: Psychology raises two distinct sorts of ethical issues: how to engage responsibly in psychological research, and how best to treat patients of clinical practitioners. Because patients are often simultaneously research subjects, however, the line between research and treatment may blur, raising other ethical concerns.

When most people think of psychologists, they think of psychotherapists. These are licensed psychologists who have a private practice with individual clients or who work in settings such as hospitals, substance abuse clinics, or victim services centers. Psychotherapists (or clinical psychologists) have as their main goal helping their clients to achieve a better sense of balance, self-esteem, or mental health. To achieve this goal, they use a variety of therapeutic techniques and follow ethical guidelines intended to ensure that the clients' best interests are being met as well as possible.

Not all psychologists, however, are therapists. Psychologists are found in a variety of nonclinical settings where they must follow ethical guidelines as they apply their psychological knowledge and skills. Research psychologists must ensure the well-being of their animal or human experimental subjects, while psychologists who work in industrial, educational, and government settings try to ensure the well-being of those with whom and for whom they work: employees, students, and citizens in general.

The American Psychological Association (APA), the largest U.S. professional organization for psychologists, has formulated and published ethical guidelines for psychologists in each of these settings. It also maintains several committees that answer questions, make suggestions, and sometimes investigate psychologists who have been reported for malpractice or other unethical behavior.

ETHICS IN THERAPY

The relationship between therapist and client is complex and potentially fraught with ethical dilemmas. In many instances, the reason the client is seeking help is, in and of itself, sensitive information; clients may be embarrassed or ashamed about a problem or behavior, such as phobia, bulimia, or sexual dysfunction. In other circumstances, a client may feel that his or her job, marriage, or even personal liberty may be in jeopardy if the issues that are brought up in therapy somehow become public knowledge. Clearly, one of the primary concerns of any clinician is to establish an open and trusting relationship with the client, and in most cases, that can be done only when confidentiality is ensured.

Therapists try to ensure confidentiality whenever possible, but a promise of complete confidentiality may put the therapist at risk for other kinds of ethical infractions. What if, for example, a client reports repeated fantasies of murdering his former girlfriend and the therapist feels that the reported fantasies may be based upon a real motive and plan? What if the client brings up a history of child abuse and then admits to being a perpetrator as well as a victim? These and other such ethical quandaries are more than hypothetical, and, after a real case in which a client did murder his former girlfriend, the California Supreme Court ruled that the privilege of therapist-client confidentiality, like the privilege of doctor-patient confidentiality, has its limits. In cases in which it appears that the public welfare is endangered (whether it be a particular individual or the public at large), a therapist is ethically and legally required to report his or her assessment of the situation to appropriate authorities who may be able to protect the endangered individual or individuals. Rarely, however, are such decisions either straightforward or without cost.

Another attribute of the client-therapist relationship that makes it difficult to make clear-cut ethical judgments is the fact that the relationship of the therapist to the client may be, at one time or another, that of an objective expert, a friend, an authority figure, a role model, or a variety of other things; and behavior that is appropriate in some kinds of relationships may not be appropriate in others. In addition, since therapeutic sessions often involve intense emotion, there is always the potential for one or both parties to interpret the emotion as personal rather than situational and to respond to that emotion in an inappropriate way. It is not always possible to know when each type of role could be helpful and when it could be harmful; thus, it is impossible to come up with clear guidelines. Most psychologists, however, acknowledge the dangers inherent in playing multiple roles and realize that it is the psychologist, rather than the client, who should always be on the alert for such dangers.

A common but undesirable type of relationship between therapist and client is one of client emotional dependence upon, or indebtedness to, the therapist. While in such a relationship, the client may make it easy for the therapist to take undue advantages that are not in the client's best interest—for example, overcharging, extending the period of therapy beyond what is necessary, accepting favors, or even entering into a sexual relationship with the client. Such outcomes are antithetical to the goal of developing a better sense of self-esteem and well-being in the client, and they should be avoided at all costs; once developed, however, such relationships are often difficult to undo without additional psychological pain or damage.

Licensed therapists are also expected to maintain professional standards in other areas, such as maintaining and upgrading their education and competence, avoiding conflicts of interest, being able to make appropriate referrals when necessary, and being truthful in their advertising and other public statements.

ETHICS IN THE COURTROOM

Psychologists are more and more frequently being called as expert witnesses in the courts. One increasingly common practice is the use of psychologists to present evidence about the validity of certain types of testimony. Psychologists may address, for example, the accuracy (or lack thereof) of eyewitness testimony of witnesses of different ages (as in child abuse cases), or of memory elicited while the witness was under hypnosis, or the likelihood of different types of errors made by "lie detectors." They may also be asked to address special issues such as child development (as in custody cases), victimology, post-traumatic stress disorder, or "brainwashing." Testimony should be unbiased and, to be accepted by the court, should be based upon accepted knowledge and standards.

Psychologists are also sometimes called upon to make judgments that could affect a person's legal status. As expert witnesses in court, they may be asked to give their opinion on a person's mental status and ability to stand trial ("competence"), on a person's likely mental status at the time of a crime ("sanity"), or on the likelihood that a particular convicted criminal will respond positively to treatment or rehabilitation. This type of testimony cannot, like the types discussed above, be based solely upon accepted scientific standards and "facts"; because each case is unique, the psychologist must rely on clinical and personal judgment as well as scientific and statistical data.

Clearly, the impact of such judgments can be of great consequence, both to the public and to the person being judged. Therefore, both ethical and legal guidelines exist in order to help psychologists (and others involved in the criminal justice system) make decisions about a person's psychological competence and legal status. Despite U.S. society's long, traditional belief in personal liberty and the pursuit of happiness, that liberty can be taken away if a person is perceived to be a threat to himself or herself or to the public; whenever such drastic measures are considered, the ethical as well as the practical consequences must be addressed.

In some cases, a person is perceived to have lost the capacity to make free, rational choices—not as a result of incarceration, but as a result of severe physical or mental illness. Psychologists must often testify regarding a person's mental status and abilities when questions arise regarding the legitimacy and enforceability of a contested will, contract, or other legal document, or the involuntary commitment of an individual to a mental treatment facility. Both ethical and legal guidelines exist that allow a guardian or other legally designated individual to make decisions in the best interests of an "incompetent" individual,

but it is difficult to determine when, if ever, a person should lose the legal right to make decisions, even when those decisions may seem irrational to an observer.

Although it is a minority opinion, some psychologists share the view of Thomas Szasz, who argues that all psychiatric and psychological diagnoses of mental disorders are simply negative labels that the majority give to those in the minority who have a different view, or kind of life. Szasz argues that simply because someone may be statistically abnormal and doesn't function the way that society expects, that does not make him or her any less of a person, even in terms of legal rights and status. Clearly, what one considers "ethical" depends substantially upon one's philosophy.

ETHICS IN EDUCATION AND THE WORKPLACE

Unlike clinical psychologists, psychologists in educational and industrial settings are unlikely to be working with clients with mental illness, yet there exist in these settings many sensitive issues that require ethical consideration. Perhaps foremost among these are the issues surrounding testing. Students, workers, or potential job applicants may be tested for a variety of things, including honesty, aptitudes and abilities, attitudes, and personality. Such tests are thought to predict academic or job performance and are thus often used to "track" people into particular classes or careers.

One of the most controversial ethical issues surrounding testing is the phenomenon of labeling. Although many of the tests used in academic and industrial settings do have predictive validity (that is, they can predict people's performance at better than chance levels), no test is perfect, so sometimes a person's performance is estimated at a much lower level than it actually is. Since the tests are thought to measure stable attributes of individuals, they are usually not given more than once; thus, a person whose test score underestimated his or her abilities would likely be tracked into an area that would underutilize that person's skills and understimulate his or her intellect. Once the person is labeled as unlikely to succeed in other, perhaps more demanding areas, it is unlikely that such opportunities will be made available. At the same time, the person may self-label and enter into what is called a "self-fulfilling prophecy"; the person will assume that the test is accurate and that he or she is not cut out for other kinds of challenges, and thus will not try more challenging things. Since many skills really reflect the phrase "use it or lose it," if the person ceases to try new things and practice skills, his or her competence level may truly drop. Thus, as a result of being labeled by a test, the person may in fact become more like what the test originally (incorrectly) suggested.

The ethical quandary surrounding test use is whether the benefits that the tests confer to the educational or business institution outweigh the potential losses to the individuals being tested. Since some tests are statistically valid, they can save institutions time and money by tracking people quickly and efficiently into areas in which they will perform well; they also can be beneficial for those students or workers who are unhappy and want professional advice about what kind of study or job may suit them better. The costs of labeling someone, however, are unmeasurable.

As an example, consider honesty testing. Some honesty tests, such as the polygraph test, are statistically better than chance at ferreting out dishonest individuals as long as the tester/interpreter is honest and well trained. By giving a polygraph test to all potential employees, a business may save thousands of dollars by screening out some people who might embezzle, steal equipment, or sell company secrets. For each dishonest person who is caught by polygraph testing, however, there are several honest people who will also be weeded out and labeled by the test. Although the institution may save money by giving the test, many innocent (honest) people will suffer—they will not get the job, they may have something negative put in their files, or they may even be told that they failed the test, and may become depressed, hopeless, angry, or otherwise emotionally scarred. Because of these human costs, the U.S. Congress has outlawed the use of polygraphs in some settings, but where they are still allowed, the psychologists involved must consider the ethical issues each time the test is administered.

Unlike the polygraph test, not all tests used in educational and work settings are even statistically valid. Sometimes tests go out of date as society and culture change. Even those that are valid for one population (for example, adult males) may not be valid for another population (for example, adolescent males). Good psychologists must constantly keep up to date about the strengths, weaknesses, and limitations of the tests they use. Like their clinical counterparts, industrial and educational psychologists must realize that their tests are not always accurate, that there are dangers in mislabeling just as there are in misdiagnosing, and that a person is more than the sum of his or her test scores.

ETHICS IN RESEARCH

Psychologists who do research are subject to federal regulations that ensure that subjects' rights are not abused. According to federal guidelines, each research institute must set up an ethics committee to monitor animal research and another to monitor human research. Each committee must include not only research scientists but also at least one individual who has studied ethics and at least one person who can represent the views of the local community. Research using both animal and human subjects must be approved by the relevant committees before it is begun.

Researchers using animal subjects must ensure that animals are housed, fed, and transported in a humane manner; government-employed veterinarians make unannounced visits to make sure that each facility is operating in compliance with federal animal welfare guidelines. Researchers must also ensure that animals' pain and suffering is minimized, and that all alternative research techniques have been considered before any painful procedures are planned. The number and species of animals that are used must also be justified. On an annual basis, each committee presents a summary report of the institution's research activities to the federal government.

Researchers using human subjects must do much more in order to get a project approved by the local committee. Each researcher must demonstrate that all subjects are informed, in writing, of all possible risks of participation; that each subject signs a written consent form (or has a legal guardian sign instead); that subjects are never pressured to participate in a study and know that they are free to withdraw from the study at any time; that counseling is available for anyone who does somehow feel injured by participation in the study; that all data are kept confidential at all phases of the study; and that all subjects receive a written "debriefing" at the end of the study, which not only thanks them for their participation but also gives them any information about the study that may have been withheld or disguised in the consent form.

Withholding or disguising information in the consent form is called "deception." Deception is kept at a minimum but sometimes is necessary in order to prevent subject bias. For example, subjects may sign up to participate in a study that is supposedly on reading, but is really on helping behavior. While the subjects are sitting in what they think is a waiting room, the experimenter may stage an "accident" and observe how many subjects try to help the accident "victim" and under what conditions. It is likely that subjects would behave in a different way under these fairly realistic circumstances if they knew that the "accident" was staged and that they were really in a study of helping behavior. All research deception must be approved by the ethics committee in advance, and the debriefing must explain to the subjects why the deception was necessary. Studies that involve major or prolonged deception are generally not approved, even though they might provide useful information.

Linda Mealey

FURTHER READING

American Psychological Association. "Ethical Principles of Psychologists." *American Psychologist* 36 (June, 1981): 633-638. Principles one through eight cover ethics for practicing psychologists, number nine is on research using human participants, and number ten is on research using animals.

Bersoff, Donald N., ed. *Ethical Conflicts in Psychology*. 3d ed. Washington, D.C.: American Psychological Association, 2003. Combines official ethical documents and guidelines of the APA, legal decisions affecting the profession, and scholarly articles on psychological ethics.

Keith-Spiegel, Patricia, and Gerald P. Koocher. *Ethics in Psychology: Professional Standards and Cases*. 2d ed. New York: Oxford University Press, 1998. Co-written by one of the original formulators of the ten ethical principles, this book gives detailed descriptions, justifications, and examples regarding APA ethical guidelines for therapy, testing, advertising, publishing, finances, and conflicts of interest.

Meyer, Robert G., E. Rhett Landis, and J. Ray Hays. *Law for the Psychotherapist*. New York: W. W. Norton, 1988. Organized as a handbook for practicing therapists, this text is still accessible to nonprofessionals. Covers many sensitive areas, including courtroom testimony, involuntary commitment, treatment issues, and malpractice.

Slife, Brent, ed. *Taking Sides: Clashing Views on Controversial Psychological Issues*. 8th ed. Guilford, Conn.: Dushkin, 1994. Each edition of this series includes a "yes" and a "no" essay from experts debating a variety of controversial issues in psychology; includes ethical issues, such as research ethics, therapy effectiveness, behavior modification, intelligence testing, the insanity defense, and the consequences of diagnostic labeling.

Szasz, Thomas Stephen. *Thomas Szasz: Primary Values and Major Contentions*. Edited by Richard E. Vatz and Lee S. Weinberg. Buffalo, N.Y.: Prometheus, 1983. An excellent summary of Szasz's works, their critiques, and his rejoinders. Puts Szasz's views in the contexts of "psychiatric wisdom" and conventional public thinking.

SEE ALSO: Behavior therapy; Behaviorism; Electroshock therapy; Ethical Principles of Psychologists; Family therapy; Freud, Sigmund; Institutionalization of patients; Intelligence testing; Jung, Carl; Mental illness; Therapist-patient relationship.

Psychopharmacology

DEFINITION: Study of the effects that drugs have on emotion, thought, and behavior

TYPE OF ETHICS: Psychological ethics

SIGNIFICANCE: Psychopharmacology is the basis for the medical treatment of mental illness. As such, it raises ethical questions involving the rights of the mentally ill to determine their own course of treatment or to refuse medication, as well as the long-term risks of medications that produce short-term benefits.

While many physicians and biologically oriented psychiatrists have had a long-standing commitment to the use of psychotropic medications for the treatment of some emotional disorders, others have questioned their use in particular cases. From an ethical perspective, some people have questioned whether such interventions are demonstrably superior to other treatment forms—such as psychotherapy, for example—in view of the known side effects of medications. In addition, it is not always clear that patients are able to give fully informed consent, and it is not always clear that patients are fully informed of all the risks inherent in psychopharmacological interventions.

HISTORY

While the use of psychoactive drugs designed to treat mental disorders is relatively recent, the use of drugs as pain relievers and sleep producers goes back for many hundreds of years. Alcohol and opiates are good examples of drugs that have been used for such purposes. The use by the medical community of drugs to treat mental symptoms goes back to the 1840's, when bromides were first used to treat anxiety. Later in the nineteenth century, Sigmund Freud, the father of psychoanalysis, suggested that cocaine was a psychoactive drug that could be helpful, and in the first part of the twentieth century, barbiturates were introduced to treat anxiety.

Alan Gelenberg, Ellen Bassuk, and Stephen Schoonover point out in their book *The Practitioner's Guide to Psychoactive Drugs* (3d ed., 1991) that in 1949, with the synthesis of chlorpromazine, the medical community began to focus on the use of drugs to treat mental illness. At about the same time that chlorpromazine was developed, reserpine (another tranquilizer synthesized from the root of the plant *Rauwolfia serpentina*) came into use. Lithium chloride was used as early as 1940, but its ability to counter manic behavior was not established until 1949 and lithium itself was not approved for use in the United States until 1970.

PRESCRIPTION PRIVILEGES

While physicians and some other health professionals (for example, nurse practitioners and optometrists) do have the authority to prescribe medications, nonphysicians, including psychologists, do not have prescription privileges, although on the federal level psychologists have legally prescribed within the Indian Health Service. Since the 1990's, there has been a spirited debate among psychologists regarding whether prescription privileges should be sought by psychologists on a state-by-state basis. The focus of the argument has been on psychotropic medications and their judicious use. Some people have argued that nursing home residents are often treated with drugs that are designed to treat mental disorders when, in fact, most of these patients are not mentally ill. Conversely, while there is agreement that some children with symptoms of hyperactivity and/or attention deficit disorder should be treated with psychotropic medications, it is important to diagnose such problems carefully, since such problems may involve parents' ineffectiveness in coping with the child.

OBJECTIONS TO PSYCHOTROPIC DRUGS

In his book *Toxic Psychiatry* (1991), Peter Breggin argues that many patients may not have been fully apprised of the negative (addictive and dangerous) side effects of many psychotropic medications. In addition, he argues that the use of drugs even for the severely mentally ill is not unequivocally supported by research and that the results of positive drug studies are countermanded by evidence that some psychotropic drugs cause brain impairment. Mary Lee Smith, Gene Glass, and Thomas Miller, in their book *The Benefits of Psychotherapy* (1980), analyzed 112 experiments that studied the separate and combined effects of drug therapy and psychotherapy. They found that even for serious psychological disorders, psychotherapy was nearly even with drug therapy in terms of overall effectiveness. While drug therapy and psychotherapy taken together produced greater effects than did either drug therapy or psychotherapy alone, the effects of these therapies in combination were only slightly greater than their separate effects.

THE COMBINED USE OF PHARMACOTHERAPY AND PSYCHOTHERAPY

In his book *The Psychotherapist's Guide to Psychopharmacology* (1990), Michael J. Gitlin raises the question of whether there are negative interactions between drug therapy and psychotherapy. To the extent that successful drug therapy reduces symptoms, some patients may not wish to continue in psychotherapy for their emotional problems. There is also concern that dependence on drugs may make patients unusually passive and relatively unwilling to explore their problems in psychotherapy. Finally, some patients may become distressed at the notion that they could benefit from medications in addition to psychotherapy, since they may perceive medications as a kind of crutch. Some patients, however, are convinced that they have some kind of chemical imbalance that needs to be "fixed" by means of psychotropic drugs. These patients do not believe that it is important to explore their problems in psychotherapy.

Gitlin also describes who should have a medication consultation. He points out that patients with such psychiatric symptoms as delusions, hallucinations, or psychosis should be considered, as well as patients with appetite or sleep disturbances and those with significant suicidal tendencies. Patients with significant medical disorders and patients with a family history of more than minor psychiatric disorders are candidates for drug therapy. Finally, patients presenting confusion, concentration problems, and other cognitive symptoms are also good candidates for medication consultations.

THE RIGHT TO REFUSE TREATMENT

In his book *Law, Psychiatry, and Morality* (1984), Alan Stone raises an important moral and ethical issue. Should hospitalized mentally ill patients be required to take antipsychotic medications? Critics of forcing hospitalized patients to take antipsychotic medications argue that this is an invasion of privacy or that these drugs are mind altering and thus violate First Amendment rights. It is known, for example, that some antipsychotic drugs can affect speech and thought. Stone cites a case in which the court was asked to decide whether the state can impose the use of antipsychotic drugs in the absence of an emergency. In that case (*Rogers v. Commissioner of Mental Health*), a federal judge decided that the patient did have the right to refuse medication, since the patient was not likely to harm himself or others. Stone argues that the real issue that should be addressed is whether a patient's mental illness will respond to antipsychotic medications, rather than assuming that antipsychotic drugs are chemical restraints. Some organizations, such as the National Association for the Mentally Ill, strongly agree with Stone. Others, including many psychologists, agree with the judge's decision. Time will tell how this topic will be resolved.

Norman Abeles

FURTHER READING

Breggin, Peter. *Toxic Psychiatry.* New York: St. Martin's Press, 1991.
Gelenberg, Alan J., and Ellen L. Bassuk, eds. *The Practitioner's Guide to Psychoactive Drugs.* 4th ed. New York: Plenum, 1997.
Ghaemi, S. Nassir, ed. *Polypharmacy in Psychiatry.* New York: Dekker, 2002.
Gitlin, Michael J. *The Psychotherapist's Guide to Psychopharmacology.* New York: Free Press, 1990.
Smith, Mary L., Gene V. Glass, and Thomas I. Miller. *The Benefits of Psychotherapy.* Baltimore: Johns Hopkins University Press, 1980.
Stone, Alan A. *Law, Psychiatry, and Morality.* Washington, D.C.: American Psychiatric Press, 1984.

SEE ALSO: Diagnosis; Drug abuse; Electroshock therapy; Institutionalization of patients; Jung, Carl; Psychology; Therapist-patient relationship.

Public interest

DEFINITION: Common good of all members of a society

TYPE OF ETHICS: Personal and social ethics

SIGNIFICANCE: Theoretically, the interests of every single member of a society may conflict with the interests of the public considered as a whole. The notion of public interest therefore requires weighing the theoretical rights of the individual against the rights of the collective, as well as considering practical claims of specific individuals or groups in specific situations.

For Plato and Aristotle, the concept of public interest arises together with the following fundamental questions: What is justice? What is the best structure of society? What is the proper role of government? The same concept, under the term "commonwealth," underlies the social contract theories of Thomas Hobbes (*Leviathan*, 1651), John Locke (*Second Treatise of Government*, 1689), and nineteenth century progressivism.

In 1907, U.S. president Theodore Roosevelt signed the Pure Food and Drug Act, quieting decades of outcry against dangerous consumer products that were perceived as resulting from unregulated pursuit of the profit motive. The 1930's saw renewed interest in the government's mission to benefit society, and a plethora of public-interest legislation resulted. During the 1960's and 1970's, legislation addressed to public health and safety introduced a new level of regulation of private enterprise, fueled by the growing consumer and environmental movements. In response to business objections, there was a partial rollback of regulation during the 1980's. The longer-term trend, however, has been the evolution of a closer identification between private enterprise and public needs, partly reversing the traditional view that free enterprise and the public interest are inherently at odds.

D. Gosselin Nakeeb

SEE ALSO: Altruism; Bentham, Jeremy; Common good; Consumerism; Environmental Protection Agency; Future-oriented ethics; Whistleblowing.

Public's right to know

DEFINITION: Notion that government agencies, and some private companies, have an obligation to disclose their plans and actions to the public

TYPE OF ETHICS: Media ethics

SIGNIFICANCE: A guiding principle behind the public's right to know is the idea that citizens in a representative democracy have the inherent right to be informed about decisions, especially those of government, that may affect them and their communities.

On July 4, 1967, President Lyndon B. Johnson signed the Freedom of Information Act (FOIA). That law effectively required the federal government and, by implication, the various state and local governments, to provide fuller disclosure of their actions and decisions to citizens, especially through the news media. The law was the logical result of a long series of campaigns to enact "sunshine laws" ensuring that government would be conducted more in the public view. Those campaigns also grew to include information about significant activities of private corporations that could have impacts on potential health hazards in the air, water, and land, as well as in food and other consumer products. The concept of the public's right to know is not confined to the United States; however, it and the FOIA have special relevance in the United States because of direct connections to the free press clause of Article I of the U.S. Constitution's Bill of Rights.

As the concept is generally accepted, the public's right to know covers several broad categories. The first is that maximum disclosure is favored over partial revelations. Protected areas may include trade secrets and other exceptions, but supporters of the right to know say exceptions should be kept to an absolute minimum. A second broad category is the promotion of open government, the "sunshine" portion of FOIA. Wherever possible, government decisions should be discussed and made in public meetings freely reported by the media.

A fourth area covered by most FOIA and right-to-know legislation is the imperative for government agencies to facilitate use of their information by the news media and citizens. This goal should be achieved through open meetings, limited costs to copy requested documents, and processes that help spread information freely. These are required obligations on the part of government—and, to some extent, the private sector as well. Finally, protection is often afforded to "whistleblowers," those individuals who come forward with previously withheld information covered by the right to know provisions of the law.

There are opponents to the principle of the public's right to know, especially in sensitive areas involving national security or competitiveness. However, courts have generally been favorable to the concept, perhaps shown nowhere more clearly than in the U.S. Supreme Court's ruling that the government could not use prior restraint to prevent *The New York Times* (1971) from publishing excerpts from the Pentagon Papers that revealed how the United States became secretly and heavily involved in the Vietnam War. The ethical obligations of a democracy to inform its citizens as fully as possible, especially about decisions that affect public policy, has clearly been established as a keystone of media operations, although there are those in and out of government who remain unhappy with the concept and its application.

Michael Witkoski

FURTHER READING

Gorman, Lyn, and David McLean. *Media and Society in the Twentieth Century.* Oxford, England: Blackwell Publishing, 2003.

Kovach, Bill, and Tom Rosentiel. *The Elements of Journalism.* New York: Crown Publishers, 2001.

Levy, Beth, and Denis M. Bonilla, eds. *The Power of the Press*. New York: H. W. Wilson, 1999.

Pavik, John. *Journalism and the New Media*. New York: Columbia University Press, 2001.

SEE ALSO: Ethics in Government Act; Freedom of Information Act; Information access; Journalistic ethics; Pentagon Papers.

Punishment

DEFINITION: Penalty suffered as a result of transgression

TYPE OF ETHICS: Beliefs and practices

SIGNIFICANCE: The legitimate purposes of punishment are a source of ongoing debate. Is it permissible, for example, to punish out of a need for revenge, or only as a deterrent to future wrongdoing? To what extent are punishment and rehabilitation compatible or incompatible goals? What limits if any should society place upon parents' rights to punish their children, or employers' rights to punish their employees, in the manner in which they see fit?

Punishment, along with crime, appears to be as old as human society. Punishment involves doing harm to supposed offenders in order to prevent the harm caused by crime. It is a crucial means used to promote social control, order, and, presumably, justice. While punishment has been endemic to human society, it is morally problematic in theory as well as practice. Therefore, it retains the status of a necessary evil. A society in which punishment is clearly obsolete has yet to evolve.

HISTORY OF THE CONCEPT

The idea and practice of punishment are as old as civilized societies. Various histories make it clear that punishment has been a basic component of human society, past and present. Indeed, one measure of advancing civilization has been the codification of law, including criminal offenses and sanctions. Punishment is treated conceptually in Western philosophy, at least from the time of Plato, and is prominent in Asian philosophy as well (for example, the Chinese Legalists). The Bible and the Qur'ān contain many passages and parables involving punishment. With the coming of the Enlightenment (in the eighteenth century), social reformers sought to rationalize and humanize punishments, making penalties proportional to offenses and arguing against particularly brutal sanctions. The Ninth Amendment to the U.S. Constitution, for example, prohibits (though it does not define) "cruel and unusual" punishment.

Punishment may be classified into several types. Corporal punishment involves physical sanctions such as beating, flogging, or the amputation of limbs. Capital punishment involves the execution of offenders and is limited to the most heinous of crimes. Incarceration, the most common modern sanction for serious offenders, involves forced restraint in a prison setting. (Incarceration also may involve forced labor, though this has become less common.) Less-serious offenders may be subjected to fines, house arrest, probation, or community service.

MORAL BASES FOR PUNISHMENT

Punishment involves doing harm to people, restraining their freedom, inflicting pain, or even taking their lives. Because of this, it requires moral justification. The primary justification is "retributive justice" (or just deserts). This means that the harm of punishment may legitimately be inflicted because the victims of punishment deserve punishment. In addition, punishment may be defended as a "deterrent." The swift and certain punishment of offenders discourages other people from breaking laws.

Two defenses of punishment try to minimize the harm inherent in the concept. "Incapacitation" suggests the morally neutral restraint of prolific criminals until they have passed the age of peak criminal activity. "Rehabilitation" suggests that punishment can be beneficial. Here, restraint is used to reform the offender in a way that serves his or her best interests as well as society's. The problem with these last two rationales is that both involve the radical restraint of freedom. (In addition, incapacitation involves massive allocation of social resources and rehabilitation has yet to be proved effective in practice.)

MORAL DILEMMAS

Punishment is morally problematic in both practical and theoretical terms. In practice, the criminal sanction is often utilized to punish real or imagined "political" crimes against autocratic or tyrannical regimes. It is also sometimes meted out by unruly mobs, as in vigilante justice. In addition, real-life punishment is often brutal, even for minor offenses. The remedies for these ills are guarantees of due process and, as mentioned above, the prohibition of cruel punishments. Even when it is formally correct, however, the criminal process is disconcertingly imperfect.

Theoretically, punishment is marred by the problematic nature of culpability and criminal responsibility. Punishment can be legitimate only if offenders deserve to be punished. To be so deserving requires the presumption of free will. Free will, however, is philosophically and sociologically problematic. Where free will is not assumed (as, for example, in cases of criminal insanity), criminal responsibility is mitigated to the extent that temporarily insane defendants may even escape punishment or medical restraint altogether. While insanity is the extreme case, people are compelled in their behavior by all sorts of factors. Thus, free will is not an absolute. Indeed, its very existence is impossible to prove. There are also important social limits to the concept of criminal culpability, particularly where crime is heavily associated with a segment of the population that is in a disadvantaged social position. In such a case, social responsibility becomes confounded with criminal responsibility. As a result, the entire criminal process, including punishment, becomes morally suspect.

LIMITED EFFECTIVENESS OF PUNISHMENT

In addition to the moral dilemmas of punishment, there are practical limits to punishment's effectiveness as a means of maintaining order. Punishment is, at best, only half of the equation when it comes to social order. The other half is the availability to all strata of society of sufficient rewards for legal pursuits. Societies that permit crime-producing socioeconomic disparities are not able to ensure social order by means of the criminal sanction. This means that a society can simultaneously have harsh punishments and high crime rates, as exhibited by the United States during the last third of the twentieth century. Thus, punishment is most accurately seen only as a corollary means of maintaining social order, one that complements the teaching of solid social values and an abundance of opportunity for legitimate gain.

THE FUTURE OF PUNISHMENT

Despite its moral and practical limits, punishment appears to be an indispensable mechanism for dealing with certain kinds of behavior. For centuries, utopian thinkers have held out the hope for a society so well ordered that punishment would become obsolete. Such a condition has yet to emerge. Until it does, people can still attempt to minimize the role of punishment in preserving order and producing justice.

Ira Smolensky

FURTHER READING

Foucault, Michel. *Discipline and Punish: The Birth of the Prison.* Translated by Alan Sheridan. New York: Vintage Books, 1979.

Garland, David. *Punishment in Modern Society: A Study in Social Theory.* Chicago: University of Chicago Press, 1990.

Matravers, Matt, ed. *Punishment and Political Theory.* Portland, Oreg.: Hart, 1999.

Matson, Johnny, and Thomas M. DiLorenzo. *Punishment and Its Alternatives: A New Perspective for Behavior Modification.* New York: Springer, 1984.

Norrie, Alan. *Punishment, Responsibility, and Justice: A Relational Critique.* New York: Oxford University Press, 2000.

Packer, Herbert L. *The Limits of the Criminal Sanction.* Stanford, Calif.: Stanford University Press, 1968.

Paul, Ellen F., et al., eds. *Crime, Culpability, and Remedy.* Cambridge, Mass.: Blackwell, 1990.

Primoratz, Igor. *Justifying Legal Punishment.* Atlantic Highlands, N.J.: Humanities Press, 1989.

Tam, Henry, ed. *Punishment, Excuses, and Moral Development.* Brookfield, Vt.: Avebury, 1996.

Ten, C. L. *Crime, Guilt, and Punishment: A Philosophical Introduction.* New York: Oxford University Press, 1987.

Van den Haag, Ernest. *Punishing Criminals: Concerning a Very Old and Painful Question.* Lanham, Md.: University Press of America, 1991.

SEE ALSO: Bentham, Jeremy; Capital punishment; Confidentiality; Criminal punishment; Foucault, Michel; Law; Mercy; Nietzsche, Friedrich; Parole of convicted prisoners; Social justice and responsibility; Three-strikes laws.

Q

Quinlan, Karen Ann

IDENTIFICATION: Comatose patient who was the focus of a well-publicized ethical controversy

BORN: March 29, 1954, Scranton, Pennsylvania

DIED: June 11, 1985, Morris Plains, New Jersey

TYPE OF ETHICS: Bioethics

SIGNIFICANCE: Despite the fact that Karen Ann Quinlan remained alive for almost ten years after she was taken off life support, the removal of her respirator set an important precedent for legal battles over euthanasia.

Karen Ann Quinlan. (AP/Wide World Photos)

On April 15, 1975, Karen Ann Quinlan, then twenty-one years old, was taken to a hospital in a critical comatose state. She had had a few drinks, passed out, and temporarily quit breathing. There was a small amount of alcohol in her body as well as a nontoxic level of aspirin and Valium. Part of her brain had died because of oxygen depletion. She was moved to St. Clare's Hospital in Denville, New Jersey, where it was determined that she had extensive brain damage. Karen began to deteriorate physically and coiled into a fetal position. She was attached to an MA-1 respirator.

In July, Quinlan's parents asked that the respirator be removed and signed papers absolving the hospital from legal liability. The doctors refused. Karen was twenty-one, so her parents were not her legal guardians. Joseph Quinlan went to court to be appointed guardian so that he could have the respirator removed. The lower court ruled against the Quinlans, but the New Jersey Supreme Court ruled in their favor. Six weeks later, Karen was still on the respirator; however, the doctors agreed to wean her from it. She continued to breathe without the respirator. In June, 1976, she was moved to a nursing home where she was given high-nutrient feedings and antibiotics. She lived for ten years in a persistent vegetative state. Her case is important in discussions of the right to die, the ordinary/extraordinary care distinction, the active/passive euthanasia distinction, and the need for a living will.

Rita C. Hinton

SEE ALSO: Death and dying; Euthanasia; Life and death; "Playing god" in medical decision making; Right to die.

Qur'ān

IDENTIFICATION: Holy book of Islam
DATE: Revealed to Muḥammad between 609 and
632
TYPE OF ETHICS: Religious ethics
SIGNIFICANCE: The Qur'ān is the central text of Is-
lam. It is believed to have been revealed to the
Prophet Muḥammad by God through the angel
Gabriel over a period of twenty-two years.

Muslims believe that the Qur'ān was revealed by God
to the Prophet Muḥammad through the angel Gabriel. At the age of forty, Muḥammad began to receive messages from God. Muḥammad had the habit
of retiring to secluded places outside Mecca in order
to pray and think.

During one of these periods of seclusion, the angel Gabriel first appeared to Muḥammad. Gabriel
shook Muḥammad several times and ordered him to
repeat after him, to "recite in the name of the Creator"
(the literal meaning of the word *Qur'ān* is "to recite"). Muḥammad's relationship with the angel Gabriel was to last the rest of his life, and the Qur'ān was
revealed piece by piece. The actual compilation of
the holy book was undertaken by the third caliph,
'Uthmān.

FORM AND CONTENTS

The Qur'ān contains 114 chapters, or *sūras*,
which are further divided into thirty parts, or *ajza*.
The order of the chapters, which is not chronological,
was decided by Zayd ibn Tabi, who was one of
Muḥammad's close associates. Zayd is believed to
have collected all the verses from various sources—
some in written form and others orally, from those
who knew them by heart.

Some scholars believe that the current form of the
Qur'ān took shape many centuries after the death of
the Prophet Muḥammad. The accepted belief among
Muslims, however, is that the book was compiled in
its original form by the order of caliph 'Uthmān.
When the compilation had been completed, 'Uthmān
sent copies to the principal centers of the Muslim empire—Damascus, Basra, and Kufa—ordering that all
previous versions be destroyed. According to one account, the people of Kufa preferred another version
that had been compiled by Ibn Mas'ud.

Orthodox Muslims believe that Islam is a complete code of life and that the Qur'ān contains answers for all conceivable questions. The Qur'ān is the
fundamental authority on all matters. (If no clear answer is found in the holy book, the next source is the
Ḥadīth, or sayings, that grew up around the life of the
Prophet Muḥammad.)

The Qur'ān is written in verse, and it is considered
to be the ultimate example of Arabic poetry—a standard against which all other literature must be
judged. It deals with all kinds of subjects, ranging
from property and family law to the way in which
prisoners should be treated during a war. The book is
written with remarkable fluency and great style, and
with a wide range of vocabulary. Because of the
Qur'ān's literary quality, many skeptics challenged
Muḥammad's claim that he did not know how to read
and write. Several Christian and Jewish scholars
claimed that Muḥammad borrowed concepts from
their religions and had help from scholars in presenting his message to his followers. Muslims, however,
claim that only a divine message could be so beautiful and poetic.

It is a fact that Muḥammad traveled extensively
for business purposes. He is said to have visited several centers of knowledge of the time, including Palestine, Egypt, and Lebanon. These are the places
where he is said to have met scholars and to have
learned about other religions. Western scholars believe that this is how Muḥammad formulated his
ideas.

One important concept contained in the Qur'ān is
that the other so-called "religions of the book"—
Christianity and Judaism—are valid because they are
based on true prophets such as Moses and Jesus, who
were sent by God. According to Islamic belief, God
sent various prophets to show people the true path.
After some time had passed, the people would be led
astray by Satan, and God would send another
prophet. Muslims believe, however, that God chose
Muḥammad to bring the final message of God for all
people. One of the Five Pillars of Islam is the belief
that there is no God but Allah, and Muḥammad is the
prophet of Allah; there will be no prophets after
Muḥammad.

Some of the most important ideas of Islam are
similar to those of Judaism and Christianity. Both Judaism and Christianity are monotheistic, and in both,
the ideas of heaven and hell are similar to those found
in Islam. Many of the episodes described in the

Qur'ān are the same as those found in the Old Testament; for example, the versions of the story of Abraham's willingness to sacrifice his son at God's command and the story of Noah's Ark are quite similar in the two books. One of the central themes of the Qur'ān is the day of judgment, which is described in various verses throughout the book. On that day, all human beings will be resurrected and made to answer for all their actions on Earth. Muslims will be expected to have followed the dictates of Islam to the letter.

There are various ways of interpreting parts of the Qur'ān, and these have led to the development of various schools of thought within Islam. Although there are two main sects in Islam—Sunnīs and Shī'ites—there are also several subsects that differ in fundamental ways regarding certain crucial concepts. In the modern Islamic world, for example, there is fierce debate regarding women's rights, laws of inheritance, interest-free banking, and many other subjects. There is a major struggle between a desire for modernity and the requirement to follow Islamic precepts to the letter. In the early twenty-first century, Iran and Saudi Arabia represented Orthodox Islam,

whereas Turkey and Egypt represented more pragmatic, modern varieties of Islam.

Khalid N. Mahmood

FURTHER READING

Ali, Ahmed. *Al-Qur'an: A Contemporary Translation*. Final rev. ed. Princeton, N.J.: Princeton University Press, 1994.

Cook, Michael. *Commanding Right and Forbidding Wrong in Islamic Thought*. New York: Cambridge University Press, 2000.

Cragg, Kenneth, and R. Marston Speight. *The House of Islam*. 3d ed. Belmont, Calif.: Wadsworth, 1988.

Denny, Frederick Mathewson. *Islam and the Muslim Community*. San Francisco: Harper & Row, 1987.

Esposito, John L. *Islam: The Straight Path*. New York: Oxford University Press, 1988.

Hashmi, Sohail H., ed. *Islamic Political Ethics: Civil Society, Pluralism, and Conflict*. Princeton, N.J.: Princeton University Press, 2002.

SEE ALSO: Abū Ḥanīfah; Būkhārī, al-; *Ḥadīth*; Islamic ethics; Jihad; Muḥammad; Shī'a; Sunnīs.

R

Rābiʿah al-ʿAdawīyah

IDENTIFICATION: Arab mystical poet
BORN: 712, Basra (now in Iraq)
DIED: 801, Basra (now in Iraq)
TYPE OF ETHICS: Religious ethics
SIGNIFICANCE: Composer of numerous religious poems, Rābiʿah was a formative influence in the development of devotional Sufism. Because her life stands as an exemplum of religious devotion, she is one of the most important women in the history of Islamic ethics.

Rābiʿah's life is a metaphor for her thought: She was a slave who was set free by her master. She was a joyful ascetic who was freed from attachment to or desire for things of this world, even from the selfish desires of attaining Paradise and avoiding Hell. Her life was completely filled with immediate love of God for God's own sake. Hers was a jealous God who would countenance no other loves: There was no remaining room for marriage, worldly gain, self, or even any special reverence for the Prophet Muḥammad. She produced no treatises or other lengthy works, but her brief sayings, her short poems in awe and celebration of God's beauty, and stories of her life made a dramatic impact and played an important part in transforming the severe asceticism of early Sufism into a mysticism focused on divine love. She inspired devotional poets such as al-Rūmī and was celebrated by ʿAṭṭār as "a second spotless Mary." She remains a popular ideal of devotion to God.

Thomas Gaskill

SEE ALSO: Asceticism; Islamic ethics; Mysticism; Rūmī, Jalāl al-Dīn; Sufism.

Racial prejudice

DEFINITION: Irrational hostility toward, or baseless preconceptions about, persons of other races
TYPE OF ETHICS: Race and ethnicity
SIGNIFICANCE: Racial prejudice is commonly thought to be wrong in modern society, but it is also believed that one should not be punished for one's thoughts. There is thus a conflict between the desire to eradicate prejudice and the desire to respect freedom of conscience. Moreover, because it is no longer socially acceptable to express racial prejudice in public, it is difficult to gauge the extent to which prejudice is disappearing in modern society and the extent to which it has simply moved underground.

Racial prejudice stems from the mistaken notion that superficial physical differences among people reflect inherited differences in character, personality, motivation, intelligence, and potential. Racial prejudice leads to interpersonal conflict and to discrimination in housing, jobs, and services. Laws designed to end the effects of prejudice have been enacted in many countries, though large numbers of people continue to harbor prejudiced views.

Racial prejudice is often confused with ethnocentrism, the presumed superiority of one's own culture over the cultures of other people. Traditional animosity between the Chinese and Japanese, for example, is sometimes interpreted as racist, but this hostility is more likely the result of cultural bias.

HISTORY

On the basis of historical records, it is difficult to distinguish racial prejudice from nationalism and ethnocentrism. An undoubted case of racial prejudice, however, developed among the Tutsi, Hutu, and Twa peoples of Rwanda and Burundi in Central Africa during the fourteenth century. This region was originally settled by the Twa, who were very short hunters and potters. At some time before the fourteenth century, the Hutu, who were agriculturalists of medium stature, moved into the region and asserted dominance over the Twa. Then the Tutsi, who were unusually tall people, immigrated to the area and assumed sovereignty over *both* the Hutu and the Twa. Physical stature played an important role in the development and maintenance of this prejudicial hierarchical system.

Racial prejudice also played a role in the histories of South Africa and the United States, countries in which white European settlers achieved cultural dominance over indigenous, darker-skinned peoples. The South African system of apartheid, which was dismantled during the early 1990's in response to years of political turmoil and international boycott, was designed by the ruling Dutch colonialists to maintain separate white and black cultures. Blacks and other nonwhites, who accounted for more than four-fifths of the population, experienced restrictions in travel, education, land ownership, and voting privileges.

In the United States, centuries of tension and misunderstanding between whites and Native Americans developed into bitter racist resentments during the nineteenth century. As a result, Native Americans were forcibly removed by the federal government to reservations where they still live. Racial prejudice was also directed against Hispanics, Asians, African Americans, Jews, and other ethnic minorities in America. White supremacist organizations such as the Ku Klux Klan used beatings, lynchings, and other terrorist tactics to maintain the low social status of racial minorities. In response to the social activism of the 1950's and 1960's, however, the Civil Rights Act of 1964 outlawed racial segregation and other forms of discrimination in public establishments. Despite this and other government reforms, white supremacists continue to foster racial prejudice in America.

One of the most chilling examples of racial prejudice resulted in Nazi Germany's attempt to exterminate the Jews during the 1930's and 1940's. Adolf Hitler believed that Jews were innately inferior to Germans and other members of the so-called Aryan race. Because Jews competed for food and other resources that his own "superior" people deserved, Hitler believed that it was his duty to eliminate Jews and other unworthy competitors. Hitler's intense race hatred led to the systematic killing of millions of Jews during the Holocaust. Similar genocidal campaigns have been mounted by the Turks against the Armenians, the Iraqis against the Kurds, and the Serbians against the Bosnian Muslims.

JUSTIFICATIONS FOR RACIAL PREJUDICE

While social scientists believe that racial prejudice is a learned response, the roots of racial prejudice often remain obscure. The justifications used by people to defend racist attitudes, however, are well documented. Ironically, the most influential justifications for racial prejudice have come from two unlikely sources: science and religion.

Racial prejudice was almost universal among Western Europeans and Americans during the nineteenth century. White scientists felt compelled to provide empirical evidence for the assumed superiority of their race. Craniometricians, for example, believed that brain size and intelligence were causally linked—the larger the brain, the more intelligent the person. Despite a lack of objective support for this hypothesis, craniometry became very popular. Brains of famous people were measured, compared, and preserved after their owners' deaths, and the average cranial capacities of skulls from people of different racial groups were computed. The results suggested that whites were more intelligent than members of other races. When IQ tests were developed during the early twentieth century, these were also employed by psychologists to reinforce the notion of white superiority. Recent studies have shown that attempts by craniometricians and psychologists to provide scientific support for racist views were flawed by unconscious bias or outright fraud.

Religious notions have also provided powerful justifications for prejudiced attitudes, especially against African Americans. For example, biblical fundamentalists have taught that the descendants of Noah's son Ham developed "inferior" traits such as dark skin and kinky hair as the result of a divine curse. Others have ascribed the origin of these traits to the activities of the devil. Still others believed that blacks originated as a result of sinful cross-breeding between humans and animals. Because of distorted ideas such as these, many white Christian congregations in America refused to admit African Americans to their services, denominationally operated hospitals denied care to dark-skinned patients, and church schools closed their doors to black children.

ERADICATING RACIAL PREJUDICE

Deeply ingrained racial prejudice is difficult but not impossible to eradicate in individuals and societies. The mass media can play an important role in reshaping societal attitudes. Political activism can promote legislative changes favoring nondiscriminatory practices. Children can learn to appreciate racial diversity if they are taught the value of human variation early in life. Individuals can overcome prejudice by associating with members of other racial groups on a regular basis.

James L. Hayward

FURTHER READING

Ehrlich, Howard J. *The Social Psychology of Prejudice*. New York: John Wiley & Sons, 1973.

Gould, Stephen J. *The Mismeasure of Man*. New York: W. W. Norton, 1981.

Kevles, Daniel J. *In the Name of Eugenics: Genetics and the Uses of Human Heredity*. Cambridge, Mass.: Harvard University Press, 1995.

Moss, Donald, ed. *Hating in the First Person Plural: Psychoanalytic Essays on Racism, Homophobia, Misogyny, and Terror*. New York: Other Press, 2003.

Stangor, Charles, ed. *Stereotypes and Prejudice: Essential Readings*. Philadelphia: Psychology Press, 2000.

Stein, George J. "Biological Science and the Roots of Nazism." *American Scientist* 76 (January/February, 1988): 50-58.

Watson, Peter, ed. *Psychology and Race*. Chicago: Aldine, 1973.

SEE ALSO: Anti-Semitism; Apartheid; Bigotry; Civil Rights movement; Genocide and democide; Oppression; Racism; Segregation.

Racism

DEFINITION: Racial prejudice that is overtly or covertly supported by institutional power structures
TYPE OF ETHICS: Race and ethnicity
SIGNIFICANCE: Racism became a justification for slavery in the Western Hemisphere and for the subsequent denial of human and civil rights to people of color.

The concept of race is an invention of the early modern world. The ancient and medieval worlds did not identify persons by race. Individuals were recognized during these earlier periods in geographic terms. Hence, an African would be called Ethiopian or Egyptian as opposed to being called black or "Negro."

ORIGINS

Racial emphasis came into use as a support for imperialism and its accompanying institution of slavery. Although the origin of the word "race" is obscure, experts believe that it began as a loose description of similar groups. This description originally was not restricted to biologically similar people. For example, in 1678, John Bunyan in *Pilgrim's Progress* wrote of a "race of saints."

The first English record of the use of the word "race" was in 1508. In that year, William Dunbar in a poem spoke of "bakbyttaris if sindry racis" (backbiters of sundry races). However, it was not until 1684 that the term "race" was used to designate skin color and other distinguishable physical features. It was then used by the Frenchman François Bernier, who used his experiences as a traveler and physician to employ such an application.

It appears, however, that such classifications did not become commonplace immediately. It was only after science adopted the concept of race as an explanation for human variation that it became a broadly accepted means of classification.

Some scholars, such as Winthrop Jordan and Joseph Harris, have documented evidence of racial prejudice all the way back to the earliest contact between whites and nonwhites. These actions appear to be based more on geographic differences than on color differences. For example, fantastic fables about Africans circulated among Europeans. Equally preposterous stories about some Europeans, however, circulated in the ancient and medieval world among other Europeans. Thus, such views seem to be the products of encounters between different peoples in an age that was characterized by superstition and fear of the unknown.

SCIENTIFIC APPLICATIONS

The year 1798 has been cited as marking the beginning of scientific racism. This later form of racism was not restricted to skin color alone. It was used to slight Jews and Catholics as well as nonwhite people.

In its earliest use, scientific racism was employed mainly as a justification of economic inertia. Thus, it was said that human deprivation could not be relieved through charitable donations. According to the proponents of scientific racism, government volunteer agencies or individuals would simply be throwing money away if they were to spend it on the segment of humanity that was hopelessly and irretrievably at the bottom of the social and economic status of society.

This employment of a pseudoscientific justification for racism was expanded with the introduction of Social Darwinism during the late nineteenth century. Purveyors of this doctrine imported Charles Darwin's theory of evolution from biology and placed it into a social context. Whereas Darwin himself had only theorized about species, the Social Darwinists declared that one race was superior to another because it had evolved further and faster than had the inferior group. A chain of evolutionary progress was created that placed the black race at the bottom and whites of the Nordic pedigree at the summit of humanity. Thus, black people were portrayed as animalistic, subhuman, and therefore incapable of higher thought, while Nordic Europeans were said to be natural leaders.

The use of science to prop up racism has probably been the most pernicious development in the history of racism. When zoology, anatomy, and other fields of scientific study advanced explanations of human differences, they were given serious hearings. Consequently, the layperson has accepted the scientist's word as authoritative in spite of its theoretical and unproved claims.

RELIGIOUS APPLICATIONS

From the beginning of the European enslavement of Africans, religion was an element in the process. As early as 1442, Pope Eugenia IV granted absolution to Portuguese seamen who, under the direction of Prince Henry the Navigator, took African "souls" and sold them. Within ten years, however, it became unnecessary to ask for absolution, because Pope Nicholas V gave the king of Spain his blessing to enslave "pagans." Christopher Columbus's writings show that he used this same justification for the enslavement of Native Americans.

Chapels were included in most of the slave factories, also known as "castles," which were erected along the west coast of Africa. Their presence was indicative of organized Christianity's approval of slavery.

At first, the Spanish provided for enslaved Africans to be manumitted upon their conversion to Christianity, since it was considered wrong for one Christian to hold another Christian in bondage regardless of the bondsman's race. As conversions to Christianity became commonplace among African slaves, however, manumissions became uncommon. At least by the middle of the seventeenth century, Europeans began to identify black skin with a lifetime of slavery.

The Bible was used to "prove" that blacks were a cursed people. A favorite scriptural citation for this purpose was Noah's curse upon his grandson Canaan because his father Ham had mocked his own father Noah (Genesis 9:20-27). This scripture was given a racial interpretation by the slavocracy's hermeneutists. They declared that Ham was the father of the black race and that Noah's specific condemnation of Canaan should be expanded to include all black people. Thus, religious justification for the enslavement of blacks evolved from the belief that it was immoral for a Christian to enslave another Christian, regardless of race, to the nineteenth century idea that the African was eternally condemned to be a servant of others. By the nineteenth century, proponents of slavery declared that it simply was the natural order for the African to be "a hewer of wood and drawer of water" for the more advanced races.

This progression is illustrative of slavery and the resulting racism's evolving ethics. As the "peculiar institution" became more prevalent, the argument to legitimate it—especially from a religious perspective—became more vindictive toward nonwhite lands.

Sermons were preached to both slaves and their masters regarding the merits of African chattel property. Especially in the southern United States, both whites and blacks were taught that anyone who espoused any form of equality between the races was actually guilty of violating the divine order of nature. Such indoctrination was extremely effective, and people's attitudes did not change when laws were passed stating otherwise. Religious justifications for racism have continued to be employed by individuals and by such hate groups as the Ku Klux Klan in the United States long after the passage of the Emancipation Proclamation, the Thirteenth Amendment to the Constitution, and even the Civil Rights Act of 1964.

CULTURAL APPLICATION

Both slavery and imperialism used cultural arguments to control other races. The doctrine of the "white man's burden" said that Europeans had a moral responsibility to expose deprived nonwhites to the superior culture of the whites. Thus, Africans who were kept on a plantation were thought to benefit from their close association with their masters. It was said that Africans, if left alone, would languish in retrogressive ignorance and backwardness.

This paternal view was not unique to American slavery. Both Europe and the United States used the concept of the white man's burden to justify the usurpation of the lands of nonwhite people. In each territory, the indigenous people were characterized as savage and uncivilized. Only exposure to the white man's superior culture would save such people.

This attitude of superiority legitimated the takeover of others' lands. It was believed that the white man knew best what to do with those lands. His takeover therefore not only helped the real estate to be put to better use but also better served the native people. This view reflected the belief that many whites held during the age of imperialism. They saw themselves as God's gift to humanity. Officially, this concept came to be known as "manifest destiny." This meant that the imperialists believed that they had a mission to expand beyond others' borders to uplift those people to the imperialists' level.

This view of a neglected or minimal culture among nonwhite people was predicated upon a Eurocentric view of history. This meant that unless Europeans were leading and shaping a culture, it was not worthy of study. This attitude was arrogant and discriminatory in its highlighting of historical contributions. Anything of note that had been done by nonwhite people was ignored, while every important aspect of human civilization was always in some way considered a product of white genius. Such a polemical view of culture helped to solidify white supremacy and the existence of racism.

ECONOMIC APPLICATION

Similar to the use of culture was the introduction of economics as a prop for racism. During slavery, the argument was advanced that the institution was necessary for the benefit of black people. It was declared that they were childlike and incapable of self-support. As long as they remained on the plantation,

they had a haven that protected them from want. Slavery's defenders in the face of abolitionists' demands used this argument to portray slavery as being quite advantageous to the slaves. Even after the U.S. Civil War, many southern historians continued to use the economic argument to show that slavery was an economic boon to blacks. They pointed to postbellum vagabondage and government dependency among freed slaves as proofs that black people were better off on the plantation, where they were given food, clothing, and shelter.

Such writers never considered that it was the years of exploitation and neglect on the plantation that had contributed to the freed slaves' deplorable condition. Also, they never addressed the freed slaves and antebellum free blacks who, in the face of tremendous difficulties, still managed not only to support themselves and their families but also to become entrepreneurs, landowners, and employers, sometimes even of whites.

In the twentieth century, economics was used as a defense for South Africa's apartheid policy and the continued business transactions carried on there by American and European corporations. In the wake of an international call for divestiture, these companies argued that their continued operation in South Africa was for the good of the blacks and colored people at the bottom of the economic ladder. Divestiture would deprive these two groups of a livable wage. Therefore, it was prudent for nonwhite people to continue to work for these corporations while the corporations used their influence to effect change.

The South African argument was as paternalistic as the American slaver's position. In both instances, the true benefactors of exploited labor declared that they had a higher mission than that of simple selfishness. Instead, they declared that their activities were for the good of nonwhite workers, who could not fend for themselves without white paternalism.

SOCIAL APPLICATION

After the American Civil War and Reconstruction, Jim Crow laws were instituted throughout the southern United States. These laws segregated society on the basis of race in practically every area of life. Except in menial jobs, African Americans could not enter white restaurants, hotels, schools, or any other "white only" public facility. When they were allowed in the same buildings as whites, they had separate, well-defined places such as balconies or basements to occupy.

Most southern states reinforced their segregation policies with laws that prohibited interracial marriages. Propagandists repeatedly warned that having one drop of African blood meant that one was a "negro." To the racist, amalgamation was a deadly sin.

Resulting from such hysteria was a negrophobia that frequently manifested itself in the worst imaginable forms of brutalization. During the late nineteenth century and the first half of the twentieth century, it was common for African Americans to be lynched. The most common offense leading to lynching was the violation of white women, real or imagined. Frequently, it was the latter. A celebrated case of this sort occurred when fourteen-year-old Emmett Till was murdered in Money, Mississippi, in 1955. Apparently, his only offense was that he called a white woman "baby."

A Lynching Case That Cannot Be Forgotten

In May, 2004, the U.S. Justice Department announced that it was reopening its investigation into the notorious murder of teenager Emmett Till, who was lynched in Mississippi in 1955 for allegedly whistling at a white woman. The two men originally tried for Till's murder had been acquitted of all charges and had since died. However, evidence remained implicating other, still living, men in Till's lynching. The five-year federal statue of limitations had long since lapsed, but anyone charged with the murder could still be tried in a state court. R. Alexander Acosta, the Justice Department assistant attorney general for civil rights leading the Till investigation, said, "We owe it to Emmett Till, we owe it to his mother and to his family, and we owe it to ourselves to see if, after all these years, any additional measure of justice is still possible."

INSTITUTIONAL APPLICATIONS

With the massive urbanization of African Americans in the United States in the twentieth century and the resulting residential segregation in cities, the stage was set for the emergence of institutional racism. This form of racism was more covert than was individual racism, which was emotional and blunt. Institutional racism resulted in a denial of equal ac-

cess to goods and services by predominantly black sections of the cities. For example, higher prices and less-desirable products were more often found in the predominantly black and Hispanic inner cities than in the white suburbs.

Since this type of discrimination manifested itself through institutions and was not individually accountable, many people were simply oblivious to its existence. In addition, because of diminished interracial contact in urban areas, many suburbanites, as a result of ignorance of the ways in which societal institutions discriminate, are prone to blame deplorable living conditions within inner cities on the residents' lack of initiative and concern rather than on institutional biases.

Nevertheless, institutional racism can at least help to explain a disproportionate number of nonwhites being unemployed, underemployed, and incarcerated in prisons. Despite affirmative action policies and legal gains that have taken place during the twentieth century, African Americans and other minorities are excluded and ignored by many institutions, such as employers, lenders, and investment agencies. A prime example is the absence of stockbrokers' and other investment advertisements in African American-oriented media.

EXPANSION

Although racism had been sporadically applied to various groups from its inception, its primary application had been toward blacks of African ancestry. In their role as America's permanent bondspeople, African Americans were ridiculed and ostracized in a way that condemned everything associated with them. In the post-World War I world, however, racist attitudes began to be manifested toward others on a systematic basis. By the 1920's, the Ku Klux Klan had begun campaigns against not only African Americans but also Asians, Jews, Catholics, and all persons born outside the United States. The hatred that had originally been primarily aimed at African Americans overflowed to such an extent that it found other victims as well. Anyone who was not Anglo-Saxon and Protestant was susceptible to racism's venom.

The following decade of the 1930's saw this expansion reach global proportions. The rise of Adolf Hitler's Nazi regime in Germany was based upon the concept of Aryan supremacy. All other groups were considered inferior and unfit. Unfortunately, this form of expanded ethnic bigotry reached such an extent that 6 million Jews perished at the hands of the Nazis during World War II.

NEW CONFLICTS

Many African American leaders have argued that it is impossible for black people to be racist. They believe that they can be prejudiced, but not racist, because they lack the power to enforce their prejudice.

While this position has been advanced by the African American left, the white right has charged that group with reverse racism. Some white conservatives contended that government affirmative action programs and the preferential treatment accorded minorities since the passage of civil rights legislation victimize whites in the same way that nonwhites previously were discriminated against by white supremacists.

Persons of goodwill have seen the wisdom in freeing humanity of racial bigotry. Although racism has been opposed since its inception, the most celebrated and concentrated efforts began with the modern Civil Rights movement, which began with the bus boycott in Montgomery, Alabama, in 1955. Under the nonviolent leadership of Martin Luther King, Jr., racism was exposed as morally wrong. King's philosophy accentuated the brotherhood of humanity and love for one's neighbor, regardless of race, nationality, or ethnicity.

By developing an integrated coalition and marching peacefully under King's leadership, King's followers erected a workable model of human cooperation that could be emulated throughout the world. In contrast, those who brutalized these nonviolent protesters with police dogs and fire hoses convinced many people throughout the world that racism was an insidious evil that should be stamped out.

As a result, people have become more reluctant to be known as racists. Instead, racially sensitive issues have been adopted as code words to describe positions. Racism continues to flourish, but it has become more institutional than individual.

Randolph Meade Walker

FURTHER READING

Banton, Michael, and Jonathan Harwood. *The Race Concept.* New York: Praeger, 1975. A general discussion of the evolution of the idea of race. Although it allows that the origin of the race concept is obscure, it is certain that the prevalent use of racial divisions of humanity coincided with the spread of early slavery.

Barzun, Jacques. *Race: A Study in Superstition.* Rev. ed. New York: Harper & Row, 1965. An interesting refutation of Nazi teachings that addresses the expanded use of race beyond color applications. A scholarly exposure of scientific racism's absurdity.

Chase, Allan. *The Legacy of Malthus: The Social Costs of the New Scientific Racism.* New York: Alfred A. Knopf, 1977. A thorough treatment of scientific racism. Discusses its destructive effects and offers a means for its eradication.

Conrad, Earl. *The Invention of the Negro.* New York: Paul S. Eriksson, 1967. A revealing look at the newness of the despised status of the "Negro." This work contends that black Africans did not suffer extreme degradation until the slave trade became big business in the Americas.

Jordan, Winthrop D. *White over Black: American Attitudes Toward the Negro, 1550-1812.* New York: W. W. Norton, 1977. A thoroughly documented study of early European perceptions of black Africans. This study provides an interesting contrast to Conrad's thesis. It contends that racism produced slavery.

Lubiano, Wahneema. "Like Being Mugged by a Metaphor: Multiculturalism and State Narratives." In *Mapping Multiculturalism*, edited by Avery F. Gordon and Christopher Newfield. Minneapolis: University of Minnesota Press, 1996. A crucial essay for understanding the relationship between the state, ideology, and racism. Addresses the question of what black American intellectuals can and should do to resist contemporary racist structures.

_____, ed. *The House That Race Built: Black Americans, U.S. Terrain.* New York: Pantheon, 1997. An anthology of essays by many of the leading scholars of race, including Toni Morrison, Angela Y. Davis, Cornel West, Stuart Hall, and Patricia J. Williams.

SEE ALSO: Anti-Semitism; Apartheid; Bigotry; Ethno-centrism; Hate crime and hate speech; Human rights; Lynching; Racial prejudice; Reverse racism; Slavery.

Rain forests

DEFINITION: Large wooded areas characterized by more than one hundred inches of rainfall annually and tall evergreen trees that provide a high canopy

TYPE OF ETHICS: Environmental ethics

SIGNIFICANCE: The potential destruction of the rain forests by humans became both a symbolic issue and a grave practical concern for the environmental movement of the late twentieth and early twenty-first centuries.

The rain forests provide indigenous peoples and the world with a rich source of actual and potential benefits. In their natural state, the rain forests act as filters for the global atmosphere, provide habitats for animal and plant species, and provide food for humans. The rain forests are also harvested as a source of fuel, with the resulting cleared land providing a rich soil for farming. Finding a balance between altering the rain forests for temporary benefit and using them in their natural and sustainable state is the heart of the rain forest debate.

In their naturally occurring state, the rain forests of the world act as watersheds for the surrounding land. The rich soil and dense foliage of the forests act as a natural sponge, capturing rainfall and runoff. These trapped waters are slowly released, recharging aquifers, streams, and natural reservoirs. It is this trapping and slow releasing of water that controls both flooding and erosion in the forests and surrounding areas. When the rain forest is clear-cut and removed, streams, lakes, rivers, and other natural waterways are quickly filled with runoff sediment and lost.

Along with playing an important role in the water cycle, the rain forest is critical in the conversion of carbon dioxide into oxygen. The loss of one of the earth's natural air filters cannot be replaced in any manner. This loss threatens not only to affect local areas but also to have global air-quality effects. With the removal of rain forests, the local area immedi-ately is affected by an alteration in the moisture content of the air and a disturbance in the water cycle. The long-term effects of this disturbance could be the development of arid savanna or desert.

Although the rain forests cover only slightly more than 7 percent of the land masses of the world, they provide habitats for more than 50 percent of the animal and plant species found on the planet. The destruction of plant life in the rain forest not only threatens the water cycle and the planet's carbon dioxide/oxygen cycle but also removes plant species that may provide important medical benefits. This loss of potential medicines is another example of local action's having worldwide effects. Rain forest plants have already contributed aspirin and many other pharmaceuticals, some of which are used in the treatment of leukemia and Hodgkin's disease. The loss of this rich pharmaceutical research possibility is not recoverable in any way.

DEPLETION

The reasons for rain forest destruction are myriad; primarily, however, it is a matter of economics and survival. Nearly half of all the trees cut in the forests are used for fuel to cook and heat homes. The vast majority of rain forests are found in less-developed countries where alternative fuels such as fossil fuels, solar power, or hydroelectric power are not available in remote and isolated areas. Yet while the forests provide a rich supply of fuel, local people nevertheless are not able to cut and secure adequate fuel supplies to meet their basic survival needs. Although globally there exist several other fuel sources, local people lack the economic strength to secure these sources of fuel. As a result, the forests are cut and sold for timber products, providing poor communities with a bit of economic freedom.

The newly cleared land, with its rich and fertile soil, is used for farming until it is depleted of all nutrition—usually, within five years. Although the agricultural use of the land is limited to such a short duration, it again provides the community with much-needed economic benefits. After the soil has been used to exhaustion, the farmer cuts more of the forest, sells the timber, and farms the new land until it also is depleted. When the trees have been cut and the soil has been depleted, the forest on that land is gone and the soil can no longer support the life that existed upon it six or seven years earlier.

Clearly, the economic benefits derived from using the forests in such a destructive short-term manner are enough to drive the process on. It is important to present to local people a means of using the forest in its natural and sustainable state that will provide them comparable economic benefit for the long term. There are several possibilities, such as harvesting and selling fruits and nuts from the forests, tourism, and a tax for the use of the rain forests for medical research.

It is the resolution of this dichotomy—the forest in its natural state providing water, oxygen, medicine, and habitat versus the economic and existence needs of local peoples—that must be effected. It is estimated that one tree, over a period of fifty years, provides $196,250 worth of benefits by producing oxygen, reducing erosion, recycling water, and creating habitats. The same tree, when sold for lumber, is worth approximately $600. The $600 is actual and usable currency, however, while the nearly $200,000 value exists in the form of benefits. It is the need for hard currency that must be addressed if preservation of the rain forest is to occur and continue. This economic need must be addressed not only by world leaders but also by indigenous peoples. Ultimately, the entire world will suffer the consequences of rain forest destruction; however, it is the local people who will be the first to suffer, and the local people have little economic capability to adjust.

Tod Murphy

FURTHER READING

Aiken, S. Robert. *Vanishing Rain Forests: The Ecological Transition in Malaysia.* New York: Oxford University Press, 1992.

Attfield, Robin. *Environmental Ethics: An Overview for the Twenty-first Century.* Malden, Mass.: Blackwell, 2003.

Gunn, Alastair S. "Environmental Ethics and Tropical Rain Forests: Should Greens Have Standing?" In *Environmental Ethics and Forestry: A Reader,* edited by Peter C. List. Philadelphia: Temple University Press, 2000.

Kilaparti, Ramakrishna, and George M. Woodwell, eds. *World Forests for the Future: Their Use and Conservation.* New Haven, Conn.: Yale University Press, 1993.

Miller, Kenton, and Laura Tangley. *Trees of Life: Saving Tropical Rain Forests and Their Biological Wealth.* Boston: Beacon Press, 1991.

Park, Chris. *Tropical Rainforests.* New York: Routledge, 1992.

Pimm, Stuart. *The Balance of Nature? Ecological Issues in the Conservation of Species and Communities.* Chicago: University of Chicago Press, 1991.

SEE ALSO: Deep ecology; Deforestation; Ecology; Endangered species; Environmental ethics; Global warming; Greenhouse effect.

Rand, Ayn

IDENTIFICATION: Russian American novelist and philosopher

BORN: Alisa Rosenbaum; February 2, 1905, St. Petersburg, Russia

DIED: March 6, 1982, New York, New York

TYPE OF ETHICS: Modern history

SIGNIFICANCE: An important philosopher and advocate of rational egoism and libertarianism, Rand expressed her philosophy in both fictional and nonfictional works, including *The Fountainhead* (1943), *Atlas Shrugged* (1957), *The Virtue of Selfishness: A New Concept of Egoism* (1964), and *Capitalism: The Unknown Ideal* (1966).

Rand advocated an ethics of rational self-interest. The hero of her best-selling *Atlas Shrugged* states, "I swear—by my life and my love of it—that I will never live for the sake of another man, nor ask another man to live for mine." The moral purpose of anyone's life is his or her own happiness; he or she exists to serve no other individual or group. The moral standard by which one guides one's actions is set by the objective requirements of human life. Thus, Rand rejected two common theses in ethical theory: that selfless sacrifice is moral and that acting in one's self-interest means doing whatever one feels like. She rejected as "moral cannibalism" any form of altruism—that is, any claim that the selfless sacrifice of some humans for the benefit of others is moral. She also argued that, since feelings are not tools of cognition, they are not reliable guides to action; hence, one must rationally define the principles of action that will allow one to achieve the values necessary to sustain one's life.

Rand extended her ethics to politics. In a social context, an individual's achievement of values requires freedom from coercion. Hence, every individual has a right to his or her own life, liberty, and property, and these rights provide a moral foundation for free enterprise and constitutionally limited government.

Stephen R. C. Hicks

SEE ALSO: Altruism; Capitalism; Consequentialism; Egoism; Free enterprise; Libertarianism; Objectivism; Selfishness.

Rape

DEFINITION: Nonconsensual sexual intercourse imposed on one person by another
TYPE OF ETHICS: Sex and gender issues
SIGNIFICANCE: Sometimes euphemistically referred to as a "fate worse than death," in some cultures forcible rape is considered the ultimate transgression. Despite this judgment, rape remains a pervasive crime in modern society, one which is rendered all the more difficult to combat by the shame often experienced by its victims and by the public distrust they often encounter if they decide to report the crime.

Rape is legally defined as any form of sexual intercourse forcibly imposed by one or more persons upon another person without the consent of the victim or victims. Mary Koss and Mary Harvey consider rape to represent the end point of a continuum of sexual victimization that includes attempted rape (the attempt to use force or the threat of force to have sexual intercourse without the victim's consent), sexual harassment (nonconsensual sexual intercourse obtained through the abuse of power or authority by the offender in a job or school setting), sexual imposition (the use of force or threats to obtain sexual acts other than intercourse, such as kissing), and sexual contact (nonconsensual touching of the victim's intimate body parts).

Koss and Harvey distinguish five types of rape: stranger rape (the rapist is unknown to the victim), acquaintance rape (the rapist is recognized by the victim), date rape (rape occurs during a consensually agreed upon social encounter), marital rape (one spouse is sexually assaulted by the other), and child sexual abuse (sexual contact that occurs to a child as a result of force, threat, deceit, or the exploitation of an authority relationship).

INCIDENCE OF RAPE

In the vast majority of cases, rapists are men and the victims are female. The Federal Bureau of Investigation's definition of rape specifies that the victim is female, and according to Koss and Harvey, 100 percent of reported rapes involve a male offender and female victim. Consequently, almost all the rape literature focuses on female victims, although the dynamics of rape are similar when the victim is male.

Rape is a persistent, serious, and frequently occurring social problem. The number of reported rapes in the United States increased more than fivefold from 1960 to 1989 (from 16,680 to 94,504); and in 2002 the number approached 248,000 rape victims. However, the number of reported rapes is undoubtedly significantly lower than the true number, because most occurrences are never reported. Koss and Harvey did a number of studies that revealed much higher rates than those officially reported. For example, in one study, 44 percent of the interviewed sample reported rape or attempted rape, and the report rates for other forms of sexual victimization were less than 1 percent. A study of female adolescents between the ages of eleven and seventeen in 1976 and 1977 revealed that 1 to 2 percent reported sexual assault by peers. Two percent translates into 540,000 sexual assaults nationwide. If children are considered, Koss and Harvey cite data that one-fifth to one-third of all women have had a sexual encounter with an adult male during childhood.

The incidence of rape is geographically influenced. Larry Baron and Murray A. Straus found significant differences in the frequency of rape among individual U.S. states. The states with the highest incidences of rape had five to ten times as many cases of rape compared to the states with the lowest incidences. Although the incidences of reported rapes have increased dramatically in all states over the years, this incidence ratio of five to ten has remained quite constant. Rapes occur much more frequently (rapes per 100,000 population) in the West, followed by the South, the North-Central region, and the Northeast. Within each state, rape occurs more frequently

In a manifestation of growing public awareness of the problem of rape, an Alabama state politician joins members of a state antirape organization addressing rape issues in March, 2004. (AP/Wide World Photos)

in urban than in rural areas, and states with a high ratio of males to females show higher rates of rapes. Rape rates were not related to the degree of income inequality in a state or to the percentage of a state's population that is black, the percentage of individuals aged 18 to 24, the percentage of single males aged 15 or older, or the level of unemployment.

CHARACTERISTICS OF RAPISTS

Susan Brownmiller made the interesting observation that when other crimes of violence are compared to rape, the rapist falls midway between aggravated assault and robbery—the rapist is "the man in the middle." The typical rapist has the following characteristics: He is slightly younger than the assaultive offender and slightly older than the robber; uses less physical force than the assaulter but more than the robber; drinks less prior to the rape than the assaulter but more than the robber; and is less likely to commit rape in his neighborhood than assault, but does not commit robbery. Rape is also more frequently committed against a total stranger than is assault but less

frequently than is robbery. Brownmiller believes that rape "borrows" from these two other crimes; rape is an act of sexual assault and robbery (the rapist "acquires" the woman's body).

Brownmiller also pointed out that the rapist has the least sharp image, and generalizations about rapists are difficult to come by. Rape is committed primarily by young poor men, and its victims tend to be young poor women. Otherwise, research comparing rapists to other groups (such as convicts, other sex offenders, and college males) has not supported significant psychological differences between these groups. In fact, along almost every dimension examined with sophisticated psychological tests, rapists are not significantly different from other males. This fact, combined with their wide variety of backgrounds, prevents making any sweeping generalizations.

Ann Wolbert Burgess's review of her and others' research suggests that a more meaningful way of typing rapists may be in terms of their motivation to commit rape. Burgess distinguishes four motivations for rape.

(1) *Aggression.* Rape is an aggressive activity that enhances the rapist's sense of power, masculinity, or self-esteem, or permits him to express feelings of mastery and conquest. He tends to be manipulative and impulsive, maintains unstable interpersonal relationships, and lacks a sense of empathy. (2) *Anger.* Rape is committed out of anger and contempt toward women and allows the rapist to hurt, humiliate, and degrade his victim. He may also, however, feel some concern for his victim and may even attempt restitution. (3) *Sadism.* The sadistic rapist is sexually aroused in response to violence, and the act of his assault, which is very brutal, may be bizarre. (4) *Impulsivity.* Rape is but one part of a pervasive exploitative, predatory, and antisocial lifestyle in an individual with an extensive criminal history.

THEORIES OF RAPE

On the face of it, it might seem that the frequency with which rape occurs is perplexing. There are easier, often perfectly legal and less risky, ways to satisfy motives of aggression, anger, sadism, and impulsivity. Why then do women so frequently become the objects of these motives? A number of theories have been developed, and these are now briefly reviewed.

The psychiatric theory of rape has dominated explanations of rape since the 1930's. (This is not to say that the theory is correct; vehement objections have been raised against it, which will be discussed.) Diana Scully and Joseph Marolla state that psychiatry explains rape as being caused by, singly or in combination: (1) irresistible impulse, (2) mental disorder, (3) momentary loss of control caused by use of alcohol and drugs, and (4) victim precipitation. In the irresistible impulse, rape is seen as an expression of an urge beyond the rapist's self-control, without logic or reason, and is experienced as a strong and overpowering drive to rape.

To view rape as a mental disorder is to explain it as a significant impairment in normal personal and social functioning. The impairment is most probably caused by faulty upbringing that produced an abnormal childhood; in particular, a sadistic personality and a hatred of the rapist's mother. The basis of the sadistic personality is a combination of the motives of sex and aggression, the two key motives in Sigmund Freud's psychoanalytic theory. Sexual intercourse becomes bound to aggression. The rapist's mother, to whom the rapist was sexually attracted as a

child as part of his oedipal wish, is simultaneously seductive and rejecting. The rapist never resolves his oedipal wish and grows up sexually attracted to his mother but also has strong feelings of aggression toward her. The offender displaces his aggression upon a woman via the act of sex. Symbolically, the rape forces his seductive but rejecting mother into submission. Additionally, some psychoanalysts believe the rapist to be a latent homosexual, which contributes to his hostility toward women.

The use of alcohol or drugs by rapists prior to the rape has been mentioned frequently in the literature. Consumption of alcohol presumably removes or reduces social restraints, allowing the sexual-aggressive drive to overwhelm rapists and lead them to commit rape. Alternatively, the rapist may claim that, although he was not under the influence of drugs, his victim was, thus inviting the rapist to take sexual advantage of her.

Victim precipitation refers to the rape victim's being functionally responsible for the rape by behaving in a way that provokes the rapist to rape her. Commissive behavior would actively encourage the rape by, for example, encouraging but then denying a sexual advance at the last possible moment or by voluntarily agreeing to drink with or ride in a car with the rapist. Omissive behavior involves failing to use preventive measures, such as failing to react sufficiently strongly to sexual overtures or dressing in a sexually suggestive way so as to attract attention and encourage sexual advances. All these acts to invite the rapist are, according to psychoanalysis, expressions of a universal, unconscious, masochistic wish on the part of women to be raped and humiliated.

The evidence to support these psychiatric-psychoanalytic theories is flimsy at best and in most cases nonexistent. The great majority of rapes are premeditated rather than the result of an irresistible impulse. The relationship between rape and alcohol or drugs as a releaser of sexual inhibitions has not been empirically demonstrated. There is also no evidence whatsoever firmly linking rape to latent homosexuality or the family dynamics described by psychoanalysis.

BIOLOGICAL THEORIES

According to Randy Wilsen, Nancy Wilsen Thornhill, and Gerard Dizinno, rape is a behavior that is performed by men who are relatively unsuccessful in competing for the status and resources necessary to attract and successfully reproduce with desirable mates. Rape is a category of sexual conflict in which males seek to control female sexual behavior and therefore is placed squarely in the purview of comparative biology and evolutionary theory. Rape is an evolved mating strategy used by those males ("big losers") who otherwise would not be able to compete with more successful males. What once may have been an adaptive behavior is now maladaptive, however, since the adaptive costs of reproduction exceed its benefits.

The authors base their theory on a comparative study of forced sexual intercourse in animals and certain statistical data about rape—that it is directed primarily at young (hence fertile), poor women primarily by young, poor ("big losers") men. This evolutionary theory is interesting. The authors have made predictions from their theory that have been supported. The theory is very new, however, and needs to be tested further. Also, making analogies between human and animal behaviors and selecting certain data on rape that support the theory are open to criticism. For example, that rapists are mostly poor young men may not necessarily mean that they rape because they are "big losers"; it may be that they rape because it is a safe way of displacing antagonism and resentment at their social status onto women or as a way of asserting their masculinity as a substitute for their lack of economic success.

SOCIETAL AND CULTURAL THEORIES

It was noted previously that there are large differences in the rates of rape among individual states and between regions of states. Through complex statistical analyses, Baron and Straus accounted for these differences in terms of three sociocultural variables: gender inequality, pornography, and social disorganization. Specifically, the lower the status of women relative to men, the higher the rate of rape. Gender inequality is part of a social milieu that is conducive to rape. Also, the higher the circulation of pornographic literature, the higher the rate of rape. The authors interpret this finding to suggest that pornography is more likely to be part of "a hypermasculine or macho culture pattern" that condones violence and force, believes in male supremacy, and degrades women. The level of social disorganization is directly related to the level of rape. The social forces that control violent behavior are weakened. In a sociocultural milieu

characterized by sexism and violence, loss of social controls permits easier outlets for rape.

Baron and Straus have identified important social contributors to rape that suggest that rape is more than simply a psychiatric problem confined to the individual male and his upbringing or a biologically based behavior.

FEMINIST THEORY

This theory stands in stark contrast to psychiatric theory and is, in part, a reaction against the psychiatric explanation of rape. According to Burgess and Maggie Humm, rape is an act of social control as well as a social institution that perpetuates the patriarchal domination of women and functions to keep women in their place through sexual degradation, violence, and assault. Rape is viewed as the logical conclusion of sexism and is an especially pernicious form of social control and coercion because it constantly reminds women of their vulnerability to men. Rape is a cultural and social behavior that is institutionalized in law and custom and is the symbolic expression of a white male hierarchy. Rape is an extension of normal sexual aggression acted out within the context of male sexual expectations and hostility toward women.

Feminist theory thus views rape as normative rather than deviant, as does psychiatric theory. Traditional male socialization encourages males to associate dominance, strength, virility, and power with being masculine, but submissiveness, passivity, weakness, and inferiority with being feminine. Thus women are viewed from legal, social, and religious contexts as male property to do with what they will.

Accompanying this attitude is the development by males of what Scully and Marolla refer to as a "vocabulary of motive" to diminish their responsibility and justify and excuse rape. For example, the psychiatrist Benjamin Karpman stated that rapists were sick but were not responsible for their behavior. They did not *consciously* and deliberately rape. Rather, they were victims of a disease from which they may suffer more than their victims. Therefore, since the rapist is "sick," he cannot be held responsible for his behavior. As another example, linking rape to latent homosexuality serves to place rapists in a group of deviant outsiders. By segregating rapists from "normal" men, the label of latent homosexuality serves to protect the interests of males.

Feminist theory has been criticized for a lack of data to support its contentions. Rather, it is supported by no more than "ideological furor." For example, if rape is normal, socially sanctioned behavior, then it would be predicted that rapists should be equally represented in all walks of life and age categories. The data show, however, that rapists are mostly young, poor males.

However valid feminist theory eventually proves to be, it has been of critical importance in the consciousness raising of males (or at least some males) concerning how they regard and act toward women. For example, in their 1984 textbook *Abnormal Psychology*, David L. Rosenhan (a psychiatrist) and Martin E. P. Seligman (a clinical psychologist) state:

> Rape is a major crime, an act for which it is imperative that society hold the individual responsible, punishing him accordingly. If we were to include rape as a *disorder* . . . , there would be some tendency to excuse the act and lighten the burden of the rapist's individual responsibility—even if there was not a shred of evidence other than the rape itself that indicated psychological abnormality. The acts of murder, assault and theft are not automatically thought of as psychological disorders unless there is additional evidence of abnormality, and we believe rape should be thought of in the same way. The expression "only a sick man could have done that," when applied to rape . . . seems to us deeply and insidiously confused.

ETHICAL ISSUES

Ross Harrison observed that "Rape is obviously bad, indeed a horrific thing. It belongs to the real world in which people are hurt, humiliated and abused . . . it is unproblematic that rape is a bad thing." A 1983 study of rape in New Zealand stated, "Rape is an experience which shakes the foundations of the lives of the victims. For many its effect is a long-term one, impairing their capacity for personal relationships, altering their behavior and values and generating fear."

The symptoms and signs of rape trauma are well documented: physical (injury, disease), emotional (anxiety, fear, depression, shame, anger), cognitive (flashbacks, memories, impaired concentration), psy-chological (lessened self-esteem, disruption in social relations, withdrawal, isolation, aggression), and sexual (sexual attitudes, impaired sexual functioning). Rape, then, represents a total assault on the very being and essence of what it is to be a person. Rape is horrifying and is not to be tolerated, and the rapist must be held responsible for his act.

Laurence Miller

FURTHER READING

Baron, Larry, and Murray A. Straus. *Four Theories of Rape in American Society*. New Haven, Conn.: Yale University Press, 1989. A detailed and excellent discussion of the sociocultural factors that influence rape.

Brownmiller, Susan. *Against Our Will*. New York: Simon & Schuster, 1975. A seminal work of the feminist theory of rape. Powerful, compelling, and convincing.

Burgess, Ann Wolbert, ed. *Rape and Sexual Assault: A Research Handbook*. 3d ed. New York: Garland, 1991. Provides thorough, comprehensive presentations of rape and its relationship to social institutions and issues.

Cahill, Ann J. *Rethinking Rape*. Ithaca, N.Y.: Cornell University Press, 2001. An important critique of the notion that rape is simply about power and not sex. Cahill argues that the sexuality of the body is of crucial importance to understanding the effects of rape, not just upon its survivors, but upon all women in patriarchal society.

Koss, Mary, and Mary Harvey. *The Rape Victim: Clinical and Community Approaches to Treatment*. Lexington, Mass.: Stephen Greene Press, 1987. Defines rape; also discusses rape trauma and social and community issues.

Tomaselli, Sylvana, and Roy Porter, eds. *Rape*. New York: Basil Blackwell, 1986. Philosophical discussions of rape within various contexts, including feminism, popular culture and art, psychoanalysis, mythology, and general philosophical issues.

SEE ALSO: Abuse; Aggression; Incest; Pornography; Rape and political domination; Roman Catholic priests scandal; Sexism; Sexual abuse and harassment; Victims' rights; Violence.

Rape and political domination

DEFINITION: Use of rape and other sexual crimes to keep women politically, socially, and economically subordinated in society

TYPE OF ETHICS: Sex and gender issues

SIGNIFICANCE: As a weapon of political domination, rape violates the ethical principles of gender and race equality, sexual autonomy, and bodily integrity.

Rape has traditionally been seen as a crime, not as an act of political domination. The women's movement of the 1970's and 1980's redefined rape as a social act of white male dominance in a sex- and race-unequal society. In this view, rape is an injury of gender and race inequality that has little or nothing to do with sexual anatomy or biology as such. The view that rape is implicated in women's second-class civil and economic status remains central to feminist ethics, grounding efforts to change norms and laws concerning rape, sexual harassment, dating, marriage, prostitution and other sex work, and pornography.

ETHIC OF EQUALITY

Rape violates the ethical principle of race and gender equality. Most rape victims are women or girls. One in four women in the United States reports subjection to a completed rape (the Federal Bureau of Investigation contends that 90 percent of rapes are not reported). Forty-four percent of women in the United States report having been subjected to rape or attempted rape at least once in their lives. African American women are subjected to an even higher in-

A woman protesting for peace in Liberia in September 2003 cries out in front of the United Nations headquarters in Monrovia, begging for an end to the killing, rape, torture, and looting by soldiers during Liberia's bloody civil war. (AP/Wide World Photos)

A Legacy of Rape

According to a United Nations report released in 1996, between 500,000 and one million Tutsi women had been raped in the Rwanda genocide two years earlier. Many had been repeatedly gang-raped. Not immediately known, however, was the fact that tens of thousands of the surviving rape victims were carrying the human immunodeficiency virus (HIV). In 2004, Amnesty International estimated that of 100,000 Rwandans in need of antiretroviral drugs, only two thousand were receiving them. Moreover, many of the people who were receiving the drugs were Hutu perpetrators of the genocide and mass rapes then serving time in prison; most of the surviving rape victims were receiving no treatments at all. This human rights crisis was magnified by the fact that many rape victims facing imminent death from acquired immunodeficiency syndrome (AIDS) were indigent widows with children who were the progeny of rape.

cidence of rape than white women. Men who are convicted of raping black women typically receive more lenient sentences than men who rape white women. That rape disproportionately and unfairly falls on women and women of color is evidence of women's continued second-class citizenship in that it continues the state's greater regard for the interests of men over those of women.

Women's rights advocates contend that the state is implicated in the reality of rape as political domination in at least two important ways. First, women's injuries from rape are often trivialized and rendered invisible by political and legal institutions. Most reported rapes are not prosecuted, most prosecuted rapes do not result in convictions, and sentences for convicted rapists are often short. The vast majority of rapists are never held to account for their crimes in any way. Second, widespread restrictions on marital rape prosecution constitute a denial of the Fourteenth Amendment's equal protection of its law. They also express women's unequal citizenship and the diminished personhood of wives.

Criminal law has failed to take the social context of sex inequality into account in defining and adjudi-

cating rape. That rape may be a form of political domination, its injury a harm of gender group membership, remains relatively unexplored in law.

BODILY INTEGRITY AND SEXUAL AUTONOMY

A core constituent of human freedom and personhood is sexual autonomy. Rape violates women's ability to control their own bodies and sexuality. Without physical and sexual security, women's public contributions and their private lives are stunted, not only by personal fears but also by public knowledge of women's legal and physical vulnerability.

Women's rights lawyers argue that existing rape law, which focuses on force and nonconsent as the most significant components of rape, should be reconfigured. In this view, nonviolent abuse or sexual cooperation resulting from extortion, economic threats, and deception impair women's sexual autonomy as much as, if not more than, violent rape. According to Catherine MacKinnon, women experience commonalties between what is legally defined as rape and what is considered normal sex. The legal dividing line between rape and sex does not correspond with women's experience of violence. MacKinnon contends that the pervasive effect of male dominance makes it impossible to say definitively that some of women's sexual relations with men (called sex) are "free" and others (called rape) are "coerced." How the law should identify, within this context of political domination, which sexual acts are criminal and which crimes deserve more severe punishment remains undecided.

Susan L. Thomas

FURTHER READING

Buchwald, Emilie, ed. *Transforming a Rape Culture.* Minneapolis: Milkweed Editions, 1995.

Burgess, Ann Wolbert, ed. *Rape and Sexual Assault: A Research Handbook.* 3d ed. New York: Garland, 1991.

Cahill, Ann J. *Rethinking Rape.* Ithaca, N.Y.: Cornell University Press, 2001.

MacKinnon, Catherine. *Sex Equality: Rape Law.* New York: Foundation Press, 2001.

SEE ALSO: Lynching; Pogroms; Pornography; Rape; Scottsboro case; Sexual abuse and harassment; Violence.

Rawls, John

IDENTIFICATION: American philosopher
BORN: February 21, 1921, Baltimore, Maryland
DIED: November 24, 2002, Lexington, Massachusetts
TYPE OF ETHICS: Modern history
SIGNIFICANCE: Rawls was widely regarded as the most important political philosopher of the twentieth century. His *A Theory of Justice* (1971) presented an egalitarian theory of justice, based on social contract theory.

John Rawls taught at Harvard University from 1962 until his retirement following a stroke he suffered in 1995. He is best known for *A Theory of Justice* (1971). In that book, Rawls defended a theory of justice that sought to strike a compromise between the democratic ideals of equality and liberty. The theory was in the social contract tradition associated with John Locke and Jean-Jacques Rousseau, but Rawls introduced the idea that the contract would establish abstract principles of justice rather than specific laws or arrangements. Rawls's contract was a hypothetical one involving agents who have been idealized in certain ways to create what he called an "original position."

Rawls argued that the agents in this original position should be ignorant of their own abilities and prospects in order to ensure that the principles they choose will be fair ones. The result, he argued, would be egalitarian principles that would maximize the position of the worst-off persons rather than maximize overall utility and that would protect certain basic liberties. Rawls is also known for the idea that any theory should be judged on the basis of whether it is the result of a process of "reflective equilibrium" in which one considers competing theories and their implications, testing these against one's intuitions about general principles and cases.

Eric H. Gampel
Updated by the editors

SEE ALSO: Consent; Corporate compensation; Deontological ethics; Distributive justice; Fairness; Ideal observer; Kantian ethics; Minimum-wage laws; Nozick, Robert; Poverty; Social justice and responsibility; *Theory of Justice, A.*

al-Razi

IDENTIFICATION: Arab philosopher and physician
BORN: c. 864, Rayy, Persia (now Iran)
DIED: c. 925, Rayy, Persia (now Iran)
TYPE OF ETHICS: Religious ethics
SIGNIFICANCE: As a trained philosopher and a practicing physician, al-Razi epitomized the man of knowledge devoted to both the ethical aspects of medicine and metaphysical speculations concerning life itself. He produced a comprehensive medical encyclopedia in twelve volumes; *The Book of Spiritual Physick* (c. 920), his principal ethical treatise; and the apologetic *The Philosopher's Way of Life* (c. 920).

Early in his life, al-Razi was educated in the fields of traditional Arabic literature, mathematics, astronomy, and philosophy. In the formation of his religious ideas, it is probable that a distinctly nonorthodox teacher, Iranshahri, played a major role. As a physician, al-Razi displays in his medical treatises the careful, methodical temperament of the empiricist, though a sense of genuine empathy is always present. According to al-Razi, some humans have been endowed with divine reason to awaken their souls to ultimate spiritual return with the Creator; others have not. Just as the Creator never seeks to harm humans, people too ought to seek only their own and others' betterment. Al-Razi believed in the transmigration of souls, the sacredness of all life, and the universal possibility of salvation through reason and philosophy, the latter position being fiercely opposed by religious scholars of his own day.

Craig L. Hanson

SEE ALSO: Bioethics; Medical ethics.

Reality television

DEFINITION: Television programs that involve real-life people engaging in contrived nonfiction situations
TYPE OF ETHICS: Media ethics
SIGNIFICANCE: Much of reality television consists of programs that encourage subjects to compete in actions that might be deemed as violating common social norms.

Members of the cast of Survivor: Pearl Island *pose with Mark Burnett (center), the creator of the popular reality show, when he accepted the People's Choice Award for the best reality-based television program of the year, in January, 2004.* (AP/Wide World Photos)

During the early twenty-first century, reality television programs emerged as a staple of American television network programming because they were comparatively inexpensive to produce and often attracted large audiences. So-called reality programs might be subdivided into four genres: competitive game shows, such as *Survivor*, *Big Brother*, and Donald Trump's *The Apprentice*; romantic or sexually oriented competitions such as *ElimiDATE*, *Who Wants to Marry a Multi-Millionaire?*, and *For Love or Money*; talk shows such as *Jerry Springer* and *Maury*; and crime dramas such as *Cops* and *America's Most Wanted*. Beyond depicting real-life people, what many reality television shows have in common is that their main theme is to portray subjects engaging in behaviors that tend to violate social norms.

Like traditional competitions, reality game shows generally pit contestants against one another, but with a fundamental difference: Their contestants are encouraged to engage in devious, unsportsmanlike conduct that frequently crosses common moral boundaries, in exchange for success—which is typically measured in large cash prizes. Romantic and sexually oriented competitions are often similar in nature, requiring participants to change or violate loyalties or social contracts, or engage in morally compromising behaviors, in order to win.

Reality talk shows take a different approach, depicting subjects who have allegedly already violated some form of social contract or norm—such as those against marital infidelity, abuse, or abandonment—and confronting them with their victims. Just as critics have assailed reality game and romance shows, critics have contended that ubiquitous portrayals of inappropriate behaviors on reality talk shows tend to normalize or glamorize misconduct.

Reality crime dramas depict real-life criminals or suspects by reenacting or documenting actual crimes. Similarly, some shows, such as *Cheaters*, act as on-air private investigators. While supporters claim that such shows may serve as deterrents to inappropriate behaviors, other critics argue that such shows depict society's "tawdry underbelly," and like reality talk shows, tend to normalize or overemphasize morally ambiguous or contradictory behaviors, leading the public to believe that crimes occur more frequently than they actually do.

Cheryl Pawlowski

SEE ALSO: Accuracy in Media; Advertising; Children's television; Media ownership; Skepticism; Tabloid journalism; Televangelists.

Realpolitik

DEFINITION: Doctrine holding that governments should eschew abstract moral codes and instead follow whatever course of action will most effectively protect and achieve their own practical interests

TYPE OF ETHICS: International relations

SIGNIFICANCE: Realpolitik is a starkly materialistic theory of international and domestic politics. Adherents to this philosophy deny that considerations such as human rights and safeguarding the environment, or even honesty and justice, should enter into political decision making or international affairs.

To a practitioner of realpolitik, the end always justifies the means. Lying, cheating, stealing, murder, and war are perfectly acceptable means to achieve the desired results. Historians and political scientists often associate the term realpolitik and its underlying tenets with Otto von Bismarck, chancellor of Germany from 1870 to 1890.

THEORY OF REALPOLITIK

The realpolitik theory rests on several premises, including strategic interests, geographic realities, mutually exclusive goals, and competition and conflict over these goals. According to this theory, states have strategic interests upon which their relative securities depend. The most basic of these interests is the security to continue to exist as independent states, which requires that they achieve power. Leaders must pursue policies that will ultimately increase the power of their state or decrease the power of real or potential enemies. Without power, there can be no true security, because the state's continued existence would rest on other states' lack of interest in destroying it, rather than on its ability to defend itself. Therefore, states must constantly attempt to increase their power relative to the power of competitors. Increasing power may take the form of expanding their armed forces, developing revolutionary new weapons, or expanding their industrial production capacity.

Political leaders also have attempted to increase the power of their nations through imperialistic expansion in order to gain access to markets and raw materials, and to acquire areas into which the excess population of their nations may expand. Power also may be increased through alliances and international agreements. Attempts by political leaders to increase the power of their states and to limit the power of other states resulted in the explosion of imperialistic expansion during the late nineteenth and early twentieth centuries. Most major Western European states, the United States, and Japan became involved in a race for colonies. Imperialistic competition became a primary factor in the massive world wars of the twentieth century, as did the complex web of entangling alliances that virtually guaranteed that any minor conflict between nations would escalate into a global war.

According to the precepts of realpolitik, leaders of states must attempt to increase the power of their state based on strategic interests and geographic realities. For example, if the state's industrial growth depends on a commodity not present within the area it controls, its leaders must attempt to secure access to areas where that commodity is present. Any means necessary to achieve that strategic interest, including war, must be pursued. Geographic realities determine most strategic interests. For example, a completely landlocked nation cannot compete in global trade, and thus increase its power, unless it secures access to a deep-water port. Its leaders may secure such access through negotiation, treaty, or international agreement. If attempts at negotiation fail, the leaders of such a nation may resort to war. Human lives mean nothing to the practitioners of realpolitik, as long as the desired end is achieved.

DOMESTIC DIMENSIONS

Realpolitik also has a domestic political dimension. Since security is the primary goal of all state policies, politicians must suppress what they conceive to be internal threats to the state, which they often interpret as any threat to their continued exercise of power. Political leaders in many different countries frequently have disregarded the constitutional rights of their citizens in suppressing political, religious, and social movements they consider subversive. Political leaders have also eliminated or neutralized individuals whom they considered dangerous to the state, often violating the laws of their nation in the process. Political leaders in all countries, including the United States, often have resorted to the use of realpolitik in domestic affairs.

Political leaders have been practicing realpolitik since the beginning of recorded history. The principles of this essentially amoral political philosophy have contributed to, if not caused, every war in human history and all the suffering associated with those wars. Political leaders have used those principles to justify murder, tyranny, slavery, and injustice.

Cynics argue that the basic premises of realpolitik continue to dominate the international and domestic policies of most twenty-first century world leaders. They maintain that politicians care nothing for issues such as human rights or protection of the global environment; instead, politicians use those issues as tools to gain advantage over real or potential enemies. Constitutional guarantees, the cynics say, are ignored by politicians in their pursuit of security and power. Certainly, many events in the 1990's and the early twenty-first century have suggested that the cynics are not entirely wrong.

If the cynics are correct, humanity would seem to be doomed to the recurrent cycle of war and tyranny that has marked history from its beginning. Unless informed citizens insist that their political leaders base foreign and domestic policies on principles such as justice and human rights, those leaders will continue to follow, consciously or unconsciously, the amoral philosophy of realpolitik.

Paul Madden
Updated by the Editors

FURTHER READING

Cusack, Thomas R. *Exploring Realpolitik: Probing International Relations Theory with Computer Simulation.* Boulder, Colo.: Lynne Rienner, 1990.

Haslam, Jonathan. *No Virtue Like Necessity: Realist Thought in International Relations Since Machiavelli.* New Haven, Conn.: Yale University Press, 2002.

Jensen, Kenneth, and Elizabeth Faulkner, eds. *Morality and Foreign Policy: Realpolitik Revisited.* Washington, D.C.: U.S. Institute of Peace, 1991.

Johnston, Douglas. *Faith-Based Diplomacy: Trumping Realpolitik.* New York: Oxford University Press, 2003.

McKay, David H., David Houghton, and Andrew Wroe. "Manifest Destiny and Realpolitik: Realism Versus Idealism in Foreign Policy." In *Controversies in American Politics and Society.* Malden, Mass.: Blackwell, 2002.

SEE ALSO: Cold War; Intervention; Just war theory; Machiavelli, Niccolò; Nationalism; Private vs. public morality; Sovereignty.

Reason and rationality

DEFINITION: Faculty that comprehends and makes sense of the world through the application of logic

TYPE OF ETHICS: Theory of ethics

SIGNIFICANCE: Reason is often opposed to emotion and intuition, and the relative importance of each to ethics is a matter of debate. Some philosophers have asserted that reason is the only possible basis for objective moral judgment. Other thinkers believe that logic falsifies a fundamentally irrational world and that the imposition of reason upon reality is itself an immoral act.

Common sense holds that being reasonable is a good thing. Being reasonable means taking account of all relevant evidence when deciding what to believe and do, and when establishing principles by which to live. It means settling disagreements by appeal to evidence, which involves being willing to change one's mind based on the evidence. If one is rational, one will discover what is true and false, and if one discovers what is true and false, one will be able to act so as to live the good life. In short, reason is commonly held to be the primary method of learning truths, including truths about morality; accordingly, rationality is held to be a virtue.

Rational theories of morality are marked by several features. They hold that there are moral facts; that those facts are universal, or true for everyone; that reason is capable of identifying those facts; and that disagreements over moral issues are resolvable by rational investigation.

Such accounts of morality, however, face challenges by accounts that hold that morality is not fundamentally rational.

IRRATIONALISM

One problem is the seeming interminability of debates about moral issues. If moral truths are rationally verifiable, why are moral disagreements so rampant? In genuinely cognitive disciplines, such as mathematics and science, methods exist with which to settle disagreements rationally, but it seems that no such methods exist in morals.

A second problem is the emotionalism that moral issues evoke. Since many people cannot be swayed from their moral beliefs by appeals to reason, perhaps morals are based on some nonrational source.

THE IS/OUGHT PROBLEM

A third consideration is the famous "is/ought" problem. David Hume argued that normative ("ought") conclusions cannot be deduced from descriptive ("is") premises. In a valid argument, terms cannot appear in the conclusion that do not appear in the premises. Therefore, if morality is concerned with facts, then normative conclusions must be deduced from fundamental statements of fact that contain "ought" terms. Sensation is the only fundamental source of factual information, however, and people do not seem to sense goodness and badness, merely colors, sounds, and so on.

Following Hume's reasoning, G. E. Moore argued that any attempt to derive moral statements from physical, biological, or psychological facts commits the "naturalistic fallacy."

While irrationalists agree that morality is not fundamentally rational—that, at most, reason helps to figure out how to satisfy moral commitments made on a nonrational basis—they disagree about the fundamental source of moral commitments.

Religious irrationalism holds that God's commands are the source of morals. Many religions hold that ethics is a matter of obeying divine commands, whether one understands them or not. The story of

Abraham in the Hebrew Scriptures (Genesis 22) is an example. God commands Abraham to sacrifice his son Isaac. From a rational perspective, obeying would be immoral: It would mean murdering an innocent boy, and it would cause Abraham and his wife great emotional suffering. Yet all Abraham believes that he needs to know is that God has commanded, so he is prepared to kill. Hence, morality for Abraham means obeying without question commands that do not necessarily make sense.

Secular irrationalism comes in several varieties. According to emotivists, such as Bertrand Russell and A. J. Ayer, moral statements express attitudes that are based on subjective emotional states. According to existentialists, such as Albert Camus and Jean-Paul Sartre, moral attitudes are based on arbitrarily chosen commitments.

Irrationalism is thus strongly linked with moral relativism—the thesis that moral values are not universal. If morals are not rationally based, then consistency is not necessary. If morals are based on subjective emotions, faith, or arbitrary commitments, then, since these are highly variable, morals will be highly variable.

REASON'S ROLE

For rational theories of ethics, then, the challenge is to find and validate a rational source of ethics. The history of ethics contains four major types of attempts to do so.

Intuitionists hold that good and bad are properties of external things themselves, in the same way that colors, textures, and sounds are properties of things. Just as people have sense organs to detect color and sound properties, they have a moral sense to detect moral properties. Moral properties are therefore independent of subjective states, they can be identified accurately, and thus they provide data for rational moral reflection and action.

Hedonists hold that moral properties are based on facts about human nature itself: Humans are born with pleasure/pain mechanisms. What causes sensations of pleasure and pain is not a matter of subjective choice. Sensations of pleasure and pain provide the data for rational moral reflection and action. Morality is a matter of calculating which actions will maximize pleasures and minimize pains.

Kantians hold that morality is based on the nature of reason itself. Noumenal reason projects a priori laws to one's phenomenal self. Since one is human, one should act in accordance with one's distinguishing feature: reason. Since reason demands consistency, morality means using one's reason to determine which maxims of action are consistently realizable, and then acting according to those maxims.

Objectivists hold that morality is based on relational facts about human nature and its environment. Human beings are organisms of a specific nature, and their nature and their environment jointly specify requirements that must be satisfied for them to survive. Good thus is identified fundamentally with what is necessary for survival, and bad with that which leads to death. Reason is a capacity whose function is to identify those survival requirements and to direct the actions of the organism in ways appropriate to fulfilling them.

Stephen R. C. Hicks

FURTHER READING

Audi, Robert. *The Architecture of Reason: The Structure and Substance of Rationality*. New York: Oxford University Press, 2001.

Camus, Albert. *The Myth of Sisyphus*. Translated by Justin O'Brien. Introduction by James Wood. London: Penguin, 2000.

Foucault, Michel. *Madness and Civilization: A History of Insanity in the Age of Reason*. Translated by Richard Howard. 1965. Reprint. New York: Vintage Books, 1988.

Hare, R. M. *Freedom and Reason*. Oxford, England: Clarendon Press, 1963.

Holt, Lynn. *Apprehension: Reason in the Absence of Rules*. Burlington, Vt.: Ashgate, 2002.

Kant, Immanuel. *Critique of Practical Reason*. Edited and translated by Lewis W. Beck. 3d ed. New York: Maxwell Macmillan, 1993.

Kierkegaard, Søren. *"Fear and Trembling" and "The Book on Adler."* Translated by Walter Lowrie. Introduction by George Steiner. London: Everyman's Library, 1994.

Kracauer, Siegfried. "The Mass Ornament." In *The Mass Ornament: Weimar Essays*, translated and edited by Thomas Y. Levin. Cambridge, Mass.: Harvard University Press, 1995.

SEE ALSO: Deconstruction; Emotivist ethics; Intuitionist ethics; Kant, Immanuel; Metaethics; Nagel, Thomas; Passions and emotions; Rand, Ayn.

Reconciliation

DEFINITION: Restoration of relationships between wrongdoers and the wronged persons or parties
TYPE OF ETHICS: Personal and social ethics
SIGNIFICANCE: Reconciliation is a central concept in the network of moral and ethical transactions having to do with how individual persons or groups respond to wrongs done to them.

Forgiveness is one's setting aside of feelings of indignation or resentment directed toward another person who has done one a moral injury. As such, forgiveness is a matter of how one feels about the wrongdoer, rather than how one treats that person. In this respect, it differs from the moral transaction of mercy. To show mercy is to treat a person with less harshness than he or she deserves. Justice is treating a person with the appropriate measure of punishment for the offense done. A person may be treated both justly and without mercy and yet be forgiven. For example, if someone used another person's credit card without permission, the owner might forgive that person while still insisting that the other person repay the money needed to cover charges made on the card. The wronged person in this instance would put aside personal resentment and thereby forgive the thief, while not showing mercy by relieving the wrongdoer of responsibility for making good the loss. In contrast, the owner of the charge card account may absolve the thief of any obligation to repay the funds, thus showing mercy while continuing to resent the thief, thereby show that no forgiveness has taken place.

Reconciliation, unlike these other interactions, is a restoration of the relationship between the wrongdoer and the wronged. Such an interaction may be based on forgiveness but does not necessarily require it. Reconciliation may or may not include the showing of mercy. Reconciliation occurs when the relationship between the injured person and the wrongdoer becomes one of substantive moral mutuality. It is not merely a restoration to the previous position between the persons, as it imposes responsibilities on both the person wronged and the wrongdoer. Reconciliation requires that moral work by both parties.

It is possible that forgiveness will not lead to reconciliation. Indeed, reconciliation can be brought about without forgiveness, although this is difficult. Neither forgiveness nor mercy necessarily requires the cooperation of the wrongdoer, although a confession, apology, or restitution by a wrongdoer may make reconciliation easier. However, reconciliation can be reached only through the mutual commitment and cooperation of both the wronged party and the wrongdoer.

Reconciliation is a community-building activity. It depends on the interconnectedness of persons and reinforces the sinew that binds persons together. It is integrally related to the performance of good deeds to the benefit of each party. When positive benefits are enacted mutually between wronged and wrongdoer, these good deeds are reconciliation, they are not merely a means to it.

Ronnie Littlejohn

FURTHER READING

Barkan, Elazar. *The Guilt of Nations: Restitution and Negotiating Historical Injustices.* Baltimore: Johns Hopkins University Press, 2001.

Cochrane, James, et al., eds. *Facing the Truth: South African Faith Communities and the Truth and Reconciliation Committee.* Columbus: Ohio University Center for International Studies, 1999.

Minow, Marta, and Nancy Rosenblum. *Breaking the Cycles of Hatred: Memory, Law, and Repair.* Princeton, N.J.: Princeton University Press, 2003.

Wink, Walter. *Peace Is the Way: Writings on Nonviolence from the Fellowship of Reconciliation.* New York: Orbis Books, 2000.

SEE ALSO: Forgiveness; King, Martin Luther, Jr.; Mercy; Parole of convicted prisoners; Revenge; South Africa's Truth and Reconciliation Commission.

Redlining

DEFINITION: Systematic exclusion of residents of certain areas, especially low-income, inner-city neighborhoods, from home mortgage lending and property insurance coverage

TYPE OF ETHICS: Business and labor ethics

SIGNIFICANCE: Critics charge that redlining is an unjust practice, because it denies opportunities to those who could qualify for financial services simply because they reside in particular areas; it results in *de facto* discrimination. Practitioners of redlining defend the practice on the grounds that

it is based on what they claim to be objective economic science.

In looking for an efficient way to screen out high-risk applications for home mortgages, rehabilitation loans, and home and auto insurance, banks and insurance companies adopted the practice of "redlining," which involves excluding entire low-income neighborhoods from consideration or charging excessively high prices in these areas. Predictably, the burden of these practices fell most heavily on poor African Americans, and civil rights organizations charged that this amounted to systematic discrimination.

The U.S. Congress passed the Community Reinvestment Act in 1977, followed by the Home Mortgage Disclosure Act, to deal with redlining and the more general problem of directing loans and insurance coverage to low-income areas. The former requires banks and thrifts to make a certain proportion of their loans in the areas where their depositors live, and the latter requires them to report their mortgage lending by census tract. The question remains, however, how much responsibility banks should take for providing loans to low-income borrowers as a matter of social policy, especially if such loans conflict with sound business practice.

D. Kirk Davidson

SEE ALSO: Civil rights and liberties; Discrimination; Economics; Fairness.

Refugees and stateless people

IDENTIFICATION: Persons uprooted from their places of origin—usually as a result of wars or other violent civil disturbances

TYPE OF ETHICS: Human rights

SIGNIFICANCE: In a world of international conflicts, civil wars, and repressive regimes, the plight of refugees and others driven from their homeland poses an ethical challenge to the ability of the more fortunate to ease the suffering of growing millions.

Refugees have fled war zones ever since the losers were routinely put to death or enslaved. History is replete with tales of vulnerable stateless peoples. Jews and Gypsies, for example, were frequently expelled

Refugee camp that housed about eighty thousand of the estimated two million Afghans living in Pakistan in September, 2001. After the United States began retaliating against Afghanistan's Taliban regime for its support of al-Qaeda, which launched the September 11, 2001, terrorist attacks on the United States, even more Afghans fled their homeland. (AP/Wide World Photos)

en masse from medieval and post-Renaissance states in Europe. In modern history, however, the numbers, visibility, and suffering of the displaced have significantly increased. In part, these developments reflect the modern world of global news networks, which have carried images of the powerless victims of warfare into the living rooms of developed societies. They also reflect the greater destructiveness of modern warfare, with its widespread use of mortars and antipersonnel land mines. Above all, these trends have reflected the artificial nature of and tensions within so many of the newer states in today's world.

During the colonial era of the early twentieth century, European nations drew boundaries within their empires with little regard to the presence of the diverse communities living within their colonial realms. In many instances, the colonial powers widened the differences separating the diverse groups

present by economically advancing some communities more rapidly than others. On some occasions, they imported diversity, as in the case of the Asians whom Great Britain brought to Uganda to provide what the British regarded as "industrious" labor. At independence the populations of most of the new states in Asia and Africa contained groups with little in common with one another and often with pre-colonial histories of mutual animosity. Civil wars, the repression of ethnic minorities, and even massacres subsequently ensued, all ejecting streams of refugees into neighboring areas.

Until the violent breakup of Yugoslavia during the early 1990's, the problems of refugees and those internally displaced in their countries of residence were primarily perceived as humanitarian issues limited to developing states. That image was rudely shattered by the reports of "ethnic cleansing," mass graves, and atrocities committed by all of the parties involved in the conflicts in the new states that separated from Yugoslavia: first Croatia, then Bosnia, and finally Kosovo during the 1990's.

The plight of these unsettled peoples has not gone unattended. Nongovernmental organizations, the United Nations, and other international bodies and individual countries have tendered humanitarian aid and, in some instances, have militarily intervened to halt conflicts generating large numbers of refugees and internally displaced persons. However, those needing assistance have multiplied faster than the funds available for their relief, and the political problems of returning them to a safe and normal life have often proven insurmountable. Thus, for example, three years after the Kosovo conflict ended, fewer than three hundred of the more than 230,000 Romany and Serbian refugees generated by that conflict had been returned to their homes.

Joseph R. Rudolph, Jr.

FURTHER READING

Cohen, Roberta, and Francis M. Deng. *Masses in Flight: The Global Crisis of Internal Displacement.* Washington, D.C.: Brookings Institution, 1998.

Dummett, Michael. *On Immigration and Refugees.* London: Routledge, 2001.

International Crisis Group. *Return to Uncertainty: Kosovo's Internally Displaced and the Return Process.* Pristina, Kosovo: Author, 2002.

SEE ALSO: Citizenship; Ethnic cleansing; Human rights; Immigration; Israeli-Palestinian conflict; Kosovo; Land mines; Peacekeeping missions; Vietnam War.

Relativism

DEFINITION: Belief that there are no absolute or universal moral standards and that what is morally right or wrong is relative to an individual, group, or culture

TYPE OF ETHICS: Theory of ethics

SIGNIFICANCE: Relativism represents a rejection of both absolutism and pluralism. It eschews the notion that moral judgments can be grounded or ver-

ified in any way, so that moral reasoning becomes a completely subjective endeavor.

Ethical relativism is related to but distinct from general philosophical relativism and epistemological skepticism. According to this position, the human mind is incapable of attaining any genuine or objective truth. Hence, knowledge is subjective and "relative" to the knower.

The ethical relativist is skeptical of determining some truth about moral matters. This position can be traced to the Greek sophists, who were the objects of Socrates' criticism in Plato's famous dialogues. Thus, sophists such as Callicles and Gorgias contended that morality was relative and that what was right for one person or group was not necessarily right for another. They rejected ethical universalism, the notion that what is morally right and wrong is basically the same for everyone, viewing ethical or moral judgments as matters of convention or personal taste.

In contrast to the sophists, most philosophers, such as Plato, Aristotle, Thomas Aquinas, Immanuel Kant, and G. W. F. Hegel, have decisively rejected this extreme position and embraced the equally extreme idea that there are universal, moral absolutes transcending time and place. Some modern thinkers, however, have resurrected the position of moral skepticism and relativism.

TYPES OF ETHICAL RELATIVISM

In general, it is possible to distinguish between two types of ethical relativism: cultural relativism and the more extreme individualistic relativism. The latter represents the viewpoint that moral values or norms differ among individuals within a society or culture. In other words, moral judgments are purely subjective; they are simply a matter of one's personal tastes or an individual's conscience. If someone believes that euthanasia is morally permissible, one's judgment in this regard must be considered valid and tenable. Likewise, if someone else considers euthanasia to be wrong, that too is a reasonable judgment. Thus, extreme relativists accept that valid ethical judgments can be inconsistent with one another.

This notion of extreme relativism is expressed in the work of modern ethicists such as John Mackie. In *Ethics: Inventing Right and Wrong* (1977), Mackie argues that there is nothing truly good or bad or right or wrong. Rather, these categories must be "invented" in order to have any ethics. Mackie believes that the seeds of this position could be found in the works of his predecessors, such as David Hume and Thomas Hobbes. For Mackie, moral language, with its reference to "right" and "wrong," creates the illusion of objectivity, but in reality objectivity in the realm of ethics is impossible.

Cultural relativism represents the more moderate viewpoint that moral values differ from one society or culture to another. It admits that within a society some valid moral standards are possible, but those standards will sometimes differ from one culture to another. As a result, principles that are considered central and vital in one society might be on the periphery of another culture's value system. Moreover, the cultural relativist proclaims that there are no fixed or immutable standards that can serve as the ultimate guide to a society's moral code. All moral norms are conditional, completely dependent on time, place, and circumstances.

Cultural relativists also differentiate between descriptive cultural relativism and normative cultural relativism. The former version of relativism is summed up in the incontrovertible proposition that moral beliefs and practices differ from one culture to another. It affirms the findings of anthropologists and historians who have discovered that different peoples have different values. For example, while some societies practice polygamy, others prohibit the practice. Similarly, a society's moral values may evolve over the course of time. Slavery was once legal and was commonly accepted in American society, but now it is regarded as offensive and grossly immoral. The descriptive relativist simply uncovers and "describes" this cultural diversity, along with a society's evolving standards.

NORMATIVE CULTURAL RELATIVISM

Normative cultural relativism represents the philosophical position that there are no transcultural, universal moral norms and that prevailing moral judgments in different cultures are equally valid. Thus, the moral judgment "bribery is wrong" in one culture is just as valid as the judgment "bribery is right" in another culture. According to normative ethical relativism, each moral judgment must include a qualifier such as the following: "Bribery is wrong *in society X*." To a certain extent, the normative relativist regards moral values as equivalent to customs in that both have only local validity instead of universal validity. The normative relativist adheres to the dictum "when in Rome do as the Romans do" when it comes to matters of custom and morality.

On the surface, normative cultural relativism seems to be plausible, especially since it is quite apparent that different societies do have different moral codes, but there are some salient difficulties with this position as well as with the more extreme view of individualistic relativism. For philosophers who believe in objective truth, if there is no absolute standard of some sort and all moral codes are valid, it becomes impossible to criticize other cultures or contend that the morals of some societies are inferior to those of other societies. Ironically, relativists would have no problem criticizing other cultures, since they would merely be expressing their equally valid judgment of that culture. But they would recognize that there is no way to ground or render objective such judgments. Similarly, if one embraces cultural relativism, the notion of objective moral progress becomes unintelligible. Progress implies improvement, but if there is no general, independent, transcultural standard, the only people qualified to measure a given culture's progress are the people inside that culture who share its evolving values.

Finally, and perhaps most significantly, the idea of cultural relativism depends upon the belief that there are distinct cultures with identifiable boundaries between them. Globalism and multiculturalism have rendered this view less and less tenable, however. As cultures mix and come mutually to influence one another, the ability of relativists to demarcate the zones in which a given set of values does or does not operate breaks down. In postmodern society, it becomes impossible to tell where one culture begins and another ends. Ironically, this may mean that postmodernism, often attacked as synonymous with moral relativism, may be the moral relativists' greatest enemy.

Richard A. Spinello
Updated by the editors

FURTHER READING

Brandt, R. B. *Ethical Theory.* Englewood Cliffs, N.J.: Prentice-Hall, 1959.
Cook, John W. *Morality and Cultural Differences.* New York: Oxford University Press, 1999.

Hales, Steven D., and Rex Welshon. *Nietzsche's Perspectivism*. Urbana: University of Illinois, 2000.

Ladd, John. *Ethical Relativism*. Belmont, Calif.: Wadsworth, 1973.

Leiser, Burton. *Custom, Law, and Morality*. Garden City, N.Y.: Anchor Books, 1969.

Levy, Neil. *Moral Relativism: A Short Introduction*. Oxford, England: Oneworld, 2002.

Lukes, Steven. *Liberals and Cannibals: The Implications of Diversity*. New York: Verso, 2003.

Mackie, John. *Ethics: Inventing Right and Wrong*. New York: Penguin Books, 1977.

Rachels, James. *The Elements of Moral Philosophy*. 3d ed. Boston: McGraw-Hill, 1999.

SEE ALSO: Absolutism; Anthropological ethics; Diversity; Ethics/morality distinction; Morality; Pluralism; Postmodernism; Prescriptivism; Russell, Bertrand; Sophists.

Religion

DEFINITION: Faithful devotion to a divine or supernatural entity, pantheon, or principle

TYPE OF ETHICS: Religious ethics

SIGNIFICANCE: Every modern religion both professes and serves as the foundation for a specific set of ethical values. The observable behavior of a religion's followers, however, is not always consistent with that religion's ethics.

The relationship of religion to ethics is controversial, especially in cultures influenced by Islam, Christianity, or Judaism. The range of opinion is wide. For some, religion destroys ethics. For others, ethics depends upon religion. For still others, religion and ethics are the same.

Religion might destroy ethics in two ways. Perhaps an omniscient God makes morality pointless, since it does away with the freedom of persons to do other than God has foreseen. A loving, forgiving deity may render obedience to moral laws optional from a practical point of view. Ethics might depend upon religion because religion provides the only effective motivation for persons to obey moral law, as opposed to pursuing their own self-interest. Perhaps God's will determines legislatively right and wrong action, in which case religion and ethics are identical.

Ethics and morality will herein be considered synonymous. Influential persons have argued for a sharp theoretical distinction, claiming that ethics is the broader notion, including much that falls outside morality. The distinction is not so much theoretical as historical, serving unnecessarily to separate ancient and modern ethical work.

DIFFERENCE ARGUMENTS

That religion and ethics are not co-identical can be shown in at least four ways. The first way is to note that connections between religion and ethics in any particular society are matters of convention. Greek polytheism and Christianity may be used to illustrate this point.

In Plato's dialogue *Euthyphro* (399-390 B.C.E.), a priest of Apollo in Athens suggests to Socrates that piety is what is loved by the gods. This is the conventional answer to the question "What is piety?" in fifth century B.C.E. Athens. Socrates then asks whether piety is pious because it is loved by the gods or is loved by the gods because it is pious. The difference is enormous. Something carried is so because someone carries it, not vice versa. The priest, Euthyphro, becomes convinced that piety is loved by the gods because it is pious. Socrates points out that this communicates that the gods love piety, but not why they love piety or what piety is. Euthyphro is thrown into confusion, not knowing how to cope with the consequences of admitting criteria for piety that are not religious. Piety is a Greek virtue. The difference between this virtue and what the gods love shows at least that arguments separating ethics and religion were known to Plato, though Athenian convention considered them identical.

The argument in *Euthyphro* is generalizable. In a Jewish, Christian, or Islamic context, it involves the awareness that answering the question "Why should I obey God's commands?" with "Because He is good" involves a vacuous circularity unless the word "good" is defined in terms other than those of obedience to God. Therefore, criteria of goodness must be independent of an awareness of divinity. Also, if people possess such criteria, they are in a position to judge good and evil on their own, without consulting divine commandments. This does not mean that the divine commands do not embody norms that are in fact good according to human criteria. They may embody such norms, which raises the second difference argument.

A second way to show that ethics and religion are different is to recognize that all nonprimal world faiths accept the Mosaic decalogue's ethical prohibitions against lying, stealing, murder, and adultery. The "nonprimal world faiths" include Islam, Christianity, Judaism, Buddhism, Confucianism, and Daoism. Clearly, these religions do not share religious doctrines or beliefs. Nevertheless, the different religions embrace the same basic codes of ethics.

Huston Smith, in his influential book *The World's Religions* (1991), refers not only to these ethical prohibitions as common denominators of world faiths but also to their shared endorsement of three basic virtues: humility, charity, and veracity. There are three common aspects of traditional religious vision as well: Things are more integrated than they seem, better than they seem, and more mysterious than they seem. Smith uses the phrase "wisdom tradition vision" rather than "traditional religious vision" in order to include Western philosophy up to René Descartes in his analysis of commonalities. This shows that ethics is much more stable in its content than is religion and is therefore different from religion.

P. H. Nowell-Smith states that cultural relativism is based on the failure to recognize this distinction between religion and ethics. "If these are lumped together, it is easy to pass from the true premise that religious rules are everywhere different to the false conclusion that moral rules are different too."

A third way to separate religion and ethics is to note that connections between them are generally absent from primal, or pretechnological, societies. The ideas that primal peoples derived their beliefs concerning right and wrong from shamans or holy people who spoke for the gods, and that religion and ethics were separated only in later, more complex and secularized stages of development in those societies, are clearly mistaken. One might use the Australian Aborigines as an example to undergird this point, but one might as easily use the ancient Greeks and Romans, the Vikings, the Druids, the Japanese (Shintō), or any of a dozen Native American tribes.

AUSTRALIA'S ABORIGINES

The Australian Aborigines use a word that means, so far as anyone can tell, "everywhen." Everywhen is the time an individual spends engaged in activity that is central to the survival or flourishing of the clan-grouping. The essential things are food, shelter, procreation, and such. When I, as an Aborigine, build my house according to the ancient plan, or hunt, or fish, or produce children, I become the first person ever to accomplish these acts successfully, and therefore one of a number of first persons. First persons are not gods to be imitated. The time difference between myself and the first persons is gone when I enter everywhen, as my children will, and their children after them. In these sacred, eternal acts, I overcome the accidents and misfortunes that occur as the normal seasons pass. This is my religion.

The native Australians are quite aware of linear time. Their notion of everywhen accomplishes the same religious work for them that the last judgment of God accomplishes for Muslims and Christians: the domination of linear history. Linear, causal history contains much injustice, accident, disease, and disaster. In it, good things happen to bad people and bad things happen to good people. Religion must offer hope in the form of an understanding that dominates these facts, or it is not a successful religion.

The critical thing to note regarding any connection between ethics and religion for the Aborigines is that judgments concerning where I am entitled to build my house, where I can hunt or fish, and with whom I produce children are not related to everywhen. These are ethical decisions made among humans, by humans, and for humans. No one speaks for the archetypes on these matters. Religion proper has nothing to say about them, and only points to the necessity of the acts themselves.

Thus, primal societies do not exhibit the kind of connection between religion and ethics that some developmental views present. They also do not subsume ethical commandments under religious teaching, as the nonprimal world faiths do. This is obscured in nonprimal religions by the fact that all but one (Hinduism) were founded by some individual. Such an individual is, of course, an integrated human being, usually highly so. He exhibits ethical as well as religious integration in his expressions, judgments, and so on, clouding the fact that religion and ethics are different.

A fourth way to show ethics and religion to be different is to consider the problem of saying just what ethical system is required by any specific religion;

for example, Judaism and/or Christianity. The Judeo-Christian religion has operated, and operates today, as a religious basis in vastly different societies or cultures. Any such religion will offer behaviors that are relatively independent of particular, specific forms of social life. It will also exhibit enormous flexibility regarding moral standards in different cultures and at different times. Historically, Judeo-Christianity has served as the religion of Hebraic tribalism, Hellenistic aristocracy, Roman imperial monarchy, Constantinian bureaucracy, the Third Reich, and American republican capitalism. As Alasdair MacIntyre says, "it will perhaps come as a relief to consider that the whole problem of Christian morality is to discover just what it is."

It is perhaps worth noting that the comparative stability of ethical norms as opposed to religious beliefs pointed out in the second difference argument above can be rendered inconsequential by classifying a group as nonhuman, as the Third Reich did in the case of the Jews, in order to kill them without violating the prohibition against murder.

Taken together, the difference arguments make identity claims hard to defend. This does not mean that individuals who recognize the difference do not themselves integrate religious and ethical beliefs and norms. Plato presents Socrates as not accepting the conventional wisdom, or the institutional understanding of a priest, regarding piety. Just as clearly, Socrates accepts piety as a personal virtue. Plato's Socrates also exhibits religious beliefs when speaking for himself and not engaged in dialectic, particularly in *Phaedo* (388-368 B.C.E.).

DEPENDENCE ARGUMENTS

One need not stray from Plato for a model for arguments that render ethics dependent upon religion for motivation. Plato entertains this line of thought in *Republic* (388-368 B.C.E.), his utopian rendering of the ideal state.

The religion of the Greeks was contained in the narratives and poetry of Homer, Hesiod, and others. These stories were considered by Plato as unsuitable subject matter for the education of the young in *Republic*, because they present the divine as capricious, immoral, and even cruel. The divine nature must be, for Plato, good, not a source of evil. This brings to the fore Plato's attitude toward the truth. It should be noted that the Greek word *pseudos* need not have the

deprecatory connotations of "false" or "lying." The stories *(mythoi)* told to children are in general fictitious *(pseudoi)*. What Plato insists upon is that these stories be "true" by not misrepresenting the divine character.

In *Republic* there is a discussion to the effect that, although outright lying is despicable, "spoken falsehood" may be useful; for example, militarily or to save a friend from himself or herself. This passage ends with an analogy to medical practice: As medicine should be administered by a physician only for the good of the patient, so also falsehoods should be employed by rulers only for the good of the state. Plato then passes into a myth for his own purposes. His practical, ethical purposes in this myth are to bind persons to both their land and one another. The myth has it that the rulers, guardians, and workers sprang full-grown from Mother Earth, who nurtured, formed, and educated them.

This sequence of passages has long been used to question or condemn Plato's ethics. Such condemnation has prompted heartfelt defenses also, such as that of Francis Cornford, who despises those who would "suggest that he [Plato] would countenance the lies, for the most part ignoble, now called propaganda." These reactions are extreme because Plato is toying with the controversial notion that a religious creation story is necessary to provide a level of solidarity and fellow-feeling that might serve to glue humans together in community, actual or utopian, and motivate them to follow ethical norms.

Plato is *not* here countenancing propaganda of any crude sort, since he clearly intends for both the guardians and rulers to be convinced of the truth of the myth. Neither group is particularly credulous, and Socrates does not express much confidence in his ability to secure their belief.

This argument and others like it concern motivation, not ethical content. Ethical content is fairly constant between religious cultures. Dependence arguments harp on motivating persons through religion to observe ethical content. Some say that only religion will work, while others say that religion is unnecessary or irrelevant. It is in this standoff that destruction arguments become relevant.

DESTRUCTION ARGUMENTS

Some who claim that religion is unnecessary for or irrelevant to ethical motivation are neutral about or committed to a religious point of view, but others are not. Some are convinced that religion is the cause of most ill will and violence between persons in the world. They catalog the historical abuses of secular power by ecclesiastical authorities. They cite the enmity in Northern Ireland between Protestants and Catholics. They cite fanatical acts by Christian or Islamic fundamentalists. They are morally nauseated by these facts. Their nausea motivates them to mount arguments that religion destroys ethics, such as those mentioned at the beginning of this article. Quite naturally, such persons react strongly against any suggestion that ethics is dependent upon religion, because the two tend in opposite directions in their minds.

The two sides of this conflict will never touch. One side clings to direct experience with the divine. The other clings just as tenaciously to the trouble caused by organized, and therefore politically effective, religious groups, not to mention clinging to objections to the metaphysics of religious beliefs. Intelligent religious folk are not motivated to refute claims that religion has been the cause of all manner of evil in the world, because it does not threaten the status of their direct experience with the divine. For religious folk, the fact that such experience becomes perverse when constituted as a conflict-producing political platform is a manifestation of human corruption, not divine corruption. This response sometimes incenses those who want religious people to take responsibility for the carnage their religious organization causes, presently or historically. But this is heat, not light. Closed religious people hide behind their belief that without God, all is permitted. Closed humanists hide behind their belief that all religious people have been lobotomized. The two groups never speak directly to each other.

THOMISM

Is there any hope for resolution, anything better than this heated darkness? Some religious persons and humanists think there is a positive answer: Thomism. Although Thomas Aquinas was a Roman Catholic theologian, open, secular persons are not put off by Thomism. MacIntyre says, "Aquinas' theological ethics is such as to preserve the nontheological meaning of the word good." This is true, for Thomas Aquinas defines good as "that toward which desire tends." MacIntyre allows Thomas Aquinas's faith because, in it, calling God good is naming him as the object of

desire. This means that God and good are not defined in terms of each other. Therefore, "'God is good' is a synthetic proposition, and to cite God's goodness is to give a reason for obeying his commandments."

This reason, the nature of goodness, is naturally desired and as available to nonbelievers as believers, so both groups have access to accurate beliefs about goodness. Believers must regard unbelievers as possessed of natural reason, because of, not in spite of, their own faith. God created this natural reason, acknowledged or not, in every person. Believers and unbelievers are even in terms of practical rationality and can learn from each other in making ethical decisions. MacIntyre, in turn, does not consider religious folk ethically irrelevant; only their religious beliefs are ethically irrelevant.

Clearly it matters more, regarding ethics, whether a religious person is open or closed than whether he or she is religious or nonreligious. The same is true of a nonreligious person. MacIntyre goes as far as to say, "Thomist Christianity . . . exhibits more of a kinship with certain kinds of secular rationalism than with certain kinds of Christian irrationalism."

Thomism is Thomas Aquinas's version of Aristotle. Neither of these thinkers separates virtue from happiness, acting well from doing well. Modern ethicists, religious and nonreligious, have separated virtue and happiness. Modern ethics texts take the crucial issue to be the reconciliation of altruism with self-interest. This presupposes that to be virtuous is not to be happy, if "happy" means satisfying one's natural desires, and that to be happy is to be not virtuous. The invention and acceptance of modern individualism by Martin Luther, Niccolò Machiavelli, Thomas Hobbes, and Immanuel Kant was necessary to accomplish this separation. Modern individualism presupposes that basic opposition between self-centeredness and virtuous behavior that prompts requiring virtuous behavior to be motivated by the power of religion. According to Hobbes and Luther, humanity is depraved by nature. Thomas Aquinas and MacIntyre refuse to allow this presupposition.

Thomism cannot be expected to solve much in Islamic or Jewish cultures unless it is properly translated. Such translation and synthesis await an appropriate time or champion. It is difficult, however, to ignore a sophisticated, open theology in a time of oppression and violence caused partly by closed religion. The significance of Thomism is underrated in the academy's postmodern reflection in proportion to the overrating of the necessary demise of religion and/or closed humanism.

Joe Frank Jones III

FURTHER READING

Buckman, Robert. *Can We Be Good Without God? Biology, Behavior, and the Need to Believe.* Amherst, N.Y.: Prometheus Books, 2002. Argues that the need to believe in transcendent principles may have a biological basis, but that it is nevertheless useful to assume that there is no God when constructing practical moral systems.

Byrne, Peter. *The Philosophical and Theological Foundations of Ethics: An Introduction to Moral Theory and Its Relation to Religious Belief.* 2d ed. New York: St. Martin's Press, 1999. A general survey of moral theory as seen through the lens of the relationship between ethics and religion.

Gilby, Thomas. "Thomism." In *The Encyclopedia of Philosophy*, edited by Paul Edwards. New York: Macmillan, 1972. A brief but excellent introduction to Thomism, with an explanation of its attractiveness to nonreligious ethicists and statesmen.

Hudson, Yeager. "The Independence of Ethics from Religion." In *The Philosophy of Religion.* Compiled by Yeager Hudson. Mountain View, Calif.: Mayfield, 1991. Contains useful discussion of primitive societies, developmental issues, and Thomist natural law. Hudson fleshes out the relation between rational and religious ethics in a manner acceptable to religious Thomists and secular rationalists alike.

MacIntyre, Alasdair. *After Virtue: A Study in Moral Theory.* 2d ed. Notre Dame, Ind.: University of Notre Dame Press, 1984. MacIntyre critiques Kant for attempting to preserve a religious moral category (Original Sin) within the framework of a secularized moral system. Without the Christian notion of redemption to make sense of it, MacIntyre demonstrates, Kant's notion of inherent sinfulness damages his moral philosophy irreparably.

_____. *A Short History of Ethics: A History of Moral Philosophy from the Homeric Age to the Twentieth Century.* 2d ed. London: Routledge, 1998. A historical study of how ethical thinking in the West got where it is. It is standing the test of time well.

Nielsen, Kai, and Hendrik Hart. *Search for Community in a Withering Tradition: Conversations Between a Marxian Atheist and a Calvinian Christian.* Lanham, Md.: University Press of America, 1990. For those interested in pursuing the relation between ethics and religion in postmodern dialogue.

Nowell-Smith, P. H. "Religion and Morality." In *The Encyclopedia of Philosophy*, edited by Paul Edwards. New York: Macmillan, 1972. Excellent discussion, with more room for detail than the present article, but without serious consideration of the rapprochement offered by Thomism.

Smith, Huston. *The World's Religions.* San Francisco: HarperCollins, 1991. Acknowledged almost universally in the West as the best, most accurate, brief textbook on world religions.

SEE ALSO: Atheism; Christian ethics; Church-state separation; Deism; God; Hindu ethics; Islamic ethics; Jain ethics; Jesus Christ; Jewish ethics; Revelation; Secular ethics; Zoroastrian ethics.

Religion and violence

DEFINITION: Relationship between religious ethics and acts of violence carried out in the name of religion

TYPE OF ETHICS: Religious ethics

SIGNIFICANCE: From its earliest conception, religion has been linked with violence. Because religious violence is a pronounced aspect of contemporary societies and international politics, exploring the ethical connections between religion and violence is critical.

Religion and violence are intimately linked. The earliest archaeological records show evidence of apparently religiously motivated animal sacrifices and, later, human sacrifices, as in Mexico's Aztec culture. The biblical story of Abraham and Isaac is the repudiation of human sacrifice in Judaism, but animal sacrifice remained. In Christianity, the central symbol, the cross, is related to an act of violent sacrifice. Likewise, the historical and mythological stories of the world's religions are steeped in war and violence, from Hinduism's *Bhagavadgītā* to the conquest of the Holy Land in Judaism.

There are many explanations for interconnections between religion and violence. Religion involves human responses to the ongoing struggle between life and death. Primal religions saw all life as interconnected. For life and generation to continue, the forces responsible for the continuance and renewal of life had to be appeased. Sacrifice was seen as necessary for the continuance of the life cycle. A second explanation focuses on the social animosities that develop in any culture. To maintain social stability, animosities are focused on a sacrificial "scapegoat." The act of violent sacrifice defuses social tensions, guaranteeing continued social cohesion.

As human societies evolved into urban-based cultures, religion became a legitimatization for both violent forms of punishment and warfare. The laws of the state were presented as the laws of the gods. To break a law was to insult the sacred. Violent punishment was required to appease the gods and set right the moral order. Jesus' death on the cross was presented as such a sacrifice.

Warfare was also given divine sanction under the rubric of "holy war." Nation states were representatives of particular gods. In the name of those gods, urban civilizations made war on each other. To kill or to die in the service of a god was seen as a great honor and brought the promise of great rewards. The use of war, having a common enemy, is also viewed as an extension of the scapegoat theory, a means for creating social cohesion. These dynamics are still current in many modern conflicts.

STRUCTURAL VIOLENCE

Religion has also legitimated various forms of structural violence, violence that is a product of social laws and institutions. Religion has been used to justify caste systems, such as that in India, which left those in the lowest class (the untouchables) destitute and powerless. In Western Protestant societies, aid for the poor was withdrawn, as their poverty was viewed as God's punishment for their immoral behavior.

Religions also justified racial oppression and discrimination. Most notable was the claim by Europeans that the blackness of Africans was a sign of God's punishment, thus justifying slavery. Whiteness was also equated with purity and being God's chosen people. A similar theology was expressed in apartheid concepts in South Africa.

Likewise, women have been oppressed, often quite brutally, in all cultures. Such oppression has been justified by religious myths and teachings. In traditional India, widows were sometimes burned alive, along with their dead husbands, as part of funeral services. Some African groups practice female genital mutilation. In most societies, until recently, women could not vote, own property, or hold public jobs. Such restrictions based on religious continue in many countries and cultures.

As the twentieth century progressed, there was a widespread belief that religion was diminishing in terms of its social influence and so would cease to be a contributing force for violence (secularization theory). In reality, religion has become increasingly prominent in many societies and in the realm of international politics. Most early twenty-first century international conflicts have religious components. Examples include Hindus versus Muslims in the India-Pakistan conflict, Christians versus Muslims in the United States-Iraqi conflict, and Jews versus Muslims in the Israel-Palestine conflict. Religion has also become a source of violence inside many countries as conflict between religious groups has intensified and religious extremism has become more prominent, most notably in Northern Ireland, the Sudan, and the "ethnic cleansing" in Serbia and Bosnia.

RELIGIOUS FUNDAMENTALISM

Increasing religious violence in the world has several sources. In some cases conflicts arise over disputed sacred territories, such as Jerusalem and the site of the former Babri Mosque in India. In others it is a continuance of religious legitimation of certain forms of structural violence such as racism and the oppression of women. More pronounced, however, has been the rise of various forms of religious fundamentalism that have come to be part of many cultures and most religious traditions.

While most religious fundamentalists do not engage in violent activity, fundamentalism presents a worldview that encourages and legitimates violence. Religious fundamentalism develops in reaction to aspects of modern culture and politics, and its adherents define themselves oppositionally. In addition, religious fundamentalists typically claim to have precise understandings of God's will and see themselves as God's "chosen" agents. Additionally, fundamentalists view the world dualistically: as a battle between forces of good and evil. The opposition is by definition evil and so becomes a religiously sanctioned target of violence. This is evident in events such as the 1995 bombing of the Oklahoma City Federal Building and the September 11, 2001, terrorist attacks on the Pentagon and the World Trade Center.

Charles L. Kammer III

FURTHER READING

Appleby, R. Scott. *The Ambivalence of the Sacred: Religion, Violence, and Reconciliation.* Lanham, Md.: Rowman & Littlefield, 2000.

Beuken, Wim, and Karl-Josef Kuschel, eds. *Religion as a Source of Violence?* Maryknoll, N.Y.: Orbis Books, 1997.

Gopin, Marc. *Between Eden and Armageddon: The Future of World Religions, Violence, and Peacemaking.* Oxford, England: Oxford University Press, 2000.

Huntington, Samuel. *Clash of Civilizations and the Remaking of World Order.* Riverside, N.J.: Simon & Schuster, 1997.

Jeurgensmeyer, Mark. *Terror in the Mind of God: The Global Rise of Religious Violence.* Berkeley: University of California Press, 2001.

SEE ALSO: Christian ethics; Hate crime and hate speech; Holy war; Israeli-Palestinian conflict; Jihad; Nonviolence; Pacifism; Religion; Secular ethics; Violence.

Reparations for past social wrongs

DEFINITION: Compensation, typically in money, for injuries or damage done to members of groups or their ancestors

TYPE OF ETHICS: Race and ethnicity

SIGNIFICANCE: The concept of paying reparations for past social wrongs involves such ethical issues as justice and fairness, and the moral obligation to atone for wrongs committed.

International law firmly dictates that the victims of human rights violations have a right to compensation. In recognizing this right, several nation-states have provided reparations to members of groups whose human rights were violated. The two most recognized cases are those involving the provision of reparations to the Jewish people by the German government for crimes committed against them during the Holocaust, and the provision of reparations to Japanese Americans by the government of the United States following their internment in World War II.

The most highly debated case for reparations involves zAfrican Americans. While it is generally agreed that slavery was morally wrong, several unique ethical issues are involved. The reparations issue is complicated by the fact that slavery happened so far in the past. In the cases of victims of the Holocaust and Japanese American internees, many of the perpetrators of the violations were still alive when the reparations were offered, as were many victims. In the case of slavery, both the original perpetrators and the original victims are long dead. Who, then, should be the recipients of reparations for slavery? Who would be responsible? Can crimes committed so long ago be judged in terms of modern standards of morality?

From a relativistic perspective, human rights violations that were committed in the past cannot be judged by the moral standards of the present day. Thus, while contemporary moral standards hold slavery to be a crime, relativists argue that it is unfair to judge past behavior by current standards. However, others argue that human rights are universal; they transcend time and space. Therefore, successor nations have a moral obligation to compensate the victims of crimes that were committed long ago. Actions by the U.S. government in the late 1990's supported this latter perspective. For example, the Sand Creek Massacre National Study Site Act of 1998 provided reparations for an 1864 attack on a Cheyenne village.

THE VICTIMS OF SLAVERY

The injuries sustained by slaves are unquestioned. Slaves were denied freedom, treated as chattel property, physically punished, killed, denied their own cultures and languages, denied marriage rights, and made to suffer other abuses. The slaves provided their owners free labor. While former slaves were promised compensation at the end of the slavery (for example, the Southern Homestead Act of 1866 promised "forty acres and a mule"), that promise was never realized. Therefore, a case for former slaves can be made quite easily. However, those who served as slaves are deceased. Who, then, would be the beneficiaries of reparations?

Essentially, there are two possible beneficiaries in this case. First, the direct descendants of slaves could receive reparations. Proponents argue that the legacy of slavery has been sustained by a number of factors, one of which is a lack of wealth. Wealth is generally passed down from one generation to the next. Since slaves were unable to obtain wealth, they had almost nothing pass along to their descendants, thereby handicapping their descendants by making it more difficult for them to compete fairly in the economic market. This option is criticized on the grounds that it is unjust, since the descendants were not slaves themselves. It is also criticized on the basis that it encourages African Americans to view themselves as victims, denying them self-esteem and dignity.

The other possible beneficiary could be African Americans as a group. The system of slavery was jus-

tified by negative stereotypes of blacks as a whole. Since stereotypes are applied to groups and tend to be sustained over long periods of time, all African Americans may be regarded as having to suffer the negative consequences of slavery. Also, the Jim Crow system of discrimination that existed after slavery affected all members of the group, not merely former slaves. Even when legalized discrimination ended, institutional discrimination remained. The counterargument is that all African Americans have not suffered equally. By the early twenty-first century many African Americans were doing quite well. The conditions of African Americans as a group have improved substantially over time. By providing reparations to all African Americans, it is argued, the beneficiaries would be treated on the basis of race as a primary characteristic. This is, by definition, racist. This option, like the first, may also encourage African Americans to view themselves as victims.

Andrew Robinson-Gaither, a Los Angeles pastor, speaking at a Washington, D.C., demonstration in favor of reparations for slavery in August, 2002. (AP/Wide World Photos)

A final criticism of this approach is based on the primacy of individual rights over those of groups. Since the Enlightenment, notions of justice have been based on individual rights. Therefore, it would be unjust to pay reparations to those who are not the direct descendants of slaves. However, justice was extended to groups through civil rights legislation. Contemporary justice includes group rights.

WHO IS RESPONSIBLE?

The perpetrators of slavery are deceased. Who, then, should be responsible for paying reparations? Again, there are two primary options. One group that could be held responsible is those who inherited the wealth produced by slaves. The descendants of slave owners would be included, as would corporations that significantly increased their assets during the slavery era. However, these descendants were not directly involved in slavery, and it is argued that it would be unfair to hold them directly responsible.

The federal and state governments are the other possible option, since they allowed the human rights violations to occur. This option would, in essence, hold the whole nation accountable. It is argued that white Americans, as a group, have benefited from slavery and the ensuing discrimination and therefore have a collective responsibility to compensate the victims. Just as negative stereotypes hurt black Americans, they advantaged white Americans. The main argument against this approach again deals with an individualistic notion of justice. Not all white Americans living in the time of slavery participated directly in slavery, nor did any of the immigrants who arrived after slavery ended. In addition, it is argued that judging all whites simply on the basis of skin color is racist in itself, and therefore unjust.

Amy J. Orr

FURTHER READING

America, Richard F. *The Wealth of Races*. New York: Greenwood Press, 1990.

Barkan, Elazar. *The Guilt of Nations*. Baltimore: Johns Hopkins University Press, 2000.

Brooks, Roy L., ed. *When Sorry Isn't Enough*. New York: New York University Press, 1999.

Robinson, Randall. *The Debt*. New York: Penguin Putnam, 2000.

Winbush, Raymond A., ed. *Should America Pay?* New York: HarperCollins, 2003.

SEE ALSO: Anti-Semitism; Apologizing for past wrongs; Collective guilt; Developing world; Holocaust; Japanese American internment; Native American genocide; Relativism; Slavery; South Africa's Truth and Reconciliation Commission; Victims' rights.

Republic

IDENTIFICATION: Book by Plato (c. 427-347 B.C.E.)

DATE: *Politeia*, wr. c. 388-368 B.C.E. (*Republic*, 1701)

TYPE OF ETHICS: Classical history

SIGNIFICANCE: *Republic* is arguably the single most influential work of ancient Greek philosophy. It is a dramatic meditation on the nature and value of justice and on the social structure best suited to achieve it.

Republic consists of a lengthy discussion of the advantages of choosing justice rather than injustice. In order to persuade his interlocutors, Socrates, the protagonist of *Republic*, uses every rhetorical device available to him, blending images and arguments into a whole that is worthy of the name "cosmos." Included in the work are fictional regimes, noble lies, an analogy of the good, allegories exposing human ignorance, geometrical explanations of knowledge, an image of the soul in speech, and a myth. The interlocutors, however, remain skeptical. They see no reason to believe that the soul has conflicting powers that are in need of intelligent governance, and they doubt that a philosopher-king would rule the city more successfully than would a greedy tyrant who might agree to satisfy the interlocutors' own greed.

Framed among the most refined set of images available to philosophy, Socrates' failure to persuade is also a success. So rich is Socrates' ability to demonstrate the truth of his claim that it has provoked innumerable commentaries. The power of the dialogue lies in its drama. Captured at the end of a religious festival, Socrates is forced to argue the merits of justice and the disadvantages of injustice. Under the tyrannical rule of Cephalus, who believes that justice is good only for those whose appetites have become dull with time, Socrates gives in to his craving for arguments and must find a way out of his own injustice.

Cephalus leaves the discussion and hands his power to his son Polemarchus, who claims that justice is good for collecting debts. Thrasymachus, a guest, believes that justice proves advantageous for strong persons who can use justice to subdue the weak.

SOCRATES ON JUSTICE

Aware that justice has been shattered and that each speaker has taken from it what suits his preference, Socrates does justice to justice. Since justice requires the ordering of many parts into a unity governed without tyranny and with concern for the well-being of both the parts and the whole, the philosopher must attempt to educate his interlocutors. The hardest to persuade are Thrasymachus and Adeimantus, who are men of appetites; like the appetites that govern them, they are insatiable unless they are restrained but are also fragile and can be destroyed easily by excessive discipline. In respect to the city, the larger picture of the soul, this is tantamount to saying that Socrates must convince the artisans, or the masses, to accept the rule of the philosopher-king. Appetites and artisans respond to whatever appears to be pleasurable. The philosopher, therefore, must carefully select images that are simultaneously appealing and restraining. The story of Gyges and the tale of Er meet this need, awakening desire for the pleasures of justice and rejection of the pain that follows injustice.

Spiritedness, in turn, receives a strong dose of fiction. Intelligence thrives on the divided line. In order to educate whole souls and entire cities, one must use didactic devices that function as a whole. *Republic* itself is that whole. It should be kept in mind, however, that this whole is not available to the *dramatis personae* of the work. Therefore, the fact that the interlocutors are not persuaded by Socrates does not diminish the power of the drama. *Republic* is written in the first person and is presumed to be Socrates' recollection of past events. In fact, only the unnamed audience must be truly persuaded.

Socrates' instruction relies on two parallel triads, each of whose parallel terms are presumed to share a common virtue. The intelligence of the soul corresponds to the ruler of the city, and their common virtue is wisdom. The spiritedness of the soul corresponds to the guardians of the city, and their common virtue is courage. Finally, the appetites of the soul correspond to the artisans of the city, and their common virtue is moderation. Justice is the virtue of the city and the soul taken as a whole. Training into moderation proceeds through imitation, courage comes about through fictions, and wisdom (rational thought) arises from the study of music and geometry. Geometry satisfies intelligence's desire to look into the nature and structure of things, and music prepares intelligence to govern the many, forming a beautiful unity that never neglects the well-being of its parts. Justice, then, is learned through music. Presumably, music keeps intelligence in touch with the whole soul, for "someone properly reared in rhythm and harmony would have the sharpest sense of what has been left out or what is not a beautiful product of craft or what is not a fine product of nature." When intelligence matures in reason, or *logos*, music takes the form of dialectic. This claim makes good sense if one recalls that Greek is a language with pitch and rhythm.

Dialectic harmonizes. If one analyzes the divided line musically, one notices that its center is a continuous note that is interrupted by pauses marked by the lines that divide images from sensations and thoughts from truths. At the end of sensation, one sees a longer pause that is analogous to the rest that is inspired in the soul by the trust that seeing an object causes. When the object that is being observed causes a contrapuntal sensation, the soul, which is provoked to think, continues the melody. The sensation in question provokes thought by "tending to go over to the opposite." Seeing the index finger, the middle finger, and the little finger, one is satisfied to call them fingers. One pauses. Their relationship, however, gives mixed messages, calling the index finger both large and small.

What is required is a measure, a gathering of the parts into a harmonious whole that is analogous to the organization that is required by the parts of the city and the powers of the soul. The dialectician is the one who grasps the explanation of the being, or *ousia*, of each thing and unifies the many according to their nature. He provides a melody, conducts the orchestra, and hears and cherishes every note that is played, but never imposes an interpretation on the players. He governs by minding his own business. That minding of one's own business precisely defines what justice is. It should not surprise one then, that the best ruler of both the city and the soul is the philosopher-king.

Anne Freire Ashbaugh

FURTHER READING

Annas, Julia. *An Introduction to Plato's "Republic."* Oxford, England: Clarendon Press, 1981.

Crombie, I. M. *An Examination of Plato's Doctrines.* London: Routledge & Kegan Paul, 1963.

Mayhew, Robert. *Aristotle's Criticism of Plato's "Republic."* Lanham, Md.: Rowman & Littlefield, 1997.

Naddaff, Ramona A. *Exiling the Poets: The Production of Censorship in Plato's "Republic."* Chicago: University of Chicago Press, 2002.

Reeve, C. D. C. *Women in the Academy: Dialogues on Themes from Plato's "Republic."* Indianapolis, Ind.: Hackett, 2001.

Rice, Daryl H. *A Guide to Plato's "Republic."* New York: Oxford University Press, 1998.

Roochnik, David. *Beautiful City: The Dialectical Character of Plato's "Republic."* Ithaca, N.Y.: Cornell University Press, 2003.

SEE ALSO: Constitutional government; Excellence; Idealist ethics; Justice; Plato; Platonic ethics; Public interest; Religion; Socrates; *Utopia*; Virtue.

Responsibility

DEFINITION: Legal or moral liability for one's acts or omissions

TYPE OF ETHICS: Beliefs and practices

SIGNIFICANCE: Responsibility is a precondition for moral regard. People are usually judged morally praiseworthy or blameworthy only if they are responsible for their actions.

The concept of responsibility is a focus of long-standing dispute in metaphysics and moral philosophy. There is widespread disagreement about whether and in what sense persons are morally responsible for their actions. Some philosophers believe that to be morally responsible an agent must be free. Others think that responsibility obtains independently of the question of free will. Among those who regard freedom as essential to responsibility there are various theories about whether and in what sense persons are free. To understand the philosophical background of dispute about the concept of responsibility, it is nec-

essary to sketch out the main lines of controversy and evaluate the strengths and weaknesses of some of the most influential positions.

FREEDOM AND RESPONSIBILITY

It is commonly said that people can reasonably be held responsible for what they do only if their actions are done freely. In moral evaluation and legal decision making, persons are usually excused from responsibility for their actions if the evidence suggests that they acted without the ability or opportunity to choose to act differently.

People with severe mental disabilities or mental illness and those under extreme duress are routinely exempted from moral responsibility. The law similarly draws commonsense distinctions between murder in the first degree and manslaughter, in which an agent is said to have acted in the heat of passion. The idea is that under circumstances of extraordinary confusion or stress, the average person is not capable of acting freely; therefore, moral responsibility is at least temporarily diminished or suspended. A victim coerced by threat of violence to commit a moral offense in conditions in which most persons would find they have no choice but to comply is often seen as a mitigating circumstance absolving the agent of moral responsibility.

The same reasoning applies to the exclusion of severely mentally retarded or insane persons from the category of moral responsibility. Persons with such disorders are usually judged unable to reason about their actions and the consequences of those actions. They are thought not to act freely or to act with such limited freedom that they cannot be considered moral agents, and their actions are not judged morally right or wrong. More morally and legally controversial cases concern substance abuse addicts and others under the influence of biochemical compulsions who may be involved in wrongful actions but who seem to lack the necessary self-control to be considered responsible.

DETERMINISM

If these examples prove that responsibility entails freedom, then moral responsibility for action is problematic. There are scientific and philosophical reasons for doubting that humans are free enough in a deeper metaphysical sense to support the traditional concept of moral responsibility. The freedom to choose to act or to refrain from acting is challenged by causal, logical-semantic, and theological kinds of determinism. These theories maintain, on different grounds, that persons cannot act otherwise than they in fact do. Logical-semantic determinism holds that agents are determined in what they do by the eternal abstract truth conditions of propositions describing their future actions.

Theological determinism makes similar claims from the assumption of God's perfect omniscience of what agents will do and how they will choose to act. Since causal determinism is thought to pose the most serious threat to free action, however, it is convenient in what follows to limit discussion to it. Causal determinism arises from the conception of human beings as physical systems, subject, like other macrophysical entities, to deterministic natural laws. If persons are determined by the laws of physics, then they are no more free to choose and act than nonliving things are. If moral responsibility entails causal freedom, then persons are not morally responsible.

There is a spectrum of degrees of freedom and responsibility in the ordinary, nonphilosophical, sense. It begins, on the low end, with nonhuman animals and severely retarded or insane persons, who are believed to have no moral responsibility at all. Then come addicts and persons under the direction of psychopathological compulsions; they are intermediate cases, who are typically thought to have some, but less than normal, moral responsibility. Finally, there are normal human adults, who, other things being equal, are usually regarded as morally responsible agents. If nonhuman animals, the severely retarded, and insane persons lack responsibility, and if addicts and compulsives have diminished responsibility because they cannot exercise sufficient self-control, the same reasoning coupled with philosophical arguments for determinism suggests that no one anywhere in the spectrum is morally responsible.

If human beings are merely complicated physical systems, then even normal human adults are not freely in control of what they do. They cannot do other than what they do, but are merely manipulated through body chemistry and the environment by the same cause-and-effect relations that govern all other natural phenomena in the universe. If this is true, and if moral responsibility entails causal freedom, then no person is morally responsible, and there is no justification for regarding normal human adults as more

morally responsible than nonliving things, nonhuman animals, the severely retarded or insane, addicts, or compulsives.

Accordingly, to preserve moral responsibility in the light of the challenge of determinism, some philosophers have argued that freedom is not necessary for moral responsibility. They interpret responsibility as mere accountability. By this they mean that to be morally responsible is to be the person causally responsible for a certain event, capable of explaining one's reasons for acting, and perhaps able and willing to accept approval for a good result and accept blame for or rectify an unwanted outcome. It is in this pragmatic sense that airlines are held responsible for damage to a passenger's luggage, and it is at this level that legal responsibility generally functions, without raising deep metaphysical issues about whether airline employees act freely in the sense of being causally undetermined.

METAPHYSICS OF RESPONSIBLE ACTION

There are two main types of theories of moral responsibility, which can be referred to as compatibilist and incompatibilist. Compatibilist theories of responsibility hold that responsibility is independent of the problem of freedom, or that responsibility is logically compatible with causal determinism, so that agents can be responsible in the pragmatic sense even if they are not free. Incompatibilist theories insist that whether agents are morally responsible logically depends on whether and in what sense they are free, and that responsibility is logically incompatible with causal determinism. Incompatibilism further divides into responsibilist and nonresponsibilist theories. Responsibilist incompatibilism is the position that responsibility is incompatible with determinism but that agents are responsible precisely because they are not causally determined. Nonresponsibilist incompatibilism is the view that responsibility is incompatible with determinism, but since agents are causally determined, they are not responsible. Nonresponsibilist incompatibilism implies that an agent's feeling of responsibility, sometimes manifested as pride, guilt, or stirrings of conscience, is illusory.

The distinction is reflected above in cases involving compatibilist responsibility, such as an airline's collective accountability for a passenger's luggage, and the incompatibilist judgment that if agents are not causally free in a deeper metaphysical sense, then they are no more responsible for what they do than are nonhuman animals or even nonliving physical things. The advantage of compatibilism is that it assumes no burden of challenging the modern scientific world outlook according to which all natural phenomena are supposed to be reductively causally explainable by the laws of physics. Yet it preserves a pragmatic sense in which it is intelligible to hold normal human adults responsible, while morally excusing and excluding from responsibility nonhuman animals, the severely retarded or insane, and related commonsense and legally recognized exceptions.

The advantage of responsibilist incompatibilism, if it can be convincingly defended, is that it accords with traditional moral thinking about the dignity of mind and the difference between human beings and other natural systems, and especially with the conception that an agent in acting responsibly could have chosen to act differently. From the standpoint of responsibilist incompatibilism, compatibilism offers an intellectually unsatisfying diluted sense of responsibility that is insufficient to sustain moral judgment and justify the social mechanisms of praise and blame, reward and punishment. From a nonresponsibilist incompatibilist standpoint, such judgments and practices cannot be justified, because they are based on false assumptions about the freedom of action.

To resolve the metaphysics of freedom and responsibility requires an investigation of concepts in philosophical psychology or the philosophy of mind. The freedom of the will is accepted by substance dualist theories of mind, in which the mind or soul is said to be a spiritual substance distinct from the body's material substance. If the mind is immaterial, then it is causally free and undetermined by causal necessity. Unfortunately, substance dualism cannot satisfactorily explain causal interaction between body and mind. If mind and body are causally independent of each other, and if only the body is subject to causation, then the mind cannot be causally responsible, and hence cannot be morally responsible, for actions involving body movements. If, however, mind and body are identical, and if the body, like other purely physical systems, is subject to causal determinism, then so is the mind; therefore, the problem of the causal determinism of action remains on incompatibilist assumptions to threaten moral responsibility. The dilemma is that if the mind is part of the body's causal nexus, then it is causally deter-

mined and therefore not morally responsible for its actions; if the mind is not part of the body's causal nexus, then the mind is not causally responsible, and again therefore not morally responsible for its actions.

There is another theory of mind that allows both mind-body causal interaction and incompatibilist freedom of will and moral responsibility. Instead of regarding mind as a spiritual substance distinct from but somehow interacting with the body's physical substance, persons can be understood as physical substances with both physical and nonphysical aspects, or properties. This alternative to classical substance dualism is known as aspect, or property, dualism. If the mind is not an immaterial substance, then the problem of its causal interaction with the material body does not arise. If mental properties are irreducible to purely physical properties, then there is a sense in which persons are not merely physical entities. The nonphysical or physically irreducible properties of persons constitute an aspect of persons by virtue of which they do not fully fall under deterministic causal laws. The difference between the mind and ordinary purely physical systems postulated by this kind of theory permits minds to be causally undetermined in the contracausally free ethical decision making for which they are morally responsible.

ACCEPTING RESPONSIBILITY

There are social as well as metaphysical dimensions of the concept of responsibility. To be judged morally responsible for the consequences of an action, an agent must intend to act, intend that the action result in the consequences for which the agent is responsible, and be aware of or remember having done the action when held accountable for it. A shared sense of values in taking responsibility and holding others responsible is also presupposed. These factors impose additional intentional conditions on the concept of moral responsibility.

The importance of these additional conditions can be illustrated by a commonsense example. Suppose that an agent freely decides to turn on a light switch. The agent is responsible for the immediate action of turning on the light but not necessarily responsible for its further unforeseen consequences. If turning on the light enables a killer to see a victim in the room, then the agent's turning on the light may in some sense be causally responsible for the victim's murder.

If the agent has no knowledge that the killer is present or that the person in the room might be a target for murder, however, and has no acquired responsibility to act as the victim's guardian, then the correct judgment seems to be that the agent is at most partly causally responsible, but not morally responsible, for the victim's death. This condition can be formulated by saying that an agent must intend the consequences of an action in order to be morally responsible for it. The agent in the example intends to turn on the light and is, as far as moral considerations are relevant, morally responsible for doing so. The agent does not intend that the victim be killed, however, and therefore is not morally responsible for the fact that this occurs in part as a consequence of turning on the light. The killer intends to murder the victim and is morally responsible for that action, for which the light's being turned on merely affords an opportunity.

AWARENESS OF CONSEQUENCES

A related though more controversial condition is that the agent recognize or be aware of doing an action or of its effects at the time when held responsible for it. Persons who have committed what would otherwise be regarded as a moral offense are sometimes acquitted of responsibility by the consideration that they have no memory of having so acted. If an agent acts and then suffers amnesia permanently affecting memory of the action, it may be inappropriate to hold the person morally responsible thereafter, even if at the time the agent would have been rightly judged morally responsible. It seems pointless to praise, blame, reward, or punish persons for actions they have no memory of doing.

It may be equally pointless to hold persons morally responsible, in the sense of morally praising, blaming, rewarding, or punishing them, if they do not share at least some of the relevant values of those judging them. This is a normative condition that can be explained as the agent's intending to do an action in a certain way, as a morally good, bad, or indifferent act. The light switcher may intend to turn on the light as a morally indifferent act. The killer presumably intends to murder the victim as a morally wrong act.

If, however, the killer has values so different from those of the persons who judge the murder that the act is not intended to be something morally wrong, but instead something morally good or indifferent, and if there is no prospect of altering the killer's behavior or

values by moral censure or punishment, then, regardless of legal proceedings taken against the person for the safety of others, it may be inappropriate to regard the killer as morally responsible. A more realistic example concerns the incompatible attitudes of those persons who value the private possession of property and those who share all things in common. If members of two such opposite cultures meet and the sharers take and use a possessor's property, it is arguably unjustified to hold the sharers morally responsible for committing an act of theft. The fact that moral responsibility is seldom overridden by normative considerations testifies to prevailing agreement among human cultures at least about the most basic moral values. The normative element is nevertheless an important part of the complete philosophical analysis of the concept of moral responsibility.

LIMITS OF RESPONSIBILITY

If there are some things for which agents are morally responsible, there are still others for which they clearly are not responsible. Some existentialist philosophers maintain that each person is morally responsible for the state of the entire universe, including its past history and future.

The exact meaning of this extravagant thesis is obscure, but the claim seems to be that in accepting the fact that the universe exists, the individual participates in the fact of its existence in such a way as to comply with and constitute the universe as existent. The individual's acceptance is an intentional mental act, involving the person as agent in adopting a certain attitude toward the world. The consequence of the act is that the universe exists and would otherwise not exist for the individual who accepts the fact. If persons are morally responsible for the intended consequences of their acts, then an individual who accepts the existence of the universe becomes morally responsible for it.

The existentialist argument seems confused. Agents are morally responsible only for intended events for which they are causally responsible, provided that memory and normative conditions are also satisfied. Accepting the fact that the world exists does not make the agent causally responsible for its existence, and the agent certainly cannot be causally responsible and hence is not morally responsible for any part of the world's past history. Assuredly, no human agent correctly remembers having caused the

universe to exist. In the present analysis of moral responsibility, there is no sound basis for existential
guilt, despair, and anxiety about the state of the world
as the burden of one's personal responsibility. By the
same token, no person can be morally responsible for
what another does, except insofar as an agent acts as
an instrument of another's will. This is not an exception to the analysis, but an application of the definition of moral responsibility by which a person is indirectly but still ultimately causally responsible for an
event undertaken by another person acting as dele-
gate.

Dale Jacquette

FURTHER READING

Berofsky, Bernard. *Freedom from Necessity: The
Metaphysical Basis of Responsibility.* London:
Routledge & Kegan Paul, 1987. A detailed discussion of the metaphysical presuppositions of
moral accountability. Philosophical analysis of
addictive and compulsive behavior, necessity, un-
alterability, autonomy, and psychopathology.

Cane, Peter. *Responsibility in Law and Morality.*
Portland, Oreg.: Hart, 2002. An examination of
responsibility in law and ethics. Explores the relationship between moral philosophy and legal philosophy, as well as the impact of theory upon
practice.

Edwards, R. B. *Freedom, Responsibility, and Obligation.* The Hague: Martinus Nijhoff, 1970. Examines central issues of the concept of responsibility as it relates to the problem of human
freedom.

Fingarette, Herbert. *On Responsibility.* New York:
Basic Books, 1967. An exact but nontechnical
inquiry into the role of responsibility in practical
reasoning, including the development of self-
realization and the sense of responsibility and
guilt.

Fischer, John M., ed. *Moral Responsibility.* Ithaca,
N.Y.: Cornell University Press, 1986. A useful
collection of papers by contemporary philosophers on the nature of agency and responsibility
for action.

Glover, Jonathan. *Responsibility.* London: Routledge & Kegan Paul, 1970. A balanced treatment
of theoretical and practical topics. Emphasizes
problems in the traditional conflict between determinism and moral responsibility, blamewor-

thiness, and excusability, with special application
to mental illness and criminal responsibility.

Jacquette, Dale. *Philosophy of Mind.* Englewood
Cliffs, N.J.: Prentice-Hall, 1994. Discusses property dualism as a solution to the mind-body problem and its implications for contracausal freedom
of will and action, moral responsibility, and the
dignity of mind.

Shotter, John. *Social Accountability and Selfhood.*
Oxford, England: Basil Blackwell, 1984. An investigation of the concept of responsibility to
others and the development of the sense of responsibility from the standpoint of developmental psychology.

Widerker, David, and Michael McKenna, eds. *Moral
Responsibility and Alternative Possibilities: Essays on the Importance of Alternative Possibilities.* Burlington, Vt.: Ashgate, 2003. An anthology exploring the relationship between free will
and responsibility. Interrogates the notion that
one must have available alternative choices in order to be held responsible for the choice one
makes.

SEE ALSO: Accountability; Bad faith; Conscience;
Determinism and freedom; Dignity; Existentialism;
Freedom and liberty; Future-oriented ethics; Intention; Moral responsibility; Social justice and responsibility.

Resumés

DEFINITION: Written summaries, or inventories, of
job-seekers' qualifications and experiences
TYPE OF ETHICS: Personal and social ethics
SIGNIFICANCE: Accurate and honest resumés are valuable tools for job applicants; not only can they influence applicants' current and future employment, they also reflect the ethics and integrity of
the applicants.

Ethical principles define behavior as good, right, and
proper. An ethical person uses these principles when
making personal and professional decisions. Making
ethical decisions leads to self-esteem and respect
from others. However, many obstacles can intrude on
ethical decision making. One obstacle is self-interest,

by which every decision a person makes is based on a risk-reward calculation: Is one willing to do the right thing even when it is not in one's self-interest to do so?

Life is full of choices and an import aspect of choice is intent—why one engages in a particular action. The answer is that one's actions matter. Individuals are morally—and often legally—responsible for the outcomes of their decisions. Responsible people are in charge of their own choices and can be held accountable. One area in which ethical issues may arise is in the writing of a resumé. A resumé is a concise summary of a person's work history, education, skills, and experience. Because of its value to the employment process, accuracy and honesty are important features of a resumé. Accurate, honest and ethical resumés can influence their writers at three moments: When they are written, during the job applicants' interviews, and after the applicants take up their new employment.

People tend to compartmentalize ethics into occupational and private categories, and when it comes to resumés they often underestimate the cost of lying. Many people think that ethically questionable behaviors are justified when they see other people doing them, when no one appears to be hurt, or when the misbehavior seems to be trivial. However, since ethical decisions generate and sustain trust and demonstrate respect for societal rules, any ethical violation can have serious consequences. Thus, regardless of qualifications, many employers want to be sure they are hiring applicants whom they can trust.

There are many examples of people who have lost their jobs after it is discovered that they had lied about their experiences or are found to have presented false credentials. Examples include people who have gotten their degrees from diploma mills or who claim to have earned college degrees when, in fact, they have not. Other examples include people who fail to report criminal convictions or lie about their past employment records to cover gaps in their employment history.

Ethical decision making plays an important role in the development and use of resumés. Employers spend time and money checking the accuracy of resumés. Inaccuracies can lead not only to a loss of trust but also to an applicant's loss of employment.

Janice G. Rienerth

FURTHER READING

Citrin, James, and Richard Smith. *The Five Patterns of Extraordinary Careers: The Guide for Achieving Success and Satisfaction.* New York: Crown Business, 2003.

Gostick, Adrian, and Dana Telford. *The Integrity Advantage.* New York: Gibbs Smith, 2003.

Maxwell, John. *There's No Such Thing as Business Ethics: There Is Only One Rule for Making Decisions.* New York: Warner Books, 2003.

SEE ALSO: Cheating; College applications; Drug testing; Hiring practices; Honesty; Identity theft; Lying; Merit; Self-interest; Self-respect.

Retirement funds

DEFINITION: Savings that individuals invest in stock markets and other places in the expectation that their investments will steadily grow and provide them with secure income after they retire from working

TYPE OF ETHICS: Business and labor ethics

SIGNIFICANCE: When working people invest funds for their retirement, they understand the risks but also expect to be treated fairly and count on government agencies to regulate the ethical practices of the security firms in which they place their investments.

Until the Great Depression of the 1930's, American security firms regulated themselves, and the result was that influential investors received preferential treatment and had access to information not made available to the general public. However, after the collapse of the New York Stock Exchange in 1929, it became painfully clear to the public that the stock market was effectively rigged to favor certain investors over others. Those who had inside information about the impending collapse of stock values sold their shares before the crash occurred, while average investors lost their investments. Although investors lost much of their faith in the stock market, President Herbert Hoover was philosophically opposed to government regulation of security markets. Things changed, however, after Franklin D. Roosevelt's inauguration in March, 1933.

Roosevelt realized that the federal government needed to regulate the stock market in order to save capitalism by restoring public trust in the market. During his first two terms, he signed three important bills that imposed ethical values on the security industry and created a Securities and Exchange Commission (SEC) with the power to regulate the security industry and to punish violators with fines and jail terms. These laws were the Securities Act of 1933, the Securities Exchange Act of 1934, and the Investment Company Act of 1940. Among other things the new laws made fraudulent financial reports, insider trading, unequal treatment of investors, and deceptive selling techniques federal crimes. The SEC also created the National Association of Security Dealers (NASD) to regulate securities representatives.

RESPONSIBILITIES OF SECURITIES REPRESENTATIVES

Candidates for certification as securities representatives must pass a qualifying examination that tests their understanding of what a representative can and cannot do. About one-quarter of the examination deals with ethical issues. For example, when securities representatives advise investors, they must propose stocks, bonds, or mutual funds that are appropriate to the specific investors' needs. For investors who are opposed to risks or who are elderly, appropriate investments might be government bonds or conservative bond funds.

By contrast, significantly younger investors who are willing to accept higher risks in the hope of reaping high returns in the future might be directed toward such riskier investments as growth or international mutual funds, junk bonds, or stocks in unproven new companies. In all presentations to their clients, securities representatives must make appropriate recommendations and repeatedly remind investors that investments in stock markets are not guaranteed and that they might even lose their principal.

MANAGING RETIREMENT FUNDS

Investment companies and security companies must also behave in an ethical manner in managing retirement funds. Many investors choose to invest in mutual funds and not in individual stocks because they wish to spread out risks over the many different companies in which individual mutual funds invest their members' money. The federal Investment Company Act of 1940 requires that mutual funds establish the values of their shares right every day, immediately after the closing of stock markets. This regulation was designed to prevent insider trading and to make sure that all investors receive equal treatment.

Mutual fund managers must also adhere to the philosophies announced in their prospectuses. For example, a mutual fund that states that its intention is to invest 70 percent of its funds in blue-chip American companies and 30 percent in government guaranteed bonds cannot suddenly decide to invest it funds in foreign companies or in junk bonds. If managers of such funds do not respect their announced approaches, the SEC can bring criminal charges against them, and investors can sue such managers for losses caused by investments that contradict the announced goals and philosophies of a specific fund.

These ethical and legal protections are important because they give investors legal rights and remedies. A scandal that became public in 2003 illustrates the importance of such protection. Managers of several mutual funds, including the Putnam and Strong funds, made illegal trades after the 4:00 P.M. closing time of the New York Stock Exchange that gave them profits that were not shared by other investors. Not only were these managers and their investment companies forced to pay large fines to state and federal regulators, but individual investors in the funds also had the legal right to sue the mutual fund companies and their managers for real losses and punitive damages.

Some investors oppose investments of their retirement finds in industries that may conflict with their ethical beliefs. Many people, for example, do not want their money used to support the production and sale of alcoholic or tobacco products because of their opposition to tobacco and alcohol for personal or religious reasons. Many investment companies offer such mutual funds, which are often called "social choice" funds, that do not invest any funds in tobacco or alcohol companies. In this way, investors can be sure that their retirement funds are not being used to promote activities that are incompatible with their ethical beliefs.

Edmund J. Campion

FURTHER READING

Braithwaite, Valerie, and Margaret Levi, eds. *Trust and Governance.* New York: Russell Sage, 1998.

Dardi, YoDav. *Misbehavior in Organizations.* Mahwah, N.J.: Lawrence Erlbaum, 2004.

Davis, E. P. *Pension Funds.* New York: Oxford University Press, 1999.

Machan, Tibor R. *Primer on Business Ethics.* Lanham, Md.: Rowman & Littlefield, 2002.

Mitchell, Olivia, ed. *Innovations in Retirement Financing.* Philadelphia: University of Pennsylvania Press, 2002.

Soule, Edward. *Morality and Markets: The Ethics of Government Regulations.* Lanham, Md.: Rowman & Littlefield, 2003.

SEE ALSO: Ageism; Gray Panthers; Income distribution; Insider trading; Profit taking.

Revelation

DEFINITION: Communication or disclosure of absolute truth to humans by a divine being

TYPE OF ETHICS: Beliefs and practices

SIGNIFICANCE: If instances of divine revelation have in fact occurred, they establish the existence of God and of an objective moral law. They do not, however, guarantee that God's law is known or knowable on Earth, because it may not be possible for the human mind to encompass or comprehend divine truth.

While the earliest reflections on the nature of ethical conduct were rooted in religion, the philosophical treatment of ethics has led many people to assume the autonomy of ethics. This is the idea that ethics is not in any way dependent on revelation. Thus, a wedge has been driven between moral philosophy and theological or revealed ethics. There are, however, interesting and persistent questions about a possible relation between the two.

Since revelation means, at the highest level of generality, divine disclosure, questions about the relationship between revelation and ethics are part of a larger network of more general questions about the relationship between God and morality. Those questions that focus expressly on the significance of revelation for the moral life arise for any religious tradition that holds that God has revealed himself in some way that bears upon the human moral situation, but revelation may be understood in different ways.

THE MEANING OF REVELATION

First, revelation may take the form of general information about divine reality gleaned from the pattern of the natural world order created by God. Here, divine truth is disclosed indirectly through the effects of divine activity—especially the activity of creation. This is often called "general revelation." Some philosophers, such as Thomas Aquinas, have argued that general revelation is an ample source of knowledge about the foundations, principles, and sanctions of ethics. This view is known as the natural law tradition in ethics.

Second, revelation may refer to an intersubjective encounter between God and humanity that is entirely lacking in the overt transmission of any truths. The propositional content of what may be called "personal revelation" is at most implicit in the divine-human encounter. The possibility of basing ethics on revelation depends on what is concretely implied by the character of one's religious experience. It would be difficult to justify the universalizability of moral principles derived in this fashion since religious experience is in principle a very private matter.

Third, revelation may be understood as the direct divine disclosure to humans of truths in propositional form. The great "revealed religions"—Judaism, Christianity, and Islam—hold that their respective scriptures are a deposit of divine revelation. Theologians have called this sense of divine revelation "special revelation" to distinguish it from general revelation. It is special revelation that is usually in view in discussions about the relationship between revelation and ethics.

ETHICS AND REVELATION

There are at least three views about the general relationship between revelation and ethics. First is the view that a system of ethics must be based on (special) revelation. This claim is defended by a developed account of the implications of divine sovereignty and of human sinfulness and by the attempt to refute all secular systems of ethics. The sovereignty of God implies that the content of morality is determined by the will of God. Moreover, human depravity involves rebellion against the will of God, resulting in a failure even to know the will of God. Finally, all secular theories of ethics provide empirical evidence of the corruption of human thought about ethics.

A second approach affirms the complete, or nearly complete, autonomy of ethics. Goodness cannot be determined by the will of God, for it can be meaningfully asked: Is the will of God itself good? Those who define goodness in terms of God's will are no better off than those who define goodness in terms of some natural property such as pleasure. To define goodness, which is an irreducible property, in terms of something else is always a mistake.

The suggestion that ethics is autonomous must be qualified, for, as British philosopher G. E. Moore observed, one's metaphysics will have a bearing upon the practical question "What ought I to do?" "If, for example, Metaphysics could tell us not only that we are immortal, but also, in any degree, what effects our actions in this life will have upon our condition in a future one, such information will have an undoubted bearing upon the question what we ought to do. The Christian doctrines of heaven and hell are in this way highly relevant to practical Ethics." Since revelation might provide the sort of metaphysics that Moore refers to here, one cannot strictly rule out the bearing of revelation upon ethics, even if goodness is a non-natural and unanalyzable property.

In any case, there is an important difference between that which makes an action right or wrong and the way in which one is to know that the action is right or wrong. One is an ontological problem; the other is an epistemological question. Even if the moral quality of an action is not ontologically determined by the will of God, God, if he is omniscient and wills the goodness of humans, may elect to reveal the nature and content of that morality which does not strictly depend upon his will.

According to the third view, ethics enjoys a limited range of autonomy from special revelation, though ethics is supplemented or completed by special revelation. Natural law theories are typical examples of this approach. To be sure, they envision a link between revelation and all correct ethical thinking, but much of the content of a true ethical system can be known without the aid of special revelation, since general revelation is also an important source of moral knowledge.

THREE ADDITIONAL QUESTIONS

Does moral experience establish a need for revelation? Background knowledge about the existence and nature of God, together with an awareness that humans are faced with a complex set of moral difficulties, may be thought to justify the expectation of some further revelation from God that would address the moral needs and concerns of the human community.

This raises a second question: Is God a member of the moral community? If God exists, then it is quite possible that God himself is a member of the moral community, and that human persons have moral obligations toward God as well as toward other humans. It may even be that God has moral responsibilities toward humans about which it would be useful for humans to know. Suppose, for example, that God should make a promise to act in a certain way on behalf of humans and thus obligate himself to them. How should humans know of his promise apart from revelation, and what would be the force of a promise of which humans were not aware? Suppose, further, that the promise takes effect only if humans act in a particular way. In that case, the conditions must be revealed as well.

Finally, it needs to be asked, What effect might revelation have upon moral theory? If it turns out that there is a good argument for the need for revelation given the quality of human moral experience, then people can expect that any revelation answering this need will deeply inform, perhaps even overturn, much of human moral theory. The supposition of a revelation that addresses human moral experience implies that morality may be deeply affected by revelation.

H. Richard Niebuhr has noted four changes to the moral law caused by divine revelation: the prescriptive force of the moral law is discovered to be absolute in that humans are revealed to be beholden to the sovereign of the universe; the application of the moral law is discovered to be wider ranging than any secular ethics and timelessly in force; the moral law is discovered to be unexceptionable, providing an external corrective to any corruptible human system of morality; and the eventual transformation of human persons into freely loving agents is discovered to be a real possibility.

R. Douglas Geivett

FURTHER READING

Adams, Robert M. *The Virtue of Faith*. New York: Oxford University Press, 1987.
Gracia, Jorge J. E. *How Can We Know What God*

Means? The Interpretation of Revelation. New York: Palgrave, 2001.

Grisez, Germain. *Christian Moral Principles.* Vol. 1 in *The Way of the Lord.* Chicago: Franciscan Herald Press, 1983.

Gustafson, James M. *Ethics from a Theocentric Perspective.* 2 vols. Chicago: University of Chicago Press, 1981-1984.

Lefebure, Leo D. *Revelation, the Religions, and Violence.* Maryknoll, N.Y.: Orbis Books, 2000.

McInerny, Ralph. *Ethica Thomistica: The Moral Philosophy of Thomas Aquinas.* Washington, D.C.: Catholic University of America Press, 1982.

Mitchell, Basil. *Morality: Religious and Secular.* Oxford, England: Clarendon Press, 1985.

Moore, G. E. *Principia Ethica.* Rev. ed. New York: Cambridge University Press, 1996.

Niebuhr, H. Richard. *The Meaning of Revelation.* New York: Macmillan, 1970.

Swinburne, Richard. *Revelation: From Metaphor to Analogy.* Oxford, England: Clarendon Press, 1992.

SEE ALSO: Christian ethics; Divine command theory; Epistemological ethics; Ethical monotheism; God; Jewish ethics; Moore, G. E.; Muḥammad; Naturalistic fallacy; Religion; Ten Commandments.

Revenge

DEFINITION: Response in kind for a wrong done to oneself; punishment inflicted in retaliation for an offense

TYPE OF ETHICS: Personal and social ethics

SIGNIFICANCE: Many moral codes, including Jewish and Christian ethics, consider revenge to be wrong. Social philosophers have questioned whether systems of criminal justice are genuinely interested in rehabilitation and deterrence, or whether they are actually state-sanctioned systems of revenge in disguise.

Pietro Marongiu and Graeme Newman proclaim in *Vengeance* (1987) that "Vengeance has the power of an instinct. The 'lust for vengeance,' the 'thirst for revenge' are so powerful that they rival all other human needs." Revenge is a form of the universal motive of aggression in which reciprocity is sought to avenge injuries to oneself or to restore a sense of equality.

Revenge is often considered to be neurotic, aberrant behavior. In the words of the psychoanalyst Karen Horney, "Every vindictiveness damages the core of the whole being," implying resentment, spite, malice, or righteousness. Revenge is the basest of human motives. At the other end of the continuum stands forgiveness, the act of pardoning another person for any unpleasant or hostile behavior committed against oneself. In contrast to revenge, forgiveness is good and represents the noblest manifestation of human nature.

THE FUNCTION OF REVENGE

The dichotomy between revenge and forgiveness obscures certain facts about the place of revenge in the human psyche, according to Susan Jacoby (*Wild Justice*, 1983). If revenge is a universal human need, then to forgive requires conscious suppression of the need to make others suffer as one has suffered. Humanity's long history is characterized by injury being inflicted on and sustained by others. That humanity seems to prefer revenge to forgiveness gives revenge a certain importance.

In fact, both Jacoby and Marongiu and Newman argue that revenge is not abnormal or aberrant behavior but a legitimate human need. Underlying this legitimacy is, as Jacoby says, "the profound sense of moral equilibrium impelling us to demand that people pay for the harm they have done to others." Revenge serves both moral and utilitarian roles. It is an example to society and a means of dealing with an offender. By making an example of an offender through revenge, society demonstrates to its members that certain behaviors are serious violations of the social order, are morally repugnant, and will produce unpleasant consequences for the perpetrator. Thus, revenge has deterrent, exemplary (it shows the public that society's well-being is being addressed), and moral aspects. In 1976, the U.S. Supreme Court legitimized the death penalty by proclaiming that revenge was an acceptable legal objective. That capital punishment was appropriate under certain circumstances reflected society's belief that some crimes are so terrible that the only adequate penalty for them is death.

THE DOCTRINES OF POLLUTION AND PROPORTIONALITY

The use of the term "revenge" may produce a disquieting sense of unease and discomfort. "Revenge" seems to be pejorative. If the words "justice," "restitution," "punishment," or "retribution" are substituted for revenge, however, the pejorative connotation disappears. Looked at in this way, the issue is not whether revenge is aberrant or evil behavior, but the establishment of a just and proper relationship between the nature of the act and the severity of the revenge. Finding such a relationship has been an ongoing matter of concern in literature, religion, and law since antiquity.

The two key concepts in striking this appropriate balance are the doctrines of pollution and proportionality. In ancient times, revenge was carried out as an individual vendetta or at the tribal level. The religious and political doctrine of pollution that developed among the ancient Greeks and Hebrews viewed certain acts, such as murder, as offenses against the whole society. This doctrine was an important point of transition between tribalism and written law. By means of this doctrine, the primacy of the state and of its gods and laws over the individual and tribe in enforcing punishment for acts of pollution was established.

The doctrine of proportionality states that the revenge extracted for an act of pollution shall be neither excessive nor trivial but shall match or be proportional to the seriousness of the act. This statement establishes a distinction between constructive revenge and destructive revenge. Limits are placed on the imposition of extreme forms of legalized revenge for lesser transgressions by forbidding penalties greater than the original crime and making the punishment fit the crime. "If men strive, and hurt a woman with child, so that her fruit depart from her . . . and he shall pay as the judges determine . . . thou shalt give life for life, eye for eye, tooth for tooth, hand for hand, foot for foot, burning for burning, wound for wound, stripe for stripe" (Exodus 21:22-25).

REVENGE AS A QUANDARY AND A DILEMMA

The doctrines of pollution and proportionality establish that certain acts shall be met by revenge meted out by the state and that this revenge shall be proportional to the offending act. Pollution is relatively straightforward in that there will be a relatively high level of agreement among people regarding what acts pollute. Proportionality is often very difficult to determine, however, as is indicated by the wide variation in prison sentences handed out for the same crime in different states and the controversy surrounding the issue of capital punishment. Thus, the pollution aspect can be viewed as a quandary (a question for which no single undisputed answer or consensus can be attained), but the proportionality aspect is often a dilemma (in which more than one ethical position is possible). Since revenge seems to be inherent in the human condition, these issues will have to be faced continually.

Laurence Miller

FURTHER READING

Aase, Tor, ed. *Tournaments of Power: Honor and Revenge in the Contemporary World.* Burlington, Vt.: Ashgate, 2002.

Ayers, Edward L. *Vengeance and Justice.* New York: Oxford University Press, 1984.

Barton, Charles K. B. *Getting Even: Revenge as a Form of Justice.* Chicago: Open Court, 1999.

French, Peter A. *The Virtues of Vengeance.* Lawrence: University of Kansas Press, 2001.

Govier, Trudy. *Forgiveness and Revenge.* New York: Routledge, 2002.

Jacoby, Susan. *Wild Justice.* New York: Harper & Row, 1983.

Marongiu, Pietro, and Graeme Newman. *Vengeance.* Totowa, N.J.: Rowman & Littlefield, 1987.

Nietzsche, Friedrich. *On the Genealogy of Morals.* Edited and translated by Walter Kaufmann. New York: Vintage Books, 1967.

SEE ALSO: Criminal punishment; Forgiveness; Justice; Mercy; Reconciliation; Violence.

Reverse racism

DEFINITION: Racial prejudice directed by a minority group that lacks institutional power toward the racial or ethnic majority; or, pejorative term for institutionally sanctioned racial preference systems, such as affirmative action, designed to counteract the effects of racism

TYPE OF ETHICS: Race and ethnicity

SIGNIFICANCE: Reverse racism is often used as a term of disapprobation for a politically controversial set of practices, including affirmative action and consideration of race in college admissions. Debate continues over whether such practices are just or unjust.

Reverse racism is a term for government-supported programs designed to remedy past injustices caused by racial discrimination. It is a term employed only by people who disagree with such programs. Remedies such as hiring quotas and affirmative action favor one race at the expense of another to make up for privileges that the second race has traditionally enjoyed at the expense of the first. In the simplest terms, such policies have been questioned on the basis of whether two wrongs can make a right. The term "reverse racism" has also been used to attack racial consciousness-raising methods among minority groups that use the denigration of the majority racial group as a means of attaining intraracial solidarity. These methods are practiced by minority political and religious figures such as the Nation of Islam's Louis Farrakhan and academics such as Leonard Jeffries, head of the African American Studies Department of City College of New York, who has told his classes that the lack of melanin in the skin of whites has rendered them inferior to blacks.

William L. Howard
Updated by the editors

SEE ALSO: Affirmative action; Political correctness; Racism.

Revolution

DEFINITION: Overthrow of an existing ruler or political system and replacement with a new ruler or political system, accomplished by or in accordance with the will of the governed

TYPE OF ETHICS: Politico-economic ethics

SIGNIFICANCE: The term "revolution" carries a strong connotation of a popular or majority movement. The sudden and violent overthrow of a government by a minority, or of one ruler by another, is usually referred to as a *coup d'état*. Unlike a coup, revolutions usually involve the transformation of the entire social order and of the society's central values.

During the late twentieth and early twenty-first centuries, the term "revolution" was invoked so frequently as to lose its currency. The word has come to be used to describe dramatic changes in virtually any area of human activity. Thus, one may read about a "revolution" in fashion, a "sexual revolution," a "women's revolution," or a "revolution" in the arts. While revolution in its traditional sense may involve change in any or all of these activities, it is a term whose classical application is properly limited to a few events of enormous political and social magnitude. It is not to be confused with a rebellion, a revolt, or a *coup d'état*, in which only political power is transferred from one group to another. While it includes a shift in political power, its transforming effects are not limited to politics. They involve rapid and enduring social, cultural, and economic change as well as political change.

In its original sense, the word "revolution" had nothing to do with politics or with violent or rapid social and political change. Rather, the word was part of the scientific vocabulary and meant to return to a proper, prescribed course. Therefore, for example, in 1543, a posthumously published book by the Polish astronomer Nicholas Copernicus was titled *The Revolutions of the Celestial Spheres*. Copernicus was using the word "revolution" in its accepted sense—something proceeding according to a proper, prescribed course. The planets, he contended, proceeded according to such a course around the sun. Revolution, then, meant literally revolving. In retrospect, Copernicus's book was revolutionary in a more modern sense—it transformed the human view of the world by postulating a theory of a heliocentric universe in place of the geocentric universe that was dominant until that time.

The association of the term "revolution" with the political events of the seventeenth century began to transform the term's meaning. Even then, the word continued to retain its earlier meaning of persisting in a prescribed course or returning to a designated course from which there had been a departure. The events of 1688-1689 in England provide an example of this usage. They were called the Glorious, or Bloodless, Revolution, by which was meant that, after the improper actions of King Charles II and

James II, England returned to its proper, designated course with the replacement of King James II by William and Mary.

In this sense, revolution was political but conservative; that is, the revolutionaries were restoring things, returning them to a proper course. The American Revolution was also sometimes justified in this way. Americans thought that they were deprived first of the "rights of Englishmen"—then of the "rights of man." They were restoring something that they claimed they already had but that King George III had allegedly taken from them. Insofar as war for American independence was not accompanied by a radical social transformation, some historians argue that it was not a revolution in the classic sense.

THE FRENCH REVOLUTION

The French Revolution, which began in 1789, became the model for revolution, not only for historians but also for later revolutionaries of the nineteenth and twentieth centuries. They would try to emulate the French Revolution. Even the Chinese, who began

their revolution in the second decade of the twentieth century, thought first in terms of the French example, and the French Revolution was only later displaced by the model of the Russian, or Bolshevik, Revolution of 1917.

The French Revolution, even in its early stages, was characterized by Edmund Burke, its harsh critic, as a social revolution, "a revolution in sentiments, manners and moral opinions." It challenged and overturned the values of society. What was most appalling to Burke was that the French Revolution rejected the past. The French Revolutionary generation rather quickly adopted the phrase "old régime" to designate the society that it was rejecting. The revolutionaries were sweeping away the old order of privilege and inequality and were replacing it with something new and, presumably, better. The best example of this repudiation of the past was the attempted institution, however unsuccessful, of a new calendar. The French Revolutionaries established the year 1 to be dated from the beginning of the Republic in 1792. History was starting over. Religion and the Church

Bolshevik soldiers during the Russian Revolution. (Library of Congress)

were repudiated. The social order of the old society was abolished. Even established fashion changed, as with the *sans culottes* (those who wore no britches), who repudiated the dress that was associated with the corrupt aristocracy.

REPUDIATING THE PAST

The extent to which the past is repudiated may differ with different revolutions, but it is not only the political order that is transformed. Along with their repudiation of the past, revolutionaries need a vision of a future, however vague. They must be convinced that they are building a better world. The vision of the future may be drawn from the writings of a generation of social critics, as the French Revolutionaries drew upon the *philosophes* of the eighteenth century, or from a more systematic theory of society, such as that of Karl Marx and Vladimir Lenin, whose work influenced the Bolshevik revolutionaries in Russia in 1917. Although they are influenced by theories developed in the past, revolutions are future oriented, insofar as they are ordinarily conceived as inaugurating a period of enduring progress, equality, and justice.

In this connection, revolution is related to the humanism of the Western tradition, since revolutionaries assume that humankind can improve the human condition. This optimism and fervor are evident in the sense of passion and zeal that is displayed by revolutionaries and even those nonparticipant contemporaries who are transported by the intensity of their times. So, for example, William Wordsworth could write of 1789, "Bliss was it in that dawn to be alive/ But to be young was very heaven."

Revolutionaries have often been aware of the importance of their own times and instilled with a sense of the righteousness of their actions. Accordingly, their deeds are often accompanied by eloquent justifications, such as the American Declaration of Independence or the French Declaration of the Rights of Man and the Citizen.

Revolution has been a modern phenomenon, insofar as it requires an organized state against which to rebel. While it was also a Western phenomenon, it has in the twentieth century been transported to other areas of the world, such as China. Given their dimensions and their transforming effects, revolutions are relatively rare. Many historians would include the English Revolution of the 1640's along with the American and French Revolutions in the following

Time Line of Major World Revolutions	
1688	England
1776	United States
1789	France
1804	Haiti
1848	Europe
1910	Mexico
1917	Russia
1949	China
1959	Cuba
1979	Iran

century among the few pre-twentieth century revolutions. In the twentieth century, after the Russian Revolution, the upheavals in China and Cuba qualify as revolutions given the magnitude of the social changes that they generated. The Iranian Revolution appears to be unique in that it was not future oriented. It rejected the immediate past, which had been influenced and supposedly corrupted by the West, in order to return to a more purified condition that ostensibly obtained before Western influence was exerted.

Abraham D. Kriegel

FURTHER READING

Arendt, Hannah. *On Revolution*. 1963. Reprint. New York: Viking Press, 1990.

Best, Geoffrey, ed. *The Permanent Revolution: The French Revolution and Its Legacy*. Chicago: University of Chicago Press, 1989.

Billington, James. *Fire in the Minds of Men: Origins of the Revolutionary Faith*. New York: Basic Books, 1980.

Bookchin, Murray. *The Third Revolution: Popular Movements in the Revolutionary Era*. 2 vols. New York: Cassell, 1996-1998.

Brinton, Crane. *The Anatomy of Revolution*. Rev. and exp. ed. New York: Vintage Books, 1965.

Dunn, John. *Modern Revolutions: An Introduction to the Analysis of a Political Phenomenon*. Cambridge, England: Cambridge University Press, 1972.

Gunnemann, Jon P. *The Moral Meaning of Revolution*. New Haven, Conn.: Yale University Press, 1979.

Kouvelakis, Stathis. *Philosophy and Revolution: From Kant to Marx*. Translated by Geoffrey Goshgarian. Preface by Frederic Jameson. New York: Verso, 2003.

SEE ALSO: Anarchy; Burke, Edmund; Civil disobedience; Class struggle; Communism; Declaration of Independence; Marxism; Political liberty; Social contract theory; Socialism.

Right and wrong

DEFINITION: Right: in accordance with the ethical values of justice and goodness—moral; wrong: violating or transgressing those values—immoral

TYPE OF ETHICS: Theory of ethics

SIGNIFICANCE: Perhaps the oldest and most central of all ethical questions is how best to determine the difference between right and wrong.

Since the days of the ancient Greek philosophers Socrates, Plato, and Aristotle, thinkers have searched for a way to distinguish between right and wrong. One twentieth century thinker who adopted and further developed the Aristotelian position was William D. Ross. He made the case for intuitionism, arguing that the moral convictions of well-educated, reasonable, and thoughtful people were the data of ethics, just as sense perceptions are the data of the sciences. He rejected both ethical subjectivism and utilitarianism, arguing instead that duty was the key to ethics. For Ross, right and good had distinct objective qualities. The former had to do with acts, while the latter had to do with motives.

Another modern philosopher who accepted Ross's argument was James Rachels, who added that morality—the attempt to discern right from wrong, good from bad—must be guided by reason. One should do whatever one has the best reasons for doing while keeping in mind the worth and interests of all those people who will be affected by one's actions. When considering a course of action, the conscientious moral individual will analyze the possible choices, measuring the implications of certain choices. After such deliberation, the moral individual will take the best possible course of action. Not all thinkers, however, agree with the above appeal to reason.

THE PROBLEM OF ETHICAL SUBJECTIVISM

Scholars such as Ross and Rachels refused to accept subjectivism, which holds that everything is relative. To a subjectivist, nothing is right or wrong. Rather, moral judgments about good and bad and right and wrong are simply personal opinions based on an individual's "feelings" and nothing more. Even "truth" to an individual is truth according to "feelings." Thus, subjectivists reject the role of reason in making moral judgments. Furthermore, cultural subjectivism or relativism addresses a similar point, arguing that morals and values vary from culture to culture. Thus, there is no one standard of right and wrong. Regarding both ethical and cultural subjectivism, Ross and Rachels responded that reason and reasons are central, for truths in morals are truths of reason; that is, moral judgments that are correct must be backed by better reasons than an alternative judgment. Subjectivists are right that feelings and opinions are important to an individual, but to consider only those factors in making judgments is, in effect, to opt out of moral thinking, for moral thinking must weigh the reasons for and consequences of potential actions.

RIGHT, WRONG, AND RELIGION

In the United States, most laypersons would list ministers, priests, and rabbis if they were asked to name moral "experts." Unfortunately, such laypersons regard morality and religion as inseparable when, in fact, religious leaders appear to be no better and no worse judges than are people in other "walks" of life. Nevertheless, many people embrace what some theologians call the divine command theory, which holds that what is morally right is commanded by God and what is wrong is condemned and forbidden by God. A positive result of such a view is that it immediately solves the problem of subjectivism.

Atheists and agnostics reject the divine command argument. Even the noted Christian Thomas Aquinas rejected it. One reason why philosophers object to the theory is that it poses an unsolvable dilemma, for the following question must be asked: Is conduct right because God commands it or does God command it because it is right? To answer the question, one might take the example of truthfulness. The Hebrew God commands it in the book of Exodus; therefore, people should be truthful because God orders them to be so. It is God's command that makes telling the truth necessary, and without such a command, truth would be neither right nor wrong, neither good nor bad. This view makes God's commands seem arbitrary, meaning that God could have given another command (to lie, for example) that would then have been right. Such logic reduces the goodness of God to unintelligible nonsense, for believers think that in addition to being all-knowing and all-powerful, God is also all-good.

A second analysis of the divine command theory takes another path. God commands truthfulness, other virtues, and right action simply because they are right. Thus, he commands people not to lie, not to kill, not to steal, and so on because such actions are simply wrong, while their opposites are simply right. This views avoids the dilemma mentioned in the above paragraph. The goodness of God is maintained. Upon reflection, however, one sees that this second view abandons the theological definitions of right and wrong, for it is saying that there are standards of right conduct and right thinking that are independent of God and that rightness existed prior to God's affirmation of it.

Because of the above contradictions, most theologians do not stress the divine command theory. Instead, they embrace the theory of natural law, which holds that reason determines moral judgments of right and wrong. Were the natural law theory to end there, modern philosophers such as Ross and Rachels could likely accept the position. Theologians explain, however, that God is still involved, for he is a perfectly rational entity. He created a rational order in the universe and gave humans the power to be rational and to use powers of reason. Thus, in this view, moral questions of right and wrong still depend on God.

The natural law theory seems to hold up well in minor matters but appears to falter whenever moral dilemmas emerge. Since the 1970's, for example, an ongoing struggle has been waged on the issue of abortion. Good, sincere, reasoning people have disagreed on the subject. Many religious people are on opposite sides of the issue. Whither the natural law theory? It does not provide the answer. A further criticism includes the fact that if God gave humans the power to reason, he obviously did not give all people equal reasoning skills. Simple observation demonstrates that not all people are equal when it comes to intelligence, skills, and so on.

PSYCHOLOGICAL AND ETHICAL EGOISM

Any "system" of morality discerns rights and wrongs and also asks people to behave unselfishly. Before one acts, one must consider the consequences. Will anyone be hurt by the course of action? Unless one can answer no, a proposed action should be forestalled. Psychological egoism attacks the just-stated point. Once widely held by philosophers, psychologists, and others, the theory of human nature holds that, indeed, people will act selfishly as they pursue their own self-interest. Furthermore, the theory holds that it is unreasonable to expect people to act otherwise, for pure altruism has never existed except in myth.

Psychological egoism leads to a reinterpretation of motives for being right and good. For example, if a wealthy man or woman donates much time and money to charitable work that benefits hundreds or thousands of people, that person is really only showing his or her superiority, for he or she is publicly demonstrating how successful he or she is. The unspoken statement is this: "Look at me. Not only can I

Egoism of Abraham Lincoln

According to legend, even Abraham Lincoln was a psychological egoist. Once, while riding a stagecoach, he remarked to a fellow passenger that he thought most men were motivated by selfishness. Just as the other passenger was collecting his thoughts to rebut Lincoln's statement, the coach passed over a bridge and the two men heard a sow below the bridge making horrible noises. Her piglets were mired in water and mud and were threatened with drowning Lincoln called out to the driver to stop, then got out of the coach, ran down below the bridge, and pulled the young pigs to safety on a dry bank. As Lincoln climbed back into the coach, the other passenger asked him what had happened to the selfishness. Abe supposedly replied that had he not saved the pigs, he would have worried about it for days, so he had actually acted out of self-interest.

take adequate care of myself, but I have much left over and will share with those who are failures and who are therefore inferior to me."

Perhaps another person, John Doe, also gives money to charity. His motive is likely selfish, for his religion teaches him that he will be rewarded in Heaven, and John is trying to buy his way in. Or, again, a hero saves several families from a burning apartment complex. Had it not been for her valor, all would have perished in a most horrible way. While the mayor gives the hero the key to the city, a psychological egoist points out that the hero acted not out of concern for the innocent families but to gain public acclaim.

It is actually the unselfish person who derives great satisfaction from helping others, whereas the truly selfish person does not. If one wishes for others to be happy (or fed, or given health care, or given a job, or saved from a burning building) and acts on that thought, then one is indeed unselfish and altruistic. Psychological egoism is only the act of reinterpreting "right" motives to make them seem "wrong," while straining the English language and the meaning of its words.

A close cousin of psychological egoism, ethical egoism says that there is only one principle of conduct: self-interest. All questions of morality, of right and wrong, of good and bad must be subordinate to that principle. Occasionally, however, it might be that one cooperates with others, keeps promises, completes duties, and so on because one's self-interest might be compatible with the self-interest of others. Furthermore, ethical egoism also sees a boundary between self-interest and self-indulgence. Indulgence might lead to a life of drug use, drinking, gambling, and so on; ethical egoists would frown on all such lifestyles, arguing that such vices are definitely not in a person's true self-interest.

Ayn Rand was one thinker who embraced a form of ethical egoism. She argued that striving for one's own self-interest is the only way one can make one's life valuable. True altruism, she argued, would lead one to see that one's own life was nothing but a "thing" to be sacrificed for the sake of doing good deeds for others. Altruism, she concluded, does not "teach" one how to live one's life, only how to sacrifice it. Although Rand was not a trained philosopher, her ideas, which were most popular during the 1960's and 1970's, still have some force.

Among the problems of Rand's view is the problem of extremism. In her writings, she pushed ideas to their absolute extremes. To her, altruism implied that one's life had no value at all because one had to sacrifice everything upon any demand made by others; for example, when considering the starving poor, one would give all one's food and all one's money to those unfortunates and would then, of course, become one of them. Altruism does not necessarily push one to that extreme. One can help others within reason. Additionally, ethical egoism cannot be correct, for it cannot provide true solutions to the many different people whose self-interests are in conflict. In real conflicts, all cannot "win" unless moral rules are adopted, which Rand condemned.

UTILITARIANISM AND THE SOCIAL CONTRACT

Utilitarians in the mold of David Hume, Jeremy Bentham, and John Stuart Mill hold that one should follow the course that brings the greatest good to the greatest number; in other words, one should follow a course that will create happiness for the greatest number. The problem? Utilitarianism can soon lead to hedonism, a philosophy that accepts no moral rules whatsoever. Whatever feels good and makes one happy is all that counts.

With extreme utilitarianism, all moral rights and rules are tossed aside. Consider, for example, the case of Mr. X, who lives in a small town where everyone knows everyone else. All other adults in town hate Mr. X because he is always dirty, never takes a bath, and shows up for all occasions in tattered clothes; worse, there is always alcohol on his breath. What an awful example he is to the youngsters in the community, especially since the children love him, for he always has time to stop and tell them stories about elves, fairies, and leprechauns. One morning the police find Mr. X shot to death. A strict, no-exceptions utilitarian would conclude that the murder of X was right, for it brought happiness to the adults of the community and it saved the children from the influence of a degenerate. In this way, extreme utilitarianism can be used to condone murder.

Those who believe that they can find rules for right-wrong, good-bad in the social contract may be close to the mark in developing a moral ethical society. They hold that people are naturally social and want to live among their kind for mutual benefits such as group protection from danger, companionship, a more interesting social and cultural life, and so on. When people enter the social contract, however, they agree that certain moral rules are necessary if the group is to survive and flourish. Personal violence and murder are not permitted, nor are untruthfulness, theft, child abuse, adultery, and so on. Those vices are not permitted because they would tear the group-society asunder.

IMMANUEL KANT

Aspects of Kant's philosophy can, in a manner of speaking, be used to buttress the argument for the social contract theory of right and wrong. His categorical imperatives remain potent in this modern age. His imperatives are not relative and are unchanging over time. He held that people should say and do things that could be accepted as "universal" laws that could be followed by all people, everywhere. Thus, is it right or good to steal the goods of others? No, for society would revert to violent chaos if all stole from all. Can one be a habitually violent person, perhaps even a murderer? No, for if everyone behaved in that way, the war of one against all and all against all would commence as society collapsed. One should not lie because that would be an announcement that universal lying was permissible. Yet such behavior would be self-defeating, for if all people lied, no one would ever believe anyone again, including the first liar who started it all. Modern philosophers will not press Kant's views to the extreme, however, for they hold that exceptional circumstances may, if only rarely, mitigate any of his imperatives.

CONCLUSIONS

There are many approaches to finding an answer to the question of moral right-wrong, good-bad, and several are complementary. Modern philosophers such as Ross and Rachels stress that ethics is a product of reason, not merely of feelings or opinions. Certainly, they are correct. Many voices call for less selfishness, holding that one must also think of others and their welfare if they will be affected by an action. Concern for others, then, is desired. Certainly, this, too, is correct. The utilitarian's belief in the greatest good for the greatest number can also be a guide, but one with limits—limits that must include concern for duty and justice. Equally, the social contract's view of moral rules for civilized living, rules that can hold a society together, are also valid. Finally, all of Kant's

categorical imperatives (with room for exceptions) could be interwoven with the ideas of reason, good, and the social contract to add more strength to the doctrine of right and wrong. Rejected then would be relativism of any kind, egoism in any form, and reliance on God, for God's true commands are unknowable.

James Smallwood

FURTHER READING

Adler, Mortimer J. *Desires, Right and Wrong: The Ethics of Enough.* New York: Macmillan, 1991. Adler focuses on the ethics of right and wrong and on overwhelming desires that tempt "right." He ends by arguing for moderation or for what he called the ethics of "enough."

Black, Donald. *The Social Structure of Right and Wrong.* Rev. ed. San Diego, Calif.: Academic Press, 1998. This up-to-date volume examines social conflict, conflict management, and social control—all within the framework of right and wrong.

Cabot, Richard C. *Honesty.* New York: Macmillan, 1938. After generally examining honesty and "right" thinking and behaving, Cabot examines wrongs under such headings as prevarications, self-deceit, and dishonesty.

_____. *The Meaning of Right and Wrong.* Rev. ed. New York: Macmillan, 1936. This volume began Cabot's examination of various ethical issues and problems relating to the idea of "right" and "wrong."

Greider, William. *Who Will Tell the People: The Betrayal of American Democracy.* New York: Simon & Schuster, 1992. A journalist rather than a trained philosopher, Greider nevertheless does a good job of exposing many of the wrongs in American society, including government and business scandals. He seems to conclude that there are many more wrongs in modern America than there are rights.

Payne, Robert. *The Corrupt Society: From Ancient Greece to Present-Day America.* New York: Praeger, 1975. Writing just after the Watergate scandal of the 1970's, Payne examines frauds, falsehoods, dishonesty, and other wrongs as well.

Rachels, James. *The Elements of Moral Philosophy.* 3d ed. Boston: McGraw-Hill, 1999. A trained philosopher, Rachels examines various issues in ethical moral philosophy, including such elements as relativism, utilitarianism, and the question of right and wrong.

Ross, William D. *The Right and the Good.* New ed. New York: Oxford University Press, 2002. This seminal work in ethical intuitionism distinguishes between what is right and what is good in order to come to conclusions about the proper ways to live and act.

Scanlon, T. M. *What We Owe to Each Other.* Cambridge, Mass.: Belknap Press of Harvard University Press, 1998. Scanlon makes a contractualist argument, claiming that right and wrong should be defined in terms of our ability to justify ourselves to others.

Taylor, A. E. *The Problem of Conduct: A Study in the Phenomenology of Ethics.* New York: Macmillan, 1901. This older work is still valuable because Taylor focuses on dishonesty and other wrong behaviors while upholding ethical behavior.

SEE ALSO: Dilemmas, moral; Evil; Integrity; Morality; Sin; Virtue.

Right to die

DEFINITION: Just or legitimate claim to be allowed to die rather than submit to necessary medical treatment

TYPE OF ETHICS: Bioethics

SIGNIFICANCE: Claims that terminally ill persons have a right to die are founded upon the notion of human dignity. Proponents claim that forcing someone to stay alive and to continue suffering against their will violates their dignity, whereas allowing them to die restores or preserves it. Opponents may assert that suicide, even passive suicide, is an absolute moral wrong, or they may point out that extremely ill people are often not in their right minds and may not be competent to make such a difficult and irrevocable decision.

"Right to Die" was the title of a debate in the journal *Forum* on legalizing euthanasia. Later, the term was used to refer solely to voluntary euthanasia. Viewed narrowly, the right to die is merely the application of autonomy-based legal principles of self-determina-

tion and informed consent developed in the nineteenth century: If treatment cannot be given without consent, even for the individual's own good, then the individual must have a right to refuse treatment. During the 1970's and 1980's, the right to die was used in this sense, as a synonym for voluntary passive euthanasia.

HISTORY

After World War II, several factors led to the recognition of the right to die. Medical advances and social prosperity reduced sudden deaths, resulting in a growing population of older people, greater incidence of senility, and greater incidence of death from degenerative diseases. Meanwhile, health care costs soared and smaller, more dispersed families led to increased institutionalization of older people. By means of respirators and other forms of technology, life could be continued indefinitely despite failing organs. Although the number of patients in "a limbo between life and death" had increased, these issues remained private as physicians discontinued treatment or withheld resuscitation for some hopelessly ill patients. With the advent of transplants, however, particularly heart transplants, the established definition of death became inadequate. Public debate began with a Harvard committee's 1968 recommendation that brain death be included in the "definition" of death. Meanwhile, civil and human rights movements emphasizing self-determination, bodily integrity, and individual empowerment were reflected in a movement away from "mercy killing" to a focus on voluntary euthanasia.

Then, in 1975, the case of Karen Ann Quinlan galvanized the public consciousness in the battle for end-of-life decision-making control. The family sued to have Karen, who was in a persistent vegetative state (a coma with minimal brain function and no anticipated recovery of consciousness), removed from a respirator. The New Jersey Supreme Court held in 1976 that under the Constitution, acceptance or refusal of any treatment was to be made by the patient, or in the case of incompetency, by her guardians in accordance with her expressed desire. The Quinlan case also suggested that "ethics committees" could assist families and physicians in medical decision making. Such committees, staffed by physicians, ethicists, and lawyers, later became common.

Afterward, courts consistently found a "right" to

die in the common law or federal or state constitutions. In 1990, the U.S. Supreme Court confirmed a federal constitutional "liberty" basis for the right to refuse life-sustaining treatment, including possibly artificial nutrition and hydration.

ETHICAL ISSUES

Society has long held legal and moral prohibitions against the taking of human life. Early discussions centered on whether allowing a human being to die when that death could be prevented or forestalled was tantamount to killing. In 1957, Pope Pius XII distinguished between permissible forgoing of treatment in "hopeless cases" and active euthanasia, which was killing or suicide, but who was to determine which was which? The pope intimated that the individual's duty to accept, and society's duty to provide, medical treatment extended to ordinary treatment but not to extraordinary (or "heroic") measures. Although popular during the 1970's, these categories were later dismissed as unworkable. Other attempts to distinguish killing from permitting "natural death," distinguishing between withholding and withdrawing treatment and between acts and omissions, were also rejected as morally indefensible and tending to discourage the initiation of treatment. Committing suicide cannot be distinguished from refusing treatment on the basis of an action versus nonaction distinction. Thus, the fundamental question is whether an individual should ever be allowed to forgo life-sustaining treatment.

The right to die is often justified along utilitarian grounds and opposed on the basis of deontological, beneficence-based principles. Some utilitarians oppose any euthanasia, however, believing that the harms from potential abuse and from accepting incursions into the sanctity of life outweigh the benefits. Conversely, some deontologists support the right to die by defining "benefit" to encompass not only prolonged life but also freedom from suffering, or the protection of individuals' liberty interests. Some suggest that autonomy cannot be overridden, others that decisions in extremis are not autonomous.

OPPONENTS OF EUTHANASIA

Opponents of euthanasia often argue the "slippery slope"—that allowing some to die will lead to further "justified" endings of lives. Some cite various eugenics movements as evidence for this view. Proponents counter that all moral choices involve drawing lines with a potential for abuse. Another objection raised is that the slippery slope entails accepting a recognized evil, disregarding the autonomy, dignity, and suffering of the dying patient in favor of possible future evils.

Some argue that human life is inviolable and that acceptance of a decision to forgo any amount of life necessarily requires a societal recognition that some lives are not worth living. Others counter that this inviolability is negated by causes throughout history that have been deemed worthy of self-sacrifice. Some fear that passive euthanasia will insidiously change the treatment of older people and dying; individuals may be subtly coerced into dying because they perceive themselves as burdens to their families, or because they see others who are younger, healthier, or even in comparable positions refusing treatment.

Passive euthanasia for the terminally ill enjoys overwhelming societal and judicial support, though popularity in the polls does not foreclose the need to address the ethical concerns surrounding the issue. The public and the media characterize the issue as one of not unduly "prolonging life" or of allowing individuals to die "naturally" and "with dignity"; such characterizations beg the question of what is a dignified and natural death in the context of advancing medical technology.

Even if passive euthanasia is acceptable, a number of issues remain unresolved: Can the right be invoked on behalf of incompetent patients? For formerly competent individuals, treatment decisions can be made on the basis of previously expressed wishes. For the never competent (including children), recognizing an equal right to refuse treatment produces thornier questions of how to carry out that right without committing involuntary euthanasia.

Is a slow, painful, and lingering death or an indefinite existence under sedation dignified? Can artificially administered nutrition and hydration be withheld to hasten the end? Are feeding tubes or intravenous drips another form of medical treatment? Is it dignified to allow individuals to starve to death? Does the right to die include the right to assistance in suicide? Finally, should the right to die be extended to individuals suffering from painful chronic or degenerative illnesses?

Ileana Dominguez-Urban

FURTHER READING

Beauchamp, Tom L., and Robert M. Veatch, eds. *Ethical Issues in Death and Dying.* 2d ed. Upper Saddle River, N.J.: Prentice Hall, 1996.

Humphry, Derek, and Ann Wickett. *The Right to Die: Understanding Euthanasia.* New York: Harper & Row, 1986.

Kleespies, Phillip M. *Life and Death Decisions: Psychological and Ethical Considerations in End-of-Life Care.* Washington, D.C.: American Psychological Association, 2004.

Meisel, Alan. *The Right to Die.* New York: John Wiley & Sons, 1993.

Rothman, David J. *Strangers at the Bedside: A History of How Law and Bioethics Transformed Medical Decision Making.* New York: Basic Books, 1991.

Russell, O. Ruth. *Freedom to Die: Moral and Legal Aspects of Euthanasia.* New York: Human Sciences Press, 1975.

United States President's Commission for the Study of Ethical Problems in Medicine and Biomedical and Behavioral Research. *Deciding to Forgo Life-Sustaining Treatment: A Report on the Ethical, Medical, and Legal Issues in Treatment Decisions.* Washington, D.C.: GPO, 1983.

SEE ALSO: Euthanasia; Infanticide; Institutionalization of patients; Life and death; Medical ethics; Quinlan, Karen Ann; Right to life; Suicide; Suicide assistance.

Right to life

DEFINITION: Just or legitimate claim of an unborn child to be carried to term and allowed to live, rather than being aborted

TYPE OF ETHICS: Bioethics

SIGNIFICANCE: Another name for the pro-life movement, the right-to-life movement argues that abortion impermissibly violates the inalienable right of a fetus to be born. The term sometimes, but not always, implies an embrace of a consistent ethic opposed to killing under all circumstances, including abortion, capital punishment, warfare, and even the killing of animals for food.

Ethical conflict over abortion has faced humanity throughout history. On one hand, sociological problems, maternal health, woman's rights, and the fear of overpopulation have led many people to espouse abortion. On the other hand, religious and biological issues have led others to favor antiabortion (right-to-life) concepts. Finding sensible, ethical solutions to the problem of abortion is essential to society. Appropriate solutions must satisfy mothers, prevent the murder of humans still in the uterus, and avoid exploitation of individual population sectors while permitting abortions that are deemed acceptable.

METHODOLOGY AND CONCEPTS

Many nonabortive birth control methods are widely used. These include abstinence, coitus interruptus (male withdrawal), rhythm (intercourse during safe portions of the menses), pessaries (for example, condoms), birth control pills, and surgical intervention by tubal ligation or vasectomy. Despite these methods, many unplanned pregnancies present the moral dilemma of whether to abort.

Those favoring abortion argue that it is fitting during the time period when a fetus is not a person, though precisely when humanity occurs is uncertain. Many people argue that any abortion is correct when carrying a fetus to term will cause a mother death, severe psychological damage, or impinged human rights. Another point of view is that when a fetus is found to be severely physically or mentally damaged, abortion is merited. Still other abortion advocates note that abortion stops overpopulation.

The antiabortion viewpoint—right to life—also varies greatly. Some advocates preach that sexual abstinence is the only suitable birth control method and that conception always engenders the right to life. Others believe that once egg and sperm join, a human has been produced, and that the abortion of unborn people—they claim that tens of millions of such operations have been carried out—exceeds the worst planned race or religious genocide ever carried out. At the other end of the right-to-life group spectrum are those who espouse factoring into the decision the age—yet to be determined—at which a fetus becomes a person, potential problems for the mother, and societal aspects.

HISTORY

Many people believe that abortion is a product of modern medicine and that the debate—nowadays very antagonistic—regarding whether to abort and why or when to do so is a modern phenomenon. This belief is the result of clashes between pro-choice and pro-life factions who espouse appropriate abortion and no abortion, respectively. In fact, the Greek, Roman, and Jewish philosophers of antiquity codified abortion and its use. For example, Plato and Aristotle favored abortion when it was for the good of society, and Aristotle defined human life as present forty or ninety days after conception for males and females, respectively. Neither philosopher, however, would have set those times as upper limits for abortion.

With the development of Christianity, strong antiabortion sentiment arose (for example, Roman emperor Constantine outlawed abortion). As the power of Christianity grew, so did sanctions against abortion. Even among theologians, however, there were—and continue to be—various degrees of condemnation. Some declared that any abortion was murder, others saw it as murder beginning forty days after conception (a holdover from Aristotle?), and some believed that abortion was acceptable to save a mother's life.

In more modern times, English common law stated that abortion was legal until mothers felt movement in the womb—"quickening"—and this view persisted well into the eighteenth century throughout the British Empire and the nations that arose from it. Hence, in the colonial United States, quickening was viewed as the time when abortion became illegal. On this basis, despite the unchanged view of Christian ministers and priests, abortion became a common mode of birth control. The practice, which was so widespread that abortionists often advertised their services in newspapers, led to antiabortion sentiment. First, the American Medical Association (c. 1850) condemned it. Soon, feminist movements joined in, denouncing abortion as a tool of male domination.

This segment of the abortion debate was relatively mild and died out by the twentieth century. In fact, it was so quiescent that beginning during the 1950's, many abortions were made legal, a legality supported by the American Medical Association, the National Organization for Women, many states, and the federal government. Adding to the popularity of abortion legality was fear—fanned by the media—that population growth would soon cause the world to starve to death.

It was at this time, with most Americans in favor of therapeutic abortion, that the right-to-life move-

ment came into being. The polarization between pro- and antiabortionists has grown hugely, and the debate has become more and more radical. In 1973, the Supreme Court case *Roe v. Wade* assured women the right to decide whether to terminate pregnancy. Then, in 1989, in *Webster v. Reproductive Health Services*, the Supreme Court reversed its position. The attempts by Operation Rescue to stop legal abortions by picketing and by harassing those choosing abortion and physicians performing abortion have further confused the issue, polarizing public opinion even more.

CONCLUSIONS

Two thorny ethical issues concerning abortion are whether it is ever appropriate to stop the occurrence of a human life and whether a woman should determine what happens to her body. Advocates of both issues propose that if their point of view is unheeded, the consequences, aside from unethical decision making, will cause horrible outcomes for society. Antiabortionists state that the murder of fetuses will lead to other equivalent crimes (such as genocide). Those who favor abortion fear that following absolute criminalization will come restrictive legislation that will diminish human rights and produce a model of minority persecution. It seems possible that both these views are extreme and that ethical compromise could give both sides some of their desires, with much flexibility. One model for use could be that of Western Europe, which promises respect for every human life and permits abortion under conditions deemed appropriate in a well-thought-out, ethical fashion. Abortion programs also must be designed so that inequities (such as limitation to less-advantaged classes) are avoided and informed consent is guaranteed.

Sanford S. Singer

FURTHER READING

McMahan, Jeff. *The Ethics of Killing: Problems at the Margins of Life.* New York: Oxford University Press, 2002.

Merton, Andrew H. *Enemies of Choice.* Boston: Beacon Press, 1981.

Paige, Connie. *The Right to Lifers.* New York: Summit Books, 1983.

Reeder, John P., Jr. *Killing and Saving: Abortion, Hunger, and War.* University Park: Pennsylvania State University Press, 1996.

Rice, Charles E. *No Exceptions*. Gaithersburg, Md.: Human Life International, 1990.

Rosenblatt, Roger. *Life Itself*. New York: Random House, 1992.

Whitney, Catherine. *Whose Life?* New York: William Morrow, 1991.

Williams, Mary E., ed. *Abortion: Opposing Viewpoints*. San Diego, Calif.: Greenhaven Press, 2002.

SEE ALSO: Abortion; Bioethics; Birth control; Christian ethics; Family; Jewish ethics; Pro-choice movement; Pro-life movement; Right to die.

Rights and obligations

DEFINITION: Concepts of what people are allowed to do or are expected to refrain from doing are rights, and concepts of what people should ought or should not do are obligations

TYPE OF ETHICS: Theory of ethics

SIGNIFICANCE: Ethics deals with moral judgments of the behavior of individuals and groups. Questions surrounding what the rights and obligations of these moral actors are lie at the heart of ethics.

Rights may be seen from several different perspectives. They can be seen as claims to perform or refrain from certain acts without interference by others, or they may be claims to have certain acts performed or refrained from by others, or they may be claims to have certain entitlements honored. The basis of such entitlements may be by law, such as legal rights or claims to state welfare benefits, such as health care. Likewise, rights may be claims made on moral grounds alone, such as the right to have an item of trifling monetary value returned that someone has been given with the understanding that it was not a gift but would be returned. In this case, the right has been created by an express or tacit promise.

Obligations are acts that one ought or ought not to perform. However, "ought" has more than one meaning. Consequently, there are various kinds of obligation. Moral obligations are those generally believed to deserve some degree of social condemnation when they are not kept. Such condemnation may be mild or strong, depending on public judgment of the act—or omission of the act—in question. In instances of strong condemnation for violation of certain moral obligations, people believe serious consequences should follow. Those who violate certain primary or fundamental obligations, such as violating the right of others to life, are generally thought to be wicked or evil. Another way of saying this is that people generally believe that there should be serious social pressure brought to bear on those found violating moral obligations.

Other kinds of obligations include prudential obligations, which individuals are morally free to perform or not, as they please. If someone says that you ought to leave for the theater if you wish to avoid missing the last show, there is no suggestion that it is morally wrong for you to fail to leave. All "prudential" obligations can be put in an "if, then" format: If you wish to get top grades in school, then you "ought" to study hard. However, people who possess superior talent in fields such as music or sports that restrict their study time or people who choose to take some time away from their studies each week to perform charitable work are not usually considered to be morally worse than those who spent all their free time studying. General laziness, however, is usually condemned.

A final form of obligation be considered is rational obligation. This form of obligation states that one must accept such propositions as the mathematical equation that "two plus two equals four." Certain propositions of symbolic or ordinary logic, geometry, and similar disciplines also fall into this category. In the context of ethics, however, only moral obligation is relevant

RECIPROCITY OF RIGHTS AND OBLIGATIONS

Most rights and obligations are interrelated in particular ways. Most rights, for example, involve what is called reciprocity. That is, one's claim to certain rights necessarily involves recognition of an obligation to respect the same or similar rights of others. Failure to recognize reciprocal obligations places one in a situation of untenable self-contradiction or irrationality. Thus if one claims a right to one's own wallet but refuses to respect the rights of other persons to their own wallets, such a person would be in a state of self-contradiction. For the claim of a right that everyone ought to respect necessarily involves recognition of a reciprocal right held by others. That is, claiming a right necessarily involves an obligation to respects similar rights of others. Thus rights and obligations usually are intimately related in this way.

One class of rights, however, involves no such relationship. This class involves rights in certain cases of competition among individuals or groups, for example sporting competitions. Each team in a football game has a right to win the game, but there is no obligation on the part of either team to respect the right of the opposing team by allowing the other team to win. *Both* teams have a right to win. This is a situation of a right versus a right. However, such situations often involve obligations consisting of adherence to sets of rules. Each football team has a right to win, but not by any means. The teams are obligated to win in accordance with mutually agreed rules and not otherwise.

SOURCES OF RIGHTS AND OBLIGATIONS

A principal source of both rights and obligations is law. Valid law is created by those individuals or bodies such as legislatures that are authorized to make law by politically organized societies. Such bodies must act in accordance with a rule of recognition that describes the procedures that a legal system has laid down as valid for creating law.

In Western societies, it is generally agreed that there are limits to the obligation to obey law. Such limits are usually said to be moral limits as determined by the concept of justice or other moral limits such as those set by religious doctrine. Moral limits based on strictly secular sources are also often recognized. Those refusing to obey military conscription laws obliging persons to join armies cite either religious doctrines or secular equivalents.

Among the most common sources of both rights and obligations is the institution of promising. Since the meaning of the word "promise" is a requirement that must be met, promises are universally accepted as sources of obligation. Those who make promises incur obligations by the act of promising. By the same token, those to whom promises are made gain rights—the right that the promise be kept.

Promising takes a variety of forms, some more formal and others less so. Everyone is familiar with informal acts of promising found in everyday life, such as agreeing to meet someone at a specified place and time. More formal acts of promising include varieties of contract, often written documents enforceable by courts. Contracts may be oral or written; written contracts (and some oral ones) tend to stipulate

the exact nature of the rights and obligations incurred by the agreeing parties. Creating new rights and obligations is something people do every day.

Another familiar form of promising is the institution of marriage. In some societies, the institution of marriage has even included formal marriage contracts. In modern American society, certain rights and obligations of many marriages are set forth in detail prior to the marriage ceremony through contracts known as prenuptial (premarital) agreements.

All acts of promising that create valid rights and obligations raise legitimate expectations on the part of those being promised that such expectations will be fulfilled. On the other hand, promises that raise no legitimate expectations create neither rights nor obligations. Thus if someone known not to be wealthy promises to give another person a million dollars, it is not reasonable that those promised (knowing the promisor lacks resources) expect to receive the money. Accordingly, recipients of such promises thus have no legitimate expectations, and the promises themselves create no rights or obligations.

Another aspect of understanding the institution of promising as a principal means of creating rights and obligations is the distinction between tacit and express promises, or consent to acquire obligations. Tacit consent is consent—that is, promising—that is understood from the context of situations or the implications of acts or statements. The idea that "silence is consent" expresses this idea.

Another common form of tacit consent occurs when one travels to another country. It is commonly understood that entrance of foreigners into the territory of a state entails the traveler's tacit consent to obey the country's laws. There may, indeed, be various exceptions to this idea based on moral rules that foreign laws may violate; however, the tacit consent to obey has been generally accepted for centuries.

INTERNATIONAL LAW AND HUMAN RIGHTS

In addition to the domestic laws of a country and various forms of promises, two other sources of rights claimed in the modern world stand out. One is rights (with corresponding obligations) based upon international law. International law is based on several sources. One is treaties, conventions, and other kinds of formal agreements among states. In making such treaties, nations consent to follow them. In consenting they acquire obligations.

Conflicting Obligations

During World War II, a member of the French Resistance approached philosopher Jean-Paul Sartre to ask his advice: Should he devote his energy to fighting against Nazi tyranny in Occupied France, or should he, an only child, care for his aged, invalid mother? Sartre replied, "Choose!"

Another important source of international law, and therefore of legal obligation, is custom. In that case, standard, certain well-established practices are recognized by many courts dealing with international law as valid law when not contradicted by positive (written) law, especially by international treaty.

A further source is obligation is human rights, which are rights said to be conferred upon human beings solely on account of their humanity, as opposed to rights gained from written laws. Human rights are modern versions of the "unalienable rights" of the Declaration of Independence. Such rights are said to be "natural rights," based on human nature and the nature of society. Their successor category, "human rights," have been recognized as legitimate since the Nuremberg Trials of Nazi war criminals after World War II.

Some Nazi actions, especially the Holocaust, in which an estimated eight million people—mostly Jews—were exterminated, were unprecedented in human history. Existing laws did not describe these acts; however, common decency and moral right cried out for their judicial condemnation. The concept of "crimes against humanity" was therefore created to deal with such colossal crimes. Soon afterward, in 1948, a Universal Declaration of Human Rights was issued by the newly established United Nations Organization.

Controversy, however, surrounds the concept of human rights. Not all philosophers agree that such rights exist or even make sense. Moreover, all rights, including human rights, are either negative—in the sense that people have the right to be protected against certain acts—or are positive—in the sense that holders of the rights have entitlements, such as the right to health care or housing. Some philosophers argue that positive rights give the state excessive and dangerous power. Others insist that positive rights are legitimate.

CONFLICTS AMONG RIGHTS AND AMONG OBLIGATIONS

Conflicts can occur among rights as well as among obligations. In the case of rights, the right to freedom of speech may conflict with a right of privacy, for example, or it may endanger rights to life and property if mob action is incited. Or the right to religious freedom can conflict with children's right to life, if parents withhold medical care on religious grounds. Numerous such conflicts exist.

Similarly, conflicts among obligations are common. On an everyday level, employees' obligations to their employers may conflict with their obligations to their own families. On another plane, obligations to perform military service may conflict with religious obligations; or obligations to enforce law may conflict with moral obligations to family members, and so on. On many occasions, processes of moral reasoning may satisfactorily determine which obligations are stronger, but not always.

Charles F. Bahmueller

FURTHER READING

Attfield, Robin. *A Theory of Value and Obligation.* New York: Croom Helm, 1987.

Cane, Peter, and Jane Stapelton, eds. *The Law of Obligations: Essays in Celebration of John Fleming.* New York: Oxford University Press, 1998.

Dworkin, Ronald. *Taking Rights Seriously.* Cambridge, Mass.: Harvard University Press, 1978. In a groundbreaking work, a legal philosopher presents a theory of rights that includes a definition of rights and a discussion of types of rights, and applies his theory of rights to law.

Locke, John. *The Second Treatise of Government.* Edited by Peter Laslett. Cambridge, England: Cambridge University Press, 1988. This timeless work establishes the philosophical basis for the Declaration of Independence, arguing that rights and obligations are rooted in both consent and nature.

Simmons, A. John. *Moral Principles and Political Obligations.* Princeton, N.J.: Princeton University Press, 2000. A philosopher dissects arguments for political obligation and challenges each in turn. He discusses major theories of obligation from liberal classical writers including John Locke and David Hume and twentieth century figures such as John Rawls and Robert Novick.

Walzer, Michael. *Obligations: Essays on Disobedience, War and Citizenship*. Cambridge, Mass.: Harvard University Press, 1982. A distinguished political philosopher discusses the idea that the obligation derives from consent and applies it to practical situations, including obligation to fight during wartime and civil disobedience.

Zimmerman, Michael J. *The Concept of Moral Obligation*. New York: Cambridge University Press, 1996.

SEE ALSO: Citizenship; Civil rights and liberties; Custom; Deontological ethics; Human rights; Law; Natural rights; Promises; Universal Declaration of Human Rights.

Robotics

DEFINITION: Science and technology of creating machines that mimic the ways in which humans perform tasks

DATE: Originated during the 1940's

TYPE OF ETHICS: Scientific ethics

SIGNIFICANCE: The existence of machines that are capable of replacing humans in various activities has a far-reaching impact on society and may eventually redefine humankind's role in the world

The word "robot" was first used in 1921 in *R.U.R., or Rossum's Universal Robots*, a play by the Czech writer Karel Čapek. In that dramatic work, the term was used to describe machines that performed the work of humans. The word itself is derived from the Czech word *robota*, which means slave labor. Čapek's play is a story of mechanical laborers who revolt against their human masters.

The science of robotics draws on two technologies: automatic machine control and artificial intelligence. Devices for automatic machine control, which are called servomechanisms, work by feeding information about a machine's location, speed, and direction back to a computer-based control unit that automatically makes adjustments.

By the 1950's, mathematicians began to explore the possibilities of emulating human logic and behavior in computer programs. In 1956, John McCarthy, then at Dartmouth College, gave this discipline its name—artificial intelligence. The first artificial intelligence researchers began to program computers to play games, prove mathematical theorems, and even play the role of ersatz psychologists. Later efforts focused on the building of robots. The first patent for an industrial robot was awarded to Joseph Engelberger in 1961. His machine, which was called the Unimate, used a feedback control system that was attached to a computer. The Unimate robots were first used to control die-casting machines.

ROBOTICS DEVELOPMENT AND APPLICATIONS

Robotics has continued its development through two approaches to design. The first of these is the top-down approach, which focuses on a specific task to be done by the machine. Industrial robots that pick parts from a bin, paint auto body parts, or do welding, drilling, grinding, routing, or riveting from a fixed position on a factory floor are examples of top-down design. Computer programs called expert systems also employ the top-down approach to perform tasks focused in a narrow field—such as identifying mineral deposits or advising doctors about blood diseases—by consulting a body of knowledge in the form of rules.

A more difficult approach to robot design is the bottom-up approach, in which the goal is to build general-purpose machines. Robots of this type tend to be mobile, use camera systems to see the world around them, and employ electronic sensors for touch. They may be programmed to accomplish a variety of tasks. Computer programs for these machines simulate learning by adding observations and experience to their models of the world.

Reliable, quick industrial robots have become regular components of industrial processes. Some applications combine two conventional robotic arms to work together to perform complex assembly tasks, including maintenance operations for nuclear reactors, removal of toxic waste, and loading and unloading machine tools—tasks that are dangerous for humans to perform.

In the medical field, heart surgery is being performed without opening the patients' chests by using robotic arms that are inserted into the chest region through three or four holes, each less than a centimeter in diameter. One robot has a camera for transmitting images to a computer console, while the others are fitted with operating instruments. The robotic movements are guided by a surgeon sitting at a computer, on whose monitor a magnified image of the operating area appears. Bypass surgery and repairs of heart murmurs and valve defects have been successfully performed with this alternative approach to conventional surgery. Similar applications are being used with brain and lung surgeries.

Much of the focus of robotics researchers is on the development of autonomous robots. In the first years of the twenty-first century, robotics researchers at Cardiff University in Wales were developing agile, versatile robots fitted with the latest Pentium-based

control systems, vision sensors, video links, and a Global Positioning System for navigation. One application allows farmers to use these robots to check on distant herds of animals, unload feed in selected fields, and inspect gates and fencing. Other applications include robotic wheelchairs and cleaning and security devices.

Another robot, a hexapod, is a two-foot long, six-legged, self-propelled machine that can avoid obstacles and negotiate rough terrain. This robot has sensors to monitor its position and a charge-coupled device camera and laser to generate a three-dimensional map of the surrounding terrain.

Numerous military applications for robotics are also being explored. An intelligent, mobile robot known as Rhino was developed at the University of

One of the practical applications of using robotics to protect human lives is this remote-controlled device designed to handle and neutralize terrorist explosives at the 2004 Olympic Games at Athens. (AP/Wide World Photos)

Bonn and has been used to conduct guided tours at a museum in Bonn, Germany. Mobile robots have also been used to explore the earth's seafloor and the surface of Mars.

ETHICAL ISSUES

The ethical issues of robotics arise from several areas. One fundamental concern is what kind of ethical principles should be built into robots. Science-fiction author Isaac Asimov began to explore this issue in the 1940's with a series of stories about intelligent robots, which were collected in *I, Robot* (1950) and other books. Asimov's robots had "positronic brains," circuits based on what he called the Three Laws of Robotics, whose principles were protecting the well-being of humans, obeying human orders, and self-preservation—in that order.

Asimov's principles are tested when considering the social consequences of replacing human labor with machine labor. Large-scale factory automation has resulted in the permanent loss of millions of unskilled jobs throughout the industrialized world. As robots continue to be refined and used in more applications, they will replace humans in jobs requiring ever greater degrees of skill. The economic benefits of robot automation reach a point of diminishing returns when the social costs of the unemployed workers—government subsidies, poverty, crime, and political unrest—become too high.

Some experts think that general-purpose humanoid robots will remain too expensive ever to reach widespread use. They contend that society is working itself through an inevitable turbulent period in the wake of the robot automation of industry and will evolve into a period in which skilled workers are used instead of robots. Others believe that advances in computer and robotics technology will inevitably lead to a convergence of the specialized, expert approach and the general-purpose, mobile, artificial intelligence approach. Such a convergence would lead to the development of self-aware machines with sophisticated models of their worlds and the ability to increase their knowledge.

Other ethical issues arise from the prospect of robots becoming more and more like humans in appearance and behavior. Such issues raise questions that have no answers, because there is no way to know what will happen until sentient machines actually make their appearance. Until then, the cost effec-

tiveness of such development is likely to remain a major obstacle.

By 1993, chess computers were playing at tournament level, and in 1997, Deep Blue became the first computer to defeat the reigning world chess champion, Garry Kasparov, in a classical chess match. Given the possibility of intelligent, humanlike robots, what should be their place in human society? Should they be allowed to coexist with people, with their own fundamental rights protected by law, or should they be regarded as a disposable race of slaves?

LEGAL ISSUES

Many questions have been raised about the legal status of intelligent robots. If they are accorded rights under the law, should they also have responsibilities? For example, might robots ever manage human workers, serve on juries, or run for elected office? Will they ever vote? Who would be blamed if a robot's "negligence" were to cause the accidental death of a human being? (Many of these issues are raised in Asimov's fictional robot stories.)

On May 17, 1992, an industrial robot called Robbie CX30 killed its operator, Bart Matthews, at the Cybernetics corporation in Silicon Heights, California. Authorities concluded that a software module written by a computer programmer from Silicon Techtronics was responsible for the robot oscillating out of control and killing Matthews. The programmer was charged with negligence. Further investigation revealed that the interface design combined with flawed software was probably the real culprit. That tragic incident emphasized the need to supply robot designers and programmers with guidelines and handbooks that deal with the ethical issues and principles that should be incorporated into future robot development.

Some robotics experts predict that intelligent machines will eventually be capable of building other, even more intelligent machines. Although robotics research and development currently models robots based upon human senses, actions, and abilities, as the future continues to unfold, people may confront some very disturbing prospects if the machines they have created become more intelligent and powerful than they are themselves. Because machine technology develops millions of times faster than biological evolution, the capabilities of robots could someday so far surpass human ones that the human race could become extinct—not because of war, pestilence, or famine, but because of a lack of purpose. Consequently, future robotics research and development should be carefully governed by the ethical principles advocated by Asimov.

Charles E. Sutphen
Updated by Alvin K. Benson

FURTHER READING

Brooks, Rodney A. *Flesh and Machines: How Robots Will Change Us.* New York: Pantheon Books, 2002.

Katic, Dusko. *Intelligent Control of Robotic Systems.* Boston, Mass.: Kluwer Academic Publishers, 2003.

Mulhall, Douglas. *Our Molecular Future: How Nanotechnology, Robotics, Genetics, and Artificial Intelligence Will Transform Our World.* Amherst, N.Y.: Prometheus Books, 2002.

Nehmzow, Ulrich. *Mobile Robotics: A Practical Introduction.* New York: Springer, 2003.

Warwick, Kevin. *March of the Machines: Why the New Race of Robots Will Rule the World.* London: Century, 1997.

Winston, Patrick Henry. *Artificial Intelligence.* 3d ed. Reading, Mass.: Addison-Wesley, 1992.

Zylinska, Joanna, ed. *The Cyborg Experiments: The Extensions of the Body in the Media Age.* New York: Continuum, 2002.

SEE ALSO: Animal rights; Artificial intelligence; Computer technology; Dominion over nature, human; Exploitation; Sentience; Technology; Virtual reality.

Roe v. Wade

THE EVENT: U.S. Supreme Court decision legalizing a woman's right to choose to terminate her pregnancy through abortion

DATE: Decided on January 22, 1973

TYPE OF ETHICS: Sex and gender issues

SIGNIFICANCE: The Court's decision ruled that under the Constitution, a woman's right to choose to terminate a pregnancy is a fundamental part of the right of privacy, and only a compelling reason will allow the government to interfere with or abridge that right.

In January, 1973, Justice Harry A. Blackmun delivered the 7-2 opinion of the Court, which upheld a woman's right to choose to terminate a pregnancy. That right, however, was not absolute. The Court divided the full term of a normal nine-month pregnancy into three three-month-long trimesters. During the first trimester, the decision to terminate a pregnancy rests with the woman and her physician. The government may not interfere, except to mandate that any abortion is performed by a licensed physician.

In the second trimester the government has the power to regulate abortion only in ways designed to protect and preserve the health of the *woman*. The Court stated that this objective becomes compelling at the end of the first trimester because before that time abortion is less hazardous than childbirth. During that time period, the only permissible abortion regulations are those designed to ensure that the procedure is performed safely.

At approximately the beginning of the third and final trimester, the fetus becomes viable, or capable of surviving outside the womb. At that time, protection of fetal life also becomes a compelling reason sufficient to justify interference by the government to regulate or even prohibit abortion in order to protect fetal life unless the abortion is necessary to preserve the life or health of the woman.

The Court ruled that the "liberty" interest of the Fourteenth Amendment was broad enough to encompass a woman's decision to terminate her pregnancy. According to the Court, a woman's right to abortion outweighs the rights of a nonviable fetus and generally prohibits government interference.

SOCIAL CLIMATE

The central figure in the *Roe v. Wade* case was "Jane Roe," a twenty-one-year-old panhandler who claimed that her unwanted pregnancy was the product of rape. In order safely and legally to end that pregnancy, she filed a lawsuit against Henry Wade, a Dallas county prosecutor and state official charged to enforce a Texas law forbidding abortion. Along with the laws of approximately two-thirds of U.S. states at that time, Texas law outlawed abortion. The social climate of the early 1970's was being transformed by a breakdown of traditional moral and ethical norms governing sexual behavior, and a rise in family disruption. At the same time, the medical profession had been performing elective abortions in states that permitted the procedure, but physicians were concerned with possible criminal and civil liability. The decision, therefore, shielded physicians.

Roe, who later revealed that her true name was Norma McCorvey, was the mother of two children prior to her lawsuit, and she later worked in abortion facilities. In 1995, however, she denounced abortion, became a Christian, and founded a pro-life ministry called "Roe No More." Her original story that her unwanted pregnancy was the product of rape proved to be false, as was her claim to have been unmarried. In reality, her mother had adopted her first child, and her second child had been adopted by its natural father.

AFTERMATH

The main consequence of the decision in *Roe v. Wade* was to revive a right-to-life movement that had predated the case but which became well organized largely by virtue of the Supreme Court's decision. The pro-life group elected public officials who believed, as its members did, that abortion was a form of murder that should be outlawed. The members of the movement also attempted to remake the federal judiciary by seating new judges who would interpret the Constitution as not protecting abortion rights. They hoped ultimately to seat a majority of pro-life justices on the Supreme Court who would overrule *Roe v. Wade*. President Ronald Reagan, a right-to-life advocate, appointed more than half of the members of the federal judiciary and three Supreme Court justices. Numerous cases subsequent to *Roe v. Wade* sought its reversal.

On June 17, 2003, Norma McCorvey filed an appeal to the Fifth Circuit Court of Appeal requesting that it reopen and overturn *Roe v. Wade*. In her accompanying affidavit, she alleged that the original case had been wrongly decided and caused great harm to women and children. She also alleged that she had been exploited and deceived by the legal system and did not understand the meaning and consequences of abortion at the time of her own abortion. The Texas District Court dismissed her motion.

Despite the tenuous nature of the constitutional right to choose to terminate a pregnancy, and the

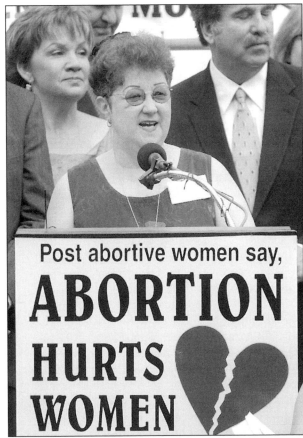

Norma McCorvey, the "Jane Roe" of Roe v. Wade, *speaking at an antiabortion rally in Dallas, Texas, in June, 2003.* (AP/Wide World Photos)

complex moral sentiments in America, that right still existed at the beginning of the twenty-first century. Meanwhile, several cases concerning abortion had led to notable court decisions. These include *Webster v. Reproductive Health Services* (1989), in which the Supreme Court examined the time line for the viability of fetuses, advancing it to twenty-four weeks, with testing to determine viability to be performed at twenty weeks' gestation. In *Planned Parenthood of Southeastern Pennsylvania v. Casey* (1992), the Court also upheld a state law requiring a mandatory twenty-four-hour delay following information conveyed by a doctor to a patient and before an abortion can be performed because the waiting period did not constitute an "undue burden" on a woman who chooses abortion by placing substantial obstacles in her path.

THE ABORTION DEBATE

The debate between the so-called pro-life and pro-choice factions entails such ethical issues as autonomy (independent decision making) and non-maleficence (doing no harm). Pro-life feminists have challenged the claims of pro-choice feminist that abortion rights are prerequisites for women's social equality and full development. Pro-lifers argue that women can never achieve fulfillment of their role of motherhood in a society that permits abortion. Pro-choice advocates assert that the unrestricted right to choose to terminate a pregnancy is a moral imperative and an integral part of women's reproductive freedom.

Stating the argument otherwise, the pro-lifers argue that abortion does not equate with the moral right to control one's own body. That concept, they feel, belongs to cases of organ transplantation, contraception, sterilization, and mastectomies. They distinguish pregnancy because it involves not one, but two, individuals, and point to the wrongfulness of harming others, no matter how immature or powerless.

The pro-choice position rests on the concept of individual autonomy, or one's own decision-making capacity, and advocates that if a woman does not wish to continue a pregnancy for whatever reason, that pregnancy should be terminated. Philosophers have made the argument that a woman's body is her property, to do with as she chooses. If pregnancy and childbearing impede her living a particular kind of life, she is therefore justified in seeking abortion. The permissiveness of abortion law is often greeted with the reaction that it is unethical, juxtaposed against the argument that one person cannot ethically impose her individual opinion on others. The ethical and moral dilemma, therefore, continues.

DIVISION IN RELIGIOUS CIRCLES

Abortion is not only a feminist issue, but a divisive religious issue as well. In religious circles, especially the Roman Catholic Church, those who disapprove of abortion point to the "sacredness and sanctity of life" and often argue that life begins at conception. Abortion advocates, however, counter with the argument that viability is evidence of life. Prior to the time of viability, a fetus is not a "person" entitled to the full cadre of rights.

Critics assert that the due process clause of the Fourteenth Amendment, which prohibits a state from depriving any person of life, liberty, or property, does not give a woman the right to abort her fetus. Instead, they contend that the amendment protects all life and does not distinguish between unborn and living persons. It should be noted that when mentioned in *Roe v. Wade*, the Supreme Court referred to "person" in the postnatal sense.

Marcia J. Weiss

FURTHER READING

Baird, Robert M., and Stuart E. Rosenbaum, eds. *The Ethics of Abortion: Pro-Life v. Pro-Choice.* Buffalo, N.Y.: Prometheus Books, 1993.

Hull, N. E. H., and Peter Charles Hoffer. *Roe v. Wade: The Abortion Rights Controversy in American History.* Lawrence: University Press of Kansas, 2001.

Knapp, Lynette, ed. *The Abortion Controversy.* San Diego, Calif.: Greenwood Press, 2001.

Reiman, Jeffrey. *Abortion and the Ways We Value Human Life.* Lanham, Md.: Rowman & Littlefield, 1999.

Shrage, Laurie. *Abortion and Social Responsibility: Depolarizing the Debate.* New York: Oxford University Press, 2003.

Tribe, Laurence H. *Abortion: The Clash of Absolutes.* New York: W. W. Norton, 1990.

Williams, Mary E., ed. *Abortion: Opposing Viewpoints.* San Diego, Calif.: Greenwood Press, 2002.

SEE ALSO: Abortion; Privacy; Pro-choice movement; Right to life.

Role models

DEFINITION: Persons whose behavior in particular roles is admired and imitated by others, especially by the young

TYPE OF ETHICS: Personal and social ethics

SIGNIFICANCE: Individuals whose character or vocations are in the process of formation are inclined to emulate those whom they regard as admirable, giving those who are regarded as role models special ethical responsibilities.

The value of role models has been recognized at least since the time of Aristotle, the ancient Greek philoso-

Public Opinion on Successful Cheaters

An opinion poll conducted by the Massachusetts Mutual Life Insurance Company in 1991 asked a cross-section of Americans how strongly they agreed with the statement that society looks up to people who succeed by cheating and breaking rules, so long as they make a lot of money.

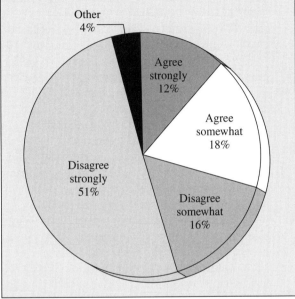

Other 4%
Agree strongly 12%
Agree somewhat 18%
Disagree strongly 51%
Disagree somewhat 16%

Source: The Roper Center for Public Opinion Research. Figures based on responses of 1,200 adult Americans surveyed in September, 1991.

athletes. Images in the mass media—motion pictures, television, and the Internet—have greatly intensified the influence of such heroes. Propelled thus into prominence, these influential achievers are often reminded of their responsibilities to conduct themselves in a manner worthy of emulation, as they have been selected as role models by legions of the young. There can be little doubt that for children, misbehavior on the part of their heroes can be a shattering experience.

From the viewpoint of successful athletes, performers, and other prominent individuals who have become role models without consciously seeking such status, the high expectations of their fans are likely to seem unreasonable. Athletic or artistic excellence, though frequently the result of the exercise of self-discipline and other virtues, does not guarantee overall moral excellence. Many in the limelight have proven to be either unable or unwilling to serve adequately as models for would-be emulators they have never met. Whether a prominent athlete or entertainer should feel any obligation in this matter, the fact that the frequently large incomes of such persons derive from the approval of their admirers constitutes an argument for their accepting some measure of responsibility. Because such arguments in many

pher who asserted that human beings learn to be virtuous by imitating the behavior of moral people. Since virtue was for Aristotle an activity, it is important to be able to observe worthy actions. Beginning also in the ancient world, books such as Plutarch's biographies of famous Greeks and Romans were emphatically moral in their purpose. Biographies written for children in particular have historically served the purpose of inspiring children with impressive models of behavior. Other than in reading material, role models throughout history have generally been people close in time and space to their admirers and might thus be expected to recognize their ethical responsibility to set positive examples for their admirers.

Although worthy role models are desirable at any age, they are particularly important for children and adolescents. From the late twentieth century into the early twenty-first century, young Americans have increasingly grown to admire popular entertainers and

"I am not a role model"

In 1993 basketball star Charles Barkley caused a minor sensation in the sports world when he appeared in a television commercial for Nike shoes in which he declared, "I am not a role model." Although Barkley was known for his outspokenness and occasionally ill-mannered public behavior, his statement surprised many people because of the possible damage that it might do to his career, particularly in off-court endeavors, such as commercial endorsements. Barkley's statement had the positive effect of promoting public discussion of issues such as the merits of young people making sports and entertainment heroes their role models and the responsibilities of public figures to their young admirers.

cases go unrecognized, however, parents, teachers, and counselors must exercise their responsibility to advise the young as to which habits of their heroes are worthy of imitation.

Robert P. Ellis

FURTHER READING

Andrews, David L., and Steven J. Jackson, eds. *Sport Stars: The Cultural Politics of Sporting Celebrity.* New York: Routledge, 2001.

Reynolds, Barbara A. *And Still We Rise: Interviews with Fifty Black Role Models.* Washington: USA Today Books, 1988.

SEE ALSO: Aristotelian ethics; Confucian ethics; "Everyone does it"; Godparents; Heroism; Leadership; Merit; Narrative ethics; Political liberty; Virtue ethics.

Roman Catholic priests scandal

THE EVENT: Revelations of widespread and long-term sexual abuse of children by Roman Catholic priests that first gained national attention in Massachusetts

DATE: First publicized in January, 2002

TYPE OF ETHICS: Religious ethics

SIGNIFICANCE: This church scandal has raised questions about the Roman Catholic Church's authoritarian structure, and how it may have interfered with the church's capacity to discharge its responsibility to protect its members, as well as the psychosexual dynamics of sexual abuse.

The Roman Catholic priests sex abuse scandal first captured public attention when a sensational story hit the front pages of the *Boston Globe* in January, 2002. The *Globe* story contained shocking revelations concerning John Geoghan, a defrocked Boston priest and convicted child sex abuser, who had been transferred from parish to parish by his church superiors, despite their knowledge that he had been sexually abusing children. The story immediately raised questions about how such a thing could happen. As the outraged public responded, there was no shortage of culprits whom people alleged to be responsible. Some people blamed a church hierarchy that they re-

garded as more zealous to protect its church's reputation than to protect the lives of the church's youngest members.

Other people responded to the story by suggesting that the church's requirement of priestly celibacy imposed impossibly difficult rules and thus invited priests to violate the rules. Some people even claimed that the problem could only have occurred in the context of an all-male clergy. That view, while unproven, does in fact conform with statistics on sexual abuse, which suggest that it is a male specialization.

Observers on the right argued that the villain was homosexuality, which was known to be widespread among Roman Catholic priests. However, that argument also presupposed a connection between homosexuality and pedophilia, which, though perhaps cherished in the popular heterosexual imagination, has no scientific basis. In any case, the vast majority of offenders were never accused of pedophilia at all. Typical cases involved inappropriate touching of post-pubescent boys. Such behavior constituted a legal offense, a religious transgression, and perhaps signs of underlying psychological disorders, but not necessarily pedophilia.

When the dust finally settled on the initial revelations of priestly misconduct, the essence of the "scandal" appeared to center more on the church's attempts to cover up the story than on the priests' crimes. One result of this collective redefinition was a public call for the resignation of Bernard Cardinal Law, the archbishop of Boston and a key player in the cover-up. Law retired under pressure in December, 2002.

THE QUESTION OF CELIBACY

The most interesting, difficult, and profound questions arising from the scandal relate to sex and gender. Understandably, members of the Roman Catholic Church have tended to focus more on ecclesiastical matters, such as the question of reforming policies for reporting abuse and disciplining abusers. However, the complex question of the relation between ecclesiastical and legal norms has also received widespread attention. Only at the outset did the public raise the question of the nature and meaning of the abuses themselves.

The fact that the perpetrators and most of their victims were male might lead observers to conclude that the underlying cause of the problem was homosexuality. However, if the problem were defined as one of repressed homosexuality that expressed itself, desperately, in furtive encounters with helpless, compliant victims who were predisposed to keep things secret, then what needs to be addressed is not homosexuality but homophobia—both within the church and society in general. It is presumed that persons with what are considered normal sexual outlets would not be driven to have sex with young people entrusted to their professional care. In this regard, the subject may be less about homosexuality than about heterosexuality.

If the central problem is priestly celibacy, one might expect that heterosexual abuse would be as rampant within the Roman Catholic Church as homosexual abuse, which is not the case. On the other hand, opportunities for homosexual abuse in the church are much more common than opportunities for heterosexual abuse, as priests are more likely to lead same-sex outings, such as camping trips, than to lead mixed-sex outings. However, the relative scarcity of heterosexual abuse cases in the church does not prove an absence of motivation. Indeed, since in the various cases of same-sex abuse that came to light, perpetrators have not necessarily been homosexuals but may have acted as they did because of the opportunities that were presented to them. The underlying cause would seem to be sexual repression and not necessarily homosexuality.

The church's main response to the scandal has been to promise to be more vigilant in enforcing its celibacy rules and to punish transgressors, rather than to revisit its own rules themselves. It is important to note that this represents a particular position regarding the rule of celibacy. Drug laws present a relevant analogy. One could argue either that drug abuse is caused by lax enforcement of drug laws or that the very existence of drug laws encourages people to abuse them. If one believes that any kind of use is immoral then the problem is clearly one of enforcement.

GENDER NORMS

Another approach to the problem involves examining gender norms. Interestingly, there has been no reluctance on the part of the church's critics—both inside and outside the church—to assert that the cover-up could only have been perpetrated by an all-male authority structure. By contrast, little has been said about the possibly inherent relation between masculinity and sexual abuse. Sex abuse is abnormal—as abnormal as abuse of power.

An act that is abnormal is not necessarily the opposite of a normal act. Indeed, it may not differ qualitatively from normal behavior at all, as it merely violates a boundary that may have been established for purely practical purposes. For example, while it is legal to "hard sell" a product, it is illegal to sell something by making fraudulent claims. The question is whether there is a qualitative difference between fraud and exaggeration. There is a legal distinction between the two. However, what if the difference between normal male sexuality and sex abuse were similar? What if a potential for sex abuse—such as sexual harassment—were built into the structure of male sexuality as a deviant expression of it? The sex abuse crisis in the church would then look similar to what happens when men are in charge without anyone to whom to answer. In that sense, the ethical questions raised by the problem of sex abuse and those raised by the cover-up are essentially the same.

Jay Mullin

FURTHER READING

Butterfield, Fox. "789 Children Abused by Priests Since 1940, Massachusetts Says." *The New York Times*, July 24, 2003, p. 1.

France, David. *Our Fathers: The Secret Life of the Catholic Church in an Age of Scandal.* New York: Broadway, 2004.

Jenkins, Philip. *Pedophiles and Priests: Anatomy of a Contemporary Crisis.* New York: Oxford University Press, 2001.

McCabe, Kimberly A. *Child Abuse and the Criminal Justice System.* New York: Peter Lang, 2003.

Plante, Thomas G. *Bless Me Father for I Have Sinned: Perspectives on Sexual Abuse Committed by Roman Catholic Priests.* New York: Praeger, 1999.

Thigpen, Paul, ed. *Shaken by Scandals: Catholics Speak Out About Priests' Sexual Abuse.* Atlanta, Ga.: Charis Books, 2002.

Wakin, Daniel J. "Secrecy over Abusive Priests Comes Back to Haunt Church." *The New York Times*, March 12, 2002, p. 1.

SEE ALSO: Abuse; Child abuse; Homosexuality; Hypocrisy; Incest; Prostitution; Rape; Sexual abuse and harassment.

Rorty, Richard

IDENTIFICATION: American philosopher and author
BORN: October 4, 1931, New York, New York
TYPE OF ETHICS: Modern history
SIGNIFICANCE: One of America's best-known contemporary philosophers, Rorty has developed a theory of ethics that encompasses such issues as immigration, the obligations of citizens, contemporary liberalism, the politics of gender, and democracy's role in world politics.

Renowned for the breadth of his philosophical interests and publications, Richard Rorty is the son of intellectuals with leftist leanings. He entered the University of Chicago when the university's Great Books Program permitted its students to master the curriculum at their own paces. Rorty completed his bachelor's degree at Chicago before he was eighteen, stayed on for a master's degree, then entered Yale University, where he earned a doctorate in philosophy before his twenty-fifth birthday.

A committed lifelong liberal, Rorty focused on ontology—the philosophy of being—in his doctoral dissertation. In his earliest book, *Philosophy and the Mirror of Nature* (1979), he concerned himself with the ways in which individuals form the perspectives through which they view the world. In that book he comments on the relativity of such eternal verities and ethical concerns as truth, good, and evil. As a liberal thinker, Rorty was prepared to accept the absolutism of many earlier philosophers who dealt with theories of being and defined ethical behavior absolutely.

Rorty is best known, however, through his essays collected in *Contingency, Irony, and Solidarity* (1989), which has been translated into several languages. In that work, Rorty calls himself a "liberal ironist," one who views society as determined by a combination of history and of nominalism. However, these factors coexist with factors that, in all humans, have individual moral and ethical bases.

Rorty's appeal is accounted for largely by his relatively accessible prose. He is centrally concerned with developing a theory of ethics that encompasses such burning contemporary issues as immigration, the obligations of citizens, contemporary liberalism, the politics of gender, and democracy's role in world politics.

R. Baird Shuman

SEE ALSO: Ayer, A. J.; Derrida, Jacques; Gender bias; Hobbes, Thomas; Immigration; Liberalism.

Rousseau, Jean-Jacques

IDENTIFICATION: French philosopher
BORN: June 28, 1712, Geneva (now in Switzerland)
DIED: July 2, 1778, Ermenonville, France
TYPE OF ETHICS: Enlightenment history
SIGNIFICANCE: The author of *A Treatise on the Social Contract: Or, The Principles of Politic Law* (*Du contrat social: Ou, Principes du droit politique*, 1762), Rousseau was one of the most influential proponents of social contract theory. Based on an optimistic notion of the state of nature, he believed that humanity was naturally innocent, and that a legitimate and genuine social contract could help to recover the innocence humans had lost when they entered society.

Rousseau's philosophical writings and novels, all of them rich in ethical content, inspired a major shift in Western thought during the eighteenth century and part of the nineteenth century. They substantially undercut the Age of Reason and inspired a new Age of Romanticism. In the process, Rousseau's eighteenth century lifestyle and work influenced manners and morals, the reevaluation of education, conceptions of the state and of politics, and the reassertion of religious values. His philosophical genius led the way to new views of human nature, liberty, free creative expression, violence, the character of children, and the vital human and cultural importance of women.

FOUNDATIONS OF ROUSSEAU'S ETHICS

Rousseau's ethics were rooted in his moral and religious perceptions about human nature, human behavior, and human society. In *Discourse on the Sciences and the Arts* (*Discours sur les sciences et les arts*, 1750), *Discourse on the Origin of Inequality* (*Discours sur l'inégalité*, 1755), and *Social Contract* (1762), he systematically traced his thoughts on each of these subjects. Humanity, Rousseau believed, was fundamentally good. Originally living alone, simply, and in a state of nature, humanity was free, healthy, and happy. As a result of living in society, however, humanity acquired property along with the aggressiveness required for securing and defending that property. Depraved conditions, ignoble passions, and vices soon were rampant: pride in possessions, false inequalities, affectations, greed, envy, lust, and jealousy, which were attended by insecurity, personal violence, and war. Thus, although humanity was by nature good, society itself was innately corrupt. Humanity, Rousseau concluded, had been corrupted by society. What most educated eighteenth century observers viewed as the rise of civilization, Rousseau viewed as its decline.

Rousseau's own experiences were responsible for this assessment of society, even though the assessment itself was laced with idealism. He had begun life orphaned, poor, and vagrant. Unhappily struggling through menial posts and an apprenticeship, he subsequently rose to notoriety, thanks to the help of generous and sensitive patrons, many of them women. He became familiar with sophisticated intellectuals and with the rich, yet eventually he abandoned this level of society for a life of simplicity and honest, if irrational, emotions. His style and philosophy repudiated society's standards, its affectations, its belief in the indefinite improvement of humanity, and its philosophical addiction to stark reason and utilitarianism.

Rousseau's Social Contract

Rousseau believed that humanity had descended from a natural state of innocence to an artificial state of corruption—a state made worse by what he regarded as the stupidity and self-delusion of most of his contemporaries. He fully understood that any hopes of returning to humanity's ancient innocence were chimerical. Nevertheless, the values that he cherished—freedom, simplicity, honestly expressed emotions, and individualism—were still in some measure attainable as the best of a poor bargain. In his *Social Contract*, he indicated how the liberty that humanity had lost in the descent to "civilization" could be recovered in the future.

Recovery could be achieved by means of humanity's acceptance of a new and genuine social contract that would replace the false one to which Rousseau believed humanity was chained. Thus, while humanity was born free and was possessed of individual will, its freedom and will had become victims of a fraudulent society. People could, however, surrender their independent wills to a "general will"; that is, to

Rousseau's abstract conception of society as an artificial person. In doing so, people could exchange their natural independence for a new form of liberty that would be expressed through liberal, republican political institutions. The general will, a composite of individual wills, pledged people to devote themselves to advancing the common good. The integrity of their new social contract and new society would depend upon their individual self-discipline, their self-sacrifice, and an obedience imposed on them by fear of the general will.

Religious and Educational Ethics

The history of republican Geneva, Rousseau's birthplace, imbued him with a lifelong admiration of republican virtues, but neither the eighteenth century Calvinism of Geneva nor Catholicism, Rousseau believed, fostered the kind of character that would be required for the republican life that he imagined under the "Social Contract." In his view, Catholicism, for example, directed people's attention to otherworldly goals, while Calvinism had succumbed to a soft and passive Christianity that was devoid of the puritanical rigor and innocence that had once characterized it and that Rousseau admired. Rousseau, on the contrary, advocated the cultivation of this-worldly civil values that were appropriate for a vigorous republican society: self-discipline, simplicity, honesty, courage, and virility. His proposed civic religion, stripped of much theological content, was intended to fortify these values as well as to enhance patriotism and a martial spirit.

Rousseau's educational ideas, like his religious proposals, sought to inculcate republican civic virtues by directing people toward freedom, nature, and God. Small children were to be unsaddled and given physical freedom. Children from five to twelve were to be taught more by direct experience and by exposure to nature than by books. Adolescents should learn to work and should study morality and religion. Education, Rousseau argued in his classic *Émile* (1762), should teach people about the good in themselves and nature, and should prepare them to live simple, republican lives.

Clifton K. Yearley

Further Reading

Broome, J. H. *Rousseau: A Study of His Thought.* New York: Barnes & Noble, 1963.

Froese, Katrin. *Rousseau and Nietzsche: Toward an Aesthetic Morality.* Lanham, Md.: Lexington Books, 2001.

Grimsley, Ronald. *Jean-Jacques Rousseau.* Brighton, England: Harvest Press, 1983.

Guéhenno, Jean. *Jean-Jacques Rousseau.* 2 vols. Translated by John and Doreen Weightman. London: Routledge & Kegan Paul, 1966.

Havens, George R. *Jean-Jacques Rousseau.* Boston: Twayne, 1978.

Kelly, Christopher. *Rousseau as Author: Consecrating One's Life to Truth.* Chicago: University of Chicago Press, 2003.

Lange, Lynda, ed. *Feminist Interpretations of Jean-Jacques Rousseau.* University Park: Pennsylvania State University Press, 2002.

Reisert, Joseph R. *Jean-Jacques Rousseau: A Friend of Virtue.* Ithaca, N.Y.: Cornell University Press, 2003.

Rousseau, Jean-Jacques. *"The Social Contract" and "The First and Second Discourses."* Edited by Susan Dunn. New Haven, Conn.: Yale University Press, 2002.

SEE ALSO: Citizenship; Corruption; Courage; Democracy; Enlightenment ethics; Honor; Obedience; Self-control; Social contract theory; Voltaire.

Royce, Josiah

IDENTIFICATION: American philosopher
BORN: November 20, 1855, Grass Valley, California
DIED: September 14, 1916, Cambridge, Massachusetts
TYPE OF ETHICS: Modern history
SIGNIFICANCE: In such works as *The World and the Individual* (1899-1901) and *The Philosophy of Loyalty* (1908), Royce developed an ethic based on his "philosophy of loyalty," which emphasized that human beings are not isolated individuals but are members of communities.

After teaching in San Francisco and at the University of California at Berkeley, Josiah Royce moved to Cambridge, Massachusetts, in 1882 and distinguished himself as a professor of philosophy at Harvard University. There he became close friends with the American pragmatist William James, although Royce's philosophy differed fundamentally from that of his famous colleague.

Royce's philosophical idealism stressed that a human self is a center of purpose and striving; therefore, human life involves suffering and a struggle with evil. Royce affirmed, however, that in facing these obstacles courageously, in achieving success wherever one can, and in recognizing that one's relationship with the Absolute, or God, entails the overcoming of every evil, one can experience positive meaning and joy.

According to Royce, such human fulfillment depends on loyalty, which he defined as "the willing and practical and thoroughgoing devotion of a person to a cause." Not all causes are good ones, but Royce believed that the act of being loyal is good whenever it does occur. He concluded that the most fundamental principle of the moral life ought to be that of being loyal to loyalty. This principle points toward a community where all individuals are free, where they use their abilities and cultivate their interests, and where all these persons and factors encourage and support one another.

John K. Roth

SEE ALSO: Common good; Idealist ethics; James, William; Loyalty; Loyalty oaths; Social justice and responsibility; Universalizability.

Rūmī, Jalāl al-Dīn

IDENTIFICATION: Afghan mystical poet
BORN: c. September 30, 1207, Balkh (now in Afghanistan)
DIED: December 17, 1273, Konya, Asia Minor (now in Turkey)
TYPE OF ETHICS: Religious ethics
SIGNIFICANCE: Rūmī was the most influential mystical poet in the Persian language and the eponymous founder of the Mevlevī Sufi order. He wrote numerous mystical and philosophical poetic works, including *Mathnavī* (1259-1273).

Rūmī was an extraordinarily prolific Persian poet, best known for his *Mathnavī*, which is arguably the most important single work in Persian literature. Although the *Mathnavī* is massive in scope (26,000 verses), it focuses on Rūmī's primary concerns: the longing of the soul for its beloved and the loss of self in a love for God so absolute that only God exists. He emphasized the cycle of the origination of all things from God and their return through extinguishing the self. The highest possible achievement of the soul is longing for God, beyond which there is annihilation of individuality. Rūmī frequently reworked traditional stories or used metaphors of intoxication and/or human love, and, disdaining discursive thought and logical argument, he saw himself as being in the spiritual tradition of al-Hallāj, Sanā'ī, and ʿAṭṭār.

BIOGRAPHY

Rūmī's family left Balkh when he was quite young, fleeing the invading forces of Genghis Khan. In 1228, he moved to Konya, where his father, the noted theologian Bahā' al-Dīn Walad, taught. Rūmī took over those teaching duties after his father's death. In 1244, he met the famed Sufi Shams al-Dīn Tabrīzī in Konya (they may have met previously in Syria), and the two became inseparable partners in the rapture of absolute, mystical love of God. This relationship seems to have been the cause of Rūmī's turn to mystical poetry. Rūmī's relationship with Shams dominated his life, eclipsing responsibilities to family and students, who exiled Shams to Syria. Rūmī's eldest son, Sultan Walad, recalled Shams because the separation was heartbreaking for Rūmī. Their previous behavior resumed, leading another of Rūmī's sons to conspire successfully with his students to murder Shams. Soon thereafter, Rūmī entered into a similar relationship with Salāh al-Dīn Zarkūb.

LEGACY

After Rūmī's death, Sultan Walad organized the Mevlevī (Turkish for Rūmī's title, *maulānā*, or master) order of Sufis, in which dancing in circles is an important spiritual exercise. The Mevlevī (the "whirling dervishes" of European writers) have been a significant popular, devotional alternative to more legalistic Islamic orthopraxy, and Rūmī's tomb remains a focus of popular religion and pilgrimage. His poetry was influential as far away as Bengal and has remained influential to the present day. Among those moved by his poetry were the Mughal emperor

Akbar, the Chistī Sufi saint Nizām al-Dīn Auliyā, and the twentieth century poet Muhammad Iqbal.

Thomas Gaskill

SEE ALSO: Hallāj, al-; Rābiʿah al-ʿAdawīyah; Sufism.

Russell, Bertrand

IDENTIFICATION: English mathematician and philosopher
BORN: May 18, 1872, Trelleck, Monmouthshire, Wales
DIED: February 2, 1970, Plas Penrhyn, near Penrhyndeudraeth, Wales
TYPE OF ETHICS: Modern history
SIGNIFICANCE: Although primarily a logician, Russell developed a subjectivist ethical position in the belief that human beings could choose good over evil. His most important ethical works include *On Education* (1926), *Why I Am Not a Christian* (1927), *Marriage and Morals* (1929), *Education and the Social Order* (1932), *Religion and Science* (1935), and *Human Society and Ethics* (1955).

Bertrand Russell's early work centered on mathematics and logic, culminating in a book he coauthored with Alfred North Whitehead, *Principia Mathematica* (1910-1913). Twice, however, he was dramatically drawn into issues of values and ethics. The first occasion came in 1901, when a "quasi-religious experience" brought home to him the isolation of the individual and led to his advocacy of humane policies in education, the punishment of criminals, and personal relationships. He published an essay, "A Free Man's Worship" (1903), but was too involved in his work on logic to devote much time to these ideas. The second and lasting shift was prompted by World War I, which he opposed, though he would later support the opposition to Nazism in World War II.

The horrors of the world wars prompted Russell to consider how humankind might change. He was convinced that the key was education, because childhood experience molded adult attitudes, including the acceptance of violence. In his writings and at Beacon Hill School, which he founded, he advocated the disciplined but kindly treatment of students. Ultimately, however, he realized that values were matters of opinion, and he never found an objective way to prove that his values were best. He argued powerfully, however, for his humane approach to education, as well as to sexual relationships, religion, and other important aspects of social life.

Fred R. van Hartesveldt

SEE ALSO: Humanism; Idealist ethics; Reason and rationality; Relativism; Subjectivism; Whitehead, Alfred North.

Rwanda genocide

THE EVENT: Ethnic conflict in which as many as 800,000 Rwandans—mostly Tutsis—were killed
DATE: April-July, 1994
PLACE: Rwanda, Central Africa
TYPE OF ETHICS: Human rights

SIGNIFICANCE: In addition to the obviously horrific slaughter of hundreds of thousands of innocent people, the Rwandan genocide raised troubling questions about the ethical responsibility of the world's nations to intervene in the affairs of other nations.

Covering more than ten thousand square miles in the heart of Africa, Rwanda has a population made up of three distinct peoples. The Hutu constitute the majority of the population and are traditionally subsistence farmers; the minority Tutsi were traditionally cattle herders and provided the country's rulers; and the Twa, who constituted only about 2 percent of the total population, were traditionally potters. After Germany and Belgium colonized Rwanda and neighbor Burundi around the turn of the twentieth century, colonial rule reinforced and exacerbated the distinctions among Rwanda's three groups.

Under Belgian rule, which lasted from 1916 until 1962, colonial administrators favored the Tutsis, sin-

During his 1998 visit to Rwanda, United Nations secretary general Kofi Annan (right) visited a memorial site at which the skulls of thousands of victims of genocide were on display. (AP/Wide World Photos)

gling them out for greater access to education and government jobs. By 1959, however, the majority Hutus were powerful enough to force out the last Tutsi king. Thousands of Tutsi supporters went into exile to neighboring Uganda at that time. After Rwanda declared its independence from Belgium, a government headed by Hutus came to power. In 1973, a Hutu general, Juvenal Habyarimana, seized power in a coup and a dictatorship was established that lasted until his death in 1994, when an airplane on which he and the president of Burundi were traveling crashed, killing both leaders. Suspicion that the airplane had been shot down by Tutsi opponents of the Hutu government touched off the genocide that ensued against the Tutsis in Rwanda.

A few years before Habyarimana's death, a civil war had begun, between the Rwanda Patriotic Front (RPF), representing the Tutsis and operating out of Uganda, and the Hutu government. Habyarimana was also under pressure from the international community to democratize Rwandan politics and ameliorate the country's economic condition, which was dismal. In 1992, he agreed to conditions that led to a cease-fire between the two sides. Since the negotiations leading to the cease-fire took

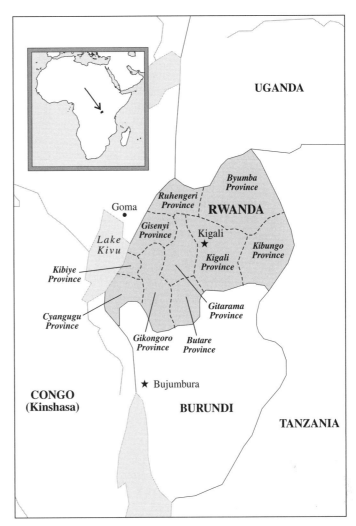

place in Arusha, Tanzania, they were referred to as the Arusha Accords. A power-sharing schedule was drawn up that included the eventual holding of elections. Many within Habyarimana's government were angry at the conditions imposed by the Arusha Accords, charging that the Tutsis would maximize their power under the agreement. With so many unhappy within the ranks of his own government and with Habyarimana trying to simultaneously appease his people as well as appear to be moving forward under the accords, political unrest grew.

GENOCIDE IN RWANDA

On April 6, 1994, Habyarimana's plane crashed in Rwanda's capital city, Kigali, and he was instantly killed. Blame for the apparently sabotaged plane was

never finally established; Hutus claimed that Tutsis were responsible, and Tutsis claimed that extremist elements within the Hutu government had killed their own leader. The Hutu-dominated army seized upon the crash as a pretext to move against all Tutsis, organizing ruthless killings of the RPF and all Tutsis in an attempt to eliminate them from Rwanda. Ordinary Hutus were exhorted to kill "Tutsi vermin" in radio broadcasts throughout the country, and many did.

Human rights abuses that dehumanized the other side and portrayed them as animals were common on the part of the Hutus as the genocide spread. Over the next three months, the RPF advanced in the north and was eventually able to take control of large parts of the country and form an interim government. A Tutsi government still ruled the country a decade later.

Meanwhile, however, three months of genocide had taken around 800,000 lives, the majority of whom were Tutsi. Many Hutus, including members of the former government and militias, fled to refugee camps in the neighboring Democratic Republic of the Congo (then called Zaire) and Tanzania.

The genocide in Rwanda was a sober lesson to the world community in how rapidly civil violence could spread and how deadly its effects could be. The debates over what ethical and moral responsibility the world community had in stopping the genocide were still being voiced a decade later. The United Nations had only a small force in the country on the eve of the violence and failed miserably to stop the genocide, although the Canadian commander of the U.N. peacekeeping mission, Roméo Dallaire, tried to alert U.N. officers to the need for additional help.

Ethical questions have also been raised about the reluctance of the United Nations to get involved in the conflict until after the genocide had occurred. In 2004, Rwanda was still limping back to normalcy after trials for crimes against humanity were held against Hutus responsible for the killings. The country's first election after the genocide, held in August, 2003, resulted in the maintaining of power by President Paul Kagame, although there have been charges of voter intimidation by his opponents.

Tinaz Pavri

FURTHER READING

Dallaire, Roméo. *Shake Hands with the Devil: The Failure of Humanity in Rwanda.* Toronto: Random House Canada, 2003.

Gourevitch, Philip. *We Wish to Inform You That Tomorrow We Will Be Killed with Our Families: Stories from Rwanda.* New York: Picador, 1999.

Off, Carol. *The Lion, the Fox and the Eagle: A Story of Generals and Justice in Yugoslavia and Rwanda.* Toronto: Random House Canada, 2000.

SEE ALSO: African ethics; Dallaire, Roméo; Genocide and democide; Holocaust; Peacekeeping missions; United Nations; United Nations Convention on the Prevention and Punishment of the Crime of Genocide; War crimes trials.

S

Sales ethics

DEFINITION: Formal and informal codes of conduct defining the morally proper and improper ways to sell things to people.

TYPE OF ETHICS: Business and labor ethics

SIGNIFICANCE: Sales is often perceived, by both buyers and sellers, as the art of convincing people to purchase things they do not really need or to pay more for a commodity than it is really worth. This act raises ethical concerns involving who is ultimately responsible for the decisions of consumers and the extent to which purveyors of commodities can or cannot be said to manipulate buyers or the marketplace itself.

The selling of goods and services has long been the subject of moral and, sometimes, theological concern. Economic theorists at least since the time of Adam Smith have assured people that when a buyer and a seller with equal knowledge of a product reach agreement and a transaction occurs in the marketplace, the situations of both buyer and seller are improved; otherwise, one or the other would not have agreed to the transaction. Nevertheless, since both buyer and seller are seeking to maximize their positions and since their interests are diametrically opposed, one seeking the lowest possible price and the other seeking the highest, it is natural to expect each to try to take advantage of the other, sometimes unfairly. The problem is rooted in whether buyer and seller have equal knowledge; as products and services have become increasingly complex and as manufacturers and sellers have grown into multibillion-dollar corporations, equal knowledge, and therefore equal power, in the marketplace has become the exception rather than the rule.

MARKETING ETHICS

The ethics of marketing, a broader and more current interpretation of sales, can be viewed in terms of the natural dimensions of the marketing function.

The first concerns the safety and appropriateness of the product or service being marketed, normally considered under the subject of product liability. Here the question is: Who has responsibility and liability for any harm done to individuals or to society by the product? This has become an enormously complex and rapidly changing area of the law and of moral concern as well. Traditionally, common law and social thought relied on contract theory, which holds that buyer and seller come as equals to the marketplace, and once the deal has been struck, the buyer is responsible for the product, including any harm it might cause. Especially since the 1950's, however, more and more of the responsibility and liability have been placed on the seller and, particularly, the manufacturer. It has been argued that the manufacturer has the most knowledge of the product, is in the best position to prevent harm from occurring, and is better able to bear the financial liability for harm than is the buyer, especially when the latter is an individual consumer. No longer is it necessary to show that manufacturers have been negligent in any way; they are now expected to anticipate any potential hazards or possible misuse by customers.

PRICING AND PROMOTION ISSUES

Ethical questions can arise also in the pricing function of marketing. Here the question is whether a price is considered fair, especially when the product is a necessity such as a basic food item, housing, or medical care. The introduction of revolutionary pharmaceutical products—for example, Burroughs Wellcome's AZT for the treatment of acquired immunodeficiency syndrome (AIDS) patients and Genentech's TPA for heart attack victims—has often triggered complaints that the manufacturer's high price puts an unfair burden on the buyer. Some retailers have been accused of unfairly charging prices in low-income areas that are higher than those that they charge in more affluent neighborhoods for the identical merchandise.

Sophisticated advertising and other promotional

tactics are often the subject of ethical questioning. Critics charge that advertisers, usually the manufacturers, manipulate and exploit consumers, and thus use unfair means to encourage them to buy. Manufacturers and some social scientists respond that unless the advertising is actually dishonest, and therefore illegal, consumers cannot be coerced by legal advertising messages into buying anything that they do not really want to buy. This issue takes on added significance when so-called "vulnerable" groups are the target. Cigarette companies have been criticized for targeting African Americans and women; breweries for targeting young, inner-city African Americans for high-alcohol-content beverages; breakfast cereal and toy manufacturers for targeting children; and door-to-door sellers of safety devices for targeting older people. Other ethical questions raised about advertising include the promotion of inappropriate values; for example, materialism and the exploitation of women by emphasizing sex.

In the distribution function of marketing, ethical questions are raised when retailers close stores in inner-city areas (for example, after the Los Angeles riots of May, 1992), when major food retailers collect "slotting fees" from manufacturers just for agreeing to carry new products, and when direct marketers buy and use confidential demographic and consumer behavior information in compiling lists of potential customers.

CORRECTIVE ACTION

Action to correct these ethical problems comes from three sources. First, various industries and business associations agree to exercise self-restraint through company-wide or industry-wide codes of conduct and through the formation of organizations such as the Better Business Bureaus to monitor corporate behavior. Second, dozens of watchdog consumer organizations, such as the Center for Auto Safety, Co-op America, and the Center for Science in the Public Interest, have been formed to guard consumers' interests and call attention to what they perceive as improper behavior on the part of sellers. Third, since the 1970's, many laws have been passed to help protect consumers, such as the Consumers Products Safety Act, the Child Protection and Safety Act, and the Hazardous Substances Act at the federal level.

D. Kirk Davidson

FURTHER READING

Davidson, D. Kirk. *The Moral Dimension of Marketing: Essays on Business Ethics.* Chicago: American Marketing Association, 2002.

Galbraith, John Kenneth. *The Affluent Society.* 40th anniversary ed. Boston: Houghton Mifflin, 1998.

Hunt, Shelby D., and Lawrence B. Chonko. "Marketing and Machiavellianism." *Journal of Marketing* 48 (Summer, 1984): 30-42.

Laczniak, Gene R., and Patrick E. Murphy. *Marketing Ethics: Guidelines for Managers.* Lexington, Mass.: Lexington Books, 1985.

Levitt, Theodore. "The Morality (?) of Advertising." *Harvard Business Review,* July-August, 1970: 84-92.

Milne, George R., and Maria-Eugenia Boza. *A Business Perspective on Database Marketing and Consumer Privacy Practices.* Cambridge, Mass.: Marketing Science Institute, 1998.

Schlegelmilch, Bodo B. *Marketing Ethics: An International Perspective.* Boston: International Thomson Business Press, 1998.

Smith, N. Craig, and John A. Quelch. *Ethics in Marketing.* Homewood, Ill.: Richard D. Irwin, 1993.

SEE ALSO: Advertising; Business ethics; Consumerism; Marketing; Price fixing; Telemarketing; Warranties and guarantees.

SALT treaties

IDENTIFICATION: Cold War treaties designed to curb the nuclear arms race and to place limits on the development of antiballistic missile defenses

DATES: SALT I, May 26, 1972; SALT II, June 18, 1979

TYPE OF ETHICS: International relations

SIGNIFICANCE: The Strategic Arms Limitation Treaties (SALT I and SALT II) began the process of mutual U.S. and Soviet nuclear weapons reduction, in recognition of the dangers posed to the long-term security of all nations by unfettered nuclear stockpiling.

After several years of preliminary efforts, negotiations between the United States and the Soviet Union regarding reducing strategic nuclear weapons began on November 17, 1969. Several factors spurred both states toward an agreement. The United States was anxious to stop the steady Soviet buildup of intercontinental ballistic missiles (ICBMs), which in 1970 for the first time exceeded those of the United States. By the early 1970's, the Soviet Union was approaching numerical parity with the United States in the total number of strategic nuclear delivery vehicles.

For its part, the Soviet Union was anxious to avoid a competition with the United States in building antiballistic missile (ABM) defenses. In 1967, the U.S. Lyndon Johnson administration decided to proceed with a pilot ABM system, as did the succeeding Richard Nixon administration. Another factor was that both countries had committed themselves to nuclear weapons reductions as part of their effort to persuade non-nuclear weapons states to sign the Nonproliferation Treaty. Finally, during the early 1970's, the two superpowers were moving toward improved relations, which both sides recognized would be dramatically symbolized by significant arms control agreements.

SALT Treaties Time Line

Date	Event
September 18, 1967	U.S. secretary of defense Robert McNamara announces limited U.S. ABM system.
July 1, 1968	U.S. president Lyndon B. Johnson announces preliminary SALT discussions.
November 17, 1969	SALT negotiations begin in Helsinki, Finland.
May 26, 1972	SALT I agreements are signed in Moscow, Russia.
July 1, 1972	Moratorium on offensive missiles begins.
September 30, 1972	ABM Treaty is ratified by United States.
October 3, 1972	SALT I agreements take effect.
November 21, 1972	SALT II negotiations begin.
November, 1974	Ford-Brezhnev accord begins at Vladivostok summit.
March 12, 1977	U.S. president Jimmy Carter endorses comprehensive plan.
October 1, 1977	Missile moratorium expires.
June 18, 1979	SALT II Treaty is signed in Vienna.
December, 1979	Soviet Union invades Afghanistan.
January, 1980	U.S. president Jimmy Carter withdraws SALT II Treaty from Senate consideration.
March, 1983	U.S. president Ronald Reagan proposes Strategic Defense Initiative (Star Wars).

SALT I

Between November, 1969, and May, 1972, seven negotiating sessions were held, alternating between the cities of Helsinki and Vienna. Completion of the SALT I package was not achieved until May, 1972, when Richard Nixon and Leonid Brezhnev met in their first summit session in Moscow. The fundamental compromise of SALT I was embodied in two agreements: an ABM Treaty limiting defensive weapons (the primary concern of the Soviet Union) and a moratorium on the deployment of offensive weapons (the principal U.S. objective).

The ABM Treaty was the more important of the two agreements. It provided that each party would refrain from building a nationwide antiballistic missile defense and would limit the construction of ABM site defenses to only two specific sites. (Subsequently, the treaty was modified to limit site defense to a single site.) The site defenses were intended to permit both sides to protect their national capitals and one ICBM site. The Soviet Union had already begun construction of an ABM defense of Moscow, and the United States was free to do the same for Washington, D.C. (which it never did). An important provision of the ABM Treaty stipulated that "Each Party undertakes not to develop, test, or deploy ABM systems or components which are sea-based, air-based, space-based, or mobile land-based." More than a decade later, this prohibition would be used to criticize as illegal the proposal of the Ronald Reagan administration for a "strategic defense initiative." The ABM Treaty, which was ratified by the United States on September 30, 1972, is of unlimited duration, although it is subject to review every five years.

The other part of SALT I was an Interim Agreement not to construct any new fixed, land-based ICBM missile launchers for a five-year period beginning July 1, 1972. This five-year moratorium was formalized as an Executive Agreement rather than as a treaty. Both parties could modernize and replace their strategic offensive missiles and launchers, but they could not increase their total number. Thus, the United States was limited to 1,054 ICBMs and the Soviet Union to 1,618. A protocol to the Interim Agreement limited the United States to a maximum of 710 submarine-launched ballistic missiles (SLBMs) and the Soviet Union to 950 launchers. The rationale for this agreement was that while both parties possessed a different mix of weapons, they were nevertheless roughly in a state of parity. While in certain categories of missiles the Soviet Union possessed more, the United States had the advantage of technological superiority. It was assumed that before the moratorium expired, both governments would negotiate a follow-on agreement (SALT II) that would begin the process of inventory reduction.

SALT II

SALT II proved to be considerably more difficult to negotiate than SALT I had been. In October, 1977, the five-year moratorium ended and no follow-on agreement was in sight. Both governments unilaterally and simultaneously announced their intention to abide by the constraints of the Interim Agreement, pending a new accord. Not until May, 1979, was SALT II completed, and then it was never ratified. There were three principal reasons for the protracted negotiations of SALT II. First, during the 1970's, technological improvements in weapons systems made verification of an agreement extremely difficult. The development of cruise missiles by the United States, the deployment of mobile launchers by the Soviet Union, and the deployment of multiple independently targeted reentry vehicles (MIRVs) by both sides required intrusive and cooperative monitoring measures that both sides were reluctant to accept.

Second, the détente relationship of the early 1970's collapsed as the decade passed. Soviet-American conflicts in the Third World fueled suspicions that the Soviet Union was determined to expand at Western expense. Soviet-Cuban involvement in Angola and Ethiopia during the mid- to late 1970's particularly angered the United States. The Soviet invasion of Afghanistan in December, 1979, induced U.S. president Jimmy Carter to abandon the effort to ratify SALT II. Third, negotiations were complicated by domestic politics, particularly in the United States. President Nixon was disabled by the Watergate crisis, which forced his resignation in 1974. President Carter was slow to move the negotiations because of both overambition to produce drastic cuts and diplomatic ineptitude.

In 1974, President Gerald Ford met Leonid Brezhnev in Vladivostok to devise a general framework for a SALT II treaty. They agreed that each side would be permitted a total of 2,400 strategic delivery vehicles, of which 1,320 could be MIRVs. Five years later, under a different American administration, an agreement was reached. It was signed by Carter and Brezhnev at a summit meeting in Vienna.

Unlike SALT I, SALT II is a long and complicated agreement. The documents include a Treaty to remain in force through 1985, a Protocol of three years' duration, and a Joint Statement of Principles to serve as a guideline for future negotiations. The main terms of the agreement can be summarized as follows: a ceiling of 2,400 strategic launchers, to decline to 2,250 by 1981; a limit of 1,320 on MIRV missiles and bombers; a further subceiling of 1,200 for MIRVs, ICBMs, and SLBMs; a further subceiling of 820 for MIRV ICBMs; a limit on the number of warheads on MIRV missiles; limits on the deployment of mobile missiles and cruise missiles; and a limit on Soviet production of the Backfire bomber.

By the time SALT II was signed, relations between the superpowers had deteriorated, making ratification in the United States politically difficult. Reagan, who was elected U.S. president in 1980, opposed the ratification of SALT II, though throughout his administration he adhered to its provisions (as did the Soviet Union). During the 1980's, U.S.-Soviet relations radically improved, and subsequently the two states did agree on arms control measures that went breathtakingly beyond both SALT I and SALT II. The threat of nuclear devastation was substantially reduced by these agreements.

Joseph L. Nogee

FURTHER READING

Arms Control and Disarmament Agreements: Texts and Histories of Negotiations. Washington, D.C.: U.S. Arms Control and Disarmament Agency, 1982.

Graham, Thomas, Jr. *Disarmament Sketches: Three Decades of Arms Control and International Law.* Seattle: Institute for Global and Regional Security Studies/University of Washington Press, 2002.

Hopmann, P. Terrence. "Strategic Arms Control Negotiations: SALT and START." In *Containing the Atom,* edited by Rudolf Avenhaus, Victor Kremenyuk, and Gunnar Sjöstedt. Lanham, Md.: Lexington Books, 2002.

Newhouse, John. *Cold Dawn: The Story of SALT.* New York: Holt, Rinehart & Winston, 1973.

Stanford Arms Control Group. *International Arms Control: Issues and Agreements.* 2d ed. Stanford, Calif.: Stanford University Press, 1984.

Talbott, Strobe. *Endgame: The Inside Story of SALT II.* New York: Harper & Row, 1979.

Wolfe, Thomas. *The SALT Experience.* Cambridge, Mass.: Ballinger, 1979.

SEE ALSO: Cold War; International law; Mutually Assured Destruction; Nuclear arms race; Union of Concerned Scientists.

Sanctions

DEFINITION: Political, economic, or military measures adopted by one or more nations designed to coerce another nation into obeying international law or otherwise acceding to the coercive nations' will

TYPE OF ETHICS: International relations

SIGNIFICANCE: Sanctions provide a means short of full-scale warfare to encourage compliance with international law, but they may still be seen as violating the sovereignty of the nation being sanctioned.

International relations are marked by the lack of centralized mechanisms for maintaining order and punishing violations of international law. For this reason, states, in both their individual capacities and as collective groups, have relied on sanctions to punish of-

fending governments. Sanctions take a variety of forms, including the imposition of trade boycotts and embargoes, the freezing of assets held in foreign banks, the suspension of foreign aid or investment activity, the breaking of diplomatic relations, the establishment of blockades, and even the limited use of military force. Economic sanctions are not always effective in achieving compliance from the offending government. Their success is most likely when a large number of states that have commercial and economic ties to the offending state act quickly and firmly to impose sanctions, when the offending state is economically weak and unable to withstand the sanctions, and when third parties are unlikely to come to the offender's assistance. Historically, sanctions took the form of unilateral retaliation by the injured state against the offender. In the twentieth century, with the rise of international organizations such as the League of Nations and the United Nations, sanctions have been adopted as a multilateral mechanism for taking action against renegade states that violate international law.

HISTORY

Sanctions have always been present in international relations as a means of punishing violators of international law. In effect, an injured state, having no capacity to appeal to a higher authority, relied on its own resources to take action against governments that injured it by violating treaty obligations or customary international law. Several principles, however, placed ethical, moral, and legal constraints on how states could use retaliatory force and how much force they could use as a sanction against the offender. Three basic principles were involved. First, it was assumed that one could retaliate legally only when the action was in response to a prior illegal action or provocation. Second, it was assumed that the injured party would allow some time to resolve the dispute peacefully. Third, it was required that any retaliation would be proportional in character and degree to the original offense. Excessive retaliatory force was considered illegal, and restraint in the course of retaliation was expected.

With the emergence of global and regional collective security organizations in the twentieth century, governments moved toward the multilateral use of sanctions. Collective security organizations require their members to resolve disputes among themselves peacefully; that is, to avoid the use of force against one another. When a member of a collective security treaty such as the United Nations illegally uses force against another member, other member states are expected collectively to resist and punish such aggression. Sanctions are typically employed to deal with such situations, although the severity of the sanctions and their effectiveness have varied substantially in actual practice, and in many instances there has not been adequate consensus to employ any sanctions at all. This happens when there is doubt about which state was actually the author of aggression and in cases in which a clear aggressor has powerful allies that will oppose efforts by collective security bodies such as the United Nations to take any action. In such cases, individual states are free to impose sanctions of their own against a state that has violated international law. Multilateral sanctions, in other words, have not replaced self-help by individual states but have supplemented it. When, how, and whether sanctions are imposed ultimately depends more on political realities than on ethical, moral, or legal considerations.

ETHICAL ISSUES

International relations are marked primarily by the principle that states are sovereign. This principle calls for nonintervention in the domestic affairs of a state. It calls for each state to recognize the independence, territorial integrity, and equality of other states. How then can sanctions be justified against a state? When should sanctions be imposed? Under collective security treaties to which governments have voluntarily subscribed, sanctions are justified when one state violates the territorial integrity of another state and, at least under the United Nations Charter, when such violations threaten international peace and security. In other words, if states have a right to territorial integrity and noninterference in their domestic affairs, then they have a duty to respect other states' independence and territorial integrity. Where clear-cut aggression occurs, sanctions are ethically, morally, and legally justified. The U.N. Security Council can act only if a majority of its members (that is, nine states, including the five permanent members who have veto power) agree to impose sanctions. If they fail to do so, then states are left to decide how to proceed to protect their rights and interests.

One of the most ticklish issues concerning sanctions turns on the question of their use against states for actions that are primarily domestic in character and that may not clearly threaten international peace and security. May the international community, for example, interfere in the domestic affairs of a state to punish it for mistreatment of its own citizens? States have, for example, imposed sanctions on their own, and at the request of the United Nations, to oppose South Africa's domestic policy of apartheid. Sanctions were imposed on Rhodesia when a white minority unilaterally declared independence during the 1960's. Such cases are, however, rare. Usually, sanctions are imposed when the domestic actions of states begin to have serious international consequences. When domestic instability produces civil war, refugee flows into neighboring states, boundary incursions, and the like, then states are more likely to impose sanctions.

Another problem with economic sanctions is that they often hurt the innocent population of a country without damaging or removing the culpable government, as happened in Iraq in the late twentieth century. For how long should states impose sanctions that are hurtful to the innocent? Here, ethical and humanitarian considerations must be weighed in the balance with political judgment.

CONCLUSION

Sanctions are imposed by states for many reasons. Sometimes they are meant to punish an aggressor, sometimes to pressure an outlaw state into compliance with international law, sometimes to prevent the further spread of conflict, and sometimes simply to express the moral indignation or outrage that the people and government of one country feel about the actions of another country's government. In the latter case, the imposition of sanctions fulfills its purpose in the very act of implementation even if the offending state fails to desist from its objectionable behavior.

Robert F. Gorman

FURTHER READING

Bennett, A. LeRoy. *International Organizations: Principles and Issues.* 6th ed. Englewood Cliffs, N.J.: Prentice Hall, 1995.

Cortright, David, and George A. Lopez, eds. *Smart Sanctions: Targeting Economic Statecraft.* Lanham, Md.: Rowman & Littlefield, 2002.

Daoudi, Mohammed, and Munther Dajani. *Economic Sanctions: Ideals and Experience*. London: Routledge & Kegan Paul, 1983.

Harrelson, Max. *Fires All Around the Horizon: The U.N.'s Uphill Battle to Preserve the Peace*. New York: Praeger, 1989.

Henkin, Louis, et al. *Right v. Might: International Law and the Use of Force*. 2d ed. New York: Council on Foreign Relations Press, 1991.

Hufbauer, Gary C., and Jeffrey Schott. *Economic Sanctions Reconsidered: History and Current Policy*. Washington, D.C.: Institute for International Economics, 1985.

Weiss, Thomas G., ed. *Political Gain and Civilian Pain: Humanitarian Impacts of Economic Sanctions*. Lanham, Md.: Rowman & Littlefield, 1997.

SEE ALSO: Deterrence; Economics; International justice; International law; Intervention; Limited war; Power; Sovereignty.

Śaṅkara

IDENTIFICATION: Early Indian philosopher
BORN: c. 700, Kāladi, Kerala, India
DIED: 750, Himalayas
TYPE OF ETHICS: Religious ethics
SIGNIFICANCE: In his commentaries on the Hindu religious canon (the Prasthānatraya), Śaṅkara advocated monistic or Advaita Vedānta philosophy, which explains how to achieve the ultimate reality, or *Brāhmin*. He founded four Indian *mathas*, or monasteries.

The most influential philosopher of the Advaita, or nondualistic, school of Vedānta philosophy in India. Śaṅkara was considered the incarnation of the god Śiva. His view is representative of the main teachings of the Upaniṣads, which do not portray any consistent view of the universe and of reality. Śaṅkara detected a synthesis underlying the Upaniṣads and insisted on interpreting them in a single coherent manner. He tried to revive the intellectual speculation of the Upaniṣads through his reaction against the ascetic tendency of Buddhism and the devotional tendencies stressed by the Mīmāṃsa school. The central position of Śaṅkara's philosophy is that all is one; only the ultimate principle has any real existence, and everything else is an illusion (*māyā*). The basic teaching of Advaita Vedānta is that the direct method of realization of *Brāhmin* is the path of knowledge, which consists of getting instruction from a teacher, reflecting on its meaning, and meditating on truth with single-minded devotion. For Śaṅkara, philosophical discrimination and renunciation of the unreal are the basic disciplines for the realization of *Brāhmin*. Finite humanity can catch a glimpse of *Brāhmin* through a personal god, who is the highest manifestation of the infinite.

The self, or *ātman*, according to Śaṅkara, is pure subject and is never an object of consciousness. It is not a duality; it is different from the phenomenal, the spatial, the temporal, and the sensible. It is assumed to be foundational but it is in no sense a substance. Self is the ever-existent and self-existent first principle. It is not something that is unknown. One must come to the realization that one is *Brāhmin*. This is self-knowledge, the knowledge of self being the self of all things. One must realize one's identity as *Brāhmin*, for *Brāhmin* is knowledge. Self-knowledge and realization are one and the same. From the level of *Brāhmin*, nothing is seen to be real—not the existential self that people view as ego, not the worlds, and not the universes.

According to Advaita Vedānta philosophy, the highest good consists in breaking down the bonds that shut one out of the reality that one is. It is only the realization of *Brāhmin* that can give one permanent satisfaction. Śaṅkara wrote, "Attaining the Knowledge of Reality, one sees the universe as the nondual *Brāhmin*, Existence-Knowledge-Bliss Absolute." It is not possible for everyone to achieve this highest state, yet everyone can try to achieve it progressively, through his or her inner light. It is up to the individual to choose any course of action (karma) that is of value to that person. When one clings to the world, one looks for rewards for action and feels disappointed when the objects of desire are not achieved. This applies even to praiseworthy actions such as worship and giving alms. If these actions are performed with desire or attachment, they cause bondage. Therefore, nonattachment must be cultivated if one wants to progress to the highest good.

It is often believed that Śaṅkara discourages the performance of duties and advocates the discipline of nonaction for the realization of truth. This is not true, however, because Śaṅkara's position is that because of *māyā*, or ignorance, one does not recognize one's true nature and finds oneself involved with the relative world of good and evil, life and death, and other pairs of opposites. Therefore, one tries to avoid evil and to do good, rising and falling according to the results of one's actions. Gradually, one discovers that it is impossible to attain lasting happiness and peace by clinging to rewards and realizes that work performed in the spirit of surrendering the results to God, in the spirit of calm, unattached by love or hate, by reward or punishment, purifies the heart and makes it inclined toward the cultivation of meditation and self-knowledge. The liberated person engages in service to humanity but not in an egoistic way, because a liberated person is above good and evil, above morality.

Release from the wheel of birth and rebirth comes through *jñāna*, or knowledge or insight, which lifts one out of one's individuality into the oneness of the infinite. At the beginning stage, one learns the art of concentration through the worship of the personal God and acquires purity of heart through performance of unselfish duties. In the next stage, one acquires knowledge of *Brāhmin* and realizes the impersonal absolute. The way of devotion (*bhakti mārga*) must be transcended if one is to realize the supreme good, the realization of self as *Brāhmin*. It is at this level that one becomes liberated from the endless sufferings of the world. This level can be achieved during one's lifetime. This freed soul does not have anything more to achieve but still continues to work for the welfare of the world. The liberated person does not negate his or her relationship to the finite world, since there is a direct relationship between the spiritual and the ethical. The freed soul (*jivan-mukta*) follows the moral code set down by his or her society, because he or she is unattached and freed from desires.

Krishna Mallick

FURTHER READING

Deussen, Paul. *The System of the Vedānta*. Translated by Charles Johnston. Chicago: Open Court, 1912. Reprint. New Delhi: Banarsi Das, 1979.

Hiriyanna, Mysore. *The Essentials of Indian Philosophy*. London: Allen & Unwin, 1949.

Koller, John M. *The Indian Way*. New York: Macmillan, 1982.

Marcaurelle, Roger. *Freedom Through Inner Renun-ciation: Śaṅkara's Philosophy in a New Light*. Albany: State University of New York Press, 2000.

Radhakrishnan, Sarvepalli. *Indian Philosophy*. 2 vols. New York: Macmillan, 1958.

Smith, Huston. *The Religions of Man*. New York: Harper & Row, 1958.

Victor, P. George. *Life and Teachings of Ādi Śaṅkarācārya*. New Delhi: D. K. Printworld, 2002.

SEE ALSO: Aurobindo, Sri; Karma; Tagore, Rabindranath; Upaniṣads; Vedānta.

Santayana, George

IDENTIFICATION: Spanish philosopher, poet, and novelist
BORN: December 16, 1863, Madrid, Spain
DIED: September 26, 1952, Rome, Italy
TYPE OF ETHICS: Modern history
SIGNIFICANCE: The author of *The Life of Reason: Or, the Phases of Human Progress* (1905-1906), *Scepticism and Animal Faith* (1923), and *Realms of Being* (1927-1940), Santayana posited an evolution of ethics that led to lifestyles that emphasized detachment, contemplation, kindness, faith, and a sense of irony about human failings.

A materialist and a gentle skeptic, George Santayana expressed himself as sensitively in his extensive formal and philosophical writings as he did in his poetry and novels. Pushing doubt as far as he could, he ended his explorations believing that everything could be doubted except, possibly, faith. Such "animal faith" sprang, he explained, from humankind's survival instincts. Santayana's somewhat Platonic ideal world arose from primitive magic and science and took a higher form in religion. The ethics that he derived from his philosophizing were explained as the results of a three-phase historical evolution. Early, or prerational, morality, although culturally rich, was crude and without consistent application. Its refinement, rational morality, was a vital outgrowth of humankind's general adherence to the dictates of reason and, as the nineteenth century well understood, to a belief in progress.

The horrendous effects of two world wars, however, supplanted the positivism of rational morality with postrational pessimism. With little that was positive distinguishing this world, humankind's attention shifted to the promise of otherworldliness—for Santayana, the sad end of ethical development. After years of teaching at Harvard University, Santayana, the recipient of an inheritance, took up residence in Rome, thereafter exemplifying a lifestyle that conformed with his ethics. It was a contemplative existence marked by a kindly, tolerant skepticism and detachment. Able to cultivate the interrelated values of science, art, and religion, he came as close as a doubter could to assessing the benefits of his ideal society.

Clifton K. Yearley

SEE ALSO: Comte, Auguste; Morality; Pessimism and optimism.

Sartre, Jean-Paul

IDENTIFICATION: French philosopher, playwright, and novelist
BORN: June 21, 1905, Paris, France
DIED: April 15, 1980, Paris, France
TYPE OF ETHICS: Modern history
SIGNIFICANCE: The leading proponent of modern existentialist thought, Sartre departed from traditional ethical theory with his subjectivist perception of human morality. He is the author of *Being and Nothingness* (*L'Être et le néant*, 1943), *Existentialism and Humanism* (*L'Existentialisme est un Humanisme*, 1946), and various plays and novels reflecting existentialist themes.

At the heart of Sartrean ethics is the same basic premise that defines Jean-Paul Sartre's larger existentialist philosophy: that humanity makes itself. There is no created human nature and thus no prescribed grounds for behavior apart from what the individual chooses. This is not to say that ethics was peripheral to Sartre, or simply an afterthought. Even during the formative days of his philosophical career, before World War II, he emphasized the need for "authenticity" in human behavior, which is one of the cardinal tenets of his theory of morality.

His first novel, *Nausea* (*La Nausée*, 1938), is the story of a young scholar seeking to learn more about

an obscure historical figure, and his research leads him to face the universal human tendency to distort real identity. For Sartre, this "unauthenticity" precluded genuine morality by denying the most elemental truth. Sartre's experiences in World War II—witnessing the defeat of France by Germany and his own imprisonment in a Nazi camp—further convinced him that morality must emanate from candidly facing the truth about one's existence.

EXISTENCE PRECEDES ESSENCE

In Sartre's thought, there was no higher being, no God who had created human nature, and thus no transcendent basis for ethics. "There is no human nature," he wrote, "since there is no God to conceive it." Candidly atheistic, Sartre turned away from traditional religion. An individual, he argued, exists before he or she has a nature (essence), and the essence that a person acquires is the result of his or her own choices and their translation into action. The pivotal emphasis is upon action, for intentions alone do not shape essence.

Jean-Paul Sartre. (Library of Congress)

1313

If this seems to place Sartre clearly within a relativist genre of ethics, other factors qualify the apparent radical individualism of his thinking about morality. The first is his unflagging zeal for human responsibility. Although one does shape one's own essence, one is also responsible—for the sake of authenticity—to be consistent with the goals of one's chosen way of life. For example, one who eschews dishonesty can hardly spend his or her life lying or otherwise deceiving others. Responsibility in Sartrean ethics is tantamount to commitment, a view that has an interesting correlation with more conventional ethical thinking in the Judeo-Christian and other great major religious traditions.

A second dimension of Sartrean ethical thought that limits extreme relativism and individualism is Sartre's perception of "bad faith" (*mauvaise foi*). It is bad faith, to Sartre, to pretend—particularly to oneself—to be something that one is not. Social role-playing such as "being" a student, professor, worker, or attorney is one level of such bad faith, but so is assuming that one's being is exhausted by such a definition. People are more than the social roles they play, and morality is much more than being good at performing the expected behavior patterns. Although there is no one in the final analysis to help one make choices, one is responsible to one's past and anticipated future to be sincerely what one is.

Furthermore, Sartre defined individual existence in terms of broader human existence. Just as a person is the product of the past, he or she is also relational. The surrounding world of things, as well as other people, is an integral part of one's existence and therefore morality. In the play *No Exit* (*Huis clos*, pr. 1944, pb. 1945), the characters are in Hell, which is symbolized by a small room where each is subjected to the piercing gaze of the others. One of them, Ines, is a lesbian who is responsible for the death of her friend's husband. Like Garcin, a deserter, and Estelle, a child-killer, Ines can find no escape from the others' eyes and presumed judgment.

No less a philosopher than Immanuel Kant had raised similar moral issues, but he did so in terms of the question of whether a person could legitimately want his behavior to be universal. Kant's "categorical imperative," as it is called, assumed a universal transcendent moral order. Sartre did not, but neither did he advocate behavior that did not in some sense aid the existence of others. If Sartre thus seemed to ap-proximate such concepts as love and universal moral premises, he remained humanistic in his ethical theory. The significance of others in one's ethics is that they also objectively exist and are part of the individual's responsibility.

BEING-FOR-ITSELF

Basic to this line of ethical reasoning is Sartre's distinction between being-for-itself (*pour-soi*) and being-in-itself (*en-soi*). Being-in-itself is the type of existence that defines things. A rock's essence and being are identical. There is no self-conscious reflection, no selfhood at stake. In short, there are no choices to be made by things. Human existence is radically different, a being-for-itself; that is, the human mode of existence is one of active choices and bearing the responsibilities for the outcome of those choices. In that sense, it is being-for-itself. Humanity also exists "*en-soi*," however, and this dual nature demands responsibility. A tree or rock cannot decide, either for itself or for other things, what to do or be. Humans can and must. The individual is in the present, facing the de facto past and facing a future that requires continued decision making and acting on those decisions responsibly.

IMPLICATIONS FOR ETHICAL CONDUCT

In the Sartrean view of human life, nothing counts more than responsibility. Indeed, responsibility is the essence of being human. With no higher moral order either to shape one's essence or by which to judge one's actions, one must face squarely individual responsibility as well as the possible impact that one's behavior might have on others. Sartre's own estimation of the ethical implications of his ideas focused on the notion that the individual's quest for being is related to that of humanity as a whole. People are, he argued, agents "by whom the world comes into being." Lacking in Sartrean ethics is a transcendent source of value, but there are good reasons in the existentialist perspective to love, to help others, and to discipline one's actions.

Thomas R. Peake

FURTHER READING

Catalano, Joseph S. *Good Faith, and Other Essays: Perspectives on a Sartrean Ethics*. Lanham, Md.: Rowman & Littlefield, 1996.

Greene, Norman Nathaniel. *Jean-Paul Sartre: The*

Existentialist Ethic. Westport, Conn.: Greenwood Press, 1980.

McBride, William L., ed. *Existentialist Ethics*. New York: Garland, 1997.

Meszaros, Istvan. *Search for Freedom*. Vol. 1 in *The Work of Sartre*. Atlantic Highlands, N.J.: Humanities Press, 1979.

Nass, Arne. *Four Modern Philosophers: Carnap, Wittgenstein, Heidegger, Sartre*. Translated by Alastair Hannay. Chicago: University of Chicago Press, 1968.

Richter, Liselotte. *Jean-Paul Sartre*. Translated by Fred D. Wieck. New York: Frederick Ungar, 1970.

Warnock, Mary. *Existentialist Ethics*. New York: St. Martin's Press, 1967.

SEE ALSO: Absurd, The; Beauvoir, Simone de; *Being and Nothingness*; Existentialism; Heidegger, Martin; Intersubjectivity; Subjectivism.

Schindler, Oskar

IDENTIFICATION: German industrialist
BORN: April 28, 1908, Zwittau, Moravia, Austria-Hungary
DIED: October 9, 1974, Frankfurt, Germany
TYPE OF ETHICS: Human rights
SIGNIFICANCE: Schindler saved eleven hundred Jews from certain death during the Holocaust. His actions testify that ordinary people facing extreme danger can act in an ethical manner.

Nothing in Oskar Schindler's early life suggested that he would one day become a moral hero. A poor student, he was expelled from school at the age of sixteen for playing pranks. After marrying in 1928, Schindler soon became bored with his wife; he frequented taverns and took up with other women. After his father went bankrupt in 1935, Schindler became a salesman for the Moravian Electrotechnic Company. In 1938 he joined a local branch of Adolf Hitler's Nazi Party. During that same year, the German intelligence service recruited Schindler to gather military information during his business travels in Poland.

One month after the German army occupied Poland in September, 1939, Schindler arrived at

Oskar Schindler in 1968. (AP/Wide World Photos)

Krakow looking for moneymaking opportunities. In Krakow he acquired a Polish enamelware company that the Nazis had confiscated from its Jewish owner. Cultivating the friendship of high-ranking Nazi officials, Schindler showered them with gifts and in early 1940 received contracts to produce field kitchenware for the German army. The Jewish slave labor that Schindler used in his plant made his contracts particularly lucrative. Schindler became wealthy and lived lavishly, supporting several mistresses.

At first, Schindler objected to Nazi mistreatment of Jews because arbitrary abuse of his workers interfered with efficient operation of his factory. However, after he realized, in mid-1942, that the Nazis intended to kill all Jews, Schindler's opposition became more principled, more far-reaching, and increasingly dangerous to him. He was arrested on three separate occasions, but each time he managed to be released. Schindler then began deliberately staffing his factory with Jews who appeared to be in greatest danger of being sent to Nazi death camps. He certified children, intellectuals, and the elderly as machinists whose labor was vital to the German war effort.

SCHINDLER'S LIST

After the Germans eliminated Krakow's Jewish ghetto, Schindler, at his own expense, set up a sub-camp around his factory so that his workers could avoid living in the terrifying Plaszow labor camp. In September, 1944, Schindler learned that the Plaszow camp was about to close; all its inmates were to be sent to death camps. Through cajolery and bribery, he received permission to move his factory to Moravia, in eastern Czechoslovakia, taking his workers with him. The names of the laborers who were to go with him made up the famous "Schindler's list" of eight hundred men and three hundred women who survived the Holocaust because of Schindler's efforts. When the women on Schindler's list were mistakenly sent to the Auschwitz death camp, Schindler personally arranged for their release—the only mass rescue reported by Holocaust survivors.

Why Schindler, ostensibly an unscrupulous fortune hunter, risked losing his life and wealth to aid the Polish Jews is unclear. He afterward said it was the human thing to do; however, few others in positions similar to his acted as he did. When Schindler arrived in the American Zone of Austria in 1945, he was penniless, and he never again succeeded in business.

During the final decades of his life, Schindler lived on donations from the Jews whose lives he once had saved. In 1993, nearly two decades after Schindler died, director Stephen Spielberg told the story of his heroism in *Schindler's List*, a film honored with several Academy Awards, including best picture.

Milton Berman

FURTHER READING

Brecher, Elinor J. *Schindler's Legacy: True Stories of the List Survivors*. New York: Dutton, 1994.

Keneally, Thomas. *Schindler's List*. New York: Simon & Schuster, 1982.

Roberts, Jack L. *The Importance of Oskar Schindler*. San Diego, Calif.: Lucent Books, 1996.

SEE ALSO: Anti-Semitism; Bystanders; Concentration camps; Genocide and democide; Heroism; Holocaust; Nazi science; Nazism; Nuremberg Trials; Slavery.

Schopenhauer, Arthur

IDENTIFICATION: German philosopher
BORN: February 22, 1788, Danzig (now Gdańsk), Poland
DIED: September 21, 1860, Frankfurt am Main (now in Germany)
TYPE OF ETHICS: Modern history
SIGNIFICANCE: Schopenhauer's pessimistic philosophy, put forward in *The World as Will and Representation* (*Die Welt als Wille und Vorstellung*, 1819), advocated an ethics of asceticism, yet his emphasis on the primacy of will influenced both will-to-power thinkers and modern existentialists.

Financial independence enabled Arthur Schopenhauer to devote his life to philosophy, and he developed his pessimistic system as a follower of Immanuel Kant. In *The World as Will and Representation*, he identifies the will as the Kantian thing-in-itself that comprehends the external world through the mental constructs of time, space, and causality. As Schopenhauer understood it, will comprises intellect, personality, and the potential for growth and development. Although powerful, it is not free but is controlled by causation like all else that exists.

Confronting a meaningless existence and a godless universe, Schopenhauer concluded that ethical behavior requires withdrawal from the pleasures of life in favor of contemplation. The individual must tame the will so that it becomes less insistent on its egoistic desires, which lead only to further desires. Where others are concerned, the proper attitude is compassion, since they too suffer an identical fate. The truth of Christianity, according to Schopenhauer, lies in its early emphasis on renunciation of the world and an ascetic life. Although he failed to clarify how this asceticism could be achieved in the absence of freedom, Schopenhauer's work includes a strong suggestion. Because human actions are explicable through motives, he equates motive with cause. Thus, causation may be rooted in intellectual concepts. As the individual recognizes the futility of existence, he or she can become compassionate toward others and accept the futility of desire.

Stanley Archer

SEE ALSO: Asceticism; *Beyond Good and Evil*; Compassion; Pessimism and optimism; Wickedness; Will.

Schweitzer, Albert

IDENTIFICATION: German theologian and missionary
BORN: January 14, 1875, Kaysersberg, Upper
    Alsace, Germany (now in France)
DIED: September 4, 1965, Lambaréné, Gabon
TYPE OF ETHICS: Modern history
SIGNIFICANCE: A important theologian who was al-
    ways interested in public affairs, Schweitzer used
    his *Philosophy of Civilization* (*Kulturphilosophie
    I: Verfall und Wiederaufbau der Kultur,* 1923) to
    explore the ways in which civilization had be-
    come "self-destroying." He received the 1952
    Nobel Peace Prize.

In his early adulthood, Albert Schweitzer was an
organist, a music scholar, and a world figure in theological studies. In 1905, Schweitzer began studying to be a physician so that he could be a mission
doctor in equatorial Africa. In 1913, he opened a
clinic in Gabon, doing much of the building with his
own hands. He lived there for most of the rest of his
life.

Schweitzer's work in Africa caused him to contemplate world civilization as a whole. He developed
an ethics that he called "Reverence for Life." He believed that life itself was of the highest value, but that
life is harsh and self-destructive. People should treat
every form of life with the same reverence that they
afford their own. They should do this by trying to
reach their own highest level of perfection and by
helping their society reach perfection. These two
goals are often contradictory: In raising the individual, one must keep in mind one's responsibilities
to the society. In addition, because humans destroy
something or someone by their every act, every action taken to attain perfection also results in destruction. This awareness drove Schweitzer's philan-
thropy but also made him an unhappy man.

Cynthia A. Bily

SEE ALSO: Ahiṁsā; Morality; Nobel Peace Prizes.

Science

DEFINITION: Formal theorization and experimenta-
    tion designed to produce objective knowledge,
    especially knowledge of the general laws govern-
    ing the natural world.
TYPE OF ETHICS: Scientific ethics
SIGNIFICANCE: Modern standards of scientific in-
    quiry require science to be conducted as far as
    possible in an impartial, disinterested fashion, but
    most forms of science cannot be conducted at all
    without major sources of funding which may in-
    fluence inquiry either directly or indirectly. Ethi-
    cal issues raised by science also include appropri-
    ate treatment of living research subjects and the
    practical effects upon the real world of scientific
    discovery.

Science, ethics, and philosophy interact in a range of
arenas. The development of ethical standards—that
is, codes of behavior that govern moral decisions—
has been a major issue for the great philosophers and
thinkers throughout time. Traditionally, metaphysical hypotheses and religious beliefs have governed
the attempts of humankind to fathom the unfathom-
able, to come to grips with mortality, and to hold
themselves to a set of standards of conduct. The science of the twentieth century influenced this search,
in some cases incorporating, in some cases rejecting,
religion as a part of that effort.

The writings of Albert Einstein epitomize the attempt to reconcile science with religion. Einstein
holds a central place in modern history because of
his groundbreaking ideas on theoretical physics. He
writes, "To know what is impenetrable to us really
exists, manifesting itself as the highest wisdom and
the most radiant beauty which our dull faculties can
comprehend only in their most primitive forms—this
knowledge, this feeling, is at the center of true reli-
giousness."

At the same time, the achievements of science and
technology have posed their own moral dilemmas.
For example, the theory of relativity, developed by
Einstein during the early twentieth century, set the
stage for the development of the atom bomb. In the
face of a creation with such awesome destructive potential, however, the question is posed: To what extent should scientists involve themselves in the ultimate consequences of their research?

For this generation and for generations to come, the advances in the fields of genetics and biomedicine are likely to give rise to similar dilemmas. The much-seen film *Jurassic Park* (1993) focused the popular consciousness on the risks inherent in bioengineering technology. With all their inherent potential for good, genetic technologies may carry as yet unknown risks and consequences.

The limited amount of funding available for scientific research has forced both scientists and those responsible for science policy to make choices regarding which projects to fund. Should "big" projects such as the Human Genome Project or the Superconducting Supercollider (SSC) be funded or should many smaller but important projects receive government or private monies? Where should these "big" projects be located? Should basic research be targeted in the hope of eventual payoff or should applications research be the major focus? Are political and economic concerns playing a too-important role in the funding process? To what extent should science and mathematics education be considered a priority?

During the late 1980's and early 1990's, the spotlight turned on ethical conduct and misconduct in scientific research. A major challenge to both the scientific community and the community at large is this: What is the appropriate response to scientific fraud and misconduct? What should be the response to the "gray areas" of even more problematical situations of conflict of interest or "honest mistakes"?

PHILOSOPHICAL ISSUES

As a guide in an attempt to deal with the range of ethical issues involved in scientific research, the scientific community and the community at large might look to philosophical thinkers who have dealt with issues in this field. In fact, from antiquity through the beginning of the twenty-first century, the great thinkers concerned themselves with issues not only of philosophy, ethics, and morality but also with those of science. Aristotle, René Descartes, and Immanuel Kant made major contributions not only to philosophy but also to the sciences. Wolfgang von Goethe, although best known for his literary works, also wrote extensively on the natural sciences.

At the same time, science has had a major, sometimes even a revolutionary, impact on the values and the worldview of society. The theories of Galileo and Isaac Newton on planetary motion and the views of Charles Darwin on the evolution of species had that kind of revolutionary impact. Similarly, the development of the atom bomb strongly influenced the political and social climate of the latter half of the twentieth century. It is likely that major advances in computer science and bioengineering now taking place will have their impact well into the twenty-first century. It is equally likely that scientists and society will have to deal with the ethical dilemmas posed by the positive and negative capabilities of these technologies.

The analysis of moral and ethical decisions in science might make use of following principles of ethics and philosophy.

The value neutrality of science is epitomized by the vision of the scientist as the ceaseless seeker motivated only by the search for truth. This theory has its basis in features first introduced in the seventeenth and eighteenth century. The theory of the scientific method, which is known as inductivism, has relied on this concept and postulates that science begins with the collection of data, goes on to generalize about laws and theories, and makes predictions that can be proved. The theory of inductivism had its roots in the writings of Francis Bacon in the sixteenth and seventeenth century and in the empiricist theories developed by David Hume in the eighteenth century. The inductivist view was supported by the Cambridge school of Bertrand Russell during the early twentieth century and the Vienna circle of the 1920's and 1930's.

Critics of the Vienna circle and of inductivism have included Karl Popper. Popper maintains that the concepts and postulates (which are ultimately proved or disproved by experimentation) are the products not necessarily of observations but of potentially "unjustified (and unjustifiable) anticipations, by guesses, by tentative solutions to our problems, by conjectures. The conjectures are controlled by criticism; that is, by attempted refutations, which include severely critical tests." The source of the hypothesis is irrelevant; the originator of the hypothesis or postulate joins in the criticism and testing of the hypothesis that he or she has proposed. Popper is considered to have inaugurated the current era in the philosophy of science.

MISCONDUCT IN SCIENCE

The embarrassment of the "honest mistake" is far surpassed by the violation of the ethos of science of the outright fraud. Fraud in science impugns the integrity of the research process and destroys the trust on which scientific achievement is built. At the same time, intentionally fraudulent actions undermine the confidence of society and the body politic in science and scientific inquiry. Potentially, the effects of fraud may be horrific; if, for example, a medical treatment should be based on fraudulent results.

Many scientists base their codes of conduct on the example of role models and on what some have termed the "school of hard knocks." A more systematic approach has been contributed by professional organizations who have contributed their expertise. A recent contribution is a 1989 publication of the National Academy of Science, *On Being a Scientist.* Other resources include a 1992 report, likewise from the National Academy of Sciences, called *Responsible Science: Ensuring the Integrity of the Research Process.* These publications and others often cite as examples of fraud and misconduct the actions of William Summerlin at Sloan-Kettering during the 1970's, those of John Darsee at Harvard and those of Stephen E. Breuning in Pittsburgh during the early 1980's, and those of Thereza Imanishi-Kari and Nobel laureate David Baltimore during the late 1980's.

A well-known and rather tragic example of fraud was that of William Summerlin. During the early 1970's, Summerlin came to the Sloan-Kettering Institute as the chief of a laboratory working on transplantation immunology. A laboratory assistant noticed that the supposedly black grafts on white mice could be washed off with ethanol. It turned out that Summerlin had used a black felt-tipped marker to mimic the appearance of black grafts. Additional discrepancies regarding Summerlin's results on corneal transplantations led an internal committee to recommend that Summerlin take a medical leave of absence and to condemn Summerlin's behavior as irresponsible.

During the early 1980's, John Darsee had worked under the supervision of Eugene Braunwauld, a well-known cardiologist at Harvard University. At Harvard, three coworkers apparently observed Darsee fake data for an experiment. An internal investigation for the next few months found no discrepancies. A subsequent National Institutes of Health (NIH) investigation, however, demonstrated that virtually every paper that Darsee had produced was fabricated.

Another episode involved a professor at the University of Pittsburgh, Stephen E. Breuning, who had become prominent for his expertise in the medical treatment of mental retardation. In 1983, Breuning's former mentor, Robert Sprague, questioned the veracity of his student's research. Eventually, it turned out that much of Breuning's data came from experiments that had not been performed on subjects that had not even been tested.

An exceptionally disturbing case was that of Thereza Imanishi-Kari and Nobel laureate David Baltimore of the Massachusettes Intitute of Technology (MIT). A postdoctoral fellow at Imanishi-Kari's laboratory, Margot O'Toole, uncovered evidence that Imanishi-Kari may have fabricated certain results appearing in a paper in *Cell* on gene transplantation, a paper that was also coauthored by Baltimore. University inquiries at MIT dismissed O'Toole's concerns, but a few years later, the concerns resurfaced, resulting in ultimate retraction of the *Cell* paper and investigations by the NIH, Congressman John Dingell, and the Secret Service. While the U.S. attorney in the case declined to prosecute Imanishi-Kari, as of this writing, clouds continued to obscure her career and that of Baltimore.

During the late 1980's and the early 1990's, more than two hundred allegations of misconduct in science were received by the U.S. government. One study has indicated that approximately 40 percent of the deans of graduate schools knew of cases of misconduct at their institutions. A survey sponsored by the American Association for the Advancement of Science likewise indicated that during the first ten years, 27 percent of scientists indicated that they had personally encountered incidences of falsified, fabricated, or plagiarized research.

In fact, by the late 1980's and into the early 1990's, articles on misconduct in science continued to constitute the vast majority of references on science ethics produced by computerized literature searches. During the late 1980's, incidents of apparent fraud, plagiarism, and misconduct drew the attention of the Subcommittee on Oversight and Investigations of the U.S. House of Representatives, chaired by Congressman John D. Dingell. The threat not only to the research process but also to the autonomy of the scientific community posed by examples of abuse has challenged scientists to develop ways of dealing with misconduct within their ranks. Congressman Dingell himself acknowledged the drawbacks of resolving issues of misconduct in the congressional hearing.

"Encouraging science to police itself is far preferable to the alternatives . . . But with every case [which is] is covered up or mishandled, pressure builds for such extreme measures."

GRAY AREAS

Certain instances of apparent fraud violate any accepted standards of moral or ethical conduct. Many other situations, however, fall into what might be termed a "gray area."

For example, a vexing question concerns the allocation of credit for scientific achievements. The bitter dispute between Newton and Gottfried Wilhelm Leibniz over who first discovered the calculus is paralleled by the twentieth century quarrel between Robert Gallo, the renowned acquired immunodeficiency syndrome (AIDS) researcher at the NIH, and his counterpart at the Pasteur Institute, Luc Montagnier, over the discovery of the AIDS virus.

Also in what might be termed a "gray area" are issues of "conflict of interest." (Outright bribery to promote fabrication of results would violate most standards of conduct.) By the late 1980's and early 1990's, doubts over the degree to which scientists' findings might be influenced by funding sources led journals such as *Science, JAMA,* and the *New England Journal of Medicine (NEJM)* to adopt standards of disclosure for potential conflicts of interest. The *JAMA* and *NEJM* standards stressed financial conflicts; the *Science* standards also include a range of other relationships that might possibly have influenced the scientist's work. The possibility of abuse inherent in these kinds of standards has led to a "backlash" as scientists and physicians engaged in medical research talked of a "New McCarthyism in Science" and evoked the possibility that not only financial conflicts but also such factors as religion and sexual orientation might be included in the disclosure standards. Kenneth J. Rothman, writing in the *Journal of the American Medical Association,* cites Popper (*The Open Society and Its Enemies,* 1966) in noting the impossibility of achieving full objectivity in any scientific endeavor.

Equally problematical for the scientist—and also in a "gray area"—are the new ethical problems created by scientific discoveries. Are scientists responsible for the ethical and moral uses of their discoveries? For example, should decisions about the use of the atom bomb have been in the hands of the scien-

tists or, as actually occurred, in the hands of the politicians? Should scientists attempt to exert any kind of control over the uses of their discoveries?

A tradition of political neutrality governed science from the seventeenth century through World War I. Bacon, for example, conceived of science as a "new instrument." The chemist Robert Hooke warned the founders of the Royal Society of London that their business was to "improve the natural knowledge of things, not meddling with Divinity, Metaphysics, Moralls, Politicks, Grammar, Rhetorick or Logic." World War I, however, disrupted the tradition of neutrality as technological solutions not only made up for the losses of raw materials caused by the war but also played a major role in enhancing the lethal effect of explosive and chemical weapons.

Political authorities continued to come into the scientific arena with the advocacy by Joseph Stalin's regime of the 1930's and 1940's of the genetic theories of T. D. Lysenko. Nazi Germany purged its Jewish and left-wing scientists. Some disapproving scientists left the country, but others remained, adhering to a tradition that held no place for social responsibility and hoping to exert influence on the Nazi regime. World War II gave impetus to research in a range of areas, as synthetics replaced raw materials and new drugs such as penicillin became available. Refugee scientists from Nazi Germany encouraged preliminary research on an atom bomb. The ensuing success of the Manhattan Project resulted in the explosion of the atom bombs over Hiroshima and Nagasaki, which was followed by the development of atomic capability by the Soviet Union in 1949.

The dilemma for scientists is this: To what extent should they concern themselves with the ultimate consequences of their discoveries? Is scientific knowledge and discovery an inherent good? Are the risks of scientific and technological advances as important as the potential benefits?

The challenges posed by the development of the atom bomb are paralleled by issues raised by the scientific advances of the 1980's and 1990's. The development of computer and electronic technology raises some important issues of privacy and the possibility of social control. Equally problematical are issues raised by advances in the biological and medical sciences.

An additional ethical issue concerns the eradication of racism and sexism in science. For example, a particularly shocking example of racism involved the Tuskegee syphilis experiment. During a forty-year study that received federal funds, African American victims of syphilis were denied treatment even after penicillin became available. The apparent justification was that the denial of treatment was essential to the study of the progress of the disease.

A challenge for researchers is to design studies of common illnesses (for example, myocardial infarction, diabetes) that not only provide sufficient data on the white middle-class male population but also include information on which to base the treatment of minority and female patients.

ALLOCATION OF RESOURCES

Scientific research in the United States is funded to a large extent by the U.S. government. Major corporations, such as large pharmaceutical companies, support much of the rest. What are the implications of these facts?

The marriage of science and government dates back to World War II and Vannevar Bush, who then headed the Office of Scientific Research and Development. In the system that evolved, research proposals are initiated by the researcher, who usually works in a university or institute setting. At the same time, funding was a federal responsibility, and although some research was taking place in government laboratories, most basic research was undertaken in universities. There arose not a single funding agency, as envisioned by Bush, but a multiplicity of agencies— responsible for funding basic research.

By the late 1980's, the numbers of individuals involved in basic research had increased, while the pool of dollars available stayed the same. The result was that a far smaller proportion of grant proposals were being funded. For example, in 1980, the NIH approved up to one in three "meritorious" grants for funding, while by the 1990's, fewer than one in five grants received approval. The system in place through the latter half of the twentieth century achieved scientific productivity, as measured by the numbers of citations; prestige, measured by the numbers of Nobel Prizes; and some degree of economic productivity.

During the late 1980's and early 1990's, the lessened availability of funding and the potential for political abuse and "pork-barrel" science led some experts to question the current criteria for funding

scientific research. At the same time, the costs of new technologies and issues relating to the use of those technologies have led some people to question the direction of public policy on science issues. This position has yet to be adopted by public policy makers. The direction of governmental policy at the beginning of the 1990's is reiterated by Donna Shalala, Secretary of the federal department of Health and Human Services. Shalala states:

> The last thing we should try to do is try to curb technology in our attempt to deal with costs or to slow down our investment in research. . . . The issue is how you use technology, far more than whether we should keep producing technology. Rather than beating up on technology, we need to get scientists and administrators to think about the more appropriate use of it.

Adele Lubell

FURTHER READING

Bell, Robert. *Impure Science: Fraud, Compromise and Political Influence in Scientific Research.* New York: John Wiley & Sons, 1992. The author claims to document how some members of the scientific community have fostered influence, misconduct, and fraud in scientific research. The volume is most valuable for its account of some less-well-known examples of alleged fraud or misconduct.

Claude, Richard Pierre. *Science in the Service of Human Rights.* Philadelphia: University of Pennsylvania Press, 2002. Seeks to address the political and ethical dimensions of science and the scientific dimensions of socio-political ethics. Examines such issues as cloning and the rights of African people with AIDS to have access to pharmaceutical treatment.

Dingell, J. D. "Shattuck Lecture: Misconduct in Medical Research." *New England Journal of Medicine* 328 (June 3, 1993): 1610-1615. Congressman Dingell is best known for his role as chairman of the Subcommittee on Oversight and Investigations of the U.S. House of Representatives. Dingell played a major role in governmental investigation into scientific misconduct during the late 1980's and early 1990's. The article is the address he gave to the Massachussetts Medical Society in Boston in May, 1992.

Gillies, Donald. *Philosophy of Science in the Twentieth Century.* Cambridge, Mass.: Blackwell Scientific, 1993. The author discusses some important trends in the philosophy of science in the twentieth century. He particularly focuses on the ideas of Karl Popper, with whom Gillies studied during the late 1960's.

Martino, J. P. *Science Funding.* New Brunswick, N.J.: Transaction, 1992. This volume documents the history and current status of trends in the funding of scientific research, from Vannevar Bush to the present.

Mosedale, F. E., ed. *Philosophy and Science.* Englewood Cliffs, N.J.: Prentice-Hall, 1979. Includes the writings of philosophers, scientists, and others on important issues in science. Many selections discuss ethical and moral concerns.

National Academy of Sciences. Committee on the Conduct of Science. *On Being a Scientist.* Washington, D.C.: National Academy Press, 1989. A booklet that offers the beginning and active scientist an introduction to the ethos of science.

Seebauer, Edmund G., and Robert L. Barry. *Fundamentals of Ethics for Scientists and Engineers.* New York: Oxford University Press, 2001. Practical textbook designed for the student of ethics or of engineering that takes a hands-on approach to scientific ethics. Contains many specific examples of ethical dilemmas in science, some actual and some fictionalized, in order to illustrate the virtue-based principles of ethical practice endorsed by the authors.

United States Committee on Science, Engineering, and Public Policy's Panel on Scientific Responsibility and the Conduct of Research. *Responsible Science: Ensuring the Integrity of the Research Process.* 2 vols. Washington, D.C.: National Academy Press, 1992-1993. Comprehensive volumes that attempt to delineate issues around integrity in science research and devise appropriate procedures for dealing with misconduct.

SEE ALSO: Bacon, Francis; Bioethics; Darwin, Charles; Experimentation; Hume, David; Industrial research; Manhattan Project; Nazi science; Psychology; Technology.

Scientology

DEFINITION: Controversial modern religious organization

DATES: Founded as a church in 1954

TYPE OF ETHICS: Religious ethics

SIGNIFICANCE: Many former members of the Church of Scientology have accused the organization of such cultlike practices as brainwashing, intimidation, and financially controlling its members. Many people also question Scientology's claims to be a religion, accusing its leaders of using the church as a ruse to exploit the tax-exempt status and other privileges afforded to religious organizations.

The foundation of any new "religion" is an audacious undertaking, as most people's notions of spirituality are inextricably linked to the traditions of their cultural legacies, making the exact characteristics of the concept difficult to define. Nonetheless, religions are generally regarded as systems of belief in which spiritual values are held in higher regard than material values.

During the early 1950's science-fiction novelist L. Ron Hubbard attempted to found an entirely new church based on a belief system that he called "dianetics." Difficult to describe succinctly, dianetics is a practice that combines elements of Buddhism, psychology, and new age mysticism into an eclectic philosophy that is characterized by its penchant for forms of discipline and systematization. In this regard, dianetics is more akin to the pragmatic, materialistic focus of modern scientific thought than to what Hubbard viewed as the metaphysical vagaries and superstitions of traditional religion. The Church of Scientology that Hubbard formed in 1954 takes its name from its ostensibly unique synthesis of traditional spiritual principles and scientific rationality. It focuses especially on efforts to control negative emotions that, according to Hubbard, impede the individual's progress toward inner peace, satisfying interactions with others, intellectual growth, and material prosperity.

As dianetics and Scientology became well known during the 1960's and 1970's, so did the controversies surrounding these new belief systems. Detractors of Scientology dismissed it as a legal entity rather than a spiritual one, many claiming that Scientologists merely organized a "church" in order to receive tax-exempt status. Critics cited the ambiguities and secrecy that make it difficult for outsiders to understand Scientology's organization and belief system, as well as the organization's apparent emphasis on material success as a measure of its members' spiritual growth.

By the late 1960's, the church's net worth was estimated at one billion dollars. The fact that that sum rivaled the assets of many major traditional religious institutions called Scientology's financial practices into question. Scientology became the target of media criticism and eventually litigation by those claiming that the group brainwashed its members, required them to pay large sums of money to advance to the higher levels of membership, expected them aggressively to recruit new members, and systematically alienated them from relatives and friends who were not involved with the church.

Critics of Scientology also cited the group's penchant for science-fiction symbolism and imagery as casting serious doubts on its authenticity as a genuine religious institution. Although the symbolism of Scientology evokes elements a variety of traditional belief systems, images of spacecraft and extraterrestrial life abound in its rituals and mythos. Scientology's popularity demonstrates that many followers throughout the world believe that they have benefited from its rationalistic and original approach to spiritual enlightenment. However, those who accuse Scientology of being a cult that manipulates its members to its own self-serving ends cite such things as its references to space travel and extraterrestrial life and its eclectic and allegedly haphazard reinterpretation of traditional religious ideas. Nevertheless, Scientology remains widely discussed and debated as a development in the evolution of contemporary religious thought and practice.

FURTHER READING

Corydon, Bent. *L. Ron Hubbard: Messiah or Madman?* Fort Lee, N.J.: Barricade Books, 1992.

Hubbard, L. Ron. *Dianetics: The Modern Science of Mental Health.* Los Angeles: Bridge Publications, 1986.

Theology and Practice of a Contemporary Religion: Scientology. Los Angeles: Bridge Publications, 1998.

Gregory D. Horn

SEE ALSO: Buddhist ethics; Mysticism; Psychology; Religion; Science; Taxes.

Scorched-earth policies

DEFINITION: Military strategies calling for the destruction of the natural environment, particularly food resources, as a deliberate means of waging warfare

TYPE OF ETHICS: Military ethics

SIGNIFICANCE: Whether offensive or defensive, scorched-earth tactics do harm to noncombatants and cause environmental and economic damage that can outlast by years the war of which they are a part. They raise the fundamental issue of the ethical limits of warfare and whether warring parties have any moral obligations to limit the ill effects of their actions or whether belief in such obligations is unrealistic in the context of war.

In its narrow sense of setting the grass of the plains on fire, the practice of scorched-earth warfare is particularly associated with the steppelands of Russia and the Ukraine. The first attested example of the practice occurred during a war between the Scythians and the Persians in 512 B.C.E. (recorded by Herodotus in 440 B.C.E.). The Scythians, a nation of nomadic horsemen, lured the Persian army of Darius ever deeper into the steppe by retreating before the Persians. Some Scythians then doubled back, destroying the grass and poisoning the wells along the Persians' original route, believing that this would prevent the Persian cavalry's escape (since their horses would be deprived of food). As the Scythians candidly recalled, however, their plan backfired. The Persians escaped by retracing their footsteps, despite the devastation they encountered.

MODERN WARFARE

Analogous tactics were used more than two millennia later. During the Russian retreat before the invading army of Napoleon Bonaparte in 1812, the Russians themselves burned Moscow and the croplands along the route of Napoleon's advance. When the tide of battle turned, the French army had to retreat through a devastated countryside that offered no food or shelter. This successful use of the scorched-earth policy as a patriotic and defensive tactic—enhanced by Leo Tolstoy's epic depiction of Russian sacrifices during 1812 in his historical novel *War and Peace* (1865-1869)—lent it an enduring positive aura, at least in the Russian context.

More typically, however, scorched-earth tactics used defensively have backfired. If one goes along with environmentalist Arthur Westing's interpretation that deliberate destruction of the land by other means, such as flooding, is also scorched-earth policy, then the most cataclysmic example in the twentieth century occurred during the second Sino-Japanese War (1937-1945). In 1938, as a defensive measure, the Chinese dynamited a major dam on the Yellow River. This temporarily halted the Japanese advance and resulted in several thousand Japanese casualties; in the long run, however, several hundred thousand Chinese, mainly civilians, drowned, and damage from flooding continued for a decade.

Scorched-earth tactics used offensively have tended to be successful in the short run. Major incidents of deliberate crop destruction as a means of offensive warfare have abounded throughout history. During the Peloponnesian Wars (431-404 B.C.E.), the Spartans repeatedly destroyed the Athenian grain crops (and, not incidentally, won the war); the Athenians did not choose to employ a tactic that until then had been used only by barbarians. Widespread crop destruction, in large part deliberate, accompanied the ravages of the Huns, the Vandals, and the Mongolian conquests (1213-1224). The Mongolian conquerors of Mesopotamia destroyed the ancient irrigation works on which agriculture had depended for millennia, and the Fertile Crescent became a desert. In the Thirty Years' War (1618-1638), the majority of Czech casualties (up to 75 percent of the population of Bohemia) resulted from starvation and disease caused by crop destruction.

The use of scorched-earth tactics increased in the modern era, and it came to be morally justified as a humane means of bringing war to a swifter conclusion. The theory was formulated in the American context during the U.S. Civil War (1861-1865) by two Union generals, Philip Sheridan and William Tecumseh Sherman. One of the many ways in which this war transformed civilization was an increased consideration of all factors that contributed to the war effort, including food itself. As part of a conscious policy of bringing the war home to the civilians who supported the soldiers, in order to make the war end quickly, Sheridan oversaw the destruction of about 2,700 square miles of agricultural land in the Shenandoah Valley, and Sherman's troops laid waste to about 15,000 square miles of rural Georgia (1864). As a result, the war did indeed end quickly. In view of the success of these tactics, they were incorporated into U.S. policy during late federal government wars with Native Americans and again during the U.S. intervention in the Philippine Insurrection around the turn of the twentieth century.

NUCLEAR WAR AS AN ALTERNATIVE

The apotheosis of the scorched-earth policy as a fast way to end a war, justified by the idea that there would be fewer total casualties, was the atom bombing of Hiroshima and Nagasaki in Japan in 1945. This action immediately ended Japanese participation in World War II, but it raised ethical questions that cannot be easily answered.

The ultimate scorched-earth policy would be a nuclear war, after which the affected parts of the earth would be so scorched as to be uninhabitable for thousands of years. The ultimate scorched-earth policy thus brings one back to the discovery made by the cunning Scythians who may be credited with inventing it in the first place: It tends to backfire. Defenders who employ the tactic find that they have a tiger by the tail: Both immediately and in the long run, they may do far more damage to themselves than to the invading enemy. Those who employ scorched-earth tactics offensively stand to lose on many counts: They put themselves in an extremely weak position in world opinion, since the policy will justifiably be termed barbaric; they are destroying the earth's resources, thereby impoverishing themselves as well as others; and they are moving in the direction of total war, which tends to blur distinctions not only between combatants and noncombatants but also between the opposing sides.

D. Gosselin Nakeeb

FURTHER READING

Chandler, D. G. *The Campaigns of Napoleon.* New York: Macmillan, 1966.

Levandowsky, Michael. "Environmental Consequences of Nuclear War." In *Security vs. Survival: The Nuclear Arms Race,* edited by Theresa C. Smith and Indu B. Singh. Boulder, Colo.: Lynne Rienner, 1985.

Liddell Hart, B. H. *Sherman: Soldier, Realist, American*. New York: Dodd, Mead, 1929.

Nash, J. R. *Darkest Hours: A Narrative Encyclopedia of Worldwide Disasters from Ancient Times to the Present*. Chicago: Nelson-Hall, 1976.

Thomas, William. *Scorched Earth: The Military's Assault on the Environment*. Philadelphia: New Society, 1995.

Westing, A. H. *Warfare in a Fragile World: Military Impact on the Human Environment*. London: Taylor & Francis, 1980.

_____, ed. *Environmental Warfare: A Technical, Legal, and Policy Appraisal*. London: Taylor & Francis, 1984.

SEE ALSO: Bioethics; Environmental ethics; Land mines; Military ethics; War.

Scott v. Sandford

THE EVENT: U.S. Supreme Court decision placing limits on Congress's ability to control slavery and determining that African Americans were not eligible to become U.S. citizens

DATE: Ruling made on March 6-7, 1857

TYPE OF ETHICS: Modern history

SIGNIFICANCE: The Supreme Court's decision in *Scott* strengthened slaveholders' claims that they had unlimited property rights to slaves and affirmed that slaves were legally incapable in principle of ever gaining the protections of the Bill of Rights.

Scott v. Sandford was the result of a suit for freedom by the slave Dred Scott. Scott's master had taken Scott to serve him during an army posting in the northern part of the Louisiana Purchase, where slavery had been prohibited by Congress. Eventually, Scott's master returned Scott to the slave state of Missouri. Scott sued for his freedom on the basis of his residence in a territory where slavery did not exist. Chief Justice Roger B. Taney ruled that Scott was still a slave and that Congress had no authority to prohibit slavery in American territories.

Congress had denied southerners due process of law under the Fifth Amendment by singling out their property, and not that of northerners, for restriction.

Furthermore, Taney ruled, the case was not properly before the Supreme Court. No person of African descent—whether slave or free—was a citizen of the United States with rights to bring suit in federal court. This case strengthened the power of slaveholders and undercut antislavery activists who were seeking a general abolition of slavery in U.S. territories.

Harold D. Tallant

SEE ALSO: Bill of Rights, U.S.; Citizenship; Civil rights and liberties; Slavery; Supreme Court, U.S.

Scottsboro case

THE EVENT: U.S. Supreme Court decision holding that states must provide counsel for indigent or ignorant defendants in capital cases

DATE: Ruling made on November 7, 1932

TYPE OF ETHICS: Race and ethnicity

SIGNIFICANCE: The Supreme Court's finding in the Scottsboro case, that deprivation of counsel in a capital case had denied the defendant a fair hearing, represented the first time the Court had held that a state criminal trial was defective under the due process clause of the Fourteenth Amendment. It thereby set a crucial precedent and paved the way for the general extension of the rights of the accused contained in the Bill of Rights, from federal to state courts.

The Scottsboro case (known technically as *Powell v. Alabama*) was one of several sensational cases that arose from the arrest and trial of seven young black men for the rape of two white women in Alabama. The men were quickly tried and sentenced to death in an atmosphere of great public excitement; units of the Alabama National Guard had to be called up to prevent the defendants from being lynched. At trial, no effective assignment or employment of counsel had been made, as the Supreme Court later found.

By a 7-2 vote, the Supreme Court ruled that the trial court's failure to assure effective representation of the defendants had deprived them of a fair hearing. Since notice and hearing are the central elements of due process, the convictions were reversed. This case provided a particularly significant precedent because the Court showed itself willing for the first time to in-

Clarence Norris, one of the men convicted in the Scottsboro case, leaving his Alabama prison cell in 1946—fifteen years after his wrongful arrest. (Library of Congress)

voke the due process clause of the Fourteenth Amendment to hold that a state criminal proceeding had deprived a defendant of a fundamental right.

Robert Jacobs

SEE ALSO: Bill of Rights, U.S.; Civil rights and liberties; Due process; Erroneous convictions; Rape; Supreme Court, U.S.

The Second Sex

IDENTIFICATION: Book by Simone de Beauvoir (1908-1986)
DATE: *Le Deuxième Sexe*, 1949 (English translation, 1953)
TYPE OF ETHICS: Sex and gender issues
SIGNIFICANCE: *The Second Sex* attempts to explain why women as a class remain oppressed. It advocates a constructivist view of gender, rejecting the essentialist view that gender traits are determined by biology.

Simone de Beauvoir rejects the Aristotelian position that women, because of their biological characteristics, must play a limited role in society. She further rejects Freudian psychology's position that woman's natural state is passive while man's is active because of the physical characteristics of the genitalia. She posits that women are limited primarily by the conditioning imposed on them by a male-dominated society, not by any biologic weakness or inferiority.

Because the behavior of human beings is based in large part on rationality and choice instead of on instinct, Beauvoir suggests that human behavior is not fixed and immutable but should be based on the individual's rational decision to behave in a particular way in a given situation. Beauvoir then expands on that stance, using Jean-Paul Sartre's belief that to be fully human, each person must be free to choose what he or she will become and that the process of choosing never ends. She further asserts that the sexual identity assigned to girls by modern Western society, which prepares them primarily to become wives, mothers, and housewives, destroys women's creative potential and leads to self-alienation and destruction of the psyche.

Mary Johnson

SEE ALSO: Beauvoir, Simone de; Sexism; Sexual stereotypes; Sexuality and sexual ethics; Women's ethics; Women's liberation movement.

Secular ethics

DEFINITION: Any set of moral principles or school of moral philosophy whose values do not derive from religion or belief in the supernatural
TYPE OF ETHICS: Theory of ethics
SIGNIFICANCE: A secular ethics may directly attack religious ethics as ill-advised or untrue, or it may simply ignore religious systems altogether.

"If God is dead, then everything is permitted." Toward the end of the nineteenth century, Fyodor Dostoevski expressed his despair at the disrepute into which religious ethics had fallen. The enormous prestige of science had led many thinkers to believe that science had supplanted religion as the proper source of answers to questions about the universe and humanity's place in it. Ethics, many believed, should follow the path of other disciplines—such as astronomy, physics, and biology—and become secular; that is, shorn of its traditional religious context.

Traditional religious ethics claim that without a god, ethics is meaningless. Three considerations motivate this claim. First, the fact that humans have argued about ethics for several millennia without reaching agreement is evidence that humans are not able to discover, by their own efforts, what is good and bad. Second, the fact that many people do things that they believe are unethical is evidence that humans are weak by nature and therefore are not competent to be good by their own efforts. Third, the fact that many evil-doers are never brought to justice is evidence that humans are not competent to administer justice effectively. Without a god, therefore, humans would wallow in ignorance and sin, and evil would often triumph over good. Accordingly, the religious account argues, a being greater than humanity—a powerful, knowledgeable, and good being—is needed to tell humans what to do, to make sure they do it, and to administer ultimate justice.

CRITICISMS OF RELIGION

One major difficulty of the religious view is proving the existence of a god. Even supposing that the existence of a god could be proved, however, religion still would face serious difficulties. For, even if there is reason to believe there is a god, why should humans do what that god says?

The fact that the god was powerful would not guarantee that what it said was in fact good, for it could be both powerful and evil or both powerful and uninformed. To do what it says simply because it ordered one to do so would be to commit a logical fallacy—the appeal to force.

The fact that the god was knowledgeable also would not be a sufficient guarantee—for it could be both knowledgeable and evil—and to do what it says simply because it is knowledgeable would be to appeal to authority.

Finally, that the god is good cannot be determined without circularity, for the religious approach claims that humans do not know what is good before the god

tells them so; they would have to know what was good, however, before they could judge whether the god was good and therefore whether they could trust its commands. If humans can distinguish good and evil, then they do not need a god to tell them which is which, but if humans cannot distinguish good and evil, then they have no way of knowing whether a god is telling them to do good things or bad things.

According to these objections, religion fails to ground ethics rationally. Advocates of religion may reject rationality and fall back on faith, but irrational faith is a precarious thing. Without evidence, one has no way of knowing whether one's faith is true, and therefore one has no way of knowing whether the principles upon which one acts are moral. Since different individuals believe different things on the basis of faith, faith leads to social difficulties. Without appealing to rationality and evidence, members of different faiths cannot resolve disagreements peacefully. History provides ample evidence that disagreements over articles of faith regularly lead to violence.

The above epistemological criticisms are sometimes supplemented by criticisms of the central content of religious ethics. By placing the sources of value in a supernatural realm, religion devalues life on Earth. Evidence for this view can be found in the fact that virtually all religions emphasize sacrifice rather than achievement, suffering rather than pleasure, and self-denial rather than self-affirmation.

SECULAR SOURCES

These criticisms of religious ethics have given impetus to secular accounts of ethics. By appealing to natural phenomena, secular approaches try to solve the problems that have traditionally motivated religious ethics.

One such problem is finding a source for universal ethical principles; that is, principles that are true for everyone. Religion attempts to solve this problem by claiming that a god establishes rules and stipulates that they hold for everyone. Some secular theorists (relativists) attempt to solve this problem by rejecting the assumption that there are universal ethical principles. Relativists argue that ethics is based on individual or group feelings or traditions. If ethics is primarily a matter of feeling, however, then the obvious fact that feelings vary radically rules out universality. If ethics is primarily a matter of social traditions, history and anthropology provide evidence of a wide range of radically different social traditions.

Other secular theorists, however, accept the challenge of finding a universal source for values by identifying natural facts that are universal. For example, some theorists (Hedonists) note that all humans have a pleasure/pain mechanism, and therefore they argue that people should define "good" and "bad" in terms of pleasure and pain. Other theorists (the Kantians) note that all humans have a rational faculty, and therefore they argue that morality should be defined in terms of the rational consistency of action. Other theorists (objectivists) note that all humans have the same fundamental survival needs, and therefore they argue that people should define "bad" in terms of what leads to death and "good" in terms of that which makes human life possible.

Stephen R. C. Hicks

FURTHER READING

Asad, Talal. *Formations of the Secular: Christianity, Islam, Modernity.* Stanford, Calif.: Stanford University Press, 2003.

Grayling, A. C. *Meditations for the Humanist: Ethics for a Secular Age.* New York: Oxford University Press, 2002.

Smith, George. *Atheism: The Case Against God.* Buffalo, N.Y.: Prometheus, 1979.

Warnock, Mary. *Existentialist Ethics.* New York: St. Martin's Press, 1967.

SEE ALSO: Aristotle; Atheism; Dostoevski, Fyodor; Existentialism; God; Kant, Immanuel; Mill, John Stuart; Nietzsche, Friedrich; Rand, Ayn; Religion; Sartre, Jean-Paul.

Sedition

DEFINITION: Criminally inciting others to resist or overthrow their government

TYPE OF ETHICS: Politico-economic ethics

SIGNIFICANCE: Because it incites people to violent action rather than merely expressing dissent, sedition is one of the few types of speech not protected by the First Amendment. In order to ensure that the right of political dissent is preserved, current definitions of sedition include only direct incitements of violence.

The first sedition laws in the United States were the Alien and Sedition Acts of 1798, which were passed during the administration of President John Adams. These laws defined sedition very broadly; many believed them to be unconstitutional. They were certainly impolitic and unpopular, and they were repealed under the Thomas Jefferson administration in 1801. In the United States today, sedition consists of advocacy of the illegal or violent overthrow of the government; it is more than mere defamation of the government or government officials. Because the essence of sedition is speech or publication, the crime as it is defined in most American jurisdictions always involves free speech issues. By the latter part of the twentieth century, rules set by the U.S. Supreme Court made it nearly impossible to convict anyone of sedition unless the government could show that the defendant's speech or publication explicitly advocated illegal acts and that it created a "clear and present danger" that the acts would take place. These rules place so heavy a burden on the prosecution that there were no successful federal sedition prosecutions in the United States between 1953 and 1993.

Robert Jacobs

SEE ALSO: Constitution, U.S.; First Amendment; Loyalty; Sedition Act of 1798; Treason.

Sedition Act of 1798

IDENTIFICATION: One of four "Alien and Sedition Acts" designed to suppress domestic opposition to Federalist policies during a period of European anti-American aggression

DATE: Passed in 1798

TYPE OF ETHICS: Media ethics

SIGNIFICANCE: The Sedition Act challenged the First Amendment's guarantees of free speech and a free press, an attempt that ultimately served to broaden the scope of both rights and to limit governmental restraint of political dissent.

The Sedition Act was prompted by Federalist fears that growing Republican opposition to Federalist policy would weaken popular support and lead to the end of Federalist control at a time when the United States was caught between rival international powers. The act sought to apply the English common-law tradition of "seditious libel" by making it unlawful to "write, print, utter, or publish . . . any false, scandalous, or malicious writing . . . against the government of the United States . . . or to bring [it] . . . into contempt or disrepute." On that basis, ten newspaper editors were convicted, one of them a congressman, by courts made up exclusively of Federalist judges.

Advocates justified the act by interpreting the First Amendment as pertaining only to "prior restraint," meaning that the government could not prevent the publication of dissent but could prosecute the result. Opponents protested that the First Amendment prevented the government from suppressing political speech at any stage, and they pronounced the act unconstitutional. Republican opposition was carried out through the Kentucky and Virginia Resolutions (written by Thomas Jefferson and James Madison, respectively), which asserted the right of states to "nullify" unwanted federal intrusions on individual rights. The act expired with the inauguration of Thomas Jefferson, and no subsequent attempt to suppress political dissent has ultimately been successful.

SEE ALSO: Constitution, U.S.; First Amendment; Freedom of expression; Jefferson, Thomas; Politics; Sedition.

Segregation

DEFINITION: Physical separation of one group, especially a racial or ethnic group, from another
TYPE OF ETHICS: Race and ethnicity; Civil rights
SIGNIFICANCE: Now deemed to be unconstitutional, racial segregation in the United States was originally the product of overt and unapologetic racist ideologies. When racism and white supremacy initially became less defensible as legal principles, however, segregation remained in place, but it was justified on grounds of social harmony. It was argued that maintaining separate but equal facilities and institutions would prevent the disorder that racial mixing would supposedly produce.

Segregation, historically, was born in the colonial era when the "majority" practiced de facto segregation. When most black Americans were slaves, free blacks suffered de facto segregation in housing and social segregation based on "custom" and "folkways." As the northern colonies abolished slavery, de facto segregation sometimes became de jure separation supported by local ordinances and state law.

As long as the South maintained slavery, that institution "regulated" race relations, and de jure segregation was not needed. In 1865, however, the southern slaves were set free, and legal segregation made its appearance. After the Civil War, most southern states passed legislation known as black codes, which resembled the old slave codes. Under the new codes, social segregation was often spelled out. For example, most states moved immediately to segregate public transportation lines. By the end of the Reconstruction (1865-1877), race lines had hardened, and social segregation was the rule rather than the exception.

UNSUCCESSFUL CHALLENGES

Some African Americans challenged segregationist laws. In 1896, blacks from Louisiana sued a public transportation company (railroad) that operated segregated passenger cars, as stipulated by Louisiana's state laws. Black leaders argued that the state laws and the railroad's actions violated the Thirteenth and Fourteenth Amendments to the Constitution. The case, *Plessy v. Ferguson* (1896), reached the U.S. Supreme Court, which ruled that segregation was "legal" as long as "separate but equal" facilities were made available for minorities. A lone dissenter, Justice John M. Harlan, who happened to be a white southerner, rejected the majority opinion, saying that the Constitution should be "color-blind" and that it should not tolerate "classes" among the citizens, who were all equal.

Despite Harlan's dissent, the *Plessy* decision gave absolute legal sanction to a practice that many states, including some in the North, were already practicing by custom and tradition: *Plessy* "froze" segregation into the highest law of the land. Thereafter, segregationists, especially those in the South, used their legislatures to pass a host of new laws that extended the supposed "separate but equal" doctrine to all areas of life. For example, restaurants, hotels, and theaters became segregated by law, not only by custom. Railroad cars and railroad stations divided the races; hospitals, doctors' offices, and even cemeteries became segregated.

The laws of some southern states called for segregated prisons, while prisons in other states took criminals from both races but separated them within their facilities. At least one state passed a law that forbade a white and a black prisoner to look out the same prison window at the same time. If the prisoners were physically close enough to look out at the same time, they were too close to please segregationists.

As the United States matured during the twentieth century, segregation was extended whenever "technology" made it seem necessary. For example, in 1915, Oklahoma became the first state in the Union to require segregated public "pay" telephone booths. When motor cars were first used as a "taxi" service, taxi companies were segregated—a "white" taxi serving whites only and a "black" taxi serving African Americans only. Public water fountains became segregated, as did public restroom facilities.

Another problem became associated with segregation. Often, there was *no* separate facility for blacks, who were denied service altogether. For example, as late as the 1960's, President Lyndon B. Johnson's personal maid and butler-handyman experienced difficulty traveling by car from Washington, D.C., back to Johnson's Texas home. There were few if any "motels" along the way that would rent rooms to African Americans.

SUCCESSFUL CHALLENGES

Eventually, the National Association for the Advancement of Colored People (NAACP) launched new attacks against segregationist laws—especially in circumstances in which no separate facilities existed for African Americans.

For example, in *Gaines v. Missouri* (1938) and *Sweatt v. Painter* (1949; a Texas case), the Supreme Court ruled that blacks could attend white law schools because no separate school was available in state for African Americans. In 1950, in *McLaurin v. Oklahoma*, the NAACP tested the same concept and won another court battle. As *McLaurin* showed, the University of Oklahoma had admitted a black student to its graduate program but then had segregated him on campus. After the high court ruled that such segregation was unfair and illegal because it denied

Typical "white only" sign of the Jim Crow era. (Library of Congress)

"equal" education, Thurgood Marshall of the NAACP became even more determined to challenge segregation. He did so successfully when, in *Brown v. Board of Education* (1954), the Court declared segregated public education illegal.

If segregation was unjust and unconstitutional in education, it seemed clear that it was also unjust in other areas of life. Thus, in 1955, under the leadership of Martin Luther King, Jr., and others, a nonviolent protest movement took to the streets and eventually won victories that included new laws such as the Civil Rights Act of 1964 and the Voter Registration Act of 1965.

Ultimately, a limited social and economic "revolution" occurred that condemned segregation and, in part, created a new American society.

James Smallwood

FURTHER READING

Blauner, Bob. *Racial Oppression in America*. New York: Harper & Row, 1972.

Branch, Taylor. *Parting the Waters: America in the King Years, 1954-1963*. New York: Simon & Schuster, 1988.

Feagin, Joe R., and Clairece Booher Feagin. *Racial and Ethnic Relations*. 7th ed. Upper Saddle River, N.J.: Prentice Hall, 2003.

Forman, James. *The Making of Black Revolutionaries*. Ill. ed. Forward by Julian Bond. Seattle: University of Washington Press, 1997.

Garrow, David J., ed. *We Shall Overcome: The Civil Rights Movement in the United States in the 1950's and 1960's*. 3 vols. Brooklyn, N.Y.: Carlson, 1989.

Hacker, Andrew. *Two Nations: Black and White, Separate, Hostile, Unequal*. New York: Scribner, 2003.

Powledge, Fred. *Free at Last? The Civil Rights Movement and the People Who Made It*. Boston: Little, Brown, 1991.

Schnell, Izhak, and Wim Ostendorf, eds. *Studies in Segregation and Desegregation*. Burlington, Vt.: Ashgate, 2002.

Sitkoff, Harvard. *The Struggle for Black Equality, 1954-1992*. New York: Hill & Wang, 1993.

SEE ALSO: Apartheid; Bigotry; *Brown v. Board of Education*; Caste system, Hindu; Civil Rights movement; Integration; *Plessy v. Ferguson*; Racial prejudice; Racism; Slavery.

Self-control

DEFINITION: Discipline or restraint exercised upon one's own actions or emotions in frustration of one's impulses or desires

TYPE OF ETHICS: Personal and social ethics

SIGNIFICANCE: Self-control may be seen as a necessary characteristic for maintaining virtue and resisting temptation, or it may be seen as a virtue in itself, especially in value systems in which desire and bodily impulses are represented as inherently sinful.

The concept of self-control as a modern moral and psychological trait is directly rooted in the Greek concept of *sōphrosynī*, which is usually translated as "temperance," although there is no exact English equivalent. Although a number of concepts capture facets of what the Greeks meant by *sōphrosynī*—balance, limit, proportion, order, equilibrium, harmony, restraint, moderation, sobriety—none defines it completely. Yet the concept of self-control, complemented by self-knowledge, lies at its core, being a virtue crucial to the achievement of order and moderation in life. In contrast to it is *hybris* (hubris), the vice of arrogance, excessive behavior, unrestrained passion, and other extremes.

Sōphrosynī was not only a personal virtue for the Greeks but a civic one as well; in addition to being a standard of individual behavior and character, it was, especially for Athenians, a measure of the political and social health of the *polis*, lying between the extremes of tyranny and anarchy. Just as the individual was responsible for maintaining the proper order among the elements of the soul by means of the intelligent control of its baser parts, the rulers were responsible for maintaining the proper order among the various segments of society by the wise governance of its lower echelons. Plato utilizes this concept of self-control in his *Republic*. An individual must control the influence of spirit (feelings) and passion (desire) by subjecting them to the constraints of reason (intelligence), the highest element of the soul. The philosopher-king, using the judgment that comes from philosophical wisdom, must maintain order among the lower elements of society so that the self-control proper to a virtuous individual is amplified in the polis as a whole.

Aristotle understands self-control, the virtue of

"temperance," more narrowly. In the *Nicomachean Ethics*, self-control is marked by the disciplined enjoyment of eating, drinking, and sexual intercourse, as opposed to the correlative vices of excessive indulgence and insufficient sensitivity to physical pleasure. Although Aristotle cites temperance as a separate virtue, however, it possesses a generic component that is fundamental to the other virtues as well. Every Aristotelian virtue requires self-control. For example, courage is the exercise of bravery in the right way at the right time for the right reason and to the right degree. To misjudge the proper measure of courage—to be brave to the point of foolhardiness, or to be cowardly when courage is required—is to be wrongly controlled by either ambition on the one hand or fear on the other, which happens when one loses control over oneself and allows intelligent judgment to be subdued by one's nonrational faculties.

Sōphrosynī was central to Stoic moral teaching during the Hellenistic period. The Stoics viewed it as essentially the exercise of wise and practical judgment in matters of indulgence and abstinence, preserving the traditional Greek association between *sōphrosynī* and self-control. The Romans eventually absorbed *sōphrosynī* into their ethical canon, where it figures prominently in the writings of Cicero, who identifies *temperantia*, or "self-control," as its most important component and contrasts it to *luxuria* United States ("excess") and *avaritia* (greed), which he believed were the worst vices of Roman citizens. Early Christianity, although at first eschewing anything associated with paganism, eventually assimilated *sōphrosynī*, along with other classical virtues, into its own ethical structure, since these virtues were consistent with Christian ethics. Christians made chastity the defining feature of *sōphrosynī*, however, almost eclipsing its other aspects.

MODERN VIEWS

Sōphrosynī was absorbed by the modern mind in essentially its original Greek form, with a continued emphasis on self-control. It is recognizable in Michel de Montaigne's essay "Of Husbanding Your Will," in which Montaigne extols the virtues of a moderate lifestyle: "One must moderate oneself between hatred of pain and love of pleasure; and Plato prescribes a middle way of life between the two." Undue absorption with personal and public affairs is to be avoided if one wishes to live serenely. In addition, the

more possessions one acquires, the more likely one is to suffer the bad luck that is an inherent aspect of material acquisition and ownership. One's energy should be expended chiefly on what one can control; namely, oneself and one's personal affairs: "The range of our desires should be circumscribed and restrained to a narrow limit . . . and moreover their course should be directed not in a straight line that ends up elsewhere, but in a circle whose two extremities . . . terminate in ourselves." Balance and moderation are the keys to tranquillity.

Because of its inward, quasi-psychological nature, self-control, like some of the other traditional virtues of character, has been largely neglected by most modern philosophers. Some thinkers, however, have attempted to reinstate consideration of the traditional virtues as an essential feature of moral discourse. Anthony Quinton (1993), for example, defines moral character as self-control or self-discipline, which is required to maintain one's determination toward a goal and to avoid being distracted by "passing impulses" and unproductive pursuits. It is the essential element in moral development, even though the self-control necessary to good moral character may be used for bad purposes as well. According to Quinton, modern people would do well to emulate the vigorous moral rectitude of the Victorians, whose incorporation of self-control into their character made them worthy models of moral uprightness.

Barbara Forrest

FURTHER READING

Aristotle. *Nicomachean Ethics*. Translated and edited by Roger Crisp. New York: Cambridge University Press, 2000.

Kennett, Jeanette. *Agency and Responsibility: A Common-Sense Moral Psychology*. New York: Oxford University Press, 2001.

Montaigne, Michel de. "Of Husbanding Your Will." Translated by Donald M. Frame. In *The Complete Works: Essays, Travel Journal, Letters*. New York: Alfred A. Knopf, 2003.

North, Helen F. "Temperance (Sōphrosynī) and the Canon of the Cardinal Virtues." In *Dictionary of the History of Ideas: Studies of Selected Pivotal Ideas*, edited by Philip P. Wiener. Vol. 4. New York: Charles Scribner's Sons, 1973.

Plato. "Charmides." In *The Collected Dialogues of*

Plato, edited by Edith Hamilton and Huntington Cairns. 1961. Reprint. Princeton, N.J.: Princeton University Press, 1984.

_____. *The Republic*. Translated by Desmond Lee. 2d ed. New York: Penguin Books, 2003.

Quinton, Anthony. "Character and Culture." In *Vice and Virtue in Everyday Life: Introductory Readings in Ethics*, edited by Christina Sommers and Fred Sommers. 4th ed. Fort Worth, Tex.: Harcourt Brace College, 1997.

Stroud, Sarah, and Christine Tappolet, eds. *Weakness of Will and Practical Irrationality*. New York: Oxford University Press, 2003.

SEE ALSO: Character; Passions and emotions; Perfectionism; Stoic ethics; Temperance; Virtue ethics.

Self-deception

DEFINITION: Conscious or unconscious clinging to a belief that one knows on some level to be false

TYPE OF ETHICS: Personal and social ethics

SIGNIFICANCE: Self-deception often facilitates immoral action, but some philosophers have posited that some forms of self-deception may be necessary to survival.

A person is tempted to self-deceive whenever the reasons for accepting a certain thought as true are better than the reasons for not accepting it and the person does not want the thought to be true. If the individual in such a situation avoids acknowledging a fact that is supported by evidence because of the intimated advantage of doing so, then the person self-deceives. Since this act violates a basic principle of rational cognition (to assent to what is supported by the evidence), the self-deceiver will further self-deceive about the very activity of self-deceiving. Hence, people who in fact are deceiving themselves will vehemently deny to themselves and to others that they are doing so.

In this general process, the person need not fully embrace utter falsehoods. Self-deception essentially occurs by avoiding the recognition of some important and well-supported conception. The person can be held accountable for this evasion because there is tacit awareness of the good reasons for not evading

acknowledgment; "deep down," the self-deceiver "knows better." This paradoxical nature of being self-deceived is manifested in inconsistencies in conduct and in speech; on some occasions, action will be based on what is "really known," and on other occasions, it will be based on self-deception.

Self-deception is morally problematical for three reasons. First, it is a practice of untruthfulness, and to the extent that being truthful is inherently good, self-deception is always wrong. This is true even if the deceiving involves a morally neutral issue.

Second, deceiving oneself can have deleterious effects on one's conscience and the ability to understand oneself. Conscience is corrupted because self-deception (especially if it is habitual) can involve overlooking moral failures in one's past and avoiding consideration of moral obligations to which one is bound in the present. The ability to understand oneself is damaged because self-deception (again, especially if it is habitual) can direct attention away from realities of oneself that are important but are very difficult to accept.

Third, self-deceiving can have harmful effects on others. Being able to deceive oneself about a topic greatly facilitates deceiving others about that same topic (by masking from them one's own disbelief). In addition, deceiving oneself about the harm that one is causing for others makes it easier to harm them (by precluding scruples arising from one's own conscience). If this type of self-deceiving becomes habitual, then one can become completely oblivious to the harmful effects of one's conduct on others.

FAILURE TO TAKE RESPONSIBILITY

A prevalent type of self-deception with deleterious effects on self and others involves not taking responsibility for one's own actions. People tend to deceive themselves concerning how able they are to act in a manner other than the manner in which they act when they do something wrong. Shunning avowal of the immediately evident reality of their own free will, they focus instead on how "pressing" their needs and wants appear to be to them. This type of self-deceiving subverts the sense of being in control of one's own impulses, which in turn results in those impulses being less controlled. It thereby becomes likely that the individual does whatever he or she wants to do, in spite of obvious immorality and harm to others.

The diminishment in self-control brought on by

chronic self-deception about one's own responsibility can also affect the degree of control that one has over the very impulse to deceive oneself. This in turn can make it difficult to distinguish voluntary self-deception from pathological self-delusion. In the latter case, the person is incapable of admitting the truth and is not subject to moral censure. Only if a person is able to abstain from self-deception and admit to the truth is the act of self-deception subject to moral evaluation. If it is controllable and wrong, it should be avoided.

In order to avoid deceiving oneself, one must be aware of the subjects about which there is temptation to deceive oneself. Since all people want to think highly of themselves and want to avoid making costly sacrifices, the strongest enticements to self-deceive arise when people assess their moral imperfections or are subject to demanding moral obligations. To prevent self-deception when one confronts such topics, it is necessary to keep clearly in mind the good of authentic self-understanding and the evils that can result from deceiving oneself. There are, however, issues about which a measure of self-deception could be harmless or even beneficial. For example, if one deceives oneself into thinking that one is less afraid than one actually is about delivering an impending public address, then one may be better able to deliver the speech. Nevertheless, in such situations, self-deception is rarely the only means available to achieve the beneficial results. Since self-deceiving can become a habit and habitual self-deception carries with it the dangers noted earlier, it is probably best to always avoid deceiving oneself.

Mark Stephen Pestana

FURTHER READING

Dupuy, Jean-Pierre, ed. *Self-Deception and Paradoxes of Rationality*. Stanford, Calif.: CSLI, 1998.

Giannetti, Eduardo. *Lies We Live By: The Art of Self-Deception*. London: Bloomsbury, 2000.

McLaughlin, Brian P., and Amelie Oksenberg Rorty, eds. *Perspectives on Self-Deception*. Berkeley: University of California Press, 1988.

Martin, Mike W. *Self-Deception and Morality*. Lawrence: University Press of Kansas, 1986.

Mele, Alfred R. *Irrationality: An Essay on Akrasia, Self-Deception, and Self-Control*. New York: Oxford University Press, 1987.

Murphy, Gardner. *Outgrowing Self-Deception*. New York: Basic Books, 1975.

Sartre, Jean-Paul. *Being and Nothingness: A Phenomenological Essay on Ontology*. Translated by Hazel E. Barnes. New York: Washington Square Press, 1992.

SEE ALSO: Existentialism; Freud, Sigmund; Hypocrisy; Integrity; Lying; Sartre, Jean-Paul; Self-righteousness; Truth.

Self-interest

DEFINITION: Concern for one's own success, well-being, goals, and projects
TYPE OF ETHICS: Personal and social ethics
SIGNIFICANCE: Self-interest is the opposite of altruism; it is valued by those who disparage altruism and attacked by those who see altruism as a moral good. Philosophers also disagree as to whether one's own interests and the interests of one's community are necessarily compatible, are necessarily incompatible, or have no necessary relationship.

Although Plato in his *Republic* was the first to raise the issue of the role that self-interest plays in ethics, it was Thomas Hobbes's treatment of the concept in *Leviathan* (1651) that cast the discussion of the relationship between ethics and self-interest in modern terms.

VARIETIES OF SELF-INTEREST

Philosophers generally speak of two kinds of self-interest: enlightened and unenlightened. This distinction is made by those who think that self-interest has a significant contribution to make to ethics. Interests can be classified as being either short-term or long-term, and sometimes what may be in one's short-term interest may not be in one's long-term interest. Short-term interests are those that are immediate consequences of the action performed and are of immediate benefit to the individual who is acting. Long-term interests, however, are future consequences of the action, and the benefit to the individual may not matter for quite some time.

Almost no one would advocate that one should pursue short-term interests exclusively. Rather, those who believe that self-interest and ethics are related encourage the pursuit of long-term interests. Emphasizing the pursuit of long-term as opposed to short-term interests is called enlightened (or rational) self-interest, while emphasizing the pursuit of short-term interests is called unenlightened self-interest.

One can appreciate the different positions regarding the relationship between self-interest and ethics by reflecting on the answers to the following question. Do the demands of enlightened self-interest ever correspond to the dictates of ethics? There is a theory of ethics that answers this question in the affirmative: egoism. This theory claims that self-interest plays a crucial role in determining ethically appropriate action. There are two kinds of egoism, depending in part on the role that is assigned to self-interest.

PSYCHOLOGICAL EGOISM

This theory claims that human beings by their very nature must act in their own self-interest. According to this view, human beings cannot help but act in their own interest. That is how they are constituted.

Technically, this is not an ethical theory but rather a scientific or psychological theory about human nature. In fact, a psychological egoist would contend that ethics as traditionally conceived is impossible, since traditional ethics requires a person to act altruistically, to act in the interests of others, and human beings are simply psychologically incapable of doing that. Psychological egoism advocates that ethics should be revamped to take into account this important fact about human nature. Once this is done, the goal of this redefined ethics is to persuade people to pursue enlightened rather than unenlightened self-interest. Thomas Hobbes is the person most often associated with psychological egoism.

ETHICAL EGOISM

The other brand of egoism is called ethical egoism. In contrast with psychological egoism, ethical egoism is a traditional ethical or normative theory that acknowledges that people have the ability to act altruistically. It contends that, although people can act in the interests of others, they should not. Ethical egoism claims that one should pursue one's enlightened self-interest exclusively. It contends that the

only time one should take into consideration the interests of others is when it is in one's interest to do so.

A number of reasons have been offered by ethical egoists to explain why one should act in one's own self-interest. For one thing, it just makes good sense. People should know what is in their own interest better than they know what is in the interest of others, and it is always good to act on as much information as possible. For another, if everyone pursued his or her own interests exclusively and did not meddle in other people's business, everyone would be better off.

Two major branches of ethics—namely, utilitarianism and deontological ethics—answer the above question in the negative. They both claim that acting solely in the light of one's own self-interest is never ethically acceptable. They contend that one of the goals of an ethical theory is to persuade an agent to put aside self-interested pursuit, whether enlightened or not, and act altruistically. These groups, however, deal with self-interested behavior in different ways.

UTILITARIANISM

Utilitarianism claims that, in determining what the morally appropriate action is, one should take into consideration the interests of everyone who is affected by the action, and no one person's interest should count more than anyone else's. The right action is the one that will produce the greatest good for the greatest number of people. Notice that this theory still uses the concept of self-interest, though in a much-diminished capacity. One's interests do matter, but they matter only as much as everyone else's. This theory requires that one may have to sacrifice one's interest for the interests of others (the common good).

DEONTOLOGICAL THEORIES

Both egoism and utilitarianism determine right and wrong by looking at the consequences of an action. Deontological theories look to something other than consequences to determine right and wrong. For that reason, these theories go a step further than utilitarianism does, banishing self-interest in any form. According to these theories, acting in self-interest automatically removes the agent from the ethical realm. Self-interest is something that must be controlled or defeated in order for true ethical behavior to take place.

John H. Serembus

FURTHER READING

Engelmann, Stephen G. *Imagining Interest in Political Thought: Origins of Economic Rationality.* Durham, N.C.: Duke University Press, 2003.

Gauthier, David P., ed. *Morality and Rational Self-Interest.* Englewood Cliffs, N.J.: Prentice-Hall, 1970.

Hobbes, Thomas. *Leviathan.* Edited by Richard Tuck. Rev. student ed. New York: Cambridge University Press, 1996.

Holley, David M. *Self-Interest and Beyond.* St. Paul, Minn.: Paragon House, 1999.

Olson, Robert. *The Morality of Self-Interest.* New York: Harcourt, Brace & World, 1965.

Rachels, James. *The Elements of Moral Philosophy.* 3d ed. Boston: McGraw-Hill, 1999.

SEE ALSO: Altruism; Egoism; Egotist; Hobbes, Thomas; Human nature; *Leviathan*; Selfishness; Self-love.

Selfishness

DEFINITION: Concern with and pursuit of one's own interests and desires without regard to or in conflict with the interests and desires of others

TYPE OF ETHICS: Personal and social ethics

SIGNIFICANCE: Always a pejorative term, unreflective or excessive selfishness may be opposed to altruism or selflessness on the one hand and to mere self-interest or ethical egoism on the other.

Selfishness is construed as a vice or character flaw. All one has to do to see this is to reflect on the common usage of the term. To be labeled "selfish" is to be censured and held in low regard. Such labeling is a condemnation. Ethical theorists also share this disdain, though Ayn Rand with her philosophical theory of objectivism may appear to be an exception. Selfishness plays an important role in her ethical theory.

If someone is acting selfishly, that person is not acting ethically. Traditionally, the goals of ethics and those of selfishness are antithetical. Even those theories of ethics that advocate acting in one's own interest—namely, the various versions of egoism—would never endorse constant selfish behavior. For this rea-son, it will be helpful to explore the relationship between selfishness and self-interest.

SELFISHNESS AND SELF-INTEREST

Are acting selfishly and acting self-interestedly identical? Critics of egoism, which is the ethical theory that claims that one should always act in one's own interest, answer this question in the affirmative. They find egoism morally repugnant because they find selfishness morally repugnant. Certainly, selfish behavior does involve some form of self-interested behavior. A selfish act is performed because the person expects to satisfy some current need or desire. Does self-interested behavior, however, necessarily involve selfish behavior? In other words, can there be behavior that is self-interested yet unselfish? Defenders of egoism say yes. For example, they insist that it is not in one's interest to act purely selfishly all the time, though there are some egoists who maintain that it is acceptable to act selfishly on occasion. Egoists distinguish between short-term and long-term self-interests.

SHORT- VS. LONG-TERM INTERESTS

Short-term interests are those that are met immediately, while long-term interests are those that will be satisfied in the future. When one acts selfishly, one is acting on the basis of short-term self-interests exclusively. When one acts selfishly, one does not take into account the impact of the pursuit of one's short-term interests on others; hence, one does not take into account the impact on one's own long-term interests. Since interfering with others in their pursuit of their interests may lead them to hinder one's own pursuit of future interests, such interference may have a negative impact on one's long-term interests. What this means, then, is that acting selfishly, though it is in one's short-term interest to do so, may have consequences that will hinder the pursuit of one's long-term interests.

Conversely, it may be in one's long-term interest to act unselfishly, since acting unselfishly would not anger others and would give them no reason to interfere with one's future goals. Thus, an egoist could simultaneously advocate the exclusive pursuit of self-interest and avoid the charge of selfishness by insisting that it is the pursuit of one's long-term as opposed to short-term self-interest that is at the heart of egoism. Aiming for the long-term is described as acting in one's rational self-interest. This means that it is not generally rational to act selfishly, although an egoist could still advocate selfish behavior as long as that behavior did not interfere with one's long-term interests.

AYN RAND AND OBJECTIVISM

In *The Virtue of Selfishness* (1961), Ayn Rand seems to be contradicting the claim made at the start that ethics views selfish behavior with disdain and contempt. It seems that she encourages selfish behavior, believing that it is at the core of true ethical behavior. By calling selfishness a virtue, she seems to be sanctioning that kind of behavior.

It turns out, however, that her position is not far from that of the ethical mainstream. Her title is intended to capture and hold the reader's attention. As a title for a treatise on ethics it is misleading. What she is really advocating is that the definition of selfishness should be stripped of all its negative connotations. She suspects that there has been some kind of moral conspiracy on the part of the ethics of altruism, which advocates that one needs sometimes to put one's own interests aside and act for the interests of others, and which demeans and belittles anyone who dares to act in his or her own interest exclusively.

The goal of her theory, known as objectivism, is to expose this conspiracy and to show that there is nothing wrong with acting in one's own interest exclusively. What does selfishness, denuded of its negative connotations, look like? It is nothing other than what traditional egoists call rational self-interest. Hence, her position on selfishness is consistent with the ordinary one, and her own ethical theory is just another version of egoism. Although she claims the contrary, the point is essentially a semantic one. For Rand, then, selfish behavior and self-interest are identical, but selfishness should be stripped of its negative connotations. For traditional egoists, however, selfishness, and self-interest are not identical. They discourage selfishness and encourage the pursuit of rational self-interest.

John H. Serembus

FURTHER READING

Campbell, Richmond. *Self-Love and Self-Respect: A Philosophical Study of Egoism.* Ottawa, Canada: Canadian Library of Philosophy, 1979.

Dawkins, Richard. *The Selfish Gene.* New ed. New York: Oxford University Press, 1999.

Elster, Jon. "Selfishness and Altruism." In *Economics, Ethics, and Public Policy*, edited by Charles K. Wilber. Lanham, Md.: Rowman & Littlefield, 1998.

Gauthier, David P., ed. *Morality and Rational Self-Interest.* Englewood Cliffs, N.J.: Prentice-Hall, 1970.

Olson, Robert. *The Morality of Self-Interest.* New York: Harcourt, Brace & World, 1965.

Rand, Ayn. *The Virtue of Selfishness: A New Concept of Egoism.* New York: New American Library, 1964.

Rescher, Nicholas. *Unselfishness: The Role of the Vicarious Affects in Moral Philosophy and Social Theory.* Pittsburgh: University of Pittsburgh Press, 1975.

SEE ALSO: Egoism; Egotist; Greed; Objectivism; Rand, Ayn; Self-interest; Self-love; Self-preservation.

Self-love

DEFINITION: Pursuit of actual or apparent goods for oneself, or, narcissism

TYPE OF ETHICS: Personal and social ethics

SIGNIFICANCE: Self-love is considered by different writers to be essential to an ethical life, to be the greatest opponent of ethics, or to lie somewhere between these extremes.

The best approach to understanding the relationship between self-love and ethics is to study its history. Aristotle, in his *Nicomachean Ethics* (c. 330 B.C.E.), addresses the question of whether ethical or unethical persons love themselves more. His answer is that, although most people believe that unethical persons love themselves more than do ethical persons, precisely the opposite is actually true. He defends this position by making an analogy between self-love and the friendship of two persons. The type of friendship he has in mind is not a superficial one, but rather a strong relationship between two ethically mature persons. He identifies five characteristics of such a friendship: (1) wishing and doing what one believes to be good for the friend, (2) wishing the friend to continue living, (3) finding it pleasant to spend time with the friend, (4) desiring the same things as does the friend, and (5) sharing the friend's sorrows and joys.

Aristotle then writes that if one is ethical, one will have an analogous relationship with oneself: (1) wishing and doing what one believes to be good for oneself, (2) wishing oneself to continue living, (3) finding it pleasant to spend time with oneself, (4) having consistent desires, and (5) sharing one's own sorrows and joys consistently. Aristotle then contrasts this type of self-love with the self-love of one who is unethical: (1) wishing and doing for oneself what is pleasant to the senses, rather than what is good for oneself; (2) hating one's own life, because of painful memories of evil actions; (3) seeking the company of other persons in order to be distracted from the memory of past evil actions and the expectation of future evil actions; (4) having inconsistent desires; and (5) being torn by the internal conflict of both regretting one's evil actions and remembering them as pleasurable.

Aristotle goes on to explain that most people have false beliefs about self-love. There is a sense in which "selfish" people, those who seek the greatest share of such contested goods as money, honors, and bodily pleasures for themselves, love themselves. This is what most people mean by "self-love." It is, however, an inferior type of self-love that deserves condemnation. In contrast, persons who sacrifice the inferior goods of money, honors, and bodily pleasures in order to benefit others are the ones who genuinely love themselves. Aristotle believes that this is true even in the case of what most people consider the ultimate sacrifice: that of one's life. He maintains that the true self-lover prefers dying in defense of friends and country to living a long life with the memory of having been a coward.

These two types of self-love, sometimes distinguished from each other and sometimes not, appear frequently within post-Aristotelian discussions of ethics. For example, both of the following passages are found in Saint Augustine's *The City of God* (413-427):

> The two cities were created by two kinds of love: the earthly city was created by self-love reaching the point of contempt for God, the Heavenly City by the love of God carried as far as contempt of self.

> God, our master, teaches two chief precepts, love of God and love of neighbor; and in them man finds three objects for his love: God, himself, and his neighbor; and a man who loves God is not wrong in loving himself.

Although one could conclude that Augustine is inconsistent, a more reasonable conclusion (perhaps supported by the fact that he uses different Latin words for "love" in the two passages) is that there is a qualitative difference between the two self-loves.

In more recent ethical theory, however, the trend is toward viewing self-love as being opposed to ethics. Joseph Butler, in his *Fifteen Sermons Preached at the Rolls Chapel*, maintains that both the "principle of benevolence" and the "principle of self-love" are natural to human persons. Furthermore, he does not see them as being in competition with each other: "Though benevolence and self-love are different; though the former tends most directly to public good,

The eighteenth century English cleric Joseph Butler wrote that the principles of both benevolence and self-love are natural to human beings. (Library of Congress)

and the latter to private: yet they are so perfectly coincident, that the greatest satisfactions to ourselves depend upon our having benevolence in a due degree; and that self-love is one chief security of our right behavior toward society." He also states, however, that in his discussion of these two principles, "they must be considered as entirely distinct." He explains that "there can no comparison be made, without considering the things compared as distinct and different."

Although Butler argues at length that benevolence and self-love promote each other, many of his successors maintain that the two principles are indeed distinct and that they frequently oppose each other. This understanding of the relationship between self-love and ethics is quite different from Aristotle's. For Aristotle, people are confronted with the choice between loving themselves improperly and loving themselves properly. Because to love oneself properly is to love others, however, one does not have to choose between proper self-love and love of others. According to what has become the dominant position of eighteenth to twentieth century ethical theory, however, one is confronted with a choice between loving oneself and loving others. Although few writers hold that one should have no self-love, many argue that ethics requires that one decrease one's self-love and increase one's love for others.

One example of a twentieth century writer who is committed to what is now the dominant view is William K. Frankena. Despite the fact that both Saint Augustine and Joseph Butler were Christian bishops, and even though the mainstream of the Christian moral tradition has considered proper self-love to be the basis of obedience to the biblical command "love your neighbor as yourself," Frankena writes in *Ethics* (1973): "In the Judeo-Christian tradition, self-love, even of an enlightened kind, has generally been regarded as the essence of immorality, at least when it is made the primary basis of action and judgment." Although there is room to debate the meanings of "enlightened self-love" and "primary basis," Frankena's statement is at best misleading and at worst false.

David W. Lutz

FURTHER READING

Aristotle. *Nicomachean Ethics*. Translated and edited by Roger Crisp. New York: Cambridge University Press, 2000.

Augustine, Saint. *The City of God Against the Pagans*. Edited and translated by R. W. Dyson. New York: Cambridge University Press, 1998.

Butler, Joseph. *Fifteen Sermons Preached at the Rolls Chapel and A Dissertation upon the Nature of Virtue*. London: G. Bell, 1964.

Magno, Joseph A. *Self-Love: The Heart of Healing*. Lanham, Md.: University Press of America, 2000.

Sidgwick, Henry. *The Methods of Ethics*. 7th ed. 1907. Reprint. Foreword by John Rawls. Indianapolis: Hackett, 1981.

Thomas Aquinas, Saint. *The Summa Theologica*. Translated by Laurence Shapcote. 2d ed. 2 vols. Chicago: Encyclopaedia Britannica, 1990.

SEE ALSO: Altruism; Augustine, Saint; Butler, Joseph; Egoism; Friendship; Love; Narcissism; Prudence; Self-interest; Selfishness.

Self-preservation

DEFINITION: Activity in which a being works to perpetuate its existence or to avoid harm

TYPE OF ETHICS: Personal and social ethics

SIGNIFICANCE: The instinct for self-preservation can motivate and perhaps be used to justify drastic and immoral actions under extreme circumstances. Acts of heroism often require one to mitigate if not ignore such instincts.

On July 20, 1993, a Pennsylvania logger named Don Wyman found himself trapped in the wilderness, his left leg broken and pinned underneath a fallen tree. For an hour, Wyman called for help and attempted to dig his leg out, both to no avail. Aware that he was continuing to lose blood from his injuries, the trapped logger began pursuing what he perceived to be his only chance to escape. Using a bootlace as a tourniquet, Wyman proceeded to amputate his leg just below the knee with a pocket knife. Thus freeing himself from the tree, he crawled two hundred yards up a steep slope to a bulldozer, drove the bulldozer some three hundred yards to his pickup truck, and drove the truck to a farm two miles away, where an ambulance was called.

The case of Wyman is a dramatic illustration of the drive for self-preservation that is a fundamental inclination of human nature. Interestingly, philosophers reflecting on this natural inclination have reached very different conclusions concerning its moral significance. Especially noteworthy in this regard is the contrast between the advocacy of suicide by Stoicism and the absolute prohibition of suicide by some schools of natural law morality.

Fourth century B.C.E. Stoic philosophers such as Zeno of Citium and Cleanthes of Assos were committed to following the demands of nature and were equally aware of the inclination for self-preservation that permeates the natural order. In the case of human beings, they understood the inclination for self-preservation as a demand to perfect one's nature. Taking rationality to be definitive of human nature, the Stoics advocated the soul's complete governance by reason as the epitome of virtue. Strong passions and appetites, however, were symptomatic of a diseased soul and thus were regarded as states of mind that needed to be expunged in the quest to achieve true virtue. Because a soul's attachment to the affairs and goods of the external world is what causes it to be governed by emotions and desires, the Stoics prescribed a rational indifference to the vicissitudes of life. So strong was their commitment to this indifference that the Stoics saw the rational choice of one's own death as a morally legitimate expression of indifference to the affairs of the world, a conviction upon which both Zeno and Cleanthes are believed to have acted. Although it is not obviously inconsistent, it is at least ironic that a philosophy that recognizes the natural inclination toward self-preservation as a basic moral principle should come to the conclusion that suicide is a morally permissible option.

NATURAL LAW MORALISTS

Also recognizing the natural inclination toward self-preservation, Thomas Aquinas and other natural law moralists reach the conclusion—in direct opposition to that of the Stoics—that it is always impermissible to commit suicide. According to the natural law ethics of Thomas Aquinas, God has created the natural order according to a plan and has placed within natural beings a tendency to work toward the fulfillment of that plan. Human beings, like all other natural beings, have divinely implanted inclinations that point the way to their fulfillment. Unlike other natural beings, however, human beings have been given the gift of freedom and thus can choose to act

either in accordance with God's plan or in opposition to it. In order to live a virtuous life, then, human beings must reflect upon their God-given nature and freely act so as to fulfill that nature. Insofar as he viewed the drive for self-preservation as one of the fundamental inclinations of human nature, Thomas Aquinas arrived at the conclusion that it is always impermissible intentionally to terminate or shorten one's own life.

In order to understand fully Thomas Aquinas's position, it is important to note that he did think that there are circumstances in which it would be morally permissible to perform an action that one foresees will result in one's own death. For example, it would be morally praiseworthy for a soldier to throw himself or herself on a hand-grenade to save the lives of fellow combatants. That such cases do not contradict the absolute prohibition of suicide is found in the fact that a true case of suicide requires that one intend to kill oneself, whereas the heroic soldier intends only to save the lives of others and does not intend his or her own death.

One of the strongest objections to the natural law defense of an absolute moral prohibition of suicide is that formulated by the Scottish philosopher David Hume. Hume maintained that the inclination for self-preservation is not a fundamental inclination, because it is grounded in the more comprehensive inclination to achieve happiness. Therefore, suicide does not violate a human beings' natural inclinations if the continuance of the individual's life promises more hardship than happiness.

James Petrik

FURTHER READING

Beauchamp, Tom L., and Robert M. Veatch, eds. *Ethical Issues in Death and Dying*. 2d ed. Upper Saddle River, N.J.: Prentice Hall, 1996.

Brody, Baruch A., ed. *Suicide and Euthanasia: Historical and Contemporary Themes*. Dordrecht, Netherlands: Kluwer, 1989.

Freud, Sigmund. *Beyond the Pleasure Principle*. Translated and edited by James Strachey. New York: Norton, 1989.

Horan, Dennis J., and David Mall, eds. *Death, Dying, and Euthanasia*. Frederick, Md.: University Publications of America, 1980.

Johnston, Darlene M. "Native Rights as Collective Rights: A Question of Group Self-Preservation."

In *The Rights of Minority Cultures*, edited by Will Kymlicka. New York: Oxford University Press, 1995.

Kant, Immanuel. *Groundwork for the Metaphysics of Morals*. Edited and translated by Allen W. Wood. New Haven, Conn.: Yale University Press, 2002.

Novak, David. *Suicide and Morality: The Theories of Plato, Aquinas, and Kant and Their Relevance for Suicidology*. New York: Scholars Studies, 1975.

SEE ALSO: Euthanasia; Hobbes, Thomas; Hume, David; Kant, Immanuel; Kevorkian, Jack; Self-interest; Selfishness; Stoic ethics; Suicide; Thomas Aquinas.

Self-regulation

DEFINITION: Imposition of a code of conduct or set of ethical standards by an organization or profession upon its own members

TYPE OF ETHICS: Business and labor ethics

SIGNIFICANCE: The term self-regulation generally implies that measures have been taken to preempt or otherwise render superfluous government intervention or statutory regulation of an industry. Essentially, a group promises to act ethically in order to avoid being forced to act legally. To the extent that members of the group may disagree with the action taken on their behalf, self-regulation raises issues about individual autonomy.

During the late nineteenth century, social critics began to promote increased government regulation of business, industry, and various professions. In an attempt to stave off additional government intrusion into commercial affairs, many Self-Regulatory Organizations (SROs) were formed. SROs function as private rule-making and enforcement bodies that govern the activities of their members. Exemplary among such SROs is the American Institute of Certified Public Accountants (AICPA), which was founded in 1887 to self-regulate the accounting profession. The AICPA states that its mission is to "provide standards of professional conduct and performance," "monitor professional performance," and "promote public confidence in the integrity, objectivity, competence, and professionalism" of public accountants. SROs such as the AICPA possess the

power to censure or disbar their members from practice if they violate professional standards of conduct. Proponents of SROs contend that voluntary professional organizations are inherently more capable of encouraging ethical behavior than is a centralized government agency. Critics of SROs charge that the organizations merely act in the self-interest of their members rather than in the interest of society at large.

W. Jackson Parham, Jr.

SEE ALSO: Mozi; Price fixing; Professional ethics.

Self-respect

DEFINITION: Recognition of and behavior in accord with one's own intrinsic worth

TYPE OF ETHICS: Personal and social ethics

SIGNIFICANCE: Self-respect is usually opposed to self-degradation. That is, lack of self-respect results in treating oneself, or allowing someone else to treat one, as an object or a means, rather than as a subject or an end in oneself.

According to Immanuel Kant, self-respect is the most important of one's moral duties to oneself and is the prerequisite for the fulfillment of one's duties to others. To transgress this duty is to forfeit the intrinsic worth that one possesses as a human being. Being human confers upon one a uniquely significant status: One possesses the gift of reason, and only rational beings can engage in moral deliberation. Consequently, only rational beings can recognize the concept of duty and act in recognition of universal moral law. Since the moral law commands the respect of rational beings by virtue of its absolute power over them, each rational being must acknowledge and respect this power of recognition in every rational being. One owes one's fellow humans respect as rational, moral beings; likewise, one owes oneself respect insofar as one is human and, therefore, rational and moral.

FORFEITURE OF SELF-RESPECT

There are actions that result in the forfeiture of one's self-respect and the respect of others. Drunkenness robs a person of dignity insofar as it makes that person an object of ridicule, unable to act responsibly or to exercise the powers of rational deliberation. "Cringing servility" is likewise degrading, and it detracts from one's special status as human, as does lying. A liar, though possibly harming no one, becomes tainted by the intrinsic vileness of the lie. One who becomes the instrument or plaything of another, and who may do so for gain or profit, forfeits the respect that humans owe to themselves and to which they are entitled from others. Since all persons are equal by virtue of their common humanity, any act that places a person in a subservient position relative to someone else diminishes that person's self-respect. Accepting favors or charity places one in a permanently subordinate position relative to one's benefactor, a position in which the recipient remains even after repaying the debt.

Suicide, however, is the most serious violation of one's duty to oneself because it constitutes the use of oneself as an instrument, a means to an end, violating the supreme moral duty to treat every human being, including oneself, as an end rather than a means. To end one's life, even to escape intolerable suffering, is an abuse of the ennobling freedom that gives humans the capacity for virtue. Finally, just as this freedom is the source of human virtue, so is it also the source of human depravity, which springs from actions that not only dehumanize the perpetrators but also degrade them below the level of animals. Such an action is the *crimen carnis contra naturam*, an unnatural crime of the flesh, exemplified by an offense so abominable that it arouses nausea and contempt in one who merely contemplates it. In the light of the potential for depravity through the abuse of humanity's freedom, each person has a special responsibility to use that freedom to bring credit to himself or herself as an individual representative of humanity, for when one degrades oneself individually, one degrades humanity as a whole. According to Kant, respect for humanity as exemplified in oneself reveals one's respect for the moral law.

From the standpoint of modern moral psychology, self-respect may be viewed as being somewhat different from "self-esteem." Whereas self-respect is rooted in the moral quality of one's character, self-esteem refers to a positive assessment of oneself that may come from traits such as appearance, personality, talents, and so forth. The difference is evident in the fact that a negative appraisal of oneself with respect to characteristics such as physical appearance or talent does not necessarily result in an unwillingness to recognize one's value and rights as a human being.

MODERN MORAL PSYCHOLOGY

Self-respect, in addition to being an important theme in modern moral psychology, occupies a prominent place in the ethical thought of modern moral philosophers after Kant. Thomas Hill, Jr., allows self-respect to retain its Kantian significance when he contrasts it with servility. Servility, which is marked by a refusal to insist on respect from others and by a willingness to submit to public humiliation, is morally blameworthy when it springs from laziness, timidity, or the desire to retain some relatively unimportant advantage. The moral wrongness of this kind of servility results from the fact that in refusing to stand up for one's rights, one devalues oneself as a human being. In doing so, one devalues the moral law, which humans have a unique duty to uphold.

Self-respect serves as an important component in a well-ordered society, according to John Rawls in *A Theory of Justice* (1971). Rawls distinguishes self-respect as the most important primary good, a primary good being something that a rational individual would want regardless of the kind of life the person lives or whatever else that person wants. The just society, in recognizing the importance of each individual, provides a strong foundation for self-respect. A person who has a secure sense of self-worth is more likely to carry out life plans successfully, since the value of those plans is derived to a significant degree from the self-respect that comes from having one's personal value acknowledged by society.

Barbara Forrest

FURTHER READING

Darwall, Stephen L. "Two Kinds of Respect." In *Ethics and Personality: Essays in Moral Psychology*, edited by John Deigh. Chicago: University of Chicago Press, 1992.

Deigh, John. "Shame and Self-Esteem: A Critique." In *Ethics and Personality: Essays in Moral Psychology*. Chicago: University of Chicago Press, 1992.

Didion, Joan. "On Self-Respect." In *Slouching Towards Bethlehem*. New York: Noonday Press, 1990.

Hill, Thomas, Jr. "Servility and Self-Respect." In *Vice and Virtue in Everyday Life: Introductory*

Readings in Ethics, edited by Christina Sommers and Fred Sommers. 4th ed. Fort Worth, Tex.: Harcourt Brace College, 1997.

hooks, bell. *Rock My Soul: Black People and Self-Esteem*. New York: Atria Books, 2003.

Kant, Immanuel. *Lectures on Ethics*. Edited by Peter Heath and J. B. Schneewind. Translated by Peter Heath. New York: Cambridge University Press, 2001.

Owens, Timothy J., Sheldon Stryker, and Norman Goodman, eds. *Extending Self-Esteem Theory and Research: Sociological and Psychological Currents*. New York: Cambridge University Press, 2001.

Rawls, John. *A Theory of Justice*. Rev. ed. Cambridge, Mass.: Belknap Press of Harvard University Press, 1999.

SEE ALSO: Character; Dignity; Duty; Guilt and shame; Honor; Kant, Immanuel; Perfectionism; Pride; Psychology.

Self-righteousness

DEFINITION: Belief that one's own moral values are superior to those of others or that one's own actions comport better with a common value system than do those of others; narrow-mindedly or self-importantly preachy

TYPE OF ETHICS: Personal and social ethics

SIGNIFICANCE: Self-righteousness is commonly associated with lack of sympathy or compassion for others. It connotes an inability to put oneself in another person's shoes and an utter lack of nuance in applying abstract moral rules to concrete, complex, flawed human reality.

Self-righteousness can be condemned as involving either or both of two moral faults: hypocrisy (one does not measure up to one's avowed standards) or pride (one treats others with disdain or makes ostentatious displays of one's accomplishments). In the first case, one's claim to being righteous is vitiated by unacknowledged moral faults; in the second case, by behavior toward other persons designed to make them feel inferior and to enhance one's own self-image by comparison.

Christian thinking has typically opposed finding one's righteousness in oneself in favor of finding it through faith in Jesus. Self-righteousness can, however, be understood more positively as the reasonable conviction that one indeed does adhere of one's own will to a defensible moral code and thus deserves self-approval. Such self-approval, however, does not warrant requiring others to accept that judgment. Also, Jesus' condemnation of the Pharisees as hypocrites for attending to external rather than internal matters of law and morality (Matt. 23) points to the possibility of self-deception that is inherent in thinking of oneself as righteous.

Paul L. Redditt

SEE ALSO: Character; Hypocrisy; Pride; Self-deception.

Sentience

DEFINITION: Capacity to feel pain and pleasure; consciousness

TYPE OF ETHICS: Animal rights

SIGNIFICANCE: Some animal rights advocates assert that sentience is a necessary and sufficient condition for moral standing, because morality requires that all creatures capable of suffering be prevented from suffering, as much as possible. Many philosophers, however, believe that consciousness alone is insufficient, and the actual condition of moral standing is *self*-consciousness. They assert, in other words, that only moral agents, those capable of making moral decisions, have full moral worth.

Derived from the Latin verb *sentīre*, meaning to feel or perceive, the term "sentient" was used as early as 1632 to describe a being as conscious. The concept of sentience (the quality of being sentient) became crucial to the animal rights movement after Peter Singer took it to be a necessary and sufficient condition for having interests in his book *Animal Liberation* (1975). Singer's view was that all (and only) beings that are capable of feeling pain or conscious suffering have interests that matter from the moral point of view. The question "Which beings are sentient?" is answered by using an analogy. The more relevant behavioral and neurophysiological similarities there are between a given organism and a human being, the stronger is the case for saying that the organism is sentient. In *Animal Liberation*, Singer speculated that (with the exception of cephalopods like octopi, squid, and cuttlefish) probably only animals above the phylogenetic "level" of mollusks are conscious. While excluding insects, this does include crustaceans (such as shrimp and lobsters).

Many who have examined the available evidence have concluded that although all vertebrates probably are capable of feeling pain, invertebrates probably are not (again, with the exception of cephalopods).

Gary E. Varner

SEE ALSO: Animal consciousness; Animal research; Animal rights; Artificial intelligence; Brain death; Moral status of animals; Pain; Robotics; Singer, Peter; Vivisection.

Service to others

DEFINITION: Helping others without expectation of reciprocity

TYPE OF ETHICS: Personal and social ethics

SIGNIFICANCE: Service to others is denying one's own self-interests in order to serve the interests of others. Such service may be motivated by a personal sense of civic obligation, moral or religious obligation, or some calculated social utility. A service-to-others ethic in Western civilization is built upon the foundations of classical Greek and Roman civic philosophy as well as Judeo-Christian moral philosophy.

In classical Greek and Roman thought the ideal citizen serves society and other citizens selflessly—a requirement that weighed especially heavily upon the privileged classes. The Greeks and Romans understood that citizenship required individual sacrifices in order to provide for the common good. Without such sacrifices, society would degenerate into a chaos of self-interest in which the strong would dominate the weak, thereby destroying social cohesion. Both the values of honor and duty underscored the classical notion of service to others. The most honored Greek citizens were not necessarily the wealthiest or most beautiful or most wise but those who heroically sacrificed and performed their civic duty to society.

The Judeo-Christian tradition built upon the classical tradition by adding a layer of moral obligation to the service ethic. In the Judeo-Christian tradition, service to one's neighbor is not merely a civic obligation for the sake of social cohesion but also a religious obligation imposed by God. In other words, to serve others is to serve God. The Bible, both Old and New Testaments, is replete with examples of how the faithful are called to serve others. The powerful have a special obligation to protect and help the weak. In a way, service to others becomes a test of religious devotion.

A more economic or utilitarian approach would argue that by serving others one improves one's own lot however distant or vague the benefit may be. Under the rubric of conditional altruism, one's interest in serving others in conditional upon others (not necessarily the beneficiary of one's own actions) doing the same. For example, a person may be more likely to donate money to public television knowing that others are willing to do the same. Or even more broadly, one may be more likely to help the homeless if one knows that others are also serving the homeless or at least using their resources to alleviate social problems.

A person's service is conditional upon the service of others because one recognizes that the likelihood of success in any social endeavor is greater if more people are involved, as combining their resources increases the likelihood of success. Moreover, when there is greater level of social involvement by others—even on different problems—individual persons calculate that they will ultimately reap some benefit, however distant or indirect, such as safer streets or better schools.

Steve Neiheisel

FURTHER READING

Bellah, Robert, et al. *Habits of the Heart: Individualism and Commitment in American Life*. Berkeley: University of California Press, 1996.

Bellah, Robert, William M. Sullivan, and Ann Swidler. *The Good Society*. Knopf, 1992.

Gomes, Peter. *The Good Life*. San Francisco: HarperSanFrancisco, 2002.

SEE ALSO: Altruism; Benevolence; Charity; Common good; Maximal vs. minimal ethics; Objectivism; Peace Corps; Selfishness; Tipping; Virtue.

Sex therapy

DEFINITION: Mental and emotional treatment of sexual disorders

TYPE OF ETHICS: Psychological ethics

SIGNIFICANCE: For many people, sex therapy can conflict with personal or intimate codes of ethics, because it involves talking about activity that they feel should remain private or because they believe it entails seeking artificial help with something that should be utterly natural. In addition, sex therapy raises all of the ethical issues of therapy and intimate relations generally, including confidentiality, mutual respect between partners, and the nature of the therapist-patient relationship.

Sexual therapy was pioneered by William H. Masters and Virginia E. Johnson, although other therapists have also created many important techniques. Sex therapy generally focuses on reducing performance anxiety, changing self-defeating expectations, and fostering sexual skills or competencies. Both sex partners are often involved in therapy, although individual treatment is possible. Because sexual dysfunction may be linked to drug effects, sex therapists must be knowledgeable to some degree about pharmacology. Sex therapists educate the couple and guide them through a series of homework assignments. They also treat interpersonal problems.

TYPES OF SEXUAL DISORDERS

Three main sexual disorders treated by sex therapy are arousal and erectile disorders, premature ejaculation, and inhibited orgasm. Two causes are predominant: people's tendency to adopt a spectator role during intercourse, which causes them to examine their own performance; and the fear of performing inadequately. Either of these problems can create inhibitions against enjoying the normal sensations that lead to sexual satisfaction.

Arousal and erectile disorders are of two types: primary and secondary erectile dysfunction. Primary erectile dysfunction means that a man has never had an erection of sufficient strength for sexual intercourse. Fear and unusual sensitivity or anxiety regarding sexual incidents that have happened early in life may contribute to primary erectile dysfunction. Secondary erectile dysfunction means that the man has had successful sexual intercourse in the past but now fails to achieve penile erection in 25 percent or more of his sexual attempts. Secondary erectile dysfunction can be a vicious cycle: One or a few incidents of impotence can lead a man to become overanxious and abnormally sensitive, so that the next

(AP/Wide World Photos)

Masters and Johnson

Using scientific measuring equipment, William H. Masters and his wife, Virginia E. Johnson, recorded physiological responses to sexual stimulations in men and women engaging in sexual activity. In 1966 they published the results of an eleven-year-long research project in the best-selling book *Human Sexual Response*. Their other books include *Homosexuality in Perspective* (1979), Crisis: *Heterosexual Behavior in the Age of AIDS* (1988), *The Pleasure Bond: A New Look at Sexuality and Commitment* (1975), and *Textbook of Sexual Medicine* (1979).

attempts at intercourse are also failures. Next, an interpersonal component enters the picture. Almost any response by the man's partner exacerbates the problem. If she continues to be physically affectionate, he may interpret her actions as a demand for sexual intercourse, a demand that he fears he is unable to satisfy. If she is less affectionate physically, he may defensively interpret her behavior as a rejection of his sexually inadequate self.

Sensate focus, which is a basic element of treatment of arousal and erectile disorders (as well as inhibited orgasm), involves directing attention away from intercourse and toward other behaviors that feel pleasurable to the partner, such as caressing the neck or massaging the back. Intercourse is initially forbidden by the therapist, so these exercises take on importance, allowing the couple to experience sexuality in a relaxed, non-performance-oriented manner. Gradually, more and more involved sexual activities are allowed, and the couple is eventually told that intercourse is permissible. Typically, such treatment is successful. Improvement rates for primary erectile dysfunction are about 60 percent, and for secondary erectile dysfunction, they are 74 percent.

Premature ejaculation occurs when a man cannot delay ejaculation long enough to satisfy his sexual partner during at least half of his sexual encounters. Premature ejaculation is usually caused by emotional and psychological factors. The most common treatment is the squeeze technique, in which the man's sexual partner stimulates him manually until he signals that ejaculation is about to occur. Then, the partner firmly squeezes the tip of his penis to inhibit orgasm. When he feels that he has control, stimulation is repeated. Gradually, he acquires the ability to delay orgasm sufficiently for satisfactory intercourse.

Inhibited orgasm is of two types: primary and secondary. Primary orgasmic dysfunction means that a woman never achieves an orgasm through any method of sexual stimulation. Although many causes are physical, more often they are psychological and are grounded in extreme religious orthodoxy, unfavorable communication about sexual activities, or some childhood trauma. Secondary orgasmic dysfunction is the inability of a woman who has achieved orgasm by one technique or another in the past to achieve it in a given situation. Secondary orgasmic dysfunction may occur when a woman is unable to accept her partner because she finds him sexually un-

attractive, undesirable, or in some other way unacceptable. In addition, many women find that orgasm brings about feelings of guilt, shame, and fear.

Tʀᴇᴀᴛᴍᴇɴᴛ

Treatment of primary and secondary orgasmic disorders involves understanding the woman's sexual value system and the reasons for her inability or unwillingness to achieve orgasm. Using her value system, the therapist teaches her to respond to sexual stimulation. Often, she is encouraged to focus on sexual responsiveness through masturbation or vigorous stimulation by a partner. Initially, the couple is directed to avoid intercourse but is taken through a series of treatment sessions involving an increasing amount of erotic pleasure. Orgasm is not the focus of these sessions, but ultimately it is achieved in an unhurried situation in which pressure to perform is removed from both partners.

Treatment of both male and female disorders involves teaching people not to fear failure and helping them to be free from anxiety. Both the man and woman are taught the art of giving pleasure in order to receive pleasure. They are encouraged to relax and to enjoy touching, feeling, and being sexual. The therapist may arrange desensitization experiences in real sexual encounters between the couple. Eventually, natural processes will take control and intercourse will follow in due time.

A central aspect of treatment of both male and female sexual disorders is communication. Couples must learn to communicate their sexual needs without embarrassment and misinterpretation. Such communication may be difficult. Also, for sex therapy to be successful, the sexual partners must be flexible individuals who are willing to accommodate the directive- and sometimes value-laden features of sex therapy. In addition, both partners need to develop a better understanding of male and female sexual response cues. Sex therapy may involve a specific technique, such as the squeeze technique, or an overall treatment of the couple's relationship.

Lillian M. Range

Fᴜʀᴛʜᴇʀ Rᴇᴀᴅɪɴɢ

Arentewicz, Gerd, and Gunter Schmidt, eds. *The Treatment of Sexual Disorders*. New York: Basic Books, 1983.

Hyde, Janet S, and John D. DeLamater. *Understand-*

ing *Human Sexuality.* 8th ed. New York: McGraw-Hill, 2003.

Kaplan, Helen S. *Disorders of Sexual Desire and Other New Concepts and Techniques in Sex Therapy.* New York: Simon & Schuster, 1979.

Kleinplatz, Peggy J., ed. *New Directions in Sex Therapy: Innovations and Alternatives.* Philadelphia: Brunner-Routledge, 2001.

Masters, William H., and Virginia E. Johnson. *Human Sexual Inadequacy.* Boston: Little, Brown, 1970.

Wade, Carole, and Sarah Cirese *Study Guide to Accompany Human Sexuality.* 2d ed. Chicago: Harcourt Brace Jovanovich, 1991.

SEE ALSO: Lust; Marriage; Promiscuity; Psychology; Sexuality and sexual ethics.

Sexism

DEFINITION: Bias toward people on the basis of their sex

TYPE OF ETHICS: Sex and gender issues

SIGNIFICANCE: Like racism, sexism most commonly refers to instances of sexual prejudice that are supported or validated by institutional power structures. Sexism is, in fact, perhaps the clearest demonstration of the importance of such covert power structures in enforcing prejudice, since sexism against women remains common in societies in which women comprise a majority.

A person is sexist who believes, for example, that women cannot be competent doctors or that men cannot be competent nursery school teachers. Institutions, as well as individuals, can be sexist. Sexism can be revealed in stereotypes (beliefs about people based on gender), prejudice (negatively prejudging a person solely on the basis of gender), or discrimination (acting in accordance with prejudice).

Sexism influences perceptions and behavior from birth. In one classic study, fathers described their first babies almost immediately after they were born; mothers described their babies during their first twenty-four hours. Despite objective hospital records that showed that these baby boys and girls were almost identical in color, muscle tone, reflex re-sponses, weight, and length, parents described them differently. Baby girls were perceived as relatively softer, finer-featured, smaller, and less attentive. Fathers in particular were susceptible to this type of selective perception. Children and adults learn from these types of messages what society expects of women and men.

Sexism can be blatant, as it is when a female premedical student is told that women belong at home rather than at work or a male home economics student is told that men belong at work rather than at home. Sexism can also be subtle, as it is when people interpret the same behavior in different ways depending on whether it is exhibited by women or men. People may see a man as assertive but a woman as pushy, a man as flexible but a woman as fickle, a woman as sensitive but a man as a sissy, or a woman as polite but a man as passive. For example, in one research project, college students rated the quality of professional articles in several fields. When an article was attributed to a woman, it received lower ratings than it did when it was attributed to a man. Furthermore, women raters were as guilty as men at assuming male superiority. Therefore, sexism influences both women and men in a variety of blatant and subtle ways.

Although sexism is typically most damaging to women, men can also be victims. Even in the current era, for example, people are more willing to hire a man for a "man's job" and to hire a woman for a "woman's job."

Sexism extends to the way in which people use language. Benjamin Whorf advocated the concept of linguistic relativity, the theory that the properties of language shape perceptions of the world. His classic example compared English and Eskimo views of snow. English has only one word for snow, whereas Eskimo has many words that distinguish falling snow, slushy snow, and so forth. In recent years, the idea that language influences people's perceptions of the world has extended to the way in which sexist terms are used. Although the masculine forms are supposed to refer to both men and women, most people think of men when they are used. For this reason, some scholars substitute gender-neutral terms such as "firefighter" for gender-laden terms such as "fireman" and avoid using the terms "lady" and "girl" on the ground that they perpetuate the view of women as frivolous and childish. The American Psychological Association's *Publication Manual* contains guidelines for avoiding sexist language that include using the plural whenever appropriate, using "his and her" rather than "his," and using parallel construction (for example, "husband and wife" rather than "man and wife").

Sexist language harms people in two different ways. First, women may reach adulthood feeling inferior because of the more frequent references in language to males. For example, in an analysis of children's books published after 1972, most of the fictional characters were male, whether the stories were about children, adults, or even animals. Furthermore, boys were characterized as curious, clever, and adventurous, whereas girls were characterized as fearful and incompetent. Such bias takes a heavy toll on female self-esteem. Second, the use of certain terms may lead women and men to believe that certain occupations are beyond their capabilities. The harm done by this type of language can be avoided if writers and speakers are aware of the problem and motivated to change the gender-laden terms they are accustomed to using.

Lillian M. Range

FURTHER READING

American Psychological Association. *Publication Manual of the American Psychological Association.* 5th ed. Washington, D.C.: Author, 2001.

Bem, Sandra L. "Gender Schema Theory: A Cognitive Account of Sex Typing." *Psychological Review* 88, no. 4 (July, 1981): 354-364.

Bourdieu, Pierre. *Masculine Domination.* Translated by Richard Nice. Stanford, Calif.: Stanford University Press, 2001.

Maccoby, Eleanor E., and Carol N. Jacklin. *The Psychology of Sex Differences.* Stanford, Calif.: Stanford University Press, 1974.

Matlin, Margaret W. *The Psychology of Women.* New York: Holt, Rinehart and Winston, 1987.

Moss, Donald, ed. *Hating in the First Person Plural: Psychoanalytic Essays on Racism, Homophobia, Misogyny, and Terror.* New York: Other Press, 2003.

Rubin, Jeffrey Z., Frank J. Provenzano, and Zella Luria. "The Eye of the Beholder: Parents' Views on Sex of Newborns." *American Journal of Orthopsychiatry* 44 (July, 1974): 512-519.

Swim, Janet, Eugene Borgida, and Geoffrey Maruyama. "Joan McKay Versus John McKay: Do Gender Stereotypes Bias Evaluations?" *Psychological Bulletin* 105, no. 3 (May, 1989): 409-429.

Tavris, Carol, and Carole Offir. *The Longest War.* New York: Harcourt Brace Jovanovich, 1977.

Whorf, Benjamin L. *Language, Thought, and Reality: Selected Writings of Benjamin Lee Whorf.* Edited and introduction by John B. Carroll. Foreword by Stuart Chase. Cambridge, Mass.: The MIT Press, 1967.

SEE ALSO: Beauvoir, Simone de; Homophobia; *Second Sex, The*; Sexual abuse and harassment; Sexual stereotypes; Suffrage.

Sexual abuse and harassment

DEFINITION: Inappropriate sexual behavior or speech directed toward a professional colleague or subordinate, or otherwise engaged in under color of social or institutional authority

TYPE OF ETHICS: Sex and gender issues

SIGNIFICANCE: Sexual abuse and harassment involve such moral issues as the moral worth of a person, gender inequality, and the social distribution of power, authority, and opportunities.

Both the perpetrator of sexual harassment and the victim of sexual harassment may be either male or female as well as being either heterosexual or homosexual. In the vast majority of incidents of sexual harassment, however, the victim is female and the perpetrator is a male heterosexual. This is true primarily because gender inequality is endemic in virtually every culture on earth. That is, the history of the social roles of men as compared with women is such that men, owing only to an accident of birth, are granted significantly more power and authority in society and enjoy the full complement of opportunities that a particular society makes available. (Clearly, there are other factors, many of which are also accidents of birth, that might preclude some segments of a society's male population from this privileged status, such as skin color, religious affiliation, and so forth.)

Women, by contrast, are granted significantly less power and authority in society (in some cases, historically, none) and suffer severe restrictions with respect to the availability of opportunities offered by the society. The result of such an institutionalized imbalance of power and opportunities between the genders is an insidious development of social expectations according to which women literally come to be viewed (even by one another) as second-class citizens.

To the extent that these traditional distinctions between the social roles of men and women come to be seen as "the norm" and to the extent that the members of society (male and female), even if only implicitly, recognize that such distinctions are attributable only to the difference in gender, a social climate is created in which any abuse of an individual who happens to be female—simply because she is female—is taken less seriously than it would be were the same type of abuse to be directed at a male person. The rationale for this difference in response is based on the abused individual's status as a member of the privileged or the nonprivileged gender.

THE IMPORTANCE OF SOCIAL SETTINGS

It should come as no surprise, then, that social settings in which the imbalance of power and opportunities between the genders is most prevalent are ripe for sexual abuse or harassment; two such examples are the work and educational environments.

In the typical work environment, positions of power and authority are held, for the most part, by men, while women usually hold positions of less power and authority. This tradition has been maintained, in large part, because of an institutionalized lack of opportunity for women even to be considered eligible for positions of greater power and authority. Given this fact, it is not at all uncommon for women in the workplace to be the victims of sexual harassment. Such harassment typically involves a male perpetrator of sexual harassment who holds a position of authority over the female victim of sexual harassment. In the work environment, sexual harassment can also take other forms; for example, the perpetrator might be the male client of a female employee who is the victim.

The most obvious imbalance of power and authority in the educational environment is the fact that the instructor determines the grades of the students. Given this fact, there is always the potential for an instructor to abuse the educational system by sexually harassing a student. Although, in theory, the possibility is greater here for both the perpetrator and the victim to be of either gender and of either sexual orientation, in practice, more often than not, the victim is female and the perpetrator is male (heterosexual). The fact that, more often than not, the perpetrator in this environment is male and heterosexual is explained fundamentally (but not completely) by the fact that although female instructors, within the student-instructor relationship, possess the power to assign student grades, in the society at large, they are still members of the nonprivileged gender, which fact has great influence on their social behavior. Furthermore, in the society at large, there are far more heterosexual males than there are homosexual males.

Additional environments in which sexual harassment occurs are the therapeutic environment and the religious environment. Incidents of sexual harassment in the therapeutic environment are usually similar to those that take place in the educational environment, while incidents of sexual harassment in the religious environment are usually similar to those that take place in the work environment.

Having recognized some examples of specific social environments that allow for above-average potential for sexual harassment because of their very one-sided imbalance of power and opportunities between perpetrator and victim, it is important to acknowledge that any social setting is a potential stage for sexual harassment. Moreover, sexual harassment is not restricted to relationships that involve only one perpetrator and only one victim, and it is not restricted to a private setting. For example, two or more perpetrators of sexual harassment might together verbally abuse several other persons at the same time and might do so in a public forum.

TYPES OF HARASSMENT

Some specific types of sexual harassment are sexist comments (remarks or jokes that stereotype or disparage a single gender), unwelcome attention (uninvited flirtations), body language (fixed eye contact on specific body parts of another), physical sexual advances (pinching, fondling, and so forth), verbal sexual advances (such as nonspecific verbal expressions of sexual interest), explicit sexual propositions (unambiguous invitations for sexual encounters), and sexual coercion or bribery (unambiguous invitations for sexual encounters with the implicit or explicit promise of rewards for acceding or the threat of punishment for refusing).

What makes sexual harassment morally repugnant is that the victim is devalued as a person, in that the victim's dignity as a person is abused, and that such harassment inhibits the victim's ability to pursue whatever activities he or she was engaged in prior to the occurrence of the incident. Any defense that has ever been offered by a perpetrator of sexual harassment, after the fact, has involved the idea that the fact of harassment, or the offense that it engenders, depends upon the person; that is, what offends one person might not offend another, even another of the same gender in the same circumstances. Although it can be granted that sexual harassment is, in a sense, "in the eye of the beholder," this in no way morally excuses it. In the final analysis, the determining factor for what constitutes sexual harassment must be the interpretation of the victim as reasonably construed from the victim's perspective.

Stephen C. Taylor

FURTHER READING

Dodds, Susan M., et al. "Sexual Harassment." *Social Theory and Practice* 14 (Summer, 1988): 111-130.

Hughes, John C., and Larry May. "Sexual Harassment." *Social Theory and Practice* 6 (Fall, 1980): 249-280.

MacKinnon, Catharine A. *Sexual Harassment of Working Women.* New Haven, Conn.: Yale University Press, 1979.

Neville, Kathleen. *Internal Affairs: The Abuse of Power, Sexual Harassment, and Hypocrisy in the Workplace.* New York: McGraw-Hill, 2000.

Skaine, Rosemarie. *Power and Gender: Issues in Sexual Dominance and Harassment.* Jefferson, N.C.: McFarland & Co., 1996.

Thomas, Alison M., and Celian Kitzinger, eds. *Sexual Harassment: Contemporary Feminist Perspectives.* Bristol, Pa.: Open University Press, 1997.

Wall, Edmund. "The Definition of Sexual Harassment." *Public Affairs Quarterly* 5 (October, 1991): 371-385.

Wise, Sue, and Liz Stanley. *Georgie Porgie: Sexual Harassment in Everyday Life.* London: Pandora, 1987.

SEE ALSO: Abuse; Child abuse; Coercion; Incest; Internet chat rooms; Rape; Rape and political domination; Roman Catholic priests scandal; Sexism; Sexual stereotypes; Victims' rights.

Sexual revolution

THE EVENT: Social movement involving the relaxation of sexual mores and inhibitions, especially regarding premarital and nonmonogamous sexual relations, and a more open embrace of sexuality generally

DATE: 1960's

TYPE OF ETHICS: Sex and gender issues

SIGNIFICANCE: The sexual revolution has been variously described as liberating people from im-

The sexual revolution of the 1960's was closely identified with the free-spirited "hippie" movement, which reached its apotheosis at the Woodstock music festival, near Bethel, New York, in August, 1969. (AP/Wide World Photos)

proper or artificial ethical restrictions, or as an immoral movement that degraded human beings and human relations. One of the central issues raised by debates over the meaning of the movement is the proper source of sexual morality. Is it a matter of personal ethical intuition and values guiding intimate behavior, or is it a matter of general moral rules regulating such behavior?

During the 1940's and 1950's, the United States and most other Western countries were sexually restrictive. Prepubertal sexuality was ignored or denied, marital sex was considered the only legitimate sexual outlet, and other forms of sexual expression were condemned or prohibited by law.

During the 1960's, with the development of reliable contraceptive methods, sexual activities became less restricted. Premarital intercourse became more acceptable and more frequent, the latter particularly so among women. Young people became more sexually active at younger ages, and society tolerated a wider variety of sexual behavior than had been tolerated in the past. This change, the sexual revolution, was most prominent among women.

During the 1990's, however, despite any so-called revolution, adolescent boys still reported more sexual activity than adolescent girls, with about 80 percent of boys and 70 percent of girls reporting sexual intercourse before the end of adolescence. Also, a double standard for sexual behavior existed: Males were subtly encouraged to engage in sexual behavior but females were subtly discouraged from engaging in sexual activity. Additionally, the life-threatening disease acquired immunodeficiency syndrome (AIDS) made people aware that sexual activity could result in death. Finally, society in general became more conservative. The sexual revolution changed, with sexual activity and attitudes becoming more conservative, and some differences between men and women remained present.

Lillian M. Range

SEE ALSO: *Griswold v. Connecticut*; Premarital sex; Promiscuity; Sexism; Sexuality and sexual ethics; Sexually transmitted diseases.

Sexual stereotypes

DEFINITION: Preconceptions about the capacities, values, characteristics, or desires of persons based on their sex or gender

TYPE OF ETHICS: Sex and gender issues

SIGNIFICANCE: Sexual stereotypes can prevent men and women from seeing themselves and each other clearly, interfering with moral imperatives to know oneself, to recognize others, and to treat others as dignified subjects or ends in themselves rather than as objects or means to one's ends.

Sexual stereotypes are based on the idea that all females are alike in personality, interests, and abilities, and that males also constitute a homogeneous group. The masculine stereotype includes the characteristics of aggressiveness, achievement orientation, dominance, rationality, independence, high sexual interest, and physical strength. The feminine stereotype emphasizes passivity, submissiveness, emotionality, nurturance, modesty, low sexual interest, and physical weakness. Although stereotypes are an easy way of categorizing people, they are extreme generalizations. They destroy individuality and lead to discriminatory behavior and the victimization of women in the forms of domestic abuse, rape, and pornography.

HISTORY

Male and female sexual stereotypes have existed in European civilization since ancient Greece and probably even earlier. Aristotle, Paul of Tarsus and other leaders of the Christian church, and civil authorities have endorsed the idea that women share typical characteristics. The concept of women as evil was an important rationale for the witch-hunts of the sixteenth and seventeenth centuries. European males typically considered women the "weaker sex," not only physically but also intellectually and morally.

Criticism of sexual stereotypes grew out of John Locke's political philosophy of natural rights. Mary Wollstonecraft's treatise *On the Subjection of Women* (1792) was an early statement about the effects of sexual stereotypes on the liberty and personal growth of women. Elizabeth Cady Stanton and other leaders of the mid-nineteenth century women's movement in the United States worked chiefly for civil liberties and intellectual parity. The negative effects of sexual stereotypes were restated by Simone de Beauvior in *The Second Sex* in 1949. They were an important concern in the women's liberation movement and in social science research during the second half of the twentieth century.

ETHICAL PRINCIPLES

Sexual stereotypes are attitudes about a group of individuals. These attitudes are ethically significant because they often lead to discrimination. Women were denied political liberty because they were regarded as incapable of rational thinking. Thus, strongly held stereotypes typically imply an infringement on the liberty of individuals.

Furthermore, stereotypes lead to various problems in social equity, including educational and job discrimination and the denial of economic power. The stereotyped differences between men and women are assumed to be innate rather than cultural or socially acquired. Historically, women have been denied access to educational opportunities at the precollege, college, and graduate level. Lessened opportunities are reflected in lower salaries, less prestige and influence, and fewer opportunities to advance. Job discrimination in hiring and promotions results from stereotypes about what work is appropriate for women. Accordingly, stereotypes can be used to justify denying civil and economic rights to women and granting preferential treatment to men.

Stereotypes of women as passive—even masochistic—and of men as aggressive and sexually driven contribute to the victimization of women by means of domestic abuse, rape, and pornography. These stereotypes are reflected in the psychoanalytic theories of Sigmund Freud and other psychodynamic theorists. "Natural" male aggression can be used as justification for violence; this argument removes ethical responsibility for actions from the aggressor. Stereotypes can even be used to suggest that the victim should be blamed for inappropriate conduct that led to the offense; for example, it may be suggested that a woman who enters a bar alone is inviting rape.

ETHICAL ISSUES

The controversy regarding whether to emphasize equality between the sexes, or to recognize true gender differences remains an issue. Whether women should seek equality with men by attempting to reduce stereotypes to a minimum or should challenge

male domination with a different, feminine ideology is unclear. For example, Carol Gilligan has proposed that there are clear ethical differences in the kinds of reasoning that men and women use to analyze ethical dilemmas. Males usually describe their reasoning as being based on principles that are applicable to every situation. Females frequently make ethical decisions that are strongly weighted by a consideration of the particular situation and, especially, by social relationships and responsibilities. Although it is important to reduce stereotypes, it may also be important to maintain a diversity of gender perspectives.

Annette Baier proposes that a particularly feminine ethical stance is that of trust. Trust underlies cooperation and thus is significant for ethical interpersonal relations. Trust is significant in family relations, between husband and wife as well as between parent and child. Because trust is part of the feminine stereotype, however, it has been largely ignored by philosophy.

OTHER FORMS OF STEREOTYPING

Sexual stereotypes; racial, ethnic, and religious stereotypes; and age stereotypes are similar. People who rigidly hold one kind of stereotype frequently espouse other stereotypes. Because such attitudes lead to discriminatory behavior, all such stereotypes tend to deny equality and opportunity to members of a stigmatized group. In Western society, older minority women experience a triple oppression because of stereotypes and discrimination.

Prejudice against homosexual males and lesbian women is also related to sexual stereotyping. Some prejudicial attitudes result from a perception that homosexual males and lesbians do not act in accord with commonly held stereotypes. Social stigmatization and other forms of harassment frequently result from such views.

Mary M. Vandendorpe

FURTHER READING

Baier, Annette. *Postures of the Mind.* Minneapolis: University of Minnesota Press, 1985.

Davis, Angela Yvonne. *Women, Race, and Class.* New York: Random House, 1981.

Faludi, Susan. *Backlash: The Undeclared War Against American Women.* New York: Crown, 1991.

Gilligan, Carol. *In a Different Voice: Psychological*

Theory and Women's Development. Cambridge, Mass.: Harvard University Press, 1982.

Haskell, Molly. *From Reverence to Rape: The Treatment of Women in the Movies.* 2d ed. Chicago: University of Chicago Press, 1987.

Irigaray, Luce. *This Sex Which Is Not One.* Translated by Catherine Porter and and Carolyn Burke. Ithaca, N.Y.: Cornell University Press, 1985.

Jaggar, Alison M. *Feminist Politics and Human Nature.* Totowa, N.J.: Rowman & Littlefield, 1988.

Kaschak, Ellyn. *Engendered Lives.* New York: Basic Books, 1992.

Kittay, Eva Feder, and Diana T. Meyers, eds. *Women and Moral Theory.* Totowa, N.J.: Rowman & Littlefield, 1987.

Lloyd, Genevieve. *The Man of Reason: "Male" and "Female" in Western Philosophy.* 2d ed. Minneapolis: University of Minnesota Press, 1993.

Stangor, Charles, ed. *Stereotypes and Prejudice: Essential Readings.* Philadelphia: Psychology Press, 2000.

SEE ALSO: Ageism; Bigotry; *Feminine Mystique, The*; Homophobia; Pornography; Rape; *Second Sex, The*; Sexism; Sexual abuse and harassment; Social justice and responsibility.

Sexuality and sexual ethics

DEFINITION: Sexuality: aspects of people's desires, perceptions, actions, interactions, and identities that influence or constitute their sexual behavior; sexual ethics: formal and informal codes of conduct governing the moral permissibility of specific acts and expressions of sexuality

TYPE OF ETHICS: Sex and gender issues

SIGNIFICANCE: Sexuality is one of the most fundamental aspects of human identity and motivation. Even that statement is potentially controversial, however, because the proper relationship of one's sexual identity and experience to one's identity as a whole is a matter of ethical debate. Sexual ethics thus includes not merely the ethics of sexual activity and intimate relationships, but the ethically proper way to incorporate sexuality into one's life.

Men and women have most things in common. In that sense, the biblical view that one sex comes from the middle of the other is very appropriate. The biological view that the male is a modified female also indicates this strong commonality. Concepts of sexuality, however, focus on the differences associated with gender. Sexual assignment and the many behaviors associated with it are basic to personality. The most fundamental difference between male and female is that males produce sperm and females produce eggs, but to be classified as male or female does not involve merely the obvious differences in anatomy; sexuality has profound effects on how a person feels, thinks, communicates, and acts.

Attraction between the sexes and the pleasure inherent in the sex act constitute an efficient biological design that tends to continue the species, but sex is more than reproduction, and most human sex does not involve producing babies. Sex involves the desire for a meaningful, close relationship with another, and it involves the most pleasurable short-term act of which the body is capable. The intimacy of the sex act calls for trust and commitment. The philosopher Richard Solomon has stated, "To think that one can indulge in the traditionally most powerful symbolic activity in almost every culture without its meaning anything is an extravagant self-deception."

HUMAN ASPECTS OF SEXUALITY

Several biological factors are unique to human sex. First, humans are apparently the only creatures that consciously understand that sex is linked to reproduction. Other animals do not know that intercourse may cause pregnancy. Second, human females may be sexually receptive at any time. In contrast, many mammals mate only seasonally, when the hormonal levels, especially of estrogens, cause females to signal their receptivity to males. At that time females are said to be in "heat." Some mammals have more frequent periods of heat. The sexual interest and activity of human females, however, is different. It is influenced, but not limited to, specific hormone-dependent times. Circumstances, judgments, cultural norms, mood, and emotions play larger roles than do hormones when it comes to the timing of the sex act by humans. A third factor is that humans often have sex face-to-face, which seems to be significant in that it promotes bonding and commitment for the protection of possible offspring.

Childhood experiences affect the choice of a mate. Certain characteristics come to be valued. If a person meets and gets to know another person and this person meets many of the desired characteristics, attraction occurs. At that point, the brain is affected by chemicals (especially phenylethylamine) that are similar to amphetamines. The person experiences a chemical high that can last several years, causing the feelings of being in love. The continued presence of a partner causes endorphins to be released internally, causing feelings of calmness and security. This promotes long-term attachment. Finally, another chemical, oxytocin, is released. This chemical is thought to cause cuddling and to enhance pleasure in sex.

There is much that is not known, but sexual behavior is definitely more than simply genes and chemical reactions. Human sexuality is formed by a complicated interplay and overlap of genetics, culture, experiences, and free will. The roles of these elements are difficult to define. One can always argue about the extent to which females are biologically bound to be passive, coy, and monogamous. Likewise, one can question the extent to which males are dealing with genes that compel them to be aggressive, dominating, risk-taking, and promiscuous. How much weight should people give to genetics? How free are human actions?

GENETIC DETERMINATION

Genes, mainly but not exclusively, determine the production of hormones that cause the development of the sex organs and the various secondary physical differences such as body size, percentages of fat, tilt of the pelvis, muscle thickness, voice pitch, and thickness of body hair. Even the development of the brain and patterns of behavior are affected by the sex genes. Normally, two X chromosomes will basically program a woman, while having both an X and a Y chromosome will produce male characteristics.

In 1987, geneticist David C. Page and his colleagues found that there is a particular gene on the Y chromosome that is required to produce a male offspring. In a study of abnormal cases, Page found that a twelve-year-old girl was XY but that the Y chromosome was not complete, apparently lacking the male gene. About one in twenty thousand men is XX but also has inherited a small piece of the Y chromosome that includes the sex gene, causing him to develop as a male. Such XX males and XY females are usually infertile. The location of the sex gene on the Y chromosome (and the additional discovery of a similar sex gene on the X chromosome) indicates that genetic factors in sex determination are not completely understood. While further study is needed, questions about whether homosexuality is a matter of choice or inheritance are being raised. Preliminary investigation indicates that a gene for homosexuality may also exist. Other studies also indicate a physical difference in the structure of the brain when homosexuals and heterosexuals are compared.

CULTURAL INFLUENCE

Length of hair, type of dress, vocational choices, and many sexual behaviors seem to be mainly cultural values. Because every society has legitimate interests in sexual conduct, certain standards and norms of behavior are maintained. These may vary from culture to culture, but both religion and government tend to be involved, often reinforcing each other, as in the case of requiring marriage to be formalized as a way of providing family structure for the nurturing of children. Within a family, male and female children are usually raised quite differently. At times, these standards within a culture may change.

Many behaviors have more than one cause. For example, self-assertiveness, the ability to communicate openly and honestly in a functional way, appears to be related to gender. Hormones can certainly be given some credit for male aggressiveness in many activities, but women seem to be encouraged by society to be quiet, polite, and considerate of others' feelings, while men are encouraged to take charge. Change in this area can certainly be made by means of teaching and practicing communication techniques that allow both sexes to communicate openly and freely about their feelings, needs, and desires.

Only in the late twentieth century did significant numbers of girls and women begin participating in competitive sports. The positive results have shown that cultures may have mistaken ideas about fixed or natural sexual limits and roles.

FREE WILL

One can argue that all behavior and even culture is programmed by genetics, but biological determinism is a gloomy mechanistic view of life. Are people free to choose or do they merely respond in programmed ways to various signals? Free will allows people to accept, augment, or reject both nature and nurture. Individuals may choose to modify sexual characteristics, whether they are biological or cultural. One can shave hair or allow it to grow. One can wear high-heeled shoes that accent side movement in walking. A person may consciously choose to dress and act in ways that a society may generally see as part of the role of the opposite sex. Yet perhaps what is perceived as freedom is an illusion. Perhaps such modifications are also programmed. Are humans trapped by their biology? Biology is certainly not irrelevant to social behavior; however, as biologist Richard Lewontin has argued, there is simply not enough DNA to code for all the situations that humans face. Patterns of behavior can only be very generally coded. Humans do have choices.

AREAS OF CONCERN

Sexual ethics is concerned with questions about how sexuality might influence one's behavior, how basic biology might require careful thought and control, and how the common good might be preserved. Sexuality can have many goals, but even if sex and reproduction could be completely divorced, sex and morality cannot. Sex almost always involves another person. Sex, or the choice not to have sex, involves valuing others as ends in themselves, not merely as the means to selfish pleasure. This is not a new principle, even with Immanuel Kant, but goes back to the ancient Jewish and Christian command to love one's neighbor: to be concerned for the emotional and physical welfare of others. Beyond being a means of procreation, sex is a form of communication.

Sex involves much of ethics: trust, truth telling, commitment, friendship, and fairness. There really is no special variety of sexual ethics, but ethics in the sexual realm is very special. This is because sexual behaviors reflect the core of one's personality and can allow the most intimate knowledge of one's being. At the same time, the way in which sexuality is treated profoundly affects all interactions in a society. If the most personal relationships are unethical, then all relationships are at risk.

Societies have a justifiable interest in the area of sexuality. Children need good parents to care for them. The spread of sexually transmitted diseases (STDs) should be prevented; casual sex can carry mortal risk. The education of teenagers should not be interrupted by extramarital pregnancy. Respect for persons requires that sex should never be forced on another person.

ADULTERY

If two people consent to have sexual intercourse outside marriage, is this immoral? If it is a private matter between consenting adults, what is the harm? Richard Wasserstrom argues that this activity involves the breaking of an important promise. First, the breaking of this promise involves deep hurt and pain to the innocent spouse. Second, such activity almost always involves deception about where a person was and about what was occurring. Third, sexual intimacy should reflect a person's real feelings for another. Western culture teaches that sexual intercourse involves the strongest feelings that one person can have for another. Therefore, the restriction of sexual intercourse to a marriage is logical.

To engage in extramarital sex involves the deepest deception about true feelings, toward either the innocent spouse or the extramarital partner. Society has yet to answer various questions. Can one separate sexual activity from its deep meanings of commitment to a single person? What is sexual love? How could it be different? What price would people pay if sexual relations came to mean something else? Would the institution of marriage be lost and the nurture and protection of children suffer?

NATURAL OR UNNATURAL

Sometimes in arguments about sexual matters, a judgment will be made regarding whether an activity or behavior is natural. The implication is that perhaps "the laws of nature" can be violated, but the laws of nature are only descriptive and by their nature cannot be violated. They are not prescriptive for behavior, and life would be gloomy if it were so. As Sarah Blaffer Hrdy has said, people need to rise above nature in sexual ethics. Arguments that will convince the general population must be based on ethical traditions that consider the consequences of an action (teleological theories) or traditions that maintain that people have duties (deontological theories).

SEXISM

False assumptions about the intrinsic worth of either females or males often cause trouble in society. Children of the "wrong sex" may be devalued and even aborted. Programs or instruction in schools should not favor one sex. Equal work and responsibility calls for equal pay and equal opportunities for promotion. To use biological differences such as sex or race, over which a person has no control, as a systematic basis for denying anyone their rights violates individual human dignity and autonomy.

A most serious danger is to describe one sex as setting the standards for the species. When this is done, the other sex is viewed as not fully developed, abnormal, and therefore is devalued. For example, during the nineteenth century, Paul Broca claimed that female brains were smaller than normal ("normal" was a European white man's brain) and therefore not capable of higher learning. Educational policies and women's aspirations were affected until this view was overcome, when people realized that general body size and many other factors must be considered. Female brains are normal for females. Female intelligence is not limited by sexuality.

GAY RIGHTS

Although the issue of respect for privacy discourages and complicates the enforcement of laws that regulate sexual behavior, the courts are not silent regarding such matters. In 1993, a Virginia County Circuit Court found that a woman's lesbian relationship made her "an unfit parent." The judge noted that the woman admitted to engaging in oral sex, which is a felony in Virginia, concluded that her conduct was immoral, and left the woman's child in the custody of the grandmother. The grandmother testified that the child might grow up confused about sexuality. The judge cited a 1985 Virginia Supreme Court ruling that said that a parent's homosexuality is a legitimate reason for losing parental rights. Since 1985, however, more than one hundred gay people have gained parental rights through the Virginia courts by means of what is called coparent, second-parent, or same-gender adoption. The issue is far from settled.

SEX SELLS

Advertising plays an important role in society. The device of associating a product with a beautiful or handsome model raises the issue of honesty. The ethics of using sexuality to sell products and to promote messages is questionable and is demeaning to the persons so used. Interesting cases have developed involving the hiring of women as newscasters. What is really going on when management tells a female newsperson to wear her hair differently?

Billions of dollars are spent annually on cosmetics, especially by women, to enhance beauty and sexuality. (The testing of cosmetic products on animals is an ethical issue in itself.) The clothing fashion industry is also keyed to promoting attractiveness. Models are selected to promote particular images of female body shape and beauty. These images may be unrealistic for most females and may lead to the development of low self-esteem or even serious illness (anorexia, bulimia). Furthermore, Cornel West has pointed out that the ideology of white female beauty even tends to permeate black thinking. "The ideal of female beauty in this country puts a premium on lightness and softness mythically associated with white women and downplays the rich stylistic manners associated with black women." Damaged self-image and lack of self-confidence can cause fundamental harm to a whole race.

How sexuality is treated in society and how individual humans act sexually involves all of ethics. Making responsible decisions in this area may be more difficult than in others because of the effects of biology and culture. Nevertheless, the effort must be made to affirm sexuality, to recognize it as fundamental to human existence. In all its uses, however, sexuality also needs to be disciplined to communicate truth. William Starr has pointed out that one can have purely casual sex. There is pleasure in it or the act would not be performed. "But what sort of pleasure is it?" Starr continues. "It is short term, transitory, lacks lasting value, lacks continuity with the rest of one's life . . . and adds nothing to the quality of one's life." Sexual relations with a person who is loved, however, represent "a part of the ongoing process of the enhancement of one's existence."

Paul R. Boehlke

FURTHER READING

Baker, Robert B., Kathleen J. Wininger, and Frederick A. Elliston, eds. *Philosophy and Sex.* 3d ed. Amherst, N.Y.: Prometheus Books, 1998. An essential reference for anyone interested in sexual ethics, this extremely comprehensive anthology contains essays by authors ranging from Pope Paul VI and Thomas Aquinas to Michel Foucault and Luce Irigaray, on topics from gay marriage to linguistics.

Goodwin, Robin, and Duncan Cramer, eds. *Inappropriate Relationships: The Unconventional, the Disapproved, and the Forbidden.* Mahwah, N.J.: Lawrence Erlbaum Associates, 2002. Anthology of essays about various kinds of "inappropriate" sexual relationships, ranging from the outright taboo (necrophilia) to the mildly disapproved (marriages between Grateful Dead fans and non-fans).

Gould, Stephen Jay. *The Mismeasure of Man.* New York: W. W. Norton, 1981. Gould shows how society and science can impose imagined gifts and limits on people according to nature. His section on Broca's studies of women's and men's brains shows that both society and science can err.

Hrdy, Sarah Blaffer. "The Primate Origins of Human Sexuality." In *The Evolution of Sex: Nobel Conference XXIII*, edited by Robert Bellig and George Stevens. San Francisco: Harper & Row, 1988. Hrdy indicates that some aspects of human sexuality are not entirely unique, especially when primate behavior is studied. She concludes that, ethically, humans need to rise above nature.

LaFont, Suzanne, ed. *Constructing Sexualities: Readings in Sexuality, Gender, and Culture.* Upper Saddle River, N.J.: Prentice Hall, 2003. An anthology of essays on sexuality and culture, including work on transgender issues, internet sex, and the cultural construction of categories of sexual identity.

MacKinnon, Catharine A. *Feminism Unmodified: Discourses on Life and Law.* Cambridge, Mass.: Harvard University Press, 1987. The chapter "Sex and Violence" describes the nature of rape, sexual harassment, pornography, and battery.

Solomon, Robert C. "Sex, Conception, and the Conception of Sex." In *Thirteen Questions in Ethics*, edited by G. Lee Bowie et al. Fort Worth, Tex.: Harcourt Brace Jovanovich College Publishers, 1992. Solomon concludes that sex cannot be free from morals, because it allows for the deepest interpersonal expressions.

Toufexis, Anastasia. "The Right Chemistry." *Time* 141 (February 15, 1993): 49-51. Discusses the evolutionary roots, experiences, and chemicals involved in falling in love. The experiences and people of childhood apparently lead one to select a particular person to love. Internal chemicals cause a natural high. Toufexis argues that nature's love lasts about four years and is not exclusive.

West, Cornel. *Race Matters*. Boston: Beacon, 1993. The whole book is fascinating, but the chapter on black sexuality is particularly significant regarding the effects of culture.

SEE ALSO: Clinton, Bill; Dress codes; Equal Rights Amendment; Gay rights; Homosexuality; Marriage; Personal relationships; Rape; *Second Sex, The*; Sexual revolution; Sexually transmitted diseases.

Sexually transmitted diseases

DEFINITION: Venereal and other diseases that are often, but not exclusively, spread by sexual contact

TYPE OF ETHICS: Bioethics

SIGNIFICANCE: The existence of sexually transmitted diseases (STDs) complicates sexual ethics in general, because it further raises the stakes of an already ethically charged relationship. In addition to this broad theoretical complication, definite knowledge that one or one's partner has an STD may have specific, practical ethical consequences.

Sexually transmitted diseases, whose incidence is rapidly increasing, are caused mainly by specific bacteria and viruses. Gonorrhea, chlamydia, and syphilis are bacterial and can be treated with antibiotics. Untreated cases of these diseases can result in sterility, infections of newborn children, and other serious problems. Among the viral infections are herpes 2, genital warts, and acquired immunodeficiency syndrome (AIDS). Herpes 2 and AIDS have no cures. Herpes 2 causes painful sores on the sex organs that heal but reappear. A mother can infect her child with herpes 2 at birth. Genital warts may lead to cancer of the cervix and other tumors.

Although all STDs are serious, AIDS is devastating. The human immunodeficiency virus (HIV) damages the immune system by taking over and killing CD4 white blood cells. A person is said to have AIDS when his or her CD4 count falls below 200 per microliter (normal is 800-1,200 per microliter). At that point, the victim is likely to die from various opportunistic infections.

The risk of getting any STD varies with behavior. Practicing abstinence until marriage is the best safeguard against STDs. Risk increases with the number of sexual partners. Latex condoms offer some protection but are not perfect.

About 64 percent of AIDS cases in the United States involve homosexual men and correlate with high-risk anal intercourse. Another 28 percent of AIDS cases are caused by the sharing of contaminated needles during drug abuse. About 3 percent are the result of receiving transfusions of infected blood. HIV can also cross the placenta or be in a mother's milk and infect a baby. HIV transmission by heterosexual intercourse is increasing. The risk of HIV infection increases ten to one hundred times if sores from another STD are present.

ETHICAL PRINCIPLES

In *Grounding for the Metaphysics of Morals* (1785), Immanuel Kant wrote that people must not treat others only as a means to some end. All people must be valued as ends in themselves. Respect for persons, fairness, truth telling, and promise keeping are vital to meaningful sexual behavior. Margaret Farley of Yale University concluded that sexual desire without interpersonal love leads to disappointment and loss of meaning. Justice must discipline sexuality so that no one is harmed and the common good is considered. Farley added that sexuality should be freed and nurtured while also being channeled and controlled. One cannot allow that "anything goes" even between consenting adults. Society has legitimate interests regarding the care of offspring, the limiting of extramarital pregnancies, and the control of disease.

ETHICAL ISSUES

To transmit disease carelessly by sexual means violates standards of love, commitment, respect, fairness, and honesty. Consider, for example, that a man might, through extramarital affairs, give his wife HIV. What are the responsibilities of any sexual partner?

In 1991, Kimberly Bergalis died at age twenty-three from a nonsexual HIV infection transmitted to her from her dentist. Other patients were also infected. Before her death, Bergalis asked that health workers be tested and their conditions be made public. Should health workers be tested? Are health workers in greater danger from their patients? Are these private matters? Often, privacy must be balanced with other concerns. Should an infected person reveal or tell all previous sexual partners? Should

even the fact that a person has been tested be kept private?

In many cases, fear of AIDS has fed apathy and discrimination. The parents of the late Ryan White, who contracted HIV from a blood transfusion, had to file a discrimination suit against his school to allow him to attend. Many STD clinics fail to act sympathetically toward patients. Homosexuals are thought by some to deserve AIDS as punishment. How should people act when others carry an infectious disease? Should research monies be allocated for prevention or cure? Preventive and therapeutic HIV vaccines will need to be tested on animals and humans. What concerns will have to be met?

LEGAL ISSUES

Individuals can sue former partners for damages caused by STDs. Such civil actions are based on tort law. A tort is a wrongful act or injury that is committed either intentionally or negligently. Furthermore, many states have passed laws against STD transmission that set fines and prison terms.

In a 1979 landmark case, Margaret Housen of Washington, D.C., was awarded $1.3 million in compensatory and punitive damages for a gonorrhea infection. Also, when movie star Rock Hudson died of AIDS in 1985, his homosexual lover, Marc Christian, sued Hudson's estate. Christian was found to be HIV negative but was awarded $21.75 million for "grave emotional distress."

In sum, individuals must inform a sexual partner of possible infection. Noninfected partners are under no obligation to ask. Consenting to have sex does not imply consenting to being exposed to an STD. In a landmark legal case in 1993, it was decided that a Texas woman who was raped at knife point was not consenting to have sex merely because she asked the assailant to wear a condom. In another case, a prisoner with AIDS was convicted of attempted murder because he bit the hand of a prison guard.

ETHICAL DECISION MAKING

The "sexual revolution" of the 1960's, which involved improved contraception, sexual behavioral studies, the women's movement, and trends toward openness, challenged the traditional structures of monogamous relationship: marriage and the family. Mixed messages in the popular culture often neglect birth control and concern for the partner.

Meanwhile, the Centers for Disease Control (1992) reported that 73 percent of U.S. high school seniors have experienced sex and that 4 percent of secondary students have STDs. The World Health Organization (WHO) reported in 1992 that 350,000 cases of STDs were being transmitted each day worldwide. The only current disease that is more infectious is the common cold.

A pandemic makes ethical considerations seem like a luxury. Nevertheless, some experts place hope not in medical breakthroughs but in changes in sexual behavior. As Robert Ashmore of Marquette University has stated, "we must not lose sight of the idea that the purpose of moral inquiry is practical." Can people who are "in love" be rational? Making responsible decisions in an area involving biological desires, peer pressure, society's concerns, moral standards, and individual autonomy may be a formidable task, but it is a necessary one.

Paul R. Boehlke

FURTHER READING

Allen, Peter Lewis. *The Wages of Sin: Sex and Disease, Past and Present*. Chicago: University of Chicago Press, 2000.

Ashmore, Robert B. *Building a Moral System*. Englewood Cliffs, N.J.: Prentice-Hall, 1987.

Farley, Margaret A. "Sexual Ethics." In *Encyclopedia of Bioethics*, edited by Warren T. Reich. Rev. ed. Vol. 5. New York: Macmillan, 1995.

Gibbs, Nancy. "How Should We Teach Our Children About Sex?" *Time* 141 (May 24, 1993): 60-66.

Green, Richard. *Sexual Science and the Law*. Cambridge, Mass.: Harvard University Press, 1992.

Lerman, Evelyn. *Safer Sex: The New Morality*. Buena Park, Calif.: Morning Glory Press, 2000.

Merson, Michael H. "Slowing the Spread of HIV: Agenda for the 1990s." *Science* 260 (May 28, 1993): 1266-1268.

Thielicke, Helmut. *The Ethics of Sex*. Translated by John W. Doberstein. Grand Rapids, Mich.: Baker Book House, 1975.

SEE ALSO: Acquired immunodeficiency syndrome (AIDS); Marriage; Promiscuity; Self-control; Self-respect; Sexual revolution; Sexuality and sexual ethics.

Shaftesbury, third earl of

IDENTIFICATION: English philosopher
BORN: Anthony Ashley Cooper; February 26, 1671, London, England
DIED: February 15, 1713, Naples, Italy
TYPE OF ETHICS: Renaissance and Restoration history
SIGNIFICANCE: In *Characteristics of Men, Manners, Opinions, Times* (1711), Shaftesbury argued that the source of human morality was an innate "moral sense" that was allied with, and promoted, the good of society.

The third earl of Shaftesbury's education was placed in the hands of the philosopher John Locke by the boy's grandfather, the first earl of Shaftesbury. He was fluent in classical Latin and Greek in his early youth, as well as in modern French; in his later youth, he spent three years on the European Continent and became thoroughly familiar there with art and music. His later writings, in fact, are of equal importance in both aesthetic and moral philosophy. In Shaftesbury's time, English moral philosophy was heavily influenced by Thomas Hobbes, who maintained that human nature is essentially selfish and that unless they are coerced by society, people will not cooperate to act decently.

In direct contradiction of Hobbes, Shaftesbury maintained that the very existence of society demonstrates a predisposition for moral cooperation—the "moral sense" that he was the first to name. Because it was bound up with society, the moral sense found its greatest virtue in pursuing the public interest. Shaftesbury also believed that morality and religion were separable, which enhanced the status of the moral sense as an innate human attribute. Shaftesbury's views directly influenced the British philosophers Francis Hutcheson and David Hume.

Robert M. Hawthorne, Jr.

SEE ALSO: Hobbes, Thomas; Hume, David; *Leviathan*; Locke, John; Moral-sense theories; Secular ethics; Selfishness.

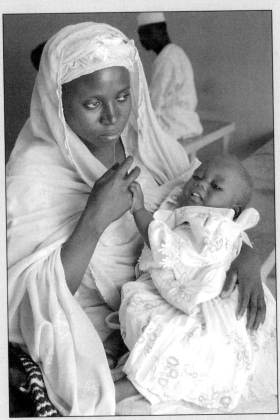

Amina Lawal, one of the women sentenced to be stoned to death for adultery in northern Nigeria, in early 2003. (AP/ Wide World Photos)

The Price of Adultery in Northern Nigeria

In 2002, the conservative Islamic legal traditions still in force in northern Nigeria made headlines around the world as word got out that two young women were sentenced to be stoned to death for committing adultery. Northern Nigeria's twelve predominantly Muslim states all practiced Sharī'a law, which calls for death by stoning of Muslims convicted of adultery or rape. Plans to execute the young women might have gone unnoticed by the outside world, had not Nigeria been about to host the Miss World beauty pageant, which brought large numbers of foreign journalists into the country. Under growing pressure from other world governments, Nigeria's secular national government ordered the Islamic executions stopped. Meanwhile, continuing strains between conservative Muslims of the north and non-Muslims, including Christians, of the south were leading to violent clashes in which thousands of Nigerians were dying.

Sharī'a

DEFINITION: Any of the several traditions of Islamic law

TYPE OF ETHICS: Religious ethics

SIGNIFICANCE: All of Islamic ethics— including personal ethics—is connected to *sharī'a*, since Islam does not separate the private, political, and religious realms of behavior.

Within Islam, no clear distinctions can be made between law and ethics. they are seen, instead, as facets of the single effort to build a community that is guided by the will of God. The Qur'ān (the primary source of Islamic law), for example, provides religious law ("Set not up with Allah any other God"), moral rules ("come not near unto adultery"), social regulations (on fiduciary management of the property of orphans), and guidance for the development of good character—all intermingled in *sūra* 17:22-39.

In issues not addressed by the Qur'ān and its exegesis, the next recourse is usually to the traditions in *Ḥadīth* of the life of Muḥammad. There is a broad diversity of views about possible additional sources of law, which could include '*ijmā* (consensus among the learned, which is important in Sunnī traditions) or the imām (the leader of the faithful, who is important in Shī'a traditions). There can be no "wall of separation" (Thomas Jefferson's phrase) between church and state in Islam, since all sovereignty resides with God and human authorities administer only through his will.

SEE ALSO: *Ḥadīth*; Islamic ethics; Law; Muḥammad.

Shīʿa

DEFINITION: One of the two main sects of Islam
DATE: Founded around 661-680
TYPE OF ETHICS: Religious ethics
SIGNIFICANCE: Shīʿa Islam provides a different interpretation of Islam and its tenets from that supplied by the Sunnī majority.

Islamic religion is divided into two main sects: Sunnīs and Shīʿites. Shīʿites are followers of ʿAlī ibn Abī Ṭālib, a cousin and son-in-law of the Prophet Muhammad, and ʿAlī's sons, Ḥasan and Ḥusayn. Shīʿites contend that ʿAlī should have succeeded Muhammad at his death. They view the other three caliphs, Abū Bakr, ʿUthmān, and ʿUmar, as usurpers. ʿAlī was chosen caliph after the third caliph, ʿUthmān, was assassinated.

After ʿAlī's death, Muʿawiyya assumed the caliphate despite opposition from many followers of ʿAlī, who considered ʿAlī's sons, Ḥasan and Ḥusayn, the rightful successors. After Muʿawiyya's death, his son Yazid succeeded him. ʿAlī's second son, Ḥusayn, tried to claim the caliphate but was defeated and killed by Yazid's forces. The anniversary of Ḥusayn's death is commemorated by Shīʿites as a major religious event.

There are two main branches of Shīʿites: the Twelvers, or Imāmis, and the Seveners, or Ismāʿīlites. The Twelvers believe that there were twelve Imāms, or leaders, after ʿAlī, each chosen by his predecessor. The twelfth Imām disappeared when he was a small child. Shīʿites believe that he will appear at an appropriate time as Mahdī, or savior, to rescue the world and restore the glory of Islam. The Ismāʿīlites believe that Ismāʿīl should have succeeded Imām Jafar, the sixth Imām. Ismāʿīl was Jafar's son. The Twelvers are the predominant branch of Shiism. Currently approximately 10 percent of the world's Muslim population is Shīʿite.

Khalid N. Mahmood

SEE ALSO: Abū Bakr; Islamic ethics; Sunnīs.

Shinran

IDENTIFICATION: Japanese Buddhist monk
BORN: Matsuwaka-Maru; 1173, near Kyōto, Japan
DIED: November 28, 1262, Kyōto, Japan
TYPE OF ETHICS: Religious ethics
SIGNIFICANCE: Shinran founded the True Pure Land Sect (Jōdo Shinshū) of Japanese Mahāyānist Buddhism. His teaching differentiated between real truth (faith), the gift of salvation in the next world; and common truth (morality), one's duty to society in this world.

A monk at Mount Hiei from age nine to age twenty-nine, Shinran had a vision in which Kannon (Avalokiteśvara, the bodhisattva of compassion) directed him to follow the teachings of Hōnen. Both men taught that salvation could be achieved through reciting the nembutsu, the phrase "Hail [or 'I place . . . my faith in'], Amida Buddha." Amida was understood as a Buddha who lived in the Western Paradise and would bring there all persons who came to him in faith. While Hōnen thought that the nembutsu should be repeated over and over, Shinran thought that it was sufficient to pray sincerely to Amida once, since reciting the nembutsu was an act of gratitude for the gift of salvation, not a work by which one earned salvation. In the salvation experience, the believer experiences undoubting faith in Amida and simultaneously utters the nembutsu. Upon death, the devotee is reborn in the Western Paradise, which Shinran identified with nirvana. There the devotee would become a Buddha and return to the earth to enable others to achieve salvation. Shinran broke with his master over the celibacy of monks, married, and fathered six children.

Paul L. Redditt

SEE ALSO: Avalokiteśvara; Bodhisattva ideal; Buddhist ethics.

Shintō ethics

DEFINITION: Moral values central to the dominant religious system of Japan
TYPE OF ETHICS: Religious ethics
SIGNIFICANCE: Shintō ethics played a major role in the development of the national state of Japan and of Japanese nationalist ideology. It emphasizes

that there is no timeless and universal formula guiding moral action. Rather, the context of each action must be thoroughly considered before a decision is made.

Shintō, the "Way of the Gods," is the indigenous religion of Japan. After several centuries of development of traditions, rituals, and observances, it evolved into an organized religion between the third and sixth centuries. Shintō is best described as a religion of daily life. Love and respect for spirits and ancestors are far more important than is appeasement of deities or immortality.

History

From the beginning, Shintō was influenced by or through China. Confucianism infiltrated Japan from northern China in the third century and was followed in the sixth century by Buddhism. Buddhism, when united with Shintō, gave Japanese religion renewed vitality, universal ideals, and transcendental speculation. Confucianism, which is basically an ethical system, provided the ethical foundation for the social and political development of Japan.

In spite of the infusion of Confucianism, Western scholars have had difficulty in discovering concrete ethical principles in Shintō. Although earlier Shintō reveals very little ethical thought, Confucian contributions brought a major increase in ethical thinking.

This growing ethical consciousness experienced great change and adaptation in later centuries. One of the most serious changes was the Meiji ("enlightened government") Restoration in 1868. This event officially established Shintō as the state religion of Japan and set the nation on a path of imperialism and conquest. The ethical consequences of this path are abundant. Shintō ethics, as used by the state, helped to formulate the conduct and blind obedience of Japanese military personnel during World War II. Negative examples of such behavior include the brutal treatment of prisoners by the Japanese on the Bataan Death March and the work of the Kamikaze suicide pilots near the end of the war. State Shintō was disestablished after the national humiliation of military defeat in 1945, but it was not eliminated as a national faith.

Ethical Principles

A careful study of Shintō ethics reveals at least eight principles that are dominant influences on the daily lives of the Japanese people. The foundational principle of Shintō ethics is embodied in the Three Sacred Treasures of Shintō. These treasures, to which are attached moral and ethical values, are displayed in all significant Shintō shrines. The mirror stands for wisdom, integrity, purity, and righteousness. The sword reflects valor and justice. The last treasure, the stone necklace, symbolizes benevolence, affection, and obedience.

The second principle is tribal ethics, or the authority of the community. In this ethic, the individual melts into unreasoning submission to communal authority. At key points in Japanese history, this has been the power that solidified the people, but it also has been used to justify aggressive national conduct. Tribal ethics fosters a tendency to refer ethical decisions to government offices. It emphasizes a contextual approach and glorifies the ethics of intention.

A strong social ethic is built on the position of the emperor as a direct descendant of the sun goddess and also as the head of a giant family. The roof over the family has often been extended to include the entire world. This ethic has established an almost unbreakable relationship between the emperor and the people, with very few attempts at revolutionary change.

Consistent with the situational nature of Shintō ethics is the concept of *makoto*, or "truth." Truth is relative, thus in Shintō there is no ultimate truth. *Makoto* involves an inner heart-searching while confronting any ethical issue.

Related to *makoto* is the principle that all evil is external. When a person is untrue to himself or herself or to others, it is only a result of a lack of awareness caused by external influences.

The Shintō ethic of guilt is better understood as shame. A person who fails to fulfill his or her proper role, as determined by the communal authority, is often consumed by an overwhelming shame, even to the point of suicide.

A unique principle of Shintō ethics is *naka-ima*, or the "middle present." *Naka-ima*, which first appeared in the imperial edicts of the eighth century, means that the present moment is the most important moment of all times. Shintōists are thus exhorted to make each moment as true and as worthy as possible.

The last ethic of Shintō is a strong concept of racial superiority. This concept became extremely important after the inauguration of State Shintō in the nineteenth century. It produced a jealous contempt for all non-Japanese culture and a major attempt to keep such influences out of Japanese life. Officially, this principle was abolished by imperial decree on January 1, 1946.

CONCLUSION

Japan's military defeat in 1945 unleashed long-suppressed forces of change. The embodiment of moral and ethical truth in the community headed by the emperor was forever broken. Replacing that sentiment was a feeling of individual cooperation by morally responsible citizens of the community. Although many traditional Japanese values have been retained, there is now more freedom to accept the ethical principles of other cultures.

Problems related to State Shintō did not all disappear in 1945. The ethics involved in shrine worship—particularly the Yasukuni Shrine, which honors as deities more than two million war dead—remained as a continual dilemma for many Japanese people. The basic ethical nature of State Shintō has, however, been replaced by the ethic of world peace and an attempt to contribute to the well-being and advancement of all world cultures.

Glenn L. Swygart

FURTHER READING

Anesaki, Masaharu. *History of Japanese Religion.* Rutland, Vt.: Charles E. Tuttle, 1963.

Bocking, Brian. *The Oracles of the Three Shrines: Window on Japanese Religion.* Richmond, England: Curzon, 2001.

Holtom, D. C. *Modern Japan and Shintf Nationalism.* Chicago: University of Chicago Press, 1943.

Kisala, Robert. *Prophets of Peace: Pacifism and Cultural Identity in Japan's New Religions.* Honolulu: University of Hawai'i Press, 1999.

Mason, J. W. T. *The Meaning of Shinto: The Primæval Foundation of Creative Spirit in Modern Japan.* Port Washington, N.Y.: Kennikat Press, 1967.

Ono, Sokyo. *Shinto: The Kami Way.* Rutland, Vt.: Charles E. Tuttle, 1962.

Ross, Floyd Hiatt. *Shinto: The Way of Japan.* Boston: Beacon Press, 1965.

SEE ALSO: Buddhist ethics; Christian ethics; Daoist ethics; Religion; Situational ethics.

Sidgwick, Henry

IDENTIFICATION: English philosopher
BORN: May 31, 1838, Skipton, Yorkshire, England
DIED: August 28, 1900, Cambridge, Cambridgeshire, England
TYPE OF ETHICS: Modern history
SIGNIFICANCE: Sidgwick attempted, in *Methods of Ethics* (1874), to discover a rational means of making ethical decisions and further developed the utilitarian ideas of John Stuart Mill by applying to them Immanuel Kant's notion of the categorical imperative. His work is considered by some scholars to be the most important English-language work on ethics of the nineteenth century.

In *Methods of Ethics*, his greatest book, Henry Sidgwick argues that there are no grounds for rational action in judging an act either on the basis of the happiness it brings to the actor (egoism) or on the basis of criteria other than the promotion of happiness (intuitionism). Instead, he proposes a system of "universal hedonism" in which one seeks to reconcile the conflict between one's own pleasures and those of others. His argument is similar to that of Kant and is parallel to the latter's "categorical imperative."

Sidgwick's interests went beyond formal systems of ethics; he also engaged in psychic research and studied political economy. Among his works are *Principles of Political Economy* (1883), *Elements of Politics* (1891), and *The Development of European Polity* (1903), which was published after his death.

Robert Jacobs

SEE ALSO: Egoism; Golden rule; Hedonism; Intuitionist ethics; Kant, Immanuel; Mill, John Stuart; Utilitarianism.

Sierra Club

IDENTIFICATION: Oldest and largest environmental organization in the United States
DATE: Founded in 1892
TYPE OF ETHICS: Environmental ethics
SIGNIFICANCE: Since the organization's foundation, the mission of the Sierra Club has been to protect the natural environment.

The Sierra Club was founded on May 28, 1892, with an initial membership of 182 persons. Naturalist John Muir was selected as the club's first president. Many of the organization's early activities were concerned with the preservation of natural resources and the establishment of national parks in the United States. Its initial campaign in 1892 focused on defeating a proposed reduction of the boundaries of Yosemite National Park in California.

From this beginning, the Sierra Club grew to an international organization claiming a membership of approximately 700,000 people at the beginning of the twenty-first century. It retained as its primary mission today the protection and enhancement of Earth's natural environment by sustaining natural life-support systems, facilitating the survival of species, establishing and protecting natural reserves, controlling population growth and pollution, developing responsible technology managing resources and educating the public about environmental protection.

Critics of the Sierra Club have charged that the organization's policies to preserve and protect the environment may sometimes infringe on individual rights and restrict public access to property. Some critics also assert that the Sierra Club is composed of an economic, social, and political elite interested in preserving the wilderness for a select few who are not sincerely concerned with environmental justice at the grass-roots level. For example, in 1972 the club opposed the attempt by Walt Disney Enterprises to build a highway through Sequoia National Park in California to a proposed ski resort that was expected to attract fourteen thousand visitors a day. The club argued that the valley should be kept in its natural state for its own sake. The club has also advocated breaching the Glen Canyon Dam on the Colorado River and draining Lake Powell in order to return the region to its natural state. The dam provides flood control and electricity for four million people, and Lake Powell is one of the most popular camping sites in the United States. Controversies such as these illustrate an ethical dilemma repeatedly faced by the Sierra Club: how to balance individual rights and the protection of the environment for all people.

William V. Moore

SEE ALSO: Animal rights; Bioethics; Conservation; Deep ecology; Ecology; Environmental movement;

Leopold, Aldo; Muir, John; National Park System, U.S.; Pollution.

Sikh ethics

DEFINITION: Monotheistic ethical system centered in Punjab, India, that espouses the equality of all people

TYPE OF ETHICS: Religious ethics

SIGNIFICANCE: Sikhism presents a challenge to the Hindu conceptions of polytheism and caste hierarchy that predominate in India. It offers the model of the "saint-soldier" for whom spiritual insight and physical courage are complementary virtues.

The Sikhs are a religious group that constitute approximately 2 percent of the total population of India. The majority of the Sikhs live in the state of Punjab in the northwest, but followers of the Sikh faith are also in diaspora across north India and in the United States, the United Kingdom, and Canada. By the turn of the twenty-first century, there were about sixteen million Sikhs living throughout the world.

Sikhism, which began in the fifteenth century, draws from elements of both Hinduism and Islam, the predominant religions of the Indian subcontinent. Persecuted by both Hindu and Muslim rulers at various points in their history, the Sikhs have developed a firm sense of themselves as a separate community and have recently begun agitating for separate nationhood. Issues concerning the use of violence in maintaining Sikh autonomy are at the forefront of ethical debates within the Sikh community.

DEVELOPMENT OF SIKHISM

Sikhism as a system of faith was initiated by Nānak, the first of a series of ten Sikh gurus, or teachers. Guru Nānak, drawing on meditative traditions within Hinduism but rejecting its elaborate ritualism, gathered a group of disciples (*sikhs*) around him to form a community called the *Panth*. Within the *Panth*, caste differences were eradicated, as were inequalities between men and women. In addition, the multiple deities of Hinduism were replaced by devotion to a single god something like that of Islam.

Sikhism quickly acquired converts from the lower-caste levels of the Hindu system. In this, it followed the pattern of several other heterodox religious movements of India, notably Buddhism and Jainism. For many, however, Sikhism remained heavily intertwined with Hinduism, with many villages and even many families incorporating both Sikhs and Hindus in relative harmony.

Guru Nānak himself is venerated not only as the religion's founding figure but also as a kind of mediator between the human and the divine. He was followed by a succession of nine other gurus who took up the leadership of the Panth. Two of these in particular left a lasting stamp on the nature of the Sikh faith. Hargobind, the sixth guru, donned the double-edged sword that has become symbolic of the Sikhs, representing the recognition that Sikhism must wield both spiritual and temporal power to be successful. This theme was carried further by the tenth and last guru, Guru Gobind Singh, who, after years of persecution, came to the conclusion that the Sikhs had to become militant to defend their religious beliefs and social order.

Guru Gobind Singh created a brotherhood of militant Sikhs called the Khalsa, or "pure," who were ready to die in defense of their faith. They all took on the surname of Singh ("lion") and adopted the five symbols of Sikh identity: uncut hair, comb, breeches, sword, and steel bangle. One effect of these five signs was to make Khalsa Sikhs highly visible, with the characteristic turbans into which their uncut hair was bound their outstanding feature. Probably this innovation was related to an awareness of the fate of other rebellious religious movements in Indian history, which tended to become merged into the overarching Hindu framework. Guru Gobind Singh believed, however, that physical violence on the part of the Khalsa was to be used only in *defense* of the Sikh faith, and only after all other means had failed.

Sikh communities in India and abroad cluster

Sikh temple in El Centro, a California town near the border with Mexico. (National Archives)

The Five Signs of the Sikh (Five "K's" in Punjabi)	
1. *kesh*	uncut hair
2. *kangi*	comb
3. *kachch*	breeches
4. *kirpan*	sword
5. *kara*	steel bangle

around their *gurudwaras*, or temples (literally, "gateways to the Guru"). The communal kitchen is a key feature of the Sikh community, symbolic of the Sikhs' rejection of caste rules forbidding interdining. (The kettle and the sword are said to be representative of Sikh beliefs—the kettle for feeding the hungry and the sword for defending the weak.) Worship services at Sikh *gurudwaras* may involve readings from their scripture, the Guru Granth Sahib, as well as the singing of hymns, recitation of poetry, or other kinds of contributions from community members including, recently, political statements.

The holy city of the Sikhs and center of the Sikh faith is Amritsar in Punjab, India. (*Amrit* is the nectar stirred by the sword and drunk to consecrate a commitment; Amritsar is the "pool of nectar.") The so-called "Golden Temple" is the main Sikh shrine at Amritsar, and it has been the focal point of the dispute between the Sikhs and the government of India. In 1984, the Golden Temple complex was the scene of intense fighting between the Indian army and Sikh insurgents agitating for an independent state of Khalistan ("Land of the Pure"). The perceived desecration of this shrine by Indian troops and the Hindu-Sikh rioting that followed pushed many Sikhs to take a more militant political posture. Upheaval has continued in Punjab, and it is one of the major security concerns of the Indian government. Human rights issues surrounding India's handling of the Punjab problem have become a focus of several international investigations.

Eᴛʜɪᴄᴀʟ Issᴜᴇs ᴏꜰ Cᴏɴᴛᴇᴍᴘᴏʀᴀʀʏ Sɪᴋʜɪsᴍ

Sikhism is at its heart an ethical system as well as a theology and a design for living. The foundation of Sikh ethics is the principle of equality, which is better understood as an ideal than as an accomplishment.

(Aspects of caste still persist in Sikh communities, and relationships between women and men remain inequitable in many ways.) Other ethical precepts followed by Sikhs include admonitions against theft, lying, and adultery, and a ban on smoking. Many Sikhs regard charity and courage as among the noblest virtues; the "saint-soldier" is the model emulated by many.

The most problematic issue for modern Sikhs, given the political violence endemic in the Punjab, is that of legitimate defense of the faith. Sikhism has never advocated a policy of "turning the other cheek," but it does seek to restrain the aggressive, as opposed to the defensive, use of force. Whether actions in which noncombatants are killed fall within the realm of defensive violence, and whether the Sikh community is actually under a threat substantial enough to evoke the use of force, are deeply disturbing questions for many Sikhs. For outsiders, conditions in the Punjab are very difficult to evaluate because of extreme limitations on press coverage and travel in the region. It is clear, however, that many thousands of Sikhs were killed during the 1980's and 1990's and that there is a strong feeling of being a community under siege on the part of both Indian and overseas Sikhs.

Cynthia Keppley Mahmood

Fᴜʀᴛʜᴇʀ Rᴇᴀᴅɪɴɢ

Cole, W. Owen. *The Sikhs: Their Religious Beliefs and Practices*. Boston: Routledge & Kegan Paul, 1978.

Fox, Richard G. *Lions of the Punjab: Culture in the Making*. Berkeley: University of California Press, 1985.

Kapur, Rajiv. *Sikh Separatism: The Politics of Faith*. London: Allen & Unwin, 1986.

Kaur, Gurnam, ed. *The Sikh Perspective of Human Values*. Patiala, India: Publication Bureau, Punjabi University, 1998.

McLeod, W. H. *The Sikhs: History, Religion, and Society*. New York: Columbia University Press, 1989.

Rai, Priya Muhar. *Sikhism and the Sikhs: An Annotated Bibliography*. New York: Greenwood, 1989.

Singh, Khushwant. *A History of the Sikhs*. Princeton, N.J.: Princeton University Press, 1966.

Sᴇᴇ ᴀʟsᴏ: Hindu ethics; Nānak; Religion.

Silent Spring

IDENTIFICATION: Book by Rachel Carson (1907-1964)

DATE: Published in 1962

TYPE OF ETHICS: Environmental ethics

SIGNIFICANCE: *Silent Spring* increased popular awareness of chemical pollution by illustrating the demise and death of organisms that had once been a part of a rural spring.

During the late 1950's, a proliferation of the manufacturing and use of chemical agents as insecticides and herbicides seemed to stimulate the agricultural industry. Initially, these chemicals provided relief to farmers who could now control and obliterate insect pests and weeds from cropland. Insufficient testing and monitoring of the use of these chemicals, however, led to widespread contamination of water and land, resulting in the destruction of a great variety of animals and plants.

The popular book *Silent Spring* aroused public awareness of a sinister development in which streams and springs became silent as birds, frogs, fish, and other organisms died from the toxic chemicals used in adjacent fields. Ethically, the realization that humans can quickly and easily pollute and blight large regions through the careless use of chemicals illustrated the necessity for good stewardship of natural resources. As an alternative to control insect pests, Rachel Carson suggested the use of nonchemical methods that were more environmentally wholesome. Carson's landmark book led to the formation of numerous environmental groups that have committed themselves to protecting natural resources.

Roman J. Miller

SEE ALSO: Clean Air Act; Clean Water Act; Conservation; Earth and humanity; Environmental ethics; Environmental movement; Environmental Protection Agency; Nature, rights of; Pollution; Toxic waste.

Sin

DEFINITION: Violation of religious moral law

TYPE OF ETHICS: Religious ethics

SIGNIFICANCE: Although sometimes used in a secular context, sin carries strong connotations of transgression against the ethical system of a monotheistic religion. The term therefore implies that one's actions are objectively wrong and that they constitute a rejection or failure of one's duty to God. Sin also evokes the Christian concept of Original Sin, the notion that all people are inherently guilty from the moment of their birth.

The concept of sin has its origin in the prehistoric past in the magical attempt to deal with the forces of nature. Some of these forces are taboo—that is, dangerous to handle. The breaking of taboos is not essentially sinful, since the behavior is typically unavoidable. In ancient Mesopotamia, a moral dimension entered the picture. The creation myth, the *Enuma elish*, explained that humans were created to serve the gods. The *Gilgamesh Epic* took that thinking further. It tells of the creation of Enkidu, a savage of whom the other beasts knew no fear. Enticed to participate in civilization by a prostitute, he lost his innocence, joined with the hero Gilgamesh, put on clothing, and learned to eat and drink in proper proportions. In short, he became human and ultimately met the fate of all humans: death. The Greeks further developed the idea of moral guilt. Plato saw moral failure as a matter of error; no one who knew what is best would choose to do otherwise. It was, however, the Judeo-Christian tradition that more fully developed the notion of sin.

SIN IN THE HEBREW BIBLE

The story of the origin of sin occupies the third chapter of the Bible, and its scope, effects, and forgiveness occupy much of the remainder. Sin is introduced in Genesis 3 as a deliberate act of disobedience by Adam and Eve. Sin was experienced both as the rupture of their relationship with God and as a power that grasped them. It spread to all other humans like a contagious disease, disrupting both the natural and the social order as well as the standing of each sinner before God. Forgiveness for sin in the Hebrew Bible could involve animal sacrifice coupled with human contrition or intercession by a prophet or priest.

The biblical Hebrew language employed about twenty different words for sin, but four in particular stand out. The first root (the basic form of a word from which various parts of speech can be derived) was used 457 times and originally meant to "miss" a target or "fail" to follow the proper order. Hence, sin was understood as the failure to comply with moral standards or obligations. This failure might include obligations to another person (parent, superior, spouse) or to God. Still other sins constituted a failure toward both: for example, murder, robbery, adultery, giving false testimony, and perverting justice.

The second root, which appears 136 times, originally meant "breach" and is used of sin in the sense of a breach of a covenant or "rebellion." Hence, sin carried with it the idea of persons revolting and dissolving the relationship between themselves and God. A sinner not only commits wrong acts but also lives in a state of rebellion against God.

The third and fourth roots can be dealt with more quickly. The third, used more than 254 times, originally meant "bend" and emphasized the condition of guilt as a consequence of bending the rules. The fourth, used 19 times, meant to "err" and emphasized that the sinner had gone astray and become lost.

The later idea of moral (or cardinal) sins derived from passages in the Hebrew Bible that associated death with the commission of certain sins (for example, premeditated murder, striking one's father, kidnapping, bestiality, and sorcery). Some passages associated a more general state of sinfulness with death (for example, Ezek. 18:20: "The soul that sins shall die").

Atonement for sins in the Hebrew Bible was conceived as a covering for sin. It was achieved primarily through sacrifice. The "sin offering" was made for unintentional offenses that broke a person's relationship with God and endangered the welfare of the community. The "guilt offering" atoned for offenses that required restitution along with a sacrifice. Less bloody means were also used. On the Day of Atonement, the high priest would symbolically lay the sins of the people upon the scapegoat and drive it out of the community, carrying their sins with it. Exodus 30:16 suggests that money could be given for the same purpose. Finally, the Hebrew Bible also speaks of prophets and priests interceding for sinners. For genuinely minor sins, penitents might pray for themselves.

Sin in Rabbinic Judaism

The rabbis, who led Judaism to think through its theology after the destruction of Jerusalem by the Romans in 70 C.E., used a term meaning "pass over" for sin. They spoke of two inclinations within humans. Literally, the names of these inclinations can be translated the "good inclination" and the "bad inclination," but these translations are misleading. The so-called "good" inclination consisted of characteristics humans were thought to share with the angels: They walk upright, have eyes on the fronts of their faces, reason, and speak. By contrast, the "evil" inclination consisted of characteristics humans share with animals: eating and drinking, voiding, mating, and dying. Clearly, none of these latter characteristics is "evil" in a moral sense, though several may lead to sin if not held in check. Just as clearly, Rabbinic Judaism did not derive from Genesis 3 a doctrine of Original Sin as Christianity did.

The rabbis also thought in terms of sins as transgressions of the individual commandments of the law. Thus, all sins constituted rebellion against God. Even so, the rabbis distinguished between light and severe sins. The most serious were murder, idolatry, adultery, and incest. They also distinguished sins of omission (in which one failed to follow a commandment) from sins of commission (in which one committed a prohibited act). Sins of commission generally were thought to be worse.

Sin in the New Testament

The New Testament employed two words for sin. The first originally indicated missing a target and was a near equivalent of the first word discussed above in connection with the Hebrew Bible. The second word designated lawlessness and usually indicated a state of hostility toward God.

The books of Matthew, Mark, Luke, and Acts did not speak of the nature of sin but of specific wrong deeds. The angel informed Joseph that Jesus would save his people from their sins (Matt. 1:21), and Jesus said that he came to call sinners to repentance (Matt. 9:13). A person who recognized Jesus' mission through the Holy Spirit but refused to confess Jesus and the salvation he brought committed a sin that both Matthew and Mark declared unpardonable. The Gospel of John conceptualized the mission of Jesus in terms of the sacrificial victim of the Hebrew

Bible: The sinless lamb of God took sin upon itself and carried it away.

The apostle Paul extended further the New Testament conceptualization of sin by raising the issue of the power of sin over human nature and the world. Paul argued that sin entered the world through Adam's act of opposition of God in the Garden of Eden. This opposition arose from Adam's freedom. Sin brought death into the world with it. Indeed, Paul portrayed death as the wages paid by sin, the workmaster. For Paul, then, sin consisted of more than individual misdeeds; it was a state of self-assertive rebellion against God in which all humans lived. An act was sinful insofar as it was a rejection of God or his law. He argued (in Rom. 1-3) that Gentiles had refused to accept God as the origin of good, and Jews (who had the law and should have known better) had rejected the law. The result was that all human beings were enslaved to sin.

With such a view of sin and humankind's entanglement in it, the New Testament considered its proclamation of forgiveness for sin "good news." Furthermore, it employed a number of analogies to explain the role of Jesus in that forgiveness. Three examples follow. The first analogy has been mentioned already: sacrifice. Jesus' death was understood as atoning for sins in the same way that sacrifices did in the Hebrew Bible. The book of Hebrews carried that thought further by conceiving of Jesus as both the perfect High Priest (because he was sinless) and the perfect victim (because he was offered once only and for all sins). Another analogy was that of ransom; Jesus' death was understood as the ransom price paid to set sinners free. Third, Paul employed legal language in speaking of atonement as justification; the death of Jesus delivers the sinner from sin, finitude, and death.

SIN IN MUSLIM THOUGHT

Sin is also an important concept in Islam, which derives its ideas on the subject more from the Hebrew Bible and Rabbinic Judaism than from the New Testament and Christianity. Human beings are not considered inherently evil, as in Christianity. Rather, in thinking akin to the rabbinic notion of the two inclinations, Muslim doctrine holds that humans have both a lower nature to which evil spirits appeal and a higher nature to which angelic creatures appeal. People sin by disobeying God's commands and thus committing individual misdeeds.

SIN IN EARLY AND MEDIEVAL CHRISTIANITY

The first Christian to write a systematic account of his theology was Saint Augustine. In his book *The Enchiridion on Faith, Hope and Love* (421 C.E.), he defined sin as a word, deed, or desire in opposition to the eternal law of God. Sin began with Adam's turning away from God, who was unchangeably good. The fall left Adam ignorant of his duty and lustful for what was harmful. Through Adam's fall, all humans were corrupted and were born under the penalty of death. Augustine's thinking on Original Sin was echoed by the Roman Catholic Church at the Council of Trent (1545-1563): The transmission of sin comes by propagation, not by the imitation of others.

Augustine is well known for his ideas about concupiscence. Concupiscence is a characteristic considered unique to human beings, who—unlike either angels or animals—are a mixture of flesh and spirit. Concupiscence grows out of that mixture. It is the fruit of past sin, part of the punishment for that sin, and the seed of future sin. Concupiscence in the first two senses is the result of Original Sin and the sins of one's parents as well as of one's own past sins. Concupiscence in the third sense is a nondeliberate desire pitted against a person's freedom to choose. Hence, it is the seed of future sins, without itself being a sin. It is not, however, exclusively an impulse to act immorally. Even less can it simply be equated with the sexual drive, though it was that aspect of concupiscence that concerned Augustine most.

Augustine recognized that not all sins were of equal severity, but he thought that distinguishing trivial from heinous sins should be left to God. Later churchmen did not share his caution. They distinguished between mortal (or cardinal) sins, which disrupt one's relationship with God, and venial sins, which only introduce disorder into one's relationship with God. Mortal sins merit eternal punishment, while venial sins merit only temporal punishment. Mortal sins must be confessed; venial sins need not be. Cardinal sins are not the same as the mortal sins of the Hebrew Bible or Rabbinic Judaism, but are characteristics that render the sinner liable for Hell and are forgivable only through penance. Enumerated as seven as early as 604 C.E., they have typically included pride, covetousness, lust, anger, gluttony, envy, and sloth.

Redemption from sin was the work of God through the death of the mediator Jesus. Furthermore, Augustine thought that God's grace was ultimately irresistible; if God chose a person to receive it, sooner or later that person would do so. Pardon for sin is offered through the church, specifically through three sacraments. Baptism was held to remove Original Sin and personal sins in cases other than those of infants. Confession removes sins one commits along the way. Extreme unction (now often called the sacrament for the sick) offered the opportunity for final confession or (for unconscious persons) complete final absolution.

SIN IN REFORMATION THOUGHT

The reformers reacted against much in Roman Catholic thinking; for example, limiting the sacraments to two (or three) and denying that baptism cleanses one from Original Sin. They differed little, however, on the doctrine of sin per se. Indeed, John Calvin, one of the leaders of the Swiss Reform movement, developed the thinking of Augustine to its logical conclusion. In his *Christianae religionis Institutio* (1536; *Institutes of the Christian Religion*), he too accepted the idea of Original Sin and the imputation of guilt to all of Adam's descendants. In speaking of total depravity, he said that everything in humanity (specifically including understanding, will, soul, and body) is polluted and engrossed by concupiscence. In short, human beings are corrupt through and through. Calvin drew from this analysis the further conclusion that everything the sinner does is accounted by God as sin.

Calvin also pushed Augustine's thinking on irresistible grace. Both men applied the idea of omnipotence to the idea of grace, concluding that God would not be omnipotent if his grace could be rejected. Calvin carried the thinking one step further: If humans are thoroughly corrupt and incapable of turning from sin, and if God chooses those who will receive grace, by implication, he also chooses those who will not receive grace.

Not all Protestants agreed with Calvin. In the Dutch Reform movement, Jacobus Arminius (d. 1609) opposed Calvin's view of predestination as too harsh in favor of what he called "conditional election," which he thought placed greater emphasis on the mercy of God. Arminius argued that God elects to eternal life those he knows will freely respond in faith to his offer of grace. His thinking was more influential in England than in Holland. Anglicans, General

Baptists, and Methodists followed him instead of Calvin. American Protestantism, even within the Reform or Presbyterian tradition, generally speaking stands closer to Arminius than to Calvin, though one can still find staunch defenders of Calvin's view of Original Sin and the imputation of Adam's sin to his descendants.

SIN IN MODERN THOUGHT

The concept of sin has continued to occupy some of the best thinkers, particularly theologians, of the modern period. One theologian deserving mention is Paul Tillich, who reinterpreted Christianity in terms of existentialist philosophy. For Tillich, humans find themselves in a state of estrangement from God, from others, and from themselves. Tillich retains the word "sin" to characterize this estrangement precisely because it includes the personal act of turning away from God. Hence, human estrangement is sin. The New Testament scholar Rudolf Bultmann also speaks of sin in existentialist terms by saying that being divided against oneself is the essence of human existence under sin.

Modern philosophers have been interested in the concept of sin because of its importance to ethics. Two examples must suffice. The first is the nineteenth century Danish philosopher of religion Søren Kierkegaard. As one of the founders of existentialism, he exercised great influence over Tillich, Bultmann, and many others. He argued that despair (in the sense of not willing to be oneself) is as much a form of sin as murder, theft, unchastity, and the like. It is sin because it constitutes a lack of faith in God not to be all that one could be. Likewise, he denied that sinfulness is inherited through biological generation; he did, however, find its presupposition in the anxiety common to all people. This anxiety is caused by the awareness of one's finitude and the threat of nonbeing. In their condition of anxiety, humans commit sinful deeds.

The second philosopher is Richard Swinburne, who defines sin as failure in one's duty toward God, the creator. He is more concerned, however, with the idea of Original Sin. Swinburne argues that one may not be held accountable for that over which one has no control. Original Sin properly may be said to have begun with the first hominid (who might even be called Adam), but it arose out of characteristics inherited in the process of human evolution. Adam's responsibility lay solely in initiating a historical and social process. Furthermore, sin arises within every hominid, whether descended from Adam or not; it is not a consequence of choices by one's forebears. It is also not the case that all humans who come after Adam are held accountable (guilty) for Adam's choices.

Kierkegaard and Swinburne have reinterpreted the concept of sin in the light of modern life and thought. Other thinkers, however, see less value in the concept of sin. Reacting against them, the psychologist Karl Menninger has complained about what he sees as the result of ignoring the concept of sin: a society that more and more has difficulty in finding grounds to condemn any behavior.

Paul L. Redditt

FURTHER READING

Foster, Durwood, and Paul Mojzes, eds. *Society and Original Sin.* New York: Paragon, 1985. A collection of essays from a variety of disciplines and from Jewish, Christian, Muslim, and Unification church thinkers on the problem of sin in general and Original Sin in particular.

Greeley, Andrew M., Jacob Neusner, and Mary Greeley Durkin. *Virtues and Vices: Stories of the Moral Life.* Louisville, Ky.: Westminster John Knox Press, 1999. A collection of stories by a liberal Catholic priest and a conservative rabbi exploring the nature of sin and moral choices.

MacIntyre, Alasdair. *After Virtue: A Study in Moral Theory.* 2d ed. Notre Dame, Ind.: University of Notre Dame Press, 1984. MacIntyre critiques Immanuel Kant for attempting to preserve the religious category of Original Sin within the framework of a secularized moral system. Without the Christian notion of redemption to make sense of it, MacIntyre demonstrates, Kant's notion of inherent sinfulness damages his moral philosophy irreparably.

Menninger, Karl. *Whatever Became of Sin?* New York: Hawthorn, 1973. A popularly written discussion of changes in the understanding of morality in American society. Menninger argues that, increasingly, "sin" has been explained in psychological or other terms, which has led to a moral malaise in which nothing (or very little) is clearly immoral.

Ricour, Paul. *The Symbolism of Evil.* Translated by Emerson Buchanan. New York: Harper & Row, 1967. A thorough study of sin and guilt within the larger context of its presentation in mythology. The chapter on sin provides an excellent discussion of the subject within theism in general and the Bible in particular.

Smith, H. Shelton. *Changing Conceptions of Original Sin.* New York: Scribner's, 1955. A clearly written study of diverse views in American theology from 1750 to 1950 about the idea of Original Sin.

Swinburne, Richard. *Responsibility and Atonement.* Oxford, England: Clarendon Press, 1989. A defense of a self-proclaimed "liberal" Christian understanding of morality, sin, and atonement by a leading religious philosopher.

SEE ALSO: Augustine, Saint; Calvin, John; Christian ethics; Guilt and shame; Islamic ethics; Jewish ethics; Right and wrong; Taboos.

Singer, Peter

IDENTIFICATION: Australian philosopher and ethicist
BORN: July 6, 1946, Melbourne, Australia
TYPE OF ETHICS: Animal rights
SIGNIFICANCE: A prolific author, Singer is a leading spokesperson for the modern animal rights movement and is also the leading utilitarian bioethicist of his generation.

Peter Singer is best known for his work in two areas of ethics, the first of which is animal rights. His book *Animal Liberation* (1975) builds a case for an animal rights movement similar to the civil and women's rights movements of mid-twentieth century America. His arguments rest upon his belief in equality as a foundational principle of ethics. This is evidenced by the many parallels Singer draws between speciesism—the treatment of nonhuman species in ways that would be considered unethical or immoral to treat human beings—and human racism and sexism. Singer asserts that all forms of animal subjugation are immoral, including domestication, experimentation, and raising animals for food.

A second area of moral thought in which Singer has worked is bioethics. His book *Practical Ethics* (1970) reveals that he holds to pure consequentialist

Peter Singer in 2001. (AP/Wide World Photos)

utilitarian ethics, regarding acts as moral if they produce more happiness, or equality, for all affected parties than do alternative courses of action. In the field of bioethics, Singer has generated much controversy as his ethics have resulted in his endorsement of many beginning-of-life issues such as in vitro fertilization, cloning, and sex selection, as well as many end-of-life practices such as abortion, euthanasia, and infanticide for disabled children.

Singer's views regarding end-of-life issues, such as euthanasia and infanticide, have engendered the greatest amount of discussion. Regarding such issues, it is important to note that Singer does not advocate taking a person's life against the persons' expressed will—or that of the person's guardians. Moreover, in line with his consequentialist utilitarian ethics, the rationale behind Singer's endorsement of end-of-life issues rests upon the notion that end-of-life practices can sometimes result in happiness for the greatest number of people—oftentimes including the individual who is put to death instead of being forced to endure a substandard life.

David W. Jones

SEE ALSO: Animal research; Animal rights; Euthanasia; Exploitation; Infanticide; Lifeboat ethics; Merit; People for the Ethical Treatment of Animals; Sentience; Vegetarianism.

Situational ethics

DEFINITION: Process of making moral decisions based upon particular contexts and individual circumstances rather than universal moral laws

TYPE OF ETHICS: Theory of ethics

SIGNIFICANCE: Situational ethics differs from applied ethics, as the latter involves taking pre-constituted values, universal laws, or inflexible rules and applying them to a given situation. Situational ethics, on the other hand, derives both ethical principles and fundamental values from a given moral context, and so involves no ground beyond the situation itself. In colloquial speech, "situational ethics" has become a euphemism for lack of ethics, for doing whatever one wants without regard to right and wrong.

Situational (or contextual) ethics is largely a reaction against legalism, the so-called "old morality" of reliance on laws and rules as dependable guides to conduct. Situational ethics emphasizes love rather than law; it begins with the unique elements of a specific ethical situation rather than with any set of laws or rules that are to be applied in every situation. Situational ethics thus takes an inductive rather than a deductive approach to ethical decision making.

JOSEPH FLETCHER

Situational ethics was popularized in 1966 by the publication of Joseph Fletcher's *Situation Ethics: The New Morality*. In this best-selling book, Fletcher states his belief that there are only three basic approaches to ethical decision making; legalism, antinomianism (the rejection of all laws and principles, sometimes called subjectivism), and situational ethics. He depicted situational ethics as being "in between" the other two extremes. The primary purpose of *Situation Ethics* was to oppose legalism, because Fletcher believed that almost all people in Western culture, especially Christians, are and have been legalistic.

Fletcher, along with other proponents of situational ethics, insisted that both Jesus and Paul taught this approach to ethical decision making. Other persons, however, find the roots of situational ethics in the philosophical approaches of existentialism and utilitarianism. Existentialist ethics has often emphasized the free choice of persons as the only avenue leading to authentic existence; such free choice is denied by any reliance on principles and rules in ethical decision making. Although Fletcher tended to categorize existentialist ethics as "antinomian," he readily incorporated into his approach the utilitarian principle of "the greatest good for the greatest number." He thus translated the principle of love into the principle of utility; the moral quality of actions derives directly from their consequences. The most loving thing to do in any ethical decision-making situation is determined by a kind of utilitarian calculus: What course of action will bring about the most good for the most people?

Among the many Christian theologians who influenced Fletcher and others who subscribe to situational ethics, Rudolf Bultmann and Paul Tillich stand out. Bultmann held that a Christian can, in love, perceive a neighbor's greatest need through a kind of moral intuition. Similarly, Tillich believed that moral judgments are based on an intuitive grasp of the potentialities of being. Fletcher quoted with approval Tillich's statement that "The law of love is the ultimate law because it is the negation of law. . . . The absolutism of love is its power to go into the concrete situation, to discover what is demanded by the predicament of the concrete to which it turns" (Tillich, *Systematic Theology*, 1951-1963).

FLETCHER'S SIX PROPOSITIONS

The heart of situational ethics, according to Fletcher, is found in six propositions that demonstrate how the principle of love works itself out in concrete situations involving ethical decision making. These propositions are:

(1) "Only one thing is intrinsically good; namely, love: nothing else at all." No law, principle, or value is good in and of itself—not even life, truth, chastity, property, or marriage. (2) "The ruling norm of Christian decision is love: nothing else." Fletcher, using several admittedly extreme examples, attempted to demonstrate how the most loving thing to do might involve violating each of the Ten Commandments.

(3) "Love and justice are the same, for justice is love distributed, nothing else." Justice is love working itself out in particular situations; it is Christian love "using its head." (4) "Love wills the neighbor's good whether we like him or not." Loving and liking are not the same thing; according to Fletcher, there is nothing sentimental about love. Love is attitudinal rather than emotional; therefore, it can be commanded. (5) "Only the end justifies the means; nothing else." Fletcher contested the classical Christian dictum that the end does not justify the means. In a world of relativities and uncertainties, one may do what would normally be considered evil if good results come from it. (6) "Love's decisions are made situationally, not prescriptively." The rightness or wrongness of an action does not reside in the act itself, but in the whole complex of all the factors in the situation.

Situational ethics has been, and remains, extremely controversial. In 1952, Pope Pius XII condemned "situation ethics" as an individualistic and subjective appeal to the concrete circumstances of actions in order to justify decisions that are in opposition to natural law or God's revealed will. Fletcher and others, however, represent a serious attempt to develop a Christian ethic that is based on the principle of love yet is free from the restrictions of a moral code.

In response to his critics, Fletcher said that he would "personally would adopt nearly all the norms or action-principles ordinarily held in Christian ethics." Yet he added, "I refuse, on the other hand, to treat their norms as idols—as divinely finalized. I can take 'em or leave 'em, depending on the situation. Norms are advisers without veto power."

C. Fitzhugh Spragins

FURTHER READING

Bennett, John C., et al. *Storm over Ethics*. Philadelphia: United Church Press, 1967.

Cox, Harvey, ed. *The Situation Ethics Debate*. Philadelphia: Westminster Press, 1968.

Cunningham, Robert L. *Situationism and the New Morality*. New York: Appleton-Century-Crofts, 1970.

Fletcher, Joseph. *Moral Responsibility: Situation Ethics at Work*. Philadelphia: Westminster Press, 1967. Reprint. Louisville, Ky.: Westminster John Knox Press, 1997.

_____. *Situation Ethics: The New Morality.* Philadelphia: Westminster Press, 1966.

O'Neil, Shane. *Impartiality in Context: Grounding Justice in a Pluralist World.* Albany: State University of New York Press, 1997.

Outka, Gene H., and Paul Ramsey, eds. *Norm and Context in Christian Ethics.* New York: Charles Scribner's Sons, 1968.

Ramsey, Paul. *Deeds and Rules in Christian Ethics.* 2d ed. Lanham, Md.: University Press of America, 1983.

Robinson, J. A. T. *Christian Morals Today.* Philadelphia: Westminster Press, 1964.

SEE ALSO: Absolutism; Bentham, Jeremy; Consequentialism; Distributive justice; Existentialism; Mill, John Stuart; Pluralism; Relativism; Subjectivism; Tillich, Paul; Utilitarianism.

Skepticism

DEFINITION: Method of philosophical inquiry involving rigorous or systematic doubt of apparent truths

TYPE OF ETHICS: Theory of ethics

SIGNIFICANCE: Philosophical skepticism always represents a self-conscious investigation of the foundations of knowledge, but it can lead to very different results for different philosophers. Some skeptics seek to doubt self-evident beliefs temporarily, in order ultimately to prove that they are indeed objectively valid. Others seek to demonstrate that knowledge has no foundation and that all values and beliefs are therefore necessarily subjective.

A society and the individuals who constitute it confront many situations that have moral significance, such as those involving abortion, euthanasia, racism, and war. Morally these situations involve decisions concerning the goodness of actions and the value of life that is reflected in those decision. A practical perspective is to view ethics as a summation of the decisions made by individuals and groups in those situations. A theoretical perspective is to derive ethics from a set of first principles, such as "All pleasure is good" or "The only unconditionally good thing is good" or "The only unconditionally good thing is a good will." Skepticism is not primarily concerned with the practical perspective. Ethical skepticism mainly involves theories about the nature of goodness, and especially the status that is accorded first principles (that they be absolutely certain or necessarily true).

CLASSICAL SKEPTICISM

The origins of Western philosophy are typically traced to Greece and Socrates in the fifth century B.C.E. Greek society at that time was undergoing many pervasive and rapid changes, in large part because of successes in commerce and trade that had been made possible by the defeat of the Persians and the advent of writing. These changes represented a challenge to accepted beliefs and values. A group of professional teachers known as Sophists made a living by offering Greek citizens a variety of theories concerning the ultimate nature of reality and the good life.

In Sextus Empiricus's *Outlines of Pyrrhonism* (c. 200), skeptical responses to exaggerated claims about hidden realities are elaborated. For Sextus, something is considered questionable and worthy of inquiry if it is not an immediate sensory presentation. Inquirers do not generally question appearances. Inquirers are interested in observing something that has not been observed or in reasoning beyond appearances to determine underlying and unobservable phenomena in order to explain something that has been observed. Skeptical inquirers are reluctant to exceed the evidence of the senses, and when they do, they hold those views with some degree of doubt. For example, a skeptic might claim that suspending judgment with regard to imperceptible realities leads to peace of mind but might admit that this may not always hold true.

Sextus imagines three possible outcomes of an inquiry: The object of the search is found; the object being sought is declared inapprehensible; or the search continues. When the thing being sought is beyond the limits of human perception, Sextus calls the first position *dogmatic*, the second *academic*, and the third *skeptical*. Ironically, only the skeptic's position leaves room for more inquiry, yet skeptics are often accused of shutting the doors to speculation.

NONEVIDENT REALITIES

A nonevident reality is one that does not make itself immediately manifest to the inquirer. There are several ways in which things might be nonevident. Referenced items might be temporarily hidden from view, as in this claim: "There is a pen locked in this desk drawer." Another way of being nonevident involves the need for special instruments of observation, such as an electron microscope or a radio telescope. Because the things being observed are extremely small or distant, there is still some uncertainty about what has been observed. Such uncertainty is evident in conclusions such as this: "There was something there, but what it was and where it is now are difficult to determine." Subatomic particles and distant quasars are less manifest and obvious than is the pen in the desk drawer.

Philosophical skeptics are not generally concerned with realities that could be made manifest to an inquirer. Instead, they are concerned with claims made about things that are permanently hidden from an inquirer's view. For example, no person can observe all things. Consequently, claims made about all things remain somewhat doubtful (unless these claims are meant only as definitions). It follows that claiming to know that "all pleasures are good" or that "only a good will is unconditionally good" is a form of exaggeration.

SKEPTICISM IN ETHICS

Skepticism is properly elaborated in response to a particular dogmatic position. It is possible, however, to identify patterns of skeptical argumentation. One positivist challenge to absolute ethics is that ethical claims are without definite meaning. Ethical claims lack meaning because, unlike ordinary factual claims, they are neither verifiable nor refutable. At the most general level, ethics is about the value or the sense of the world, of everything. That value or sense, if it exists, is something transcendental, beyond this world. Therefore, ethics may be thought of as being about something higher, but something that remains beyond words.

The emotivist challenge to the language of an absolute ethics is that ethical claims such as "All abortions are evil" can be interpreted as an expression of the speaker's likes and dislikes. Ethical claims are not true or false; they merely communicate the speaker's attitudes.

The subjectivist attack is based on the argument that the ultimate criterion of an ethical truth is the individual. Differences in ethical beliefs have existed since recorded history and seem likely to continue far into the future. People choose, and thus create, their own individual ethics.

These patterns of skeptical argumentation are responses to a dogmatically held absolute ethics. Any of these views can be transformed from a skeptical response into a dogma. For example, the statement "the individual is the criterion of ethical truth" can become exaggerated and changed into the statement "there is no higher or transcendental reality."

J. Michael Spector

FURTHER READING

Brandt, Richard B. *Ethical Theory: The Problems of Normative and Critical Ethics.* Englewood Cliffs, N.J.: Prentice-Hall, 1959.

Cavell, Stanley. *The Claim of Reason: Wittgenstein, Skepticism, Morality, and Tragedy.* New ed. New York: Oxford University Press, 1999.

Empiricus, Sextus. *Sextus Empiricus.* 4 vols. Translated by R. G. Bury. Cambridge, Mass: Harvard University Press, 1949-1957.

Hume, David. *Enquiries Concerning Human Understanding and Concerning the Principles of Morals.* 3d ed. Oxford, England: Clarendon Press, 1975.

Lom, Petr. *The Limits of Doubt: The Moral and Political Implications of Skepticism.* Albany: State University of New York Press, 2001.

Nietzsche, Friedrich. *On the Genealogy of Morals.* Edited and translated by Walter Kaufmann. New York: Vintage Books, 1967.

Teichman, Jenny. *Ethics and Reality: Collected Essays.* Burlington, Vt.: Ashgate, 2001.

Werkmeister, W. H. *Theories of Ethics: A Study in Moral Obligation.* Lincoln, Nebr.: Johnsen, 1961.

Wittgenstein, Ludwig. *Tractatus Logico-Philosophicus.* Translated by D. F. Pears and B. F. McGuinness. Introduction by Bertrand Russell. New York: Routledge, 2001.

SEE ALSO: Emotivist ethics; Epistemological ethics; Hume, David; Intrinsic good; Relativism; Socrates; Subjectivism; Wittgenstein, Ludwig.

Slavery

DEFINITION: System in which human beings are owned as property by other human beings and forced to perform labor for their masters

TYPE OF ETHICS: Human rights

SIGNIFICANCE: Slavery has historically constituted a significant denial of human rights and has a particularly significance in the human rights history of the United States.

One of the oldest institutions of human society, slavery was present in the earliest human civilizations, those of ancient Mesopotamia and Egypt, and it has continued to exist in several parts of the world into the twenty-first century. Despite the near universality of slavery, however, there is no consensus regarding what distinctive practices constitute slavery. In Western societies, slaves typically were persons who were owned as property by other people and forced to perform labor for their owners. This definition, however, breaks down when applied to non-Western forms of slavery. In some African societies, for example, slaves were not owned as property by individual persons but were thought of as belonging to kinship groups. Such slaves could be sold, but so too could nonslave members of the kinship group. In some African societies, slaves were exempted from labor and were used solely to bring honor to their masters by demonstrating the masters' absolute power over other human beings.

Sociologist Orlando Patterson suggested that slavery is best understood as an institution designed to increase the power of masters or ruling groups. Slaves can perform that function by laboring to make their masters rich; however, they can also do that simply by bringing honor to their masters. One of the defining, universal characteristics of slavery is that individual slaves cannot exist as socially meaningful persons. Slaves relate to their surrounding societies only through their masters. Slavery includes many mechanisms to remove slaves from membership in any groups, such as families, through which slaves might derive independent senses of identity. By placing masters in a dominant position over other human beings, slavery is believed to increase the honor and power of the master. The status of slaves is usually permanent and is typically passed down to the slaves' children.

HISTORY OF THE INSTITUTION

The use of slavery was widespread in the ancient Western world, especially in Greece and Italy. During the classical ages of Greek and Roman society, slaves constituted about one-third of the population. Following the collapse of the Roman Empire in Western Europe during the fifth and sixth centuries, declining economic conditions destroyed the profitability of slavery and provided employers with large numbers of impoverished peasants who could be employed more cheaply than slaves. Over the next seven hundred years, slavery slowly gave way to serfdom. Although serfs, like slaves, were unfree laborers, serfs generally had more legal rights and a higher social standing than slaves.

Familiarity with the institution of slavery did not, however, disappear in Western Europe. A trickle of slaves from Eastern Europe and even from Africa continued to flow into England, France, and Germany. Western Europeans retained their familiarity with large-scale slave systems through contacts with southern Italy, Spain, and Portugal, and with the Byzantine Empire and the Muslim world, in which slavery flourished. Western Europeans also inherited from their Roman forebears the body of Roman law, with its elaborate slave code. During the later Middle Ages, Europeans who were familiar with Muslim sugar plantations in the Near East sought to begin sugar production with slave labor on the islands of the Mediterranean.

As Western Europe entered the age of exploration and colonization, Europeans had an intimate knowledge of slavery and a ready-made code of laws to govern slaves. During the sixteenth century, as European nations sought to establish silver mines and sugar plantations in their new colonies in the Western Hemisphere, heavy labor demands led to efforts to enslave Native Americans. This supply of laborers was inadequate because of the rapid decline of the Indian population following the introduction of European diseases into the Western Hemisphere. The Spanish and Portuguese then turned to Africa, the next most readily available source of slave laborers. Between 1500 and 1900, European slave traders imported perhaps nine million African laborers into the Western Hemisphere. Every European colony eventually used slave labor, which became the principal form of labor in the Western Hemisphere. Because the wealth of several modern nations was created by slave labor, some modern African Americans have claimed the right to receive reparations payments from nations such as the United States, which continue to enjoy the wealth accumulated originally by slave laborers.

SLAVERY AND RACE

The large-scale use of African slaves by European masters raised new moral issues regarding race. There is no necessary connection between slavery and race. A massive survey by Orlando Patterson of slave societies throughout history found that within three-quarters of societies with slavery, both the masters and their slaves were of the same race. Slavery in the Western Hemisphere was unusual in human history because European slaves were drawn almost exclusively from Africa.

In most colonies of the Western Hemisphere, the use of African slaves was accompanied by the rise of racism, which some scholars claim was a new, unprecedented phenomenon caused by slavery. Scholars seeking to understand modern race relations in the United States have been intrigued by the rise of prejudice in new slave societies. Did Europeans enslave Africans merely because they needed slaves and Africa was the most accessible source of slaves? If so, then prejudice probably originated as a learned association between race and subservience. Modern racial prejudice in the United States might be broken down through integration and affirmative action programs aimed at helping whites to witness the success of African Americans in positions of authority. Did Europeans enslave Africans because they saw the Africans as inferior persons ideally suited for slavery? If so, then modern racism may be a deeply rooted cultural phenomenon that is not likely to disappear for generations to come. African Americans will receive justice only if the government establishes permanent compensatory programs aimed at equalizing power between the races.

Historical research has not resolved these issues. Sixteenth century Europeans apparently did view Africans as inferior beings, even before the colonization of the Western Hemisphere. Their racial antipathies were minor, however, in comparison to modern rac-

ism. Emancipated slaves in early settled colonies experienced little racial discrimination. The experience of slavery apparently increased the European settlers' sense of racial superiority over Africans.

After the slave systems of the Western Hemisphere became fully developed, racial arguments became the foundation of the proslavery argument. Supporters of slavery claimed that persons of African descent were so degraded and inferior to whites that it would be dangerous for society to release the slaves from the control of a master. In the United States, some proslavery theorists pushed the racial argument to extreme levels. In explaining the contradiction between slavery and the American ideal that all persons should be free, writers such as Josiah Nott and Samuel Cartwright claimed that black African were not

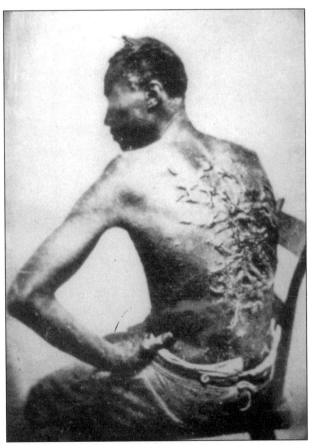

This Louisiana man named Peter had been severely whipped by a plantation overseer while he was a slave. Peter's owner discharged the overseer—probably not for wanton cruelty, but for damaging his valuable property. (National Archives)

fully human and, therefore, did not deserve all the rights belonging to humanity.

A minority of proslavery writers rejected the racial argument and the effort to reconcile slavery and American egalitarian ideals. Writers such as George Fitzhugh claimed that all societies were organized hierarchically by classes and that slavery was the most benevolent system for organizing an unequal class structure. Slavery bound together masters and slaves through a system of mutual rights and obligations. Unlike the "wage slaves" of industrial society, chattel slaves had certain access to food, clothing, shelter, and medical care, all because the master's ownership of the slaves' bodies made him diligent in caring for his property. Slavery was depicted by some proslavery theorists as the ideal condition for the white working class.

THE ANTISLAVERY MOVEMENT

From the dawning of recorded human history until the middle of the eighteenth century, few persons appear to have questioned the morality of slavery as an institution. Although some persons had earlier raised moral objections to certain features of slavery, almost no one appears to have questioned the overall morality of slavery as a system before the middle of the eighteenth century. Around 1750, however, an antislavery movement began to appear in Britain, France, and America.

The sudden rise of antislavery opinion appears to be related to the rise of a humanitarian ethos during the Enlightenment that encouraged people to consider the welfare of humans beyond their kin groups. The rise of the antislavery movement was also related to the growing popularity of new forms of evangelical and pietistic religious sects such as the Baptists, Methodists, and Quakers, which tended to view slave-holding as sinful materialism and slaves as persons worthy of God's love. The rise of antislavery was encouraged by the American and French Revolutions, whose democratic political philosophies promoted a belief in the equality of individuals. The rise of antislavery also coincided in time with the rise of industrial capitalism. The West Indian historian and statesman Eric Williams argued in *Capitalism and Slavery* (1944) that the economic and class interests of industrial capitalists rather than the moral scruples of humanitarians gave rise to the antislavery movement.

Antislavery activism initially focused on the abolition of the Atlantic slave trade. Reformers succeeded in prompting Britain and the United States to abolish the slave trade in 1807. Other nations followed this lead over the next half century until the Atlantic slave trade was virtually eliminated.

The campaign to abolish the slave trade achieved early success because it joined together moral concerns and self-interest. Many persons in the late eighteenth and early nineteenth centuries were prepared to accept the end of the slave trade while opposing the end of slavery itself. Even slaveholders were angered by the living conditions endured by slaves on crowded, disease-infested slave ships. Some masters, in fact, attempted to justify their ownership of slaves by claiming that the conditions on their plantations were more humane than the conditions on slave-trading ships or in allegedly primitive Africa. Some slaveholders supported the abolition of the slave trade because they realized that limiting the supply of new slaves from Africa would increase the value of the existing slave population. Finally, many persons believed that it was wrong for slave traders to deny liberty to freeborn Africans, but that it was not wrong for slave masters to exercise control over persons who were born into slavery. Indeed, supporters of slavery argued that the well-being of society required masters to exercise control over persons who had no preparation for freedom and might be a threat to society if emancipated.

The campaign to eradicate slavery itself was more difficult and was accompanied by significant political upheavals and, in the case of Haiti and the United States, revolution and warfare. British reformers such as William Wilberforce, Thomas Clarkson, and Granville Sharp made perhaps the most significant contributions to the organization of a worldwide antislavery movement. In 1823, British activists formed the London Antislavery Committee, soon to be renamed the British and Foreign Antislavery Society. The Antislavery Society spearheaded a successful campaign to abolish slavery in the British Empire and, eventually, worldwide. The society remained in existence into the 1990's. Known by the name Antislavery International, the society had the distinction of being the world's oldest human rights organization. Antislavery reformers were also active in the United States. From the 1830's through the 1860's, abolitionists such as William

Slave and Free States and Territories in 1861

Free states

Slave states controlled by the United States

Slave states in the Confederacy

Territories under Union control

Territories aligned with the Confederacy

Source: Adapted from Eric Foner and John A. Garraty, eds., *The Reader's Companion to American History.* Boston: Houghton Mifflin, 1991.

Lloyd Garrison, Wendell Phillips, and Frederick Douglass sought to arouse the moral anger of Americans against slavery. More effective, however, were politicians such as Abraham Lincoln, Charles Sumner, and Salmon P. Chase, whose antislavery messages were a mixture of idealism, self-interest, and expedience.

EMANCIPATION

Beginning in the late eighteenth century and accelerating through the nineteenth century, slavery was abolished throughout the Western Hemisphere. This was followed in the late nineteenth and twentieth centuries by the legal abolition of slavery in Africa and Asia.

In evaluating the success of abolition in any society, it is necessary to distinguish between legal and de facto emancipation. Changing the legal status of a slave to that of a free person is not the same thing as freeing the slave from the control of a master. Legal emancipation often has little impact on persons held as slaves if the governments of their societies fail to enforce abolition, For example, Great Britain outlawed slavery throughout its colonial empire during the nineteenth century. However, fearing a disruption of economic production in some of its colonies, its colonial administrations simply abstained from enforcing the country's own abolition laws until pressure from reformers put an end to slavery.

A similar situation existed in Mauritania, where slavery was prohibited by law three separate times:

1905, 1960, and 1980. However, neither the colonial nor the independent governments of Mauritania enacted penalties against masters who kept slaves in violation of the emancipation law, and the governments waged no campaigns to inform slaves of their emancipation. As a result, journalists and investigators for the International Labour Organisation found de facto slavery still flourishing in Mauritania during the 1990's.

Even within societies that vigorously enforced their acts of abolition, legal emancipation was usually followed by periods of transition in which former slaves were held in a state resembling that of slavery. The Abolition of Slavery Act of 1833, which outlawed slavery in most colonies of the British Empire, provided that slaves would serve as apprentices to their former masters for periods of four to six years. In the American South after the Civil War, former slaves were subject for a time to "black codes" that greatly reduced their freedom of movement and required them to work on the plantations of former slave masters. After the Civil Rights Act of 1866 and the Fourteenth Amendment outlawed such practices, southerners created the sharecropping and crop-lien systems that allowed planters to control the labor of many African Americans through a form of debt bondage.

Efforts of former masters to control the labor of former slaves in all former slaveholding countries were a part of a larger effort by post-emancipation societies to determine what rights freemen should exercise. In the United States, for example, legal emancipation raised many questions regarding the general rights of citizens, the answers to which often remained elusive more than a century after the abolition of slavery. Should freemen be considered citizens with basic rights equal to other citizens? How far should equality of citizenship rights extend? Should equality of rights be kept at a minimum level, perhaps limited to freedom of movement, the right to own property, and the right to make contracts and enforce them in a court of law? Should citizenship rights be extended to the political realm, with guarantees of the right to vote, serve on juries, and hold political office? Should citizenship rights be extended to the social realm, with the protection for the right to live wherever one wanted, to use public spaces without discrimination, and to marry persons of another race?

ANTISLAVERY AND IMPERIALISM

Ironically, the international effort to abolish slavery raised troubling new moral issues. During the last quarter of the nineteenth century, in the name of suppressing the African slave trade at its source, Great Britain and other European nations demanded of African rulers certain police powers within sovereign African domains. The Europeans also organized new African industries to encourage the shift from the slave trade to the "legitimate trade" in other commodities. In this manner, the humanitarian impulse of antislavery combined with less humane motives to produce the New Imperialism of the 1880's through the 1910's. During this thirty-year period, nearly all of Africa fell under European domination. Time and again, the campaign to suppress the slave trade became a cloak for the imperialist ambitions of the European powers. It is worth remembering that the two international conferences in which the European powers agreed to carve up Africa among themselves, the Berlin Conference of 1884-1885 and the Brussels Conference of 1889-1890, both devised significant agreements for ending the African slave trade.

SLAVERY IN THE MODERN WORLD

During the twentieth century, most Westerners believed slavery to be nothing more than a memory of the past. Major international treaties such as the Slavery Convention of the League of Nations (1926), the Universal Declaration on Human Rights (1948), and the United Nations (U.N.) Supplementary Convention on the Abolition of Slavery (1956) seemed to indicate the emergence of an international consensus that slavery in all its forms should be eradicated. In reality, throughout the twentieth century, new forms of slavery continued to appear. The U.N. Supplementary Convention defined debt bondage, serfdom, bridewealth (bride-price), and child labor as modern forms of slavery. Many persons considered the use of compulsory labor by authoritarian regimes such as those of Nazi Germany and the Soviet Union to be forms of slavery.

International cooperation toward ending slavery in the twentieth century sometimes faltered because of Cold War rivalries. Communist states were often hostile to the antislavery work of the United Nations because Westerners sought to define the compulsory labor systems in several communist states as a form of slavery. The Soviets, likewise, charged that the wage system of capitalist countries constituted a type of slavery, since the wage system compelled people to work in jobs they did not like out of fear of starvation.

At the end of the twentieth century, investigations by international human rights organizations and journalists found that millions of people still served as slaves in Haiti, the Dominican Republic, Brazil, Peru, Sudan, South Africa, Mauritania, Kuwait, Pakistan, India, Bangladesh, Thailand, and China. Even in countries such as the United States, where slavery had long been actively suppressed by the government, isolated cases of the enslavement of workers occasionally came to light with regard to migrant farmworkers and illegal aliens.

SLAVERY IN THE TWENTY-FIRST CENTURY

In the early twenty-first century, human rights organizations continued to report a few examples of traditional forms of slavery from various impoverished, traditional Southeast Asian and African countries, such as Sudan. Sometimes the governments of the countries in which the abuses occurred opposed slavery but lacked the resources to bring such practices to an end. A variety of international groups targeted these practices, with or without the help of the governments in question.

Meanwhile, it was becoming increasingly clear that it was no longer helpful to think of slavery as the public recognition of the private ownership of property in the form of other human beings. Almost nowhere on the globe did a government exist that officially allowed slavery. However, that did not mean that conditions close to slavery did not continue to exist in a number of countries, The world had a growing awareness of these conditions and the fact that they occurred in some of the most advanced nations on the globe.

The first of these conditions is what was once known in the United States by the name of "white slavery"—the domination, if not ownership of a person, for sexual purposes. This was not, strictly speaking, the same as prostitution, a trade that a person could enter voluntarily and retain the freedom later to quit. As a modern form of slavery, there was a recognition that many sexual workers had no such freedom. People forced into sexual employment generally have so little choice in the matter that they may be considered slaves in an ethical, if not a legal sense.

The very term "white slavery" betrayed its racial past. During the slave era in the United States, when only the ownership of African Americans was allowed, the term "white slavery" applied indiscriminately to all female sexual workers (of whatever race), while ignoring the prostitution of young males, especially children. The stigma attached to such work often reinforced the power the controller of the prostitute had over the sexual worker.

In the United States and some advanced countries in Western Europe, the prospect of improved economic conditions to people from poorer countries was so great that the entering those countries illegally was a risk worth taking. However, undocumented aliens were especially susceptible to extortion and sometimes found themselves virtually enslaved in their new homes. Moreover, if they attempted to flee their situations, they were themselves subject to prosecution for violating immigration law. Thus, facing either deportation or imprisonment, they endured their slavery silently. Even children tend to remain silent, although legal authorities are likely to offer them protection rather than prosecution. Sexual workers were not alone in this. Frequent reports of slavery, or near slavery, occurred in the domestic and household care industries and in industrial settings, such as the sweatshops that produce clothing. Illegal immigrants were often controlled as completely by their employers as they would be if they were owned legally. There have also been reports of such workers being bought and sold in the United States and advanced European nations.

Such conditions so closely approximated traditional slavery that the early twenty-first century opened the door to a new phase in the ethical debate over slavery. There was a curious similarity in the arguments of pre-Civil War American slavery apologists and the political masters in communist nations before the end of the Cold War. Both sought to divert attention from their own failings by pointing out the domination they saw as inherent for wage-earners in free enterprise economies. To the extent that wage earners are not free because of conditions resembling extortion, they may be considered "slaves" in a new sense, and the ethical debate shifts to ways in which improper domination can be exposed and eliminated.

Harold D. Tallant
Updated by Richard L. Wilson

FURTHER READING

Bales, Kevin. *New Slavery: A Reference Handbook*. Santa Barbara, Calif.: ABC-Clio, 2001. Broad coverage of slavery in history and in modern times in a reference book written for middle school and high school students. Includes discussion of the manufacture of modern American consumer goods by slave laborers in other countries.

Bender, Thomas, ed. *The Antislavery Debate: Capitalism and Abolitionism as a Problem in Historical Interpretation*. Berkeley: University of California Press, 1992. A collection of essays that debate the question of whether the rise of industrial capitalism caused the emergence of the antislavery movement.

Bush, M. L. *Servitude in Modern Times*. Cambridge, England: Polity Press, 2000. Comparative analysis of systems of slavery and servitude in the world since 1500.

Davis, David Brion. *The Problem of Slavery in the Age of Revolution, 1770-1823*. Ithaca, N.Y.: Cornell University Press, 1975. A Pulitzer Prize-winning study of the intellectual background of the rise of the antislavery movement.

_____. *Slavery and Human Progress*. New York: Oxford University Press, 1984. An excellent introduction to many of the ethical issues regarding slavery organized around a discussion of changing concepts of progress.

Finley, Moses I. *Ancient Slavery and Modern Ideology*. New York: Viking Press, 1980. A study of the moral, intellectual, and social foundations of slavery by the leading expert on ancient slavery. The book is especially helpful in showing the relationships between ancient and modern forms of slavery.

Foner, Eric. *Nothing but Freedom: Emancipation and Its Legacy*. Baton Rouge: Louisiana State University Press, 1983. A brief but thought-provoking study of the problems associated with emancipation in several countries. The principal focus of the book is emancipation in the United States.

Miers, Suzanne. *Slavery in the Twentieth Century: The Evolution of a Global Problem*. New York: Rowman & Littlefield, 2003. Examination of modern slavery in its historical context and ongoing efforts to eradicate slavery in the modern world.

Newman, Richard S. *The Transformation of American Abolitionism: Fighting Slavery in the Early Republic*. Chapel Hill: University of North Carolina Press, 2002. Study of the antislavery movement during the early nineteenth century.

Patterson, Orlando. *Slavery and Social Death: A Comparative Study*. Cambridge, Mass.: Harvard University Press, 1982. The most important study of slavery in its various forms. The book is based on a massive survey of slave societies on all continents from the beginning of history to the present.

Phillips, William D. *Slavery from Roman Times to the Early Transatlantic Trade*. Minneapolis: University of Minnesota Press, 1985. A highly readable historical survey of the transition from ancient slavery to modern slavery. The book includes an excellent chapter on problems in defining slavery in different historical and cultural settings.

SEE ALSO: Abolition; Apologizing for past wrongs; Colonialism and imperialism; Developing world; Emancipation Proclamation; Lincoln, Abraham; Racism; Reparations for past social wrongs; *Scott v. Sandford*; *Uncle Tom's Cabin*.

"Slippery-slope" arguments

DEFINITION: Arguments objecting to actions on the grounds that once such actions are taken, they may lead to other actions that proceed down a "slippery slope" until some undesirable consequence results

TYPE OF ETHICS: Theory of ethics

SIGNIFICANCE: Slippery-slope arguments arise frequently in applied ethics debates, particularly, in debates concerning bioethics issues such as euthanasia and embryo experimentation.

Slippery-slope arguments attempt to prove that objectionable initial actions will inevitably lead to worse actions and that the latter will lead to other and even worse actions, all the way down a "slippery slope" to terrible calamities at the bottom. In slippery-slope arguments, whatever would justify the first step would also justify all the others, but since the last step is not justified, the first one is not either. The final dangerous step, as the last link in the chain, is presented as a reason for rejecting the first step.

Baseball, Spider-Man, and the Slippery Slope

In May, 2004, millions of American baseball fans were dismayed to learn that Major League Baseball had made a deal to sell advertising space on its playing fields to promote the release of the new film *Spider-Man 2* in June. Having commercial advertisements inside ballparks was nothing new. What shocked fans was the plan to put Spider-Man web logos on the bases and on-deck circles. Although the logos were to appear for only a single weekend, many commentators decried the plan, charging that it was merely the first step on the "slippery slope" to unrestricted advertising that would culminate in the players wearing uniforms with as much advertising on them as NASCAR drivers wore. In response to a massive public backlash, Major League Baseball commissioner Bud Selig quickly announced that Spider-Man logos would not be placed on bases after all.

STRUCTURE OF THE ARGUMENTS

Slippery-slope arguments are constructed in either logical or causal chains, or both together. The logical form shows that accepting *A* rationally commits one to accepting *B*, *C*, and finally *N*. The causal variant predicts that adopting *A* causes *B*, which in turn causes *C* and ultimately *N*. However, actions of type *N* are always undesirable, either for intrinsic reasons, or because of their bad consequences, or both.

There are four basic types of slippery-slope arguments. Precedent arguments involve the warning that if some new step is permitted, it will function as a precedent that will set another precedent, and so on until a disastrous outcome results.

Causal arguments involve the claim that once a certain action is performed, it will cause a second event, that will in turn precipitate a causal sequence of increasingly worse consequences.

Sorites arguments involve the observation that an argument contains a critical concept that is vague and difficult to define precisely, thus leading to paradoxical consequences.

Combined arguments combine all the previous types to suggest that taking the first step will trigger a contagious series of steps, eventually ending in a "parade of horrors"—a horror such as a police state or ecological annihilation.

ASSESSMENT OF THE ARGUMENT

The tendency to treat slippery-slope arguments as fallacious is not fully warranted. Slippery-slope arguments can, in fact, be used correctly as a reasonable type of argumentation to shift a burden of proof in a critical discussion. For example, when school-based health clinics were first introduced to American schools, some parents complained that they represented a first step toward the distribution of birth-control devices through the schools. That argument proved to be valid, as many school-based health clinics eventually did begin offering birth control and reproductive counselling.

A slippery-slope argument might be misused because of logical or causal gaps in the sequence; however, the argument should be judged fallacious only if it is advanced to prevent posing appropriate critical questions in the course of dialogue. Slippery-slope arguments are commonly strong or weak in particular respects, but they are seldom so bad to be fallacious. Generally, they are as strong as the weakest links in their chains.

Majid Amini

FURTHER READING

Govier, Trudy, and John Hoaglund, eds. *The Philosophy of Argument*. Newport News, Va.: Vale Press, 1999.

Walton, Douglas. *Slippery Slope Arguments*. Oxford, England: Clarendon Press, 1992.

SEE ALSO: Euthanasia; Medical ethics; Photojournalism; "Playing god" in medical decision making; Right to die.

Smith, Adam

IDENTIFICATION: Scottish economist
BORN: June 5, 1723, Kirkcaldy, Fifeshire, Scotland
DIED: July 17, 1790, Edinburgh, Scotland
TYPE OF ETHICS: Enlightenment history
SIGNIFICANCE: The author of *The Theory of Moral Sentiments* (1759), and *An Inquiry into the Nature*

and Causes of the Wealth of Nations (1776), Smith was one of the inventors of the field of political economy and a major advocate of laissez-faire economics and the division of labor.

Born in Calvinist Scotland, bereft by the early death of his father, and extremely precocious, Adam Smith spent his life trying to reconcile Providence with the needs of the individual and the greater society. He became professor of moral philosophy at the University of Glasgow in 1752, and it was there that he completed his first important work.

THE THEORY OF MORAL SENTIMENTS

During Smith's time, moral philosophy embraced a series of disciplines in what today would be considered the humanities and the social sciences. At that time, philosophers of the Enlightenment were developing the discrete social sciences, especially psychology and economics.

Although basically a skeptic, Smith never became completely skeptical, as did his close friend David Hume. Smith took Providence into account when formulating his theories of personal and social ethics, especially in the field of economics, in which he became most famous.

Smith sought to reconcile humankind's selfish nature and self-love with its dependence on the greater society. There is in human nature, believed Smith, some principle that makes the fortune of others and their happiness agreeable, even necessary. The individual has a capacity for sympathy and the ability to put himself or herself into another's place and to observe that other as an "impartial observer." Hence individuals, while not compromising their own selfish needs, are able to approve of and to support that which makes others happy and to disapprove of measures that have a negative effect. Self-interest, however, remains dominant. For Smith, self-interest accounted for the habits of economy, industry, discretion, attention, and application of thought.

Smith's theories were well received, but had he written only *The Theory of Moral Sentiments*, he would have become no more than a footnote in the history of philosophy. A trip to France between 1764 and 1766, however, was to change both his outlook and his life. There he met many of the Physiocrats, early economists who began to challenge the prevail-

ing theory that economic wealth was a static commodity and that one nation could grow rich only by impoverishing others. The Physiocrats were free traders who sought to end governmental control of the economy. Smith also had cause to observe the effect of a controlled economy on England's American colonies. What disturbed Smith was the emphasis the Physiocrats placed on land as the major source of wealth. Were this true, then Scotland, with its thin rocky soil, would be forever condemned to poverty. Smith also had occasion to observe the work of the skilled French artisans and to see that the export of their wares provided a major source of revenue for the French state. Smith became convinced that it is labor rather than land or commodities such as bullion that is the true source of wealth.

THE WEALTH OF NATIONS

Smith's monumental and seminal work, *An Inquiry into the Nature and Causes of the Wealth of Nations*, appeared in 1776, the year of the Declaration of Independence by Britain's American colonies. In it, Smith posited three important points: that wealth is created by labor and is thus organic or growing, that the division of labor can enormously increase productivity, and that free trade among states or nations can vastly improve the welfare of humankind. By "wealth," Smith did not mean accumulated treasure, but rather the minimal amount of money needed to keep human beings decently fed, clothed, and housed.

Smith's great problem was the reconciliation of his theory of ethics with theories of economics. He reconciled these theories by emphasizing the selfish nature of humankind, the impulse of self-interest, the greed for material gain. He stated his position succinctly when he wrote that it was not the benevolence or sympathy of the butcher, the brewer, and the baker that put the dinner on one's table, but rather their self-interest. One speaks to them not of one's necessities, but of their advantage.

Smith would remove all bureaucratic impediments and permit individuals and nations alike to pursue what they do best economically. The result, and here Smith waxed lyrical, again falling back on Providence, would be that a wonderful universal machine would be created and a "hidden hand" would distribute equitably the ever-increasing bounty of the earth and with it the greatest possible happiness.

Smith's name is inextricably linked to what came to be called laissez-faire economics, or free trade.

IMPLICATIONS FOR ETHICAL CONDUCT

It would seem that Smith condoned any individual action as long as it benefited the economy. Indeed, Smith's theories were often used to justify the most extreme kind of "rugged individualism" and the unconscionable exploitation of labor; economics was well on the way to becoming the "dismal science." Smith recognized the danger and exhorted that the laws of justice not be violated, appealing to instinctive human feelings of sympathy for others. He realized that his division of labor by concentrating on a single mindless operation could result in the brutalization of labor, and he called upon governments, through education, to ameliorate the lot of workers.

Nis Petersen

FURTHER READING

Bronowski, Jacob, and Bruce Mazlish. "Adam Smith." In *The Western Intellectual Tradition from Leonardo to Hegel*. New York: Harper & Row, 1962.

Dougherty, Peter J. *Who's Afraid of Adam Smith? How the Market Got Its Soul*. New York: J. Wiley, 2002.

Glahe, Fred R., ed. *Adam Smith and "The Wealth of Nations," 1776-1975: Bicentennial Essays*. Boulder: Colorado Associated University Press, 1978.

Jones, Peter, and Andrew S. Skinner, eds. *Adam Smith Reviewed*. Edinburgh: Edinburgh University Press, 1992.

Lux, Kenneth. *Adam Smith's Mistake: How a Moral Philosopher Invented Economics and Ended Morality*. New York: Random House, 1990.

Otteson, James R. *Adam Smith's Marketplace of Life*. New York: Cambridge University Press, 2002.

Smith, Adam. *An Inquiry into the Nature and Causes of the Wealth of Nations: A Selected Edition*. Edited by Kathryn Sutherland. New York: Oxford University Press, 1998.

_____. *The Theory of Moral Sentiments*. Edited by Knud Haakonssen. New York: Cambridge University Press, 2002.

SEE ALSO: Capitalism; Christian ethics; Economics; Exploitation; Free enterprise; Hume, David; Marxism; Self-interest; Utilitarianism.

Social contract theory

DEFINITION: Philosophical system positing that legitimate governments are formed when individuals freely and rationally agree to cede their political sovereignty to the state or that all members of civil society are implicit parties to such an agreement

TYPE OF ETHICS: Politico-economic ethics

SIGNIFICANCE: Social contract theory, in all its forms, strongly asserts that it is the individual will, subject to reason, that is the ultimate source of morality.

Social contract theory is a framework for understanding the origin and organization of human society. It begins with the basic assumption that people are autonomous rational moral agents who agree to give up some of their individual power to do as they please in order to live in cooperation with others who also agree to give up some of their individual power. This theory is discussed in the works of many philosophers but is probably given its clearest and most powerful voice in the works of Thomas Hobbes, John Locke, and Jean-Jacques Rousseau. It is a theory that underlies many aspects of modern political life; for example, the U.S. Constitution and Bill of Rights, the United Nations, trade agreements, and military treaties.

THOMAS HOBBES

According to Thomas Hobbes, perhaps the clearest enunciator of social contract theory, people are naturally inclined to be in the society of others. In society, however, it is necessary that there exist a sovereign to protect each person against every other person. Without such protection, people are in what Hobbes identifies as the state of nature. In the state of nature, people have two basic rights: the right to self-preservation and the right to take anything they have the power to take. In the state of nature, there is a war of all against all as people seek to exercise these rights. Each person experiences the constant threat of violence against his or her self and property. In fact, to secure their rights, people will begin to act in anticipation of their being abrogated. They will kill those who are perceived as potential threats.

This insecurity is ever-present and makes society something to be avoided rather than enjoyed. Life in this state of nature is "solitary, poor, nasty, brutish, and short." Reason leads people to find this situation intolerable. Therefore, as rational autonomous individuals, people agree to form a contract, giving up some of their power to a sovereign in return for that sovereign's protection. They are then bound, absolutely, by that sovereign's laws. This contract is formed out of logical self-interest.

JOHN LOCKE

John Locke offers a kinder picture of the state of nature but reaches much the same conclusion as Hobbes. For Locke, the state of nature is a state of plenty in which each person is able to fulfill his or her needs. Each has a right to as much of anything as he or she can use, if enough is left for others. The only real limitation on how much a person should take is the fact that most goods will spoil if they are not used promptly. With the introduction of money, a nonperishable unit of exchange, the limits on consumption are removed and hoarding and competition begin.

This state of an unbounded right to property would be chaotic except that each person possesses reason. The state of nature is not necessarily synonymous with the state of war (as it is for Hobbes) because of the use of reason. Reason dictates a state in which people seek peace, a state in which the natural rights of life, liberty, and property are honored. This state requires that judgments be made concerning what threatens the life, liberty, and property of an individual. There is the danger here that if one person misjudges what is necessary for his or her own safety or the safety of others and becomes preoccupied with achieving security, he or she may act in anticipation of harm and threaten the security of others.

For Locke, it is the absence of a common judge that distinguishes the state of nature and causes uncertainty and potential disharmony. To protect against misjudgment, people form a contract. This contract is to form a government that will hold the power of the people in trust. It will act as a judge, and it must act to preserve its citizens. The purpose of civil society is to provide each person with security.

JEAN-JACQUES ROUSSEAU

Jean-Jacques Rousseau offers an approach that differs significantly from those of Hobbes and

---

Alienation and Social Contract Theory

Jean-Jacques Rousseau grappled with the problem of how human beings can form a society in which sovereignty would be legitimate, yet one in which the governed would not lose their autonomy or alienate their freedom. He believed that he found the solution in the social contract. In order to form a social contract, each person would alienate his or her rights to the entire community, to the general will. Such alienation would not entail the loss of autonomy or liberty, however, because each member, as a part of the general will, would be governed by laws to which each person consented. Legitimate authority and individual freedom would be guaranteed by the accord between private wills and the general will.

Locke. Rousseau idealizes the state of nature. People are pure and innocent in the state of nature, whose typical inhabitant is the noble savage. It is civil society itself that has corrupted people and led to strife. In the state of nature, people's wants and needs are simple and easily satisfied. Furthermore, Rousseau's goal is not so much to show the legitimate power of the individual (though he does intend to do this as well) to achieve the collective good—the general will.

Rousseau begins with the assumption that nature is good and that those things that have gone wrong are the result of the wrong actions of human society. He seeks not to explain the origins of civil society, but to create a state in which people can retain their original freedom. One should not be dependent on the opinion or will of others; one should also not be dependent on possessing power over and above one's needs or at another's expense. The general will requires that each person be free from these particular dependencies. One should not come to believe, however, that this freedom entails being independent in the sense of being free from influence or obligation.

Rousseau's individual has a duty to be aware of the general well-being, act in accord with it, and make sure that others do so as well. There is no greater sense of social obligation. Each individual feels an obligation to society through the realization of individual interdependence and equality. Rousseau thinks that as a result of showing individuals that ultimately there is no difference in vulnerability among people—that they are equal—rationality and feeling will then direct such people to form a community that is in the interest of all. Provided that they have been instilled with the correct sentiments, reason will lead to the formation of a general will in which each is bound only by his or her own will and therefore is not enslaved.

CRITIQUE

The social contract tradition has its critics. Some challenge the notion that it is possible for free, autonomous, rational people to form a contract at all. Such challengers argue that no one is free from pressure and coercion; therefore, it is not possible to tell if the contract is valid or for whom it is valid.

One particular example of this problem is the place of women in the contract. In the writings of the main proponents of the social contract theory, it is made clear that it is free, autonomous, rational men who form the primary contract, though women, children, and slaves are somehow to be bound by it as well. Carole Pateman offers an interesting reading of this issue in her book *The Sexual Contract* (1988).

Erin McKenna

FURTHER READING

Hobbes, Thomas. *Leviathan.* Edited by Richard Tuck. Rev. student ed. New York: Cambridge University Press, 1996.

Joseph, Jonathan. *Social Theory: Conflict, Cohesion, and Consent.* Edinburgh: Edinburgh University Press, 2003.

Locke, John. *Two Treatises of Government.* Edited by Peter Laslett. New York: Cambridge University Press, 1988.

Macpherson, C. B. *The Political Theory of Possessive Individualism: Hobbes to Locke.* Oxford, England: Oxford University Press, 1988.

Pateman, Carole. *The Sexual Contract.* Stanford, Calif.: Stanford University Press, 1988.

Rousseau, Jean-Jacques. *"The Social Contract" and "The First and Second Discourses,"* edited by Susan Dunn. New Haven, Conn.: Yale University Press, 2002.

Sample, Ruth. "Sexual Exploitation and the Social Contract." In *Feminist Moral Philosophy,* edited by Samantha Brennan. Calgary, Alta.: University of Calgary Press, 2002.

Wittig, Monique. "On the Social Contract." In *Feminist Interpretations of Jean-Jacques Rousseau,* edited by Lynda Lange. University Park: Pennsylvania State University Press, 2002.

SEE ALSO: Capitalism; Civil rights and liberties; Enlightenment ethics; Environmental ethics; Hobbes, Thomas; Human rights; Individualism; Locke, John; Natural law; Rousseau, Jean-Jacques; *Theory of Justice, A.*

Social Darwinism

DEFINITION: Application of Charles Darwin's theory of biological evolution by means of natural selection to the development of society and human social behavior
DATE: Concept coined during the late nineteenth century
TYPE OF ETHICS: Modern history
SIGNIFICANCE: Social Darwinism, used in the nineteenth and twentieth centuries to justify the mistreatment of colonial and working-class peoples and various forms of racism, is described by some sociologists as a misapplication of Darwin's theory based on an extremely dubious analogy between biological species on the one hand and social or economic groups on the other.

Western colonialism and imperialism and the Industrial Revolution of the late nineteenth century did little to benefit all people equally. Disparity in access to resources, wealth, and social status was nothing new, but as non-Western peoples and their natural resources were exploited by those in the West, a justification for such behavior was sought. Western governments were motivated to expand their political and economic power and influence, while industrialists sought to fulfill their desires for wealth and fame. The Western clergy, in turn, saw colonial expansion as an opportunity to consummate their mission of spreading the Gospel.

HERBERT SPENCER

In 1857, Herbert Spencer, a British social philosopher, published "Progress: Its Laws and Causes," in which he expressed his early ideas on social evolution. Later, after Charles Darwin had published *On the Origin of Species* (1859), Spencer sought to apply the ideas outlined by Darwin to human society. Spencer's ideas then were used to perpetuate the conservative status quo of the unequal distribution of wealth associated with the changing capitalist environment. Indeed, it was Spencer and not Darwin who coined the metaphors "struggle for existence" and "survival of the fittest," which Darwin later incorporated into his fifth edition of *On the Origin of Species* (1869).

Darwin's ideas on natural selection were employed to account for biological evolution. Specifically, Darwin demonstrated to the world that evolution took place and that its requirements were variation, inheritance, natural selection, and time. Since Darwin's ideas preceded those of the pioneering geneticist Gregor Mendel by six years, Darwin believed that the environment was critical to explaining variation and that biological success was measured by the frequency with which one reproduced. Successful reproduction in turn was influenced by various environmental forces. For Darwin, the term "struggle" was illustrated by the subtleties of environmental influence. Simply stated, although animals and plants attempted to survive heat, cold, wind, rain, and competition with other species, they were not involved in within-species warfare and bloodshed, as was implied by those who later promoted Social Darwinism as a natural and expected precondition of human social evolution.

When Spencer introduced the groundwork for what became known as Social Darwinism, he failed to recognize the importance of Darwin's subtleties. Spencer included various value and moral judgments in his suggestion that the struggle for existence within society or between societies was a natural condition for cultural evolution. He believed that societies were comparable to biological organisms, slowly evolving from simple to complex by means of competition for resources, and that such competition was natural and to be expected within and between societies. Social Darwinists believed that those individuals, institutions, and societies that attained the greatest political and economic power were by definition more fit, while those that did not were by their nature less fit.

WILLIAM GRAHAM SUMNER

William Graham Sumner, an American sociologist and economist, became a strong advocate of Spencer's ideas. He was a supporter of laissez-faire economic policy, arguing that people were not born equal and that millionaires were a product of natural selection. Typical of the industrialists who accepted Social Darwinism was John D. Rockefeller, Sr., the rugged individualist and successful capitalist who founded the Standard Oil Corporation. Rockefeller is quoted in Hofstadter (1959) as having said, "The growth of a large business is merely a survival of the fittest. . . . It is merely the working-out of a law of nature and a law of God." His statements express the attitude of many Social Darwinists. Indeed, Spencer and Sumner opposed social and economic planning and any attempts to offer social assistance to the poor because of their belief that such practices interfered with the natural process of social evolution.

Sumner argued in his book *Folkways* (1906) that customs and morals were instinctive responses to drives such as fear, sex, and hunger. Thus, Social Darwinists sought scientific justification from nature to promote individual competition and the exploitation of the poor by the rich classes. Because the concept and its followers supposed that social progress demanded that competitive struggle occur between nations, states, and races, Social Darwinism was used to justify Western ethnocentrism, racism, and eugenics. Such ideas were carried to a horrifying extreme by Nazis in Germany during World War II. Under Adolf Hitler, the Nazi belief in a master race and the inferiority of Gypsies and Jews led to the genocide of millions of people who were believed to be inferior. It was partly because of the world's revulsion toward the acts of the Nazis that the popularity of Social Darwinism and racism began its decline.

Turhon A. Murad

FURTHER READING

Brantlinger, Patrick. *Dark Vanishings: Discourse on the Extinction of Primitive Races, 1800-1930.* Ithaca, N.Y.: Cornell University Press, 2003.

Dickens, Peter. *Social Darwinism: Linking Evolutionary Thought to Social Theory.* Philadelphia: Open University Press, 2000.

Garbarino, Merwyn S. *Sociocultural Theory in Anthropology: A Short History.* New York: Holt, Rinehart and Winston, 1977.

Hofstadter, Richard. *Social Darwinism in American Thought.* New York: George Braziller, 1959.

Rosenberg, Alexander. *Darwinism in Philosophy, Social Science, and Policy.* New York: Cambridge University Press, 2000.

Spencer, Herbert. *The Evolution of Society: Selections from Herbert Spencer's "Principles of Sociology."* Edited by Robert L. Carneiro. Chicago: University of Chicago Press, 1967.

Sumner, William G. *Folkways: A Study of the Sociological Importance of Usages, Manners, Customs, Mores, and Morals.* Boston: Ginn, 1940. Reprint. New York: Arno, 1979.

SEE ALSO: Anthropological ethics; Colonialism and imperialism; Darwin, Charles; Ethnocentrism; Eugenics; Evolutionary theory; Genocide and democide; Human rights; Humanism; Marxism; Nazism; Normative vs. descriptive ethics.

Social justice and responsibility

DEFINITION: Moral obligations to participate in or ensure the fair and equitable distribution of wealth and resources throughout a society or across all existing human societies

TYPE OF ETHICS: Personal and social ethics

SIGNIFICANCE: The values of social justice and responsibility represent ethical responses to liberal individualism and to rights-centered theories of morality.

Rights-centered theories of morality assert individual and collective obligations to allocate resources as fairly as possible, both within and between nations, and they presuppose that the economic realm is a central and appropriate venue for considerations of justice. Most individualist and rights-centered ethics would respond to these assertions by saying that, while distribution of resources to those who lack them may be a morally admirable act, it is certainly not one that is in any sense required, as such a requirement would infringe upon such values as merit, individual sovereignty, and a conception of fairness that concentrates on opportunity rather than outcome.

Questions about justice and responsibility arise because different needs, conflicting interests, and scarce resources exist in human society. There are conflicting demands upon society's scarce resources and there is uncertainty about who has the responsibility to meet those needs. How is it possible to adjudicate among competing claims to determine the just distribution of resources? Is it right to tax the rich to provide for the poor? Does society have an obligation to take care of the needy? These questions deal mainly with a form of justice called distributive justice.

Responsibility, too, can be interpreted in different ways. First, responsibility can refer to the character of a person. To say that a person is responsible in this sense means that the person has uprightness of character, can be trusted, and has a sense of duty. Second, responsibility means the same thing as the ability and capacity to perform some task. Third, responsibility also refers to the issues of praise and blame. Fourth, responsibility refers to position or office in accordance with which a person is entrusted with the performance of a particular task. The latter is closely tied to the question of social justice, because the concept of justice implies that someone is responsible for being just.

Distributive justice deals with the fair allotment of society's goods and services and presupposes the complementary issues of responsibility, equality, and the good society. A theory of distributive justice should determine what needs should be met and what goods individuals should give up for the common good. These issues can also be encompassed in the questions of entitlement, desert or merit, and equality.

PHILOSOPHICAL VIEWS

Plato, who was not an egalitarian, developed a vision of a just society along lines of unequal status. In the *Republic*, Plato attempted to define the *dikaios*, the "just person," and the *kallipolis*, the "good city." The just person is one who possesses the virtues of wisdom, moderation, and courage. The just city is divided into three classes: the working class, the warriors, and the philosopher-rulers. The city is just if it is based on an aristocratic constitution and the three social classes embody their respective virtues. The aristocratic class is wisdom-loving, the warriors are courageous lovers of honor, and the artisans exercise moderation in their pleasure seeking. Each individual and each class, by responsibly fulfilling its duty, contributes to the existence of a just society.

Another approach to social justice and responsibility has been offered by social contract theory, which holds that justice and society are produced by a general agreement—a social contract. People are obligated to obey rules and the government because they have agreed to do so. They have made a contract to live by certain rules because it suits their self-interest. The general will of the people creates rules, laws, and government. Individuals give up certain rights and privileges for the protections and mutual advantages of the state.

Jean-Jacques Rousseau wrote an essay called "On the Social Contract," whose purpose was to explain the nature of authority. It was based on an optimistic view of human nature but a negative view about society. For Rousseau, human beings are born good, but they are corrupted by society. Social contract theory argues that human beings give up or alienate their rights by transferring them to society. The state becomes the sole possessor of political authority. The state is a legitimate power and guarantees the freedom and autonomy of its citizens through a social contract—a voluntary, unanimous agreement of all people of a society to form a united political community. Popular sovereignty is called general will.

Immanuel Kant formulated, in *Foundations of the Metaphysics of Morals* (1785), the categorical imperative, which holds that one should act only on that maxim that one can will to become a universal law. Kant presupposes that persons are rational creatures, that they have an infinite worth of dignity (that is, that they are ends in themselves), and that they are authors of moral law, or are autonomous. In short, human beings are ends in themselves. Therefore, Kant envisions society as a kingdom of ends.

Utilitarianism adheres to the rule that one should always try to make as many people happy as possible. This "greatest happiness principle" states that one ought to act so as to maximize pleasure and minimize pain. The principle of utility, which is derived from the happiness principle, is a rule that determines moral norms and actions according their ability to maximize or minimize happiness. Rule utilitarianism means that governments are to use this rule in establishing general laws and are to treat individuals

according to existing rules. In his essay *On Liberty* (1859), John Stuart Mill stated that society could progress to a higher state of civilization on the basis of what he called the basic principle—that individuals, groups of individuals, and the mass of people must refrain from interfering with the thoughts, expressions, and actions of any individual. The second principle, which is known as the "harm to others principle," holds that government may not interfere in private life except to prevent harm to others. These principles function as regulative criteria for developing public policy that preserves individual rights, limits government intervention, and fosters general well-being.

Michael Candelaria

FURTHER READING

Gautier, Jeffrey A. *Hegel and Feminist Social Criticism: Justice, Recognition, and the Feminine.* Albany: State University of New York Press, 1997.

Jacobs, Lesley A. *Pursuing Equal Opportunities: The Theory and Practice of Egalitarian Justice.* New York: Cambridge University Press, 2004.

Marx, Karl, and Friedrich Engels. *The Marx-Engels Reader.* Edited by Robert C. Tucker. 2d ed. New York: W. W. Norton, 1978.

Mill, John Stuart. *"Utilitarianism"; "On Liberty"; "Considerations on Representative Government"; "Remarks on Bentham's Philosophy."* Edited by Geraint Williams. London: Dent, 1993.

Plato. *The Collected Dialogues of Plato.* Edited by Edith Hamilton and Huntington Cairns. 1961. Reprint. Princeton, N.J.: Princeton University Press, 1984.

Rousseau, Jean-Jacques. *"The Social Contract" and "The First and Second Discourses,"* edited by Susan Dunn. New Haven, Conn.: Yale University Press, 2002.

Selborne, David. *The Principle of Duty: An Essay on the Foundations of the Civic Order.* Notre Dame, Ind.: University of Notre Dame Press, 2001.

Vallentyne, Peter, ed. *Equality and Justice.* New York: Routledge, 2003.

SEE ALSO: Accountability; Hegel, Georg Wilhelm Friedrich; Justice; Mill, John Stuart; Plato; Responsibility; Rousseau, Jean-Jacques; Socialism; Utilitarianism; Welfare rights.

Socialism

DEFINITION: Political and economic system characterized by collective ownership of the means of
production and equitable distribution of goods
and resources

DATE: Developed during the late nineteenth century

TYPE OF ETHICS: Politico-economic ethics

SIGNIFICANCE: Socialism represents an alternative
vision for social ethics in which justice is realized
through material equality and the eradication of
exploitation, leaving all members of society free
to associate in common productive efforts aimed
at satisfying social needs.

Socialism is based in a positive conception of freedom, defined as a way of life that allows all humans
to realize and express their inherent potential through
their labor. This definition is generally in conflict
with definitions of freedom based on individual
rights and choice and with capitalist notions of labor
as productive of increased wealth rather than expressive of humanity.

Socialism is a politico-economic system in which
the struggle to eradicate social inequality is the highest ethical pursuit. Socialist morality generally extols
the collective pursuits of the larger community and
asserts that the vast potential latent in the human species can be fully realized only through freely associated, nonexploitative social relations. Throughout
history, socialism has developed from its origins in
the romantic visions of intellectuals and philosophers to an alternative social system that has been
struggled for by exploited classes in virtually all corners of the globe. The legacy of socialism persists in
the modern world, both as an ethical critique of capitalist values and as an alternative prescription for social justice.

UTOPIAN SOCIALISM

Although some of the key ethical elements within
socialism can be traced back to ancient times, their
consolidation into a unified vision occurred at the beginning of the nineteenth century in what has since
become referred to as utopian socialism. Claude Henri
Saint-Simon, Charles Fourier, and Robert Owen,
among others, created a comprehensive critique of
early capitalist society as it entered its industrial
phase. Although the socialist visions of each thinker

differed, all the utopian socialists shared a preoccu-
pation with the morally bankrupt character of early
industrial capitalism and saw the need for a more
communal and egalitarian society in which an ethic
of cooperation would prevail over individual greed.

Equally representative of utopian socialism was
the notion that a socialist world could somehow be
achieved through enlightened choice. Later socialists, such as Karl Marx and Friedrich Engels, argued
that this idea amounted to a lack of a revolutionary
strategy for realizing the utopian vision. Utopian socialists generally saw political violence as the historical baggage of presocialist society and believed that
it would be unnecessary in a world that was being
gradually civilized by means of emerging socialist
values. In short, their moral critique of bourgeois society was not accompanied by an analysis of the way
in which capitalist domination could be decisively
broken.

Emile Durkheim, one of the founders of modern
sociology, argued in his posthumously published
work *Socialism* (1928) that Saint-Simon conceptually linked the ethical failures of the social era born of
the Enlightenment with the urgent call for a consciously managed society—one in which production
is cooperatively organized and the interests of the exploited classes are advanced through the socialization of industry. Saint-Simon's call for a "New Christianity" that would emphasize public concerns rather
than the pursuit of individual self-interest made his
utopian vision a complete one from Durkheim's perspective.

Robert Owen likewise espoused the notion that
once socialist principles became enacted and shared,
socialism's intrinsic desirability would automatically lead to its promulgation. Owen's contributions
to socialism were vast, because of his agitation for reforms on behalf of the English proletariat as well as
his sponsoring of experimental socialist communes
that were based on socialist morality and cooperative
business ventures. Charles Fourier added to the utopian socialist vision with his critique of the family
and his agitation for sexual liberation. He became famous for his expression that the best measure of social freedom is the existing degree of women's freedom. Fourier argued that industrial bourgeois society
repressed the human passion for love. Liberation
could be gained only through smashing the prohibitions against human sexual expression, according to

Fourier, and the larger community needed to guarantee all of its members the support necessary for "basic" sexual and well as economic satisfaction.

REVOLUTIONARY SOCIALISM

Utopian visions of socialism ultimately became overshadowed by the emergence of the revolutionary socialism pioneered by Karl Marx and Friedrich Engels. Marx, a German thinker, transformed socialism into a practical program for struggle out of which organized social classes within industrial capitalist societies could create a socialist society through revolution. Marx and Engels's point of departure is their social class analysis, which argues that only the exploited working class is capable of successfully carrying out a socialist revolution. The ethical basis of what later became known as Marxian socialism is to be found in revolutionary "praxis," or practical activity, designed to overthrow bourgeois domination. The moral basis for revolutionary activity, including armed struggle, was to be found in the larger historical mission of the working class, which was the ending of class exploitation.

An important distinction of Marxian socialism is its dialectical conception of ethics, which views all systems of morality as historically situated and dynamic insofar as morality changes in accordance with the ongoing struggle of social classes. The "contradictory" nature of morality thus rests in the notion that what is ethical at one stage of history becomes outmoded as human social relations continue to change and develop. The ethical basis of revolutionary armed struggle, for example, becomes transformed once new social circumstances become achieved and the need for violence has been surpassed. As Engels argued in *Anti-Duhring* (1878), a fully humanized morality can be achieved only after a socialist revolution has overcome social class inequalities and after the former system of morality has vanished from the collective memory.

MODERN SOCIALISM

The twentieth century could be largely characterized by the struggle between the competing systems of capitalism and socialism. Even the fall of the socialist bloc countries during the late 1980's and early 1990's can be related to an ethical crisis of particular political regimes and their relative inability to realize socialist goals. In the twenty-first century, most modern nations continue to experience political tensions between the status quo and powerful critics who argue for socialistic reforms or the need for a socialist revolution. The socialist critique of race, gender-based, and social class exploitation remains relevant in the modern era, and its advocates remain influential in world affairs.

Richard A. Dello Buono

FURTHER READING

Berki, R. N. *Socialism*. New York: St. Martin's Press, 1975.

Bottomore, T. B., and Maximilien Rubel, eds. *Karl Marx: Selected Writings in Sociology and Social Philosophy*. New York: McGraw-Hill, 1964.

Durkheim, Emile. *Socialism*. New York: Collier Books, 1962.

Fromm, Erich, ed. *Socialist Humanism: An International Symposium*. Garden City, N.Y.: Doubleday, 1965.

Levine, Andrew. *A Future for Marxism? Althusser, the Analytical Turn, and the Revival of Socialist Theory*. London: Pluto, 2003.

McLellan, David. *The Thought of Karl Marx: An Introduction*. New York: Harper & Row, 1971.

Marx, Karl, and Friedrich Engels. *The Marx-Engels Reader*. Edited by Robert C. Tucker. 2d ed. New York: W. W. Norton, 1978.

Selsam, Howard, and Harry Martel, eds. *Reader in Marxist Philosophy: From the Writings of Marx, Engels and Lenin*. New York: International, 1963.

Williams, D. T. *Capitalism, Socialism, Christianity, and Poverty*. Cape Town, South Africa: J. L. van Schaik, 1998.

SEE ALSO: Capitalism; Communism; Communitarianism; Durkheim, Émile; Freedom and liberty; Individualism; Marx, Karl; Marxism; Revolution; Social justice and responsibility; *Utopia*.

Society for the Prevention of Cruelty to Animals

IDENTIFICATION: Organization created by humanitarians to oppose the mistreatment of animals

DATE: Founded in 1824

TYPE OF ETHICS: Animal rights

SIGNIFICANCE: As the first animal welfare organization in England or Continental Europe, the Society for the Prevention of Cruelty to Animals (SPCA) influenced all future western humane organizations.

According to the seventeenth century philosopher René Descartes, animals were soulless, God-created automatons lacking consciousness and the ability to feel pain. Any human use of animals was therefore justifiable. By the late eighteenth century, other philosophers challenged humanity's right to absolute dominion over animals, thus heralding the birth of the anticruelty movement. These new convictions were best summarized by the utilitarian philosopher Jeremy Bentham, who wrote in 1789, "The question is not, can they *Reason*? Nor can they *Talk*? But can they *Suffer*?"

Reflecting increasing concern over animal welfare, M. P. Richard "Humanity Dick" Martin in 1822 submitted and successfully promoted the passage of a bill protecting domestic farm animals from cruelty. Meanwhile, encouraged by the Martin Act, humane activists formed the SPCA, which began policing slaughterhouses, markets, and private citizens for animal abuse. With the bestowal of royal patronage in 1835, the organization became the Royal Society for the Prevention of Cruelty to Animals (RSPCA). During the late twentieth century, the United Kingdom remains a principal center of advocacy of animal rights.

Mary E. Virginia

SEE ALSO: Animal rights; Cruelty to animals; Humane Society of the United States; People for the Ethical Treatment of Animals; World Society for the Protection of Animals.

Sociobiology

DEFINITION: Study of the evolutionary basis of human social behavior

DATE: Originated around 1975

TYPE OF ETHICS: Scientific ethics

SIGNIFICANCE: Sociobiological studies of humans are based on the premise that human behavior is the result of evolution. Thus, sociobiologists argue that morality has evolutionary value, and indeed that it results from processes of natural selection. This argument has been attacked, however, as a form of biological determinism.

In 1975, E. O. Wilson, a Harvard professor and world-renowned expert on ants, published a massive book in which he tied together decades of empirical research by animal behaviorists with decades of theoretical work by geneticists and evolutionary biologists. In so doing, he defined a new academic discipline, "sociobiology," the name of which is taken from the title of his book, *Sociobiology: The New Synthesis*.

The thesis of Wilson's book was that behavior, like any other attribute of an animal, has some of its basis in genetics, and therefore scientists should study behavior in the same way they do anatomy, physiology, or any other observable feature of an animal; that is, they should not only describe it but also try to figure out its function and the reasons why it evolved. Most biologists found no fault with this logic, and the discipline grew very rapidly, spawning hundreds of books and thousands of articles. Many predictions generated from this new perspective were corroborated, and many previously unexplained behaviors started to make sense.

The majority of biologists were rapidly convinced that this new approach was both useful and valid. Other scientists, however, as well as many sociopolitical organizations and representatives, immediately took a stand against it. In his book, Wilson had included a closing chapter on the sociobiology of human behavior, and his critics believed that the principles and methods used to study nonhuman animals simply could not be applied to humans. Academic critics tended to be psychologists, sociologists, anthropologists, and political scientists who believed that learning and culture, not evolution and genetics, determine most human behavior. Nonacademic critics tended to be either philosophers and theologians who believed that the human spirit makes people qualitatively different from other animals or left-leaning political organizations who believed that violent, discriminatory, and oppressive human behaviors might somehow be justified by calling attention to the existence of similar behaviors in other animals.

THE ALTRUISM DEBATE

The first, and perhaps most significant, debate over sociobiology as it applied to humans involved explanations for altruism. Altruism, by definition, is behavior that helps another individual or group at some cost to the altruist. Since altruistic behavior would appear to help nonaltruistic recipients of altruism to survive and pass on their genes but not help altruists themselves, any genetic tendency toward altruism should rapidly die out; which would imply that altruistic behavior must be nonevolved; that is, either culturally learned or spiritually motivated, as the critics claimed.

Biologists, however, had documented altruistic behavior in a wide variety of nonhuman animals, suggesting either that other animals must also have cultural or spiritual motives (suggestions not accepted by most of the critics) or that altruism really must, somehow, increase the altruist's ability to survive and pass on genes, not merely help the nonaltruistic recipient. Two theoreticians provided explanations for how this might have occurred.

W. D. Hamilton proposed an evolutionary model based on the concept of "kin selection"; according to this model, altruistic behavior does not have to increase the altruist's chances of survival and reproduction, as long as it increases the survival and reproduction of the altruist's relatives. Since relatives share genes, even though an altruist may decrease his or her own chances of survival and reproduction, the genetic tendency for altruism can be passed on to subsequent generations because the altruist has increased the total number of his or her genes in the next generation by increasing the number of collateral, or nondirect, descendants.

Later, Robert Trivers proposed a model based on the concept of "reciprocal altruism"; according to this model, altruists do increase their own chances of survival and reproduction, because the recipients of their altruism remember them and help them out when the tables are turned. (This is often referred to colloquially as the "You scratch my back and I'll scratch yours" model.)

Largely on the basis of these two models of altruism, sociobiologists argued that even the most complex and seemingly spiritually motivated behaviors of humans could be explained solely by evolutionary biology. This notion was widely publicized in Richard Dawkins's book *The Selfish Gene* (1976), E. O. Wilson's subsequent book *On Human Nature* (1978), and Richard Alexander's *The Biology of Moral Systems* (1987).

Although many anthropologists and psychologists have converted to the evolutionary perspective and found it fruitful, many remain antagonistic to it, and sociologists, philosophers, and theologians, in particular, remain highly critical. Their argument continues to be that human behavior is qualitatively different from that of other animals because of the complexity of human culture and spirituality. They argue that a reductionist approach to human behavior will inevitably miss the most important features of human nature and social interactions.

In addition, many individuals and political groups remain hostile to sociobiology because of the widespread belief that if something is genetic, it is inevitable and justifiable. Although these conclusions are not logically valid, there is legitimate concern that some people might use sociobiological arguments to try to undermine moral teaching or to promote or rationalize nepotism, aggression, racism, or sexism. To the extent that sociobiology is perceived as an ideological tool rather than a scientific enterprise, it has been argued that sociobiological research should not be funded or otherwise promoted by public institutions (such as universities). The debate has thus become one of politics and social goals as well as one of scientific philosophy and method.

Linda Mealey

FURTHER READING

Alexander, Richard D. *The Biology of Moral Systems*. Hawthorne, N.Y.: Aldine De Gruyter, 1987.

Cameron, Donald. *The Purpose of Life: Human Purpose and Morality from an Evolutionary Perspective*. Bristol, England: Woodhill, 2001.

Caplan, Arthur L., ed. *The Sociobiology Debate: Readings on Ethical and Scientific Issues*. New York: Harper & Row, 1978.

Casebeer, William D. *Natural Ethical Facts: Evolu-*

tion, Connectionism, and Moral Cognition. Cambridge, Mass.: MIT Press, 2003.

Dawkins, Richard. *The Selfish Gene.* New ed. New York: Oxford University Press, 1999.

Kitcher, Phillip. *Vaulting Ambition: Sociobiology and the Quest for Human Nature.* Cambridge, Mass.: MIT Press, 1985.

Montagu, Ashley, ed. *Sociobiology Examined.* New York: Oxford University Press, 1980.

Ruse, Michael. *Sociobiology: Sense or Nonsense?* Boston: D. Reidel, 1979.

Thompson, Paul, ed. *Issues in Evolutionary Ethics.* Albany: State University of New York Press, 1995.

Wilson, E. O. *Sociobiology: The New Synthesis.* Cambridge, Mass.: Belknap/Harvard University Press, 1975.

SEE ALSO: Academic freedom; Altruism; Anthropological ethics; Darwin, Charles; Determinism and freedom; Evolutionary theory; Ideology; Political correctness; Social Darwinism; Taboos.

Socrates

IDENTIFICATION: Ancient Greek philosopher
BORN: c. 470 B.C.E., Athens, Greece
DIED: 399 B.C.E., Athens, Greece
TYPE OF ETHICS: Classical history
SIGNIFICANCE: Socrates objected to written language because he believed that it was inherently removed from truth, and he therefore never produced any written works. Thus, he is known primarily as a character in the dramatic philosophical dialogues of Plato, his greatest student. Socrates is believed to have shifted the focus of Greek philosophy from the natural world to the human psyche and ethics and to have argued that moral goodness is based on objective knowledge.

Socrates' views on ethics must be understood against the background of his main opponents, the Sophists. They were moral relativists who believed that ethical beliefs could never be more than a matter of convention and subjective human opinions. In contrast, Socrates thought that ethical truths were universal and objective and concerned the way in which humans should best live. He said that the goal in human life was not simply living but "living well." To make an excellent ship, one must understand the purpose of ships and what constitutes the standard of excellence for a ship. Similarly, to live life well, one must understand what constitutes human excellence. For this reason, Socrates said that "the unexamined life is not worth living."

For Socrates, the goal of ethics was not obedience to some set of abstract duties. The whole purpose of ethics was to flourish as a human being, to fulfill one's true function, to achieve happiness. Hence, "Why should I be moral?" was a foolish question, for it was like asking, "Why should I live a happy, fulfilled life?" The problem is, Socrates said, that people tend to identify themselves with their bodies, and this gives them a false picture of what is the true goal in life. The body is, however, merely the outward shell, or instrument, of the soul. The immortal, nonphysical soul within one is the real person. The proper goal in life, therefore, is to "care for one's soul," to make it as good as possible, and this is achieved by striving to achieve wisdom.

Socrates' position is sometimes called "ethical intellectualism," because he believed that ethics is a matter of the intellect and that the moral person is one who has correct moral knowledge. Socrates' ethical conclusions are often called the "Socratic paradoxes" because they seem to contradict normal moral intuitions. Two of the key Socratic teachings are that virtue is knowledge and that no one knowingly does what is wrong.

VIRTUE IS KNOWLEDGE

In the Greek language, the word for "virtue" has a much broader meaning than does its English counterpart. For anything to have "virtue" meant that it was excellent at its task or fulfilled its function well. Hence, the virtue of a shipbuilder is the skill of making high-quality ships. Human beings engage in many different and specific tasks (making music, playing sports, practicing medicine), and each activity has its appropriate goal and requires a certain sort of knowledge. Socrates believed, however, that people are all engaged in the more general task of living human life, and this is something that can be done poorly or well, depending on how well one understands this task. Hence, being a moral person requires having knowledge of what is genuinely valuable.

For Socrates, there is a difference between genuine knowledge and correct belief. Someone can be told the correct answer to a mathematics problem without really knowing why it is the correct answer. Similarly, simply having the correct moral beliefs is not enough. To truly have moral knowledge of the right way to live requires that one understand why that way is best. Socrates claimed that the end of human life is the achieving of wisdom; only wisdom will make one a morally excellent person.

No One Knowingly Does What Is Wrong

Since moral goodness is knowledge of how to live well and flourish, it was inconceivable to Socrates that anyone could have this knowledge and not follow it. Since doing what is wrong will harm the soul, however, those who do evil do so through error, thinking that they are pursuing what is good for them. For example, a thief steals because he or she believes that money is the ultimate value. By starting out with this false assumption about what is important in life, the thief logically concludes that it is good to obtain money in any way possible. What is wrong with the thief, Socrates would say, is that he or she lacks a correct understanding of what is genuinely valuable. Still, it may seem that sometimes people knowingly do what is wrong. Socrates would say, however, that when one performs an action that is morally wrong and harmful to one's soul, one does so because one's mind is blinded by desire. In that moment, one actually believes that the pleasure of the moment is a better goal to pursue than one's long-range satisfaction. For the person who has wisdom and the true vision of life, reason will guide the emotions in the right direction in the same way that a chariot driver guides his horses.

Implications for Ethical Conduct

For Socrates, being a moral person was more than simply doing the right thing. It also did not mean simply following a list of rules or duties. Instead, morality was a matter of making one's inner self as excellent as possible. This required an understanding of what is of enduring value in life as opposed to what is merely transitory and peripheral. One can gain this understanding by means of a process of self-examination in which one critiques the values by which one lives, abandoning those values that prove to be worthless, and getting a clear understanding of those

values that lead to human excellence. Once one's soul has a vision of what is truly good, one will have no reason to do anything else but to steer one's life in that direction.

William F. Lawhead

Further Reading

Green, Ricky K. *Democratic Virtue in the Trial and Death of Socrates: Resistance to Imperialism in Classical Athens*. New York: Peter Lang, 2001.

Guthrie, W. K. C. *Socrates*. London: Cambridge University Press, 1971.

Lutz, Mark J. *Socrates' Education to Virtue: Learning the Love of the Noble*. Albany: State University of New York Press, 1998.

Plato. *The Collected Dialogues of Plato*. Edited by Edith Hamilton and Huntington Cairns. 1961. Reprint. Princeton, N.J.: Princeton University Press, 1984.

Santas, G. X. *Socrates: Philosophy in Plato's Early Dialogues*. London: Routledge & Kegan Paul, 1979.

Taylor, A. E. *Socrates*. Garden City, N.Y.: Doubleday, 1953. Reprint. Westport, Conn.: Hyperion Press, 1979.

Vlastos, Gregory, ed. *The Philosophy of Socrates: A Collection of Critical Essays*. Garden City, N.Y.: Anchor Books, 1971.

_____. *Socrates: Ironist and Moral Philosopher*. Ithaca, N.Y.: Cornell University Press, 1991.

See also: *Apology*; Cyrenaics; Paradoxes in ethics; Plato; Platonic ethics; *Republic*; Sophists; Virtue ethics; Wisdom.

Solzhenitsyn, Aleksandr

Identification: Russian novelist and historian
Born: December 11, 1918, Kislovodsk, U.S.S.R.
Type of ethics: Modern history
Significance: Recipient of the 1970 Nobel Prize in Literature, Solzhenitsyn produced both literary works, including *One Day in the Life of Ivan Denisovich* (*Odin den' Ivana Denisovicha*, 1962), *The First Circle* (*V kruge pervom*, 1968), and *Cancer Ward* (*Rakovy korpus*, 1968), and historical works such as *The Gulag Archipelago, 1918-*

1956: An Experiment in Literary Investigation (*Arkhipelag GULag, 1918-1956: Opyt khudozhestvennogo issledovaniya*, 1973-1975). In all his work, he advanced the idea of the mutuality of communal and individual ethics within the context of the Russian Christian tradition.

While confronted with mounting censorship from Soviet authorities during the 1960's and his eventual arrest and forced exile in 1974, Aleksandr Solzhenitsyn maintained an ethical identity with his homeland and his image of its historical traditions. Solzhenitsyn's ethical base was predicated on a renewal of traditional Russian Christian values; he was not attracted to the individualism or democratic institutions of the West.

Solzhenitsyn condemned the oppression of the Soviet (and especially the Stalinist) phase in Russian history and described the ethical and moral bankruptcy of the Soviet regime and its institutions. In particular, he condemned the depersonalization of Russian life under the Soviets. He advanced the cause of the individual living within a free but ethically based and directed society. Solzhenitsyn's exile came to an end in 1994, when he returned home to live in Russia. Although all the Solzhenitsyn canon is worthy of study, his most significant works from the standpoint of ethics are *One Day in the Life of Ivan Denisovich* and *The Gulag Archipelago*.

William T. Walker
Updated by the editors

SEE ALSO: Art; Christian ethics; Communism; *Gulag Archipelago*; Stalin, Joseph.

Song lyrics

DEFINITION: Expressions of a wide range of subjects by means of words set to music
TYPE OF ETHICS: Arts and censorship
SIGNIFICANCE: The lyrics of contemporary popular music challenge the boundaries of taste and public notions of propriety and are central to the debate over limits to free expression.

Bawdy and subversive lyrics are as old as music, and the impulse to suppress them is as old as social hier-archy. There is an ancient underground tradition of songs that defy the prevailing order, satirize the ruling class, and challenge commonly accepted precepts. Anthems such as France's "Marseillaise" and the communist "Internationale" began as often-banned incitements to revolution. In nineteenth century Italy, the politics of the reunification movement, the Risorgimento, circumscribed the texts of Giuseppi Verdi operas. Richard Strauss's opera *Salome* was shut down after one performance in New York in 1908, in part because of its allegedly indecent German libretto, which was based on a play by Oscar Wilde.

MODERN POPULAR CULTURE

With the invention of sound recording and the advent of broadcast media, arguments favoring limits to the content of commercially distributed songs gained currency in the United States. Before the 1950's, most censorship incidents involved the proscription or laundering of Harlem Renaissance blues lyrics or Broadway show tunes such as Cole Porter's "Let's Do It." On occasion, records such as the Andrews Sisters' "Rum and Coca-Cola," whose unexpurgated lyrics refer to a mother-and-daughter team of Trinidadian prostitutes "working for the Yankee dollar," would be banned from the radio. During the Joseph McCarthy era, the socially conscious lyrics of leftist folksingers such as Woody Guthrie were widely suppressed as "communist" propaganda.

With the rise of rock and roll during the 1950's, the verbal content of popular music began to ignite moral panic. Rock, which evolved from African American rhythm and blues in the early 1950's, was considered "jungle music," a destructive combination of primitive rhythms and lewd lyrics. Early antirock music campaigns were sometimes unapologetically racist and always maintained that the music spread violence and promiscuity. The lyrics of some songs, such as the Kingsmen's "Louie Louie," did not even have to be decipherable to be deemed obscene by the Federal Bureau of Investigation and the Federal Communications Commission.

Although the sexual frankness that crept into pop lyrics as the 1960's progressed became increasingly overt, rock songs of that decade were most commonly censored or banned because of real or imagined references to drugs. The Beatles' "Lucy in the Sky with Diamonds" (1967), for example, was reviled in some quarters because it was assumed to describe the effects of LSD. More overt allusions to drug use, such as the Jefferson Airplane's "White Rabbit" (1967), with its exhortations to "feed your head," often caused the song to be denied radio play. Drug-culture jargon and four-letter words at times provided authorities with convenient excuses to keep antiwar and social protest songs off the air.

Within the United States, organized efforts to clean up rock music lyrics have come from across the political spectrum. Leaders of such campaigns have ranged from right-wing ideologue David Noebel to civil rights activist Jesse Jackson. In the late 1970's, the messages of punk bands such as the Sex Pistols, along with the continuing popularity of "heavy metal" music among young teenagers, created concern that "morbid" and "occult" lyrics were causing a rise in teenage suicide. In the late 1980's, artists were threatened with legal action by bereaved parents and in some cases sued. Evangelists and radio personalities such as Bob Larson popularized the idea that satanic messages were encoded in rock lyrics or subliminally injected into certain albums through sound engineering.

Upset by masturbation references in Prince's song "Darling Nikki" in 1985, Tipper Gore, the wife of future vice president Albert Gore, cofounded the Parents Music Resource Center (PMRC), an organization aimed at curbing the excesses of popular music. Congressional hearings held at PMRC's request resulted immediately in censorship activity at the state level. By 1990, the Recording Industry of America (RIAA) was pressured into instituting a voluntary warning-label system whereby some records would carry stickers with the label "Parental Advisory/Explicit Lyrics." The labeling scheme created a climate of censorship within the music industry and provided a foundation for efforts to restrict sales and criminalize certain lyrics in Louisiana, Washington state, and elsewhere.

The Demonization of Rap

In the late 1980's, Florida attorney Jack Thompson began enlisting allies in a campaign against rap, an African American art form that he considered an affront to "traditional values." Thompson helped to inspire the arrest and obscenity conviction of a record-store owner who was guilty of selling the Miami rap group 2 Live Crew's album *Nasty as They*

Wanna Be (1990); the band itself was arrested in Fort Lauderdale following a live performance of such songs as "Me So Horny." Although 2 Live Crew was acquitted, Thompson continued to hound them and other outspoken rap musicians—especially NWA (Niggas With Attitude)—across the country and as far as the United Kingdom, where 22,000 copies of an NWA album were impounded.

Hysteria over "gangsta" rap reached fever pitch in 1992 with the release of Ice-T's *Body Count* album (technically a heavy metal record), an outpouring of rage over forms of racism. Its climactic song, "Cop Killer," was condemned for its venom:

> I got my twelve gauge sawed off.
> I got my headlights turned off.
> I'm 'bout to bust some shots off.
> I'm 'bout to dust some cops off.
> COP KILLER, it's better you than me.
> COP KILLER, f—— police brutality!

Iran-Contra figure Oliver North retained Jack Thompson as counsel in July, 1992, for the express purpose of mobilizing his lobbying operation, Freedom Alliance, against musicians. North's strategy included encouraging police organizations to use various means to eliminate the sale, broadcast, or commercial release of "seditious" music. Ice-T and his distributor, Time Warner, were finally driven to excise "Cop Killer" from future pressings of the *Body Count* album. Other artists who were legally threatened or economically pressured included Ice Cube, Tupac Shakur, Almighty RSO, and Paris, whose "Bush Killa" vented rage at the White House.

Censorship During the 1990's

In 1994, mounting a fresh campaign to force the recording industry to clean up rap and heavy metal lyrics, the PMRC created the unlikely team of liberal Democrat C. Delores Tucker, chairman of the National Political Congress of Black Women, and conservative Republican William J. Bennett, secretary of education under President Ronald Reagan. In joint press releases, op-ed columns, and public appearances, Tucker and Bennett decried "lyrics from the gutter" while paying little attention to actual content. In 1995, Tucker and Bennett successfully pressured Time Warner to drop its controlling interest in

Interscope Records, which carried such controversial artists as Snoop Doggy Dogg.

U.S. senators Joseph Lieberman of Connecticut and Sam Nunn of Georgia joined Tucker and Bennett in public condemnation of "obscene music," citing such songs as Dove Shack's "Slap a Ho." In 1997, Senator Sam Brownback of Kansas held hearings designed to showcase complaints about objectionable lyrics and other elements of what Senator Lieberman, in testimony, called our "broken culture." In Brownback's media-tailored forum, the voices of artists, serious analysts of American culture, and free-speech advocates were almost absent; witnesses who deplored the moral turpitude of popular music were welcomed warmly. As Congress continued its attack, the Recording Industry Association of America, once fiercely opposed to censorship, began wavering in its support for freedom of expression.

By the mid-1990's, the $12 billion U.S. recording industry began backing away from nonmainstream music. The climate of censorship was aggravated by pressure from retailers and distributors. Wal-Mart, the largest record retailer in the nation, refused to sell albums with "parental-advisory" warning stickers and went so far as to demand censored versions of certain record albums, with problematic songs edited for content or dropped altogether.

After students gunned down fellow classmates at Littleton, Colorado's Columbine High School in 1999, and similar incidents occurred elsewhere, the campaigners against rock and rap were eager to blame the incidents on the troubled teenagers' taste in music. When it was erroneously reported that the Columbine shooters were fans of "goth-rock" singer Marilyn Manson, Senator Brownback and nine of his colleagues demanded that Seagram's, which owned

Eminem (Marshall Mathers III) accepting a Grammy Award for best rap album of the year, in February, 2003. (AP/Wide World Photos)

Manson's record label, put an end to the performer's career. They also called for an investigation into popular culture by the U.S. surgeon general.

In an era during which commercial music veered away from political content, the popular art being demonized was often material daring to critique contemporary American life. The so-called gangsta rap genre vented the outrage of an underclass whose real grievances received scant attention in congressional hearings. Critic Lawrence Stanley describes gangsta rap an "unmistakably black art form" that emerged at a time when white institutions were indifferent, if not hostile, to the concerns of African Americans.

For young people of all races who felt numbed by American middle-class life, Marilyn Manson offered an invigorating challenge to traditional gender roles, religious fundamentalism, and pressure to conform. White rapper Marshall Mathers III, who performs under the name Eminem, was vociferously condemned by everyone from Joan Garry of the Gay and Lesbian Alliance Against Discrimination (GLAAD) to Republican activist Lynne Cheney, wife of future vice president Dick Cheney, when his *Marshall Mathers LP* (2000) gained popularity, praise, and award nominations. Accused of nihilistic, misogynist ranting, Eminem was in fact an articulate chronicler of the ills of working-class Detroit. Describing the blighted industrial city in his song "Amityville," Eminem sings:

> we don't call it Detroit, we call it Amityville ('Ville). You can get capped just having a cavity filled (filled). Ahahahaha, that's why we're crowned the murder capital still (still). This ain't Detroit, this is m———n' Hamburger Hill (Hill!). We don't do drivebys, we park in front of houses and shoot. and when the police come we f———n' shoot it out with them too! That's the mentality here (here), that's the reality here (here). . . .

Through the 1990's, song-lyric censorship in the United States was opposed by the National Campaign for Freedom of Expression, the National Coalition Against Censorship, and grassroots advocacy groups such as Rock Out Censorship and the Massachusetts Music Industry Coalition. The American Civil Liberties Union (ACLU) Arts Censorship Project worked to provide legal aid to embattled musi-

cians, producers, and retailers, helping to overturn an "erotic music" law in Washington state and to defend record stores across the country. Citing federal court rulings on speech, ACLU attorneys maintained that song lyrics, even if they extolled armed rebellion, did not constitute a direct and imminent threat—and that First Amendment protections did indeed apply to such works as "Cop Killer." The irreconcilable disagreements in this controversy illustrated a growing rift between opposing visions of American democracy.

Inspired by a growing worldwide concern about content restrictions on music, activists and musicians held the first World Conference on Music and Censorship in Copenhagen, Denmark, in November, 1998. In the twenty-first century, the debate over song lyrics and other popular expressive media pitted human aspirations toward freedom against a perceived need, real or imagined, for increased authoritarian social control in response to a growing terrorist menace.

James D'Entremont

Further Reading

Blecha, Peter. *Taboo Tunes: A History of Banned Bands and Censored Songs*. San Francisco: Backbeat Books, 2004.

Cloonan, Martin. *Policing Pop*. Philadelphia: Temple University Press, 2003.

Gore, Tipper. *Raising PG Kids in an X-Rated Society*. Nashville, Tenn.: Abingdon Press, 1987.

Korpe, Marie, ed. *Shoot the Singer: Music Censorship Today*. London: Zed Books, 2004.

Martin, Linda, and Kerry Segrave. *Anti-Rock: The Opposition to Rock 'n' Roll*. Hamden, Conn.: Archon Books, 1988.

Nuzum, Eric D. *Parental Advisory: Music Censorship in America*. New York: Perennia, 2001.

Petley, Julian, et al. "Smashed Hits." *Index on Censorship* 27, no. 6. London: Writers and Scholars International, 1998.

Stanley, Lawrence A, ed. *Rap: The Lyrics*. New York: Penguin Books, 1992.

See also: Art and public policy; Book banning; Children's television; Freedom of expression; Internet piracy; Jackson, Jesse; Napster; Pornography; Violence.

Sophists

DEFINITION: Group of professional teachers active in ancient Greece and generally based in Athens

DATE: Fifth and fourth centuries B.C.E.

TYPE OF ETHICS: Classical history

SIGNIFICANCE: Known largely through their caricature in the work of Plato, the Sophists trained their students in rhetoric and oratory, among other subjects, and used formal logic to criticize traditional Greek values. For this reason, they are often represented as having believed that truth is irrelevant, morality is an empty construct, and the point of philosophical and legal argument is simply to win no matter what side one is on. Whether this is a fair assessment of some or all of the Sophists is a matter of ongoing debate.

First appearing in Greece during the period of Athenian empire-building (the *Pentekontaetia*), the Sophists established a general intellectual climate rather than a well-defined school of thought. The Sophists furthered the *Pentekontaetia*'s process of dynamic change by declaring that traditions were based on optional arrangements. In an era of sharpened competition, they also claimed that the value of actions varied according to circumstances, that knowledge was necessarily imperfect, and that truth was relative. Their relativistic, individualistic, and skeptical outlook was epitomized by their foremost representative, Protagoras of Abdera, who declared that "man is the measure of all things." The Sophists' ethical relativism was sharply attacked by a new philosophical movement, led by Socrates, reaffirming absolute values. Socrates and his followers, however, adopted the Sophists' critical spirit and concern with ethical issues; by further exploring Sophist topics such as the nature of truth and the justification of values, the Socratics built upon and partially perpetuated their work.

Michael J. Fontenot

SEE ALSO: Aristotelian ethics; Deconstruction; Derrida, Jacques; Plato; Platonic ethics; Situational ethics; Socrates.

South Africa's Truth and Reconciliation Commission

IDENTIFICATION: Government commission established to investigate human rights abuse that occurred under the former apartheid regime

DATE: Established in July, 1995

TYPE OF ETHICS: Human rights

SIGNIFICANCE: The work of the Truth and Reconciliation Commission established that it is possible to negotiate a peaceful transition from a repressive, authoritarian regime to an open, democratic civil society and that restorative justice is achievable through public truth telling, dialogue, and reparations to victims, while extending amnesty to perpetrators of a previous brutal regime.

After centuries of white-minority rule, South Africa elected its first nonracial government in 1994 and put a final end to the notoriously rigid segregation policy known as apartheid. Under an agreement worked out between the outgoing National Party leaders of the old government and the incoming leaders from the nonracial African National Congress (ANC), the Truth and Reconciliation Commission was created to investigate human rights abuses perpetrated by all factions over the previous forty-four years—the period of time from South Africa's 1960 Sharpeville massacre to the inauguration of Nelson Mandela as president in 1994.

The commission was officially created by the 1995 Promotion of National Unity Act, which defined the commission's goals. Under its chairman, Archbishop Desmond Tutu, a winner of the Nobel Peace Prize and a long-time advocate of human rights in South Africa, the commission conducted its work from April, 1996, through July, 1998. Over that four-year span, it heard testimony from more than 21,000 victims of apartheid and received more than 7,000 petitions for amnesty from prosecution for crimes committed under apartheid. By 1998, the commission had rejected 4,500 of those petitions and granted only 125 amnesties. In October, 1998, it issued a 3,500-page report on its findings.

BACKGROUND

During the early 1990's, shortly before the leaders of the National Party agreed to cede power to the

African National Congress, they demanded a general amnesty for the members of the government military and paramilitary forces responsible for atrocities, tortures, and human rights abuses under the past regime. That request was deemed unacceptable, but the interim parliament instead crafted a unique amnesty provision that found its way into South Africa's interim constitution of 1993. The amnesty provision provided for the establishment of a Truth and Reconciliation Commission by the new government that would deal with issues related to human rights abuses during the apartheid regime. The commission was tasked to serve as an outlet for citizens who were willing publicly to disclose details of gross violations of human rights they had committed during the apartheid regime and in turn were to be granted amnesty.

The Truth and Reconciliation Commission's Mandate

The South African legislation that created the commission charged it with promoting national unity and reconciliation in a spirit that transcended conflicts and divisions of the past. The commission was specifically charged with these goals:

1. Establishing as complete a picture as possible of the causes, nature, and extent of the gross violations of human rights committed under apartheid through investigations and hearings.

2. Facilitating the granting of amnesty to persons who fully disclose all relevant facts relating to acts associated with political objectives and who comply with the requirements of this act.

3. Establishing and making known the fate or whereabouts of victims of past abuses and restoring the human and civil dignity of such victims by granting them opportunities to relate their accounts of the violations of which they were victims, and recommending reparation measures.

4. Compiling a report providing as comprehensive an account as possible of the activities and findings of the commission and offering recommendations of measures to prevent future human rights violations.

The more than seven thousand amnesty petitions filed with the commission revealed details of atrocities committed by agents of the apartheid regime and, to a much lesser extent, by members of the African National Congress. Those applying for amnesty included the perpetrators of some of apartheid's most publicized crimes, such as the murder of Stephen Biko in 1977. They testified before the commission and thereby escaped prosecution for their actions. Some critics decried this process of swapping "truth for justice" as unconscionable and immoral.

The legislation that established the Truth and Reconciliation Commission was the outcome of a confluence of political and social developments negotiated during South Africa's transition to democracy. The key political tensions were between the outgoing government's demands to protect members of the old regime and the liberation movement's insistence to hold the leadership of the apartheid government accountable for past wrongs. As a part of the transitional constitutional arrangements, both sides accepted the creation of a truth commission. Details of the exact balance between punishment and indemnity and accountability and impunity had to be negotiated as well. In the end, the final agreement produced a compromise that obligated the incoming majority-rule government to provide amnesty to human rights abusers in exchange for their "honest" contrition of what happened. The Truth and Reconciliation Commission was thus shaped more by the national political agendas at the time of its creation than by the needs of victims of historical abuses.

SHORTCOMINGS

Despite the laudable aims of the legislation that created the commission, the act was not clear on how the commission was to achieve the lofty goal of promoting "national unity and reconciliation in the spirit of understanding that transcends the conflicts and past divisions." The commission achieved the goal of restoring dignity to victims of apartheid abuses primarily by engaging communities in the process of collecting statements from local victims during community human rights hearings. Community hearings thus became the dominant focus during the first fourteen months of the commission's work, during which eight community hearings were held. The hearings focused on victims—giving them opportunities to tell their stories. The hearings provided forums for open discussions that helped promote understanding among different political parties and different ethnic groups. The community hearings also provided powerful media images that could be conveyed throughout the country.

The more difficult challenge of the commission was the goal of promoting justice and reconciliation. This facet of the commission's work proved a contentious point, as it was interpreted differently by various political parties and communities through the life of the commission. It could be argued that the commission actually denied justice through its very structure. For example, its amnesty provision robbed victims of their right to seek justice through a criminal and civil process.

Following the commission's final report in 1998, studies of the commission found a wide range of opinions on its work. While some community members, particularly the Inkatha Freedom Fighters opposed the commission in principle, most community members had mixed feelings about the process. Almost every aspect of the commission's work caused some level of controversy.

Marc Georges Pufong

FURTHER READING

Hamber, B., D. Nageng, and G. O'Malley. "Telling It Like It Is . . . Understanding the TRC from the Perspective of Survivors." *Psychology in Society* 6 (2000).

Kollapen, N. "Accountability: The Debate in South Africa." *Journal of African Law* 37, no. 1 (1993): 1-9.

Minow, Martha. *Between Vengeance and Forgiveness.* Boston: Beacon Press, 1998.

Rotberg, Robert I., and Dennis Thompson, eds. *Truth v. Justice: The Morality of Truth Commissions.* Princeton, N.J.: Princeton University Press, 2000.

Van der Merwe, Hugo. "Some Insights from a Case Study of Duduza." Published as section of the *TRC Final Report*, vol 5, chapter 9, pp. 423-429, Cape Town, South Africa, Junta, 1998.

SEE ALSO: Apartheid; Collective guilt; Dirty hands; Forgiveness; Justice; Mandela, Nelson; Reconciliation; Torture; Truth; Tutu, Desmond.

Sovereignty

DEFINITION: Legitimate and exclusive possession of autonomous political authority over a particular territory or citizenry

TYPE OF ETHICS: International relations

SIGNIFICANCE: National sovereignty, essentially the right to demand that other countries respect a nation's absolute authority within its own borders, raises significant moral issues involving the limits of a government's right to remain unmolested if it mistreats its own people, as well as the ethical limits of a benevolent government's right to harm the people of other nations in order to preserve its own power. Internally, claims of sovereignty raise the moral questions of when and why one ought to obey the sovereign.

Sovereignty is a central concept in domestic and international law as well as in political theory, and its ethical implications are enormous.

To be sovereign in international law, a nation must be completely self-governing—recognizing no exterior legal authority to have the right to control its actions. The form of a national government is not an issue in determining sovereignty; a democracy, an absolute monarchy, a military junta, or a communist dictatorship may be sovereign if it submits to no higher, external legal authority.

In international affairs, one often contrasts de jure with de facto sovereignty, sovereignty in law versus sovereignty in fact. Some nations have been officially self-governing but have been, in fact, controlled by another. During the 1930's and 1940's, for example, Egypt was officially an independent nation but was, in fact, ruled by the British Empire in an arrangement that some historians have called an "informal empire."

Alternatively, some nations are nominally under foreign control but do, in fact, govern themselves. Such was clearly the case between the Balfour Declaration of 1926, wherein the British government promised not to interfere in the self-government of the dominions, and the Statute of Westminster (1931), which granted the dominions de jure independence.

During civil wars and wars of independence, questions of sovereignty are often blurred. The American colonies declared their independence from the British crown on July 4, 1776, but the Crown did not recognize that independence until the Treaty of Paris

(1783). When did sovereignty pass from the king in Parliament to the Continental Congress (or, more exactly, to the several states)?

Legally, such issues of sovereignty in international law are often solved by resort to competing interpretations by domestic law. American law views the date of the Declaration of Independence as the effective date of American sovereignty for all legal purposes, while in British law, the Treaty of Paris marks the end of British sovereignty in the thirteen American colonies.

In international law, land without a sovereignty over it is called *terra nullius* (or *territorium nullius*)—empty land—even though it may have a substantial human population. *Terra nullius* is open for annexation by existing sovereignties under international law on the theory that land without a sovereign is dangerously susceptible of producing lawlessness, such as piracy or terrorism, or armed conflicts between existing nations. Given the new dispensation in international affairs under the United Nations Charter, it is likely that an area of *terra nullius* that contained a large population but had not developed (or had lost) a governmental structure capable of asserting an "international legal personality" would be put in a trusteeship relationship with an established nation until such time as it might be capable of asserting sovereignty. By this means, the aura of direct colonialism might be averted.

SOVEREIGNTY AND POLITICAL PHILOSOPHY

The concept of sovereignty has application in political philosophy as well as in international law. Sovereignty is not only a claim of a right to rule made vis-à-vis other sovereignties but also one made domestically in regard to those subject to a governmental authority.

Political philosophers as divergent as Thomas Hobbes and Jean-Jacques Rousseau have recognized the essential truth that sovereignty is illimitable and indivisible. By the late twentieth century, these observations had fallen into general disuse, perhaps in the aftermath of the rise of the American Republic. In the British system, whatever Parliament passed and the king signed was law, without question and without limitation. Political theorists spoke of the legal omnipotence of the king-in-Parliament.

With the development of the U.S. Constitution, with its division of powers and its system of checks and balances between the executive, legislative, and judicial branches, it may, perhaps, have seemed that sovereignty could be divided and limited. Writing in the *Federalist Papers*, Alexander Hamilton, James Madison, and John Jay propounded the new sovereignty, which was tamed not only by the relationships of the branches of the national government but also by a federalism that preserved a sphere for the power of states and a system of enumerated rights that protected the citizen from governmental abuse.

In fact, in the U.S. Constitution, as in all political systems, sovereignty remains undivided and without limitation. Within the constitutional order, an ordinary sovereignty operates with divisions and limitations of power, but an extraordinary sovereignty resides also. The process of constitutional amendment could create a monarchy, establish an official church, authorize torture, eliminate elections, abolish the Supreme Court, and so forth. Seeming limitations, such as the prohibition upon depriving a state of its equal suffrage in the Senate, prove to be only procedural variants, because an amendment reducing the senatorial representation of a particular state would need ratification by that state, and an amendment to abolish the Senate would require unanimous ratification by the states.

In all approaches to sovereignty, there are underlying implications of a moral right to rule, in addition to a legal right and a practical power to rule. Even with legal positivism, in which moral questions are not directly injected into the pure theory of law—in which law is seen as merely "the command of the sovereign"—morality reenters through the questions of why, when, and whether the subject ought to obey the sovereign.

Also concerned in the ethical issues surrounding sovereignty has been its origin: Is sovereignty natural, or is it the construct of a social contract arising out of a state of nature? Anarchists, furthermore, including theoretical anarchists, such as Robert Paul Wolff, have viewed sovereignty as a morally dangerous illusion.

Patrick M. O'Neil

FURTHER READING

Austin, John. *The Province of Jurisprudence Determined and the Uses of the Study of Jurisprudence.* London: Weidenfeld & Nicolson, 1954.

Broomhall, Bruce. *International Justice and the In-*

ternational Criminal Court: Between Sovereignty and the Rule of Law. New York: Oxford University Press, 2003.

Brown, Chris. *Sovereignty, Rights, and Justice: International Political Theory Today.* Malden, Mass.: Blackwell, 2002.

Bryce, James. *Studies in History and Jurisprudence.* Vol. 2. Oxford, England: Clarendon Press, 1901.

Lugo, Luis E., ed. *Sovereignty at the Crossroads? Morality and International Politics in the Post-Cold War Era.* Lanham, Md.: Rowman & Littlefield, 1996.

Marshall, Geoffrey. *Constitutional Theory.* Oxford, England: Clarendon Press, 1971.

SEE ALSO: Anarchy; Constitution, U.S.; Hobbes, Thomas; International law; Intervention; *Leviathan*; National security and sovereignty; Nationalism; Social contract theory; *Two Treatises of Government.*

Soviet psychiatry

DEFINITION: Use of psychiatric techniques and facilities in the Soviet Union as tools of political oppression

DATE: Approximately 1862 to the 1990's

TYPE OF ETHICS: Psychological ethics

SIGNIFICANCE: The confinement of religious and political dissidents by Soviet psychiatrists was been a vivid reminder of the ways in which a profession can function unethically as an agent of social control.

The persecution of both political and religious dissidents by mental health authorities in the former Soviet Union was long a source of great concern to organizations that monitor human rights violations. Extensive evidence exists that hundreds if not thousands of mentally healthy dissidents were involuntarily committed to Soviet psychiatric hospitals. These individuals were committed in order to remove them from society and thus suppress their dissenting ideas and opinions.

HISTORY

Although psychiatric facilities in the Soviet Union practiced this type of abusive social control for many years, Soviet psychiatry was not always an eth-

ically compromised profession. The field of psychiatry was founded in the Soviet Union by Ivan Belinski, a Russian physician, who formed the first Russian psychiatric society in 1862. Belinski promoted psychiatric training and worked to establish outpatient treatment for the mentally ill. Under his leadership, the profession of psychiatry grew rapidly. In 1887, the first Congress of Russian Psychiatrists met in Moscow and endorsed the humane, scientifically informed treatment of mental patients as well as the notion that, if possible, psychiatric patients should be cared for in their home environments. Such ideas put Russian psychiatrists on an equal plane with their fellow practitioners in the rest of the world.

Positive developments continued to take place in the field of Soviet psychiatry after the Communist Revolution of 1917. At the time of the revolution, a People's Commissariat of Health was formed, with a special division devoted to psychiatry. Under the commissariat's leadership, many types of services were offered free of charge to the mentally ill, such as crisis intervention, sheltered workshops, and home care programs. Many Soviet psychiatrists also began to develop an interest in the young field of psychoanalysis, and the major works of Sigmund Freud were widely distributed.

THE ADVENT OF ABUSE

Problems began to develop during the late 1920's, as Joseph Stalin consolidated his hold on the government of the Soviet Union. Stalin had little concern for the rights of the mentally ill, and he viewed involuntary psychiatric commitments as an effective way to control his ideological opponents. Although psychiatric hospitals continued to treat individuals who suffered from genuine forms of mental illness, they also became a place of involuntary confinement for individuals who openly disagreed with the political or religious doctrine of the government. Labor organizers and artists who advocated creative freedom were favorite targets of the psychiatric establishment. Placing such dissidents in psychiatric facilities served both to remove them from society and to discredit their ideas by allowing the government to label them as insane.

A special diagnostic category, known as "sluggish schizophrenia," was developed. Anatoly Snezhnevsky, a notorious Russian psychiatrist who rose to a position of high authority under the Stalinist regime, defined sluggish schizophrenia as delusions of reforming the country's social system in the mind of an otherwise normal individual. This type of false diagnosis enabled psychiatrists such as Snezhnevsky to label mentally stable individuals as insane and have them involuntarily committed to psychiatric facilities. Even if such an individual was eventually fortunate enough to be discharged, his or her name was maintained on a national list of mental patients. This registry was distributed to prospective employers and schools, ensuring that the individual would suffer from lifelong discrimination. Doctors who refused to follow the unethical practices of this system were routinely disciplined or even imprisoned. Over time, Soviet psychiatrists became virtual servants of the state, with no professional autonomy and little room for ethical judgment.

THE USE OF TORTURE

Psychiatric treatment in the Soviet Union eventually became so abusive that some dissidents were actually tortured during their hospitalization. A convincing account of such treatment has been provided by Anatoly Koryagin, a Soviet psychiatrist who was himself hospitalized involuntarily because he refused to carry out government policy. Throughout his fifteen-month hospitalization, Koryagin was kept on a virtual starvation diet, so that he was severely emaciated and in a constant state of hunger. He was forced to take various psychiatric medications and also reports having had a probe smeared with acid placed in his stomach in order to induce excruciating pain. This type of torture was apparently designed to force Koryagin and other dissidents to renounce their ideological beliefs. Because of such extreme violations of human rights, the World Psychiatric Association (WPA) condemned Soviet psychiatry in 1977. Six years later, the All-Union Society of Soviet Psychiatrists resigned from the WPA rather than face certain expulsion.

Such international condemnation, however, did little to change the field of psychiatry in the Soviet Union. Peter Reddaway, a political scientist who has written extensively about Soviet psychiatric abuse, has noted that only *glasnost* and the reorganization of Soviet society has brought about genuine reform. In what was once the Soviet Union, the reorganized profession of psychiatry appears to be returning to its humanitarian roots.

Steven C. Abell

FURTHER READING

Amnesty International, USA. *Political Abuse of Psychiatry in the USSR: An Amnesty International Briefing.* New York: Author, 1983.

Bloch, Sidney, and Peter Reddaway. *Psychiatric Terror: How Soviet Psychiatry Is Used to Suppress Dissent.* New York: Basic Books, 1977.

_____. *Soviet Psychiatric Abuse: The Shadow over World Psychiatry.* Boulder, Colo.: Westview Press, 1985.

Fireside, Harvey. *Soviet Psychoprisons.* New York: W. W. Norton, 1979.

Kanas, Nick. "Contemporary Psychiatry: Psychiatry in Leningrad." *Psychiatric Annals* 22 (April, 1992): 212-220.

Koryagin, Anatoly. "The Involvement of Soviet Psychiatry in the Persecution of Dissenters." *British Journal of Psychiatry* 154 (March, 1989): 336-340.

Smith, Theresa C., and Thomas A. Oleszczuk. *No Asylum: State Psychiatric Repression in the Former USSR.* New York: New York University Press, 1996.

SEE ALSO: Farrakhan, Louis; Human rights; Institutionalization of patients; Mental illness; Oppression; Psychology; Stalin, Joseph.

Sperm banks

DEFINITION: Places in which human sperm cells are frozen and stored for later use in artificial insemination and in vitro fertilization techniques

DATE: First established during the late twentieth century

TYPE OF ETHICS: Bioethics

SIGNIFICANCE: Although most often used to ensure that couples will be able to reproduce in the future, sperm banks can also be used as sources of anonymous genetic material for infertile couples, lesbian couples, or women who want to become single mothers. This application raises ethical issues involving genetic manipulation, as well as the rights and responsibilities of the genetic father of a child produced with donated sperm.

The freezing of tissue, or cryopreservation, is a procedure that is used to delay the normal degenerative

In 1983, the Sperm Bank of California became the first such facility in the United States to ask donors if they would be willing to be contacted by the offspring of their donated sperm after the latter reached legal adulthood. In early 2002, a young woman named Claire, seen here (at left) with her mother, made plans to become the first person to take advantage of the sperm bank's policy by contacting her anonymous father to learn about her genetic history. (AP/Wide World Photos)

processes that occur when a tissue is removed from the body. Sperm banks acquire sperm from male donors and then deep freeze the sperm in liquid nitrogen, where they can be preserved for more than a decade. When needed, the sperm can be thawed out and used in processes such as artificial insemination and in vitro fertilization. Some sperm donors are husbands who cannot have children with their wives by ordinary means. Others are men who face sterilization through vasectomies or as the result of chemotherapy drugs for cancer. Still others are healthy men who donate their sperm for the money.

Those interested in obtaining donor sperm can often choose the sperm based on the physical characteristics, hobbies, and/or intellectual capacities of the donor. This technology tends to tempt persons to manipulate the gene pool so as to create a superior class of persons, avoid individuals with undesirable traits, and attempt to create the "perfect child." One problem involves determining the true father of the child—the biological donor or the parent who raises the child but did not donate the sperm. Additionally, some people believe that the commercialism inherent in the business of sperm banking tends to lessen the value of procreation.

Roman J. Miller

SEE ALSO: Bioethics; Eugenics; In vitro fertilization; Parenting; Surrogate motherhood.

Spinoza, Baruch

IDENTIFICATION: Dutch philosopher
BORN: November 24, 1632, Amsterdam, United
    Provinces (now the Netherlands)
DIED: February 21, 1677, The Hague, United
    Provinces (now the Netherlands)
TYPE OF ETHICS: Renaissance and Restoration
    history
SIGNIFICANCE: In such works as *A Theologico-Political Treatise* (*Tractatus theologico-politicus*, 1670) and *Ethics* (*Ethica*, 1677), Spinoza constructed a monistic philosophy of God and nature in which ethical behavior would follow naturally from understanding reality as a unified whole.

In the seventeenth century, academic Scholasticism, with its syllogistic reasoning and its Aristotelian epistemology, was withering away after a milennium of dominance. The empirical scientific methods of Nicholas Copernicus, Johann Kepler, and Galileo showed a new direction of philosophical understanding, and a rising interest in mathematics suggested new types of philosophical proof based on the methods of Euclidian geometry. Baruch Spinoza played a part in the movement that resulted, together with such notable thinkers as Francis Bacon, Thomas Hobbes, René Descartes, and Gottfried Leibniz.

LIFE

Spinoza was born into a family of prosperous Jewish merchants in Amsterdam, an area with a tolerance for religious practice and dissent in advance of its time. His education was in the Hebraic tradition of his community, with studies of the Old Testament and the Talmud, as well as of Scholastic philosophy and theology. Preparing to become a rabbi, he continued his studies after finishing school, becoming acquainted with the Kabbala and the thinking of medieval Jewish philosophers. His own views, fueled by a determination to think everything through ab initio, diverged from orthodoxy to the point that he was expelled from the Jewish community (by civil, not religious, authority) in 1656. He renounced his Hebrew name, Baruch, and was thenceforward known as Benedict (de) Spinoza. He continued in Amsterdam for a time, studying Latin, Greek, physics, geometry, and the philosophy of Descartes, and associating with members of a number of free-thinking Christian sects such as the Mennonites, the Collegiants, and the Remonstrants.

In 1660, Spinoza left Amsterdam to live successively in Rijnsburg, Voorburg, and finally The Hague (all on an axis of approximately thirty miles between Amsterdam and The Hague). In these places, he supported himself as an expert lens grinder and met for discussion with groups of philosophically minded friends. This activity led to his early writings, in which he set forth his views on God, humanity, and the universe, and produced an account of Descartes's philosophy. These were original and powerful enough that his reputation quickly spread beyond his immediate circle, and within a few years he was in correspondence with major philosophers in Europe and England, including Leibniz and the physicist Christiaan Huygens on the Continent, and in England Henry Oldenburg, secretary of the Royal Society of London, and the scientist Robert Boyle. *A Theologico-Political Treatise* was published anonymously in 1670 and was widely condemned for its religious skepticism. All of Spinoza's other works, including his major production, the *Ethics*, were published posthumously by his friends.

In 1672, the French general Condé (Prince Louis II of Bourbon) invited Spinoza to visit, possibly with a position in mind, but no position was forthcoming. In the following year, he was offered a position at Heidelberg University, but he declined it. Spinoza's last years were spent virtually as an invalid, and at the age of forty-four he died of consumption, probably aggravated by the silica dust from his lens-grinding activities.

EARLY THOUGHT AND WORK

The *Short Treatise* of 1660 and the exposition of Descartes's philosophy were written when Spinoza's thinking was developing into the mature expression of the *Ethics*. The Descartes work, written for a group of students, was expressly not his own thinking. Nevertheless, he derived valuable ideas from it through reaction, notably his rejection of the dualism of mind and body (or spirit and matter) and his affirmation that the individual must form his own judgments in political and religious matters, free from the pressures of church and state alike. It was this conviction, as expressed in *A Theologico-Political Treatise*, that first aroused opposition that later became virulent. Spinoza's notion of freedom of thought and action is absolute, a position that does not sit well with religious or political authority.

ETHICS

The reason for this absolute freedom becomes evident in the *Ethics*. Laid out in Euclidian fashion with definitions and axioms, and propositions deduced from them, the *Ethics* first deals with God and nature, which are one. God/nature is its own cause, requiring no prior cause and encompassing all that is, including humankind. Properly understood, this eternally existing unity admits of no internal contradictions. It also admits of no free will and is absolutely impersonal about the fate of humankind. These last conclusions led to Spinoza's condemnation as a dangerous atheist, although his God informs his entire system of morality and ethics. In his deterministic universe, the ethical imperative is unending rational inquiry to learn the true nature of things. The free individual perceives what he or she must do and acts accordingly. Those with confused ideas about their universe are in some degree not free, and they act not through understanding but because they cannot help themselves.

SIGNIFICANCE AND INFLUENCE

Morality and ethics are individual matters for Spinoza, and they lead to political and religious consensus only when enough people, made free by rational and empirical inquiry, act on the understanding they have gained. Spinoza's philosophical system is remarkably complete and self-contained, which has led to much misunderstanding by later thinkers who tried to extract and develop portions of it. This misunderstanding, together with the charge of atheism, produced an almost total lack of influence of Spinoza's work for more than a century. Only in the nineteenth century, in the time of rejection of monarchy and despotism, were his ideas taken up by the German and English romantics and idealists. No school of thought has grown from his writings, and his influence on philosophy has been more catalytic than structural.

Robert M. Hawthorne, Jr.

FURTHER READING

Allison, Henry E. *Benedict de Spinoza: An Introduction.* Rev. ed. New Haven, Conn.: Yale University Press, 1987.

De Djin, Herman. *Spinoza: The Way to Wisdom.* West Lafayette, Ind.: Purdue University Press, 1996.

Donagan, Alan. *Spinoza.* Chicago: University of Chicago Press, l989.

Garrett, Aaron V. *Meaning in Spinoza's Method.* New York: Cambridge University Press, 2003.

Hampshire, Stuart. *Spinoza.* New York: Penguin Books, 1987.

Harris, Errol E. *Spinoza's Philosophy: An Outline.* Atlantic Highlands, N.J.: Humanities Press International, 1992.

MacIntyre, Alasdair. "Spinoza, Benedict (Baruch)." In *The Encyclopedia of Philosophy*, edited by Paul Edwards. Vol. 7. New York: Macmillan, 1972.

Scruton, Roger. *Spinoza.* New York: Routledge, 1999.

Spinoza, Benedictus de. *The Collected Works of Spinoza.* Edited and translated by Edwin Curley. Princeton, N.J.: Princeton University Press, 1985-.

SEE ALSO: Descartes, René; Ethics; Jewish ethics; Perry, R. B.; Truth.

Stalin, Joseph

IDENTIFICATION: Soviet political leader

BORN: Joseph Vissarionovich Dzhugashvili; December 21, 1879, Gori, Georgia, Russian Empire

DIED: March 5, 1953, Kuntsevo, U.S.S.R.

TYPE OF ETHICS: Modern history

SIGNIFICANCE: Stalin was the leader of the Communist Party of the Soviet Union from 1928 to 1953, during which time he directed the transformation of the Soviet Union into a repressive totalitarian state and led the country in the Great Patriotic War against Nazi Germany.

Joseph Stalin was one of the most powerful leaders of the twentieth century. His rule would have a permanent impact upon not only the Soviet Union but also the entire international system. Stalin governed his political behavior according to the Marxist-Leninist tenet that the ends—the transformation of society along the lines anticipated by Karl Marx and Vladimir Ilich Lenin toward socialism, under the undisputed leadership of the Communist Party of the Soviet Union (CPSU)—justified whatever means were deemed to be appropriate by the party leadership.

In addition, Stalin accelerated and eventually fully implemented many of the policies and trends initiated during the period of Lenin's active rule in the Soviet Union (1917-1922). These included the complete consolidation of CPSU totalitarian intrusion into all social, economic, cultural, political, and even personal aspects of life in the Soviet Union, as well as the acceleration and eventually the institutionalization of the centralizing, bureaucratic, authoritarian trends within the party itself. Finally, Stalin directed the industrialization of the Soviet Union, led the Soviet Union's tenacious defense during World War II, and significantly buttressed Soviet security in the war's aftermath. In doing so, however, Stalin applied a degree of mass coercion and terror rarely equaled in human history.

STALIN AND TOTALITARIAN RULE

Following the 1917 Revolution, Stalin rose rapidly to power largely as a result of his early institutional control over the CPSU Apparat via his position as general secretary of the party's Central Committee, as well as his membership in the party's top decision-making organs. As a result of these institutional positions, particularly that of general secretary, Stalin was able to assign personal allies and protégés to strategic leadership positions not only within the CPSU organization itself but also throughout the Soviet state bureaucracy. Since that development was framed against the rapid expansion of CPSU and Soviet state totalitarian control over all aspects of Soviet public and even private life, by 1928, Stalin had successfully placed his lieutenants in virtually all key positions of power throughout the Soviet Union. Simultaneously, by the end of the 1920's, he had isolated and effectively eliminated or rendered politically powerless all of his political rivals from the early post-Revolutionary period.

Between 1928 and his death in 1953, Stalin was unquestionably the most powerful person within the Soviet leadership. As power increasingly concentrated at the highest level of the party hierarchy, Stalin continuously, but with extreme skill and perception, coalesced a sufficiently powerful, though ever-changing, body of allies and supporters to enable him

to remain the dominant Soviet leader, despite periodic challenges to his ruling position from within the party elite.

Conversely, within this dynamic but largely shrouded framework of coalitions and counter-coalitions that characterized Soviet politics at the political center, Stalin aggressively purged real or imagined policy dissidents and individuals who appeared to threaten his personal leadership from positions of power and authority. Although Stalin's practice of purging the ranks of the party can be traced to the precedent of Lenin's theory and practices regarding the enforcement of party discipline, the massive scope and degree of Stalin's use of terror, imprisonment, and physical liquidation within the CPSU were both qualitatively and quantitatively unprecedented in party annals prior to the 1930's.

Although the precise or even approximate number of party members and affiliated individuals purged during the Stalin period will never be known, it has been estimated that during the period of the 1930's alone, approximately one million party members perished. Furthermore, in addition to the physical decimation of the party's ranks caused by the purges of the Stalin era, the terror engendered within the party created a tone of fear, denunciation, and paralysis of individual initiative and willingness to assume personal responsibility that permanently influenced the character of the CPSU and the attitudes of its members.

Stalin's use of arbitrary arrest, imprisonment, torture, execution, and terror were not confined to the ranks of the party, but were extended on a much larger scale throughout the entirety of Soviet society. Indeed, as the tentacles of party control and the domain of its self-assigned responsibilities extended throughout the whole of the Soviet public and private sectors, and, further, as the Stalin-led Party leadership moved to reshape the entire character of the Soviet Union, those who individually or collectively offered actual or perceived resistance to the party's policies or who could be utilized by the party as scapegoats for the CPSU's failures to fulfill promises in return for societal sacrifices felt the harsh, cold, bureaucratic, deadly wrath of the authorities. Hence, tens of millions of Soviet citizens were killed or imprisoned, or simply disappeared during the two and a half decades of Stalin's rule. Between ten and fifteen million perished during the 1930's alone, not including the victims of the famine associated with the collectivization of agriculture.

TRANSFORMATION OF THE SOVIET UNION

As the CPSU increasingly established totalitarian control over the entire Soviet Union, the tone, direction, and specific policies adopted in every sector of Soviet life were increasingly determined by Stalin and the party leadership. One of the aspects of Soviet life most transformed during the Stalin era was the Soviet economy. Stalin inaugurated and directed the collectivization of Soviet agriculture, which, though enormously costly in both human life and material resources, was designed to break permanently the politico-economic power of the Russian peasantry and to secure the agricultural resources necessary to sustain the accompanying industrialization effort.

The industrialization of the Soviet Union under the rubric of a series of centrally formulated and administered Five Year Plans, which were inaugurated during the late 1920's, rapidly expanded the Soviet Union's heavy industrial and defense output. As with the agrarian sector, the dramatic expansion of Soviet capital output was accomplished at a very high human, material, and environmental cost. Overall, the Stalinist economy left a legacy of over-centralization of economic direction; imbalances between sectors of the economy, with most resources dedicated to the priority heavy industrial and defense components of the economy at the expense of consumer industries and agriculture; and a resultant lack of material incentives for Soviet workers. Notwithstanding these human, material, and long-term systemic and environmental costs, however, in 1928 Stalin inherited an economy during the early stages of industrialization and transformed it into a major heavy industrial and defense production power by the time of his death in 1953.

In addition to directing the transformation of the Soviet economy and virtually every other aspect of Soviet domestic life, Stalin also orchestrated the successful defense of the Soviet Union during the 1941-1945 war against Nazi Germany—"The Great Patriotic War." Notwithstanding the initial successes enjoyed by the Germans following their massive surprise attack upon the Soviet Union on June 22, 1941, a combination of German politico-strategic-operational errors, combined with the tenacious resistance of the Soviets themselves, enabled the Red Army to halt and drive the Germans back at the gates of Moscow in December, 1941, and on the banks of the Volga River, at Stalingrad, in late 1942 and early 1943.

Following the Soviet victory at the Battle of Kursk in July, 1943, the offensive capability of the German Army on the Eastern Front was permanently broken and the Soviet forces surged relentlessly westward. By mid-1944, when the Western allies successfully landed their armies on the beaches of Normandy, the Soviets had successfully liberated most of the pre-1939 Soviet territory. Finally, throughout the remainder of 1944 and into 1945, the Red Army fiercely fought across Poland and into the eastern portion of Germany, as well as up the Danube River Valley into

Joseph Stalin. (Library of Congress)

Austria and Czechoslovakia. The war, the largest land conflict in human history, left a tremendous wake of devastation throughout most of the western portion of the Soviet Union. Within the Soviet Union alone, between twenty-five and forty million Soviet citizens had died, tens of millions more were wounded in body or spirit, and massive urban, industrial, and agrarian destruction extended throughout the European half of the country.

THE POSTWAR WORLD

By the conclusion of hostilities in Europe, the Red Army dominated eastern and much of central Europe. Capitalizing upon this unprecedented level of military power, combined with the inability of the United States and Great Britain to counter effectively Soviet postwar designs on the areas it dominated, Stalin not only successfully secured de facto Western acknowledgment of the Soviet annexation of Estonia, Latvia, and Lithuania, as well as portions of Finland, Poland, Czechoslovakia, and Romania, but also imposed Soviet satellite regimes in Poland, Czechoslovakia, Hungary, Albania, Rumania, and Bulgaria. These measures, combined with the establishment of a Soviet zone of occupation within prewar German territory, significantly enhanced Soviet security against the threat of future overland invasion from the West and extended Soviet influence over a large portion of Europe.

Similarly, in the Far East, in return for the Soviet Union's entry into the war against Japan in August, 1945, Stalin obtained direct Soviet control over the Kurile Islands and the southern half of Sakhalin Island. In addition, he oversaw the erection of satellite regimes in North Korea and, in 1949, over the entirety of mainland China. Finally, Stalin encouraged the prompt development and acquisition of atomic and thermonuclear weapons. In short, by the time of his death in 1953, Stalin had not only greatly enhanced the geo-strategic security of the Soviet Union but also had expanded Soviet influence to engulf a significant portion of the Eurasian landmass. Indeed, the entire character of the post-World War II international system was shaped, in large measure, by the policies of Stalin.

On March 5, 1953, Stalin died in circumstances that remain shrouded in mystery. True to the ethics of Marxism-Leninism, Stalin used any and all means necessary to reshape the Soviet Union in accord with

his plan for the advancement of the historical process toward his vision of socialism. Ultimately, however, after two and a half decades of Stalinist rule, the means had clearly consumed the ends, thereby permanently marring the achievements of the Stalin era.

Howard M. Hensel

FURTHER READING

Conquest, Robert. *The Great Terror: A Reassessment.* New York: Oxford University Press, 1990.

Kun, Miklós. *Stalin: An Unknown Portrait.* New York: Central European University Press, 2003.

Mawdsley, Evan. *The Stalin Years: The Soviet Union 1929-1953.* New York: Palgrave, 2003.

Medvedev, Roy. *Let History Judge.* Rev. and exp. ed. Edited and translated by George Shriver. New York: Columbia University Press, 1989.

Tucker, Robert C. *Stalin as Revolutionary, 1879-1929.* New York: W. W. Norton, 1973.

_____. *Stalin in Power: The Revolution from Above, 1928-1941.* New York: W. W. Norton, 1990.

Ulam, Adam B. *Stalin.* New York: Viking Press, 1973.

Volkogonov, Dmitrii. *Stalin: Triumph and Tragedy.* Edited and translated by Harold Shukman. New York: Grove Weidenfeld, 1991.

SEE ALSO: Cold War; Communism; Dictatorship; Fascism; Lenin, Vladimir Ilich; Orwell, George; Potsdam Conference; Solzhenitsyn, Aleksandr; Trustworthiness.

Stanton, Elizabeth Cady

IDENTIFICATION: Pioneering American suffragist leader

BORN: November 12, 1815, Johnstown, New York

DIED: October 26, 1902, New York, New York

TYPE OF ETHICS: Sex and gender issues

SIGNIFICANCE: Stanton advocated woman's suffrage as necessary to achieve full moral and social equality between men and women.

Elizabeth Cady Stanton was one of the first Americans to call vociferously for full equality between women and men. After marrying abolitionist Henry

Stanton in 1840, she traveled with him to the World Antislavery Convention. As a woman, she was denied a voice or voting privileges at the convention, an experience that convinced her that women's rights must be promoted. She helped organize the first Woman's Rights Convention in Seneca Falls, New York, in 1848. She also contributed to the convention's principal document, the Declaration of Sentiments, which decried the oppression that made women irresponsible moral beings by denying them freedom to choose and act. More progressive than some of her contemporary suffragists, Stanton believed women and men were moral and social equals and called for woman's suffrage to achieve full equality.

As Stanton grew increasingly convinced of religion's role in oppressing women, she led a committee of women that prepared *The Woman's Bible*, a two-volume commentary on biblical passages dealing with women. The first volume, published in 1895, was criticized soundly by clergy and many other suffragist leaders. Despite opposition from the National-American Woman Suffrage Association, for which Stanton had previously served as president, Stanton and the committee published the second volume in 1898.

Following her death, Stanton was remembered as a great leader of the suffrage movement, a pioneer in feminist theology, and a woman committed to the ethical principle of the fundamental equality of women and men in all aspects of their moral lives and social relationships.

L. Dean Allen

SEE ALSO: Equal Rights Amendment; Feminist ethics; Gender bias; League of Women Voters; Sexual stereotypes; Suffrage; Women's ethics; Women's liberation movement.

State of nature

DEFINITION: Theoretical formulation of the conditions of existence of individual persons prior to the advent of any social order

DATE: Concepted developed during the seventeenth and eighteenth centuries

TYPE OF ETHICS: Politico-economic ethics

SIGNIFICANCE: The concept of a pre-social state of nature was used by political philosophers to provide a foundation for social contract theory. It was meant to illustrate the motives behind and the alternative to the social contract.

The state of nature describes those conditions in which individuals find themselves prior to the existence of any society or government. To envision the state of nature, try to imagine what conditions would be like if there were no law, no society, and no government. The resulting image captures what is meant by the state of nature.

Thomas Hobbes, John Locke, and Jean-Jacques Rousseau make extensive use of the concept in their political writings to explain the origin of society and government. The resulting theory is known as the social contract theory. One goal of the social contract theory is to explain how and why individuals moved from the state of nature to form society and government. Their explanations, though they have the common thread of the social contract, vary as a result of their differing conceptions of the state of nature.

THOMAS HOBBES

In *Leviathan* (1651), Thomas Hobbes spells out his account of the state of nature. Since there is no society, there is no right or wrong. There are no constraints, whatsoever, except for physical limitations, on human actions. Human beings, then, are completely free. In addition, human beings are essentially equal. There is an equality of need. All humans need more or less the same things; for example, food, clothing, and shelter. There is, however, a scarcity of the things that are needed. Resources are limited. All human beings have an equality of power. Although one individual may be physically stronger than another, no one person is so strong that he or she cannot be conquered, through cunning, intelligence, conspiracy, or other means, by another. Finally, there is limited altruism. In this state of nature, people will think and act for themselves first and rarely act for others.

According to this view, the state of nature is bleak and intolerable. Nothing productive could be done for fear that what one produced would be taken. Commerce and trading could not take place because there would be no guarantees that people would be fair in their dealings with one another. In short, people would live in constant fear. Hobbes labels these conditions a state of war, and life in such a state would be unbearable.

It is no wonder, then, that individuals want out of the state of nature. Hobbes shows that the way to escape the state of nature is for individuals to cooperate with one another. The way to ensure cooperation is to have a strong government that will guarantee that individuals will coexist peaceably in society.

JOHN LOCKE

In his *Second Treatise on Civil Government* (1690), John Locke also makes use of the state of nature to explain the origin of society and government, but his account is far different from that of Hobbes. In fact, one could make the case that the *Second Treatise on Civil Government* was written in response to and as a criticism of Hobbes's account. Locke disputes Hobbes's claim that the state of nature is identified with the state of war. Locke believes the state of nature to be peaceful, because he thinks that human beings by nature are rational and that there is a natural moral law that reason can discover. In Hobbes's account, there are absolutely no laws that bind individuals in the state of nature, while Locke contends that there are natural laws that individuals as rational agents will discover and follow. Such laws hold that one should not infringe on another's life, liberty, or property. The state of war comes about only when individuals fail to heed the dictates of the natural moral laws.

There is, then, for Locke, less of a motivation to escape the state of nature and form society. For Hobbes, conditions were quite intolerable. Locke can imagine, however, that conditions would be quite comfortable if everyone followed the natural laws. Unfortunately, what individuals ought to do and what they actually do are two different things. The individuals in Locke's state of nature get together to form society to ensure that those individuals who do not obey the natural law because it is a rational thing to do so will obey it because they will be punished if they do not.

JEAN-JACQUES ROUSSEAU

In *A Discourse upon the Origin and Foundation of the Inequality Among Men* (1758), Jean-Jacques Rousseau spells out his version of the state of nature. It has elements in common with the thought of both Hobbes and Locke but also is different in significant ways. Like Hobbes, Rousseau claims that individuals in the state of nature are motivated by self-interest and are not bound by laws of any kind. Unlike Hobbes, however, Rousseau does not believe that this will lead to intolerable conditions. Rousseau believes that humans are naturally good and will feel compassion for, not animosity toward, their fellow humans. This compassion is a by-product of an individual's self-interest. Unlike Hobbes, Rousseau acknowledges that natural inequalities of physical strength and talent exist, but he does not think that this will lead to problems because of the existence of compassion. Hence, the state of nature is not tantamount to the state of war but is an idyllic state that is to be sought and envied.

Like Locke, Rousseau believes that individuals possess a special quality that makes them noble and their situation tolerable. For Locke, that quality is rationality. For him, the individual is a noble thinker. For Rousseau, that quality is the sense of freedom. For him, the individual is a noble savage. Rousseau thinks that individuals in the state of nature live off the land, coming and going as they please, enjoying their freedom and self-indulgence while having natural compassion for all other individuals.

Why, then, would individuals give up this life and choose to live in society? For Hobbes and Locke, the formation of society was a positive step. For Rousseau, it entailed mixed blessings at best. Individuals in the state of nature noticed that their freedoms were secured and sometimes enhanced by engaging in social behavior. They entered naively into the social contract to form society without seeing the dangers to freedom that would result. In particular, they failed to recognize that the political, economic, and moral inequalities that forming a society generate would ultimately curtail rather than expand their freedom. Rousseau thought that the state of war that both Hobbes and Locke claimed arose in the state of nature could exist only after the formation of society.

John H. Serembus

FURTHER READING

Edwards, Paul, ed. *The Encyclopedia of Philosophy.* New York: Macmillan, 1967.

Hobbes, Thomas. *Leviathan.* Edited by Richard Tuck. Rev. student ed. New York: Cambridge University Press, 1996.

Locke, John. *Two Treatises of Government.* Edited by Peter Laslett. New York: Cambridge University Press, 1988.

Rousseau, Jean-Jacques. *"The Social Contract" and "The First and Second Discourses."* Edited by Susan Dunn. New Haven, Conn.: Yale University Press, 2002.

Simmons, A. John. "Locke's State of Nature." In *The Social Contract Theorists: Critical Essays on Hobbes, Locke, and Rousseau,* edited by Christopher W. Morris. Lanham, Md.: Rowman & Littlefield, 1999.

Slomp, Gabriella. *Thomas Hobbes and the Political Philosophy of Glory.* New York: St. Martin's Press, 2000.

Solomon, Robert. *A Passion for Justice: Emotions and the Origins of the Social Contract.* Reading, Mass.: Addison-Wesley, 1990.

SEE ALSO: Hobbes, Thomas; Hume, David; *Leviathan*; Locke, John; Rousseau, Jean-Jacques; Social contract theory; *Two Treatises of Government.*

Stem cell research

DEFINITION: Scientific studies of undifferentiated cells derived from fertilized human embryos less than one week old that have the ability to develop into virtually any other human cell

DATE: First discoveries announced in November, 1998

TYPE OF ETHICS: Bioethics

SIGNIFICANCE: Stem cells are uniquely valuable to medical research because they can be directed to become specific types of cells or tissues useful to treat such diseases as juvenile diabetes and heart disease. They can also yield new methods for screening and testing new drugs and provide insights into the earliest stages of human development. However, they are at the center of a major ethical debate over definitions of the beginning of human life.

In 1998, biologist John Gearhart of John Hopkins University and researcher James Thomson of the University of Wisconsin announced that they had isolated embryonic stem cells and induced them to

Actor Michael J. Fox with former first lady Nancy Reagan at the Juvenile Diabetes Research Foundation dinner at which Reagan spoke out in support of stem cell research. (AP/Wide World Photos)

Nancy Reagan's Endorsement of Stem Cell Research

During a May, 2004, fund-raising event for juvenile diabetes research in Beverly Hills, California, former first lady Nancy Reagan spoke out publicly for the first time in favor of human embryonic research. Alluding to her Alzheimer-stricken husband, former president Ronald Reagan (who died the following month), she said, "Ronnie's long journey has finally taken him to a distant place where I can no longer reach him. Because of this I'm determined to do whatever I can to save other families from this pain. I just don't see how we can turn our backs on this."

At the same event, actors Harrison Ford and Calista Flockhart read letters from former presidents Gerald Ford, Jimmy Carter, and Bill Clinton that endorsed her support of embryonic stem cell research.

begin copying themselves without turning into anything else. They had apparently discovered how to manufacture cells that could become human tissue.

Both Gearhart and Thomson called on the U.S. Congress to enact clear legal guidelines for future stem cell research. Instead, Congress placed a moratorium on federal funding for experimentation on most fetal tissue. However, no law governed what scientists could do using private funding. A situation then arose in which most stem cell research was in the hands of corporate-backed researchers. This proved to be a mixed blessing. While the situation permitted stem cell research to continue, albeit more slowly, the research was being done by privately funded scientists and was therefore not subjected to the multiple levels of peer review and disclosure normally required of publicly funded researchers. Producing even greater anxiety was the fact that stem cell research can make human cloning possible.

Because stem cell research uses cells from human embryos, controversy developed over the ethical question of when human life begins. Roman Catholic, evangelical, and Islamic religious theorists say that life begins at the moment sperm meets egg. By this view, a single cell can have sacred rights. Scientists counter, however, that technically that process is not what happens. DNA (deoxyribonucleic acid) sets from egg and sperm do not in fact immediately merge, as the egg divides once before the onset of genetic recombination.

Obstetricians sometimes mark the time when life begins at about two weeks after conception—when the fertilized egg implants itself in the mother's womb. *Roe v. Wade*, the 1973 Supreme Court decision permitting women to choose to terminate their pregnancies through abortion, held that viability (the moment when the fetus is capable of existing outside the mother) was significant. Other authorities argue that life begins at the moment when fetal brain activity commences, around the twenty-fifth

George W. Bush on Stem Cell Research

Extracts from his August 9, 2001, speech in Crawford, Texas:

Research on embryonic stem cells raises profound ethical questions, because extracting the stem cell destroys the embryo, and thus destroys its potential for life. Like a snowflake, each of these embryos is unique, with the unique genetic potential of an individual human being.

As I thought through this issue I kept returning to two fundamental questions. First, are these frozen embryos human life and therefore something precious to be protected? And second, if they're going to be destroyed anyway, shouldn't they be used for a greater good, for research that has the potential to save and improve other lives?

I've asked those questions and others of scientists, scholars, bio-ethicists, religious leaders, doctors, researchers, members of Congress, my Cabinet and my friends. I have read heartfelt letters from many Americans. I have given this issue a great deal of thought, prayer, and considerable reflection, and I have found widespread disagreement.

On the first issue, are these embryos human life? Well, one researcher told me he believes this five-day-old cluster of cells is not an embryo, not yet an individual but a pre-embryo. He argued that it has the potential for life, but it is not a life because it cannot develop on its own.

An ethicist dismissed that as a callous attempt at rationalization. "Make no mistake," he told me, "that cluster of cells is the same way you and I, and all the rest of us, started our lives. One goes with a heavy heart if we use these," he said, "because we are dealing with the seeds of the next generation."

And to the other crucial question—If these are going to be destroyed anyway, why not use them for good purpose?—I also found different answers. Many of these embryos are by-products of a process that helps create life and we should allow couples to donate them to science so they can be used for good purpose instead of wasting their potential. . . .

As the discoveries of modern science create tremendous hope, they also lay vast ethical mine fields. My position on these issues is shaped by deeply held beliefs. I'm a strong supporter of science and technology, and believe they have the potential for incredible good—to improve lives, to save life, to conquer disease. . . .

I have concluded that we should allow federal funds to be used for research on these existing stem cell lines, where the life-and-death decision has already been made. . . .

week of gestation, indicating that the fetus has become human.

THE CLINTON ADMINISTRATION

In September, 1999, the National Bioethics Advisory Commission appointed by President Bill Clinton released its final report recommending federal funding for research on the derivation and use of human embryonic stem cells. The commission recommended that voluntary consent to the research should be sought only from individuals or couples who have already decided to discard their embryos instead of storing them or donating them to other couples. It further recommended that the sale of embryos remain illegal, and that professional standards should be developed to discourage fertility clinics from increasing the numbers of embryos remaining after infertility treatments that might subsequently become eligible for research.

Ethical and moral problems are associated with manufacturing embryos in the laboratory to be used in research. Most members of American society do not want to see embryos treated as products or as mere objects, fearing that such a development will diminish the importance of parenting, risk commercialization of procreation, and trivialize procreation. Society, it is argued, has granted embryos a special standing in American law and culture because of their potential to become human beings. Manufacturing embryos for stem cell research would violate that status.

During the early years of the twenty-first century, several clinical trials were utilizing mature stem calls taken from adult human beings. There were, however, severe limitations to this line of research because adult cells are already functionally specialized and their potential to regenerate damaged tissue is thus limited. Adults do not have stem cells in many vital organs, so when those tissues become damaged, scar tissue develops. Only embryonic stem cells, which have the capacity to transform into any kind of human tissue, have the potential to repair vital organs. Moreover, embryonic stem cells have the ability to reproduce indefinitely in laboratories, while adult stem cells are difficult to grow, and their potential to reproduce diminishes with age. In 2003, a

study indicated that deciduous (baby) teeth were a source of stem cells. Research is ongoing.

BUSH ADMINISTRATION AND STEM CELL RESEARCH

In a speech delivered on August 9, 2001, President George W. Bush announced that he would allow research on only existing human embryonic stem cell lines, provided that the stem cells came from embryos that no longer had the possibility of developing into human beings. He specifically referred to organs and tissues "harvested" from executed Chinese prisoners and stated that he was limiting federal subsidies to the more than sixty genetically diverse stem cell lines that already existed. (At the time of Bush's speech, the National Institutes of Health identified thirty diverse stem cell lines). Some commentators applauded Bush's decision because it could be used to justify policies such as organ harvesting. Others denounced it because they felt it justified the taking of human life.

Marcia J. Weiss

FURTHER READING

Engendorf, Laura K., ed. *Medicine: Opposing Viewpoints.* Farmington Hills, Mich.: Greenhaven Press, 2003.

Holland, Suzanne, Karen Lebacqz, and Laurie Zoloth, eds. *The Human Embryonic Stem Cell Debate: Science, Ethics, and Public Policy.* Cambridge, Mass.: MIT Press, 2001.

Kristol, William, and Eric Cohen, eds. *The Future Is Now: American Confronts the New Genetics.* Lanham, Md.: Rowman and Littlefield, 2002.

Ruse, Michael, and Christopher A. Pynes, eds. *The Stem Cell Controversy: Debating the Issues.* Amherst, N.Y.: Prometheus Books, 2003.

Torr, James D., ed. *Medical Ethics: Current Controversies.* San Diego, Calif.: Greenhaven Press, 2000.

SEE ALSO: Bioethics; Biotechnology; Brain death; Cloning; Genetic engineering; Human Genome Project; Life, meaning of; Life and death; Medical research; "Playing god" in medical decision making; Pro-life movement.

Sterilization of women

DEFINITION: Medical procedure—including hysterectomies and surgical and chemical blocking of the Fallopian tubes—that render women incapable of bearing children

TYPE OF ETHICS: Sex and gender issues; Bioethics

SIGNIFICANCE: Whether sterilization is involuntary or voluntary, the procedure raises ethical questions about respect for the autonomy of individuals in making decisions about their own bodies.

Involuntary sterilization may be performed against the express wishes—or even without the knowledge—of the women who are sterilized. Sterilization may be more subtle, though still involuntary, when social conditions prevent subjects from making autonomous decisions. Justifications for involuntary sterilization include the desire to protect society from the financial burdens imposed by so-called degenerate or inferior types of people, to achieve ideals of "racial purity," or to curb population growth, often of poor or racial minorities. Additional justifications for subtle coercion include economic constraints and birth control. Sterilization may also be a voluntary choice, and both involuntary and voluntary sterilization raise the issue of informed consent.

The earliest American laws permitting involuntary sterilization were inspired by the nineteenth century eugenics movement, a combination of scientific and social beliefs that aimed to improve society. The main assumptions of the eugenics movement were that all human defects, including feeblemindedness, insanity, criminality, drug and alcohol addiction, and even epilepsy were determined by genetics and that people so afflicted constituted a threat to society and the very viability of humanity. The threat was often conceived in terms of cost, though arguments that sterilization improved the victim's own life also appeared as if to soften the criticism that those sterilized were injured. As institutionalization proved too costly and limited, eugenicists turned to sterilization to achieve their goals.

EUGENIC STERILIZATION IN THE UNITED STATES

The earliest eugenic measures targeted men because medical technology at the turn of the twentieth century could not sterilize women safely and inexpensively. Twelve state laws passed between 1907 and 1917 authorized sterilization, generally by vasectomies, for institutionalized men—criminal, rapists, and those regarded as imbeciles and idiots. However, seven of those state laws were challenged and found to be unconstitutional. For example, the New Jersey supreme court found that the sterilization approved in 1912 for Alice Smith, an epileptic and resident of a state facility, to violate the constitutional principle of equal protection. Meanwhile, by contrast, California's sterilization laws remained unchallenged from 1909 through 1921, during which time more than 2,500 people were sterilized—a figure constituting nearly 80 percent of the total for the entire United States.

During the 1920's, renewed efforts for sterilization laws succeeded in thirty states. A leading eugenicist, Harry Hamilton Laughlin found a way to avoid the unconstitutional aspects of the earlier laws that were imposed mainly on institutionalized people. He formulated a plan for appointing a state eugenicist who would examine the entire population to identify citizens who were unsuitable for reproduction. Hearings and jury trials would be held to recommend sterilizations, followed by the possibility of legal appeals. In a famous 1924 appeal case of Carrie Buck, the seventeen-year-old mother of a child conceived after she was raped, the U.S. Supreme Court upheld the law.

Most sterilizations in the United States were performed during the 1930's. After a slowing down during World War II, sterilizations increased moderately. By the 1940's, it also became apparent the hereditarian assumptions concerning the sources of mental weakness were false. However, in the 1950's, involuntary sterilization took a racist turn, with the "Mississippi appendectomy"—sterilization of many southern African American women and girls without their knowledge. Only during the 1970's did coercive sterilization became a central concern of the movement for reproductive rights after abuses of Native American, Mexican, African American, and Puerto Rican women became publicly known. Activists pushed for the enactment of rigorous measures requiring informed consent.

STERILIZATION IN OTHER NATIONS

The successes of eugenics advocates in the United States inspired other nations, including Canada, Denmark, Germany, Sweden, Norway, Finland,

Mexico, Japan, and France to pass involuntary sterilization laws during the 1920's and 1930's. Only in Great Britain were such laws soundly rejected. In 1933, the German government enacted a comprehensive sterilization law. By some estimates, Germany sterilized 3.5 million people between then and 1945.

In many nations outside Western Europe and North America, sterilization was illegal until the late twentieth century. In developing countries, such as Peru, sterilization became legal and was used by governments as a means of coerced population control of the poor and minorities, especially indigenous peoples. China's official population control policies involve the employment of coercive means, including forced abortions and sterilization.

SUBTLE ABUSES AND INFORMED CONSENT

Many pressures on women to choose sterilization have existed. Where access to abortion or birth control is limited, women may have only the option of sterilization for family planning. Sometimes subtle forms of coercion are economic. For example, in 1978, the American Cyanamid Company in the economically depressed area of Willow Island, West Virginia, required women employees working in its lead-pigment department to be surgically sterilized; five women underwent the procedure. The ostensible purpose of the company's policy was to prevent fetuses from exposure to lead poisoning.

Other subtle reasons for sterilization include inadequate medical care. Undesired sterility can be caused by sexually transmitted diseases and by pelvic inflammatory disease caused by the use of intrauterine devices. The burden of these problems falls most heavily on the less advantaged.

Medical ethicists and legal scholars have argued that sterilization, whether surgical or chemical, may be performed only if the person has given informed consent, a criterion extended to repeat sex offenders. The standards of informed consent include two major principles. First, patients must make medical decisions voluntarily, as free from coercion as possible. The American College of Obstetrics and Gynecology advises physicians to refrain from making recommendations to patients that reflect their own values, social goals, or racial, ethnic or socioeconomic factors.

Informed consent also requires that patients must be fully advised concerning the risks and benefits of sterilization procedures. They must understand that sterilization is irreversible. While informed consent may rest on a utilitarian principle that patients benefit from participation in decision-making processes, it is more often justified by appeals to respect for individuals' autonomy. Special difficulties arise with certain persons, such as those with chronic mental illnesses or mental disabilities—both of which are variable conditions. The permissibility of sterilization or its denial may be determined through extensive interviews with trained psychologists, according to definitions of legal competence, possibly in conjunction with court decisions.

Kristen L. Zacharias

FURTHER READING

Black, Edwin. *War Against the Weak: Eugenics and America's Campaign to Create a Master Race.* New York: Four Walls Windows, 2003.

Kevles, Daniel J. *In the Name of Eugenics: Genetics and the Uses of Human Heredity.* Cambridge, Mass.: Harvard University Press 1995.

Kline, Wendy. *Building a Better Race.* University of California Press, 2001.

Larson, Edward J. *Sex, Race and Science: Eugenics in the Deep South.* Baltimore: Johns Hopkins University Press, 1995.

Reilly, Philip R. *The Surgical Solution: A History of Involuntary Sterilization in the United States.* Baltimore: Johns Hopkins University Press, 1991.

SEE ALSO: Birth control; Eugenics; Genocide and democide; Institutionalization of patients; Nazi science; Sperm banks.

Stewart, Martha

IDENTIFICATION: Entrepreneur and television personality

BORN: August 3, 1941, Jersey City, New Jersey

TYPE OF ETHICS: Business and labor ethics

SIGNIFICANCE: Stewart parlayed her homemaking and fashion skills into a multimillion dollar business empire and became a national icon of style and domesticity, but her ethical reputation took a severe blow when she was charged with insider trading and other offenses and was convicted on all counts in 2004.

Martha Stewart, immediately after learning that she has been convicted on all charges in March, 2004. (AP/ Wide World Photos)

Beginning with a modest catering service in 1976, Martha Stewart gradually built a homemaking and style empire of books, articles, syndicated television shows, magazines. and a line of products sold through her own mail-order business and at Kmart department stores all over the United States. Her total worth after she consolidated her enterprises as Martha Stewart Living Omnimedia and went public in 1999 put her for two years running on *Forbes Magazine*'s list of the four hundred wealthiest citizens of the United States.

In December, 2001, the day before the stock of the ImClone company fell sharply because the Federal Drug Administration had refused to approve ImClone's anticancer drug, Erbitux, Stewart sold her ImClone shares. Her timely move gave the appearance of having been improperly influenced by inside information. Federal investigators were led to Stewart because of the arrest of Samuel Waksal, the chief

executive officer of ImClone and a personal friend of Stewart's, on insider trading charges in the summer of 2002. Now suspected of insider trading herself, Stewart told investigators that she had ordered her broker to sell her ImClone stock if the price per share went down to sixty dollars. The broker corroborated her statement, but his assistant, who had handled the sale, later said that he knew of no "stop-loss" order in this case. Stewart protested her innocence of any wrongdoing.

On June 4, 2003, Stewart was indicted, not for insider trading, but for conspiracy, making false statements, obstruction of justice, and securities fraud. The last charge was based on the allegation that she defrauded investors in Martha Stewart Living Omnimedia by making false statements about her company's worth. Stewart again maintained her innocence of all charges but immediately resigned from the directorship of Omnimedia, though she remained on its board as "creative director."

Stewart's indictment occasioned much speculation about the reason for federal interest in a case involving a stock transaction worth less than forty-six thousand dollars—a tiny fraction of Stewart's total assets—when nothing was being done about more serious cases, such as the multimillion dollar misdeeds of Kenneth Lay, the former chief executive officer of Enron. Many claimed that Stewart was singled out for attention not because she had committed a major transgression, but because she was a self-made and eminently successful businesswoman and a celebrity or because prosecutors believed that they would win an easy conviction.

Other speculation centered around the reasons why the original basis of the investigation of Stewart for insider trading was abandoned for the lesser, and perhaps farfetched, charge of misleading her investors. That charge was based on Stewart's public claim in June, 2002, that she had done no wrong. It was also suggested that charges of insider trading are notoriously difficult to prove and more easily left to the jurisdiction of the Securities and Exchange Commission.

Before the scandal over ImClone broke, Stewart had been regarded as a paragon of competence, style and good taste. However, the apparent inconsistencies in the three accounts of the sale of her ImClone stock tarnished her reputation for honesty and forthright dealing, and her financial worth began to decline. CBS-TV cancelled her regular appearances on its weekday *Early Show* and relegated her popular daily homemaking show, *Martha Stewart Living*, to a 2 A.M. time slot.

Although Stewart retained the enthusiastic support of tens of thousands of her admirers and experienced no immediate decline in her line of products sold at Kmart stores, the popularity of her formerly best-selling magazine, *Living*, fell precipitously. Most damaging, however, was the nearly 50 percent fall between June of 2002 and June of 2003 in the value of Omnimedia stock, of which Stewart herself was the major shareholder. This was especially damaging because Stewart's image and that of her company were virtually identical. Recovery of a lost reputation under such a circumstance is extremely difficult, if not impossible.

On March 5, 2004, Stewart and her stockbroker were convicted on all charges of obstructing justice

and lying to the government about her stock sale. In July, she was fined thirty thousand dollars and sentenced to five months in a federal prison. She began serving her term in a West Virginia minimum-security facility on October 8, 2004.

Margaret Duggan

FURTHER READING

Byron, Christopher M. *Martha Inc.: The Incredible Story of Martha Stewart Living Omnimedia.* New York: John Wiley & Sons, 2002.

SEE ALSO: Corporate scandal; Insider trading.

Stoic ethics

DEFINITION: School of ancient Greek philosophy that defined happiness as the result of making wise moral choices

DATE: Fourth century B.C.E. to third century C.E.

TYPE OF ETHICS: Classical history

SIGNIFICANCE: Stoic ethics are typical of and influential upon traditional Western philosophy, in that they begin from the premise that emotion is deceptive or untrustworthy and that reason is the only legitimate basis for moral choice. While this premise was generally accepted for many years, the critique of reason and "logocentrism" launched by feminism and poststructuralism in the second half of the twentieth century left it open to debate.

Stoicism was one of the most significant philosophical movements of the Hellenistic Age. The founder of Stoicism was the fourth century B.C.E. Greek philosopher Zeno, who lived and taught in Athens. He taught his disciples in the *stoa poikilī*, the painted colonnade of the market place, from which the name of this movement was derived. Stoicism, like most philosophies in the ancient world, was concerned not only with abstract concepts but also with how an individual behaved in society. Therefore, the teachings and writings of Zeno and his later followers had a major ethical component.

The basic goal that undergirds Stoic ethics is humanity's search for happiness. Happiness is not defined in the sense of emotional well-being, but is a description of living with what is good and moral. In the Stoic system, this goal of happiness is ultimately achieved by making wise choices that are based upon nature. For the Stoics, the ultimate virtue was to live harmoniously with nature, which would result in a lifestyle that would guarantee happiness.

BASIC BELIEFS

The Stoics believed that a person was constantly engaged by his or her passions. These passions were generated by outside images that would entice a person's internal impulses to choose that which was undesirable. The goal for the wise person in Stoicism was to allow the logos (the reason or intellect within a person) to rule. When the logos ruled, then one could choose what was best and be free of the passions. This freedom does not mean that one is unfeeling or is unpassionate, but that a person does not let these areas interfere with making the right and logical judgments in the ethical realms of life.

This decision-making process can be taught to a certain extent. There are those things in the world that can be classified as good, evil, and indifferent. The indifferent would be those areas such as death, life, fame, scandal, hardship, lust, wealth, poverty, sickness, and health. If one considers these areas as indifferent to one's life, these areas have no bearing upon the experience of happiness. Because of their indifference to such areas of life, the Stoics were often incorrectly labeled as passionless and perhaps unfeeling individuals. This perception has carried over into the modern usage of the word "stoic," when it is applied to a person who, in the face of what appears to be a traumatic and emotional event, does not express feelings.

The process of choosing between good and evil is more difficult and more intuitive in the Stoic system. This intuitive decision making of right judgments is assisted, however, when the wise person uses nature as a guide or criterion. The good is that which is in harmony with nature; the bad or evil is that which is against or in tension with nature. For the Stoics, nature becomes the all-encompassing norm that enables one to evaluate situations and make decisions. In observing nature, a Stoic could make some rational deduction regarding what is natural in relationship to plants, animals, and humanity. For example, it is not inherent in nature for a person to starve; it is unnatural. Therefore, the Stoics would render the logical action of feeding starving people. When one attempts to live according to nature, one practices a strong social ethic. Therefore, a Stoic individual honors the kinship networks and his or her native land.

When events or situations occur within nature that do appear as natural, these only help to reinforce what is the norm. For example, the birth of a six-legged cat is an anomaly that helps illustrate that in nature, cats have four legs. The Stoic system illustrates that one considers the whole on the basis of its parts. When nature is considered as a whole, it becomes clear that it is perfect. It is humanity's task to strive for that perfection and to live in harmony with nature.

The founder of Stoicism, Zeno, used a metaphor to illustrate the choice that humanity could make regarding living in this harmonious relationship with nature. He compared the situation of humanity to that of a dog tied behind a cart. The dog has the choice to run freely with the cart or to be dragged along. The choice is the dog's to make. To freely follow along behind is to live in harmony with nature and to ensure one's happiness. To be dragged is to live contrary to nature and to ensure one's misery.

To live in harmony with nature was the ultimate goal for a Stoic because it culimated in happiness. Yet followers of the Stoic tradition lived with the realization that they could never truly attain this goal. The ideal toward which to strive was to become a sage who, when faced with a choice, would invariably choose the good. In the Stoic system, one always attempted to reach the level of sage, but it was a rare feat. One of the later Stoic teachers, Seneca, remarked that a good man (a sage) appeared only once every five hundred years.

CONCLUSION

Although Stoicism as a movement no longer exists, its influence is evident in many areas of ethics and human behavior. The Stoics placed a great deal of emphasis upon those things that are indifferent, and one natural outcome of this emphasis is a form of asceticism. Groups that practice forms of abstinence or austerities often employ some of the ideological framework of Stoicism. Also, one can see traces of Stoicism in Immanuel Kant's categorical imperative: "Always act in such a manner that your actions can be taken as a universal maxim." Kant's emphasis is upon reason, which Stoics valued in all decision making.

David M. May

FURTHER READING

Colish, Marcia L. *The Stoic Tradition from Antiquity to the Early Middle Ages.* 2 vols. Leiden, the Netherlands: E. J. Brill, 1985.

Ierodiakonou, Katerina, ed. *Topics in Stoic Philosophy.* New York: Oxford University Press, 1999.

Inwood, Brad, ed. *The Cambridge Companion to the Stoics.* New York: Cambridge University Press, 2003.

Long, A. A. *Hellenistic Philosophy: Stoics, Epicureans, Sceptics.* 2d ed. Berkeley: University of California Press, 1986.

_____, ed. *Problems in Stoicism.* London: Athlone Press, 1971.

Rist, John M. *Stoic Philosophy.* Cambridge, England: Cambridge University Press, 1977.

Wenley, Robert. *Stoicism and Its Influence.* New York: Cooper Square, 1963.

SEE ALSO: Aristotelian ethics; Choice; Cynicism; Descartes, René; Epictetus; Marcus Aurelius; Natural law; Nussbaum, Martha; Platonic ethics; Reason and rationality.

The fact that New York's Stonewall Inn riots left a worldwide legacy is evident in the thirtieth-anniversary celebrations held around the world in 1999. Among the celebrations was a Lesbian and Gay Pride Parade held in Paris on June 26, 1999. An estimated 100,000 people participated in the event. (Notre-Dame Cathedral is visible in the background.) (AP/ Wide World Photos)

Stonewall Inn riots

THE EVENT: Uprising by gay men and lesbians in Greenwich Village sparked by police harassment

DATE: Began on June 28, 1969

PLACE: Greenwich Village, New York City, New York

TYPE OF ETHICS: Sex and gender issues

SIGNIFICANCE: Named for the New York bar at which they began, the Stonewall Inn riots signaled the beginning of what would eventually become the modern gay rights movement. It was the first response by the queer community as a group to the harassment and oppression of its members.

There are moments in history when conditions come together to create the impetus for great social change. Although the roots of the social movement for gay, lesbian, and bisexual equality date back to mid-nine-teenth century Germany, many historians and activists place the beginning of the modern movement at the Stonewall Inn, a small bar in New York City's Greenwich Village that was frequented by drag queens, gay and lesbian street people, students, and others.

At approximately 1:20 A.M. on June 28, 1969, Deputy Inspector Seymour Pine, along with seven other officers from the Public Morals Section of the First Division of the New York City Police Department, conducted a routine raid on the bar on the basis of the trumped-up charge that the owners had been selling alcohol without a license.

Police raids on gay and lesbian bars were a frequent occurrence in New York City; for example, laws were enacted for the express purpose of closing establishments that catered to a gay and lesbian clientele. Statutes forbade more than "three homosexuals at a bar at any given time," behavior that was considered "campy," and same-sex dancing, touching, and kissing. It was also required that bar patrons wear at least three "gender-appropriate" garments.

Although small pockets of resistance to police raids on gay and lesbian bars had occurred before June 28, 1969, bar patrons usually accommodated officials. This time, however, was different. Believing that they had been harassed for far too long, bar patrons and others challenged police officers with varying degrees of intensity for the next five days, flinging bottles, rocks, bricks, and trash cans, and using parking meters as battering rams.

The Stonewall Inn riots occurred in a larger social and political context of enormous upheaval and change. It is also probably no coincidence that the riot began only a few hours after the funeral of Judy Garland, a longtime cultural icon to gay and lesbian people.

The events that occurred at the Stonewall Inn would lead to the development of a number of both militant and mainstream groups that jointly would constitute a new, highly visible movement. In commemoration of the riots, June is designated each year as "Gay, Lesbian, and Bisexual Pride (or History) Month," and marches and various celebrations are held during that month.

Warren J. Blumenfeld

SEE ALSO: Gay rights; Homophobia; Homosexuality; Police brutality; Sexual stereotypes.

Subjectivism

DEFINITION: View that knowledge of the external world of objects is dependent upon the perspective and disposition of the knowing subject

TYPE OF ETHICS: Theory of ethics

SIGNIFICANCE: Subjectivism maintains that perspective is constitutive of knowledge, so that "objective knowledge" is a contradiction in terms. Thus, ethical judgments and moral norms are a function of the standpoint and disposition of the person making the judgment.

Epistemological subjectivism is the belief that the objects of knowledge are constituted by consciousness. In this doctrine, reality, truth, knowledge, meaning, and understanding are limited to the subjective states of the subject of knowledge. Metaphysical subjectivism leads directly to solipsism, the idea that the world exists only for the self, or to subjective idealism, which reduces the world to the realm of ideas found in an individual consciousness.

In epistemology, the "subject" is the agent or apprehender of the knowing process. The "subject" may be understood as a conscious ego, a transcendental ego, mind, the cognitive state, the self, and so forth. "Object" refers to that which is being apprehended, known, or being attended to by an act of perception, cognition, or understanding. Simply put, the subject is the perceiver and the object is what is perceived. "Objective" means possessing the character of a real object existing independently of the knowing mind.

ETHICAL SUBJECTIVISM

Ethical subjectivism holds that ethical judgments refer directly to certain feelings, attitudes, and beliefs of individuals or groups; namely, feelings of approval or disapproval with regard to some person or action or quality. Ethical judgments are regarded either as meaningless or as relative to the individual who holds them. Bertrand Russell maintained that differences about values are really differences about tastes. Ethical judgments really express feelings of approval or disapproval. This is the doctrine called emotivism. Ethical judgments are neither true nor false, but are simply expressions of feelings of approval or disapproval.

The Sophists believed that the senses were the only source of knowledge about the world and that reality was in a constant process of change. Everything that exists is only a matter of appearance. Therefore, the Sophists believed in the relativity of knowledge and were skeptical regarding truth. They questioned the validity of ethical principles and claimed that morality was a matter of social convention. Protagoras of Abdera said, "Man is the measure of all things, of things that are, that they are, of things that are not, that they are not." This philosophy relativizes truth and morality. Interestingly, it ends up justifying democracy and equal rights, because it holds that each individual must decide for himself or herself.

Epicurus held that pleasure is the sole good. This doctrine is known as hedonism. The view that people value pleasure above all else is known as psychological hedonism. Ethical hedonism goes a step further and holds that people not only seek pleasure but ought to seek pleasure. Since pleasure is relative to an individual's experience, feelings, and tastes, however, hedonism amounts to ethical subjectivism.

Bishop George Berkeley believed in the doctrine called immaterialism, which denied the existence of the immaterial world. Whatever exists, exists in the mind–*esse est percipe* ("to be is to be perceived"). This doctrine amounts to solipsism, the idea that nothing exists but one's mind and its ideas.

Immanuel Kant held to a motivistic theory of ethics. According to this doctrine, the rightness or wrongness of an act depends upon the motives and intentions of the moral agent, not upon the intrinsic character of the act or the consequences of an act.

Johann Gottlieb Fichte believed that the ego, which is pure creative activity, makes possible not only the awareness of self but also that of the nonego (whatever is not regarded as self). According to Fichte, the conscious mind creates the objects of the world because they exist only in the mind's knowledge of those objects. Therefore, both subject and object are generated by a creative ego. It is the ego that makes the world intelligible.

EXISTENTIALISM AND PHENOMENOLOGY

Søren Kierkegaard adhered to the doctrine that truth is subjectivity. Truth involves passion. There is no objective absolute truth. Truth is that on which the individual acts, a way of existence. Truth does not consist in what is said but in how it is said. Because there is no absolute truth, uncertainty accompanies subjectivity, calling for a leap of faith.

Jean-Paul Sartre claimed that humanity is condemned to freedom. People are absolutely free and morality is relative. One creates one's own values.

Edmund Husserl employed a philosophical method called phenomenological reduction that considered only the pure phenomena of consciousness—that is, self-evident, certain, and intuitive thoughts and ideas of consciousness. Phenomenological reduction revealed three elements of knowledge: the pheno-

menological ego, which is identical to the stream of consciousness; thinking activities; and the objects of thought. Husserl's doctrine of intentionality claimed that every act of consciousness was a consciousness of something and that that something was a mental entity. Therefore, knowledge of the world is purely subjective.

ETHICAL PROBLEMS

If moral standards are merely subjective, there seems to be no objective way of settling ethical disputes and disagreements regarding moral behavior. Mistakes about values are impossible to make. What becomes of the sense of duty in this scenario? Sometimes, the sense of acting out of duty to others means acting against one's own inclinations. Finally, subjectivism seems to contradict ordinary language and common sense, in which it is assumed that "good," "bad," "right," and "wrong" have the same meanings for everyone.

Michael R. Candelaria

FURTHER READING

Ayer, A. J. *Language, Truth, and Logic.* London: V. Gollancz, 1936. Reprint. Introduction by Ben Rogers. London: Penguin, 2001.

Behler, Ernst, ed. *Philosophy of German Idealism.* New York: Continuum, 1987.

Haraway, Donna J. "Situated Knowledges: The Science Question in Feminism and the Privilege of Partial Perspective." In *The Blackwell Reader in Contemporary Social Theory*, edited by Anthony Elliott. Malden, Mass.: Blackwell, 1999.

Hegel, Georg Wilhelm Friedrich. *The Phenomenology of Spirit.* Translated by A. V. Miller. Oxford, England: Oxford University Press, 1977.

Husserl, Edmund. *Cartesian Meditations: An Introduction to Phenomenology.* Translated by Dorion Cairns. The Hague: Martinus Nijhoff, 1988.

Kant, Immanuel. *Critique of Pure Reason.* Translated by Norman Kemp Smith. Introduction by Howard Caygill. Rev. 2d ed. New York: Palgrave Macmillan, 2003.

Nietzsche, Friedrich. *On the Genealogy of Morals.* Edited and translated by Walter Kaufmann. New York: Vintage Books, 1967.

Smith, Thomas Vernon. *Berkeley, Hume, and Kant.* Edited by T. V. Smith and Marjorie Grene. Chicago: University of Chicago Press, 1967.

SEE ALSO: Emotivist ethics; Epicurus; Epistemological ethics; Existentialism; Hedonism; Idealist ethics; Kant, Immanuel; Kierkegaard, Søren; *Phenomenology of Spirit*; Pluralism; Sartre, Jean-Paul; Sophists.

Suffrage

DEFINITION: Right to vote in government elections
TYPE OF ETHICS: Sex and gender issues
SIGNIFICANCE: Suffrage is the central right and responsibility of each full citizen in a democratic government. Lack of suffrage marks one as less than a full member of such a society. In the nineteenth century, "suffrage" became a common shorthand for woman suffrage specifically and for the movement to gain full citizenship for women.

Woman suffrage is the basis of political power for women. From the nineteenth and early twentieth century campaigns for woman suffrage in the United States and Great Britain, the issue of suffrage spread worldwide. By the late twentieth century, women could vote in most countries.

HISTORY

Participation in the political process through voting was either nonexistent or limited to a small elite until the nineteenth and twentieth centuries (the United States removed all property qualifications for voting during the 1830's). Suffrage in the colonial United States was limited to white, male property owners, and women did not vote or, if married, even exist legally.

Because of the eighteenth century revolutionary movements that were active in America and parts of Europe, the question arose whether the rights of man should not also apply to women. In England, Mary Wollstonecraft, in *A Vindication of the Rights of Woman* (1792), asserted that women could be good citizens of the state if men would let them participate. The state constitutions in the new United States of America, however, prohibited women from voting except in New Jersey, which allowed all property owners to vote. Spinsters and widows who owned property voted until 1807 when New Jersey restricted suffrage to white male property owners. By

the 1830's, however, there was universal adult white male suffrage throughout the United States, while women and racial minorities remained disfranchised.

During the early nineteenth century, many women in the northern states embraced reform movements, including the antislavery movement. The antislavery movement split during the 1830's over the proper role for women within its organizations and within society as a whole. In 1840, American women delegates to the World Anti-Slavery Convention in London, England, were excluded from the convention and relegated to a curtained gallery to observe deliberations. As a result, Elizabeth Cady Stanton and Lucretia Mott decided that women needed to work for their own rights.

They organized a women's rights convention on July 19 and 20, 1848, in Seneca Falls, New York. Stanton wrote the document that was adopted by the convention, the most controversial resolution of which was a demand for woman suffrage. Other women's rights conventions followed. Susan B. Anthony and Lucy Stone joined the cause in 1851, with Anthony doing most of the work before the Civil War.

The women's rights movement interrupted its activities during the Civil War, but its members felt betrayed when their antislavery male allies proved to be more interested in securing rights for freedmen than for women. When the Fourteenth Amendment (1869) introduced the term "male inhabitants" into the Constitution, suffragists were alarmed, and the proposed Fifteenth Amendment, extending suffrage to black men but not to women, divided the woman suffrage movement. In 1869, Stanton and Anthony formed the National Woman Suffrage Association, which advocated a wide range of women's rights and advocated a federal amendment to achieve woman suffrage. The American Woman Suffrage Association, headed by Stone, focused on suffrage and worked on campaigns at the state and local level.

Suffragists campaigned for woman suffrage between 1867 (Kansas referendum) and the 1920 ratification of the Nineteenth Amendment. They participated in state referenda campaigns (mostly unsuccessfully) and petitioned and lobbied legislatures and state constitutional conventions, while continuing to advocate a federal amendment. In the western United States, some women were voting, beginning in the Wyoming (1870-1890) and Utah (1870-1887) territories. By 1900, women had the vote in four Rocky Mountain states: Wyoming (statehood, 1890), Colorado (referendum, 1893), Utah (statehood, 1896) and Idaho (state constitutional amendment, 1896). In some areas, women had limited suffrage (school board or municipal or presidential elections). In 1890, the rival suffrage organizations merged, becoming the National American Woman Suffrage Association (NAWSA).

TWENTIETH CENTURY MOVEMENTS

In 1903, Emmeline Pankhurst organized the Women's Social and Political Union to demand woman suffrage in England. The group quickly adopted militant tactics, resulting in arrests of the Suffragettes. In January, 1918, Parliament passed a law granting suffrage to women thirty years of age or older who met specified property qualifications (in 1928 suffrage was extended to all women older than twenty-one). By 1918, women also had the right to vote in New Zealand (1893), Australia (1902), Finland (1906), Mexico (1917), and Russia (1917), and suffrage was extended in 1918 to Austria, Canada, Czechoslovakia, Germany, Hungary, Ireland, Poland, Scotland, and Wales.

Carrie Chapman Catt, president of NAWSA (1900-1904 and 1916-1920), designed the "Winning Plan." This plan involved state campaigns that would continue until women were able to vote in thirty-six states (the number needed to ratify a federal amendment), after which there would be a campaign to pass the "Anthony Amendment" for woman suffrage. Suffragists became more visible, adopting some of the tactics of the English Suffragettes. Catt believed that, although it was important that women support the involvement of the United States in World War I (1917-1918), they should continue working for suffrage during the war.

The radical National Woman's Party, headed by Alice Paul and Lucy Burns, opposed the war, and its members picketed the White House for suffrage, with some of them being arrested. Catt secured the support of President Woodrow Wilson for the "Anthony Amendment" in 1918. Congress passed the Nineteenth Amendment in June, 1919. On August 24, 1920, Tennessee became the thirty-sixth state to ratify the Nineteenth Amendment, thereby enfranchising women in the United States.

During the twentieth century, woman suffrage extended throughout the world. In 1954, the United Nations Convention on Equal Political Rights affirmed women's right to suffrage and political activity. By 1985, only in Saudi Arabia and the Gulf States were women still completely disfranchised.

Judith A. Parsons

FURTHER READING

Baker, Jean H., ed. *Votes for Women: The Struggle for Suffrage Revisited.* New York: Oxford University Press, 2002.

Clift, Eleanor. *Founding Sisters and the Nineteenth Amendment.* Hoboken, N.J.: John Wiley & Sons, 2003.

Flexner, Eleanor. *Century of Struggle: The Woman's Rights Movement in the United States.* New York: Atheneum, 1968.

Frost, Elizabeth, and Kathryn Cullen-DuPont. *Women's Suffrage in America: An Eyewitness History.* New York: Facts On File, 1992.

Giele, Janet Zollinger, and Audrey Chapman Smock, eds. *Women: Roles and Status in Eight Countries.* New York: John Wiley & Sons, 1977.

Mackenzie, Midge, ed. *Shoulder to Shoulder.* New York: Alfred A. Knopf, 1975.

Rhoodie, Eschel M. *Discrimination Against Women: A Global Survey of the Economic, Educational, Social, and Political Status of Women.* Jefferson, N.C.: McFarland, 1989.

SEE ALSO: Campaign finance reform; Civil rights and liberties; Equality; League of Women Voters; Mill, John Stuart; Political liberty; Poll taxes; Stanton, Elizabeth Cady; Voting fraud; Wollstonecraft, Mary; Women's liberation movement.

Sufism

DEFINITION: Mystical practices and traditions associated with Islam

TYPE OF ETHICS: Religious ethics

SIGNIFICANCE: Sufism encompasses many important paths of spiritual and ethical discipline and has been important in the global dissemination of Islam.

Sufism embraces so many mystical traditions that many scholars debate whether there is one referent to "Sufism" and whether some Sufi traditions are Islamic. Sufi mystics emphasize the importance of extreme, ascetic adherence to *sharīʿa* (Islamic law), or ecstatic union with God (sometimes associated with antinomianism), or a middle ground between those extremes. Some Sufis believe legalistic and antinomian traditions to be mutually exclusive. Others view them as aspects of a single, larger truth, as did Sanāʾī in his famous claim that "the veils are many, but the Bride is One."

Most often, Sufis abjure worldly goods and follow a "path" (*ṭarīqa*) of exercises for spiritual discipline and purification. Along the path, the Sufi attains "stations" (*maqāmat*) or plateaus of spiritual development, to each of which there is a proper "state" (*ḥāl*). The ultimate state to which Sufis aspire is variously indicated as "love" (*mahabbat*), "gnosis" (*maʿrifat*), "annihilation" (*fanāʾ*), or "union" (*ittiḥād* or *tauḥīd*). These goals sometimes have attracted the condemnation of Islamic legists who have argued that these states imply pantheism or, at least, a denial of the absolute transcendence of God.

In its early history, Sufism was the private spiritual effort of individual Sufis. In the eighth century, groups of students or disciples began to assemble informally around prominent Sufis. In the eleventh century, these informal associations began to formalize as clearly defined Sufi orders, with distinctive sets of spiritual practices, and these orders often were housed in a compound at the tomb of an important Sufi whose spiritual power (*barakat*) remains at the tomb.

Sufism provides popular ethical guidance in several ways. The keepers of Sufi tombs, to which many turn (for practical needs) in order to avail themselves of *barakat*, are a source of popular religious and ethical guidance. Reverence for individual Sufis such as Rābiʿah serves as a frequent reminder of the importance of detachment from worldly goods and of love of God. Sufi poetry and hagiography have been extremely popular and have been important in transmitting Islam and Sufi spiritualism in vernacular languages. Sufism's devotionalism and instrumental religion associated with *barakat* often have been more accessible than the sometimes-austere Islamic legalism, and often have served to gradually assimilate popular culture to Islam.

Philosophical treatises are not prevalent in Sufism, but some Sufis (notably al-Ghazālī and Ibn ʿArabī) have made significant contributions to ethical theory, especially through analyses of moral psychology and the epistemic status of direct apprehension of God.

Thomas Gaskill

SEE ALSO: Baḥya ben Joseph ibn Paḳuda; Ghazālī, al-; *Ḥadīth*; Ḥallāj, al-; Ibn al-ʿArabī; Islamic ethics; Mysticism; Rābiʿah al-ʿAdawīyah; Rūmī, Jalāl al-Dīn.

Suicide

DEFINITION: Self-initiated, intentional act directed toward, and resulting in, the ending of one's own life

TYPE OF ETHICS: Personal and social ethics

SIGNIFICANCE: Most religions condemn suicide as immoral; however, humanitarian organizations argue that persons have a right to choose death rather than suffer by remaining alive. Some ethicists have raised questions, though, as to whether a person in physical or mental anguish is competent to make the decision to commit suicide or whether their suffering constitutes a form of duress.

French writer and philosopher Albert Camus, in *The Myth of Sisyphus* (1955), asserted that the core philosophical question is whether to choose suicide. Existential suicide is founded on the idea that as a person comes to the insight that life is an empty absurdity, he or she must confront suicide as an option.

Deaths by suicide are notoriously underreported, even in countries that do not strongly condemn the act. In countries where there are adverse sanctions related to suicide, powerful pressures exist to cover up suicidal deaths. Therefore, caution must be used in interpreting officially recorded suicide statistics.

In 1985, conservative estimates held that, worldwide, more than 400,000 persons committed suicide. Although suicide is a major problem in the United States, which had more than 30,000 documented suicides in 1988, the suicide rate in the United States is notably lower than are those of many developed countries. According to the World Health Organization, many countries have suicide rates that are double that of the United States (Hungary, Denmark, Finland, and others), and many others have rates, which, although not double, are substantially higher (Japan, Czechoslovakia, China, Sweden, Switzerland, and others). Of particular concern in the United States was the near tripling of the suicide rates of adolescents and young adults between the 1950's and the 1980's. As of 1990, suicide was the second leading cause of death of adolescents and the third leading cause of death among adults aged twenty to twenty-four in the United States.

Western opinions concerning the morality of suicide have been heavily influenced by the teachings of Judaism and Christianity. Although the Old Testament of the Bible provides no condemnation as it records the suicides of several important persons (Abimelech, Saul, Samson, and others), rabbis and theologians have rebuked suicide as a violation of the sixth commandment: Thou shalt not kill. According to the fifth century Christian theologian Saint Augustine, no degree of torment, no physical injury or disease, no threat to personal safety, and no amount of personal suffering can justify suicide.

Although many of the world's other major religions condemn suicide, some do not. Islam damns the person who commits suicide, although exceptions are made for suicides that are part of a holy war or for a woman to protect her virginity. For the Baha'i, suicide is forbidden, and anyone who commits suicide will suffer spiritually in the afterlife. Buddhism rejects suicide on the principle that all life is sacred. Still, there have been cases in which Buddhist priests have used self-immolation as a method to draw attention to morally intolerable situations.

While Hindus and Sikhs reject most suicides because they interfere with reincarnations, both religions concede special circumstances in which suicide is either allowed or encouraged. For example, in the Hindu rite of suttee, a widow is encouraged to die in her husband's funeral pyre. Although honoring a person who commits suttee is illegal in India, instances of the practice continue to be reported.

EUTHANASIA

Any discussion of suicide becomes confused when the practice of euthanasia is brought into the

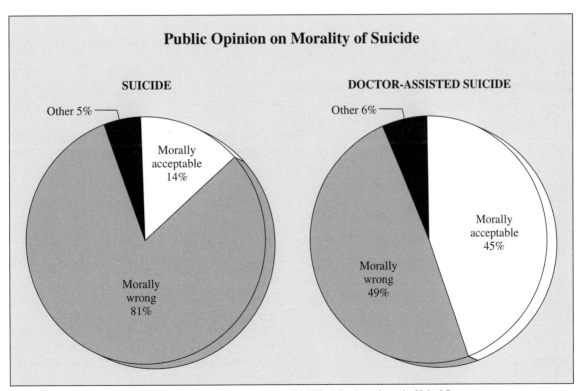

Public Opinion on Morality of Suicide

SUICIDE

Other 5%

Morally acceptable 14%

Morally wrong 81%

DOCTOR-ASSISTED SUICIDE

Other 6%

Morally acceptable 45%

Morally wrong 49%

Source: Gallup Poll, May 5-7, 2003. Figures summarize responses of 1,005 adults throughout the United States.

deliberation. Euthanasia has been variously defined as the good death, death with dignity, mercy killing, and the deliberate putting to death of a person suffering intolerable life circumstances. The two most commonly discussed forms of euthanasia are passive euthanasia and active euthanasia.

Initially, passive euthanasia was defined as including the refusal of life-sustaining medications, requests that resuscitation not be provided, and other solicitations related to not being subjected to unwanted medical procedures. Later, the concept of passive euthanasia was broadened to include a variety of alterations or abatements of medical treatments that might hasten death. Therefore, disconnecting a patient from a respirator, provision of adequate dosages of pain-relieving narcotics, and the termination of forced feeding were included as examples of passive euthanasia. Most religions accept all but the last practice (termination of feeding) as acceptable choices. These practices are not viewed as murder or suicide because a natural course of events is being allowed to unfold.

Active euthanasia, however, the administration of a lethal agent or the initiation of a process that will prove fatal, is condemned by most religions. Furthermore, if a second person aids in the commission of active euthanasia, the second person may be charged with homicide or held responsible under a statute that makes aiding suicide illegal.

During the 1980's, many U.S. states broadened patients' rights in regard to living wills and the right to refuse unwanted treatments. Despite the fact that most states either allow or are mute regarding the right of a competent person to terminate his or her life, they all permit the involuntary commitment and forced treatment of suicidal persons deemed to be suffering mental diseases. According to the American psychiatrist Thomas Szasz, "in treating desires as disease, we only end up treating man as a slave." Although he does not oppose treating the person who voluntarily seeks psychiatric assistance, Szasz concludes, "if the prevention of death by any means necessary is the physician's therapeutic mandate, then the proper remedy for suicide is indeed liberticide."

Bruce E. Bailey

FURTHER READING

Berger, Arthur S., and Joyce Berger, eds. *To Die or Not to Die? Cross-Disciplinary, Cultural, and Legal Perspectives on the Right to Choose Death.* New York: Praeger, 1990.

Fairbairn, Gavin J. *Contemplating Suicide: The Language and Ethics of Self-Harm.* New York: Routledge, 1995.

Larue, Gerald A. *Euthanasia and Religion: A Survey of the Attitudes of World Religions to the Right to Die.* Los Angeles: The Hemlock Society, 1985.

Lester, David. *Why People Kill Themselves: A 2000 Summary of Research Findings on Suicide.* 4th ed. Springfield, Ill.: C. C. Thomas, 2000.

Pohier, Jacques, and Dietmar Mieth, eds. *Suicide and the Right to Die.* Edinburgh: T & T Clark, 1985.

Rachels, James. *The End of Life: Euthanasia and Morality.* New York: Oxford University Press, 1986.

Roleff, Tamara L., ed. *Suicide: Opposing Viewpoints.* San Diego, Calif.: Greenhaven Press, 1998.

SEE ALSO: Bushido; Death and dying; Durkheim, Émile; Euthanasia; Existentialism; Kevorkian, Jack; Life and death; Mental illness; Nihilism; Right to die; Self-preservation; Suicide assistance.

Suicide assistance

DEFINITION: Active provision of help to a person committing suicide

TYPE OF ETHICS: Bioethics

SIGNIFICANCE: Decisions to assist other human beings end their own lives pose difficult moral dilemmas, and suicide assistance is illegal in most U.S. states.

Terminally ill patients often openly express the wish to hasten their deaths. Such requests may pose dilemmas for persons in the position to assist with the suicides. Historically, the self-induction of death among persons who are severely ill and suffering has been justified by a number of philosophers including Plato, Seneca, and David Hume. The concept of having a physician assist with a patient's suicide was not widely discussed until after the twentieth century discovery of analgesics and anesthetics. When administered in sufficient quantities, these substances permit the inducement of painless deaths.

Assistance to commit suicide became an increas-

Arguments for and Against Physician-Assisted Suicide

Arguments for	*Arguments against*
Decisions about time and circumstances of death are personal; competent persons should have the autonomous right to choose death.	Assisted suicide is morally wrong because it contradicts strong religious and secular traditions supporting the sanctity of life.
Like cases should be treated alike. If competent, terminally ill patients may hasten death by refusing treatment, those for whom treatment refusal will not hasten death should be allowed the option of assisted death.	There is an important difference between passively letting someone die and actively killing a person. The two options are not equivalent.
Suffering may go beyond physical pain; there are other physical and psychological burdens for which physician-assisted suicide may be a compassionate response to suffering.	There is a potential for abuse; persons lacking access to care and support may be pushed into assisted death; moreover, assisted death may become a cost-containment strategy.
Although society has a strong interest in preserving life, that interest lessens when a person becomes terminally ill and has a strong desire to end life. A complete prohibition on assisted death excessively limits personal liberty.	Physicians have a long ethical tradition against taking life. Their Hippocratic oath pledges them not to "administer poison to anyone where asked" and to "be of benefit, or at least do no harm."
Assisted deaths already occur secretly, as when the administration of morphine may be a covert form of euthanasia. Legalization of physician-assisted suicide would promote open discussion of the subject.	Physicians occasionally make mistakes, and there may be uncertainties in diagnoses, and the state has an obligation to protect lives from such mistakes.

Source: Ethics in Medicine, University of Washington School of Medicine (http://eduserv.hscer.washington.edu/bioethics/topics/pas.html).

ingly important issue as Americans began to grow significantly older and advances in health care extended life spans among terminally ill patients. Over the second half of the twentieth century, a shift from dying in the home to dying in clinical-care settings and hospitals developed. By the early twenty-first century, approximately 80 percent of American deaths were occurring in medical-care settings. Consequently an increasing number of persons have begun seeking ways to die with dignity and in physical comfort. There has been a growing demand for modern medicine to provide comfortable, pain-free deaths and merciful ends of lives. Studies have shown that approximately 70 percent of the American public favors legalization of physician-assisted suicides or aids in dying. Health-care proxies and advance directives routinely include provisions to ensure that individual patients retain autonomy and control over their dying.

Although committing suicide is not in itself a crime, assisting or failing to take steps to prevent a person's suicide can result in ethical and legal actions. The double effect of providing medications that relieve suffering while at the same time inadvertently shortening a patient's life is an ethically accepted part of medical practice. The withdrawal of life-sustaining but burdensome treatments that leads to death is also an accepted part of medical care, even when such actions hasten death. However, in 2004, *voluntary* active euthanasia was illegal in the United States, and assisted suicide was against the law in the majority of states.

In June, 1977, the U.S. Supreme Court ruled that persons have no right to assistance in committing suicide. However, the Court did not rule out the possibility that state law could legalize physician-assisted suicide. The ruling addressed a narrow federal constitutional question that affects the mentally competent, terminally ill patient who seeks the assistance from a physician to prescribe medication for the purpose of committing suicide. However, states were permitted the right to publicly debate the issue and pass laws that either prohibit or allow physician-assisted suicide. At the federal level, this Supreme Court decision clarified the role of the physician in handling requests from a patient to hasten death. The Supreme Court did not address the role of other health care professionals such as social workers and psychologists. Following the Court's decision, a law to legally sanction physician-assisted suicide in the state of Oregon was passed.

Frank J. Prerost

FURTHER READING

Humphry, Derek. *Final Exit: The Practicalities of Self-Deliverance and Assisted Suicide for the Dying.* 2d ed. New York: Dell, 1996.

Quill, T. *Caring for Patients at the End of Life: Facing an Uncertain Future Together.* Boston: Oxford University Press, 2001.

Snyder, Lawrence, and T. Quill, eds. *Physician Guide to End-of-Life Care.* New York: ACP-ASIM Publishing, 2001.

SEE ALSO: Death and dying; Dilemmas, moral; Euthanasia; Homicide; Infanticide; Kevorkian, Jack; Right to die; Self-preservation; Suicide.

Summa Theologica

IDENTIFICATION: Book by Thomas Aquinas (c. 1225-1274)

DATE: *Summa theologiae*, wr. c. 1265-1273 (English translation, 1911-1921)

TYPE OF ETHICS: Medieval history

SIGNIFICANCE: The *Summa Theologica* encompassed, modified, and extended the ethics of Aristotle within a Christian framework. It advanced the view that Christian morality was rationally defensible.

Thomas Aquinas intended the *Summa Theologica* to provide instruction to students in Roman Catholic theological schools who not only studied the Old and New Testaments of the Bible but also participated in oral disputations concerning controversial theological questions. The *Summa Theologica* is a written, if condensed, version of these theological debates.

The work was also intended to reform the teaching of sacred doctrine, which for Thomas Aquinas involved not only the exposition of those religious tenets known through revelation—such as the nature of salvation—but also the aspects of the Christian faith that are accessible to reason—such as the question of God's existence. Reducing the confusing number of topics, arguments, and distinctions that were often arbitrarily arranged in the standard theological texts, the *Summa Theologica* argues its way point by point through questions concerning first the nature of God, then "the rational creature's movement towards God," and finally Jesus Christ (a person's way to God).

Thomas Aquinas died before finishing the third part; a supplement, drawn from his earlier writings, completes the plan of the work. Part 1 is divided into three parts (the divine essence, the persons of the Trinity, and creation), and part 2 into two parts (part 2-1, the general treatment of virtues of vices, and part 2-2, their specific treatment). Part 3 deals with Jesus Christ, the sacraments of the Church, and with resurrection and eternity.

THE NATURE OF TRUE HAPPINESS

For Thomas Aquinas, and for Aristotle (whom the *Summa Theologica* calls "the Philosopher"), everything in the universe has a purpose, an "end," a teleology. The purpose of a saw is to cut; the purpose of the acorn is to grow into a tree. Since human beings can reason and act, they are able to choose what they think will fulfill their desire for the perfect good; human moral choices, by their nature, are oriented toward this "last end." Happiness is the fulfillment of human desire for the perfect good, but as both Thomas Aquinas and Aristotle point out, happiness is not equivalent to wealth, honor, power, or pleasure. Instead, since human beings share a common human nature, happiness involves a life full of all the things that all human beings really need, in the right order and the right proportion. For Thomas Aquinas, the perfect happiness is in the life to come and consists of the contemplation of God's essence. In this life, however, happiness involves not only (imperfect) contemplation but also the development of practical reason to direct human actions and feelings into a life of choosing what is truly—not apparently—good, and learning to enjoy those choices.

In Thomas Aquinas's Aristotelian view, morality touches all of life; everyday choices tend to develop in the individual either virtue (human excellence) or vice. "Right reasons" must direct human activity to acquire that which is objectively good for human beings (such as knowledge). These goods are intrinsically to be desired, but their acquisition is also a means of building the kind of stable character with which God is pleased. Without courage, for example, a person would be unable to act in accordance with right reason.

Thomas Aquinas took Aristotle's view to be complementary to his own, not competitive. Unaided by supernatural grace, Thomas Aquinas said, reason could discern the kind of character that a human being ought to have, but a complete picture of an individual required God's grace, which would provide the theological direction that human beings could not discover through philosophic reflection alone. Already in this life, God was suffusing human beings with faith, hope, and charity (love), the three theological virtues, which were given not by human action but by the Holy Spirit. They prepared a believer for the vision of God in the life to come.

Central to the *Summa Theologica*'s discussion of true happiness and the final end is the concept of law. A law is made by reason for the common good by those in charge of a community, and persons cannot become truly virtuous independent of society. God's eternal law—his divine plan—governs the universe; the natural moral law, which is made up of those precepts that human beings discern through the use of right reason, reflects the eternal law. Actions that oppose the natural moral law are forbidden not because God arbitrarily says they are wrong, but because they are contrary to the development of full human potential. In addition, there is positive divine law, in which God wills that individuals receive grace through the sacraments, and those are positive human laws, in which communities or states restrain actions that are detrimental to society and promote obedience to the natural moral law; unjust laws do not have to be obeyed. Governments exist not only to provide peace

and protection but also to nurture the common good. In times of need, the resources of a community become "common property," and thus it is not sinful for someone to take bread to feed a starving child. People may resist tyrannies and overthrow them, unless there is good reason to believe rebellion would make matters worse.

The *Summa Theologica* presents a synthesis of faith and reason that was declared to be of permanent value to the Roman Catholic Church by Pope Leo XIII in 1879.

DIVISIONS OF THE WORK

The three parts of the *Summa Theologica* (as well as the supplement to the third part) are divided into questions dealing with the main subtopics of each part; in turn, every question is divided into several articles. Each of the 3,112 articles in the work is a stylized disputation beginning with an assertion of the position contrary to the one that Thomas Aquinas will take and a presentation of several objections to Thomas Aquinas's position. Thomas Aquinas answers by supplying a relevant quotation from the Bible or a Church father (such as Saint Augustine), followed by his own argument. The point here is to show that reason (that is, Thomas Aquinas's reply) is in harmony with sacred Scripture and the theologians of the Church. Finally, there are specific replies to each objection.

Dan Barnett

FURTHER READING

Coplestan, F. C. *Aquinas*. Harmondsworth, England: Penguin Books, 1955.

Eschmann, Ignatius Theodore. *The Ethics of Saint Thomas Aquinas: Two Courses*. Edited by Edward A. Synan. Toronto: Pontifical Institute of Mediaeval Studies, 1997.

Glenn, Paul J. *A Tour of the Summa*. St. Paul, Minn.: B. Herder, 1960.

Kreeft, Peter, ed. *Summas of the Summa: The Essential Philosophical Passages of St. Thomas Aquinas' "Summa Theologica" Edited and Explained for Beginners*. San Francisco: Ignatius Press, 1990.

McInerny, Ralph. *A First Glance at St. Thomas Aquinas: A Handbook for Peeping Thomists*. Notre Dame, Ind.: University of Notre Dame Press, 1990.

Sigmund, Paul E., ed. *St. Thomas Aquinas on Politics and Ethics*. New York: W. W. Norton, 1988.

SEE ALSO: Aristotelian ethics; Christian ethics; Jesus Christ; Natural law; Reason and rationality; Thomas Aquinas.

Sunnīs

DEFINITION: One of the two main sects of Islam
TYPE OF ETHICS: Religious ethics
SIGNIFICANCE: The majority of the world's Muslims belong to the Sunnī sect of Islam.

Sunnī Muslims in Baghdad protest the intrusion of occupying U.S. troops in their mosque during their Friday prayers. (AP/Wide World Photos)

Islamic religion is divided into two main sects: Sunnīs and Shīʿites. Sunnī Islam developed over many centuries. An important distinction between the two sects is that the Shīʿites relied on Imāms to provide spiritual guidance, while the Sunnīs emphasize the Qurʾān; the Sunna, or examples, from Muḥammad's life and his practice of Islam; and interpretations of these sources by eminent religious scholars. The interpretation of Islamic concepts by these scholars led to the emergence of several schools of thought. Four of the most important of these schools were led by Imām Abū-Hanīfa, Mālik ibn-Anas, al-Shafiʿi, and Ahmad ibn-Hanbal.

With the passage of time and expansion of the newly emerging Muslim empire, numerous issues relating to the meaning of the various religious concepts emerged. One such issue that ultimately helped to define the Sunnīs was the definition of a Muslim. A group of people known as Khārijites believed that only those who strictly adhered to the teachings of the Qurʾān and Sunna could be called Muslims, and those who did not should be declared non-Muslims and expelled from the community of Muslims. Others thought that even sinners should be considered Muslims and that the punishment for their sins should be left to God. People belonging to the latter school were ultimately defined as Sunnīs.

Khalid N. Mahmood

SEE ALSO: Abū Ḥanīfah; ʿAlī ibn Abī Ṭālib; Islamic ethics; Qurʾān; Shīʿa.

Supererogation

DEFINITION: Doing what is morally praiseworthy beyond what is required by duty or what is required to be free of moral blame
TYPE OF ETHICS: Theory of ethics
SIGNIFICANCE: If supererogation is possible, then moral goodness is not exhaustively describable as the fulfillment of moral duty; it is possible to go above and beyond the call of duty.

The term "supererogation" derives from the Latin verb *supererogare*, which means "to overspend" or "to spend in addition." The first known appearance of this verb is in the Latin Vulgate biblical account of the Good Samaritan (the tenth chapter of the Book of Luke). The modern notion of supererogation is based upon the idea of making an expenditure of one's goods or energy over and above what is required of one by moral duty. More precisely, the modern notion requires that an act satisfy three conditions to qualify as an act of supererogation. First, the performance of the act must be morally praiseworthy. Second, the performance of the act must not fulfill moral duty. Third, the omission of the act must not be morally blameworthy.

Although the idea of rising above and beyond the call of duty is familiar to most people, there has for centuries been great opposition to this idea. The major figures of the Protestant Reformation associated the idea of supererogation with the detested practice in the Roman Catholic Church of selling indulgences, which was based upon the idea that the good actions of the saints create a treasury of merit. The Protestants Martin Luther, John Calvin, and Philipp Melanchthon taught, on the contrary, that God requires all people to do what is good or praiseworthy; hence, it is impossible to do good over and above the requirements of duty. No matter how saintly or heroic one's behavior is, even to the point of sacrificing one's life, one is simply doing what God requires as a matter of duty.

The Protestant Reformers were also bitterly opposed to the Scholastic distinction between the commandments of God and the counsels of God. According to Thomas Aquinas and other Scholastics, the commandments of God are obligatory to obey, but the counsels of God are optional recommendations. Although Christians are not required to obey the counsels of God, such as renouncing riches and carnal pleasures, following them is recommended to those who wish to lead more perfect lives. Clearly, this distinction opens the door to the possibility of supererogation, and the Reformers refused to acknowledge that there are any counsels of God apart from what God demands as obligatory. If it is good to renounce wealth or carnal pleasure, that is exactly what one is required to do.

Opposition to the idea that supererogation is possible has more recently come from two of the major modern traditions in ethics: Kantian ethics and act utilitarianism. According to Kantian ethics, an act can be a moral act only if it is performed in obedience to moral duty. Thus, if an act is performed that goes beyond the requirements of duty, Kantians dismiss it as an act that falls outside the sphere of ethics or morality. One cannot, according to their view, act morally in a way that transcends duty.

ACT UTILITARIANISM

Act utilitarianism is based roughly upon the idea that persons ought at a given time to perform whatever act produces the greatest benefits for the greatest number of persons. In this view, duty requires one to choose the alternative that maximizes benefits. If a person chooses this alternative and acts accordingly, the person has fulfilled his or her duty. If the person chooses another alternative and acts accordingly, the person has violated his or her duty. In both cases, however there is no possibility of doing what is praiseworthy without fulfilling duty. Either one's act fulfills duty or it does not, but if it does not fulfill duty, it is the violation of duty and hence cannot be praiseworthy.

In spite of all the opposition to the idea that acts of supererogation are possible in human life, there is also much support for the idea. An article by J. O. Urmson entitled "Saints and Heroes," published in 1958, has been particularly significant in restoring popularity to the notion of supererogation. Urmson, a philosophical ethicist, presents several persuasive arguments to show that saintly and heroic behavior cannot plausibly be regarded as the fulfillment of duty. In one example, Urmson describes a soldier who throws himself upon a live grenade to save the lives of his comrades. Surely it would be wrong to judge that the soldier has a duty to perform this act, and surely it would be wrong to blame him for deciding not to perform it. Yet it is clearly a morally praiseworthy act, and hence it qualifies as an act of supererogation.

Urmson admits that saints and heroes often regard their own behavior as the fulfillment of duty. People frequently reply that they were only doing their duty when congratulated for performing acts of saintliness or heroism, and this is a phenomenon that has led many people to conclude that there really are no acts of supererogation in human life. Urmson argues, however, that people who react to their own saintly or heroic acts in this manner are simply mistaken. They have subjected themselves to a standard of duty that is unrealistically rigorous, and they have in reality gone beyond the call of duty.

David Heyd has argued that, in addition to heroism and saintliness, there are five other categories of acts that are capable of qualifying as supererogatory. First, there are acts of beneficence, such as acts of charity, generosity, and gift giving; second, doing favors for others; third, volunteering or promising something; fourth, forbearing to do what is within one's rights; and fifth, forgiving, pardoning, and showing mercy. In each of these categories there is room for performing acts of supererogation.

Although acts of supererogation are almost always portrayed in dramatic fashion, it is important to realize that small acts of generosity, courtesy, or kindness can satisfy the three conditions required of being supererogatory. Thus, it can be supererogatory to buy lunch for a coworker who has arrived at work without any money, to put in a good word about someone else to a person in authority, or to offer to cover the office phone while everyone else is downstairs at the office Christmas party.

Gregory F. Mellema

FURTHER READING

Attfield, Robin. *A Theory of Value and Obligation.* New York: Croom Helm, 1987.

Heyd, David. *Supererogation.* Cambridge, England: Cambridge University Press, 1982.

May, Todd. *The Moral Theory of Poststructuralism.* University Park: Pennsylvania State University, 1995.

Mellema, Gregory. *Beyond the Call of Duty: Supererogation, Obligation, and Offense.* Albany: State University of New York Press, 1991.

Urmson, J. O. "Saints and Heroes." In *Moral Concepts,* edited by Joel Feinberg. London: Oxford University Press, 1969.

Zimmerman, Michael J. *The Concept of Moral Obligation.* New York: Cambridge University Press, 1996.

SEE ALSO: Calvin, John; Christian ethics; Duty; Good, the; Kantian ethics; Maximal vs. minimal ethics; Utilitarianism.

Supreme Court, U.S.

DEFINITION: The highest court in the United States

DATE: Established in 1789

TYPE OF ETHICS: Legal and judicial ethics

SIGNIFICANCE: The U.S. Supreme Court has the authority to make final decisions in all judicial cases relating to the U.S. Constitution and federal legislation.

The U.S. Constitution mandated the creation of the Supreme Court and outlined its basic powers and duties. The first Congress then established the Court's organizational structure and determined the number of its justices. The Court itself decides most of its own procedures, such as allowing both dissenting and concurring justices to publish signed opinions of the cases on which the Court rules. The major function of the Court is to review the decisions of state courts and lower federal courts. Each year, out of approximately four thousand appeals, the Court chooses to give detailed examination and render judgments in about 150 cases.

The Supreme Court's central role in the American system of government is primarily a result of its long-standing practice of judicial review, which includes the power to make judgments about the constitutionality of congressional legislation and executive actions. The Court's precedents are binding on lower courts, and those relating to constitutional interpretations are recognized as constitutional law.

ETHICAL ISSUES

The Supreme Court frequently decides controversial cases dealing with such values as equality, individual freedom, and fairness. When making its decisions, the Court must interpret many ambiguous terms in the Constitution, including "cruel and unusual punishment," "establishment of religion," and "unreasonable search and seizure." Because such terms are value-laden, liberal and conservative justices tend to disagree about their meanings in particular situations.

In the realm of individual liberty, the Court's most important judgments are usually based on the First Amendment, which prohibits government from abridging freedom of expression, religion, and assembly. The Court has never held that these freedoms are absolute, but during the second half of the twentieth century, the Court greatly expanded constitutional protections for matters such as pornography, subversive speech, and unpopular religious practices. In looking at these and other issues, the Court's jurisprudence includes subtle "line-drawing." After 1962, for instance, the Court consistently held that prayer ceremonies in the public schools are unconstitutional, even though the Court allows such ceremonies in sessions of Congress and state legislatures.

In the area of equality, the Court has made a large number of important decisions relating to the Fourteenth Amendment's requirement that government must provide persons with an "equal protection of the law." In the 1896 case of *Plessy v. Ferguson*, for example, the Court decided that the Constitution's equal protection clause allowed states to mandate racial segregation, based on the doctrine of separate but equal. One-half century later, however, in *Brown v. Board of Education* (1954), the Court reversed *Plessy v. Ferguson* and held that racially segregated

public schools were inherently unequal and therefore unconstitutional. In later years, cases dealing with affirmative action and reverse discrimination engendered heated controversy.

The Court has frequently examined ethical issues of law enforcement. For instance, the Fifth Amendment mandates that defendants may not be forced to testify against themselves in criminal trials. The Court has broadly interpreted this provision as applying to suspects from the moment that police officers begin their interrogations. In the famous case, *Miranda v. Arizona* (1966), the Court found that the only way to ensure a confession was voluntary was to require the police to notify suspects of their basic constitutional rights. Many conservatives have denounced the decision as legislative rather than interpretative, while liberals insist that it is entirely consistent with the Fifth Amendment's purpose of preventing police coercion.

Some of the Court's most notable value-laden

The U.S. Supreme Court under Chief Justice William H. Taft (center front), former president of the United States, in 1921. (Library of Congress)

cases have dealt with the right to privacy, which is based on an expansive interpretation of the reference to "liberty" in the Fifth and Fourteenth Amendments. Using this interpretation, the Court held in *Roe v. Wade* (1973) that women have a constitutional right to abortions during the early stages of a pregnancy. Likewise, in 2003 the Court ruled that states may not punish homosexual acts between consenting adults in private homes. Critics have charged that the decisions went beyond the text of the Constitution and ignored moral traditions.

APPROACHES TO DECISION MAKING

Supreme Court justices frequently disagree with one another about the theoretical approaches that they should apply to interpreting the Constitution and the laws. Most justices claim to make decisions without reference to their personal preferences for public policy but do not deny that their theories about jurisprudence have a profound impact on their decisions.

There is considerable disagreement about whether the justices should concentrate on the literal words of the text in contrast to the "spirit" and structure of the Constitution. These two views are often labeled "strict constructionism" and "broad constructionism." A related question is the extent to which the justices base their interpretations on the "original intent" of framers of the Constitution. Critics of this approach prefer to look at the contemporary meanings of the words, which is the idea of a "living Constitution." Still another distinction relates to whether constitutional interpretations should be informed by philosophical conceptions of justice and natural law.

Because continued application of the Court's previous decisions gives stability and predictability to the laws, the justices are hesitant to overturn the Court's own precedents, especially those that are longstanding. However, the justices have different views about the extent to which they should follow the common-law practice of *stare decisis* (literally "let the decision continue"). While some justices tend to minimize the importance of precedents, others believe they should defer to them except when the arguments to do otherwise are extremely compelling. Likewise, the justices differ in the extent to which they defer to judgments of Congress and the state legislatures.

The polemical term "judicial activism" is commonly used to refer to justices who make expansive interpretations, ignore the intent of the Constitution's framers, emphasize philosophical concepts of justice, and do not give much deference to Court precedents and legislative judgments. The contrasting label, "judicial self-restraint," refers to the alternative approaches to jurisprudence. Around the turn of the twenty-first century, liberal justices were tending to be somewhat more activist than conservative justices, but clearly the latter were not consistently practicing self-restraint themselves.

Thomas Tandy Lewis

FURTHER READING

Abraham, Henry, and Barbara Perry. *Freedom and the Court: Civil Rights and Liberties in the United States.* 8th ed. Lawrence: University of Kansas Press, 1998.

Biskupic, Joan, and Elder Witt. *The Supreme Court and Individual Rights.* Washington, D.C.: Congressional Quarterly, 1996.

Dworkin, Ronald. *Freedom's Law: The Moral Reading of the American Constitution.* Cambridge, Mass.: Harvard University Press, 1996.

Hensley, Thomas, Christopher Smith, and Joyce Baugh. *The Changing Supreme Court: Constitutional Rights and Liberties.* Minneapolis: West Publishing, 1997.

Irons, Peter. *People's History of the Supreme Court.* New York: Penguin Group, 2000.

Lewis, Thomas T., and Richard L. Wilson, eds. *Encyclopedia of the U.S. Supreme Court.* 3 vols. Pasadena, Calif.: Salem Press, 2000.

O'Brien, David. *Storm Center: The Supreme Court in American Politics.* 6th ed. New York: W. W. Norton, 2002.

O'Connor, Sandra Day. *The Majesty of the Law: Reflections of a Supreme Court Justice.* New York: Random House, 2003.

SEE ALSO: Affirmative action; Bill of Rights, U.S.; Brandeis, Louis D.; *Brown v. Board of Education*; Capital punishment; Constitution, U.S.; Constitutional government; Judicial conduct code; Jurisprudence; Justice; Supreme Court justice selection.

Supreme Court justice selection

DEFINITION: Processes by means of which Supreme
  Court justices are chosen

TYPE OF ETHICS: Legal and judicial ethics

SIGNIFICANCE: The U.S. Supreme Court is meant to
  be an apolitical and impartial body entirely populated by political appointees. As a result, selecting
  justices to sit on the bench is a complex and politically charged process. The Supreme Court attempts to resolve many of the most important and
  controversial issues in the United States, and in
  doing so, it shapes government policy in areas as
  diverse as civil rights and environmental protection. Generally, conservative presidents appoint
  conservative justices and liberal presidents appoint
  liberal justices, but because those terms have substantially different meanings in the context of
  constitutional scholarship than they do in the context of legislative politics, justices frequently act
  in unpredictable ways once they reach the Court.

Article II, Section 2, of the U.S. Constitution states
that the president of the United States shall have the
power, with the advice and consent of the Senate, to
nominate and appoint justices of the Supreme Court
of the United States. Supreme Court justices are appointed for life by the president of the United States
and confirmed by the Senate. The nomination process has become very publicized in recent years because the decision making of the Court has had an increasing effect on the lives of all American citizens
and has become an important factor in presidential
politics. People are more aware now more than ever
that an elected president will nominate Supreme
Court justices who generally (though not always)
support his political views and will make their decisions based on these views, often for a long period of
time after the president has left office. Although most
judges make their decisions based on facts as opposed to ideological precepts, they often use their
own ideological precepts to guide them in interpreting facts.

The selection of judges to the U.S. Supreme Court
is one of the most important responsibilities of the republic. Their decisions are very rarely, if ever, overturned, and the policies that are set by them have a
profound effect on the entire nation, collectively and
individually.

There are no set qualifications to be a judge or justice on the federal bench. The courts were set up by
the Constitution as the third branch of the government in order to ensure the separation of powers.
They were to be an independent, impartial branch of
government that would serve, as Alexander Hamilton wrote in *The Federalist* "as bulwarks of a limited
Constitution, as an intermediate body between the
people and the legislature, in order, among other
things, to keep the latter within the limits assigned to
their authority." This principle was embraced by
Chief Justice John Marshall, who established the
power of judicial review in the 1803 case *Marbury v.
Madison*, giving the Supreme Court the power to declare legislative acts and laws unconstitutional.

JUDICIAL INDEPENDENCE

Although the Court is an impartial judicial branch,
each of its members has been nominated by a president who is a political figure. Any president will try
to select Supreme Court justices who share his outlook. To demand minute particulars, however, would
make impossible the president's real task: to find
men and women of learning, character, and wisdom.
The most important factor shaping the Court's policies at any given time is the identity of its members,
which is why the nomination process so clearly reflects the potential justice's views on the direction
that the laws need to take in order to reflect the values
and priorities of the society that he or she serves.

The Supreme Court makes policy through the interpretation of the law, but the way in which this goal
is achieved raises an ethical dilemma. Issues of public policy come to the Court through legal questions
that the court is asked to resolve. Two parties bring a
dispute before the Court and ask the Court to review
it. The Court reviews it and makes a judgment about
the specific dispute brought to it, gives an interpretation of the legal issues involved in that dispute, and
takes a position on the policy questions that are connected to the legal issues. Although the function of
the Supreme Court is not that of a legislative body,
should the Court be free to overturn and thwart legislatures because of what the justices perceive to be unjust or unfair results of a case as applied to the existing laws and precedents? That is the main question
that is posed in discussions of the ethics of selecting
Supreme Court justices.

The extent to which judges should be bound by

statutes and case precedents as against their own ethical ideas and concepts of social, political, and economic policy involves the question of which should prevail when justice and the law appear to the judges to be out of alignment with one another. Some judicial lawmaking is inevitable, but to what extent? Should the ideological agenda of a judge or a group of people be imposed through judicial decree rather than through directly elected officials? Should the Senate and the president of the United States ask a particular nominee how he or she would rule on a controversial issue of law, such as abortion, prior to appointment and should his or her answer be grounds for disqualification? Should judges be more concerned with granting new civil liberties that they perceive to be fair or with interpreting the Constitution? Does interpreting the Constitution mean relying upon the original intent of the Founders for guidance, or does the Constitution change as society changes and becomes more open and permissive? Is the job of the judge to adhere to the law or to do justice? If there is an injustice in society and Congress and the states have failed to act, should the Supreme Court fill the void? What is the main source of societal change: judges or the people? How far should the Supreme Court go in using its substantial power of the citizens?

These are all questions that are answered many different ways by many different judicial nominees, based on their philosophy of law and their experiences. Although there is no denying that judicial nominees to the Supreme Court must adhere to the highest standards of personal conduct, there are vast differences in judicial philosophy and interpretations of the role of the Court that present ethical dilemmas that will always be with the United States in the nomination of justices to the highest Court in the land.

Amy Bloom

FURTHER READING

Abraham, Henry J. *Justices, Presidents, and Senators: A History of the U.S. Supreme Court Appointments from Washington to Clinton.* 4th rev. ed. Lanham, Md.: Rowman & Littlefield, 1999.

Baugh, Joyce A. *Supreme Court Justices in the Post-Bork Era: Confirmation Politics and Judicial Performance.* New York: P. Lang, 2002.

Chase, Harold W. *Federal Judges: The Appointing Process.* Minneapolis: University of Minnesota Press, 1972.

Danelski, David J. *A Supreme Court Justice Is Appointed.* New York: Random House, 1964.

King, Gary. "Presidential Appointments to the Supreme Court: Adding Systematic Explanation of Probabilistic Description." *American Politics Quarterly* 15 (July, 1987): 373-386.

Perry, Barbara A. *A Representative Supreme Court? The Impact of Race, Religion, and Gender on Appointments.* New York: Greenwood Press, 1991.

Stewart, Alva W. *U.S. Supreme Court Appointments, 1961-1986: A Brief Bibliography.* Monticello, Ill.: Vance Bibliographies, 1987.

SEE ALSO: Brandeis, Louis D.; Constitution, U.S.; Jurisprudence; Law; Supreme Court, U.S.

Surrogate motherhood

DEFINITION: Bearing of a child by one person for another person

DATE: Term coined in 1976

TYPE OF ETHICS: Bioethics

SIGNIFICANCE: Also known as surrogacy, surrogate motherhood touches on many moral and ethical issues, ranging from adultery; exploitation of infertile couples, surrogate mothers, and children by baby brokers; to buying and selling of babies; dehumanization of reproduction; privacy rights; and custody and identity problems.

Infertile couples and others may seek the services of surrogate mothers if other reproductive procedures, such as artificial insemination, in vitro fertilization, or adoption, are not options for them. Two forms of surrogacy are in common use. The first method involves using artificial insemination of the surrogate mother with sperm provided by the prospective father. This technique is called traditional surrogacy.

The second method depends on in vitro fertilization (IVF). In this procedure, sperm and eggs provided by the intended parents or third-party donors, are used to produce embryos that are implanted into the surrogate mothers. This method, which is known as gestational surrogacy, is the more common of the two, and it produces what have been dubbed "test-tube babies."

Surrogate Motherhood Time Line

1975   First publicized artificial insemination of a surrogate under contract performed by California physician Harris F. Simonds.

1981   In *Doe v. Kelly*, Michigan's appellate court rules that surrogate motherhood is legal but that a state statute prohibits monetary compensation for such purposes.

1986   In *Surrogate Parenting Associates, Inc. v. Kentucky*, Kentucky's supreme court rules that its state attorney general cannot revoke the corporate charter of the defendant because the state legislature has not yet addressed the legality of surrogate motherhood contracts.

1987   Louisiana passes the first state law prohibiting surrogacy. Over the following five years, eighteen additional states pass similar legislation.

1987   The Roman Catholic Church condemns surrogacy arrangements.

1988   In *Mary Beth Whitehead v. William and Elizabeth Stern* (the "Baby M" case), New Jersey's supreme court rules that surrogate contracts are invalid and against public policy when payments are involved and when surrogate mothers are required to give up their babies.

1988   Florida, Indiana, Kentucky, Michigan, and Nebraska pass laws regulating surrogacy contracts.

1993   In *Anna L. Johnson v. Mark and Crispina Calvert*, California's supreme court becomes the first state judicial body to validate a gestational surrogacy agreement in a case in which the surrogate mother refuses to surrender a test tube-conceived baby. The California court places a high value on the preconception intents of individuals entering into surrogacy contracts, that is, the women who intend to bring about the birth and raise the children are considered to be the natural mothers, not the surrogates.

2001   Helen Beasley from Britain sues a California couple, Charles Wheeler and Martha Berman, in order to terminate their parental rights so that she can allow the twins she is carrying to be adopted. Wheeler and Berman become dissatisfied when Beasley does not abort one of the twins.

2002   *Redbook Magazine* reports that surrogate motherhood is quietly booming.

ARGUMENTS FOR AND AGAINST

Traditional surrogacy is ethically objectionable to some people on the grounds that it removes procreation from marriage, replaces natural processes with artificial ones, and introduces third parties—the surrogate mothers—whose presence can create potentially damaging personal relationships within both the adopting families and the surrogates' own families.

Some critics also question whether surrogate motherhood is a form of adultery. Moreover, one might question whether it is ethical for a surrogate mother to conceive a child whom she has no intention of raising. When the surrogates provide the eggs used to create embryos, new complications often arise when the surrogates develop strong emotional attachments to their fetuses.

By contrast, supporters of surrogate motherhood argue that artificial processes are often medical necessities for those who are infertile. Moreover, the individual's right to self-determination includes freedom to reproduce by unconventional means.

Similar ethical arguments can be made for and against the gestational surrogacy, which involves in vitro fertilization and embryo transfer. In these cases, the surrogates are carriers, or incubators, and do not contribute genetic material to the embryos; they therefore are less likely to develop possessive feelings toward the resulting children.

Those who object to this form of surrogate motherhood say that the procedure removes the act of reproduction from marriage by using artificial means and enlists the services of a third-party surrogate.

In addition, the in vitro technique requires that the embryos be cultured and evaluated for periods of time. Defective embryos are discarded, some may be frozen for future use, and others are implanted into the hosts. If more than one embryo implants, or an implanted embryo has defects, selective reduction techniques—namely, abortion—may be used to remove the unwanted embryos from the surrogates' uteruses.

Opponents say that gestational surrogacy places human life in peril and allows medical professionals to make God-like decisions concerning life and death. Those who support this type of surrogacy say that the parents' natural desire to have children outweighs the ethical arguments against it and that progress in medical science will eventually free humans from all the constraints of infertility.

LEGAL CONSIDERATIONS

In 2003, it was estimated that more than fifteen thousand surrogate births had taken place in the United States alone since the first recorded case in 1976. During that period, more than twenty U.S. states passed laws dealing with surrogacy. The legalization and widespread use of surrogacy raises other ethical, legal, and social questions. One concern is the right to privacy as interpreted by the U.S. Supreme Court in cases involving reproduction and abortion. For example, do the intended parents and the surrogates have the right to be free from governmental interference when they enter into a contract involving reproduction? Several states have laws regulating such contracts, and many prohibit compensation for surrogate mothers and brokers. Another matter is the right to privacy when a contract keeps the intended parents or the surrogates anonymous, thus leaving them open to potential harm later if their identity is revealed.

Another concern is allocation of responsibility. Who is responsible for medical costs during the pregnancy? What about the behavior of the surrogate during pregnancy? Do the intended parents have the right to meet and choose the surrogate and monitor her behavior? Will the surrogate be allowed to drink alcohol, smoke, or engage in other activities that may harm the baby? The intended parents might justifiably insist such behaviors be curtailed during the contract period with the surrogate.

If the children of surrogate mothers are determined not to be the biological offspring of their intended fathers in traditional surrogacies, or if they have birth defects, can the intended parents refuse to take responsibility for them? Are biological fathers financially responsible for the children of surrogates, even when the surrogates elect to keep the children themselves?

Baby M

An unforeseen problem in surrogate motherhood that has come to the forefront is custody. Surrogate mothers sometimes become so emotionally attached to the babies they carry that they refuse to surrender them to the couples with whom they have contractual relationships.

The best-known case is that of "Baby M.," who was born in New Jersey in 1986. A year earlier, William and Elizabeth Stern contacted with Mary Beth Whitehead to bear a child for them using William Stern's semen by means of artificial insemination. After a girl they named Melissa was born, a custody battle developed between Whitehead and the Sterns. A New Jersey court eventually ruled that Whitehead had no parental rights, but it granted her visitation rights.

WOMEN'S ISSUES

Will the popularization of surrogacy lead to the exploitation of women? Opponents argue that surrogacy might become another low-paying, high-risk job for underprivileged women, and that it degrades women by commercializing pregnancy and childbirth. Opponents also say that surrogacy subjects women to social and economic exploitation because the surrogate mothers are essentially under the control of the brokers and the sperm donors during their pregnancies. Advocates argue that women of various socioeconomic backgrounds become surrogates of their own will and often do so without compensation out of a sense of sympathy for the infertile couple.

Will the surrogate be able to cope with the emotional and medical stresses of surrogate motherhood?

Will the surrogate mother suffer from psychological or physical harm due to the pregnancy and parting with the child at birth? Potential surrogates often go through both psychological and medical screening to help ensure successful and positive outcomes. Controversial components of such screening are efforts to determine if the women being considered as surrogates will easily detach themselves psychologically from the children they carry in their wombs and readily give up visitation rights after the children are born.

WHOM SHOULD SURROGATE MOTHERHOOD SERVE?

Will surrogacy be regulated so that only those in dire need of the procedure have access to it, or should any couple who can afford it, whether they are infertile or not, be allowed to use it? Should surrogacy be deemed appropriate in some situations but not others? What about the interests of the children? The children may end up having various psychological and social problems, such as lack of identity and self-worth and mistrust in adults.

Some critics have argued that hiring a surrogate can be equated to purchasing a baby. They say that the legalization of surrogacy will encourage the development of an industry of baby brokering. Those opposed to surrogacy say that treating human babies as commodities to be bought and sold constitutes a type of dehumanization that is similar to slavery.

Are reproductive medical services, sperm, eggs, embryos, and surrogate mothers becoming commodities that can be bought and sold? Many think these procedures and natural products need to be regulated in a manner similar to organs for transplantation. Advocates say that surrogacy should be viewed in the same light as foster care or adoption and that cash payments to surrogate mothers are merely compensation for the lost time and inconvenience of the surrogates and are not payments for the children themselves.

Identity is another serious issue in surrogate motherhood. Who is the child's legal mother—its gestational mother, its genetic mother, or its caregiving mother? This confusion creates identity problems similar to those experienced by adopted children.

Rodney C. Mowbray

FURTHER READING

Alpern, Kenneth D., ed. *The Ethics of Reproductive Technology.* New York: Oxford University Press, 1992.

Blank, Robert, and Janna C. Merrick. *Human Reproduction, Emerging Technologies, and Conflicting Rights.* Washington, D.C.: Congressional Quarterly, 1995.

Cook, Rachel, and Shelley Day Sclater, eds. *Surrogate Motherhood: International Perspectives.* Oxford, England: Hart Publishing, 2003.

Field, Martha A. *Surrogate Motherhood.* Cambridge, Mass.: Harvard University Press, 1990.

Gostin, Larry, ed. *Surrogate Motherhood.* Bloomington: Indiana University Press, 1990.

Landaue, Elaine. *Surrogate Mothers.* Edited by Iris Rosoff. New York: Franklin Watts, 1988.

Meyer, Cheryl L. *The Wandering Uterus: Politics and the Reproductive Rights of Women.* New York: New York University Press, 1997.

Sloan, Irving J., ed. *The Law of Adoption and Surrogate Parenting.* New York: Oceana, 1988.

Wekesser, Carol, ed. *Reproductive Technologies.* San Diego, Calif.: Greenhaven Press, 1996.

SEE ALSO: Children; Genetic testing; In vitro fertilization; Sperm banks.

Sustainability of resources

DEFINITION: Ability of natural environments to maintain constant levels of resources in the face of human exploitation

TYPE OF ETHICS: Environmental ethics

SIGNIFICANCE: There is no scientific consensus on how many human beings Earth's natural resources can support because the intensity of resource use varies across societies and regions. Developing ethical principles to guide human interactions with the environment is important to ensure the sustainability of resources and environmental quality across national and cultural boundaries.

Modern societies create enduring tensions between development and conservation. Development is often considered as the means to improve economic growth with the ultimate goal of improving human welfare and quality of life. As populations grow and demands for higher quality of life increase, society's demands for natural resources increase, leading inevitably to further exploration and exploitation of environments that may otherwise be preserved. Moreover, there is substantial evidence that current practices to obtain and redistribute natural resources are adversely affecting the environment, potentially resulting in the depletion of certain essential resources, extinctions of biological species, and the pollution of air, water, and soil to extents that are detrimental to the welfare of human societies. The application of environmental ethics to sustainability science aims to discover globally acceptable standards and practices for balancing development with the conservation of natural resources.

ETHICAL ISSUES IN RESOURCE CONSERVATION

How many natural resources should the average human being consume? Should societies provide for each individual at the risk of depleting natural resources? The answers to such questions may play a role in determining the fate of human societies on Earth. Innovative scientific approaches to these questions are being developed, but convincing answers will most likely transcend disciplinary science, as ethical issues play greater roles in providing robust guidance.

Nutritional foods, clean water, and clean air are all essential for the growth and development of both individual human beings and human societies. Keeping these most basic resources available requires the expenditure of energy, which was still dominated by combustion of such fossil fuels as coal, petroleum, and natural gas at the beginning of the twenty-first century. Supplies of these resources are finite, and their distribution is uneven across national boundaries. Toxic waste products from industrial development that relies on these sources of energy also threaten communities worldwide, but their impacts are also unevenly distributed, with poor communities and nations suffering more than affluent ones. These problems have raised the profile of equity as a dominant topic of debate among environmental ethicists. Equity issues in resource conservation transcend geographical, generational, and phylogenetic boundaries.

GEOGRAPHICAL AND GENERATIONAL DIVIDES

Concerns over global climate change, including its causes, impacts, and mitigation strategies are fundamentally different between industrialized countries of the Northern Hemisphere and the less developed countries of the Southern Hemisphere. Therefore, questions of ethics, fairness, equity, and environmental justice have often stalled agreements at international summits aiming to design long-term solutions to problems associated with global environmental change.

The likelihood that certain natural resources may be depleted in one or two generations and the storage of radioactive waste materials with long half-lives have raised the questions about trans-generational ethics and equity. How should humans living today protect and reserve natural resources and conserve good environmental quality for those who will live tomorrow? Whereas most people will agree that societies should reserve the benefits of abundant natural resources and clean environments for future generations, there is wide disagreement on how much sacrifice individuals and societies must make in the present to ensure satisfactory levels of resources in the future.

Most contributions made by ethicists on these questions have been theoretical, but the time has arrived for practical applications of solutions that have emerged from ethical debates. Indeed, at the beginning of the twenty-first century, some of those applications were being proposed in international conventions on the environment.

THE PHYLOGENETIC DIVIDE

Perhaps the most difficult of the numerous ethical questions in resource conservation and global sustainability arises from the phylogenetic divide that forces humans to set monetary values on other organisms. What values should humans place on biological diversity and the extinction of species? Non-human organisms rely on humans to make their case for conservation. Therefore, there is an inherent bias in protection and conservation practices that favor organisms that humans find useful or appealing for aesthetic reasons. Given that most of the biological diversity on Earth remains to be classified, while rates of urbanization, desertification, and deforestation are increasing, there is clearly an urgent need for a coherent system of resource conservation that is based on sound ethical principles.

There is a global challenge to resolve the difficult issues surrounding the concept of sustainable development. Is economic development possible without compromising the sustainability of natural resources and a clean environment? The relatively new disciplines of industrial ecology and sustainability science have highlighted the path to possible solutions, but it is imperative for these discussions to include innovations in the study of ethics and human character—if the recommended scientific solutions are expected to be widely accepted and sustainable.

O. A. Ogunseitan

FURTHER READING

Armstrong, Susan J., and Richard G. Botzler. *Environmental Ethics: Divergence and Convergence.* New York: McGraw-Hill, 1993.

Boochkin, Murray. *The Philosophy of Social Ecology.* Montreal: Black Rose Books, 1990.

Des Jardins, Joseph R. *Environmental Ethics: An Introduction to Environmental Philosophy.* Belmont, Calif.: Wadsworth/Thomson Learning, 2001.

Dobson, Andrew, ed. *Fairness and Futurity: Essays on Sustainability and Social Justice.* New York: Oxford University Press, 1999.

Kates, Robert W., et al. "Sustainability Science." *Science* 292 (2001): 641-642.

Myers, N., and J. Kent. *New Consumers: The Influence of Affluence on the Environment.* Proceedings of the National Academy of Science (U.S.A.) 100: 4963-4968, 2003.

Ruttan, V. W. *Technology, Growth, and Development.* New York: Oxford University Press, 2001.

SEE ALSO: Bioethics; Conservation; Deep ecology; Deforestation; Earth and humanity; Ecofeminism; Ecology; Environmental movement; Genetic engineering.

T

Tabloid journalism

IDENTIFICATION: Popular form of news reporting in weekly newspapers and television programs
DATE: First emerged during the 1920's
TYPE OF ETHICS: Media ethics
SIGNIFICANCE: Tabloid journalism provides readers with news in condensed and highly sensationalized forms that often sacrifice journalistic integrity for marketability.

The term "tabloid" originally referred to the physical size of tabloid newspaper pages, which were smaller than the standard twelve-by-twenty-four-inch pages of broadsheet papers. During the 1920's, when tabloid newspapers first arose to significance, the term "tabloid" expanded to include the content of the newspapers as well as their size, especially referring to the papers' preference for stories involving crime, scandals, and sexual escapades of celebrities. Among the most famous and influential of the early tabloid newspapers were the *New York Daily News*, the *Daily Graphic*, and the *Daily Mirror*—all of which were published in New York City. During a well-publicized "war of the tabs" those three newspapers established the tabloid format and style that have continued into the twenty-first century.

Although the tabloids never entirely disappeared—indeed, the *New York Daily News* enjoyed one of the largest circulations in the nation—they faded in importance during the 1950's and 1960's. Then, toward the end of the 1960's, tabloids began to re-emerge, this time in a weekly format with greater attention given to celebrities, such as television and movie

stars, and an emphasis on the private lives of their subjects. The tabloids also generally included highly sensationalized stories about alleged alien abductions, births of monstrous babies, prophecies of coming disasters, and similar items. Buoyed by such content and filled with often lurid photographs, individual tabloids such as the *Star* and the *National Enquirer* achieved enormous circulation figures through their national sales, often at the checkout lines of supermarkets.

Tabloid newspapers trade on a mixture of familiar celebrity names and sensational revelations about the celebrities' misbehavior. (AP/Wide World Photos)

A spin-off phenomenon was known as "tabloid television," or shows which featured stories about celebrities, especially their more scandalous activities. Highly visible and publicized crimes, such as the murder of O. J. Simpson's former wife, were also key elements of television tabloid journalism. Like their newspaper tabloid counterparts, these television programs featured stories that were short, sensational, long on illustrations, and short on reliable factual information.

The ethical standards of both print and televised tabloids have been low. Representatives of both forms have been remarkably unconcerned with the actual truth of the stories on which they report, as they freely report rumor and innuendo as fact. Both forms have traditions of paying large amounts for "inside" information, often obtained from relatives and friends of the lead characters in their stories. Photographs and film of intimate moments, including the aftermath of shocking crimes, are highly prized and have included such dubious achievements as the *National Enquirer*'s printing photographs of the dead body of Elvis Presley in a Memphis morgue.

No matter how low the standards of tabloid journalism, however, there is a pervasive fear among media watchers that, because of their high circulation and ratings, the tabloids' methods and outlook may in time be copied by the more mainstream media.

Michael Witkoski

FURTHER READING

Fox, Richard, and Robert Van Sickel. *Tabloid Justice*. Boulder, Colo.: Lynne Rienner, 2001.

Gorman, Lyn, and David McLean. *Media and Society in the Twentieth Century*. Oxford, England: Blackwell, 2003.

Levy, Beth, and Denis M. Bonilla, eds. *The Power of the Press*. New York: H. W. Wilson, 1999.

Mott, Frank Luther. *American Journalism*. 3d ed. New York: Macmillan, 1962.

Pavlik, John V. *Journalism and New Media*. New York: Columbia University Press, 2001.

SEE ALSO: Advice columnists; American Society of Newspaper Editors; Invasion of privacy; Journalistic entrapment; Journalistic ethics; News sources; Photojournalism; Reality television; Truth.

Taboos

DEFINITION: Practices proscribed by the moral or religious codes of a community

TYPE OF ETHICS: Beliefs and practices

SIGNIFICANCE: Taboos are often the foundation stones of ethical systems and moral codes that are built on proscriptive principles of tradition or religious belief, as opposed to rational inquiry.

There are two senses, two related concepts, that are signified by the term "taboo." The older sense, derived from the Polynesian *tapu* and its applied meaning, refers to that which is paradoxically both sacred but also potentially harmful, and pure but subject to defilement. In the second, more generic and familiar sense, a taboo is a practice or behavior that is forbidden by the mores of a particular culture.

TWO SENSES OF TABOO

In the first sense, "taboo" is used, for example, to refer to the former untouchables of the Hindu caste system. It can also be used to refer to religious or quasi-religious objects with alleged magical powers, such as the Holy Grail of medieval legend, or sacred places, such as tribal burial grounds.

In general, the term applies to objects of primal power that have an ambiguous potential to harm or destroy and to heal or empower, and therefore refers to things both feared and venerated. The concept thus relates to the dual religious potential both to injure and heal, punish and reward.

In the second sense, most directly relating to applied ethics codified as law, the term is applied to any practice beyond a society's moral pale. In this sense, common taboos are incest and cannibalism, which are nearly universal examples; thus, the term relates more to an act than an object or place.

There is an inherent relationship between the two meanings derived from the attitude toward taboos in primitive cultures. In the Polynesian culture, a taboo object was so powerful that it was sacrosanct and could be approached only by a priest or shaman. If the taboo were violated—touched by an uninitiated intruder, for example—it could require purification through a ritual that could include the death of the offender.

In many primitive cultures, taboos are revealed as part of a rite of passage through significant stages of life, such as birth, marriage, and death, and are recorded on a tribal or clan totem as formulas or symbols, frequently depicted as animals or plants. Thus, the term "totem" is often linked to "taboo" and is sometimes used to refer to folk customs, such as rules of courtship and mourning, as opposed to taboos or moral prohibitions of a specific culture.

Some taboo objects in primitive societies were anathema, or cursed and therefore feared, which relates to the revulsion experienced in the violation of a taboo in the second meaning of the word. In many cultures, moral repugnancy is associated with such acts as cannibalism or incest, or even with violations of strict dietary laws or sexual practices.

ETHICAL IMPLICATIONS

Many taboos are so deeply and strongly rooted in the beliefs and practices of a folk as to be a priori foundation stones that preclude the need for their iteration in ethical coda, a prime example being the Judaic-Christian Decalogue, which carries no prohibitions against either cannibalism or incest, both of which are fundamental taboos in Western culture.

Canonical, civil, and criminal laws have all addressed taboo issues, often in vague terms such as "crimes against nature" that reflect a historical unwillingness to be explicit in legal formulations dealing with them, in part because the graphic language necessary for describing taboo acts may itself be taboo. Statutes written in indefinite language have increasingly come under judicial review and have been revised, particularly in those cases in which human behavior has denuded a taboo of its inhibitive power.

Although some taboos, such as those against cannibalism and incest, have in many cultures been rigidly observed for centuries, others, such as those against sodomy and miscegenation, have been modified if not completely abandoned. Law, of course, is always slow to reflect changing mores; therefore, much condoned social behavior remains technically condemned by law.

In societies where personal freedom has evolved and the right to privacy has been ensured, many taboos have been gradually depleted of their force. Even the most permissive societies, however, have some taboos and impose legal or social penalties for their violation. Moreover, scientific and technological advances have greatly muddied the ethical waters by introducing new imponderables that must be re-

solved in philosophical thought before being distilled into practical legal codes. For example, scientific evidence revealing that sexual preference is a matter not of choice but of inherited, genetic makeup has had profound ethical implications and has forced the liberalization of laws against sodomy based on principles of scriptural sanctions, moral choice, or "natural" behavior.

The modification or abandonment of a traditional taboo may result from a war that is waged on a moral battleground between forces deeply committed to inherited values, often based in religious convictions, and those embracing new attitudes supported by modern science and medicine. Two notable examples are the practices of abortion and euthanasia, which were almost universally condemned in the past but now have been condoned by many people as both appropriate and ethical in at least some instances.

John W. Fiero

FURTHER READING

Brain, James Lewton. *The Last Taboo: Sex and the Fear of Death.* Garden City, N.Y.: Anchor Press, 1979.

Browne, Ray Broadus, ed. *Forbidden Fruits: Taboos and Tabooism in Culture.* Bowling Green, Ohio: Bowling Green University Popular Press, 1984.

Douglas, Mary. *Purity and Danger: An Analysis of the Concepts of Pollution and Taboo.* New York: Routledge, 2002.

Frazer, Sir James George. *The Golden Bough: A Study in Magic and Religion.* Reprint. New York: Oxford University Press, 1994.

Freud, Sigmund. *Totem and Taboo: Some Points of Agreement Between the Mental Lives of Savages and Neurotics.* Translated and edited by James Strachey. Introduction by Peter Gay. New York: W. W. Norton, 1989.

Fryer, Peter. *Mrs. Grundy: Studies in English Prudery.* New York: London House & Maxwell, 1964.

Hardin, Garrett James. *Stalking the Wild Taboo.* Los Altos, Calif.: W. Kaufmann, 1973.

Steiner, Franz Baerman. *Taboo, Truth, and Religion.* Vol. 1 of *Selected Writings,* edited by Jeremy Adler and Richard Farndon. New York: Berghahn Books, 1999.

Webster, Hutton. *Taboo: A Sociological Study.* New York: Octagon Books, 1973

SEE ALSO: Anthropological ethics; Cannibalism; Custom; Euthanasia; Evolutionary theory; Freud, Sigmund; Homophobia; Homosexuality; Incest; Sociobiology.

Tagore, Rabindranath

IDENTIFICATION: Indian writer and philosopher
BORN: May 7, 1861, Calcutta, India
DIED: August 7, 1941, Calcutta, India
TYPE OF ETHICS: Modern history
SIGNIFICANCE: One of the most famous Indian (Bengali) poets of the twentieth century and recipient of the Nobel Prize in Literature in 1913, Tagore worked to promote mutual understanding between India and the West and founded Vishvabharati University in Shantiniketan, India. *Gitanjali* (song offerings, 1910) is his best-known work in the West.

Tagore began to write poetry as a child. His first book was published when he was seventeen years old. After returning to India from a trip to England in 1878 to study law, he became the most popular author of the colonial era. Through the short stories, novels, and plays that he wrote, he conveyed his belief that truth lies in seeing the harmony of apparently contrary forces. He was not interested in building a philosophical system; instead he wanted to deepen mutual Indian and Western cultural understanding.

Tagore was very much influenced by the Upaniṣads but interpreted them theistically. His artistic nature made him more of a follower of the way of *bhakti*, or "devotion," than of the way of jñāna, or "knowledge," of Advaita Vedānta. Because he believed in the harmony of complementary forces, however, he did not reject the Advaita, or monistic, view of Vedānta. In Tagore's view, both the one and the many are real. The doctrine of *māyā*, or illusion, points to the false belief that the world is independently real. God, humanity, and the world are interrelated. Tagore viewed life in a positive way, as the discovery of the divine nature of humanity.

Krishna Mallick

SEE ALSO: Śaṅkara; Upaniṣads; Vedānta.

Talmud

IDENTIFICATION: Holy scripture of Judaism
DATE: Written between the early second century B.C.E. and c. 500 C.E.
TYPE OF ETHICS: Religious ethics
SIGNIFICANCE: The Talmud is a repository of ideas and wisdom reflecting Jewish religious and cultural activity as interpreted by centuries of sages who lived in Eretz Israel and Babylonia (today part of Iraq) from before the common era to the beginning of the Middle Ages. As the primary source for post-biblical Jewish law and lore, the Talmud is second only to the Bible in religious and moral authority.

If the Hebrew Bible, or Tanak, is the cornerstone of Judaism, then the Talmud is its magnificent edifice. Its bricks and mortar are shaped by the revelation of the written Torah as represented, understood, and lived by the sages who molded Israel's salvific apparatus from the ruins of the Second Temple (destroyed by the Romans in 70 C.E.) until the beginning of the Middle Ages. Their accomplishment, the Mishnah, and its commentary, the Gemarah, which together form the Talmud, became the dominant structure of Judaism.

The Talmud is not easily classified in any literary genre. This is because of its encyclopedic range of topics, including law, legend, philosophy, science, and some history; its pragmatic treatment of everyday life issues alongside flights into abstract and ethereal problems; its multiple and varied methodologies, equally logical and fanciful; its terse writing style, which is reminiscent of note taking; and the meticulous final editing of pedantic redactions, themselves based on free-flowing ideas composed centuries earlier.

More a library than a single book, the Talmud is an anthology of national expression responding to the Roman catastrophe of the first and second centuries, and it is more meaningful when it is learned and studied than it is when it is read. The association between one idea and another, a rabbi in Galilee and another in Babylon, the first century and the fifth century, is tenuous at first, but persistent study connects the diverse pieces of knowledge in a way that is reminiscent of the links of a chain—the chain of tradition. The thought of the sages is like a winding stream of consciousness that flows into the "sea of the Talmud" and nurtures the religious and national life of a people. Accordingly, though not surprising, forces hostile to Israel as "a light unto the nations" have maligned the Talmud, prohibited its study, and consigned its pages to flames countless times during the Middle Ages, in *fin de siècle* Europe, and during the Nazi era. From such horrendous acts, a *talmud* (in a limited sense, the word means "instruction") has been revealed: Strip the Talmud from the "people of the Book," and chances for Israel's spiritual and, ultimately, physical survival are almost nonexistent.

MISHNAH

The Mishnah is the core document of the rabbinic system of philosophy and legalism traditionally called *Torah shehbe'al peh* (oral Torah). The quintessential "tradition of the elders," it represents a Pharisian application of the written Torah in the life of the people. Inevitably, as a living interpretation, reflecting changing times and events, it added, subtracted, and modified the written teaching of God. Humility (many teachings are given anonymously), respect for sanctity of the teaching of Moses, and concern that the rabbinic spirit might replace the letter of the Torah in the eyes of the people (for example, *mamon tahat ayin* [monetary compensation for bodily injury] in place of *ayin tahat ayin* [an eye for an eye]; near abolition of the death penalty; introduction of a court administered *prosbul* to overcome the cancellation of debts during the year of release) inhibited individual schools of rabbis from writing down their decisions.

Ultimately, successful dissension within greater Judaism (for example, Jewish Christianity) and greater Roman oppressiveness in response to ill-fated Jewish wars led to conditions of exile and set the stage for the redaction of the Mishnah. Rabbi Judah the Prince collated the unwritten rules, customs, interpretations, and traditions of multiple masters, pre-70 and post-70, into a written guide. The Mishnah ("repetition" or "recapitulation" of the revelation at Sinai) claimed an authoritative affinity to Sinai ("everything which a sage will ask in the fu-

ture is already known to Moses at Sinai") and also claimed to be its living successor ("We teach more Torah [than] received at Sinai"). Therefore, the Mishnah designates the transition from Israelite religion to the system now called Judaism in the same manner that the New Testament points the way from Israelite religion to Christianity.

The Mishnah is divided into six orders (*sedarim*), which are subdivided into sixty-three topical sections (*massekhtot*), with each *massekhet* containing multiple chapters (*perakim*). The Mishnah, also known as *SHaS*, an acronym for the six orders (*shishah*

Six Orders of the Mishnah

1. "Seeds" (*Zeraim*) — Agricultural rulings (gleanings, tithes, the Sabbatical year, and so forth), though the first *massekhet* is a discussion on "Benedictions" (*Berakhot*).

2. "Appointed Festivals" (*Mo'ed*) — Regulations governing holy time, such as the Sabbath, the holidays, and their respective festival offerings.

3. "Women" (*Nashim*) — Ordinances on marriage, divorce, and vows, and related exceptional cases, such as Levirate marriage, suspected adulteresses, and the Nazarite vow.

4. "Damages" (*Nezikim*) — Civil and criminal decrees, and the conduct of and conduct before an ecclesiastical court of law. Includes the tractate *Avot* ("Founders"), a selection of maxims and ethical statements given in the names of sixty *tannaim* (Aramaic for "repeaters," or teachers) of the oral Torah; its five chapters (and a sixth one, added centuries later) are traditionally studied on the six Sabbath afternoons between Passover and Pentecost.

5. "Sacred Things" (*Kodashim*) — Holy things of the Temple, pertaining mainly to animal, fowl, and meal offerings.

6. "Purifications" (*Tohorot*) — Conduct dealing with cultic and domestic purity and defilement.

An Israeli man armed with an assault rifle holds a copy of the Talmud while serving on a border patrol in a Jewish settlement in the disputed West Bank region. (AP/Wide World Photos)

sedarim), covers a range of Pentateuchal legislative topics.

The Mishnah is an enigmatic corpus. It claims the authority of revelation but it was not admitted by the rabbis into the canon of Holy Scriptures. Written in Hebrew, it departs from the style and syntax of biblical Hebrew. It does not speak of an eschatological future (stable material in the holy writings of world religions), and it fuses a cultic past (the Temple), regarding which it has no direct access, into a present that is dubious and fanciful. Its many *halakhot* (laws) regulate an "existing" priesthood, Jewish government, and courts, totally oblivious to the ruin of these institutions during the first and second centuries. Other *halakhot* relate to religious practices that have no bearing on the Judaism of the day. It purports to be a code of law, but it is actually a compilation of unre-

solved legal disputations together with biblical exegesis (*midrash*) and nonlegal material (*aggadot*). Despite these facts, however, the Mishnah's paradoxical complexity is justified by its objective: the restoration of the peoplehood of Israel when all signs, internal and external, pointed to its disintegration. In the end, the Mishnah represents a beginning: the initiation of a salvation grounded more in polity survival than in personal salvation.

GEMARAH

In the generation following its appearance, the Mishnah proved to be the focus of increasingly involved discussions by groups of rabbis and their students. The first generation (early third century) clarified obscure passages, and the succeeding generations developed and expanded principles and rules of conduct from the extant mishnaic material as they applied to situations arising in their own societal setting. In due time, new tributaries of oral Torah called *gemarah* ("completion," "learning tradition") in Aramaic and *talmud* ("learning") in Hebrew gushed forth from academies in Galilee and in Babylonia.

Decades of *gemarah* expansion became a virtual reservoir of oral Torah, and the need arose to legitimate the process by editing inconsistencies, curtailing new interpretations, and showing coherent linkage between *gemarah* and Mishnah. In addition, the abrupt Roman closure of Galilean schools of learning during the mid-fourth century and the exile of Jewish communities from Babylonia hastened the pace of selection and collation. The informed result was the creation of two Talmuds, each named after the place of redaction: Yerushalmi (a product of the land of Israel, not Jerusalem, as the name would suggest), circa 400 C.E., and Bavli (Babylonia), circa 500 C.E.

The Talmuds share the same Mishnah (for the most part), but their *gemarah* are written in different dialects of Aramaic (Yerushalmi in Western Aramaic, with a considerable mixture of Greek words; Bavli in Eastern Aramaic, with many Hebrew loan words). They differ in length (Bavli is about twice the length of Yerushalmi), style, syntax, and methodological principles. Their diverse emphasis and *halakhot* may be explained by their places of composition. For example, the Yerushalmi, serving Palestinian Jewry, has *gemarah* for all tractates dealing with agriculture in the Order *Zeraim*, but this is lacking in the Bavli, a product of diaspora *amoraim* (Aramaic for "interpreters" of the Mishnah). Similarly, the Bavli records that the fourth century Amora, Mar Samuel of Nehardea, laid down the principle *Dina deMalkhuta Dina*, which holds that, in civil matters, the law of the land (Jews were a minority in Babylonia) is as binding on Jews as are the commandments of the written Torah.

A dwindling Jewish community in Eretz Israel, stunted in its growth in oral Torah, and a growing diaspora Jewry, which drew succor and moral support from the Babylonian sages, combined to make the Bavli the Talmud of authority during the past 1,500 years of Jewish life and learning, and conceivably for the future as well. For all practical purposes, the Yerushalmi has become a closed book; its many obscure passages have become the objects of antiquarian research. The reclamation of the Temple Mount by the Israelis in the Six-Day War (June, 1967), however, has renewed interest in the Yerushalmi by groups of religious nationalists, who believe that the Talmud of the land of Israel holds the key for the rebuilding of the Third Temple and proper worship therein.

Temple building and its complementary idea, Israel's messiah, however, were conceived by the framers of the Talmud in an ahistorical framework. The main purpose of the oral Torah is to emphasize the holiness of everyday acts and thoughts, which are the way to achieve individual and group happiness and survival. The Talmud successfully preserved the teachings of earlier generations so that later generations could continue them. Its directive "Go forth and study!" is heard to this day.

Zev Garber

FURTHER READING

Danby, Herbert, ed. and trans. *The Mishnah*. 1933. Reprint. New York: Oxford University Press, 1977.

Katz, Jacob. *Divine Law in Human Hands: Case Studies in Halakhic Flexibility*. Jerusalem: The Magnes Press, The Hebrew University, 1998.

Maccoby, Hyam. *Early Rabbinic Writings*. New York: Cambridge University Press, 1988.

_____. *The Philosophy of the Talmud*. Richmond, England: Curzon, 2002.

Montefiore, Claude G., and Herbert M. Loewe, eds. *A Rabbinic Anthology*. New York: Meridian Books, 1960.

Neusner, Jacob. *Judaism: The Evidence of the Mishnah*. Chicago: University of Chicago Press, 1981.

_____. *Judaism in Society: The Evidence of the Yerushalmi*. Chicago: University of Chicago Press, 1983.

_____. *Judaism, the Classical Statement: The Evidence of the Bavli*. Chicago: University of Chicago Press, 1986.

Urbach, Efraim E. *The Sages: Their Concepts and Beliefs*. Jerusalem: Magnes Press, Hebrew University, 1975.

SEE ALSO: Hebrew Bible; Jewish ethics; Kabbala; Messianism; Torah; *Tzaddik*.

Taxes

DEFINITION: Compulsory payments levied for support of government

TYPE OF ETHICS: Politico-economic ethics

SIGNIFICANCE: Taxes can have a major impact on the profitability of businesses and the disposable incomes of millions of people, and every discussion of tax-rate changes raises ethical questions about fairness.

To individual citizens, most taxes appear to be coerced payments. The benefits that individual taxpayers receive from government services are seldom proportional to the tax payments that the individuals make, and taxpayer are sometimes tempted to be "free-riders" by trying to minimize their tax liability, often by crying "unfair." There are many possible ways to determine the fairness of taxes, and they sometimes contradict one another.

TAX STRUCTURES AND FUNCTIONS

Most people agree that taxes should be fair, but the taxes should also be functional. The ostensible purpose of taxes is to raise funds to finance government expenditures. However, governments do not really need to collect money, which they can print cheaply. What governments need are goods and services that they purchase from the private sectors of the economy. Taxes serve to reduce the amount of goods and services used by the private sectors and thus make them more available for government uses.

The willingness of citizens to pay taxes is a measure of the citizens' willingness to permit resources to be used by the government rather than the private sectors. However, some taxpayers may think that they experience injustice when government conducts programs against which they have strong objections—most notably wars. By this view, taxes imposed to support immoral governments, such as those of Adolf Hitler, Joseph Stalin, or Saddam Hussein, are inherently immoral.

Libertarians who believe that government is too large favor taxes that are painful, so that the public will favor smaller government. In this view, "taxation without tyranny is misrepresentation," and high taxes are intrinsically unfair. When U.S. president Ronald Reagan successfully pressed for reductions in federal income tax rates during the early 1980's, part of his argument was that this was a method of restraining growth in federal expenditures—"starving the beast," in the jargon of the times.

Many observers would also raise moral objections against situations in which most tax revenues are taken from a small minority of citizens and used for programs that benefit other people who do not pay taxes. During the eighteenth and nineteenth centuries, this concern was often raised as an argument against the establishment of majoritarian democracy. Modern democratic governments rely on tax systems that are complex and require high degrees of voluntary compliance. If a large portion of taxpayers believe that a tax system is unfair, voluntary compliance may not occur. In extreme cases, individuals and business firms may relocate to more favorable tax environments.

The feasibility of specific types of tax depends on the structure of the economic system. Modern industrial countries rely on taxes on incomes and on corporate profits. These systems require extensive formal financial record-keeping and are not suitable for countries in which most people are self-employed farmers or shopkeepers. Before 1900, the revenue of the U.S. federal government was based primarily on import tariffs, commodity excise taxes, and property taxes.

Property taxes are a major financial support of local governments, as they are location-specific taxes. Such taxes create a special problem of fairness when property tax revenues are used to finance local schools. Rural areas generally have less tax potential per resident than urban areas, which contain expensive commercial and industrial real estate. As a result, many state governments face pressures from their rural areas to provide financial supplements to property tax revenues.

ASSESSING FAIRNESS

Assessing the fairness of taxes is complicated by difficulty in identifying who are ultimate payers of the taxes and by the possibility that the burden of tax may differ from the distribution of revenue raised by the government. One of the most substantial federal taxes in the United States is the wage tax that finances Social Security. In 2003, the rate was 7.25 percent of each wage earner's taxable income assessed against the wage earner and 7.25 percent of the same income assessed against the employer. Although one part of that tax is taken out of the wage earners' take-home pay, employers view both parts of the tax as effectively a part of their payroll costs, a fact that reduces their demand for labor. Part of that tax falls on workers, but the cost of the tax is also reflected in higher product prices paid by consumers. Similarly, economists believe much of the tax on corporate profits is shifted to consumers in the form of higher prices, or to workers as lower wages. However, the burden of personal income taxes falls primarily on the individual taxpayers who pay them.

Taxes on fixed assets have additional complications. For example, increasing a tax on a rental property will lower the property's net income, causing its price to fall. The owner of the property may, in effect, bear the entire future burden of the tax. Similar effects can befall corporate stockholders if profits taxes are increased, lowering the prices of their stock. This impact on asset prices is called capitalization.

Economists apply the term "excess burden" to situations occurring when a tax places a burden on public income that is greater than the amount it increases government revenue. An example is an import tariff that is so high that it yields little revenue, while contributing to an inefficient pattern of resource use that reduces national output. A common source of excess burden involves compliance costs. The federal income tax system is so complex that more than half of American taxpayers engage professional tax preparers to do their taxes for them. In 2002, the four largest tax-preparation firms alone collected seven billion dollars for performing tax services. All the money that goes to tax-preparation services is a burden on taxpayers that contributes nothing to government revenues.

ABILITY TO PAY

One traditional standard of fairness in taxation is the idea that families with more income and wealth should pay more taxes—and even pay higher percentages of their incomes—than poorer people. The concept of higher tax rates for higher incomes is called progressive taxation. The federal income tax in the United States is a progressive tax because higher incomes are taxed at higher rates. The progressive rate structure is reflected in the fact that in the year 2000, the top 25 percent of personal income receivers—those with incomes of $55,000 or more—provided 84 percent of the federal income tax revenues.

Some economists favor progressive income taxes because they act as "automatic stabilizers" against business fluctuations. During economic recessions, declining incomes cause income tax collections to decline, and this in turn helps cushions the decline in incomes.

Persons who favor progressive taxation are also likely to favor taxing inherited property. Not only do inheritances provide the means to pay the taxes, but inheritance revenue also may be considered as unearned by its recipients. Moreover, only a small portion of the population is wealthy enough to bequeath substantial estates. President George W. Bush pressed Congress to eliminate or reduce the federal inheritance tax. A major objection to such taxes is that they can create major problems for family-owned business firms and farms, which may have to be dissolved to meet inheritance-tax liabilities.

Nobel laureate Milton Friedman recommended that the federal government provide a "negative income tax," one under which families whose exemptions and deductions exceed their incomes would receive cash payments. That proposal was, in fact, enacted in the earned income credit law, which provides cash benefits for low-income wage earners.

One of the corollaries of taxing on the principle of ability to pay is that persons in substantially equal financial conditions should be taxed equally. However, the complex federal personal income tax clearly fails that standard.

Avoidable Taxes

Some taxes may be considered voluntary because people can avoid them simply by not purchasing the goods or services on which the taxes are assessed. Taxes on cigarettes and alcohol are notable examples. Indeed, part of the rationale for such taxes is to discourage people from consuming harmful products. The amounts that individuals pay into such taxes can be considerable. For example, smokers in New York City paid three dollars a pack in taxes for cigarettes (half goes to the city, half to the state) in 2004. Two-pack-a-day smokers thus paid six dollars a day, or nearly $2,200 a year, in taxes that nonsmokers did not have to pay.

PROTECTING INCENTIVES

A major objection to progressive taxation of incomes and wealth is that high incomes are considered rewards for high productivity and are thus considered by many people to be fair. Most incomes are payments for personal services, and high personal incomes tend to go to managers of business firms and professional persons such as doctors and lawyers. Imposing high tax rates on high incomes may impair the incentives for persons to enter these occupations, since professional education requires much time and expense. Indeed, newly qualified physicians often begin their professional careers with heavy burdens of student loans to pay off.

High tax rates on wealth, or on incomes generated by wealth, may also impair savings and investments. If the national economy is to grow and create more and better jobs and more and better goods and services, people must be willing to save and invest in new equipment and technology. Most saving and investment is done by persons in the highest income brackets. Persons concerned with economic growth sometimes argue that tax burdens should rest more on consumption and can be heavier on low-income persons and still be fair because over time economic growth will help raise wages and reduce poverty. Examples of taxes on consumption are the value-added taxes (VAT) levied by many European countries. A value-added tax is a kind of sales tax, structured so that it does not become excessive when collected at various stages in production and distribution.

Supporters of progressive taxation argue that high incomes are often products of unfair advantages gained by persons who are born into high-income families or who are born with special physical gifts or talents—such as those possessed by professional athletes and entertainers. However, there is not much evidence that high tax rates on high-income persons have substantially impaired the flow of persons into high-income professions.

OTHER ASPECTS OF TAXATION

Some taxes can advantageously be linked with specific government programs. One example is the wage tax that finances Social Security. Although the benefit to any individual is not closely linked to the

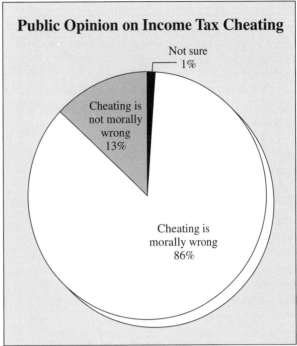

Public Opinion on Income Tax Cheating

Not sure
1%

Cheating is not morally wrong 13%

Cheating is morally wrong 86%

Source: Roper Center for Public Opinion Research, University of Connecticut. *Time* magazine survey, January, 1987. Figures based on interviews with 1,014 adult Americans.

amount of tax paid, taxpayers believe there is a connection. This reduces the risk that politicians will enact further large increases in benefits. Another "benefit tax" is the gasoline tax, revenues from which are generally used for highway programs, which are of clear advantage to users of gasoline. When increased highway use leads to increases in gasoline tax revenues, legislators generally conclude that new highway expenditures are appropriate.

As concern for the environment has increased, many tax programs and proposals have been developed to encourage environmental protection. For example, taxes on pollution can be used to deter polluters. A common recommendation is to impose excise taxes on fossil fuels such as coal and gasoline, which are major sources of carbon dioxide and particulates. This could produce a gasoline tax much higher than needed for highway financing.

A MORAL OBLIGATION?

U.S. Supreme Court justice Oliver Wendell Holmes once remarked that "taxes are what we pay for civilized society." On the other hand, Chief Justice John Marshall earlier pointed out that "the power to tax involves the power to destroy." The many different criteria for determining tax fairness illustrate why there are many opportunities for conflicts of goals. Such conflicts were much in evidence in 2003, when President Bush persuaded Congress to reduce tax rates even though the federal government was already running a deficit, spending more than it took in. Bush wanted to stimulate the economy by giving consumers more disposable income during a recession that had resulted from weak growth in spending for goods and services. He succeeded in reducing taxes on dividend incomes. However, critics of his tax cuts noted that the benefits went predominantly to high-income people and that consumer spending was not likely to be stimulated much by such cuts. Bush evidently saw the tax reduction as a long-run change that would eventually encourage more saving and investment. Meanwhile many Americans believed they had a moral obligation to support American troops then fighting in the Middle East by making large tax payments to the government.

In paying taxes, as in other aspects of life, honesty is generally understood to be the best policy. However, the distinguished federal judge Learned Hand once sagely observed that "Nobody owes any public duty to pay more than the law demands: taxes are enforced exactions, not voluntary contributions."

Paul B. Trescott

FURTHER READING

Fisher, Irving, and Herbert W. Fisher. *Constructive Income Taxation: A Proposal for Reform.* New York: Harper & Row, 1942. Classic study advocating taxes that do not penalize saving and investment.

Forbes, Steve. *A New Birth of Freedom: Vision for America.* Washington, D.C.: Regnery Publishing, 1999. Forbes's proposal for a flat tax, summarized in chapter 5, was an important element in his bid for the Democratic nomination for president in 2000.

Friedman, Milton, and Rose Friedman. *Free to Choose.* New York: Avon Books, 1979. Chapter 4 puts Friedman's negative-income-tax proposal in a context of welfare-state measures.

Musgrave, Richard A. *The Theory of Public Finance.* New York: McGraw-Hill, 1959. This now-classic scholarly work devotes chapters to the benefit

principle, ability to pay, and equal treatment of equals.

Pechman, Joseph A. *Tax Reform, the Rich and the Poor.* 2d ed. Washington, D.C.: Brookings Institution, 1989. Brief, simple overview of tax issues by a leading tax researcher and strong proponent of progressive taxation.

Slemrod, Joel, ed. *Does Atlas Shrug? The Economic Consequences of Taxing the Rich.* Cambridge, Mass.: Harvard University Press, 2000. Fifteen conference papers and commentaries examine the important moral and economic aspects of the topic.

SEE ALSO: Cheating; Civil disobedience; Economic analysis; Equality; Income distribution; Lotteries; Tobacco industry.

Technology

DEFINITION: Practical application of scientific knowledge
TYPE OF ETHICS: Scientific ethics
SIGNIFICANCE: The ethics of modern technology involved reconsiderations of personal and social values to ensure the wise use of technology and to prevent dehumanization and environmental destruction.

Through technology, humans have developed the means to transcend certain physical and mental limitations of their bodies. In the process, they have modified materials and their environment to better satisfy their needs and wants. Technological change has, however, resulted in an expanded range of choices and new ethical dilemmas that necessitate a reconsideration of personal and social values. Ethical analysis of technology involves reviewing whether the social and personal impact, economic costs, environmental damage, and potential risks associated with technology are worth its benefits. Such analysis is used in combination with scientific knowledge to formulate goals and policies to help ensure the responsible development and utilization of technology.

HISTORICAL CONTEXT

Despite its profound influences on humanity and the environment, technology became a subject of ethical inquiry only relatively recently. A review of how the cultural context of science and technology has changed with time is useful in understanding why technology did not come under the scrutiny of ethical analysis earlier.

Technology is generally considered to be the application of scientific knowledge; however, technology actually preceded science. The first human use of tools and the development of agriculture were early forms of technology. The word "technology" originates from the Greek *technè*, which means "art," "craft," or "skill." In ancient times, science was equated with the search for truth and understanding of the world and of human life. The Greek philosophers were the first to formulate ideas about matter, although they never experimentally tested their ideas. Their discourse focused on determining what was real and unique about humans relative to other forms of matter.

A relationship between science and technology began in the Middle Ages with the practice of alchemy—a sort of mystical chemistry practiced by people with an interest in human health and the quality of life. Alchemists prepared elixirs in efforts to remedy ailments as well as to confer immortality. It was Francis Bacon, however, who first perpetuated the belief that knowledge obtained through science could be utilized to enrich human life through new inventions.

Bacon lived in an age when people first used instruments to collect information about nature and the universe but also considered the influence of the stars upon their destinies and believed in witchcraft. As an alternative, Bacon outlined what was to become the modern scientific method—a process characterized by induction, experiment, and the empirical study of data.

Over the next hundred years, René Descartes, Thomas Hobbes, Robert Boyle, and Sir Isaac Newton further contributed to the philosophical basis of the scientific revolution. Science was viewed as one of humanity's noblest enterprises and one of the best means for gaining an understanding of nature. Of relevance to ethics was the fact that this new image of science differed from previous philosophical thought on at least two major points. First, classical ethics assumed that there were limits on humanity's power over natural phenomena; nature and the future were controlled by fate, chance, or some divine power.

According to Bacon, however, the power obtained through knowledge would enable humans to control nature and their own destiny.

Scientific knowledge was also considered objective and tangible. Scientific judgments could be tested by observation of facts and logical analysis; one could provide clear evidence of truth. In contrast, moral judgments were seen as subjective, abstract, and incapable of being empirically tested. Ethical analyses reflected attitudes of the persons involved and were based on values held by an individual or society—all of which have a tendency to be relative to a particular culture and time. Such relativism was not thought to apply to scientific data.

Bacon could not have fully imagined the extent to which his predictions about the enhancement of human life would come true as a result of technological innovations beginning with the Industrial Revolution. By the mid-twentieth century, numerous dreaded diseases had been virtually eliminated with the discovery of antibiotics and vaccines. Fertilizers, pesticides, and animal breeding had increased and enriched the world's food supply. New materials such as plastics and fibers had brought new products into homes, industrial automation had increased leisure time, advances in transportation and communications had linked remote regions of the world, and humanity had begun to look toward outer space as a new frontier.

The public was content to leave details of scientific concepts to a perceived elite group of experts. What seemed important was that technology, the practical result of this work, was the means to improve the quality of life for the average person both by providing conveniences to simplify tasks and ease the burden of work and by offering new luxuries and expanded time for leisure. Advancements in new weaponry and synthetic pesticides that dramatically impacted the course of World War II served to further the public's positive view of technology.

CHANGING ATTITUDES

Despite the perceived benefits of technology, several events during the twentieth century contributed to changing attitudes about science and technology. The development of the assembly line in 1913, initially hailed as a means of providing affordable products for everyone, was blamed for the loss of jobs during the Great Depression. Around this same time, philosophical concerns about technological impact on humans were voiced by individuals like William F. Ogburn, Leslie White, Lewis Mumford, and C. P. Snow. They all questioned whether the machine was an amplifier of human power that challenged human productive abilities or something that placed humans into a new serfdom. Despite this, mechanization propagated as the industrial robot and other forms of automation were introduced.

The United States' use of the atom bomb during World War II raised the level of consciousness of responsibility among scientists. Afterward, they protested against nuclear weapons testing, development of antiballistic missiles, and military research being done within university settings. Additionally, scientists (most notably Rachel Carson) pointed out that science and technology had the potential to destroy the world by the irreversible damage to the environment caused by industrial pollution and the rampant use of pesticides. Such testimony by scientists and other experts led to an increased social awareness of environmental hazards resulting from technology, and for the first time, the general public began to question the value of technology.

Philosophers of the technological age, such as Herbert Marcuse, Jacques Ellul, Victor Ferkiss, and Jacob Bronowski, began to formulate the foundations of a new ethic. New methods of analysis emerged. One example was Norbert Wiener's notion of communication and feedback control processes in animals and machines that he introduced in his book *Cybernetics* (1948); it became a discipline of study in the 1960's. Several other books emerged during the middle of the twentieth century in which the authors openly questioned the value of technology. Rachel Carson's *Silent Spring* (1962) was pivotal in this respect. The evils of technology were often emphasized, and it was pointed out that technology had altered the image of humankind. Science-fiction writers portrayed the horrors of technology gone awry; for example, Kurt Vonnegut's *Player Piano* (1952) detailed the impact of technological change on the human psyche.

Public concerns about science and technology rose dramatically toward the end of the twentieth century. Nuclear energy, resource availability, biomedical and reproductive technologies, genetic engineering, animal welfare, the value of "big science"—such as space exploration, strategic defense initiatives, superconductors, and the Human Genome Project—and the economic and environmental impact of technology were all among the topics of concern. A growing reliance on computers, the Internet, and new electronic modes of communication were changing models of conducting business, accessibility to information, and perceptions of time and distances around the globe. New ethical concerns were being raised about the artificial extension of the human mind and the changing forms of human interactions. Life science research and biotechnology methodologies led to gene therapy, genetically modified foods, cloning of mammals, and the use of stem cells for research—all of which have raised to unprecedented levels public awareness of the new ethical dilemmas.

TECHNOLOGY AND PUBLIC POLICY

Despite a move in the United States to isolate scientific research from political control, the opposite situation occurred. Scientists and engineers were consulted by the government for advice on technology—especially, originally, on issues related to atomic energy. Federal government involvement in science expanded during the 1950's and early 1960's, with the formation of funding agencies such as the National Science Foundation and the National Institutes of Health.

Changing economic and political situations in the 1960's, however, led to decreased federal appropriations for research, and there was a new emphasis on accountability. Scientists were expected to be productive, and research was expected to lead to practical applications. Phrases such as "applied science" and "publish or perish" became popular, blurring the distinction between science and technology. The increased involvement of government in research and technology and the increased dependence of science on public funding severely challenged the previously held ideal that these were ethically neutral areas. Value judgments, social attitudes, and political and economic pressures were clearly influencing the national science agenda, research priorities, and public opinions of technology.

After the 1960's, the level of federal funding for science in the United States increased significantly; a large percentage of scientists rely on federal research support. Entrepreneurial partnerships between universities and business have become common, serving to further emphasize applied research and profit-making—sometimes at the expense of the traditional academic missions of education and basic research. Social priorities define where research funds are directed; this is evident in the large amounts of funding available for research related to cancer, acquired immunodeficiency syndrome (AIDS), and, in the early twenty-first century, national security—especially in the wake of the events of September 11, 2001.

During the 1970's, private institutes such as the Hastings Center in New York and government advisory groups such as the Office of Technology Assessment and the National Academy of Sciences were established to initiate discussions and studies of ethical issues in technology. Emphasis was on the personal and social impact of technology, regulatory issues, and finding ways to better inform the public about technology. International gatherings of scientists (most notably the meeting on recombinant DNA technology held at Asilomar, California, in 1975) focused on ethical dilemmas related to the safe application of new and controversial technology in scientific research, industry, and agriculture.

The national dialogue about technology and ethics expanded as professional scientific societies began to routinely include sessions on ethics at their annual national meetings. Ethics has become a required component of the curriculum of many science graduate school programs, and researchers often must address ethical issues when submitting grant proposals for federal research funds. Centers of ethics related to technology have been developed at a number of universities; the Center for Bioethics at the University of Pennsylvania and the Markkula Center for Applied Ethics at Santa Clara University in California are prominent examples.

Calls to place limits on, or even ban, certain types of research were beginning to be voiced. Initially these came largely from environmentalists and animal rights activists, but they later expanded to groups concerned about genetically modified foods and reproductive technologies, including cloning. A National Bioethics Advisory Commission was established by executive order during President Bill Clinton's initial term in office. This advisory committee examined issues related to human subjects' protection in research. Growing public concerns about human cloning and embryonic stem cell research led President George W. Bush to establish a new President's Council on Bioethics that met for the first time in January, 2002.

Ethical dilemmas related to the distribution of wealth and knowledge and environmental damage resulting from technology have become a major focus of foreign policy. This is evident in provisions of international agreements such as the Montreal and Kyoto Protocols (which focus on environmental concerns), unilateral agreements on weapons and nuclear power, and discussions about the distribution of AIDS drugs to developing nations where the disease is most prevalent. In October, 2003, the president of France, Jacques Chirac, called for an international convention to address ethics raised by advances in genetic engineering and biotechnology.

ETHICAL PRINCIPLES

Traditional ethics were anthropocentric; the fundamental nature of the human entity was presumed to be constant. Classical theories such as Immanuel Kant's theory on moral law focused on similarities between kinds of situations and people. Questions of good or evil actions toward fellow humans were confined to the foreseeable future and to individuals to whom a person was either related or was close in the sense of time or physical location. Actions toward nonhuman objects were considered to be outside the realm of ethical consideration.

Modern technology has altered these premises of classical ethics by changing the nature and the realm of human actions. Individualism and uniqueness, rather than similarities, are valued; society is pluralistic. Innovations in communication and transportation have altered perceptions of time and space, as well as changing the very nature of how humans interact with each other. Humans must think globally in terms of their actions, since they can affect not only living relatives and neighbors but also unknown people living thousands of miles away or someone who might be born several generations in the future.

Modern technology is informed by a much deeper understanding of natural phenomena, yet nature is critically vulnerable to technological intervention. Because of this, the realm of moral consideration has been expanded to include nonhuman living organisms, or even all components of the planet. This has led to the animal rights movement and the development of the field of environmental ethics. Despite this new awareness, humans continue to use technology to construct new environments and alter existing elements of nature—described by some as humans' attempt to re-create Eden.

Contemporary ethics, which emerged in the twentieth century, is usually divided into three components. Through descriptive ethics, one seeks an accurate, objective account of moral behavior or beliefs. Metaethics involves examining the meanings and uses of moral terms such as "good" or "right" and studying moral reasoning and foundations for moral judgments. In normative ethics, moral arguments about what types of conduct are right or wrong, or good or bad, are analyzed. Normative ethics is also concerned with how human beings might best lead their lives and which states of affairs ought to be furthered in society. It is this latter branch of contemporary ethics on which discussions about technology focus.

Most ethical considerations of technology are issue- or case-oriented (applied ethics) and often focus on specific areas such as bioethics or computer ethics. Ethical assessments draw on traditional ethical theory and principles when possible, but also rely on scientific evidence and psychological, political, economic, and historical factors. Traditional ethical reasoning involves consideration of utility, right, justice, common good, and virtue, and use of such standards would lead to questions such as the following when assessing technology: What are the benefits and harms of a particular technology? Who will be impacted and do individuals have free choice in determining whether they will use or be impacted, by technology? Are individuals protected from technology being used in ways they do not want? Will there be a fair distribution of the direct benefits and wealth technology brings? However, given the pace at which new information is obtained and put into application, and the inability to foresee all the consequences of technology, it is difficult to conduct such a thorough assessment.

The fundamental ethical question of whether science and its applications through technology are good or evil is frequently debated. Since goodness is a function of both personal and societal sets of values, there is no absolute set of standards from either classical or contemporary ethics that can be used in this area. Such analysis is further complicated by divided views as to whether technology is mechanical or autonomous. In the mechanical view, or instru-

mental theory, technology is seen as a tool with which to accomplish a humanly defined goal. As such, it has instrumental value depending on its usefulness to humans, and ethical judgments can be made only regarding the goals for which the tools are used. In the autonomous view, or substantive theory, technology has a life of its own and may no longer be under human control. Ethical concerns center both on whether to control or restrict technology and on the moral impact of technology on individuals and society.

NEW ETHICAL ISSUES

Fears that technology might someday begin controlling humans have long been a major ethical concern. Some people believe this to be reality. During the 1980's and 1990's, Neil Postman and Langdon Winner both described how technology had redefined social relationships, culture, ideas of space and time, individual habits, moral boundaries, and political and economic structures. Ironically, technology, which originally led to increased leisure time, has now created a mind-set in business (at least in the United States) that prioritizes efficiency and productivity and promotes a "24-7" mentality. Without free time to pursue friendships, people ironically now turn to their computers for human interaction. Some have noted that the ever-accelerating pace of new knowledge acquisition and implementation of new technologies correlates with fast-paced modern society that is characterized by temporary relationships (consider the high divorce rate, the increasing trend of frequent career changes, and the routine buyouts and mergers in business).

Many have described the seductive power of technology and society's increasing reliance on it. Ruth Conway refers to the "flick of a switch" syndrome where individuals use technology but are unaware of the workings of the machine or the environmental impact of the product and are completely disconnected from the science and creativity that went into the design. She sees this as a debilitating power of technology that can lead to a sense of powerlessness and incompetence. (Consider some people's dependence on remote controls or the common perception that younger generations can no longer do mathematical calculations without the aid of a calculator.) As technology advances, the scientific literacy of the general public lags farther behind. Given the expanding information gap between the experts and the public, who should make decisions about acceptable risks of technology, determine public policy on scientific research, or set limits on technology that threatens to cross some unacceptable moral boundary?

Humans have never before dealt with the types of ethical implications to which modern technology has given birth. Genetic engineering is a good example of a modern technology that leads to a range of new ethical dilemmas including decisions about whether humans should genetically modify themselves or other animals and uncertainties associated with scientists tinkering with evolution and natural selection. However, besides these, there are questions of whom, if anybody should profit from this technology.

In *Diamond v. Chakrabarty* (1980), the U.S. Supreme Court ruled that oil-eating bacteria produced by genetic engineering were living inventions and thus were patentable. This decision further sparked debate over whether life-forms should be engineered, much less patented, and has intensified as a result of the various genome sequencing projects and the patenting of specific DNA sequences isolated from living organisms. A scientist can patent not only a gene responsible for some desirable trait in a crop plant but also a potentially interesting abnormal gene isolated from tissue of a patient with some disease (without the patient's knowledge). Previously unimaginable businesses such as gene prospecting (from humans and other species) and trade in indigenous DNA have emerged.

Computer and communication technologies have also led to new ethical dilemmas—typically in the areas of privacy and intellectual property rights. While some parents may appreciate the ability to check in on their children electronically at a day care center, they might strongly object to the same technology being used in their workplace to monitor their own work. Global positioning systems enable products such as OnStar, which can be used to help a stranded motorist, but also allows companies to track the driving patterns and location of automobile owners without their explicit consent. The Internet and electronic mail communication have many benefits, but they also expand the availability of potential victims, as evidenced by the increase of new breeds of criminals including hackers and online sexual predators.

INTERNATIONAL ISSUES

Most countries realize that their welfare is dependent in part on their national scientific and technological capacity. In the past, the poor (including those in technological countries) have benefited least from technology. How is it possible to distribute justly the benefits of technology? Should everyone enjoy some equitable level of quality of life before further technological advances are permitted? Does the inequality in wealth and technology that exists between industrial and developing nations lead to undesirable practices such as black markets for weapons or substances such as chlorofluorocarbons (CFCs)—which were later banned by the provisions of the Montreal Protocols? Should technologically advanced countries continue to use resources obtained from less-developed countries? If so, what constitutes a fair compensation?

The British philosopher David Hume stated that a system of justice was necessary because of human passions, selfishness, and limits of resources. Ethical discussions of technology often refer to the tragedy of the commons. The commons are those provisions of the earth that humans must share; the tragedy is that human nature compels people continually to increase their well-being—often at the expense of fellow humans. Can a spirit of cooperation prevail if competition is instinctual?

Countries may be obligated to share not only the benefits of technology but also certain kinds of knowledge, such as that related to the eradication of disease. For poor countries, the information may be useless unless financial assistance for implementation is also provided. Who becomes responsible for such financial support? Other technical information, such as that linked to national security, may require protection. Who decides which information is to be shared?

New technology raises questions of priorities, especially when resources are limited. Should ending world hunger be of higher priority than having humans explore outer space? Proponents argue that technology stimulates human intellect, national prestige, and pride. Of what value are these? When a nation has a large national debt, how much technology is needed for security (whether to serve as a deterrent or for defense)? What would be the social price of not using technology?

Technology is often blamed for the depletion of

many natural resources. Can limited resources be shared or conserved? If technology cannot provide alternatives to scarce resources, what valued material goods and comforts would humans be willing to sacrifice? What alternative energy sources are acceptable substitutes when traditional ones are depleted? Innovations in agriculture enhanced the world's food supply, but overpopulation threatens the planet. Should birth control (via technological products) be mandated to bring the population back into balance with what the earth can support?

Other new ethical questions relate to responsibilities toward future generations. What impact will continued technological development have on the future of humanity and Earth's ecosystem? Are these even within the realm of human responsibility? The technology accepted in the twenty-first century or any decisions made to set limits on research and evolving technologies will likely have far-reaching consequences for many generations to come.

HAS TECHNOLOGY ALTERED HUMANS?

Early ethical considerations of technology asked whether it was a threat to the dignity of humans and whether humans were becoming slaves to machines. In contrast, others argue that the machine has freed humans from demoralizing and tedious physical labor, allowing them to more fully develop their intellectual capacities. Modern technological advances have the potential to further blur the boundary between human and machine, including artificial intelligence, neurotechnology—which involves implantable microcomputer chips connected to prosthetic devices—and nanotechnology.

Advances in computing and communication technology allow individuals to access information and regions of the world previously unattainable for the majority of people. To achieve this global connectivity, what has been lost in terms of fundamental human values of family and community? Despite the capability to access almost infinite amounts of information, computers and artificial intelligence are blamed for diminished communication skills and a loss of imagination. Are impersonal interactions and loss of privacy worth the ability to augment intellectual power?

Through technology, scientists have revealed the "secret of life" (DNA structure), and it is theoretically possible to modify humans through genetic en-

gineering. Scientists are identifying the chemical reactions that are responsible for learning, memory, behavior, and the perceptions of pleasure and pain. It has become possible to predict some future health problems, the ability to learn, or an individual's potential for criminal conduct or displaying an addictive behavior—in some cases, before a person is even born. How will such information be used, and by whom? Chemical or genetic modification of behavior, in combination with computers and artificial intelligence, will further enable the expansion of the mental capacities of humans. Researchers have the technology and most of the genetic details to redesign humans should they so choose. What impact does such knowledge have on humanity and spirituality?

Individual value systems are influenced by a person's experiences and environment. Both one's sense of self and decision-making abilities are determined by these values. What happens to human values when the factors that influence them are in constant flux? Values are known to change more slowly than the reality of human experience; what sort of crisis does this present? Humans are confronted with more choices than ever. With shifting values and no set of common societal values, how can decisions be made?

TECHNOLOGICAL RISK AND RESPONSIBILITY

Although technology provides numerous benefits to society, it also entails risks. Oftentimes, not all potential dangers resulting from technology can be foreseen, since predictive knowledge falls behind the technical knowledge and humankind's power to act. Because of this, risk-benefit analysis (a utilitarian approach) is not relevant in all cases, nor is it always possible to logically determine acceptable levels of risk. Choices must be made regarding things that humans have not yet experienced.

How should people address risk in a way that accommodates the perceptions and values of those who bear it when perceptions of the nature, magnitude, and acceptability of the risk differ tremendously among people? Is it possible to identify common values and consider objectives for technology that different cultures within a society or across international boundaries can accept?

Highly trained science experts have difficulty keeping up with developments in their own specialized areas. Couple this with the view that the general public is relatively scientifically illiterate, and how, in a democratic society, can citizens participate in wise decision making relative to technology? What responsibility do people have to educate themselves about science and technology? How does the public gain access to the relevant information? What are the obligations of scientists and technologists in disseminating complex information to the public? How do scientists and technologists balance loyalties to their employers, their profession, and the public in calling attention to potential risks arising from their work? Is it the role of journalists to provide an adequate set of facts to the public?

Even when intelligent decisions are made, errors can occur. Who becomes responsible for unexpected applications or undesirable consequences of technology? Who could have predicted that terrorists would use jets as weapons of mass destruction or samples from biomedical research for bioterrorism? The unpredictable nature of humans and the complexity of political and economic factors make it impossible to foresee all consequences. How can people know the truth about the future conditions of humankind and the earth? How can people know what might possibly be at stake? How important does trust become when regulating the power that humankind obtains through technology?

If technological change is inevitable, consideration must be given to how it should be controlled and assessed and how progress should be defined. Is continued evidence of technological progress a sufficient measure of the healthful state of modern culture? Ironically, modern decision making is dependent on the collection and analysis of data and the use of technological devices for this process; technology is used to assess and make decisions about technology. Where does ethical analysis fit into the process? Are there some areas of research and technology that simply should not be pursued? Who should determine the legitimate goals of science and technology, and who will be responsible for setting limits on scientific freedom and bans on certain technologies?

Although difficult, attempts are continually being made to evaluate technological outcomes. Modern pluralistic societies cannot agree on what ends should be served or how conflicting values should be prioritized. There is a general consensus that technology should be regulated, but the development of public

policy has been hampered by the unanswered question of who should decide what the moral boundaries should be. Values of freedom (respect for autonomy) and of individual choice conflict with ideas on what is right for society as a whole (the utilitarian perspective). Such conflict between self-interest and profit on one side and the sense of obligation for the common good on the other is typical of Western philosophy. A series of profound questions remain unanswered. What are the foundations of an ethic that is applicable to this new technological age? How should the new image of humans be defined in a technological age? How can the survival of humanity, which many people claim is permanently threatened by automation, computers, and genetic engineering, be ensured?

Diane White Husic

FURTHER READING

Burke, John G., and Marshall C. Eakin, eds. *Technology and Change.* San Francisco: Boyd & Fraser, 1979. Collection of essays dealing with ethics, attitudes toward technology, and policy issues. Includes classic excerpts from philosophers of the technological age.

Conway, Ruth. *Choices at the Heart of Technology: A Christian Perspective.* Harrisburg, Pa.: Trinity Press International, 1999. Explores how technology has changed individuals, society, and human values and summarizes several modern ethical analyses of technology.

D'Souza, Dinesh. *The Virtue of Prosperity: Finding Values in an Age of Techno-Affluence.* New York: Free Press, 2000. Analysis of the spiritual and social consequences of a new technology that has led to a mass affluent class.

Ellul, Jacques. *The Technological Society.* London: Random House, 1967. Classic treatise on how technology controls humans.

Mumford, Lewis. *Technics and Civilization.* San Diego, Calif.: Harvest Books, 1963. Classic book that provides a multidisciplinary analysis of technology.

Ophuls, William, and A. Stephen Boyan, Jr. *Ecology and the Politics of Scarcity Revisited: The Unraveling of the American Dream.* New York: W. H. Freeman, 1992. Broad look at the interweaving of ethics, science, and politics through case studies. The authors make frequent references to classical philosophers and illustrate how their ideas are relevant to modern technological issues.

Postman, Neil. *Technopoly: The Surrender of Culture to Technology.* New York: Vintage Books, 1993. Traces the evolution of technology from its origins as a support system of culture to a phenomenon that controls society.

Shrader-Frechette, Kristin, and Laura Westra, eds. *Technology and Values.* Lanham, Md.: Rowman & Littlefield, 1997. Collection of essays that examine contemporary science- and technology-related ethical issues.

Watkins, Bruce O., and Roy Meador. *Technology and Human Values: Collision and Solution.* Ann Arbor, Mich.: Ann Arbor Science, 1977. Cowritten by an engineer and a science writer, this concise book presents several ethical arguments for and against technology. Each side of the debate is critically analyzed, providing a balanced perspective.

Winner, Langdon. *The Whale and the Reactor: A Search for Limits in an Age of High Technology.* Chicago: University of Chicago Press, 1986. A series of essays that investigate technological consequences on society, politics, and philosophy.

SEE ALSO: Bacon, Francis; Biotechnology; Cloning; Computer technology; Dominion over nature, human; Electronic mail; Future-oriented ethics; Nuclear energy; Robotics; Science; Stem cell research.

Telemarketing

DEFINITION: Fast-growing international industry that reaches customers through direct telephone calls

TYPE OF ETHICS: Business and labor ethics

SIGNIFICANCE: Although it is recognized that telemarketing provides useful services to consumers, the industry is known for ethically questionable practices that annoy uninterested persons and undermine consumer trust and faith in the marketplace generally.

Telemarketing can be an efficient method of selling products, services, and philanthropic opportunities. It can also disseminate useful information to interested consumers. However, telemarketers are notorious for harming vulnerable consumers and businesses, providing misinformation, annoying people with unsolicited calls, and creating animosities and suspicions that limit the benefits of telemarketing itself. During the first years of the twenty-first century, it was estimated that the American public was losing an estimated forty billion dollars per year to fraudulent telemarketers.

Voluntary telemarketing codes of conduct and state and national criminal codes require that telemarketers make disclosures to consumers, prohibit lies, regulate hours of operation and sales tactics, and allow call recipients to request placement on do-not-call lists. Ethical issues arise when the marketing tactics are unfair, intrusive, or excessively forceful; the sellers, solicitors, buyers, or donors engage in deception or fraud; the marketing targets are vulnerable or exploited; or the products or benefits are exaggerated or misrepresented.

UNETHICAL PRACTICES

Such telemarketing tactics as after-hours or repeated calls, calls to private homes during private hours, calls that clog business telephones and message centers, and sales pitches implying negative consequences for resisting sales calls are considered both unethical and unfair. Some anti-telemarketing tactics are considered unethical. These include fraudulently accepting sales agreements or charitable pledges, injuring telemarketers' ears with loud whistles or horns, insincere and repeated requests for callbacks and written materials, and providing telemarketers with false or misleading information.

Both telemarketing callers and the people who take their calls are unknown to each other, making enforcement of applicable laws difficult to enforce. Some telemarketing companies practice what are known as fly-by-night tactics: After their unfair practices are detected and targeted for investigation, they close their operations, hide their assets, and reopen their businesses under new names with new corporate identities. Companies operating out of foreign countries may be beyond the enforcement reach of U.S. national and state authorities. At the same time, some buyers engage in equally fraudulent behavior by taking delivery of products or services for which they have no intention to pay.

Telemarketing sales pitches that target the elderly, persons with disabilities, geographically and socially

The National Do Not Call Registry

In September, 2003, the Federal Trade Commission (FTC) responded to complaints about telemarketers by establishing the National Do Not Call Registry. Its goal was to give citizens more control over their private telephones by enlisting government help to stop unsolicited commercial calls. New federal legislation made it a criminal offense for telemarketers to call any numbers on the registry and laid down guidelines for acceptable and unacceptable telephone solicitations and penalties for violations of the new law.

Meanwhile the FTC invited members of the public to register, at no charge, their telephone numbers. In late March of 2004 the FTC reported that 58.4 million phone numbers were registered and that "most telemarketers have been diligent" in complying with the law. According to an independent public opinion survey conducted by the Harris Poll in February, 2004, about 57 percent of all adults in America had registered phone numbers with the Do Not Call Registry. Moreover, more than 90 percent of those who had registered reported receiving fewer or no telemarketing calls since registering.

To sign up on the Do Not Call Registry or to get more information, visit the FTC Web site at www.ftc.gov/ donotcall/.

isolated persons, or persons with limited financial resources are considered especially unfair. Pitches exploiting the victims' greed, avarice, ego, or emotional sensitivities are also unfair but are often viewed less harshly by the public.

The Federal Trade Commission (FTC) and other enforcement agencies have been lenient in allowing puffery, exaggeration, and hyperbole in marketing. The marketing companies themselves may provide honest and forthright scripts for their callers to read to potential customers; however, they may also encourage their callers to deviate from their scripts to make sales. It is difficult to bring legal charges on oral sales pitches that are delivered by anonymous salespersons. In some cases the product, services, or charities do not even exist. Some telemarketing is a cover for credit card or identity theft, or is used to gather financial and consumer information used by other telemarketers at later dates.

Gordon Neal Diem

FURTHER READING

Ditch the Pitch: Hanging Up on Telephone Hucksters. Washington, D.C.: Federal Trade Commission, Office of Consumer and Business Education, 2001.

O'Dea, Valerie. *Better Business by Phones: A Guide to Effective Telebusiness.* West Lafayette, Ind.: Ichor Business Books, 1999.

Sisk, Kathy. *Successful Telemarketing: The Complete Handbook on Managing a Profitable Telemarketing Call Center.* New York: McGraw-Hill, 1995.

SEE ALSO: Business ethics; Electronic mail; Etiquette; Identity theft; Invasion of privacy; Marketing; Privacy; Sales ethics.

Teleological ethics

DEFINITION: Moral theories asserting that the purpose or end of an action determines the moral quality of that action, or that a moral obligation exists to fulfill one's inherent purposes or ends

TYPE OF ETHICS: Theory of ethics

SIGNIFICANCE: As a general category, teleological ethics—or ethics focused on intent or on consequences, rather than duty—constitutes one of the two major types of ethics; the other is deontological ethics. A more specific school of teleological ethics is founded upon the assumption that *teloses*, or ends, exist objectively in the world, that is, that things and people have inherent purposes the fulfillment of which should guide human action. For the narrower school, therefore, one has an ethical duty to discover and accomplish one's purpose in the world.

The term "teleological" is derived in part from the Greek word *telos*, which means end or goal. Teleological ethics refers to ethical theories that base the rightness of actions or the moral value of character traits on the ends or goals that they promote or bring about. A teleological perspective was typical in ancient and medieval ethical thought. Its classic expression is found in Aristotle's *Nicomachean Ethics*, particularly in the opening lines of chapter 2 of book 1:

> Now if there is an end which as moral agents we seek for its own sake, and which is the cause of our seeking all the other ends . . . it is clear that this must be the good, that is the absolutely good. May we not then argue from this that a knowledge of the good is a great advantage to us in the conduct of our lives?

Aristotle, like most ancient and medieval thinkers, used ends and goals to justify virtues and other character traits as well as actions. Until the recent revival of virtue-based ethics, most modern teleological ethical theorists were concerned with theories of obligation; that is, of right and wrong action.

English philosopher C. D. Broad, writing during the early part of the twentieth century, was the first to use the term "teleological" more narrowly to refer to theories of obligation. According to Broad, teleological theories hold that the "rightness or wrongness of an action is always determined by its tendency to produce certain consequences which are intrinsically good or bad."

TEOLOGY VS. DEONTOLOGY

In Broad's classification scheme, which has become standard, teleological theories are contrasted with deontological theories. The latter judge at least some actions to be right in certain circumstances, regardless of what their consequences might be. Leading deontological ethical theorists include Immanuel Kant, W. D. Ross, and John Rawls. No standard or standards of right action are agreed on by all deontologists; instead, what is common to such theorists is a denial of the teleologists' claim that the goodness of consequences is the sole right-making feature of actions or rules of action. For example, Ross insisted that some acts, such as keeping a promise, are right even if doing something else would result in a slight gain in the value of the total consequences. Ross's criticism is of a familiar type directed specifically at the aspect of teleological theories that is sometimes referred to as their "consequentialism"; that is, their requirement that right actions are those having the best consequences. The English philosopher G. E. M. Anscombe first used the term "conse-

quentialism" in a 1958 paper to classify moral theories of obligation. She objected to such theories because of their moral laxity, in that they justified violating rules if the consequences of observing the rules were sufficiently bad.

Another way of expressing the contrast between teleological theories and deontological theories is that suggested by William Frankena and John Rawls. This approach begins with the idea that the two basic moral concepts are the right (the rightness or obligatoriness of actions) and the good (the intrinsic goodness or value of things or states of affairs). Teleological theories give priority to the good over the right in that they define the good independently of the right and then define the right as that which maximizes the good. It is possible to identify what is good or has value independent of any idea of what is right. By contrast, deontological theories define the right independently of what is good, thus allowing that a right action may not necessarily maximize the good.

Looked at this way, one of the questions that teleological theories must address is: "What is good in itself, or has intrinsic value?" The theory of value that is adopted by a teleologist may judge a single kind of thing, such as pleasure, to be good, or it may hold a plurality of things to be good. Jeremy Bentham, the famous English utilitarian, was a defender of the former view, called "hedonism," while the early twentieth century English philosopher G. E. Moore subscribed to the latter, pluralist view. Another conception of value is a "perfectionist" one, according to which some ideal of human excellence is seen as valuable and worthy of pursuit. Aristotle maintained that the human good consisted of the active exercise of the distinctively human faculty of reason.

WHOSE GOOD SHOULD BE PROMOTED?

Teleological theories also provide different answers to the question of whose good it is that should be promoted. Egoistic theories contend that the relevant good is the good of the agent, the person acting, while universalistic theories hold that agents must consider the good of all those who are affected by an action. The best-known of all teleological theories is the universalistic one: utilitarianism. Developed by Jeremy Bentham during the early nineteenth century, utilitarianism has been one of the dominant ethical theories and social philosophies in the English-speaking world.

Classical utilitarians such as Bentham, John Stuart Mill, and Henry Sidgwick were hedonistic utilitarians who asserted that actions, policies, and institutions are to be judged on the basis of the amount of pleasure (as opposed to pain) they produce, considering all those affected. Other utilitarians have departed from the classical view in several ways: Some "ideal" utilitarians, such as G. E. Moore, took the position that things other than pleasure were intrinsically good, while other "rule-utilitarians" stated that rules, not actions, should be judged on the basis of goodness of consequences. While utilitarianism in its various forms remains an important system of moral thought, its once dominant position was eclipsed during the late twentieth century by other types of teleological theories—especially by deontological theories, which have regarded utilitarianism as being open to the charge of insufficiently respecting the value of individuals and allowing too easily the sacrifice of one individual for the greater good of others.

Mario Morelli

FURTHER READING

Aristotle. *Nicomachean Ethics*. Translated and edited by Roger Crisp. New York: Cambridge University Press, 2000.

Broad, C. D. *Five Types of Ethical Theory*. 1930. Reprint. London: Routledge & K. Paul, 1962.

Frankena, William. *Ethics*. 2d ed. Englewood Cliffs, N.J.: Prentice-Hall, 1973.

Mill, John Stuart. *Utilitarianism*. Edited by George Sher. 2d ed. Indianapolis: Hackett, 2001.

Rawls, John. *A Theory of Justice*. Rev. ed. Cambridge, Mass.: Belknap Press of Harvard University Press, 1999.

Rhonheimer, Martin. *Natural Law and Practical Reason: A Thomist View of Moral Autonomy*. Translated by Gerald Malsbary. New York: Fordham University Press, 2000.

Ross, William D. *The Right and the Good*. New ed. New York: Oxford University Press, 2002.

SEE ALSO: Aristotelian ethics; Aristotle; Consequentialism; Deontological ethics; Egoism; Good, the; Hegel, Georg Wilhelm Friedrich; *Phenomenology of Spirit*; Utilitarianism.

Televangelists

DEFINITION: Ministers of the Christian Gospel who conduct services and raise money on television

TYPE OF ETHICS: Religious ethics

SIGNIFICANCE: The emergence of televangelism as a cultural phenomenon in the latter half of the twentieth century raised numerous ethical issues regarding the relationship between mass media and religion.

Televangelism is a product of the evangelical movement in modern Christianity that emphasizes a strict interpretation of biblical authority and a personal commitment to Jesus Christ reinforced by specific conversion experiences. It is the conversion experience itself that televangelists seek to impart in their audiences in accordance with their evangelical mandate to spread the Christian Gospel.

Evangelical Christians were among the first religious groups to recognize and utilize the power of mass media, beginning with the advent of commercial radio during the 1920's. However, regulatory policies that encouraged noncontroversial and ecumenical religious broadcasting served to marginalize the conservative Protestant messages of evangelical broadcasters, forcing them to purchase their own airtime on mainstream media outlets and develop their own media apparatuses to spread their messages. This environment shaped the development of televised evangelist ministries during the 1950's as Billy Graham, Rex Humbard, and other early televangelists worked to create their own organizations for syndication and distribution of programming.

The growth of the television industry during the 1950's and 1960's and the emergence of cable television in the 1970's provided new opportunities for televangelists to reach their target audiences. By the 1980's, televangelism was a multimillion-dollar industry with a worldwide audience of more than twenty million viewers, but subsequent revelations of financial and sexual misconduct by Jim Bakker and Jimmy Swaggart and the failed presidential campaign of Pat Robertson led to a decline in the popularity of televangelists, prompting many Christian broadcasters to turn to family-oriented secular programming to boost their audiences. Nevertheless, the core of televangelism, with its emphasis on sermons, salvation, and solicitation of funds, remained.

RELIGIOUS ISSUES

The popularity of televangelists has raised many ethical issues within the realm of organized religion. Religious leaders of various faiths have expressed concerns about the success of televangelists in advancing Fundamentalist Christian doctrine. For example, moderate evangelical Christians have charged that the prominent role of televangelism in popular religion distorts public perceptions by creating the impression that all evangelical Christians embrace Fundamentalism. However, the prevalence of televangelists in religious broadcasting is the result of long-standing regulatory policies that many of these critics have benefited from and are loathe to alter. Many religious leaders see the growing audiences of televangelists as evidence of the increasing influence of Fundamentalism in modern religious thought. Some, however, question the success of televangelists in converting believers, arguing that they have been more successful in reinforcing the beliefs of those already converted than in winning new initiates.

Critics of televangelists often take issue with their perceived vanity, their reliance upon entertainment to capture their audiences, and the celebrity status that many of them attain. Many mainstream Christians believe that these traits are antithetical to Christian scriptures and traditions that place strong emphasis upon humility and the rejection of materialism, especially with regard to members of the clergy.

Some critics also question the tendency of prominent televangelists to use their airtime, spiritual authority, and celebrity status to advance political agendas, a practice that is arguably contrary to the teachings of Jesus Christ, whom the Christian Gospels depict as a purely spiritual leader who repeatedly refused to take positions on political issues. In response to these charges, defenders of televangelists often argue that their political stances are consistent with religious doctrine and their concern for the welfare of their communities, and that their acquisition of power and influence through celebrity serves the utilitarian purpose of winning converts.

COMMUNITY VS. INDIVIDUAL

A common criticism of televangelism is that it undermines the sense of community that is crucial not only to conventional religious worship but also to the welfare of the secular community. Since televangel-ists by nature preach to multiple audiences of individual television viewers, rather than to assembled groups of worshippers, many critics charge that televangelism changes the focus of worshippers from community to self by circumventing the fellowship and peer support that the communal worship experience provides to worshippers. Some suggest that this focus on self reinforces the emotional and cultural isolation of consumers of televangelism, placing emphasis on individual salvation and personal gain over the good of the community. By contrast, televangelists often point to the sizes of their audiences and the scopes of their ministries as evidence that they are fulfilling needs neglected by industry regulators and otherwise unrepresented in the free market by ministering to those in need of religious experience, many of whom are unable to attend conventional worship services. The validity of each of these arguments is dependent in part upon how many consumers of televangelism would be willing and able to attend conventional church services if religious broadcasts were not available to them, an indicator for which reliable data are difficult to obtain.

THE MONEY FACTOR

Perhaps the strongest and most enduring ethical criticisms of televangelists involve the solicitation and utilization of money in their ministries. Televangelist ministries, like conventional ministries, are dependent upon private donations to support their operations. Televangelists' use of the airwaves to solicit donations can thus be compared to the passing of collection plates in conventional churches. However, televangelists are often criticized for using "hard-sell" techniques to extract contributions from their viewers, many of whom are emotionally and financially vulnerable. Revelations of the financial improprieties of Jim and Tammy Faye Bakker in the 1980's coupled with the antics of Oral Roberts—who claimed that God had promised to take his life if his ministry did not meet its financial goals—lent credence to these accusations and reinforced the conventional stereotype of the vain, unethical televangelist. However, supporters of televangelism continued to argue that most televangelists do not engage in corrupt practices, and that televangelist ministries continue to provide a valuable service despite their reputations for corruption.

Michael H. Burchett

FURTHER READING

Alexander, Bobby C. *Televangelism Reconsidered: Ritual in the Search for Human Community.* Atlanta, Ga.: American Academy of Religion, 1994.

Forbes, Bruce D., and Jeffrey H. Mahan, eds. *Religion and Popular Culture in America.* Berkeley: University of California Press, 2000.

Frankl, Razelle. *Televangelism: The Marketing of Popular Religion.* Carbondale: Southern Illinois University Press, 1987.

Roof, Wade Clark, et al. *A Generation of Seekers: The Spiritual Journeys of the Baby Boom Generation.* San Francisco: Harper & Row, 1994.

Schultze, Quentin J., ed. *American Evangelicals and the Mass Media.* Grand Rapids, Mich.: Zondervan, 1990.

SEE ALSO: Christian ethics; Faith healers; Hypocrisy; Jesus Christ; Reality television; Religion.

Temperance

DEFINITION: Moderation or self-restraint, particularly in abstaining from consuming alcohol

DATE: U.S. movement flourished between the 1820's and the 1920's

TYPE OF ETHICS: Personal and social ethics

SIGNIFICANCE: The American temperance movement, culminating in the institution of Prohibition, is generally understood as an attempt to legislate morality. In other words, it advocated outlawing actions whose moral or immoral character was a matter of debate. The destructive results and repeal of Prohibition are often used by social theorists to support arguments that morality cannot be successfully legislated—that is, that social consensus about moral values and appropriate behavior cannot be imposed by rule of law.

The term "temperance" is used to refer to moderation in all activities, especially those of eating and drinking. Aristotle advised that "moderation in all things is a virtue." Temperance can also refer to the practice of not drinking alcohol at all, and that is how the term will be used in this article.

In the United States, the Prohibition Era lasted from 1920 to 1933. The violence of the underworld gangs that supplied illegal liquor and the wild activities of the men and women who defied the law and drank at illegal bars called "speakeasies" earned the decade the nickname "the Roaring Twenties."

EARLY PROHIBITION EFFORTS

During the early nineteenth century, the temperance movement began to urge Americans to avoid alcoholic beverages of all kinds. The term "temperance" as it related to this movement was a misnomer, since the members of the movement actually advocated total abstinence from alcohol. The supporters of the temperance movement were known as the "drys." They believed that alcohol endangered people's physical and mental health as well as encouraging crime and violent behavior. In 1846, Maine passed the first prohibition law, and by 1860, twelve more states had adopted prohibition. Throughout the U.S. Civil War the issue of temperance was ignored. The Women's Temperance Union and the Anti-Saloon League picked up the battle from 1875 to 1900. In 1872, the Prohibition Party was formed, and it nominated candidates for president and vice president. The zenith of the party's influence was reached in 1892, when it won 271,000 votes for its candidates. After that time, the party steadily lost ground.

By 1900, prohibitionists had lost so much ground that only five states still had prohibition laws. As a result, advocates of prohibition decided to make it a national issue, and they succeeded. In 1913, Congress passed the Webb-Kenyon Act, which forbade the shipment of alcohol from a wet to a dry state. During World War I, prohibitionists argued that using grain needed to feed soldiers to make alcohol was unpatriotic. A strong puritan strain in American culture served to support the prohibitionists' claims. In 1917, the Eighteenth Amendment to the U.S. Constitution was passed, which prohibited the import, manufacture, sale, and transport of alcoholic beverages. Congress provided enforcement power by passing the Volstead Act, which penalized violations of the Eighteenth Amendment.

LIFE WITHOUT LEGAL ALCOHOL

Hundreds of thousands of U.S. citizens disobeyed prohibition laws, claiming that they had the right to live by their own standards. They believed that the laws were unjust and violated their rights, and were thus to be ignored.

As has been the case with illegal drugs, the demand for alcohol drove prices up, and the huge profits that could be realized attracted organized crime to the alcohol trade. The most notorious profiteer was Al Capone of Chicago, who made millions of dollars selling beer and liquor. The wealth and power of the crime gangs made it possible for them to bribe police and government officials. Those who could not be bribed were threatened or even killed. Gangs controlled the governments of several U.S. cities and were difficult to oppose.

Gangs not only made alcohol themselves but also found ways of controlling alcohol made by others. It was legal to make "near beer" by brewing beer of regular strength and then weakening it. Bootleggers simply bought or stole the strong beer and sold it to the public at exorbitant prices. The government allowed industries to make alcohol for medical purposes and research. Again, the gangs either bought or stole this alcohol and converted it into beverages. The gangs also imported alcohol illegally by smuggling it into the United States from Europe, the Caribbean, or Canada. In 1924, this smuggled alcohol had an estimated worth of $40 million, a huge sum of money at the time.

The outlawing of alcohol brought about great changes in American life. In the same way that some people produce drugs in home laboratories today, some people during the Prohibition Era made liquor at home, calling it by such names as "white lightning" and "bathtub gin." Such liquor was strong and of poor quality, but it served to get people drunk. Prior to 1920, few women drank alcohol in public, but both sexes drank together in the crowded speakeasies. This made it acceptable for women to drink in bars with men. Many people carried liquor in concealed hip flasks or in purses. Because the government never had enough agents to enforce Prohibition, people found it easy and relatively safe to defy the prohibition laws. Since these laws were so unpopular with the public, many officers were reluctant to enforce them.

LEGALIZATION

Many Americans concluded that Prohibition created more harm than good. It criminalized behavior that people were determined to pursue, thereby increasing crime and making a mockery of law enforcement. In addition, the 1929 stock market crash led to the Great Depression, and Americans had problems larger than alcohol consumption to worry about. Many people wanted to end Prohibition, and they argued that legalizing alcohol would help the government recover from the Great Depression by allowing it to tax the manufacture and sale of liquor. Consequently, in 1933, the Twenty-first Amendment to the Constitution repealed the Eighteenth Amendment and ended the Prohibition Era. In 1966, the state of Mississippi became the last state to repeal its prohibition laws. Less than 2 per-

Poster for the temperance movement published in 1874. (Library of Congress)

cent of Americans live in areas that have prohibition laws. In most cases, such laws reflect the influence of churches, not prohibition or temperance groups.

By 1976, only 16,000 Americans voted for the Prohibition Party's candidate for president. In 1977, the Prohibition Party changed its name to the National Statesman Party. It works closely with the American Council on Alcohol Problems and the Anti-Saloon League. Since the repeal of the Eighteenth Amendment, such groups have been relatively ineffective in promoting the prohibition of intoxicants.

CONCLUSIONS

For most people, the subjects of intemperance, alcoholism, and addiction conjure up mental images of individuals who are out of control, who are belligerent, argumentative, and violent. Many Americans associate substance abuse with spouse and child battering, frequent fighting, crimes against persons and property, and fetal alcohol syndrome. Once it was believed that alcoholics and other addicts could overcome their addiction through heroic acts of will. Nowadays, however, many physicians believe that a predisposition to alcoholism may be hereditary. Today, society views addiction as a disease rather than as a character flaw. Medical models have replaced social models, and addicts are now seen as people who need twelve-step programs and support groups such as Alcoholics Anonymous, and medical treatment rather than criticism, incarceration, and condemnation. Addiction is a complex issue that involves physiology as much as morality.

Dallas Browne

FURTHER READING

Aristotle. *Nicomachean Ethics*. Translated and edited by Roger Crisp. New York: Cambridge University Press, 2000.

Carter, Paul. *Another Part of the Twenties*. New York: Columbia University Press, 1977.

Cashman, Sean. *Prohibition: The Lie of the Land*. New York: Free Press, 1981.

Clark, Norman. *Deliver Us from Evil: An Interpretation of American Prohibition*. New York: W. W. Norton, 1976.

Szymanski, Ann-Marie E. *Pathways to Prohibition: Radicals, Moderates, and Social Movement Outcomes*. Durham, N.C.: Duke University Press, 2003.

Thornton, Mark. *The Economics of Prohibition*. Salt Lake City: University of Utah Press, 1991.

Wagner, David. *The New Temperance: The American Obsession with Sin and Vice*. Boulder, Colo.: Westview Press, 1997.

Wallace, James. *Virtues and Vices*. Ithaca, N.Y.: Cornell University Press, 1978.

SEE ALSO: Christian ethics; Gluttony; Morality; Private vs. public morality; Self-control; Virtue.

Temptation

DEFINITION: Enticement to do something one should probably not do

TYPE OF ETHICS: Personal and social ethics

SIGNIFICANCE: Temptation includes enticement to do anything from engaging in mildly self-destructive behavior, such as eating fattening foods, all the way up to committing heinous crimes. It is associated with weakness or wickedness, because it entails acting on desires one knows and acknowledges to be wrong.

Oscar Wilde's witty descriptions of temptation help to demonstrate the tremendous power of temptation over the human will. He said: "I can resist everything except temptation" and "The only way to get rid of a temptation is to yield to it."

Temptation is closely linked conceptually to the phenomenon of the weakness of human will. Paradoxically, although stories of weakness of will are found as early as in the biblical story of Adam and Eve, many philosophers have insisted that weakness of will does not exist. Weakness of will is usually defined as action that is contrary to one's better judgment. Some people have argued that it is impossible for a rational agent to act voluntarily while simultaneously realizing that his or her best judgment condemns that very act. Others have argued that since the acts in question are voluntary, the best evidence of what an agent wanted most strongly is the act itself. Therefore, they argue, it is impossible to know that weakness of will has been involved in any observed act.

Such arguments fly in the face of ordinary human experience, but the plausibility of the arguments does make the temptation involved in weakness of will seem paradoxical. Some thinkers (such as Sterling Harwood and David McNaughton) suggest that weakness of will should be defined not as action contrary to one's better judgment but as a disposition to act against one's higher-order desires. Lower-order desires include hunger, thirst, and lust. Higher-order desires are desires that have to do with desires such as a dieter's desire for a suppressed appetite. This is one possible way to resolve the paradox, for it allows one to define the temptation in weakness of will as an unusually strong disposition to do the tempting act, whether or not one in fact succumbs to the temptation by performing that act. This conception of temptation seems to fit the hard data of human experience, which show (Fingarette, 1988) that even those who are professionally treated for alcoholism indulge their craving for drink about as often as those who are left untreated, and also show that smoking tobacco is roughly as addictive as heroin.

Sterling Harwood

FURTHER READING

Bratman, Michael E. "Toxin, Temptation, and the Stability of Intention." In *Rational Commitment and Social Justice: Essays for Gregory Kavka*, edited by Jules L. Coleman and Christopher W. Morris. New York: Cambridge University Press, 1998.

Fingarette, Herbert. *Heavy Drinking: The Myth of Alcoholism as a Disease.* Berkeley: University of California Press, 1988.

Harwood, Sterling. "For an Amoral, Dispositional Account of Weakness of Will." *Auslegung* 18 (1992): 27-38.

Kruschwitz, Robert B., and Robert C. Roberts, eds. *The Virtues: Contemporary Essays on Moral Character.* Belmont, Calif.: Wadsworth, 1987.

McNaughton, David. *Moral Vision: An Introduction to Ethics.* New York: Basil Blackwell, 1988.

Mele, Alfred R. *Irrationality: An Essay on Akrasia, Self-deception, and Self-control.* New York: Oxford University Press, 1987.

Mortimore, Geoffrey. *Weakness of Will.* New York: St. Martin's Press, 1971.

Plato. *Protagoras.* Translated by C. C. W. Taylor. Oxford, England: Clarendon Press, 1976.

SEE ALSO: Integrity; Self-control; Weakness of will; Wickedness; Will.

Ten Commandments

IDENTIFICATION: Ten absolute moral laws traditionally ascribed to the divine revelation of Moses on Mount Sinai
DATE: Proclaimed between the fifteenth and thirteenth centuries B.C.E.
TYPE OF ETHICS: Religious ethics
SIGNIFICANCE: By tradition, the Ten Commandments specify the Hebrews' responsibilities in their covenant with Yahweh. Beginning in the thirteenth century C.E., the Commandments were gradually incorporated into Christian instruction manuals and catechisms as well. Many scholars assert that they form the philosophical foundation upon which modern criminal law has been built, although many others see this notion as potentially dangerous, because it seems to combine secular and religious moral principles, weakening with the separation of church and state.

The Ten Commandments, or the Decalogue, appear twice in the Hebrew Bible (Christianity's Old Testament)—in Exodus 20:1-17 and Deuteronomy 5:6-21—with only slight variations in the wording.

The Decalogue was given within the context of Israel's deliverance from slavery and selection as the chosen nation of God. "I am the Lord thy God, which have brought thee out of the land of Egypt, out of the house of bondage" (Exod. 20:2; all biblical quotations in this article are from the King James Version). Following God's liberation of the Israelites from Egyptian servitude, God entered into a covenant relationship with them at Mount Sinai. The Lord (Yahweh) pledged to protect the Israelites and make them prosper, and they in turn vowed to honor Yahweh as their sovereign and to obey his commandments. The motivation for obedience was to be gratitude for the gracious actions of the Lord.

CONTENTS

The first four commandments deal with humanity's duties toward God; the concern of the last six is people's obligations to others. Biblical scholars generally agree that the commandments were stated originally in a concise fashion, probably as follows:

1. *Thou shalt have no other gods before me.* Allegiance to other deities is prohibited. Unlike Israel's polytheistic neighbors, the nation of Yahweh must

worship only the Lord. The first commandment establishes a practical—and perhaps a theoretical—monotheism, thus making Israel's faith unparalleled in the ancient world.

2. *Thou shalt not make unto thee any graven image.* A graven image is an idol, a visual representation of Yahweh for use in worship. Imageless worship was another unique feature of Israel's religion. The second commandment implies that Yahweh is so awesome that nothing in the physical world can represent him.

3. *Thou shalt not take the name of the Lord thy God in vain.* The term "in vain" means for an empty or worthless purpose. Forbidden here are frivolous, deceitful, and manipulative uses of the divine name. Examples of irreverent speech include profanity, magical incantations, and false oath-taking in Yahweh's name. In the Bible, the Lord's name is equivalent to his very person; therefore, the misuse of the divine name makes God himself to appear empty and worthless.

4. *Remember the sabbath day, to keep it holy.* The sabbath is the seventh day, or Saturday. To keep it holy means to observe it as a day that is different from the other days on which ordinary work is performed. Labor must cease on the sabbath; the sabbath is to be a day of rest and worship. Interestingly, this is the only commandment that is not repeated in the New Testament for Christians to observe. In commemoration of Christ's resurrection, the early church changed the day of worship from Saturday to Sunday.

5. *Honour thy father and thy mother.* Children of any age are to respect, obey, and cherish their parents. The admonition refers especially to supporting helpless old parents. They are not to be abandoned when they can no longer provide for themselves. Old and weak dependents must be cared for by their adult children.

6. *Thou shalt not kill.* Prohibited here is the unlawful killing of a human being; that is, murder. The Old Testament condemns murder as particularly heinous because it assaults the very image of God in man, a feature that makes human life unique and especially precious in the eyes of the Lord. The sixth commandment does not, however, outlaw warfare, legally sanctioned capital punishment, or the killing of animals. All these acts are clearly sanctioned elsewhere in the Hebrew Bible.

7. *Thou shalt not commit adultery.* This injunction aims to protect the sanctity of marriage and also reflects the importance that Yahweh places upon faithfulness in relationships. By implication, the seventh commandment relates to the entire range of sexual ethics. Adultery is singled out as the most pernicious sexual sin because it involves infidelity to a covenanted partner and undermines the stability of the home.

8. *Thou shalt not steal.* Theft covers all attempts to deprive an individual of his livelihood and property. In the Old Testament, property is viewed as a gift of God and necessary for earning a living. Hence, the eighth commandment implicitly upholds a person's right to own property. By extension, it also attempts to preserve human freedom, since the worst kind of theft involves kidnapping a human being and selling him or her into slavery.

9. *Thou shalt not bear false witness against thy neighbour.* To bear false witness is to lie. This commandment primarily forbids perjured testimony in a lawsuit involving a neighbor. Its application may be broadened, however, to cover any false statements that could damage a neighbor's reputation. This prohibition underscores the value that Yahweh places upon truthfulness.

10. *Thou shalt not covet any thing that is thy neighbour's.* The word "covet" refers to strong desire or craving for personal gain at the expense of one's neighbor. An Israelite was to be content with what the Lord provided. This final precept takes Yahweh's absolute ethical standard into an individual's inner life. By implication, all evil desires are prohibited. The tenth commandment reflects the teaching of the Hebrew prophets and Jesus that the source of almost all sinful behavior lies within the human heart.

Ronald W. Long

FURTHER READING

Barclay, William. *The Ten Commandments for Today.* Grand Rapids, Mich.: Wm. B. Eerdmans, 1977.

Craigie, Peter C. "The Ten Commandments." In *Evangelical Dictionary of Theology*, edited by Walter A. Elwell. Grand Rapids, Mich.: Baker Book House, 1984.

Freedman, David Noel, Jeffrey C. Geoghegan, and Michael M. Homan. *The Nine Commandments: Uncovering a Hidden Pattern of Crime and Punishment in the Hebrew Bible.* New York: Doubleday, 2000.

Harrelson, Walter J. "Ten Commandments." In *The Interpreter's Dictionary of the Bible*. Vol. 4. New York: Abingdon Press, 1962.

Kaiser, Walter C., Jr. *Toward Old Testament Ethics*. Grand Rapids, Mich.: Zondervan, 1983.

Kaye, Bruce, and Gordon Wenham, eds. *Law, Morality, and the Bible*. Downers Grove, Ill.: InterVarsity Press, 1978.

Sampey, John R. "The Ten Commandments." In *The International Standard Bible Encyclopedia*, edited by Geoffrey W. Bromiley. Rev. ed. Vol. 4. Grand Rapids, Mich.: Wm. B. Eerdmans, 1979-1995.

SEE ALSO: Christian ethics; Divine command theory; Ethical monotheism; God; Hammurabi's code; Hebrew Bible; Jewish ethics; Moses; Religion; Revelation; Torah.

Terrorism

DEFINITION: Unlawful use, or threatened use, of violence with the intent of intimidating or coercing societies or governments, often for ideological or political reasons

TYPE OF ETHICS: Military ethics

SIGNIFICANCE: While terrorist acts are widely regarded as unethical by those who are attacked, the acts themselves are typically guided by particular sets of ethics held by the attacking parties.

When Timothy McVeigh set a bomb that destroyed a federal government building in Oklahoma City in 1995, and when Middle Eastern suicide pilots hijacked the American airliners they used to attack New York City's World Trade Center and the Pentagon building outside Washington, D.C., on September 11, 2001, they all solemnly believed that the United States was an evil entity and that their actions were morally and ethically justified.

An essential element of terrorist actions is that they are attempts at communication. Through the direct material and human damage they cause, terrorists hope to convey certain "messages" that the target groups will interpret, understand, and act upon. They hope that the traumatic impact of their actions on public emotions will leave their targets emotionally ready to react as they wish. However, the September 11, 2001, attacks by al-Qaeda prompted calls by political leaders for a world "war on terrorism." For terrorists and antiterrorists alike, it has seemed appropriate to adopt the terminology of war. A terrorist attack is almost always followed by reprisals, which in turn yield further terrorist attacks, which in turn lead to further reprisals.

ETHICS

The most commonly accepted body of ethical theory applied to the study of terrorism and counterterrorism is the just war theory. In the *Summa Theologica* (1266-1273), Saint Thomas Aquinas presented the general outline of this theory. He gave both a justification of war and the kinds of activity that are permissible in war.

Just war theory has two key divisions—the *jus ad bellum* and *jus in bello*. The *jus ad bellum* gives the conditions under which resorting to war is justifiable. First, war must be declared and waged by legitimate authority. Second, there must be a just cause for going to war. War must be waged only with a right intention. It must also be a last resort. The *jus ad bellum* insists that there must be reasonable prospect of success. Finally, the violence used must be proportional to the wrong being resisted.

The *jus in bello* is concerned with the permissible methods by which legitimate wars should be waged. It offers two basic governing principles. The first, known as the principle of discrimination, limits the kinds of violence that can be used, principally by placing restrictions on what constitute legitimate targets. A major part of the discrimination principle concerns the immunity of noncombatants from direct attack. The second principle is proportionality. It limits the degree of response by requiring that the violent methods used do not inflict more damage than the original offense could require.

A common element in ethical discussions of terrorism is the observation that one faction's "terrorists" may be another faction's "freedom fighters." Placing bombs on public buses or in shopping centers or abducting, torturing, and killing civilians in order to "send messages" to adversaries are actions carried out with little consideration for the victims' ethical status, that is, whether they have done anything to deserve such treatment. In *Second Treatise of Civil Government* (1690) English philosopher John Locke said that legitimate violence should be directed only against perpetrators and not those who have no part in the offense.

SUPREME EMERGENCY

The "supreme emergency" principle attempts to justify both terrorism and counterterrorism measures by arguing that political communities that are defending themselves against external aggression—thus fulfilling the requirements of *jus ad bellum*—and that are facing dangers that are both imminent and serious may be justified in letting military necessity override the non-combatant immunity requirement of *jus in bello*.

Ethical caution—a heightened degree of making certain ethical rules are not being violated—is called for when the argument of supreme emergency is used. The fact that one's only option to achieve a goal is to use violent means does not necessarily mean that violent means are ethically justified. For example, it might be true that the only chance a man with a terminal heart problem has of surviving would require killing another person in order to have that person's heart implanted into his own body. Nevertheless, that situation does not mean that the man would be ethically justified in killing the other person.

New Yorkers flee as an explosion rocks the World Trade Center during the September 11, 2001, attacks. (AP/Wide World Photos)

When agents of national groups—such as Palestinians—that do not have states of their own commit acts of terrorism against persons nondeserving of violent treatment simply to forward their goal of national independence, they send a message to the rest of the world that theirs will be states that are likely to disrespect the rights of individuals, possibly even of those of their own people.

COUNTERMEASURES

"Counterterrorism" may be taken to refer to fights against terrorism that are themselves conducted by terrorist means. To define it properly, it should mean "measures by state agencies designed to combat terrorism." This is equivalent to the ethical necessity for the police force of any city to arrest and bring to justice murderers and robbers within its jurisdiction. Not to do so would be tantamount to accepting that some people may violate innocent citizens' most basic rights and get away with it.

Ethical criticisms of terrorists who attack innocent persons have an obvious relevance to states and agencies that employ violent military means to combat terrorism. To the extent that they do not want themselves to be regarded as perpetrators of unjustified acts of terrorism, such governments and agencies must take special care to avoid indiscriminately killing, maiming, or incarcerating people who are unrelated to the terrorist activities they are trying to end.

THE PRINCIPLE OF DOUBLE EFFECT

Following just war theory, ethically bad effects of actions that are unintended but predictable may be justifiable if the actions themselves, as well as their intended effects, are ethically permissible. This is because the indiscriminate acts of terrorists create the need for antiterrorist operations; hence, the terrorists may become ethically responsible for situations in which further innocent people may be killed as unintended effects of the resulting antiterrorist operations. This is the principle of "double effect."

However, there is a real danger that antiterrorist agencies will count all innocent victims of their operations as unintended casualties in justified wars against terrorism. This suggests that the principle of double effect should be modified by the antiterrorist agencies in a way that extends the agent's responsibility for the recipients. One such modification has been proposed by philosopher Michael Walzer, who has argued that not only should soldiers in combat try not to kill noncombatants, they should also try to protect them from being killed, even if so doing means risking their own lives. In practice, this would mean undertaking more operations on the ground and engaging in face-to-face encounters with terrorist enemies, instead of relying on bombs and rockets that may be safe from terrorist fire, but which cannot discriminate between terrorists and nonterrorists. It also means that operations against terrorist bases must be preceded by careful collecting and studying of intelligence in order to make it possible to identify legitimate targets.

ALTERNATIVES TO VIOLENCE

What sorts of responses to terrorism can be ethically legitimate? Just war theory rules out the use of terrorism to combat terrorism. The use of violence to capture or even kill terrorists can be legitimate if it accords with the conditions of the just war theory and other principles that govern the ethics of resort to war. One of the most crucial conditions is the doctrine of last resort. This doctrine is based on the idea of the ethical superiority of peace over war. Decisions to go to war must be reluctant, and realistic alternatives to violence must be considered.

A necessary element among alternatives to violence is the attempt to understand terrorist grievances. Attending to the grievances of the terrorists may be a precondition for defeating the terrorist campaign, and ignoring them may contribute to increasing the terrorist threat. Rigid refusals to negotiate with terrorists may be impediments to progress. Discussions among the parties can be helpful, but the chances of success are not assured. However, talking is sometimes the only alternative to violence, and willingness to talk with enemies is equivalent to recognizing the enemies as human beings. This tends to defuse the well-known strategy of dehumanizing adversaries and can lead to real progress.

Financial and other sanctions have been placed by many countries on organizations that directly or indirectly support terrorists. Such measures usually include restrictions on, or withdrawal of, trade rights, diplomatic ties, and membership in international or-

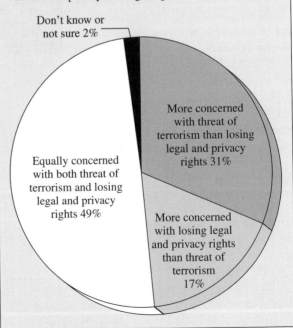

Public Concerns About Terrorism and Losing Privacy and Legal Rights

In August, 2003, a TIPP/Investor's Business Daily/ Christian Science Monitor Poll asked a cross section of Americans which of the views noted below most closely reflected their concerns about terrorism and the loss of privacy and legal rights.

Don't know or not sure 2%

Equally concerned with both threat of terrorism and losing legal and privacy rights 49%

More concerned with threat of terrorism than losing legal and privacy rights 31%

More concerned with losing legal and privacy rights than threat of terrorism 17%

Source: Roper Center for Public Opinion Research. Figures are based on responses of national sample of 901 adults.

ganizations or forums. Sanctions have been successful in gaining cooperation from some governments but were not effective with others.

Military Tribunals and Profiling

Few aspects of the war on terrorism have provoked as much criticism as U.S. president George W. Bush's military order of November, 2001, dealing with the detention, treatment, and trial of certain noncitizens in the U.S. war against terrorism. Hundreds of al-Qaeda and Taliban suspects were imprisoned on the U.S. Navy's base at Guantanamo, Cuba, and held for trial by military courts. Some attorneys representing the suspected terrorists attempted to have their trials moved to civilian courts.

Searching or screening for terrorist suspects by means of descriptive profiles has been used frequently by Israel and a few other countries. After September 11, 2001, the United States began the profiling of airline flight passengers to prevent possible terrorists from boarding planes. Profiling does not normally raise deep ethical issues for most people, but some concern was expressed regarding the Patriot Act that was passed shortly after the September 11, 2001, terrorist attacks on the United States. The fear was that the new law had little to do with catching terrorists but a lot to do with increasing the strength of the government to infiltrate and spy on organizations and individuals.

Certain rules, if followed, tend to legitimize profiled searches. First, the security of the country must be facing a clear and present danger. Next, profiled searches must be carried out by proper legitimate authorities. Finally, general privacy protection guidelines must be followed.

Calvin Henry Easterling

Further Reading

Abrams, Norman. *Anti-Terrorism and Criminal Enforcement*. St. Paul: Thomson, 2003. Examination of the practical aspects of enforcing antiterrorist measures,

Bauhn, Per. *Ethical Aspects of Terrorism*. Lund, Sweden: Lund University Press, 1989. A thoughtful treatment of terrorism, synthesizing recent world events with the ideas of major just war theorists.

Booth, Ken, and Timothy Dunne. *Worlds in Collision: Terror and the Future of Global Order*. New York: Palgrave Macmillan, 2002. Exploration of the threat to post-Cold War world peace posed by terrorism.

Christopher, Paul. *The Ethics of War and Peace: An Introduction to Legal and Moral Issues*. Englewood Cliffs, N.J.: Prentice Hall, 1998. Introduction to the ethics of war and peace that explores in depth the legal and moral issues of when and how to use force to achieve political objectives.

Cole, David. *Terrorism and the Constitution: Sacrificing Civil Liberties in the Name of National Security*. 2d ed. New York: New Press, 2002. Critical examination of the post-September 11 impulse to trade liberty for security in the United States.

Cordesman, Anthony H. *Terrorism, Asymmetric Warfare, and Weapons of Mass Destruction: Defending the U.S. Homeland*. New York: Praeger Publishers, 2001.

Dershowitz, Alan M. *Why Terrorism Works*. New Haven, Conn.: Yale University Press, 2002.

Dudonis, Kenneth J., Frank Bolz, and David P. Schultz. *The Counterterrorism Handbook: Tactics, Procedures, and Techniques*. Boca Raton, Fla.: CRC Press, 2001. Comprehensive strategy for dealing a wide range of possible terrorist threats, ranging from bombings and hostage-taking to nuclear terrorism and what would need to be done before, during, and after such events.

Ganaratna, Rohan. *Inside al-Qaeda: Global Network of Terror*. New York: Columbia University Press, 2002. Very readable examination of the leadership, ideology, structure, strategies, and tactics of the most famous terrorist organization in the early twenty-first century.

Locke, John. *The Second Treatise on Civil Government*. Amherst, N.Y.: Prometheus Books, 1986. Originally written in 1690, this classic work provides a justification for government and sets out the duties of government, including protecting its citizens from violence threats.

Maniscalco, Paul, and Hank. T. Christen. *Understanding Terrorism and Managing the Consequences*. Englewood Cliffs, N.J.: Prentice Hall, 2001. Textbook for officials who have to deal with potential terrorism that also addresses such ethical issues as biological terrorism and the use of weapons of mass destruction.

Thomas Aquinas, Saint. *The Summa Theologica*. Translated by Laurence Shapcote. 2d ed. 2 vols.

Chicago: Encyclopaedia Britannica, 1990. Written in the late thirteenth century, this classic work lays the foundation for modern just war theory.

Walzer, Michael. *Just and Unjust Wars*. New York: Basic Books, 2000. No other book has created so much discussion about just war theory. A modern classic, it deals with the essential just war theory questions. Easily readable, it contains little philosophical jargon.

SEE ALSO: Homeland defense; Jihad; Just war theory; Religion and violence.

Theory and practice

DEFINITION: Theory: systematic abstract reasoning or a rational system of thought composed of abstract principles; practice: concrete action guided by such principles or applying them to actual situations

TYPE OF ETHICS: Beliefs and practices

SIGNIFICANCE: Theory necessarily involves simplification, and arguably falsification, of the world, since rationality is not a property of the world itself, but only of human interpretations of it. Successful practice thus requires that one anticipate disjunctions between theory and reality, and develop methods of compensating for these disjunctions. The difficulties of translating theory into practice acquire moral significance when theoretical misapplication or lack of preparation leads one to cause real harm.

According to George F. Kneller, science is the pursuit of knowledge about nature. Science seeks facts; that is, events or states or things that happen. In the service of that pursuit, science has developed a powerful method of inquiry that distinguishes it from other areas of inquiry, such as philosophy, literature, art, or religion. Kneller divides this scientific method into four successive steps: observation, classification, laws, and theories.

FROM OBSERVATIONS TO LAWS AND THEORIES

By using their senses and sophisticated instruments, scientists make systematic and detailed observations about the universe, which yield facts.

As facts accumulate, classification serves the purpose of discovering commonalities among a set of facts and thus making general statements about those facts. For example, Dmitry Mendeleyev proposed in 1869 that if the various elements were arranged in order of atomic weight, they would arrange themselves into groups that have similar chemical properties.

Classification leads to laws, which are statements that describe regularities. Laws summarize a number of separate facts and enable predictions to be made. Isaac Newton's second law of thermodynamics (which states that heat cannot by itself pass from a colder to a hotter body) and Galileo's law of freely falling bodies are well-known examples of laws.

Theories stand at the pinnacle of the scientific method and are the most important part of the process. Theories organize and explain a number of known laws and also generate new predictions that can be tested. If the predictions are confirmed, new knowledge is obtained and the process begins anew. If the predictions are not confirmed, the theory will have to be revised or abandoned. Einstein's theory of relativity is a famous example of a theory that has stood the test of time and has greatly advanced our understanding of the universe.

THEORY INTO PRACTICE

Ethical issues enter into theory construction and testing in two ways. First, the knowledge that the theory generates by incorporating bodies of existing knowledge and by uncovering new knowledge can often be translated into technology and put into practice at a practical level. Technological applicability means that scientific knowledge is not necessarily neutral. It becomes part of other human purposes and endeavors and therefore can be used or misused. As long as scientific knowledge could not be applied via technology, unhampered search for the truth was a laudable goal. During the late nineteenth century, however, technology began to make significant use of scientific theory. The chemical industry, for example, used scientific theory to alter natural substances and, eventually, to synthesize new ones.

The great English scientist Francis Bacon said in the seventeenth century that science must be responsible to humanity. Since knowledge confers power, knowledge that benefits humankind should be sought. Science thus has a specific ethical, moral, and social responsibility to regulate itself that is more important than professional responsibility, personal ambition, or the advancement of science. Kneller argues that scientists should not conduct research that may pose a danger to the public or may have technological uses that are potentially more harmful than useful.

Other scientists, however, have argued that the goal of science and theory building is to seek knowledge. It is axiomatic that knowledge is good, and it is the responsibility of the scientist to seek that knowledge without concern for its consequences or practical applications. As long as ethical guidelines are followed in conducting research and constructing and testing theories, then the pursuit of knowledge should be unregulated. A potential for abuse exists in any area of research. Through vigilance and external review boards, however, this problem can be managed.

The second issue is that, in the words of Norwood Russell Hanson, "observations are infused with the concept; they are loaded with the theories." That is, theories define a phenomenon in a particular way and influence the perception of that phenomenon. For example, as Hanson observed, Tycho Brahe and Johannes Kepler may both have seen the same sun, but each saw it differently. Brahe's geocentric theory caused him to see the sun rise over the earth. Kepler's heliocentric theory led him to see the earth's horizon fall away from the sun.

To take but one example of these two issues, the reigning theory of human sexuality has for a long time stated that sexual orientation is learned. Furthermore, it was held that heterosexuality was the normal sexual orientation and homosexuality was abnormal. Because homosexuality was both abnormal and learned, homosexuality was to be treated and undone. Male and female homosexuals were subjected to a variety of therapies that were derived from this particular theory of sexuality, some that were appalling. None proved to be in the least effective, but many were continued because of the theoretical orientation regarding homosexuality.

Sexuality and Biology

Recent research suggests that sexuality is strongly influenced by biology. Sexuality is therefore not learned and normally occurs as heterosexual and homosexual. Rather than reassuring the homosexual community, this new theory has aroused considerable anxiety in some quarters. Such knowledge could be used by homophobic individuals or agencies to

once again seek a "cure" for homosexuality, this time through chemical or surgical treatment of the nervous system.

Scientists working in this field, however, reply that the potential for abuse exists in every area of biomedical research. To discontinue such work would stop efforts to construct a theory of sexual orientation, thus simultaneously forgoing the acquisition of new knowledge and the benefits that such a theory could provide.

The ethical issues involved in putting theories into practice thus constitute a dilemma. Two ethically defensible responses can be justified. The most common approach seems to be to let research and theory building progress in as unfettered a way as possible, while scrutinizing them carefully and watching for potential abuses.

Laurence Miller

Further Reading

Burr, Chandler. "Homosexuality and Biology." *The Atlantic* 271 (March, 1993): 47-65.

Hanson, Norwood Russell. *Patterns of Discovery.* Cambridge, England: Cambridge University Press, 1958.

Kneller, George F. *Science as a Human Endeavor.* New York: Columbia University Press, 1978.

Matson, Floyd W. *The Broken Image.* New York: George Braziller, 1964.

Murphy, Jeffrie G. *Character, Liberty, and Law: Kantian Essays in Theory and Practice.* Boston: Kluwer Academic, 1998.

Strewer, Nancy S. *Theory as Practice.* Chicago: University of Chicago Press, 1992.

See also: Bacon, Francis; Bioethics; Ethics; Industrial research; Intention; Medical research; Reason and rationality; Science; Technology; Weapons research.

A Theory of Justice

IDENTIFICATION: Book by John Rawls (1921-   )
DATE: Published in 1971
TYPE OF ETHICS: Politico-economic ethics
SIGNIFICANCE: Rawls's book offers a major contribution to modern thinking about the proper rela-

tionship between individual citizens and government and represents a landmark attempt to resolve the ethical dilemma created by the conflict between equality and freedom.

According to the views John Rawls expresses in *A Theory of Justice*, political society should be viewed as the product of a choice made by free, rational, and equal persons who seek fair institutions and arrangements for the governance of their relationships. His theory, therefore, develops and generalizes the social contract theories of John Locke, Jean-Jacques Rousseau, and Immanuel Kant. while insisting that principles of justice for the basic structure of society are the object of the theoretical "agreement" between people and government.

In search of the principles of justice, Rawls places every person in an original position of equality corresponding to the state of nature in traditional contract theory. In this imaginary position, all people operate behind a "veil of ignorance" shielded from any knowledge of their relative positions in society, wealth, natural assets, and abilities. No person, therefore, can know what principles or social arrangements would be to his or her advantage. In this theoretical condition of equality and ignorance, Rawls then asks what principles of justice would free and rational persons choose as a basis for their government.

By this method, Rawls deduces his two principles of justice. The first broadly addresses the issue of personal freedom: Every person should have an equal right to the most extensive basic liberty compatible with similar liberty for others. Under this principle, the primary reason for limiting personal freedom is to avoid conflict among the full range of rights individuals wish to enjoy and that political institutions are obliged to protect.

The second principle holds that social and economic inequalities should be arranged so that they are reasonably expected to be to everyone's advantage and are attached to positions and offices that are open to all. Inequalities, therefore, are unjust if some are systematically advantaged at the expense of others, or if some are systematically excluded from influence over authoritative decisions.

John R. Rink

SEE ALSO: Deontological ethics; Distributive justice; Kant, Immanuel; Kantian ethics; Locke, John;
Nozick, Robert; Rawls, John; Rousseau, Jean-Jacques; Social contract theory; Social justice and responsibility.

Therapist-patient relationship

DEFINITION: Association between a psychotherapist and client

TYPE OF ETHICS: Psychological ethics

SIGNIFICANCE: Ethical aspects of the therapist-patient relationship are governed both by codes of professional conduct and by statutory law. The relationship raises issues involving paternalism, autonomy, confidentiality, and informed consent.

There are often disagreements among therapists regarding what constitutes the best treatment for a given individual. At last count, almost three hundred different forms of treatment had been described for the alleviation of emotional disorders. Samuel Perry, Allen Frances, and John Clarkin group treatments into three broad categories in their book *A DSM-III Casebook of Differential Therapeutics* (1985). These categories are exploratory, directive, and experiential. Exploratory techniques include psychoanalysis and treatments that are not as lengthy or as frequent as psychoanalysis but utilize at least some psychoanalytic techniques. Proponents of these psychodynamic treatments argue that their treatments are useful for many patients and can be adapted to the requirements of individual patents better than can traditional psychoanalysis, which requires the patient to come to therapy four to five days a week.

Directive techniques include the use of principles derived from the study of how people learn and may utilize reward, punishment, advice giving, or other methods designed to change maladaptive behaviors. For example, some directive therapists argue that patients have learned misconceptions about themselves or others that must be unlearned. Other therapists attempt to reduce patient anxieties by gradually exposing them to frightening situations in order to reduce and eliminate the impact of the anxiety-provoking situation.

Experiential techniques utilize a different perspective. Advocates of these techniques emphasize the expression of feelings. They see little, if any, value in diagnosis or psychiatric classifications. They also object to the power differential found in most therapist-patient relationships. Instead, experiential therapy is viewed as an encounter between two equal individuals who care for each other as real people. Experiential therapists tend to focus on the present and believe that personal growth is an important aspect of therapy. Thus, it is not necessary to be emotionally disturbed to benefit from experiential treatment.

It should be pointed out that these descriptions are necessarily brief and are designed to give the reader an overview rather than a detailed understanding of techniques used in therapist-patient relationships. They are helpful, however, for providing a foundation for understanding some of the ethical issues involved in such relationships.

INFORMED CONSENT AND CONFIDENTIALITY

The American Psychological Association's "Ethical Principles and Code of Conduct" (1992) discusses a number of topics relevant to therapist-patient relationships. The code of conduct requires therapists to discuss with patients such topics as the nature and anticipated course of therapy, fees, and confidentiality. Thus, the beginning of a therapist-patient relationship involves the informed consent of the patient. Daniel R. Somberg, Gerald L. Stone, and Charles D. Claiborn (1993) suggest that this includes discussion of the potential risks of therapy, the length of treatment, the procedures to be used, alternatives to therapy, and the limits of confidentiality. Therapists need to be sure that the patient has given consent freely, and if the patient is unable to give consent legally (for example, if he or she is a young child), permission must be obtained from those who are able to give legal consent. Even with individuals who are not capable of giving informed consent, however, psychologists have an obligation to explain the proposed intervention and to seek cooperation and agreement. In addition, the therapist must take into account that person's best interest.

With regard to confidentiality, the limits of confidentiality must be discussed. In many jurisdictions, for example, there are limitations on confidentiality when treatment is done in a group or family setting. There may also be limitations on confidentiality whenever more than one therapist and one patient are present, as in marital therapy, for example. Disclosures of confidential information are not permitted without the consent of the individual unless permitted by law. Usually, disclosures are limited in order to obtain professional consultations and to provide needed professional services. In addition, disclosures can be made in order to protect a patient or others from harm. Such disclosures are discussed further under the duty to warn.

DUTY TO WARN

This requirement arose out of a suit brought by the parents of Tatiana Tarasoff in the 1970's. Tatiana had been killed by an individual who had been in treatment at the student health facility at the University of California at Berkeley. The patient had revealed to the therapist that he was extremely attached to Tatiana and that he planned to purchase a gun. The therapist, after consulting with colleagues, concluded that the patient was both mentally ill and dangerous and should be hospitalized. Police interviewed the patient and decided there was no need for hospitalization after the patient agreed not to contact Tatiana. The parents of Tatiana sued, and their attorney eventually came before the California Supreme Court, arguing that the treating therapist should have warned Tatiana Tarasoff or her family and that the patient should have been committed involuntarily to an inpatient facility. Initially, the court decided that not only did the therapist have a duty to warn because of the special relationship between therapist and patient but also that the police might be liable, since their questioning of the patient probably resulted in the patient's decision to terminate treatment.

In a later opinion, the same court broadened the duty of the therapist to protect others from dangerous actions of patients but no longer held the police liable. Since that time, a number of states have passed laws requiring therapists to breach confidentiality in the face of patient threats to harm others. Alan Stone, in his book *Law, Psychiatry, and Morality* (1984), argues that therapists are not effective in consistently evaluating the dangerousness of their patients. Nevertheless, he believes that when a therapist is convinced of the dangerousness of a patient, the special relationship between patient and therapist does justify the legal duty to protect both the patient and the public. Thus, therapists are called upon to balance the interests of society against the interests of patient-therapist relationship.

Norman Abeles

FURTHER READING

American Psychological Association. "Ethical Principles of Psychologists and Code of Conduct." *American Psychologist* 47 (December, 1992): 1597-1611.

Crits-Christoph, Paul, and Jacques P. Barber, eds. *Handbook of Short-Term Dynamic Psychotherapy.* New York: Basic Books, 1991.

Perry, Samuel, Allen Frances, and John A. Clarkin. *A DSM-III Casebook of Differential Therapeutics.* New York: Brunner/Mazel, 1985.

Slovenko, Ralph. *Psychotherapy and Confidentiality: Testimonial Privileged Communication, Breach of Confidentiality, and Reporting Duties.* Springfield, Ill.: Charles C. Thomas, 1998.

Somberg, Daniel R., Gerald L. Stone, and Charles D. Claiborn. "Informed Consent: Therapists' Beliefs and Practices." *Professional Psychology: Research and Practice* 24 (May, 1993): 153-159.

Stone, Alan A. *Law, Psychiatry, and Morality.* Washington, D.C.: American Psychiatric Press, 1984.

Syme, Gabrielle. *Dual Relationships in Couseling and Psychotherapy: Exploring the Limits.* Thousand Oaks, Calif.: Sage Publications, 2003.

SEE ALSO: Confidentiality; Diagnosis; Electroshock therapy; Group therapy; Institutionalization of patients; Medical ethics; Physician-patient relationship; *Principles of Medical Ethics with Annotations Especially Applicable to Psychiatry*; Professional ethics; Psychology; Psychopharmacology.

Thomas Aquinas

IDENTIFICATION: Italian theologian
BORN: 1224 or 1225, Roccasecca, near Naples, Kingdom of Sicily (now in Italy)
DIED: March 7, 1274, Fossanova, Latium, Papal States (now in Italy)
TYPE OF ETHICS: Medieval history
SIGNIFICANCE: In such works as *Summa Theologica* (c. 1265-1273) and *Summa Contra Gentiles* (c. 1258-1264), Thomas Aquinas combined Aristotle's philosophical ethics based on happiness and virtue with the Christian understanding of law, grace, and love of God.

The moral life, for Thomas Aquinas, consists in each person achieving human fulfillment through freely chosen actions. Presupposed is a human nature with a given, determinate structure and a corresponding determinate fulfillment or perfection. Actions are morally good if they promote this fulfillment and bad if they hinder it. In this sense, Thomas Aquinas's ethics are teleological and eudaimonistic, but unlike classical utilitarianism, the end of good action is not simply pleasure, but the perfection of the human being. Being naturally social, persons cannot attain their perfection alone, but only in community. Consequently, although the ethical life is ordered to promote personal fulfillment, it is not individualistic. Every aspect of Aquinas's ethics (good action, virtue, law, and so forth) is understood in the light of achieving one's fulfillment.

HAPPINESS AND GOOD AND EVIL ACTIONS

Aquinas recognized two levels of human fulfillment or happiness. First is the perfection of human nature simply on the natural level, which is the object of philosophical ethics. Second is the Christian understanding of human nature as raised by divine grace and destined to a supernatural end. Theological ethics treats the latter and was Aquinas's major concern. At both levels, happiness lies primarily in intellectual activity, that of knowing God. The natural end consists in knowing God by philosophical investigation, while the supernatural end consists in a direct vision of God, which is possible only after death.

Actions such as studying, educating, praying, and temperate eating are good because they are intrinsic to true human fulfillment, while acts like murder, stealing, or adultery hinder it and therefore are evil. Besides choosing and performing a good act, a person must intend a good end; friendship in itself is good, but it would not be morally good if it were chosen for the sake of vanity or ambition. Morally good action requires a good act, the right circumstances, and a good intention.

VIRTUE AND VICE

An integral part of Aquinas's ethics is his theory of virtue and vice. Both virtue and vice are "habits," steady inner dispositions inclining an agent to a certain mode of action. The virtue of courage inclines one to face dangers when reason judges that good action requires it; under the influence of the vice of

Saint Thomas Aquinas. (Library of Congress)

cowardice, one would tend to commit evil action rather than face danger. Hence, all habitual tendencies toward perfective activities are virtues and their opposites are vices. There are many different moral virtues and vices corresponding to the many different spheres of moral action: the virtue of religion is a disposition to be properly related to God, liberality is the virtue of being generous with one's wealth, truthfulness concerns speaking the truth, and so on. The chief moral virtues are the four cardinal virtues: temperance, the right disposition toward pleasures (opposed vices: gluttony, drunkenness, sexual promiscuity); courage, the right disposition toward fearful dangers (opposed vices: cowardice, recklessness); justice, the disposition to respect the rights of others and to treat them fairly (opposed vice: injustice); and prudence, the disposition to deliberate well about moral action. Since

all good action requires a good judgment about what should be done, every other virtue depends upon prudence. These moral virtues are acquired by repeatedly performing appropriate virtuous actions.

The theological virtues are infused by God and are dispositions toward actions directed to the supernatural end. By means of the three theological virtues—faith, hope, and charity (love)—a person believes, hopes in, and loves God. These virtues, for Aquinas, are higher than the moral virtues, and among them charity is the highest. Ultimately, every virtuous action is done for the love of God and therefore depends upon the virtue of charity.

MORAL LAW

Moral law is a rational principle that directs actions toward their proper ends. Lacking animal instinct, free, rational, moral agents direct themselves toward an end according to a rational conception. This is supplied by the law, which commands good acts and prohibits bad acts. Since action always occurs in singular, concrete circumstances, however, law alone is an insufficient rule. Every particular action requires a prudential judgment as its proximate rule.

There are several kinds of law. First is the divine law, the explicit commands of God, such as the Ten Commandments or the Beatitudes, which direct persons to their supernatural end. Second is the natural law, consisting of general principles of right action that are discovered by reason, which reflects on human experience and learns over time what leads to fulfillment and what does not. Because human nature is determinate and is shared by all, the general principles of the natural law are valid for everyone and for all times. Finally, there are human positive laws, the civil laws enacted by society. These are part of the moral law in that they direct moral actions, especially those related to life in society. If, however, a civil law contradicts the natural law or the divine law, it is not a true law and has no binding force. All law, Aquinas said, is ultimately part of the eternal law, the ordering wisdom of God by which he governs the whole of creation.

David M. Gallagher

FURTHER READING

Bowlin, John. *Contingency and Fortune in Aquinas's Ethics.* New York: Cambridge University Press, 1999.

Flannery, Kevin L. *Acts amid Precepts: The Aristotelian Logical Structure of Thomas Aquinas's Moral Theory.* Washington, D.C.: Catholic University of America Press, 2001.

McInerny, Ralph. *Ethica Thomistica: The Moral Philosophy of Thomas Aquinas.* Washington, D.C.: Catholic University of America Press, 1982.

Pieper, Josef. *The Four Cardinal Virtues: Prudence, Justice, Fortitude, Temperance.* Translated by Richard Winston, Clara Winston, et al. Notre Dame, Ind.: University of Notre Dame Press, 1966.

Pope, Stephen J., ed. *The Ethics of Aquinas.* Washington, D.C.: Georgetown University Press, 2002.

Rhonheimer, Martin. *Natural Law and Practical Reason: A Thomist View of Moral Autonomy.* Translated by Gerald Malsbary. New York: Fordham University Press, 2000.

Simon, Yves. *The Tradition of Natural Law.* Edited by Vukan Kuic. New York: Fordham University Press, 1992.

Thomas Aquinas, Saint. *Summa Contra Gentiles.* Translated by Anton Pegis et al. 5 vols. Notre Dame, Ind.: University of Notre Dame Press, 1975.

_____. *The Summa Theologica.* Translated by Laurence Shapcote. 2d ed. 2 vols. Chicago: Encyclopaedia Britannica, 1990.

Weisheipl, James. *Friar Thomas d'Aquino: His Life, Thought, and Work.* Washington, D.C.: Catholic University of America Press, 1983.

SEE ALSO: Aristotle; Benevolence; Christian ethics; Natural law; *Summa Theologica*; Teleological ethics; Virtue.

Thoreau, Henry David

IDENTIFICATION: American writer and philosopher
BORN: July 12, 1817, Concord, Massachusetts
DIED: May 6, 1862, Concord, Massachusetts
TYPE OF ETHICS: Modern history
SIGNIFICANCE: The most influential practitioner of New England Transcendentalism, Thoreau believed that self-reliant persons could, by using nature as a guide, live moral and productive lives without the excessive use of material goods. His most important works include "Civil Disobedience" (1849) and *Walden: Or, Life in the Woods* (1854).

Whether the words of *Walden* and "Resistance to Civil Government" ("Civil Disobedience") or the actions on which they are based have had greater influence, it is clear that Thoreau's life refutes the notion that the Transcendentalists spent their time in the clouds rather than on Earth. A skilled observer of nature as well as a citizen who spoke his mind on current ethical questions, Thoreau made the idealism of Transcendental philosophy a part of his daily life. At Walden Pond, he put into practice Ralph Waldo Emerson's advice to be self-reliant and self-directed. He built his own house, planted his own garden, and lived without a conventional job for more than two years quite contentedly and, as he goes into great detail to show, quite economically.

Thoreau believed that to mire oneself in materialism and then to sacrifice one's principles for fear of losing those material things was to sink into evil. He established that point in his essay "Resistance to Civil Government," in which he chastises his fellow citizens for grumbling about the government's war in Mexico while continuing to pay the taxes that supported it. His own refusal to pay was based not only on his moral judgment of the war but also on the questionable ethicality of a private individual's being forced to support any activity of the larger society. In "Resistance" and other essays—"A Plea for Captain John Brown," "Slavery in Massachusetts," "Life Without Principle"—Thoreau chides his fellow citizens for the disparity between their actions and their principles.

William L. Howard

SEE ALSO: Civil disobedience; Conscientious objection; Conservation; Emerson, Ralph Waldo; Environmental ethics; Transcendentalism; *Walden*.

Three-strikes laws

DEFINITION: State laws mandating twenty-five-year-to-life prison sentences—usually without possibility of parole—for persons convicted of third felony offenses

TYPE OF ETHICS: Legal and judicial ethics

SIGNIFICANCE: Designed to remove habitual offenders from society, these laws violate several classical judicial principles and minimize judicial discretion, while also contributing to falling crime rates and rising prison populations in the United States.

The term "three-strikes laws" draws on the baseball analogy that calls a batter out after accumulating three strikes before hitting the ball fairly. The concept was introduced to U.S. criminal justice during the 1990's, a period of declining national crime rates but growing concern about drug abuse and violence. A federal law was enacted during Bill Clinton's presidency by a Democratic Congress in response to hardened voter sentiment on crime control issues. The federal law requires only one previous serious violent felony and one serious drug offense for the third felony to earn a life imprisonment. By 2003, twenty-six states had also enacted three-strikes laws and some, like Georgia, enacted two-strikes laws. California's law, signed in 1994 by Governor Pete Wilson, followed outrage over the 1993 abduction-murder of twelve-year-old schoolgirl Polly Klaas by a twice-convicted kidnapper who was on parole. California's law is retroactive, reaching back before its enactment, and progressive in that second-time offenders receive double the sentences that first-time offenders would receive for their crimes, before they are sentenced to life in prison for their third felonies.

PHILOSOPHY OF PUNISHMENT

Three-strikes laws embody the principles of certainty of punishment and of protecting the public through incapacitating offenders. However, they are more consistent with eighteenth century British philosopher Jeremy Bentham's idea that repeat offenders should receive harsher sentences to outweigh the profit from offenses likely to be committed. In this, Bentham's views differed from those of his contemporary, Italian classical theorist Cesare Beccaria, whose work informed the authors of the U.S. Constitution. Indeed, three-strikes laws contradict classical ideas that punishment should fit the crime, since the lengths of sentences they impose are related to the numbers of offenses committed, rather than their seriousness. Under classical theory, punishment should be no more than deserved for a specific crime, rather than a series of crimes, and offenders should not be sentenced twice for a crime. Under the three-strikes laws, offenders receive, in effect, sentences for three crimes, even though they have already received sentences for their previous two offenses.

Three-strikes sentences are a version of mandatory sentences, meaning that they are invoked automatically on an offender's conviction. This removes a judge's discretion to set sentences based on the uniqueness of the cases, degrees of culpability, and other mitigating or aggravating circumstances. The fundamental moral question remains, should offenders be punished for the kinds of person they may be—that is, repeat offenders—or should they be punished strictly for the specific offenses they commit, with sentence lengths based on the seriousness of the harm they cause? Under a three-strikes law offenders may get life sentences, even if their previous two offenses are comparatively minor nonviolent drug offenses, and even if their third offenses are less serious than their previous two. Offenses as minor as purse-snatching and shoplifting count as "strikes" under three-strikes laws.

IMPACT AND CRITICISM

Advocates of stricter sentencing claim that the 5 percent per year decline in crime rates observed in the United States through the 1990's resulted in part from the incarceration of habitual offenders by three-strikes laws, even though thirty-five states already had other habitual-offender laws in place since 1971. They claim that crime in states such as California has gone down 40 percent since implementation of three-strikes laws in 1994. They also claim that the certainty of punishment under three-strikes laws deters would-be offenders from continuing their patterns of crime. However, the actual effectiveness of the laws has been questioned by critics, such as the Sentencing Project, who argue that some states without three-strikes laws experienced similar reductions in crime rates through the same period. New York experienced a 41 percent reduction; Massachusetts, 33 percent; and Washington, D.C., 31 percent.

Three Strikes in California

Many people argue that three-strikes laws are inherently unethical and cite cases in California, which has an especially strict law. One of the most notorious cases is that of Leandro Andrade. In 1995, he shoplifted nine videocassettes from two K-Mart stores to give to his nieces for Christmas gifts. His crime was completely nonviolent, and he did not even resist arrest. However, because he had two prior felony convictions, he was given *two* sentences of from twenty-five years to life and could not hope for release before the year 2046.

In another California case, Gary Ewing received a twenty-five-year sentence for stealing three golf clubs, worth at total of $400, from a country club.

Critics claim that three-strikes punishment is excessive and unnecessary, that it contributes to the problems of clogged courts and prison overcrowding, and that it increases the determination of third-time offenders to avoid arrest. These laws abandon the classical principle that repeat offenders are more likely to choose to commit lesser offenses. Instead, facing three-strikes laws, offenders might choose additional and more serious offenses in order to avoid apprehension and conviction.

Doug Kieso, who researched California's three-strikes laws, argues that the initial fear of "clogged courts" was based on the assumption that no plea bargaining would take place. However, he found evidence that judges and appellate courts have "looked the other way," allowing plea bargaining to take place, thereby providing added "pressure" that is used by prosecutors to force defendants to accept longer sentences, rather than risk a life sentence.

HIGHER COURTS

In 2003 the U.S. Supreme Court considered the case against a Court of Appeals ruling that California's three-strikes law was unconstitutional due to its violation of the Eighth Amendment ban on cruel and unusual punishment. Consistent with classical principles, the federal Court of Appeals had ruled that punishments for third-strike crimes cannot be grossly disproportionate to the offenses committed. How-

ever, by a 5-4 majority, the Supreme Court upheld the California law, allowing states the discretion to incapacitate repeat offenders for long periods in the interests of protecting public safety.

Whether because of state fiscal crises or a recognition of the ethical problems of "vengeance as social policy," some three-strikes states, such as Michigan, had by 2003 repealed their determinate sentences, at least for drug offending.

Stuart Henry

FURTHER READING

Abramsky, Sasha. *Hard Time Blues: How Politics Built a Prison Nation.* New York: St. Martin's Press, 2002.

Currie, Elliott. *Crime and Punishment in America.* New York: Henry Holt, 1998.

Greenwood, Peter W., ed. *Three Strikes and You're Out: Estimated Benefits and Costs of California's New Mandatory-Sentencing Law.* Los Angeles: RAND, 1994.

Herivel, Tara, and Paul Wright, eds. *Prison Nation: The Warehousing of America's Poor.* New York: Routledge, 2003.

Shichor, David, and Dale K. Sechrest, eds. *Three Strikes and You're Out: Vengeance as Social Policy.* Thousand Oaks, Calif.: Sage, 1996.

Zimring, Franklin E., Gordon Hawkins, and Sam Kamin. *Punishment and Democracy: Three Strikes and You're Out in California.* New York: Oxford University Press, 2003.

SEE ALSO: Arrest records; Criminal punishment; Erroneous convictions; Parole of convicted prisoners; Peltier conviction; Punishment.

Tillich, Paul

IDENTIFICATION: German American theologian
BORN: August 20, 1886, Starzeddel, Germany
DIED: October 22, 1965, Chicago, Illinois
TYPE OF ETHICS: Modern history
SIGNIFICANCE: Tillich was one of the leading Christian theologians of the twentieth century. In such works as *Systematic Theology* (1951-1963), *Dynamics of Faith* (1957), and *The Protestant Era* (1948), he proposed a new conduit of Christian

systematic theology that helped to facilitate essential dialogue between Protestant and Roman Catholic Christianity, and enabled the Christian faith to relate to other world religions and to the world of secularism.

Tillich was a professor of theology and philosophy at a number of German universities before he was expelled by the Nazi regime for his ties with the Religious Socialists and his vehement anti-Nazi stand. He emigrated to the United States in 1933 and taught at Union Theological Seminary in New York (1933-1955), Harvard University (1955-1962), and the University of Chicago (1962-1965).

Tillich's major teaching in *Dynamics of Faith* (1957), the classic introduction to his thought, is the significance of faith as ultimate concern, which means that the unpredictable, and often forceful, penetration of the abstract ("ultimate") into one's consciousness elicits a concrete response ("concern"), making the revelationary manageable in one's own *Weltanschauung* (worldview). The experience of ultimate concern is a continual process of unconditional correlation of opposite but related elements (subject/object, particular/universal; law/freedom, and so forth), which Tillich views as the essential-existential ground of being, intellectually and emotionally. A true ultimacy, such as God-centrism, is worthy of human commitment, and such an ultimacy is reached by means of an assemblage of rites and symbols that point to and participate in but never replace the sacredness of an ultimate concern. A false ultimacy is an ultimate commitment to that which is not ultimate (idolatry) and opens the way to the demonic. Thus, for Tillich, the absolutization of Jesus, in opposition to orthodox Christology, is a form of heresy (Christolatry).

Although Tillich's categories of thought are not easily classified, this quintessential liberal Protestant thinker always wrote in the spirit of *Ecclesia Semper Reformanda*, as his complete works and supplementary volumes (Stuttgart, 1959-1981) show clearly. In his last public address (at the Divinity School of the University of Chicago, on October 12, 1965), "The Significance of the History of Religions for the Systematic Theologian" (*The Future of Religions*, 1966), he expressed limitations both in the supersessionist view of traditional Christian theology and the modern views of neo-orthodoxy and the "God is dead"

movement, and he proposed that future Christian systematic theology needs to consider the basic insights of other world religions. He taught as he lived—"on the boundary."

Zev Garber

SEE ALSO: Buber, Martin; Christian ethics; Existentialism; Niebuhr, H. Richard; Situational ethics.

Tipping

DEFINITION: Gratuitously awarding money to persons who provide services, such as waiting on tables

TYPE OF ETHICS: Business and labor ethics

SIGNIFICANCE: From the point of view of customers, the central ethical question relating to tipping is whether the action should be regarded as voluntary or involuntary.

In modern Western societies, tipping is regarded as a custom whereby customers receiving services give to the providers additional direct compensation, usually in the form of cash. Service providers such as a taxi drivers, restaurant waiters, hairstylists, and porters are examples of workers who accept tips. Custom generally dictates that tips from satisfied customers should range from 10 to 15 percent of the cost of the services provided, not including sales taxes. Owners of businesses themselves are generally regarded as exempt from tipping. For example, taxicab owners, barbers who own their barbershops, and restaurant owners are exempt.

There are two primary ways one might consider the ethics of tipping. The first is to understand a tip to be a voluntary reward and therefore an evaluation of the service rendered. The second is to consider a tip as an expected form of additional compensation over and above what the workers receive from their employers.

If one chooses to think of tipping as a reward for good service, the giving of tips, as well as the amounts of the tips, are entirely voluntary and left to the discretion of the customer. Seen in this light, generous tips serve as signals to workers that their performance is above average. Conversely, the absence of tips or ungenerous amounts are meant to indicate

Income Tax and Tipping

Many workers who receive tips do not report their tip income when they file their tax returns. However, failure to report tipping income not only is regarded as unethical, it is illegal. Tips earned by waiters, taxi drivers, hairdressers, caddies, and other service workers are subject to the same tax liabilities as other forms of income. In 2004, all employees working in the United States who received more than twenty dollars per month in tips were required, by federal law, to report their tips in full to their employers. The employers, in turn, were required to withhold from their employees' wages the same amounts for state income tax, federal income tax, Social Security tax, and Medicare tax that they would have withheld for the same amounts of money in the employees' regular salaries.

to workers that their performance needs improvement. From this market perspective, it is ethical to tip only if performance warrants it. In Europe, where tipping is less frequent than in the United States, tipping is considered just such a signal of exemplary service and gratitude on the part of the customer.

In the United States, the public custom of tipping is more complex. Some people consider tipping, as in the European custom, a reward of exemplary service. More often however, American tipping is regarded as customary; tipping is therefore an expected and routine part of the exchange. Customers thus tip 10 to 15 percent of the costs of the services they receive, regardless of the quality of service. Since tips are viewed as part of the overall charges, they are routinely expected by workers. From this perspective, the tip as part of the compensation owed to the server is simply a portion of the total compensation provided by the customer rather than the employer.

The expectation that tipping is customary has arisen, in part, in response to minimum wage laws. Many service workers—particularly those who are most likely to be tipped—are paid below minimum wage levels. Therefore customers, and certainly the workers themselves, view tipping as a just way to close the gap.

Steve Neiheisel

FURTHER READING

Schein, John E., Edwin F. Jablonski, and Barbara R. Wohlfahrt. *The Art of Tipping*. Wausau, Wis.: Tipping International, 1984.

Segrave, Kerry. *Tipping: An American Social History of Gratuities*. Jefferson, N.C.: McFarland, 1998.

Tuckerman, Nancy, and Nancy Dunnan. *The Complete Book of Etiquette*. New York: Doubleday, 1995.

SEE ALSO: Cheating; Equal pay for equal work; Etiquette; Generosity; Income distribution; Minimum-wage laws; Service to others; Taxes.

Title IX

IDENTIFICATION: Section of the federal Education Amendments designed to ban sex discrimination at educational institutions receiving federal funds

DATE: Enacted in 1972

TYPE OF ETHICS: Sex and gender issues

SIGNIFICANCE: Title IX was based on the straightforward view that the principle of equality demands unbiased treatment of female and male students; in practice, however, its provisions have been difficult to implement and have had both positive and negative consequences.

Title IX was signed into law by President Richard M. Nixon as part of the Education Amendments of 1972. It is administered by the Office of Civil Rights of the federal Department of Education. While Title IX covers all educational institutions receiving federal aid, and all activities of those institutions, its most dramatic impact has been in college sports. Prior to the passage of Title IX, fewer than 32,000 women competed annually in intercollegiate sports. By 2003, more than 150,000 women were competing. Over that same period, the number of girls playing high school sports likewise rose dramatically.

While participation in women's sports has surged, many colleges have eliminated parts of their men's sports programs in order to pay for the women's sports. Men's programs that have been dropped have typically been such nonrevenue-generating sports as swimming, wrestling, gymnastics, and tennis. Some observers have argued that Title IX is the cause, forcing cash-strapped college athletic departments to cut men's programs in order to fund the women's programs and scholarships required under Title IX. Proponents of Title IX have countered that the real culprits are the major men's sports—principally football and basketball—whose coaches' salaries and program costs have skyrocketed.

Government enforcement of Title IX has done little to calm the waters. The Office of Civil Rights regulations have been interpreted by many legal scholars and university administrators to require a quota system for allocating funds and scholarships among men's and women's sports programs. "Quota" carries with it all the bad political baggage of late-twentieth century fights over affirmative action and reverse discrimination.

Underpinning the Title IX controversy are the uneasy relationships among education, sports, and sexuality in America. Universities are centers of learn-

ing and research, yet they also maintain huge athletic departments that are run much like business enterprises. To participate in sports, women must be aggressive and competitive, but those same women face conflicting social pressures to be demure and nurturing. Overlain on this apparent contradiction is the notion that sports is a meritocracy. Since the time of the Roman gladiators, it has been assumed that in sports only the strongest should survive. However, Title IX promotes equal participation for women, still considered in America the weaker sex.

Title IX is but a part of the intricate puzzle of modern gender discrimination. Most observers would agree that until basic cultural constraints on women—and men—are eliminated, no federal law or regulatory scheme can be expected to operate perfectly.

Robert L. Palmer

Title IX and the Women's World Cup

On July 10, 1999, the U.S. women's soccer team beat the Chinese national team, 1-0, to win the World Cup in Pasadena, California. The 90,000-plus spectators who attended the game made up the largest crowd to attend any women's sporting event in history. In the months leading up to the final match, the national media covered the U.S. team's progress through the preliminary games. Many of those games drew record crowds, some of them drew larger television audiences than National Hockey League playoff games airing at the same times, and individual players, such as Mia Hamm, became media stars. The American victory was seen as a great triumph—both for soccer in the United States and for women's sports generally. Less noticed by the public was the fact that the American team's success was also a triumph for Title IX. All twenty women on the American team had attended college on athletic scholarships they could not have dreamed of receiving if they had reached college age before Title IX came into law. Indeed, so aware were the players of their debt to that law that they nicknamed themselves the "Title IX Team."

FURTHER READING
Messner, Michael A. *Taking the Field: Women, Men, and Sports.* Minneapolis: University of Minnesota Press, 2002.
Weistart, John. "Equal Opportunity? Title IX and Intercollegiate Sports." *Brookings Review* 16, no. 4 (1998): 16-23.
Zimbalist, Andrew. *Unpaid Professionals: Commercialism and Conflict in Big-Time College Sports.* Princeton, N.J.: Princeton University Press, 1999.

SEE ALSO: Affirmative action; College applications; Discrimination; Equal pay for equal work; Equal Rights Amendment; Gender bias; Merit; Professional athlete incomes; Women's ethics.

Tobacco industry

DEFINITION: Producers and distributors of tobacco products
TYPE OF ETHICS: Business and labor ethics
SIGNIFICANCE: The American tobacco industry has come under fire for marketing products known to have links to severe health problems—a fact that raises questions as to the industry's ethical responsibility for the illnesses and deaths attributed to tobacco use. The issue also involves questions about the personal responsibility of adults who choose to use products they know are harmful.

During the 1990's, the American tobacco industry came under unprecedented attack from state and federal officials who sought compensation from the companies for the cost of medical treatments of tobacco-related illnesses. Government representatives argued that their publicly funded health care systems were swamped with payments for tobacco-related illnesses for which the tobacco industry was largely responsible.

INDUSTRY LIABILITY TO SOCIETY

Even with the addition of federal warnings of health problems associated with cigarettes, smoking remained a popular if declining activity in American culture. Prior to the 1990's the federal government conducted low-key antismoking campaigns, limited mainly to advertisements and surgeon general reports highlighting the dangers of smoking. By the early 1990's, a burst of antismoking activity broke out, starting with a 1993 Environmental Protection Agency (EPA) report, followed by congressional hearings and continuing into regulations by the Clinton administration. The impetus behind the antismoking campaign was the rising costs in government-funded health care programs.

The ballooning Medicare and Medicaid program budgets were blamed on tobacco-related illnesses including cancer and heart disease. The federal and state governments demanded that tobacco companies reimburse them for these health costs, which were partly caused by their products. This demand became part of a lawsuit filed by state governments seeking damages from the tobacco companies. A settlement was reached in 1998, with the major tobacco companies agreeing to pay more than $200 billion to the states in return for an end to lawsuits over smoking. This money was to be used to reimburse states for health care costs and to pay for antismoking campaigns.

Antismoking advocates argued that the tobacco industry owed society and the government for taking care of those made ill by cigarette smoking. This was a different argument from the one offered by individual smokers who were suing the tobacco industry for smoking-related illnesses they personally suffered. The governments' lawsuits sought reimbursement not for direct damage caused to government or society by cigarette smoking, but for indirect damage— in the form of higher health care costs brought on by

more smoking-related illnesses. This made a single industry responsible for a product voluntarily used and known by the users to be dangerous to human health.

The state governments' arguments were not entirely convincing. Governments have agreed to pay for the poor and elderly's health care costs until their death. Many of those costs would exist with or without smoking because death is inevitable. While smoking may contribute to certain types of terminal illnesses, it does not necessarily produce or increase the costs of caring for terminal patients. Forcing tobacco companies to pay government for terminal illnesses linked to their product makes those companies responsible for the inevitable: terminal illness.

The 1990's also saw another, indirect, government assault on the tobacco industry in the former of rising excise taxes on cigarettes in order to discourage people from taking up smoking and to raise revenues. For many years most states had imposed taxes of only a few cents per pack on cigarettes. By 2004, however, the average state tax on a pack of cigarettes was sixty cents, and sixteen states had raised their taxes to more than one dollar a pack. Not surprisingly, the states with the lowest tax rates were all tobacco-producing southern states. Meanwhile, smokers in New York City faced a double tax: one dollar and fifty cents went to both the city and the state, adding a total of three dollars in taxes to each pack of cigarettes. In early 2004, New York City added to smokers' difficulties by outlawing all smoking in restaurants.

INDUSTRY LIABILITY TO INDIVIDUAL SMOKERS

In addition to lawsuits filed by state and federal governments, tobacco companies faced suits from individual smokers seeking damages for their own terminal illnesses. Other companies have suffered considerable economic damages when their products were found to have contributed to illness or death of consumers. The asbestos industry, the producers of silicon breast implants, and the producers of the Dalkon Shield all paid huge sums to those who suffered medical problems from their products.

However, there was a significant difference between those products and tobacco products. For nearly forty years consumers had been aware of the dangers of cigarette smoking, while those who used the other products were unaware of potential health

State Excise Tax Rates on Cigarette Packs in 2004

Rank	State	Cents	Rank	State	Cents
1	New Jersey	205	27	Arkansas	59
2	Rhode Island	171	28	Idaho	57
3	Connecticut	151	29	Indiana	55.5
	Massachusetts	151	30	Delaware	55
5	New York*	150		Ohio	55
6	Washington	142.5		West Virginia	55
7	Hawaii	140	33	South Dakota	53
8	Oregon	128	34	New Hampshire	52
9	Michigan	125	35	Minnesota	48
10	Vermont	119	36	North Dakota	44
11	Arizona	118	37	Texas	41
12	Alaska	100	38	Georgia	37
	District of Columbia	100	39	Iowa	36
	Maine	100		Louisiana	36
	Maryland	100	41	Florida	33.9
	Pennsylvania	100	42	Oklahoma	23
17	Illinois*	98	43	Colorado	20
18	New Mexico	91		Tennessee*	20
19	California	87	45	Mississippi	18
20	Nevada	80	46	Missouri*	17
21	Kansas	79	47	Alabama*	16.5
22	Wisconsin	77	48	South Carolina	7
23	Montana	70	49	North Carolina	5
24	Utah	69.5	50	Kentucky	3
25	Nebraska	64	51	Virginia*	2.5
26	Wyoming	60			

Source: Federation of Tax Administrators. Figures reflect scheduled tax rates as of July 1, 2004. Median rate for the country was 60 cents per pack. Asterisked (*) states permitted their counties and cities to impose additional taxes, ranging up to 15 cents per pack in all jurisdictions except New York City, which imposed an additional $1.50 per pack.

problems attributed to the products' use. However, prior knowledge of the potential health problems caused by cigarette smoking can shift only part of the responsibility from the industry to the consumer.

Smokers can also attribute specific illnesses and possibly early death and considerable suffering to tobacco products. Individuals suffering because of asbestos exposure or the negligence of makers of breast implants were paid directly by the companies in-

volved. By contrast, no government claimed that it should be reimbursed for the costs of caring for those who suffered lung cancers because of asbestos exposure.

The tobacco industry also had to accept responsibility for other ingredients in cigarettes, including nicotine. Studies have shown that nicotine is an addictive drug, partly explaining the difficulty many smokers have in "kicking the habit" of cigarettes.

During the 1990's further evidence was uncovered suggesting that tobacco companies had manipulated nicotine levels in cigarettes in order to create addicted smokers of their products. If tobacco companies were guilty of adjusting nicotine levels and knew about the addictive qualities of nicotine, then that fact raises new questions about the industry's accountability for the health problems of cigarette smokers.

While an individual might be considered responsible for choosing to smoke, an addictive and dangerous product might condemn that person to serious illness or death. An addictive product, not revealed as such to the consumer, places responsibility for its effects squarely on the tobacco industry. Deliberate manipulation of nicotine levels would suggest the companies were attempting to create an addiction to a product that all knew was potentially unsafe. Health problems including disease and death traced to cigarettes and their addictive qualities would make the tobacco industry responsible for the damage caused by smoking.

The Lethal Dangers of *Not* Smoking

Tobacco-related diseases are not the only health threats that the cigarette industry poses to the public. According to a National Fire Protection Association study of fires in the United States over the twenty-five years leading up to 2004, the greatest single cause of fire-related deaths is unextinguished cigarettes. Over that period, about 25,000 Americans—including many nonsmokers—were killed by fires started by untended cigarettes. The tobacco industry admits to designing cigarettes to keep burning when not being smoked—to save smokers the trouble of relighting. However, critics note that cigarettes that burn out on their own result in more sales.

It has long been possible to manufacture cigarettes that are self-extinguishing when not being smoked. In mid-2004, New York became the first state to ban the sale of cigarettes that do not meet fire-resistance standards. The New York law was expected to inspire other states to enact similar legislation and perhaps move the U.S. Congress to create a federal law requiring self-extinguishing cigarettes.

RESPONSIBILITY TO NONSMOKERS

Another issue of responsibility for the tobacco industry is the cost to nonsmokers and their exposure to smoking. During the 1990's, the federal government and private antismoking organizations used a 1993 EPA report to warn of the dangers of what became known as secondhand smoking—the cigarette smoke inhaled by nonsmokers exposed to cigarette smoking.

The EPA report linked secondhand smoking to asthma in children or heart disease and cancer in adults. The report prompted the federal government to seek new methods of limiting exposure to smoking. Cigarette smoking was tied to the health problems of nonsmokers, breaking the chain of responsibility usually placed on smokers. Nonsmokers did not choose to smoke yet suffered negative effects of the product. They could thus blame any ill effects they suffered on the industry.

With secondhand smoking possibly contributing to negative health effects, local governments began limiting where and when people could smoke within public spaces. Starting in the mid-1990's, laws were passed prohibiting smoking in many public buildings including airports, courtrooms, and government offices. Supporters of the bans argued that nonsmokers in those buildings had no choice but to inhale cigarette smoke unless smoking was banned. The bans became broader as many cities and some states began prohibiting smoking within private businesses including bars, restaurants, and stores. These bans, initiated throughout the United States, were supported by the public based on the fear that secondhand smoke was dangerous. However, when it came to secondhand smoking, it was the antismoking advocates who faced ethical questions.

ETHICS OF TOBACCO CRITICS

When the EPA issued its 1993 report claiming that private studies linked secondhand smoking to health concerns, it did not explain the methodological problems associated with its report. The EPA report was actually a combination of nine studies, none of which showed a significant connection between secondhand smoking and health problems for nonsmokers. The EPA combined those nine studies and produced a report that contradicted the results of the nine. The greatest concern raised by this is the public policy that was based on the distorted results. Laws

Young antismoking demonstrators greet Florida governor Lawton Chiles after he returns from a trip in which he helped to negotiate a multibillion-dollar compensation agreement with the tobacco industry in August, 1997. (AP/Wide World Photos)

passed restricting public smoking were based on public belief that secondhand smoke was dangerous to nonsmokers. Lack of definitive scientific proof of this casts doubt on the wisdom of limiting the right to smoke. It also raises concerns about the tactics of antismoking advocates. Those seeking to limit smoking are limiting the rights of other individuals to pursue activities—smoking—that they enjoy. Such a limitation of freedom must be accompanied by some national goal promoting the general welfare. If smoking does not harm nonsmokers, then the rush to limit exposure to secondhand smoking may be an unnecessary limit on individual choice.

ETHICS OF ADVERTISING

Known health dangers of smoking raise questions about the ethics of tobacco advertising. Companies use advertising to create new markets for their products, drawing in new consumers. These advertise-

ments highlight the popularity of products and suggest that use of the products will enhance a person's social standing and make him or her more popular among others. Like all other advertising, cigarette advertisements promote products, attempting to attract youths into using tobacco. However, even with the warning labels attached to such ads, there is little information about the potential harms associated with smoking. Young people have less experience with those dangers.

Antismoking advocates point to print ads, sponsorship of athletic events by tobacco companies, and placement of products in television shows and movies as examples of the industry's attempt to glamorize smoking to youth. The companies clearly attempt to gloss over the dangers of smoking while highlighting its social acceptability. Those seeking to regulate cigarettes contend that smoking should never receive any positive public relations because of

1493

the serious health problems caused by it. Recruiting people to engage in smoking would expose them to the addictive nature of nicotine and possibly to higher rates of cancer and heart disease. To meet this criticism, the tobacco industry agreed to implement voluntary limitations on its advertising and mounted another ad campaign attempting to limit youth smoking. For the first time in any industry's history, the makers of products were spending money attempting to dissuade consumers from using their products.

Douglas Clouatre

FURTHER READING

Hayes, Eileen. *Tobacco U.S.A: The Industry Behind the Smoke Curtain*. New York: Twenty-first Century Books, 1999. This work focuses on the tobacco industry's attempt to hide information linking smoking to health problems while claiming that no such evidence existed.

Hilts, Philip, and Henning Gutmann, eds. *Smokescreen: The Truth Behind the Tobacco Industry Cover-up*. New York: Addison-Wesley, 1996. A series of articles attacking the tobacco industry for hiding the results of studies linking smoking to health problems.

Johnson, Paul. *The Economics of the Tobacco Industry*. Westview, Colo.: Praeger Publishing, 1998. Short work explaining how the tobacco industry remains profitable even as it comes under attack from government and private antismoking organizations.

Milloy, Steven. *Junk Science Judo: Self Defense Against Health Scares and Scams*. Washington, D.C.: Cato Institute, 2001. This work criticizes "scientific" studies used to advance a political goal. In one chapter, Milloy takes special aim at the 1993 EPA report linking secondhand smoking to heart disease and shows how the EPA manipulated data to reach its desired conclusion.

Oakley, Dan. *Slow Burn: The Great American Anti-Smoking Scam*. New York: Eyrie Press, 1999. This book takes aim at antismoking advocates and their attempts to eliminate smoking within the public sphere.

Pampel, Fred. *Tobacco Industry and Smoking*. New York: Facts On File, 2004. Evenhanded work that describes the controversy over smoking and how the tobacco industry has handled it.

Sullivan, Jacob. *"For Your Own Good": The Antismoking Crusade and the Tyranny of Public Health*. New York: Touchstone Books, 1999. Critical work on the efforts by public health officials to use studies in order to restrict smoking in public and private areas.

Zegart, Dan. *Civil Warriors: The Legal Siege on the Tobacco Industry*. New York: Delacorte Press, 1996. Examination of the work of an attorney suing the tobacco industry for damages for smokers made ill by years of smoking and the efforts of tobacco companies to win those suits at any cost.

SEE ALSO: Advertising; Business ethics; Drug abuse; Health care allocation; Medical insurance; Product safety and liability; Taxes.

Tolerance

DEFINITION: Indulgence for, or allowance of, beliefs or practices that conflict with one's own

TYPE OF ETHICS: Personal and social ethics

SIGNIFICANCE: Arguably as a consequence of ever-increasing diversity, tolerance of differing views, and especially of different religions, has become a widespread moral ideal in many Western societies. This ideal, however, is neither universally espoused nor always successfully realized by those who do embrace it.

The history of tolerance is shorter than are those of most of the concepts pertaining to personal and social ethics that are included in this work. The word itself has a long history, deriving from Latin and Greek words meaning "to bear" or "to put up with," but for centuries it referred to circumstances of physical conditions. In the sense of putting up with practices regarded as contrary to one's own, the word is not found before 1765. Although the word "toleration" was used in this general sense two centuries earlier, that term invariably referred to civil or religious bodies that were regarded as authoritative and capable of restricting the exercise of nonconforming thought. To tolerate dissident views implies the power not to tolerate them. The idea of tolerance as a personal ethical principle or general social attitude has developed much more slowly.

THE PARADOX OF TOLERANCE: EARLY ADVOCATES

Why should one have any sympathy for beliefs or practices that one believes to be wrong or wrong-headed? Throughout most of human history, the right to differ, especially in religious matters, has simply been denied. A historical survey of human behavior in such matters might raise the question of whether powerful convictions and tolerance can ever coexist.

Michel de Montaigne was a man of remarkable tolerance for his time. He first published his *Essays* in 1580, and the title of one essay, "It Is Folly to Measure the True and the False by Our Own Capacity," suggests his disinclination to pass moral judgments. Although Montaigne did not preach nonconformity, the whole tenor of his work is individualistic and nonjudgmental. A corollary of the Renaissance spirit of individualism exemplified by Montaigne is respect for others as worthwhile individuals in their own right.

An early advocate of religious tolerance was the Jewish philosopher Moses Mendelssohn (grandfather of the composer Felix Mendelssohn-Bartholdy), whose friendship with Gotthold Ephraim Lessing, a noted writer of German Protestant origin, during the mid-eighteenth century shocked most of his coreligionists. He went on to defy Mosaic law by denouncing excommunication—certainly ironic behavior for a man named Moses. He saw excommunication as the attempt to control thought, which in his view neither church nor state had the right to do.

In the nineteenth century, Harriet Taylor identified the idea of conformity as "the root of all intolerance." John Stuart Mill, much influenced by Taylor (who became his wife), made individuality the subject of the third chapter of his *On Liberty* (1859). "In proportion to the development of his individuality, each person becomes more valuable to himself, and is therefore capable of being more valuable to others," he wrote. Thus, Mill would allow the widest latitude in people's ideas and behavior as long as they do no unjustifiable harm to others. One should not oppress the individuality of another, Mill argues, although one has a right to exercise one's own individuality in opposition in various ways; for example, by avoiding the society of, or cautioning others against, a person whose views one regards as wrong or dangerous.

ORGANIZED RELIGION AND TOLERANCE

Liberal Protestant thought has tended to minimize doctrine or at least find room for considerable differences within the confines of doctrine. Like orthodox Judaism, Roman Catholicism was slower to countenance deviation from official doctrine, but since the Second Vatican Council (1962-1965) Catholicism too has shown more of an inclination to tolerate views formerly regarded as dangerous. The ecumenical movement among Christians of various denominations has subsequently fostered tolerance as a positive and spiritually enriching value.

TOLERANCE AS A MODERN CHALLENGE

Increasingly in the modern world, liberal ethical thought has condemned the attitude of intolerance on the part of those who do not or cannot actively interfere with nonconforming individualists, the point being that people can hardly be expected to act tolerantly in the social sphere if they harbor intolerant attitudes. Certainly, many people without the disposition or capacity to interfere significantly with others' liberties express their intolerance in small ways that nevertheless work hardships on nonconformists and contribute to a general milieu of intolerance.

The limits of tolerance are often manifest in the public arena. For example, abortion, though morally acceptable to millions of people, remains for other millions a horrid evil not to be tolerated. It is unlikely that the fierce opposition to abortion clinics throughout the United States can be explained merely by the objection to the expenditure of public funds on a practice believed by its opponents to be evil. Abortion is, to many of its opponents, intolerable in itself despite its acceptance by others whose ethical standards generally appear to be above reproach. Some normally law-abiding people are quite willing to break the law to prevent what they regard as the murder of innocents; others are appalled by what they regard as the blatant infringement on a woman's right not to bear unwanted children who in many cases would impose a burden on society.

It may well be that the soundest ethical basis for tolerance is to be found not in organized religion but in humanistic respect for others and their right to express themselves freely so long as their expression does not harm other individuals or society. Because it is so difficult to achieve a consensus regarding what constitutes serious and unjustifiable harm, however, the ethical value of tolerance remains controversial.

Robert P. Ellis

FURTHER READING

Creppell, Ingrid. *Toleration and Identity: Foundations in Early Modern Thought.* New York: Routledge, 2003.

Katz, Jacob. *Exclusiveness and Tolerance.* Westport, Conn.: Greenwood Press, 1980.

Mendus, Susan, ed. *Justifying Toleration: Conceptual and Historical Perspectives.* Cambridge, England: Cambridge University Press, 1988.

Mill, John Stuart. *On Liberty, and Other Essays.* Edited by John Gray. New York: Oxford University Press, 1998.

Newman, Jay. *Foundations of Religious Tolerance.* Toronto: University of Toronto Press, 1982.

Shweder, Richard A., Martha Minow, and Hazel Rose Markus, eds. *Engaging Cultural Differences: The Multicultural Challenge in Liberal Democracies.* New York: Russell Sage Foundation, 2002.

Wolff, R. P., et al. *A Critique of Pure Tolerance.* Boston: Beacon Press, 1969.

SEE ALSO: Civil rights and liberties; Diversity; Freedom of expression; Mill, John Stuart; Multiculturalism; *On Liberty*; Private vs. public morality; Religion.

Torah

IDENTIFICATION: First five books of the Hebrew Bible, or Old Testament; also, totality of Hebrew oral and written law passed down from Moses
DATE: Collected and written before 622 B.C.E.
TYPE OF ETHICS: Religious ethics
SIGNIFICANCE: Torah is a system derived from contact between the human and the divine that instructs by means of narratives, aphorisms, laws, commandments, and statutes, providing rules of life for individuals and society. The goal provided by Torah is to achieve spiritual and temporal happiness in the full realization of the divine will.

Torah is a feminine noun formation of the verbal root *yrh* ("to instruct") in its causative conjugational form; the root may be semantically related to the Arabic *rawa(y)* ("to hand down") or to the Akkadian *(w)aru* ("to guide"). The renderings of the biblical Hebrew word *torah* as *nomos* in the Greek Septuagint (first half of the third century B.C.E.) and as *lex* in the early Latin Bible translations have historically and theologically given rise to the misunderstanding that *torah* means legalism and that Torah means "Law." In essence, Torah is not supernatural revelation, religious dogma, or general self-evident propositions. It is the cumulative record of moral truths formed by the divine, and codified by humanity. In addition, modern Hebrew uses the word *torah* to designate the thinking system of a savant (for example, the *torah* of Plato, Maimonides, or Einstein) or a body of knowledge (the *torah* of mechanics).

DUAL TORAH

Various biblical verses point to the Pentateuch as Torah distinct from the rest of the Scriptures. The verse "Moses charged us with the Teaching (Torah) as the heritage of the congregation of Jacob" (Deut. 33:44) suggests the inalienable importance of Torah to Israel: It is to be transmitted from age to age, and this transmission has become the major factor for the unity of the Jewish people throughout their wanderings.

The rabbis of the Talmud kept the Torah alive and made its message relevant in different regions and times. This has been done by means of the rabbinic hermeneutic of a dual Torah that has been read into verses from the book of Exodus. Regarding God's words to Moses regarding the covenantal relationship between Himself and Israel, it is said in Exodus, "Write down [*ktav*] these words, for in accordance [*'al pi*; literally, 'by the mouth'] with these words I have made a covenant with you and with Israel" (Exod. 34:27), and, "I will give you the stone tablets with the teachings [*torah*] and commandments which I have inscribed [*ktav-ti*] to instruct [by word of mouth] them" (Exod. 24:12). The sages saw the words "write," "accordance," and "instruct" as the legitimate warrant for the written Torah (*Torah shehbiktav*) and the oral Torah (*Torah shehb'al peh*). In their view, the written Torah, the teaching of Moses, is eternal. The oral Torah is the application of the written Torah to forever changing historical situations, which continues to uncover new levels of depth and meaning and thus makes new facets of Judaism visible and meaningful in each generation.

THE PROCESS OF TORAH: REVELATION AND REASON

The ninth principle of the Creed of Maimonides (1134-1204) states, "I believe with perfect faith that this [written] Torah will not be changed, and that there never will be any other Torah from the Creator, blessed be His Name." It is clear from Maimonides' philosophical magnum opus *The Guide for the Perplexed* (c. 1200) that the written Torah is not to be taken in a literal fashion. For example, Genesis 1:26a says, "And God said, Let us make man in our image, after our likeness." If Judaism expresses strict monotheism, then what is to be made of the plural cohortative "us" and the notion that humanity and God share a "likeness"? For Maimonides, revelation teaches that God is incorporeal and ineffable, while reason imparts that humanity is finite, thus rending a nonliteral reading (that the plural is that of majesty, anthropomorphic language, figurative speech). Not only in narrative but also in legislation are revelation and reason the primary forces in understanding Torah. Take *lex talionis*, for example.

Three times the Pentateuch mentions the legislation of *lex talionis* (the law of retaliation, of an "eye for an eye"): regarding the penalty for causing a pregnant bystander to miscarry when two individuals fight (Exod. 21:23-25), the case of one who maims another (Lev. 24:19-20), and the punishment meted out to one who gives false testimony (Deut. 19: 18-21).

Although the law of "measure for measure" existed in the ancient Near East and persists today in parts of the Muslim Middle East, there is little evidence that the Torah meant that this legislation should be fulfilled literally except in the case of willful murder. "Life for life" is taken literally in cases of homicidal intention, and fair compensation is appropriate when physical injuries are not fatal. Equitable monetary compensation is deemed appropriate by the oral Torah in the case of a pregnant woman whose unborn child's life is lost and when animal life is forfeited. Indeed, the written Torah casts aside all doubts regarding the intent of the biblical *lex talionis* injunction: "And he that kills a beast shall make it good; and he that kills a man shall be put to death" (Lev. 24:21).

Rejecting the literal application of *lex talionis* puts an end to the mean-spirited charge that Judaism is "strict justice." Instead, Judaism advocates reme-

dial justice for the guilty and concern for the injured. The wisdom of *mamon tahat 'ayin*, the "value of an eye," is not arbitrary, but a principle that is central in any democratic system of torts. The modern Jew who carefully probes for the reasons behind the commandments inculcated by the Torah will see their importance not in faith alone but also in association with logic and practicality.

Nevertheless, the severe language of the written Torah's "eye for an eye" sends forth a strong reminder. There is no remuneration in the world that can properly compensate serious injury, death, or any act of serious victimization.

THE ETERNAL TORAH

The doctrine of the eternity of the Torah is implicit in verses that speak of individual teachings of the Torah in phrases such as the following: "A perpetual statute throughout your generations in all your [lands of] dwellings" (Lev. 3:17) and "throughout the ages as a covenant for all time" (Exod. 3:16). Biblical (Proverbs, in which Torah equals wisdom), Apocryphal (the wisdom of Ben Sira), and Aggadic (Genesis Rabbah) traditions speak of the preexistence of Torah in Heaven. Although the Talmud acknowledges the prerevelation existence of Torah in Heaven, which was later revealed to Moses at Sinai, it concentrates more on Torah's eternal values.

Jewish thinkers from the first century to the nineteenth century have proclaimed the Torah eternal, some in terms of metaphysics, others in terms of theology, and most in defense of Judaism against the political polemics of Christianity and Islam, which taught that aspects of Torah are temporal or have been superseded. In the first century, Philo Judaeus spoke metaphysically of the Torah as the word (*logos*) of God, the beginning of creation. In the tenth century, Saadia Gaon proclaimed that the Jews were unique only by virtue of the Torah; if the Jewish nation will endure as long as Heaven and Earth, then Torah must also be eternal. In the twelfth century, Maimonides extolled the perfection (eternity) of Torah, regarding which there is neither addition or deletion. After Maimonides, the issue of the eternity of the Torah became routine; the Torah's eternity became an undisputed article of belief. The schools of Kabbala, however, declared that the preexistent form of Torah is eternal but that the words and message of the Torah are recycled every 7,000 years.

In the nineteenth century, the *Wissenschaft des Judentums* (Scientific Study of Judaism) movement, inspired by the scholarship of biblical critics, presented a historical-critical approach to Torah study. As a result, the traditional concept of the eternity of the Torah became a non sequitur and the idea of the Torah as a human book prevailed. By the mid-twentieth century, however, responding to negative trends in higher literary criticism, which was affected by classical Christian bias and "higher" anti-Semitism, objective and critical studies by Jewish loyalists helped to reaffirm the Jewishness of the Bible's origins. No matter how a Jew views the nature of Torah—as a kind of "mythicizing history" or as a product of the people for the people or as written (inspired) by God—Torah as ultimate authority is an indisputable article of faith.

THE WAY OF TORAH: THREE PATHS

Whether the Torah is defined as the result of an exclusive encounter at Sinai or of an evolving journey from Sinai, this national treasure is traditionally understood by the response of *na'aseh ve-nishma'* ("We shall do and we shall hear [reason]"). Accordingly, the way of Torah presents three paths for the contemporary Jew:

1. One should believe that God's Torah given at Sinai is all knowledge. (*Na'aseh* alone.)

2. The Torah-at-Sinai tradition should be abandoned, and Torah should be explained in purely rationalist terms. Torah is made in the image of the Jewish people. (*Nishma'* alone.)

3. One should accept the existential position that God's teaching was shared at Sinai, face to face, with all of Israel, present and future. "Present" implies that God's revelation occurred and that Torah is the memory of this unusual theophany; "future" hints that Israel's dialogue with God is an ongoing process. This view holds that people know only a part of divine truth and that each generation seeks, makes distinctions, categorizes, and strives to discover more. (*Na'aseh ve-nishma'*.)

Na'aseh alone permits no ultimate questions; *nishma'* alone provides no ultimate answers. *Na'aseh* and *nishma'* together ask questions and attempt answers but leave many uncertainties unanswered. Yet uncertainty is truth in the making and the inevitable price for intellectual freedom.

Zev Garber

FURTHER READING

Buber, Martin. *Moses: The Revelation and the Covenant*. New York: Harper, 1958.

Cassuto, Umberto. *The Documentary Hypothesis and the Composition of the Pentateuch*. Jerusalem: Magnes Press, Hebrew University, 1961.

Hertz, Joseph H., ed. *The Pentateuch and Haftorahs*. 2d ed. London: Soncino Press, 1980.

Neusner, Jacob. *The Perfect Torah*. Boston: Brill, 2003.

_____. *The Torah and the Halakhah: The Four Relationships*. Lanham, Md.: University Press of America, 2003.

Plaut, W. Gunther. *The Torah: A Modern Commentary*. New York: Union of American Hebrew Congregations, 1974.

Segal, Moses Hirsch. *The Pentateuch: Its Composition and Its Authorship and Other Biblical Studies*. Jerusalem: Magnes Press, Hebrew University, 1967.

SEE ALSO: Baḥya ben Joseph ibn Paḳuda; Hebrew Bible; Jewish ethics; Kabbala; Maimonides, Moses; Moses; Philo of Alexandria; Talmud; Ten Commandments; *Tzaddik*.

Torture

DEFINITION: Deliberate, systematic inflicting of physical or mental pain, as a means of coercing information or confession, as a form of punishment, or out of sheer cruelty

TYPE OF ETHICS: Human rights

SIGNIFICANCE: Torture is almost universally thought of as a moral evil, but it is not always labeled as an absolute evil. Some consequentialists advocate the use of torture on terrorists or combatants in order to gain information that would save the lives of others. Even those who deem such acts to be excusable, however, would agree that they corrupt the goodness of their perpetrators.

The darker chapters in human history, including those of the modern era, have all involved torture. In fact, modern torture on a large scale, as practiced in Adolf Hitler's death camps and Joseph Stalin's gulags, has eclipsed even the horrors of the notorious

Members of the Israeli human rights group B'tselem demonstrate a torture technique they claimed was frequently used by Israeli security agents while interrogating Palestinian prisoners. The demonstration was conducted in a press conference designed to call public attention to the issue of government-inflicted torture in 1998. (AP/Wide World Photos)

Spanish Inquisition. Yet there are no places where torture is still legally sanctioned, and it is viewed as morally repugnant, if not universally, at least in more highly developed countries. That, however, has not always been the case.

JUDICIAL TORTURE

In Europe after 1300, when the Roman canon law of evidence replaced ordeal as the basis for determining criminal guilt, legal torture became widespread. Ironically, the new law, in attempting to protect the accused against capricious justice, fostered judicial torture, because the death penalty, imposed for a variety of crimes, required "full proof" (the evidence of two eyewitnesses) or "half proof" (sufficient circumstantial evidence) plus a confession. Because many crimes were not witnessed, magistrates were empowered to torture suspects to exact confessions, and

they had at their disposal the infamous devices that haunt even the modern imagination—thumb and leg screws, pressing weights, rack, iron maiden, and strappado.

Although barbaric, torture was allowed because almost all criminal offenses carried blood sanctions, from death and maiming to branding and whipping. Capital punishment, which was exacted for crimes as minor as burglary, was meted out through such gruesome means as hanging, drawing and quartering, burning at the stake, pressing, gibbeting, beheading, and impaling. Knowing what the accused faced, magistrates demanded that suspects bear witness against themselves, and they usually resorted to torture only when the suspects remained uncooperative. Torture was seldom employed in full-proof cases or when the penalties faced were less severe than execution, and its use for punishment was not widely condoned.

ABOLITION OF LEGAL TORTURE

The practice of judicial torture was gradually abandoned, partly because alternatives to death as punishment for serious criminal offenses made it less necessary. Transportation and indentured servitude, imprisonment, and conveyance to the galleys were options for judges in capital cases in which conviction was based on strong circumstantial evidence rather than incontrovertible proof. Furthermore, the validity of confessions exacted through torture had always been in doubt, and during the Enlightenment, circa 1750, that doubt was joined to the moral argu-

---

U.S. Abuse of Iraqi Prisoners

In early 2004, stunning new stories coming out of U.S.-occupied Iraq reported that U.S. military personnel had been severely and frequently abusing Iraqi prisoners under their control. The revelations were made even more shocking by the publication of photographs showing U.S. soldiers laughing and gesticulating beside such scenes as naked Iraqi men piled on top of each other and posed in positions simulating sex acts—scenes particularly abhorrent to Muslims. These revelations prompted Army and government investigations that led to changes in the command structure, the disciplining of key personnel, and criminal charges against those directly responsible for acts of abuse. Investigations and criminal proceedings continued through the year. Meanwhile, Americans were left to ponder how it was possible for fellow citizens representing the United States to participate in such unethical behavior.

Most news stories focused on Abu Ghraib, a prison near Baghdad administered by the U.S. military since the fall of Saddam Hussein's regime in early 2003. During Hussein's time, Abu Ghraib had been a notorious center of torture and secret executions of suspected government opponents. After Hussein's regime fell, Iraqi civilians gutted the prison, but the U.S. Army soon renovated the facility and began using it as a detention center for common criminals, civilians suspected of committing "crimes against the coalition," and known leaders of anticoalition insurgent movements.

Abu Ghraib's already unsavory reputation combined with the revelations of U.S. misbehavior to raise protests against the U.S. occupation to new levels both within and outside Iraq. Recognition of these acts of torture did irreparable damage to the moral reputation of the United States. As the scandal unfolded, evidence of U.S. military misconduct grew. In April, 2004, *The New Yorker* magazine obtained a copy of the official report of a secret Army investigation of the scandal written by Major General Antonio M. Taguba in February. According to Taguba, numerous instances of "sadistic, blatant, and wanton criminal abuses" had occurred at Abu Ghraib during the previous autumn.

Two Iraqi men rest in the shade of a wall decorated with graffiti condemning American treatment of prisoners. One illustration is a faithful copy of one of the most notorious photographs taken at Abu Ghraib: A hooded Iraqi standing on a flimsy box was told that if he fell off the box, he would be electrocuted by the wires attached to his body. (AP/Wide World Photos)

ments promulgated against torture by such thinkers as Voltaire. By the end of the nineteenth century, legal torture had become an anomaly, and protections against it, as provided by the "cruel and unusual punishment" injunction of the Eighth Amendment to the U.S. Constitution, were almost universally in place.

MODERN TORTURE

It is, however, one thing to abolish a practice on paper, to make it illegal, and another to curtail completely its practice. As late as 1984, when the United Nations adopted the Convention Against Torture and Other Cruel, Inhuman, or Degrading Treatment or Punishment, dozens of nations, in violation of their own laws, were secretly sanctioning its use. In recent history, it has been a particularly invidious practice during war, despite Geneva Conference protocols, and during civil unrest and insurrection, when it has been used as an instrument of persecution and suppression, as in internally troubled states such as Chile, El Salvador, South Africa, Cambodia, and the former Yugoslavian state of Bosnia-Herzegovina.

It is unlikely that torture can ever be completely eradicated. It only takes two, persecutor and victim, to dance torture's grim dance, and the potential for torture exists in any interpersonal relationship in which one party exercises physical or psychological control over another, as in, for example, familial relationships between parent and child or husband and wife.

The crude instruments of the *ancien régime* are now museum pieces, but they have been replaced by such things as psychoactive "brainwashing" drugs and electroshock, courtesy of modern science. The crude methods have not disappeared, even in the United States, as the burned, scarred, and starved bodies of abused children have testified.

Although organizations such as Amnesty International can bring before the United Nations evidence of the torture of citizens by governments, exposure of its practice under private circumstances—for example, within the family—has depended largely on the willingness of victims to complain. In the last few decades, victims have been more inclined to seek help and legal remedy, encouraged by civil rights legisla-

tion, counseling, and an awareness, fostered by media coverage of abuse, that their situation is not unique. Tragically, tortured children are often too young to know that redress is even possible.

The belief that the modern era is more humane and more morally astute than were previous eras is partly illusory. Although modern efforts to rectify human abuse and cruelty may be unprecedented, extending even to animals, modern events have repeatedly revealed and psychological studies have often documented that the sadomasochistic impulses that lie behind torture frequently accompany such fundamental human feelings as frustration, rage, guilt, and shame. The best hope for ending torture lies in legal recourse made possible by public awareness and ethical vigilance.

John W. Fiero

FURTHER READING

Amnesty International. *Report of an Amnesty International Mission to Israel and the Syrian Arab Republic to Investigate Allegations of Ill-Treatment and Torture, 10-24 October 1974*. London: Author, 1975.

_____. *Torture in the Eighties*. London: Author, 1984.

Dunér, Bertil, ed. *An End to Torture: Strategies for Its Eradication*. New York: St. Martin's Press, 1998.

Foucault, Michel. "The Body of the Condemned." In *Discipline and Punish: The Birth of the Prison*, translated by Alan Sheridan. New York: Vintage Books, 1979.

Langbein, John H. *Torture and the Law of Proof: Europe and England in the Ancien Régime*. Chicago: University of Chicago Press, 1977.

Peters, Edward. *Torture*. New York: Blackwell Publishers, 1985.

Stover, Eric, and Elena O. Nightingale, eds. *The Breaking of Bodies and Minds*. New York: W. H. Freeman, 1985.

SEE ALSO: Abuse; Amnesty International; Animal rights; Coercion; Cruelty; Electroshock therapy; Holocaust; Military ethics; Oppression; Punishment; Terrorism.

Toxic waste

DEFINITION: Poisonous or other dangerous substances needing specialized forms of disposal

TYPE OF ETHICS: Environmental ethics

SIGNIFICANCE: Ethical practices of toxic waste disposal are those that protect the environment and human life.

By the early twenty-first century, toxic waste was spreading throughout the world at an alarming rate. To protect the environment and human life, ethical practices must be employed to dispose of toxic waste materials generated by industry, agriculture, consumers, and individual persons. The numerous toxic-waste disposal abuses of the past were sometimes due to ignorance or carelessness; however, many abuses were due to the unethical practices used to save companies or individuals time and money in waste disposal. Disposed toxic substances can be highly detrimental to people, whether the people are aware that they are being exposed to the materials or not. Among other things, careless, unethical dumping of toxic waste has produced dirty streams, greasy drinking water, noxious fumes, and human suffering, disease, and death.

TOXIC SITES

During the nineteenth and twentieth centuries, many toxic waste substances were spread into the air, soil, and water. For example, Love Canal, an artificial waterway that was built near Niagara Falls, New York, during the 1890's became a site of industrial toxic waste disposal, with more than forty toxic organic compounds found in the canal and in nearby soil, water, and air samples collected during the late 1970's. In May, 1980, the federal Environmental Protection Agency released a study showing a rate of chromosome damage among babies born to people living near the Love Canal site. Among myriad other sites where dumped toxic wastes have produced documented cancer, mysterious health problems, and other devastating effects are Waukegan Harbor, Illinois; Times Beach, Missouri; Woburn, Massachusetts; Mapleton, Utah; and Bhopal, India.

Many of the more than fifty thousand toxic-waste-producing firms in the United States contract with waste-disposal companies to provide ethical, scientifically sound, legal ways to dispose of their waste materials. Some companies dump or bury their toxic wastes on-site. In many instances when problems develop, waste disposers claim that the problems are not serious and decline to spend any money to clean up disposal sites. This difficulty led the U.S. Congress to pass the Comprehensive Environmental Response, Compensation, and Liability Act in 1980, which included the establishment of the Superfund to pay for immediate cleanup of abandoned toxic-waste sites and inoperative sites where the owners refuse to clean them up.

As the numbers of toxic waste sites, the amounts and varieties of chemical contamination, and cleanup costs continue to escalate, the only feasible solutions for protecting the environment and human life and rights appear to be regulatory controls that focus on waste minimization and ethical practices of waste disposal. Grassroots organizations across America demand that the government legislate and enforce such action.

Alvin K. Benson

FURTHER READING

Crawford, Mark. *Toxic Waste Sites: An Encyclopedia of Endangered America*. Santa Barbara, Calif.: ABC-CLIO, 1997.

Girdner, Eddie J., and Jack Smith. *Killing Me Softly: Toxic Waste, Corporate Profit, and the Struggle for Environmental Justice*. New York: Monthly Review Press, 2002.

Setterberg, Fred, and Lonny Shavelson. *Toxic Nation: The Fight to Save Our Communities from Chemical Contamination*. New York: John Wiley & Sons, 1993.

SEE ALSO: Bioethics; Birth defects; Business ethics; Environmental ethics; Environmental movement; Environmental Protection Agency; "Not in my backyard"; Nuclear energy; Pollution permits; *Silent Spring*; Sustainability of resources.

Tragedy

DEFINITION: Form of literary drama and a topic of philosophical investigation that involves the extremes of human behavior in the face of life's great misfortunes

TYPE OF ETHICS: Theory of ethics

SIGNIFICANCE: Both tragedy and ethics focus on the moral value of human conduct in the face of life's conflicts and extremities.

The term "tragedy" has been used in at least two distinct senses. First, tragedy refers to a genre of literary and dramatic works originally developed in ancient Greece. Aristotle defined tragedy, in this first sense, as an imitation (a theatrical play) of an action by, typically, a noble person whose character is flawed by a single weakness (such as pride or envy) that causes him to make an error in judgment resulting in his downfall. The hero moves from a state of ignorance to one of insight generally at the cost of personal misery. Aristotle believed the spectator of a tragic drama underwent a catharsis, or cleansing, of his own emotions.

In the second sense, tragedy has been used to refer to a subject of philosophical theorizing involving the meaning of tragic literature as well as the possible existence of tragic events in the world that must be philosophically reckoned with in any worldview. It is in this latter meaning of tragedy that the primary ethical import lies. However, it is unlikely that the two senses of the term can or should be completely disentangled, since presumably literature and drama often mirror something significant about human existence.

Plato, unlike Aristotle, believed that there were several ethically undesirable consequences of Greek tragedy and drama. Plato condemned tragic poetry for making men too emotional. Tragic drama, Plato argued, implies that a good person may be undone by an accidental reversal of fortune. Tragedies thus teach the young that their well-being is contingent upon the whims and vagaries of appearance. For Plato, the world of appearance and consequently what generally passes for "tragedy" is ultimately unreal. Even one's physical death is tragic only as long as one is in ignorance. For example, Socrates, Plato's teacher, understood the immortality and superiority of the real; hence, he did not fear the hemlock poison that the Athenian town counsel required him to drink.

What appeared to be a tragedy was in actuality a great victory for the good. Tragedies, however, encourage the audience to think that a hero can be undone by an accidental reversal of fortune. Consequently, for Plato, tragedies teach falsely and inspire fear of unrealities.

THE GERMAN PHILOSOPHERS

The early nineteenth century German philosopher G. W. F. Hegel held that, in the first sense noted above, Aristotle's definition of tragedy was definitive. In the second sense, however, tragedy is motivated by a conflict of two great moral forces, both justified and both embodying the good. For example, in Sophocles' ancient Greek play *Antigone*, one protagonist—Antigone—is motivated by justifiable family values to provide a proper burial for her brother, while King Creon is equally justified by public values to prevent her from doing so. The task of the tragic hero is to attain a "synthesis" in which the claims of each side are reconciled. Antigone and Creon are both right but not right enough. Consequently, their destruction is just and reveals the absolute rule of the divine principle. Hence, in Hegel, the ethical dilemma of tragedy consists in the conflict between two goods that can be resolved only through a higher synthesis of good. In one-sidedness, the tragic hero fails to comprehend this synthesis and is justifiably overruled and destroyed by the might of absolute justice.

Arthur Schopenhauer, taking a consistently pessimistic view of human life, argued that all existence is tragic. Quoting an ancient Greek source, he noted that the greatest thing that one could ever hope for was to have never been born. A quick death would be the next most desirable event. Thus, tragic art reveals the terrible side of life, which relentlessly destroys and annihilates anything that the human spirit might cherish. For Schopenhauer, tragedy teaches that the only resolution to the arbitrary cruelties of life is total renunciation of the will.

Friedrich Nietzsche, a student of Schopenhauer, believed that Greek tragedy answered a fundamental need of human life. Greek tragedy gave the Greeks the ability to face the horrors and arbitrariness of life and yet find a basis for self-affirmation. Nietzsche, while acknowledging the reality of human suffering, rejected the excessive rationalism of Plato and the excessive pessimism of Schopenhauer. In the two

Greek gods Dionysus and Apollo, Nietzsche discovered two basic elements of human nature. Dionysus embodies excess, vitality, and passion, while Apollo represents reason, order, and balance. In the time of the ancient Greeks, the tragic art form accomplished a unification of these tendencies and enabled the Greek culture to grow strong and noble.

In Nietzsche's later work, he showed that perception of the tragic realities of life could lead in two directions: to nihilism or to the superman. The superman is an individual who declares, "Joy is deeper than woe!" He affirms life and self in full light of the ambiguities and tragic qualities to which human flesh is heir. These elite and noble "Yea-Sayers" of Nietzsche represent his answer to the ethical challenge given by the tragic aspect of life.

During the late twentieth century, there was a general concern that the tragic sense of life had been lost, to the detriment of humanity's self-image. Tragedy has generally depicted a sometimes horrifying but heroic picture of the human condition. Although in tragedy there have been great "reversals of fortune," there has also been the implication that humanity has fallen from a great height. The twentieth century did not sustain a vision of human nature that was sufficient for great tragedy. For example, in Samuel Beckett's *Waiting for Godot* (1954) and Arthur Miller's *Death of a Salesman* (1949), tragedy was superseded by the Theater of the Absurd. The protagonists of these tragicomedies minimize the horror and terror of life but also fail even to hint at its possible greatness. These antiheroes exit the stage with a "whimper," not a bang.

Some recent developments did, however, follow the ennobling promises of modernity. Miguel de Unamuno y Jugo (1864-1936), author of *The Tragic Sense of Life*, argued that humanity thirsts for a status in life that reason cannot support. People live in the tragic sense of life when they refuse to abandon either the heart or the intellect. Humanity is neither God nor worm, but something in between. Unamuno suggests that this tension is unresolvable, yet people may live authentically by refusing to deny either aspect of life. Thus, a form of "tragic optimism" appeared to be emerging in the late twentieth century. By following the guidelines of Nietzsche, Unamuno, and other twentieth century philosophers, it is possible to recapture the nobility of humanity at the expense of illusions about absolutes. In the recognition

that life is a mystery to be heroically lived and not a problem to be intellectually solved, the birth pain of a new postmodern form of tragedy may be heard.

Paul Rentz

FURTHER READING

Cavell, Stanley. *Disowning Knowledge in Seven Plays of Shakespeare.* Updated ed. New York: Cambridge University Press, 2003.

Eagleton, Terry. *Sweet Violence: The Idea of the Tragic.* Malden, Mass.: Blackwell, 2003.

Hegel, Georg Wilhelm Friedrich. *Hegel on Tragedy.* Edited by Anne Paolucci and Henry Paolucci. Smyrna, Del.: Griffon House, 2001.

Kaufmann, Walter A. *Tragedy and Philosophy.* Garden City, N.Y.: Doubleday, 1968.

Nietzsche, Friedrich. *The Birth of Tragedy.* Translated by Douglas Smith. New York: Oxford University Press, 2000.

Nussbaum, Martha C. *The Fragility of Goodness: Luck and Ethics in Greek Tragedy and Philosophy.* New York: Cambridge University Press, 1986.

Unamuno, Miguel de. *The Tragic Sense of Life in Men and Nations.* Princeton, N.J.: Princeton University Press, 1972.

Weitz, Morris. "Tragedy." In *The Encyclopedia of Philosophy*, edited by Paul Edwards. Vol. 8. New York: Macmillan, 1972.

SEE ALSO: Aristotle; Hegel, Georg Wilhelm Friedrich; Narrative ethics; Nietzsche, Friedrich; Plato; Schopenhauer, Arthur; Unamuno y Jugo, Miguel de.

Transcendentalism

DEFINITION: Philosophical belief in an objective reality that exists beyond human experience

TYPE OF ETHICS: Theory of ethics

SIGNIFICANCE: Transcendentalism holds that the structure of the mind both grounds, and determines the limits of, human knowledge, and that there is an absolute division between human knowledge and reality. Some schools of transcendentalism also believe that the gap between experience and the real world can be breached in moments of irrational spirituality that provide guidance as to the ethically proper way to live one's life. Others emphasize the rational nature of reality and assert that obeying rational moral law is the only way to achieve harmony with the objective world.

Transcendentalism was an idealistic revolt against materialist philosophies such as John Locke's empiricism, Sir Isaac Newton's mechanism, and William Paley's utilitarianism. In those materialist theories, one's code of behavior derived from a compilation of sensory experiences by means of which one determined what was good or useful. The transcendentalist, however, believed that one's code of behavior preceded his or her experiences, that the structure of ideas inherent in the mind itself molded ethical conduct.

ORIGINS

Although the term "transcendental" had been employed by medieval philosophers, the Prussian philosopher Immanuel Kant first used the term in its modern meaning during the late eighteenth century. His *Critique of Pure Reason* (1781) addressed a fundamental philosophical question: Does all knowledge come from the senses' interactions with the world, or is some knowledge embedded in the mind prior to sensory experiences? He concluded that there were ideas that "transcended" experience and that ethical conduct was a matter of the mind's inherent desire to act consistently with itself.

Philosophers and literary figures in Germany, France, Great Britain, and the United States who were seeking a liberating idealism believed that they had found it in Kant's work. His idea that the mind contained a set of moral ideas that helped mold a person's relationship to the universe made his theories a welcome alternative to materialistically based ones. His idea that one's primary ethical duty was to remain faithful to the ethical laws dictated by one's own mind appealed to those who were hungry for a more spiritually and individually based set of ethics. Many strongly believed that this set of transcendent ideas was humankind's connection to God, in which its highest and noblest aspirations could be found.

AMERICAN TRANSCENDENTALISM

Among those who were influenced by Kant were the American Transcendentalists, although they received his philosophy secondhand through the works of the British authors Samuel Taylor Coleridge and Thomas Carlyle. This group consisted generally of New Englanders, many of them Unitarian ministers or former ministers, who were most influential from the first meeting of the Transcendental Club in 1836 until the American Civil War. Prominent members of the movement were Bronson Alcott, George Ripley, Theodore Parker, William H. Channing, Margaret Fuller, Henry David Thoreau, and Ralph Waldo Emerson, most of whom also contributed to the literary journal *The Dial*.

A popular idea among the group was Coleridge's simplified version of Kant's theory that the mind was divided into a higher faculty, called "reason," that sought to systematize and unify the various impressions collected and analyzed by the lower faculty, termed the "understanding." The works of Emerson and Thoreau both emphasize reason. "Higher laws" or "spiritual laws," as they called them, ranked above the mechanical rules of cause and effect in the material world and gave unity and ethical purpose to human activities. The permanence of the higher laws appealed to these thinkers, who deplored the utilitarian values and relative ethics that seemed to have replaced principled behavior. They also liked Kant's idea that the source of morals, and thus the closest link to God, was found in one's own mind. From this premise, they developed their influential concept of self-reliance.

Many of the major works of American Transcendentalism appropriated Kant's idea that morality exists in the mind and fused it with a mystical belief that a divine spirit was prevalent in nature. In *Nature* (1836), Emerson argued that ethics and the natural world were inextricably linked: "the moral law lies at the centre of nature. . . . All things with which we deal, preach to us. What is a farm but a mute gospel?" Thoreau expressed similar thoughts in *Walden* (1854). He spent two years at Walden Pond, where he built his own house, planted and harvested his own food, and yet reserved ample time for reflection. He consistently linked the simple acts of his daily life, such as hoeing a bean field or plumbing the depths of the pond, to the immanence of a universal spirit.

Although they resisted the trendiness of social movements, the American Transcendentalists were attracted to the moral issues raised by those movements. Margaret Fuller, in *Woman in the Nineteenth Century* (1845), argued the case for women's rights.

Thoreau went to jail rather than pay taxes that supported an immoral war, an experience that he chronicled in "Resistance to Civil Government" (1849), and in "Slavery in Massachusetts" (1854), he opposed slavery and the moral irresponsibility of those who allowed themselves to become accomplices to its evil.

Aside from the major political events of their time, the Transcendentalists were also concerned with the ethical content of their own day-to-day lives and those of their fellow citizens. In "The Transcendentalist" (1842), Emerson seemed almost to plead with his audience that it "tolerate one or two solitary voices in the land, speaking for thoughts and principles not marketable or perishable." Thoreau, in "Life Without Principle" (1863), makes a similar case for the role of principles in the too often materialistic lives of the populace.

After several centuries of empirically based philosophy, Transcendentalism provided strong evidence that humankind still recognized a spiritual element in its personality. The Transcendentalists believed that innate spiritual insights were essential in directing ethical judgments.

William L. Howard

FURTHER READING

Boller, Paul F. *American Transcendentalism, 1830-1860: An Intellectual Inquiry.* New York: Putnam, 1974.

Cavell, Stanley. *Emerson's Transcendental Etudes.* Stanford, Calif.: Stanford University Press, 2003.

Emerson, Ralph Waldo. *Essays and Lectures.* New York: Viking Press, 1983.

Frothingham, Octavius Brooks. *Transcendentalism in New England: A History.* New York: Harper, 1959.

Illies, Christian F. R. *The Grounds of Ethical Judgment: New Transcendental Arguments in Moral Philosophy.* New York: Oxford University Press, 2003.

Kant, Immanuel. *Critique of Pure Reason.* Translated by Norman Kemp Smith. Introduction by Howard Caygill. Rev. 2d ed. New York: Palgrave Macmillan, 2003.

Koster, Donald N. *Transcendentalism in America.* Boston: Twayne, 1975.

Malpas, Jeff, ed. *From Kant to Davidson: Philosophy and the Idea of the Transcendental.* New York: Routledge, 2003.

Thoreau, Henry David. *"Walden" and "Civil Disobedience": Complete Texts with Introduction, Historical Contexts, Critical Essays.* Edited by Paul Lauter. Boston: Houghton Mifflin, 2000.

SEE ALSO: Emerson, Ralph Waldo; Idealist ethics; Kant, Immanuel; Kantian ethics; Thoreau, Henry David; *Walden*.

Treason

DEFINITION: Betrayal of one's nation or one's government to its enemies, foreign or domestic
TYPE OF ETHICS: Politico-economic ethics
SIGNIFICANCE: Essentially a crime of disloyalty, treason raises the issue of the relative importance or precedence of competing types of loyalty, including loyalty to one's nation, ideals, family, religion, racial or ethnic group, class, gender, and self. The more idealized or mythologized a national government becomes, the more heinous acts of treason against it will seem.

The U.S. Constitution defines treason as "giving aid and comfort to the enemies of the United States." In most legal systems, however, treason consists also in attempting to overthrow the legal government within the state, and it may be supplemented by crimes such as espionage and sedition. Most ethical systems see one as having moral obligations, including loyalty, to one's nation and to its rulers. Treason, therefore, is ordinarily a seriously blameworthy act, and the attendant horrors of foreign military conquest or revolutionary upheaval add to its inherent evils.

An anarchist could scarcely acknowledge the legitimacy of the concept of treason, but supporters of natural law and Kantian ethics, for example, would advocate a strong degree of deference owed to the sovereign but would also acknowledge that the sovereign may be defied, overthrown, or even assassinated if he or she commands or commits great evil.

Although there is almost universal opprobrium attached to treason done for profit or advancement, other cases of treason are muddied by the contrast of the objective evaluation of the ideology, religion, or philosophy prompting the act with the subjective element of the traitor's personal commitment to that belief.

Noted Historical Figures Charged with Treason

Name	Basis of treason charges
Niccolò Machiavelli	Tried for treason for opposing Florence's Medici family and sent into exile in 1512.
Guy Fawkes	Executed for plot to blow up England's Parliament and king in 1605.
James Scott, Duke of Monmouth	Executed for rebelling against England's King James II in 1685.
John Locke	Branded a traitor for his association with Monmouth; went into exile in the Netherlands.
Benedict Arnold	U.S. general who plotted to surrender West Point to British forces in 1780.
Aaron Burr	Allegedly conspired to take over western territories of United States during Thomas Jefferson's administration.
Sir Roger Casement	Executed in 1916 for plotting with Germany to obtain arms for Irish rebels.
Mildred Gillars, a.k.a. "Axis Sally"	American who broadcast propaganda for Germany during World War II.
Iva Toguri, a.k.a. "Tokyo Rose"	American who allegedly broadcast propaganda for Japan during World War II.
Ezra Pound	American who broadcast propaganda for Italy during World War II.
William Joyce, a.k.a. "Lord Haw-Haw"	British subject who broadcast propaganda for Germany during World War II.
Henri-Philippe Pétain and Pierre Laval	French leaders who collaborated with German occupation forces during World War II.
Vidkun Quisling	Norwegian officer executed in 1945 for collaborating with German occupation forces during World War II; his name afteward became synonymous with "traitor."
Alger Hiss	Allegedly spied on United States for the Soviet Union during the 1930's-1940's.
Julius Rosenberg and Ethel Rosenberg	Executed in 1953 for allegedly spying on U.S. atom bomb project for the Soviet Union.
Klaus Emil J. Fuchs	Stole British and U.S. atomic secrets for the Soviet Union during the 1940's.
Guy Burgess, Kim Philby, and Donald Maclean	Spied on British intelligence operations for the Soviet Union during the 1940's-1950's.
Sir Anthony Blunt	Spied on Britain for the Soviet Union durng the 1930's-1950's.
John Anthony Walker	Spied on U.S. military for the Soviet Union 1970's-1980's.

Treaty of Versailles

Henri-Philippe Pétain (1856-1951) was one of France's greatest military heroes during World War I, but for collaborating with Nazi Germany by heading the puppet Vichy regime during World War II he was branded a traitor. After the war, he was convicted of treason; his sentence was commuted to life imprisonment, and he died in disgrace at the age of ninety-five. (Library of Congress)

The "judgment of history" often seems particularly amoral. To cite one example, Adolf Hitler is never labeled a traitor despite his having tried unsuccessfully to overthrow the Bavarian state government in the Munich "Beerhall Putsch," because his eventual capture of the German government a decade later seems to have extinguished the guilt of treason in that view.

Patrick M. O'Neil

SEE ALSO: Citizenship; Duty; Espionage; Nationalism; Patriotism; Politics; Revolution; Sedition.

IDENTIFICATION: Treaty that formally ended the state of war between Germany and the Entente powers, concluding World War I
DATE: Ratified on June 28, 1919
TYPE OF ETHICS: International relations
SIGNIFICANCE: The Treaty of Versailles imposed harsh, economically disruptive conditions upon Germany aimed at permanently reducing its ability to wage war upon other nations and to act as a world power. These conditions undermined democracy in Germany and arguably fostered the nationalistic excesses that produced Nazi totalitarianism, state terrorism, and renewed global warfare.

The treaty encouraged the rise of German fascism and was an underlying cause of World War II. The German surrender in 1918 was based on a general acceptance of President Woodrow Wilson's Fourteen Points. In formulating the peace terms, the British and French ignored most of those points.

The treaty stripped Germany of human and material resources, in violation of its avowed goals of national self-determination and respect for territorial integrity, and reduced the German armed forces to a level that was incompatible with national defense. It also imposed crushing indemnities upon Germany and forced Germans to accept sole war guilt. The treaty's blatant unfairness and economically destabilizing consequences, further aggravated by the onset of the Great Depression in 1931, aided the success of Adolf Hitler's revanchist, extremist National Socialist (Nazi) Party. Hitler's sustained efforts to reverse the Versailles treaty provoked World War II, the most devastating conflict in history.

Michael J. Fontenot

SEE ALSO: Fascism; Hitler, Adolf; League of Nations; Nationalism.

Triage

DEFINITION: Process of sorting victims of war, accident, or disaster to determine priority of medical treatment

TYPE OF ETHICS: Bioethics

SIGNIFICANCE: Triage is perhaps the most extreme single instance of ethically difficult resource allocation. It requires immediate, life-and-death decisions to be made about whose injuries will be treated first and who will be left to wait. The major ethical question raised by triage is whether severity of injury is the only appropriate criterion for determining priority, or whether other considerations such as age, occupation, social status, membership in the enemy military, and criminal record may be considered.

Triage employs a utilitarian calculation concerning how to do the most good with whatever resources are available, determining which patients will be helped at all, and in which order those to be helped will be treated. Triage may be employed in any situation in which all the injured, sick, or wounded cannot be treated: on the battlefield, at the site of a natural disaster, in the first moments of a traffic accident, in the emergency room of a large hospital, or in a country suffering from mass starvation. Triage is more easily defended than are some other types of utilitarian calculations, since there is no intent to sacrifice the innocent for the greater good of the majority. Since triage does require that one make a "quality of life" judgment before one decides which victims will be helped, however, it may be an ethically objectionable practice. If it is wrong to judge who is worth helping and who is not, then it is arguable that triage should be replaced with a "first-come-first-helped" principle.

Daniel G. Baker

SEE ALSO: Lifeboat ethics; Medical ethics; Military ethics; "Playing god" in medical decision making; Utilitarianism.

Truman Doctrine

IDENTIFICATION: Foreign policy initiative undertaken by the U.S. president Harry S. Truman's administration to prevent the spread of Soviet communism into Greece and Turkey

DATE: Promulgated on March 12, 1947

TYPE OF ETHICS: International relations

SIGNIFICANCE: The Truman Doctrine signaled a shift in American foreign policy. It proclaimed a sphere of influence in the Middle East, which had never been a traditional interest of the United States.

The Truman Doctrine was prompted by the British government's announcement that it would withdraw from Greece after the British had liberated the country from the Nazis in 1944. After World War II, the Soviet Union was a threat to the Balkan Peninsula, and the Eastern European communist regimes were aiding the Greek communists in their civil war against the Greek government. To offset this communist threat, Truman asked the Congress for $400 million for military and economic aid to Greece and Turkey.

Bill Manikas

SEE ALSO: Cold War; Communism; International justice; International law; North Atlantic Treaty Organization; Potsdam Conference.

Trustworthiness

DEFINITION: Disposition of character that leads people to do reliably what others have a right to expect of them

TYPE OF ETHICS: Personal and social ethics

SIGNIFICANCE: Trustworthiness is a crucial virtue for people living together in a community, in which personal, commercial, and professional relationships depend on it

Trustworthiness involves both words and conduct. A trustworthy person speaks truthfully to others, and therefore the words of such a person are to be trusted. Also, a trustworthy person is willing to make commitments concerning future behavior, and can and will keep whatever commitments have been entered into; therefore, the conduct of such a person is to be relied upon. A trustworthy mechanic, for example, can be counted on both to tell one truthfully what repairs one's automobile needs and to fulfill the terms of any contract that he or she enters into to do the work.

Trustworthiness is an admirable trait of character because it is socially useful. Hence, it is appropriate to classify it as a moral virtue, even though it has been little discussed by traditional ethical theorists, the word "trustworthy" having entered English only in the nineteenth century.

The term "trustworthy" is ambiguous because it does not specify whether it refers to trustworthiness in some specific respect or trustworthiness as a pervasive disposition of a person's character. When one calls a mechanic trustworthy, one is usually speaking only of trustworthiness regarding automotive repairs, though one could mean to say that the person is trustworthy in all aspects of life. Marital fidelity and honesty in paying income tax will count as evidence of trustworthiness in a mechanic only when the second, broader meaning is intended.

RELATIONSHIP TO OTHER VIRTUES

Trustworthiness is akin to and overlaps such other virtues as truthfulness, honesty, and fidelity, but it is distinguishable from each of these. Trustworthiness differs from truthfulness in that the latter pertains only to communication, while the former can relate to a much wider range of behavior. Trustworthiness differs from honesty in that it can concern the keeping of commitments of any kind, not merely those the breach of which would be dishonest. It differs from fidelity in that trustworthiness requires greater effectiveness in the carrying out of commitments than is needed for fidelity; thus, a loyal but incompetent person can be faithful without being trustworthy.

Trustworthiness must also be distinguished from trustfulness (which is not, in general, a virtue) and from the appropriate degrees of trust that ought to pervade various relationships (these degrees of trust often arise only in proportion as the participants are properly trustworthy, yet this proportionality is merely contingent).

Within the family and in personal relationships generally, trustworthiness is required if all is to go well. When a husband is worthy of his wife's trust and she of his, this makes it likelier that they will indeed trust each other and that their affections will remain firm and their responsibilities will be effectively shared. Lovers, friends, neighbors, and acquaintances all will find that their relationships tend to be strengthened when there are appropriate degrees of trustworthiness on each side.

Some feminist thinkers have particularly focused on the importance of trustworthiness. Sara Ruddick, for example, writes of trustworthiness as one of the virtues especially needed by a mother who is to have a sound relationship with her child. She stresses that the child must be able to rely on the mother to stand up for it against the father, against intrusive government, and against the archaic mores of society. Ruddick's emphasis is controversial, and one might wish to add that children also need to find their fathers trustworthy and need to be taught to be trustworthy themselves. In any case, trustworthiness on all sides seems to be indispensable for good family relationships.

Is trustworthiness more prized in men by women than it is in women by men? There may be some truth in Arthur Schopenhauer's view that women prize stability (and hence trustworthiness) in their liaisons, while men tend to seek variety. Yet such sweeping generalizations carry little weight.

TRUSTWORTHINESS IN BUSINESS

It is in the world of business, however, that trustworthiness finds its most distinctive place in modern life, especially in connection with the provision of financial services. Banking activities of a recognizable kind seem to have had their origin during the Renaissance in the dealings of merchant families, among whom the Medici and the Fuggers were leaders. Initially, these families had merely bought and sold on their own account, but then gradually they began to provide financial services to others, transferring money from one city to another, holding deposits, making commercial loans, and insuring against the loss of ships and shipments. The availability of these services became enormously helpful to commerce and set the stage for the rise of capitalism.

It was essential that the providers of such services should develop strong reputations for trustworthiness, since no merchant wanted to deposit funds except with a banker who could be relied upon to handle them as promised. The concept of trust (Latin, *fiducia*) has been central to the activities of banking and insurance from the start. Members of these businesses always have sought to cultivate favorable reputations and have found that the most reliable way of doing so is by actually being trustworthy. Since the eighteenth century, the fiduciary trustworthiness of corporate entities has come to be even more important than that of individuals and families (some corporate entities even came to be called "trusts"). Without fiduciary trust, the economic world as it is known could not exist.

In the professions, such as medicine and law, trustworthiness also has come to play a central role. The patient or client is not equipped to make independent judgments about the complex technicalities of medicine or law and therefore must rely on the knowledge and technical skill of the professional, as well as on the professional's motivation to serve well. Only professionals who acquire reputations for trustworthiness are likely to be successful in the long run. Part of the role of professional organizations has been to promote trustworthy behavior by members of the professions and to encourage potential patients and clients to trust them.

Stephen F. Barker

FURTHER READING

Baier, Annette. "Trust and Antitrust." *Ethics* 96, no. 2 (January, 1986): 231-260.

Bok, Sissela. *Lying: Moral Choice in Public and Private Life.* 2d ed. New York: Vintage Books, 1999.

Golin, Al. *Trust or Consequences: Build Trust Today or Lose Your Market Tomorrow.* New York: American Management Association, 2004.

Murphy, Kevin R. *Honesty in the Workplace.* Pacific Grove, Calif.: Brooks/Cole, 1993.

Pellegrino, Edmund D., et al., eds. *Ethics, Trust, and the Professions.* Washington, D.C.: Georgetown University Press, 1991.

Potter, Nancy Nyquist. *How Can I Be Trusted?: A Virtue Theory of Trustworthiness.* Lanham, Md.: Rowman & Littlefield, 2002.

Ruddick, Sara. *Maternal Thinking: Toward a Politics of Peace.* Boston: Beacon Press, 1995.

SEE ALSO: Business ethics; Feminist ethics; Honesty; Loyalty; Personal relationships; Professional ethics; Promises; Truth; Virtue.

Truth

DEFINITION: Factual, actual, and real
TYPE OF ETHICS: Theory of ethics
SIGNIFICANCE: Truth is the central object of philosophical inquiry, and no consensus exists as to any aspect of it. At one extreme lies the belief that there is an objective reality, and objective truth exists either in the world or beyond it. At the other lies the belief that truth merely names the set of conventional beliefs and common metaphors in circulation in a given society, and it is generated by rhetoric rather than reality.

Truth is a feature of propositions—assertions, statements, and claims. If one claims that one's notebook is on a desk, and it is, one's claim is true. The desk is not true and the notebook is not true: They simply exist. If one removes the notebook but makes the same assertion as before, the assertion is false, but falseness would still not be a characteristic of the desk or the notebook. Equally, the number nine is neither true or false, but the equation $9 + 5 = 14$ is true, while $9 + 15 = 23$ is false.

Truthful statements or assertions represent "things" as they are—reality. False assertions do not depict things as they are. Truthful statements and falsehoods depend on those things as they are, not on a person's (or a society's) beliefs, desires, wishes, or prejudices. Furthermore, at the elemental level of logic, the "law of the excluded middle" is operative. According to that law, it is assumed that statements or claims have only two possible conditions: A claim is either true or false.

Throughout history, philosophers have attempted to develop sweeping theories to explain the nature of truth and its opposite, falsehood.

COHERENCE THEORY

Several philosophical theories of truth are extant, one being the coherence theory. Its groundbreakers include such thinkers as Baruch Spinoza, G. W. F. Hegel, and Gottfried Leibniz, and it is associated with the great rationalist system-making metaphysicians. In coherence theory, when one says that a statement or judgment is true or false, one means that the statement coheres or does not cohere with other statements, which, taken together, create a "system" that is held together either by logic or by pure mathematics. To be called "true," a statement must fit into a comprehensive account of the universe and its reality. In everyday language, people often reject outlandish assertions (such as someone claiming that he or she sees ghosts or claiming that God visits him or her every day) because the assertions do not cohere with other scientific views or even with common sense.

Believers in the coherence theory justify their position, in part, on the basis of their view of the theory of knowledge and also, in part, on the basis of a priori reasoning such as that found in such fields as mathematics and logic. They believe that all knowledge is a vastly organized and logically expressed interlocking series of statements or judgments.

Critics who reject the coherence theory point out that a priori statements that are typical of mathematics and physics are unlike empirical statements about observations of everyday life, and thus they give priority to empirical evidence rather than a priori judgments. For example, scientists may have determined by observation that water boils at 100 degrees Celsius but may, after further observation, learn that the statement is true of water at sea level but is not true of water at higher altitudes; either way, empirical evidence is the key to "the truth."

CORRESPONDENCE THEORY

Influenced by Bertrand Russell, many modern philosophers embrace the correspondence theory of truth, which holds that the truth corresponds to reality. As Russell defined the term, truth exists in some form of correspondence between belief and fact (reality). Actually, the lineage of this belief can be traced back to Aristotle, who held that "A" is always "A" and "non-A" is never "A." By the "facts" of a case, the case is true if the "facts" are true or is false if the "facts" are untrue. The "liar's paradox," however, bedevils those who embrace this theory. Eubulides, a Megarian philosopher, a near contemporary of Aristotle, first formulated the paradox: "I am a liar, and what I'm now saying is false." Correspondence theorists would have to reason that the statement is true if the man is a liar; that is, it is true if it itself is false, but false if it is true.

Writing after the turn of the twentieth century, G. E. Moore justified the correspondence theory on the grounds that statements that reflect reality are true and those that do not reflect reality are false.

Moore held that truth is agreement between belief and fact. If the former is true, there is a "fact" in the universe to which the belief corresponds; if the belief were false, there would be no "fact" to which it could correspond. Bertrand Russell added that there can be no incompatibility among "real" facts, but there are many incompatibilities among falsehoods.

PRAGMATIC THEORY

Pragmatic theory holds that the truth is the satisfactory solution to a problematic situation. This theory developed, in part, as a reaction against Cartesian logic. René Descartes considered matters individually and subjectively, believing that an idea was clear and true if it seemed to him to be clear and true, never considering that an idea might seem clear and true even though it was false. Pragmatists such as Charles S. Peirce, who wrote during the late nineteenth and early twentieth centuries, argued that truth had a public rather than an individual character and that it should never be severed from the practicality and reality of human life or from the human pursuit of knowledge. Peirce then defined scientific truth as a learned judgment ultimately agreed upon by all who investigate a certain statement, issue, or problem.

John Dewey's definition of pragmatic theory differed from that of Peirce; Dewey held that truth originates with doubt, which in turn prompts an investigation. First, relevant "facts" are gathered and applied; they mark off what seems safe and secure (true). Investigation then begins, lasting until "reality" (truth) is verified. Russell disagreed with Dewey, however, holding that truth is still truth even if it is not verified by an investigator. Another critic formed an example of what Russell meant: Smith committed a crime on Monday that was not discovered until Friday. The truth (the crime), "happened" on Monday and became reality then even if the authorities did not verify that truth until later.

Another pragmatist, William James, developed his own views of truth, holding that truth was expedient—it was whatever put one in a satisfactory position with the world. James came under attack from others who objected to his amoral approach, for if truth was only an expedient and a satisfactory position then lies might become truth, good might become bad, and all definitions of truth would be torn asunder.

Many pragmatists are also empiricists. For example, Isaac Newton's theory of gravitation is true because Newton's ideas lead to computations that agree with observations. The old corpuscular theory of light was eventually rejected because certain of its ideas did not agree with experience and observation.

EARLY EVOLUTION OF THE PHILOSOPHICAL CONCERN FOR THE TRUTH

Many early philosophers, in addition to those mentioned above, decided that objective truth existed. Plato's ideas included elements of both the correspondence and coherence theories, and, as mentioned above, Aristotle also developed the correspondence model. Challenges and criticisms of this idea were made by the early Sophists, who held that the truth was relative, and early skeptics, who argued that the real truth is not knowable by humans and that people should therefore live in a state of suspension of judgment.

During the Middle Ages, the doctrine of double truth was in vogue, largely because it appeared to save theology from philosophy. Those who stressed double truth claimed that what might be true in philosophy might be false for religion. Thomas Aquinas contributed to the debate by modifying the correspondence theory. He held that truth was the "adequation" of thought to things, and added that since truth is a transcendental concept, the highest truth was that of God. In the modern era, the double truth doctrine remains in vogue, as would-be religionists allow science and theology to coexist.

Later philosophers added depth to the search for truth. Baruch Spinoza, for example, argued that truth was the standard literally of itself and of the false as well. Leibniz drew a distinction between truths of reason and truths of facts (today's analytic-synthetic distinction). The former relied on the principle of identity and the latter simply on "sufficient" reason. John Locke joined the debate by drawing distinctions between truths of thought and truths of words; the former rested on the agreement of ideas with things, the latter on the agreement of ideas. Hegel explored what he called the "historical truth" versus formal truth, with the former relating to concrete existence and the latter to mathematics.

TRUTH, ERROR, LOGIC, AND MORALITY

Formal logic holds that a proposition or a fact is true if it reports, portrays, or describes "things" as they are (reality). A true idea corresponds in structure to reality. Formal logic, however, cannot account for certain types of falsehoods or errors, especially those that have moral or ethical overtones. Out of prejudice, ignorance, willfulness, or "feelings," people may embrace error. Many, for example, are superstitious; some deny certain scientific "truths" because they are not in accord with feelings or beliefs. Others embrace patently false philosophies and doubtful theological heresies because such heresies make them "feel" better. Worse, humans who are ignorant of "facts" experience a certain type of a void or a vacuum, and they often fill in their void or vacuum with errors.

Volitional untruth often leads to immorality and/or unethical behavior. Many a liar, for example, justifies his or her falsehoods with the phrase "everyone does it." Many a politician justifies the courting and the accepting of bribes because "everyone does it." Many a priest, preacher, or rabbi professes goodness while leading a private life that no "good" God could condone. Unfortunately, religion provides fertile ground for volitional untruth. Religionists believe in doctrines and ideas that are impossible to prove true. Yet many religionists still persecute and discriminate against those who do not embrace their unprovable assertions.

Prejudice appears to be a major source of volitional untruth that causes great harm. Historical examples could include the Holocaust, the German slaughter of at least six million Jews; Joseph Stalin's mass murders before and during World War II; and Serbia's "ethnic cleansing," a euphemism for attacks (that led to much destruction and many deaths) on other ethnic groups in what used to be Yugoslavia. It is clear that, worldwide, much racism and rabid ethnocentrism still exists.

TRUTH AS COMMON SENSE

When "common" people, living in the real world, use the term "common sense," they generally contrast the term with its opposite, nonsense, for what is opposed to common sense is nonsensical. Generally, people who have common sense tend to trust their five senses of perception and therefore to trust the observations about reality that their senses record. Common sense as a form of truth is usually opposed to "high" and obvious paradox, and it offers people protection from gross absurdity. For example, a person with common sense probably will not give much consideration to the following question: "if a tree falls in the forest, does it make a noise if no one is there to hear it?" Common sense dictates that one should disregard that question, because it involves only mental gymnastics. Likewise, most people do not attempt to determine how many angels can stand on the head of a pin.

In terms of the truth (or philosophy) of common sense, Aristotle was one of the first to stress "A" and "non-A" and to argue that the reality of the world was for the most part exactly what it seemed to be. Some modern philosophers echo Aristotle's dictum. For example, G. E. Moore developed "truisms" that implied the correctness of common sense: Earth has existed many years in time and in space; human beings have also existed for many years and have related to the material Earth and to each other. Thus, Moore condemned philosophers who tried to deny the existence of material things, of space, and of time. Some woebegone philosophers, Moore complained, had even denied the existence of minds other than their own; thus, they had to convince their listeners or their readers that they—the listeners and readers—did not exist, but if they did not exist, how could they hear of or read about the philosopher's opinions in the first place?

Commonsense observations do, of course, have limitations. Common sense can produce error. Primitive humans probably could not have believed the modern "view" that the earth is always revolving in an orbit around the Sun. Trusting their powers of observation, primitives would likely laugh at such a statement because the earth under their feet was not moving. Philosophers who stress common sense, however, argue that such error is always temporary because common sense evolves as more is learned about the world and reality.

TRUTH AND UNTRUTH IN THE WORLD OF POLITICS AND ECONOMICS

In the real world in which people live, falsehoods and unethical behavior abound (caused by, for example, personal character flaws or someone's drive for power). Nowhere is this more evident than in the United States' political system and economic system. In politics, for example, in recent decades Americans have witnessed something of a public circus. The Watergate scandal of the early 1970's disgusted many people, especially after certain tapes revealed that President Richard Nixon, in speaking to aides, acted much like a Mafia chieftain who plotted the destruction of his political enemies (real or imagined). The tapes also proved that Nixon was deeply involved in the scandal, not blameless as he had earlier maintained.

The 1980's and early 1990's witnessed such episodes as the "Iran-Contra" affair, which tainted President Ronald Reagan, and various congressional scandals involving the House of Representatives' "bank," its "post office," and its restaurant. Concerning economics, people witnessed such developments as the savings and loan scandal, a scandal that cost billions of dollars, most of which the general public ultimately will have to pay.

If one multiplied the examples above by one hundred, one might begin to approach the number of scandals that have occurred in modern America. The root cause has to do with unethical behavior, with falsehood rather than truth, with "bad" rather than "good." So wrong have things gone that many people have despaired and become apathetic, not knowing whom to trust. Furthermore, many analysts from different academic fields now talk about the decline of American civilization.

James Smallwood

FURTHER READING

Broad, William, and Nicholas Wade. *Betrayers of the Truth.* New York: Simon & Schuster, 1982. Broad's work examines various fields of science and finds so many examples of fraud that it leads one to question many aspects of those sciences.

Engel, Pascal. *The Norm of Truth: An Introduction to the Philosophy of Logic.* Buffalo, N.Y.: University of Toronto Press, 1991. Engel analyzes truth from the vantage points of philosophy and logic.

Goleman, Daniel. *Vital Lies, Simple Truths: The Psychology of Self-Deception.* New York: Simon & Schuster, 1985. This study examines the nature of cognition and of "social" truths, "psychological" truths, and psychological defense mechanisms for denying truth.

Haack, Susan. *Philosophy of Logics.* New York: Cambridge University Press, 1978. Contains a superb discussion and critique of the coherence, correspondence, and pragmatic theories of truth.

Künne, Wolfgang. *Conceptions of Truth.* New York: Clarendon, 2003. A comprehensive survey of the major theories of truth, from the Greeks to the present day. Includes the author's own attempt to define truth in a fashion which is both plausible and useful to philosophical inquiry and daily life.

Munitz, Milton Karl. *The Question of Reality*. Princeton, N.J.: Princeton University Press, 1990. Wide in scope, Munitz's volume considers events and ideas relevant to creation, to reality, and to the theory of knowledge.

Nietzsche, Friedrich. "On Truth and the Lie in an Extra-Moral Sense." In *Philosophy and Truth: Selections from Nietzsche's Notebooks of the Early 1870s*, edited and translated by Daniel Breazeale. Atlantic Highlands, N.J.: Humanities Press, 1979. A seminal essay arguing that truth is a matter of linguistic and cultural convention, rather than having anything to do with the real.

Quine, W. V. *Pursuit of Truth*. Cambridge, Mass.: Harvard University Press, 1990. A well-written book of much breadth, this volume examines "truth" from the standpoint of meaning and semantics and also considers the theory of knowledge.

Rorty, Richard. *Objectivity, Relativism, and Truth*. New York: Cambridge University Press, 1991. Rorty's work examines the relationships among truth, "representation" (in philosophy), relativity, objectivity, and postmodernism.

Sartre, Jean-Paul. *Truth and Existence*. Chicago: University of Chicago Press, 1992. The existentialist philosopher focuses on the relationships among reality, knowledge, and existentialism.

SEE ALSO: Absolutism; Aristotle; Deconstruction; Epistemological ethics; Moral realism; Objectivism; Platonic ethics; Pluralism; Pragmatism; Relativism; Subjectivism.

Tutu, Desmond

IDENTIFICATION: South African cleric and rights activist

BORN: October 7, 1931, Klerksdorp, Transvaal, South Africa

TYPE OF ETHICS: Religious ethics

SIGNIFICANCE: As an Anglican cleric, Tutu contributed moral force to help end South Africa's racial segregation.

Of native African heritage, Desmond Tutu grew up in Johannesburg, South Africa, under the rigid racial segregation system of apartheid. After training to become a teacher in black Africans schools, he left that profession because of the country's inherently unequal educational system. Eventually convinced only a moral challenge to apartheid could forcefully combat the system, he became a priest in the Anglican Church in 1961. The church was a worldwide body known for its forthright opposition to racism. Tutu spoke against the inhumanity of racial segregation to increasingly sympathetic listeners in South Africa and abroad. While the South African government used repressive force against violators of segregation laws, Tutu advised his followers to respond with the greater moral force of nonviolence.

After being appointed a bishop, Tutu became secretary-general of the South African Council of Churches in 1978. From that national platform, he courageously

Archbishop Desmond Tutu (right) shakes hands with former South African president P. W. Botha in 1996. (AP/Wide World Photos)

transmitted his message of nonviolent opposition to racism and published a series of books, the first of which, *Hope and Suffering*, appeared in 1983. For his sustained nonviolent challenge to apartheid, he received the Nobel Peace Prize in 1984.

Ten years later apartheid definitively ended when South Africa elected its first black majority government and Nelson Mandela became president of the country. By then Tutu was archbishop of Cape Town. In 1995 he was selected to preside over the government's Truth and Reconciliation Commission. Requiring a firm sense of moral balance, the commission investigated atrocities by all factions in the struggle against apartheid. When the commission presented its final report in 1998, it concluded that primary blame lay with the former apartheid government, but that all sides were guilty of outrages. Tutu himself later spoke out against Israeli treatment of Palestinians, calling it a form of apartheid.

Edward A. Riedinger

SEE ALSO: Apartheid; Mandela, Nelson; Nobel Peace Prizes; Nonviolence; South Africa's Truth and Reconciliation Commission.

Two Treatises of Government

IDENTIFICATION: Book by John Locke (1632-1704)
DATE: Published in 1690
TYPE OF ETHICS: Enlightenment history
SIGNIFICANCE: A seminal work of classical liberalism, the *Treatises* argued for natural rights, private property ownership, limited government, and the construction of legitimate government on the basis of consent and a social contract.

Two Treatises of Government was supportive of the political agenda of the Whigs and articulated a revolutionary sophisticated political theory of classical liberalism. John Locke's political theory and political ethical arguments were derived from his interpretation of the natural and rational human self-interests to survive and to acquire private property. The moral premises of universal natural rights and government's ethical obligation to protect such rights underpinned Locke's interpretation of natural law.

The law of nature was a source of rational moral political principles and a universal code of ethics. It was morally obligatory for all individuals to consult and comply with these moral precepts. Because of partiality, self-interest, and the personal pursuit of private property, however, humans often misunderstood the law of nature. The law of nature required all individuals to preserve their own lives and property, and "no one ought to harm another in his life, health, liberty, or possessions."

Locke asserted a moral objectivist perspective, based on his assumption that the law of nature had universal applicability and transcended any particular historical or social context. In the state of nature, because of the lack of public authority each individual was responsible for the interpretation and implementation of the law of nature as well as for the punishment of transgressors. Although individuals were relatively equal, free, and independent rational moral agents who pursued property in the state of nature, inconveniences and disputes regarding property transactions prompted individuals to unite by means of a social contract to institute a civil society.

The concept of a state of nature was viewed by Locke as a fictional contrivance that served to demonstrate the normative basis of legitimate political authority. Unlike Thomas Hobbes's political ethical theory that humans were primarily motivated by fear of violent death to fulfill their moral obligations to the state, Locke's moral political philosophy held that individuals were guided by reason in the creation of their social and political institutions. Locke interpreted the political authority relationship as being derived from the consent of citizens to government. Governments were entrusted specifically to protect the natural rights (particularly of private property) of individuals.

Locke's *First Treatise* rejected the political theory of royal absolutism, monarchical prerogative, patriarchalism, and divine right of kings advocated by Sir Robert Filmer's *Patriarcha*. In contrast to Hobbes's theory of political absolutism, which was based upon the passive obedience of citizens, Locke's political theory of classical liberalism was grounded in the normative principles of limited government, governmental accountability, and the active moral assessment by citizens of public authority. Locke justified rebellion against an arbitrary, tyrannical sovereign who ruled by absolute power and existed in a state of war with the people. In addition to simply being a moral justification of an individual's natural right to mix his or her labor with material objects and thereby claim exclusive property ownership, Locke's labor theory of value and concept of property were broadly identified with the ethical principle of individual moral autonomy.

Mitchel Gerber

SEE ALSO: Constitution, U.S.; Hobbes, Thomas; *Leviathan*; Liberalism; Locke, John; Natural law; Social contract theory.

Tyranny

DEFINITION: Oppressive power unjustly exerted by a government over its people

TYPE OF ETHICS: Politico-economic ethics

SIGNIFICANCE: Classically, there are three forms of political tyranny: dictatorship, or tyranny by an individual; oligarchy, or tyranny by a group; and nonrepublican democracy, or tyranny of the majority. Each form has been condemned on the grounds that it abridges the right to self-determination.

In seventh century B.C.E. Greece, aristocrats ruled city-states called *poleis*, whose citizens obeyed the laws made by kings and governing councils, called *archons* in Athens. The first tyrant was Cypseleus, who took power by force in Corinth in 657 B.C.E. Pisistratus overthrew the political leadership in Athens with his army and ruled as a tyrant from 546 B.C.E. to his death in 528 B.C.E. A Greek tyrant was not necessarily feared or hated. Pisistratus, for example, built temples, sponsored festivals, and was admired, if not loved, by many Athenians. Tyranny, however, was established through extralegal means, and even if the tyrant later obtained popular approval, he still imposed his will on the people. It is this aspect of tyranny that has been emphasized in criticisms of rulers from George III of England by the Americans to Czar Nicholas II by the Russian revolutionaries. Tyranny implies the use of force by a powerful leader to control the people. It results in the denial of freedom and the imposition of the will of the ruler.

James A. Baer

SEE ALSO: Arendt, Hannah; Assassination; Dictatorship; Fascism; Hitler, Adolf; Hussein, Saddam; *Leviathan*; Machiavelli, Niccolò; Oppression; *Two Treatises of Government*.

Tzaddik

DEFINITION: Jewish ideal of a person who is just, righteous, pious, and virtuous, or an action that is morally correct

TYPE OF ETHICS: Religious ethics

SIGNIFICANCE: The concept of the *tzaddik* provides Jews with an ideal model of moral and ethical behavior. In Hasidism, it is synonymous with the *rebbe*, the leader of a Hasidic court.

The Bible considers the *tzaddik*, who lives by faith, to be an abomination to the wicked and holds that the actions of the *tzaddik* can influence others to be righteous. Several of the prophets, however, along with the books of Ecclesiastes and Job, suggest a dilemma: The *tzaddik* is rewarded with material prosperity and divine blessings but suffers tribulations; his merit may endure forever, but he may perish in his righteousness. For the rationalist rabbis, the concept of absolute righteousness is unattainable. In their opinion, however, the *tzaddik* is to be praised more than are the ministering angels; his creative acts are coequal with those of God, and he is capable of canceling or at least minimizing the stern decrees of Heaven and Earth.

Indeed, it is because of the sustaining merit of the *tzaddikim*, rather than psychological determinism and mechanics, that the world exists. The Kabbala teaches that the soul of the *tzaddik* exhibits a harmonious relationship between the hidden aspect of the divine and the divine as it is manifested. The *tzaddik*'s life, therefore, suggests that the inner turmoil of one's soul is not a problem that defies solution but a mystery that can be resolved if, following the *tzaddik*'s narrow path to otherworldliness, one loves and fears God in joy. In the words of one talmudist-kabbalist, "The justification of [man's] life is that, at every moment, he burns in the consuming fire of the Lord, for his soul is the candle of God."

A central concept in the Kabbala is the symbiotic interaction of God and humanity, in which the actions of the lower world have an impact on the higher world. In the Hasidic world, this developed into the complementary roles of the *rebbe/tzaddik* and the *hasid* ("pious"). During the Shoah (the Holocaust), for example, the cadres of *rebbeim/tzaddikim* were a source of *hithazqut* ("encouragement"), which served to diminish despair (*ye'ush*) among the Hasidim. The *rebbeim/tzaddikim* acted as a kind of sponge for misery, absorbing pain and cruelty before they spilled out and overcame all else. They taught that multiple acts of holiness in the service of God and humanity help to restore dignity and self-respect, and can bring sanity to a shattered world. This view provides a marked contrast to the "theology of suffering," which views sainthood in terms of martyrdom.

Zev Garber

SEE ALSO: Hasidism; Hebrew Bible; Jewish ethics; Kabbala; Talmud; Torah.

U

Unamuno y Jugo, Miguel de

IDENTIFICATION: Spanish philosopher
BORN: September 29, 1864, Bilbao, Spain
DIED: December 31, 1936, Salamanca, Spain
TYPE OF ETHICS: Modern history
SIGNIFICANCE: In such works as *The Life of Don Quixote and Sancho* (*Vida de Don Quijote y Sancho según Miguel de Cervantes Saavedra, explicada y comentada por Miguel de Unamuno*, 1905), *The Tragic Sense of Life in Men and Peoples* (*Del sentimiento trágico de la vida en los hombres y en los pueblos*, 1913), and *The Agony of Christianity* (*La agonía del Cristianismo*, 1925), Unamuno explored his own soul in an attempt to understand humankind's quest for immortality. He believed that faith and emotion were the best tools with which to explore the tragedy of life.

Subjectivity, individualism, an acknowledgment of the role of irrationality, and a sense of life's anguish and tragedy were among the existential values that Miguel de Unamuno y Jugo shared with Søren Kierkegaard, Martin Heidegger, and Friedrich Nietzsche. Although he gave his own distinctive accent to their concept of the tragic sense of life, Unamuno rejected their idea that life was nothingness. He found meaning in his own passionate desire to escape annihilation by questing for the immortality of body and soul, and he concluded that this quest was common to all people. This perception was not derived from the principal philosophical systems of the day. Those systems were too abstract for Unamuno because they yielded only dehumanized ideas about human nature and human beings themselves: "thinking man," "economic man," or "freedom-seeking man."

Having devoted his intellect to exploring his inner self, Unamuno viewed humanity as a creature of flesh and bones, not as a philosophical object or an academic construct. Real humans were driven by passions and by faith. Since reason could explain neither the human search for immortality nor its own existence, Unamuno viewed humanity as being caught in a tragic struggle between reason and faith—faith being simply the hope that death does not bring annihilation. Unamuno's faith had, as Catholic theologians say, a "vital" religious base that also provided a foundation for his subjectivity and his intense individualism. Regarding most political systems as, at best, cloaks for civil privateering or masks for tyranny, and remaining innately suspicious of ethical and scientific ideals, he was a lifelong champion of the divine rights of individuals and of the battle for the human spirit.

Clifton K. Yearley

SEE ALSO: *Being and Nothingness*; *Beyond Good and Evil*; Hare, R. M.; Heidegger, Martin; Kierkegaard, Søren; Ortega y Gasset, José; Tillich, Paul.

Uncle Tom's Cabin

IDENTIFICATION: Novel by Harriet Beecher Stowe (1811-1896)
DATE: Published in 1852
TYPE OF ETHICS: Race and ethnicity
SIGNIFICANCE: One of the most influential and best-selling didactic novels in American history, *Uncle Tom's Cabin* used Christian ethics to attack slavery as immoral and to arouse popular sentiment against it.

Harriet Beecher Stowe's best-selling novel was the most influential antislavery work published in the years just prior to the American Civil War. It was a direct response to the moral concessions in the Compromise of 1850, and particularly the Fugitive Slave Law, which required citizens of northern states to return runaway slaves to their southern owners. The novel also refuted some contemporary religious arguments that attempted to justify slavery through biblical evidence.

Notice posted in Boston in 1851—the year before Uncle Tom's Cabin *was published in book form—warning African Americans about the dangers of slave catchers.* (Library of Congress)

Stowe was committed to exposing slavery as anti-family and atheistic. She believed that the materialistic values of mid-nineteenth century commerce had numbed Americans' moral sense and blinded them to the tragic consequences of the slave trade. Stowe believed that the Christian, domestic values embodied by wives and mothers were the best antidote for this evil, and her book makes numerous appeals to American women to use their humanizing influence to end slavery. Another ethical issue raised by the novel is the appropriate response of slaves to oppression. Although some modern readers question the docility of the titular hero, Stowe's purpose was to create a

Christ-like figure who embodied superior character traits, such as humility, goodness, and submission to God's will, that were essential in Stowe's Christian value system.

William L. Howard

SEE ALSO: Abolition; Narrative ethics; Racism; Slavery.

Unconditional surrender

DEFINITION: Total military capitulation in which the losing side has no power to negotiate and must accept any conditions that are imposed upon it by the victor

TYPE OF ETHICS: Military ethics

SIGNIFICANCE: Refusal to accept anything less than unconditional surrender may significantly prolong military conflicts or increase the destruction they cause, raising ethical questions about the permissible or justifiable scope of warfare.

During some of the most critical days of World War II, American president Franklin D. Roosevelt and British prime minister Winston S. Churchill met in January, 1943, in Casablanca, Morocco. Their intent was to plan future Allied operations and to reassure their hard-pressed Soviet ally that they would make no diplomatic deals with the common Axis enemy. Concluding this Allied North African Conference (ANFA), Roosevelt publicly announced that the war against Nazi Germany, Japan, and Italy would end only with the "unconditional surrender" of those countries. Roosevelt made it clear that the Allies were conducting war not against the peoples of these enemy nations but against their governments and military machines. Enunciated after Great Britain had been at war for nearly four years and the United States had been at war for two, the doctrine of unconditional surrender signaled the Allied resolve to fight the war to the finish. Roosevelt's announcement surprised some of his own military chiefs, as well as Churchill, and it subsequently proved to be a source of confusion and controversy.

THE DOCTRINE'S ORIGINS

Just as the French Revolution introduced Europeans to the realities of the beginnings of total war, so too did the U.S. Civil War introduce Americans to them. In February, 1862, the previously little-known Brigadier General Ulysses S. Grant gained recognition by demanding the "unconditional surrender" of Confederate Fort Donelson. One year later, in January, 1863, he gained fame for demanding unconditional surrender at Vicksburg, when the commander of Confederate forces holding the town, Simon Bolivar Buckner, requested terms of surrender from Grant. Buckner had reason to expect generosity, for he and Grant had been friends at West Point. Grant's reply, however, was "unconditional surrender." In making this reply, Grant expressed his, and the Union's, acceptance of a grinding, bloody total war. In terms of doctrine, it hardly mattered that Grant later allowed his exhausted and starving Confederate prisoners to go home on parole or that the terms that Grant offered to Confederate general Robert E. Lee, which ended the war at Appomattox, were extremely generous.

THE DOCTRINE'S EVOLUTION

The diplomacy preceding and during warfare was something with which Americans had little experience between the Civil War and the nation's participation in the last years of World War I. The issuance of President Woodrow Wilson's Fourteen Points in January, 1918, marked a fresh and controversial approach to settling with the enemy, chiefly Wilhelminian Germany. An armistice was predicated on the overthrow of Kaiser Wilhelm and his government and the installation of a government that represented the German people—one that thereby became acceptable to Wilson. On November 9, 1918, the kaiser abdicated and a new government was formed; on November 11, an armistice ended the fighting. Subsequently, Wilson's detailed peace plans were compromised and the planned American participation in a League of Nations failed to materialize. Supporters of Wilson believed that Wilson's Fourteen Points and armistice terms, by separating the German people from the policies of the kaiser's government, had helped to shorten the war.

Many people believed, however, that Germany should have been crushed, that Berlin and most of Germany should have been occupied by the United States and its allies. By the mid-1930's, American disappointment over its wartime experience, combined with the new presence of a rearmed and militant Hitlerian Germany, led to the conclusion that Germany had profited from too much leniency in 1918. The unlimited warfare unleashed by Germany, Japan, and their allies in World War II provided ample grounds for reviving Grant's concept of unconditional surrender.

THE DOCTRINE DURING WORLD WAR II

President Roosevelt's reassertion of unconditional surrender at Casablanca was aimed at attaining several immediate objectives. A global war had reached a critical stage. A long string of unbroken Allied defeats had just been ended. The Battle of the Atlantic was still being lost. Mistrust persisted between Britain and the United States, on one hand, and their invaluable ally the Soviet Union, on the other. Thus, the doctrine was intended to raise Allied morale, reassure the Russians, and signal Allied resolve to the enemy. Scholars later noted that of all the Allied statements, this was the only one that Adolf Hitler believed completely.

In 1943, Roosevelt's military chieftains apparently had little or no prior knowledge of the unconditional surrender doctrine. Initially, therefore, the doctrine did not represent a military initiative. Roosevelt probably drew upon the recommendations of a 1942 State Department Advisory Committee on Postwar Policy that had been passed on to him by Committee Chairman Norman Davis. The recommendation was that "nothing short of unconditional surrender by the principal enemies, Germany and Japan, could be accepted" (The way was left open for a "negotiated peace" with Italy.) Amid the drama of Casablanca, Roosevelt apparently recalled the Committee's recommendation.

After the Allies won a number of victories in 1944, Roosevelt and his military commanders decided that German resistance had been stiffened by the doctrine, thus prolonging the war, but Winston Churchill adamantly refused to abandon the doctrine. Consequently, in order to preserve harmony within the Grand Alliance, unconditional surrender was retained.

ETHICAL IMPLICATIONS

The questions of whether the doctrine of unconditional surrender lengthened the war, whether it was necessary for military victory, and whether it was morally justifiable continued to be controversial after the war's end. Did the ruthless acts of the Axis nations make it ethically permissible to match total war and terror with more total war and terror? No conclusive answers to this question have been found. American Cold War doctrine (1946 to 1986) in reaction to Soviet policy indicated, however, that if war came, the United States and its allies were prepared for a nuclear war of mutually assured destruction (MAD). Logically, the doctrine of unconditional surrender meant annihilation.

Clifton K. Yearley

FURTHER READING

Armstrong, Anne. *Unconditional Surrender.* New Brunswick, N.J.: Rutgers University Press, 1961.

Casey, Steven. *Cautious Crusade: Franklin D. Roosevelt, American Public Opinion, and the War Against Nazi Germany.* New York: Oxford University Press, 2001.

Eisenhower, David. *Eisenhower at War, 1943-1945.* New York: Random House, 1986.

Grob, Gerald N., ed. *Statesmen and Statecraft of the Modern West.* Barre, Mass.: Barre, 1967.

Harris, William C. "Toward Appomattox, Toward Unconditional Surrender?" In *The Lincoln Enigma: The Changing Faces of an American Icon*, edited by Gabor Boritt. New York: Oxford University Press, 2001.

Matloff, Maurice. *Strategic Planning for Coalition Warfare, 1943-1944.* Washington, D.C.: Office of the Chief Military History Department of the Army, 1959.

Pogue, Forrest. *George C. Marshall.* New York: Viking Press, 1963-1987.

SEE ALSO: Hiroshima and Nagasaki bombings; Limited war; Military ethics; Mutually Assured Destruction; *On War*; War.

UNESCO Declaration on the Human Genome and Human Rights

IDENTIFICATION: First universal instrument in the field of biology and ethics

DATE: Adopted on November 11, 1997

TYPE OF ETHICS: Bioethics

SIGNIFICANCE: Written in several iterations by representatives from around the world, this statement aims at striking a balance between the rights and freedoms of human beings and the goal of ensuring freedom of research.

In early 1995 the Bioethics Unit of the United Nations Educational, Scientific, and Cultural Organization (UNESCO) prepared a draft declaration regarding human genome research. The purpose was to prepare a universal instrument designed to safeguard cultural diversity while presenting an ethical stand on genetic research. In September, 1995, that draft was revised by a committee that met in Paris. The revised draft was given to the meeting of government experts in July, 1997, for their comments. The fifth session of the UNESCO International Bioethics Committee reconvened in October, 1997, in Cape Town, South Africa. The final version that emerged was the Universal Declaration on the Human Genome and Human Rights, which was adopted unanimously by the 188 members of the general conference of UNESCO on November 11, 1997. Five years later, the International Society for Bioethics (SIBI) awarded its SIBI Award to UNESCO for the declaration.

The preamble of the declaration presents UNESCO's mandate and previous declarations regarding human rights, discrimination, research, and related issues ratified by member states. The declaration's first section is about human dignity and the human genome. It underscores the unity of all human beings and calls for scientists to respect their subjects, not reduce individuals to genetic characteristics or base their work solely on financial gain. The second section, about the rights of concerned persons, calls for informed consent, rigorous preliminary research, nondiscrimination, confidentiality, and punitive damages for violation of an individual's genome.

The third section is about research on the human genome and has three articles that call for respect of human rights over research; forbidding practices contrary to human dignity, such as human cloning and making universally available the results of research. The fourth section deals with the conditions under which scientific research is conducted. Its four articles pertain to meticulousness in inquiry, intellectual freedom, restriction of uses to peaceful purposes, and committee assessments. The fifth section pertains to solidarity and international cooperation, with two articles about global cooperation. The sixth section is about the promotion of principles in the declaration, and the final section is about implementation of the declaration by each of the member states.

Manoj Sharma

FURTHER READING

Boon, Kevin Alexander. *The Human Genome Project: What Does Decoding DNA Mean for Us?* Berkeley Heights, N.J.: Enslow, 2002.

Roberts, Leslie. "Controversial from the Start." *Science* 291 (2001): 1182-1188.

Sulston, John, and Georgina Ferry. *The Common Thread: A Story of Science, Politics, Ethics and the Human Genome.* New York: Bantam, 2002.

Toriello, James. *The Human Genome Project.* New York: The Rosen Publishing Group, 2003.

SEE ALSO: Biotechnology; Genetic engineering; Genetic testing; Human Genome Project; International Covenant on Civil and Political Rights.

Union of Concerned Scientists

IDENTIFICATION: Organization established to examine the uses and hazards of nuclear energy
DATE: Founded in 1969
TYPE OF ETHICS: Scientific ethics
SIGNIFICANCE: The Union of Concerned Scientists pursues a vigorous program of public advocacy and education concerning the effects of advanced technology on society and public policy.

At the end of the 1960's, the testing of nuclear weapons had been suspended by the United States, the Soviet Union, and other nations with nuclear arms, but the Strategic Arms Limitation Treaty (SALT) talks that would halt the construction of weapons had not

yet begun. In addition, the first nuclear power plants were either on the drawing boards or actually under construction. The Union of Concerned Scientists (USC) was founded at this time to gather information on the nuclear arms race, arms control, nuclear reactor safety, energy policy, and other related matters. (Although the membership of the USC is not made up exclusively of scientists, a core of technically competent professionals makes its studies definitive and disinterested.)

The USC's findings are made available in its own periodicals, in conferences, in public presentations, in the media, in speaking engagements, and in educational packets provided for school use. The USC also provides court testimony and appearances at hearings such as those conducted by the U.S. Nuclear Regulatory Commission (NRC) regarding the relicensing of atomic power plants. More recently, the USC has broadened its scope to deal with the impact of advanced technology in general on society and has organized scientists on a worldwide basis out of concern for the earth's ecology.

Robert M. Hawthorne, Jr.

SEE ALSO: Atom bomb; Atomic Energy Commission; Earth and humanity; Mutually Assured Destruction; Nuclear energy; Nuclear Regulatory Commission; SALT treaties; Science.

United Nations

IDENTIFICATION: Intergovernmental world organization established for the promotion of international peace and security
DATE: Established in 1945
TYPE OF ETHICS: International relations
SIGNIFICANCE: As an international mechanism for collective security, conflict resolution, and promotion of prosperity and humanitarian welfare, the United Nations is frequently involved in disputes that bring the competing goals and varying ethical standards of different nations into conflict.

Established at San Francisco by fifty world governments in 1945, the United Nations (U.N.) represented an effort to foster international cooperation, to encourage peaceful settlement of disputes, to prevent war, to punish aggression, and to control conflict through a collective security system. After the widespread destruction of World War II, which left tens of millions of people dead, governments realized a need to prevent and control conflict through legal and diplomatic means, while addressing the underlying causes of conflict, such as poverty, ignorance, cultural misunderstanding, injustice, and disrespect for the dignity of the human person, human rights, and fundamental freedoms.

The United Nations was designed to be a comprehensive venue in which causes of conflict could be identified and addressed by governments so as to reduce the propensity to war among nations, and as a place where imminent threats to peace or threats of aggression could be prevented or managed. The U.N. General Assembly, comprising all member states, was charged with overall coordination of U.N. activities, while the Security Council, comprising a smaller number of states—including five great powers as permanent members—was established as the primary U.N. body for maintaining international peace. To address the promotion of human rights, humanitarian assistance, and economic development the Economic and Social Council (ECOSOC) was also established.

BASIC ETHICAL PRINCIPLES

The U.N. system is rooted in several important ethical principles. The U.N. Charter recognizes the principle of the sovereign equality of its members, who are called to cooperate with one another through common efforts to achieve a better world. This reflects the important ethical principle of solidarity. The cooperation is to be achieved by the mutual efforts of governments within their own domestic systems of government. This represents the ethical principle of subsidiarity, which is reflected in the sovereignty, territorial integrity, and political independence of each member state.

The United Nations is not an overarching or all-powerful world government, but rather a system through which politically independent and legally sovereign nations can cooperate to achieve common objectives such as collective security, peace, and greater social and economic advancement. To advance these goals, U.N. member states agree to refrain from the threat or use of force against fellow member states, and to cooperate with other members in punishing member states that violate their obliga-

tions to resolve disputes peacefully. The United Nations is rooted in the ethical principles of charity and preventing harm. However, charity can hurt as well as help and preventing harm often involves threats of harm against those who would inflict harm unjustly. U.N. efforts to oppose aggression may involve the use of force to punish egregious violations of Charter obligations. Wherever it turns the United Nations faces ethical dilemmas.

HUMAN RIGHTS AND SELF-DETERMINATION

Although member states may expect no interference in their domestic affairs or infringement upon their territorial integrity, the U.N. Charter does provide for the promotion of human rights, and it recognizes the principle of self-determination of peoples. If a member state engages in gross violation of human rights, may it expect the United Nations to refrain from any form of intervention? If a member state faces a civil war in which a portion of its population expresses a desire for self-determination, should the United Nations support the existing legal sovereign or should it honor the principle of self-determination of peoples?

These tensions complicate the work of the United Nations, which as a general rule has honored the principle of national sovereignty over that of human rights. The United Nations worked aggressively for the principle of self-determination for colonial areas, which rapidly gained independence and U.N. membership. However, many of these newly independent member states proved to be politically unstable, economically weak, and badly divided along ethnic lines from within. When civil wars and human rights abuses erupted in many of these countries, the tendency of the United Nations was to honor the principle of sovereignty to the detriment of human rights and self-determination. The civil wars were seen as largely domestic disputes lying outside the competence of U.N. collective security efforts, which were designed primarily to prevent international conflicts. There were exceptions to this, as when the United Nations intervened after the independence of the Congo in 1960 to put down civil wars and prevent the self-determination claims of the resource-rich Katanga Province.

As a rule, the Cold War that swiftly overtook international relations after World War II led to a stalemate among the permanent members of the Security Council that possessed veto power and could thus prevent common action against international security threats. Not until the end of the Cold War in the late 1980's and early 1990's did the Security Council emerge as an active enforcer of collective security, and when it did so, it confronted primarily civil war situations where conflicting claims to self-determination complicated its work.

SOLIDARITY AND SUBSIDIARITY

At the very heart of the U.N. system is the mutual link between the principles of solidarity and subsidiarity. Solidarity is a quality of mutual support, cooperation, loyalty, and fellow feeling. It is most profoundly characteristic of families, where mutual love and support are most deeply felt. It is characteristic of local communities, of church groups, and of clan associations. It is also often exhibited in the feelings of patriotism of citizens toward their country, although in many parts of the world such a national sense of solidarity has never developed, which leaves such countries vulnerable to civil disturbance among competing groups with high levels of solidarity. Finally, the United Nations reflects an effort to develop a sense of global solidarity, in terms of achieving international peace and security. Clearly, solidarity is weakest at this international level, and it will likely always remain so. Still, a degree of solidarity is necessary at this level to encourage basic international cooperation in the interest of collective security and international justice.

Closely coupled with the principle of solidarity is that of subsidiarity, which acknowledges the proper independence of each level of human activity, from individuals and families, to local associations and civic bodies, to provincial and national political life, and to international associations. Subsidiarity asserts that each sphere of human activity should be left to its proper pursuit of human goods. Each person should be respected as endowed with fundamental rights and freedoms. Families have a right to beget and raise children into human maturity and to serve as the first educators and primary teachers of ethics and of solidarity to their children. However, individuals and families cannot provide for all things. Thus local governments come into being to promote the safety, security, and good public order in which individuals and families can thrive.

National governments arise to promote the general welfare, to provide for common defense, and to

support, not to displace, the efforts of local governments and of families in their primary duties. Similarly, history shows that nations must cooperate to maintain international peace and security and prevent humanitarian disasters. Global tasks require a concomitantly global organization to promote cooperation. The aim should be support rather than to dictate to governments how they must order their domestic life. Every level of human organization has an appropriate role to play in advancing the human good and in supporting those institutions that are best suited to achieve those goods.

SUBSIDIARITY IN PEACEMAKING

The U.N. Charter acknowledges the principle of subsidiarity in two ways: first, in honoring the principle of sovereignty and the inherent right of each member state to act in self-defense when facing imminent threats to security, and second, in providing for regional collective security organizations. The seventh chapter of the U.N. Charter provides that member states may join together in regional organizations to promote regional peace and security.

Member states have an obligation to keep the U.N. Security Council informed of acts of self-defense and regional collective security actions, but they are free to act in situations in which delay or even the impossibility of the Security Council to reach consensus on a decision to act would compromise their national safety and security. Thus, the U.S. action in Afghanistan to remove terrorist threats after the September 11, 2001, attacks, though controversial, won the general endorsement of the United Nations. The United States, Great Britain, Spain, and several other U.N. members, though failing to win explicit U.N. endorsement, justified the use of force against Iraq in 2003 on grounds of peremptory self-defense.

SUBSIDIARITY IN SOCIAL AND HUMANITARIAN POLICY

The promotion of human rights, the achievement of social and economic advancement, and the application of humanitarian assistance are primarily the right and duty of national governments, not of the United Nations itself, whose role is supportive. Similarly no government of a country can promote such causes without vigorous local action and implementation. When there is a disastrous breakdown in the capacity of local or national efforts to achieve such goals, countries often turn to the United Nations for assistance. This happens during famines, natural disasters, or widespread civil disturbances. Normally, local nongovernmental organizations (NGOs), religious groups, private enterprises, and businesses in cooperation with governments of countries are the institutions in healthy civic settings where this work is more directly and effectively accomplished. If U.N. bodies or international nongovernmental organizations lose respect for these local capacities and cultural values and resources, or when they attempt to monopolize or co-opt them, even during an emergency, the principle of subsidiarity is compromised.

The spectacular growth in the numbers of NGOs and international advocacy groups, coupled with the growing number of U.N.-sponsored conferences to which such groups are now routinely invited along with governments, has created situations where the principle of subsidiarity can be violated. Some NGOs advance ideas and principles in such settings that could not gain legislative support within their own nations. Examples include various attempts at international conferences to redefine the traditional family values, to advance abortion as a human right, and to advance population control in ways that violate local cultural and religious norms. Such issues are politically controversial, culturally explosive, and deeply personal ones that beg for local and personal resolution in keeping with the principle of subsidiarity.

CONCLUSION

Questions concerning the cardinal virtues of justice, prudence, temperance, and fortitude populate the U.N. agenda. Just as individuals and governments must reflect these virtues, so must the United Nations wrestle in its often highly controversial debates with matters of public policy and ethics. It does so imperfectly. It is often unable to achieve consensus on appropriate action, leaving member states to accommodate as best they can.

When, how, and whether to intervene where human rights abuses of a member state shock civilized consciences remains a question of both politics and prudence. The failure of the United Nations and its members to effectively intervene in the Rwandan genocide of 1994 left hundreds of thousands dead, when minimal action might have saved countless lives. Ineffective though well-intentioned U.N. inter-

vention in Bosnia in the early 1990's contributed to human suffering in that strife-torn country. U.N. economic sanctions in Iraq and Haiti did little to force intransigent regimes to change invidious policies but imposed considerable hardship on innocent populations. On the other hand, U.N. economic sanctions were instrumental in paving the way to the demise of the racist apartheid system and the attainment of majority rule in South Africa, and U.N. charitable aid for starving peoples and displaced refugees has saved tens of millions of lives over the decades. The U.N. record is one of mixed failure and success that nonetheless illustrates the need for international institutions aware of both their limits and their potential in advancing the human good.

Robert F. Gorman

FURTHER READING

Amstutz, Mark R. *International Ethics: Concepts, Theories, and Cases in Global Politics*. Lanham, Md.: Rowman & Littlefield, 1999. A thoughtful assessment of the limits and possibilities of the use of force and sanctions in international politics.

Anderson, Mary B. *Do Ho Harm: How Aid Can Support Peace—Or War*. Boulder, Colo.: Lynne Rienner, 1999. An experienced practitioner offers insights about how agencies should approach humanitarian work in the context of violent complex emergencies that advance peaceful outcomes rather than deepening hostilities.

Gorman, Robert F. *Great Debates at the United Nations: An Encyclopedia of Fifty Key Issues, 1945-2000*. New York: Greenwood Press, 2001. Includes a history of the U.N. system, summaries of debates on fifty key political and ethical questions, a time line, a glossary, and a bibliographic essay.

Henkin, Louis, et al. *Right v. Might: International Law and the Use of Force*. New York: Council on Foreign Relations, 1989. An anthology of opposing views on the state of development of international law in regard to the use of force.

Minow, Martha. *Between Vengeance and Forgiveness: Facing History After Genocide and Mass Violence*. Boston: Beacon Press, 1998. Reflections on how U.N. trials, national truth commissions, reparations, and the like can contribute to or detract from the attainment of justice and reconciliation in countries badly scarred by gross violations of human rights.

Moore, Jonathan, ed. *Hard Choices: Moral Dilemmas in Humanitarian Intervention*. Lanham, Md.: Rowman & Littlefield, 1998. A varied collection of essays on the moral choices facing governments, U.N. agencies, and NGOs in advancing human rights and humanitarian policy in civil war settings.

SEE ALSO: Conflict resolution; Human rights; International Covenant on Civil and Political Rights; League of Nations; North Atlantic Treaty Organization; Peacekeeping missions; United Nations Convention on the Prevention and Punishment of the Crime of Genocide; United Nations Declaration of the Rights of the Child; United Nations Declaration on the Rights of Disabled Persons; Universal Declaration of Human Rights; World Trade Organization.

United Nations Convention on the Prevention and Punishment of the Crime of Genocide

IDENTIFICATION: International treaty

DATE: Adopted on December 9, 1948; became law on January 12, 1951

TYPE OF ETHICS: Human rights

SIGNIFICANCE: The United Nations (U.N.) convention allows all the nations that sign it to take appropriate actions against countries and individuals implementing genocide.

At the end of World War II, the horrifying visible evidence of the Holocaust illustrated to the world the effects of genocide on a massive scale. In 1948, when the General Assembly of the United Nations unanimously adopted the Convention on the Prevention and Punishment of the Crime of Genocide, it provided a way to inhibit this crime in the future. The intent of the framers of the convention was to establish a system of collective security for designated groups. Under the terms of the convention, any attempt to destroy a national, ethnic, racial, or religious group should result in the United Nations taking appropriate steps to stop the genocide. Moreover, charges should be filed against those attempting to develop or implement such a policy.

Ethically, it seems like a simple and straightforward process to eliminate genocide. However, the U.N. attempt to achieve what seemed to be a simple ethical goal has raised many other issues. For example, should political groups or others that are not specifically national ethnic, racial, or religious groups also be afforded protection? Is it possible to practice genocide against members of one's own group—which is what some people have said that the Khmer Rouge did in Cambodia during the 1970's?

Within the context of the convention, only the physical destruction of a group—by killing, inflicting bodily or mental harm, imposing intolerably harsh living conditions, or preventing births or taking away children—is considered genocide. Should other acts, such as cultural assimilation, be considered genocide? The convention states that for policies to be genocidal, they must intend to "destroy, in whole or in part" a protected group. How many members of a group must be killed or harmed to consider a policy one of genocide?

Two other, somewhat opposite, ethical considerations also relate to the convention. The agreement gives only the contracting parties that have signed the convention the right to invoke its provisions. That limitation leaves many groups at risk with no recourse against genocide. Do signatories of the convention have any responsibility for protecting them? How extreme must the circumstance get before other countries are willing to intervene? What does this do to the traditional ideal of national sovereignty?

At the other extreme, some countries are worried about false charges being brought against their citizens. This concern is the principal reason that the United States did not ratify the convention until 1988, even though it was one of the original signatories. What protection can be afforded innocent countries or individuals in these cases?

Donald A. Watt

FURTHER READING

Neier, Aryeh. *War Crimes: Brutality, Genocide, Terror, and the Struggle for Justice*. New York: Times Books, 1998.

Power, Samantha. *A Problem from Hell: America and the Age of Genocide*. New York: Basic Books, 2002.

Schabas, William A. *Genocide in International Law: The Crimes of Crimes*. New York: Cambridge University Press, 2000.

SEE ALSO: Geneva conventions; Genocide and democide; Genocide, cultural; Genocide, frustration-aggression theory of; International law; Lemkin, Raphael; Peacekeeping missions; Rwanda genocide; United Nations; Universal Declaration of Human Rights.

United Nations Declaration of the Rights of the Child

IDENTIFICATION: Official edict laying out ten principles under which individuals, organizations, and governments should aid and protect children
DATE: Promulgated in 1959
TYPE OF ETHICS: Children's rights

SIGNIFICANCE: The U.N. Declaration of the Rights of the Child formally recognized the ethical obligations of governments toward children. It paved the way for the Convention on the Rights of the Child, in which the nations of the world agreed to honor those theoretical obligations in practice.

The Declaration of the Rights of the Child grew out of earlier international accords: the 1924 League of Nations Declaration of the Rights of the Child and the 1948 Universal Declaration of Human Rights. The 1959 declaration reiterates that all people—regardless of race, color, religion, sex, and so on—have rights and freedoms simply because they are human. Children are often neglected or abused, however, because they cannot stand up and claim their basic human rights. Therefore, it is the duty of every

Ten Principles of the U.N. Declaration of the Rights of the Child

1. All children shall enjoy all the rights set forth in the declaration, without regard to race, color, sex, language, religion, political or other opinion, national or social origin, property, birth or other status.

2. All children shall enjoy special protection and be given opportunities and facilities, by law and by other means, to enable them to develop physically, mentally, morally, spiritually and socially in a healthy and normal manner and in conditions of freedom and dignity.

3. Every child shall be entitled from birth to a name and a nationality.

4. Every child shall enjoy the benefits of social security and be entitled to grow and develop in health and have the right to adequate nutrition, housing, recreation and medical services.

5. Children who have physical, mental or social disabilities shall be given the special treatment, education and care required by their conditions.

6. All children shall, wherever possible, grow up in the care and under the responsibility of their parents, and always in an atmosphere of affection and of moral and material security.

7. All children are entitled to education, which shall be free and compulsory, at least in the elementary stages.

8. Children shall in all circumstances be among the first to receive protection and relief.

9. Children shall be protected against all forms of neglect, cruelty and exploitation and shall not be admitted to employment before an appropriate minimum age or be placed in any occupation or employment that might prejudice their health, education, or physical, mental or moral development.

10. Children shall be protected from practices that may foster racial, religious or any other forms of discrimination. They shall be brought up in a spirit of understanding, tolerance, friendship among peoples, peace and universal brotherhood, and in full consciousness that their energy and talents should be devoted to the service of fellow human beings.

Source: Markkula Center for Applied Ethics.

person and every government to take extra steps to guarantee the rights of children. The declaration spells out principles to guide this effort. All children are entitled to a name, a nationality, medical care, nutrition, housing, education, and recreation. Handicapped children have rights to special care. Governments should assist families in caring for children, and children without families are entitled to care. Children should not be subject to discrimination or taught to discriminate.

The declaration remained the primary United Nations statement on the rights of children until 1989, when a formal convention was adopted and opened for ratification by member nations. The Convention on the Rights of the Child was ratified by the requisite twenty states and entered into force on September 2, 1990. This convention listed thirty-eight rights of children that ratifying nations must respect, and it established an international oversight committee to which all such nations must periodically report. By the end of 1995, 185 nations had ratified the convention, making it both the most universally adopted and the most quickly ratified human rights treaty in history. Additionally, the U.N. adopted two Optional Protocols to the Convention on May 25, 2000. These protocols, which signatories to the convention could join at their discretion, banned child slavery, prostitution, and pornography, and also raised from fifteen to eighteen the minimum age for military service.

Cynthia A. Bily

SEE ALSO: Child labor legislation; Child soldiers; Children; Children's Bureau; Children's rights; Head Start; International Covenant on Civil and Political Rights; United Nations; Universal Declaration of Human Rights.

United Nations Declaration on the Rights of Disabled Persons

IDENTIFICATION: Official proclamation stating that people with physical disabilities have the same rights that other human beings have
DATE: Promulgated in 1975
TYPE OF ETHICS: Civil rights
SIGNIFICANCE: The declaration was the first of several attempts by the United Nations to address the specific rights and needs of people with physical disabilities.

Adopted in 1975, the U.N. Declaration on the Rights of Disabled Persons confirmed and expanded the 1971 Declaration on the Rights of Mentally Retarded Persons. Although the preferred terminology has changed since these declarations were made, their intention was to recognize the humanity of mentally and physically challenged people. The 1975 declaration defines "disabled person" as anyone who is prevented, because of a physical or mental deficiency, from pursuing a normal life.

The declaration promises the same rights to persons with disabilities that other human beings share and recognizes that delivering on these promises may mean providing special programs. People with disabilities are entitled to proper medical care, physical therapy, education, and training. They have a right to economic security. They have a right to guardians and advisers, when needed, and the right to be protected from abuse and exploitation. The adoption of the declaration led to further study and action by the United Nations, which sponsored an International Year of the Disabled (1981) and a U.N. Decade of Disabled Persons (1983-1992).

Cynthia A. Bily

SEE ALSO: Americans with Disabilities Act; Disability rights; International Covenant on Civil and Political Rights; United Nations.

Universal Declaration of Human Rights

IDENTIFICATION: Formal proclamation of fundamental principles of human rights to which all nations should adhere
DATE: Promulgated on December 10, 1948
TYPE OF ETHICS: Human rights
SIGNIFICANCE: The Universal Declaration of Human Rights, as an unbinding statement of basic principles, provided common standards of basic rights for all persons. This theoretical statement of standards later became the basis of binding agreements meant to enforce the principles laid out in the declaration.

The charter of the United Nations affirms the world organization's faith "in fundamental human rights" and its commitment to promote and encourage "respect for human rights." To fulfill that responsibility, the U.N. formed a Commission on Human Rights in 1946 to begin drafting an international bill of rights. On December 10, 1948, the General Assembly of the United Nations adopted the Universal Declaration of Human Rights. This declaration was not legally binding on member nations, but it established the fundamental principles upon which legally binding treaties would be based.

The declaration proclaimed several principles of civil and political rights that were already found in many declarations and constitutions: that all human beings are free and equally valuable; that everyone is entitled to freedom regardless of race, color, nationality, political opinion, and so on; that humans have rights to life, liberty, and security; and that all people are entitled to freedom from torture, freedom to travel, and freedom to own property. The declaration was unusual in also proclaiming several principles of economic, social, and cultural rights. These two sets of principles were regulated in 1966 by U.N. Covenants, which are legal treaties.

Cynthia A. Bily

SEE ALSO: Human rights; Human Rights Watch; International Covenant on Civil and Political Rights; International justice; International law; United Nations; United Nations Convention on the Prevention and Punishment of the Crime of Genocide; United Nations Declaration of the Rights of the Child.

Universalizability

DEFINITION: Logical possibility of making the motive behind a moral decision into a general moral law

TYPE OF ETHICS: Theory of ethics

SIGNIFICANCE: A key concept for German philosopher Immanuel Kant, universalizability is founded upon Kant's notion that the only valid moral law is one that has the formal structure of law as such, regardless of content. If it is possible to turn an individual's motive into a universal maxim without contradicting the laws of reason,

Kant argued, then that motive has a logical structure which validates it ethically.

Immanuel Kant's ethical theory is called a deontological or nonconsequential or duty-based ethical theory. According to Kant, an action is right if it follows from duty; that is, an action should be done not because of its consequences but because it is the right thing to do. The principle that one follows must be universalizable; in other words, it should be possible to argue that everyone ought to act the same way in a similar situation. For example, the rules that promises should not be broken by anyone, that no one should kill others, and that no one should cheat should be followed by everyone always. There are certain moral rights that everyone possesses.

Kant uses the example of making a false promise to make his point. In a particular situation, making a false promise might suit one's purpose, yet one cannot make the principle of making a false promise into a universal law, because then the concept of promising would have no meaning.

Krishna Mallick

SEE ALSO: Consistency; Deontological ethics; Golden rule; Kant, Immanuel; Moral principles, rules, and imperatives; Promises; Utilitarianism.

Upaniṣads

IDENTIFICATION: Ancient Hindu scriptures

DATE: Written between 1000 and 400 B.C.E.

TYPE OF ETHICS: Religious ethics

SIGNIFICANCE: The Upaniṣads stress the importance of physical, mental, ethical, and spiritual disciplines as the prerequisites for the realization of the knowledge of *Brāhmin*, or ultimate reality.

The Upaniṣads, literally meaning "to sit near someone," constitute the concluding portion of the Vedas, the first original Hindu scripture, which has four sections: Saṃhitās or collections—hymns, prayers, and formulas of sacrifice; Brāhmaṇas—prose treatises discussing the significance of sacrificial rites and ceremonies; Āraṇyakas, or forest texts; and the Upaniṣads, or later Vedas. The Upaniṣads are the main basis for the Vedānta school of philosophy. The doctrines of the Upaniṣads were imparted orally. Groups of students sat near the teacher to learn from him the truths by which ignorance could be destroyed. The authors of the Upaniṣads, of which there are more than two hundred, are not known.

The principal Upaniṣads are the *Īsa, Kena, Katha, Praśna, Muṇḍaka, Māṇkya, Taittirīya, Aitareya, Chāndogya,* and *Bṛhadāraṇyaka* Upaniṣads. Śaṅkara, a Vedānta philosopher, wrote commentaries on the above ten and on the *Śvetāśvatara Upaniṣad*. In addition, the *Kauṣitaki, Mahānārāyaṇa,* and *Maitri* are also considered principal Upaniṣads. These Upaniṣads were written partly in prose and partly in verse.

The Upaniṣads are concerned with the meaning of the sacrificial rites, and in the process of discussing them, they introduce some profound metaphysical and religious ideas. With the Upaniṣads began the period of speculative research into human nature and the individual's position in the universe. The practical result of the Upaniṣads was to depersonalize the universe and to minimize the importance of earlier Vedic gods. The Upaniṣads were not philosophical treatises, but they contained certain fundamental ideas that form the basis of a philosophical system out of which the orthodox schools of Indian philosophy—Sāṃkhya, Yoga, Nyāya, Vaíśeṣika, Mīmāṃsā, and Vedānta—developed their systems.

The Upaniṣads have for their ideal the realization of *Brāhmin*, becoming one with God. The world is not an end in itself. It comes from God, through his mysterious power, and it ends in God. Everything in the phenomenal world, including the individual, must realize the infinite, must strive to reclaim the highest. The Absolute is the highest and most desirable ideal. The performance of duty is necessary if one is to achieve the highest perfection. Morality is valuable because it leads one toward this highest perfection. Inner purity is more important than outer conformity. The ethics of the Upaniṣads insist on the transformation of the whole person. In the process of this transformation, one knows that one's liberation from the phenomenal appearance depends on oneself and not upon the grace of transcendent deity. The idea of rebirth, the idea that the individual who has not gained the ultimate reality will be subject to the cycle of birth and death, is also presented for the first time in the Upaniṣads.

Krishna Mallick

SEE ALSO: Ahiṁsā; Asceticism; Aurobindo, Sri; Ḥallāj, al-; Hindu ethics; Mysticism; Śaṅkara; Tagore, Rabindranath; Vedānta.

Utilitarianism

DEFINITION: School of philosophy that defines the good as that which is useful

TYPE OF ETHICS: Theory of ethics

SIGNIFICANCE: Utilitarianism marks an early attempt to devise a secular, rational, scientific moral system; its influence can be attributed to its simplicity, its adaptability, and the talent of its defenders. Its most important ethical ideas are that individuals should strive for maximum pleasure and minimum pain and that society should strive to achieve the greatest amount of happiness for the greatest number of people.

Utilitarianism is a decision procedure for normative ethics that holds that the rightness (or wrongness) of human actions, policies, or rules is determined by their effects on the general welfare. Since the late eighteenth century, it has been one of the most prominent moral theories. In addition, utilitarian principles have become major factors in shaping social policy and have given rise to numerous applications, ranging from behaviorist psychology to cost-benefit analysis. Utilitarianism has undergone many changes, and it exists in many forms. Consequently, there are many versions of utilitarianism, which makes it difficult to discuss in general terms.

JEREMY BENTHAM

The dominant version was developed and articulated by Jeremy Bentham, who applied it to the reformation of the legal, political, social, educational, penal, and economic institutions of Britain and other countries. His principle of utility formed the standard by which actions are judged: "It is the greatest happiness of the greatest number that is the measure of right and wrong." Classical utilitarianism is based on a hedonistic theory of value. Happiness (that is, pleasure and the absence of pain) is the only thing that is intrinsically good. Other things are valuable only to the extent that they bring happiness. Thus, moral actions result in producing the greatest balance of pleasure over pain. Bentham held that pleasure and pain (in the basic, feeling sense) are quantifiable, and he devised a "felicific calculus" to measure the utility of acts numerically and to make comparisons among them.

Utilitarianism is consequentialist, not deontological: Actions are evaluated by their outcomes and not by the agent's intentions or motives. This is consistent with Bentham's desire to devise a system that would be objective and scientific. Although one can empirically ascertain the results of people's actions, one can only guess regarding their intentions. Utilitarianism is universalist rather than egoistic. One should seek to maximize the pleasure of all, not act selfishly to maximize one's own pleasure at the expense of others. Hence, utilitarianism is egalitarian, since each person's happiness is of equal value. Even the feelings of animals can be taken into account. Bentham claims that the principle of utility is not susceptible to direct proof, because it is the principle that is used to prove everything else.

Bentham's moral system drew storms of protest. Many critics complained that an ethics based on hedonism legitimized crass self-indulgence and base animal pleasures. Christians were troubled by utilitarianism's secularism. Critics also complained that utilitarianism reduced ethics to cold, impersonal calculations; that it was too difficult and demanding; that it was too simplistic and easy; and that it could easily lead to rights violations and injustices. The history of utilitarianism since Bentham consists of the ways in which its advocates have reacted to critics by reshaping and improving the theory.

JOHN STUART MILL

Bentham's chosen successor was his godson John Stuart Mill. In his major ethical work, *Utilitarianism* (1861), Mill responded to the aforementioned charges. He defended utilitarianism (to varying degrees of success), but he also changed Bentham's hedonism in significant ways. Responding to Thomas Carlyle, whose distaste for ethical hedonism led him to denounce utilitarianism as a "sordid pig-philosophy," Mill argued that pleasures differed qualitatively and that some pleasures are superior to others. Another significant change came forty years later, when G. E. Moore articulated his "ideal utilitarianism," which allows for the intrinsic goodness and desirability of other values besides happiness.

Charges that utilitarianism could lead to injustice have persisted despite the explanations of Bentham, Mill, and a host of others. The strong claim that one should always do whatever results in the greatest utility has prompted critics to imagine scenarios in which utilitarianism is construed to endorse such detestable actions as gladiator fights (if the aggregate pleasure of the multitudinous spectators outweighs the pain of the participants), the punishing of innocents (if convicting someone of committing a sensational crime appeases the masses, staves off riots, and restores faith in the system), torture (if torture could force a captured terrorist to confess where a bomb has been planted), and even murder (if surgeons harvest an individual's organs for transplant in other patients, thus improving and saving several lives).

Such problems have led to the distinction between act- and rule-utilitarianism and the view that utilitarianism is more effective as a formula for developing basic rules than as a method for rationalizing the best action in a particular case. John Rawls has argued that utilitarianism neglects basic principles of justice and fairness by ignoring the distinction between persons and the distribution of goods. He believes that emphasizing the sum total of happiness or average utility not only leads to inequalities but also legitimizes them. Utilitarians maintain that there is a natural dynamic that favors egalitarianism, in that a given sum of money will likely have greater utility value for a poor person than for a wealthy person. Moreover, utilitarians claim that it is unlikely that an extremely inegalitarian distribution of resources or benefits would bring about the greatest possible amount of happiness.

The success of utilitarianism is remarkable. Few persons regard themselves as utilitarians, yet utilitarianism remains among the dominant schools of ethical theory. Its influence extends beyond ethics into social sciences and formal decision theory. Thanks to its able advocates, its appeal to basic rational principles, and its flexibility, utilitarianism has adjusted to the challenges of critics and maintained its prominence.

Don A. Habibi

FURTHER READING

Allison, Lincoln, ed. *The Utilitarian Response: The Contemporary Viability of Utilitarian Political Philosophy.* London: Sage, 1990.

Bentham, Jeremy. *An Introduction to the Principles of Morals and Legislation.* Edited by J. H. Burns and H. L. A. Hart. New York: Methuen, 1982.

Dinwiddy, John. *Bentham: Selected Writings of John Dinwiddy.* Edited by William Twining. Stanford, Calif.: Stanford University Press, 2004.

Glover, Jonathan, ed. *Utilitarianism and Its Critics.* New York: Macmillan, 1990.

Lyons, David. *The Forms and Limits of Utilitarianism.* Oxford, England: Clarendon Press, 1965.

Mill, John Stuart. *Utilitarianism.* Edited by George Sher. 2d ed. Indianapolis: Hackett, 2001.

Shaw, William H. *Contemporary Ethics: Taking Account of Utilitarianism.* Malden, Mass.: Blackwell, 1999.

SEE ALSO: Bentham, Jeremy; Consequentialism; Cost-benefit analysis; Distributive justice; Epicurus; Hedonism; Mill, John Stuart; Moore, G. E.; Pragmatism; Sidgwick, Henry; Universalizability.

Utopia

IDENTIFICATION: Book by Sir Thomas More (1478-1535)

DATE: Published in 1516

TYPE OF ETHICS: Medieval history

SIGNIFICANCE: A description of a supposedly ideal society, *Utopia* revitalized ethical thinking on social planning, prompting a flood of utopian literature over the ensuing centuries.

Thomas More coined the word "utopia" for this book and simultaneously provided a noun to describe an ideal society and an adjective—utopian—to signify a hopelessly impractical approach to living. The word "utopia" derives from the Greek for "no place," but it is also a pun on "good place." With this play on words, More sowed the seeds of argument regarding his book: Was he serious? Was he a communist, a liberal, an autocrat? Was he an advocate of euthanasia and divorce?

Utopia shows many influences. More was a classical scholar of high standing—a product of the Renaissance. He also pursued a career in law with great success. Amerigo Vespucci's writings on America inspired him with references to paradisiacal lands

Sir Thomas More. (Library of Congress)

and the communal ownership of property. The Roman Catholic Church was the dominant influence of his boyhood, and perhaps of his whole life. Interestingly, More wrote *Utopia* in a lull before the Reformation; one year after its publication, Martin Luther defied the Church by nailing his ninety-five theses to the door of All Saints Church in Wittenberg.

UTOPIAN PRACTICES AND ETHICS

Book 1 of *Utopia* describes meeting a man called Hythloday, who first castigates European society and then proceeds in book 2 to describe Utopia with heartfelt admiration. Hythloday condemns the idle of Europe, including noblemen and their servants. He asserts that rulers wage war, not peace, and that ministers at court do not listen to arguments, but indulge in politics for their own gain. His remedies for economic ills include stopping the enclosure and monopoly of land by the rich. With strong words, he condemns the execution of thieves as unfair and ineffective, stating that it incites men to kill, since murder carries the same penalty.

Book 2 describes More's fictional state in detail. The Utopians live a regulated, standardized life. All the cities are beautiful and identical. All citizens wear the same simple clothes, with some modifications for gender. They live together in families of specific size and work six hours a day, spending their leisure time reading and attending lectures. Women may marry at the age of eighteen, men at twenty-two. Adultery is strongly condemned and can result in slavery or even execution. In extreme circumstances of recurrent adultery or perversion, however, divorce is permitted.

Utopia is a state founded on compassion and altruism. No one wants for material goods. Health care is universal, though few get sick. Society gently encourages euthanasia when a mortally ill person suffers from great pain. All property is owned communally. Every ten years, a family exchanges its house, which is supposed to encourage people to take proper care for the next tenant. Even their eating takes place in a large hall that holds as many as thirty households.

Ultimately, authoritarianism is a strong feature of this model state. No one has the freedom to remain idle. Everyone needs permission to travel. Any discussion of government matters outside official meeting-places is punishable by death. Utopia also has rigid hierarchies: children defer to adults, women to men, younger to older, and families to their elected representatives. Paradoxically, however, Utopia has strong democratic elements, including voting for all key political posts, though people are barred from canvassing votes, to minimize corruption. Slavery replaces hanging as the deterrent for deviant behavior. Serious criminal behavior leads to slavery, which entails working constantly in chains, performing the meanest labor.

Citizens may practice any religion, but strong proselytizing is barred for fear that it may lead to argument. Certain tenets must be held by all: belief in a wise Providence and an afterlife. Utopians pursue pleasure as natural and logical, but they abhor vanity and pomp and place no value on gold and silver, even while storing it for economic advantage and for trade. They avoid war whenever possible but conduct military training for both sexes. When threatened by another nation, they offer rewards to kill the ruler of the opposing nation. Failing that, they sow contention in that nation and, as a last resort, hire mercenaries to fight alongside their own soldiers.

Discussion

More uses this book to debate opposing viewpoints for intellectual stimulation. For example, when Hythloday says that as long as there is property there will be no justice, More counters that in a communist society people would not work or have any in-

centive to better themselves. Hythloday contrasts the greed and selfishness of Europe with Utopia's communism based on a harmony of purpose, with the family unit at its core. Utopia also, however, has internal contradictions. The residents' humanistic values—respecting individual inquiry and religious freedom—contrast with the total conformity of their lives and the fact that certain basic beliefs must be held by all.

Utopia is a commentary on More's own society, a combination of monasticism and feudalism, but Utopia is founded on reason, not Christianity. More is pleading: If they can do so well without divine revelation, why can Europe not do better with it? It is impossible to believe that More meant *Utopia* as a blueprint for an ideal society. Elements that support this conclusion include the deadpan humor (Anider, a river, means "no water"; Utopians use gold in making chamber pots) and the contrast with More's own religious convictions (he persecuted heretics and chose execution rather than compromise his opposition to divorce). Ultimately, *Utopia* is not so much interesting or original in itself as it is noteworthy because it stimulated discussion regarding "social engineering" as a remedy for society's ills.

Philip Magnier

Further Reading

Baker-Smith, Dominic. *More's "Utopia."* Toronto: University of Toronto Press, 2000.

Constable, George, ed. *Utopian Visions: Mysteries of the Unknown.* Alexandria, Va.: Time-Life, 1991.

More, Thomas. *Utopia: A Revised Translation, Backgrounds, Criticism.* 2d ed. New York: Norton, 1992.

Negley, Glenn, and J. Max Patrick. *The Quest for Utopia.* College Park, Md.: McGrath, 1971.

Nelson, William. *Twentieth Century Interpretations of Utopia.* Englewood Cliffs, N.J.: Prentice-Hall, 1968.

Tod, Ian, and Michael Wheeler. *Utopia.* New York: Harmony Books, 1978.

See also: Common good; Communism; Communitarianism; Criminal punishment; Democracy; Euthanasia; Family values; Humanism; Luther, Martin; Platonic ethics; *Republic*; Socialism.

V

Value

DEFINITION: Relative level of worth, goodness, significance, or utility possessed by an entity, attribute, or event; or, an intangible quality or attribute that has intrinsic worth in itself

TYPE OF ETHICS: Theory of ethics

SIGNIFICANCE: For an objectivist, value is the basis of judgment. For a subjectivist, value is the thing produced by judgment. Thus, all moral judgment involves either assigning value to an action, person, or thing, or accurately perceiving the value that exists within an action, person, or thing.

Values are of signal importance; without them, human life would be drained of significance, a bland and textureless existence without differentiation. Academic disciplines focus on value in a variety of ways: The arts explore expressions of value; sociology, anthropology, and history all examine the ways in which values are embedded in society's structures; and psychology, including the work of philosophical psychologists such as Friedrich Nietzsche, looks at the ways in which individuals acquire their beliefs about values and the roles these beliefs play in their psyches. The philosophical study of value, axiology, tries to step back from these particular inquiries and look instead at the question "What is value?" Axiology has been a central focus of philosophical inquiry throughout the history of the discipline. For all that, however, little consensus has emerged, although certain positions tend to run as threads throughout the discussion.

Answers to the question "What is value?" take two possible forms. The first and simplest provides a list of values, such as courage, honesty, beauty, and compassion. The second attempts to answer the question "What is value in general?" It may seem relatively simple to compile a list of values, but history and anthropology reveal that such lists vary considerably at different times and in different cultures. Homeric heroes were applauded for their ability to lie

and dissimulate, and classical Japanese samurai were expected to test a new sword by slicing through an unlucky wayfarer from the shoulder to the opposite flank. The honor of both the samurai and the swordmaker depended on a clean bisection.

Assuming that a list of values can be compiled, the inevitable next question is "What exactly is meant by 'courage' or 'beauty' or 'friendship'?" The ancient Greek philosopher Plato focused on questions of this "What is X?" form in his early dialogues. The *Laches* seeks the definition of courage, the *Euthyphro* that of piety, and the *Lysis* that of friendship. Although these dialogues are notorious for providing few answers and for clearly showing how quickly simplistic answers become tangled in their own contradictions, one important implication becomes clear: One cannot know what particular values are unless one knows the nature of value in general.

SUBJECTIVISM/OBJECTIVISM

Plato begins to address the question "What is value in general?" in the Meno, and it is a central theme in many of his other dialogues. One view to which he is clearly attracted is that personal excellence is knowledge; that view, however, is replaced in later dialogues, notably his *Republic*, by the view that there is a source of excellence, for both people and objects, that can be known. He argues that, since all instances of a certain value—for example, beauty or courage—share some property, there must be something, the "form" of that excellence, that they make manifest. Forms for Plato are separable essences, with an independent existence, that infuse the objects or people who display them. Objects or people are excellent or have value insofar as they make manifest the form of a particular value. There are, therefore, forms of all excellences, and the highest of these is the form of the good. One's own particular excellence or excellences are produced by one's knowledge of the good, and it is this knowledge that is the ultimate goal of all philosophical inquiry. This emphasis on an external source of value is one of the threads that runs through all discussions of value.

The second thread arises from the indubitable fact that people have emotional responses to instances of value. Humans are moved by compassion and repulsed by wanton cruelty; they admire bravery and appreciate beauty. This raises the following question. Do people have these responses to these actions and objects because they have the value they do or do they have the value they do because people have these responses to them? In this article, "subjectivism" is taken to be the position that human emotional responses to actions, character traits, or objects are what endow them with value.

"Objectivism" is taken to be the position that there is some source or standard of value that is separate from the emotions; emotional responses to actions, character traits, or objects are prompted by, but in no way contribute to, their having value. Both negative and positive values are included in these analyses. Plato clearly took the objectivist path, and in this he was followed by many other great thinkers: Saint Thomas Aquinas, echoing Aristotle, said in his *In Divinus Nominibus* (1265), "It is not that a thing is beautiful because we love it, but we love it because it is beautiful and good." Other philosophers, however, have argued powerfully that what makes something valuable is the act of valuing it; perhaps the greatest of these thinkers is David Hume.

DAVID HUME

Hume drew an important distinction between matters of fact and matters of value. In a famous passage from his *Treatise of Human Nature* (1739-1740), he said,

> In every system of morality . . . I have always remark'd, that the author proceeds for some time in the ordinary way of reasoning . . . when of a sudden I am surpriz'd to find, that instead of the usual copulations of propositions, *is*, and *is not*, I meet with no proposition that is not connected with an *ought*, or an *ought not*. This change is imperceptible; but is, however, of the last consequence. For as this *ought*, or *ought not*, expresses some new relation or affirmation, 'tis necessary . . . a reason should be given, for what seems altogether inconceivable, how this new relation can be a deduction from others which are entirely different from it.

The illegitimacy of deriving value (ought) statements from factual (is) propositions alone was later labeled the "naturalistic fallacy" by G. E. Moore.

Hume's views on human psychology are an integral part of his answer to how one moves from matters of fact to matters of value. He identifies two distinct psychological processes: reason and sentiment. Reason establishes matters of fact, while sentiment, or the passions, provide a motive for action. For example, one's reason may tell one that one is standing on a railway line, that a train is coming, and that if one does not move one will be crushed, but it is only one's desire not to be crushed that provides the motive force to move. Given that moral judgments provide motives for action, Hume reasoned that they must be the result of sentiment "gilding and staining all natural objects with [its] colours."

Distinguishing between matters of fact and matters of value and locating the source of value in human sentiment—usually some form of happiness or pleasure—are integral parts of the subjectivist position. People value, and ascribe value to, those things that make them happy or sad, or that cause them pleasure or pain. Although the notion of what constitutes happiness or pleasure can be somewhat crude (Aristippus opted for immediate physical pleasures, whereas Epicurus advocated philosophical reflection and a diet of bread, cheese, and milk), in the hands of someone like David Hume, it is a subtle and many-layered aspect of the psyche.

Although subjectivism holds that all positive value has its source in positive human sentiment, the corollary does not hold; not everything in which people find happiness or pleasure is good. Pulling the wings off flies is not good simply because generations of small children have relished it; there are better and worse pleasures. John Stuart Mill recognized this distinction in the quality of pleasures, and in *Utilitarianism* (1863) he wrote that

> Few human creatures would consent to be changed into any of the lower animals, for a promise of the fullest allowance of that beast's pleasures; no intelligent human being would consent to be a fool, no instructed person would be an ignoramus, no person of feeling and conscience would be base, even though they should be persuaded that the fool, the dunce or the rascal is better satisfied with his lot than they are with theirs.

For Mill, the good life was founded on the refined pleasures of the higher faculties. The pleasures of a life of intelligent understanding, fine feeling, and elevated conscience are better than the pleasures of a life of ignorance, selfishness, and lack of restraint. His evidence for this is the fact that those who have had a chance to experience both types of life overwhelmingly prefer the more refined variety.

OBJECTIONS AND REPLIES

Locating the source of value in refined human sentiments brings with it three serious problems. The first is that, as G. E. Moore pointed out in an application of the naturalistic fallacy, simply because people *do* seek and value what provides them with pleasure does not mean that they *ought* to seek it. Subjectivists, including Mill and Hume, have tried to get around this objection by asserting that happiness is the only good in itself and that all else is sought as a means of obtaining it, but this fails to answer the thrust of Moore's objection. Even if everything else is sought as a means to happiness, it still does not mean that happiness is that which people ought to seek. The second problem is the parochialism of the idea of refined sentiment. While everyone can recognize what is wrong with the sadist who relishes inflicting pain, it is harder to say with any credibility that someone whose life is dedicated to a sybaritic wallow in the pleasures of the flesh is doing something *wrong*. (There is, of course, the issue of harm to others caused by this indulgence, but that is a separate question.) With this parochialism comes a potentially disturbing paternalism; if the refined pleasures are somehow better, then I may have some moral grounds for forcing unenlightened others to enjoy them. There are undertones of this view in Mill's *On Liberty* (1859).

Finally, there is the problem that if the source of value lies within the sentiments, then the value of an individual to others depends on their, the others', sentiments. X's value to Y depends on Y's feelings about X, not on some source of value possessed by X, and this does not seem to capture what philosophers mean when they talk about the moral value of persons. People, as Immanuel Kant pointed out, are valuable as ends in themselves, not simply as means to another's ends (in this case, the enjoyment of certain individual or social passions). These considerations have led many thinkers to reject the subjectiv-

ist source for value and to seek instead a source external to the human psyche. Plato identified the form of the good as this source, and generations of theistic writers including Thomas Aquinas and Saint Augustine of Hippo have taken a similar line by identifying God as the source of all value. Immanuel Kant saw the dictates of pure practical reason as the test for what was good and bad, and Moore argued that the good was an unanalyzable nonnatural property that one came to know by means of ethical intuition.

Although there is a problem of relativism with this position similar to that of subjectivism (Which religion or religious person has heard God's word correctly? Whose intuition has apprehended the good?), objectivism at least has a ready reply: Although humans may have an imperfect understanding of the good, there is nevertheless one right answer that they must find. A second difficulty is what J. L. Mackie in *Ethics* (1977) called the problem of "queerness." If there is an external, objective value, what would it look like; what kind of existence would it have? Clearly, it would have to be unlike anything else anyone has ever come across. The third and more serious problem comes by way, once again, of the naturalistic fallacy. Even supposing that there is a standard of right and wrong, a source of objective value, why should it necessarily be the case that we should accede to it? Assuming that God decrees compassion to be a valuable character trait, one still must decide, presumably by some separate standard, whether one ought to follow God's word. As Hume would say, the fact that God approves of compassion has no power over one's action unless one already wants to, or feels one ought to, obey God. Kant tries to argue that duty, one's motive force for obeying the dictates of pure practical reason, is not a sentiment, because it is produced by internal reason and not by fear or desire of external conditions, but this answer is extremely thin.

OTHER ALTERNATIVES

Faced with the seeming failure of both objectivism and subjectivism to provide an unequivocal and palatable answer to the question "What is value?" philosophers have tried other approaches. Existentialists such as Søren Kierkegaard, Jean-Paul Sartre, and Albert Camus focused on the fundamental choices and commitments by which people create value in the face of an absurd world. In the analytic school during the mid-twentieth century, axiology waned as the focus switched to analyzing the meaningfulness of value language. A. J. Ayer and Charles L. Stevenson both argued that value language had no literal meaning, that it described no real property or object, and that it was rather an expression of emotion. Saying "Justice is good" was semantically equivalent to saying "Justice—hooray," and the theory quickly became known as the "boo hooray" theory.

The problem at the heart of this issue is that both the factual aspects of actions or character traits and human emotional responses to them are important elements in valuation. The sharp division in Western philosophy between reason and emotion means that the issue has usually been framed as a dichotomy: The source of value is either in the emotions or in some objective standard. One way around this disjunction is to deny the dichotomy and to see value as an emergent property arising from the interaction between factual characteristics and beliefs about, and emotional responses to, those characteristics. Emergent properties are those properties that exist as part of a dynamic system and are not reducible to any part or additive combination of parts of that system. Therefore, people appreciate a beautiful object or a noble deed because it exhibits certain characteristics, and it is those characteristics that make it beautiful or noble. What isolates those characteristics from the total description of the action or object, groups them together, and endows them with significance, however, are one's beliefs about and emotional responses to them. These responses, in turn, are shaped and guided by the characteristics that one perceives as significant.

In observing a bullfight, for example, one can isolate and describe many of the natural features of the event: the size and color of the bull, the number of people in the crowd, the blood of the bull on the sand, the color of the matador's trousers, the pleasure experienced by the crowd, the day of the week, the pain experienced by the bull, the color of the sky, and so on. Only some of these features will be relevant to an ethical assessment of the value of a bullfight, and the network of beliefs and emotions through which we perceive them will group some of those features together and endow them with significance. For most observers, the pain of the bull will be relevant, while the color of the sky will not. The way in which that pain is interpreted, however, will vary depending on

the beliefs of the observer; it may be seen as evidence of the nobility of the bull and the bullfight or as evidence of the cruelty of both the event and the matador. It is not that the source of the value lies solely in the beliefs and emotions of the observers or solely in the natural features of the bullfight that one groups together, but rather in the interaction between the two. Such a process will, as Hume says, "raise, in a manner, a new creation." Out of the vast array of features, beliefs, and emotions will rise a morally significant event, an odious or noble bullfight.

Robert Halliday

FURTHER READING

Hume, David. *An Enquiry Concerning the Principles of Morals*. Edited by J. B. Schneewind. Indianapolis: Hackett, 1983. The standard edition of this seminal work in which Hume develops the ideas postulated in his *Treatise of Human Nature*.

MacIntyre, Alasdair. *After Virtue: A Study in Moral Theory*. 2d ed. Notre Dame, Ind.: University of Notre Dame Press, 1984. An extremely influential book that argues that virtues can be understood only in the context of a social practice.

Mill, John Stuart. *Utilitarianism*. Edited by George Sher. 2d ed. Indianapolis: Hackett, 2001. Mill's classic discussion of happiness as the source of all values includes his distinction between higher and lower happiness.

Nietzsche, Friedrich. *Beyond Good and Evil*. Translated by Walter Kaufmann. New York: Vintage, 1989.

_____. *On the Genealogy of Morals*. Edited and translated by Walter Kaufmann. New York: Vintage Books, 1967. Nietzsche asserts that one of philosophy's most important projects is to analyze the "value of values," to determine where value comes from and what effects it has, rather than merely assuming that "good" is always better than "bad." This is the first step in the "revaluation of all values," the construction of a new set of values which will fit the needs of humankind.

Plato. *The Republic*. Translated by Desmond Lee. 2d ed. New York: Penguin Books, 2003. A mature Platonic dialogue in which the idea of the good is explicated and defended. One of the great classics in moral and political philosophy.

Railton, Peter. *Facts, Values, and Norms: Essays Toward a Morality of Consequence*. New York:

Cambridge University Press, 2003. A contemporary objectivist attempt to ground moral value through naturalistic argument.

Sartre, Jean-Paul. *Existentialism and Humanism.* Edited and translated by Phillip Mairet. Brooklyn: Haskell House, 1977. A short lecture in which Sartre addresses the foundations of existentialism. Provides a more accessible introduction to existential commitment than does his giant *Being and Nothingness* (1956).

SEE ALSO: Absolutism; Epicurus; Good, the; Kierkegaard, Søren; Morality; Naturalistic fallacy; Objectivism; Relativism; Right and wrong; Subjectivism; Values clarification.

Values clarification

DEFINITION: Series of strategies designed to help individuals who have mutually exclusive values

TYPE OF ETHICS: Theory of ethics

SIGNIFICANCE: Values clarification seeks to develop an umbrella set of ethical values that will be able to reconcile conflicts between more specific values. This overall ethical framework, once developed, guides one's individual decisions and helps one to lead the kind of life one desires.

Traditionally, educators have taught values development through such strategies as didactic moralizing, prescriptive modeling, inspiring, and appealing to conscience. Yet these traditional strategies have not noticeably produced the desired results—at least, so believe the proponents of values clarification, who advocate a different set of strategies to develop effective values consciousness.

BACKGROUND

Values clarification evolved during the mid-1960's, when American activists challenged the war in Vietnam, along with the political system, and promoted civil rights for minorities. Concurrently, critics attacked the schools for ignoring the teaching of values in a time of crises. Noting that parents and religious institutions had little impact, critics believed that the media, particularly television, adversely affected the values of the young. Hence, they argued that education should teach the young how to develop appropriate values.

The first major book on values clarification, Louis Raths's *Values and Teaching* (1966), argued that Western pluralistic society made it impossible to inculcate a uniform set of values. Instead, Rath wanted to teach individuals the processes through which values emerge and may be acted upon. Rath and his associates proceeded to devise the theoretical construct of values clarification and create appropriate strategies.

The clarifying stage is most crucial because clarification cannot occur unless values collide with competing values. Suppose that one strongly believes in the importance of sustaining life. Place that value in a particular situation, such as that of an elder suffering unbearable pain caused by an incurable disease. Two values thus conflict: the importance of sustaining life and the importance of lessening or eliminating pain. To clarify and then resolve the conflict of what to do, one must proceed through the seven-question framework established by Raths.

Louis Rath's Seven-Question Framework

1. What are the alternatives, given the choices?

2. What are the consequences of each alternative?

3. Can one's choices be made independently?

4. What are one's value preferences?

5. Can one declare one's preferences publicly?

6. Once decisions are made, can one act upon one's choices?

7. Can one develop a values stance that is consistent with a long-term framework of personal conduct?

The goals of values clarification are to help individuals select and reflect on the values chosen that best suit a particular situation. Borrowing from John Dewey the basic tenet that values are not fixed but change as life situations change, advocates of values clarification perceive all values as relative.

To engage in values clarification, its advocates recommend the workshop, with small informal groups providing an interchange of ideas. The leader-teacher stimulates the moral reasoning within the group, often providing some subject for the values discussion; for example, a story, poem, cartoon, game, or news event. After recapping the subject's content, the leader-teacher and the group probe both the intrinsic values of the material itself and the values of the group.

Three Stages of Values Clarification

1. identifying and analyzing values

2. clarifying the values

3. internalizing or acting upon the reconstituted values

VALUES CLARIFICATION AND ETHICS

Values clarification was initially regarded as an exciting area in education, filled with potential. Later, values clarification became an explosive educational issue.

Protest activists of the mid-1960's brought values-clarification techniques to the attention of the public through media events. Suddenly values clarification was "in." Teachers, too, reported that it stimulated students because of its wide applications to everyday experiences. Students not only learned to deal with their feelings but also practiced communication and decision-making skills and articulated their value judgments.

Values clarification advocates such as Sidney Simon, Howard Kirschenbaum, and Jack Fraenkel created innovative strategies. Both teachers and students delighted in using value ladders, role playing, value grids, rank-order and forced-choice dilemmas, time diaries, and so forth.

LATER REACTIONS

Once the novelty of values clarification lessened, some educators raised warning flags. For example, hard research data on its effectiveness was nonexistent. Because values clarification deals with feelings and emotions, some critics equated it with "touchy-

feely" activities found in sensitivity training. Others questioned the idea that values-clarification strategies are value free, noting that the valuing process itself, the seven-step criteria, held hidden values.

Likewise, inexperienced teachers allowed values discussions to drift and, on occasion, because of cultural differences, provoked unsettling confrontations among participants. Peer pressures among youngsters often discouraged the open, free exchange of ideas, while teachers were uncertain as to how far they should go in accepting all values. Were all values equal?

Parents, once aware that their children were engaging in values clarification, complained the children were not mature enough to participate in such complex processes. Moreover, if all values were viewed as equal, children were not learning right from wrong.

Pressure groups increasingly charged that values-clarification practices confused children because schools and teachers lacked standards of conduct. They also claimed that the schools brainwashed the children, insisting that teachers cannot remain ethically neutral and that they manipulate student values—inadvertently or by design.

When pressure groups offered values-clarification activities as evidence that schools were practicing "secular humanism," many school boards banned books and workshops on values clarification. The real conflict was over whose values should be taught and how.

Since the late 1970's, educators have sought compromise, attempting to balance the clarification of personal values with the transmission of lawful societal values. In sum, the major contribution of values clarification to the field of ethics has been the development of innovative exercises and strategies designed to allow individuals to clarify their values.

Richard Whitworth

FURTHER READING

Cummings, William K., Maria Teresa Tatto, and John Hawkins, eds. *Values Education for Dynamic Societies: Individualism or Collectivism.* Hong Kong: Comparative Education Research Centre, University of Hong Kong, 2001.

Fraenkel, Jack. *How to Teach About Values: An Analytic Approach.* Englewood Cliffs, N.J.: Prentice-Hall, 1977.

Kirschenbaum, Howard, and Sidney Simon. *Readings in Values Clarification*. Minneapolis, Minn.: Winston Press, 1973.

Monges, Miriam Ma'at-Ka-Re. "Beyond the Melting Pot: A Values Clarification Exercise for Teachers and Human Service Professionals." In *Teaching About Culture, Ethnicity, and Diversity: Exercises and Planned Activities*, edited by Theodore M. Singelis. Thousand Oaks, Calif.: Sage, 1998.

Raths, Louis, et al. *Values and Teaching*. 2d ed. Columbus, Ohio: Charles E. Merrill, 1978.

Simon, Sidney, et al. *Values and Teaching: Working with Values in the Classroom*. Sunderland, Mass.: Values Press, 1991.

_____. *Values Clarification: A Handbook of Practical Strategies for Teachers and Students*. Sunderland, Mass.: Values Press, 1991.

SEE ALSO: Dewey, John; Humanism; Moral education; Nagel, Thomas; Perry, R. B.; Value.

Vardhamāna

IDENTIFICATION: Ancient Indian religious reformer
BORN: c. 599 B.C.E., Kundagrama, Bihar, Magadha (now in India)
DIED: 527 B.C.E., Pavapuri, Bihar, Magadha (now in India)
TYPE OF ETHICS: Religious ethics
SIGNIFICANCE: Vardhamānŭ was the founder of the Jain religion and an important teacher of the ethical values of nonviolence and spirituality.

Once, when he was attacked by a powerful man, Vardhamāna, also known as Mahāvīra, responded not with violence, anger, or fear but with love. This approach conquered his assailant, and thus Mahāvīra discovered the power of nonviolence. A new religion in India, Jainism, arose from the flames of Mahāvīra's love. In a world of destructive force, Mahāvīra bequeathed a great weapon to those seeking peace and justice: moral force. This moral force influenced the peace, civil rights, and animal rights movements.

In the sixth century B.C.E., India was dominated by Hinduism and the caste system. Mahāvīra rebelled against this system, and at age thirty he re-nounced wealth, position, and his own family to seek spiritual fulfillment. Practicing an extreme asceticism, in twelve years he became a perfected soul, a *jina*, or "conqueror," of passions. The focus of his teaching was love of *all* life. To Mahāvīra, true justice meant to cause no suffering for any life, and thus required the practice of vegetarianism.

Salvation required the three jewels of the soul: right knowledge, right conviction, and right conduct. Mahāvīra regarded right conduct as the most precious jewel of the three. It consists of five vows: no killing of any living creature, no lying, no stealing, no sexual pleasure or alcohol, and no desire or attachments.

Mahāvīra believed that no harm could ever befall a good man. Ritual, prayer, sacrifice, and social power could not make one worthy. The only value is the good life, which must be realized by right conduct.

Mahāvīra and the Jains so loved life that they would not even harm insects. At a time when life has become cheap, perhaps nothing is more ethically relevant than the reverence for all life that Mahāvīra so fervently practiced.

T. E. Katen

FURTHER READING

Jain, Hiralal, and A. N. Upadhye. *Mahāvīra: His Times and His Philosophy of Life*. 3d ed. New Delhi: Bharatiya Jnanpith, 1998.

Jaini, Jagomandar Lal. *Outlines of Jainism*. Westport, Conn.: Hyperion Press, 1982.

Stevenson, Mrs. Sinclair. *The Heart of Jainism*. New York: Oxford University Press, 1915. Reprint. New Delhi: Munshiram Manoharial, 1970.

SEE ALSO: Ahiṁsā; Animal rights; Environmental ethics; Hindu ethics; Jain ethics; Vegetarianism.

Vedānta

DEFINITION: Major school of Indian philosophy associated with monism, transcendentalism, and mysticism
TYPE OF ETHICS: Religious ethics
SIGNIFICANCE: The goal of Vedānta is to achieve the ultimate reality, or *Brāhmin*, by breaking the cy-

cle of birth and rebirth in three different ways: the way of knowledge, or *jñāna*; the way of devotion, or *bhakti*; and the way of action, or karma.

Vedānta, literally meaning the "end of the Vedas," is a school of Indian philosophy. The Upaniṣads, *Bhagavadgītā*, and Brahma Sūtra, together with their commentaries, form the essence of the Vedānta philosophy.

ADVAITA, OR NONDUALISTIC, VEDĀNTA

Śaṅkara (788-850) is considered the most powerful advocate of pure monism, or Advaita. Śaṅkara advocates the way of knowledge, or *jñāna*, as the only way to attain liberation, or *mokṣa*. The basic question of Advaita is the nature of *Brāhmin*, or ultimate reality. *Brāhmin* is pure consciousness, devoid of attributes. *Brāhmin* is nondual (*advaita*) and transcends the distinction between the knower, knowledge, and the known. The world is not real; it is an illusion, or *māyā*. It appears to be real because of ignorance, or *avidyā*, but when one comes to the realization of *Brāhmin*, one realizes the illusoriness of the world. In understanding Indian philosophy, one must realize that it believes in different levels of being. Therefore, one who comes to the realization of *Brāhmin* becomes identical with *Brāhmin* and is, therefore, at the highest level of being and has the highest reality. Every individual has a phenomenal self, which is empirically real, since it is a part of his or her experience, and a real self, or *ātman*, which is transcendentally real and is one with *Brāhmin*.

VIŚIṢṬADVAITA, OR QUALIFIED MONISM

The early twelfth century philosopher Ramanuja refutes the absolute monism of Śaṅkara and denies that the world is illusory, or *māyā*, and emphasizes *bhakti*, or worship, as a means of liberation. He advocated the way of devotion as opposed to the way of knowledge advocated by Advaita Vedāntins. For Ramanuja, *Brāhmin*, or ultimate reality, is spirit but has attributes. *Brāhmin* has self-consciousness and has a conscious will to create the world and bestow salvation. For Ramanuja, *Brāhmin* is a whole consisting of interrelated elements. There is no pure, undifferentiated consciousness. *Brāhmin*, for Ramanuja, is not a formless entity but a supreme person qualified by matter and souls. Matter (*achit*), soul (*chit*), and God (Iśvara) are real, but matter and soul are de-

pendent on God. God (Iśvara) is *Brāhmin*, and he manifests himself in various forms for his devotees. Souls are in bondage because of ignorance. Liberation can be achieved, according to Ramanuja, by the intuitive realization that the soul is a mode of God. The soul that is liberated is not identical with *Brāhmin* because soul is always finite and God is infinite. That is why Ramanuja believes that liberation can be achieved only after death, when the soul is separated from the body. Ramanuja's view opened the way for theism, especially Vaiśnavism, within Vedānta.

DVAITA, OR DUALISTIC, VEDĀNTA

During the thirteenth century, Mādhava developed the philosophical view called Dvaita, or dualistic, Vedānta, and he was outspoken against Advaita Vedānta philosophy. Mādhava was considered an incarnation of the god Viṣṇu. He stressed duality and, like Ramanuja, advocated the way of devotion, or *bhakti*. For Mādhava, God is distinct from individual souls and matter, an individual soul is distinct from another individual soul, the individual soul is distinct from matter, and when matter is divided, each part of that matter is distinct from each other. According to Mādhava, souls can be classified into three groups: those who are devoted to God alone and are bound to achieve liberation, those who will never attain liberation and are destined to perpetual rebirth, and those who revile Viṣṇu and are subject to damnation. Mādhava believed that there are different degrees of knowledge and enjoyment of bliss in liberated souls. The worship of Viṣṇu in thought, word, and deed was for him the way to liberation.

MODERN VEDĀNTA

During the early twentieth century, Sri Aurobindo made a unique contribution to Vedānta philosophy. His view is popularly called the Philosophy of Integralism, or Integral Nondualism. His teaching is that the Absolute, God, world, and souls are One. His philosophy is a reinterpretation of traditional Vedānta that applies it to the social context. According to Aurobindo, human life can be transformed into the highest form of spiritual reality by practicing yoga. If one searches for the divine force that is within one and accordingly transforms all dimensions of life, one will be able to live in the highest possible divine way. Society should also be reshaped in such a way that is helpful to this transformation of life.

Vivekānanda, a late ninteenth century disciple of Ramakrishna, organized the Ramakrishna Mission (it is also called the Vedānta Society in the United States). Vivekānanda considered himself an *advaitin*, but his Advaita viewpoint did not lead to inactive meditation; it was instead a call to action. He viewed knowledge, devotion, and action as three paths leading in different directions but reinforcing each other. He stressed practical work to achieve liberation. Since a person is identical with God, one should seek to abolish the indignities of the world.

The Indian philosopher Sarvepalli Radhakrishnan, who served as the second president of India (1962-1967), contributed to Advaita Vedānta philosophy by providing a positive approach to *Brāhmin* in which human values were preserved. He argued that the phenomenal world is temporal, which does not mean that it is unreal and does not have any meaning and significance. Karma should not be interpreted pessimistically. It is true that the past cannot be changed, but the past does not determine the future. An individual is still free to act within the limits of the past. He emphasized that one can lead a meaningful life here and now. His view constitutes a spiritual democracy that allows everyone to work side by side. He stressed unity rather than diversity. He conveyed his teaching to the West by stating that each religion is valid to the extent that it helps one to achieve spiritual realization.

Krishna Mallick

FURTHER READING

Fowler, Jeaneane. *Perspectives of Reality: An Introduction to the Philosophy of Hinduism*. Portland, Oreg.: Sussex Academic Press, 2002.

Isherwood, Christopher. *Vedanta for the Western World*. Hollywood, Calif.: Marcel Rodd, 1945.

Panda, R. K., ed. *Studies in Vedānta Philosophy*. Delhi: Bharatiya Kala Prakashan, 2002.

Reyna, Ruth. *The Concept of Maya from the Vedas to the Twentieth Century*. Bombay, India: Asia, 1962.

Schweitzer, Albert. *Indian Thought and Its Development*. Translated by Mrs. Charles E. B. Russell. Gloucester, Mass.: Peter Smith, 1977.

Zaehner, R. C. *Hinduism*. London: Oxford University Press, 1962.

Zimmer, Heinrich. *Philosophies of India*. Edited by Joseph Campbell. Princeton, N.J.: Princeton University Press, 1967.

SEE ALSO: Aurobindo, Sri; Hindu ethics; Karma; Mysticism; Śaṅkara; Tagore, Rabindranath; Upaniṣads.

Vegetarianism

DEFINITION: Dietary practice of subsisting primarily or entirely without eating meat, especially red meat or poultry
TYPE OF ETHICS: Animal rights
SIGNIFICANCE: Vegetarian diets have been advocated on ethical grounds, because they are believed to prevent famine, animal suffering, and environmental degradation.

Although vegetarian diets have been advocated for ethical reasons since ancient times, the English term "vegetarian" came into general use upon the founding of the Vegetarian Society at Ramsgate, England, in 1847.

TYPES OF VEGETARIANS

Modern nutritionists recognize several categories of vegetarians. Vegans are strict vegetarians who consume neither meat nor meat "by-products" (animal-based foods, such as dairy products and eggs, that can be obtained without slaughtering the animal). Among less strict vegetarians, *lactovegetarians* eat no meat or eggs but do eat dairy products, *ovovegetarians* eat no meat but do eat eggs, and *lacto-ovovegetarians* eat no meat, but do eat both dairy products and eggs. *Pescovegetarians* eat fish but neither poultry nor red meat (from mammals), and *semi-vegetarians* eat dairy products and eggs, and some poultry and fish, but no red meat.

ETHICAL ARGUMENTS FOR VEGETARIANISM

Several kinds of ethical arguments have been given for adopting vegetarian diets. These arguments differ in terms of the entities for which they express concern (human beings versus nonhuman animals and/or ecosystems) and which kinds of vegetarianism they support (semi-vegetarianism or lacto-ovovegetarianism versus veganism, for example).

Arguments from human health are based on scientific studies of the effects of vegetarian diets on human health. During the 1970's and 1980's, evidence accumulated that diets high in saturated fats contribute to cardiovascular disease and that diets emphasizing vegetables might help to prevent certain cancers. Jeremy Rifkin and John Robbins emphasized these concerns in popular books which combined this human health argument with concerns about famine, ecology, and animal welfare related to diets heavy in meat and animal by-products.

Although a broad consensus emerged that Americans were eating too much red meat for their own good, arguments from human health do not decisively support veganism so much as semi-vegetarian, pescovegetarian, or lacto-ovovegetarian diets, for two reasons.

First, even lacto-ovovegetarian diets can be high in saturated fats (if one eats a lot of cheese and eggs, for example), and saturated fat can be reduced significantly without eliminating meat. As beef consumption dropped during the 1980's, consumption of poultry and fish (which are lower in fat) increased, butchers began removing more fat from cuts of meat, and farmers experimented with leaner breeds of pigs and cattle.

Second, some nutritionists believe that vegan diets are inordinately risky, especially for women and young children. Vegans commonly are cautioned to plan their diets carefully in order to avoid deficiencies of nutrients such as iron and calcium, which are either less prevalent in or less efficiently absorbed from nonanimal sources, and vitamin B, which is present only in animal products. Nutrition researchers have tended, however, to identify vegans with members of religions and cults who eat extremely simplified diets and eschew medical supervision and nutritionally fortified foods, and research on these individuals may not accurately portray the risks and benefits of a vegan diet.

Two other arguments support limited vegetarianism. The argument from famine, popularized by Frances Moore Lappé, stresses that vegetarian diets are a particularly efficient way to feed the hungry. More people could live by virtue of grains and vegetables that could be produced on the good farm land that is now used to raise feed grains supporting only feedlot cattle. Related ecological arguments oppose the consumption of meat, especially beef, produced by razing Third World rain forests or in other ecologically unsustainable ways. Both arguments, however, support only semi-vegetarian or pescovegetarian diets. Two alternative ways to help alleviate hunger would be to harvest fish from the oceans and to raise livestock on rangelands unsuitable for row crop production, and neither of these practices is necessarily ecologically unsustainable.

Ethical support for stricter vegetarian diets comes from animal rights and animal welfare arguments, such as those popularized by Peter Singer and Tom Regan, whose arguments were criticized in detail by Raymond Frey. Many in the animal rights movement became vegetarians because they believed either that intensive, "factory" farming is inhumane (an animal welfare perspective) or that it is inherently wrong to slaughter animals for food, no matter how humanely they may have been treated (a true animal rights perspective).

Although primarily concerned with slaughter, the animal rights movement also targeted egg production as a particularly inhumane form of animal agriculture. Following World War II, economies of scale were achieved by confining laying hens in crowded "battery" cages in highly mechanized operations, in which the entire flock is slaughtered and replaced when average egg production drops below a certain level (approximately every twelve to fifteen months). Consequently, more than 90 percent of American laying hens were caged by 1990.

Dairy products also came under fire from some in the animal rights movement, because of intensification (epitomized by the development of bovine growth hormone during the 1980's and 1990's) and because of ties between the dairy industry and the veal and beef industries. Male offspring of dairy cattle are sold as veal calves, and dairy cows themselves spend only three to four years (on average) in production, after which they are slaughtered as low-grade beef. On these grounds, animal rights and animal welfare arguments are used to support not only lacto-ovovegetarianism but also veganism.

Gary E. Varner

FURTHER READING

Frey, Raymond G. *Rights, Killing, and Suffering: Moral Vegetarianism and Applied Ethics*. Oxford, England: Basil Blackwell, 1983.

George, Kathryn Paxton. *Animal, Vegetable, or Woman? A Feminist Critique of Ethical Vegetarianism.* Albany: State University of New York Press, 2000.

Lappé, Frances Moore. *Diet for a Small Planet.* 10th anniversary ed. New York: Ballantine Books, 1982.

Regan, Tom. *The Case for Animal Rights.* Berkeley: University of California Press, 1983.

Rifkin, Jeremy. *Beyond Beef.* New York: Dutton, 1992.

Robbins, John. *Diet for a New America.* Walpole, N.H.: Stillpoint, 1987.

Singer, Peter. *Animal Liberation.* New York: Ecco, 2002.

Walters, Kerry S., and Lisa Portmess, eds. *Ethical Vegetarianism: From Pythagoras to Peter Singer.* Albany: State University of New York Press, 1999.

SEE ALSO: Ahiṁsā; Animal rights; Cruelty to animals; Environmental ethics; Famine; Hunger; Singer, Peter; Vivisection.

Veterans' rights

DEFINITION: Special rights due to former members of the military services

TYPE OF ETHICS: Politico-economic ethics

SIGNIFICANCE: The citizens of most nations recognize the principle that those who serve to protect their countries—and especially those who risk their lives in combat—deserve special privileges and should be accorded special respect.

Before 1636, wounded soldiers were not considered to be the responsibility of either the military branches in which they served or the governments that oversaw the military branches. During that year, the government of Plymouth Colony passed a law providing for the government to provide financial support to soldiers who were disabled in the recent war with the Pequot Indians. That colonial legislation was the first recognition of the ethical principle that a government has an obligation to care for soldiers after they have honorably served it in armed combat.

In 1776, the Continental Congress provided pensions for soldiers who were disabled. The thirteen colonies that became states of the United States also gave direct medical and hospital care to their veterans. In 1811, the U.S. Congress set up the first home and medical facility for military veterans. After the mid-century Civil War, Congress authorized benefits and pensions not only for veterans, but also for their widows and dependents. At the same time, many state governments established veterans' homes to provide medical treatment for all injuries and diseases incurred by veterans, even ailments not related to the veterans' military service.

After the Civil War, the idea arose that veterans should not be penalized for the time taken away from their civilian jobs while they are serving their country, so they were accorded veterans preferences in employment. These meant that the veterans were to be the first applicants hired and the last to be laid off among other qualified job applicants and holders. By the beginning of the twenty-first century, veterans of the United States military were entitled to get back their former civilian jobs, with the same pay increases and seniority they would have received if they had never left their jobs.

In 1917, the U.S. Congress established veterans programs for disability compensation, insurance, and vocational rehabilitation for veterans with disabilities. In 1944, Congress passed the G.I. Bill, which provided veterans with funds to complete their educations, including college education. By the end of the century, the educational benefits of the bill applied to veterans of military service even if they were never involved in armed combat.

The modern United States has the world's most comprehensive veterans assistance. Some programs are considered entitlements that the government is required to provide; others are incentives offered to encourage new enlistments. Distinctions between rights, or entitlements, and incentives is not always clear, however.

One of the principles of veterans' rights is that they are granted only to those who receive honorable discharges when they leave military service. Since the opinions of superior officers about what constitutes good and bad conduct can be arbitrary, veterans who receive dishonorable discharges have the right to have their discharges reviewed before impartial adjudicative bodies.

What are considered veterans' rights in one country may not be so perceived in another. Within some countries, local jurisdictions may provide more generous programs for veterans than those of their national governments. Thus, the determination of veterans' rights ultimately depends more on what political leaders believe that veterans are entitled to receive than on abstract ethical principles.

Michael Haas

FURTHER READING

Addlestone, David F., Susan H. Hewman, and Frederic J. Gross. *The Rights of Veterans*. New York: Avon Books, 1978.

Armstrong, R. E., and Terry P. Rizzuti. *Veteran's Benefits: A Guide to State Programs*. Westport, Conn.: Greenwood Press, 2001.

Stichman, Barton F., Ronald B. Abrams, and David F. Addlestone, eds. *Veterans Benefits Manual*. Charlottesville, Va.: Lexis, 2002.

SEE ALSO: Americans with Disabilities Act; Biochemical weapons; Chemical warfare; Child soldiers; Disability rights; Mercenary soldiers; Military ethics.

Vice

DEFINITION: Indulgence in immoral or depraved sources of pleasure, or a specific moral flaw or inherent depravity of character

TYPE OF ETHICS: Personal and social ethics

SIGNIFICANCE: The term "a vice" usually refers to a minor foible or weakness, such as smoking or buying lottery tickets. This type of vice, while possibly a subject of negative moral judgment, is rarely a criminal offense. Vice as a collective noun, however, can refer to much more serious moral and legal transgressions.

Deriving from the Latin word for "flaw," "vice" originally meant any defect of the will predisposing an individual toward socially unacceptable behavior. The opposite term, "virtue," also refers to habitual behavior. The so-called "seven deadly sins" of medieval moralists—pride, envy, anger, sloth, avarice, gluttony, and lust—are more properly termed cardinal vices, because they are habitual character defects that affect large numbers of people

The general concept of vice can be derived from observation and is not culture-specific, but the list of vices and the gravity ascribed to each vary markedly from culture to culture and historically within a culture. For example, masturbation, which was regarded as an exceedingly grave vice in early twentieth century European and American society, is ignored by many traditional cultures and has become acceptable in Western culture in recent years; attitudes toward homosexuality similarly range from acceptance to extreme condemnation.

Vice can involve any habitual act or attitude, but the vices that plague society are the common ones—those that tempt the average person and that the perpetrator may recognize as unwise, illegal, and potentially damaging, but not as heinous or depraved.

VICE AND CRIMINAL JUSTICE

In modern U.S. law enforcement, vice has come to be roughly synonymous with victimless crimes, including alcohol and drug abuse, prostitution, gambling, pornography, and sexually deviant behavior between consenting adults. This catalog of modern vices includes behavior that is damaging to the perpetrator, to society as a whole, and to indirect targets (notably, the family of the perpetrator), rather than to a specific intended victim. Such vices are typically psychologically if not physically addictive. Indeed, the medieval concept of vice and the modern concept of psychological addiction are surprisingly close.

Efforts to combat vice through the criminal justice system have a poor record of success and a tendency to co-opt the machinery of justice. Strong psychological, physiological, and financial motivations to persist in exercising proscribed vices have created a powerful underground subculture capable of corrupting and intimidating police and government officials. The collapse of communism in the Soviet Union demonstrated that even a regimented totalitarian regime is more effective at hiding than at suppressing vice, which blossomed with amazing rapidity once controls were loosened.

VICE AND BIOLOGY

The question of the origin of vice has long been a subject of debate and speculation, and, like most complex questions of human nature, probably has no single answer. The concept is not simply an artifact created by human prejudice; it is a product of long experience identifying what is harmful in a particular social context. Prejudice and changing conditions, however, can and often do cause harmless actions to be labeled as vices.

The prevalent medieval view of vice (exemplified by Thomas Aquinas) stated that human beings, having free will, are free to choose evil, and they acquire vices by repeatedly performing evil acts. Since people are also free to choose virtue, vices can be overcome through grace, the exercise of virtue, knowledge, and prayer. Restated in modern terms, vice is learned, self-reinforcing behavior that can be overcome by education and behavior modification.

The alternative view, that vice is an innate, congenital quality, possibly suppressible but ultimately incurable, is in its earliest formulation a corollary of predestination: The qualities that damn the sinner are preordained by God, and neither petition nor the exercise of virtuous acts can change the underlying reality.

During the early part of the twentieth century, the popularization of Charles Darwin's theory of evolution and especially of Social Darwinism, the application of Darwinian biological models to society and psychology, led to a revival of the idea of vice as an innate quality. The Italian criminologist Cesare Lombroso proposed the theory of atavism, which gained wide currency. According to this theory, vices are relics of a lower state of evolution, are inherited, and are correlated with apelike physiognomy. Such a model readily lends itself to the labeling of non-European physical characteristics as atavistic, citing them as proof of the moral inferiority of other ethnic groups, and atavism was accepted as scientific dogma in Nazi Germany. Sociobiology also hypothesizes that certain types of habitual antisocial behavior (such as lust and aggression) may be a legacy from primitive hominid ancestors, but it does not postulate that atavism is more pronounced in any race or social group.

There is also some recent evidence that specific genetic factors may predispose individuals to vice. A large Danish study of children of criminal parents adopted at birth showed a high incidence of crime in this population, and a study of men with a doubled Y chromosome suggested that this group was prone to violence. The precise physiologic mechanisms for this behavior are unknown, however. Human personality is complex and malleable, and a genetic predisposition toward particular behavior is not equivalent to a mandate.

Martha Sherwood-Pike

FURTHER READING

Blackburn, Simon. *Lust: The Seven Deadly Sins.* New York: Oxford University Press, 2004.

Bloomfield, Morton W. *The Seven Deadly Sins: An Introduction to the History of a Religious Concept, with Special Reference to Medieval English Literature.* East Lansing: Michigan State College Press, 1952.

Cook, Philip J. "An Introduction to Vice." *Law and Contemporary Problems* 51 (Winter, 1988): 1-7.

McCracken, Robert J. *What Is Sin? What Is Virtue?* New York: Harper & Row, 1966.

Paul, Ellen Frankel, Fred D. Miller, Jr., and Jeffrey Paul, eds. *Virtue and Vice.* New York: Cambridge University Press, 1998.

Pick, Daniel. *Faces of Degeneration: A European Disorder, c. 1848-c. 1918.* New York: Cambridge University Press, 1989.

SEE ALSO: Agreement for the Suppression of White Slave Traffic; Betting on sports; Drug abuse; Private vs. public morality; Prostitution; Sexuality and sexual ethics; Social Darwinism; Virtue.

Victims' rights

DEFINITION: Special legal and moral rights of victims of crimes

TYPE OF ETHICS: Legal and judicial ethics

SIGNIFICANCE: The recognition or failure of recognition of victims' rights shapes in part what and when legal proceedings are affected by victim testimony. For supporters of victims' rights, their recognition helps balance the legal and moral concerns of victims with those of offenders. For critics of victims' rights, their recognition contaminates the presumption of innocence and due legal process.

By early 2003, two-thirds of the states in the United States had constitutional amendments recognizing and identifying specific rights of crime victims. In addition, a bill had been proposed in the U.S. Senate to amend the U.S. Constitution with a Victims' Rights Amendment. That bill addressed a concern felt by many people that the legal criminal system had long emphasized the rights of the accused over the rights of victims. For example, while persons accused of crimes have the legal right to speedy trials by juries of their peers and a legal right to be present throughout their trials, the victims of the accused have no legal right to either. The issue of victims' rights, then, falls under the larger issues of retributive justice, which is concerned with punishing criminals, and restorative justice, which is concerned with restoring or compensating victims.

WHO IS THE VICTIM?

A central issue within the scope of victims' rights is who actually should be considered the victim of a crime. Although it is obvious that the persons most directly harmed are victims, other people can be and are often indirectly harmed, such as the families of murder victims. This issue becomes especially important when victim impact statements (VIS) are allowed into legal proceedings.

A VIS is a written or verbal statement of a victim's views concerning the impact the crime has had. In cases in which the direct victim cannot give a VIS, other relevant persons—notably family members—can submit them. These statements, usually offered during sentencing or release hearings, provide not only the victims' opinions on the impacts of the crimes on their lives but also their recommendations of appropriate sentences, and even what they believe may be the risks to their own persons if the accused or convicted defendants are released or are given short sentences.

RIGHTS TO WHAT?

To exactly what do, or should, victims have rights? Answers to this question vary from state to state, but they generally fall under several types of categories.

In some states, victims have the right to information about numerous concerns, such as assistance programs for victims, compensation programs, protection and safety programs, and the status and location of the offenders. Victims may also have the right to participate in the different stages of the legal proceedings involving the offenders. These may include the right to attend relevant hearings, to provide statements (including a VIS) within the context of the proceedings, to designate and confer with lawful representatives, and to contest the post-conviction releases of the offenders.

Victims may also have a right to restitution or compensation, that is, to have prosecutors ask judges to order the offenders to reimburse them for expenses incurred as a result of the offenders' crimes. Victims may also have access to special educational or employment services designed for people who, because of the crimes inflicted on them, cannot continue in their previous careers.

OBJECTIONS TO VICTIMS' RIGHTS

In spite of the apparently clear reasons for recognizing and supporting victims' rights, many people, groups, and organizations have expressed skepticism and concern over such rights and how they are to be understood. One concern is the question of who the victims are. Indirect victims, such as family members, are usually included as victims of crimes. Extending the definition of "victim" to indirect victims is usually explicit in victim impact statements.

A second concern is that allowing the views and interests of victims to be heard in a trial before a judge or jury returns a verdict contaminates the legal deliberation process and runs counter to the idea that the accused is innocent until proven guilty. Such victim testimony violates due process at two levels, say critics: first, prior to the decision about conviction,

---

Victims or Not?

A central difficulty in defining "victims" of crimes lies in drawing nonarbitrary lines between indirect victims and others. For example, if a person's home is burgled, and the next-door neighbor then purchases a home security system in order to avoid being similarly burgled, should that neighbor be considered an indirect victim? Or, suppose that a person driving into a convenience store parking lot sees an armed robbery taking place within the store and then suffers a serious injury in a collision while rushing to exit the lot to seek police help. Is that person a victim of the armed robbery crime?

and second, in sentencing after a conviction. For the determination of guilt or innocence, the burden of proof must lie with the state, but victim impact statements are not criminal evidence and so should not be allowed at this stage of legal proceedings. Once guilt is determined, victim statements can only inject emotion, perhaps simply revenge, into the process.

Critics also claim that victim impacts run counter to equal justice under the law, since the offenders are not being sentenced on objective common standards of punishment, but at least in part on how well victims can make their cases of suffering. That is, two similar or legally identical crimes might result in very dissimilar sentences because of the different eloquence of victims. Despite these objections, there has been growing support for the recognition, enunciation, and codification of victims' rights at the national level.

David Boersema

FURTHER READING

American Correctional Association. *Point/Counterpoint: Correctional Issues*. Lanham, Md.: Author, 1998.

Carrington, Frank. *Victims' Rights: Law and Litigation*. New York: M. Bender, 1989.

Fletcher, George P. *With Justice for Some: Victims' Rights in Criminal Trials*. Reading, Mass.: Addison-Wesley, 1995.

Glenn, Leigh. *Victims' Rights: A Resource Handbook*. Santa Barbara, Calif.: ABC-CLIO, 1997.

Jasper, Margaret. *Victims' Rights Law*. Dobbs Ferry, N.Y.: Oceana, 1997.

Poliny, Valiant R. W. *A Public Policy Analysis of the Emerging Victims Rights Movement*. San Francisco: Austin & Winfield, 1994.

Stark, James H., and Howard W. Goldstein. *The Rights of Crime Victims*. Carbondale: Southern Illinois University Press, 1985.

SEE ALSO: Accused, rights of; Identity theft; Incest; Psychology; Rape; Reparations for past social wrongs; Sexual abuse and harassment.

Vietnam War

THE EVENT: Civil war between North Vietnam and South Vietnam, in which the United States participated on the South Vietnamese side

DATE: August 5, 1964-April 30, 1975

TYPE OF ETHICS: Military ethics

SIGNIFICANCE: The morality of U.S. participation in the Vietnam War was questioned by many at the time it occurred and has been questioned ever since. The war's greatest legacy has arguably come in the form of its effects upon U.S. foreign policy, U.S. self-perception, and the world's perception of the United States. It was as a direct result of the Vietnam War that both the moral purity of the United States' interests and the invincibility of the U.S. military came to be questioned on a significant scale, both at home and abroad.

The question of when a powerful nation should intervene militarily in the affairs of a small country is not susceptible to a simple answer. Failure to intervene can mean that a small country will be subjected to tyranny, anarchy, or even genocide. Yet a military intervention that is bloody and inconclusive can also wreak havoc on a small country; furthermore, sending troops into a combat situation abroad means that some people will be killed or wounded. The unsuccessful end of the costly and controversial American intervention in Vietnam by no means ensured that policymakers would be spared similar dilemmas in the future.

The United States had been involved in the affairs of Vietnam ever since that country was divided, in 1954, into a communist North and an anticommunist South. As long as the American military mission in South Vietnam was small-scale, it aroused little opposition in the United States. Between 1965 and 1968, however, the number of American combat troops in Vietnam rose from 50,000 to 500,000; the casualties suffered by the troops and the monthly draft calls soared; and the loud debate at home reached an unprecedented level.

RELIGIOUS OPPOSITION TO THE WAR

Although at least one theologian (R. Paul Ramsey) did support the American military intervention in Vietnam, members of the clergy and theologians were conspicuous in the movement against

(1) France falls, 1954. (2) Tet Offensive, January, 1968. (3) Cambodian invasion, April-May, 1970. (4) Sihanouk falls, April, 1970. (5) Laotian incursion, February, 1971. (6) Areas of U.S. bombing, 1972. (7) Mining of Haiphong Harbor, May, 1972. (8) Lon Nol falls, April, 1975. (9) North Vietnamese offensive, spring, 1975. (10) South Vietnam surrenders, April 20, 1975.

such intervention. In 1966, the organization Clergy and Laymen Concerned About Vietnam was formed. Vocal opponents of the American war effort included the Protestant theologian Robert McAfee Brown; Yale University's Protestant chaplain, William Sloane Coffin; and two Roman Catholic priests, Daniel Berrigan and Philip Berrigan.

THE JUST WAR TRADITION

The just war tradition was first elaborated by the theologians of Christian Europe during the late Mid-

dle Ages. After centuries of indifference by peoples and governments, this tradition was revived by the Nuremberg War Crimes Trials of 1946, which followed the defeat of Nazi Germany in World War II (1939-1945).

The just war tradition sets forth six criteria for determining whether a particular war is just. The war must be waged for a just cause; it must be waged as a last resort; the intent behind the war must be right; there must be a reasonable hope of success; the war must be waged by a legitimate, duly constituted authority; and the harm inflicted by the war must not be disproportionate to the good that one hopes to achieve. During the Vietnam War, America's clergy, theologians, and laypersons questioned whether American military intervention in Vietnam met all or even most of these criteria for a just war.

OPPOSITION TO THE WAR

The U.S. Constitution, while making the president commander in chief of the armed forces, gives Congress the right to declare war. Yet the massive war effort in Vietnam, dissenters pointed out, had come about through presidential orders alone. The first substantial increase in troop levels in Vietnam had been announced on July 28, 1965, at a little-publicized presidential news conference. The dis-

senters did not have an airtight case, however: The Korean War (1950-1953) had also started without a congressional declaration.

The official justification for the war, given by presidents Lyndon Baines Johnson (1963-1969) and Richard M. Nixon (1969-1974), was that the American military was in South Vietnam to repel aggression launched from communist North Vietnam. Defenders of the war viewed the conflict through an ideological lens, as an assault by international communism against those who loved freedom. The moral and material support that the world's major communist states, China and the Soviet Union, gave to North Vietnam was cited as evidence for this interpretation.

The opponents of the war, by contrast, stressed the facts that both sides of the conflict were ethnic

U.S. soldiers take cover behind a wall near the Army's bachelor officer quarters in Saigon during a Viet Cong attack in 1968. (National Archives)

Vietnamese and that Vietnam had been a single country until 1954. Dissenters viewed the United States as meddling in another country's civil war and thus committing aggression itself, rather than nobly defending a victim of unprovoked aggression; hence, the war did not meet the "just cause" criterion.

The dissenters' localized view of the Vietnam conflict led them to scorn the notion that defeating the communists in South Vietnam was necessary to protect the United States itself. The dissenters saw the Vietnamese communists as nationalist defenders of Vietnamese independence, not as the Southeast Asian arm of a worldwide conspiracy against American democracy. Hence, the war, dissenters believed, did not meet the "last resort" criterion.

WAR CRIMES

Until the early 1970's, the spearhead of the communist assault on the South Vietnamese government was not the North Vietnamese Army, but the so-called National Liberation Front, or Viet Cong. The Viet Cong, drawn from communist sympathizers in the South, were not regular troops in uniform; instead, they were guerrillas who wore peasant clothing and blended in with the villagers after conducting hit-and-run raids against American or South Vietnamese troops.

It was nearly impossible for American troops to fight such an enemy without hurting some innocent civilians. The American military attacked villages whence sniper fire had come (one officer declared that he had had to destroy a village in order to save it) and decreed whole areas to be free-fire zones, where anybody who moved was assumed to be the enemy. The chemical Agent Orange was used to defoliate certain areas, in order to deprive the Viet Cong of food. Napalm, a burning jelly, was dropped on centers of enemy fire; inevitably, some children were hurt. In the My Lai massacre of March, 1968 (made public in 1969), all the people in a village were killed by American troops under the command of Lieutenant William Calley.

Such suffering led all dissenters to question whether the war met the "proportionality" criterion; some dissenters even condemned the war as genocidal. Defenders of the war effort pointed out that the Viet Cong also committed atrocities and that the perpetrators of My Lai were finally subjected to American military justice.

THE DEBATE AFTER THE WAR'S END

In April, 1975, the North Vietnamese, having signed a peace agreement with the United States in January, 1973, overran and conquered South Vietnam. As a result, the United States admitted, by airlift, a wave of refugees. Contrary to the fears of earlier American administrations, the loss of South Vietnam did not lead to a communist advance to Hawaii or even to the fall of all of eastern Asia; the only other Asian countries to become communist were Vietnam's neighbors, Laos and Cambodia. By 1979, however, the repressiveness of the communist regime led to another massive flight of refugees, this time by boat; ironically, at least a few of the new refugees were former Viet Cong. The results of defeat started a new debate in America.

In 1978, historian Guenter Lewy published a history of the Vietnam War, defending American intervention in that conflict; in 1982, magazine editor Norman Podhoretz did the same thing. Both looked back on the Vietnam War as a noble effort to defend a free people against communism; so also did the president of the United States during the 1980's, Ronald Reagan. Political philosopher Michael Walzer, in *Just and Unjust Wars* (1977), condemned the means used in the Vietnam War without thoroughly discussing the issue of the war's rationale. In 1985, former president Richard M. Nixon published *No More Vietnams* defending his administration's Vietnam policy. Podhoretz's view, that post-1975 communist repression provided a retrospective justification for the American war effort of 1965 to 1973, never won a great following among academics or the general public. By the end of the 1980's, as the Cold War ended, the question of the morality of the war was still controversial among historians and journalists.

Paul D. Mageli

FURTHER READING

Brown, Robert McAfee, Abraham Heschel, and Michael Novak. *Vietnam: Crisis of Conscience.* New York: Association Press, 1967.

Capps, Walter H. *The Unfinished War: Vietnam and the American Conscience.* Boston: Beacon Press, 1982.

Casey, William Van Etten, and Philip Nobile, eds. *The Berrigans.* New York: Praeger, 1971.

Chomsky, Noam. *For Reasons of State.* 1972. Reprint. Introduction by Arundhati Roy. New York: W. W. Norton & Co., 2003.

Daum, Andreas W., Lloyd C. Gardner, and Wilfried Mausbach, eds. *America, the Vietnam War, and the World: Comparative and International Perspectives*. New York: Cambridge University Press, 2003.

Hall, Mitchell D. *Because of Their Faith: CALCAV and Religious Opposition to the Vietnam War.* New York: Columbia University Press, 1990.

Kissinger, Henry. *Ending the Vietnam War: A Personal History of America's Involvement in and Extrication from the Vietnam War.* New York: Simon & Schuster, 2003.

Levy, David W. *The Debate over Vietnam.* 2d ed. Baltimore: Johns Hopkins University Press, 1995.

Lewy, Guenter. *America in Vietnam.* New York: Oxford University Press, 1978.

Podhoretz, Norman. *Why We Were in Vietnam.* New York: Simon & Schuster, 1982.

Woods, Randall B., ed. *Vietnam and the American Political Tradition: The Politics of Dissent.* New York: Cambridge University Press, 2003.

SEE ALSO: Civil disobedience; Cold War; Communism; Conscientious objection; International law; Military ethics; Pacifism; Sovereignty; War.

Violence

DEFINITION: Intentional infliction of physical or emotional harm or injury
TYPE OF ETHICS: Personal and social ethics
SIGNIFICANCE: It is a matter of debate whether violence is ever justified in, for example, a just war or the revolutionary overthrow of a tyrannical regime.

When people think about violence, they tend to think most often of a person being physically assaulted, raped, or murdered. As Robert McAfee Brown has noted in his book *Religion and Violence*, however, violence may be either personal or institutional, either overt or covert. Thus, personal overt violence may be physical assault. Personal covert violence could be psychological or emotional abuse of another person. Institutional overt violence may take the form of war

or revolution. Covert institutional violence may take the forms of repression, racism, or the denial of human rights. This article will be primarily concerned with issues of institutional violence—just war theory, violence and the Civil Rights movement, violence and revolution in liberation theology, and Marxism.

It is not clear whether violence or aggression is a natural part of the human species or a learned behavior. Thomas Hobbes, the author of *Leviathan* (1651), advocated a strong authoritarian government, partly using arguments based on a naturalistic concept of aggression. Chapter 13 of *Leviathan*, the famous passage on the "Natural Condition of Mankind," claims that because of a kind of natural equality, human beings are, in their natural condition, always in a state of war, a *Bellum omnium contra omnes*, a "war of all against all." He characterized the life of man as "solitary, poore, nasty, brutish and short." He held to a dim view of human nature. Behavior arises because of "aversions" from fear and want and the desires for security and gain. A commonwealth becomes a necessary antidote to the horrors of human nature.

From a psychoanalytic point of view, Sigmund Freud argued that aggression was a natural human instinct. In his early writings, he developed the idea of instinctual conflict within the human psyche between two principles: the pleasure principle and the reality principle. The pleasure principle is the most impulsive instinct in driving the organism toward immediate gratification. The reality principle, however, operates as a rational mechanism that allows the organism to defer gratification and to sublimate potentially destructive wishes by means of a redirection of energy toward work. Both principles operate to reduce stress. Freud also discovered a compulsion on the part of neurotics to repeat past negative experiences as a defensive measure that often turned self-destructive. This led Freud to postulate the death instinct, or Thanatos. The death instinct preserves the organism from threats of death. When it confronts such threats, aggression results. Directed at the self, aggression becomes self-destructive.

Konrad Lorenz worked out a theory of aggression based on Charles Darwin's theory that struggle is pervasive in nature and in evolution. It appears in the struggle for survival, the defense of offspring, and the improvement of the species. The question therefore arises, "Does aggression play a positive and necessary role in furthering the organization of the human species?" That aggression can be destructive and harmful is indisputable, but can aggression be directed rightfully for the just pursuit of good and beneficial consequences? Can violence be a force for good?

JUST WAR THEORY

Saint Augustine, in *The City of God* (413-427), argues that not all homicide is murder. Even God, the supreme authority, makes exceptions to the law against killing. The law against killing, says Augustine, is not broken by those who wage war by the authority of God or impose the death penalty by the authority of the state. Thus, Augustine sets up the state and God as authoritative and just sources of power. Here, then, is one of the criteria for waging a just war—it must be declared by a legitimate authority.

Aggression may also be justified on account of the wickedness of a neighboring nation. In Augustine's opinion, honest people do not go to war against peaceful neighbors. Thus, the cause must be just. It is not enough to wage war to increase one's borders. The increase of the empire may be justified, however, by the wickedness of those against whom war is waged.

The increase of empire was assisted by the wickedness of those against whom just wars were waged. In Augustine's words, "For it is the injustice of the opposing side that lays on the wise man the duty of waging wars; and this injustice is assuredly to be deplored by a human being."

In the thirteenth century, Thomas Aquinas gave fuller exposition to the just war theory. In answer to the question "Is it always sinful to wage war?" Aquinas set forth criteria for a just war. First, there must be a declaration on the part of a legitimate authority—the ruler of the state, for example. War may not be declared by a private individual. It is not the business of the private individual. Second, a just cause is required. Those who are attacked should be attacked because they deserve it, on account of some fault. Third, war should be waged with the right intention so that either good is advanced or evil is avoided. Fourth, the outcome of war must be peace. Fifth, a just war must avoid inordinate and perilous arms.

Martin Luther, in his political tract "Temporal Authority: to What Extent It Should be Obeyed" (1523), formulates the two-kingdoms theory, a theory obviously acquired from Augustine's *The City of God—civitas Dei* (spiritual authority) and *civitas mundi* (earthly authority). Luther attempts to answer questions concerning the division of powers between Church and state. Is the Church an earthly power? Can secular rulers claim spiritual authority? Luther recognized the secular authority of the state and the spiritual authority of the Church. Each has its own realm. Each realm is a tool of the *Regnum Dei* (Kingdom of God) to fight the *Regnum diaboli* (Kingdom of the Devil). The state's weapons are law, power, force, and authority. The Church's weapons are faith and the Gospel. In effect, the individual becomes bifurcated into a public person and a private person. As a private person the individual abides by the gospel of love, but as a public person the individual may serve the state with the sword to inflict punishment on wrongdoers. The two-kingdoms theory was used by the Lutheran State churches in Germany to remain neutral in the face of Nazism (Ansbach Decree, 1935).

VIOLENCE AND THE CIVIL RIGHTS MOVEMENT

The American civil rights leader Martin Luther King, Jr., embodied a nonviolent philosophy of social change. He was catapulted to public attention by the bus boycott in Montgomery, Alabama, in 1955. He led voter registration drives and a desegregation campaign. His famous March on Washington eventually led to the signing of the Civil Rights Act in 1963, and, in 1964, he won the Nobel Peace Prize. His influence waned after the Watts riots in 1965. He came to his philosophy of nonviolent resistance through reading Henry David Thoreau's "Civil Disobedience" (1849). He also studied Walter Rauschenbusch's *Christianity and the Social Crisis* (1907), which laid the theological foundations for Christian social action and connected socioeconomic conditions to spiritual welfare.

Karl Marx sharpened King's consciousness of the gap between superfluous wealth and abject poverty. King was also influenced by Mohandas K. Gandhi's concept of *satyagraha*—"truth force" or "love force"—which advanced a love ethic as a powerful instrument of social and collective transformation. Gandhi presented the method of nonviolent resistance as the only moral way out for oppressed people. Reinhold Niebuhr refuted the false optimism of liberalism, and his work helped King to see the destructive power of sin not only at the level of personal life but also at the social, national, and international levels. E. S. Brightman and L. Harold Dewolf, King's Boston University professors, insisted, in their philosophy of personal idealism, that personality is ultimately and cosmically real. This idea laid the ground for conceiving a personal God and the concept of cosmic backing for justice and the dignity of human beings.

King was convinced that love is an instrument of social transformation and that suffering is to be accepted without retaliation because unearned suffering is redemptive. Hate destroys, but love builds up. King set forth his method of nonviolence in the following principles: ascertain the situation of justice, attempt revolution by dialogue, undergo personal purification and accept violence, and use direct nonviolent action. In his famous "Letter from a Birmingham Jail," King also delineated several principles of nonviolent direct action: do not be cowardly; do not seek to defeat the opponent, but seek friendship and understanding; defeat the forces of evil, not people; accept suffering without retaliation; reject inward violence; and have faith that justice has a cosmic backing.

Malcolm X, King's contemporary in the leadership of the African American Civil Rights movement, rejected King's nonviolent philosophy and advocated his own brand of social revolution, which made room for violence. Malcolm X believed that when the law failed to protect African Americans, African Americans were justified in using arms to protect themselves from harm at the hands of whites. He believed that it was criminal to remain passive in the face of being attacked. He not only encouraged self-defense but also mandated it. In his own words, "I am for violence if nonviolence means we continue postponing a solution to the American black man's problem—just to avoid violence. I don't go for nonviolence if it also means a delayed solution."

VIOLENCE AND LIBERATION THEOLOGY

As has been shown, Christian thinkers have concerned themselves with the ethics of violence. Attitudes toward institutional forms of violence have included just war, holy crusades, pacifism, and civil disobedience. With liberation theology, Christian thinkers took seriously the question of a just revolution. Dom Helder Camara, a bishop in Recife, Brazil, believed that a repressive state starts a spiral of violence through institutional injustice that leads the op-

pressed to revolt. In his eyes, people had a right to revolt against an unjust government. Yet he cautioned that revolt would only lead to more repressive measures on the part of the government. Because of the fear of brutal retaliatory measures on the part of the state, Camara advocated a nonviolent approach.

A Colombian cleric, Camilio Torres, was exasperated by the brutality of the repressive state and believed in the people's right to revolt. Unlike Camara, however, Torres did not turn to passivism out of fear of the military and police apparatuses of the state. Instead, Torres left the church and joined guerrilla forces in the mountains to overthrow the unjust government. He believed that the essence of Christianity consisted in the love of one's neighbor. He also concluded that the welfare of the majority could be attained only through a revolution. Taking state power was necessary to complete the teaching of Jesus Christ to love one's neighbor. According to Torres, love must be embodied in social structures and the concern for well-being must be translated into a program for change. If those in power will not willingly share power, then the only other effective means of change is revolt. Revolution becomes obligatory for Christians in order to realize their love of humanity. In the viewpoint of Torres, there can there be a just revolution.

Hugo Assmann, a Brazilian philosopher and theologian, argues for a Third World anti-imperialistic revolution for a universal and equitable share of the world's goods and for antioligarchic revolutions for political freedom. Assmann defines the world as a world in conflict. He argues for a language of liberation denouncing domination, articulating the mechanics of dependence, opposing capitalist economic systems, and breaking with unjust political governments.

Gustavo Gutierrez, a Peruvian priest, points out that the unjust violence of the oppressor is not to be equated with the just violence of the oppressed. Thus, he makes a distinction between just violence and unjust violence. Repression is unjust, but revolt against tyranny is just. For Gutierrez, the goal of the struggle against institutional injustice is the creation of a new kind of human being. The Exodus of the Hebrew slaves from Egypt serves as the model for active participation in the building of a new society. Christian brotherhood, according to Gutierrez, must be understood within the context of class struggle. Class struggle, in his opinion, is a fact; therefore, neutrality is impossible. Universal love cannot be achieved except by resolutely opting for the oppressed, that is, by opposing the oppressive class.

In the view of José Miguez Bonino, of Argentina, history is a dialectic that implies a certain violence for the emergence of the new. Hence, violence will be accepted in the struggle for justice or rejected in the state's attempt to create law and order at all costs. Miguez Bonino agrees with Gutierrez and Assmann that class struggle is a fact. On one side, the dominant class tries to maintain the status quo; on the other, the oppressed classes struggle for a new society.

VIOLENCE AND MARXISM

The question of violence, in liberation theology, had to do with making Christian love effective in a situation of oppression. The issue of violence for Marxism has to do with the relationship between means and ends in the struggle for social transformation. That Karl Marx was a passionate and ardent revolutionary goes without saying. His advocacy of violence must be carefully regarded in the context of his writings. In his "Introduction" to *Towards a Critique of Hegel's Philosophy of Right* (1844), Marx claims that the weapon of criticism cannot supplant the criticism of weapons and that material force must be overthrown by material force.

In the famous *Communist Manifesto*, written on the eve of the 1848 revolutions, Marx clearly regarded the takeover of state power as the aim of the Communist Party: "The immediate aim of the communists is the same as that of all the other proletarian parties: formation of the proletariat into a class, overthrow of the bourgeois supremacy, conquest of political power by the proletariat."

Speaking in Amsterdam in 1872, Marx made it clear that the use of violence varies from circumstance to circumstance. In his own words, "there are countries like America, England . . . and Holland where the workers can achieve their aims by peaceful means. . . . [I]n most of the countries . . . it is force that must be the lever of our revolutions."

Marx believed that violence may be necessary to effect a socialist revolution, but he was not dogmatic and absolute about the use of violence. He also was not adamant about the velocity of the transformation to socialism. For Marx, violence was a means, not an end.

What Marx was unbending about was the fact that class struggle involves violence, coercion, and repression. Workers are exploited and alienated. Because of propertylessness, workers are coerced into selling their labor power for means of subsistence. If they try to organize themselves, mobilize, and politicize their interests, they are met with repression. Violence breeds violence. The workers' revolution may require violence.

Mikhail Bakunin, an erstwhile companion of Marx, believed that destruction was a necessary tool of social change. Georges Sorel, who lived from 1847 to 1922, was a syndicalist Marxist who denied the then-popular theory that capitalism would collapse because of its own contradictions. He espoused a radical brand of revolutionary syndicalism. In 1906, in *Reflections on Violence*, he set up class war as the very essence of socialism. Acts of violence, he believed, would create a workers' morality, destroy the bourgeoisie, and lay the foundations for socialism.

Vladimir Ilich Lenin believed that the Marxist doctrine of the dictatorship of the proletariat meant the seizing and holding of state power by the use of violence. Karl Kautsky argued in *Terrorism and Communism* (1919) that Lenin's concept of the dictatorship of the proletariat was leading away from the essence of socialism. Leon Trotsky replied, in his own book *Terrorism and Communism* (1920), that a violent revolution was necessary because parliamentary means were ineffective. The revolutionary class should attain its end by any means at its disposal—even terrorism. György Lukács decried Kautsky's peaceful transistion to socialism and denied the validity of the question of the legality or illegality of means. For him, what counted was what would be most successful in achieving social transformation. A sense of world history and the sense of the world mission of the proletariat would determine the question of tactics and ethics.

Michael R. Candelaria

FURTHER READING

Augustine, Saint. *The City of God Against the Pagans*. Edited and translated by R. W. Dyson. New York: Cambridge University Press, 1998. Augustine originally wrote this book as a response to criticism leveled against Christians after the sacking of Rome.

Brown, Robert McAfee. *Religion and Violence: A Primer for White Americans*. Philadelphia: Westminster Press, 1973. This text nicely summarizes the just war theory and offers a stimulating criticism of it. The author also argues that the criteria justifying war could be used to justify revolution.

Freud, Sigmund. *The Ego and the Id.* Translated by Joan Riviere. Edited by James Strachey. New York: W. W. Norton, 1962. Here Freud introduces the instincts he calls "Eros" and "Thanatos."

Gutierrez, Gustavo. *The Theology of Liberation.* Maryknoll, N.Y.: Orbis Books, 1973. This is the classic text of liberation theology. Here are laid down the major lines of thought that are central themes in liberation theology.

New Formations: A Journal of Culture, Theory, Politics 35 (Autumn 1998). Edited by Renata Salecl, this special issue on "The Ethics of Violence" includes essays by such major scholars as Slavoj Žižek, Parveen Adams, and Etienne Balibar.

Thomas Aquinas, Saint. *On Law, Morality, and Politics.* Edited by William P. Baumgarth and Richard J. Regan. Indianapolis: Hackett, 1988. Aquinas expounds on the just war theory more systematically and clearly than does Augustine.

SEE ALSO: Abuse; Aggression; Augustine, Saint; Civil disobedience; Coercion; Cruelty; Just war theory; Nonviolence; Police brutality; Rape; Religion and violence; Revolution.

Virtual reality

DEFINITION: Computer-generated experiences meant to resemble in form or content the perceptual experience of reality

TYPE OF ETHICS: Scientific ethics

SIGNIFICANCE: Virtual reality is designed to be the most visceral possible form of representation. It therefore raises all the issues raised by representation generally, involving responsible and irresponsible portrayals of people, social groups, and issues; the function of ideology within representation; and the ability or desirability of art to instruct people morally. In addition, virtual reality intensifies debates over whether "mere" representation is ultimately innocuous, or whether its effects on the world are significant enough to merit moral concern or even legal regulation.

Virtual reality (VR) is a computerized system of data presentation that allows the user to project himself or herself into a simulated three-dimensional space and move about in that space, introduce other objects into it, change the positions and shapes of objects already there, and interact with animate objects in the space. VR was made possible by the enormous increase in computer memory and data-processing capacity, even in personal computers (PCs), and by the development of miniaturized video and audio devices and motion sensors that give the illusion of motion and of touching and manipulating material objects. Other descriptive names for this technology are artificial reality, virtual environment, telepresence, and immersive simulation, but VR is the preferred term.

SOFTWARE AND PRESENTATION DEVICES

The memory software of VR consists of many, many points of a three-dimensional grid, built from either an actual scene or a computer-generated space. The array of coordinates must be complete enough to allow the space to be rotated on three axes and the viewpoint to be moved similarly. In addition, other objects, animate and inanimate, must be held in memory with complete manipulability (including the tactile sensing of shape, inertia, texture, and so forth); and provision must be made for the creation of new objects with equal flexibility. Clearly, this technology calls for enormous memory capacity and complex programs to accomplish the apparent motion.

VR presentations can be very simple, such as viewing a scene on a PC monitor, or very complex, such as donning a helmet containing a miniature television screen for each eye, to give stereoscopic vision; headphones for directional sound; motion sensors to slew the scene left or right, up or down as the viewer's head moves; and a so-called Dataglove both to accept motion commands from the hand and to give back pressure information to define objects, motion, and so forth. Presentations between the simple and the complex seem to be missing; at the upper end, a whole-body sensing suit is expected to be available in the future. This very brief description of equipment may suggest why VR had to wait until microchip technology made the necessary memory available within reasonably sized computers.

Positive Applications of Virtual Reality

Many uses of VR raise few if any ethical questions. It is used, for example, to train surgical students on a "virtual" patient before they actually perform an operation. Experienced surgeons can practice a complex new procedure before using it in the operating room. Operators of heavy construction equipment can train on VR devices, and in some cases controls have been redesigned for greater simplicity and efficiency on the basis of such experience. Physiological chemists can manipulate molecules in VR to see—or feel—how they fit together in three dimensions. Attractions and repulsions of functional groups in the molecules are programmed into memory, and the user can actually feel, through the Dataglove, when a drug molecule fits or fails to fit in a cellular structure, or when a virus clicks into place on a cell receptor. Pilots can be trained in VR simulations so lifelike that an hour of training is considered as effective as an hour of actual flying time. In fact, the Air Force was an early major developer of VR presentations. Architects and their clients can stroll through a building that has yet to be built, to get the feel of it and to identify where the design needs to be changed for greater comfort. These are all fairly unexceptional applications.

Possible Ethically Negative Aspects

One of the most frequently voiced criticisms of VR is that it makes possible what might be called participatory pornography—not simply reading, video viewing, or telephone talk, but all these combined but together with the tactile feedback of a whole body suit that will allow virtual sexual experience of all varieties. Some designers and marketers of VR equipment speak enthusiastically of such pornography as an exciting prospect for the future. Critics view it as a real moral menace in a society that is already awash in casual sexuality. Others believe that it is merely an extension of the pornography that has always existed.

One commentator spoke sourly of "the myth that sex and pornography are the keys to understanding the growth of all new technologies." Perhaps the real menace here is that VR can be a powerful new device for furthering the alienation of individuals by making artificial experience easier and more exciting than actual human contact. This is true not only of VR sex but also potentially of all VR experience except training applications. Another aspect of this ethical concern lies in the enormous amount of time and attention that could be wasted because of VR. In a society that already spends a tenth of its time in front of television, imagine what the effect would be if every household had its own VR.

Other questions raised by VR that are perhaps medical rather than ethical but are worth mentioning: Can the tactile feedback become vigorous enough to cause physical damage? VR causes physical reactions for some users (such as nausea and actual vomiting in flight simulations); can it cause mental damage as well? Is this a technology that should be kept away from the undeveloped psyches of children and restricted to adults? All these ethical questions have yet to be addressed.

In sum, VR appears to be simply another new technology that can be used well or badly. Its capacities for good and evil seem not much greater than those of electric power, the automobile, or the telephone. The decisions lie, as always, in human hands.

Robert M. Hawthorne, Jr.

Further Reading

Churbuck, David C. "Applied Reality." *Forbes* 150 (September 14, 1992): 486-489.

Dvorak, John C. "America, Are You Ready for Simulated Sex and Virtual Reality?" *PC Computing* 5 (May, 1992): 78.

Earnshaw, Rae, Huw Jones, and Mike Gigante. *Virtual Reality Systems*. San Diego, Calif.: Academic Press, 1993.

Hayles, N. Katherine. *How We Became Posthuman: Virtual Bodies in Cybernetics, Literature, and Informatics*. Chicago: University of Chicago Press, 1999.

Hsu, Jeffrey, "Virtual Reality." *Compute* 15 (February, 1993): 101-104.

Rheingold, Howard. *Virtual Reality*. New York: Summit Books, 1991.

Spinello, Richard A. *CyberEthics: Morality and Law in Cyberspace*. 2d ed. Boston: Jones and Bartlett, 2003.

Woolley, Benjamin. "Being and Believing: Ethics of Virtual Reality." *The Lancet* 338 (August 3, 1991): 283-284.

_____. *Virtual Worlds: A Journey in Hype and Hyperreality*. Cambridge, Mass.: Blackwell Scientific, 1992.

Žižek, Slavoj. "Cyberspace: Or, The Unbearable

Closure of Being." In *The Plague of Fantasies.* New York: Verso, 1997.

_____. "From Virtual Reality to the Virtualization of Reality." In *Electronic Culture: Technology and Visual Representation*, edited by Tim Druckrey. New York: Aperture, 1996.

SEE ALSO: Art; Artificial intelligence; Computer technology; Narrative ethics; Pornography; Robotics; Science; Technology.

Virtue

DEFINITION: Moral excellence, or a specific morally admirable quality, value, or characteristic
TYPE OF ETHICS: Personal and social ethics
SIGNIFICANCE: In most classical ethical systems, virtue both constitutes morality and stands as its ultimate goal or aim—an idea encapsulated in the phrase "virtue is its own reward."

Each thought and act a person takes sets in motion two tendencies: a greater likelihood to engage in similar thoughts and acts, and a change in the character of the person. Thinking and action that lead a person away from life, goodness, and perfection of inner nature create *vice*—evil or wicked behavior and character. Conversely, those thoughts and acts that are life-promoting, aim for goodness, and work to perfect the inner nature lead to *virtue*—moral excellence of behavior and character. When people choose vice, their inner natures change and it becomes easier for them to choose the bad and more difficult for them to choose the good. In contrast, choosing virtue changes the inner nature so that it becomes easier, and more natural, to choose good rather than evil. Furthermore, this same principle appears to be operative with groups of individuals. For example, it seems quite logical that if a society wishes to prosper and to promote the well-being of its members, it should teach and encourage those people to pursue that which is virtuous. After all, is it possible to have a good society without good people? It is, therefore, in the best interests of both the individual and society to identify, promote, and practice those principles that work toward the ultimate good.

Numerous lists of virtuous principles have been put forth by diverse cultures over thousands of years to serve as moral guidelines for those particular cultures. One such list, the Seven Virtues, which includes the cardinal and the theological virtues, has been particularly influential in Western thought. Although the Seven Virtues deserve special attention, it is important to consider conceptions arising from other cultures. Only by doing so can the attempt be made to identify virtues that are both universal and, perhaps, eternal.

CONFUCIAN VIRTUE

Confucius, who lived in the sixth century B.C.E., was the most influential person in the shaping of Chinese ethics. In *The Confucian Analects*, he describes himself as a transmitter of ancient wisdom, particularly in regard to distinctions between right and wrong and the characteristics of a virtuous character. In *The Doctrine of the Mean*, Confucius considers virtue to be a mean between the extremes of excess and deficiency. In the short treatise known as *The Great Learning*, steps for promoting personal and governmental virtue are described.

Confucianists believe that there are five primary virtues: charity, righteousness, propriety, wisdom, and sincerity. All these virtues are described in detail in *The Confucian Analects*. Charity is the virtue of human relations, the practice of benevolence and respect to others. Confucius believed that this virtue was summed up in the most important principle guiding a person's life: the golden rule (Do unto others as you would have them do unto you). Righteousness is the virtue of public affairs: duty, responsibility, and the following of just principles. Propriety is concerned with fitting and proper behavior in human affairs. Confucius taught that propriety must always be accompanied by charity to keep a person from pride. Wisdom about humans, divine commands, and language is extolled by Confucius as the virtue of personal growth that comes only from study and practice. The final virtue, sincerity, is concerned with truthfulness and faithfulness in interactions with others.

BUDDHISTIC VIRTUE

Siddhārtha Gautama, who lived in India in the sixth century B.C.E., taught that right thinking and self-denial would enable a person to reach true wisdom and, ultimately, nirvana—a state free of all suffering and sorrow. Gautama was given the title of Buddha—one who embodies the divine characteristics of virtue and wisdom. The Eightfold Path, consisting of rightness of views, speech, thoughts, actions, living, recall, exertion, and meditation, was taught by the Buddha as the way to nirvana. In the Dhammapada, a collection of proverbs and moral principles, it is said that a person can rightly be called a *brāhmin*—a Hindu of the priestly class—if that individual leads a life that expresses such virtues as patience, self-restraint, contentment, sympathy, and mildness. As precepts for all Buddhists, the Buddha set forth five commandments: Abstain from killing, stealing, adultery, lying, and strong drink. An interesting feature of Buddha's teaching was that these moral principles were interpreted particularly stringently for those aspiring to be monks or nuns. Thus, while the ordinary person was enjoined to simply refrain from adultery, absolute abstinence from all sexual activity was required of monks and nuns.

The closest Buddhist teaching to a list of virtues is contained in the six *pāramitās*—perfections of character. The pāramitās are virtues of love, morality, patience, courage, meditation, and knowledge. Followers of the Buddha are enjoined to exercise these virtues perfectly.

MUḤAMMAD AND ISLAM

The Arabian prophet Muḥammad, who lived from 570 to 632, wrote in the Qurʾān (the sacred book of Muslims) that it is the duty of all people to believe in Allah (the Muslim name for God) and to live a life of high moral standards. Although the Qurʾān presents numerous moral principles such as kindness to parents, kin, and strangers, the sum of Muḥammad's teaching consists of believing in Allah and living a virtuous life according to the Five Pillars of Islamic law: the creed, the prayer ritual, beneficence (loving acts to others), fasting, and the pilgrimage, or *hajj*, to Mecca. The golden rule was also taught by Muḥammad and could plausibly be considered a sixth primary moral duty.

TEUTONIC VIRTUES

Tacitus, the Roman historian of the first and second centuries C.E., describes in his book *Germania* the social and moral lives of the Teutonic peoples—inhabitants of northern Europe. The Teutonic virtues identified by Tacitus in the first century have been greatly influential in the shaping of Western ideals in the succeeding centuries. Eight of these virtues have particular relevance to nobility of character: endurance (of purpose), loyalty, generosity, hospitality, truthfulness, modesty, marital purity (abstinence from adultery), and courage—considered the most important virtue by the Teutons.

VIRTUE IN CLASSICAL GREEK PHILOSOPHY

The great Greek philosophers of the fifth and fourth centuries B.C.E., Socrates, Plato, and Aristotle, devoted much attention to the subject of virtue. Their teachings on virtue have a timeless quality, shaping and stimulating modern thinking on moral matters. The ideas of Aristotle will be discussed first; Socrates and Plato will be dealt with in the discourse on the Seven Virtues.

In the *Nicomachean Ethics*, Aristotle distinguished between theoretical and practical virtues. The three theoretical virtues included wisdom (the ability to order knowledge into an ultimate system of truth), science (the ability to draw knowledge from demonstrations), and understanding (the ability to apprehend the truths that lie at the roots of knowledge). The two practical virtues were art (the ability to know how to produce or create things) and prudence (the ability to know how to act well in life's affairs). Prudence is considered to be the virtue most applicable to living a good moral life.

Like Confucius, Aristotle also proposed a doctrine of the mean, arguing that the essence of virtue is a middle ground between the vices of excess and deficiency. Thus, the virtue of courage can be considered the middle ground between cowardice on one hand and impulsiveness on the other. Aristotle did not intend to convey the notion that people should therefore look for the middle ground between leading a moral versus an immoral life. On the contrary, he said that people should find virtue and live it to the fullest. For example, the soldier should not settle for a middle ground between rashness and cowardice, but instead should serve as courageously as possible.

THE SEVEN VIRTUES IN WESTERN THINKING

Socrates, according to Plato in the *Republic* (book 4), contends that the ideal state would exemplify and promote four main qualities: wisdom, courage, temperance, and justice. Although the implication in the *Republic* is that these virtues were known and taught by the predecessors of Socrates, it is Plato who first identifies these as the core components of the noble moral character. The four qualities are called the cardinal virtues (from the Latin word *cardo*, meaning "hinge"), because all other virtues are seen to hinge, or be dependent, on them. These four virtues, according to Plato, promote health and harmony of the soul—Plato's definition of virtue. These virtues also correspond to Plato's conception of the soul: Wisdom is the virtue of the intellect, courage that of the will, temperance that of feelings, and justice that of the soul's relation to others—that is, society.

The acceptance of the four cardinal virtues as primary qualities of the moral life can be seen in the writings of subsequent Greek and Christian philosophers. Aristotle centered his *Nicomachean Ethics* on them, although he opposed the Platonic idea of innate virtue, arguing instead that they are acquired through experience. The Stoic school, opposing the Epicureans, who were promoting pleasure as the ultimate good, contended that virtue is the only good. The fourth century B.C.E. Stoic philosopher Zeno of Citium taught that people should live their lives in accordance with the divine plan of nature and that virtue alone was important in living the good life.

Among the early Christian writers, Origen, born in 185, taught that science and philosophy could be in accord with Christian teachings, and was among the first Christian writers to argue that the four cardinal virtues were essential to the Christian moral character. The crucial step in Christianizing the cardinal virtues was taken by Saint Augustine, who interpreted the cardinal virtues in light of the love of God: prudence is love's discernment; courage, love's endurance; temperance, love's purity; and justice is the service of God's love. It is in the teachings of Saint Augustine that the cardinal virtues are placed alongside the theological virtues of the New Testament (I Corinthians 13): faith, hope, and love. Among later Christian philosophers, Saint Thomas Aquinas in the thirteenth century, preeminent as a champion of the virtuous life, presents in works such as *Summa Theologica* the seven virtues as the chief signs of the Christian moral character. More recently, the great Christian author of the twentieth century, C. S. Lewis, in his classic defense of the Christian faith, *Mere Christianity* (1943), wrote that proper Christian behavior manifests the qualities of the seven virtues.

THE SEVEN VIRTUES DESCRIBED

Prudence means exercising common sense and sound judgment in practical matters, carefully considering the consequences of one's actions. It involves forethought, caution, discretion, discernment, and circumspection. It is not the same thing as intelligence; great geniuses may act imprudently. The prudent person can speak the "fitting" word at the proper time, knows when and how to promote the interests of both self and others, and knows how to arrange his or her affairs for the greatest benefit.

Temperance refers to moderation and self-restraint in the pursuit and expression of all pleasures. The essence of temperance is self-control, not, generally speaking, complete abstinence. It involves moderation with food, chastity with sexuality, and humility with great success. A person lacking in temperance would be given to gluttony, promiscuity, and arrogance. Conversely, too much restraint would leave a person with austere eating habits, excessive prudishness in sexual behavior, and a self-deprecating personality.

Justice demands that affairs among people be guided by fairness, impartiality, and equality. Aristotle divided justice into general and particular categories. General justice can be construed as a social justice in which societies are organized in such a way that all members contribute to and benefit from the common good. Particular justice is subdivided into corrective justice—the fulfilling of contracts between people—and distributive justice—fairness and impartiality in the distribution of goods and burdens. The just person is honest, is truthful, stands for what is right, and keeps his or her word.

Courage is the ability to face danger and distress with endurance and purpose of heart. Courage involves not only withstanding evil but also attacking it and working to overcome it. The courageous person will stand for the moral right and persevere in it no matter how unpopular that may be. Bravery, determination, sturdiness, and tenacity are the characteristics of those who are courageous. Courageous people are not those who lack fear. Courageous people act in spite of fear, work to overcome their fears, and triumph in the face of fear.

Faith, according to the New Testament writer Paul (Heb. 11:1), is "the substance of things hoped for, the evidence of things not seen." Faith, in the theological sense, involves apprehending, trusting, and holding on to spiritual truth. Although the context of faith in the writings of the apostle Paul certainly emphasizes the divine dimension, the importance of faith in the human condition cannot be ignored. The faithful person demonstrates the traits of loyalty, steadfastness, dependability, and trustworthiness. Faith works to bring and keep people together in marriage, politics, and religion (with God). It is the glue that binds one human heart to another. Infidelities of all sorts serve to separate even the closest of human relationships.

Hope is the expectation that one's desires will be realized. Hope is forward-looking, giving direction, purpose, and energy to life. The apostle Paul (Heb. 6:19) describes hope as the "anchor of the soul, both sure and steadfast." The person who hopes is stimulated to greater personal growth, works toward a better society, and believes in something better to come. Lack of hope—apathy, helplessness, and pessimism—saps life from individuals, brings stagnation to civilizations, and empties religion of its meaning.

Love is a transcending devotion to another. In his great discourse on love in I Corinthians 13:4-8, the apostle Paul describes love as "always patient and kind; it is never jealous; love is never boastful or conceited; it is never rude or selfish; it does not take offense, and is not resentful. Love takes no pleasure in other people's sins but delights in the truth; it is always ready to excuse, to trust, to hope, and to endure whatever comes. Love does not come to an end." Love is affective; it involves feelings of closeness, tenderness, and passion. Love is behavioral; it has to do with how one person acts and intends to act toward another. Love is cognitive; it involves knowing another, wishing for and thinking of another's best. The loving person cares for others, is benevolent, and stands against hatred and malice wherever it appears. In I Corinthians 13:13, love is considered to be preeminent over faith and hope. Indeed, many have called love the greatest of the seven virtues.

It is notable that in religiously inspired lists of virtues, love is almost always included and occupies a prominent position. In many secular lists, such as the cardinal virtues, love is often absent or is only indirectly mentioned. Perhaps to consider the greatest good, God, necessitates the consideration of the greatest virtue, love.

Paul J. Chara, Jr.

FURTHER READING

Aristotle. *On Man in the Universe.* Introduced and edited by Louise Ropes Loomis. New York: W. L. Black, 1943. English translations of five of Aristotle's greatest works are presented: *Metaphysics, Parts of Animals, Nicomachean Ethics, Politics,* and *Poetics.* The first seven books of *Nicomachean Ethics* are particularly concerned with virtue and closely related issues.

Darwall, Stephen, ed. *Virtue Ethics.* Malden, Mass.: Blackwell, 2002. Anthology collecting the major classical texts in virtue-based ethical theory (Aristotle, Hutcheson, Hume), as well as contemporary essays by Philippa Foot, Alasdair MacIntyre, and others.

Erikson, Erik H., ed. *Adulthood.* New York: W. W. Norton, 1978. Erikson's theory of personality development is one of the few modern psychological theories to integrate the notion of virtue into psychological growth. Erikson's description of the virtues attainable in each development stage is presented in the first chapter of the book, "Dr. Borg's Life Cycle."

Fagothey, Austin. *Fagothey's Right and Reason: Ethics in Theory and Practice.* 9th ed. Columbus, Ohio: Merrill, 1989. A general introduction to the study of ethics written in a style accessible to the novice reader. Many of the chapters are relevant to the topic of virtue; however, the sixteenth chapter, "Habit," specifically goes into detail regarding the cardinal virtues.

Lewis, C. S. *Mere Christianity.* London: Collins, 1988. This book, written by a Cambridge scholar, is a lucid exposition of the Christian faith and is considered to be among the greatest Christian works ever penned. Book 3, "Christian Behavior," relates each of the seven virtues to Christian living.

MacIntyre, Alasdair. *After Virtue: A Study in Moral Theory.* 2d ed. Notre Dame, Ind.: University of Notre Dame Press, 1984. One of the most significant works of twentieth century moral philosophy. In an attempt to revitalize moral theory, MacIntyre redefines a "virtue" as a value necessary to the preservation of a specific institution of social practice.

Plato. *The Collected Dialogues of Plato.* Edited by Edith Hamilton and Huntington Cairns. 1961. Reprint. Princeton, N.J.: Princeton University Press,

1984. English translations of five of Plato's greatest works are presented: *Apology*, *Crito*, *Phaedo*, *Symposium*, and *Republic*. Book 4 of the *Republic* deals specifically with the cardinal virtues. It is here that these virtues are first accepted as the standard virtues of the ancient world.

SEE ALSO: Aristotelian ethics; Augustine, Saint; Buddhist ethics; Christian ethics; Confucian ethics; Plato; Platonic ethics; Socrates; Thomas Aquinas; Vice; Virtue ethics.

Virtue ethics

DEFINITION: Practical approach to both understanding and living the good life that is based on conceptions of moral excellence
TYPE OF ETHICS: Theory of ethics
SIGNIFICANCE: Virtue ethics eschews or minimizes talk of rules, principles, obligation, duty, or consequences. Instead, it focuses primarily on the notion of the good or virtuous person: It seeks to develop a concrete and nuanced understanding of what such a person is like, and then to use that theoretical exemplar to guide actual behavior.

Everyday life and the actions that constitute it involve patterns of interaction. People do good and perform right actions not so much as a consequence of individual acts of moral reasoning but as a consequence of inherited patterns of right and wrong, good and bad. It is in taking responsibility for these inherited patterns that meaningful ethical life takes place, not in esoteric discussions and tentative moral actions related to new technologies, fads, and lifestyles that seek ethical justification. Certainly, discussions of new ethical challenges must take place, but support for and recognition of the importance of character, values, and virtues in everyday life must be recognized as imperative.

One's point of view is expressed in one's thoughts and actions. Actions manifest one's values, commitment, and character. Good character is not an accident. It requires discipline, reflection, and responsibility. A virtue is a reflection of good character because it is a pattern of action. It should not be suggested, however, that one's ethical life is isolated and is developed apart from other people. One's virtues depend on others for their origin and sustenance—for their origin, because one usually inherits the virtues of parents, peers, and significant others; for their sustenance, because to sustain a pattern of action over a prolonged period of time, one needs encouragement and positive reinforcement.

FOCUSING ON HUMAN LIFE RATHER THAN HUMAN RULES

Much of modern ethics focuses on specific acts that are justified by rules or consequences. Virtue ethics focuses on good judgment as a consequence of good character. Beliefs, sensitivity, and experience are of more importance than are rules and consequences for determining one's ethical life. Because its focus is on human life rather than on human rules, virtue ethics becomes involved with various psychologies of ethics as well as with the ways in which gender, race, ethnicity, economics, and power shape character and thus the experience of virtue.

How is one fulfilled as a human being? Does fulfillment vary on the basis of gender, race, ethnicity, and economic position? The answer to these questions is of vital importance to virtue ethics.

DIFFICULTIES

Since virtue ethics gives a significant role to feelings in the ethical life, many wonder where the consistency necessary for ethical living, independent of the subjectivity of daily life and transitory human feelings, exists. If feeling is central to virtue, then the ethical life is built on the shifting sands of human emotion. Those who practice virtue ethics recognize this difficulty and agree with the thrust of the critique. Yet it must be recognized that one reason for the growth of virtue ethics is that "rules and consequences ethics" leaves out an essential part of human life—feelings. All ethical theories and practice must deal with the whole person: mind and feelings, rules and consequences.

Virtue ethics presupposes that one will be drawn to the personally perceived good. Christians suggest, however, based on the doctrine of Original Sin, that humans are more attracted to the bad than to the good. The increase in the prison population as well as daily experience may cause many non-Christians to fear an ethic based on human perfectibility. One cannot say, "I will be good someday, but not today," they claim. One must see one's duty and do it. These individual acts are important and cannot wait to become part of some overall pattern of living.

Virtue ethics, while reaffirming that people readily deceive themselves when searching for the good, prefers to speak about development. Human perfectibility is the base principle. Vice will always be part of that journey of perfectibility. Virtue is gained only in dealing with vices, but it is gained, say virtue ethicists, only because virtue is seen as better than vice.

Some virtues are part of any listing of virtues: justice, prudence, generosity, courage, temperance, magnanimity, gentleness, magnificence, wisdom. Yet there is no agreed-upon list of virtues. Some authors point out that there may be conflicts between some virtues—gentleness and justice, for example—that cannot be resolved. These authors suggest that the only way to resolve such conflicts is to give primacy to "rule and consequences ethics" rather than virtue ethics. Yet the challenge of human living is to deal with conflict in a constructive way, and virtue ethics holds that dealing with such conflicts will lead to growth in a person's ethical character.

Nathan R. Kollar

FURTHER READING

Carr, David. *Educating the Virtues: An Essay on the Philosophical Psychology of Moral Development and Education.* New York: Routledge, 1991.

Darwall, Stephen, ed. *Virtue Ethics.* Malden, Mass.: Blackwell, 2002.

Donahue, James A. "The Use of Virtue and Character in Applied Ethics." *Horizons* 17 (Fall, 1990): 228-243.

Hauerwas, Stanley. *Vision and Virtue: Essays in Christian Ethical Reflection.* Notre Dame, Ind.: University of Notre Dame Press, 1981.

Hauerwas, Stanley, and Charles Pinches. *Christians Among the Virtues: Theological Conversations with Ancient and Modern Ethics.* Notre Dame, Ind.: University of Notre Dame Press, 1997.

Kruschwitz, Robert B., and Robert C. Roberts, eds. *The Virtues: Contemporary Essays on Moral Character.* Belmont, Calif.: Wadsworth, 1987.

MacIntyre, Alasdair. *After Virtue: A Study in Moral Theory.* 2d ed. Notre Dame, Ind.: University of Notre Dame Press, 1984.

_____. *Whose Justice? Which Rationality?* Notre Dame, Ind.: University of Notre Dame Press, 1988.

Smith, R. Scott. *Virtue Ethics and Moral Knowledge: Philosophy of Language After MacIntyre and Hauerwas.* Burlington, Vt.: Ashgate, 2003.

Yearley, Lee H. "Recent Work on Virtue." *Religious Studies Review* 16 (January, 1990): 1-9.

SEE ALSO: Benevolence; Good, the; Morality; Role models; Sin; Vice; Virtue.

Vivisection

DEFINITION: Invasive surgical experimentation upon living animals

TYPE OF ETHICS: Animal rights

SIGNIFICANCE: In current usage, "vivisection" carries a strong negative connotation. It is used by people opposed to the practice of animal experimentation in general, or by people condemning a specific experiment as cruel or unnecessary.

Formed from the Latin words *vīvi* (living) and *sectio* (cutting), the word "vivisection" was used as early as 1707 to refer to an operation performed on a living animal. In both the nineteenth and twentieth centuries, people opposed to research on animals organized under the heading of "antivivisection" (for example, the National Anti-Vivisection Society). Since animal rights activists do not necessarily oppose all animal experimentation, however, "vivisection" usually is taken to refer specifically to operations performed without anesthesia or for trivial reasons.

Many or most scientists (and some animal rights advocates) assume that if the animals involved feel no pain or distress (for example, they are anesthetized), then no moral issues are raised by their use. The development of paralytic drugs in modern medicine created a problem. These strong muscle relaxants thoroughly immobilize the subject, allowing very delicate operations (like open heart surgery) to be performed, but when used alone (a practice called "chemical restraint"), they do not deaden sensations of pain. Chemical restraint is sometimes practiced on animals and human infants.

Gary E. Varner

SEE ALSO: Animal consciousness; Animal research; Animal rights; Cruelty to animals; National Anti-Vivisection Society; Sentience; Society for the Prevention of Cruelty to Animals.

Voltaire

IDENTIFICATION: French writer and philosopher

BORN: François-Marie Arouet; November 21, 1694, Paris, France

DIED: May 30, 1778, Paris, France

TYPE OF ETHICS: Enlightenment history

SIGNIFICANCE: The author of *Candide: Or, All for the Best* (*Candide: Ou, L'Optimisme,* 1759), Voltaire viewed morality as a commitment to justice and humanity that was based on the universal ethical precepts of natural law.

Voltaire. (Library of Congress)

One of France's greatest writers, Voltaire distinguished himself as a historian, novelist, dramatist, poet, philosopher, and crusader against religious intolerance. As a rationalist and Deist, he rejected the traditional Christian view of God and belief in the immortality of the soul. He adhered to a natural religion, believing in an impersonal, remote deity whose attributes were beyond human understanding but who inspired a great sense of awe. Voltaire shared the belief of fellow Deists who considered the essence of religion to be morality, a commitment to justice and humanity.

Voltaire strongly believed that universal ethical principles were inherent in natural law and that the merit of human laws was determined by the extent to which they reflected such just and humane standards. Even though all religions derived from a universal rational source, the teachings of theologians and priests distorted the common truth, divided humanity, and perpetuated intolerance. Only under the guidance of enlightened thinkers who rose above superstition and prejudice could a rational morality be cultivated that would bring about human brotherhood.

In practice, Voltaire promoted a social ethic that was conducive to the harmonious interests of the entire society. In pursuing this goal, he was quite willing to accept socially useful beliefs that he personally rejected. Thus, he held that, even though the deity probably did not concern himself with human affairs, it was good for the people to believe that there are rewards and punishments for human actions. Among his deepest concerns was the happiness of the individual in society. In *Candide*, he satirized the view that this is the best of all possible worlds, but he nevertheless imagined that in time reason and enlightenment would lessen superstition and fanaticism and bring about a more harmonious social order. To this end, Voltaire remained a passionate advocate of individuals who had been denied justice, especially by the power of the Church, and of judicial reform.

George P. Blum

SEE ALSO: Deism; Enlightenment ethics; God; Humanism; Hume, David; Leibniz, Gottfried Wilhelm; Locke, John; Montesquieu; Natural law; Rousseau, Jean-Jacques; Social justice and responsibility.

Voting fraud

DEFINITION: Violations of laws governing the privilege of voting

TYPE OF ETHICS: Politico-economic ethics

SIGNIFICANCE: Voting fraud can not only unfairly affect the outcomes of elections but also contribute to corrosion of the basic legitimacy of democratic society. American courts have responded by passing down decisions that expand definitions of fraud and stress the importance of legitimacy.

To have the privilege of casting a ballot in the United States, a person must be an American citizen over the age of eighteen years and comply with relevant federal, state, and local statutes. The individual states set the conditions for voting under a basic framework laid down by the U.S. Constitution and its amendments. For example, a state may insist on voters registering before they vote but may not deny the right to vote to a person on any grounds prohibited by the Fourteenth, Fifteenth, Nineteenth, Twenty-fourth, and Twenty-sixth Amendments to the U.S. Constitution. The prohibitions include denying persons the vote because of their race or sex.

Moreover, while the individual states grant voting privileges, or the franchise, they must also comply with the Fourteenth Amendment's equal protection clause by setting and applying equal conditions to every person eligible to vote. In the United States, the franchise is thus considered a legal right, though it is not considered a basic human right.

THE ETHICS OF EQUAL PROTECTION

While the concept of equal protection has served as a potential legal standard for determining vote fraud for years, the Supreme Court first made that standard explicit in its 2000 *Bush v. Gore* decision. The Court made its ruling at a moment when charges and counter-charges of voting fraud were swirling around Florida's tightly contested presidential election. The Court's ruling applied the equal protection clause to stop a recount of votes in Florida, effectively giving the national election to George W. Bush. The Court asserted that Bush and his supporters would be denied equal protection if Florida counted some, but not all, Florida ballots. At the same time, the Court did not consider other equal protection issues, such as whether Florida's African American voters might be denied equal protection because of discriminatory voting-list purges, absentee ballot irregularities, and possible misuse of certain kinds of voting machines and ballots.

While the U.S. Supreme Court majority attempted to limit the scope of their judgment to the specific facts of the case, it is unlikely that the logic of equal protection can be so easily contained. Equal protection has become a complicated, demanding standard posing serious ethical issues relating to all aspects of voting and elections throughout the nation's fifty states, with their diverse voting laws. The new standard has expanded the scope of fraud, making many laws open to legal challenge. What were once limited questions to be resolved by state courts are now national constitutional fraud issues. In the years immediately following the 2000 presidential election, the final outcome of this ethical debate remained far from clear.

Richard L. Wilson

FURTHER READING

Dionne, E. J., Jr., and William Kristol, eds. *Bush v. Gore: The Court Cases and Commentary.* Washington, D.C.: Brookings Institution, 2001.

Rakove, Jack N. *The Unfinished Election of 2000: Leading Scholars Examine America's Strangest Election.* New York: Basic Books, 2001.

Rubin, Barry. *A Citizen's Guide to Politics in America: Expanded Edition.* Armonk, N.Y.: M. E. Sharpe, 2000.

Scher, Richard K., Jon L. Mills, and John J. Hotaling. *Voting Rights and Democracy.* Chicago: Nelson-Hall, 1997.

SEE ALSO: Campaign finance reform; Fraud; Nader, Ralph; Poll taxes; Suffrage.

Wage discrimination

DEFINITION: Payment of different wages to members of different social groups for reasons unconnected with job performance

TYPE OF ETHICS: Sex and gender issues

SIGNIFICANCE: Taken in the aggregate, wage discrimination violates such values as fairness, equity, and social justice. It is difficult to combat, however, because any single instance of the practice may seem justifiable to an employer, who may point to factors other than social identity that influenced the wages of a particular individual.

During the 1960's, various disadvantaged groups asserted their rights in the job market. The Equal Employment Opportunity Commission and various laws provided for equal access to jobs in the United States, but little was said about the compensation for those jobs. Studies quickly established that white men in the United States earned more than people of any other race-and-sex combination.

Business advocates quickly postulated reasons for the discrepancies, including differences in experience, intelligence, education, on-the-job training, occupational choice, and attachment to the labor force. Many studies focused on women, who, it was argued, are more prone to periodic absences resulting from child care responsibilities and also are more likely to leave their jobs for long periods, or permanently, to have children. These propensities make them less valuable in the long run, even if their daily performance while on the job is identical to that of men. Employers defended their right to invest less in workers who were less likely to stay around and pay back the investment. One argument thus became circular: Women were paid less because they had less training, and they were given less training because they were women. Defenses of lower wages for minority workers rested primarily on lack of experience and lower levels of education and training.

Various studies explored these reasons for wage differences. They typically found about half of the differences between men's and women's wages to be explained by objective factors, leaving the other half of the difference unexplained, possibly a result of discrimination.

A. J. Sobczak

SEE ALSO: Affirmative action; Equal pay for equal work; Equal Rights Amendment; Hiring practices; Inequality; Minimum-wage laws; Social justice and responsibility.

Walden

IDENTIFICATION: Book by Henry David Thoreau (1817-1862)

DATE: Published in 1854

TYPE OF ETHICS: Environmental ethics

SIGNIFICANCE: *Walden* provides a model of the proper ethical treatment of nature and serves almost as a handbook for an environmental ethics.

Henry David Thoreau's two-year experiment of living at Massachusetts's Walden Pond was on one level an effort to determine whether a person really needed the material possessions that were considered essential in mid-nineteenth century America. His book demonstrated that one could attain the good life by living in harmony with nature supplied only with the bare necessities. The first chapter, entitled "Economy," demonstrates that human needs are few; thus, there is no need to exploit nature to attain them. Much of the rest of the book attacks the acquisitive spirit. At bottom, Thoreau argues, materialistic values indicate not enterprise but a basic lack of spiritual self-reliance. In Thoreau's ethic, ownership of the land is invalid. Humans should act as stewards rather than squires.

Thoreau's own love of nature is illustrated in the intricate detail with which he describes the seasons, flora and fauna, natural processes, and Walden Pond itself. If he measures and documents, plumbs the depths of the lake, scrupulously counts every penny spent in the building of his house, and ponders his profit after selling produce from his garden, it is to show that empirical science does have a use, but that it should be subordinate to a guiding spirit that respects and loves the natural environment rather than exploits it. *Walden* continually demonstrates "correspondences"; that is, clear relationships between the ethical life of humankind and nature, an interconnectedness that Thoreau believed deserved more acknowledgment and respect.

William L. Howard

SEE ALSO: Earth and humanity; Nature, rights of; Thoreau, Henry David; Transcendentalism.

Wang Yangming

IDENTIFICATION: Chinese philosopher
BORN: November 30, 1472, Youyao, Zhejiang, China
DIED: January 9, 1529, Nanen, Jiangxi, China
TYPE OF ETHICS: Medieval history
SIGNIFICANCE: In *Instructions for Practical Living* (*Zhuan xi lu*, 1527), Wang rejected the Confucian dualism of principle and material force, insisting instead on the unity of knowledge and action in human affairs.

At the time that Wang developed his ideas, Confucianism had been a major religion in China for more than 1,700 years, from the time when the ideas of Confucius were gathered, along with commentaries, during the Han Dynasty (256 B.C.E.-220 C.E.). Confucianism was a secular religion emphasizing proper conduct and relationships learned by observation of exemplary individuals.

The eclectic writings of Confucianism were codified in the twelfth century C.E. by Zhu Xi, who clarified the notion of principle (*li*, somewhat like the Platonic "idea"), which acted through the mind and material things to create the world, physical and moral, that people perceive. Wang regarded this as an unacceptable dualism, insisting that principle and mind are one, that knowledge and action are inseparable and are related to principle and mind, and that

the way to understand these things is not through study of canonic writings, as Zhu Xi taught, but by direct investigation of one's own mind to find the knowledge of the good that resides there. These ideas led to the practice of a Zen-like form of meditation. Wang's ideas were influential in Chinese Confucianism well into the eighteenth century, and even later in Japan.

Robert M. Hawthorne, Jr.

SEE ALSO: Confucian ethics; Confucius; Secular ethics; Theory and practice; Zhu Xi.

War

DEFINITION: State of armed combat between enemy states
TYPE OF ETHICS: Military ethics
SIGNIFICANCE: War raises many ethical questions, including attempts to determine when—and if ever—waging war is morally permissible and what means combatants may use to gain their objectives.

The starting point of all discussions of the philosophy of war is the just war theory first articulated by the fourth-fifth century North African philosopher Saint Augustine and developed by later medieval philosophers, including Saint Thomas Aquinas. According to that theory, waging war is morally permissible if and only if seven conditions pertain.

The first condition is that the war must be declared legally by rightful authority. Second, the war must be pursued for a morally just cause. Next, the war must be undertaken with a morally permissible intention. This condition rules out waging war for reasons of greed, cruelty, mere vengeance, or hatred. The fourth requirement is that the just cause behind the war must be reasonably probable. This condition aspires to limit the unnecessary, purposeless slaughter of human lives. The fifth requirement is that war must be waged only as a last resort. While this condition cannot be taken literally—for nations almost always have one more available maneuver prior to declaring war—the principle requires that all reasonable efforts be made to resolve disputes peacefully before resorting to violence.

The sixth and seventh requirements concern the actual conduct of war. Any war must achieve a good that is greater than the amount of harm produced by military action. Finally, a war must be fought by means that are not inherently immoral. This condition precludes directly killing innocent people, inflicting more injuries than necessary, torturing people unjustifiably, and otherwise not undertaking actions that go beyond the immediate necessities of successful combat.

Ethical Questions Posed by Just War Theory

- Is it possible to measure the benefits and devastation of war even though numerous elements of each are not comparable? For example, how can lives lost in present combat be weighed against future possible gains in liberty?

- Do the "rightful" authorities that are permitted to declare war include *all* legally established governments? Or, must such governments themselves be morally rightful authorities?

- Must the intentions animating declarations of war be entirely pure? Or, can they be mixed, so long as the primary intentions are morally permissible?

- Is it inherently wrong for a nation or a group of soldiers to fight for a just cause that is likely to be crushed by a more powerful and evil enemy?

DOCTRINE OF DOUBLE EFFECT

Just war theory addresses two aspects of the justification of war: the reasons and causes for fighting (*jus ad bellum*) and the means used to secure military objectives (*jus in bello*). Even if a nation is morally justified in waging war it may be morally unjustified in the way it conducts the war. The doctrine, or principle, of double effect is sometimes invoked to justify means that may be morally troubling that are used to secure military objectives. According to this doctrine, acts that bring about foreseen evil effects, such as the deaths of innocent people, are morally permis-

sible if and only if those same acts also produce good effects that outweigh the bad ones. Such acts are not inherently immoral because the evil effects are not the means to the good effects, and only the good effects are intended.

To understand this doctrine, suppose that a nation passes the conditions of just war theory pertaining to *jus ad bellum*. The nation decides to bomb its evil enemy even though its leaders foresee that their attack will kill people who are clearly innocent, such as children, people with mental disabilities, and civilians who oppose the wrongful objectives of their own leaders. At first view, the foreseen killing of innocent human beings contaminates the attacking nation in terms of *jus in bello*, even though the nation may be morally justified in waging war. The doctrine of double effect, however, justifies the bombing when all its conditions are fulfilled.

The doctrine of double effect, however, invites serious questions. Is it possibly truly to distinguish a combatant's intentions when they are mixed? Is it not intuitively obvious that the more closely the two effects of the act—one focused on securing legitimate military objectives, the other centered on the foreseen killing of innocent human beings—are connected, the less plausible is the moral agent's claim to intend one but not the other effect? Also, is it clear when the evil effects—for example, the killing of innocent human beings—are not the means to the good effects of attaining justified military goals?

THE REALIST ARGUMENT

The seemingly insurmountable moral puzzles surrounding the waging and conduct of war lead some thinkers to conclude that moral theorizing is irrelevant in the context of military action. The realist argument claims that nations at war operate within a Hobbesian state of nature, a condition in which moral notions are unenforceable because no force is powerful enough to guarantee compliance. Moral notions bear currency only within civilized settings in which contractual promises are enforceable. Talk of neither fairness nor unfairness is coherent in a state of nature.

The realist argument tends to exaggerate the global conditions surrounding war. Numerous international treaties pertaining to the conduct of war affirm that talk of a state of nature is extravagant. Even during times of war, nations are not fully independent

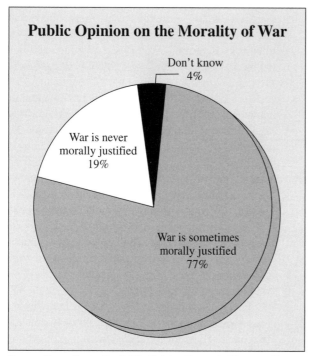

Public Opinion on the Morality of War

Don't know
4%

War is never
morally justified
19%

War is sometimes
morally justified
77%

Source: Roper Center for Public Opinion Research. Figures reflect responses of 1,032 adults surveyed by Pew Research Center in March, 2003.

of all other nations. World opinion still bears moral currency as some warring nations are praised and others are disparaged for their reasons for waging war and their use of means to attain military objectives. The realist argument would be persuasive only in a global moral vacuum in which all nations renounce all efforts to make moral distinctions. However, such a moral vacuum did not occur even during the waging of the two great world wars of the twentieth century.

THE ARGUMENT FROM INNOCENCE

Beginning from a Kantian premise that it is never morally permissible to kill innocent human beings directly, the argument from innocence holds that the use of certain modern weapons, such as nuclear arms, is morally impermissible. Noncombatants are nonthreatening bystanders to war and thus innocent people. The notion that it is morally impermissible to treat human beings as a mere means to one's ends is a generally accepted Kantian maxim. People may not treat others as less than they themselves are, regard them as mere instruments for their own purposes, or

disregard their moral status to achieve their own goals. If a state harms nonthreatening bystanders to achieve its legitimate military goals, it wrongfully uses those innocent people as mere means to its (rightful) ends. Accordingly, the use of modern weapons that have a high probability of killing numerous noncombatants is morally impermissible because such use foreseeably and directly exploits innocent people.

The argument from innocence places a limit on *jus in bello*. Those who advocate the use of modern weapons despite the fact that noncombatants will thereby be foreseeably harmed sometimes appeal to the doctrine of double effect. The loss of innocent lives is not directly intended, but only a foreseen, unavoidable side effect of attaining a justified military objective. Only the good effect is intended, and the death of innocent people is not the means to secure the good effect. All other conditions of the doctrine of double effect are also satisfied. Advocates of modern weapons point out the differences between intentionally and wrongfully using innocent persons as, for example, human shields against an enemy, and foreseeably and indirectly killing noncombatants as an unintended consequence of an otherwise legitimate military attack.

The argument from innocence bears considerable moral currency. However, it must refine its notion of innocence. The combatant/noncombatant distinction is too crude. Not all combatants are soldiers by choice, while numerous noncombatants directly support the war efforts of their national leaders through the work they do, their advocacy of war, and money they give to their governments. Moreover, the argument from innocence resists all appeals to consequences. What if foreseeably and indirectly, or even directly, killing a few noncombatants might result in a faster ending of a war than otherwise available, in favor of a just cause that would lessen the number of overall war casualties?

PACIFISM

Some thinkers, such as the philosopher Robert Holmes, use the argument from innocence to conclude that all modern wars are presumptively immoral because they invariably and foreseeably result in the direct killing of numerous innocent people.

Holmes denies a sharp distinction between *jus ad bellum* and *jus in bello*. He argues that it is not possible morally to assess the justice of waging war in isolation from the inevitable means used to conduct modern wars.

Holmes understands the fragility of identifying the wrongfulness of war with the killing of noncombatants. Instead of stressing combatant/noncombatant distinctions, he advances innocent/noninnocent distinctions. People are innocent to the degree that they lack responsibility for wrongful aggression. Most initiators of wrongdoing, such as governmental leaders, and some agents of wrongdoing, such as military commanders and combat soldiers, are noninnocents because they are morally responsible for wrongful aggression. Some contributors to war efforts, such as munitions workers, military researchers, and taxpayers, and some who otherwise approve of the war are less morally responsible for wrongful aggression,

but are not clearly innocents. Clearly innocent are noncontributors to, and nonsupporters of, the wrongdoing such as young children, the insane, and active opponents of the war who refuse to pay taxes or are jailed for refusing induction into the armed forces.

In assessing these categories, one should pay special attention to the enormous social pressures upon citizens deciding whether to consent to their nations' military actions. Citizens are inclined to support their governments because of their habits of obedience to their governments, the psychological forces of patriotism, the moral investments they typically make in their nations, the misinformation and limitations on information typically provided to them by their governments, and, very often, fears that opposition to official policies will bring governmental and social retaliation.

Holmes argues that even a wrongfully aggressive nation—one that is deficient from the vantage point

Children take shelter under a makeshift bomb shelter in a Karen refugee camp, into which guerilla allies of Myanmar's military government began firing mortar rounds in early 1998. As in other civil wars around the world, children endured a disproportionate amount of the suffering. (AP/Wide World Photos)

of *jus ad bellum*—includes numerous innocent people. At least some of those people will necessarily be killed in modern warfare, regardless of the intentions and motivations of the opposing sides. A morally righteous nation, for example, cannot be expected adequately to distinguish innocent from noninnocent members of its enemy. Moreover, the killing done by the wrongfully aggressive nation is the killing of innocents because it involves killing those who have done no wrong relative to the war. The morally righteous nation, presumably, contains only innocent people focused on morally permissible self-defense.

Virtually all members of a morally righteous side and many members of the wrongfully aggressive side can be considered innocent people. Given the inability of opposing sides clearly to distinguish innocent from noninnocent enemies, and given the nature of modern weapons, it is clear that waging modern war will inevitably kill innocent people. The impossibility of *jus in bello* destroys the possibility of *jus ad bellum*. Accordingly, modern war is presumptively wrong because it inevitably destroys innocent lives. As an antidote, Holmes champions nonviolent resistance as a way of life.

One might ask whether Holmes mistakenly reduces complex moral questions about the nature of war to only one of their components, the killing of innocent people. Does he take an unreasonably absolutist position on the notion that killing innocent people is always wrong? Is there a practical, less violent alternative to war when confronting wrongfully aggressive enemies? Moreover, is it possible that even innocent people might sometimes pose threats to the well-being of others that permit a right to self-defense? Finally, what would be the transition costs of moving to national pacifism?

WALZER'S ALTERNATIVE.

Michael Walzer, influenced by just war theory, offers an alternative to Holmes. He argues that the knowing, foreseeable, but merely incidental killing of noncombatant innocents of the aggressive nation is justified only when killing such people prevents the loss of a greater number of innocent lives; when such killing is done as a last resort; when the killers minimize the evil involved, including the manner and number of killings; and when the killers accept reasonable risks and costs to themselves in minimizing the evil. If successful, Walzer's alternative permits at least the theoretical possibility that a morally righteous nation could fulfill the standards of both *jus ad bellum* and *jus in bello*.

Raymond Angelo Belliotti

FURTHER READING

Augustine, Saint. *The Political Writings of St. Augustine.* Edited by Henry Paolucci. Chicago: Gateway Editions, 1987. Early work on the justification of war.

Belliotti, Raymond Angelo. "Are All Modern Wars Morally Wrong?" *Journal of Social Philosophy* 26, no. 2 (1995): 17-31. Analysis of the just war theory.

Clausewitz, Karl von. *On War.* Princeton, N.J.: Princeton University Press, 1976. Classic work arguing that there is theoretically no moral limit to the conduct of war and no practical limit other than a nation's will and capabilities.

Holmes, Robert L. *On War and Morality.* Princeton, N.J.: Princeton University Press, 1989. One of the strongest and clearest arguments that social pacifism is morally required and that all modern wars are presumptively wrong.

Johnson, James Turner. *Can Modern War Be Just?* New Haven, Conn.: Yale University Press, 1984. Defends the relevance of just war theory in the modern nuclear age.

Thomas Aquinas, Saint. *The Summa Theologica.* Translated by Laurence Shapcote. 2d ed. 2 vols. Chicago: Encyclopaedia Britannica, 1990. Medieval refinement to Saint Augustine's just war theory.

Walzer, Michael. *Just and Unjust Wars.* New York: Basic Books, 1977. A moral argument, with historical illustrations, that just and unjust military action are distinguishable.

SEE ALSO: *Art of War, The*; Chemical warfare; Geneva conventions; Holy war; Just war theory; Limited war; Military ethics; *On War*; Peacekeeping missions; Scorched-earth policies; Unconditional surrender; Vietnam War.

War crimes trials

DEFINITION: International tribunals convened to try persons responsible for genocide and other gross violations of human rights during military conflicts

DATE: First trial began in 1945

TYPE OF ETHICS: Human rights

SIGNIFICANCE: Trying war criminals for their acts has developed into an important way to confront and perhaps deter some of the worst atrocities of war, but the ethics of war crime trials themselves have been challenged.

The idea of crimes of war and the legal prosecution of war criminals have had a brief and troubled history. Traditionally, moral and legal sanctions have been considered out of place in times of war, in which the rape and murder of innocents has been considered standard practice—and, in some eras, regarded as spoils of war—and thus beyond the boundaries of law. While it is true that since antiquity ethical objections have occasionally been raised about the conduct of war, only during the twentieth century did individuals begin to face criminal trials and punishment for their deeds.

The first major war crimes trials were in Nuremberg, Germany, and Tokyo, Japan, to try Axis leaders after World War II. After a five-decade silence during the ensuing Cold War, war crime trials returned in the wake of mass atrocities in Yugoslavia and Rwanda. Further, the International Criminal Court, which was established in The Hague in 2002, has the authority to prosecute war criminals who fall under its jurisdiction.

The laws of war crimes originate primarily through two series of treaties: The Hague Conventions of 1899 and 1907 and the Geneva Conventions of 1949. These collected treaties, along with other treaties, United Nations conventions, and precedents set by the post-World War II trials, established a framework for defining which acts are permissible in wartime and which merit prosecution. Among the war crimes that merit consideration for prosecution are waging aggressive warfare, genocide, deliberately targeting civilians, mistreating prisoners of war, and using such banned weapons as chemical and biological agents.

Numerous ethical and moral issues arise from war crime trials. Many observers have questioned the ap-

propriateness of trials for acts carried out under the stresses of war. They argue that the concept of the trials represents a civilian bias against the horrible military necessities of war. Others have wondered whether criminal trials for war crimes can ever be fair, as the trials usually lack objective courts, and their verdicts resemble punishments inflicted by victors on the vanquished. This criticism has led to charges of "victor's justice" and a lingering bitter-

(Library of Congress)

Adolf Eichmann

One of Nazi Germany's bloodiest war criminals, Adolf Eichmann was responsible for sending millions of people to extermination camps during World War II. After escaping from Allied troops when the war ended, he fled to Italy and eventually settled in Argentina, where he assumed the name "Ricardo Klement" and lived quietly as a Buenos Aires factory worker. In 1960, agents of the Israeli Security Service found him and brought him to Israel, where he was tried for his war crimes in a sensational tribunal that was televised around the world. He was found guilty and hanged in Israel on May 31, 1962.

ness over some of the trials. Some would argue that it would be better to have a postwar amnesty, or even summary executions of enemy leaders, than apply peacetime civilian notions of right and wrong to the horrors of war.

Traditionally, theories of criminal justice have implied that punishments are somehow equal to the crimes for which they are inflicted, that punishments somehow restore the moral balance that the criminals have disrupted, and that punishment puts things "right." However, in cases in which criminals have taken hundreds or thousands or even millions of lives, it is difficult to imagine how punishing a few individual criminals—no matter how harshly—can provide satisfaction for the victims.

Aaron Fichtelberg

FURTHER READING
Bass, Gary. *Stay the Hand of Vengeance: The Politics of War Crimes Tribunals*. Princeton, N.J.: Princeton University Press, 2002.

Gutman, Roy, and David Rieff, ed. *Crimes of War: What the Public Should Know*. New York: W. W. Norton, 1999.

Robertson, Geoffrey. *Crimes Against Humanity: The Struggle for Global Justice*. New York: The New Press, 2000.

SEE ALSO: Concentration camps; Geneva conventions; Hitler, Adolf; Holocaust; International Criminal Court; International law; Kosovo; Nuremberg Trials; Rwanda genocide.

Warranties and guarantees

DEFINITION: Assurances made by manufactuers or dealers to consumers that if the products or services they sell fail to meet certain standards, they will repair or replace the goods or otherwise compensate buyers

TYPE OF ETHICS: Business and labor ethics

SIGNIFICANCE: In modern society, warranties and guarantees represent legally binding contracts between manufacturers and consumers. Ethical issues relating to warranties include consumer fraud (a consumer may pretend that a product had a defect when it was really damaged through care-

lessness), evasion of duty (a company may pretend that damage resulted from consumer carelessness rather than defect), and the proper calculation of a fair and reasonable warranty period.

The terms "guarantee" and "warranty" are virtually synonymous in their marketplace meanings. Laws in the United States generally use the term "warranty," while "guarantee" is perhaps more common in everyday speech. Both terms imply some sort of assurance of quality or standards to the buyer of a product or service. Sellers of products have probably always offered some form of guarantee, if nothing more than their reputation. During the Middle Ages, guilds for various professions set standards for the training and qualifications of their members. This could be considered to be the first formal type of guarantee.

FORMS OF WARRANTIES
Product warranties can take the form of written or oral statements. Some warranties are implied and are in force even though they are not directly communicated from seller to buyer. Sellers have some protection, in that they can specify that products are warrantied only for "reasonable use" or can attach warnings that products are not suited for particular uses. Many product liability lawsuits hinge on the meaning of "reasonable use" and whether a product is as safe as could reasonably have been expected.

In the United States, written warranties are covered by the Magnuson-Moss Warranty Act of 1975. According to the provisions of that act, a warranty must describe the specific coverage offered and what the purchaser of a product has to do to obtain it, as well as what the warrantor must do to remedy a problem. Prior to passage of the act, a warranty could be used to limit the seller's responsibility to what was stated on the warranty, thus breaking some reasonable expectations on the part of the buyer. The act states that warranties must be available in writing and must be available for purchasers to read before a purchase is made.

The Magnuson-Moss Warranty Act specifies two types of implied warranties that almost always are in force even though they are not stated in a seller's written warranty. In most cases, sellers are not able to release themselves from these implied warranties. The implied warranty of merchantability states that the product or service is suited for ordinary use. The implied warranty of fitness for a particular purpose states that sellers are responsible for providing correct information regarding particular uses to which a buyer might put a product. Sellers in this case represent themselves as experts whom consumers can trust for advice. For example, a consumer might tell a vacuum-cleaner salesperson what types of carpets the vacuum cleaner is being purchased to clean. The salesperson then would make a recommendation based on this information. The consumer has a right to expect that the vacuum cleaner will perform, even if the use to which it is put is not ordinary.

Warranties can be either full or limited. The Magnuson-Moss Warranty Act states conditions that must be met for a warranty to be labeled as "full." Limited warranties restrict the promises made by sellers. They can include clauses calling for payment of labor charges by the purchaser, reinstallation charges, or pro-rata refunds based on how long the product had been in use.

Many warranties apply only to new products. Consumers have less protection when they buy used goods, particularly if the goods are specifically sold "as is." Implied warranties most often do not apply to such sales.

ETHICAL IMPLICATIONS

Warranties and guarantees protect consumers both from unscrupulous behavior and from unanticipated consequences. An honest seller may unintentionally sell a defective product. His or her guarantee to the purchaser may be a simple oral statement that the product can be returned if it is defective. It may also take a formal contractual form. In either case, buyers face little risk when dealing with honest sellers.

Written warranties protect consumers from sellers who misrepresent their products, perhaps lying about the characteristics or expected performance of the product or about what the sellers will do to remedy defects or other consumer dissatisfaction. In the absence of enforceable warranties, sellers would be able to make any claims about their products, and consumers would have no way of making judgments other than basing them on the reputation of the seller. Unscrupulous sellers could then make sales based on exaggerated claims, then refuse to back those claims. The marketplace might even offer an incentive for such behavior, since consumers would be drawn to products for which exaggerated claims had been made, at least until the sellers' dishonesty had been established.

Warranties thus provide protection against dishonest marketplace behavior. They serve to make marketplaces more efficient, because consumers can be more certain of the information provided to them rather than having to rely on reputation. Warranties also increase the rewards to honest sellers, who are not faced with dishonest competitors who can make sales through false claims about their products. Warranties thus serve to enforce and reward ethical behavior.

A. J. Sobczak

FURTHER READING

Eiler, Andrew. *The Consumer Protection Manual.* New York: Facts On File, 1984.

Eisenberger, Kenneth. *The Expert Consumer: A Complete Handbook.* Englewood Cliffs, N.J.: Prentice-Hall, 1977.

Kurer, Martin, et al., eds. *Warranties and Disclaimers: Limitation of Liability in Consumer-Related Transactions.* New York: Kluwer Law International, 2002.

Maynes, E. Scott. *Decision-Making for Consumers: An Introduction to Consumer Economics.* New York: Macmillan, 1976.

Sapolsky, Harvey M., ed. *Consuming Fears: The Politics of Product Risks.* New York: Basic Books, 1986.

Weinstein, Alvin S., et al. *Products Liability and the Reasonably Safe Product: A Guide for Management, Design, and Marketing.* New York: John Wiley & Sons, 1978.

SEE ALSO: Business ethics; Consumerism; Product safety and liability; Sales ethics.

Washington, Booker T.

IDENTIFICATION: American educator
BORN: April 5, 1856, Hale's Ford, Virginia
DIED: November 14, 1915, Tuskegee, Alabama
TYPE OF ETHICS: Race and ethnicity
SIGNIFICANCE: Washington was the founder and principal of Tuskegee Normal and Industrial Institute and author of *Up from Slavery* (1901). He

interpreted human actions by utilitarian and pragmatic principles, focusing on their results rather than their motives.

Booker T. Washington's ethical position is set against the cultural, political, and societal forces of the late nineteenth and early twentieth centuries. His life corresponded with the Reconstruction years and their aftermath, when the South was adjusting to the post-Civil War trauma. The United States was emerging as a powerful industrial nation, and few restraints had been placed on economic competition. The era was dominated by industrialists who amassed great wealth through hard work and shrewd business practices. Some of the wealth, however, was diverted to select philanthropic causes.

By 1881, when Washington became principal of the Tuskegee Normal and Industrial Institute, the status of African Americans, particularly in the South, had eroded. Jim Crow laws, supporting racially discriminatory practices, proliferated. There was grow-

ing support in all sections of the country for disenfranchisement. The U.S. Supreme Court, in 1883, overturned that portion of the 1875 Civil Rights Act that had prohibited racial discrimination in the public sector. In 1896, the Court held in *Plessy v. Ferguson* that "separate but equal" public facilities were constitutional. In this context, Washington lived and developed his ethical and social views.

THE INTERNATIONAL EXPOSITION ADDRESS

Washington's speech at an exposition in Atlanta, Georgia, on September 18, 1895, established him as a spokesperson for many African Americans, those he called the "masses of my race." The speech summarized his position on race relations, and it found an enthusiastic audience, especially among white listeners. Thereafter, he was in great demand as a speaker and a national symbol for his race, being publicly recognized by presidents William McKinley, Theodore Roosevelt, and William Howard Taft as well as Queen Victoria of England.

In his Atlanta address, Washington proposed a compromise through which demands for full political and civil rights of African Americans would be exchanged for a share in the economic benefits that were expected to arise out of industrial development in the South. Instead of appealing for political power and recognition, he urged African Americans to establish respect by developing marketable vocational skills. He asserted that prosperity would come "in proportion as we learn to dignify and glorify common labor and put brains and skills into the common occupations of life." Without confrontation and with practical skills, African Americans could present themselves as law-abiding and nonoffensive citizens so that the social standards of the South would not be challenged.

In a separate-but-equal appeal, Washington found a willing audience when he said, "In all things purely social we can be as separate as the fingers, yet one as the hand in all things essential to mutual progress." Social equality was rejected in exchange for "material prosperity [which] will bring into our beloved South a new heaven and a new earth." Later, when he proposed greater economic cooperation between the races, he was reminded by the white

Booker T. Washington. (Library of Congress)

establishment that even business relationships were social and therefore should be treated as separate. His correspondence, however, reveals that Washington was secretly working to combat disenfranchisement and segregation.

Although Washington's Atlanta address brought him praise and fame as a nonthreatening voice for African Americans, he was never able to move significantly from the compromise position he had so convincingly established in the speech. Strong opposition to his philosophy of accommodation was vocalized by W. E. B. Du Bois, founder of the Niagara Movement, and, later, executive secretary of the National Association for the Advancement of Colored People. Du Bois was a staunch advocate of full social, civil, political, and economic opportunities and recognition for all African Americans.

UP FROM SLAVERY

Since there was widespread interest in Washington's life, his 1901 autobiography presented the story of his rise from slavery, his diligent effort to receive an education, particularly at Hampton Institute, and his ensuing dedication to the development of Tuskegee and his race.

His story became a sacred text for many of his readers, and he was regarded as a hero, even a messianic figure. The autobiography was widely translated and was read in Africa, Asia, and Europe. Some regarded his story as an inspirational example of success against great odds, but others saw it as a safe statement intended for a white audience. Washington saw himself, however, as a moral leader who was capable of guiding both races to a new level of racial justice. He verbalized the traditional views of American society toward nonwhites, presenting an uncomplicated and childlike image of African Americans.

ETHICAL IMPLICATIONS

Washington's strategy was both utilitarian and pragmatic. His prevailing view was that economic success was the key to success in other areas of life. He was convinced that manual labor brought dignity and self-esteem. He wanted to send each of his graduates into society "feeling and knowing that labor is dignified and beautiful." Success came as a result of using practical principles to meet racial goals. Although some of his critics insisted that he was perpetuating a caste system, he insisted that industrial, vo-

cational, and agricultural education were morally valuable. He strongly believed that it was the duty of an African American "to deport himself modestly in regard to political claims, depending upon the slow but sure influences that proceed from the possession of property, intelligence, and high character for the full recognition of his political rights." Washington's pragmatic approach deemphasized claims to inherent rights.

At the conclusion of his autobiography, although he was optimistic about the future, Washington recognized that there was an ongoing struggle "in the hearts of both southern white people and their former slaves to free themselves from racial prejudice." Washington left no successor to guide the Tuskegee enterprise, and because his dreams were rooted in the past, his influence on the resolution of twentieth century racial complexities was marginal.

Coleman C. Markham

FURTHER READING

Evans, James H., Jr. *Spiritual Empowerment in Afro-American Literature*. Lewiston, N.Y.: Edwin Mellen, 1987.

Harlan, Louis R. *Booker T. Washington: The Making of a Black Leader, 1856-1901*. New York: Oxford University Press, 1972.

_____. *Booker T. Washington: The Wizard of Tuskegee, 1901-1915*. New York: Oxford University Press, 1983.

_____. *Booker T. Washington in Perspective: Essays of Louis R. Harlan*. Edited by Raymond W. Smock. Jackson: University Press of Mississippi, 1988.

Mansfield, Stephen. *Then Darkness Fled: The Liberating Wisdom of Booker T. Washington*. Nashville, Tenn.: Cumberland House, 1999.

Meier, August. *Negro Thought in America, 1880-1915: Racial Ideologies in the Age of Booker T. Washington*. Ann Arbor: University of Michigan Press, 1963.

Verney, Kevern. *The Art of the Possible: Booker T. Washington and Black Leadership in the United States, 1881-1925*. New York: Routledge, 2001.

Washington, Booker T. *The Booker T. Washington Papers*. 14 vols. Edited by Louis R. Harlan. Urbana: University of Illinois Press, 1972-1989.

_____. *Story of My Life & Work*. Irvine, Calif.: Reprint Services Corporation, 1991.

————. *Up from Slavery.* New York: Penguin Books, 1986.

SEE ALSO: Civil rights and liberties; Discrimination; Du Bois, W. E. B.; National Association for the Advancement of Colored People; Pragmatism; Segregation; Utilitarianism.

Watergate scandal

THE EVENT: Burglary of Democratic presidential campaign headquarters by agents working for Republican incumbent president Richard M. Nixon
DATE: June 17, 1972
TYPE OF ETHICS: Politico-economic ethics
SIGNIFICANCE: The Watergate break-in scandalized the American people and caused them to question the ethics of all politicians and the fairness of the electoral process. It provided the national vernacular with a new suffix, "-gate," which has since adorned several major political scandals, such as "Irangate," "Whitewatergate," and "Debategate."

In early 1972, on behalf of President Richard M. Nixon's reelection campaign, a group of so-called "plumbers" broke into the Democratic national headquarters, which was located in the Watergate complex in Washington. They photographed various documents and "bugged," or tapped, the phone lines. Later, the plumbers broke in again to photograph more material, but the second time they were caught by an observant security guard.

Although the Watergate crisis seemed to drag on forever, eventually some of the truth finally came out in the courts and in the U.S. Senate Watergate hearings; the crusading newspapermen Bob Woodward and Carl Bernstein managed to learn some of the truth because they would not give up on the story. Eventually, investigators learned that President Nixon had approved of the Watergate break-in.

Many people who were linked to the break-in served terms in prison, including several high-ranking Nixon associates. After Nixon was pardoned by Gerald Ford, the public's esteem for politicians (most of them lawyers) fell to an all-time low.

James Smallwood

SEE ALSO: Corruption; Freedom of Information Act; Pentagon Papers; Political realism; Politics; Private vs. public morality; Truth.

Weakness of will

DEFINITION: Inability to act on what one knows to be the best course of action
TYPE OF ETHICS: Theory of ethics
SIGNIFICANCE: Weakness of will creates questions not only in ethics and generally in philosophy of mind about the notion of rational action, but also in economics and psychology about the notions of rational choice and cognition.

To act deliberately against one's better judgment is to fall prey to weakness of will in action. This is also known as incontinence, or *akrasia*, in its Greek form. Adam and Eve of the Bible knew that they ought not to eat the forbidden fruit but ate it all the same. Their behavior is an example of what the Roman poet Ovid called seeing and approving the better course and yet following the worse course. Similar experiences are well known to those who wish to give up bad habits but yield to temptation. Since the time of the early Greek Plato, philosophers have been interested in this phenomenon as a problem in morality. They ask questions such as, What leads a rational person to perform an action he or she believes to be wrong? However, the difficulty posed by such questions goes beyond morality by focusing attention on the very idea of rational action.

Rational actions are not those that deserve praise for their intelligence or logicality, but those that are rational in the light of their agents' beliefs, desires, and intentions—the ingredients of what are thought to be an agent's reasons. According to the principles of rational agency, insofar as an agent regards one of two courses of action as better, then that agent wants most to do that which is better and will in fact do it. However, according to this conception of rational agency, weakness of will is impossible, since an incontinent agent does something intentionally while believing there to be another available course of action which, all things considered, the agent deems as genuinely better. Few instances are needed to show that *akrasia*, far from being impossible, is commonplace in people's lives.

Weakness of will is, therefore, a form of inconsistency, since the agents' actions are not of the kind specified in their practical reasoning. However, inconsistency is itself a form of irrationality, and, thus, *akrasia* is a type of irrationality. It is an irrationality that at least involves an evaluative inconsistency between one's judgment about what is best to do and what one actually does.

There is no universally agreed approach to the problem of incontinence, and intuitions vary on its source and solution. However, there is a consensus that the phenomenon poses problems in general conceptions of what it is to act for reasons, thus creating a scope that straddles the frontiers between philosophy, psychology, and economics. As a kind of irrationality, incontinence has interested economists because of its impact on the rationality/irrationality of human choices and deliberations. Many issues in psychology are also germane. Those most closely allied with weakness of will include compulsiveness, self-deception, unconscious motivation, and the possibility of dividing the human mind into a multiplicity of interacting subsystems. Generally, the problem highlights the complexity of mind and its activities.

Majid Amini

FURTHER READING

Charlton, William. *Weakness of Will*. Oxford, England: Basil Blackwell, 1988.

Kane, Robert, ed. *The Oxford Handbook of Free Will*. Oxford, England: Oxford University Press, 2002.

SEE ALSO: Consistency; Good, the; Kant, Immanuel; Morality; Nietzsche, Friedrich; Temptation; Will.

Weapons research

DEFINITION: Investigation and experimentation to develop more effective means of waging war

TYPE OF ETHICS: Military ethics

SIGNIFICANCE: Perhaps more than any other branch of science, weapons research raises the question of the ethical relationship between theory and practice. In other words, when new forms of weaponry are used on the battlefield, does the responsibility for the effects of those weapons lie with their inventors, or does it lie only with their wielders?

The ethical stance used to justify research into developing more efficient weapon systems is nearly the same as that used to justify standing military forces—defense. The theory is that a society with a well-trained and well-equipped military force is the one best prepared to defend itself from outside aggression. Historically, the most efficient means to promote a military force's victory is to provide it with quality leadership and supply it with weapon systems superior to those of the adversary. Traditionally, any participation in the defense of one's nation and its people is seen as a moral, noble, and patriotic act. These reasons often motivate members of the scientific community to participate in defense projects in much the same way that they inspire other people to enter diplomatic or military service.

ETHICAL JUSTIFICATIONS

Ethical justification for any defense-oriented service to one's nation is readily accepted if the motivating force is to provide protection of way of life, family, sovereignty, territorial integrity, political agenda, or philosophical belief. On occasion, however, the missions of defensive weapons have been redefined or new weapons have been sought for purely offensive purposes in order to foster a society's political, territorial, or philosophical agenda. While the use of such weapons may be ethically and morally justified by those seeking to expand their political or philosophical influence, these weapons present many science professionals with an ethical dilemma involving their personal beliefs and the demands of their vocation: Do their personal or professional ethics conflict with the research that society demands of them, and if so, should they withhold their expertise and skills, or should they set aside personal beliefs and allow the ends to justify the means?

In an idealistic world, science professionals would work only on projects that conformed to their personal ethical standards. As a community, science professionals abide by a code of ethics governing scientific methodology, and adherence to this code influences their dedication, discipline, and loyalty in the pursuit of scientific goals. As individuals, however, science professionals are like all other citizens in that they are members of society and by their choice of vocation have become providers of unique services to that society: They are educators, inventors, engineers, physicians, explorers, and theoretical and applied researchers in all fields. For this reason, science professionals have been asked throughout history to help solve problems for humanity. In most instances, society's requests of science pose little ethical difficulty: finding cures for disease, improving crop yields, designing safe products.

Another of society's requests, however, is that science professionals commit their knowledge and skills to aid in the defense of their society. As a result, many scientific discoveries are transformed into weapons systems providing more effective means for nations to defend themselves. Intellectually, science professionals participating in weapons research projects know that their work, if used, may cause the death of other living things, but this knowledge is complicated by a paradox: Technologies specifically developed for weapon systems have resulted in products that improve the quality of life, and, conversely, research done for totally benign purposes has resulted in very effective weapons.

Some examples are lasers, whose use has revolutionized both medical surgery and the delivery of explosive ordnance; computer systems that speed computations and communication yet also control weapons systems; materials research that provides energy savings, durability, and protection in commercial packaging as well as for armored vehicles; and aircraft designs that improve the performance of both civilian and military aircraft. The multiple uses of modern technologies make it nearly impossible to predict their long-term applications.

ETHICAL CODES OF PROFESSIONALS

Science professionals understand that the specialized educations and skills that they possess do not come with an inherent moral or ethical code, and each time they consider participating in a research project, their decision to participate or not is based on their perception of the research's possible ramifications. Each individual's choice may be influenced by theological beliefs, personal values, professional agendas, political motives, emotions, patriotism, or societal demands. These personal values have influenced many science professionals to turn away from all weapons research.

After World War II, many scientists and engineers, appalled by the massive civilian casualties resulting from the uncontrollable destructive force of tactical nuclear weapons, refused to continue working on weapons research. Other science professionals, who are opposed to the use of tactical nuclear weapons but aware of their society's defensive needs, have chosen to engage in "smart bomb" research, designing nonnuclear explosive ordnance that can be directed to point-specific military targets with minimal danger to civilian noncombatants.

Science professionals understand that the discoveries, inventions, and technologies that arise from their scientific inquiries are in themselves amoral. They view their input in the development and perfecting of new weapon technologies as something quite separate from the production and use of these technologies. Science and military professionals do not operate with carte blanche in the field of weapons research. It is society and its representatives, based on their interpretation of perceived threats, that establish a weapons research agenda. Society utilizes the services of science and military professionals to ensure that its defense agenda is fulfilled. It is also society that instructs these professionals to use weapon systems to make war. All too often, society proves reluctant to accept the ethical burdens and responsibilities resulting from war, and science and military professionals find themselves blamed for the efficiency with which they have carried out the will of their nation.

Randall L. Milstein

FURTHER READING

Atiyah, Michael. "Science and the Military." In *Science and Technology Ethics*, edited by Raymond E. Spier. New York: Routledge, 2002.

Barke, Richard. *Science, Technology, and Public Policy*. Washington, D.C.: Congressional Quarterly, 1986.

Bronowski, Jacob. *Science and Human Values*. Rev. ed. New York: Harper & Row, 1965.

Dyson, Freeman. *Disturbing the Universe*. New York: Harper & Row, 1979.

Florman, Samuel C. *Blaming Technology: The Irrational Search for Scapegoats*. New York: St. Martin's Press, 1981.

Lakoff, Sanford A., ed. *Science and Ethical Responsibility*. Reading, Mass.: Addison-Wesley, 1980.

Rose, Hilary, and Steven Rose, eds. *The Political Economy of Science: Ideology of/in the Natural Sciences.* London: Macmillan, 1976.

SEE ALSO: Atom bomb; Industrial research; Manhattan Project; Military ethics; Nuclear arms race; Nuclear energy; Science; Technology; War.

Weber, Max

IDENTIFICATION: German sociologist
BORN: April 21, 1864, Erfurt, Prussia (now in Germany)
DIED: June 14, 1920, Munich, Germany
TYPE OF ETHICS: Modern history
SIGNIFICANCE: Weber was one of the most prominent social scientists of the early twentieth century. His *The Protestant Ethic and the Spirit of Capitalism* (*Die protestantische Ethik und der Geist des Kapitalismus*, 1904-1905) explored the ways in which Protestant religious and ethical beliefs influenced the development of modern capitalism.

Max Weber. (Library of Congress)

Weber is considered to be one of the founders of modern social science. His intellectual achievement reflected extraordinary breadth, including original studies of economy and law, social structure, comparative civilizations, and methods of the social sciences. He is best known for *The Protestant Ethic and the Spirit of Capitalism*, in which he analyzed human motives—that is, beliefs and values determining action—in the development of capitalism and concluded that certain religious beliefs could be linked to economic trends.

The Calvinist doctrine of predestination held that God had singled out humans before their births either to be saved by grace or to be damned. The uncertainty of not knowing whether believers were saved or damned prompted them to exhibit controlled and methodical conduct in the pursuit of their worldly calling, which Weber called "inner-worldly asceticism." Many Calvinists came to regard economic success, including the accumulation of capital, as a possible sign of God's grace and salvation, which often had been achieved by abstinence from "unnecessary"

consumption, leading to savings and reinvestment in economic growth. Weber did not deny that other material and psychological factors were conducive to the development of capitalism, but he pointed out that never before the advent of capitalism had religious beliefs viewed economic success as a sign of God's grace.

In studies of world religions, Weber attempted to explain how religious beliefs shaped a people's social and political institutions and economic activities. He argued, for example, that in Confucianism and Hinduism particular doctrines inhibited economic advance under conditions that were otherwise favorable to economic pursuit. Such a finding, he hoped, would make more convincing the uniqueness of religious and ethical factors in the development of Western European capitalism.

George P. Blum

SEE ALSO: Calvin, John; Capitalism; Economics; Luther, Martin; Marxism.

Welfare programs

DEFINITION: Publicly funded, state-run distribution of money or material resources to those in need

TYPE OF ETHICS: Human rights

SIGNIFICANCE: Welfare programs are designed to ensure that all members of a given society enjoy a minimum standard of living. They raise theoretical issues about the responsibility of the state toward its citizens and the responsibility of individuals to support themselves, as well as practical concerns about the liability of welfare systems to fraudulent claims and their tendency to motivate people to remain unemployed or otherwise dependent on the state.

One of the first compulsory national programs of social insurance was instituted in Austria in 1854, but societies have always recognized responsibilities to less fortunate members. Welfare programs simply institutionalize society's responses to the various problems that individuals face.

PRIVATE VS. PUBLIC PROGRAMS

Many of the tasks of national or state welfare programs have been, and still are, performed by smaller groups. Many families care for their sick, old, or unemployed members. In other cases, individuals form voluntary organizations to protect their standards of living. Insurance companies and mutual aid societies are examples of individuals agreeing to provide for others in exchange for a guarantee that they will be provided for if necessary. Governments step in when families or other larger groups are unwilling to or cannot provide what is deemed to be an adequate standard of living.

Private systems of contracting sometimes break down, or the scale of programs becomes so large that government provision becomes the least costly means of delivery. In other cases, society may declare that a condition is desirable, in opposition to individuals. One example concerns child labor and education. Poor families may decide that having a child work and provide an income is preferable to having the child become educated. Society as a whole may enforce education and prohibit child labor, both for the children's immediate good and to break a cycle of poverty in which uneducated children grow up unable to earn a living.

TYPES OF WELFARE

The most basic welfare programs provide cash grants so that recipients can buy what they need. Concerned that welfare recipients may make poor choices, welfare providers sometimes provide goods "in kind"; for example, food stamps and housing vouchers that can be used only for those specific goods or services. These restrictions on welfare are sometimes justified on the basis of the argument that the adult direct recipients of welfare may not, in the absence of restrictions, pass on benefits to indirect recipients such as children.

Welfare programs correct a variety of individual problems. People may be unable to work because of illness or injury, or simply because they cannot find jobs. They may have the responsibility of caring for someone else. Perhaps society deems that people above a certain age should not have to work. In any of these cases, welfare programs may provide income to take the place of wages or salaries.

Programs can also provide particular goods and services. Provision of food, housing, health care, and education is common. Health care and education programs have become so institutionalized that many people do not consider them to be welfare. In many cases, however, these services are provided to consumers at a price lower than would exist in a free, competitive market.

INTERNATIONAL COMPARISONS

Typically, the countries of Western Europe have the most extensive welfare systems. Great Britain, for example, has a national health care system. Several Western European countries provide widespread housing allowances. Switzerland went so far as to provide that local governments would plant rosebushes on graves if the friends or relatives of the deceased were unwilling or unable to do so. Clearly, different governments have differing definitions of an adequate standard of living and how far government should go to provide it. It is not uncommon for a Western European government to spend 20 percent or more of its gross national product on welfare programs. Much of this spending takes the place of private spending, as in the case of housing allowances, but the figure still illustrates a deep commitment to social welfare.

In less developed countries, an adequate standard of living may mean simply having enough food to avoid starvation. These countries cannot afford to set higher standards, even though such standards obviously are desirable. Some of the wealthier countries therefore have extended welfare programs to encompass foreign aid.

ETHICAL ISSUES

Ethical issues arise regarding both the acceptance and the provision of welfare. Acceptance of welfare implies a moral choice. Numerous cases exist in which people have abused welfare systems by claiming benefits for which they have no true need, perhaps choosing not to work when they are able and when jobs exist. Some programs insist that able-bodied welfare recipients either work or enroll in training programs to enhance their job skills.

Welfare providers must make choices. Money spent to achieve one standard of living cannot be spent on another goal, and money spent on one family cannot be spent on another. Some system of priorities therefore is necessary. A further trade-off is that money spent on welfare programs cannot be spent on other types of programs such as national defense or research. Finally, money given to one person must be taken from someone else. Governments must decide how much redistribution is equitable and must be concerned that taking money from those who work discourages them from working.

A different set of issues concerns the goals of welfare programs. An obvious goal is ensuring that individuals achieve a minimum standard of living. Means of achieving that goal, however, differ in their consequences. Providing aid to someone, for example, may destroy private initiative. People may become dependent on welfare. Rules of welfare programs may also instigate a "cycle of poverty" in which children raised on welfare learn the rules of that system but do not learn how to earn a living on their own. Welfare rules that provide extra payments to families may encourage women to have children, thus locking them in to child care and dependence on the welfare system. Welfare planners must consider such unintended consequences.

A. J. Sobczak

FURTHER READING

Bryner, Gary. *Politics and Public Morality: The Great American Welfare Reform Debate.* New York: W. W. Norton, 1998.

Davis, Kenneth S., ed. *The Paradox of Poverty in America.* New York: H. W. Wilson, 1969.

Glazer, Nathan. *The Limits of Social Policy.* Cambridge, Mass.: Harvard University Press, 1988.

Gregg, Pauline. *The Welfare State: An Economic and Social History of Great Britain from 1945 to the Present Day.* Amherst: University of Massachusetts Press, 1969.

Levitan, Sar A., and Clifford M. Johnson. *Beyond the Safety Net: Reviving the Promise of Opportunity in America.* Cambridge, Mass.: Ballinger, 1984.

Lutz, Mark A., and Kenneth Lux. *The Challenge of Humanistic Economics.* Menlo Park, Calif.: Benjamin/Cummings, 1979.

Moynihan, Daniel P. *The Politics of a Guaranteed Income: The Nixon Administration and the Family Assistance Plan.* New York: Random House, 1973.

SEE ALSO: Altruism; Entitlements; Generosity; Homeless care; Hunger; Social justice and responsibility; Utilitarianism; Welfare rights.

Welfare rights

DEFINITION: Legitimate claim of all persons, regardless of status, to the basic economic resources needed to maintain well-being

TYPE OF ETHICS: Human rights; Politico-economic ethics; Religious ethics

SIGNIFICANCE: The principle of welfare rights is central to many modern arguments about the nature and scope of justice and human rights.

In traditional (precapitalist) societies, persons recognized a mutual obligation to meet the essential economic needs of all other members of the community. This obligation is asserted in Judaism, Christianity, Islam, Hinduism, Buddhism, Daoism, and Confucianism. In African and Native American traditions, moral development was demonstrated by giving away personal wealth during festivals. All these various traditions operated with a kinship model of ethics (in which all members of the community are to be treated as family). As these traditions developed, their morality was universalized so that all humanity was to be regarded as family. Based on these religious foundations, peasants in feudal societies retained certain economic rights (subsistence rights) vis-à-vis the nobility. The modern concept of welfare rights draws on this earlier, highly developed concept of community obligation.

MODERN HISTORY

The rise of industrial capitalism in the nineteenth century destroyed the earlier model. Modern individualism and laissez-faire economics separated the individual from the community and made survival dependent upon individual employment, effort, opportunity, and reward. In the process, poverty was reconceptualized as being self-caused and the poor were denigrated as being lazy and immoral. Consequently, society renounced any moral obligation to help the poor. A distinction was drawn between the deserving poor (disabled and orphans) and the undeserving, but programs to help the poor became a matter of optional private charity, not of justice and social policy.

The right to accumulate unlimited personal wealth by almost any means, regardless of social cost, was given moral priority over meeting the needs of all persons in the community. In response, protest against the widespread harsh forms of poverty generated by capitalism developed. Recognizing that the primary causes of poverty were economic cycles of depression and unemployment, exploitation of workers, low wages, and lack of educational opportunity, socialist movements reasserted the right of all to basic economic security. Karl Marx proposed an economic system based on the following principle: "From each according to ability, to each according to need." Frightened by threats of socialist revolution and labor unrest, models of capitalism were proposed that included welfare rights, a guaranteed level of subsistence for all. A rudimentary welfare state was implemented in Germany in 1871.

This model gained influence during the 1930's in response to the Great Depression. U.S. president Franklin D. Roosevelt's New Deal incorporated many of the elements of the welfare state. The actual term "welfare state" was first employed in 1941 by British archbishop William Temple. Following World War II, most European nations adopted systems based on a recognition of welfare rights, which included health care, adequate diet and housing, and

guaranteed employment or a guaranteed minimum annual income for all. Such policies were endorsed by the United Nations Declaration on Human Rights (1948). The United States was one of the few developed nations to reject such rights.

The 1960's recognized the emergence of a new period of social activism on behalf of welfare rights. Socialist revolutions erupted in numerous developing nations. In the United States, George Wiley formed the National Welfare Rights Organization (NWRO) and Lyndon Johnson initiated the War on Poverty, expanding welfare programs. In 1966, the United Nations ratified the Covenant on Economic, Social, and Cultural Rights, giving universal validation to the concept of welfare rights. Welfare rights, however, continue to conflict with the basic premises of American individualism and laissez-faire economics.

The United States did not endorse the United Nations' covenant and during the 1980's began a conservative attack on welfare programs and welfare rights. Nineteenth century arguments against helping the poor and distinctions between the deserving and the undeserving were resurrected and used to shape social policy. The number of the poor and severity of their conditions increased dramatically. This attack was resisted by liberal religious groups that instituted programs to feed and house the poor. They also reaffirmed the centrality of the moral obligation to meet the needs of the poor. Third World liberation theologians and the U.S. Catholic Bishops' pastoral *Economic Justice for All* (1986) cite a "preferential option for the poor" that should inform all social policy. A similar concept is articulated by philosopher John Rawls in his earlier work *A Theory of Justice* (1971). The central issue remains the relative rights and obligations of persons in a community to one another.

ETHICAL ARGUMENTS EMPLOYED

(1) Basic economic needs (food, shelter, education, health care) must be met, since they are necessary for survival and development. (2) All persons have equal worth. (For religious persons, all are created equal.) (3) Greed and personal pleasure are not sufficient reasons for depriving others of resources needed for human survival. (For religious persons, God created the world to benefit all.) (4) The primary causes of poverty are a function of chance (place of

birth, social location, innate capabilities, economic cycles). Therefore, there exists a moral obligation to meet the basic needs of others. (5) For religious persons, the primary moral requirement "Love your neighbor" obligates persons to meet others' needs. (6) As part of a community that provides myriad benefits, members of the community have a moral obligation to ensure the economic subsistence of all other members. (7) Fulfilling welfare rights improves the quality of life for all by reducing crime, reducing class antagonisms and conflicts, and providing a healthy, well-educated workforce.

Charles L. Kammer III

FURTHER READING

Abramovitz, Mimi. *Under Attack, Fighting Back: Women and Welfare in the United States.* New York: Monthly Review Press, 1996.

Brown, Robert McAfee, and Sydney Thomson Brown, eds. *A Cry for Justice: The Churches and Synagogues Speak.* New York: Paulist Press, 1989.

Kingfisher, Catherine Pélissier. *Women in the American Welfare Trap.* Philadelphia: University of Pennsylvania Press, 1996.

Moon, J. Donald, ed. *Responsibility, Rights, and Welfare: The Theory of the Welfare State.* Boulder, Colo.: Westview Press, 1988.

Piven, Frances Fox, and Richard A. Cloward. *The New Class War: Reagan's Attack on the Welfare State and Its Consequences.* New York: Pantheon Books, 1982.

Schorr, Alvin. *Common Decency: Domestic Policies After Reagan.* New Haven, Conn.: Yale University Press, 1986.

Winston, Morton E., ed. *The Philosophy of Human Rights.* Belmont, Calif.: Wadsworth, 1989.

SEE ALSO: Capitalism; Economics; Homeless care; Human rights; Social justice and responsibility; Socialism; Universal Declaration of Human Rights; Welfare programs.

Whistleblowing

DEFINITION: Publicly revealing, or reporting to appropriate authorities, that one's employer is guilty of corporate or professional wrongdoing

TYPE OF ETHICS: Business and labor ethics

SIGNIFICANCE: Whistleblowing may violate both ethical values, such as loyalty and confidentiality, and specific legal requirements, such as nondisclosure agreements. It is generally defended, however, on the grounds that it serves the public interest and protects third parties from harm. Whistleblowing laws have been passed in many states to protect whistleblowers from corporate reprisals such as lawsuits, dismissal, or demotion.

Blowing the whistle on a person or activity is intended to bring to a halt some activity that will cause harm to the public. Since it is generally recognized that one should prevent harm to others if one can do so without causing great harm to oneself, whistleblowing would seem to be morally required. It is also generally recognized, however, that one should be loyal to one's employers and professional colleagues. Since whistleblowing by an employee appears to breach this loyalty by reporting the harmful activity to those outside the organization, the employee who discovers misconduct is faced with a moral dilemma.

Some writers argue that such "ratting" on one's employer is always wrong. Others argue that those who are willing to risk their futures to expose wrongdoing are heroes. Still others assess individual acts of whistleblowing by asking various questions: Have all the internal reporting channels been exhausted without results? Is the harm to the public without a report significantly greater than the harm to the organization with a report? What is the likelihood that the report will actually prevent the harm; that is, is the report believable and substantiable?

Ruth B. Heizer

SEE ALSO: Business ethics; Confidentiality; Corporate responsibility; Corporate scandal; Loyalty; Obedience; Professional ethics.

White-collar crime

DEFINITION: Criminal activity in the corporate, commercial, professional, and political arenas
TYPE OF ETHICS: Business and labor ethics
SIGNIFICANCE: The treatment of white-collar crime both by law enforcement officials and by the media raises fundamental issues of social justice and equal treatment under the law, since such crime is often under-prosecuted in comparison with similar crimes committed by working-class people.

White-collar crimes are distinguished by the fact that they most commonly take place at the workplace and involve activities related to otherwise legitimate occupations. In addition, white-collar criminals rarely use violence or weapons.

The lowest level of white-collar crime, and the one easiest to identify and prosecute, is employee theft, ranging from taking office supplies for nonwork use to the theft of products intended for sale. Higher levels of white-collar crime typically involve manipulations of bookkeeping accounts or legal documents. These crimes are more difficult to trace, particularly as more records are kept in electronic form, with fewer "paper trails" to identify wrongdoing. A variation of this type of crime involves violating the terms of a business contract or law with the intent of earning a profit in a way not intended by the other contracting parties or by society. An example is insider trading, in which stock, bond, or commodity traders use information they have learned earlier than other traders in order to make a profit in their trading. This example points out a difficulty in prosecuting some white-collar crime: It is difficult to say what information is illegal to use, since financial markets are designed to reward those who make effective use of information. The lines of ethical and legal behavior are also difficult to draw in cases of political corruption; "constituent service" to one person might be considered to be political favoritism or graft to another.

A. J. Sobczak

SEE ALSO: Business ethics; Corporate responsibility; Corporate scandal; Corruption; "Everyone does it"; Fraud; Insider trading.

Whitehead, Alfred North

IDENTIFICATION: English mathematician and philosopher
BORN: February 15, 1861, Ramsgate, Isle of Thanet, Kent, England
DIED: December 30, 1947, Cambridge, Massachusetts
TYPE OF ETHICS: Modern history
SIGNIFICANCE: In such works as *Science and the Modern World* (1925), *Religion in the Making* (1926), *Process and Reality: An Essay in Cosmology* (1929), *Symbolism: Its Meaning and Effect* (1927), and *Adventures of Ideas* (1933), Whitehead applied mathematical and scientific principles to philosophical ethics.

In 1924, at the age of sixty-three and nearing compulsory retirement at the Imperial College, London, Whitehead accepted an appointment to teach philosophy at Harvard University in Cambridge, Massachusetts. For the next thirteen years, he lectured and developed his metaphysics. Influenced by the thought of Henri Bergson and, at the same time, an erstwhile Platonist, Whitehead considered the requirements for an ethical society through an analysis of religion (*Religion in the Making*) and the fundamental requirements for a dynamic society (*Adventures of Ideas*). He argued that religion—realized only through profound human reflection—contributed to an ethical understanding of the relationship of the individual in society and the universe.

After earlier affiliations with Anglicanism and Roman Catholicism, Whitehead did not identify with any organized religion; he did not consider religion as a societal institution to be very meaningful. *Adventures of Ideas* constituted Whitehead's most comprehensive statement of his philosophy and has been his most widely acclaimed and read book. Individual freedom required an ordered society; Whitehead was not sympathetic to anarchism, which frequently advanced values similar to his. Whitehead was concerned with the nature of beauty, art, and peace, predicated upon an ethics that recognized the fundamental primacy of the individual within the context of Western civilization.

William T. Walker

SEE ALSO: Bergson, Henri; Hartshorne, Charles; Idealist ethics; Plato; Platonic ethics; Russell, Bertrand.

Wickedness

DEFINITION: Quality of desiring to do wrong for its own sake; evil

TYPE OF ETHICS: Theory of ethics

SIGNIFICANCE: Wickedness, far more than vice, is the precise opposite of virtue. It is the positive valuation of evil as its own reward.

The problem of evil is an ancient problem in philosophy and religion. In religion, the problem consists in explaining why God, who is all good, can allow for evil in the world; in philosophy, the problem entails accounting for the motives that lead people to do evil things. Socrates, for example, denies that people are motivated to do evil; he claims that people are motivated to do what is good and that it is only from ignorance of what is good that people do evil. Thus, people do not knowingly do wrong. Others have taken a similar stance with respect to God, arguing that God does not allow for evil and that it is only the inadequate and finite human knowledge of God that leads people to think that evil exists. Both these responses to the problem of evil, therefore, simply deny the existence of evil. In the philosophical discussion that has surrounded the topic of wickedness, however, there has been an acceptance of the fact that evil does indeed exist; because of this acceptance, the problem of why people are wicked (the problem of evil) reappears with all its force.

In Immanuel Kant's article "Of the Indwelling of the Bad Principle Along with the Good" (1927), he argues that evil results when people are not properly motivated. By being properly motivated, Kant means that one should be motivated to act out of respect for the moral law (that is, universal moral principles), not from self-interest. It is when one's moral principles follow from one's self-interest, and not the other way around as it should be, that one can be wicked and evil. Despite this account of why people do evil, Kant nevertheless believes that evil actions are to be understood in the light of the good that motivates them—that is, the good as perceived in terms of self-interest rather than of the universal moral law. Kant consequently does not believe that people are ever wicked or do evil for the sake of wickedness or evil, and thus he is part of the tradition that denies the existence of evil as such.

Arthur Schopenhauer, in his book *The World as Will and Representation* (1818), denies the traditional rejection of evil and sets forth the notion of "pure wickedness" as an act done solely for the sake of evil. Citing the character Iago from William Shakespeare's play *Othello*, Schopenhauer claims that people can be wicked because they derive disinterested pleasure from the suffering of others or because they are motivated to act by evil.

TYPES OF WICKEDNESS

S. I. Benn has set forth a more detailed typology and discussion of wickedness in his article "Wickedness" (1985). Benn cites two ways in which one can be wicked: either one is wicked in pursuing what one perceives to be good, or one is wicked in acting for the sake of evil. Benn further divides the first class of wickedness into "self-centered," "conscientious," and "heteronomous" wickedness. With self-centered wickedness, one acts in order to promote the interests of oneself or one's family, company, or nation, but does so with a ruthless disregard for others. With conscientious wickedness, one believes that the good that one pursues is universally valid, not only valid for oneself, and pursues this good ruthlessly while excluding others. A Nazi, for example, may act according to a good that he or she believes to be universally valid, but will exclude others to the point of genocide. Heteronomous wickedness entails choosing to act according to another's principles—principles that can be seen to be evil.

The second class of wickedness that Benn discusses, acting for the sake of evil, corresponds to Schopenhauer's idea of "pure wickedness"; Benn labels it "malignity" or "unalloyed wickedness." In discussing this class of wickedness, Benn turns to the problem of evil: Why are people wicked if they are not motivated by self-interest or by something that is thought of as good? Benn's answer to this question consists largely of showing the inadequacy of attempts to subsume all evil actions under a motivation to do good; when it comes to stating why one would be motivated to do evil because it is evil, however, Benn for the most part avoids the issue.

The problem of why people are wicked, or why evil is pursued as an evil and not as a good, is the central theme of Mary Midgley's book *Wickedness: A Philosophical Essay* (1984). Midgley argues that wickedness cannot be explained by referring it to external, social causes or by denying it exists. Wickedness, she argues, is a real potential that all people have. This potential results from what Midgley takes to be a perversion of natural hostilities and conflicts with others. Midgley claims that this perversion is not the same thing as Sigmund Freud's concept of the "death-instinct" (which is an instinct that serves to bring about death and destruction). People have motives that aim toward negative, destructive ends (such as eliminating enemies and threats), and the perversion of such motives leads to the pursuit of negative ends for their own sake. In short, this perversion entails doing something evil simply because it is evil; it is, as Midgley and others have understood it, wickedness.

Jeff Bell

FURTHER READING

Benn, S. I. "Wickedness." In *Ethics and Personality: Essays in Moral Psychology*, edited by John Deigh. Chicago: University of Chicago Press, 1992.

Fromm, Erich. *The Anatomy of Human Destructiveness*. New York: Holt, Rinehart and Winston, 1973.

Kant, Immanuel. "Of the Indwelling of the Bad Principle Along with the Good." In *Kant's Theory of Ethics*, translated by T. K. Abbot. London: Longman, Green, 1927.

Midgley, Mary. *Wickedness: A Philosophical Essay*. Boston: Routledge & Kegan Paul, 1984.

Milo, Ronald D. "Virtue, Knowledge, and Wickedness." In *Virtue and Vice*, edited by Ellen Frankel Paul, Fred D. Miller, Jr., and Jeffrey Paul. New York: Cambridge University Press, 1998.

Schopenhauer, Arthur. *The World as Will and Representation*. Translated by E. F. J. Payne. 2 vols. 1958. Reprint. New York: Dover, 1969.

Waddell, Terrie, ed. *Cultural Expressions of Evil and Wickedness: Wrath, Sex, Crime*. New York: Rodopi, 2003.

SEE ALSO: Cruelty; Evil; Fascism; Good, the; Kant, Immanuel; Kantian ethics; Schopenhauer, Arthur; Temptation; Virtue.

Wiesel, Elie

IDENTIFICATION: Romanian-born author and rights activist

BORN: September 30, 1928, Sighet, Transylvania

TYPE OF ETHICS: Modern history

SIGNIFICANCE: Wiesel, an outstanding defender of human rights and a pioneer interpreter of the Shoah (Holocaust), is the author of *Night* (*Un di Velt hot geshvign*, 1956), one of the most important and widely read memoirs of a concentration camp survivor. In that and other works, he explores ways in which the faith of Holocaust survivors can be used to help heal the post-Holocaust world. Wiesel was awarded the Nobel Peace Prize in 1986.

Elie Wiesel. (Copyright *Washington Post*, reprinted by permission of the Washington, D.C., Public Library)

Elie Wiesel's writings have made him the messenger of the Jewish Holocaust dead and the prophetic muse of the post-Auschwitz age. This fact may explain why he wrote his first published memoir, *Night*, in Yiddish, the *lingua franca* of the murdered Jewish people, rather than in French, the language in which he wrote all of his other works. Wiesel writes masterfully, with a Kafkaesque pen, and his themes include pogroms, the destruction of the *shtetls* (Jewish villages), songs of mourning and exile, the madness of the Messiah, divine love and silence, and the guilt and obligation of survival, all of which are interwoven with threads of Hasidic tales, Kabbalistic mysticism, talmudic wisdom, and pietistic folklore.

Theologically, Wiesel's testimony is a continuous *Din Torah* (a disputation based on the judgment of the Torah) with God, who allowed Auschwitz to occur, and with radical dehumanization, the existence of which raises the possibility that the world is either not listening to or does not care about the lessons that can be learned from the Shoah. Wiesel has done more than anyone to establish "Holocaust" (a word that invokes images of fire and burnt offerings) as the accepted term for the Judeocide that occurred during World War II. Because the term is associated with the *akedah*, or "binding," of Isaac in the biblical story in which Abraham is tested and Isaac is victimized (Gen. 22), the use of the term permits Wiesel to question the intentions of God. This act of questioning does not diminish the paradox of the Shoah, but serves to make the issue more significant and more troubling, and therefore also more full of hope. Wiesel has strongly advocated that the specific lessons of the Shoah should never be lost. His eyewitness approach to the issue, which is rooted in the redemptive quality of memory, carries the message that one can survive with morality, a message that will appeal to all those who have suffered or will suffer.

Zev Garber

SEE ALSO: Anti-Semitism; Concentration camps; Hasidism; Holocaust; Jewish ethics; Lemkin, Raphael; Nobel Peace Prizes.

Wilderness Act of 1964

IDENTIFICATION: Federal law setting aside specific tracts of land to be preserved and managed so that the natural conditions of the wilderness ecosystem remain unaltered

DATE: Enacted on September 3, 1964

TYPE OF ETHICS: Environmental ethics

SIGNIFICANCE: Designed to ensure that wilderness would be available as a resource for future generations, the Wilderness Act brought into federal law for the first time the principle that nature is valuable for its own sake, not only for the uses to which humans can put it.

A wilderness bill was first introduced in the U.S. Senate in 1956, but because of conflicts between economic interests and conservationists regarding the appropriate uses of land in areas set aside for wilderness, it was not until 1964 that the Wilderness Act was finally made law. The Wilderness Act of 1964 defines wilderness as "an area where the earth and community of life are untrammeled by man, where man himself is a visitor who does not remain."

The act does allow prospecting for minerals and protects mining interests that existed as of January 1, 1964, but it does not allow any new mineral patents after that date. This was a compromise that was difficult to effect. No motorized equipment, motor vehicles, motorboats, or commercial enterprises are allowed in wilderness areas. Supporters of the act stated that these exclusions did not violate the multiple-use principle, which calls for public lands to be used for their highest and best use, but indeed applied the principle by reserving some lands for the whole of the community to enjoy. The act embodies the principle that nature should not be managed, in these wilderness areas, merely to suit people, but so as to preserve and protect the land in its natural condition in accordance with wilderness values.

Sandra L. Christensen

SEE ALSO: Conservation; Ecology; Environmental movement; Future generations; Leopold, Aldo; Muir, John; National Park System, U.S.; Sierra Club.

Will

DEFINITION: Mental faculty used by conscious beings to initiate autonomous action

TYPE OF ETHICS: Theory of ethics

SIGNIFICANCE: In traditional philosophical models of the mind, reason is used to evaluate one's desires to determine whether or not they should be acted upon, and will is the faculty that carries out those decisions once they have been made. Thus, it is the will in conjunction with reason that makes morality possible on a practical level by preventing people from becoming automatons ruled solely by brute impulse and instinct.

One of the presuppositions of morality is the belief that a human being is a special kind of agent that is to be held morally responsible for its actions. A boulder that tumbles from a precipice and crushes the leg of a climber is an agent, because the energy that it has acquired is a source of change, the crushing of the climber's leg. Nevertheless, the boulder is not held responsible for its actions, since it is not deemed a moral agent. Although there have been periods when animals other than human beings have been treated as moral agents, it is generally true that human beings alone are held morally responsible for their actions and thus are taken to be the only moral agents within the natural order. (This remark must be confined to the natural order, since many theists believe that God and other spiritual beings—angels, demons, and so forth—are moral agents.) The conviction that a human being is an agent in this special way is often explained by claiming that a human being has a will, a capacity to initiate action through the formation of mental events (volitions) that prompt the desired action.

NATURE OF THE WILL

Although philosophers who believe in the will are in agreement concerning its importance to moral responsibility, there is considerable disagreement over what kind of thing it is. Some philosophers (for example, Plato, Saint Augustine, and Thomas Aquinas) maintain that the will is a faculty that is literally a part of the soul. The will, according to this view, is distinct from other mental faculties such as the intellect and also distinct from its volitions.

Other philosophers (such as Baruch Spinoza and David Hume) reject the notion that the will is literally a part of the soul. These thinkers maintain that the attribution of a will to human beings is simply a shorthand way of saying that the human soul can form volitions and that these volitions can initiate action. In this view, there is no distinct faculty or part of the soul that stands behind its volitions; rather, the will is simply the sum total of all the soul's volitions.

Regardless of the stand that one takes on the precise nature of the will, one still must deal with the two most difficult issues confronting any adequate theory of the will. The first issue is that of explaining the mechanism whereby volitions exert their influence. This issue is one aspect of the larger philosophical problem of explaining how the mind and the body interact—the so-called "problem of interaction." The second issue is that of specifying what it is about the will's agency that distinguishes it from other agents in a morally significant way. This second issue is that of the will's freedom or autonomy.

PROBLEM OF INTERACTION

Experience seems to indicate that bodily events can cause mental events and that mental events can cause bodily events. The unfortunate climber mentioned at the beginning of this essay experienced the bodily event of a broken leg and then experienced the pain, a mental event, caused by this physical trauma. In fact, all sensations, all cases of tasting, touching, seeing, smelling, and hearing, seem, at least uncritically, to involve bodily events (in which the physical environment acts upon one's sensory organs) that cause mental events (the actual sensory experiences). By the same token, experience indicates that mental events cause bodily events. The mental event of willing to raise one's hand does, under normal circumstances, lead to the bodily event of one's hand raising. The problem of interaction refers to the challenge of explaining this apparent causal interplay between the mind and the body. With regard to the will, the problem of interaction arises in terms of the need to explain how the mind's volitions can give rise to bodily actions.

Although the problem of interaction was explicitly formulated at least as early as the fourth century B.C.E. in Aristotle's *De anima*, attention to it intensified dramatically in the seventeenth century in response to René Descartes's promulgation of substance dualism. Substance dualism is a theory of human nature that holds that human beings are composed of two radically different kinds of substances: mind and body. Descartes conceived of the mind as an immaterial (spatially unextended) substance and the body as a material (spatially extended) substance. In addition, he maintained that the mind and the body can exist apart from each other.

Although the Cartesian philosophy grew in popularity during the late seventeenth and early eighteenth centuries, concern over the problem of interaction grew as well. The radical heterogeneity of the mind and the body upheld by Cartesian dualism led thinkers to wonder how such radically different substances could interact. Descartes himself never fully came to grips with this issue; however, a number of solutions were developed by those who were either avowed Cartesians or were at least heavily influenced by Descartes's philosophy.

The late-seventeenth century French philosopher Nicholas Malebranche attempted to solve the problem by conceding that the mind and the body do not really interact. The reason that mental events appear to cause bodily events is that God creates these events so that they exhibit the correlation that people experience. Thus, the connections between willing to raise one's arm and the subsequent act of arm raising must be explained in terms of God's causing the arm to raise on the occasion of the volition that it be raised. Insofar as it implies that mental events and bodily events are not true causes but are only occasions upon which God acts as a cause, this view is known as occasionalism.

The late-seventeenth century German philosopher Gottfried Wilhelm Leibniz worried that the occasionalists' supposition of God's ongoing intervention in the world was an unjustifiably complex assumption that would destroy the possibility of there being laws of nature. He preferred his own view of pre-established harmony. Like occasionalism, pre-established harmony conceded that the mind and the body do not really interact. Unlike the occasionalists, however, Leibniz explained the correlation between mental and bodily events by supposing that the events occurring within a substance result from an internal principle of development that God placed in the substance from the outset and designed so that the events unfolding in the mind would be in harmony with the events unfolding in the body.

A third response to the problem of interaction was that of rejecting the dualism that gave rise to the problem. In the seventeenth century, this solution was attempted in two very different theories. First, the seventeenth century British philosopher Thomas Hobbes maintained that the very concept of an immaterial substance was a contradiction in terms, for substance could only mean body. According to this materialism, then, mental events are nothing other than internal bodily events; thus, the interaction of the mind with the body is always nothing more than matter acting upon matter.

Also rejecting the dualism of Descartes was the seventeenth century Dutch philosopher Baruch Spinoza. Like Hobbes, Spinoza maintained that there is only one substance in the universe. Unlike Hobbes, however, he maintained that this substance should not be characterized exclusively as material, for spatial extension and thought are both attributes of the single substance constituting the universe. In keeping with this dual-aspect theory, Spinoza maintained that correlated mental and bodily events are really the same event viewed from different standpoints: the standpoints of thought and extension. Insofar as there is, at bottom, only one event behind any given mind-body correlation, the problem of explaining the interaction of distinct events dissolves in Spinoza's system.

Regardless of which of these avenues one chooses to explain the efficacy of volitions, one still must undertake the task of explaining why the agency manifested by the will is of a special type that can support the attribution of moral responsibility. Although recognition of the will's special agency is commonly made by referring to it as free and autonomous, there is considerable disagreement concerning the nature of this freedom and autonomy.

FREEDOM AND AUTONOMY

Numerous theories of human freedom have been defended throughout the history of philosophy; however, it does not do excessive violence to the subtleties of these theories to classify them all in one of the two following categories: voluntarism and compatibilism.

Advocates of voluntarism note that people normally do not punish others for actions that they could not have altered, and they thus maintain that the agency underpinning moral responsibility cannot be one that is governed by causal necessity. With this in mind, voluntarists (also known as incompatibilists and indeterminists) maintain that the will's freedom entails that its volition not be necessitated by antecedent causes or conditions. According to the voluntarist, if one could reproduce the external and internal conditions immediately preceding an individual's choice, the individual would still be free to choose otherwise than he or she actually did. Thus it is that voluntarists such as John Duns Scotus (c. 1265-1308) and William of Ockham (c. 1280-1347) explain the will's freedom in terms of its complete independence of causally determining factors.

In direct opposition to voluntarism, compatibilism maintains that it is possible for certain human actions to be both free and causally determined. Also known as soft determinism and necessitarianism, compatibilism admits that all human actions are causally determined; it maintains, however, that certain human actions are still free insofar as they are free from external constraint and compulsion. One's walking to the corner to mail a letter is, in this view, free, even though it is causally determined by one's beliefs, desires, and character traits. Were another individual to force one to post the letter and drop it in the box, however, one's action would be compelled and hence not free. Freedom thus does not consist in an absence of all causes; rather, it consists in being caused by the right kind of causes: beliefs, desires, and character traits.

COMPATIBILIST DEFINITIONS OF "FREE"

Fully aware that their attempt to reconcile freedom with causal determinism seems to amount to nothing more than inventing a new meaning for the term "free," the compatibilists are quick to point out that it is their definition of "free," not that of the voluntarists, that makes sense of moral responsibility. According to the compatibilist, voluntarism makes free choice a random affair, since it implies that no sufficient explanation can be given for an individual's choices. This is problematic, according to the compatibilist, because people do not hold others morally accountable for actions that happen randomly or by chance. People do not think that the lottery official who randomly pulls the ticket of a destitute mother is more charitable than is the official who randomly draws the name of a tycoon. These events happen by chance and are thus to neither official's moral credit or discredit. For this reason, the compatibilist charges the voluntarist with having reduced human freedom to a kind of internal lottery, a lottery that undermines the very moral responsibility that freedom is supposed to explain.

In defense of their own definition of "free," compatibilists point out that people do think it appropriate to punish those whose actions flowed from wicked wants or a wicked character and to praise those whose actions flowed from virtuous wants or a virtuous character. This fact shows, they argue, that people do not hesitate to hold people responsible for actions that are caused, provided they are caused by the appropriate internal states.

The debate is not thus decided in favor of the compatibilist, however, for the voluntarist will note that the compatibilists' attempt to uphold freedom only succeeds while one focuses upon the immediate causes of free action, the agent's beliefs, desires, and character traits. When one considers the causes of these internal states, one quickly sees that compatibilism implies that they are ultimately caused by factors that are wholly external to the individual in question, factors that obtained even before the individual was born. The voluntarist therefore notes that the causal determinism that is part of compatibilism undermines its attempt to redefine freedom. Since determinism implies that all of an agent's actions are ultimately the results of wholly external causes, it turns out that no actions are free even according to the compatibilists' definition of "free."

Convinced of the inability of both voluntarism and compatibilism to offer a satisfactory account of moral responsibility, some philosophers have resisted the call to offer a theory of freedom. Such hard determinists as the late-eighteenth century English philosopher Joseph Priestley resist the call by simply denying that there is any such thing as free agency. Freedom, they insist, is merely an illusion created by one's ignorance of those causal factors that have determined the way that one will act on a given occasion. Other philosophers, such as Immanuel Kant, see freedom as a necessary condition of moral responsibility and thus are not willing to dismiss it; nevertheless, they resist the call to supply a theory of freedom by maintaining that the nature of free agency is a mystery that cannot be penetrated by human reason.

Although philosophical discussion of the will's freedom and autonomy normally focuses on the degree to which the will must be immune from determining factors, an interesting sidelight to this debate concerns the possibility that an individual can, freely and knowingly, choose evil.

WEAKNESS OF WILL

Acting in a way that is contrary to one's moral obligation while one is fully aware of that obligation constitutes weakness of will. Sometimes called moral weakness or incontinence, weakness of will seems to be a part of most individuals' experience. What is philosophically interesting about incontinence is that some philosophers have been unconvinced by the abundance of experiential evidence for its occurrence and have insisted that it never actually happens.

Probably the best-known advocate of the impossibility of incontinence is Socrates. He rejected incontinence on the grounds that no person wants to be miserable and that the surest way to make oneself miserable is by disregarding the demands of morality. Having accepted these points, Socrates was led to explain those who do choose lives of vice by supposing that they must be ignorant of the true nature of a virtuous life.

Other philosophers (such as R. M. Hare) have rejected incontinence on the grounds that it is impossible to act contrary to the moral principles that one holds insofar as the only true indicators of one's moral principles are the actions that one performs. According to this view, it is what a person does and not what he or she says that reveals his or her actual moral principles. It is only because people delude themselves into thinking that they hold certain moral principles that the illusion of incontinence is so prevalent.

James M. Petrik

FURTHER READING

Bergson, Henri. *Time and Free Will*. New York: Macmillan, 1959. This work contains an influential defense of voluntarism.

Bourke, Vernon. *Will in Western Thought*. New York: Sheed & Ward, 1964. Arguably the best introduction to philosophical thought on the will, Bourke's book identifies and analyzes eight distinct conceptions of the will that have been prevalent in the history of Western philosophy.

Kane, Robert, ed. *The Oxford Handbook of Free Will*. New York: Oxford University Press, 2002. Includes essays on all aspects of free will and determinism written by many contemporary experts in the field.

Kenny, Anthony. *Will, Freedom, and Power*. New York: Barnes & Noble Books, 1976. Provides a clearly argued defense of an Aristotelian/Thomistic conception of freedom.

Mortimore, Geoffrey. *Weakness of Will*. London: Macmillan, 1971. This anthology includes selections from a broad historical spectrum and is a helpful introduction to the issue of moral weakness.

New York University Institute of Philosophy. *Determinism and Freedom in the Age of Modern Science*. Edited by Sidney Hook. New York: Collier, 1961. This work offers an understanding of the dialectical interplay among the theories of hard determinism, soft determinism, and voluntarism.

Nietzsche, Friedrich. *The Will to Power*. Translated by Walter Kaufmann and R. J. Hollingdale. New York: Vintage Books, 1968. Contains Nietzsche's famous and enigmatic declaration that the world is composed of will to power "and nothing else besides."

O'Shaughnessy, Brian. *The Will: A Dual Aspect Theory*. 2 vols. Cambridge, England: Cambridge University Press, 1980. Perhaps the most sustained treatment of the will offered in the twentieth century, O'Shaughnessy's book is a development and defense of a dual-aspect theory. Although very difficult, this work will repay a careful reading.

Ryle, Gilbert. *The Concept of Mind*. New York: Barnes & Noble, 1949. Considered by many to be the definitive critique of Cartesian dualism and its theory of volitions, it is also an excellent example of ordinary-language philosophy, one of the dominant philosophical schools of the twentieth century.

Schopenhauer, Arthur. *The World as Will and Representation*. Translated by E. F. J. Payne. 2 vols. 1958. Reprint. New York: Dover, 1969. This seminal work of pessimistic idealism views the will as determining both experience and reality.

Thorp, John. *Free Will: A Defence Against Neurophysiological Determinism*. London: Routledge & Kegan Paul, 1980. A clearly written attack on neurophysiological determinism that includes an interesting attempt to delineate between incompatibilist freedom and randomness.

SEE ALSO: Aristotle; Augustine, Saint; Autonomy; Descartes, René; Determinism and freedom; Freedom and liberty; Hare, R. M.; Nietzsche, Friedrich; Plato; Thomas Aquinas; Weakness of will.

Wisdom

DEFINITION: Accumulated knowledge and the ability to exercise sound judgment, especially in difficult ethical cases

TYPE OF ETHICS: Personal and social ethics

SIGNIFICANCE: Traditionally regarded as a cardinal virtue, wisdom remains a moral ideal, although modern critics reject the concept as elitist or arbitrary.

Wisdom, or good judgment, comprises both knowledge about facts and values and the ability to apply relevant knowledge appropriately in decision making and action. Wise judges possess discernment, fairness, and openness. They discern hidden possibilities and discover among conflicting interests unsuspected options for compromise. This ability requires patience and a tolerance for ambiguity. Aristotle emphasizes that fairness or "equity" prevents sacrificing the spirit of a rule in order to adhere to its letter. Wise judgment requires a flexible approach to rules, so the wise path may appear foolish. A long tradition concerning the so-called "wisdom of the fool" testifies to the shifting boundary between wisdom and folly. If wisdom turns into clichés, slogans, and rigid dichotomies, it may take a foolish mental openness—what in Zen Buddhism is called "emptiness"—to reveal what is truly real.

Prudence or practical wisdom (Aristotle's *phronesis*) is considered the key virtue necessary for living a morally good life. Theoretical wisdom (*sophia*) by itself is insufficient, as amply illustrated by such familiar Platonic examples as foolish theorists falling into wells or selfish sophists claiming that might makes right. In Aristotle's analysis of moral virtue as a mean between contrary vices of too much and too little, the correct judgment (*orthos lo-gos*) required to determine what is "just right" depends on the *phronesis* of the morally serious judge (*spoudaios*). However, Aristotle's arbitrary characterization of this judge and moral mistakes like his defense of "natural slavery" create doubt about his "wisdom."

Contests among competing "experts" in lawsuits and on opposing sides of almost every political debate give rise to suspicion that their show of knowledge is merely a power struggle. Philosophers such as Friedrich Nietzsche and Michel Foucault make suspicion about the uses of disguised power central to their interpretations of ethical discourse. Traditional appeals to knowledge, truth, or wisdom appear as rhetorical maneuvers for foisting one's preferred definitions of reality upon those whom one wishes to control. Suspicion provides a way of changing the subject and challenging the moral status quo.

Wisdom allows those who are—or believe they are—oppressed to challenge their oppressors' claims to deference, based on sex, race, age, or other categories. Attacks on conventional beliefs as "pseudo-wisdom" have figured prominently in social debates over civil rights, multiculturalism, feminism, sexual preference, and other areas. Attacks on the objectivity of science, in the work of Thomas Kuhn and others, have indirectly raised doubts about wisdom regarding human values, as have the social scientific ideas of David Hume and Max Weber.

Edward Johnson

FURTHER READING

Kekes, John. *Moral Wisdom and Good Lives*. Ithaca, N.Y.: Cornell University Press, 1996.

Roszak, Theodore. *America the Wise: The Longevity Revolution and the True Wealth of Nations*. Boston: Houghton Mifflin, 1998.

Sternberg, Robert J., ed. *Wisdom: Its Nature, Origins, and Development*. New York: Cambridge University Press, 1990.

SEE ALSO: Aristotelian ethics; Avalokiteśvara; Daoist ethics; Hume, David; Platonic ethics; Prudence; Socrates; Weber, Max.

Wittgenstein, Ludwig

IDENTIFICATION: Austrian-born British philosopher
BORN: April 26, 1889, Vienna, Austro-Hungarian
    Empire (now in Austria)
DIED: April 29, 1951, Cambridge, England
TYPE OF ETHICS: Modern history
SIGNIFICANCE: The author of *Tractatus Logico-*
    Philosophicus ("Logisch-philosophische Abhand-
    lung," 1921) and *Philosophical Investigations*
    (*Philosophische Untersuchungen/Philosophical*
    Investigations, 1953), and one of the most impor-
    tant philosophers of the first half of the twentieth
    century, Wittgenstein argued that value, including
    moral value, falls outside the purview of philo-
    sophy, which he viewed as an activity that is pri-
    marily concerned with the explanation and de-
    limitation of meaning to facilitate purely factual
    descriptions of the world.

Wittgenstein's philosophy is divided into early and
later periods. The early period is marked by his interest in the formal semantics for possible languages.
Wittgenstein believed that language could be meaningful only if sentences are analyzable into ultimate
atomic constituents that, in a one-to-one correspondence, exactly mirror possible facts, thereby providing a picture of the world. The sentence that describes
a fact about the world is a concatenation of names for
simple objects that corresponds to a juxtaposition of
the named objects. The implication is that language
is meaningful only if it describes contingent empirical states of affairs. This means that sentences that
purport to express moral judgments and values are
literally meaningless.

Wittgenstein regards this conclusion as showing
that ethics must be transcendent, by which he means
that value—right and wrong, good and evil—is neither part of the world nor a truth about the world.
From this it follows that there simply is no matter of
fact about whether it is right or wrong to do something; instead, moral value is a function of subjective
attitude, aesthetic taste, or emotional response to the
facts of the world. It is in this sense that Wittgenstein,
in the *Tractatus* (6.421), enigmatically declares: "It
is clear that ethics cannot be expressed. Ethics is transcendental. (Ethics and aesthetics are one)." Wittgenstein sees the mind's transcendent moral stance
toward the world of facts as vitally important to phi-

losophy and the conduct of life, despite the claims
that value statements are literally meaningless and
that value judgments cannot be stated, but only shown.

In his later development, Wittgenstein rejected
the picture theory of meaning but continued to regard
ethics as being deeply rooted in common social practices, or forms of life. There can be no adequate
reductive philosophical theory of forms of life, because they are too basic, and they constitute the foundation in Wittgenstein's later work for the philosophical explanation of the meaningfulness of discourse.
After rejecting the semantic theory of the *Tractatus*,
Wittgenstein, in the *Philosophical Investigations* and
other posthumously published writings, continued to
regard philosophy as a kind of therapy for eliminating problems that arise through the misunderstanding of language. It is not the function of philosophy to
offer a positive doctrine of right and wrong, of good
and evil, but only to explain what Wittgenstein calls
the philosophical grammar of these terms as they can
permissibly be used in the language of ethics. The
business of philosophy is to arrive at a correct understanding of meaning, not to formulate and defend
substantive commitments to particular doctrines of
morally justified action or the good.

Dale Jacquette

SEE ALSO: Art; Intersubjectivity; Language; Right
and wrong; Skepticism; Transcendentalism; Truth;
Value.

Wollstonecraft, Mary

IDENTIFICATION: English journalist and educator
BORN: April 27, 1759, London, England
DIED: September 10, 1797, London, England
TYPE OF ETHICS: Sex and gender issues
SIGNIFICANCE: Wollstonecraft's *Vindication of the*
    Rights of Woman (1792) brought together her in-
    terests in women's education and democratic hu-
    man rights to argue that women deserve an educa-
    tion equal to that of men.

Wollstonecraft's significant public activities included running a girls' school and working with radical political groups that supported the French Revolution. She wrote many articles that were published

Mary Wollstonecraft. (Library of Congress)

in left-wing periodicals as well as eight books, including novels, educational manuals, and partisan political treatises. In her most famous work, *A Vindication of the Rights of Woman*, Wollstonecraft criticized the view that women should learn only how to keep house and be attractive. Being admired for one's beauty and vocational skills, she said, is demeaning to a human being. Human beings, both male and female, are distinguished from animals in that they were created by God with the ability to shape their emotions and morals through reason. All human beings deserve an education that cultivates their reason. If all people had such an education, they would be able to respect one another as self-controlled, independent, moral, and rational beings. Mutual respect of this sort between husbands and wives is the only route to a happy marriage. In her second-most-famous work, *A Vindication of the Rights of Men* (1790), Wollstonecraft argued that mutual respect of this sort between social classes is the route to a just society.

Laura Duhan Kaplan

SEE ALSO: Equal pay for equal work; Equal Rights Amendment; Suffrage; Women's ethics; Women's liberation movement.

Women's ethics

DEFINITION: Study or advocacy of distinctively feminine or feminist ethical values
TYPE OF ETHICS: Sex and gender issues
SIGNIFICANCE: Women's ethics has challenged the traditional emphasis on reason, impartiality, autonomy, and universal principles, arguing that traditional moral philosophy has portrayed as universal values which are actually masculine or masculinist. The question of what makes a value feminine or masculine—whether it is a matter of essential biological difference, or of the particular processes of socialization prevalent in a given culture—is a matter of significant controversy.

The inclusion of women's experience and the increasing number of women philosophers have had an impact on ethical theory and practice. This impact has been enormous and varied. It is difficult to identify "women's experience." Women are not only women alone, but also belong to socioeconomic classes, racial groups, religions, geographical areas, and cultures. What is common to women's ethics is that experience matters. Just as women's experience is varied, so is women's ethical theory and practice varied.

The common classifications of women's ethical theory are maternal, psychoanalytic, liberal, socialist, Marxist, radical, and lesbian. Each of these views can be divided further among those who extol some aspect of the "feminine" as the highest virtue, those who accept the traditional "masculine" values but seek to redefine them as human, and those who propose a challenge to the idea of feminine and masculine virtues and seek to generate new concepts of morality.

Women's ethics, of any variety, recognizes "traditional" ethical theories as male centered. These theories either intentionally exclude women (and people of certain races and classes) from moral experience or unintentionally use certain male moral experience as the standard for all moral experience, thus effectively excluding women (and people of certain races and classes). The result of such exclusion is a tradition that generally favors reason over emotion, impartiality over partiality, autonomy over interdependence or dependence, the abstract over the concrete, the universal over the particular, and justice over caring. In response to this exclusion, and the resulting tradition, women's ethics consciously considers women's experiences.

MATERNAL ETHICS

Maternal ethics, also referred to as the ethic of care, holds that women's unique experiences as mothers (biological or social) lead to an ethic that focuses on relationships and interdependence, and includes self-sacrifice and care for others as primary moral qualities. Whether they believe women are specially suited for such moral action by biology or by socialization, proponents of such theories believe that it is these moral characteristics that women should be recognized as having. Celebrating women's differences from men leads some theorists to suggest that women's morality is different from but complementary to the more male voice of justice. Others suggest that the feminine voice is superior and should be the model for all humanity.

PSYCHOANALYTIC ETHICS

Psychoanalytic feminists see the family arrangement, in which it is primarily the woman who stays with and cares for the children, as problematic. They believe that it is this arrangement that leads to sharp gender distinctions and inequalities. Because girls stay attached to the same-sex parent and never learn to define themselves as selves, they remain dependent. Boys, however, must define themselves in opposition to the mother and therefore become excessively autonomous. These differences have played out in power struggles in which boys learn to break away and be independent and girls learn to compromise and save relationships. These gender distinctions could be minimized, such feminists believe, by increasing dual parenting. This approach challenges the tradition by questioning the moral superiority of autonomy over interdependence.

POLITICAL ETHICS

The liberal feminist generally calls for the equal education of women and equal opportunity to pursue traditionally male occupations. It is at times summa-

rized as fighting for the opportunity for women to become men. Liberal feminism does not go too far in challenging the traditional approach to ethics; instead, it asks that women be included as human under the same definition as men—as rational, autonomous moral agents.

Marxist feminists see the power imbalance as primarily economic. If the marketplace is changed, women will no longer be available to be possessions of men and equality will emerge. Socialist feminists share this concern about the need to change the market but also believe that it will be necessary to change education, the home, media, and women's self-images if equality is to emerge. These approaches also accept much of the tradition and ask that conditions be changed so that women too can be rational autonomous actors.

Radical and lesbian feminists call for women to separate from men (the length and extent of the called-for separation vary). They claim that women cannot know who they are or what they believe unless they define themselves in terms of relationships with other women rather than relationships with men. If they are to avoid copying the oppression and power inequalities of patriarchy, they must first break out of it. This approach seeks to challenge the tradition at its very foundation, by rejecting it and calling women to build a separate tradition for themselves that is based on their own rich and varied experiences.

CONCLUSION

Despite the variations in theories of women's ethics, they do pose some common challenges to the tradition. These theories bring to the forefront the dynamics of power that are present in almost any given situation. The solutions that they offer to address the power imbalance between men and women vary, but they all suggest a reevaluation of the assumption that moral decisions are faced by, or made by, people with real or perceived power. They ask people to evaluate traditional "universal values" from the point of view of the disempowered and ask if they still appear to be universal values. They force people to see that being inclusive of many different viewpoints requires a willingness to be critical of the canon of traditional ethics in ways not previously attempted. It would be a mistake to remove the word "man" and replace it with "human." The differences between men and women must be addressed.

1597

Some of these possible differences include seeing relationships and interdependence as the moral starting point and questioning the ideals of impartiality and autonomy as absolute moral values. Women's ethics forces people to rethink the concept of the moral agent and the moral act. It is necessary to see the connectedness of feeling and thinking and to broaden the notion of what counts as moral.

Erin McKenna

FURTHER READING

Brennan, Samantha, ed. *Feminist Moral Philosophy.* Calgary, Alta.: University of Calgary Press, 2002.

Gilligan, Carol. *In a Different Voice: Psychological Theory and Women's Development.* Cambridge, Mass.: Harvard University Press, 1982.

Irigaray, Luce. *This Sex Which Is Not One.* Translated by Catherine Porter and Carolyn Burke. Ithaca, N.Y.: Cornell University Press, 1985.

Jaggar, Alison M. *Feminist Politics and Human Nature.* Totowa, N.J.: Rowman & Littlefield, 1988.

Kittay, Eva Feder, and Diana T. Meyers, eds. *Women and Moral Theory.* Totowa, N.J.: Rowman & Littlefield, 1987.

Pearsall, Marilyn, ed. *Women and Values: Readings in Recent Feminist Philosophy.* Belmont, Calif.: Wadsworth, 1986.

Tong, Rosemarie. *Feminine and Feminist Ethics.* Belmont, Calif.: Wadsworth, 1993.

SEE ALSO: Ecofeminism; Environmental ethics; Equal Rights Amendment; Feminist ethics; Gender bias; Human rights; Personal relationships; Title IX; Women's liberation movement.

Women's liberation movement

DEFINITION: Set of social and political movements resisting patriarchy and advocating the interests of women

TYPE OF ETHICS: Sex and gender issues

SIGNIFICANCE: The women's liberation movement began by seeking to achieve equal rights and equal treatment for women and men. Later, however, this model of liberation became controversial, as some feminists began to question the assumption behind it that men and women share the same basic values. The response of this so-called Second Wave of feminism was to advocate treating feminine values as just as legitimate as masculine values, rather than pretending that one set of values fits both genders equally.

Women's liberation is the dominant version of feminism in modern American society. Women's liberation emerged in the political context of the American New Left during the 1960's. Prior to this time, the earlier feminist movement, often called the "Old Wave" or "First Wave," referred to the formation of the suffrage movement in the United States and in Britain between about 1840 and 1920. The suffrage movement stressed reforms for women in family law, economic opportunity, and obtaining the right to vote.

First Wave feminists of the 1960's carried on the suffrage movement tradition by promoting a vision of equality between men and women. They spoke and thought in terms of equality of rights, nondiscrimination, equity, and fair treatment for everyone, and they worked for constitutional changes to guarantee equal opportunity, especially in politics and education. For example, a prominent First Wave advocate, Supreme Court Justice Ruth Bader Ginsburg, championed a vision of women's liberation during the 1970's that rejected the traditional belief that men and women lived in separate and different spheres. Laws based on this distinction were designed to seemingly protect the "weaker sex" by, for example, limiting work hours or acceptable occupations. These laws created the perception that women could not take care of themselves and needed special legal protection. Ginsburg and other feminists, however, argued that such laws only justified legal subordination. They attacked laws that treated men and women differently and demanded that men and women be given equal rather than special treatment. The accomplishments of this contemporary First Wave women's liberation constitute a great and significant American success story.

SECOND WAVE WOMEN'S LIBERATION

During the 1960's and 1970's, a different and more radical women's liberation movement evolved. Self-examination in consciousness-raising groups caused the unifying theme to emerge that women were systematically and thoroughly dominated, con-

Milestones in Women's Liberation

Year	Event	Significance
1848	Declaration of Sentiments at Seneca Falls Convention	Crucial document of nineteenth century feminism.
1848	Geneva Falls Convention of Women	First women's rights convention.
1869	American and National Suffrage Associations	Early Old Wave feminist organizations founded.
1869	Wyoming grants woman suffrage	First woman suffrage law in the United States.
1920	Nineteenth Amendment is ratified	Women given the right to vote.
1937	U.S. Supreme Court upholds Washington States's minimum wage law for women.	Women workers given new legal supports.
1947	*Fay v. New York*	Supreme Court rules that women are equally qualified to serve with men on juries.
1963	*The Feminine Mystique*	Pioneering First Wave book by Betty Friedan.
1963	President's Commission on the Status of Women	Recommends appointment of women to important political positions.
1964	Title VII of the Civil Rights Act	Prohibits employment discrimination on the basis of race, color, religion, national origin, or sex.
1966	National Organization of Women (NOW) is founded	Influential contemporary women's organization.
1968	Executive Order 11246	Prohibits sex discrimination by government contractors.
1970	*The Female Eunuch*	Important Second Wave book by Germaine Greer which focused media attention on women's oppression.
1972	Equal Rights Amendment (ERA) is passed by Congress and sent to the states for ratification	Takes an important step toward guaranteeing equal rights to all women.
1972	National Women's Political Caucus is organized	Pioneering group for involving women in the political process.
1972	Title IX is passed by Congress	Prohibits discrimination based on sex in schools receiving federal monies.
1973	*Roe v. Wade*	Supreme Court ruling affirming a woman's right to abortion via her right to privacy.
1975	*Signs: Journal of Women, Culture and Society* founded	Groundbreaking forum for publication of feminist scholarship and theory.

(continued)

Milestones in Women's Liberation — continued

Year	Event	Significance
1976	Democratic National Convention	A rule is made that women must make up half of all delegates.
1978	Pregnancy Discrimination Act	Bans job discrimination against expectant mothers.
1981-1989	Reagan administration	The administration's antifeminist tone causes many setbacks for women's movement.
1981	Greenham	All-women's peace camp is set up at an Air Force base; positive use of feminist theory.
1981	Sandra Day O'Connor is appointed to U.S. Supreme Court	First woman Supreme Court justice.
1982	ERA is defeated	Not ratified by enough states.
1984	Geraldine Ferraro runs for vice president on the Democratic ticket	First woman to run for national office on a major party ticket.
1991	Anita Hill-Clarence Thomas hearings	Catalyzed the women's movement; key event in consciousness-raising.
1992	*Casey v. Planned Parenthood*	Abortion rights somewhat limited.
1992-1993	"Year of the Woman"	Historic number of women run for and are elected to Congress.
1993-2000	Clinton administration	Many women appointed to important positions, including secretary of state and attorney general.
1993	Ruth Bader Ginsburg is appointed to U.S. Supreme Court	Second woman Supreme Court justice.
1993	Violence Against Women Act	Enhances penalties for crimes motivated by gender.
1994	Gender Equity in Education Act	Federal law to train teachers in gender equity.
	Violence Against Women Act	Funds services for rape and domestic violence victims.
1996	*United States v. Virginia*	Supreme Court rules that male-only admission policy of the state-supported Virginia Military Institute (VMI) is unconstitutional.
1996	Summer Olympic Games in Atlanta	Spectacular successes of U.S. women are credited to advances in women's sports fostered by Title IX.
1997	Reinterpretation of Title IX	Supreme Court rules that college sports programs must involve roughly equal numbers of men and women.
2000	*United States v. Morrison*	Supreme Court permits victims of rape and domestic violence to sue their attackers in federal courts.

trolled, victimized, and oppressed legally, economically, and culturally by a male-dominated social structure ("andro-centricity," "hetero-patriarchy," or "sex-gender system"). As part of consciousness-raising, women would come to realize that this oppression and victimization on an individual level could form the basis for collective action, activism, and political change at a group level. This shift from stressing equity and fair treatment for everyone to stressing the oppression and victimization of women by men and the differences between men and women characterizes the "Second Wave" of women's liberation, a term coined by Marsha Weinman Lear in 1968.

COMPARING THE TWO WAVES

The First and Second Waves of women's liberation are similar in that they both believe that sexual politics is central in the struggle for women's rights. Many of their goals are the same in terms of improving the position of women in society. Certainly, both waves have had a profound effect on American politics and society, American consciousness, and awareness of gender roles and the relationship between men and women. The fundamental difference between the First and Second Waves is that the Second Wave is, as Maggie Humm pointed out, an ideology whose purpose is to create an environment for women that transcends social equity. That is, the Second Wave stresses the separateness of and differences between women and men and the communality between women, and it seeks to provide for the emancipation of women from their yoke of male oppression, victimization, and dominance. A major goal is to challenge and change the relevant social institutions and their practices, which have created and perpetuated these oppressive systems.

These goals of Second Wave feminism can be accomplished only by developing "gynaesthesia," a term coined by Mary Daley in 1978 to describe the radically new and altered perception and understanding that occur in women when they become Second Wave feminists. Christina Hoff Sommers describes this situation as a "gyncentric prism"; that is, a sharing among women of certain women-centered beliefs and social organizations. Rather than viewing men and women as equals, Second Wave feminists generally believe that equality is impossible to achieve given the patriarchical structure and orienta-

tion of American society. To adhere to equality between men and women would be like sleeping with the enemy. Men are the enemies of women, and there is a gender war in progress. The difference between the First and Second Waves is starkly defined in three statements, two by First Wave feminists Betty Friedan and Iris Murdoch, and one by Germaine Greer, a Second Wave feminist. According to Betty Friedan, "We must not let feminism be co-opted as a mask for cynical corruption by women or by men. We must resist that polarization of us against them (women against other women, even women against men) with our new vision of community that puts first the real needs of people in life." Iris Murdoch says, "to lay claim to [Second Wave feminism] . . . is to set up a new female ghetto. . . . It is a dead end in danger of simply separating women from the mainstream thinking of the human race." According to Germaine Greer, however, "male hostility to women is a constant; all men hate all women some of the time; some men hate all women all of the time; some men hate some women all of the time. . . . What is remarkable, given the implacability of male hostility to uppity women, is that we have survived."

Laurence Miller

FURTHER READING

Berkeley, Kathleen C. *The Women's Liberation Movement in America.* Westport, Conn.: Greenwood Press, 1999.

Cobble, Dorothy Sue. *The Other Women's Movement: Workplace Justice and Social Rights in Modern America.* Princeton, N.J.: Princeton University Press, 2004.

DuBois, Ellen Carol. *Feminism and Suffrage: The Emergence of an Independent Women's Movement in America, 1848-1869.* Ithaca, N.Y.: Cornell University Press, 1999.

DuPlessis, Rachel Blau, and Ann Snitow, eds. *The Feminist Memoir Project: Voices from Women's Liberation.* New York: Three Rivers Press, 1998.

Hole, Judith, and Ellen Levine. *Rebirth of Feminism.* New York: Quadrangle Books, 1971.

Kessler-Harris, Alice. *In Pursuit of Equity: Women, Men, and the Quest for Economic Citizenship in Twentieth-Century America.* New York: Oxford University Press, 2001.

McGlen, Nancy E., and Karen O'Connor. *Women's Rights.* New York: Praeger, 1983.

Matthews, Jean V. *The Rise of the New Woman: The Women's Movement in America, 1875-1930.* Chicago: Ivan R. Dee, 2003.

SEE ALSO: Ecofeminism; Equal Rights Amendment; *Feminine Mystique, The*; Feminist ethics; Gender bias; Suffrage; Women's ethics.

Work

DEFINITION: Exertion of effort to perform a task or accomplish a goal, especially habitually as one's means of livelihood; labor

TYPE OF ETHICS: Beliefs and practices

SIGNIFICANCE: The meaning or function of work, for an individual and for a society, is one of the central problems of social philosophy. Many philosophers ascribe to work either an inherent ethical value—seeing all work as a good in itself—or a potential ethical value—seeing work as potentially expressive of human freedom when performed under the proper circumstances or in the ideal society.

The Hebrew Bible, known to Christians as the Old Testament, in the mythology of creation in Genesis and in the pessimistic poetry of Ecclesiastes, evinces both a positive and a negative attitude toward work. According to the Genesis myth, God commanded the first human pair to subdue and have dominion over the earth (Gen. 1:28). God placed Adam in the Garden of Eden "to dress it and keep it" (Gen. 2:5). Thus, work was considered a necessary and integral part of human life in this world.

According to the Genesis myth, however, because of the sin of Adam and Eve, work would be filled with hardship and toil:

> Cursed is the ground for thy sake; in sorrow shalt thou eat of it all the days of thy life. Thorns also and thistles shalt it bring forth to thee; and thou shalt eat the herb of it all the days of thy life; In the sweat of thy face shalt thou eat bread, till thou return unto the ground; for out of it was thou taken; for dust thou art, and unto dust shalt thou return. . . . Therefore, the Lord God sent him forth from the garden of Eden to till the ground from whence he was taken (Gen. 3:17-19, 23).

This ambivalent attitude toward work also appears in Hebrew wisdom literature. The author of Ecclesiastes, an anonymous Hebrew poet, rhetorically asks with a pessimistic tone, "What profit hath a man of all his labour which he taketh under the Sun?" (Eccles. 1:3). Human labor appears to be empty and futile. "Then I looked on all the works that my hands had wrought, and on the labour that I had laboured to do: and behold, all was vanity and vexation of spirit, and there was no profit under the sun." The poet, who is traditionally held to be Solomon, also expresses a positive attitude, and, in the end, seems to be as ambivalent as are the Genesis myths. "There is nothing better for a man, than that he should make his soul enjoy good in his labour. This also I saw, that it was from the hand of God."

The ancient Greeks were just as ambivalent toward work as were the Hebrews, although, overall, the Greek attitude toward work, especially manual labor, was pessimistic. Plato, writing in the *Statesman*, depicts primordial life in the mythical time of Chronos as idyllic. Work was not necessary in those days because the earth, unaided by human cultivation, brought forth fruits from trees that no human had planted. The seasons were mild, the air was fresh, and the people were naked and lounged on couches of grass. In the *Laws* (book 4), Plato called the time of Chronos a "blessed rule" in which humans were happy and provisions were abundant and spontaneously generated.

Not only the ancients but also the moderns were unsure about the role of work in early human life. Jean-Jacques Rousseau postulated an early state of nature in which the needs of human beings were provided for by a generous, benevolent world: "The produce of the earth furnished him with all he needed, and instinct told him how to use it" (*A Discourse upon the Origin and Foundation of Inequality Among Mankind*, 1761). Georg Wilhelm Friedrich Hegel, even though he castigated early human beings as lazy, regarded toil as a universal feature of human activity intended to satisfy need (*Philosophy of Right*, 1875).

WORK AS NECESSITY

Even the fanciful and speculative ancient Greeks realized that labor was necessary in order to make leisure and happiness possible. Plato, in *Critias*, stated that mythology and intellectual inquiry were possible only after the necessities of life had been provided for. In the *Metaphysics*, Aristotle claimed that the arts of recreation, which were more esteemed than the arts of life's necessities, could be practiced only in an environment of leisure. In book 10 of the *Ethics*, Aristotle opined that happiness depended upon leisure and that people occupied themselves in work in order to have leisure. In book 1 of the *Politics*, he made the commonsense claim that one cannot live well until the necessities of life are provided for.

Hegel, in the *Philosophy of History*, held that the worker, in diligently providing for his or her needs, created his or her dignity. Montesquieu, in the *Spirit of the Laws* (1748), wrote that the activity of an "industrious" people was the source of their "blessing." Adam Smith held that the industriousness of even the lowest type of worker made possible the necessities and conveniences of life.

THE NATURE AND END OF WORK

Usually, a distinction has been made between types of work. One distinction was between honorable and dishonorable types of work. In *Charmides*, Plato quoted Hesiod, who held that work is no disgrace. In fact, Plato made reference to things nobly and usefully made as works, although he explicitly excluded such ignominious activities as shoemaking and pickle selling. Plato's distinction seems to be based on the belief that things that serve a utilitarian purpose are mundane and therefore ignoble. Plato, in *Republic* and *Timaeus*, separated the class of husbandmen and artisans from the class of guardians. In *Laws*, Plato strictly forbade artisans from participating in politics and citizens from occupying themselves in the handicraft arts. The craft of citizenship requires much study and knowledge, and no individual could occupy himself well with two different arts.

In the *Politics*, Aristotle agreed with Plato and insisted that the citizen refrain from the trades and crafts; otherwise, there would be no distinction between master and slave. According to Aristotle, the food-producing class and the artisans provide for the necessities of life and thus are necessary elements of the life of the state, but the state has a higher end: providing for the greater good. Aristotle also deemed the mastercraftsman more honorable and wiser than the manual laborer because the former has thorough knowledge about his activity, whereas the latter

works in ignorance. In *Politics*, Aristotle wrote that some duties are necessary but others are more honorable.

In the *Critique of Judgment* (1790), Immanuel Kant made a similar distinction between artistic production and manual labor. Artistic production is distinguished from labor in that the former is free and the latter is drudgery.

Hegel, however, was not so pessimistic about the nature of labor. He believed that adults, in working, devoted their lives to labor for definite intelligent and objective aims. Adam Smith echoed the ancient Greeks in his claim that people who pursue trades for a livelihood that others pursue merely as diversions are inferior people. Smith also made a distinction between productive and nonproductive labor that would figure prominently in the thought of classical political economy. Labor that adds value to the product is productive labor, and labor that merely renders a service but fails to add value to a product is nonproductive labor. This distinction yielded ethical advantages for the advocates of capitalism, who wanted to justify the social utility and ethical value of wage labor.

Thomas Hobbes's attitude toward work was practical and utilitarian. He advocated the creation of laws that would force those with strong bodies to be employed in useful arts and manufacture. Rousseau, with his negative attitude toward the stultifying and dehumanizing aspects of modern civilization, deplored the unhealthy trades because they shortened human life and destroyed human bodies.

WORK AND PROPERTY

Jesus said that "The workman is worthy of his hire" (Matt. 10:10). The social philosophy embedded in this pithy epigram simply sets forth the ethical principle that the worker deserves just compensation, in some form, for his or her labor. Each deserves what is proper. Property means what properly belongs to a person. Views on property have ranged from the communitarianism of Plato and Karl Marx to the concepts of private ownership found in John Locke.

In *Laws*, Plato advocated communal ownership of property and cited the old saying that "Friends have all things in common." The communal state, according to Plato, is the ideal state. Plato argued that in the ideal state there should exist neither the extreme of poverty nor that of wealth, for they produce social evils. Aristotle modified Plato's concept of property ownership. Property should be common but private. In other words, the production of property should be social but ownership should be private.

Aristotle presumes that individuals will be more industrious if they look out for their own property and attend to their own business. Yet extreme poverty should not be allowed, because it lowers the character of democracy. People should be given the opportunity to start a farm or learn a trade. As Hobbes saw it, accident and fortune may make it impossible for some to sustain themselves by means of their labor; therefore, the state must force the physically fit to work, thereby creating social resources to be distributed to the unfortunate. Rousseau, like Plato and Aristotle, believed that government should prevent inequality by denying individuals the ability and opportunity to accumulate wealth. Rousseau believed that society enslaved the poor and empowered the rich, thereby destroying natural human liberty. Property laws and inequality worked for the advantage of the few and subjected the many.

Rousseau claimed that he could not conceive how property could come about except for manual labor. John Locke appears to agree with Rousseau, but in the end Locke took a decidedly opposing stand. In the *Second Treatise of Government* (1690), Locke began the section on property by ostensibly arguing for limited appropriation on the basis that an object that was created by means of one's labor was one's property. Yet, as he saw it, the introduction of money allowed the unlimited appropriation of property. According to Hegel, what makes an object the property of a person is that the person stamps his or her will into the thing. Hegel believed that property could be alienated only because it was external to the essential being of the worker. An individual may alienate—give up, sell, set aside, yield, or abandon—any possession, because it is external to the personality of the individual. Personality, ethical character, morality, and faith are essential characteristics of the self and therefore may not be alienated. Hegel believed that an individual could alienate his or her abilities to another person for a restricted period but not for a whole lifetime, because that would amount to making the essence of the self into a thing.

Even Adam Smith conceded that the entire product of labor does not belong to the laborer. According to Smith, in the original state of nature the entire product belonged to the producer; he deplored the condition in modern society in which, all the lands having been converted into private property, the landlords reaped where they did not sow.

MARXISM AND WORK

Karl Marx condemned capitalism because it ripped away the meaningfulness of work from the worker and, through the imposition of alienated labor, dehumanized the worker. For Marx, the question of work is central to the social question, because the mode of production of material life determines the social, political, and cultural aspects of life. Work is essential to human nature, first of all, because it provides for the physical existence of human life. Work is not, however, only a means for physical existence; work is valuable for its own sake. Work is human life-activity itself. It is the realization and the fulfillment of human capacities and drives.

By means of work, human beings objectify themselves and create a human world, an environment that is conducive to the full development and flowering of all human potentials and capacities. The object of labor is not only to create a product but also to build the objective social world. The construction of the human world is the primary end of work.

Under capitalism, however, human work becomes alienated labor. Alienated labor dehumanizes the worker by enslaving the worker to an activity in which the worker becomes a passive object rather than an active agent. The worker becomes a slave of work because work is given by the capitalist and because work becomes necessary in order to maintain existence as a physical organism. The alienation of labor stems from the fact that the human being is not realized or fulfilled in work; such work does not affirm the humanity of the worker but denies it. Work is not freely entered into but is coerced. In the modern industrial world, the worker becomes a commodity, because the worker not only produces commodities but also is a commodity.

Alienated labor presupposes private property. Therefore, the emancipation from alienation, the process of dealienation, entails the abolition of private property. Dealienated labor becomes the foundation for the formulation of just political institutions and social arrangements and must be included in any conception of justice. Work is essential to human nature, a necessary expression of human life-activity and the form of human self-realization. Finally, work is the foundation of culture. By means of their work, human beings shape and construct a human world in all its aspects: culture, politics, society, and so forth.

Herbert Marcuse, in *Eros and Civilization* (1955), viewed emancipation in terms of the play impulse. The character of work itself could be changed in accord with the nondistorted needs of the life instincts. The very character of production could change as a result of instinctual transformation entering into the relations of production. The character of the working day would change, causing the elimination of the distinction between necessary time and leisure time. Human production and self-creation would lose their antithetical character. Technological advancement would allow labor to be transformed into a realm of freedom within the realm of necessity. Rationality of gratification would inform new science and new technology. It would require a new worker and a new sensibility that would abolish the distinction between productive utilitarian labor and the creative aspects of work. The new sensibility would unite work and play. Such a unity can come about, however, only if it becomes a basic need of human nature.

In *An Essay on Liberation* (1965), Marcuse stated that aim-inhibited sexuality develops in individuals a sense of what is permissible and what is not—the reality principle. Repression is heightened in advanced capitalism to prevent human beings from enjoying emancipatory possibilities; it keeps them in productive gear. In socialism, a properly repressed libido will emerge in new human relations and in culture-building activities. The prospect of automation suggests the elimination of the distinction between labor and leisure.

CHRISTIANITY AND THE SOCIAL QUESTION OF WORK

Saint Paul enjoined Christians to work and not be idle. The Cistercians' *ora et labora* cautioned the faithful to pray and work. Martin Luther interpreted the call to salvation as being inextricably tied to the position that one held in society. One's call to salvation was also a call to accept work as vocation. John Calvin interpreted work as enterprise and held that success justifies work. Max Weber demonstrated that, for Calvinist Protestants, successful work proved God's election. This idea found fertile soil in the Puritan ethos, where frugality and hard work

were believed to be the keys to success. Weber called this Protestant ethic the "spirit of capitalism." Jürgen Moltmann interprets work as participation in God's history. Work is not only self-supporting but also self-realizing. Work affirms existence; therefore, work is a right that presupposes freedom. Work must allow for self-formation. Work requiring cooperation helps in the socialization of the individual. Therefore, work should be understood as part of the socialization process. Through work, people participate in creating or destroying the world. Thus, work has eschatological significance.

In *Laborem exercens* (1982), Pope John Paul II strongly emphasized the central role that work plays in solving social ills. Making life more human presupposes making work more human. Men and women participate with God in creation by carrying out the mandate given in Genesis to subdue and dominate the earth. Men and women are created in the image of the Creator. Therefore, human beings are creative subjects and agents who are capable of planning and rationally deciding about the future.

Men and women are not only workers but also the subjects of work. They are persons apart from their work. Thus, work should realize their humanity. From this idea is derived the ethical idea of work. Work is ethical because in it, and by means of it, human beings realize their humanity and rationally decide to bring about their future. The dignity of work therefore is based on the subjectivity of the person who works. Accordingly, Pope John Paul II stressed the primacy of work over capital, the priority of human beings over things. Work is also considered to be a means toward self-realization, as is expressed in the Vatican II documents *Mater et Magistra* (1961) and *Gaudium et Spes* (1965). The Roman Catholic Church views the commodification of the worker, the treatment of the worker as a mere means of production, as a denial of human dignity.

Pope John Paul II also affirmed the world-shaping power of work. It is the foundation of the family and society. It is foundational for the family because it provides for the subsistence of the family. Work, combined with the virtue of industriousness, influences the process of family education. In Roman Catholic social teaching, work has been considered as a fundamental force shaping the world of culture and society in a human and rational manner.

Michael R. Candelaria

FURTHER READING

John Paul II, Pope. *Laborem exercens*. Boston: St. Paul Editions, 1981. *Laborem exercens* sums up centuries of Catholic social teaching on work and characteristically takes up a middle position between capitalism and socialism. It is crystal clear in its call for the right to meaningful work.

Marcuse, Herbert. *Eros and Civilization: A Philosophical Inquiry into Freud*. Boston: Beacon, 1974. Using Freudian categories, Marcuse argues that advanced capitalism represses the fundamental creative powers of human beings. He sets forth the idea that the very nature of work should change and that work and leisure should not be so radically distinguished.

_____. *An Essay on Liberation*. Boston: Beacon Press, 1969. Written in the turbulent late 1960's, *An Essay on Liberation* offers a new vision of socialism in which unchained aesthetic sensibilities would unleash creative productive powers that would make possible an environment of freedom. Work is interpreted as being playful.

Marx, Karl. *Selected Writings*. Edited by David McLellan. 2d ed. New York: Oxford University Press, 2000. Includes the *Economic and Philosophical Manuscripts of 1844*, in which Marx develops his fullest expression of both free and alienated labor, as well as selections from *Capital* on the labor theory of value.

Plato. *The Republic*. Translated by Desmond Lee. 2d ed. New York: Penguin Books, 2003. This book captures Plato's vision of the good city, which is divided into three classes with three varieties of duty.

Schaff, Kory, ed. *Philosophy and the Problems of Work: A Reader*. Lanham, Md.: Rowman & Littlefield, 2001. An anthology collecting a wide-ranging group of texts by scholars of every political stripe, covering such subjects as work and technology, market socialism, exploitation, and the welfare state.

Weber, Max. *The Protestant Ethic and the Spirit of Capitalism*. Translated by Talcott Parsons. Introduction by Anthony Giddens. New York: Routledge, 2001. This classic text successfully demonstrates the power of ideas to influence social and economic structures. It does not quite refute Marx's materialist concept of history but does a convincing job of linking the origins of capitalism with the Calvinistic-Puritan work ethic.

SEE ALSO: Calvin, John; Capitalism; Communism; Economics; Freedom and liberty; Hegel, Georg Wilhelm Friedrich; Marx, Karl; Smith, Adam; Socialism.

World Health Organization

IDENTIFICATION: International agency that initiates and coordinates efforts to solve global health problems

DATE: Founded in 1948

TYPE OF ETHICS: Bioethics

SIGNIFICANCE: Also known as WHO, the World Health Organization was founded in response to the perceived need for an entity capable of addressing medical and health problems that cross national boundaries to affect entire regions, continents, or the planet as a whole.

International health organizations have existed from the first decade of the twentieth century, but WHO's scale is far larger than that of anything that existed earlier. It admits and provides services to all states, regardless of whether they are U.N. members. Its tasks fall by their nature into three categories. The first, carried out mainly at headquarters in Geneva, might be called "minding the store": maintaining international drug standards and sanitary and quarantine regulations, and disseminating information regarding epidemics, drug addiction, chemical residues, radiation hazards, and so forth. The second involves providing education and technical assistance for member nations, experts to help plan and set up local health centers, teachers, temporary medical personnel, and so forth. The third is mobilization to deal with specific diseases, including services provided by the central organization, national health bodies, medical laboratories, and other entities.

Smallpox was declared eradicated from the world in 1980. The list of other diseases that WHO has targeted for eradication is striking. In 1988, the organization set the year 2000 as the target date for eradicating polio. That goal was not met, but by the year 2004, only 530 cases of polio were reported worldwide, and those cases were confined to six nations: India, Pakistan, and Afghanistan in South Asia, and Nigeria, Niger, and Egypt in Africa. WHO also set

2000 as the target date for eradicating leprosy. Progress in eradicating that bacterial disease has not been nearly as dramatic as has been the case for polio, but the incidence of leprosy through the world was dramatically reduced by 2004 and was continuing to decline. Other diseases that WHO has targeted for eradication include AIDS, tuberculosis, malaria, yellow fever, cholera, and diphtheria.

In the nondisease category, WHO's goals include the providing of new contraceptives, chemical and mechanical, male and female; the promotion of health practices for mothers and children in developing countries; and even antismoking campaigns. As its charter states, WHO aims for "the highest possible level of health" for all people.

Robert M. Hawthorne, Jr.

SEE ALSO: Bioethics; Geneva conventions; International Red Cross; League of Nations; United Nations.

World Society for the Protection of Animals

IDENTIFICATION: International organization dedicated to the protection of domestic and wild animals, including their natural habitats

DATE: Founded in 1981

TYPE OF ETHICS: Animal rights

SIGNIFICANCE: The World Society for the Protection of Animals (WSPA), which has more than 460 member organizations, as well as offices in twelve countries, monitors and intervenes in cases of animal cruelty and detrimental ecological practices.

Formed by the merger of two international organizations, the World Federation for the Protection of Animals (founded in 1950) and the International Society for the Protection of Animals (founded in 1959), and by absorbing the International Council Against Bullfighting in 1984, the World Society for the Protection of Animals has more than 100,000 international members. The society studies international animal welfare laws and intervenes in a diverse variety of cases involving cruelty. In 1990, for example, WSPA activities included a campaign against the annual Texas rattlesnake roundup, which was condemned because of the suffering of the snakes and because of adverse ecological effects.

The society also operates an emergency rescue service for individual distressed animals, which took action, for example, in 1989, when Colombian peasants discovered and aided a wounded Andean condor. The WSPA engineered the condor's removal to a Bogotá zoo and found a sponsor to pay for its extensive medical treatment.

Mary E. Virginia

SEE ALSO: Animal rights; Conservation; Ecology; Humane Society of the United States; Society for the Prevention of Cruelty to Animals.

World Trade Organization

IDENTIFICATION: International body that promotes and enforces trade laws and regulations

DATE: Began operating in 1995

TYPE OF ETHICS: International relations

SIGNIFICANCE: A global international body, the World Trade Organization manages the rules of trade among nations; its international ethics have come under attack because critics argue that its trade rules are undemocratic and affect not only people from member countries but the environment as well.

The World Trade Organization (WTO) was created in 1994 to replace the General Agreement on Tariffs and Trade (GATT). The WTO began officially functioning the following year, with its headquarters in Geneva, Switzerland. By the beginning of the twenty-first century, it had nearly 150 member countries.

The WTO's mission is to help those who produce goods and services, including importers and exporters, conduct their business. WTO agreements ensure member countries that their exports will be treated fairly in other countries' markets. Similarly, member countries promise to do the same for imports into their own markets. Supporters of the WTO argue that the organization adheres to ethical principles: It handles disputes constructively, it provides training and technical assistance for developing countries, and it provides more choices of products and qualities.

Mounted Australian police run down protestors demonstrating against a meeting of World Trade Organization trade ministers in Sydney in November, 2002. (AP/Wide World Photos)

The world trade that it fosters raises income levels and stimulates economic growth, cuts the costs of living, promotes peace, and encourages good government.

Critics argue that the WTO is too powerful because it can declare the laws and regulations of sovereign nations in violation of trade rules. They allege that the WTO pressures nations into changing trade laws. Developing countries that are WTO members complain that a few powerful member countries dominate WTO discussions. Other critics maintain that WTO trade rules do not adequately protect work-ers' rights, the environment, or human health. United States consumer advocate Ralph Nader believes that WTO policies are undemocratic because they erase national laws and move far beyond settling disputes over tariffs and import quotas. An activist group called the Global Trade Watch wants the WTO to restore each nation's right to make its own decisions about goods sold in its own domestic market and to allow individual nations to set their own environmental and health standards. Environmentalists have initiated the most powerful lobbying efforts against WTO policies. They argue that the WTO has canceled modern environmental protection by nullifying pollution prevention efforts through the use of bans.

When WTO leaders met to discuss trade policy in Seattle, Washington, in late 1999, thousands of people gathered there to protest against the organization. The protesters maintained that the organization neglected poor countries and endangered the environment with its policies.

Legal observers have pointed out significant gaps in WTO agreements and treaties. These include unclear definitions and articles, and contradictory elements within them that have become sources of disagreement among WTO members. The challenge for the WTO in the future is to become an ethically sound bargaining forum because of changing mixes of cooperation and aggressive unilateralism present in many countries.

David Treviño

FURTHER READING

Barfield, Claude E. *Free Trade, Sovereignty, Democracy: The Future of the World Trade Organization.* Washington, D.C.: American Enterprise Institution, 2001.

Cockburn, Alexander, and Jeffrey St. Clair. *Five Days That Shook the World: Seattle and Beyond.* London: Verso, 2000.

Danaher, Kevin, and Roger Burbach, eds. *Globalize This! The Battle Against the World Trade Organization and Corporate Rule.* Monroe, Me.: Common Courage Press, 2000.

Rugman, Alan M., and Gavin Boyd, eds. *The World Trade Organization in the New Global Economy: Trade and Investment Issues in the Millennium Round.* Cheltenham, England: Edward Elgar, 2001.

Sampson, Gary P., ed. *The Role of the World Trade Organization in Global Governance.* New York: United Nations University Press, 2001.

Wallach, Lori, and Michelle Sforza. *The WTO: Five Years of Reasons to Resist Corporate Globalization.* New York: Seven Stories Press, 1999.

SEE ALSO: Developing world; Free enterprise; Globalization; International Monetary Fund; Multinational corporations; Nader, Ralph; Poverty and wealth.

The Wretched of the Earth

IDENTIFICATION: Book by Frantz Fanon (1925-1961)

DATE: *Les Damnés de la terre*, 1961 (*The Damned*, 1963; better known as *The Wretched of the Earth*, 1965)

TYPE OF ETHICS: International relations

SIGNIFICANCE: Focusing on Africa, *The Wretched of the Earth* condemns colonialism and neocolonialism from a Marxist perspective and calls for natives to rise in violence against foreign settlers.

Frantz Fanon indicted colonialist countries for using force to exploit raw materials and labor from colonized countries. Attempting to justify their actions, colonialists stereotyped natives as savages and referred to natives' "precolonial barbarism." Colonialists proclaimed that European culture was the ideal for native peoples to emulate and used violence and divide-and-conquer strategies to keep the natives down. Fanon advocated violence against the settlers as the way for colonized people to regain their sense of self-respect. Although he was a psychiatrist, Fanon did not show that such violence would be psychologically liberating. Instead, he cited cases in which such violence led to psychological degeneration. Even if anticolonial violence were the only way to regain a sense of self-respect, however, such violence would not be automatically justifiable. Rape is not justifiable, for example, even if it appears to be the only way for a person to gain a feeling of self-respect. Thus, it is a mistake to think that Fanon has adequately justified terrorist attacks on the innocent. Fanon encouraged the colonized to reject the dehumanizing domination of Western culture. He claimed that Western culture corrupted the leaders of the decolonized state, making them put their own interests above the interests of the people. He urged former colonial powers to compensate their former colonies instead of continuing to exploit them.

Gregory P. Rich

SEE ALSO: Colonialism and imperialism; Revolution; Violence.

X

Xunzi

IDENTIFICATION: Ancient Chinese philosopher
BORN: c. 307 B.C.E., Zhao Kingdom, China
DIED: c. 235 B.C.E., Lanling, Chu, China
TYPE OF ETHICS: Religious ethics
SIGNIFICANCE: Xunzi (Hsün Tzu in Wade-Giles spelling) superseded Mencius (371-289 B.C.E.) as the foremost interpreter of Confucius. His humanistic philosophy was primarily concerned with the moral education and training necessary to cultivate the self and develop character, whereas Mencius had held that people are inherently good from birth and that they should depend on transcendental power and project universal love.

Xunzi's philosophy was primarily humanistic and realistic, being focused on humanity and the investigation of things. He rejected human dependence on any transcendental power or spirit, such as heaven (*tian*). Instead, he recommended that people depend on their own proper actions as spelled out by the rules of right conduct (*li*), especially in the *Li ji* (*The Book of Rites*), and by justice (*yi*), combined with their own experience. Although people are born evil—that is, "uncivilized"—and are moved by desire, like other animals, they have intelligence and sympathy, which are beyond the abilities of other animals, and can learn to act righteously through knowledge and wisdom acquired by education, self-cultivation, and moral training. They can thus control their animal drives by an act of will and sense of discipline.

Xunzi thought that Mencius's idea of universal love (*jian ai*), which involved loving everyone in the world equally, was unrealistic and impractical. Instead, he held that knowledge gained by study (*xue*) and wisdom (*zhi*) would enable people to control their desires. He also realized that the basis of education was the proper understanding of language and a rational approach. Hence, he stressed the importance of linguistic analysis under the rubric of "the rectification of names."

Richard P. Benton

SEE ALSO: Confucian ethics; Daoist ethics; Humanism; Mencius.

Z

Zen

DEFINITION: Buddhist school of thought whose adherents seek direct, unmediated knowledge of reality through meditation

TYPE OF ETHICS: Religious ethics

SIGNIFICANCE: A major religion in its own right, Zen Buddhism adheres to principles that have also been extremely influential in secularized form as the basis for various nondenominational spiritual philosophies.

Zen, or Zen Buddhism, is a major religion of China and Japan. The name (*Chan* in Chinese, *Zen* in Japanese) means "meditation." Zen is one branch of the Mahāyāna School of Buddhism. Buddhism originated in India before 500 B.C.E. The historical Buddha ("Enlightened Being")—whose sculpted image is familiar worldwide—taught followers to meditate to gain understanding of the true self, or Buddhanature. Bodhidharma, the legendary founder of Zen in China, came from India during the late fifth century C.E.

Great teachers and Daoist doctrine helped shape Zen, and two Chinese schools developed, with different methods of seeking enlightenment and using meditation; these had entered Japan by the fourteenth century as Rinzai and Sōtō. Temples and monasteries arose, and Zen influenced Japanese military life, poetry, art, and landscape gardening. In the twentieth century, writings by Daisetz Teitaro Suzuki and Alan Watts helped to popularize Zen in the West.

ETHICAL IMPLICATIONS

A compassionate realist, Buddha hoped to control suffering and eliminate possessiveness, greed, and self-centeredness. Nirvana, freedom from all earthly ties, was a spiritual goal. Although Buddha avoided specific ethical rules, his Eightfold Path sought to cure humanity's "dislocation" with right views, right aspiration, right speech, right conduct, right vocation, right effort, right mind control, and right meditation. Still central to Zen, these steps encourage careful, truthful thought and speech; respect for basic moral laws; useful work that hurts no one; and suppression of physical appetites and materialism. Although Zenists have sometimes been stereotyped as "happy have-nothings," one traditional Zen precept has been daily work.

Zen stresses inwardness over altruism or social interaction, assuming that people who are at peace with themselves will harmonize with the world and others. Zen tries to eliminate selfishness by curbing ego, teaching that the intuitively wise person is compassionate and humane. It encourages restraint, humility, patience, and quietness. It emphasizes the symbiotic continuity of life and the connectedness of thought and action.

Roy Neil Graves

FURTHER READING

Abe, Masao. *Zen and Western Thought*. Edited by William R. LaFleur. Honolulu: University of Hawaii Press, 1985.

Katagiri, Dainin. *You Have to Say Something: Manifesting Zen Insight*. Boston: Shambhala, 1998.

Kopf, Gereon. *Beyond Personal Idenity: Dōgen, Nishida, and a Phenomenology of No-Self*. Richmond, Surrey, England: Curzon, 2001.

Ross, Nancy Wilson. *Three Ways of Asian Wisdom: Hinduism, Buddhism, Zen, and Their Significance for the West*. New York: Simon & Schuster, 1966.

Suzuki, Daisetz Teitaro. *Zen Buddhism: Selected Writings*. Edited by William Barrett. Garden City, N.Y.: Doubleday, 1956.

Suzuki, Shunryu. *Zen Mind, Beginner's Mind*. Edited by Trudy Dixon. Rev. ed. New York: Weatherhill, 1999.

Watts, Alan W. *The Way of Zen*. New York: Vintage Books, 1999.

SEE ALSO: Bodhidharma; Buddhist ethics; Bushido; Daoist ethics; Dōgen; Five precepts of Buddhism; Huineng; Mādhyamaka.

Zero-base ethics

DEFINITION: Moral theory arising from the premise that one person's gain is always balanced by another's loss

TYPE OF ETHICS: Legal and judicial ethics

SIGNIFICANCE: Zero-base ethics takes zero-base, or zero-sum, economics as an axiom and attempts to ascertain the moral consequences of this axiom. In particular, it develops models and principles to guide decisions about who should suffer and who should benefit in the economic realm, given the assumption that for one person to benefit, another must necessarily suffer.

The zero-base concept is an economic concept that is often illustrated by means of the "fixed pie" analogy: The pie is of a fixed size, so if one person gets a larger piece, another person must get a smaller piece; if one person gets a piece at all, someone else must get none.

Zero-base economics has two major implications for ethics. First, it primarily involves the distribution of resources, not their production. Second, the question of distribution becomes the problem of deciding whose interests must be sacrificed so that others' may be satisfied.

Those who accept zero-base economics often use "lifeboat" scenarios to illustrate the essence of ethics. If eight people are on a lifeboat that contains provisions only for six, then the task is to decide which two must be sacrificed, voluntarily or not, so that the other six can live.

Zero-base economics is contrasted to the "expanding pie," or "win/win," model of production and distribution. Advocates of the expanding pie model argue that the production of wealth can be a dynamic, ever-increasing process, and therefore that ethics is fundamentally about production, not distribution. They point out, for example, that between the years 1750 and 2000, the world's population increased by roughly a factor of 6, yet during that time the world's production increased roughly by a factor of 1,600.

Stephen R. C. Hicks

SEE ALSO: Conflict of interest; Distributive justice; Economic analysis; Economics; Lifeboat ethics; Population control; Poverty and wealth.

Zhu Xi

IDENTIFICATION: Medieval Chinese philosopher

BORN: October 18, 1130, Yougi, Fujian, China

DIED: April 23, 1200, Jianyang, Fujian, China

TYPE OF ETHICS: Medieval history

SIGNIFICANCE: An influential historian and philosopher, Zhu Xi (Chu Hsi in Wade-Giles spelling) advocated extending knowledge "through the investigation of things" ("*dan jin zai ge wu*"), which referred particularly to the study of ethical conduct in and out of government. His neo-Confucianism dominated the intellectual life of China into the first decade of the twentieth century and was influential in Korea and Japan as well.

Zhu Xi's major works are virtually all revisions of, compilations of, or commentaries upon the work of others. His *Outline and Digest of the General Mirror* (1172) is a revision of Sima Qian's history of China, *Comprehensive Mirror for Aid in Government* (late eleventh century), and his philosophy is put forward in commentaries upon the texts of his precedessors, especially Confucius and Mencius. Possibly his most famous work, *Reflections on Things at Hand* (1175), collects the writings of the foremost neo-Confucian philosophers.

Zhu Xi's own neo-Confucianism embraces cosmology and metaphysics as well as ethics and a theory of evil. What he calls the supreme ultimate (*tai ji*) is the summation of emptiness, or the realm of no-things (*li*), which is "above shapes"; it is the ideal prototype and standard that determines the nature of things. The concrete physical world is determined by the vital force (*qi*; literally, "breath"), which is "within shapes." It individuates each thing. In this way, each thing has a nature (*li*) and a specific character (*qi*). Every single thing is instilled with the supreme ultimate, which is the totality of *li* in all things. Every man can cultivate *tai ji* through earnest investigation of things and extend his knowledge of *li*; such research includes the study of the *Four Books* (*Si Shu*) of Confucianism and the study of ethical conduct. People are born with either good or bad *qi*: If it is pure and clear, they are talented and wise; if it is impure and turgid, they are foolish and degenerate. In China, Zhu Xi's philosophy was called the school of *li* (*li xue*). From a Western point of view, it is a variety of idealism.

Richard P. Benton

SEE ALSO: Confucian ethics; Daoist ethics; Mencius; Wang Yangming.

Zhuangzi

IDENTIFICATION: Ancient Chinese philosopher
BORN: c. 369 B.C.E., Meng, Kingdom of Song, China
DIED: 286 B.C.E., Nanhua Hill, Caozhou, Kingdom of Qi, China
TYPE OF ETHICS: Classical history
SIGNIFICANCE: Zhuangzi (Chuang Chou in Wade-Giles spelling) developed relativism and introduced naturalism and individualism into Daoist philosophy.

Zhuangzi criticized the other schools of thought in feudal China, such as Confucianism, Mohism, and Legalism, for their artificiality. He argued that their political and social ethics were conducive to the very disharmony that their proponents appeared to be combating. Words such as "duty" and "righteousness," as well as concepts of "good" and "evil," were the unnatural products of thinkers who were ignoring the real nature of humanity and its place in the universe. The way, or *dao*, of the universe was nonjudgmental. Nothing was either good or bad. In fact, the concept "good" could not exist without the concept "bad," and thus any effort to promote one of these concepts led to the unwitting encouragement of the other. As the *Zhuangzi* (his collected works) states, "The Dao is hidden by meaningless disputation, and speech is subsumed by artificiality. The Confucians and Mohists argue endlessly that each school is 'right' and the other 'wrong,' but the Dao is universal and does not recognize right or wrong."

ZHUANGZI

The text of the *Zhuangzi* has been corrupted by additions and emendations, and there is much controversy regarding which parts constitute the inner core of Zhuangzi's thought. Despite this uncertainty, it is possible to perceive several consistent themes in the work. Zhuangzi was continuing the Daoist relativism of the *Dao De Jing*, a work attributed to a philosopher by the name of Laozi ("Master Lao"). The essence of this work is that there is a *dao*, or "way of the universe," which encompasses all things and cannot be reduced into words, which have parameters. The dao is not subject to parameters of any kind. The first paragraph in this short work states that the dao that can be spoken about or identified cannot be the true dao. Nevertheless, Laozi's book has eighty subsequent chapters that attempt to identify the manifestations of the dao. The *Dao De Jing* implies that if left alone, people are naturally peaceful and harmonious, but if they are harangued by moral argumentation, they can change for the worse. Just as concepts of shape, size, and aesthetics are all relative, so too are ethical dictates that become counterproductive because of the relativity of language.

In a sense, Zhuangzi's writing is more consistent with Laozi's injunction against trying to verbalize or even conceptualize the dao than is any other work of Daoism. Instead of sermonizing, Zhuangzi's work primarily relates anecdotes and parables, leaving the reader to intuit the universality of the dao. Reality and illusion are integral parts of the dao, and the sage does not try to distinguish between the two. Thus, Zhuangzi states simply that, on a given night, he dreamed that he was a butterfly but wondered if he were a butterfly dreaming that he was a man. In order for skepticism to be in accord with the dao, it must be an all-inclusive skepticism that doubts even doubt itself.

Instead of despairing at this uncertainty, Zhuangzi suggests that one should act as if what one is doing is real and important but should also know that it might be an illusion. This is an important point in understanding Zhuangzi's ethics. He does not dismiss moral behavior, and he frequently suggests that one should live simply and harmoniously with others. What he does dismiss, however, is the act of attributing much importance to what one does. According to Zhuangzi, therefore, ceremonies and sermons do nothing to induce moral behavior. Simplicity, and by inference what is "good," can be achieved only by "getting closer to the dao."

When Zhuangzi's wife died and he beat on a drum instead of mourning for her, he answered his critics by explaining that perhaps his wife had evolved into a happier existence than that which she had enjoyed while in human form. It was not wrong to have loved her and to miss her, but it was wrong to mourn her change from one form to another. Zhuangzi's parables point out that one cannot be certain what is best

1613

for other people and that one should therefore avoid imposing tentative and uncertain values on others.

In several tales in the *Zhuangzi*, men who, because they are criminals, have been punished by amputation seem to possess considerable wisdom, most of which has to do with not valuing things, including their limbs. Zhuangzi suggests that these men are in some ways more honest than others and have attained contentment and even "virtue" by losing that which other people strive so desperately to keep.

Zhuangzi also ridiculed those who would try to define the dao as a philosophy of action or ethics, perhaps anticipating the plethora of "The Zen of . . ." and the "Dao of . . ." literature that abounds today. A famous bandit by the name of "Robber Zhi," to whom an entire chapter of the *Zhuangzi* is devoted, is said to have argued that there is even a dao of stealing: "There is cleverness in locating the booty, courage and heroism in taking it, and the intelligence of plotting the theft. Finally, there is the honesty of dividing it fairly."

Although Zhuangzi calls for individualism and skeptical relativity, he does not argue in favor of selfishness or dissipation. Instead, his ethics consist of leaving other people to decide for themselves what is right and wrong and having no state, religion, or social organization make such determinations. To Zhuangzi, one could best perfect oneself by blending with nature and not competing with it. Only when people ceased to interfere with nature or with other people could there be peace.

Hilel B. Salomon

FURTHER READING

Allinson, Robert. *Chuang-Tzu for Spiritual Transformation.* Albany: State University of New York Press, 1989.

Giles, Herbert Allen, trans. *Chuang Tzu: Taoist Philosopher and Chinese Mystic.* 2d rev. ed. London: Allen & Unwin, 1961.

Hansen, Chad. *A Daoist Theory of Chinese Thought: A Philosophical Interpretation.* New York: Oxford University Press, 2000.

Kjellberg, Paul, and Philip J. Ivanhoe, eds. *Essays on Skepticism, Relativism, and Ethics in the "Zhuangzi."* New York: State University of New York Press, 1996.

Waley, Arthur. *Three Ways of Thought in Ancient China.* Garden City, N.Y.: Doubleday, 1956.

Watson, Burton, trans. *The Complete Works of Chuang Tzu.* New York: Columbia University Press, 1968.

Wu, Kuang-ming. *The Butterfly as Companion: Meditations on the First Three Chapters of the Chuang Tzu.* Albany: State University of New York Press, 1990.

SEE ALSO: Confucian ethics; Confucius; Daoist ethics; Laozi.

Zionism

IDENTIFICATION: Historical movement to establish a national Jewish state in Palestine, or, the political movement supporting the national and international interests of modern Israel

DATE: Formally established on August 29, 1897

TYPE OF ETHICS: Race and ethnicity

SIGNIFICANCE: The original Zionists believed that the reestablishment of a Jewish state was the only realistic means of escaping virulent anti-Semitism and the only way that Jews could fully implement Judaism as a way of life. Modern day Zionism is a form of nationalism which is closely associated with the extreme complexity and moral ambiguities of the Israeli-Palestinian conflict.

In 1882, after a series of pogroms (organized persecutions of Jews) in Russia, Russian Jewish youths formed a group called the Ḥovevei Ẓiyyon ("Lovers of Zion") to promote immigration to Palestine. "Zion" is the ancient Hebrew poetic term for the abode of the faithful; specifically, Jerusalem and the Holy Land. The Ḥovevei Ẓiyyon began what was called "practical Zionism."

In 1896, after witnessing anti-Semitic demonstrations in Paris resulting from the Dreyfus affair, Theodor Herzl wrote *The Jewish State*, in which he reasoned that if the Jewish army officer Alfred Dreyfus could be falsely convicted of treason in a country supposedly as enlightened and ethical as France simply because he was Jewish, there was no hope for Jews to live in peace anywhere except in an independent Jewish national state. Subsequently, Herzl organized "political Zionism" on a worldwide scale at the First Zionist Congress in Basel, Switzerland, in 1897.

After Herzl's death in 1904, Zionist leaders worked tirelessly in the face of Arab hostility and the horrors of the Holocaust to bring about the founding of the state of Israel on May 14, 1948. By the 1980's, practically all Jews of the Diaspora had become committed to Zionism, or at least to its mission of supporting Israel and human rights for Jews.

Andrew C. Skinner

SEE ALSO: Anti-Semitism; Bigotry; Hitler, Adolf; Holocaust; Israeli-Palestinian conflict; Nationalism; Nazism; Oppression; Pogroms.

Zoroastrian ethics

DEFINITION: Ethical values and principles of the Zoroastrian religion

TYPE OF ETHICS: Religious ethics

SIGNIFICANCE: Zoroastrian ethics emphasizes personal free choice and individual responsibility for good or evil behavior, measured according to a person's effects in the world. It has heavily influenced the ethical doctrines of Judaism, Christianity, Islam, and Buddhism.

Zoroastrian doctrine teaches that human beings freely choose right or wrong behavior and are personally responsible for their conduct. To achieve lasting happiness, people should recognize and engage in right conduct as it is defined in Zoroastrian teachings. At death, the good and evil thoughts, words, and actions of each person are judged by God; the good souls are rewarded in Paradise, while the bad are punished in Hell. Right and wrong conduct, which are clearly defined in Zoroastrian texts, encompass thoughts, words, and actions.

The basic doctrines of Zoroastrianism were first expressed in the *Gathas* (inspired poems, or *manthra*), which were composed from approximately 1700 to 1500 B.C.E. Their author, Zoroaster (Zarathustra), was a priest in a preliterate society probably in eastern Iran, where he experienced a series of divine visions and a call to teach all people a new spiritual way that would become the first divinely revealed world religion.

This way emphasizes right conduct and teaches a cosmic duality of two opposing divine spirits: the All-Wise and Good God (Ahura Mazda) and the All-Ignorant and Evil Adversary (Angra Mainyu). During Zoroaster's life, a system of rituals and customs developed as part of the new religion, many of them adapted from the older polytheistic religion that he had practiced. These rituals and customs are strikingly similar to early Hindu religious observances, suggesting a common origin of Hinduism and Zoroastrianism.

By 600 B.C.E., Zoroastrianism had become the state religion of the widespread Persian Empire and eventually was adapted by peoples from the borders of Greece in the West to those of India and China in the East. It remained the official state religion of Persia until around 700 C.E., when Islam replaced it. Through the twelve centuries that followed, it gradually lost both prestige and membership. It continues to be practiced in small communities, chiefly in Iran and India.

ETHICAL DOCTRINE

Human conduct plays a crucial role in the fate of the world, according to Zoroastrian teachings. By choosing the right conduct defined by Zoroaster, humans join the All-Wise God and the accompanying six holy immortal ones and other divinities (*yazatas*), including Mithra, in an ongoing cosmic battle against the Adversary and his followers, the race of evil ones.

This battle, which began when the Adversary attacked the newly created world, will continue to rage until righteousness finally overcomes evil, the savior of the world appears, and the day of final judgment arrives. Therefore, the personal choices in daily human life are a battleground of good and evil forces. When individuals choose good thoughts, words, and actions, they support the All-Wise One and strengthen the world's prosperity, growth, and natural order: the power of the just (*asha*). When individuals choose evil thoughts, words, and actions, they support the Adversary and increase distortion, decay, and conflict in the world: the power of the evil force (*drug*). Followers of this teaching must, therefore, recognize and follow right conduct, resist the temptations of wrong conduct, and purify themselves when they think, say, or do evil.

Human conduct not only influences the outcome of the cosmic battle of good and evil but also is the

Zoroastrians reading their holy book, Avesta, at a festival in Iran in early 2002. (AP/Wide World Photos)

sole basis of individual reward or punishment in life after death. After death, humans continue to exist in a spiritual state and are judged by the All-Wise God regarding their right or wrong conduct; good and evil conduct are placed on the scale of justice to determine reward or punishment in an afterlife of paradise or hell, with a shadowy place for the indeterminate ones.

Thus, good conduct leads to a place of joy and peace, while evil conduct leads to a place of suffering and conflict. Another judgment and a permanent assignment occur on the day of resurrection and judgment, when all living and dead people meet and are finally judged based on their conduct to be sent to either eternal life in a perfect material paradise or final destruction.

RIGHT CONDUCT

Since both individual and world salvation depend on the sum of an individual's own thoughts, words, and actions, the precepts of right conduct are paramount. They are the means of both fighting evil and supporting good in daily life. Good thoughts include intention and effort to preserve good and oppose evil. Good words include prayers, agreements, and promises. Good actions include protection of the natural world, a perfect creation of the All-Wise God.

These precepts entail many rituals that are found in other religions: daily prayer, careful preparation of food, and caring for the poor and sick. Other, less common practices include marrying next of kin (brother-sister, father-daughter), conserving land and vegetation, protecting water and fire from pollution, and treating carefully dead bodies and waste material. Conserving the purity found in nature (vegetation, lakes, and so forth) and purifying unclean pollutants (decaying flesh, sewage, and so forth) become the basis of personal and world salvation.

INFLUENCE OF ETHICS

Although Zoroastrian ethics have insignificant direct influence today, they have indirectly influenced modern societies through other religions, including Judaism, Christianity, and Buddhism, which adapted and preserved these teachings. This influence occurred when these religions came into prolonged contact with Zoroastrianism and Zoroastrian ideas gained recognition and respect.

Chief among the adapted teachings are these: Individuals are solely responsible for their own spiritual destinies; the individuals freely choose good or evil conduct; individuals can learn to support good and oppose evil conduct; conduct has permanent moral consequences; and salvation is based on the sum of thoughts, words, and actions. These ethical ideas survive today in religions practiced by millions of people.

Patricia H. Fulbright

FURTHER READING

Boyce, Mary. *Zoroastrians: Their Religious Beliefs and Practices.* London: Routledge & Kegan Paul, 1979. Reprint. New York: Routledge, 2001.

Choksy, Jamsheed K. *Evil, Good, and Gender: Facets of the Feminine in Zoroastrian Religious History.* New York: Peter Lang, 2002.

Duchesne-Guillemin, Jacques. *Symbols and Values in Zoroastrianism: Their Survival and Renewal.* New York: Harper & Row, 1966.

Frye, Richard N. *The Heritage of Persia.* Cleveland, Ohio: World Publishing, 1963.

Kriwaczek, Paul. *In Search of Zarathustra: The First Prophet and the Ideas That Changed the World.* London: Weidenfeld & Nicolson, 2002.

SEE ALSO: Akbar the Great; Buddhist ethics; Choice; Christian ethics; Hindu ethics; Islamic ethics; Jewish ethics.

Bibliography

This bibliography includes introductory texts, anthologies, and other secondary sources on general moral philosophy; a selection of primary and secondary sources in applied ethics, metaethics, and problems in ethics; primary and secondary sources on social and political philosophy; and important recent publications in general ethics that have not yet had a chance to attain canonical stature in the field. Texts are listed by subject. Some are entered under more than one category heading where appropriate, but this practice has been kept to a minimum. The most significant primary texts in ethics are listed separately in the Time Line of Primary Works in Moral and Ethical Philosophy. For narrowly focused texts on specific ethical topics, consult the Further Reading listings in individual essays.

CONTENTS

INTRODUCTORY TEXTS

Almeder, Robert. *Human Happiness and Morality: A Brief Introduction to Ethics.* Amherst, N.Y.: Prometheus Books, 2000.

Blackburn, Simon. *Being Good: An Introduction to Ethics.* Oxford, England: Oxford University Press, 2001.

_____. *Ethics: A Very Short Introduction.* Oxford, England: Oxford University Press, 2003.

Feinberg, Joel, and Russ Shafer-Landau, eds. *Reason and Responsibility: Readings in Some Basic Problems of Philosophy.* 11th ed. Belmont, Calif.: Wadsworth/Thomson Learning, 2002.

Jones, W. T., et al., eds. *Approaches to Ethics: Representative Selections from Classical Times to the Present.* 3d ed. New York: McGraw-Hill, 1977.

McNaughton, David. *Moral Vision: An Introduction to Ethics.* New York: Basil Blackwell, 1988.

Pojman, Louis P. *Ethics: Discovering Right and Wrong.* 2d ed. Belmont, Calif.: Wadsworth, 1995.

Rachels, James, ed. *The Right Thing to Do: Basic Readings in Moral Philosophy.* New York: Random House, 1989.

Solomon, Robert C. *Ethics: A Brief Introduction.* New York: McGraw-Hill, 1984.

Sommers, Christina, and Fred Sommers, eds. *Everyday Life: Introductory Readings in Ethics.* 4th ed. Fort Worth, Tex.: Harcourt Brace College, 1997.

Tännsjö, Torbjörn. *Understanding Ethics: An Introduction to Moral Theory.* Edinburgh: Edinburgh University Press, 2002.

Tiles, J. E. *Moral Measures: An Introduction to Ethics, West and East.* New York: Routledge, 2000.

Timmons, Mark. *Moral Theory: An Introduction.* Lanham, Md.: Rowman & Littlefield, 2002.

Waluchow, Wilfrid J. *The Dimensions of Ethics: An Introduction to Ethical Theory.* Peterborough, Ont.: Broadview Press, 2003.

Williams, Gerald J. *A Short Introduction to Ethics.* Lanham, Md.: University Press of America, 1999.

HISTORY OF ETHICS

SURVEYS

Becker, Lawrence C., and Charlotte B. Becker, eds. *A History of Western Ethics.* 2d ed. New York: Routledge, 2003.

Bourke, Vernon J. *History of Ethics.* 2 vols. Garden City, N.Y.: Doubleday, 1968.

Denise, Theodore C., Nicholas P. White, and Sheldon P. Peterfreund, eds. *Great Traditions in Ethics.* 10th ed. Belmont, Calif.: Wadsworth, 2002.

Langston, Douglas C. *Conscience and Other Virtues: From Bonaventure to MacIntyre.* University Park: Pennsylvania State University Press, 2001.

MacIntyre, Alasdair. *A Short History of Ethics: A History of Moral Philosophy from the Homeric Age to the Twentieth Century.* 2d ed. London: Routledge, 1998.

Payne, Robert. *The Corrupt Society: From Ancient Greece to Present-Day America.* New York: Praeger, 1975.

Robertson, Archibald. *Morals in World History.* Reprint. New York: Haskell House, 1974.

Solomon, Robert C., and Kathleen M. Higgins, eds. *From Africa to Zen: An Invitation to World Philosophy.* 2d ed. Lanham, Md.: Rowman & Littlefield, 2003.

Strauss, Leo, and Joseph Cropsey, eds. *History of Political Philosophy.* 3d ed. Chicago: University of Chicago Press, 1987.

Wagner, Michael F. *An Historical Introduction to Moral Philosophy.* Englewood Cliffs, N.J.: Prentice-Hall, 1991.

FOCUSED STUDIES

Adkins, Arthur W. H. *Merit and Responsibility: A Study in Greek Values.* New York: Oxford University Press, 1960. Reprint. Chicago: University of Chicago Press, 1975.

Baker, Robert, Dorothy Porter, and Roy Porter, eds. *The Codification of Medical Morality: Historical and Philosophical Studies of the Formalization of Western Medical Morality in the Eighteenth and Nineteenth Centuries.* Dordrecht, The Netherlands: Kluwer, 1993.

Beiser, Frederick. *The Fate of Reason: German Philosophy from Kant to Fichte.* Cambridge, Mass.: Harvard University Press, 1987.

Bloomfield, Morton W. *The Seven Deadly Sins: An Introduction to the History of a Religious Concept, with Special Reference to Medieval English Literature.* East Lansing: Michigan State College Press, 1952.

Carrick, Paul. *Medical Ethics in Antiquity: Philosophical Perspectives on Abortion and Euthanasia.* Boston: Reidel, 1985.

Cassirer, Ernst. *The Philosophy of the Enlightenment.* Translated by Fritz C. A. Koelln and James P. Pettegrove. Boston: Beacon Press, 1955.

Coons, John E., and Patrick M. Brennan. *By Nature Equal: The Anatomy of a Western Insight.* Princeton, N.J.: Princeton University Press, 1999.

Cooper, David E. *The Measure of Things: Humanism, Humility, and Mystery.* New York: Oxford University Press, 2002.

Cottingham, John. *Philosophy and the Good Life: Reason and the Passions in Greek, Cartesian, and Psychoanalytic Ethics.* New York: Cambridge University Press, 1998.

Crocker, Lester G. *Nature and Culture: Ethical Thought in the French Enlightenment.* Baltimore: Johns Hopkins University Press, 1963.

Durant, Will, and Ariel Durant. *The Age of Voltaire: A History of Civilization in Western Europe from 1715 to 1756, with Special Emphasis on the Conflict Between Religion and Philosophy.* New York: Simon & Schuster, 1965.

Gay, Peter. *The Enlightenment: An Interpretation.* 2 vols. New York: Knopf, 1966-69. Reprint. New York: Norton, 1977.

Gillespie, Michael Allen. *Nihilism Before Nietzsche.* Chicago: University of Chicago Press, 1995.

Golomb, Jacob. *In Search of Authenticity: Existentialism from Kierkegaard to Camus.* New York: Routledge, 1995.

Kouvelakis, Stathis. *Philosophy and Revolution:*

From Kant to Marx. Translated by Geoffrey Goshgarian. Preface by Frederic Jameson. New York: Verso, 2003.

Liu Xiusheng. *Mencius, Hume, and the Foundations of Ethics.* Burlington, Vt.: Ashgate, 2003.

Long, A. A. *Hellenistic Philosophy: Stoics, Epicureans, Sceptics.* 2d ed. Berkeley: University of California Press, 1986.

Malpas, Jeff, ed. *From Kant to Davidson: Philosophy and the Idea of the Transcendental.* New York: Routledge, 2003.

Myers, Milton L. *The Soul of Modern Economic Man: Ideas of Self-Interest, Thomas Hobbes to Adam Smith.* Chicago: University of Chicago Press, 1983.

Navia, Luis E. *Classical Cynicism: A Critical Study.* Westport, Conn.: Greenwood Press, 1996.

O'Manique, John. *The Origins of Justice: The Evolution of Morality, Human Rights, and Law.* Philadelphia: University of Pennsylvania Press, 2003.

Raphael, David Daiches. *British Moralists, 1650-1800.* 2 vols. Oxford, England: Clarendon Press, 1969.

Rowe, Christopher. *An Introduction to Greek Ethics.* London: Hutchinson, 1976.

Smith, H. Shelton. *Changing Conceptions of Original Sin.* New York: Scribner's, 1955.

Sorabji, Richard. *Animal Minds and Human Morals: The Origins of the Western Debate.* Ithaca, N.Y.: Cornell University Press, 1995.

Swabey, William Curtis. *Ethical Theory: From Hobbes to Kant.* New York: Philosophical Library, 1961.

Vesey, Godfrey, ed. *Idealism, Past and Present.* New York: Cambridge University Press, 1982.

Walters, Kerry S., and Lisa Portmess, eds. *Ethical Vegetarianism: From Pythagoras to Peter Singer.* Albany: State University of New York Press, 1999.

Warnock, Mary. *Ethics Since 1900.* 3d ed. New York: Oxford University Press, 1978.

Watson, John. *Hedonistic Theories from Aristippus to Spencer.* Bristol, Avon, England: Thoemmes Press, 1993.

Wenley, Robert. *Stoicism and Its Influence.* New York: Cooper Square, 1963.

Willey, Basil. *The English Moralists.* New York: W. W. Norton, 1964.

Willey, Thomas E. *Back to Kant: The Revival of Kantianism in German Social and Historical Thought, 1860-1914.* Detroit, Mich.: Wayne State University Press, 1978.

Wyatt-Brown, Bertram. *Southern Honor: Ethics and Behavior in the Old South.* New York: Oxford University Press, 1982.

CONTEMPORARY, POSTMODERN, AND POST-HOLOCAUST MORAL PHILOSOPHY

Adams, Robert Merrihew. *Finite and Infinite Goods: A Framework for Ethics.* New York: Oxford University Press, 1999.

Adorno, Theodor. *Problems of Moral Philosophy.* Edited by Thomas Schröder. Translated by Rodney Livingstone. Stanford, Calif.: Stanford University Press, 2000.

Améry, Jean. *At the Mind's Limits: Contemplations by a Survivor on Auschwitz and Its Realities.* Translated by Sidney Rosenfeld and Stella P. Rosenfeld. Bloomington: Indiana University Press, 1980.

Arkes, Hadley. *First Things: An Inquiry into the First Principles of Morals and Justice.* Princeton, N.J.: Princeton University Press, 1986.

Banki, Judith H., and John T. Pawlikowski, eds. *Ethics in the Shadow of the Holocaust: Christian and Jewish Perspectives.* Franklin, Wis.: Sheed & Ward, 2001.

Cook, John W. *Morality and Cultural Differences.* New York: Oxford University Press, 1999.

Cooper, Neil. *The Diversity of Moral Thinking.* New York: Oxford University Press, 1981.

Cunningham, Robert L. *Situationism and the New Morality.* New York: Appleton-Century-Crofts, 1970.

Demarco, Joseph P., and Richard M. Fox, eds. *New Directions in Ethics: The Challenge of Applied Ethics.* London: Routledge & Kegan Paul, 1986.

Derrida, Jacques. *Ethics, Institutions, and the Right to Philosophy.* Edited and translated by Peter Pericles Trifonas. Lanham, Md.: Rowman & Littlefield, 2002.

Donagan, Alan. *The Theory of Morality.* Chicago: University of Chicago Press, 1977.

Feldman, Fred. *Utilitarianism, Hedonism, and Desert: Essays in Moral Philosophy.* New York: Cambridge University Press, 1997.

Frankl, Viktor. *Man's Search for Meaning: An Intro-*

duction to Logotherapy. 4th ed. Boston: Beacon Press, 1992.

Garrard, Eve, and Geoffrey Scarre, eds. *Moral Philosophy and the Holocaust*. Burlington, Vt.: Ashgate, 2003.

Gert, Bernard. *The Moral Rules: A New Rational Foundation for Morality*. New York: Harper & Row, 1970.

_____. *Morality: A New Justification of the Moral Rules*. New York: Oxford University Press, 1989.

Gewirth, Alan. *Reason and Morality*. Chicago: University of Chicago Press, 1978.

Goldman, Alan H. *Moral Knowledge*. New York: Routledge, 1988.

Grayling, A. C. *Meditations for the Humanist: Ethics for a Secular Age*. New York: Oxford University Press, 2002.

Grisez, Germain G., and Russell B. Shaw. *Beyond the New Morality: The Responsibilities of Freedom*. 3d ed. Notre Dame, Ind.: University of Notre Dame Press, 1988.

Groarke, Louis. *The Good Rebel: Understanding Freedom and Morality*. Madison, N.J.: Fairleigh Dickinson University Press, 2002.

Haas, Peter J. *Morality After Auschwitz: The Radical Challenge of the Nazi Ethic*. Philadelphia: Fortress Press, 1988.

Harman, Gilbert. *The Nature of Morality*. New York: Oxford University Press, 1977.

Hatley, James. *Suffering Witness: The Quandary of Responsibility After the Irreparable*. Albany: State University of New York Press, 2000.

Hinde, Robert A. *Why Good Is Good: The Sources of Morality*. New York: Routledge, 2002.

Hocutt, Max. *Grounded Ethics: The Empirical Bases of Normative Judgments*. New Brunswick, N.J.: Transaction, 2000.

Illies, Christian F. R. *The Grounds of Ethical Judgment: New Transcendental Arguments in Moral Philosophy*. New York: Oxford University Press, 2003.

Kane, Robert. *Through the Moral Maze: Searching for Absolute Values in a Pluralistic World*. New York: Paragon House, 1994. Reprint. Armonk, N.Y.: North Castle Books, 1996.

Kruschwitz, Robert B., and Robert C. Roberts, eds. *The Virtues: Contemporary Essays on Moral Character*. Belmont, Calif.: Wadsworth, 1987.

Mackie, John. *Ethics: Inventing Right and Wrong*. New York: Penguin Books, 1977.

McShea, Robert J. *Morality and Human Nature*. Philadelphia: Temple University Press, 1990.

Madsen, Richard, and Tracy B. Strong, eds. *The Many and the One: Religious and Secular Perspectives on Ethical Pluralism in the Modern World*. Princeton, N.J.: Princeton University Press, 2003.

May, Todd. *The Moral Theory of Poststructuralism*. University Park: Pennsylvania State University, 1995.

Midgley, Mary. *Can't We Make Moral Judgments?* New York: St. Martin's Press, 1993.

Navia, Luis E., and Eugene Kelly, eds. *Ethics and the Search for Values*. New York: Prometheus Books, 1980.

Nussbaum, Martha C. *Upheavals of Thought: The Intelligence of Emotions*. New York: Cambridge University Press, 2001.

O'Neil, Shane. *Impartiality in Context: Grounding Justice in a Pluralist World*. Albany: State University of New York Press, 1997.

Outka, Gene, and John P. Reeder, eds. *Prospects for a Common Morality*. Princeton, N.J.: Princeton University Press, 1993.

Paul, Ellen Frankel, Fred D. Miller, Jr., and Jeffrey Paul, eds. *Virtue and Vice*. New York: Cambridge University Press, 1998.

Poole, Ross. *Morality and Modernity*. London: Routledge, 1991.

Prichard, H. A. *Moral Writings*. Edited by Jim MacAdam. New York: Oxford University Press, 2002.

Putnam, Hilary. *The Collapse of the Fact/Value Dichotomy, and Other Essays*. Cambridge, Mass.: Harvard University Press, 2002.

Rachels, James. *The Elements of Moral Philosophy*. 3d ed. Boston: McGraw-Hill, 1999.

_____, ed. *Moral Problems: A Collection of Philosophical Essays*. 3d ed. New York: Harper & Row, 1979.

Railton, Peter. *Facts, Values, and Norms: Essays Toward a Morality of Consequence*. New York: Cambridge University Press, 2003.

Rhonheimer, Martin. *Natural Law and Practical Reason: A Thomist View of Moral Autonomy*. Translated by Gerald Malsbary. New York: Fordham University Press, 2000.

Rorty, Richard. *Objectivity, Relativism, and Truth.* New York: Cambridge University Press, 1991.

Ross, W. D. *The Right and the Good.* New ed. New York: Oxford University Press, 2002.

Rost, H. T. D. *The Golden Rule: A Universal Ethic.* Oxford, England: George Ronald, 1986.

Roubiczek, Paul. *Ethical Values in the Age of Science.* London: Cambridge University Press, 1969.

Shaw, William H. *Contemporary Ethics: Taking Account of Utilitarianism.* Malden, Mass.: Blackwell, 1999.

Simms, Karl, ed. *Ethics and the Subject.* Atlanta: Rodopi, 1997.

Singer, Peter. *Practical Ethics.* 2d ed. New York: Cambridge University Press, 1993.

_____, ed. *A Companion to Ethics.* Cambridge, Mass.: Blackwell Reference, 1993.

Slote, Michael A. *From Morality to Virtue.* New York: Oxford University Press, 1992.

Snare, Francis. *The Nature of Moral Thinking.* London: Routledge, 1992.

Spaemann, Robert. *Basic Moral Concepts.* Translated by T. J. Armstrong. New York: Routledge, 1989.

Sprigge, Timothy. *The Rational Foundations of Ethics.* New York: Routledge, 1988.

Stout, Jeffrey. *Ethics After Babel: The Languages of Morals and Their Discontents.* Princeton, N.J.: Princeton University Press, 2001.

Stratton-Lake, Philip, ed. *Ethical Intuitionism: Reevaluations.* New York: Oxford University Press, 2002.

Teichman, Jenny. *Ethics and Reality: Collected Essays.* Burlington, Vt.: Ashgate, 2001.

Timmons, Mark. *Morality Without Foundations: A Defense of Ethical Contextualism.* New York: Oxford University Press, 1999.

Wallace, James. *Virtues and Vices.* Ithaca, N.Y.: Cornell University Press, 1978.

Wallach, Michael A., and Lise Wallach. *Rethinking Goodness.* Albany: State University of New York Press, 1990.

White, James E. *Contemporary Moral Problems.* 7th ed. Belmont, Calif.: Wadsworth, 2003.

Wyschogrod, Edith, and Gerald P. McKenny, eds. *The Ethical.* Malden, Mass.: Blackwell, 2003.

SOCIAL AND POLITICAL PHILOSOPHY

Allen, Amy. *The Power of Feminist Theory: Domination, Resistance, Solidarity.* Boulder, Colo.: Westview Press, 1999.

Allison, Lincoln, ed. *The Utilitarian Response: The Contemporary Viability of Utilitarian Political Philosophy.* London: Sage, 1990.

Anderson, Charles W. *A Deeper Freedom: Liberal Democracy as an Everyday Morality.* Madison: University of Wisconsin Press, 2002.

Arendt, Hannah. *On Revolution.* 1963. Reprint. New York: Viking Press, 1990.

_____. *The Origins of Totalitarianism.* New ed. San Diego, Calif.: Harcourt Brace, 1979.

Bakunin, Mikhail Aleksandrovich. *Bakunin on Anarchism.* Edited and translated by Sam Dolgoff. New York: Black Rose Books, 2002.

Ball, Carlos A. *The Morality of Gay Rights: An Exploration in Political Philosophy.* New York: Routledge, 2003.

Beiner, Ronald. *Liberalism, Nationalism, Citizenship: Essays on the Problem of Political Community.* Vancouver: UBC Press, 2003.

Berlin, Isaiah. *Four Essays on Liberty.* Oxford, England: Oxford University Press, 1969.

Birt, Robert E., ed. *The Quest for Community and Identity: Critical Essays in Africana Social Philosophy.* Lanham, Md.: Rowman & Littlefield, 2002.

Burke, Edmund. *Reflections on the Revolution in France.* Edited by Conor Cruise O'Brien. Harmondsworth, England: Penguin Books, 1969.

Callinicos, Alex, ed. *Marxist Theory.* New York: Oxford University Press, 1989.

Cannon, Bob. *Rethinking the Normative Content of Critical Theory: Marx, Habermas, and Beyond.* New York: Palgrave, 2001.

Carey, George W., ed. *Freedom and Virtue: The Conservative/Libertarian Debate.* Wilmington, Del.: Intercollegiate Studies Institute, 1998.

Cassirer, Ernst. *The Myth of the State.* New Haven, Conn.: Yale University Press, 1973.

Cecil, Andrew R. *Equality, Tolerance, and Loyalty: Virtues Serving the Common Purpose of Democracy.* Dallas: University of Texas at Dallas Press, 1990.

Diggs, Bernard James. *The State, Justice, and the Common Good: An Introduction to Social and*

Political Philosophy. Glenview, Ill.: Scott, Foresman, 1974.

Durkheim, Émile. *Professional Ethics and Civic Morals*. Translated by Cornelia Brookfield. Preface by Bryan S. Turner. New York: Routledge, 1992.

Dyson, Michael Eric. *The Michael Eric Dyson Reader*. New York: Basic Civitas Books, 2004.

Flathman, Richard E. *Freedom and Its Conditions: Discipline, Autonomy, and Resistance*. New York: Routledge, 2003.

Foucault, Michel. *The History of Sexuality*. Translated by Robert Hurley. New York: Vintage, 1990.
_____. *Power/Knowledge: Selected Interviews and Other Writings, 1972-1977*. Edited by Colin Gordon. Translated by Colin Gordon et al. New York: Pantheon Books, 1980.

Gautier, Jeffrey A. *Hegel and Feminist Social Criticism: Justice, Recognition, and the Feminine*. Albany: State University of New York Press, 1997.

Geuss, Raymond. *Public Goods, Private Goods*. Princeton, N.J.: Princeton University Press, 2001.

Goldman, Emma. *Anarchism, and Other Essays*. 1917. Reprint. New York: Dover, 1969.

Gordon, Avery F., and Christopher Newfield, eds. *Mapping Multiculturalism*. Minneapolis: University of Minnesota Press, 1996.

Gramsci, Antonio. *Selections from the Prison Notebooks of Antonio Gramsci*. Edited and translated by Quintin Hoare and Geoffrey Nowell Smith. New York: International, 1999.

Grant, Ruth W. *Hypocrisy and Integrity: Machiavelli, Rousseau, and the Ethics of Politics*. Chicago: University of Chicago Press, 1997.

Gregg, Samuel. *On Ordered Liberty: A Treatise on the Free Society*. Lanham, Md.: Lexington Books, 2003.

Hamilton, Alexander, James Madison, and John Jay. *The Federalist Papers*. New York: Washington Square Press, 1976.

Hamilton, Lawrence. *The Political Philosophy of Needs*. New York: Cambridge University Press, 2003.

Haraway, Donna. *The Haraway Reader*. New York: Routledge, 2004.

Hirschmann, Nancy J. *The Subject of Liberty: Toward a Feminist Theory of Freedom*. Princeton, N.J.: Princeton University Press, 2003.

Jaggar, Alison M. *Feminist Politics and Human Nature*. Totowa, N.J.: Rowman & Littlefield, 1988.

Joseph, Jonathan. *Social Theory: Conflict, Cohesion, and Consent*. Edinburgh: Edinburgh University Press, 2003.

Kaplan, Laura Duhan, and Laurence F. Bove, eds. *Philosophical Perspectives on Power and Domination: Theories and Practices*. Atlanta: Rodopi, 1997.

Kracauer, Siegfried. *The Mass Ornament: Weimar Essays*. Translated and Edited by Thomas Y. Levin. Cambridge, Mass.: Harvard University Press, 1995.

Levine, Andrew. *A Future for Marxism? Althusser, the Analytical Turn, and the Revival of Socialist Theory*. London: Pluto, 2003.

Lister, Ruth. *Citizenship: Feminist Perspectives*. 2d ed. Washington Square, N.Y.: New York University Press, 2003.

Lott, Tommy L., ed. *African-American Philosophy: Selected Readings*. Upper Saddle River, N.J.: Prentice Hall, 2002.

Lott, Tommy L., and John P. Pittman, eds. *A Companion to African-American Philosophy*. Malden, Mass.: Blackwell, 2003.

Lukacs, Georg. *History and Class Consciousness: Studies in Marxist Dialectics*. Translated by Rodney Livingstone. Cambridge, Mass.: MIT Press, 1983.

Machiavelli, Niccolò, and Francesco Guicciardini. *The Sweetness of Power: Machiavelli's "Discourses" and Guicciardini's "Considerations."* Translated by James V. Atkinson and David Sices. Dekalb: Northern Illinois University Press, 2002.

MacKenzie, Ian, and Shane O'Neill, eds. *Reconstituting Social Criticism: Political Morality in an Age of Scepticism*. New York: St. Martin's Press, 1999.

Marcuse, Herbert. *Eros and Civilization: A Philosophical Inquiry into Freud*. Boston: Beacon, 1974.

Montaigne, Michel de. *The Complete Works: Essays, Travel Journal, Letters*. Translated by Donald M. Frame. Introduction by Stuart Hampshire. New York: Alfred A. Knopf, 2003.

Nealon, Jeffrey T., and Caren Irr, eds. *Rethinking the Frankfurt School: Alternative Legacies of Cultural Critique*. Albany: State University of New York Press, 2002.

Pascal, Blaise. *"The Provincial Letters"; "Pensées"; and "Scientific Treatises."* Translated by W. F. Trotter, Thomas M'Crie, and Richard Scofield. 2d ed. Chicago: Encyclopedia Britannica, 1990.

Peirce, Charles. *The Essential Peirce: Selected Philosophical Writings.* Edited by Nathan Houser and Christian Kloesel. 2 vols. Bloomington: Indiana University Press, 1992-1998.

Pelczynski, Z. B., and John Gray, eds. *Conceptions of Liberty in Political Philosophy.* London: Athlone Press, 1984.

Rand, Ayn. *Capitalism: The Unknown Ideal.* New York: New American Library, 1966.

_____. *The Virtue of Selfishness: A New Concept of Egoism.* New York: New American Library, 1964.

Rawls, John. *Justice as Fairness: A Restatement.* Edited by Erin Kelly. Cambridge, Mass.: Belknap Press, 2001.

Read, Herbert. *Anarchy and Order: Essays in Politics.* Boston: Beacon Press, 1971.

Ricour, Paul. *Freud and Philosophy: An Essay on Interpretation.* Translated by Denis Savage. New Haven, Conn.: Yale University Press, 1970.

Santoro, Emilio. *Autonomy, Freedom, and Rights: A Critique of Liberal Subjectivity.* Boston: Kluwer Academic, 2003.

Schweitzer, Albert. *The Decay and Restoration of Civilization.* Translated by C. T. Campion. New York: Macmillan, 1953.

Selborne, David. *The Principle of Duty: An Essay on the Foundations of the Civic Order.* Notre Dame, Ind.: University of Notre Dame Press, 2001.

Sen, Amartya. *Rationality and Freedom.* Cambridge, Mass.: Belknap Press, 2002.

Sevenhuijsen, Selma. *Citizenship and the Ethics of Care: Feminist Considerations on Justice, Morality, and Politics.* Translated by Liz Savage. New York: Routledge, 1998.

Shweder, Richard A., Martha Minow, and Hazel Rose Markus, eds. *Engaging Cultural Differences: The Multicultural Challenge in Liberal Democracies.* New York: Russell Sage Foundation, 2002.

Solomon, Robert. *A Passion for Justice: Emotions and the Origins of the Social Contract.* Reading, Mass.: Addison-Wesley, 1990.

Stewart, Robert M., ed. *Readings in Social and Political Philosophy.* 2d ed. New York: Oxford University Press, 1996.

Tocqueville, Alexis de. *Democracy in America.* In *"Democracy in America" and Two Essays on America.* Translated by Gerald E. Bevan. Introduction by Isaac Kramnick. London: Penguin, 2003.

West, Cornel. *The Cornel West Reader.* New York: Basic Civitas Books, 1999.

Ziarek, Ewa Płonowska. *An Ethics of Dissensus: Postmodernity, Feminism, and the Politics of Radical Democracy.* Stanford, Calif.: Stanford University Press, 2001.

ALTERNATIVE VIEWPOINTS AND CRITIQUES OF TRADITIONAL ETHICS

Alexander, Richard D. *The Biology of Moral Systems.* Hawthorne, N.Y.: Aldine De Gruyter, 1987.

Brennan, Samantha, ed. *Feminist Moral Philosophy.* Calgary, Alta.: University of Calgary Press, 2002.

Bujo, Bénézet. *Foundations of an African Ethic: Beyond the Universal Claims of Western Morality.* Translated by Brian McNeil. New York: Crossroad, 2001.

Cameron, Donald. *The Purpose of Life: Human Purpose and Morality from an Evolutionary Perspective.* Bristol, England: Woodhill, 2001.

Casebeer, William D. *Natural Ethical Facts: Evolution, Connectionism, and Moral Cognition.* Cambridge, Mass.: MIT Press, 2003.

Daly, Mary. *Gynecology: The Metaethics of Radical Feminism.* Boston: Beacon Press, 1978.

Frazer, Elizabeth, Jennifer Hornsby, and Sabina Lovibond, eds. *Ethics: A Feminist Reader.* New York: Oxford University Press, 1992.

Friedman, Marilyn. *What Are Friends For? Feminist Perspectives on Personal Relationships and Moral Theory.* Ithaca, N.Y.: Cornell University Press, 1993.

Gill, Jerry H. *Native American Worldviews: An Introduction.* Amherst, N.Y.: Humanity Books, 2002.

Hallowell, A. Irving. *Ojibwa Ontology, Behavior, and World View.* Indianapolis: Bobbs-Merrill, 1960.

Held, Virginia. *Feminist Morality.* Chicago: University of Chicago Press, 1993.

Irigaray, Luce. *This Sex Which Is Not One.* Translated by Catherine Porter and Carolyn Burke. Ithaca, N.Y.: Cornell University Press, 1985.

Kittay, Eva Feder, and Diana T. Meyers, eds. *Women and Moral Theory.* Totowa, N.J.: Rowman & Littlefield, 1987.

Li Chenyang, ed. *The Sage and the Second Sex: Confucianism, Ethics, and Gender.* Foreword by Patricia Ebrey. Chicago: Open Court, 2000.

Lloyd, Genevieve. *The Man of Reason: "Male" and "Female" in Western Philosophy.* 2d ed. Minneapolis: University of Minnesota Press, 1993.

MacIntyre, Alasdair. *Whose Justice? Which Rationality?* Notre Dame, Ind.: University of Notre Dame Press, 1988.

May, Larry, and Shari Collins Sharratt. *Applied Ethics: A Multicultural Approach.* Englewood Cliffs, N.J.: Prentice-Hall, 1994.

Pearsall, Marilyn, ed. *Women and Values: Readings in Recent Feminist Philosophy.* Belmont, Calif.: Wadsworth, 1986.

Prokhovnik, Raia. *Rational Woman: A Feminist Critique of Dichotomy.* New York: Routledge, 1999.

Ruddick, Sara. *Maternal Thinking: Toward a Politics of Peace.* Boston: Beacon Press, 1995.

Sterba, James P. *Three Challenges to Ethics: Environmentalism, Feminism, and Multiculturalism.* New York: Oxford University Press, 2001.

_____, ed. *Ethics: Classical Western Texts in Feminist and Multicultural Perspectives.* New York: Oxford University Press, 2000.

Tong, Rosemarie. *Feminine and Feminist Ethics.* Belmont, Calif.: Wadsworth, 1993.

Waters, Anne, ed. *American Indian Thought: Philosophical Essays.* Malden, Mass.: Blackwell, 2004.

PERSONAL AND INTERPERSONAL ETHICS

Allen, Anita L. *Why Privacy Isn't Everything: Feminist Reflections on Personal Accountability.* Lanham, Md.: Rowman & Littlefield, 2003.

Baker, Robert B., Kathleen J. Wininger, and Frederick A. Elliston, eds. *Philosophy and Sex.* 3d ed. Amherst, N.Y.: Prometheus Books, 1998.

Benjamin, Martin. *Splitting the Difference: Compromise and Integrity in Ethics and Politics.* Lawrence: University of Kansas Press, 1990.

Blum, Lawrence A. *Friendship, Altruism, and Morality.* London: Routledge & Kegan Paul, 1980.

Bok, Sissela. *Lying: Moral Choice in Public and Private Life.* 2d ed. New York: Vintage Books, 1999.

Campbell, Richmond. *Self-Love and Self-Respect: A Philosophical Study of Egoism.* Ottawa, Canada: Canadian Library of Philosophy, 1979.

Cates, Diana Fritz. *Choosing to Feel: Virtue, Friendship, and Compassion for Friends.* Notre Dame, Ind.: University of Notre Dame Press, 1997.

Cox, Damian, Marguerite La Caze, and Michael P. Levine. *Integrity and the Fragile Self.* Burlington, Vt.: Ashgate, 2003.

Dobel, J. Patrick. *Public Integrity.* Baltimore: Johns Hopkins University Press, 1999.

Doris, John M. *Lack of Character: Personality and Moral Behavior.* New York: Cambridge University Press, 2002.

Edwards, R. B. *Freedom, Responsibility, and Obligation.* The Hague: Martinus Nijhoff, 1970.

Etzioni, Amitai. *The Spirit of Community: Rights, Responsibilities, and the Communitarian Agenda.* New York: Crown, 1993.

Feezell, Randolph M., and Curtis L. Hancock. *How Should I Live?* New York: Paragon House, 1991.

Fingarette, Herbert. *On Responsibility.* New York: Basic Books, 1967.

_____. *Self-Deception.* New York: Humanities Press, 1969.

Fischer, John M., ed. *Moral Responsibility.* Ithaca, N.Y.: Cornell University Press, 1986.

Fishkin, James S. *The Limits of Obligation.* New Haven, Conn.: Yale University Press, 1982.

Fox, Richard M., and Joseph P. DeMarco. *The Immorality of Promising.* Amherst, N.Y.: Humanity Books, 2001.

Friedman, Marilyn. *What Are Friends For? Feminist Perspectives on Personal Relationships and Moral Theory.* Ithaca, N.Y.: Cornell University Press, 1993.

Gauthier, David P., ed. *Morality and Rational Self-Interest.* Englewood Cliffs, N.J.: Prentice-Hall, 1970.

Giannetti, Eduardo. *Lies We Live By: The Art of Self-Deception.* London: Bloomsbury, 2000.

Gilligan, Carol. *The Birth of Pleasure.* New York: Alfred A. Knopf, 2002.

Grunebaum, James O. *Friendship: Liberty, Equality, and Utility.* Albany: State University of New York Press, 2003.

Hocker, Joyce L., and William M. Wilmot. *Interpersonal Conflict.* 5th ed. Boston: McGraw-Hill, 1998.

Kreiglstein, Werner J. *Compassion: A New Philosophy of the Other.* Amsterdam: Rodopi, 2002.

Lerman, Evelyn. *Safer Sex: The New Morality.* Buena Park, Calif.: Morning Glory Press, 2000.

Little, Adrian. *The Politics of Community: Theory and Practice.* Edinburgh: Edinburgh University Press, 2002.

Lomasky, Loren. *Persons, Rights, and the Moral Community.* New York: Oxford University Press, 1987.

Mappes, Thomas A., and Jane S. Zembaty, eds. *Social Ethics.* New York: McGraw-Hill, 1977.

Martin, Mike W. *Self-Deception and Morality.* Lawrence: University Press of Kansas, 1986.

Mellema, Gregory. *Beyond the Call of Duty: Supererogation, Obligation, and Offense.* Albany: State University of New York Press, 1991.

Morris, Herbert. *Freedom and Responsibility.* Stanford, Calif.: Stanford University Press, 1961.

Murphy, Jeffrie G. *Getting Even: Forgiveness and Its Limits.* New York: Oxford University Press, 2003.

Murphy, Jeffrie G., and Jean Hampton. *Forgiveness and Mercy.* New York: Cambridge University Press, 1988.

Olson, Robert. *The Morality of Self-Interest.* New York: Harcourt, Brace & World, 1965.

Pittman, Frank S. *Private Lies: Infidelity and the Betrayal of Intimacy.* New York: Norton, 1990.

Plummer, Kenneth. *Intimate Citizenship: Private Decisions and Public Dialogues.* Seattle: University of Washington Press, 2003.

Russell, Bertrand. *Marriage and Morals.* 1929. Reprint. New York: H. Liveright, 1957.

Scanlon, T. M. *What We Owe to Each Other.* Cambridge, Mass.: Belknap Press of Harvard University Press, 1998.

Spiegel, James S. *Hypocrisy: Moral Fraud and Other Vices.* Grand Rapids, Mich.: Baker Books, 1999.

Stoltenberg, John. *Refusing to Be a Man: Essays on Sex and Justice.* Rev. ed. New York: UCL Press, 2000

Thielicke, Helmut. *The Ethics of Sex.* Translated by John W. Doberstein. Grand Rapids, Mich.: Baker Book House, 1975.

Thomas, Laurence. *Living Morally: A Psychology of Moral Character.* Philadelphia: Temple University Press, 1989.

Zimmerman, Michael J. *The Concept of Moral Obligation.* New York: Cambridge University Press, 1996.

RELIGION

GENERAL AND COMPARATIVE STUDIES

Adams, Robert M. *The Virtue of Faith.* New York: Oxford University Press, 1987.

Asad, Talal. *Formations of the Secular: Christianity, Islam, Modernity.* Stanford, Calif.: Stanford University Press, 2003.

Barclay, William. *The Ten Commandments for Today.* Grand Rapids, Mich.: Wm. B. Eerdmans, 1977.

Barnard, G. William, and Jeffrey J. Kripal, eds. *Crossing Boundaries: Essays on the Ethical Status of Mysticism.* New York: Seven Bridges Press, 2002.

Brown, Robert McAfee, and Sydney Thomson Brown, eds. *A Cry for Justice: The Churches and Synagogues Speak.* New York: Paulist Press, 1989.

Buckman, Robert. *Can We Be Good Without God? Biology, Behavior, and the Need to Believe.* Amherst, N.Y.: Prometheus Books, 2002.

Byrne, Peter. *The Philosophical and Theological Foundations of Ethics: An Introduction to Moral Theory and Its Relation to Religious Belief.* 2d ed. New York: St. Martin's Press, 1999.

Crawford, S. Cromwell, ed. *World Religions and Global Ethics.* New York: Paragon House, 1989.

Dewey, John. *A Common Faith.* New Haven, Conn.: Yale University Press, 1991.

Evans, Donald. *Faith, Authenticity, and Morality.* Toronto: University of Toronto Press, 1980.

Greeley, Andrew M., Jacob Neusner, and Mary Greeley Durkin. *Virtues and Vices: Stories of the Moral Life.* Louisville, Ky.: Westminster John Knox Press, 1999.

Gustafson, James M. *Ethics from a Theocentric Perspective.* 2 vols. Chicago: University of Chicago Press, 1981-1984.

Kaiser, Walter C., Jr. *Toward Old Testament Ethics.* Grand Rapids, Mich.: Zondervan, 1983.

Maston, Thomas Bufford. *Biblical Ethics: A Guide to the Ethical Message of Scriptures from Genesis Through Revelation.* Macon, Ga.: Mercer University Press, 1982.

Mitchell, Basil. *Morality: Religious and Secular.* Oxford, England: Clarendon Press, 1985.

Nielsen, Kai, and Hendrik Hart. *Search for Community in a Withering Tradition: Conversations Between a Marxian Atheist and a Calvinian Christian.* Lanham, Md.: University Press of America, 1990.

Pike, E. Royston. *Ethics of the Great Religions.* London: C. A. Watts, 1948.

Smurl, James F. *Religious Ethics: A Systems Approach.* Englewood Cliffs, N.J.: Prentice-Hall, 1972.

Wright, Christopher J. H. *Living as the People of God: The Relevance of Old Testament Ethics.* Leicester, England: InterVarsity Press, 1983.

CHRISTIANITY

Blount, Brian K. *Then the Whisper Put on Flesh: New Testament Ethics in an African American Context.* Nashville, Tenn.: Abingdon Press, 2001.

Boff, Leonardo, and Clodovis Boff. *Introducing Liberation Theology.* Translated by Paul Burns. Maryknoll, N.Y.: Orbis Books, 1987.

Bonhoeffer, Dietrich. *Ethics.* Edited by Eberhard Bethge. Translated by Neville H. Smith. London: SCM Press, 1971.

_____. *Letters and Papers from Prison.* Enl. ed. Edited by Eberhard Bethge. Translated by R. H. Fuller. New York: Macmillan, 1972.

Butler, Joseph. *Fifteen Sermons Preached at the Rolls Chapel and A Dissertation upon the Nature of Virtue.* London: G. Bell, 1964.

Davis, Henry. *Moral and Pastoral Theology.* New York: Sheed & Ward, 1952.

Feuerbach, Ludwig. *The Essence of Christianity.* Translated by George Eliot. New York: Harper & Row, 1957.

Grisez, Germain. *Christian Moral Principles.* Vol. 1 in *The Way of the Lord.* Chicago: Franciscan Herald Press, 1983.

Hare, John E. *God's Call: Moral Realism, God's Commands, and Human Autonomy.* Grand Rapids, Mich.: W. B. Eerdmans, 2001.

Hauerwas, Stanley. *The Peaceable Kingdom: A Primer in Christian Ethics.* Notre Dame, Ind.: University of Notre Dame Press, 1983.

Kirkpatrick, Frank G. *A Moral Ontology for a Theistic Ethic: Gathering the Nations in Love and Justice.* Burlington, Vt.: Ashgate, 2003.

Lewis, C. S. *The Four Loves.* New York: Harcourt Brace Jovanovich, 1991.

_____. *Mere Christianity.* London: Collins, 1988.

McFaul, Thomas R. *Transformation Ethics: Developing the Christian Moral Imagination.* Lanham, Md.: University Press of America, 2003.

Pinn, Anthony B., ed. *Moral Evil and Redemptive Suffering: A History of Theodicy in African-American Religious Thought.* Gainesville: University Press of Florida, 2002.

Ramsey, Paul. *Deeds and Rules in Christian Ethics.* 2d ed. Lanham, Md.: University Press of America, 1983.

Robinson, J. A. T. *Christian Morals Today.* Philadelphia: Westminster Press, 1964.

Rooney, Paul. *Divine Command Morality.* Brookfield, Vt.: Avebury, 1996.

Scott, Ernest F. *The Ethical Teaching of Jesus.* 1924. Reprint. New York: Macmillan, 1936.

Spohn, William C. *Go and Do Likewise: Jesus and Ethics.* New York: Continuum, 1999.

Stassen, Glen H., and David P. Gushee. *Kingdom Ethics: Following Jesus in Contemporary Context.* Downers Grove, Ill.: InterVarsity Press, 2003.

OTHER FAITHS

Bocking, Brian. *The Oracles of the Three Shrines: Window on Japanese Religion.* Richmond, England: Curzon, 2001.

Boyce, Mary. *Zoroastrians: Their Religious Beliefs and Practices.* London: Routledge & Kegan Paul, 1979. Reprint. New York: Routledge, 2001.

Brandt, Richard B. *Hopi Ethics: A Theoretical Analysis.* Chicago: University of Chicago Press, 1954.

Bstan-dzin Rgya-mtsho [Fourteenth Dalai Lama]. *Buddha Heart, Buddha Mind: Living the Four Noble Truths.* Translated by Robert R. Barr. New York: Crossland, 2000.

Casey, John. *Pagan Virtue: An Essay in Ethics.* Oxford, England: Clarendon Press, 1991.

Cook, Michael. *Commanding Right and Forbidding Wrong in Islamic Thought.* New York: Cambridge University Press, 2000.

Dan, Joseph. *Jewish Mysticism and Jewish Ethics.* Seattle: University of Washington Press, 1986.

Danto, Arthur C. *Mysticism and Morality: Oriental Thought and Moral Philosophy.* New York: Basic Books, 1972.

Dharmasiri, Gunapala. *Fundamentals of Buddhist Ethics*. Antioch, Calif.: Golden Leaves, 1989.

Esposito, John L. *Islam: The Straight Path*. New York: Oxford University Press, 1988.

Harrod, Howard. *Renewing the World: Plains Indian Religion and Morality*. Tucson: University of Arizona Press, 1987.

Harvey, Peter. *An Introduction to Buddhist Ethics: Foundations, Values, and Issues*. New York: Cambridge University Press, 2000.

Hashmi, Sohail H., ed. *Islamic Political Ethics: Civil Society, Pluralism, and Conflict*. Princeton, N.J.: Princeton University Press, 2002.

Horne, James R. *The Moral Mystic*. Waterloo, Ont.: Wilfrid Laurier University Press, 1983.

Kamali, Mohammad Hashim. *The Dignity of Man: An Islamic Perspective*. Cambridge, England: Islamic Texts Society, 2002.

Kasenene, Peter. *Religious Ethics in Africa*. Kampala, Uganda: Fountain, 1998.

Kaur, Gurnam, ed. *The Sikh Perspective of Human Values*. Patiala, India: Publication Bureau, Punjabi University, 1998.

Keown, Damien. *The Nature of Buddhist Ethics*. New York: St. Martin's Press, 1992.

King, Winston L. *In the Hope of Nibbana: An Essay on Theravada Buddhist Ethics*. Lasalle, Ill.: Open Court, 1964.

Maccoby, Hyam. *The Philosophy of the Talmud*. Richmond, England: Curzon, 2002.

Martin, Michael. *Atheism, Morality, and Meaning*. Amherst, N.Y.: Prometheus Books, 2002.

Mbiti, John S. *African Religions and Philosophy*. 2d rev. ed. Portsmouth, N.H.: Heinemann, 1990.

Muilenburg, James. *An Eye for An Eye: The Place of Old Testament Ethics Today*. Downers Grove, Ill.: InterVarsity Press, 1983.

Perrett, Roy W. *Hindu Ethics: A Philosophical Study*. Honolulu: University of Hawaii Press, 1998.

Ravi, Illa. *Foundations of Indian Ethics*. New Delhi: Kaveri Books, 2002.

Ruether, Rosemary. *Gaia and God: An Ecofeminist Theology of Earth Healing*. San Francisco: HarperSanFrancisco, 1992.

Saddhatissa, H. *Buddhist Ethics: Essence of Buddhism*. London: Allen & Unwin, 1970.

Sangharakshita. *The Bodhisattva Ideal: Wisdom and Compassion in Buddhism*. Birmingham, England: Windhorse, 1999.

Sharma, I. C. *Ethical Philosophies of India*. Edited and revised by Stanley M. Daugert. New York: Harper & Row, 1970.

Steinsaltz, Adin. *Opening the "Tanya": Discovering the Moral and Mystical Teachings of a Classic Work of Kabbalah*. Translated by Yaacov Tauber. San Francisco: Jossey-Bass, 2003.

Tachibana, Shundo. *The Ethics of Buddhism*. London: Oxford University Press, 1926. Reprint. Richmond, Surrey, England: Curzon Press, 1992.

Wainwright, William J. *Mysticism: A Study of Its Nature, Cognitive Value, and Moral Implications*. Madison: University of Wisconsin Press, 1981.

MORAL EDUCATION AND DEVELOPMENT

Allman, Dwight D., and Michael D. Beaty, eds. *Cultivating Citizens: Soulcraft and Citizens in Contemporary America*. Lanham, Md.: Lexington Books, 2002.

Carr, David. *Educating the Virtues: An Essay on the Philosophical Psychology of Moral Development and Education*. New York: Routledge, 1991.

Cummings, William K., Maria Teresa Tatto, and John Hawkins, eds. *Values Education for Dynamic Societies: Individualism or Collectivism*. Hong Kong: Comparative Education Research Centre, University of Hong Kong, 2001.

Deigh, John. *The Sources of Moral Agency: Essays in Moral Psychology and Freudian Theory*. New York: Cambridge University Press, 1996.

Fleishman, Joel L., and Bruce L. Payne. *Ethical Dilemmas and the Education of Policymakers*. Hastings-on-Hudson, N.Y.: Hastings Center, Institute of Society, Ethics, and the Life Sciences, 1980.

Fraenkel, Jack. *How to Teach About Values: An Analytic Approach*. Englewood Cliffs, N.J.: Prentice-Hall, 1977.

Freire, Paulo. *Education for Critical Consciousness*. New York: Seabury Press, 1973.

Freud, Sigmund. "The Dissolution of the Oedipus Complex." In *The Standard Edition of the Complete Psychological Works of Sigmund Freud*, edited by James Strachey. Vol. 19. London: Hogarth, 1953-1974.

_____. "Femininity." In *New Introductory Lectures on Psychoanalysis*. Translated and edited by James Strachey. New York: W. W. Norton, 1965.

_____. "On Some Psychical Consequences of the Anatomical Distinction Between the Sexes." In *The Standard Edition of the Complete Psychological Works of Sigmund Freud*, edited by James Strachey. Vol. 19. London: Hogarth, 1953-1974.

_____. *Three Essays on the Theory of Sexuality*. Translated and edited by James Strachey. Foreword by Nancy J. Chodorow. New York: Basic Books, 2000.

Ivanhoe, Philip J. *Confucian Moral Self Cultivation*. 2d ed. Indianapolis: Hackett, 2000.

Jarrett, James L. *The Teaching of Values: Caring and Appreciation*. New York: Routledge, 1991.

Kohlberg, Lawrence. *The Philosophy of Moral Development: Moral Stages and the Idea of Justice*. San Francisco, Calif.: Harper & Row, 1981.

_____. *The Psychology of Moral Development: The Nature and Validity of Moral Stages*. San Francisco, Calif.: Harper & Row, 1984.

McGinnis, James, and Kathleen McGinnis. *Parenting for Peace and Justice*. Maryknoll, N.Y.: Orbis Books, 1981.

Montessori, Maria. *Education and Peace*. Chicago: Regnery, 1972.

Nelson, C. Ellis, ed. *Conscience: Theological and Psychological Perspectives*. New York: Newman Press, 1973.

Noddings, Nel. *Caring: A Feminine Approach to Ethics and Moral Education*. Berkeley: University of California Press, 1984.

Pritchard, Ivor. *Moral Education and Character*. Washington, D.C.: U.S. Department of Education, 1988.

Raths, Louis, et al. *Values and Teaching*. 2d ed. Columbus, Ohio: Charles E. Merrill, 1978.

Reardon, Betty. *Comprehensive Peace Education: Educating for Global Responsibility*. New York: Teachers College Press, 1988.

_____. *Education for a Culture of Peace in a Gender Perspective*. Paris: UNESCO, 2001.

Salomon, Gavriel, and Baruch Nevo, eds. *Peace Education: The Concept, Principles, and Practices Around the World*. Mahwah, N.J.: Lawrence Erlbaum Associates, 2002.

Shotter, John. *Social Accountability and Selfhood*. Oxford, England: Basil Blackwell, 1984.

Sichel, Betty A. *Moral Education: Character, Community, and Ideals*. Philadelphia: Temple University Press, 1988.

Simon, Sidney, et al. *Values and Teaching: Working with Values in the Classroom*. Sunderland, Mass.: Values Press, 1991.

Sterba, James P. *How to Make People Just: A Practical Reconciliation of Alternative Conceptions of Justice*. Totowa, N.J.: Rowman & Littlefield, 1988.

Tam, Henry, ed. *Punishment, Excuses, and Moral Development*. Brookfield, Vt.: Avebury, 1996.

AESTHETICS, LANGUAGE, AND REPRESENTATION

Benjamin, Walter. *Illuminations*. London: Pimlico, 1999.

Cavell, Stanley. *Disowning Knowledge in Seven Plays of Shakespeare*. Updated ed. New York: Cambridge University Press, 2003.

_____. *The World Viewed: Reflections on the Ontology of Film*. Enl ed. Cambridge, Mass.: Harvard University Press, 1979.

Clor, Harry M. *Obscenity and Public Morality: Censorship in a Liberal Society*. Chicago: University of Chicago Press, 1969.

Cohen-Almagor, Raphael. *Speech, Media, and Ethics—The Limits of Free Expression: Critical Studies on Freedom of Expression, Freedom of the Press, and the Public's Right to Know*. New York: Palgrave, 2001.

Collingwood, R. G. *The Principles of Art*. Reprint. London: Oxford University Press, 1970.

Cornell, Drucilla, ed. *Feminism and Pornography*. New York: Oxford University Press, 2000.

Danto, Arthur C. *The Transfiguration of the Commonplace: A Philosophy of Art*. Cambridge, Mass.: Harvard University Press, 1981.

Eagleton, Terry. *Ideology: An Introduction*. New York: Verso, 1991.

_____. *Sweet Violence: The Idea of the Tragic*. Malden, Mass.: Blackwell, 2003.

Eldridge, Richard. *The Persistence of Romanticism: Essays in Philosophy and Literature*. New York: Cambridge University Press, 2001.

Englehardt, Elaine E., and Ralph D. Barney. *Media and Ethics: Principles for Moral Decisions*.

Belmont, Calif.: Wadsworth Thomson Learning, 2002.

Freeden, Michael. *Ideology.* Oxford, England: Oxford University Press, 2003.

Froese, Katrin. *Rousseau and Nietzsche: Toward an Aesthetic Morality.* Lanham, Md.: Lexington Books, 2001.

Haapala, Arto, and Oiva Kuisma, eds. *Aesthetic Experience and the Ethical Dimension: Essays on Moral Problems in Aesthetics.* Helsinki: Philosophical Society of Finland, 2003.

Habermas, Jürgen. *Moral Consciousness and Communicative Action.* Translated by Christian Lenhardt and Shierry Weber Nicholsen. Cambridge, Mass.: MIT Press, 1990.

Hegel, Georg Wilhelm Friedrich. *Hegel on Tragedy.* Edited by Anne Paolucci and Henry Paolucci. Smyrna, Del.: Griffon House, 2001.

Hygen, Johan B. *Morality and the Muses.* Translated by Harris E. Kaasa. Minneapolis, Minn.: Augsburg, 1965.

Johnson, Barbara. *A World of Difference.* Baltimore: Johns Hopkins University Press, 1987.

Juffer, Jane. *At Home with Pornography: Women, Sex, and Everyday Life.* New York: New York University Press, 1998.

Künne, Wolfgang. *Conceptions of Truth.* New York: Clarendon, 2003.

Marcuse, Herbert. *The Aesthetic Dimension: Toward a Critique of Marxist Aesthetics.* Boston: Beacon Press, 1978.

Mulvey, Laura. *Visual and Other Pleasures.* Bloomington: Indiana University Press, 1989.

Nussbaum, Martha C. *The Fragility of Goodness: Luck and Ethics in Greek Tragedy and Philosophy.* New York: Cambridge University Press, 1986.

Quine, W. V. *Pursuit of Truth.* Cambridge, Mass.: Harvard University Press, 1990.

Rorty, Richard. *Objectivity, Relativism, and Truth.* New York: Cambridge University Press, 1991.

Smart, John Jamieson C. *Ethics, Persuasion, and Truth.* Boston: Routledge & Kegan Paul, 1984.

Smith, R. Scott. *Virtue Ethics and Moral Knowledge: Philosophy of Language After MacIntyre and Hauerwas.* Burlington, Vt.: Ashgate, 2003.

Stevenson, Charles L. *Ethics and Language.* New Haven, Conn.: Yale University Press, 1960.

Whorf, Benjamin L. *Language, Thought, and Reality: Selected Writings of Benjamin Lee Whorf.* Edited and introduction by John B. Carroll. Foreword by Stuart Chase. Cambridge, Mass.: The MIT Press, 1967.

Žižek, Slavoj. *The Sublime Object of Ideology.* New York: Verso, 1997.

_____, ed. *Mapping Ideology.* New York: Verso, 1995.

APPLIED ETHICS

ANIMALS AND THE ENVIRONMENT

Allsopp, Bruce. *Ecological Morality.* London: Frederick Muller, 1972.

Attfield, Robin. *Environmental Ethics: An Overview for the Twenty-First Century.* Malden, Mass.: Blackwell, 2003.

Cooper, David E., and Jay A. Palmer, eds. *The Environment in Question: Ethics and Global Issues.* New York: Routledge, 1992.

Cothran, Helen, ed. *Animal Experimentation: Opposing Viewpoints.* San Diego, Calif.: Greenhaven Press, 2002.

Dower, Nigel, ed. *Ethics and the Environmental Responsibility.* Brookfield, Vt.: Avebury, 1989.

Fox, Michael A. *The Case for Animal Experimentation: An Evolutionary and Ethical Perspective.* Berkeley: University of California Press, 1986.

Frey, R. G. *Interests and Rights: The Case Against Animals.* Oxford, England: Clarendon Press, 1980.

Fritsch, Albert J., et al. *Environmental Ethics: Choices for Concerned Citizens.* Garden City, N.Y.: Anchor Press, 1980.

George, Kathryn Paxton. *Animal, Vegetable, or Woman? A Feminist Critique of Ethical Vegetarianism.* Albany: State University of New York Press, 2000.

Kealey, Daniel. *Revisioning Environmental Ethics.* Albany: State University of New York Press, 1990.

Light, Andrew, and Holmes Rolston III, eds. *Environmental Ethics: An Anthology.* Malden, Mass.: Blackwell, 2003.

Linzey, Andrew. *Christianity and the Rights of Animals.* New York: Crossroad, 1987.

Regan, Tom. *The Case for Animal Rights.* Berkeley: University of California Press, 1983.

_____, ed. *Earthbound: New Introductory*

Essays in Environmental Ethics. New York: Random House, 1984.

Regan, Tom, and Peter Singer, eds. *Animal Rights and Human Obligations.* 2d ed. Englewood Cliffs, N.J.: Prentice-Hall, 1989.

Rolston, Holmes, III. *Environmental Ethics: Duties to and Values in the Natural World.* Philadelphia: Temple University Press, 1988.

Scherer, Donald, ed. *Upstream/Downstream: Issues in Environmental Ethics.* Philadelphia: Temple University Press, 1990.

Scherer, Donald, and Thomas Attig, eds. *Ethics and the Environment.* Englewood Cliffs, N.J.: Prentice-Hall, 1983.

Scully, Matthew. *Dominion: The Power of Man, the Suffering of Animals, and the Call to Mercy.* New York: St. Martin's Press, 2002.

Singer, Peter. *Animal Liberation.* New York: Ecco, 2002.

CORPORATE AND PROFESSIONAL CONDUCT

Adams, Julian. *Freedom and Ethics in the Press.* New York: R. Rosen Press, 1983.

Bayles, Michael. *Professional Ethics.* 2d ed. Belmont, Calif.: Wadsworth, 1989.

Cahn, Steven M. *Saints and Scamps: Ethics in Academia.* Totowa, N.J.: Rowman & Littlefield, 1986.

Callahan, Joan C., ed. *Ethical Issues in Professional Life.* New York: Oxford University Press, 1988.

Cook, Fred J. *The Corrupted Land: The Social Morality of Modern America.* New York: Macmillan, 1966.

Cooper, David E. *Ethics for Professionals in a Multicultural World.* Upper Saddle River, N.J.: Pearson/Prentice Hall, 2004.

Corey, Gerald, Marianne Schneider Corey, and Patrick Callanan. *Issues and Ethics in the Helping Professions.* Pacific Grove, Calif.: Brooks-Cole, 1993.

Davidson, D. Kirk. *The Moral Dimension of Marketing: Essays on Business Ethics.* Chicago: American Marketing Association, 2002.

De George, Richard T. *Business Ethics.* 5th ed. Upper Saddle River, N.J.: Prentice Hall, 1999.

Durkheim, Émile. *Professional Ethics and Civic Morals.* Translated by Cornelia Brookfield. Preface by Bryan S. Turner. New York: Routledge, 1992.

Elliott, Deni, ed. *Responsible Journalism.* Beverly Hills, Calif.: Sage, 1986.

Elliston, Frederick, and Michael Feldberg, eds. *Moral Issues in Police Work.* Totowa, N.J.: Rowman & Allen, 1985.

Fletcher, Joseph. *Moral Responsibility: Situation Ethics at Work.* Philadelphia: Westminster Press, 1967. Reprint. Louisville, Ky.: Westminster John Knox Press, 1997.

Gardner, Howard, Mihaly Csikszentmihalyi, and William Damon. *Good Work: When Excellence and Ethics Meet.* New York: Basic Books, 2001.

Harwood, Sterling, ed. *Business as Ethical and Business as Usual.* Boston: Jones & Bartlett, 1994.

Johnson, Larry, and Bob Phillips. *Absolute Honesty: Building a Corporate Culture That Values Straight Talk and Rewards Integrity.* New York: American Management Association, 2003.

Laczniak, Gene R., and Patrick E. Murphy. *Ethical Marketing Decisions: The Higher Road.* Boston: Allyn & Bacon, 1993.

McDowell, Banks. *Ethical Conduct and the Professional's Dilemma.* New York: Oxford University Press, 1991.

McQuail, Denis. *Media Accountability and Freedom of Publication.* Oxford, England: Oxford University Press, 2003.

Merod, Jim. *The Political Responsibility of the Critic.* Ithaca, N.Y.: Cornell University Press, 1987.

Merrill, John C., and Ralph D. Barney, eds. *Ethics and the Press: Readings in Mass Media Morality.* New York: Hastings House, 1975.

Meyer, Philip. *Ethical Journalism.* New York: Longman, 1987.

Muirhead, Sophia A., et al. *Corporate Citizenship in the New Century: Accountability, Transparency, and Global Stakeholder Engagement.* New York: Conference Board, 2002.

Murphy, Kevin R. *Honesty in the Workplace.* Pacific Grove, Calif.: Brooks/Cole, 1993.

Neville, Kathleen. *Internal Affairs: The Abuse of Power, Sexual Harassment, and Hypocrisy in the Workplace.* New York: McGraw-Hill, 2000.

Parker, Donn B., Susan Swope, and Bruce N. Baker. *Ethical Conflicts in Information and Computer Science, Technology, and Business.* Wellesley, Mass.: QED Information Sciences, 1990.

Pellegrino, Edmund D., et al., eds. *Ethics, Trust, and*

the Professions. Washington, D.C.: Georgetown University Press, 1991.

Pritchard, David, ed. *Holding the Media Accountable: Citizens, Ethics, and the Law.* Bloomington: Indiana University Press, 2000.

Schlegelmilch, Bodo B. *Marketing Ethics: An International Perspective.* Boston: International Thomson Business Press, 1998.

Seebauer, Edmund G., and Robert L. Barry. *Fundamentals of Ethics for Scientists and Engineers.* New York: Oxford University Press, 2001.

Smith, N. Craig, and John A. Quelch. *Ethics in Marketing.* Homewood, Ill.: Richard D. Irwin, 1993.

Smith, Rod F. *Groping for Ethics in Journalism.* 5th ed. Ames: Iowa State Press, 2003.

Solomon, Robert C., and Clancy Martin. *Above the Bottom Line: An Introduction to Business Ethics.* 3d ed. Belmont, Calif.: Wadsworth/Thomson Learning, 2004.

_____. *Ethics and Excellence: Cooperation and Integrity in Business.* New York: Oxford University Press, 1992.

Stuart, Iris, and Bruce Stuart. *Ethics in the Post-Enron Age.* Mason, Ohio: South-western/Thomson, 2004.

Thomas, Alison M., and Celian Kitzinger, eds. *Sexual Harassment: Contemporary Feminist Perspectives.* Bristol, Pa.: Open University Press, 1997.

HEALTH AND MEDICINE

Arras, John D., and Bonnie Steinbock, eds. *Ethical Issues in Modern Medicine.* 5th ed. Mountain View, Calif.: Mayfield, 1999.

Barker, Philip J., and Steve Baldwin, eds. *Ethical Issues in Mental Health.* London: Chapman & Hall, 1991.

Beauchamp, Tom L., and James F. Childress. *Principles of Biomedical Ethics.* 5th ed. New York: Oxford University Press, 2001.

Beauchamp, Tom L., and Robert M. Veatch, eds. *Ethical Issues in Death and Dying.* 2d ed. Upper Saddle River, N.J.: Prentice Hall, 1996.

Beauchamp, Tom L., and LeRoy Walters, eds. *Contemporary Issues in Bioethics.* 6th ed. Belmont, Calif.: Thomson/Wadsworth, 2003.

Bersoff, Donald N., ed. *Ethical Conflicts in Psychology.* 3d ed. Washington, D.C.: American Psychological Association, 2003.

Bloch, Sidney, and Paul Chodoff, eds. *Psychiatric Ethics.* New York: Oxford University Press, 1981.

Bouma, Hessel, III, et al. *Christian Faith, Health, and Medical Practice.* Grand Rapids, Mich.: Eerdmans, 1989.

Churchill, Larry R. *Rationing Health Care in America: Perspectives and Principles of Justice.* Notre Dame, Ind.: University of Notre Dame Press, 1987.

Edwards, Rem B., ed. *Psychiatry and Ethics.* Buffalo, N.Y.: Prometheus Books, 1982.

Forman, Edwin N., and Rosalind Ekman Ladd. *Ethical Dilemmas in Pediatrics.* New York: Springer-Verlag, 1991.

Foster, Claire. *The Ethics of Medical Research on Humans.* New York: Cambridge University Press, 2001.

Horan, Dennis J., and David Mall, eds. *Death, Dying, and Euthanasia.* Frederick, Md.: University Publications of America, 1980.

Jackson, Jennifer. *Truth, Trust, and Medicine.* New York: Routledge, 2001.

Keith-Spiegel, Patricia, and Gerald P. Koocher. *Ethics in Psychology: Professional Standards and Cases.* 2d ed. New York: Oxford University Press, 1998.

Kleespies, Phillip M. *Life and Death Decisions: Psychological and Ethical Considerations in End-of-Life Care.* Washington, D.C.: American Psychological Association, 2004.

Kluge, Eike-Henner W. *The Ethics of Deliberative Death.* Port Washington, N.Y.: Kennikat Press, 1981.

Ladd, John, ed. *Ethical Issues Relating to Life and Death.* New York: Oxford University Press, 1979.

Lammers, Stephen E., and Allen Verhey, eds. *On Moral Medicine: Theological Perspectives in Medical Ethics.* Grand Rapids, Mich.: William B. Eerdmans, 1987.

Roleff, Tamara L., and Laura K. Egendorf, eds. *Mental Illness: Opposing Viewpoints.* San Diego, Calif.: Greenhaven Press, 2000.

Shelp, Earl E., ed. *Virtue and Medicine.* Dordrecht, The Netherlands: D. Reidel, 1985.

Sherwin, Susan. *No Longer Patient: Feminist Ethics and Health Care.* Philadelphia, Pa.: Temple University Press, 1992.

Stein, Ronald. *Ethical Issues in Counseling.* Buffalo, N.Y.: Prometheus, 1990.

Stone, Alan A. *Law, Psychiatry, and Morality.* Washington, D.C.: American Psychiatric Press, 1984.

Veatch, Robert M. *The Patient as Partner: A Theory of Human-Experimentation Ethics.* Bloomington: Indiana University Press, 1987.

_____. *A Theory of Medical Ethics.* New York: Basic Books, 1981.

_____, ed. *Medical Ethics.* Boston: Jones & Bartlett, 1989.

Weir, Robert F., ed. *Ethical Issues in Death and Dying.* 2d ed. New York: Columbia University Press, 1986.

Welfel, Elizabeth Reynolds. *Ethics in Counseling and Psychotherapy: Standards, Research, and Emerging Issues.* 2d ed. Pacific Grove, Calif.: Brooks/Cole-Thomson Learning, 2002.

LAW, GOVERNMENT, AND PUBLIC POLICY

Abraham, Henry J., and Barbara A. Perry. *Freedom and the Court: Civil Rights and Liberties in the United States.* 8th ed. Lawrence: University of Kansas Press, 2003.

Alexy, Robert. *A Theory of Constitutional Rights.* Translated by Julian Rivers. New York: Oxford University Press, 2002.

Baird, Robert M., and Stuart E. Rosenbaum, eds. *Morality and the Law.* Buffalo, N.Y.: Prometheus Books, 1988.

Beauchamp, Tom L., and Terry P. Pinkard, eds. *Ethics and Public Policy: An Introduction to Ethics.* 2d ed. Englewood Cliffs, N.J.: Prentice-Hall, 1983.

Bodenheimer, Edgar. *Jurisprudence: The Philosophy and Method of the Law.* Rev. ed. Cambridge, Mass.: Harvard University Press, 1974.

Cane, Peter. *Responsibility in Law and Morality.* Portland, Oreg.: Hart, 2002.

Churchill, Robert Paul, ed. *The Ethics of Liberal Democracy: Morality and Democracy in Theory and Practice.* Providence, R.I.: Berg, 1994.

Donahue, Anne Marie, ed. *Ethics in Politics and Government.* New York: H. W. Wilson, 1989.

Feinberg, Joel. *Rights, Justice, and the Bounds of Liberty.* Princeton, N.J.: Princeton University Press, 1980.

Fullinwider, Robert K., and Claudia Mills, eds. *The Moral Foundations of Civil Rights.* Totowa, N.J.: Rowman & Littlefield, 1986.

Glazer, Nathan. *The Limits of Social Policy.* Cambridge, Mass.: Harvard University Press, 1988.

Goodin, Robert E. *Protecting the Vulnerable: A Reanalysis of our Social Responsibilities.* Chicago: University of Chicago Press, 1985.

Gordon, Scott. *Controlling the State: Constitutionalism from Ancient Athens to Today.* Cambridge, Mass.: Harvard University Press, 1999.

Hart, Herbert L. *Punishment and Responsibility: Essays in the Philosophy of Law.* New York: Oxford University Press, 1968.

Hashmi, Sohail H., ed. *Islamic Political Ethics: Civil Society, Pluralism, and Conflict.* Princeton, N.J.: Princeton University Press, 2002.

Kipnis, Kenneth, ed. *Philosophical Issues in Law.* Englewood Cliffs, N.J.: Prentice-Hall, 1977.

Koocher, Gerald P., and Patricia C. Keith-Spiegel. *Children, Ethics, and the Law.* Lincoln: University of Nebraska Press, 1990.

Lampen, John, ed. *No Alternative? Nonviolent Responses to Repressive Regimes.* York, England: W. Sessions, 2000.

LeBor, Adam, and Roger Boyes. *Seduced by Hitler: The Choices of a Nation and the Ethics of Survival.* Naperville, Ill.: Sourcebooks, 2001.

Linz, Juan J. *Totalitarian and Authoritarian Regimes.* Boulder, Colo.: Lynne Rienner, 2000.

Little, I. M. D. *Ethics, Economics, and Politics: Principles of Public Policy.* New York: Oxford University Press, 2002.

Lyons, David. *Ethics and the Rule of Law.* New York: Cambridge University Press, 1984.

MacKinnon, Catharine A. *Feminism Unmodified: Discourses on Life and Law.* Cambridge, Mass.: Harvard University Press, 1987.

Matravers, Matt, ed. *Punishment and Political Theory.* Portland, Oreg.: Hart, 1999.

Molotch, Harvey. *Managed Integration: Dilemmas of Doing Good in the City.* Berkeley: University of California Press, 1972.

Morris, Herbert. *On Guilt and Innocence: Essays in Legal Philosophy and Moral Psychology.* Berkeley: University of California Press, 1976.

Murphy, Jeffrie G. *Character, Liberty, and Law: Kantian Essays in Theory and Practice.* Boston: Kluwer Academic, 1998.

_____. *Philosophy of Law: An Introduction to Jurisprudence.* Rev ed. Boulder, Colo.: Westview Press, 1990.

Percy, Stephen L. *Disability, Civil Rights, and Public Policy: The Politics of Implementation.* Tuscaloosa, Ala.: University of Alabama Press, 1989.

Roberts, Robert North. *Ethics in U.S. Government: An Encyclopedia of Scandals, Reforms, and Legislation.* Westport, Conn.: Greenwood Press, 2001.

Roth, Timothy P. *The Ethics and the Economics of Minimalist Government.* Northampton, Mass.: Edward Elgar, 2002.

Shklar, Judith N. *The Faces of Injustice.* New Haven, Conn.: Yale University Press, 1990.

Soule, Edward. *Morality and Markets: The Ethics of Government Regulation.* Lanham, Md.: Rowman & Littlefield, 2003.

Sterba, James P. *How to Make People Just: A Practical Reconciliation of Alternative Conceptions of Justice.* Totowa, N.J.: Rowman & Littlefield, 1988.

Stripling, Scott R. *Capitalism, Democracy, and Morality.* Acton, Mass.: Copley, 1994.

Ten, C. L. *Crime, Guilt, and Punishment: A Philosophical Introduction.* New York: Oxford University Press, 1987.

Wasserstrom, Richard A., ed. *Morality and the Law.* Belmont, Calif.: Wadsworth, 1971.

Wilber, Charles K., ed. *Economics, Ethics, and Public Policy.* Lanham, Md.: Rowman & Littlefield, 1998.

Wilson, William J. *The Truly Disadvantaged: The Inner City, the Underclass, and Public Policy.* Chicago: University of Chicago Press, 1990.

INTERNATIONAL RELATIONS, IMPERIALISM, PEACE, AND WARFARE

Akehurst, Michael. *A Modern Introduction to International Law.* 6th ed. New York: Routledge, 1992.

Amin, Samir. *Imperialism and Unequal Development.* New York: Monthly Review Press, 1977.

Berberoglu, Berch. *Globalization of Capital and the Nation-State: Imperialism, Class Struggle, and the State in the Age of Global Capitalism.* Lanham, Md.: Rowman & Littlefield, 2003.

Best, Geoffrey. *Humanity in Warfare.* New York: Columbia University Press, 1980.

Brown, Chris. *Sovereignty, Rights, and Justice: International Political Theory Today.* Malden, Mass.: Blackwell, 2002.

Cady, Duane. *From Warism to Pacifism: A Moral Continuum.* Philadelphia: Temple University Press, 1989.

Childress, James. *Moral Responsibility in Conflicts: Essays on Nonviolence, War, and Conscience.* Baton Rouge: Louisiana State University Press, 1982.

Christopher, Paul. *The Ethics of War and Peace: An Introduction to Legal and Moral Issues.* 3d ed. Upper Saddle River, N.J.: Pearson/Prentice Hall, 2004.

Ellis, Anthony, ed. *Ethics and International Relations.* Manchester, England: Manchester University Press, 1986.

Forsythe, David. *Human Rights and World Politics.* Lincoln: University of Nebraska Press, 1983.

Gibney, Mark, ed. *Open Borders? Closed Societies? The Ethical and Political Issues.* New York: Greenwood, 1988.

Henkin, Louis, et al. *Right v. Might: International Law and the Use of Force.* 2d ed. New York: Council on Foreign Relations Press, 1991.

Hurrell, Andrew, and Ngaire Woods, eds. *Inequality, Globalization, and World Politics.* New York: Oxford University Press, 1999.

Kalshoven, Frits, and Liesbeth Zegveld. *Constraints on the Waging of War: An Introduction to International Humanitarian Law.* 3d ed. Geneva: International Committee of the Red Cross, 2001.

Kisala, Robert. *Prophets of Peace: Pacifism and Cultural Identity in Japan's New Religions.* Honolulu: University of Hawai'i Press, 1999.

Lugo, Luis E., ed. *Sovereignty at the Crossroads? Morality and International Politics in the Post-Cold War Era.* Lanham, Md.: Rowman & Littlefield, 1996.

Lynch, Cecelia, and Michael Loriaux, eds. *Law and Moral Action in World Politics.* Minneapolis: University of Minnesota Press, 2000.

McKim, Robert, and Jeff McMahan, eds. *The Morality of Nationalism.* New York: Oxford University Press, 1997.

Mayer, Peter, ed. *The Pacifist Conscience.* Chicago: Regnery, 1967.

Mendlovitz, Saul, ed. *On the Creation of a Just World Order.* New York: Free Press, 1975.

Miller, Richard. *Interpretations of Conflict: Ethics, Pacifism, and the Just-War Tradition.* Chicago: University of Chicago Press, 1991.

Monshipouri, Mahmood, et al., eds. *Constructing Human Rights in the Age of Globalization.* Armonk, N.Y.: M. E. Sharpe, 2003.

Rubin, Alfred P. *Ethics and Authority in International Law.* New York: Cambridge University Press, 1997.

Said, Edward. *Orientalism.* New York: Vintage Books, 1994.

Steger, Manfred B. *Judging Nonviolence: The Dispute Between Realists and Idealists.* New York: Routledge, 2003.

Teichman, Jenny. *Pacifism and the Just War.* New York: Basil Blackwell, 1986.

Tucker, Robert. *The Inequality of Nations.* New York: Basic Books, 1977.

Warren, Bill. *Imperialism: Pioneer of Capitalism.* Edited by John Sender. London: NLB, 1980.

Weil, Simone. *Simone Weil on Colonialism: An Ethic of the Other.* Edited and translated by J. P. Little. Lanham, Md.: Rowman & Littlefield, 2003.

Yoder, John Howard. *Nevertheless: The Varieties and Shortcomings of Religious Pacifism.* Scottdale, Pa.: Herald Press, 1976.

Zahn, Gordon. *War, Conscience, and Dissent.* New York: Hawthorn Books, 1967.

SOCIAL HIERARCHIES AND OPPRESSION

Allen, Amy. *The Power of Feminist Theory: Domination, Resistance, Solidarity.* Boulder, Colo.: Westview Press, 1999.

Ball, Carlos A. *The Morality of Gay Rights: An Exploration in Political Philosophy.* New York: Routledge, 2003.

Berrill, Kevin T., and Gregory M. Herek, eds. *Hate Crimes: Confronting Violence Against Lesbians and Gay Men.* Newbury Park, Calif.: Sage, 1992.

Bishop, Anne. *Becoming an Ally: Breaking the Cycle of Oppression in People.* 2d ed. New York: Palgrave, 2002.

Blauner, Bob. *Racial Oppression in America.* New York: Harper & Row, 1972.

Blumenfeld, Warren J., ed. *Homophobia: How We All Pay the Price.* Boston: Beacon Press, 1992.

Bonnie, Richard J., and Robert B. Wallace, eds. *Elder Mistreatment: Abuse, Neglect, and Exploitation in an Aging America.* Washington, D.C.: National Academies Press, 2003.

Bourdieu, Pierre. *Masculine Domination.* Translated by Richard Nice. Stanford, Calif.: Stanford University Press, 2001.

Boxill, Bernard R. *Blacks and Social Justice.* Totowa, N.J.: Rowman & Allanheld, 1984.

Brennan, Samantha, ed. *Feminist Moral Philosophy.* Calgary, Alta.: University of Calgary Press, 2002.

Cahill, Ann J. *Rethinking Rape.* Ithaca, N.Y.: Cornell University Press, 2001.

Cobble, Dorothy Sue. *The Other Women's Movement: Workplace Justice and Social Rights in Modern America.* Princeton, N.J.: Princeton University Press, 2004.

Davis, Angela Yvonne. *Women, Race, and Class.* New York: Random House, 1981.

Faludi, Susan. *Backlash: The Undeclared War Against American Women.* New York: Crown, 1991.

Gupta, Dipankar. *Interrogating Caste: Understanding Hierarchy and Difference in Indian Society.* New York: Penguin Books, 2000.

Hacker, Andrew. *Two Nations: Black and White, Separate, Hostile, Unequal.* New York: Scribner, 2003.

Hooks, Bell. *Rock My Soul: Black People and Self-Esteem.* New York: Atria Books, 2003.

Kymlicka, Will, ed. *The Rights of Minority Cultures.* New York: Oxford University Press, 1995.

Lubiano, Wahneema, ed. *The House That Race Built: Black Americans, U.S. Terrain.* New York: Pantheon, 1997.

McGilvray, Dennis B., ed. *Caste Ideology and Interaction.* New York: Cambridge University Press, 1982.

MacKinnon, Catharine A. *Sexual Harassment of Working Women.* New Haven, Conn.: Yale University Press, 1979.

Massey, Douglas S., and Nancy A. Denton. *American Apartheid: Segregation and the Making of the Underclass.* Cambridge, Mass.: Harvard University Press, 1993.

Moore, Margaret. *The Ethics of Nationalism.* New York: Oxford University Press, 2001.

Moss, Donald, ed. *Hating in the First Person Plural: Psychoanalytic Essays on Racism, Homophobia, Misogyny, and Terror.* New York: Other Press, 2003.

O'Connor, Peg. *Oppression and Responsibility: A Wittgensteinian Approach to Social Practices and Moral Theory.* University Park: Pennsylvania State University, 2002.

Okin, Susan Moller. *Justice, Gender, and the Family.* New York: Basic Books, 1989.

Pharr, Suzanne. *Homophobia: A Weapon of Sexism.* Inverness, Calif.: Chardon Press, 1988.

Russell, Diana E. H. *Sexual Exploitation: Rape, Child Sexual Abuse, and Workplace Harassment.* Beverly Hills, Calif.: Sage, 1989.

Sample, Ruth J. *Exploitation: What It Is and Why It's Wrong.* Lanham, Md.: Rowman & Littlefield, 2003.

Skaine, Rosemarie. *Power and Gender: Issues in Sexual Dominance and Harassment.* Jefferson, N.C.: McFarland & Co., 1996.

Wells-Barnett, Ida B. *On Lynchings.* Amherst, N.Y.: Humanity Books, 2002.

Wilson, Catherine, ed. *Civilization and Oppression.* Calgary, Alta.: University of Calgary Press, 1999.

DISTRIBUTION OF WEALTH AND RESOURCES

Aiken, William, and Hugh LaFollette, eds. *World Hunger and Moral Obligation.* Englewood Cliffs, N.J.: Prentice-Hall, 1977.

Amin, Samir. *Imperialism and Unequal Development.* New York: Monthly Review Press, 1977.

Bandow, Doug, and David L. Schindler, eds. *Wealth, Poverty, and Human Destiny.* Wilmington, Del.: ISI Books, 2003.

Bartkowski, John P., and Helen A. Regis. *Charitable Choices: Religion, Race, and Poverty in the Post Welfare Era.* New York: New York University, 2003.

Bentley, Lionel, and Spyros M. Maniatis, eds. *Intellectual Property and Ethics.* London: Sweet & Maxwell, 1998.

Berberoglu, Berch. *Globalization of Capital and the Nation-State: Imperialism, Class Struggle, and the State in the Age of Global Capitalism.* Lanham, Md.: Rowman & Littlefield, 2003.

Blinder, Alan S. *Hard Heads, Soft Hearts: Tough-Minded Economics for a Just Society.* Reading, Mass.: Addison-Wesley, 1987.

Blumenfeld, Samuel, ed. *Property in a Humane Society.* LaSalle, Ill.: Open Court, 1974.

Childs, James M., Jr., *Greed: Economics and Ethics in Conflict.* Minneapolis: Fortress Press, 2000.

Churchill, Larry R. *Rationing Health Care in America: Perspectives and Principles of Justice.* Notre Dame, Ind.: University of Notre Dame Press, 1987.

Dobson, Andrew, ed. *Fairness and Futurity: Essays on Sustainability and Social Justice.* New York: Oxford University Press, 1999.

Dougherty, Peter J. *Who's Afraid of Adam Smith? How the Market Got Its Soul.* New York: J. Wiley, 2002.

Dunning, John H., ed. *Making Globalization Good: The Moral Challenges of Global Capitalism.* New York: Oxford University Press, 2003.

Friedman, Milton, with Rose D. Friedman. *Capitalism and Freedom.* Chicago: University of Chicago Press, 1962.

Galbraith, John Kenneth. *The Affluent Society.* 40th anniversary ed. Boston: Houghton Mifflin, 1998.

Heilbroner, Robert L. *The Nature and Logic of Capitalism.* New York: Norton, 1985.

Hodgson, Bernard. *Economics as Moral Science.* New York: Springer, 2001.

Jacobs, Lesley A. *Pursuing Equal Opportunities: The Theory and Practice of Egalitarian Justice.* New York: Cambridge University Press, 2004.

Kaus, Mickey. *The End of Equality.* New York: Basic Books, 1992.

Kessler-Harris, Alice. *In Pursuit of Equity: Women, Men, and the Quest for Economic Citizenship in Twentieth-Century America.* New York: Oxford University Press, 2001.

Knitter, Paul F., and Chandra Muzaffar, eds. *Subverting Greed: Religious Perspectives on the Global Economy.* Maryknoll, N.Y.: Orbis Books, 2002.

Little, Daniel. *The Paradox of Wealth and Poverty: Mapping the Ethical Dilemmas of Global Development.* Boulder, Colo.: Westview Press, 2003.

Lucas, George R., Jr., and Thomas Ogletree, eds. *Lifeboat Ethics: The Moral Dilemmas of World Hunger.* New York: Harper & Row, 1976.

McCormick, Peter. *When Famine Returns: Ethics, Identity, and the Deep Pathos of Things.* Heidelberg, Germany: C. Winter, 2003.

McCuen, Gary E. *World Hunger and Social Justice.* Hudson, Wis.: Author, 1986.

Massey, Douglas S., and Nancy A. Denton. *American Apartheid: Segregation and the Making of the Underclass.* Cambridge, Mass.: Harvard University Press, 1993.

Moon, J. Donald, ed. *Responsibility, Rights, and Welfare: The Theory of the Welfare State.* Boulder, Colo.: Westview Press, 1988.

Mossberger, Karen, Caroline J. Tolbert, and Mary

Stansbury, eds. *Virtual Inequality: Beyond the Digital Divide.* Washington, D.C.: Georgetown University Press, 2003.

Olsaretti, Serena, ed. *Desert and Justice.* New York: Oxford University Press, 2003.

Pogge, Thomas W., ed. *Global Justice.* Malden, Mass.: Blackwell, 2001.

Pojman, Louis P., and Owen McLeod, eds. *What Do We Deserve? A Reader on Justice and Desert.* New York: Oxford University Press, 1999.

Schultz, Walter J. *The Moral Conditions of Economic Efficiency.* New York: Cambridge University Press, 2001.

Sen, Amartya. *On Ethics and Economics.* Oxford, England: Blackwell, 1987.

Sidel, Ruth. *Women and Children Last: The Plight of Poor Women in Affluent America.* New York: Penguin Books, 1987.

Singer, Joseph William. *The Edges of the Field: Lessons on the Obligations of Ownership.* Boston: Beacon Press, 2000.

Singer, Peter. *Rich and Poor.* Cambridge, England: Cambridge University Press, 1979.

Smeeding, Timothy M., Michael O'Higgins, and Lee Rainwater, eds. *Poverty, Inequality, and Income Distribution in Comparative Perspective.* Washington, D.C.: Urban Institute Press, 1990.

Stripling, Scott R. *Capitalism, Democracy, and Morality.* Acton, Mass.: Copley, 1994.

Toton, Suzanne C. *World Hunger: The Responsibility of Christian Education.* Maryknoll, N.Y.: Orbis Books, 1982.

Vallentyne, Peter, ed. *Equality and Justice.* New York: Routledge, 2003.

Wilber, Charles K., ed. *Economics, Ethics, and Public Policy.* Lanham, Md.: Rowman & Littlefield, 1998.

Williams, D. T. *Capitalism, Socialism, Christianity, and Poverty.* Cape Town: J. L. van Schaik, 1998.

Zsolnai, László, and Wojciech W. Gasparski, eds. *Ethics and the Future of Capitalism.* New Brunswick, N.J.: Transaction, 2002.

Biographical Directory

All the ethicists, philosophers, and historical figures listed here are discussed in the main body of essays. Figures whose names are printed in SMALL-CAPPED *letters are subjects of essays, which are alphabetically arranged. For additional information on all figures, see the Personages Index.*

ABELARD, PETER (c. 1079-1142): French philosopher and theologian who wrote many works on ethics, logic, philosophy, and theology.

ABŪ BAKR (c. 573-634): Arab caliph who succeeded Muḥammad. He afforded Muḥammad moral and financial support while he was in Mecca.

ABŪ ḤANĪFAH (c. 699-767): Muslim theologian and legal scholar who contributed to Islamic ethics with the creation of his legal doctrines.

Adams, John (1735-1826): Second president of the United States who believed that religion was necessary to sustain society and favored common sense over abstract theory. Adams placed society above the individual and contributed to the foundation of modern or traditionalist conservatism.

AKBAR (1542-1605): Mogul emperor who invented a new religion, called "Din-e-Ilahi," which combined parts of several religions, such as Islam and Hinduism.

ʿALĪ IBN ABĪ ṬĀLIB (600-661): The fourth and last of the Arab caliphs after Muḥammad's death. He is regarded as one of the most important leaders in early Islam because of his extensive knowledge of Islam.

ARENDT, HANNAH (1906-1975): German philosopher and author of numerous books such as *The Origins of Totalitarianism* (1951), *The Human Condition* (1958), *Eichmann in Jerusalem* (1963), and *On Revolution* (1963).

Aristippus (c. 435-365 B.C.E.): Greek philosopher who founded the Cyrenaic School of philosophy, the central component of which was hedonism.

Aristotle (384-322 B.C.E.): Greek philosopher who wrote the extremely influential *Nicomachean Ethics* (335-323 B.C.E.), the first methodical work on ethics in the Western world.

AŚOKA (c. 302-c. 230 B.C.E.): Indian emperor who fostered the spread of Buddhism and promoted public morality.

ATATÜRK (1881-1938): Atatürk launched a massive social reform movement as the founder and first president of Turkey.

AUGUSTINE, SAINT (354-430): Theologian and philosopher whose ethical teachings have influenced the Christian church for centuries. His most significant works were *Confessions* (397-400) and *City of God* (413-427).

AUROBINDO, SRI (1872-1950): Indian philosopher and a leading religious visionary who aided the spiritual and political growth of India. His works include *The Life Divine* (1914-1919) and *Synthesis of Yoga* (1948).

AVERROËS (1126-1198): Arab philosopher who wrote many studies on Aristotle's work, as well as critical interpretations on the work of Avicenna and al-Fârâbî.

AVICENNA (980-1037): Persian philosopher and important author of many works including *The Book of Healing* (early eleventh century). Avicenna is considered to be the most thoroughly regarded philosopher in the Islamic world.

AYER, A. J. (1910-1989): English philosopher who combined logical positivism and empiricism to form his own idea of ethics, which he detailed in the book *Language, Truth, and Logic* (1936).

BACON, FRANCIS (1561-1626): English philosopher whose partiality toward a naturalistic approach toward ethics governed English moral philosophy into the modern era.

BAHYA BEN JOSEPH IBN PAḲUDA (fl. second half of eleventh century): Arab philosopher who is celebrated for writing *Duties of the Heart* (c. 1080). The work is regarded as the most renowned moral-religious work of the medieval era and had a lasting influence on ensuing generations of Jewish ethical and pietistic writing. It is about the personal response needed for a sincere devotion of self to the service of God.

Bakunin, Mikhail (1814-1876): Leading Russian anarchist and author who likened violence to virtue, believing that violence would inspire social change.

BEAUVOIR, SIMONE DE (1908-1986): French existentialist philosopher and author of numerous works including *The Second Sex* (1949).

Bellah, Robert (1927-   ): American sociologist who is the leader of the Communitarianism movement—a drive toward community-based, rather than individual-based existence. Bellah believes that the fabric of the American community is in such a state of disaster that morality is essentially impossible. Author and editor of numerous books including *Habits of the Heart: Individualism and Commitment in American Life* (1985).

BENNETT, WILLIAM (1943-   ): American statesman who published *The Book of Virtues: A Treasury of Great Moral Stories* (1993). His virtuous character was questioned when it was revealed he was a high-stakes gambler.

BENTHAM, JEREMY (1748-1832): English philosopher, economist, and author of numerous works including *A Fragment on Government* (1776), *An Introduction to the Principles of Morals and Legislation* (1789), *The Rationale of Reward* (1825), and *The Rationale of Punishment* (1830). Bentham also initiated the philosophy of utilitarianism in England.

BERDYAYEV, NIKOLAY (1874-1948): Russian philosopher and author of *The Origin of Russian Communism* (1937) and editor of the journal *Put'* (path). Berdyayev used Christian existentialism to examine the function of freedom in improving the human race.

BERGSON, HENRI (1859-1941): French philosopher who promoted "process philosophy." He wrote several significant philosophical discourses, the most renowned of which was *Matter and Memory* (1896). Bergson was awarded the Nobel Prize in Literature in 1927.

Berkeley, George (1685-1753): British empiricist whose theory denied the existence of physical objects. Everything that exists is said to exist in the mind.

Binet, Alfred (1857-1911): French psychologist and physician who tried to scientifically evaluate intelligence—it was Binet who invented the expression "intelligence quotient." Binet was most concerned with how the normal mind works.

Black, Hugo L. (1886-1971): American Supreme Court associate justice (1937-1971) who attempted to delineate and in some areas expand constitutional protection of civil liberties.

BODHIDHARMA (fifth century-sixth century): Buddhist monk who founded Chinese Chan Buddhism.

BOETHIUS (c. 480-524): Roman philosopher and author of *The Consolation of Philosophy* (523) who mixed classical philosophical ideas with Christian ethics to establish a guideline for virtuous living.

BONHOEFFER, DIETRICH (1906-1945): German theologian and author of numerous works including *The Cost of Discipleship* (1937), *Ethics* (1949), and *Letters and Papers from Prison* (1951). Bonhoeffer developed a consequentialist ethical theology.

BRADLEY, F. H. (1846-1924): English philosopher and author of several works including *The Presuppositions of Critical History* (1874), *Ethical Studies* (1876), *Principles of Logic* (1883), and *Appearance and Reality: A Metaphysical Essay* (1893). Bradley's work focused on the individual's role within society.

BRANDEIS, LOUIS D. (1856-1941): American Supreme Court Justice (1916-1939) who incorporated moral values into his legal reasoning and opinions.

Brandt, Richard (1910-1997): Notable American moral philosopher of the twentieth century. His most celebrated book on ethics is *A Theory of the Good and the Right* (1979).

BUBER, MARTIN (1878-1965): Austrian philosopher and author of *I and Thou* (1923). Buber believed the core of ethics centered on the "I-Thou" personal relationship rather than the detached "I-It" relationship.

BUDDHA (c. 566-c. 486 B.C.E.): Indian religious leader who started Buddhism and developed its moral code. Buddhism is one of society's primary religious orders.

BŪKHĀRĪ, AL- (810-870): Islamic scholar who assembled the *al-Jāmi' al-Ṣaḥīḥ*, a collection of customs, or *ḥadīth* from Muḥammad's life.

Burger, Warren (1907-1995): Chief Justice of the United States Supreme Court (1969-1986) who criticized the Court for "moral neglect" because of its decisions on insanity and self-incrimination. He also helped found the American Inns of Court.

BURKE, EDMUND (1729-1797): English politician and author of *Reflections on the Revolution in France* (1790). He provided the model that serves as the foundation of modern conservatism.

Bush, George W. (1946-): President of the United States (2001-) during a time that the United States faced several significant moral issues such as the war in Iraq, stem cell research, and capital punishment.

BUTLER, JOSEPH (1692-1752): English cleric and author of *Fifteen Sermons Preached at the Rolls Chapel* (1726), in which he emphasized the significance of morals in life and decisions.

CALVIN, JOHN (1509-1564): Swiss theologian who believed in the supremacy of God's will—everyone's destiny is predetermined.

CAMUS, ALBERT (1913-1960): French Algerian journalist and author of numerous works such as *The Stranger* (1942), *The Myth of Sisyphus* (1942), *The Plague* (1947), *The Rebel* (1951), and *The Fall* (1956). Camus was an advocate of the individual and opposed to totalitarianism.

Carritt, Edgar F. (1876-1964): Twentieth century ethicist who explained his view of ethics in his *Theory of Morals* (1928).

CICERO (106-43 B.C.E.): Roman orator, politician, and writer of essays including *On the Republic* (52 B.C.E.), *On the Laws* (52 B.C.E..), *On the Chief End of Man* (45 B.C.E.), *Tusculan Disputations* (44 B.C.E.), and *On Duty* (44 B.C.E.). He believed just men dedicated their lives to public service.

Clausewitz, Carl von (1780-1831): Prussian intellectual and soldier whose *On War* (1832) is the most significant work of military philosophy—theory and strategy of warfare—in the Western world.

CLINTON, BILL (1946-): President of the United States (1993-2001) who was charged with perjury and obstruction of justice because of his role in the Monica Lewinsky scandal. Clinton's impeachment led to an ethical debate over whether a president's private life should be used as a criterion to assess his public performance.

COHEN, RANDY (1948-): American author of a syndicated column on applied ethics. Cohen has also published a collection of his columns called *The Good, the Bad, and the Difference: How to Tell Right from Wrong in Everyday Situations* (2002).

Comstock, Anthony (1844-1915): American postal official who lobbied Congress to pass the Federal Anti-Obscenity Act (1873), popularly known as the "Comstock Law." The statute prohibited the sending of materials judged "obscene, lewd, or lascivious."

COMTE, AUGUSTE (1798-1857): French philosopher who was the father of positivism. He stressed the importance of "moral progress" as a vital responsibility of society.

CONFUCIUS (551-479 B.C.E.): Chinese philosopher who stressed the idea of combining morality with the act of governing. Confucianism became the official state philosophy of China in the second century B.C.E. and it remained as the primary philosophy until the early twentieth century. Confucianism continues to be a significant influence on people throughout East Asia.

DALAI LAMA (Tenzin Gyatso; 1935-): Tibetan spiritual leader of the Buddhist community in Tibet who has ruled the government in exile because of Chinese occupation. His teachings stress the importance of mixing ethical values and ethical politics. The Dalai Lama was awarded the 1989 Nobel Peace Prize.

DALLAIRE, ROMÉO (1946-): Canadian commander of the U.N. peacekeeping force in Rwanda during that nation's 1994 genocide. Dallaire explored the world community's negligent behavior in response to the warnings about the uprisings in his *Shake Hands with the Devil: The Failure of Humanity in Rwanda* (2003).

DARWIN, CHARLES (1809-1882): English naturalist whose concept of evolution through natural selection, which he detailed in *On the Origin of Species* (1859), has been the foundation of numerous movements within ethics, such as Social Darwinism and evolutionary ethics.

de Klerk, F. W. (1936-): President of South Africa who started the process of ending the racist system of apartheid.

DERRIDA, JACQUES (1930-2004): Jewish philosopher renown for founding the deconstructionist school of philosophy. His most noted works, including *Speech and Phenomena* (1967), *Writing and Difference* (1967), and *Margins of Philosophy* (1972), offer lengthy evaluations of the metaphysical model underlying all of conventional Western philosophy. This analysis has forced philosophers to reexamine the very nature, methodology, and boundaries of the field of ethics.

DESCARTES, RENÉ (1596-1650): French mathematician and philosopher whose teachings changed philosophy from a metaphysical science to one more interested in the individual, which raised awareness in ethics and conduct.

DEWEY, JOHN (1859-1952): Notable American philosopher whose ethical theory defines ethical conduct as a function of human behavior initiated by the individual. He was the author of *Outlines of a Critical Theory of Ethics* (1891), *The Study of Ethics: A Syllabus* (1894), "Theory of the Moral Life" (1908, 1932), *Human Nature and Conduct* (1922), and *Theory of Valuation* (1939).

DŌGEN (1200-1253): Founder of Japan's Sōtō school of Zen Buddhism.

DOSTOEVSKI, FYODOR (1821-1881): Russian author whose fiction describes the individual experience of morality and its connection to Christian religion.

DU BOIS, W. E. B. (1868-1963): African American writer and social activist who was one of the founders of the National Association for the Advancement of Colored People. Du Bois examined the ethical consequences of racism.

Dunant, Jean Henri (1828-1910): Swiss founding father of the humanitarian organization the International Red Cross and cofounder of the Young Men's Christian Association.

DURKHEIM, ÉMILE (1858-1917): Founder of the French school of sociology who voiced concerns about the influence of modern society on the ethics of humankind.

EDWARDS, JONATHAN (1703-1758): American theologian and philosopher who tried to provide a sound interpretation of predestination.

EMERSON, RALPH WALDO (1803-1882): American theologian and author who was a leader of the American Transcendentalist movement.

EPICTETUS (c. 55-c. 135 C.E.): Greek philosopher who founded a school of Stoic philosophy. His ethical theory urged leading disciplined lives in accordance with natural law.

EPICURUS (341-270 B.C.E.): Greek philosopher whose ethical system is based on the belief that seeking personal pleasure results in the highest good. He founded the Garden School to put this philosophy into practice.

EVERS, MEDGAR (1925-1963): African American civil rights activist who staged an immense protest to bring attention to the unjust policies of discrimination and segregation in Mississippi. He became a martyr of the Civil Rights movement after his murder.

FĀRĀBĪ, AL- (870-950): Muslim philosopher who influenced Islamic ethics and thought in medieval Europe. He tried to reconcile the ideas of Aristotle, Plato, and Neoplatonic thought.

FARRAKHAN, LOUIS (1933-   ): African American leader of the Nation of Islam who has made statements involving Malcolm X and Jesse Jackson that have raised ethical concerns about his character.

FĀṬIMA (c. 606-632): The revered daughter of the Prophet Muḥammad who is viewed as a paragon of Islamic spirituality.

Fichte, Johann Gottlieb (1762-1814): German philosopher who provided the groundwork for the school of German Idealism.

FOUCAULT, MICHEL (1926-1984): French philosopher and author concerned with the effects of imprisonment and whose work generated reforms in the prison system. He is well known for such works as *Madness and Civilization* (1961), *The Order of Things* (1966), *The Discourse on Language* (1971), *Discipline and Punish* (1975), and his three-volume *The History of Sexuality* (1976-1984).

FREUD, SIGMUND (1856-1939): Austrian founder of psychoanalysis whose work had an enormous influence on the field of ethics.

Galen (129-c. 199): Greek physician and philosopher who was instrumental in formulating logical empiricism.

Galileo (1564-1642): Italian astronomer who was a principal figure of the early scientific revolution. His work helped develop the modern scientific methods of observation and experimentation. Galileo's *Dialogue Concerning the Two Chief World Systems* (1632) was condemned by the Vatican.

GANDHI, MOHANDAS K. (1869-1948): Indian nationalist leader who used nonviolent protests as a means to fight for Indian independence, women's rights, and the untouchables.

Garvey, Marcus (1887-1940): Jamacian-born journalist and orator who founded the Universal Negro Improvement Association. A proponent of black nationalism, he urged African Americans to move back to Africa.

Gewirth, Alan (1912-   ): Gewirth is one of the foremost American ethicists from the late twentieth century. He is renowned for his belief in the ethical commitment to respect human rights. Gewirth has written over one hundred articles on ethical, moral, political, and social philosophy and some of his books include *Reason and Morality* (1978), *Human Rights: Essays on Justification and Applications* (1982), *The Community of Rights* (1996), and *Self-Fulfillment* (1998).

GHAZĀLĪ, AL- (1058-1111): Persian author who is well known for his writings on ethics and mysticism.

Gilligan, Carol (1936-   ): American psychologist and author. Gilligan's early work focused on moral development in girls, leading to the formation of her "difference feminism"—women possess different moral and psychological inclinations than men. Her most famous book is *In a Different Voice: Psychological Theory and Women's Development* (1982).

Goldman, Emma (1869-1940): Russian-born American anarchist who criticized the capitalist and socialist systems. Goldman supported the ideals of anarchy through her fight for women's rights.

Gregory, John (1725-1773): Scottish physician who wrote *Lectures on the Duties and Qualifications of a Physician* (1772). The book stressed the virtues of the physician and described the physician's obligations.

GROTIUS, HUGO (1583-1645): Dutch philosopher who provided the framework for such pacts as the Geneva Conventions which dictate the conduct of war, through his influential book *On the Law of War and Peace* (1625).

Habermas, Jürgen (1929-   ): German philosopher who was an influential member of the Frankfurt School for Social Research. Habermas is well known for trying to articulate an inclusive theory of communication, language, and the development of society within an ethical system. His principal works include *Theory and Practice* (1963), *Knowledge and Human Interests* (1968), *The Theory of Communicative Action* (1981), *Between Facts and Norms* (1992).

ḤALLĀJ, AL- (c. 858-922): Persian mystic whose martyrdom was vital to the growth of Sufism.

Hardin, Garrett James (1915-2003): American ecologist and microbiologist. A prolific author, Hardin wrote articles and books on numerous subjects such as bioethics, ecology, ethics, immigration, and population theory. In *Filters Against Folly* (1985), he discussed the three intellectual filters necessary for a useful ethical theory. His other principal works include the essays "The Tragedy of the Commons" and "Living on a Lifeboat" and the books *Living Within Limits: Ecology, Economics and Population Taboos* (1993), *The Immigration Dilemma: Avoiding the Tragedy of the Commons* (1995), *Stalking the Wild Taboo* (1996), and *The Ostrich Factor: Our Population Myopia* (1999).

HARE, R. M. (1919-2002): English philosopher and author of *The Language of Morals* (1952), *Freedom and Reason* (1963), *Applications of Moral Philosophy* (1972), *Moral Thinking* (1981), *Essays in Ethical Theory* (1989), and *Essays on Political Morality* (1989). Hare developed a moral theory called "universal prescriptivism." He also displayed an interest in difficulties related to moral education and moral decision making.

HART, H. L. A. (1907-1992): English philosopher who wrote on numerous topics, including the nature of obligation, punishment, and the role of pardons in ethics and law. He contended that law and morality are not necessarily connected. One of his most famous works is *The Concept of Law* (1961).

HARTSHORNE, CHARLES (1897-2000): American philosopher, theologian, and author who was a proponent of a logical, germane view of ethics.

HEGEL, GEORG WILHELM FRIEDRICH (1770-1831): German philosopher who developed numerous doctrines that influenced various disciplines such as anthropology, history, psychology, political theory, and sociology.

HEIDEGGER, MARTIN (1889-1976): German philosopher whose theories were concerned with the study and meaning of "being."

HIPPOCRATES (c. 460-c. 377 B.C.E.): Greek physician known as the "father of Western medicine." He wrote the guidelines for ethical conduct within the medical profession—the Hippocratic oath—a standard for physician behavior in medicine.

HITLER, ADOLF (1889-1945): German dictator who was responsible for the death of thousands of people during the Holocaust and for triggering the events that started World War II.

HOBBES, THOMAS (1588-1679): English political philosopher well known as a proponent of political absolutism.

Holmes, Robert (1935-   ): American philosopher who inferred that all modern wars are immoral because innocent people are killed. He argued for the practice of nonviolence. Holmes is the author of *On War and Morality* (1989) and *Basic Moral Philosophy* (1992) and the editor of *Nonviolence in Theory and Practice* (1990).

HUINENG (638-713): Chinese Buddhist monk who taught that freedom is achieved when one realizes that there is no self.

HUME, DAVID (1711-1776): English philosopher who was a proponent of empiricism.

ḤUSAYN (626-680): Grandson of the Prophet Muḥammad, who served as a political and religious leader. Ḥusayn's death was a defining moment in Shīʿa Islam.

HUSSEIN, SADDAM (1937-   ): Dictatorial Arab leader of Iraq (1979-2003), who brutally repressed his people and was responsible for the death or inhuman treatment of thousands of civilians.

Hutcheson, Francis (1694-1746): Scottish moral philosoper who was celebrated for his ethical philosophy of innate moral sense. He also wrote *Inquiry into the Original of Our Ideas of Beauty and Virtue* (1725), *Essay on the Nature and Conduct of the Passions and Affections* (1728), and *System of Moral Philosophy* (1755).

Ibn al-ʿArabī (1165-1240): Arab philosopher who articulated a systematic philosophical account of Sufism that remains influential in modern practice. His writings include *Meccan Revelations* and *Gems of Wisdom* (1229).

IBN GABIROL (c. 1020-c. 1057): Arab philosopher and poet. Ibn Gabirol's version of Neoplatonism philosophy came to be intergrated within Christian Augustinian thought. He authored *The Source of Life* (eleventh century).

IBN KHALDŪN (1332-1406): Arab philosopher who was the first and one of the best philosophers in history. He produced a system of political ethics that he trusted would assist in the growth of civilization and better society. His massive work, *The Muqaddimah* (1375-1379) is the first known

work in the philosophy of social and cultural history.

JACKSON, JESSE (1941-   ): Noted African American Christian minister and civil rights leader whose ethical conduct has come into question on two occasions. Jackson has faced criticism for making disparaging racial and religious remarks and for committing adultery and fathering a child outside of his marriage.

JAMES, WILLIAM (1842-1910): American philosopher whose ethical theory is based upon humankind's freedom of choice. His most significant works include *The Principles of Psychology* (1890), *The Varieties of Religious Experience: A Study in Human Nature* (1902), *Pragmatism: A New Name for Some Old Ways of Thinking* (1907), and *A Pluralistic Universe* (1909).

Jaspers, Karl (1883-1969): Leading German philosopher who provided the foundation for the existential movement.

JEFFERSON, THOMAS (1743-1826): American philosopher and third president of the United States. Jefferson was the author of the Declaration of Independence, and he strived to expand and protect civil rights, democracy, public education, and religious freedom.

JESUS CHRIST (c. 6 B.C.E.-30 C.E.): Religious teacher who initiated Christianity and instructed that love is the consummate value and that sin may be forgiven through genuine penance.

Johnson, Lyndon B. (1908-1973): Thirty-sixth president of the United States who was a proponent of civil rights and increased the government's role in social welfare through his Great Society programs.

JUNG, CARL (1875-1961): Swiss psychologist and father of analytical psychology. Jung is probably best known for his descriptions of the orientations of the personality, "extroversion" and "introversion."

KANT, IMMANUEL (1724-1804): German philosopher who combined empiricism and rationalism into a new system of philosophical thought.

KELLER, HELEN (1880-1968): Blind and deaf American social activist who committed her life to serving disabled people. Keller was also an author who wrote *The Story of My Life* (1903), *The World I Live In* (1908), *Out of the Dark* (1913), *Helen Keller's Journal* (1938), and *Teacher: Anne Sullivan Macy* (1955).

Kennedy, John Fitzgerald (1917-1963): Thirty-fifth president of the United States who contributed to the tendency toward dishonesty within political circles when he received the Pulitzer Prize for a book he did not write.

KEVORKIAN, JACK (1928-   ): American pathologist who assisted in the suicide of many terminally ill patients. His actions were covered extensively by the media resulting in an ethical debate on the rights and wrongs of physician-assisted suicide.

KIERKEGAARD, SØREN (1813-1855): Danish philosopher and theologian who is viewed as the founder of existentialism. His most noted works include *Either/Or: A Fragment of Life* (1843), *Fear and Trembling* (1843), and *Concluding Unscientific Postscript* (1846).

KINDĪ, AL- (c. 800-866): A prolific author who wrote on many subjects, al-Kindī was the first significant Arab philosopher. He furnished the first methodical philosophical presentation of ethics and moral psychology in Arabic.

KING, MARTIN LUTHER, JR. (1929-1968): American civil rights leader. As founding president of the Southern Christian Leadership Conference, King headed the nonviolent movement that led to the 1964 Civil Rights Act and the 1965 Voting Rights Act. He was awarded the Nobel Peace Price in 1964 for his role in the nonviolent war against racial injustice and poverty.

KOHLBERG, LAWRENCE (1927-1987): American psychologist. He outlined his concept of moral development—a cognitive skill that evolves in phases—in his book *Essays on Moral Development* (1981).

KŪKAI (774-835): Born Saeki Mao, Kūkai, was a Japanese monk who established the Shingon school of Japanese Buddhism. He instructed that compliance to moral and social principles comprised the second of the ten rungs on the ladder that leads to actual Buddahood.

LAOZI (604 B.C.E.-sixth century B.C.E.): Chinese philosopher and religious figure who is widely identified as one of the primary masters of Daoism, the second of China's great philosophical schools.

LEIBNIZ, GOTTFRIED WILHELM (1646-1716): German philosopher, theologian, and historian. Leibniz contributed to the development of rationalist philosophy. His works include *Theodicy: Essays on the Goodness of God, the Freedom of Man, and the Origin of Evil* (1710) and *New Essays Concerning Human Understanding* (written 1704; published 1765).

LEMKIN, RAPHAEL (1900-1959): Renowned Polish legal scholar and political activist who defined the word genocide. His efforts to have genocide acknowledged as a crime aided the 1948 adoption of the United Nations Genocide Convention.

LENIN, VLADIMIR ILICH (1870-1924): Born Vladimir Ilich Ulyanov. Lenin, a Russian political ruler, modified Marxist theory to the politics of late imperial Russia, establishing and heading the Communist Party. He was the main architect of the new socialist state that became the model for world communism.

LEOPOLD, ALDO (1887-1948): American scientist and writer who has been called the father of modern wildlife management and ecology. He wrote the influential *A Sand County Almanac* (1949) and founded the Wilderness Society in 1935.

LEVINAS, EMMANUEL (1906-1995): Levinas fostered the idea that responsibility to others is the foundation of ethics. His writings on ethics include *Difficult Freedom: Essays on Judaism*.

LINCOLN, ABRAHAM (1809-1865): President of the United States who issued the Emancipation Proclamation and supported other legislation to deal with the ethical dilemma of slavery.

LOCKE, JOHN (1632-1704): English philosopher who mixed empiricism and theism, creating a powerful philosophy of mind and ethics. He was one of the most powerful political theorists from the Enlightenment era. His writings include *An Essay Concerning Human Understanding* (1690) and *Two Treatises of Government* (1690).

Lorenz, Konrad (1903-1989): Austrian ethologist and zoologist who was awarded the Nobel Prize in Physiology or Medicine in 1973. He was considered a principal founder of the science of ethology because of his work in correlating patterns of animal and human behavior. As a result of this work, Lorenz developed his theory of aggression which has numerous ethical implications.

LUTHER, MARTIN (1483-1546): German Protestant reformer who developed a theology and a religious movement that had a profound impact on the social, political, and religious thought of Western society.

McCarthy, Joseph R. (1908-1957): United States senator who achieved notoriety for his unethical persecution of political and entertainment figures during the 1950's.

Machiavelli, Niccolò (1469-1527): Italian political theorist who introduced a pragmatic manner of political discourse that is completely free of ethical considerations derived from traditional sources of moral authority, such as classical philosophy and Christian theology.

MacIntyre, Alasdair (1929-   ): An influential Scottish moral philosopher. In *After Virtue* (1981), MacIntyre outlines the history of Western ethical thinking, defines the moral dilemmas of the modern era, and provides a novel approach to ethical theory to face and settle those dilemmas. MacIntyre's other works include *A Short History of Ethics* (1966), *Difficulties in Christian Belief* (1959), *Marxism and Christianity* (1968), and *First Principles, Final Ends, and Contemporary Philosophical Issues* (1990).

MacKinnon, Catharine A. (1946-   ): American lawyer, professor, author, and activist. A leader in the formation of feminist legal theory, MacKinnon's argument that sexual harassment is a form of sex discrimination was later ratified.

Maimonides, Moses (1135-1204): Jewish philosopher whose works were characterized by ethical concerns, most particularly in *Mishneh Torah* (1185) and *Guide of the Perplexed* (1190).

Malcolm X (1925-1965): Born Malcolm Little. As an American religious leader and social activist, Malcolm X was a proponent of using "any means necessary" to achieve equality, justice, and freedom for African Americans. His actions spurred ethical debates about nonviolent and violent protest.

Malthus, Thomas Robert (1766-1834): English economist who encouraged controls on human reproduction in his *An Essay on the Principle of Population, as It Affects the Future Improvement of Society* (1798).

Mandela, Nelson (1918-   ): South African social activist and statesman who has been a leader or participant in many ethical issues such as apartheid, AIDS, and human rights.

Mao Zedong (1893-1976): Chinese political figure who established the People's Republic of China. His regime was one of repression and oppression that led to the mass murder of his country's people.

Mapplethorpe, Robert (1946-1989): American artist whose work was the center of controversy in disputes over censorship and public funding of the arts during the late 1980's and early 1990's.

Marcus Aurelius (121-180): Born Marcus Annius Verus. Roman emperor who produced a Stoic philosophy in his *Meditations* (c. 171-180). This work reflects the emperor's efforts to achieve the Platonic ideal of the philosopher-king and is the last great literary statement of Stoicism.

Marcuse, Herbert (1898-1979): German philosopher who was a member of the Frankfurt School for Social Research. His works included *Eros and Civilization* (1955) and *One-Dimensional Man* (1964), both of which criticized capitalist society as oppressed. In *Soviet Marxism* (1958) he was antagonistic toward bureaucratic communism.

Marx, Karl (1818-1883): German political philosopher. Marx's opinions regarding economic distribution and social class have significantly influenced theories in economic and philosophical thought and have helped form the political structure of the modern world.

Mead, George Herbert (1863-1931): American pragmatist philosopher and psychologist. His principal works include *The Philosophy of the Present* (1932), *Mind, Self, and Society* (1934), *Movements of Thought in the Nineteenth Century* (1936), and *The Philosophy of the Act* (1938).

Mencius (c. 372-c. 289 B.C.E.): Chinese philosopher born Meng Ke. Mencius explained and developed the wisdom embodied in Confucius's *Analects*, rendering Confucian ideas more accessible. His *Mengzi* transcended other interpretations of Confucius and gained acceptance as the orthodox version of Confucian thought.

Mill, John Stuart (1806-1873): English philosopher and economist who was the most renowned modern advocate of utilitarianism. His most influential works include *On Liberty* (1859), *Utilitarianism* (1863), and *The Subjection of Women* (1869).

Milošević, Slobodan (1941-   ): Serbian political leader whose ethnic cleansing policies against ethnic Albanians received widespread outrage and was eventually stopped.

Moniz, Egas António (1874-1955): Portuguese neurosurgeon who won the Nobel Prize in Physiology or Medicine in 1949 for his prefrontal leukotomy procedure. Moniz believed that his technique could be used to reduce apprehension and other emotional conditions in humans.

Montaigne, Michel de (1533-1592): French essayist who declared that European colonization of the New World was morally wrong. He also denounced animal cruelty.

MONTESQUIEU (1689-1755): French political philosopher who studied the nature of government, laws, and society. His works include *The Persian Letters* (1721) and *The Spirit of the Laws* (1748).

MOORE, G. E. (1873-1958): English philosopher who established analytic philosophy as a major system in modern philosophical thought. His work includes *Principia Ethica* (1903) and *Ethics* (1912).

MOSES (c. 1300-c. 1200 B.C.E.): Early Hebrew leader. The codification of religious and ethical laws in the Pentateuch, the first five books of the Old Testament, is traditionally attributed to him.

MOZI (c. 470-c. 391 B.C.E.): Chinese philosopher and teacher whose philosophy advocated universal love and condemned warfare. His teachings are preserved in a book, *Mozi* (fifth century B.C.E.; *The Ethical and Political Works of Motse*, 1929; also known as *Mo Tzu: Basic Writings*, 1963), compiled by his disciples.

MUḤAMMAD (c. 570-632 C.E.): Founder of Islam whose visions served as the basis for the Qurʾān. Muslims believe that Muḥammad's life serves as the premier example of an ethical existence.

MUIR, JOHN (1838-1914): Scottish American naturalist who founded the Sierra Club and played an important role in the conservation movement and the development of the national park system.

Mussolini, Benito (1883-1945): Italian dictator whose fascist regime placed the state's interests above individual human rights. Mussolini also ordered the unethical invasion and use of poison gas against Ethiopia.

NADER, RALPH (1934-   ): American advocate of consumer rights and a proponent of responsible government behavior.

Naess, Arne (1912-   ): Norwegian philosopher who founded the environmental movement known as deep ecology. His most influential work is *Ecology, Community, and Lifestyle* (1974).

NĀGĀRJUNA (c. 150-c. 250 C.E.): Indian Buddhist philosopher who founded the Mādhyamaka school of Mahāyāna Buddhism. His most important innovation was the concept of "emptiness," or *śūnyatā*—a recognition that things derived their only meaning from their relationships to other things.

NAGEL, THOMAS (1937-   ): American philosopher who devised a form of ethical realism that acknowledges objective and subjective grounds for action. He is famous for his books, *The Possibility of Altruism* (1970) and *The View from Nowhere* (1986).

NĀNAK (1469-1539): Indian religious leader who combined the basic principles of Islam and the tradition of Hinduism into a new universal religion, Sikhism. His teaching emphasizes the equality of all human beings and regards responsible social action as central to true spiritual practice.

Newton, Isaac (1642-1727): English physicist whose scientific studies served to provide an explanation of occurrences in the physical world thereby moving away from God as the explanation for these occurrences.

NIEBUHR, H. RICHARD (1894-1962): American theologian who became one of the principal Christian ethicists of the twentieth century. He wrote influential books such as *The Meaning of Revelation* (1941) and *Christ and Culture* (1951).

NIEBUHR, REINHOLD (1892-1971): American theologian who devised Neoorthodox theology. He used the political and social arenas to place the Christian faith in the center of the cultural and political world of his day.

NIETZSCHE, FRIEDRICH (1844-1900): German philosopher whose analysis of traditional ethics in *Beyond Good and Evil* (1886) and *On the Genealogy of Morals* (1887) significantly impacted the intellectual perspective of the twentieth century.

Nixon, Richard (1913-1994): Thirty-seventh president of the United States (1969-1974) who was impeached for his unethical behavior during the Watergate scandal.

Noddings, Nel (1929-   ): American professor and education theorist. Noddings is well known for her writings on caring and the part it plays in ethical behavior and moral training. Noddings's principal works include *Caring: A Feminine Approach to Ethics and Moral Education* (1984),

Educating Moral People: A Caring Alternative to Character Education (2002), and *Starting at Home: Caring and Social Policy* (2002).

NOZICK, ROBERT (1938-2002): American philosopher and author. He is most famous for his book *Anarchy, State, and Utopia* (1974).

NUSSBAUM, MARTHA (1947-   ): American scholar who believes that ethical and moral interests should always be the guiding force in international relationships.

ORTEGA Y GASSET, JOSÉ (1883-1955): Spanish philosopher whose fame helped to bring Spain out of a long period of cultural isolation and whose thought contributed greatly to his country's intellectual reawakening. He wrote the book *The Revolt of the Masses* (1929).

ORWELL, GEORGE (1903-1950): Born Eric Blair. British novelist who expressed his consideration of social concern in a diverse body of works. He believed that people should be afforded equality and justice under the law.

Paley, William (1743-1805): English theologian and author who established a moral system based on utilitarianism.

PASCAL, BLAISE (1623-1662): French philosopher who believed that one should not compromise one's ethical beliefs to achieve political or social influence. He wrote *The Provincial Letters* (1656-1657) and *Pensées* (1670).

PEIRCE, CHARLES SANDERS (1839-1914): American philosopher who is one of the fathers of pragmatism. Peirce criticized established ideas regarding truth and knowledge and made important contributions to the fields of logic and epistemology.

Percival, Thomas (1740-1804): English physician who wrote *Medical Ethics* (1803). His work laid the foundation for the first American Medical Association Code of Ethics in 1847.

PERRY, R. B. (1876-1957): American philosopher who wrote *General Theory of Value* (1926) and *Realms of Value* (1954). Perry is renowned for his development of the theory of value.

PHILO OF ALEXANDRIA (c. 20 B.C.E.-c. 45 C.E.): Egyptian philosopher who united Greek philosophy with Old Testament teaching. He wrote *The Creation of the World, That God Is Immutable,* and *On the Ten Commandments* (all early first century C.E.).

Pinchot, Gifford (1865-1946): American leader in the late nineteenth century conservation movement. He and Theodore Roosevelt wrote extensively about the conservation ethic.

Pius XII (1876-1958): Italian pope who spoke on behalf of the Church on moral issues such as euthanasia and lifesaving measures. He also denounced the practice of situational ethics.

PLATO (c. 427-347 B.C.E.): Born Aristocles, Plato was a Greek philosopher. He is one of the most influential thinkers of Western civilization. Plato used the dialogue structure in order to pose basic questions about knowledge, reality, society, and human nature. He formulated his own philosophy, Platonism, in order to answer these questions, a philosophy which has been one of the most influential thought-systems in the Western tradition.

QUINLAN, KAREN ANN (1954-1985): Comatose patient whose case is important in discussions of the right to die, the ordinary/extraordinary care distinction, the euthanasia debate, and the need for a living will. The removal of her respirator helped the fight for the right to die, and her death is important in discussions regarding whether there is a difference between active and passive euthanasia.

RĀBIᶜAH AL-ᶜADAWĪYAH (712-801): Arab mystical poet who composed several significant poems inspired by the absolute love of God. Her life represents an example of religious devotion.

RAND, AYN (1905-1982): Born Alisa Rosenbaum. A Russian American novelist and philosopher who promoted rational egoism and libertarianism. Rand declared her philosophy in works, such as *The Fountainhead* (1943), *Atlas Shrugged* (1957), *The Virtue of Selfishness: A New Concept of Egoism* (1964), and *Capitalism: The Unknown Ideal* (1966).

RAWLS, JOHN (1921-2002): American political philosopher whose theory of justice is based on the social contract theory. Rawls is best known for his works *A Theory of Justice* (1971) and *Political Liberalism* (1993).

RAZI, AL- (c. 864-c. 925): Arab philosopher and physician who set new standards for medical ethics, the clinical observation of disease, and the testing of medical treatment. His works include a comprehensive medical encyclopedia in twelve volumes; *The Book of Spiritual Physick* (c. 920), his principal ethical treatise; and the apologetic *The Philosopher's Way of Life* (c. 920).

Read, Herbert (1893-1968): English author and critic who defined the differences between the theory of liberty and personal freedom.

Reagan, Ronald (1911-2004): Fortieth president of the United States (1981-1989) whose presidency was tainted by the Iran-Contra scandal and possible cover-up. Other issues during the Reagan administration that had ethical implications were Reagan's opposition to abortion rights and his signature on a bill prohibiting the use of federal money for what many regarded as obscene works of art.

Regan, Tom (1938-   ): American philosopher, author and editor of several philosophy books on animal rights, environmental policy, ethics, and medical ethics. Regan is regarded as the "philosophical father" of the animal rights movement. Some of Regan's principal works on animal rights include *The Case for Animal Rights* (1983), *The Animal Rights Debate* (2001), and *Defending Animal Rights* (2001).

Robertson, Pat (1930-   ): American religious broadcaster and politician. He is well known as the creator of *The 700 Club*, a Christian television show, and for ethical and religious views which some view as extreme. Robertson also founded the Christian Coalition, the conservative, grassroots political organization.

Roosevelt, Franklin D. (1882-1945): Thirty-second president of the United States (1933-1945) who passed the New Deal legislation, yet also ruled the country in an imperial fashion.

Roosevelt, Theodore (1858-1919): Twenty-sixth president of the United States (1901-1909) who considered himself a moral leader and struck a balance between the collective good and individualism.

RORTY, RICHARD (1931-   ): American author and philosopher who has developed his own theory of ethics that addresses immigration, gender, and democracy among other issues.

Ross, W. D. (1877-1940): Scottish moral philosopher who denounced utilitarianism and promoted a form of intuitionism. His works include *Aristotle* (1923), *The Right and the Good* (1930), *Foundations of Ethics* (1939), *Plato's Theory of Ideas* (1951), and *Kant's Ethical Theory* (1954).

ROUSSEAU, JEAN-JACQUES (1712-1778): French philosopher who helped transform the Western world into a predominantly democratic civilization dedicated to assuring the dignity and fulfillment of the individual. He wrote *A Treatise on the Social Contract: Or, The Principles of Politic Law* (1762).

ROYCE, JOSIAH (1855-1916): American philosopher who was a proponent of philosophic idealism. His works include *The World and the Individual* (1899-1901) and *The Philosophy of Loyalty* (1908).

Ruddick, Sara (1935-   ): American feminist philosopher and author of *Maternal Thinking: Towards a Politics of Peace* (1989). Ruddick contends in her book that a focus on nurturing and educating children has an effect on their ethical decisions and actions.

RŪMĪ, JALĀL AL-DĪN (c. 1207-1273): Afghan mystical poet who was the founder of the Mevlevī Sufi order. His most influential work is *Mathnavī* (1259-1273).

Rummel, Rudolph (1932-   ): American author and professor who coined the term "democide." His works include *Death by Government* (1994), *The Miracle That Is Freedom* (1996), *Power Kills* (1997), and *Statistics of Democide* (1997).

RUSSELL, BERTRAND (1872-1970): English philosopher who believed that people could choose good over evil. His most influential ethical works include *On Education* (1926), *Why I Am Not a Christian* (1927), *Marriage and Morals* (1929), *Education and the Social Order* (1932), *Religion and Science* (1935), and *Human Society and Ethics* (1955). He won the 1950 Nobel Prize in Literature.

ŚAṄKARA (c. 700-750): Indian philosopher and commentator of Advaita Vedanta Hinduism, a religious and philosophical tradition based on a nondualist, monistic reading of the Hindu sacred texts. He is also the author of commentaries on the *Bhaghavadgītā* and the Upaniṣads and established four Indian monasteries.

SANTAYANA, GEORGE (1863-1952): Spanish philosopher, poet, and novelist who wrote *The Life of Reason: Or, The Phases of Human Progress* (1905-1906), *Scepticism and Animal Faith* (1923), and *Realms of Being* (1927-1940). Santayana's view of ethics amounted to a life that stressed detachment, reflection, generosity, and faith.

Sartre, Jean-Paul (1905-1980): French philosopher, playwright, and novelist. Sartre was a principal advocate of modern existentialist thought. His works include *Being and Nothingness* (1943) and *Existentialism and Humanism* (1946). He won the 1964 Nobel Prize in Literature.

Schindler, Oskar (1908-1974): German merchant who rescued eleven hundred Jews from death sentences during the Holocaust. He risked his life and fortune in order to act morally responsible.

Schopenhauer, Arthur (1788-1860): German philosopher who developed a pessimistic system of philosophy based upon the primacy of will. His *The World as Will and Representation* (1819), advanced his philosophy.

Schweitzer, Albert (1875-1965): German theologian and missionary who urged the public, politicians, and statesmen to come to grips with the threat of nuclear war and work for peace. He wrote the *Philosophy of Civilization* (1923). He was recipient of the 1952 Nobel Peace Prize.

Shaftesbury, Third Earl of (1671-1713): Born Anthony Ashley Cooper, he was an English philosopher who emphasized common sense as opposed to logical systems and introduced the theory of moral sense as a significant component of ethical theory. Among his most important works are *An Inquiry Concerning Virtue* (1699), *A Letter Concerning Enthusiasm* (1708), *Sensus Communis* (1709), *The Moralists* (1709), and *Characteristics of Men, Manners, Opinions, Times* (1711).

Shakespeare, William (1564-1616): English Renaissance dramatist whose plays often touched on the morality of issues such as assassination.

Shinran (1173-1262): Born Matsuwaka-Maru. Shinran was a Japanese Buddhist monk who founded the Japanese Mahāyānist Buddhist sect Jōdo Shinshū, or the True Pure Land Sect. He taught the difference between faith (salvation in the next world) and morality (one's duty to society in this world).

Sidgwick, Henry (1838-1900): English philosopher who tried to reconcile an intuitive approach to morality with that of utilitarianism. He produced *Methods of Ethics*, one of the most significant works on ethics in English, the capstone of nineteenth century British moral philosophy.

Singer, Peter (1946-   ): Australian philosopher and ethicist who wrote *Animal Liberation* (1975), *Practical Ethics* (1979), and *Rethinking Life and Death* (1994), among many other works. Singer is an eminent authority in two areas of ethics—animal rights and bioethics.

Skinner, B. F. (1904-1990): American psychologist and behaviorist primarily responsible for the development of modern behaviorism. Skinner believed that the fundamental traits of human nature are neither good nor bad but the outcome of complicated environmental interactions.

Smith, Adam (1723-1790): Scottish economist who was a leading proponent of laissez-faire economics. He wrote *The Theory of Moral Sentiments* (1759), and *An Inquiry into the Nature and Causes of the Wealth of Nations* (1776).

Socrates (c. 470-399 B.C.E.): Greek philosopher who is thought to have switched the focus of Greek philosophy from the natural world to the human mind and ethics. He believed that moral goodness is based on objective knowledge.

Solzhenitsyn, Aleksandr (1918-   ): Russian novelist and historian who promoted the idea of the mutuality of communal and individual ethics within the context of the Russian Christian tradition. He advanced this idea in literary works such as *One Day in the Life of Ivan Denisovich* (1962), *The First Circle* (1968), and *Cancer Ward* (1968), and in historical works such as *The Gulag Archipelago, 1918-1956: An Experiment in Literary Investigation* (1973-1975). He was the recipient of the 1970 Nobel Prize in Literature.

Sophocles (c. 496-406 B.C.E.): Greek dramatist, military and civil leader. His play *Antigone* (c. 441 B.C.E.) showed an awareness of the conflict between respecting civic duty versus the demands of the conscience within the individual.

Spencer, Herbert (1820-1903): British philosopher and sociologist who was one of the main defenders of evolutionary theory. He also criticized utilitarian positivism.

Spinoza, Baruch (1632-1677): Dutch philosopher who contributed much to the emergence of political and religious tolerance. His works include *A Theologico-Political Treatise* (1670) and *Ethics* (1677).

Stalin, Joseph (1879-1953): Russian political leader of the Communist Party of the Soviet Union (1928-1953). Under his leadership, the Soviet Union became a repressive totalitarian state.

STANTON, ELIZABETH CADY (1815-1902): American suffragist who was a proponent of complete moral and social equality for women.

Stevenson, Charles L. (1908-1979): American philosopher who largely developed the ethical theory of emotivism. He also wrote *Ethics and Language* (1944), one of the most pivotal works on ethics in the modern era.

STEWART, MARTHA (1941-   ): American entrepreneur whose character was questioned after a series of unethical business decisions.

TAGORE, RABINDRANATH (1861-1941): Indian poet, playwright, and philosopher. The foundation for Tagore's literary achievements is his vision of the universal man, based on his unique integration of Eastern and Western thought. *Gitanjali* (*Song Offerings*; 1910) is his best-known work in the West. He was the recipient of the Nobel Prize in Literature in 1913.

Tertullian (c. 155-160 C.E.-after 217 C.E.): Religious figure from the age of Imperial Rome who is considered the prominent spokesman for Christianity in the Latin West before Saint Augustine. Tertullian's polemical treatises set the direction for much of later Western theology. Among his personal beliefs was an opposition to vivisection.

THOMAS AQUINAS (1224 or 1225-1274): Italian theologian who combined elements of the Christian faith with Aristotle's theory of ethics that had implications for ethics, law, psychology, semantics, and the nature of reason itself. His works include *Summa Theologica* (c. 1265-1273) and *Summa Contra Gentiles* (c. 1258-1264).

THOREAU, HENRY DAVID (1817-1862): American writer, philosopher, and a major figure in the Transcendentalist movement. His most significant works include "Civil Disobedience" (1849) and *Walden: Or, Life in the Woods* (1854).

TILLICH, PAUL (1886-1965): German American theologian who introduced a unique and challenging approach to the area of theology. His works include *Systematic Theology* (1951-1963), *Dynamics of Faith* (1957), and *The Protestant Era* (1948).

Tolstoy, Leo (1828-1910): Russian author who was renowned for his fiction and later achieved prominence as a moralist, pacifist, and social activist.

TUTU, DESMOND (1931-   ): South African advocate of civil and human rights who urged the end of apartheid by appealing to the moral conscience of people worldwide.

UNAMUNO Y JUGO, MIGUEL DE (1864-1936): Spanish philosopher who was a key figure in the expression of the existentialist tension between reason and faith. He wrote such works as *The Life of Don Quixote and Sancho* (1905), *The Tragic Sense of Life in Men and Peoples* (1913), and *The Agony of Christianity* (1925).

VARDHAMĀNA (c. 599-527 B.C.E.): Indian religious reformer who established the Jain religion. He instructed on the ethical significance of nonviolence and spirituality.

VOLTAIRE (1694-1778): Born François-Marie Arouet. French writer and philosopher who believed that morality was an obligation to humanity and justice. He wrote *Candide: Or, All for the Best* (1759).

WANG YANGMING (1472-1529): Chinese philosopher who quelled rebellions and created a reign of peace in China that lasted a century. As a Neo-Confucian philosopher, he exercised tremendous influence in both China and Japan for 150 years. He wrote *Instructions for Practical Living* (1527).

WASHINGTON, BOOKER T. (1856-1915): African American educator who used utilitarian and pragmatic standards to explain human behavior. He was the author of *Up from Slavery* (1901).

WEBER, MAX (1864-1920): German social scientist and theorist widely acclaimed as the "father of sociology." Weber is best known for his thesis of the Protestant ethic, which links the psychological effects of Calvinism with the development of modern capitalism. He detailed his theory in *The Protestant Ethic and the Spirit of Capitalism* (1904-1905).

WHITEHEAD, ALFRED NORTH (1861-1947): English philosopher who applied mathematical and scientific laws to philosophical ethics. He explored his theories in works such as *Science and the Modern World* (1925), *Religion in the Making* (1926), *Process and Reality: An Essay in Cosmology* (1929), *Symbolism: Its Meaning and Effect* (1927), and *Adventures of Ideas* (1933).

WIESEL, ELIE (1928-   ): Romanian-born author and rights activist. Wiesel is a significant figure in the human rights cause and author of *Night* (1956), one of the most influential and best known memoirs of a concentration camp survivor. He was awarded the Nobel Peace Prize in 1986.

Wilson, Edward O. (1929-   ): American scholar and activist whose work introduced a new academic discipline, sociobiology. Wilson believes that behavior is rooted in genetics. He has written on numerous subjects such as animal behavior and evolutionary psychology, biodiversity, environmental ethics, and the philosophy of knowledge. Author of the Pulitzer Prize-winning *On Human Nature* (1978), Wilson went on to write numerous other books including *The Diversity of Life* (1992), *Consilience: The Unity of Knowledge* (1998), and *The Future of Life* (2002).

Wilson, Woodrow (1856-1924): Twenty-eighth president of the United States (1913-1921) and the primary architect of the League of Nations.

WITTGENSTEIN, LUDWIG (1889-1951): Austrian-born British philosopher. Wittgenstein is one of the most important and influential philosophers of the twentieth century. He believed that moral value was outside the scope of philosophy. He was the author of *Tractatus Logico-Philosophicus* (1922), and *Philosophical Investigations* (1953).

WOLLSTONECRAFT, MARY (1759-1797): English journalist and educator who developed a comprehensive feminist program. She described her beliefs in her *Vindication of the Rights of Woman* (1792).

XUNZI (c. 307-c. 235 B.C.E.): Chinese philosopher who promoted a humanistic philosophy concerned with the moral training required to enhance one's self and character.

Zeno of Citum (c. 335-c. 263 B.C.E.): Greek philosopher who founded Stoicism, the principal Hellenistic school of philosophy. Stoicism focused on abstract ideas and on how an individual functioned in the world.

ZHU XI (1130-1200): Chinese philosopher whose most important contribution to the field of ethics was his examination of ethical behavior in and out of government.

ZHUANGZI (c. 369-286 B.C.E.): Chinese philosopher who incorporated individualism and naturalism into Daoist philosophy.

Glossary

Note that many terms listed here have multiple meanings. This glossary provides only the definitions most directly relevant to ethics.

A priori. Independent of, or logically prior to, lived experience; logically deduced solely from abstract rational premises without reference to empirical evidence.

Absolutist. Advocating the belief in objective truth and universal moral values.

Absurd, the: That which points toward the ultimately meaningless character of human life.

Accountable. Answerable for a moral or ethical transgression.

Actual. Existing; real.

Adjudicate. To act as a judge in a legal proceeding; or, to judge between two conflicting ethical claims or priorities.

Adversarial. Acting as opponents in a competition.

Afterlife. Eternal existence following death, usually in a location determined by the moral quality of one's actions while alive.

Ageism. Unfair treatment of people, or unjust beliefs about them, based upon their age.

Aggression: Any behavior that is intended to harm someone, either physically or verbally.

Ahiṁsā. Hindu practice of refraining from harming living creatures.

Alienation. Unnatural emotional isolation from, or inability to comprehend or communicate with, either oneself or the external world.

Alterity. Absolute radical difference; otherness.

Altruism. Unselfish devotion to helping others.

Anarchy. Political disorder; chaos.

Anathema. Hated or attacked as being diametrically opposed to one's own values.

Anthropocentrism. Tendency to see the world solely in terms of human concerns.

Anthropomorphism of the divine: Description of God or gods in terms of properties that are typical of human beings.

Applied ethics. Branch of moral philosophy that deals with making practical ethical choices and solving actual problems in the real world.

Argument. Series of logical statements designed to prove that something is true or to persuade another person to believe something.

Aristotelian ethics. Ethics based on the values and ideas central to Aristotle, especially concern with defining the nature of the good life and with the ultimate purpose, or *telos*, of all things.

Ascetic. Strictly observant of religious rules requiring self-denial and abstinence.

Atheism. Belief that there is no god.

Attribute. Property; characteristic.

Authentic. Truly originating from oneself and not imposed by outside influences; genuine.

Authority. Legitimate right to exercise power, issue commands, have one's judgments accepted, or have one's opinions believed.

Autonomy. Complete self-sufficiency and independence.

Bad faith. Dishonesty or insincerity behind words or actions designed to win someone's trust.

Benevolent. Kind.

Bigotry. Intolerance for the opinions of others.

Binding. Imposing an inescapable obligation.

Bioethics. Branch of ethics dealing with the moral implications of science and technology for medical practices and procedures.

Bodhisattva ideal. Deferral of nirvana so that one can help other, less enlightened people on their paths to nirvana.

Bushido: Japanese military code meaning "way of the warrior" that incorporates strict ethical responsibilities with a code of physical sacrifice.

Capitalism. Economic system in which private individuals and corporations are the primary owners of the means of production, and wealth circulates in order to create more wealth.

Casuistry. Making an argument to prove something that one knows to be false; or, applying general moral principles to resolve specific questions.

Character. One's level of personal integrity.

Charity: Sharing one's property and person with others in order to alleviate their basic needs.

Chivalry: Medieval code of stressing loyalty, wisdom, courage, generosity, religious fidelity, and the virtues of courtly love.

Citizen. Person both subject to a sovereign state and enjoying the full rights and privileges accorded to the members of that state.

Civil disobedience. Intentional violation of an unjust law; or, intentional violation of laws maintaining social order to draw public attention to, or to prevent, a specific injustice.

Class. One of the broad categories of economic identity, such as upper class, middle class, lower class, bourgeoisie, aristocracy, or proletariat, that divide and categorize the members of a given society.

Code. System of rules or laws governing behavior.

Coercion. Use of intimidation or force to make someone comply with one's desires.

Cognitivism. Belief that ethical utterances constitute logical propositions that can be evaluated for truth or falsity.

Command. Instruction or order given by someone in a position of authority.

Common good. Set of interests shared by all members of a group or society.

Common sense. Beliefs that, whether actually true or false, seem to be obviously true and to require no explanation or justification.

Communism. Politico-economic system in which private property has been abolished, the means of production are controlled by everyone equally (at least in theory), and wealth merely circulates without being created or increased; or, a social theory advocating the creation of such a system.

Communitarian. Ethically concerned primarily with the common good rather than the good of each individual member of the community.

Community. Group of people, of any size and geographic distribution, whose members perceive themselves as sharing certain traits, interests, or values in common.

Comparative ethics. Study of similarities and differences between the moral theories, moral values, and moral behaviors of different cultures or communities.

Compromise. To lessen one's demands in return for similar concessions on the part of an adversary; or, to jeopardize or violate the integrity of a thing, especially of something affecting one's character or reputation.

Conduct. Behavior, especially behavior regulated by codes of etiquette or professional ethics.

Confidentiality. Secrecy of information, deriving from the nature of the relationship in which the information was shared.

Conflict of interest. Situation in which one person has two goals or desires that are mutually exclusive, especially when one goal is a private desire and the other is a public goal; or, situation in which one professional serves two clients who are in direct or indirect competition with each other.

Conscience. Intuitive sense of right and wrong influencing one's moral decisions and behavior.

Conscientious objection: Refusal to perform an action, such as military service, on moral or religious grounds.

Consent. To give permission, especially permission to perform a medical procedure.

Consequence. Effect or result.

Consequentialism. Doctrine that the morality of one's actions should be judged by the positive or negative nature of their consequences.

Conservative. Advocating or believing in traditional values and institutions; generally resistant to change.

Consistency. Unwavering adherence to a pattern of behavior or belief; lack of self-contradiction.

Constraint. Physical or mental restriction, coercion, or obligation; lack of autonomy.

Contract. Formal, morally and legally binding agreement.

Conventional. Traditionally, customarily, or commonly done, accepted or believed.

Criterion. (plural, *criteria*). Standard of judgment; yardstick.

Critique. Evaluation of the form, content, significance, and effects of a human creation, institution, or pattern of behavior.

Culpability. Worthiness of blame; guilt.

Cultural. Deriving from culture rather than nature; produced by humans; artificial.

Culture. Set of all distinctive or meaningful ways of behaving, interrelating, communicating, and living common to a given society, social group, or subgroup.

Cynicism. Distrust of the motives of others or disbelief in the ability of ethical theory to guide actual human behavior; or, more narrowly (and always capitalized) a school of ancient Greek philosophy holding that self-control is the highest good.

Daoism. Philosophical system advocating a lifestyle of extreme simplicity and harmony with nature.

Deconstruction. Literary and philosophical movement that investigates the construction and consequences of truth, meaning, and value.

Defamation. Malicious lies designed to harm a person's reputation.

Deism: Belief that it is possible to establish the existence of an intelligent and ethical supreme being on the basis of reason.

Democracy. Government in which ultimate authority is vested in the citizenry.

Deontology. Formal study of duty and moral obligations.

Descriptive. Portraying or describing factually, without making value judgments.

Desert. Just reward or punishment, or other treatment that is merited.

Determinism. Belief that human thought and action are governed by the laws of cause and effect.

Deterrent. Explicit or implicit threat of consequences meant to discourage undesirable actions.

Diagnose. To determine the root cause of a symptom.

Difference. Existence of significant, socially meaningful dissimilarities between the members of a given community; or, quality or state of having a trait that prevents one from resembling another.

Dignity. Recognition of or respect for a person's inherent worth.

Dilemma. Problem that forces one to choose between two evils, or, more broadly, an insoluble problem

"Dirty hands." Taint one one bears when performing morally or ethically questionable acts.

Discipline. Self-control or self-regulation maintained through training.

Discrimination. Illegitimate treatment of an individual based on the social category, such as race or gender, to which the individual belongs.

Disempowered. Deprived of social influence or of control over one's own life.

Dissent. Public expression of disagreement with the values, methods, actions, or ideology of one's government or of the political majority.

Distributive justice. Fair allocation of resources to all members of a community.

Diversity. Presence of multiple types of people, with fundamentally different identities or values, within the same community.

Divine command theory: Belief that the ethical values and principles binding upon human beings depend only on the commands of a higher power or god.

Doctrine. Fundamental teaching or axiom advocated by a particular religion, government, philosophical school, or other formal belief system.

Dominant values. Values or ideologies accepted or followed by the majority of members of a community, including members whose own best interests may be damaged by their acceptance.

Dualism. Belief in the existence of two absolutely irreconcilable and fundamentally opposed entities, such as the mind and the body, good and evil, or facts and values.

Duress. Coercion that compels and thus legally invalidates or mitigates an action, decision, or contract by depriving one of the ability to consent or act freely.

Duty. Commitment one is morally required to fulfill.

Egalitarian. Embracing equality as one of the fundamental moral values; treating all people in exactly the same fashion.

Ego. Portion of the psyche, both conscious and unconscious, that forms the recognizable identity or self; the "I."

Egoism. Philosophical system that asserts that self-interest is the highest good.

Egotism. Tendency to understand all aspects of life in terms of their effects upon oneself.

Elitist. Characterized by a belief that one segment of society is better than another segment, because it is more educated, richer, or otherwise more fully developed.

Emotivism. Philosophical theory that language expresses and influences emotions, rather than signifying meanings or making logical assertions.

Empirical. Based solely upon perceptual experience rather than abstract theory.

Empiricism. Doctrine that all genuine knowledge and all legitimate philosophical theories derive from perceptual experience.

End. Entity whose value comes solely from itself and not from the uses to which it may be put; or, the ultimate purpose or goal.

Enlightenment, the. Philosophical movement of the seventeenth and eighteenth centuries characterized by a belief in the power of reason, the autonomy and sovereignty of the rational individual, and the existence of natural rights.

Entity. Particular, self-contained thing.

Environmental ethics. Branch of moral philosophy dealing with the rights and obligations of human beings with respect to nature.

Epistemology. Philosophical study of knowledge and the nature of truth.

Equality. State in which all people are acknowledged to have the same moral worth and to enjoy the same fundamental rights and privileges.

Ethics. Philosophical science that deals with the rightness and wrongness of human actions; closely allied with morality.

Ethnocentrism. Belief that one's own race or ethnicity is the norm according to which all others are to be judged.

Etiquette. Formal or informal code of conduct governing proper social behavior.

Euthanasia. Killing someone, or allowing someone to die, as an act of mercy.

Evidence. Facts, details, or observations that tend to support a subjective opinion or prove the truth of an objective assertion.

Evil. Clear and extreme moral transgression for the sake of such transgression alone; or, quality of taking pleasure in such an act; or, anything that has only harmful effects.

Excellence. Quality of surpassing all or most others in skill or achievement.

Excuse. Legitimate reason for a fault or transgression.

Existentialism. School of philosophy that holds that the world lacks objective meaning or purpose, but individuals are morally obligated to create such meaning for themselves.

Explanation. Description of a state of affairs in terms of causes and effects; description meant to make something make sense.

Exploit. To treat people as a means to achieve one's own ends, or as objects rather than as subjects; or, to extract surplus value from laborers.

Expression. Act of uttering, writing, or otherwise representing one's ideas or emotions to others; communication.

Fact. Something that is objectively true.

Fair. Unbiased; equitable; just.

Fatalism: Belief that events are predetermined by forces beyond human control and that individual destinies cannot be altered.

Federal. Pertaining to the central, national government of the United States.

Feminism. Political, social, and theoretical movements resisting masculine domination and masculinist values.

First philosophy. Branch of philosophy—different according to different philosophers—that grounds all other branches and that must therefore be completed prior to any other philosophical inquiry. The Greeks believed that ontology was first philosophy. In the Enlightenment, epistemology was considered first philosophy, and for some twentieth century philosophers, philosophy of language became first philosophy.

Formal. Official, or explicitly set out in writing or in some other manner that imparts authority or validity; or, having a rigorously defined set of elements and structure, as in a system or model.

Foundationalism. Philosophical doctrine that logical or scientific methods of reasoning both can and should be used to establish the objective truth or validity of knowledge and judgment, and that this grounding should take place prior to any further reasoning or action.

Four noble truths. Buddhist belief that eliminating consciousness of the individual self will enable one to overcome desire and to eliminate all suffering in one's life.

Fraud. Unfairly depriving someone of something of value by means of deception.

Free-riding: Enjoying of benefits produced by the efforts of others without contributing one's own fair share.

Freedom. Lack of constraint; autonomy of judgment and action; or, living in a manner that allows one to realize one's true potential and to express fully one's creative impulses.

Gaia hypothesis: Belief that the earth is a living entity whose biosphere is self-regulating and capable of maintaining planetary health by controlling its chemical and physical environment.

Gender. Set of cultural meanings and values that attach to or are produced by biological sex; that is, masculinity or femininity, as opposed to maleness or femaleness.

Genocide. Mass murder based on shared cultural identity of the victims.

Golden mean. Perfect balance between extremes.

Golden rule. Always do unto others as you would have them do unto you.

Good, the. Source or embodiment of moral value; the set of all things and actions that should be desired.

Good faith. Sincere attempt to do right by one's actions, regardless of their actual outcome; or, sincere intent to honor both the letter and the spirit of contract or agreement and to ensure that both parties to the agreement benefit from it.

Ground. To demonstrate logically the objective validity of a judgment, belief, or system.

Guilt. Moral culpability for wrongdoing; or, subjective awareness of such culpability accompanied by feelings of shame and remorse.

Happiness. Joy; or, living the good life.

Hate crime: Criminal acts committed against individuals or groups because of their race, ethnicity, religion, sexual orientation, or other group affiliation.

Homophobia. Irrational hatred of nonheterosexual people, or of one's own homosocial impulses.

Honor. Self-esteem based upon one's rigorous commitment to a personal or conventional ethical code.

Human nature. Qualities, capacities, or propensities shared in common by all human beings.

Human rights. Set of basic moral rights that inhere in all people.

Humanism. Philosophy grounded in a belief in human nature and in the ethical centrality of the values and interests shared by all people.

Humility. Self-effacement or modesty arising from one's recognition of people or forces whose power, value, or significance is greater than one's own.

Hypocrisy. Practice of condemning in public what one does in private, or otherwise espousing values one does not actually possess.

Id. Portion of the psyche, residing entirely in the unconscious, that consists solely of instinct and impulse, ungoverned by reason or restraint.

Idealism. Belief in noble principles that seem to conflict with the state of the actual world; dedication to achieving extremely or unrealistically high standards.

Idealism, German. School of philosophy concerned to investigate the nature and structure of subjective experience and its relationship to material reality.

Idealism, Platonic. School of philosophy that asserts that abstract concepts such as Justice or Equality exist independently of human subjects and have actual effects in the world.

Identity. Person's fundamental continuity of experience or character over time; the specific characteristic or characteristics felt to be most important in defining one's character; sense of self.

Identity politics. Activism rooted in specific, culturally significant categories of identity, such as race, class, gender, or sexuality.

Ideology. Socially determined structures of thought that make possible the conversion of perception into meaningful experience while simultaneously limiting the range of possible meanings of that experience; or, a specific example of these structures, as capitalist ideology, communist ideology, feminist ideology, patriarchal ideology, and so on.

Immediate. Intuited or known directly, without any intervening filter or template; not mediated.

Immortality: Eternal life.

Impartial. Unbiased; objective; fair.

Imperative. Demand or requirement for action.

Imperative, categorical. Imperative that is demanded universally by all situations, as "always treat people as ends in themselves and never as means only."

Imperative, hypothetical. Imperative that is demanded by a particular situation or goal, as "in order to keep your belongings safe, lock the door behind you."

Imply. To require logically, as the existence of a watch implies the existence of a watchmaker.

Inalienable. Inherent, unquestionable, and incapable of being taken away.

Incommensurable. Lacking any common basis for comparison or exchange.

Individualism. Interpretation of human culture or history in terms of single persons rather than groups or movements; belief that a single person is a more significant moral unit than is a community.

Inherent. Permanently, definitively, inseparably, or essentially characteristic of a person or thing; innate.

Innate. Arising necessarily as a result of the fundamental nature of a person or thing; inherent.

Institution. Publicly recognized, formally structured organization or set of relationships, especially one that generates some form of authority and distributes it hierarchically among its members.

Integrity. Strength of character; moral fortitude; honesty.

Intention. Purpose or motive behind an action.

Intentionality. Property of referring to something; "aboutness."

Interest. State of relative fulfillment or attainment of a need, benefit, or advantage; or, causal connection between a particular state of affairs and such a benefit.

Intrinsic. Resulting inherently from the essential nature of a thing; inseparable; innate.

Intuition. Direct, pure, immediate perception, insight, or knowledge.

Intuitionism. Philosophical belief that moral truth can be apprehended directly through intuition, rather than being learned or deduced logically.

Investment. Expenditure of emotion, energy, or value on a person, thing, or situation, in anticipation of a desired or beneficial result.

Involuntary. Against or not as a result of one's will; unintentional.

Irrational. Not based upon or agreeing with reason; nonsensical; illogical.

Judgment. Assignment of positive or negative value, moral praise, or blame to a person, thing, or action; evaluation.

Jurisprudence. Philosophy of law.

Justice. Fundamental moral principle or ideal of perfect correspondence between desert and actual reward or punishment.

Kantian ethics. Ethics based on the values and ideas central to Immanuel Kant, especially belief in a categorical imperative and the importance of moral duty.

Karma. Positive or negative spiritual energy resulting from moral or immoral acts.

Law. Formally or institutionally authorized rule, or set of all such rules in a given society.

Legitimate. Backed up, verified, or validated by official rules or standards; lawful; just.

Liable. Legitimately responsible; answerable in court.

Libel. Written defamation.

Liberal. Open to or advocating progress and reform; disinclined to preserve traditional values for the sake of tradition.

Liberal individualism. Central political ideology in the United States and much of Europe, that portrays individuals as autonomous, rational decision makers who enjoy fundamental natural rights.

Libertarianism. Political philosophy, combining social liberalism with economic conservatism, dedicated to maximizing individual liberties and minimizing centralized government.

Liberty. Political freedom; ability to act as one sees fit without interference by government.

Limited war. Warfare involving a fraction of the total military resources of a nation, or whose goal is to defeat or control only a fraction of the enemy's military or territory.

Lobby. To attempt to persuade a legislator to vote in a particular way.

Logic. Formal system of reasoning, rational argumentation, or analysis.

Logocentrism. Belief that logic is the superior method, or the only valid method, for divining truth, producing knowledge, or communicating.

Loyalty. Unwavering dedication; faithfulness.

Luck. Randomness or arbitrariness in events that affect one's life positively or negatively; fortune.

Lust. Strong or unmanageable desire, especially sexual desire.

Mādhyamaka: School of Buddhist philosophy advocating moderation in all things.

Manichean. Divided between two absolute extremes; given to seeing things as black or white.

Materialism. Marxist school of philosophy that asserts that brute physical reality, especially economic reality, is the ultimate determinant of history, and that economic and political changes cause new ideas, not the other way around; or, philosophical rejection of spirituality in favor of beliefs that correspond with empirically verifiable experience; or, trait of caring excessively about physical objects and wealth and ignoring spiritual or intangible values.

Meaning. Source and nature of the importance of a thing, person, idea, or situation; significance.

Means. Tool or method used to accomplish some goal.

Mediate. To filter, transmit, translate, or otherwise convey in an indirect fashion.

Mercy. Leniency motivated by compassion.

Merit. Legitimate claim to recognition or reward; desert.

Messiah. Prophesied figure who is expected to deliver the Jewish people from harm; or, any such promised deliverer or savior, such as Jesus Christ.

Messianism: Belief in a messiah.

Metaethics. Branch of philosophy concerned to ground or criticize the practice of ethics.

Metaphysics. Branch of philosophy that studies the fundamental nature of the world, especially as that nature relates to and is presupposed by other branches of philosophical inquiry; or, any specific set of presumptions about the nature of reality; or, belief that the world humans experience has a hidden, objective nature lying underneath its surface.

Metaphysics of presence. Belief that the world is composed of objects or things that exist independently of one another, that these objects present themselves to equally autonomous human subjects who can experience and evaluate them without affecting or being affected by them, and that the objects, once evaluated, can be exhaustively described and understood through logical propositions; or, belief that meaning is objectively present in spoken and written language, and that language can convey this meaning immediately from one speaker to another without the need for interpretation.

Model. System of rational principles or axioms that define the nature or parameters of a particular discipline, practice, or thing.

Monotheism. Belief in a single, all-powerful god.

Moral equivalence: Equating of the morality and ethics of two entities that are not usually seen as comparable, such as Adolf Hitler and Saddam Hussein.

Moral luck. Any instance of random fortune or chance that affects a person's ethical status.

Morality. Belief in right and wrong; or, any specific set of ethical values or beliefs, especially absolute or totalizing values.

Motive. Purpose or intent behind a given action; reason for acting.

Multiculturalism. Diversity of cultural backgrounds and viewpoints within a community; or, ethical position advocating such diversity or advocating tolerance for the mixture of values and beliefs that results from it.

Mysticism. Belief in a reality or a spiritual or divine entity that normally transcends human experience, but that can be contacted and provide enlightenment under specific circumstances.

Narrative. Story.

Nation. A people unified under, or desiring to be unified under, a centralized government; or, any such centralized government that exercises or enjoys sovereignty.

Nationalism. Belief that one's national affiliation defines one's identity and that one's nation commands one's absolute loyalty.

Natural law. Moral rules derived from objective human nature and applicable to and within all societies.

Natural rights. Rights enjoyed by all people according to the principles of natural law.

Naturalistic fallacy. Any attempt to define moral good in terms of something else, rather than taking it to be an irreducible concept in itself.

Necessary. Logically mandated as a prior requirement for some proposition to be true or for some situation to prevail.

Negative. Bad; or, reactive rather than active—defined primarily in terms of an opposition to some external entity or set of values, rather than in purely internal terms.

Negligence. Failure to take proper care or otherwise to safeguard some person or interest one was morally obligated to protect.

Nihilism. Rejection of all beliefs, except the belief that all other beliefs should be rejected.

Nirvana. Buddhist spiritual enlightenment and transcendence resulting from moral virtue.

Noncognitivism. Belief that ethical utterances are irrational expressions of value rather than fact, and that they therefore are neither true nor false.

Nonviolent resistance. Passive physical interference with unjust activities; or, passive refusal by a protester to comply with the instructions or commands of law enforcement agents who are placing the protester under arrest, requiring the agents to lift or drag the protester bodily in order to accomplish the arrest.

Norm. Accepted, average, or customary state of affairs.

Normative. Prescribing rules or making value judgments about what ought to be done and what ought not to be done.

Obedience. Compliance with commands issued by someone in authority; or, general tendency or predisposition to follow such commands.

Object. Thing or person that is acted upon, thought about, or judged.

Objective. Existing independently of human perceptions, values, or interpretations; simply and undeniably true; or, unbiased or impartial.

Objectivism. Philosophical belief that objective facts exist and are the necessary starting point for any genuine philosophy.

Obligation. Moral requirement or duty.

Ontology. Philosophical study of being and the nature of existence.

Oppression. Unjust, usually systematic, exercise of power or authority to subjugate a social group.

Optimism. Tendency to interpret things in the most positive possible light or to anticipate good things happening in the future.

Other. Absolutely different from the self, especially, characterized by attributes that are diametrically opposed to one's own or one's culture's most deeply cherished values.

Pacifism. Commitment to nonviolent resolution of conflict on all scales from the personal to the international.

Panentheism: Belief system that attempts to mediate between theism and pantheism.

Pantheism: Belief that God is synonymous with the universe.

Passion. Strong and irrational emotion.

Paternalism. Practice of intrusively managing or interfering in the affairs of others, purportedly for their own good.

Perspectivism. Belief that the world has no fundamental or inherent nature, and therefore that no single point of view can be exhaustive or objectively valid.

Pessimism. Tendency to interpret things in the most negative possible light or to anticipate bad things happening in the future.

Phenomenological. Having to do with the nature of subjective experience, especially as studied or understood from the internal point of view of the subject having the experience.

Philosophy. Formal study of knowledge, truth, reality, and value.

Platonic ethics. Ethics based on the values and ideas central to Plato, especially belief in objective, ideal forms and the importance of guiding all people to lead virtuous lives.

Pleasure. Feeling produced by the satisfaction of desire; enjoyment.

Pluralism. System that fosters tolerance for multiple points of view or advocacy of a community in which diverse perspectives are accepted or celebrated; or, ethical philosophy that asserts that there is a plural but finite number of valid moral beliefs and values.

Politically correct. In accord with or advocating an informal set of conventions governing appropriate and inappropriate forms of social and political speech.

Politics. Practice or profession of exercising governmental power; or, practice of maneuvering for power in a nongovernmental institution.

Positive. Good; or, the opposite of negative; active rather than reactive—defined primarily in terms of internal traits or values, rather than in opposition to something external.

Postmodernism. Set of aesthetic and intellectual movements within late capitalist or postindustrial culture, characterized primarily by a celebration of cultural fragmentation, by disbelief in any distinction between art and popular culture, and by an extreme skepticism toward any attempt to ground values or judgments.

Poststructuralism. School of philosophy and criticism that looks at human culture as a set of texts, and that understands those texts as rule-governed but irrational, noncentered structures or systems that include among their elements the philosopher or critic who reads them.

Power. Ability to have effects in the world.

Practical. Directed toward, preparing for, informing, or influencing concrete action.

Practice. Concrete action based upon or applying theoretical principles; or, a meaningful social activity that takes place within a specific institution and that can function as an arena for achievement or excellence.

Pragmatism. School of philosophy asserting that the meaning of a word or sign is a function of its practical effects in the world, and that the truth of a belief is determined by its usefulness.

Prejudice. Preconception, especially an unfavorable preconception about an individual based upon the individual's group affiliations; bias.

Prescription. Ethical command or edict.

Prescriptivism. Belief that moral language is meant to command actions and omissions, rather than describe values or express feelings or judgments.

Principle. General law or truth governing or grounding more specific laws or truths within a particular discipline or context; or, any generally accepted rule, especially one guiding proper moral conduct.

Prior restraint. Governmental or legal action that prevents someone in advance from publishing or otherwise circulating specific information or opinions.

Privacy. Right or ability to withhold some portion of one's life from public scrutiny or to protect it from governmental interference.

Private. Pertaining to or located within the domestic or personal sphere; separated from general social interaction.

Professional ethics. Codes of conduct defined by unions or other vocational organizations, or through customary work-related interactions, that define the moral standards of behavior required or expected of all members of a particular occupation or profession.

Progressive. Dedicated to reforming and improving society, especially through grassroots movements and by lobbying or otherwise utilizing existing social and political institutions.

Propaganda. Material designed to manipulate the opinions of its audience in order to support a particular ideology.

Property. That which belongs legitimately to a particular person, group, corporation, community, or government; anything that is owned; or, quality, characteristic, or attribute.

Proscription. Command to refrain from an action; interdiction; prohibition.

Prudence. Justifiable caution; good judgment.

Public. Pertaining to or located within the professional, political, or economic sphere; occurring outside domestic space and within the general purview of society.

Pure (of reason). Prior to or independent of practical experience; based solely on abstract logical principles without reference to the actual world.

Quality. Essential characteristic or attribute that distinguishes one thing from another.

Racism. Prejudice or bias that is based on race and that exists as a structural principle within one or more social or political institutions.

Rational. Based on reason; sensical; logical.

Rationale. Reason provided to justify something, especially an empty or specious reason invented to justify a course of action already desired or settled upon, or a reason created after the fact to provide retrospective justification.

Rationalism. Doctrine that all genuine knowledge and all legitimate philosophical theories derive from abstract logic or reason.

Rationality. Faculty of logic and reason within the human psyche; or, quality of being reasonable or logical.

Realism. Moral theory that holds that values, including ethical values, have an objective existence in the world; or, set of aesthetic movements that attempt to portray objects, or to transmit meanings, without calling attention to the techniques, styles, or signs used to accomplish the portrayal or transmission.

Realpolitik. Doctrine that political policies and actions, especially in foreign affairs, should be based solely on practical considerations and should be unaffected by moral or ethical principles.

Reason. Rational faculty of the human mind that evaluates, judges, and makes sense of its experiences; logic.

Recognition. Sympathetic perception of another person that acknowledges the inherent worth both of the person and of the person's goals, projects, and desires.

Reconcile. To cause two contradictory principles to coexist or fit together.

Regulation. Formal, usually quasi-legal, rule published or circulated in an official set of guidelines or principles.

Relationship. Connection or association between two or more entities.

Relativism. Belief that the fundamental or inherent nature of the world is such that it admits of an infinite number of valid, exhaustive descriptions, or that all moral beliefs are true.

Religion. Any systematic and customary set of shared beliefs in a supernatural or divine Entity or entities that gives meaning to or provides explanations of human experience, and that generally includes a specific set of moral values and principles to guide human action.

Resources. Any materials, skills, objects, abilities, currency, or other potentially useful items of value that are in finite supply.

Responsibility. Accountability; liability; culpability.

Retaliation. Vengeful or strategic response to a wrongful or transgressive action; reprisal.

Reverse discrimination. Discrimination by members of a socially disempowered group against a socially empowered group; or, institutional discrimination in favor of a socially disempowered group designed to correct or redress traditional discrimination against that group.

Revolution. Sudden social and political change or upheaval.

Right. That which is fair, just, and proper; the set of all actions that are permissible or required by accepted moral principles.

Rights. Objectively legitimate, universally valid moral claims to privileges or entitlements; or, similar claims whose legitimacy is derived from specific laws or legal principles within a particular society.

Rule. Principle; regulation; law.

Salvation. Deliverance from the world of pain to a transcendent or paradisiacal existence, especially deliverance from and redemption of sin.

Secular. Advocating belief only in empirical reality; nonreligious.

Self. Unified entity or identity underlying all subjective experience and differentiated from the external world of objects and other subjects; ego.

Self-regulation. Voluntary passage of formal, internal rules of ethical conduct by a professional organization or other entity that might otherwise be subject to external regulation by the government.

Semiotics. Study of signs.

Sense. One of the five types of physical interface between the human perceiving mind and the external world: sight, hearing, taste, touch, or smell; or, any mental faculty that seems to convey infor-

mation or perceptions to the mind in a manner analogous to the physical senses; intuition; or, a specific feeling or intuition conveyed by such a faculty.

Sentience. Conscious awareness.

Sentiment. Feeling, sense, or emotion.

Sex. Physical distinction between two biological reproductive categories, upon which gender identities are based; that is, maleness or femaleness, as opposed to masculinity or femininity.

Sexism. Prejudice or bias that is based on sex or gender and that exists as a structural principle within one or more social or political institutions.

Sign. Any thing that conventionally symbolizes or stands for another thing or otherwise conveys or expresses meaning.

Signify. To symbolize; to mean; to stand for.

Sin. Serious moral transgression, especially transgression against religious moral laws.

Situated. Placed or located; having a particular position or perspective; partial rather than impartial.

Situation. State of affairs; context.

Situational ethics. Nonuniversal, nonabsolutist ethics based solely upon moral principles that arise from the particular context in which a moral decision or act takes place.

Skepticism. Intentional doubt of apparent or obvious truths, cultivated as a method to facilitate successful philosophical inquiry; or, unintentional doubt, or utter inability to believe in such truths.

Slander. Spoken defamation.

Slippery slope. Tendency of minor erosions of safeguards, scruples, or freedoms to escalate rapidly into major erosions and to continue escalating until the safeguards, scruples, or freedoms no longer exist.

Social. Having to do with the communal or interactive aspects of human behavior.

Social contract. Theoretical construct retroactively describing the circumstances under which society would have formed if it were formed as a result of rational, premeditated choice.

Social Darwinism. Political philosophy, modeled loosely and unscientifically after Darwin's theory of evolution by means of natural selection, that seeks to apply the theory to societies as if they were organisms.

Social justice. Fair and equitable distribution of wealth, resources, and power across all levels of society or throughout the globe, especially to counteract or ameliorate disparities produced by the division of labor.

Society. Large-scale, usually national, group of people that exists in a set of highly structured relationships, produces an identifiable culture or set of cultures, and understands itself as a community.

Sophism. Philosophical school popularly believed to have taught that rhetorical skill was more important than, or constitutive of, truth and that successful legal argumentation was more important than, or constitutive of, moral right.

Spiritual. Valuing intangible or mystical types of experience, or things of benefit to the soul, rather than wealth or other material objects and pleasures of the body.

Standard. Thing to which one compares all other things of the same class or type; basis for evaluation or judgment.

State. Unit of political sovereignty, especially a nation that enjoys a legal monopoly on the means of violence within its borders.

State of nature. Philosophical fiction describing human experience prior to or outside of any community.

Stereotype. Caricatured mental image or other preconception about members of a social group or class based upon simplification and exaggeration of features that are common among the group.

Stoicism. Ancient Greek philosophy characterized by studied indifference to joys and sorrows and advocating the use of reason alone to make moral decisions.

Subject. Self-aware, knowing, judging, willing, and communicating entity; a total self, including the conscious mind, the unconscious mind, and other aspects of identity that exceed the "I" or ego.

Subjective. Biased, partial, or otherwise based upon personal values and experience; or, perceived or experienced by a subject.

Subjectivism. Belief that knowledge is partial or perspectival by definition, and that objective knowledge is not only impossible but is an incoherent concept.

Subjectivity. Conscious, self-conscious, and unconscious rational and irrational mental processes of a sentient, social, and linguistic entity; interiority; psyche.

Sufficient. Logically adequate in itself to cause some proposition to be true or some situation to prevail.

Superego. Portion of the psyche, residing largely but not solely in the preconscious, that regulates, restrains, and redirects thoughts and desires before they can become fully conscious or before they can motivate action; conscience.

Supererogation: Doing what is morally praiseworthy beyond what is required by duty or what is required to be free of moral blame.

Supernatural. Not explainable by the scientifically accepted laws of nature.

Symptom. Perceivable sign that indicates the existence of a hidden problem, disease, or contradiction.

System. Rationally ordered set of elements, structured in well-defined relationships to one another, that forms a unitary whole.

Teleology. Belief that the world as a whole, or things in the world, have objective purposes or ends.

Telos. Greek word referring to the "final cause" or ultimate purpose of an entity.

Terror. Violence perpetrated to eliminate difference.

Theism. Belief in the existence of a higher power, or god, who is responsible for creating the earth and humankind and on whom all finite things are in some way dependent.

Theodicy. Theological explanation for the presence of evil in a world created by a benevolent deity.

Theology. Study of religion; or, a particular body of religious belief or doctrine.

Theory. Abstract rational knowledge of general rules or principles; or, a proposed fact or principle that has yet to be proven or disproven; or, a nickname (often capitalized) for a large body of academic social, literary, and cultural theory that is meant to be applicable to the interpretation and analysis of every meaningful aspect of human existence; critical theory.

Tolerance. Allowing or acceptance of difference.

Totalizing. Claiming to apply to or include everything, without exception.

Traditional. Rooted in the practices or values of the past; conventional; customary.

Transcendental. Investigating subjective experience in order to deduce facts or truths that exist beyond or prior to subjective experience.

Transgression. Violation; crime; impermissible or forbidden act.

Truth. Quality of beliefs that causes them to count as knowledge, of statements that causes them to count as honest or accurate, and of propositions that causes them to count as factual.

Tyranny. Cruel, domineering, or illegitimate rule.

Understand. To know the meaning or importance of; to comprehend.

Universal. Applying equally to all things in all times and all places.

Utilitarianism. Hedonistic social philosophy that asserts that usefulness is the highest good.

Value. Goodness or badness; worth.

Vice. An immoral or merely frowned-upon pleasure; or body of such pleasures generally.

Violence. Material or spiritual attack causing physical or emotional harm.

Virtue. An inherent moral value, or body of such values generally.

Voluntary. Caused through the exercise of will; freely chosen.

War. Large-scale combat between societies, usually nation-states or national factions.

Western. Having to do with the dominant or the traditionally dominant cultures or values shared by Western Europe and the United States.

Will. Ability intentionally to act or to refrain from action; volition.

Worth. Relative value.

Wrong. That which is unfair, unjust, or improper; the set of all actions that are impermissible or forbidden by accepted moral principles.

Zen: Buddhist school whose adherents seek an experiential perception of reality through meditation.

Andy Perry

Nobel Peace Prize Winners

Year	Recipients	Reason
1901	Jean Henri Dunant (Swiss)	Founding of International Red Cross and Geneva Convention
	Frédéric Passy (French)	Founding of first French peace society
1902	Élie Ducommun (Swiss)	Work with Permanent International Peace Bureau
	Charles Albert Gobat (Swiss)	Administration of Inter-Parliamentary Union and International Peace Bureau
1903	Sir William Cremer (British)	Founder and secretary of International Arbitration League
1904	Institute of International Law	Development of international law and studies of laws of neutrality
1905	Bertha von Suttner (Austrian)	Support of pacifist societies; founding of Austrian peace society
1906	Theodore Roosevelt (American)	Negotiations to end Russo-Japanese War
1907	Ernesto Teodoro Moneta (Italian)	Work with Lombard League for Peace
	Louis Renault (French)	Organization of peace conferences
1908	Klas Pontus Arnoldson (Swedish)	Founding of Swedish Society for Arbitration and Peace
	Fredrik Bajer (Danish)	Work with International Peace Bureau
1909	Auguste Beernaert (Belgian)	Work with Permanent Court of Arbitration
	Paul d'Estournelles de Constant (French)	Founding and direction of French Parliamentary Arbitration Committee
1910	Permanent International Peace Bureau	Promotion of international peace and arbitration
1911	Tobias Asser (Dutch)	Conferences on international law
	Alfred Fried (Austrian)	Writings on peace; editor of *Die Friedenswarte*
1912	Elihu Root (American)	Organization of Central American Peace Conference; settlement of problem of Japanese immigration into California
1913	Henri Lafontaine (Belgian)	President of International Peace Bureau
1914-1916	No awards	
1917	International Committee of the Red Cross	War relief
1918	No award	
1919	Woodrow Wilson (American)	Support for League of Nations
1920	Léon Bourgeois (French)	President, Council of League of Nations
1921	Karl Hjalmar Branting (Swedish)	Promotion of Swedish social reforms
	Christian Lous Lange (Norwegian)	Secretary-general, Inter-Parliamentary Union
1922	Fridtjof Nansen (Norwegian)	Russian relief work; originated Nansen passports for refugees
1923-1924	No awards	
1925	Sir Austen Chamberlain (British)	Locarno Peace Pact
	Charles G. Dawes (American)	Plan for German reparations
1926	Aristide Briand (French)	Locarno Peace Pact
	Gustav Stresemann (German)	German acceptance of reparation plan; development of Locarno Peace Pact
1927	Ferdinand Buisson (French)	President, League of Human Rights
	Ludwig Quidde (German)	Writings on peace; participation in peace conferences
1928	No award	

Year	Recipients	Reason
1929	Frank B. Kellogg (American)	Negotiations for Kellogg-Briand Peace Pact condemning war as means of solving international problems
1930	Nathan Söderblom (Swedish)	Writings on peace; association with ecumenical movement
1931	Jane Addams (American)	Work for international peace; president, Women's International League for Peace and Freedom
	Nicholas Murray Butler (American)	Work with Carnegie Endowment for International Peace; promoter of Kellogg-Briand Pact
1932	No award	
1933	Norman Angell (British)	Work for international peace; author of *The Great Illusion*
1934	Arthur Henderson (British)	President, World Disarmament Conference of 1932
1935	Carl von Ossietzky (German)	Promotion of international disarmament; pacifist writings
1936	Carlos Saavedra Lamas (Argentine)	Negotiation of peace settlement between Bolivia and Paraguay
1937	Lord Robert Cecil (British)	Working with peace movements; founding of International Peace Campaign
1938	Nansen International Office for Refugees	Relief work among refugees
1939-1943	No awards	
1944	International Committee of the Red Cross	War relief
1945	Cordell Hull (American)	Work for peace as United States secretary of state; work on formation of United Nations
1946	John R. Mott (American)	YMCA work/relief for displaced persons
	Emily Greene Balch (American)	President, Women's International League for Peace and Freedom
1947	Friends Service Council and the American Friends Service Committee	Humanitarian work
1948	No award	
1949	Lord John Boyd-Orr (British)	Directing United Nations Food and Agriculture Organization
1950	Ralph Bunche (American)	Mediation of Israeli War for Independence; director, Division of Trusteeship of the United Nations
1951	Léon Jouhaux (French)	Organization of national and international labor unions
1952	Albert Schweitzer (German)	Humanitarian work in Africa
1953	George C. Marshall (American)	Promotion of European Recovery Program
1954	Office of the United Nations High Commissioner for Refugees	Work on refugee problems
1955-1956	No awards	
1957	Lester B. Pearson (Canadian)	Organization of United Nations' Egyptian force; president, United Nations General Assembly
1958	Georges Pire (Belgian)	Settlement of displaced persons
1959	Philip Noel-Baker (British)	Promotion of peace; author of *The Arms Race: A Program for World Disarmament*
1960	Albert Lutuli (South African)	Campaign against South African racial segregation
1961	Dag Hammarskjöld (Swedish)	Work for peace in Congo; secretary general of United Nations
1962	Linus Pauling (American)	Work for elimination of nuclear weapons

Year	Recipients	Reason
1963	International Committee of the Red Cross and the League of Red Cross Societies	Humanitarian work
1964	Martin Luther King, Jr. (American)	Nonviolent protests in support of civil rights for blacks
1965	United Nations Children's Fund (UNICEF)	Worldwide aid for children
1966-1967	No awards	
1968	René Cassin (French)	Promotion of human rights; drafter of United Nations Declaration of Human Rights
1969	International Labour Organisation	Improvement of working conditions
1970	Norman E. Borlaug (American)	Increases in food production through development of high-yield grains of wheat and rice
1971	Willy Brandt (German)	Improvement of East-West relations and promotion of European unity
1972	No award	
1973	Henry Kissinger (American) and Le Duc Tho (Vietnamese) (Declined award)	Negotiation of Vietnam War cease-fire
1974	Seán MacBride (Irish)	Work for human rights
	Eisaku Satō (Japanese)	Work to improve international relations; work toward limitation of nuclear weapons
1975	Andrei Sakharov (Soviet)	Promotion of peace and respect for human rights for the individual
1976	Mairead Corrigan (Irish) and Betty Williams (Irish)	Organization of movement to end sectarian violence in Northern Ireland
1977	Amnesty International	Aid for political prisoners
1978	Menachem Begin (Israeli) Anwar el-Sadat (Egyptian)	Efforts in settling Middle East conflict
1979	Mother Teresa (Agnes Bojaxhiu; Albanian)	Aid and service to India's poor
1980	Adolfo Pérez Esquivel (Argentine)	Promotion of human rights and nonviolence
1981	Office of the United Nations High Commissioner for Refugees	Support for refugees
1982	Alva Myrdal (Swedish) and Alfonso García Robles (Mexican)	United Nations disarmament negotiations
1983	Lech Wałesa (Polish)	Nonviolent campaign for workers' rights in Poland
1984	Desmond Tutu (South African)	Nonviolent campaign against South African racial separation
1985	International Physicians for the Prevention of Nuclear War	Campaign on potential effects of nuclear war
1986	Elie Wiesel (American)	Efforts on behalf of victims of repression and racial discrimination
1987	Oscar Arias Sánchez (Costa Rican)	Attempts to end wars in Central America
1988	United Nations peacekeeping forces	Prevention of military conflicts
1989	The Dalai Lama (Tibetan)	Nonviolent efforts opposing Chinese occupation of Tibet
1990	Mikhail Gorbachev (Soviet)	Promotion of world peace by reducing East-West tension

Year	Recipients	Reason
1991	Aung San Suu Kyi (Burmese)	Nonviolent promotion of human rights and democracy in Burma
1992	Rigoberta Menchú (Guatemalan)	Work for social justice and recognition of the cultures of indigenous peoples
1993	Nelson Mandela and F. W. de Klerk (South African)	Work for a negotiated end to apartheid
1994	Yasir Arafat (Palestinian) and Shimon Peres and Yitzhak Rabin (Israeli)	Efforts to end the Middle East's Israeli-Palestinian conflict
1995	Joseph Rotblat (British) and Pugwash Conferences on Science and World Affairs	Development of the Russell-Einstein Manifesto, which established the annual Pugwash Conferences for limiting and ultimately eliminating nuclear weapons
1996	Carlos Filipe Ximenes Belo and José Ramos-Horta (East Timorian)	Work to end the conflict between East Timor and the government of Indonesia
1997	International Campaign to Ban Landmines; Jody Williams (American)	Work to eliminate land mines throughout the world
1998	John Hume and David Trimble (British)	Efforts to end Northern Ireland's Protestant-Roman Catholic conflict
1999	Médecins Sans Frontières	Humanitarian medical work throughout the world
2000	Kim Dae-jung (South Korean)	Work in support of human rights in South Korea and Southeast Asia
2001	Kofi Annan (Ghanaian) and United Nations	Work to resolve international conflicts
2002	Jimmy Carter (American)	Longtime efforts to find peaceful solutions to conflicts and promotion of international social and economic cooperation
2003	Shirin Ebadi (Iranian)	Championing of women's and children's rights in Iran
2004	Wangari Muta Maathai	Leading Green Belt Movement that has contributed to sustainable development in Africa by planting more than thirty million trees and campaigning for women's rights.

Organizations

Listed below are centers, institutions, organizations, and societies that dispense information, conduct research, sponsor education, and advocate policies promoting ethical issues and topics.

AARP

FOUNDED: 1958
601 E Street NW
Washington, DC 20049
PHONE: (888) 687-2277
FAX: (202) 434-2320
WEB SITE: www.aarp.org/
ETHICAL CONCERNS: Civil rights; elder rights; politico-economic ethics

Formerly known as the American Association of Retired Persons, AARP is committed to helping older Americans achieve lives of dignity, independence, and purpose. Members are afforded easy access to information on such topics as computers and the Internet, finances, health and wellness, legislative issues, and leisure activities.

Accuracy in Media (AIM)

FOUNDED: 1969
4455 Connecticut Avenue NW, Suite 330
Washington, DC 20008
PHONE: (800) 787-4567
FAX: (202) 364-4098
E-MAIL: info@aim.org
WEB SITE: www.aim.org/
ETHICAL CONCERNS: Media ethics; professional ethics

Grassroots news media monitoring group that assesses "botched and bungled" news stories and corrects the record on significant issues that have received biased coverage. AIM's intent is to promote fair and objective media coverage without bias or partisanship.

American Academy of Religion (AAR)

FOUNDED: 1909
825 Houston Mill Road NE, Suite 300
Atlanta, GA 30329-4205
PHONE: (404) 727-3049
FAX: (404) 727-7959
WEB SITE: www.aarweb.org/
ETHICAL CONCERNS: Religion; religious ethics

World's largest organization for American scholars in the field of religious studies. The Ethics Section of the AAR provides a symposium for the ethical issues all religious bodies face.

American Association of Retired Persons. See **AARP**

American Bar Association (ABA)

FOUNDED: 1878
321 North Clark Street
Chicago, IL 60610
PHONE: (312) 988-5000
E-MAIL: askaba@abanet.org
WEB SITE: w3.abanet.org/home.cfm
ETHICAL CONCERNS: Attorney conduct; legal ethics

Organization founded to serve as the voice of the legal profession. Although the ABA does not have the authority to chastise attorneys, it influences attorney behavior through its ethical guidelines. One of the ABA's goals is "to achieve the highest standards of professionalism, competence and ethical conduct." The ABA has three committees relating to ethics: the Special Committee on Bioethics and the Law, the Standing Committee on Ethics and Professional Responsibility, and the Legal Ethics and Professional Responsibility committee.

American Catholic Philosophical Association

FOUNDED: 1926
Administration Building
Fordham University
Bronx, NY 10458
PHONE: (718) 817-4081
FAX: (718) 817-5709
E-MAIL: acpa@fordham.edu
WEB SITE: www.acpa-main.org/
ETHICAL CONCERNS: Ethical issues; philosophy

The members of the association, largely composed of college and university professors of philosophy, incorporate the work of major philosophers from every era into the issues and focus of modern philosophy. Basic ethical issues are often the focus of conferences and research carried out by the association.

American Civil Liberties Union (ACLU)
FOUNDED: 1920
125 Broad Street, 18th Floor
New York, NY 10004
PHONE: (212) 344-3005
WEB SITE: www.aclu.org/
ETHICAL CONCERNS: Civil liberties; civil rights; legal ethics

Established to safeguard civil liberties, the ACLU works in communities, courts, and legislatures to defend First Amendment rights, equal protection, right to due process, and the right to privacy laws afforded to all Americans under the Constitution and Bill of Rights.

American Enterprise Institute
FOUNDED: 1943
1150 Seventeenth Street NW
Washington, DC 20036
PHONE: (202) 862-5800
FAX: (202) 862-7177
E-MAIL: info@aei.org
WEB SITE: www.aei.org
ETHICAL CONCERNS: Domestic policy; international policy; moral issues

Think tank established to uphold and enrich cultural and political values in the United States. Research on moral issues and domestic and international economic policy is conducted and published by the institute.

American Federation of Labor and Congress of Industrial Organizations (AFL-CIO)
FOUNDED: 1955
815 16th Street NW
Washington, DC 20006
PHONE: (202) 637-5000
FAX: (202) 637-5058
WEB SITE: www.aflcio.org/
ETHICAL CONCERNS: Business and labor ethics; economic justice; social justice

Formed through a merger, the AFL-CIO was created to fight for economic and social justice in the workplace and throughout the United States. It is a voluntary federation of national and international la-bor unions whose goals include empowering working families, strengthening the political voice of families, and providing a voice for workers in the global economy.

American Humanist Association (AHA)
FOUNDED: 1941
1777 T Street NW
Washington, DC 20009-7125
PHONE: (202) 238-9088
FAX: (202) 238-9003
E-MAIL: aha@americanhumanist.org
WEB SITE: www.americanhumanist.org/
ETHICAL CONCERNS: Civil liberties; education; humanism; human rights

The AHA introduces social reforms and establishes new programs. Much notable progress in the areas of civil liberties, education, human rights, humanistic psychology, and science was first proposed and supported by the AHA and by Humanists.

American Inns of Court (AIC)
FOUNDED: 1985
1229 King Street
Alexandria, VA 22314
PHONE: (703) 684-3590
FAX: (703) 684-3607
E-MAIL: info@innsofcourt.org
WEB SITE: www.innsofcourt.org/default.asp
ETHICAL CONCERNS: Legal and judicial ethics; professional ethics

Organization of legal professionals whose purpose is to enrich the abilities, ethics, and professionalism of judges and lawyers. Most inns focus on issues encompassing civil and criminal litigation. There are others that focus on administrative law, family law, federal litigation, labor law, white-collar crime, and numerous other types of law.

American Medical Association (AMA)
FOUNDED: 1847
515 North State Street
Chicago, IL 60610
PHONE: (800) 621-8335
WEB SITE: www.ama-assn.org/
ETHICAL CONCERNS: Bioethics; medical ethics; professional ethics

Principal organization of medical doctors that advocates for patients and physicians and works toward the betterment of the health care system in the United States. The AMA's code of medical ethics, first issued in 1847, underwent several substantial revisions during the twentieth century. In 1997 the AMA established the Institute for Ethics, an academic research center that conducts research on end-of-life matters, genetics, managed care, and professionalism. The institute's own Web site is located at ife@ama-assn.org. The AMA also sponsors the Ethics Resource Center, which provides students and physicians with the instruments and ability to handle ethical difficulties in a transforming health care climate. Its Web site is erc@ama-assn.org.

American Philosophical Association (APA)

FOUNDED: 1900
31 Amstel Avenue
University of Delaware
Newark, DE 19716-4797
PHONE: (302) 831-1112
FAX: (302) 831-8690
E-MAIL: apaOnline@udel.edu
WEB SITE: www.udel.edu/apa
ETHICAL CONCERNS: Ethical issues; philosophy

One of the largest philosophical societies in the world, with a membership of over 10,000. Ethical issues are a major focus of the association. The APA publishes newsletters and holds conferences related to many issues in ethics such as computer use, the environment, feminism, law, medicine, and race.

American Society for Bioethics and Humanities (ASBH)

FOUNDED: 1998
4700 West Lake
Glenview, IL 60025-1485
PHONE: (847) 375-4745
FAX: (877) 734-9385
E-MAIL: info@asbh.org
WEB SITE: www.asbh.org/
ETHICAL CONCERNS: Bioethics; professional ethics

ASBH strives to further the sharing of ideas and promote "multidisciplinary, interdisciplinary, and interprofessional scholarship, research, teaching, policy development, professional development, and collegiality" among those working in fields related to bioethics and health-associated humanities.

American Society for the Prevention of Cruelty to Animals (ASPCA)

FOUNDED: 1866
424 East 92nd Street
New York, NY 10128-6804
PHONE: (212) 876-7700
E-MAIL: napcc@aspca.org
WEB SITE: www.aspca.org/site/PageServer
ETHICAL CONCERNS: Animal rights

The ASPCA promotes respect for and humane treatment of all animals. The ASPCA conducts nationwide programs in humane education, public awareness, government advocacy, shelter support, and animal medical services and placement.

American Society of Newspaper Editors (ASNE)

FOUNDED: 1922
11690B Sunrise Valley Drive
Reston, VA 20191-1409
PHONE: (703) 453-1122
FAX: (703) 453-1133
E-MAIL: asne@asne.org
WEB SITE: www.asne.org
ETHICAL CONCERNS: Media ethics; professional ethics

The goals of the ASNE are to maintain the propriety and rights of the craft of journalism, to contemplate and institute ethical standards of professional conduct, and to exchange ideas for the promotion of professional ideals.

Amnesty International (AI)

FOUNDED: 1961
322 8th Avenue
New York, NY 10001
PHONE: (212) 807-8400
FAX: (212) 463-9193
E-MAIL: admin-us@aiusa.org
WEB SITE: www.amnesty.org/
ETHICAL CONCERNS: Death penalty; human rights; international relations

Watchdog organization established to campaign for internationally accepted human rights. AI conducts research and seeks to prevent and end human rights abuses worldwide. The following are some of the types of campaigns initiated by AI: ending violence against women, controlling arms, ending the use of child soldiers, eradicating the death penalty, ending torture, fighting for international justice, fighting for economic globalization and human rights.

Anti-Defamation League (ADL)

FOUNDED: 1913
823 United Nations Plaza
New York, NY 10017
E-MAIL: webmaster@adl.org
WEB SITE: www.adl.org/adl.asp
ETHICAL CONCERNS: Anti-Semitism; civil liberties; discrimination; prejudice

Founded to combat the vilification of Jewish people, the ADL strives to achieve fair and just treatment for all citizens. The league also monitors the activities of hate groups. In 1977, the ADL founded the Braun Center of Holocaust Studies (later renamed the Braun Holocaust Institute). It also publishes a magazine on the Holocaust, *Dimensions: A Journal of Holocaust Studies*.

Association for Practical and Professional Ethics (APPE)

FOUNDED: 1991
Indiana University
618 East Third Street
Bloomington, IN 47405-3602
PHONE: (812) 855-6450
FAX: (812) 855-3315
E-MAIL: appe@indiana.edu
WEB SITE: www.indiana.edu/~appe/
ETHICAL CONCERNS: Professional ethics

Established to foster high-caliber interdisciplinary scholarship and teaching of ethics, APPE supports this mandate by advancing communication and shared ventures among centers, colleges, and professional associations.

Association for the Prevention of Torture (APT)

FOUNDED: 1977
Route de Ferney 10
P.O. Box 2267
CH-1211 Geneva 2
Switzerland
PHONE: 41 22 919 21 70
FAX: 41 22 919 21 80
E-MAIL: apt@apt.ch
WEB SITE: www.apt.ch
ETHICAL CONCERNS: Human rights; torture

Independent nongovernmental organization working worldwide to prevent torture and inhumane treatment of prisoners.

Brookings Institution

FOUNDED: 1916
1775 Massachusetts Avenue NW
Washington, DC 20036
PHONE: (202) 797-6000
FAX: (202) 797-6004
E-MAIL: webmaster@brookings.edu
WEB SITE: www.brook.edu/
ETHICAL CONCERNS: Economics; foreign policy; government

Independent and nonpartisan think tank devoted to research, analysis, and public education, with a focus on economics, government, and foreign policy.

Carnegie Council on Ethics and International Affairs

FOUNDED: 1914
Merrill House
170 East 64th Street
New York, NY 10021-7478
PHONE: (212) 838-4120
FAX: (212) 752-2432
E-MAIL: info@cceia.org
WEB SITE: www.cceia.org
ETHICAL CONCERNS: Armed conflict; economics; environmental protection; global justice; human rights

Organization's original objective was to achieve world peace. The council has evolved into a medium for education and study in ethics and international policy. The council gathers specialists to discuss numerous ethical approaches to confusing moral problems such as environmental protection, human rights violations, and global economic disparities.

Center for Environmental Philosophy (CEP)

FOUNDED: 1989
University of North Texas
370 EESAT
P.O. Box 310980
Denton, TX 76203-0980
PHONE: (940) 565-2727
FAX: (940) 565-4439
E-MAIL: cep@unt.edu

WEB SITE: www.cep.unt.edu/
ETHICAL CONCERNS: Environmental ethics

CEP publishes the journal *Environmental Ethics*, promotes research in environmental ethics through conferences and workshops, reprints significant books through its book series *Environmental Ethics Books*, and promotes graduate and postdoctoral research and education in environmental ethics.

Center for Professional Responsibility

FOUNDED: 1978
321 North Clark Street, 15th Floor
Chicago, IL 60610
PHONE: (312) 988-5323
E-MAIL: ETHICSearch@staff.abanet.org
ETHICAL CONCERNS: Legal ethics

Established by the American Bar Association (see above), the center produces and interprets principles and academic resources in legal ethics, professional behavior, professional responsibility, and client protection mechanisms. A feature of the center is its Ethics Department, which is the nucleus for development, research, and implementation of legal and judicial ethical principles. The department distributes information in various ways, such as advising the ABA Standing Committee on Ethics and Professional Responsibility and through its use of ETHICSearch. ETHICSearch is a comprehensive research service that studies ethical predicaments and identifies suitable standards to settle the problems.

Center for Science in the Public Interest (CSPI)

FOUNDED: 1971
1875 Connecticut Avenue NW, Suite 300
Washington, DC 20009
PHONE: (202) 332-9110
FAX: (202) 265-4954
E-MAIL: cspi@cspinet.org
WEB SITE: www.cspinet.org/
ETHICAL CONCERNS: Consumer protection; health and nutrition

Consumer advocacy organization that has focused on health and nutrition and food safety issues for the American public. The CSPI conducts research on issues such as alcohol, the environment, food, and health and dispenses up-to-date, unbiased information to consumers and policymakers.

Children's Bureau

FOUNDED: 1912
330 C Street SW
Washington, DC 20447
WEB SITE: www.acf.hhs.gov/programs/cb
ETHICAL CONCERNS: Children's rights

Oldest federal organization to advocate for children's rights. Its original intent was to handle problems related to infant mortality, preventive medicine, orphanages, the juvenile justice system, and child labor. The agency's efforts have evolved to include preventing child abuse and finding new homes for children who have been removed from their homes because of neglect or abuse.

Congress of Racial Equality (CORE)

FOUNDED: 1942
817 Broadway
New York, NY 10003
PHONE: (212) 598-4000
FAX: (212) 598-4141
E-MAIL: core@core-online.org
WEB SITE: www.core-online.org/index.html
ETHICAL CONCERNS: Civil rights; equal rights; race and ethnicity

CORE's goal is to establish "equality for all people regardless of race, creed, sex, age, disability, sexual orientation, religion or ethnic background." In striving to reach its goal, CORE attempts to identify and reveal discriminatory acts in the private and civil sectors.

Council on Foreign Relations

FOUNDED: 1921
The Harold Pratt House
58 East 68th Street
New York, NY 10021
PHONE: (212) 434-9400
FAX: (212) 434-9800
WEB SITE: www.cfr.org/
ETHICAL CONCERNS: Foreign policy

Independent, nonpartisan body in which senior government officials, scholars, world leaders, and members of the council debate and examine the current significant foreign policy concerns facing the world. The council generates articles and books that analyze these concerns and recommend solutions to these policy issues. *Foreign Affairs* is a journal published by the council, covering U.S. foreign policy and international affairs. The council also supports autonomous task forces whose reports assist in setting the public foreign policy agenda.

Elie Wiesel Foundation for Humanity

FOUNDED: 1988
529 Fifth Avenue, Suite 1802
New York, NY 10017
PHONE: (212) 490-7777
FAX: (212) 490-6006
E-MAIL: info@eliewieselfoundation.org
WEB SITE: www.eliewieselfoundation.org/
ETHICAL CONCERNS: Human rights

The foundation promotes human rights by developing platforms for the debate and resolution of pressing ethical problems. The Prize in Ethics Essay Contest was started by the foundation in 1989. Each year, students from colleges and universities across the United States participate in the contest by submitting an essay on an ethics issue of their choice. The foundation also sponsors a humanitarian award, which was established to recognize notable individuals whose achievements are consistent with the aims of the foundation. Recipients of this award have included Danielle Mitterrand (1989), George H. W. Bush (1991), King Juan Carlos of Spain (1991), Hillary Rodham Clinton (1994), and Laura Bush (2002).

Environmental Protection Agency (EPA)

FOUNDED: 1970
Ariel Rios Building
1200 Pennsylvania Avenue NW
Washington, DC 20460
PHONE: (202) 272-0167
WEB SITE: www.epa.gov/epahome/
ETHICAL CONCERNS: Environment; environmental ethics

Federal government agency whose objective is to safeguard human health and the environment. Some of the functions of the EPA include developing and executing the regulations of environmental laws, conducting environmental research, and promoting environmental education.

Ethics and Public Policy Center (EPPC)

FOUNDED: 1976
1015 15th Street NW, Suite 900
Washington, DC 20005
PHONE: (202) 682-1200

FAX: (202) 408-0632
E-MAIL: Ethics@eppc.org
WEB SITE: www.eppc.org
ETHICAL CONCERNS: Public policy

The EPPC emphasizes the role of moral tradition in the area of domestic and foreign policy issues. The center has various programs, such as research, writing, publication, and conferences to encourage debate on public policy issues in the Judeo-Christian moral tradition.

Ethics Resource Center (ERC)

FOUNDED: 1977
1747 Pennsylvania Avenue NW, Suite 400
Washington, DC 20006
PHONE: (202) 737-2258
FAX: (202) 737-2227
E-MAIL: ethics@ethics.org
WEB SITE: www.ethics.org
ETHICAL CONCERNS: Global ethics

The ERC aims to support global ethical leadership through the use of education, partnerships, and research. The goals of the ERC are for individuals to act in an ethical manner toward one another, for institutions to act ethically, and for individuals and institutions to work together to encourage or nurture ethical communities. *Ethics Today* is sponsored by the ERC as a platform for examining an immense scope of business ethics and character development questions and for presenting and addressing business ethics, global ethics, and character development ideologies. It is a free monthly publication that is e-mailed to subscribers. Each issue is also posted online for a month and then stored in the *Ethics Today* archive.

Facing History and Ourselves

FOUNDED: 1976
16 Hurd Road
Brookline, MA 02445
PHONE: (617) 232-1595
FAX: (617) 232-0281
WEB SITE: www.facing.org
ETHICAL CONCERNS: Human rights; racism

Educational organization whose mission is to fight prejudice and racism and to promote human rights through the study of the Holocaust and other incidents in the history of collective violence. The organization conducts research, holds seminars, and has an extensive collection of resources available to promote critical thinking and moral behavior.

Fairness and Accuracy in Reporting (FAIR)
FOUNDED: 1986
112 West 27th Street
New York, NY 10001
PHONE: (212) 633-6700
FAX: (212) 727-7668
E-MAIL: fair@fair.org
WEB SITE: www.fair.org/
ETHICAL CONCERNS: Censorship; media bias; professional ethics

National media-monitoring group that works to vitalize the First Amendment by urging for greater diversity in the media and studying media practices that marginalize public interest, minority, and opposing views. FAIR also serves as an anticensorship organization by uncovering slighted news stories and supporting journalists who have been silenced.

Gray Panthers
FOUNDED: 1970
733 15th Street NW
Washington, DC 20005
PHONE: (800) 280-5362
FAX: (202) 737-1160
E-MAIL: info@graypanthers.org
WEB SITE: www.graypanthers.org/
ETHICAL CONCERNS: Discrimination; environmental issues; rights for the disabled

National organization of activists committed to social change. The Gray Panthers includes more than fifty local networks that advocate for antidiscrimination legislation, campaign reform, disability rights, employment, environmental issues, families, housing, and peace. The organization has helped fight mandatory retirement age regulations, revealed nursing home abuse, and has supported a national health care system.

Greenpeace International
FOUNDED: 1971
Ottho Heldringstraat 5
1066 AZ Amsterdam
The Netherlands
PHONE: 31 20 5148150
FAX: 31 20 5148151
E-MAIL: supporter.services@int.greenpeace.org
WEB SITE: www.greenpeace.org/international_en/
ETHICAL CONCERNS: Environmental protection; international relations

Global organization dedicated to protecting the earth's biodiversity and environment. Greenpeace's campaigns have included trying to stop climate change, the nuclear threat, war, and whaling; eliminating toxic chemicals; protecting ancient forests; saving the seas; encouraging sustainable trade; and saying no to genetic engineering.

Hastings Center
FOUNDED: 1969
21 Malcolm Gordon Road
Garrison, NY 10524-5555
PHONE: (845) 424-4040
FAX: (845) 424-4545
E-MAIL: mail@thehastingscenter.org
WEB SITE: www.thehastingscenter.org
ETHICAL CONCERNS: Bioethics

Bioethics research institute established to examine vital and developing questions in biotechnology, health care, and the environment. It conducts many research projects on issues that concern medical professionals, the public, and social policy such as genetics and biotechnology; ethics, science, and the environment; health care and policy; and ethics and scientific research. The Hastings Center publishes *IRB: Ethics & Human Research*, a journal that discusses the ethical issues facing administrators, investigators, participants, and others involved in research with human subjects.

Human Rights Information and Documentation Systems, International (HURIDOCS)
FOUNDED: 1982
HURIDOCS Secretariat
48, chemin du Grand-Montfleury
CH-1290 Versoix, Switzerland
PHONE: 41 22 755 52 52
FAX: 41 22 755 52 60
E-MAIL: info@huridocs.org
WEB SITE: www.huridocs.org/
ETHICAL CONCERNS: Human rights

Worldwide network of human rights organizations concerned with improving access to and dissemination of information regarding human rights. HURIDOCS organizes documentation practices and examines difficulties and procedures of data handling in this domain.

Human Rights Watch
FOUNDED: 1978
350 Fifth Avenue, 34th Floor
New York, NY 10118-3299
PHONE: (212) 290-4700
FAX: (212) 736-1300
E-MAIL: hrwnyc@hrw.org
WEB SITE: www.hrw.org/
ETHICAL CONCERNS: Arms control; children's rights; human rights; international relations; women's rights

Organization that monitors the human rights practices of more than seventy nations around the globe. It determines whether the practices are in harmony with principles recognized by agreements such as the Helsinki Accords and the United Nations Declaration of Human Rights. It also tracks children's rights, women's rights, and arms control and reports abuses. Other areas of interest for Human Rights Watch include academic freedom, drugs, international justice, prisons, and refugees.

Humane Society of the United States (HSUS)
FOUNDED: 1954
2100 L Street NW
Washington, DC 20037
PHONE: (202) 452-1100
WEB SITE: www.hsus.org/ace/352
ETHICAL CONCERNS: Animal rights

Organization that promotes the elimination of animal abuse and exploitation, protection for endangered species and their environments, and a relationship of compassion and respect for all animals. The society has become the world's largest animal protection organization and addresses global animal abuses and concerns through advocacy, education, litigation, and rehabilitation.

Institute for Global Ethics
FOUNDED: 1990
11 Main Street
P.O. Box 563
Camden, ME 04843
PHONE: (207) 236-6658
FAX: (207) 236-4014

E-MAIL: ethics@globalethics.org
WEB SITE: www.globalethics.org
ETHICAL CONCERNS: Global ethics

Organization whose goal is to foster ethical behavior in people, institutions, and the world through discussion, education, practical action, and research. The institute also publishes the weekly *Ethics Newsline*, an online source for news and information on ethics and current events.

Institute for Philosophy and Public Policy
FOUNDED: 1976
Maryland School of Public Affairs
3111 Van Munching
College Park, MD 20742
PHONE: (301) 405-4753
FAX: (301) 314-9346
WEB SITE: www.puaf.umd.edu/IPPP/
ETHICAL CONCERNS: Public policy

Established to investigate complex and ethical questions of public policy debate and formulation, this organization concentrates on issues such as the teaching of ethics, equal opportunity, and democratic values.

Intercollegiate Studies Institute (ISI)
FOUNDED: 1953
3901 Centerville Road
P.O. Box 4431
Wilmington, DE 19807-0431
PHONE: (800) 526-7022
FAX: (302) 652-1760
E-MAIL: info@isi.org
WEB SITE: www.isi.org/
ETHICAL CONCERNS: Economics; politics

Organization established to promote among collegians a deeper understanding of the economic, political, and spiritual principles that support a free and ethical society. ISI sponsors more than three hundred educational programs, such as lectures and seminars, and offers graduate fellowships to teachers.

International Business Ethics Institute (IBEI)
FOUNDED: 1994
1725 K Street NW, Suite 1207
Washington, DC 20006
PHONE: (202) 296-6938
FAX: (202) 296-5897
E-MAIL: info@business-ethics.org

WEB SITE: www.business-ethics.org
ETHICAL CONCERNS: Business ethics

Nonprofit, educational organization dedicated to elevating public understanding of international business ethics matters and distributing information about corporate responsibility through the use of educational resources. IBEI's educational resources include its Web site, its roundtable discussion series, and the publication *International Business Ethics Review*.

International Committee of the Red Cross
FOUNDED: 1863
19 avenue de la Paix
CH 1202 Geneva, Switzerland
PHONE: 41 22 734 60 01
FAX: 41 22 733 20 57
WEB SITE: www.icrc.org/
ETHICAL CONCERNS: Humanitarianism; international relations

Organization established to assist in humanitarian efforts around the globe on a neutral and impartial basis. The Red Cross visits prisoners of war to ensure they are being treated properly, searches for missing people, provides food, water, and medical assistance to people in need, and fosters regard for international humanitarian law.

International Labour Organization (ILO)
FOUNDED: 1919
4, route des Morillons
CH-1211 Geneva 22
Switzerland
PHONE: 41 22 799 61 11
FAX: 41 22 798 86 85
E-MAIL: ilo@ilo.org
WEB SITE: www.ilo.org/public/english/index.htm
ETHICAL CONCERNS: Human rights; business and labor ethics

Dedicated to fostering social justice and internationally accepted human and labor rights, the ILO creates international labor standards by setting minimum standards of basic labor rights, such as the eradication of forced labor, implementation of collective bargaining, equal opportunity and treatment, freedom of association, and freedom to organize. The ILO also advocates the growth of independent employer and employee organizations and provides advice and training services to the organizations.

JCT Center for Business Ethics & Social Responsibility
FOUNDED: 1992
P.O. Box 16031
Jerusalem 91160 Israel
PHONE: 972-2-675-1182
FAX: 972-2-642-2075
WEB SITE: www.besr.org/
ETHICAL CONCERNS: Business ethics; Jewish ethics; personal and social ethics

Center that fosters and encourages a high level of business integrity through promoting an understanding of Jewish ethical teachings. The center produces a weekly column called the "Jewish Ethicist," in which a question regarding a business dilemma is posed and answered by a rabbi who includes general standards of Jewish ethics and law into his response. The public may suggest questions for the column by submitting them to: jewishethicist@yahoo.com. The Web site offers an archive of previous questions.

Josephson Institute of Ethics
FOUNDED: 1987
9841 Airport Blvd., #300
Los Angeles, CA 90045
PHONE: (310) 846-4800
FAX: (310) 846-4857
E-MAIL: webmaster@jiethics.org
WEB SITE: www.josephsoninstitute.org/
ETHICAL CONCERNS: Business ethics; education

Established to promote the teaching of ethics in businesses, schools, and workplaces, the institute conducts numerous programs and workshops catered to influential persons, such as mayors, judges, reporters, corporate executives, and military and police officers. The institute also conducts an "Ethics in the Workplace" training seminar.

Kennedy Institute of Ethics
FOUNDED: 1971
Healy, 4th Floor
Georgetown University
Washington, DC 20057
PHONE: (202) 687-8099
FAX: (202) 687-8089
WEB SITE: www.georgetown.edu/research/kie/site/index.htm
ETHICAL CONCERNS: Bioethics

Center focuses on research and teaching on such bioethical issues as cloning, eugenics, gene therapy, and reproductive and feminist bioethics. The institute is a source of information for those who analyze and study ethics, as well as those who debate and decide public policy.

League of Women Voters (LWV)

FOUNDED: 1920
1730 M Street NW, Suite 1000
Washington, DC 20036-4508
PHONE: (202) 429-1965
FAX: (202) 429-0854
WEB SITE: www.lwv.org
ETHICAL CONCERNS: Politico-economic ethics; public policy; sex and gender issues

Nonpartisan political organization that promotes the participation of all citizens in government, works to further the understanding of significant public policy issues, and addresses public policy through advocacy and education.

Markkula Center for Applied Ethics

FOUNDED: 1986
500 El Camino Real
Santa Clara, CA 95053
PHONE: (408) 554-5319
E-MAIL: ethics@scu.edu
WEB SITE: www.scu.edu/ethics/
ETHICAL CONCERNS: Applied ethics

Established at Santa Clara University, the center focuses on the research and dialogue of ethical issues. The center fosters communication among community leaders, faculty, staff, students, and the public to face ethical issues effectively in action, teaching, and research. The center focuses on ethical issues in the fields of biotechnology and health care, business, character education, global leadership, and government. In 1996, the center launched Ethics Connection, its interactive Web site which provides information and useful tips on making ethical decisions and allows visitors to communicate with one another and the Ethics Connection staff through the use of message boards and a feedback feature. Ethics Connection also features a section on case studies, on which visitors may comment and study.

Media Institute

FOUNDED: 1979
1800 North Kent Street, Suite 1130
Arlington, VA 22209
PHONE: (703) 243-5060
FAX: (703) 243-2453
E-MAIL: info@mediainstitute.org
WEB SITE: www.mediainstitute.org/
ETHICAL CONCERNS: Media ethics; free expression

Think tank that studies the First Amendment and communications practices. The institute fosters and advances the growth of awareness and understanding of American communications and the media. The three goals of the institute are freedom of speech, a competitive communications and media industry, and virtue in journalism. The institute fosters research into the economic, ethical, legal, and political arenas of the media and communications fields.

National Anti-Vivisection Society (NAVS)

FOUNDED: 1929
53 West Jackson Boulevard, Suite 1552
Chicago, IL 60604
PHONE: (800) 888-NAVS
FAX: (312) 427-6524
E-MAIL: feedback@navs.org
WEB SITE: www.navs.org/
ETHICAL CONCERNS: Animal rights; bioethics; scientific ethics

Educational organization founded to abolish the use of animals in product testing and biomedical research. NAVS aims to educate manufacturers, physicians, researchers, teachers, and government officials about the alternatives to using animals, which will save millions of animal lives each year and still achieve the goals of these individuals.

National Association for the Advancement of Colored People (NAACP)

FOUNDED: 1909
4805 Mount Hope Drive
Baltimore, MD 21215
PHONE: (877) NAACP-98
WEB SITE: www.naacp.org/
ETHICAL CONCERNS: Civil rights; prejudice; race and ethnicity

Civil rights organization that aims to eradicate racial prejudice by ending discrimination in all areas of the public and private sectors, including business, employment, housing, the judicial system, schools, transportation, and voting.

National Conference of State Legislatures (NCSL)
FOUNDED: 1975
444 North Capital Street NW, Suite 515
Washington, DC 20001
PHONE: (202) 624-5400
FAX: (202) 737-1069
WEB SITE: www.ncsl.org/programs/ethics/overview_ethics.htm
ETHICAL CONCERNS: Government ethics

Nonpartisan, nonprofit organization established to address the loss of trust in democracy by the American people. The Ethics Center of the NCSL has assembled information from every state on legislative ethics laws in five primary areas: gifts, honoraria, lobbyists, nepotism, and revolving door policies.

National Gay and Lesbian Task Force (NGLTF)
FOUNDED: 1973
1325 Massachusetts Avenue NW, Suite 600
Washington, DC 20005
PHONE: (202) 393-5177
FAX: (202) 393-2241
E-MAIL: ngltf@ngltf.org
WEB SITE: www.thetaskforce.org/index.cfm
ETHICAL CONCERNS: Gay rights; sex and gender issues; civil rights; hate crime

Civil rights organization that directs national efforts to organize legislative actions and nationwide grassroots organizing on a number of issues of special concern to the gay, lesbian, bisexual, and transgender population, such as domestic partnership and same-sex marriage. The NGLTF also recognizes issues outside its own community such as affirmative action, aging, civil rights, families, hate crimes, and schools.

National Institute Against Prejudice and Violence. See Prejudice Institute

National Legal and Policy Center
FOUNDED: 1991
107 Park Washington Court
Falls Church, VA 22046
PHONE: (703) 237-1970
FAX: (703) 237-2090
E-MAIL: nlpc@nlpc.org

WEB SITE: www.nlpc.org
ETHICAL CONCERNS: Legal ethics

Center established to foster ethics in government and to give visibility to the Code of Ethics for Government.

National Organization for Women (NOW)
FOUNDED: 1966
733 15th Street NW
Washington, DC 20005
PHONE: (202) 628-8669
FAX: (202) 785-8576
E-MAIL: now@now.org
WEB SITE: www.now.org/
ETHICAL CONCERNS: Civil rights; feminism; sex and gender issues; women's rights

Women's rights organization established to eradicate discrimination and prejudice against women in all areas of life. The organization seeks to acquire economic equality for women and assure it through a constitutional amendment that guarantees equal rights for women; supports abortion and reproductive freedom rights; fights racism and bigotry against lesbians and gays; and opposes violence against women. NOW uses civil action, organizing marches and rallies, lawsuits, and lobbying to work toward its goals.

New York Society for the Prevention of Cruelty to Children (NYSPCC)
FOUNDED: 1875
161 William Street
New York, NY 10038
PHONE: (212) 233-5500
FAX: (212) 791-5227
WEB SITE: www.nyspcc.org/index.htm
ETHICAL CONCERNS: Children's rights

Oldest organization in the world dedicated to protecting the interests of children. The society strives to develop and introduce educational, legal, and mental health programs that assure the healthy development of children and shield them from harm.

Office of the High Commissioner for Human Rights (OHCHR)
FOUNDED: 1993
United Nations Office at Geneva
8-14 Avenue de la Paix
1211 Geneva 10
Switzerland

PHONE: 41 22 917 9000
FAX: 41 22 917 9011
E-MAIL: 1503@ohchr.org
WEB SITE: www.unhchr.ch/
ETHICAL CONCERNS: Human rights

Branch of the United Nations that strives for the international community and its member states to abide by universally agreed upon human-rights standards. The OHCHR serves as the voice of people whose human rights have been violated; it pushes the international community to thwart violations.

People for the Ethical Treatment of Animals (PETA)

FOUNDED: 1980
501 Front Street
Norfolk, VA 23510
PHONE: (757) 622-PETA
FAX: (757) 622-0457
E-MAIL: info@peta.org
WEB SITE: www.peta.org/
ETHICAL CONCERNS: Animal rights

Militant animal-rights organization committed to establishing and defending the rights of all animals. PETA's guiding principle is that "animals are not ours to eat, wear, experiment on, or use for entertainment."

Philosophy Documentation Center

FOUNDED: 1966
P.O. Box 7147
Charlottesville, VA 22906-7147
PHONE: (800) 444-2419
FAX: (434) 220-3301
E-MAIL: order@pdcnet.org
WEB SITE: www.pdcnet.org/
ETHICAL CONCERNS: Ethics; philosophy

Information center that specializes in bibliographical and other types of information pertaining to ethics, philosophy, and philosophers. It is committed to providing affordable access to these materials. The center produces academic journals, conference and reference materials, and instructional software.

Physicians Committee for Responsible Medicine (PCRM)

FOUNDED: 1985
5100 Wisconsin Avenue NW, Suite 400
Washington, DC 20016
PHONE: (202) 686-2210

FAX: (202) 686-2216
E-MAIL: pcrm@pcrm.org
WEB SITE: www.pcrm.org/
ETHICAL CONCERNS: Animal rights; medical ethics

Professional organization of physicians and laypersons working together for humane and effective "medical practice, research, and health promotion." PCRM opposes unethical human experiments and encourages alternatives to animal research.

Population Connection

FOUNDED: 1968
1400 16th Street NW, Suite 320
Washington, DC 20036
PHONE: (202) 332-2200
FAX: (202) 332-2302
E-MAIL: info@populationconnection.org
WEB SITE: www.populationconnection.org
ETHICAL CONCERNS: Environmentalism; population control

National grassroots organization that champions efforts to stabilize world population at a level that can be sustained by the earth's resources. Formerly known as Zero Population Growth, Population Connection influences political action on international, national, state, and local levels; conducts teacher education and public education programs; provides educational materials; participates in coalitions; conducts research; and provides a forecast on the effect of the population on environmental and social problems. The organization encourages measures that seek voluntary compliance.

Prejudice Institute

FOUNDED: 1985
2743 Maryland Avenue
Baltimore, MD 21218
PHONE: (410) 243-6987
E-MAIL: prejinst@aol.com
WEB SITE: www.prejudiceinstitute.org/
ETHICAL CONCERNS: Prejudice; violence

Originally known as the National Institute Against Prejudice and Violence, the institute was reincorporated as the Prejudice Institute in 1993. The institute examines and conducts research into the occurrence of prejudice and violence and its effects on the victims and society. The issue of violence surrounding anti-gay, ethnic, racial, and religious prejudice is also addressed.

President's Council on Bioethics

FOUNDED: 2001

WEB SITE: www.bioethics.gov/

ETHICAL CONCERNS: Bioethics; cloning; research ethics; stem cell research

Federal government agency that advises the president of the United States on ethical matters related to progress in biomedical science and technology. In addition to the concerns listed above, the council also deals with aging and the end of life; biotechnology and public policy; bioethics in literature; drugs, children, and behavior control; memory boosting/suppression; mood control; neuroethics; organ transplantation; and sex selection in reproductive technology.

Public Responsibility in Medicine and Research (PRIM&R)

FOUNDED: 1974

126 Brookline Avenue, Suite 202

Boston, MA 02215

PHONE: (617) 423-4112

FAX: (617) 423-1185

E-MAIL: info@primr.org

WEB SITE: www.primr.org/

ETHICAL CONCERNS: Medical ethics

Organization committed to developing, activating, and promoting the highest ethical principles in the fields of biomedical and behavioral research. It has been the prominent source for education, progress, and resource sharing in all areas relating to the ethical, regulatory, and societal considerations of research. The organization conducts educational and training programs and holds conferences to achieve its mandate.

Sierra Club

FOUNDED: 1892

85 Second Street

San Francisco, CA 94105

PHONE: (415) 977-5500

FAX: (415) 977-5799

E-MAIL: information@sierraclub.org

WEB SITE: www.sierraclub.org/

ETHICAL CONCERNS: Environmental ethics; environmentalism

Oldest, largest, and most powerful grassroots environmental organization in the world. Its aims are to foster the responsible use of the earth's resources and to foster the responsible use of the earth's resources and ecosystems, protect wild habitats, teach and recruit people to preserve and revive the natural and human environment, and use just methods to achieve these objectives. The club's top priorities are ensuring clean water, ending commercial logging, stopping sprawl, and protecting wildland. *Sierra* is a magazine published by the club.

Society for Business Ethics (SBE)

FOUNDED: 1980

School of Business Administration

Loyola University Chicago

820 North Michigan Avenue

Chicago, IL 60611

PHONE: (312) 915-6994

FAX: (312) 915-6988

E-MAIL: jboatri@luc.edu

WEB SITE: www.societyforbusinessethics.org/

ETHICAL CONCERNS: Business ethics

International organization of intellectuals who are concerned with the academic examination of business ethics. An annual meeting is held by SBE to offer research in the field. SBE publishes the journal *Business Ethics Quarterly* to distribute significant scholarship in the discipline.

Society of Christian Philosophers

FOUNDED: 1978

Department of Philosophy

Calvin College

Grand Rapids, MI 49546-4388

WEB SITE: www.siu.edu/~scp/

ETHICAL CONCERNS: Ethics; philosophy

The society promotes the exchange of information about issues relating to ethics and the philosophy of religion. *Faith and Philosophy* is published quarterly by the society and is an influential journal in the field.

Southern Poverty Law Center (SPLC)

FOUNDED: 1971

400 Washington Avenue

Montgomery, AL 36104

PHONE: (334) 956-8200

WEB SITE: www.splcenter.org/index.jsp

ETHICAL CONCERNS: Civil rights; legal rights

Organization of legal professionals established to defend and promote the legal and civil rights of indigent people through legal means and education. Frequently the SPLC's work has centered on aiding individuals harmed or intimidated by actions of the Ku Klux Klan and other white supremacist organizations.

Union of Concerned Scientists (UCS)
FOUNDED: 1969
2 Brattle Square
Cambridge, MA 02238-9105
PHONE: (617) 547-5552
FAX: (617) 864-9405
WEB SITE: www.ucsusa.org/
ETHICAL CONCERNS: Environmentalism; food safety; scientific ethics; nuclear weapons

Organization of science professionals established to guarantee that all people have clear air, energy, transportation, and food that is manufactured in a safe manner. UCS conducts studies on the impact of global warming, the risks of genetically engineered crops, renewable energy options, and other related areas.

United Nations (U.N.)
FOUNDED: 1945
United Nations
New York, NY 10017
PHONE: (212) 963-4475
FAX: (212) 963-0071
E-MAIL: inquiries@un.org
WEB SITE: www.un.org
ETHICAL CONCERNS: Human rights; international relations

International organization to which virtually every sovereign nation belongs. The United Nations, along with its many specialized branches, attempts to identify and settle international feuds that jeopardize world peace and security. A proponent of human rights, the United Nations strives to foster conditions in which justice and honor for international law and treaties can be preserved.

United States Holocaust Memorial Museum
FOUNDED: 1980
100 Raoul Wallenberg Place SW
Washington, DC 20024-2126
PHONE: (202) 488-0400
WEB SITE: www.ushmm.org/
ETHICAL CONCERNS: Genocide; moral awareness

Museum dedicated to increasing public awareness of the Holocaust, perpetuating the remembrance of those who suffered, and encouraging visitors to contemplate on the moral and spiritual considerations raised by the Holocaust. The museum aims to increase public knowledge of the Holocaust through exhibits, research, and annual Holocaust commemorations referred to as the Days of Remembrance. The museum also serves as a memorial to the millions of people who were murdered during the Holocaust.

World Health Organization (WHO)
FOUNDED: 1948
Avenue Appia 20
1211 Geneva 27
Switzerland
PHONE: 41 22 791 21 11
FAX: 41 22 791 31 11
E-MAIL: inf@who.int
WEB SITE: www.who.int/en/
ETHICAL CONCERNS: Bioethics; environmental ethics; health care; international relations

Branch of the United Nations (see above) whose goal is the highest possible level of health—total physical, mental, and social well-being by every individual inhabiting the earth.

World Society for the Protection of Animals (WSPA)
FOUNDED: 1981
34 Deloss Street
Framingham, MA 01702
PHONE: (508) 879-8350
FAX: (508) 620-0786
E-MAIL: wspa@wspausa.com
WEB SITE: www.wspa-americas.org
ETHICAL CONCERNS: Animal rights

Animal-rights organization whose goal is the worldwide advancement of animal welfare standards. The vision of the WSPA is a world in which the welfare of animals is appreciated and regarded by all peoples and safeguarded by legislation. The WSPA exposes animal abuse and dispatches animal rescue teams to save abandoned or neglected animals.

Zero Population Growth. See Population Connection

Andrea E. Miller

Time Line of Primary Works in Moral and Ethical Philosophy

This table lists works chronologically to show the historical evolution of ethical thought.

Date	Work	Author
1200-100 B.C.E.	Old Testament	Hebrew scribes
1000-400 B.C.E.	Upaniṣads	Hindu sages
800-200 B.C.E.	*Dao De Jing*	Attributed to Laozi (fl. sixth century B.C.E.)
c. 500-320 B.C.E.	*The Art of War*	Attributed to Sunzi (fl. c. 500 B.C.E.)
c. 500 B.C.E.	*The Analects of Confucius*	Confucius (c. 551-c. 479 B.C.E.)
399-390 B.C.E.	*Apology*	Plato (427-347 B.C.E.)
388-368 B.C.E.	*Republic*	
335-323 B.C.E.	*Nicomachean Ethics*	Aristotle (384-322 B.C.E.)
	Politics	
320-289 B.C.E.	*Mengzi*	Mencius (c. 372-c. 289 B.C.E.)
310-270 B.C.E.	*Principal Doctrines*	Epicurus (c. 342-c. 270 B.C.E.)
	Letter to Menoeceus	
c. 300 B.C.E.	*Zhuangzi*	Zhuangzi (c. 370-c. 285 B.C.E.)
200 B.C.E.-200 C.E.	*Bhagavadgītā*	Hindu mystic(s)
150 B.C.E.-500 C.E.	Talmud	Hebrew scholars
c. 50-350	New Testament	Christian scribes
c. 138	*The Enchiridion*	Epictetus (c. 65-c. 135)
171-180	*Meditations*	Marcus Aurelius (121-180)
c. 256-270	*Enneads*	Plotinus (c. 204-270)
397-400	*Confessions*	Saint Augustine (354-430)
413-427	*The City of God*	
c. 610-650	Qurʾān	Muḥammad (c. 570-632) and his followers
c. 677	*The Platform Scripture of the Sixth Patriarch*	Huineng (638-713)
c. 720-c. 750	*Crest Jewel of Wisdom*	Śaṅkara (c. 700-c. 750)
1022-1037	*The Book of Salvation*	Avicenna (980-1037)
1180	*The Incoherence of the Incoherence*	Averroës (1126-1198)
1190	*Guide of the Perplexed*	Moses Maimonides (1135-1204)
c. 1265-1274	*Summa Theologica*	Thomas Aquinas (c. 1225-1274)
1516	*Utopia*	Thomas More (1478-1535)
1517	*The Ninety-five Theses*	Martin Luther (1483-1546)
1532	*The Prince*	Niccolò Machiavelli (1469-1527)
1641	*Meditations on First Philosophy*	René Descartes (1596-1650)
1651	*Leviathan*	Thomas Hobbes (1588-1679)
1677	*Ethics*	Baruch Spinoza (1632-1677)
1690	*Two Treatises of Government*	John Locke (1632-1704)
1748	*The Spirit of the Laws*	Montesquieu (1689-1755)
1751	*An Enquiry Concerning the Principles of Morals*	David Hume (1711-1776)
1762	*The Social Contract*	Jean-Jacques Rousseau (1712-1778)

Date	Work	Author
1776	*An Inquiry into the Nature and Causes of the Wealth of Nations*	Adam Smith (1723-1790)
1781, 1787	*Critique of Pure Reason*	Immanuel Kant (1724-1804)
1785	*Foundations of the Metaphysics of Morals*	
1788	*Critique of Practical Reason*	
1789	*An Introduction to the Principles of Morals and Legislation*	Jeremy Bentham (1748-1832)
1791	*Rights of Man*	Thomas Paine (1737-1809)
1792	*A Vindication of the Rights of Woman*	Mary Wollstonecraft (1759-1797)
1792	*Critique of Judgment*	Immanuel Kant
1807	*Phenomenology of Spirit*	Georg Wilhelm Friedrich Hegel (1770-1831)
1819	*The World as Will and Representation*	Arthur Schopenhauer (1788-1860)
1821	*Philosophy of Right*	Georg Wilhelm Friedrich Hegel
1826	*An Essay on the Principle of Population*	Thomas Robert Malthus (1766-1834)
1832	*On War*	Carl von Clausewitz (1780-1831)
1841-1844	*Essays*	Ralph Waldo Emerson (1803-1882)
1843	*Either/Or*	Søren Kierkegaard (1813-1855)
1848	*Communist Manifesto*	Karl Marx (1818-1883)
1854	*Walden*	Henry David Thoreau (1811-1896)
1859	*On the Origin of Species*	Charles Darwin (1809-1882)
1859	*On Liberty*	John Stuart Mill (1806-1873)
1863	*Utilitarianism*	
1864	*Apologia pro Vita Sua*	John Henry Cardinal Newman (1801-1890)
1867	*Capital*	Karl Marx
1874	*Methods of Ethics*	Henry Sidgwick (1838-1900)
1886	*Beyond Good and Evil*	Friedrich Nietzsche (1844-1900)
1887	*On the Genealogy of Morals*	
1903	*Principia Ethica*	G. E. Moore (1873-1958)
1904-1905	*The Protestant Ethic and the Spirit of Capitalism*	Max Weber (1864-1920)
1905-1906	*The Life of Reason*	George Santayana (1863-1952)
1907	*Pragmatism*	William James (1842-1910)
1908	*The Philosophy of Loyalty*	Josiah Royce (1855-1916)
1922	*Tractatus Logico-Philosophicus*	Ludwig Wittgenstein (1889-1951)
1922	*Human Nature and Conduct*	John Dewey (1859-1952)
1923	*I and Thou*	Martin Buber (1878-1965)
1927	*Being and Time*	Martin Heidegger (1889-1976)
1929	*Process and Reality*	Alfred North Whitehead (1861-1947)
1930	*Civilization and Its Discontents*	Sigmund Freud (1856-1939)
1932	*The Two Sources of Morality and Religion*	Henri Bergson (1859-1941)
1932	*Moral Man and Immoral Society*	Reinhold Niebuhr (1892-1971)
1936	*Language, Truth, and Logic*	A. J. Ayer (1910-1988)

Date	Work	Author
1943	*Being and Nothingness*	Jean-Paul Sartre (1905-1980)
1944	*The Children of Light and the Children of Darkness*	Reinhold Niebuhr
1947	*Dialectic of Enlightenment*	Theodor Adorno (1903-1969) and Max Horkheimer (1895-1973)
1949	*The Second Sex*	Simone de Beauvoir (1908-1986)
1951	*The Rebel*	Albert Camus (1913-1960)
1952	*The Courage to Be*	Paul Tillich (1886-1965)
1953	*Philosophical Investigations*	Ludwig Wittgenstein
1960	*Truth and Method*	Hans-Georg Gadamer (1900-2002)
1961	*The Wretched of the Earth*	Frantz Fanon (1925-1961)
1962	*The Structural Transformation of the Public Sphere*	Jürgen Habermas (1929-)
1969	*The Possibility of Altruism*	Thomas Nagel (1937-)
1969	*Lenin and Philosophy*	Louis Althusser (1918-1990)
1971	*A Theory of Justice*	John Rawls (1921-)
1972	*Margins of Philosophy*	Jacques Derrida (1930-)
1975	*Discipline and Punish: The Birth of the Prison*	Michel Foucault (1926-1984)
1979	*The Claim of Reason*	Stanley Cavell (1926-)
1981	*After Virtue*	Alasdair MacIntyre (1929-)
1982	*In a Different Voice*	Carol Gilligan (1936-)
1985	*Ethics and the Limits of Philosophy*	Bernard Williams (1930-2003)
1990	*Love's Knowledge*	Martha Nussbaum (1947-)

ETHICS
Revised Edition

LIST OF ENTRIES BY CATEGORY

PERSONAL AND SOCIAL ETHICS

PERSONAGES INDEX

SUBJECT INDEX